CONCISE DICTIONARY
OF THE
CHRISTIAN WORLD MISSION

WORLD CHRISTIAN BOOKS

CONCISE DICTIONARY OF THE CHRISTIAN WORLD MISSION

Edited by

STEPHEN NEILL
GERALD H. ANDERSON
JOHN GOODWIN

UNITED SOCIETY FOR CHRISTIAN LITERATURE
LUTTERWORTH PRESS
LONDON

First published in 1970

COPYRIGHT © 1971 LUTTERWORTH PRESS

ISBN **0 7188 1687 0**

Printed in Great Britain
by Ebenezer Baylis and Son, Limited
The Trinity Press, Worcester, and London

PREFACE

ONLY RARELY is it possible for authors and editors to claim that they have done something that has never been done before. The editors of this Dictionary, however, believe that this is a claim they are entitled to make. There have been histories of the expansion of Christianity throughout the world, the most notable being the seven-volume work of Professor K. S. Latourette. There is an earlier *Encyclopaedia of Missions* edited by E. Bliss (1891, revised 1904); but this dealt almost exclusively with Protestant, and mainly with American, missionary work. Here for the first time an attempt has been made to provide in dictionary form somewhat comprehensive information as to the entire process through which in the last five centuries Christianity has grown from a western to a universal religion.

The limitations of this work should first be made clear. Its aim is to cover the extension of the Christian Church, and its evangelistic encounter with mankind, during the period from 1492, when Columbus first made contact with the inhabitants of lands west of the Atlantic, to the present day.

If this Dictionary was to be kept within the limits of 700 pages, it was clear that the principles of careful selection and radical exclusion of the irrelevant must be firmly adhered to. Three lists were drawn up—countries of the world; biographies of leaders drawn from every race and confession, not forgetting the younger churches, but as far as possible limited to those who had done something new and creative in missionary work; and subjects, ranging from acculturation to witchcraft. For the convenience of the reader, all articles have been arranged in alphabetical order. Furthermore, the frequent cross-references should make it possible to find information on any subject which is treated in the Dictionary, and on many themes to which no separate article is allotted.

More than two hundred experts have co-operated in the work of the Dictionary, which is genuinely international and ecumenical. Each contributor has been free to express his own point of view; but in many cases it would be hard to guess from the contents of the article to which particular Christian confession the writer adheres. The editors have had to be strict in the matter of length (though even here contributors have shown

v

an almost unexampled capacity for keeping to the limits assigned them); they have hardly ever had occasion to modify a harsh phrase or to remove signs of confessional prejudice. Concern for the proclamation of the Gospel throughout the world appears to be the best of ecumenical medicines.

This Dictionary is intended, among other things, to be an aid to further study. Therefore short bibliographical information is appended to almost all the articles. In particular, in cases in which a longer article is to be found in one of the standard works of reference, such as the *Dictionary of National Biography*, a cross reference is given; frequently a much fuller bibliography is to be found in these larger works, though naturally the older books cannot give references to the most recent work on the subjects of which they treat. One work of reference, which appeared too late to be consulted by most of the contributors to this Dictionary, is *The Encyclopedia of Modern Christian Missions: The Agencies* (edited by B. L. Goddard, Camden, New Jersey, T. Nelson & Sons, 1967). It contains much valuable information, particularly on the work of Protestant organizations in the twentieth century.

We here express our warm gratitude to our contributors; to specialists who have advised us in particular fields; to the many who kindly responded to requests for information; and to Miss Gwen Clements who has carried with enthusiasm the large secretarial labour of this enterprise.

When all the articles were in, the editors, faced with the task of reading them all through, expected to endure many tedious hours. To their surprise they found themselves held by eager and growing interest. This Dictionary is a work that can be read through with pleasure from cover to cover. Of course the alphabetical order means that the narrative leaps unpredictably from point to point; but in a strange way all the multitudinous fragments coalesce into a picture of the movement of the Spirit of God in history. The reader finds himself, like the listeners on the great day of Pentecost, in encounter with the recitation of the wonderful works of God.

It is our hope that many users of this Dictionary may find themselves led to share with us this moving and memorable experience.

S.C.N.
G.H.A.
J.F.B.G.

CONTRIBUTORS

The Rev. C. E. Abraham, MA, DD, formerly Principal of Serampore College.

The Right Rev. Oliver C. Allison, MA, Anglican Bishop in the Sudan.

The Right Rev. Hobart B. Amstutz, MA, DD, formerly Methodist Bishop in Karachi.

The Rev. Boris Anderson, Overseas Missions Secretary, Presbyterian Church of England.

The Rev. Gerald H. Anderson STB, PhD, President of Scarritt College for Christian Workers, Nashville, Tennessee.

Gonzalo Báez-Camargo, DD, Editorial writer for *Excelsior*, Mexico City.

The Rev. Frank K. Balchin, BD, ThD, formerly Dean of Trinity College, Singapore.

Mrs. Irene M. Bampton, Sunday School Secretary, Goodwyn Avenue Methodist Church, London.

Miss Natalie Barber, BA, Missionary of the Methodist Church in Bolivia.

The Rev. David B. Barrett, STM, PhD, Secretary for Research, Church of the Province of East Africa.

The Rev. R. Pierce Beaver, MA, PhD, Professor of the History of Missions in the Divinity School, University of Chicago.

The Rev. H. D. Beeby, ThD, Vice-Principal, Tainan Theological College, Taiwan.

The Rev. T. A. Beetham, MA, formerly Africa Secretary of the Conference of Missionary Societies in Great Britain and Ireland.

J. van den Berg, Dr Theol, Professor of Church History, Free University, Amsterdam.

The Rev. Peter Beyerhaus, Dr Theol, Professor of Mission Studies and Ecumenical Theology in the University of Tübingen.

The Rev. Benno M. Biermann, OP, DD, Professor of Missiology, Albertus Magnus Academy, Walberberg, Germany.

Miss Margaret R. Blemker, MA, LHD, Secretary for the Near East, United Church Board for World Ministries, New York.

The Rev. Nils Bloch-Hoell, ThD, Professor of Ecumenics and Missiology in the University of Oslo.

Harry R. Boer, ThD, Principal of the Theological College of Northern Nigeria.

The Rev. Jóse Míguez Bonino, MA, ThD, Principal of Union Theological Seminary, Buenos Aires.

The Rev. Alan R. Booth, LLB, BD, Director, Christian Aid, London.

The Rev. A. J. Boyd, MA, DD, formerly Principal of Madras Christian College.

James W. Boyd, MA, PhD, Assistant Professor in the Department of Philosophy of Colorado State University.

Raymond M. Boyle, Assistant Editor, *Maryknoll Magazine*, New York.

The Right Rev. Leslie W. Brown, DD, Bishop of St. Edmundsbury and Ipswich.

The Rev. Jean Bruls, SAM, Editor of *Eglise Vivante*, Louvain.

The Rev. Thoburn T. Brumbaugh, STB, STM, formerly Executive Secretary for East Asia Board of Missions, of the United Methodist Church, New York.

The Rev. Horst Bürkle, Dr Theol, Professor of Comparative Religion and Missiology at the University of Munich.

The Rev. J. Busse, PhD, Director of the Bethel Mission, Germany.

The Rev. A. Camps, OFM.

The Rev. Gordon K. Chapman, BD, STM, formerly Associate General Secretary of the National Christian Council of Japan.

The Rev. Lien-min Cheng, MTh, Minister of Taipei East Gate Presbyterian Church, Taiwan.

Clement C. Chesterman, MD, FRCP, Consulting Physician and President of the Medical Missionary Association, London.

The Rev. D. Ridley Chesterton, Joint General Secretary of the United Society for Christian Literature, London.

The Rev. Rolf Christiansen, Assistant to the Professor of Missions and Ecumenical Studies in the University of Hamburg.

The Rev. Paul D. Clasper, STM, ThD, Dean of the American Baptist Seminary of the West, Berkeley, California.

Sister Mary Dorita Clifford, BVM, PhD, Assistant Professor and Chairman of the Department of History, Clarke College, Dubuque, Iowa.

The Rev. Norman F. Cocks, Secretary in Australia and New Zealand of the Congregational Council for World Mission.

The Rev. Simon Conrad, OFMCap, STD.

The Rev. B. Corley, OMI, St. Mary's, Richmond Hill, Leeds.

The Right Rev. Kenneth Cragg, MA, DPhil, Assistant Bishop in the Jerusalem Archbishopric.

The Rev. W. J. Culshaw, BA, BD, formerly Translations Secretary of the United Bible Societies, London.

The Rev. Ernst Dammann, Dr Philol, Dr Theol, Professor of the History of Religions in the University of Marburg.

The Rev. Cyril J. Davey, Secretary for Home Organization, Methodist Missionary Society, London.

The Rev. F. Noel Davey, DD, Director of the Society for Promoting Christian Knowledge, London.

The Rev. James Davison, OBE, Methodist Minister, Aughnacloy, Co. Tyrone.

The Rev. Richard L. Deats, BD, PhD, Professor of Social Ethics, Union Theological Seminary, Philippines.

The Right Rev. H. B. Dehqani-Tafti, Anglican Bishop in Iran.

The Rev. L. Harold DeWolf, PhD, STD, Dean and Professor of Systematic Theology at Wesley Theological Seminary, Washington, DC.

The Rev. Peter J. Dirven, MHM, MA, MScL, Professor in Missiology at the Missionary Institute of London.

The Rev. Harry G. Dorman Jr, BD, PhD, Director, Middle East and Europe, National Council of Churches, New York.

The Rev. Ray C. Downs, BD, formerly Director of the Student Christian Center, Bangkok.

The Rev. H. F. Drake, BD, STM, Associate Overseas Secretary of the Baptist Missionary Society, London.

The Rev. D. M. Duncan, late Missionary of the Church of Scotland in Sialkot, Pakistan.

The Rev. J. Leslie Dunstan, DD, late Judson Professor of Christian Missions and World Religions, Andover Newton Theological School, Massachusetts.

The Rev. A. Theodore Eastman, BA, BD, Rector of the Church of the Mediator, Allentown, Pennsylvania.

The Rev. Nils Ehrenström, BD, ThD, Professor Emeritus of Ecumenics at Boston University School of Theology.

The Rev. Frank G. Engel, BA, BD, General Secretary, Australian Council of Churches.

The Rev. Ido H. Enklaar, Dr Theol, Principal of the Mission School of the Netherlands Reformed Church, Oegstgeest.

Edgar L. Farrow, MB, ChB, formerly Superintendent of the Edinburgh Medical Missionary Society.

The Rev. Cyril B. Firth, MA, Asia Secretary of the Conference of Missionary Societies in Great Britain and Ireland.

The Rev. John Fleming, BD, ThD, Senior Lecturer in Divinity, University of St. Andrews.

The Rev. Charles W. Forman, BD, PhD, Professor of Missions, Yale University Divinity School.

The Rev. John Foster, DD, Professor Emeritus of Church History in the University of Glasgow.

William H. Fox, formerly Executive Director of the Near East College Association, Inc., New York.

The Ven. W. A. Franklin, OBE, Archdeacon of the Episcopal Church in Colombia.

The Rev. Austin A. Fulton, PhD, DD, formerly Convener of the Foreign Mission of the Presbyterian Church in Ireland.

The Rev. H.-W. Gensichen, DTheol, ThM, Professor of the History of Religions and of Missiology in the University of Heidelberg.

The Rev. Josef Glazik, MSC, DD, Professor of Missiology in the University of Münster.

1*

The Rev. Burton L. Goddard, ThD, SM, Director of the Library, Gordon-Conwell Theological Seminary, Wenham, Massachusetts.

The Rev. James B. Goff, BD, ThD, Missionary of the United Presbyterian Church in Colombia.

The Rev. Norman Goodall, DPhil, formerly Assistant General Secretary of the World Council of Churches.

The Rev. Fred Field Goodsell, DD, formerly Executive Vice-President of the American Board of Commissioners for Foreign Missions.

The Rev. John Goodwin, MA, Vicar of Merton, Oxfordshire, and Editor of World Christian Books.

The Rev. Peter G. Gowing, ThD, PhD, Professor of Christian History and World Religions, Silliman University, Philippines.

Sir Kenneth Grubb, CMG, LLD, formerly President of the Church Missionary Society and Chairman of the Commission of the Churches on International Affairs.

Norman P. Grubb, Director, Worldwide Evangelization Crusade, Fort Washington, Pennsylvania.

The Rev. Canon Gordon M. Guinness, MA, Vicar of Christ Church, Winchester.

The Rev. Paul G. Guinness, BD, Secretary, the Manchester Council of Churches.

The Rev. M. B. Hackett, OSA, PhD, Commissary Provincial of the Augustinian Order.

The Rev. A. J. Haile, MA, formerly Missionary in Botswana.

The Rev. J. Harry Haines, DTh, MTh, Executive Secretary of the United Methodist Committee for Overseas Relief, New York.

Gordon M. Haliburton, MA, PhD, Head of History in the University of Botswana, Lesotho and Swaziland.

The Rev. Carl F. Hallencreutz, DTh, Secretary of the Church of Sweden Mission.

The Rev. H. A. Hamilton, formerly Assistant General Secretary of the World Council of Churches.

The Rev. Canon Raymond J. Hammer, MTh, PhD, Lecturer in Christian Doctrine at The Queen's College, Birmingham.

The Rev. J. T. Hardyman, BA, BD, Missionary in Madagascar.

The Rev. Per Hassing, MA, PhD, Professor of World Christian Missions in the School of Theology of Boston University.

The Rev. Victor E. W. Hayward, MA, Associate General Secretary of the World Council of Churches.

The Rev. Göte Hedenquist, Dr Theol, Director of the *Svenska Israelsmissionen*.

The Rev. I. Hislop, OP, PhD, Provincial of the Dominican Order.

Miss Katharine B. Hockin, BD, EdD, Staff Associate of the Ecumenical Institute of Canada.

Ronan Hoffman, MA, DMiss, formerly Professor of Missiology at The Catholic University of America, Washington, DC.

The Rev. W. Richey Hogg, BD, PhD, Professor of World Christianity at Perkins School of Theology in Southern Methodist University, Dallas, Texas.

The Rev. W. Holsten, DD, Professor of Missions at the University of Mainz.

The Rev. T. E. Floyd Honey, STM, DD, General Secretary of the Canadian Council of Churches.

The Rev. J. F. Hopewell, BD, PhD, Professor of African Religions, Hartford Theological Seminary, Connecticut.

The Rev. Canon F. Houtart, MA, PhD, Secretary General of the International Federation of Institutes for Social and Socio-religious Research, Louvain.

David N. Howell, BPh, BA, General Secretary of the YMCAs of Liberia.

The Rev. G. Basil Jackson, MA, Minister of Hampsthwaite Methodist Church, Yorkshire.

The Rev. R. M. C. Jeffery, AKC, BD, Secretary of the Department of Mission and Unity of the British Council of Churches.

The Rev. A. M. Jones, MA, DLitt, formerly Lecturer in African Music at the School of Oriental and African Studies in the University of London.

The Rev. Francis P. Jones, STM, ThD, formerly Consulting Editor of the Association of Theological Schools in Southeast Asia.

Sister M. Juliana, MM, Maryknoll, New York.

The Rev. J. Herbert Kane, MA, Associate Professor of Missions at Trinity Evangelical Divinity School, Deerfield, Illinois.

J. B. A. Kessler, Jr, BD, ThD, formerly a missionary in Peru of the Evangelical Union of South America.

The Rev. Chung Choon Kim, PhD, Dean of the United Graduate School of Theology, Yonsei University, Seoul.

The Rev. Noel Q. King, MA, PhD, Professor of History and Comparative Religion and Vice-Provost of the University of California, Santa Cruz.

Roland E. Kircher, STB, MS in LS, Librarian and Professor of Bibliography at Wesley Theological Seminary, Washington, DC.

The Rev. Daisuke Kitagawa, STB, DD, late Executive Secretary for Urban and Industrial Mission of the DWME of the World Council of Churches.

Etienne Kruger, Librarian of the Paris Evangelical Missionary Society.

U Kyaw Than, General Secretary of the East Asia Christian Conference, Bangkok.

The Rev. Creighton Lacy, BD, PhD, Professor of World Christianity at Duke University Divinity School, Durham, North Carolina.

The Rev. Canon R. G. P. Lamburn, MA, Priest of the Anglican Diocese of Masasi.

The Rev. Robert O. Latham, MA, BD, Associate Secretary of the Congregational Church in England and Wales.

The Rev. Kenneth Scott Latourette, DD, late Professor of Missions and Oriental History in Yale University.

The Rev. George I. Laurenson, BA, formerly General Superintendent of the Home Mission Department, Methodist Church of New Zealand.

The Rev. John Leake, MA, Assistant Warden of Chilema Lay Training Centre, Malawi.

The Rev. Henry Lefever, BD, PhD, Senior Lecturer in Divinity, University of London Goldsmiths' College.

The Rev. E. Arno Lehmann, Dr Theol, DD, Professor of Missions and Religions in the Martin Luther University, Halle.

Thomas H. Lewis, Colonel of the Salvation Army and Literary Secretary at the International Headquarters, London.

The Rev. Harold Lindsell, AM, PhD, Editor of *Christianity Today*, Washington, DC.

The Rev. Franklin H. Littell, PhD, Dr Theol, Professor at Temple University, Philadelphia.

The Rev. James C. Logan, STB, PhD, Associate Professor of Systematic Theology, Wesley Theological Seminary, Washington, DC.

The Rev. Barnerd M. Luben, MA, DD, formerly Director of RAVEMCCO, New York.

The Rev. Frank Lynch, SJ, PhD, Director, the Institute of Philippine Culture, Ateneo de Manila University.

The Rev. Arthur McCormack, MHM, MA, Aid Director of St. Joseph's College, Mill Hill.

The Rev. Donald A. McGavran, DD, LittD, Dean of the School of World Mission and Institute of Church Growth of Fuller Theological Seminary, Pasadena.

The Rev. R. T. McGlasson, Foreign Missions Secretary, Assemblies of God, Springfield, Missouri.

The Rev. Sylvester McGoldrick, OFM, Franciscan Missionary Union, London.

The Rev. Robert L. McIntire, BD, ThD, Missionary of the United Presbyterian Church in Brazil.

The Rev. Robert C. Mackie, DD, formerly Associate General Secretary of the World Council of Churches.

The Rev. W. S. McPheat, MA, DPhil, Minister of St. Andrew's Presbyterian Church, Brisbane, Australia.

The Rev. Hans Jochen Margull, Dr Theol, Professor of Missiology and Ecumenics in the University of Hamburg.

The Rev. Harold M. Martin, BD, MRE, Promotion Coordinator for the Department of Publication Services, National Council of Churches, New York.

The Rev. Marie-Louise Martin, DD, formerly Reader in Theology at the University of Botswana, Lesotho and Swaziland.

The Rev. Bernard H. Mather, BA, Principal of Bishop Hubback Theological College, Ranchi, Bihar, India.
Charles J. Mellis, Administrative Vice-President, Missionary Aviation Fellowship, Fullerton, California.
The Rev. Donald R. Mitchell, BD, PhD, Montreat, North Carolina.
The Rev. Samuel H. Moffett, ThB, PhD, Dean of the Graduate School, Presbyterian Theological Seminary, Seoul.
The Rev. J. Edward Moseley, MA, LittD, formerly Associate Editor of *Christian Crusader*, of *The Christian Evangelist* and of *World Call.*
The Rev. Heinz Motel, Dr Theol, formerly Secretary of the German branch of the Moravian Mission.
The Rev. Ralph N. Mould, General Secretary, World Council of Christian Education, Geneva.
The Rev. Harold K. Moulton, MA, Deputy Translations Secretary of the British and Foreign Bible Society.
The Rev. H. J. Müller, OSB, Superior, Procure, St. Augustine's Mission House, London.
The Rev. Theodor Müller-Krüger, DD, Secretary for Students of the Germany Missionary Council.
Geoffrey Murray, late Information Officer of DICARWS, World Council of Churches.
The Rev. O. G. Myklebust, DTheol, Professor of Missions in the Free Faculty of Theology, Oslo, and Director of the Egede Institute.
The Rev. Emerito P. Nacpil, PhD, Professor of Theology and Academic Dean, Union Theological Seminary, Philippines.
The Right Rev. Stephen Neill, FBA, DD, Professor of Philosophy and Religious Studies at the University College of Nairobi and formerly Bishop of Tinnevelly.
The Rev. J. Robert Nelson, DTheol, DD, Professor of Systematic Theology in the University of Boston.
The Rev. Wilton M. Nelson, MA, ThD, formerly President of the Seminario Bíblico Latinoamericano, San José, Costa Rica.
The Rev. Albert J. Nevins, MM, LittD, Consulter to the Maryknoll General Council on Social Communications Projects and Editor of *Our Sunday Visitor*, Huntington, Indiana.
The Rev. Esmond W. New, MBE, formerly Secretary of Aborigines and Overseas Missions, Presbyterian Church of Victoria, Australia.
The Right Rev. Lesslie Newbigin, DD, Bishop in Madras, the Church of South India.
Eugene A. Nida, MA, PhD, Executive Secretary of the Translations Department of the American Bible Society, New York.
The Rev. Erik W. Nielsen, Director of the Theological Education Fund, London.
The Rev. Cecil Northcott, MA, PhD, Editorial Secretary of the Lutterworth Press, London.
The Rev. Gerhardus C. Oosthuizen, PhD, ThD, Head of the Depart-

ment of Divinity and Comparative Religion in the University of Durban-Westville.

The Rev. Ronald K. Orchard, BA, BD, General Secretary of the Conference of Missionary Societies in Great Britain and Ireland.

The Rev. Paul R. Orjala, MA, BD, Professor of Missions at Nazarene Theological Seminary, Kansas City.

Miss Elizabeth Palmer, General Secretary of the World YWCA.

The Rev. Robert T. Parsons, BD, PhD, Professor Emeritus, Hartford Theological Seminary, Connecticut.

Robert R. Paton, MA, Senior Reference Librarian, National Library of Australia, Canberra.

Irvin Paul, BD, PhD, Professor at Hartford Theological Seminary, Connecticut.

The Rev. Matti Peltola, ThD, Lecturer in Missiology at the University of Helsinki.

Edmund F. Perry, PhD, Professor of the History and Literature of Religions at Northwestern University, Evanston, Illinois.

The Rev. John H. Piet, PhD, Professor of Bible and Missions, Western Theological Seminary, Holland, Michigan.

A. Douglas Pilcher, General Secretary to the London Council of the North Africa Mission.

Miss A. Louise Pirouet, BA, PhD, Research Fellow in the Department of Religious Studies at Makerere University College, Uganda.

The Rev. John C. Pollock, MA, formerly Rector of Horsington, Somerset.

The Rev. John Poulton, MA, Research and Development Officer, The Archbishops' Council on Evangelism, London.

The Rev. Frank Wilson Price, BD, PhD, formerly Director of the Missionary Research Library, New York.

The Rev. J. Rath, CSSp, formerly Docent of Mission History, Knechtsteden, Germany.

The Rev. Calvin H. Reber, Jr, PhD, DD, Professor of Missions at United Theological Seminary, Dayton, Ohio.

The Right Rev. David B. Reed, DD, Bishop of the Episcopal Church in Colombia.

Mrs. Harriet R. Reynolds, PhD, Associate Professo rof Socia lSciences, Silliman University, Philippines.

The Very Reverend Alan Richardson, DD, Dean of York.

The Rev. Alan C. J. Rogers, MA, Vicar of St. Alphege's, Edmonton, London.

The Rev. V. Rondelez, CICM, Secretary, CICM, Brussels.

The Rev. Horace O. Russell, MA, BD, Deputy President, United Theological College of the West Indies.

The Rev. W. Stanley Rycroft, DD, former Executive Secretary of the Latin America Department of the National Council of Churches, New York.

René A. Ryter, Associate Executive Secretary of the Committee on Agriculture and Rural Life of the National Council of Churches, New York.

The Rev. S. J. Samartha, STM, PhD, formerly Principal of Serampore College, India.

The Rev. Martin Scheel, MD, Director of the German Institute for Medical Missions, Tübingen.

The Rev. S. Paul Schilling, STB, PhD, Visiting Professor of Philosophical Theology at Wesley Theological Seminary, Washington, DC.

The Rev. Herman Schlyter, ThD, Rector of St. Peter's Church, Malmö, Sweden.

The Rev. H. Peter Schneider, MA, Adviser to the Anglican Archbishop in Jerusalem on Jewish-Christian Relations.

The Rev. Artur Schorzmann, Missionary of the Rhenish Missionary Society.

The Rev. Lothar Schreiner, MA, Dr Theol, Lecturer in Missiology, Wuppertal-Barmen.

The Rev. Roland W. Scott, BD, PhD, Professor of World Christianity at Garrett Theological Seminary, Evanston, Illinois.

The Rev. Roberto E. Seel, BA, BD, General Secretary of the Presbytery of Venezuela.

The Rev. Floyd Shacklock, PhD, DD, Acting President of the Pacific School of Religion, Berkeley, California.

Mrs. Blanche W. Shaffer, LicLitt, General Secretary of the Friends World Committee for Consultation.

The Very Rev. R. H. W. Shepherd, DD, DLitt, formerly Principal of Lovedale, South Africa.

The Rev. Ira E. Sherman, formerly Promotion Secretary of the Iglesia Metodista, Florida, Buenos Aires.

The Right Rev. Edmund K. Sherrill, DD, Bishop of Central Brazil.

Miss Margaret Sinclair, MA, formerly Editor of the *International Review of Missions*.

Ruth M. Slade, PhD (Mrs. M. Reardon), Co-Editor of the Catholic ecumenical review *One in Christ*.

William A. Smalley, PhD, United Bible Societies Regional Translations Coordinator, Asia–South Pacific.

The Rev. Donald P. Smith, STM, BD, Personnel Secretary, Commission on Ecumenical Mission and Relations, United Presbyterian Church in the USA, New York.

The Rev. Onell Soto, Vicar of St. Nicholas' Episcopal Church, Quito, Ecuador.

The Rev. Arne Sovik, BTh, PhD, Executive Secretary of the Board of World Missions of the Lutheran Church in America, New York.

The Rev. Joseph J. Spae, CICM, PhD, Director, Oriens Institute for Religious Research, Tokyo.

The Rev. William Stewart, DD, formerly Principal of Serampore College, India.

The Rev. Eugene L. Stockwell, BD, JD, Assistant General Secretary, World Division, Board of Missions of the United Methodist Church, New York.

The Ven. D. F. Stowell, MA, Vicar of Wareside, Hertfordshire and Archdeacon Emeritus of the Seychelles.

The Rev. Theo Sundermeier, Dr Theol, Missionary of the Rhenish Mission at Otjimbingue, South West Africa.

The Rev. Canon Henry Sutton, General Secretary of the South American Missionary Society, London.

The Rev. Lloyd W. Swantz, MA, BD, Adviser to the Dar es Salaam Urban/Industrial Project, Christian Council of Tanzania.

J. L. Swellengrebel, PhD, Staff Member of the Translations Department, Netherlands Bible Society.

The Rev. David M. Taylor, MA, General Secretary of the National Council of Churches in New Zealand.

John B. Taylor, MA, Reader in Islamics, Selly Oak Colleges, Birmingham.

The Rev. Canon John V. Taylor, DD, General Secretary of the Church Missionary Society, London.

The Very Rev. Cornelius P. Tholens, OSB, Abbot of St. Willibrord's Abbey, Doetingen, Holland.

The Rev. Alan C. Thomson, BD, ThD, Executive Director, The Foundation for Theological Education in South East Asia, Singapore.

The Rev. Alan R. Tippett, MA, PhD, Professor of Missionary Anthropology at Fuller Theological Seminary, Pasadena.

John M. Todd, BA, Director of Darton, Longman & Todd, publishers, London.

Herbert W. Torrance, MD, DTM & H, formerly Medical Superintendent of the Scottish Mission Hospital, Tiberias.

The Rev. Theo Tschuy, BD, Secretary for Latin America, Division of Inter-Church Aid, Refugee and World Service, World Council of Churches, Geneva.

The Rev. Harold W. Turner, DD, Lecturer in Phenomenology and History of Religion at the University of Leicester.

The Rev. Georg F. Vicedom, DD, Professor of Missiology and Science of Religions, Neuendettelsau.

The Rev. W. A. Visser't Hooft, Dr Theol, DD, Honorary President and former General Secretary of the World Council of Churches.

A. F. Walls, MA, BLitt, Senior Lecturer in Church History, University of Aberdeen.

The Rev. Canon W. H. Murray Walton, MA, formerly Editor of the *Japan Christian Quarterly*.

The Rev. Peter Wanko, DD, SAM missionary in Africa.

The Rev. Marcus Ward, MA, DD, Professor of New Testament, Richmond College, Surrey.

The Rev. Max Warren, DD, Canon of Westminster, England.

Robin Waterfield, Diocesan Literature Worker in the Anglican Diocese of Iran.

The Rev. Hans Ruedi-Weber, Dr Theol, Associate Director of the Ecumenical Institute, Bossey, Switzerland.

The Rev. Douglas Webster, DD, Canon of St. Paul's Cathedral, London.

The Rev. Kenneth E. Wells, MA, PhD, formerly Director of the Department of Christian Education and Literature for the Church of Christ in Thailand.

The Rev. Lewis L. Wilkins, Jr, Information Secretary of the World Alliance of Reformed Churches, Geneva.

The Rev. John Wilkinson, MA, Dean of Studies at St. George's College, Jerusalem.

The Rev. Bernward H. Willeke, OFM, PhD, Professor of Missiology in the University of Würzburg.

Mrs. Dorothy Clarke Wilson, Author, Playwright and Lecturer, Orono, Maine.

The Rev. Ralph Wiltgen, SVD, DMiss.

The Rev. D. Winkler, DTh, Erlangen, Germany.

Miss Glora M. Wysner, MSSe, PhD, Professor Emeritus of Christian Missions, Garrett Theological Seminary, Evanston, Illinois.

The Rev. Walter Zumbrunnen, Missionary of the Basel Mission in West Africa.

ABBREVIATIONS

AACC	All Africa Conference of Churches
ABCFM	American Board of Commissioners for Foreign Missions
ABFMS	American Baptist Foreign Mission Society
AIM	Africa Inland Mission
BCMS	Bible Churchmen's Missionary Society
BFBS	British and Foreign Bible Society
BM	*Bilan du Monde* (2 vols., Paris, Casterman, 1964)
BMS	Baptist Missionary Society
CARA	Center for Applied Research in the Apostolate (RC: Washington, DC)
CCIA	Commission of the Churches on International Affairs
CEZMS	Church of England Zenana Missionary Society
CICM	Congregation of the Immaculate Heart of Mary (Scheutist Order)
CIM	China Inland Mission
CIPBC	Church of India, Pakistan, Burma and Ceylon
CLS	Christian Literature Society
CMA	Christian and Missionary Alliance
CMJ	The Church's Ministry Among the Jews (Anglican)
CMML	Christian Missions in Many Lands
CMS	Church Missionary Society
CR	Community of the Resurrection (Anglican)
CSC	Holy Cross Fathers
CSI	Church of South India
CSM	Church of Scotland Mission
CSMV	Community of St. Mary the Virgin (Anglican)
CSSp	Holy Ghost Fathers
CSsR	Redemptorist Order
CWME	Commission on World Mission and Evangelism of the World Council of Churches
DAB	*Dictionary of American Biography* (20 vols., London and New York, Oxford University Press, 1928–36)
DICARWS	Division of Inter-Church Aid, Refugee and World Service of the World Council of Churches
DNB	*Dictionary of National Biography* (22 vols., London, Smith & Elder, 1908–09; Supplements, London, Oxford University Press, 1920–)
DRC	Dutch Reformed Church
DRM	Dutch Reformed Mission
EACC	East Asia Christian Conference
EFMA	Evangelical Foreign Missions Association

EKL	*Evangelisches Kirchenlexikon* (4 vols., Göttingen, Vandenhoek & Ruprecht, 1956–61)
ERE	*Hastings' Encyclopaedia of Religion and Ethics* (12 vols., Edinburgh, T. & T. Clark, and New York, Scribner, 1908–21)
EUSA	Evangelical Union of South America
IFMA	Interdenominational Foreign Mission Association of North America
IMC	International Missionary Council
IRM	*International Review of Mission* (Geneva, World Council of Churches, quarterly, 1912–)
IVCF	Inter-Varsity Christian Fellowship
IVF	Inter-Varsity Fellowship of Evangelical Unions
LMS	London Missionary Society
LSPCJ	London Society for the Propagation of Christianity among the Jews
LTK	*Lexikon für Theologie und Kirche* (12 vols., Freiburg, Herder, 1957–65)
LWF	Lutheran World Federation
MEP	Paris Foreign Mission Society (*Société des Missions Etrangères de Paris*)
MHM	Mill Hill Missionaries
MM	Maryknoll Mission
MMS	Methodist Missionary Society
MRL	Missionary Research Library, New York
NAM	North Africa Mission
NCC	National Christian Council
NCC	National Council of Churches
NCE	*New Catholic Encyclopedia* (15 vols., New York, McGraw-Hill, 1967)
NECC	Near East Council of Churches
NT	New Testament
ODCC	*Oxford Dictionary of the Christian Church* (London, Oxford University Press, 1957)
OESA (OSA)	Augustinian Order
OFM	Franciscan Order
OFMCap	Capuchin Order
OMF	Overseas Missionary Fellowship
OMI	Oblates of Mary Immaculate
OP	Dominican Order
OSA (OESA)	Augustinian Order
OSB	Benedictine Order
OT	Old Testament
PECUSA	Protestant Episcopal Church in the United States of America

PEMS	Paris Evangelical Missionary Society (*Société des Missions Evangéliques de Paris*)
RBMU	Regions Beyond Missionary Union
RC	Roman Catholic
RGG	*Die Religion in Geschichte und Gegenwart* (6 vols., Tübingen, J. C. B. Mohr, 1957–62)
SA	Salvation Army
SAGM	South Africa General Mission (Africa Evangelical Fellowship)
SAMS	South American Missionary Society
SCM	Student Christian Movement
SDA	Seventh Day Adventists
SIM	Sudan Interior Mission
SJ	Jesuit Order
SM	Marist Order
SMA	Society of African Missions
SPCK	Society for the Promotion of Christian Knowledge
SPG	Society for the Propagation of the Gospel in Foreign Parts
SSJE	Society of St. John the Evangelist (Anglican)
SSM	Society of the Sacred Mission (Anglican)
SUM	Sudan United Mission
SVD	Society of the Divine Word
SVM	Student Volunteer Movement for Foreign Missions
SVMU	Student Volunteer Missionary Union
TEF	Theological Education Fund
UAR	United Arab Republic
UBS	United Bible Societies
UK	United Kingdom of Great Britain and Northern Ireland
UMCA	Universities' Mission to Central Africa
UN	United Nations
US	United States of America
USA	United States of America
USCL	United Society for Christian Literature
USPG	United Society for the Propagation of the Gospel
WCC	World Council of Churches
WCH, 1968	*World Christian Handbook* (London, Lutterworth Press, and Nashville, Abingdon Press, 1968)
WEC	Worldwide Evangelization Crusade
WF	White Fathers
WKL	*Weltkirchenlexikon* (Stuttgart, Kreuz-Verlag, 1960)
WSCF	World Student Christian Federation
YMCA	Young Men's Christian Association
YWCA	Young Women's Christian Association

An asterisk * indicates that there is an article on the word or subject following it.

PEMS	Paris Evangelical Missionary Society (Société des Missions Évangéliques de Paris)
RBMU	Regions Beyond Missionary Union
RC	Roman Catholic
RGG	Die Religion in Geschichte und Gegenwart (6 vols., Tübingen: J.C.B. Mohr 1957–62)
SA	Salvation Army
SAGM	South Africa General Mission (Africa Evangelical Fellowship)
SAMS	South American Missionary Society
SCM	Student Christian Movement
SDA	Seventh Day Adventists
SIM	Sudan Interior Mission
SJ	Jesuit Order
SM	Marist Order
SMA	Society of African Missions
SPCK	Society for the Promotion of Christian Knowledge
SPG	Society for the Propagation of the Gospel in Foreign Parts
SSJE	Society of St. John the Evangelist (Anglican)
SSM	Society of the Sacred Mission (Anglican)
SUM	Sudan United Mission
SVD	Society of the Divine Word
SVM	Student Volunteer Movement for Foreign Missions
SVMU	Student Volunteer Missionary Union
TEF	Theological Education Fund
UAR	United Arab Republic
UBS	United Bible Societies
UK	United Kingdom of Great Britain and Northern Ireland
UMCA	Universities' Mission to Central Africa
UN	United Nations
US	United States of America
USA	United States of America
USCL	United Society for Christian Literature
USPG	United Society for the Propagation of the Gospel
WCC	World Council of Churches
WCH, 1968	World Christian Handbook (London: Lutterworth Press, and Nashville: Abingdon Press, 1968)
WEC	Worldwide Evangelization Crusade
WF	White Fathers
RAC	Realenzyklopädie (Stuttgart: Kreuz Verlag, 1900)
WSCF	World Student Christian Federation
YMCA	Young Men's Christian Association
YWCA	Young Women's Christian Association

An asterisk * indicates that there is an article on the word or subject following it.

A

ABDUL MASIH (c. 1765–1827), the first Indian clergyman of the Church of England in India, was born in a well-to-do Muslim family in Delhi, and named Sheikh Salih. About 1810 he heard Henry *Martyn preach to beggars in Kanpur, and was deeply impressed by what he heard. Reading the NT, he became convinced of the truth of Christianity and asked Martyn to baptize him. This Martyn would not do, but took him with him to Calcutta and recommended him to the Rev. David Brown, by whom he was baptized on Whitsunday 1811. Daniel Corrie took AM with him to Agra, where he served for eight years as a *catechist of the *CMS, winning great regard from Christians and non-Christians alike for his sincerity and skill in the presentation of Christian truth. In 1820 he was presented to Bishop Middleton of Calcutta for *ordination; but the bishop believed that he was not empowered to ordain anyone of Indian race. AM was therefore ordained by the Lutheran missionaries of the Anglican CMS. Bishop Heber, the second Bishop, had been expressly set free from the limitation adduced by Middleton. Having met AM in Agra, he decided to ordain him according to the Anglican form; this was accordingly done on 30 November 1825, not without aggrieved comment from those who recognized no defect in his Lutheran ordination.

AM was described as a remarkably handsome man, 'with an air of Asiatic dignity tempered by the sweetness of demeanour which was perfectly fascinating'. He died on 4 March 1827, leaving behind the memory of a blameless and devoted minister of the gospel.   STEPHEN NEILL

R. D. Paul: *Chosen Vessels* (Madras 1961), pp. 59–81.

ABEEL, DAVID (1804–1846), MD and clergyman. Born at New Brunswick, NJ, USA, he arrived in Bangkok 30 June 1831, the first American missionary and first appointee of the *ABCFM to Siam (Thailand). In 1830 A. had served as chaplain in Canton under the American Seamen's Friend Society, with the option of becoming an American Board missionary if he wished. He travelled from Singapore with the Rev. Jacob Tomlin of the *LMS. Tomlin and the Rev. Carl F. A. *Gützlaff had, on 23 August 1828, been the first Protestant missionaries to reach Siam. A. and Tomlin arrived in Bangkok to learn that Gützlaff had left for China twelve days earlier, ill, his family dead. The Portuguese consul in Bangkok rented a house to A. and Tomlin. Their missionary efforts were hampered by government disapproval, ill health, shortage of tracts, and lack of language proficiency. On 25 August 1831 A. wrote to his board for more missionaries. Two couples were sent from Boston 11 June 1833. Meanwhile lingering fever induced A. to sail for Singapore with Tomlin 7 January 1832. A. returned to Bangkok alone 19 May 1832 to resume medical work, worship services in his house, and the distribution of tracts to crews of Chinese junks. On 5 November 1832 he left Siam because of ill health. He served as chaplain for some months in Singapore. Still unwell, he sailed for the USA 25 May 1833, not to return.

                                    KENNETH E. WELLS

G. B. McFarland: *Historical Sketch of Protestant Missions in Siam, 1828–1928* (The Bangkok Times, pp.5–11, 1928); G. R. Williamson: *Memoir of the Rev. David Abeel, M.D.* (New York 1848); *DAB* I, 26f.

ABORIGINAL PEOPLES are races which belong to the oldest levels of human life upon the earth. In earlier times they were very widely distributed, but now they are found surviving mostly in small groups in Asia (e.g. the Veddahs in Ceylon), Australia, Africa and America. They are for the most part hunters and food gatherers, and have no knowledge either of agriculture or of cattle raising. They often make use of a wide

1

area for their hunting, and so come into conflict with the settled people (Bushmen); sometimes they live in close association with other races (Pygmies), and in a number of cases have adopted their language. Their religious and magical ideas (e.g. hunting magic) are complex, and often include very ancient features. Because of the wandering life they lead, only in a few cases has any cult of the dead developed. Popular poetry exists in large quantities. The rock paintings both of extinct and of living AP may have had their origin in magical ideas; many of them are of high artistic quality.

Missionary work among AP is very difficult. The main problems are the small numbers involved, the lack of settled dwellings, and in some cases, as with the Kindiga in Tanzania, a strange, unrelated form of speech. The future of the AP will be cared for either by the provision of reserves, where they can carry on their traditional way of life; or by their settlement on the land, and this of course involves the abandonment of their life as hunters. In Ovamboland (S.W. Africa) the Finnish Mission has had great success with the evangelization of the settled Bushmen.

ERNST DAMMANN

W. Schmidt: *Handbuch der vergleichenden Religionsgeschichte* (Münster 1930), '*Lebende Völker als Reste ältester Völker und Kulturen*' in *Historia Mundi* 1 (München 1952); *ERE* I, 33–37.

ABRAHAM, BISHOP (1880–1947). The Most Reverend Abraham Mar Thoma, MA, DD, popularly known as Bishop Abraham, was an outstanding leader of the church in India. Born at Kallooppara in Central Travancore, he committed his life to Christ as his Saviour and Lord at the age of 13. He was ordained to the ministry of the Mar Thoma Syrian Church on 30 April 1911. After undergoing theological training in Wycliffe College, Toronto, 1911–14 and engaging in parish work for a time, he was consecrated bishop in 1917. He served the church as Suffragan to the Metropolitan for 26 years and was Metropolitan of the church 1943–47.

The thirty years of A's episcopate formed a most creative period in the development of the Mar Thoma Church. Under his leadership the church became more missionary minded and more spiritual in its outlook. Through two new organizations which he helped to found—the Voluntary Evangelists' Association and the *Sevika Sanghom* (Women Workers' Guild)—the attention of the church was focused on the witness of the laity. As president of the Evangelistic Association (founded 1888) for over two decades he strengthened the missionary outreach of the church. The Mar Thoma *āshrams* working in different parts of India owe much to him. In the internal life of the church he popularized the idea of supporting the clergy and the work in the parishes by voluntary contributions, instead of by fees charged for baptisms, weddings and funerals, etc. He succeeded in recruiting many educated young men to the service of the church as evangelists and ministers. The bishop's prayer-life, sacrificial living and keenness on evangelism have been a source of inspiration to all who came in touch with him.

A. was a great supporter and organizer of the annual Marāmon Convention. His relations with Christians of many other denominations were exemplary in their openness and charity.

C. E. ABRAHAM

ABSOLUTENESS OF CHRISTIANITY. The 'absoluteness of Christianity' is Jesus Christ. Christianity means the characteristic ways in which Christians have responded individually and collectively to Jesus Christ. The responses have varied from generation to generation and from one group to another, but what has remained fixed throughout is the ultimacy of Jesus Christ for man's understanding of his total experience. The understanding of Jesus Christ has also varied and still does with the changing circumstances and new generations of Christians. The 'shape' of the responses reflects the situation from and within which Christians respond. But Jesus Christ remains the fixed and ultimate source of the

Christians' understanding of new occasions and circumstances of response.

As the fixed source of Christian understanding and response, Jesus Christ is not to be confused or equated with any or all Christian understandings or responses. Having given himself for others, having 'put himself out', in every sense of that expression (Phil.2:7), Jesus became the Christ, the ultimate man, utterly selfless. The selfless man cannot be transcended or confined. Neither existence nor history can contain him. Neither the historical Jesus nor the spiritual Christ, nor the ecclesiastical or the biblical Lord, nor the Catholic or Reformed or Evangelical tradition can fully comprehend him, although each and all of these have re-presented him.

As the man who gave himself, Jesus Christ is the end of man, the fulfilment of humanity. Whether he is the first and only man to put himself out and so fulfil humanity is not a matter of any consequence. If Christians learn that there have been others, they can only be glad. What is a matter of great consequence is that Jesus Christ is this ultimate man and does enable men in divers times and sundry conditions to give themselves. Already all men in their humanity participate in Jesus Christ, since he fulfils their humanity; so too he participates in all men by virtue of their humanity.

Christians experience Jesus Christ as unfailingly sufficient to help men give themselves to others in help. As a result of this experience, proofs for the ultimacy of Jesus Christ are found to be unnecessary for the Christian and are hindrances in the Christian's relations with others. To those outside Christianity it can only be shown that Jesus Christ has been the absolute to which all the varieties of Christianity have been relative, and that Christian understanding of ultimate human living as self-less living is relevant to, if not definitive for, others as well as Christians. As the absolute of Christianity, Jesus Christ is the inevitable subject of a Christian's discussion with Christians and others, but he is not a subject for dispute and debate.

The implication of Jesus Christ as the fixed source of Christianity is not to impose any Christian absolutisms upon either Christians or others. The implication of Selfless Humanity is not to 'lord it over others' even in discussions, but to give oneself in service to the fulfilment of humanity which is Jesus Christ.

EDMUND F. PERRY

ACADEMIES, EVANGELICAL. After the end of the second world war, a number of academies (seventeen in all), were started by the German Protestant churches, as centres in which the church could meet with the world, and in which those who had become alienated from the church could begin again to make contact with it. The best-known EAs are those of Bad Boll in Württemberg, and of Lokkum in the neighbourhood of Hamburg. The EAs served a very useful purpose, in setting up meetings between churches and representatives of a great variety of professions—lawyers, doctors, journalists, artists and so on—in the attempt to express the relevance of the Christian faith to the contemporary world. Some bridges were also built between the churches and political parties and groups which had been traditionally hostile to the church. There are signs that, after 20 years of most useful work, the EAs are beginning to lose something of their vitality.

The academies have been primarily a German phenomenon. Attempts made in other countries to develop similar institutions have not been equally successful, perhaps because the high cost of maintaining such centres, in personnel as well as in other ways, has not been taken sufficiently seriously. The Ecumenical Centre at Mindolo, Kitwe, Zambia, has some of the features of an EA, though the lavish scale on which it was at first planned has had to be considerably reduced.

STEPHEN NEILL

Articles in *RGG*[3]; *EKL*; *WKL*, 21f.: in each case with bibliography.

ACCOMMODATION is the technical term used, especially in RC missionary history, to describe attempts to adapt or assimilate the gospel to local situations, and by omission or suppression of certain Christian customs which might be regarded as offensive to non-Christians, to make the acceptance of the gospel easier for them. The two most famous instances of accommodation are the work of Matthew *Ricci in China and Robert de *Nobili in South India. In each case converts were allowed to retain much from their non-Christian inheritance, in China the worship of ancestors, in India their caste-status, which was regarded as having only social and not religious meaning. It is not clear how far these converts were aware of the real significance of the step that they had taken in becoming Christians. The question of those and other adaptations was long and fiercely debated in Rome; the question was finally settled in 1744 by the bull of Pope Benedict XIV *Omnium sollicitudinum*, in which all but the most trivial concessions to local custom were firmly forbidden.

The term is not generally used today, but the old problem is extensively discussed. How far must the gospel necessarily come to a non-Christian people as foreign? Should it not be presented as the fulfilment of their own highest hopes and expectations? Any translation of the gospel into another language involves a measure of assimilation. In the past many harmless social customs have been condemned by missionaries or rejected by converts, and thus an unnecessary cleavage has been created between Christians and non-Christians. The value of the ancient cultures has been underestimated.

All this is true, and attempts to make the gospel at home in the world of other cultures are to be commended. The difficult question to answer is at what point accommodation passes over into *syncretism and a deformation of the gospel. It seems essential that three points should be constantly borne in mind: 1. It is inevitable that to some extent the gospel should appear 'foreign', since no other religion, not even Judaism, has ever shown any signs of evolving into anything remotely resembling Christianity. 2. The gospel is the interpretation of the mighty acts of God in history, from which

it cannot be detached; it is not a system of timeless truths, which can be accepted without relation to that history in which they are expressed. 3. The relation of the Christian to Jesus Christ, as set forth in the NT, is certainly different from anything to be found in any other religion. Furthermore, cultures and religions are always in process of change. By adapting its message too closely to any existing culture, the church might eventually find itself tied to the past rather than free to listen to what at any given time the Spirit is saying to the churches.

See RICCI, MATTHEW; NOBILI, ROBERT DE.

STEPHEN NEILL

LTK I, 243; *NCE* I, 80f., 120–22; *WKL*, 24f.

ACCULTURATION is a term applied to both a process and a product of culture change. Taken as a *process*, A. refers to what goes on when 'cultures meet'. The metaphor aside (after all, people meet, not cultures), A. in this sense means what happens during contact between one or more followers of one way of life and the followers, or evidences, of another. Taken as *product*, A. refers to any significant, lasting adjustment in a way of life, or culture, made on either side as a result of culture contact. For better understanding of A. in either sense it is important to recall that the phrase 'a culture' may refer to a particular design for living possessed by an individual (culture in the concrete) or to an abstraction based on the life designs found in all or most members of a society (culture in the abstract).

Students of culture contact distinguish a number of distinct A. processes: addition, loss, substitution, *syncretism, invention, and rejection. The processes, occurring alone or in concert, affect primarily (in point of time and logic) culture in the concrete. If common enough, however, they are ultimately registered as end products in both the individual and his culture in the abstract. Where by the adding, dropping, or substituting of culture traits or complexes an individual's culture is modified toward a second culture, the individual is said to be more or less acculturated to that other culture. By the process of syncretism a *third* kind of culture, trait, or complex comes into being, shared by members of the two contacting cultures, but different from what either side had before the meeting.

Few unassailable generalizations have been offered on the subject, but most students would agree that the processes described above depend in kind and extent upon a number of conditions. Chief among them are the following: the degree of difference between the two cultures that are in contact, the circumstances and intensity of contact, the relative prestige enjoyed by the two cultures, the particular representatives, or agents, through whom the cultures meet, and the direction in which the cultural influence is encouraged to flow.

Religious beliefs and attitudes tend especially to resist change, particularly where they embody the group's traditional world view. Hence ready acceptance of new rituals and belief-formulas may signify conformity rather than conversion, a suspicion reinforced by the finding that external A. easily coexists with an unchanged personality.

FRANK LYNCH, SJ

R. L. Beals: 'Acculturation' in A. L. Kroeber, ed.: *Anthropology Today* (Chicago 1953), pp. 621–41; R. L. Beals and H. Hoijer: 'Acculturation and Applied Anthropology' in *An Introduction to Anthropology* (3rd ed., New York 1965), pp. 735–55; M. Mead: *Cultural Patterns and Technical Change* (Paris 1953).

ADAMS, NEWTON (1804–1851), was born in East Bloomfield, New York, USA. He qualified as a medical doctor and practised for two years before being sent to South Africa in 1834 by the *ABCFM. He was a skilful physician, handsome, large-hearted, modest and devoted to his vocation, known as the 'Man of Three Coats' because he was a preacher, builder and doctor. In 1835 Dingaan, the Zulu king, allowed him to build his home and a school at Umlazi. He educated the Zulus at both primary and high school level using their own language as a medium, and encouraged them in mechanical and other arts. He continued the work at his own cost but never considered medical work as his major missionary task. In December 1844 he was ordained in Cape Town at a service in which Dr John *Philip was the moderator and a prominent DRC minister Dr Abram Faure took part. In 1846 he gained his first convert, Mbulasi Makhanya. By 1850 the Board had established twelve stations in Natal. A. concentrated on education and evangelistic work, regularly visiting the people at their kraals, and was famous as a physician. He urged the establishment of boarding schools. He served on the first Natal Land Commission.

GERHARDUS C. OOSTHUIZEN

D. J. Kotzé: *Letters from the American Missionaries* (Cape Town 1950); E. W. Smith: *The Life and Times of Daniel Lindley* (London 1949).

ADAPTATION. See ACCOMMODATION.

ADMINISTRATION. See HOME BASE.

ADRIANI, NICOLAUS (1865–1926), was born in Oud-Loosdrecht, Holland; studied linguistics, subdivision 'Languages and Literatures of the East-Indian Archipelago', 1887–93 at Leyden University and was sent out by the Netherlands Bible Society, as missionary linguist, to Poso, Central Celebes. Here A. lived in intimate social intercourse with the Toradjas, to whom he was to devote the major part of his life and work, studying especially their language, called Bare'e (now Pamona), the most eastern Toradja language. In his Biblical Readers (NT 1903[1], OT 1907[1]) he transposed the stories into the Toradja way of life and story telling. His NT (completed in 1933 by Alb. C. Kruyt and Mrs. Adriani, his two lifelong colleagues, and S. J. Esser, his pupil) shows him thoroughly at home in the language, and a creative stylist in it; exegesis, however, is not his strongest point. His principal books on Bare'e are: a description of that language, its cognates and its (oral) literature (1914); a dictionary (1928), descriptive grammar (1931) and folk tales (1932–33), published by his wife and Esser.

Some of A's leading principles: (1) People cannot make the Bible fully their own, if its linguistic form reflects that of the original, or of a western version; the translator should use, as exclusively and fully as possible, the linguistic and stylistic forms of the receptor language. (2) A missionary's first and continuing task is sympathetically to study the people's central religious, cultural and psychological concepts. Only if he starts from them, in order to go beyond them, will he be able to express the message in an intelligible way. That study requires the use of the vernacular. (3) The personal attitude of the missionary is decisive (the 'one point of contact', *Kraemer would say) in his work. He should be conscious that he has continually to learn, if he wishes to have even a chance to preach. A. not merely taught but lived missionary humility—at a time when western missions were in danger of forgetting it. (4) As to missionary strategy A. advocated concentration on the animistic peoples, whose religion, he felt, would give way before long to one of the world religions; in Indonesia that will be *Islam unless a strong Christian community is already present.

                                    J. L. SWELLENGREBEL

N. Adriani: *Verzamelde Geschriften* (Haarlem 1932), Vols. I–III (with bibliography); 'Work of a Linguistic Missionary', *IRM*, XII 1923, 580–91; 'Some principles of Bible translation', *The Bible Translator* XIV (1963), 9–13; two Bare'e biblical stories, *ibid.*, XII (1961), 9–12; *RGG* I, 100.

ADVENTIST MISSIONS are very widespread, launched chiefly by small churches in America, Canada and England. Adventism, emphasizing the proclamation of the second coming of Christ, has gained a wide following in connection with the Napoleonic wars, the first and second world wars, and the sufferings of the Christians under Communism and Nazism. In the early 19th century, a number of men of eminence in the Church of England, Church of Scotland, and other communions embraced premillenial doctrines, based on expectation of the Lord's imminent return to establish his

kingdom. Some founded separate denominations; others simply emphasized one or more teachings on the signs of the times. Among them were Edward Irving (1792–1834), founder of the Catholic Apostolic Church; Henry Drummond (1786–1860) and Robert Haldane (1764–1843), leaders in missions; Andrew Fuller (1754–1815), first secretary of the BMS (f. 1792) of which William *Carey was the first missionary; William Cunninghame (1776–1849), Lewis Way (1772–1840), and Joseph Wolff (1795–1862), missionaries of the LSPCJ. Adventists have generally devoted great attention to charting the course of church history, from the fall of the primitive church into the 'Roman apostasy', through the conflict with Islam and later anti-Christian movements, to the restitution of the church by an outpouring of the Holy Spirit and restoration of NT ordinances and style of life, followed by the imminent return of Christ in glory.

Characteristic teachings are sabbatarianism, the return of the Jews to the Holy Land, believers' baptism, conscientious objection to war, strict temperance (no alcohol, tobacco, coffee or tea), strict separation of church and state (religious *liberty), lay apostolate, and a very vigorous missionary work around the world. Of several organized denominations, the largest are the SDA (f. 1844 at Exeter, NH, USA).

Of the SDA, the formative leaders were William Miller (1782–1849) and Ellen G. White (1827–1915), both deeply devoted to missions. Ellen White, a prophetess and seer, in 1848 reported her vision of a 'stream of light to encircle the globe'. The SDA in 1968 had approximately 1,500,000 baptized (i.e. adult) members in 15,000 churches around the world. They support over 2,000 foreign missionaries, with 84 sanatoria and hospitals; 265 advanced and secondary schools, and over 40 publishing houses overseas, with work in 928 languages and dialects—228 with publications and 700 orally. In every year they rank at the top or near the top of *per capita* giving among American church members. In line with their strong emphasis on service as medical orderlies rather than bearing arms in the army, and their extensive medical missions, they have developed an accredited and highly regarded medical school in California: Loma Linda University.

FRANKLIN H. LITTELL

L. E. Froom: *The Prophetic Faith of Our Fathers*, III, 449ff., IV, 761ff. (Washington 1946, 1954).

AFFONSO, MVEMBA-NZINGA, king of the Congo (c. 1455–1543), was converted to the Christian faith by the first missionaries in 1491, and in 1506 succeeded to the throne of his father after a victory over his non-Christian brother. Honestly and earnestly A. strove for the christianization of his people; he himself proclaimed the faith, built churches and schools, and sent his own son Henrique with other young men to Lisbon, in order that they might return to serve their people as priests. Henrique returned to Africa as bishop in 1521; the area, however, was put not under his jurisdiction, but that of the European bishop of San Thomé (1534). Henrique died soon after. His father prayed 'by the passion of our Saviour' ever and again for more missionaries; but the white men were eager only for slaves, copper and ivory. When A. expelled some of them from his country, he had to face the terrible experience that even a priest wished to take his life, and made an attack on him during a service held on Easter Day. A. is one of the most tragic figures in the story of the meeting of Christian Europe with the people of other lands; he asked for bread and was given stones.

JOSEF GLAZIK

A. Brasio, ed.: *Monumenta Missionaria Africana, Africa Occidental 1471–1531* (7 vols., Lisbon 1952–56) I, 87–414; II, 39–125; III, 4ff.; J. Cuvelier: *L'ancien Congo d'après les archives romaines 1518–1640* (Brussels 1954); C. P. Groves: *The Planting of Christianity in Africa* Vol. I, pp. 127–30 (London 1948).

AFGHANISTAN. A constitutional monarchy of central Asia, bounded by Iran on the west, USSR on the north and Kashmir and West Pakistan on the east. A. is c.

245,000 sq.m. in area; its population was estimated in 1966 to be 16 million. The country is mainly pastoral, only 20,000 sq.m. being under cultivation. There are no railways and few roads.

Almost all the inhabitants are Muslims and the government and legal systems are much influenced by Muslim law. A. was one of the chief centres of *Buddhism in earlier times, but *Islam became the official religion after the 10th century A.D. There are a few *Sikhs, Hindus and Jews in the larger towns.

No Christian preaching to Muslims is permitted but there are now two congregations of foreign Christians in Kabul, RC and Protestant. The penalty for apostasy from Islam is still likely to be death.

The earliest trace of Christianity in the country is the attendance of the Bishop of Herat at the Council of Seleucia in 424. There was a *Nestorian bishop of Kabul in the 13th century but the Christians were exterminated by Timur in the 14th century.

The *CMS began work in Peshawar on the NW Frontier of India in 1853 at the request of British army officers stationed there. There is no indigenous Christian community in A. A few Afghans have been converted to the Christian faith but none has found it possible to remain in his own country.

HENRY LEFEVER

S. C. Neill: *A History of Christian Missions* (London 1964), p. 461; C. H. Robinson: *History of Christian Missions* (Edinburgh 1915), pp. 274ff.; E. Stock: *History of the Church Missionary Society* (London 1899), Vols. II, III, pp. 209ff.

AFRICA is a continent about 11,500,000 sq.m. in area, extending at its furthest points some 4,600 miles from east to west and 5,000 miles from north to south. In 1969 the estimated population was about 325 million, of whom c. 105 million inhabited North A. and were mostly Muslim; of the population of Tropical and Southern A. (approximately 220 million) about one half were pagan, one quarter Muslim and one quarter Christian.

The early church quickly spread to Egypt

and North A., in the romanized coastal areas rather than the interior. When the military force of *Islam overran North A. late in the 7th century, Christian influence vanished. Only in Ethiopia did Christianity survive; but although continuous until today, the Ethiopian Orthodox Church did not evangelize the African continent. It was from western Christianity that A. south of the Sahara received the gospel. Roman Catholic chaplains at the Portuguese trading posts from the Guinea coast to the Congo reached out to neighbouring peoples from the 16th century on, but with few lasting results. Nor did the Dutch, Danish and British Protestant chaplains have any surer success.

The 18th century Evangelical Revival in Europe provided a new impetus to mission, making the first impact on A. through the freed slaves from North America who brought to Freetown (1791) and Monrovia (1822) the faith that had become theirs across the Atlantic. At about the same time Christianity broke out of the settler bridgehead at the Cape to begin to penetrate the Bantu peoples of Southern A. This movement, following *Livingstone's trail, had by 1890 planted churches across the Limpopo and Zambesi and around Lake Nyasa. Movements from east and west had by the same date brought the church to Lakes Tanganyika and Victoria and along the Congo and its tributaries. Throughout the century the church in West A. had grown steadily, but the geographical penetration of the rain forests was not as rapid as across the open plains of Central and East A.

A significant feature of the Congo Missions was the pioneer men and women who were not members of the denominational missionary societies; these proved to be the beginning of now well-known *interdominational societies. In all these areas the overseas missionary was the spearhead of advance, building the mission houses of West A. and the mission stations of Southern and Central A.; but the person to person evangelism in countless villages was the work of African Christians.

The Protestant missions were the pioneers through most of the 19th century. By the mid-century RC missions were returning with new purpose and vitality; their progress was such that today they well surpass Protestants in numbers. Opportunities, almost unparalleled elsewhere, to provide African communities with the formal education their children were seeking gave Catholics and Protestants alike an opportunity of service and a means of commending the faith. The inherent temptation to sell church membership rather than to offer Christ was not always resisted.

The 20th century has seen important developments. *Independent African churches, often protests against a western-implanted church tradition, have increased in number and size, first in Southern A., more recently in East and West; today they form an important arm of the church's mission. Among overseas missionaries are greater numbers representing a fundamentalist theology, working often in pioneer areas which the churches of Africa had been slow to enter. Among denominational churches 'mission' has given place to 'church', in *autonomous church government and in Africanization of leadership; the resulting period of consolidation is only now beginning to give way to the church's own mission to *unevangelized areas, geographically and in depth.

Today the task is one of mission to people in towns and growing industrial areas, in a countryside disillusioned by its small share in national development, in traditional family life disrupted by population movement, in education now felt to be a responsibility of secular governments. The Christian faith has to be presented alongside the strongly pressed claims of Islam and *secularism, and in terms which unite African thought-forms with modern man's technological experience. There can be no easy optimism as to the success of the church's witness. The eye of faith sees in Africa's spiritual heritage a warm response to the Teacher who said 'God is Spirit and they who worship him must worship in spirit and in truth.'

T. A. BEETHAM

C. P. Groves: *The Planting of Christianity in Africa* (4 vols., London 1948-1958); S. C. Neill: *A History of Christian Missions* (London 1964), pp. 305-317, 368-389, 422-438, etc.; A. F. Walls, ed.: 'Bibliography of the Society for African Church History—I', *Journal of Religion in Africa* I (Leiden 1967).

AFRICA INLAND MISSION, INC. See SCOTT, PETER CAMERON.

AFRICAN INDEPENDENT CHURCH MOVEMENT. Since the beginning of widespread Christian missionary activity in Africa around the year 1800, ecclesiastical schisms and related religious movements have grown in number each decade since the first in 1819, reaching by 1967 a total of over 5,000 distinct movements among 290 different tribes in thirty-three African nations and colonies and also in Madagascar, with an estimated total of 6,900,000 nominal adherents (total community). The annual increase in 1967 was over 100 new bodies, with at least 300,000 new adherents, with seven hitherto uninvolved tribes participating. This vast range of movements has created a mushrooming literature, numbering 1,500 published items in 20 languages by 1966 (see Mitchell and Turner, cited below). Terminology is extremely varied: earlier unfavourable adjectives in use for the movement, such as anti-Christian, syncretistic, nativistic, neo-pagan, sectarian, dissident, magico-religious, etc., are largely giving way to more strictly descriptive terms such as separatist, prophetic, Ethiopian, Zionist, spiritual, etc. In ecumenical circles the accepted term is the AICM (see above), though in fact the vast majority of these bodies do not know of each other's existence and are in no sense a conscious or organized movement.

These 5,000 bodies are spread across the whole of Africa south of the Sahara, but with particularly large concentrations in the Republic of South Africa (3,000), Nigeria (500), Congo-Kinshasa (500), Ghana (200) and Kenya (160). The first noticeable surge of the movement took place in the year of the Berlin Conference for the partitioning of Africa (1885), since when the movement has expanded at a remarkably even rate, involving on average three new tribes each subsequent year. Only about 10% of all bodies formed since the start of the movement are now defunct; most of these have rejoined their parent historical church or mission, have been suppressed, or have otherwise petered out. The average size of a body is only 1,370 adherents, but many are over 50,000 in size, and the largest (Church of Jesus Christ on earth through the prophet Simon Kimbangu, in Congo-Kinshasa) has an estimated 200,000 adult members, or a nominal community of half a million.

Most bodies have separated from historical (mission) churches, Catholic and Protestant, as a result of a range of immediate causes which have striking parallels from one side of the continent to the other. It is generally agreed that the major underlying cause common to all movements is the clash of three cultures (traditional, secular European, and missionary), and the resulting tension and disruption in the life of African tribes. An important factor evident in the majority of cases has been the availability of vernacular translations of the Scriptures, which have served as an independent standard of reference against which missions and missionaries could be judged. Alleged discrepancies between mission practice and biblical liberty (as e.g. over *polygamy) have caused widespread disaffection ending in numerous secessions.

In most cases bodies have attempted to christianize African traditional customs, and this has inevitably led to charges of *syncretism being levelled against them. An ecumenical assessment of their theological character would have to recognize that, although in many respects they fall short of recognized Christian orthodoxy, yet their almost universal claim to confess the historical Jesus as Lord and Saviour establishes them as genuine Christian churches. Many have in fact attempted to join the major ecumenical bodies holding this confession, including the *WCC, *AACC, and the *UBS.

What appears to be happening therefore all over the continent is that the AICM, working quite spontaneously and in the main independently, is engaged in a massive attempt to create a synthesis between the apostolic *kerygma* and authentic African insight, based on biblical insights derived from the vernacular Scriptures. Beyond the tragic spectacle of schism after schism, therefore, one can sense the emergence of a genuinely indigenous renewal of Christianity in terms that can be understood by African societies.

From many points of view the AICM is an unprecedented phenomenon, unique in the entire history of Christian missions: the immense number of schisms and adherents involved (one-fifth of the entire Christian community in Africa), its remarkably uniform spread across one-third of Africa's tribes in the last hundred years, and the paradoxical co-existence for the first time in history of four elements—strong animistic traditional societies, mass movements into the historical churches, formidable missionary assaults on traditional religion and society, and the widespread provision of vernacular Scriptures which were interpreted as vindicating much of the traditional way of life. The AICM can therefore be placed on a level with other great schismatic controversies in history—the encounter of the post-apostolic church with the Gnostic movement in the second century, the Great Schism in A.D. 1054, and the fragmentation of Christendom in Europe during the 16th century Reformation.

DAVID B. BARRETT

D. B. Barrett: *Schism and Renewal in Africa: an Analysis of 6000 Contemporary Religious Movements* (Nairobi 1968); R. C. Mitchell and H. W. Turner: *A Bibliography of Modern African Religious Movements* (Evanston 1966); B. G. M. Sundkler: *Bantu Prophets in South Africa* (2nd ed., London 1961).

AGGREY, J. E. KWEGYIR (1875–1927), was born at Anamabu, Ghana, and after education and service as a teacher in his own country, left in 1898 for the USA, which was to be his home for a quarter of a century. Always an eager student A. continued to read, and long after his ordination and his marriage to Miss Rose Douglas he entered Columbia University, hoping to proceed to the doctorate. A. early became known as an excellent expositor of the Negro point of view, and as a passionate advocate of co-operation between the races at a time at which hostility between the black man and the white was beginning to become an international problem. He was a member of both the Phelps-Stokes Commissions on education in Africa (1920 and 1924). This gave him the opportunity for wide travel in Africa, and also for service with the *WSCF; no other African speaker has ever equalled his effectiveness in handling audiences of European students. When Achimota was founded in 1924 for the higher education of young people of Ghana, it seemed right and natural that he should be appointed as one of the Vice-Principals of the school, and he took up work in October 1924. But the experiment was only in part successful. A. had been too long away from his own country, and his wife never found it possible to settle down in it. In May 1927 he departed for leave in England and America, but died in New York on 30 July of that year, his great promise only in part fulfilled.

STEPHEN NEILL

E. W. Smith: *Aggrey of Africa* (London 1929); *DAB* XXI, 14; *RGG* I, 174.

AGLIPAY y LABAYAN, GREGORIO (1860–1940), was born in Batac, a small town in northern Luzon, Philippines, of poor farm folk of RC faith. He was educated for the priesthood in Vigan and Manila, where he was ordained in December 1889. During the rebellion against Spain the Filipino clergy, A. among them, sympathized with and aided the revolution. In the later campaigns against the Americans, A. both led guerilla expeditions, and accepted office as Vicar General of the insurgent army. In 1899 he was excommunicated for failure to appear before an ecclesiastical court to answer charges of the assumption of episcopal authority. When the Philippine Independent Church was in process of formation, its leader Isabello de los *Reyes proposed in 1902 'as the supreme head of the Filipino Independent Church the most virtuous and greatest patriot, Father Aglipay'. A. rather unwillingly accepted the post, and in 1903, in the absence of any bishop to consecrate him, was consecrated as *Obispo Maximo* by a group of twelve priests. It was always the hope of A. that the Pope would accept the representations of the Filipino patriot clergy and would reorganize the church under Filipino bishops. After the failure of this hope, and the refusal of help by the American Episcopalians, the Old Catholics, and other Christian bodies, de los Reyes and A. led the church closer to a Unitarian position. By 1927, largely through the efforts of Dr John Lathrop and Curtis Reese, formal affiliation with American Unitarians was established leading to mutual co-operation and visitation which continued until the outbreak of the second world war. A. published in 1935 *Tres Discursos Notables*. A more important work is the *Catedra de la Iglesia Filipina Independente* edited by de los Reyes in 1932, which sets forth the views of that church during the lifetime of its founder.

There has been much debate as to the character and qualities of A. To some he appeared only as a self-seeking schismatic; in the eyes of others he could do no wrong. This debate is likely to continue for many years. It is, however, beyond question that he was successful in holding together the PIC, though with some secessions, from 1903 till his death in 1940, and to maintain through that long period the character of a much trusted leader.

See PHILIPPINE INDEPENDENT CHURCH.

SISTER MARY DORITA CLIFFORD, BVM
P. S. de Achútegui, SJ, and M. A. Bernad, SJ: *Religious Revolution in the Philippines* (3 vols., Manila 1960 ff.); L. B. Whittemore: *Struggle for Freedom* (Greenwich, Conn. 1961).

AGRICULTURAL MISSIONS, INC., is

an organization which, since 1930, has served the mission boards and their rural programmes overseas. Stronger relationships are being established with the national churches, Christian councils, and related agencies, as they take over responsibilities and initiative from the former missions. At the present time (1970) the staff consists of an executive secretary and two associate secretaries, one a home economist-nutritionist. All three have had previous experience on the mission fields. The offices are located at 475, Riverside Drive, New York, N.Y. 10027.

Activities. Except for special cases of a pilot nature, AM does not operate projects. It serves essentially in an advisory capacity to missions, churches and related agencies. The major areas covered by these services are: (1) *Training.* Helping to select, train and orient career missionaries and short-term volunteers; conducting an annual seminar for furloughed missionaries and national rural workers (Protestant and Catholic); arranging studies or short courses in the USA or overseas; encouraging leadership training. (2) *Co-ordination.* Promoting co-ordination between Protestant programmes and between diverse faiths and groups, also with governmental, international agencies, foundations, and research-experimental stations; organizing conferences, seminars, and workshops that encourage greater co-ordination and promote joint action. (3) *Programming.* Helping to elaborate programmes, set guide lines, and encourage professional-like approaches. (4) *Surveys, evaluations.* Conducting and participating in surveys and evaluations of projects and programmes. Frequent field trips of staff members help maintain contact and implement these objectives. (5) *Information, data, supplies.* It is impossible to serve as a 'clearing house' on a worldwide basis, and for all aspects of agriculture and rural life. AM helps all it can but advocates the fuller use of specialized and regional agencies of organizations such as FAO, ILO, WHO, Heifer Project, Inc., and foundations, universities, institutes, self-help, etc. (6) *Publications.* Two quarterlies, *Rural Missions* and *Christian Rural Fellowship Bulletin* have an average distribution of 5,000 and 2,500 respectively, about half overseas and half in the USA. (7) *Distribution of Books.* AM does distribute a few books dealing with the rural ministry by such authors as L. H. Bailey, R. A. Felton, D. J. Fleming, E. K. Ziegler, and I. W. Moomaw.

RENÉ RYTER

AIM OF MISSIONS. Difficulty has been experienced in finding any formula, summing up the aim of mission, which will be universally acceptable. 1. The Roman Catholic sees mission as the planting of the church in every country and in every people. To him the church is a clearly defined reality, centred in Rome and under the direction of the pope; this is the home which God has appointed for all the peoples upon earth. Many Protestants have objected to this definition, since to them the connection between gospel and church is much less clear than it is to the RC, and they are not convinced that the structure of the church, as it has developed in the west, will necessarily be found appropriate in other areas. 2. In many Protestant circles, the eschatological note has been strongly heard. The end cannot come until the gospel has been proclaimed to all nations. Therefore the church, by its missionary proclamation is making possible, or hastening, the second coming of Christ. Universal conversion is not necessary. God, through his church, is gathering out his elect people, to be ready in the time of the end. Some, however, have felt that this view is based on uncertain exegesis of NT texts (e.g. 2 Pet.3:12), and does not seem to give the church clear guidance as to what is to be done now. 3. A third group, including William *Carey, has laid chief stress on the kingdom. Christ has a kingdom, and his lordship must be proclaimed to all men who have been redeemed by him. His lordship is the great reality in the world; but that lordship is denied or ignored by the great majority of mankind. The *duty* of the church is clear; results can safely be left in the hands of God.

It is possible that every definition of the aim of mission will be found to fall under one of these three heads—the Church, the Coming, the Kingdom. Perhaps a fully satisfactory definition could be reached only by a combination of all three.

The slogan 'The evangelization of the world in this generation' which had great power over the minds of Christians, especially of students, for fifty years, is a statement not of missionary aim but of missionary strategy or policy. 'Evangelization' was never confused with 'conversion'. Evangelization, the preaching of the gospel, is only the first step. The aim of mission is directed to what follows—the conversion of individuals or groups, and the gathering of the converted into churches, which will themselves in due course become instruments of mission.

In the mid-twentieth century, the slogan which appears to have the best chance of general acceptance is 'the whole church bringing the whole gospel to the whole world'. If each of the three principal words is carefully defined, this may be found to include a statement both of method and of aim.

See THEOLOGY OF MISSION.

STEPHEN NEILL

ALASKA AND ALEUTIAN ISLANDS (586,400 sq.m. in area; population 253,000 in 1967) were sold by Russia to the USA in 1876, and became the 49th state in 1958. Eighteen missionaries of the Church of Russia arrived at Kodiak Is. in 1794 and baptized nearly all the Aleuts. John *Veniaminoff (later Metropolitan of Moscow) arrived at Unalaska in 1824, removed to the mainland at Sitka, and became bishop of the diocese organized in 1840. After his recall the work languished, becoming purely pastoral service to Russian descendants and those of mixed blood. Sheldon *Jackson began Protestant missions as Presbyterian superintendent in 1877. The first Indian to be ordained was Edward Marsden in 1898, who next year initiated the 'Presbyterian navy' with the launch *Marietta*. In 1966 there were sixteen Presbyterian churches. At the request of Jackson, the American Moravian Church began its mission to the Eskimos of Kuskokwin in 1885. In 1965 the baptized community numbered 3,822. The Episcopal Mission was founded at Anvik in 1887, and the Missionary District under Bishop Peter T. Rowe created in 1892. There are a few thousand Eskimo and Indian converts. The Methodist Episcopal mission to whites, Indians and Eskimos began in 1897, and has few indigenous members. Many denominations have followed their members to Alaska. In 1967 the Roman Catholic church membership was 30,319. The Sitka and Alaska diocese of the Russian Orthodox Greek Catholic Church of America, with a very small membership, is administered by the Bishop of Washington. Numerous city churches are racially integrated. Ordinations have been rare.

R. PIERCE BEAVER

H. Stuck: *Ten Thousand Miles with a Dog Sled* (New York 1920); S. H. Young: *Hall Young of Alaska, 'the Mushing Parson'* (New York 1927).

ALGERIA. A republic of N. Africa, bounded on the north by the Mediterranean Sea, on the east by Tunisia and Libya, on the south by the republics of Niger and Mali, on the south-west by Mauritania and Spanish Sahara, and on the west by Morocco. Area: 919,591 sq.m. Population (1966): 12,093,203, of whom the great majority are Arab and Berber Muslims. After 150 years of French rule the country became independent in 1962; since then of 1,000,000 French and Spanish inhabitants all but 100,000 have left; and of 150,000 Jews a large number have migrated to Israel.

Christianity, wiped out by Muslim Arabs in the 7th and 8th centuries, was later reintroduced by French and Spanish settlers. Raymond Lull, the lay *Franciscan, entered A. in 1307, was deported in 1308; he returned in 1316 but was stoned to death at Bougie. Lazarists (French RCs) were at work from 1646 to 1827.

The best known missionary, Archbishop (later Cardinal) *Lavigerie, arrived in 1867. Soon 2,000 orphans came under his care owing to cholera and famine. He provided schools, religious instruction and farming, and arranged marriages. In January 1868 he organized a society called the *White Fathers, and later the White Sisters. Their habits resembled Arab dress and they became known throughout Africa. Emphasis was placed on acquiring indigenous languages, living like the people, and ministering to their needs. The first work began in Kabylia in 1872. The first three White Fathers among the Tuaregs were martyred in 1875. Charles de *Foucauld, former French Trappist, worked among the Tuaregs from 1901 to 1916, when he was murdered.

Protestant work among Europeans was begun in 1830 by the McCall Mission (French) and the *Basel Mission. Later both withdrew. During the late 1880s the *North Africa Mission, Algiers Mission Band (see TROTTER, LILIAS), Plymouth Brethren and French Wesleyans entered A.; during the early 1900s the Roland Mission, SDA, CMML, and Danish Mission to Jews. These were independent European groups with international, interdenominational or non-denominational staffs.

The Methodist church (USA) entered in 1908, accepting responsibility for part of the work under the North Africa Mission. Rapid expansion followed until the depression in USA, when work was curtailed. The most effective work was done through homes for girls and homes for boys. The first Methodist hospital was opened in Kabylia in 1964.

Ecumenical work has proved difficult: in 1940 the Evangelical Mission Council was organized, and in 1964 reorganized as the Association of Protestant Churches and Institutions in Algeria. Two members withdrew, refusing to co-operate with groups related in any way to the *WCC. The Christian Committee for Service to Refugees in Algeria was set up in 1963.

The total RC community numbers 35,000; the total Protestant community in Algeria and Tunisia is 2,300 (WCH 1968).

GLORA M. WYSNER

ALL AFRICA CONFERENCE OF CHURCHES. In view of the very strong feeling of African unity which has followed on the end of the colonial period, it is not surprising that the African churches took to heart the example of East Asia, and took steps to plan for a similar regional organization for Africa.

The first Conference was held at Ibadan, Nigeria, in 1958, following on the Assembly of the *IMC in Ghana earlier in the same year. This appears to have been the first all-Africa conference ever held, the church this time having been ahead of the political powers. Representatives from all African territories were present, except from the small Spanish colonies. One of the difficulties experienced was the lack of a common language; English, French and Portuguese had to be accepted as common languages, and very few African Christians can speak more than one of these. It was decided to go ahead with the formation of the AACC on a permanent basis.

The constituting conference was held in Kampala in 1963. Again the African territories were represented almost without exception. There was a strong sense of fellowship, and it was unanimously agreed that the Conference should come into being, to serve as a focal point for African Christian thinking, and on occasion as the voice of the African churches. The Conference was at first located at the Ecumenical Centre at Mindolo, Kitwe, Zambia; but this was felt to be too far south, and the headquarters were moved to Nairobi, Kenya (P.O. Box 20301).

By no means all the African churches adhere to the Conference. The Roman Catholic church is not officially connected with it, though relationships have greatly improved since the Second *Vatican Council. A large number of the so-called 'Evangelical' churches and missions are suspicious of any body that is in any way related to the *WCC and so hold aloof. It is likely, however, that the influence of the Conference will continue to increase, and that it will serve an increasingly useful purpose in holding together the widely scattered churches of the African continent.

An example of the kind of service that can be rendered was the sending of a delegation to the Sudan in 1967, to discuss with the Prime Minister and other high authorities the problem of the Christian missions in the Southern Sudan. The delegation was well received, partly no doubt because all the members without exception were Africans; discussion was frank and friendly, though no immediate change in the situation was to be observed.

STEPHEN NEILL

AACC Bulletin (Kitwe 1963–1967); *Drumbeats from Kampala: Report of the First Assembly of the All Africa Conference of Churches* (London 1963).

ALLEN, ROLAND (1868–1947), was born in England, studied at Oxford University, and was ordained in the Anglican Church in 1892. In 1895 he was sent to North China by the *SPG. He was invalided out from China and in 1904 took over an English parish church. He resigned from this in 1907 because he refused to be bound as a priest of a state church to administer baptism to the child of anyone in his parish who asked for it. During the first world war he was chaplain to a hospital ship which was wrecked in the North Sea. In the 1920s he co-operated with various groups which were attempting to put new life into the missionary efforts of the churches. He carried out a series of advisory visits to churches in Canada, India, Kenya, Rhodesia and South Africa. In 1931 he went to Kenya; there he ceased from travelling, and there death overtook him.

A. wrote innumerable letters about the work of the church to correspondents in every part of the world and to newspapers. He published many articles. In his books it is possible to see an unfolding of his thought onwards from *Missionary Methods: St. Paul's or Ours* (1912, reissued 1960), through *Pentecost and the World: the Revelation of the Holy Spirit in 'The Acts of the Apostles'* (1917), onwards to *The Spontaneous Expansion of the Church and the Causes which Hinder it*, (1927, reissued 1960), and *The Case for Voluntary Clergy* (1930, a reissue of two earlier works). The key to A's thought is that he was at heart a parish priest in the Anglican tradition with a deep love for the Bible, the sacraments, the creeds, the Prayer Book, and the liturgical year. He perceived and emphasized the work of the Holy Spirit in his community, the church, sending us out to bring all men to Christ, not to make them copy us and our institutions. He asked the church whether priests must be exclusively a professional paid class: he implored her to reconsider evangelization through co-operation with governments and setting up schools: the idea of sending professional missionaries: the use of foreign money. In asking for a return to first principles, he called for a revolution.

NOEL Q. KING

D. M. Paton, ed.: *The Ministry of the Spirit, Selected writings of Roland Allen* (2nd ed., London 1965); D. M. Paton, ed.: *Reform of the Ministry. A Study in the Work of Roland Allen* (London 1968).

AMERICA, CENTRAL. The narrow strip of land, about 1,200 miles in length, which joins the North American and South American continents, and includes the republics of Guatemala, Honduras, El Salvador, Nicaragua, Costa Rica and Panama, the small British colony of British Honduras, and the Canal Zone rented by the USA from the Republic of Panama. Guatemala lays claim, continuously but so far unsuccessfully, to the whole of British Honduras. Tension between the USA and Panama has been eased by recent modifications in the agreements between them. The total land area is 200,000 sq.m., the estimated population (1969) 15 million. The general character of the culture is Spanish; but each of the small republics has a character of its own, to some extent determined by the persistence and the proportion of the Indian element. The prevailing religion is the Roman Catholic form of Christianity. Protestants are estimated (1969) at 600,000, or 4% of the population. The completion of the Panama canal in 1914 added considerably to the political significance of the area.

The Spaniards early became aware of the importance of the region. The diocese of Darien was erected as early as 1513, the fourth see to be set up west of the Atlantic, and the first on the mainland of the American continent. The evangelization of CA proved difficult, since the resistance of many of the Indian tribes to the invaders and to their religion was fanatical and long-lasting. Though the entire population is nominally Christian, over large areas christianization has been very superficial, and some tribes have hardly been touched at all. Relations between *church and state vary considerably in the different regions. In Costa Rica the RC faith is recognized as the religion of the state, though with reasonable liberty for other forms of faith and practice. In Guatemala the revolution of 1870 led to a violent separation of church and state which still continues. Since the 18th century there have been in the area manifestations of the separatist spirit, and of cults which show strange mixtures of Christian and ancient Indian ideas.

The first attempt by Protestants to penetrate the area appears to have been the appointment of D. H. Wheeler by the American Bible Society in 1856 as agent for CA; this pioneer lost his life as a result of his efforts to circulate the Scriptures. The first permanent establishment was that of the Northern Presbyterians, who reached Guatemala City in 1882, to be followed in 1890 by the Central American Mission, and then by Baptists, Friends, Adventists and all the varieties of American Protestantism. British Honduras became an Anglican diocese (in the Province of the West Indies) in 1891. Protestant effort is gravely hindered by its fragmented character. In Costa Rica, headquarters of the *Latin America Mission, pioneer of the Evangelism-in-Depth concept and of the Spanish language school for missionaries, no less than 28 Protestant organizations are listed, though the total number of Protestants is under 40,000 (WCH 1968).

See relevant sections in K. S. Latourette: *History of the Expansion of Christianity*, Vols. III, V and VII, and articles in *NCE* on each of the territories named.

EDITORS

AMERICA, LATIN, is the common name given to 20 Republics situated between Rio Grande and Cape Horn, which shook off Spanish, Portuguese and French rule in the 19th century. Today, in spite of marked geographical and racial differences, the Latin American countries progressively co-ordinate their economic, political and cultural objectives. Three major Indian civilizations existed prior to the arrival of Christopher Columbus in 1492: the Aztecs (Mexico), the Mayas (Central America) and the Incas (Ecuador, Peru, Bolivia). The Indian religious system was based on dualistic concepts: male/female, life/death, light/darkness, heat/cold, health/sickness, etc. A *polytheistic pantheon reflected this dualism (e.g. Peru's creator god Viracocha as against the earth mother Pachamama). 'Good' or 'bad' as ethical concepts were non-existent. This pre-columbian religious structure facilitated acceptance of the Iberian conquerors' religion. To the Indians 'conversion' simply meant the addition of yet another deity into their pantheon. Both Spanish and Portuguese imposed their colonial system with much brutality, often by means of genocide, occasionally tempered by a genuine concern for the welfare and conversion of new subject races. Bartholomew de *Las Casas is a good example of this other spirit. The *Jesuit missions in Paraguay and California were laudable attempts to protect the Indians and to help develop their economy. For the most part however the concentration of land ownership and the ruthless exploitation of natural resources were approved by the church; indeed she was herself one of the large beneficiaries. The continuation of this system even today is the major cause for the present wide and explosive dissatisfaction. The importation of African slaves into Brazil, Cuba and other Caribbean countries added a third racial and religious element to Latin America: West African *animism, *voodoo, chango rites, devil worship, *spiritism, etc. Thus, Indian and African sub-religions existed side by side together with rigid, official post-Tridentine Roman Catholicism. 19th century political indepen-

dence did not touch the social structures (except perhaps in Mexico). It did however introduce liberal currents of thought from abroad (e.g. Positivism), which were eagerly accepted by intellectuals and middle class merchants and manufacturers. After independence Roman Catholicism fell into disorganization and decay. Numerous dioceses became vacant, and pastoral supervision was neglected. During the liberal régimes Protestants won a tenuous foothold. Scottish immigrants (Presbyterians) entered Argentina in 1826, followed by Welsh (Anglican) sheepgrowers. Waldensians from Italy came to Uruguay in 1850. German (Lutheran) farmers settled in southern Brazil, Argentina and Chile after 1850. Anglican chaplains began to minister to British merchants and shipping agents in all major ports. The immigrant, however, did not extend church life beyond his ethnic community. With Allen *Gardiner, a former British sea captain, a new active missionary type came upon the scene. In 1844 he founded the Patagonian (later *South American) Missionary Society, evangelizing among the Indians in Patagonia, the Chaco and southern Chile. During the American-Mexican war (1846–1848) invading American soldiers distributed the Bible. A few years later they were followed by missionaries. Methodist, Baptist and Presbyterian planters, having fled to Brazil after the American Civil War (1861–1865), issued calls for missionaries. By the turn of the century, United States missionaries began to predominate, reflecting the growing political and economic role of their country in Latin America. Since the second world war conservative American missionaries have arrived in large numbers. Several missions have pioneered in education and agriculture. Until the mid-20th century most missionaries and national pastors put the emphasis on individual conversion as against formal, cultural Christianity, liberty as against autocracy, Bible reading as against devotion to saints, the latter being the marks of traditional RC piety. Protestants freely associated with circles of liberal political tendency, often even with Freemasonry. Relations with RCs were strained. These did not hesitate to use social pressure, occasionally open persecution, against Protestants. Up to the end of the 19th century the growth of Protestantism was slow. Subsequent rapid progress, from 50,000 adherents to about 10 million today, has been largely due to Pentecostal advance among the working classes in the new urban agglomerations (Brazil, Chile, Mexico, Guatemala, Haiti). With the breakdown of the old order Roman Catholicism has lost much of its rigidity. The impact of the Second *Vatican Council, the exchange of scholars and missionaries with Europe (especially France and Belgium) and North America, the creation of research centres, such as Centro Belarmino in Chile and the Centre of Inter-Cultural Formation in Cuernavaca, Mexico, the rise of open-minded prelates, an informed laity, are helping to transform the climate. A similar re-orientation is taking place within Protestantism. The social revolution is demonstrating the limitations of the individualistic approach to evangelism, education and social action. Numerous Latin Americans have studied under Karl Barth and other first-class theologians and are steeped in ecumenical literature. In dialogues with RCs and Marxists they have begun to understand the dynamics and the terrible social problems of the 20 Republics. On the basis of this new theological reflection they are formulating new concepts of social action, economic development, church structure and evangelism. Organizations such as ISAL (Church and Society in Latin America), UNELAM (Provisional Committee for Latin American Evangelical Unity) and others are making invaluable contributions to church and social renewal.

THEO TSCHUY

G. Clark: *The Coming Explosion in Latin America* (New York 1963); P. Damboriena, SJ: *El Protestantismo en America Latina* (2 vols., Fribourg/Bogotà 1962); R. C. Moore: *Los Evangélicos en Marcha . . . en América Latina* (Santiago 1959); H. Munoz: 'Visión General del Protestantismo en Latino-américa' in *Anales de la Facultad de Teologia* (Santiago) 11, 1960; E. A. Nida: 'The Indigenous Churches in Latin America' in *Practical Anthropology* (New York) May-June 1961, Vol. 8; W. R. Read *et al.*: *Evangelical Church Growth in Latin America* (Grand Rapids 1969); W. S. Rycroft and M. M. Clemmer: *A Factual Study of Latin America* (New York 1963); W. Scopes, ed.: *The Christian Ministry in Latin America* (Geneva 1962); J. H. Sinclair: *The History of Protestantism in Latin America: A Bibliographical Guide* (Austin, Texas 1968); T. Tschuy, ed.: *Explosives Lateinamerika— Der Protestantismus in der Krise* (Berlin 1969); D. Webster: *Patterns of Part Time Ministry in some Churches in Latin America* (London 1964); ISAL (Church and Society in Latin America) publications: *Encuentro y Desafio* (Report of the first Latin American Consultation on Church and Society, Huampani, Peru, 1961); Magazines: *Christianismo y Sociedad*; *Carta Latinoamericana*; *Fichas de ISAL*.

AMERICA, NORTH. In North America the spread of Christianity among those of European descent, who constituted the large majority of the population, was mostly by the ethnic communions of the settlers and their descendants. In Canada that was the Roman Catholic church, chiefly among the French and Irish, and predominantly the Anglicans, Methodists, and Presbyterians among those whose ancestry was from the British Isles. In the USA until the 19th century the large majority were of Protestant forbears and predominantly from Great Britain and the North of Ireland. Minorities were from Germany, the Netherlands, France, and Sweden. At the time of independence from England, only about five out of 100 were members of churches. In the 19th and 20th centuries the proportion of church members in the population rose fairly steadily, until by the third quarter of the 20th century it was approximately two-thirds of the population. That was partly by immigration of RCs, with the leadership mainly from the Irish and Germans, partly by the immigration of Protestants, mostly Lutheran, from Germany and Scandinavia, and strikingly by the accession of millions from the pre-independence stock, of whom the majority became Baptists, Methodists, or adherents of denominations of indigenous origin, notably the several divisions of the Christians and Disciples of Christ, and the Church of Jesus Christ of Latter Day Saints (Mormons).

In both Canada and the USA extensive missions, RC and Protestant, won a majority of the Indians to a Christian profession. The missions began in colonial days. Many were carried on with marked heroism and devotion. Since the Indians were divided into many tribes and languages, the missions were also fragmented.

Relatively few Negroes were in Canada. In the USA they were far more numerous than the Indians. All originally were slaves. By 1860 practically all those in the north were free. To those in the south emancipation was accomplished in the 1860s, during and after the Civil War. Before the Civil War some Negro denominations arose in the north, chiefly the African Methodist Episcopal Church and the African Methodist Episcopal Zion Church. In the south before emancipation Christianity spread among a minority of the Negroes, partly by the efforts of their white masters and to a less extent by Negro ministers, for the whites feared Negro insurrections and limited both the activity of Negro clergymen and the formation of Negro churches. Most of such Negroes as became Christians were members of white congregations. After emancipation the proportion of Negroes claiming the Christian name rapidly mounted. Most of these joined Negro denominations. That was chiefly because of unwillingness to be dominated by whites. The great majority became Baptists and a substantial minority Methodists. About two-thirds of the Negro Christians were members of the National Baptist Convention and the National Baptist Convention, Incorporated. Since at the outset the overwhelming majority of the Negroes were illiterate, major efforts at education were undertaken, chiefly after the Civil War. Several were by Protestant missionary societies based

in the north. Many were by Negroes themselves.

Much attention has been given in recent years by the churches to the long-neglected problem of civil rights, and the integration of Negroes into the general life of the USA. Less than due credit has been given to the steady process by which previously segregated seminaries, ministers' fraternals, and other organizations, have been progressively opened to Christians of all races. The Episcopal and RC churches, which had had less success than the Protestant bodies in securing the allegiance of Negroes, have recently taken the step of electing and consecrating Negro bishops. But the problem still remains largely unsolved, and courageous action on the part of a number of Christian leaders has not made up for the apathy and prejudice manifested by a great many Christian congregations in the past.

KENNETH SCOTT LATOURETTE

K. S. Latourette: *A History of the Expansion of Christianity*, (7 vols., New York 1937–1945), Vol. IV, pp.175–380, Vol. V, pp.3–45.

AMERICAN BOARD OF COMMISSIONERS FOR FOREIGN MISSIONS.
The first foreign mission board founded in the USA. Organized at Bradford, Mass., on 28 June 1810 by the Massachusetts General Association (Congregational) in response to a petition of four Andover Seminary students who were pledged to missionary service. Predominantly Congregationalist, the ABCFM avoided the term in its name and so served as the foreign missions agency for the Presbyterian and Dutch Reformed churches until they formed their own boards. Barely able to purchase passage and provide a year's support, the ABCFM in a courageous act of faith allowed its first five missionaries to sail for India in February 1812. Soon the spirit of missions stirred mightily in the churches, enabling the Board, with headquarters in Boston, to open work in Ceylon (1816), Tennessee (1817, among the Cherokee Indians), Hawaii (1820), Turkey and the Near East (1820–1821), China (1830) and Africa (1834). Early committed to an

institutional as well as evangelistic approach to missions, the ABCFM rendered outstanding service in the founding of schools and colleges. In 1961, five years after the formation of the *United Church of Christ, the ABCFM merged into the United Church Board for World Ministries.

PETER G. GOWING

F. F. Goodsell: *You Shall Be My Witnesses* (Boston 1959); W. E. Strong: *The Story of the American Board* (Boston 1910).

AMERICAN LEPROSY MISSIONS. See LEPROSY MISSIONS.

AMERICAN SAMOA. See PACIFIC ISLANDS.

AMERICAN UNIVERSITY AT BEIRUT. See NEAR EAST COLLEGE ASSOCIATION.

AMERICAN UNIVERSITY AT CAIRO. See NEAR EAST COLLEGE ASSOCIATION.

AMSTERDAM 1948: See ASSEMBLIES, ECUMENICAL.

ANABAPTISTS. The term was once applied to all groups which separated from the Christendom of the 16th and 17th centuries, usually symbolizing the break by believers' baptism and refusal to communicate in the Catholic and Protestant state churches. Recent research and writing, accompanied by the publication since 1930 of a number of volumes of primary sources, has led to more precise use of the term A. and to sharp distinction between several groups of early Protestant dissenters: Anti-Trinitarians (e.g. Servetus), social revolutionaries (e.g. Müntzer), individualist spiritualizers (e.g. Franck), and *Täufer* ('baptizers', e.g. Grebel, Hutter, Marpeck, Menno Simons).

The *Täufer*, or 'As' proper, were divided after the first years (1523-35) into four wings: Swiss Brethren, South German Brethren, Hutterites, and Dutch Mennonites. The movement took its start in the

2*

Evangelical circle around Ulrich Zwingli in Zürich, and broke from the major reformers in order to accomplish a radical restitution of the early church. In their view and practice the *true* church was disciplined in order and style of life, non-resistant, missionary-minded, lay supported and congregationally governed, based on a covenant sealed by adult baptism, separated from state control and support, and shunning conformity to the world. Repudiating the territorial and parochial pattern of Christendom, both Catholic and Protestant, they considered the whole known world to be missionary territory. The Constantinian Age was dominated by a 'fallen' church: a major plank in their own restitutionist platform was to make the *Great Commission binding upon all baptized Christians. During the period 1523-73 they were savagely persecuted by the state church authorities in every land except Hesse, where Philip the Magnanimous pursued a policy of toleration which won most As in his land to rejoin the established Protestant church.

Following the Martyrs' or Missionary Synod of 1527, A. missionaries travelled throughout Europe and to points as distant as Krakow, Smithfield and Salonica. Up until the destruction of the Hutterite communities in Moravia during the *Jesuit Counter-Reformation the most extensive Protestant 'home missions' of the 16th century were carried on by that wing of Anabaptism. Outstanding missioners (*Sendbote*) included Peter Ridemann (1506-1556) and Peter Walpot (1551-1578), and the missionary letters and memoranda of the Hutterites edited by Lydia Mueller (1938) and Robert Friedmann (1967) are among the most choice materials in the history of modern missions.

With persecution, the Swiss and South Germans and Hutterites were reduced to survival tactics; with toleration, in the Netherlands the Dutch Mennonites accepted *acculturation. Missionary activity receded, to be recovered only in the modern period by the American Mennonites, who claim lineal descent from the As. Anabaptist influence, however, was felt by Martin Bucer and John Calvin, and the restitutionist view of church history—which counted missions a chief mark of the true church—influenced later groups such as Quakers, Baptists, Congregationalists, Moravians and Methodists.

FRANKLIN H. LITTELL

L. Mueller, ed.: *Glaubenszeugnisse oberdeutscher Taufgesinnter*, I (Leipzig 1938); R. Friedmann, ed.: II (Gütersloh 1967); F. H. Littell: *The Origins of Sectarian Protestantism*, chap. 4, 'The Great Commission' (New York 1964); *ERE* I, 406–12; *NCE* I, 459f.

ANCESTOR WORSHIP. At one time (chiefly in the late 19th century) many argued that AW was 'the root of every religion'. They were themselves agnostics who wished to deny the reality of religious experience, and stated that the solidarity of family groups and reverence for the past led to the acceptance of ancestors as gods.

It is the fact that, in certain areas and among certain peoples, those who are now worshipped as gods were probably in origin clan heroes or successful leaders in war. But this quasi-deification of individuals should be distinguished from AW, since here the interest is not so much in the individual as in a whole clan of beings, whose influence on the fortunes of their descendants is believed to be still immense for good or evil.

The cult of ancestors in one form or another is extremely widespread. It appears to exist among the majority of African peoples, though there are important exceptions, and among a great many of the simpler peoples of the Pacific area. But there are wide variations both in belief and practice. In general it can be said that the ancestors are not regarded as gods—in many African languages the words used for the Supreme God or for other celestial beings are quite different from those which are used for the ancestors. Many African scholars object strongly to the term AW, which they regard as western and misconceived. The aim of the reverence paid to the ancestors is the maintenance of the fellowship of the tribe or clan with its own dead, who are conceived to be in some sense living, and with whom, through their appointed rituals, relationship can be established or kept in being. They are the guardians of the traditions of the people. Land is regarded as being owned by the ancestors (just as the Israelites believed that Yahweh was the sole owner of the sacred land of Israel), and therefore can never be inherited as the permanent possession of any individual. Not all the dead become ancestors. Some are too insignificant or too wicked to attain to that dignity. And, if the necessary rituals are neglected, the ancestors may become so much displeased with their descendants as to withdraw their favour entirely from them, or may be so weakened as to be unable to exercise the influence on which the welfare of the tribe depends. Thus for many peoples continuing fellowship with the ancestors is even more important than 'religion' in most of its more generally accepted forms.

The ancient Chinese believed that their ancestors, upon death, continued to exist in heaven and to exert a very definite influence upon human affairs. It was felt that the welfare of family or clan depended on the favour of the ancestral spirits. In both China and Japan the Obon festival (now linked with *Buddhism) speaks of the annual return of the ancestral spirits to their former home—there to join in fellowship with the present 'living'. What returns is the higher spiritual principle (the *Yang*), which has become a divine spirit (Chinese *Shên*, Japanese *Kami*). In the homes the spirits of ancestors are worshipped in the 'house chapel' and the eldest son is the minister of the rites. For this reason, it is the custom for eldest sons to remain (even after marriage) in their family home, and, where there is no son, but daughters in a family, an attempt is made to obtain an *adopted* son—i.e. a son-in-law who is ready to take on the family name and maintain any family cultus.

For the majority AW means little more than a feeling of self-identity with a continuing stream of existence. The fact that (in Japan) wives lose their own family ties, and are regarded as belonging exclusively to the family into which they have married, leads sometimes to the feeling that they have even lost themselves. Those of the *new religions which allow for a continuance of ancestral cults linked with their former families have gained many women adherents.

What should be the attitude of the Christian church to this feeling of intimate connection with the past expressed in AW? The general practice has been to forbid AW in any form as involving *idolatry; in many cases this has simply meant that the old rites continue to be observed, but now in secrecy and with a feeling of guilt. The RC festivals and commemorations of the saints are not felt to fill the gap, since these Christian 'ancestors' are not the ancestors of the tribe or clan. The question is much discussed today whether, through an enlargement of Christian theology, it could be found possible to make provision for some commemoration of those who are so deeply revered by the peoples, but were not themselves Christians.

RAYMOND J. HAMMER AND EDITORS

ANDERSON, JOHN (1805–1855), first Church of Scotland missionary to South India, was born in Galloway, Scotland. Ordained in 1836 after studies at Edinburgh University, he went to Madras in 1837, to take charge of a school recently opened by Scots chaplains under the inspiration of A. *Duff's work in Calcutta. A's first prospectus declared his intention 'to convey through the channel of good education as great an amount of truth as possible . . . especially of Bible truth.' Every branch of knowledge was 'to be made subservient to this desirable end'. The school grew rapidly and is still vigorously alive, as also four 'branch schools' which he opened in neighbouring towns. A. was an ardent evangelist who founded and cared for many congregations in and around Madras, but the distinguishing feature of his work is the emphasis on western-style education as an ally of evangelism. The Madras Christian College was later developed out of his school. Also notable is his insistence, in face of bitter opposition and boycott, on admitting pupils

from the despised outcaste communities. 'Thus,' said one of their recent leaders, 'he lighted a flame of knowledge and aspiration among my people which has gone on burning'.

A. J. BOYD

J. Braidwood: *True Yoke-Fellows in the Mission Field* (London 1862).

ANDERSON, RUFUS (1796–1880), was the most influential American mission statesman, both theoretician and administrator. He was born at Yarmouth, Me., USA, and educated at Bradford Academy, Bowdoin College, and Andover Seminary. Although he had volunteered for India, the *ABCFM had him ordained an evangelist to serve as assistant secretary in 1826. He was foreign secretary from 1832 to his retirement in 1866. A's theoretical writings were published as tracts, excepting *Foreign Missions: Their Relations and Claims* (New York 1869). Larger works are historical, such as *History of the Sandwich Islands Mission* (Boston 1870). Almost every American agency adopted A's aim of missions: the planting of churches which would be self-governing, self-supporting, and self-propagating. Such churches were themselves to engage in foreign missions. His visit to India in 1855 resulted in the dispersion of central stations, organization of village churches, and ordination of native pastors. All institutions were to be aimed at building up the *indigenous church. The famous ABCFM *Outline of Missionary Policy*, 1856, put A's theories into practice.

R. PIERCE BEAVER

R. P. Beaver, ed.: *To Advance the Gospel: Selections from the Writings of Rufus Anderson* (Grand Rapids 1967).

ANDES, VOICE OF THE. See BROADCASTING, CHRISTIAN.

ANDREWS, CHARLES FREER (1871–1940), Anglican missionary in India, was brought up in the Catholic Apostolic or Irvingite Church. He was ordained in the Church of England, and spent some years as Fellow and Chaplain of Pembroke College,

Cambridge. Arriving in India in 1904, he was for some years at St. Stephen's College, Delhi, in conventional missionary work. But a profound conviction of the justice of India's claims for national freedom led him into close friendship with Tagore, Gandhi and other leaders of the national movement, and into crusades on behalf of Indian people, wherever he felt that their rights were being infringed, in places as far apart as South Africa and Fiji. For a number of years A. lived at Santiniketan, the school founded by the Tagore family. He was by far the best known Christian in India, and young people rallied to him with enthusiasm. Some European friends felt that he had gone too far in espousing uncritically every Indian cause, and had thus weakened his Christian witness. But his very personal book *What I Owe to Christ* (1932, reprinted a great many times) reveals a simple Christian piety of a strongly Johannine cast.

STEPHEN NEILL

B. Chaturvedi and M. Sykes: *Charles Freer Andrews* (London 1949).

ANGLICAN MISSIONS. After the Reformation the Church of England remained in two respects what it had been before. It comprised two local provinces, with no claim to any jurisdiction outside the British Isles, and it retained intact the episcopal form of government. Anglicans outside the British Isles, e.g. in Virginia, had no bishop (except in theory the Bishop of London) and an extreme shortage of clergy, but the problems presented by such foreign outposts failed to stir to action the Church of England, preoccupied as it was with its own religious tensions until the start of the 18th century. Anglicans on plantations or in companies abroad had their own private chaplains much as noble families had them in Britain. In 1713 Queen Anne was approached with a scheme for the appointment of four bishops for the American colonies, but the scheme was shelved. There was much discussion but it was not until after the American War of Independence that the first Anglican bishop was consecrated for service outside the British Isles. Dr Samuel

Seabury, after unsuccessful application to the Archbishop of Canterbury, was duly consecrated for the newly-independent American colonies by bishops of the Scottish Episcopal Church in 1784. The Archbishop of Canterbury first consecrated a 'colonial bishop' for Nova Scotia in 1787.

Thus it was over two centuries before Anglicans acknowledged the possibility that their church might extend as a church outside the British Isles, rather than as scattered groups of expatriates with their own chaplains. Unofficially, however, both the chaplains and members of the Church of England itself had desired something more. In order to achieve their vision of the church as an agent of Christian mission to the non-Christian world they formed themselves into voluntary societies, and it was through these and not through the church as such that new Anglican groups began to establish themselves overseas. *SPCK was founded in 1699, *SPG in 1701 and *CMS in 1799. Four years after the foundation of SPG its example had inspired two Danish pastors to begin missionary work in India, and not only was the pastoral ministry in the American colonies strengthened, but mission work was done among Negroes and American Indians. Anglican societies founded in England since 1800 for missionary work overseas include LSPCJ (1809—now Church's Ministry among the Jews), Colonial (now Commonwealth) and Continental Church Society (1823), *SAMS (1844), Melanesian Mission (1849), The Missions to Seamen (1856), *UMCA (1857), Jerusalem and the East Mission (1888), BCMS (1922). Voluntary societies exist in some other parts of the Anglican Communion, but overseas missionary work is normally the responsibility of official church boards outside England, Wales and Ireland.

Anglicans were officially anxious not to make converts from among members of ancient Christian churches with whom they found that their missionaries came in contact. But this policy was not always carried out by missionaries in the field, e.g. the early Anglican mission work in Jerusalem, and in Travancore, both of which provoked strong reactions among their supporters at home.

Anglican freedom from the need to adhere to any single confession of faith is often a source of weakness. Nevertheless the fact that the unity of the Church of England began as a local unity, based on intercommunion between its constituent dioceses, has coloured the whole of Anglican mission work. Anglicans have sought to build not so much a world denomination as a network of local churches, in broad agreement in matters of doctrine, but held together neither by uniform doctrine nor by a single source of jurisdiction, but by their common communion with the Archbishop of Canterbury. There are today 27 independent churches or provinces of the Anglican Communion, though in the developing countries they still require the support in money and manpower of Anglicans in Britain. The Canadian, American, Australian and New Zealand churches have well established missionary organizations and the *younger churches have started to send missionaries beyond their own borders.

JOHN WILKINSON

H. G. G. Herklots: *Frontiers of the Church* (London 1961); S. C. Neill: *A History of Christian Missions* (London 1964); and for a modern outcome of the Anglican thinking, S. Bayne, ed.: *Mutual Responsibility and Interdependence in the Body of Christ* (London 1963).

ANGOLA. Area 471,351 sq.m. Population 5,154,000 (UN est. 1965). More than half of these adhere to traditional religions; RCs number 1,900,000, Protestants 350,000 (WCH 1968).

Christian Penetration. The arrival of the first Roman Catholic missionary party in the Congo in 1491 makes it quite likely that some Christian teaching reached A. in the years that immediately followed. *Jesuits are known to have accompanied an expedition to A. in 1560 with little result in Christian propagation. In 1574 the return of the Jesuits brought better results, for by 1584 the chief of the area professed Christianity and many of his people were baptized. Before the end of the century four monasteries were established—one by the Jesuits and three by other orders, and A. had become an episcopal see.

Summaries of the period of the first RC penetration point out the shallow nature of the propagation and the insecurity of the footholds. The evangelistic work had been hampered by the ecclesiastical monopoly of the Portuguese. The early promise of a strong response from the friendly Africans had proved deceptive. The missionary efforts had been tied too closely to the political aggressions of the period and they were too much a part of the institution of African slavery. Some church circles denounced slavery practices while others owned slaves and slave ships.

Permanent Occupation. It was not until the 17th century that continuous RC efforts were possible in the work of the *Capuchin monks. Jesuits, *Franciscans and Carmelites centred their work in Loanda. One outstanding effort for this period was the erection of the Jesuit College providing education for Africans, Portuguese and persons of mixed parentage. This college not only prepared persons for the priesthood but for the lower levels of the departments of government. Portuguese and African secular priests were responsible for most of the work in the hinterland. The 18th and 19th centuries were times of deterioration of RC missions and by 1865 it was necessary for the office of the *Propaganda to assign the French Order of the *Holy Ghost to serve in A. From this point on missionary service in A. was firmly established.

Principal Missionary Agencies. Jesuits (1560); Franciscans, Capuchins and Carmelites (1640); Holy Ghost Fathers (1865); *Benedictines (1880); *ABCFM (Congregational) (1879); *Methodist (USA) and the Brethren Mission (1884); English *Baptist (1878); United Church of Canada (1886); *SAGM (1914); SDA (1924).

Special Difficulties. The RC church over the years chose not to jeopardize her privileged position by clear-cut denunciations of injustice and of repressive measures such as forced labour. More recently the close ties between the Portuguese state and the RC church have made many priests uneasy.

Protestants worked loyally with government authorities but there were many incidents of injustice which individual missionaries endeavoured to correct in the local communities. Protestants were accused of foreignness, of having a denationalizing influence, and were blamed for giving laymen a significant part in church government.

The churches especially the Protestants were severely affected by the rebellion of 1961 under two nationalist movements that are now in exile. The Christian teachings with regard to human dignity were considered to be one of the causes of the rebellion and thus missions and churches were involved.

ROBERT T. PARSONS

Abundant Life in Changing Africa. Report of the West Central Africa Regional Conference (New York 1946); B. Davidson: *Angola* (London 1961); J. Duffy: *Portuguese Africa* (Cambridge 1959); R. von Gersdorff: *Angola* (Bonn 1960); E. M. Wolfe: *Beyond the Thirst Belt: The Story of the Ovamboland Mission* (London 1935); *BM* II, 71–77; *NCE* I, 540f.; *WKL*, 57f.

ANIMISM is the belief in personalized supernatural power. As such it contrasts with impersonal power (*mana* and related phenomena). Its manifestations range from one God as the only spirit being, through orthodox forms of the great monotheistic religions (including angels, demons, souls of the dead, and other forms of spirits), to innumerable ghosts, ancestor spirits, spirits in natural objects, and other phenomena characteristic of many **primitive'* religions.

These latter forms of A. have given rise to a popular use of the term as a name for the religons of 'primitive' or tribal peoples. Such usage has its value, so long as it remains clear that animism is a nearly universal ingredient in religions, and is not a religious system in itself. Nor is it the only ingredient in the religions called by that name.

Animistic beliefs typically include some of the following classes of spirits: 1. Spirits associated with human beings: **soul, the part of the person which wanders in dreams, spirits of ancestors, malevolent spirits of people who died under unnatural conditions. 2. Spirits associated with non-human natural objects: spirits of unusual geographic formations like waterfalls, rock outcroppings, unusually shaped trees; spirits of dangerous places like curves in a road where many accidents have taken place, or swift rapids in a river; spirits of animals, particularly powerful or dangerous ones; spirits of celestial bodies. 3. Spirits associated with natural forces: spirits of the wind, thunder, or flood. 4. Spirits more associated with social groups than with natural phenomena: gods, **demons, angels, etc.

With the belief in spirits is usually associated a sense of need to communicate with them in the hope of warding off evil, removing calamity, or insuring well-being. In some forms of mysticism, communication with the supernatural becomes a value in itself. **Cults therefore are often associated with individual spirits or classes of spirits. These may be simple **rites performed by any member of the family before a family shrine, the elaborate ritual of a *shaman* who is trained to find out from the offended spirit what he wants in order to be appeased, the 'possession' of a person who can then transmit the spirit's message, or elaborate worship in a cathedral, temple, or mosque.

That Christian missions have had their greatest successes among 'animists' (in the popular sense) is true, but not because they are animists (in the technical sense), for so are people who practise the world religions, and who remain more impervious to the Christian witness. Instead, such success is due to a variety of factors, including the lack of a developed philosophy and ethical system adequate to compete intellectually and emotionally in the modern world. Christianity, furthermore, often brings release from intense fears associated with local spirits through an acceptance of the love and protection of the Spirit who has a compassionate and human face in Jesus.

WILLIAM A. SMALLEY

W. J. Good: *Religion Among the Primitives* (Glencoe, Illinois 1951); W. A. Lessa and

E. Z. Vogt: *Reader in Comparative Religion* (New York 1965); E. A. Nida and W. A. Smalley: *Introducing Animism* (New York 1959); E. B. Tylor: *Primitive Culture* (London 1873).

ANTHROPOLOGY AND MISSIONS. A. is the study of people—culture and society —from both a cross-cultural and a functional point of view. The cross-cultural viewpoint compares and contrasts the cultures of different peoples, making possible legitimate generalizations and questioning assumptions based only on a limited number of well-known cultures. The functional point of view sees life as a whole unit with many inter-related parts which fit together, supporting each other and in tension with each other. It reveals meaning in behaviour which would otherwise seem strange, arbitrary, or point-less.

Traditionally, A. has been concerned with the study of 'primitive' peoples. Missions have most often turned to it in this role, seeking specific information about the *'customs' of a particular group or area. Some missionaries recorded their own study of the people with whom they lived, and made a contribution to anthropological information.

A. offers far more to missions, however, than this alone. As the science of culture, it studies how people within all societies, under all kinds of conditions, develop and learn shared behaviour patterns from each other, and how such patterns provide the often unconscious 'blueprints' by which they live. It studies societies under stress to find out how culture changes and is reintegrated into new patterns. It seeks the functional role of religious practice, how religion is interwoven with other aspects of life, how it supports them and gives them meaning, and how it is supported by them. It studies the differences between the way people think they should live and the way they do live. It searches for the threads of integrating social structure which give life form, and of world-view which give it meaning, as well as for the contradictory pressures and assumptions which threaten this form and this meaning.

It observes the ways in which changes come about, what stimulates or retards them.

In countless ways, then, A. is forming generalizations about human culture, leading to a more refined and complete understanding of what man is. At every turn these insights have relevance for church and mission. The study of man is as basic to a theology of mission as the study of God. With the insights of A. we can learn more of what happens when people change, how a new world view is adopted and modified in the process, how institutions start, grow, stagnate, and die, what the church is in society. These insights have inevitable bearing on how we go about the missionary task, and what we see the nature of it to be.

See ACCULTURATION.

WILLIAM A. SMALLEY

L. J. Luzbetak: *The Church and Cultures* (Techny, Illinois 1963); E. A. Nida: *Customs and Cultures* (New York 1954); W. A. Smalley: 'Anthropological Study and Missionary Scholarship' in *Practical Anthropology* Vol. VII, No. 3 (May-June 1960), pp. 113–23. *Practical Anthropology* (Tarry-town, New York, six times a year) deals regularly with anthropology and mission.

ANTI-CHRISTIAN MOVEMENTS. These have taken many different forms. Some have been based on an antipathy to all change, and foreign teachings promoting change have been suspect. The *'Boxer' Movement in China in 1900 was one such. Some have been inspired by a religious protest against Christianity as a threat to the traditional religion of the country. An illustration of this is to be found in the *Ārya Samāj move-ment in India. Some have been inspired by politico-religious theory which tended to-wards intolerance of minorities, suspecting them, not always unjustly, of being respon-sive to the intrigues of foreign powers. The Turkish attitude to the Armenian Christian minority in the 19th and early 20th centuries is an illustration of this. Atavism, with undertones of nationalism, may provoke the kind of anti-Christian outburst seen in the Mau-Mau movement in Kenya in the

1950s. Other movements have been ideologically inspired in ways as various as the anti-God movement in Russia, the generally hostile anti-religion movement in China, and the periodic anti-Christian movements in Japan. At the end of the 16th and in the first quarter of the 17th centuries there was a deliberate attempt to eliminate Christianity from Japan. And after Japan was compelled to allow foreign trade to enter the country there was another outburst in the 19th century. In the first part of this century there was considerable anti-Christian pressure from upholders of the Imperial cult. But it should be noted that in the case of both Russia and China, the movement was basically hostile to *all* religion. It was anti-Christian in Russia because of the prominent position occupied by the Orthodox Church prior to the revolution in 1917, and the fact that the overwhelming majority of Russians professed the Christian faith. In China Christianity was identified with the foreign political threat to the integrity of China. A subtler type of anti-Christian movement is to be found in areas where a more primitive people have been politically and culturally overwhelmed by a political and cultural order professing the Christian faith. The Peyote cult in North America, the Ras Tafari movement in Jamaica, the *Cargo cults of the Pacific and some of the nativistic-religious movements in Africa are of this type.

MAX WARREN

P. A. Cohen: *China and Christianity: the Missionary Movement and the Growth of Chinese Anti-foreignism 1860–1870* (Harvard 1963); V. Lanternari: *The Religions of the Oppressed—a Study of Messianic Cults* (London 1963); L. S. B. Leakey: *Defeating Mau-Mau* (London 1954).

ANTI-MISSIONARY MOVEMENT, THE, in the USA was a strange alliance of individualistic religionists—Baptists, Quakers, Methodists, Members of the 'Christian Church', Unitarians, and free-thinkers—who championed religious *liberty and rigorous separation of church and state. It was a violent reaction against the numerous missionary societies formed between 1787 and 1830, national societies auxiliary to missions (American Bible Society, American Tract Society, etc.), and the General Union for the Observance of the Christian Sabbath, 1828. Associations were feared as encroaching on the individual's right to worship and believe according to private judgment, and condemned as aiming at the national establishment of a Calvinist Congregationalist-Presbyterian order. Legislation to enforce Sunday observance would lead to further laws infringing liberty. Beginning in New England the movement passed largely to the frontier where Baptists, 'Christians' and Methodists resented the activity of educated, salaried eastern missionaries. Key figures are Elias Smith, John Leland, Theophilus Ransom Gates (who published *The Reformer*), Daniel Parker, Alexander Campbell, and John Taylor. The fear that the societies might lead to a national establishment subsided after 1840, and the movement was then confined to certain Baptists who feared authoritarian denominational organization, and themselves founded the Primitive Baptists.

R. PIERCE BEAVER

I. D. Hudgins: 'Anti-Missionary Controversy among Baptists' in *The Chronicle* XIV (October 1951), pp.147–163. The only adequate study is unpublished—B. C. Lambert: *The Rise of the Anti-Mission Baptists*, University of Chicago PhD Dissertation, 1957.

ANTISEMITISM is a term which is used with the meaning 'anti-Judaism' or 'anti-Jewishness' (though in fact the Semites include other races in addition to the Jews). The roots of A. go back to the enslavement of the Israelites in Egypt; it was increased by the separateness which they felt as the 'chosen people of God' and by their belief that the God whom they worshipped was a totally different being from the gods of the other nations.

The Christian church, from its beginnings to our own time, has never been completely free from A. The Jews were described by the mediaeval church as 'God's murderers';

they were accused of ritual murder and were penalized by laws of church and state. Church councils forced them to wear a special hat and yellow patch and to live in ghettoes, Jewish quarters divided from the Christian population by a wall and a gate closed by night. Jews were excluded from many of the professions, but were allowed some which were considered disgraceful, such as money-lending (since canon law made it difficult for Christians to get loans from one another); this made the Jews still more hated. At the end of the 13th century European nations began to drive the Jews out of their countries: England in 1290, France in 1306, some towns in Germany and Austria in the 14th and 15th centuries, Spain in 1492. The Reformation did not change this situation very much.

At the beginning of the 18th century A. increased in intensity, especially through an extraordinary falsification of the Jewish Talmud, published in 1700 by a German professor, Eisenmenger, under the title *Entdecktes Judentum* ('Judaism Revealed'). From the early 19th century Germany became the chief centre of A.; in 1819 Hundt-Radofsky's *Judensprengel* ('Jewish Mission') suggested that the Jews be killed, or the men castrated and the women transferred to brothels. In 1873 A. flared up after the Franco-Prussian war; in France the Dreyfus case, 1894, provoked E. Zola to write his *J'accuse* (1898), which seemed to open up a new outlook in Europe. But in the 20th century the horrible falsification, *The Protocols of the Elders of Zion*, translated from the Russian into German, English and other languages, and later on Hitler's *Mein Kampf*, whipped up new hatred against the Jews; this culminated in the burning of the synagogues in Germany on 11 November 1939, and in the extermination of 6 million Jews in concentration camps and gas chambers.

In several countries many Christians through the ages stood up against A. and several countries, especially in the 19th and 20th centuries provided a refuge for persecuted Jews, such as Britain, USA, Holland and Sweden. But in some other countries A. prevailed even after the Second World War and the holocaust caused by Hitler.

To understand or explain A. completely is impossible; but probably it results from an inferiority complex that occurs when men are faced by the mysterious people who have triumphantly endured suffering and persecution throughout the centuries. Perhaps their mystery consists precisely in the fact that they were chosen by God to be his witnesses and to proclaim his word to the world. At the first Assembly of the *WCC in Amsterdam, 1948, it was stated that A. 'is sin against God and man'. And in the deliberations of the Assembly it was made clear that 'no Christian can have his relation to God in order, unless his relation to the Jews is right'. The Vatican Council of 1965 took up important parts of the Assembly's declaration and made great efforts to create new relationships with the Jews all over the world. It is being made clear that the only Christian relation to Jews is one of Christian love.

GÖTE HEDENQUIST

W. Sulzbach: *Die Zwei Wurzeln und Formen des Judenhasses* (Stuttgart 1960); K. Thieme: *Judenfeindschaft* (Frankfurt 1963); WCC Amsterdam Report 1948.

APOLO. See KIVEBULAYA.

APOLOGETICS. In theology it is customary to distinguish between *apology* and *apologetics*. Both derive from the Greek verb *apologeomai* which means 'to speak in one's own defence'. An *apology*, in Christian usage, is a speech or writing in defence of the Christian faith against a specific charge or line of attack. Because the church is sent to the world to bear witness to the gospel, it encounters inquiries, misunderstandings, accusations, and attacks to which it must reply in testimony and defence and to secure a fair hearing for its message. Christians must 'always be prepared to make a defence to anyone who calls [them] to account for the hope that is in [them]' (1 Pet.3:15; cf. Mk.13:9–11 and parallels; 2 Cor.7:11; Phil.1:7,16; Acts 22, etc.). Jesus had to defend his deed and word against Jewish misunderstanding (Mk. 2:15–27; 3:20–30; Jn.8:34–59, etc.). Throughout history his followers have had to defend their faith in him. Paul had to defend his 'gospel' against Jews and Gentiles even as he proclaimed it. In the 2nd century there were Christian writers known as *Apologists;* they set forth and defended the truth and status of the Christian faith in relation to the philosophical, religious, and political claims of the times. Since then the Christian faith has never been without apologists against its 'cultured despisers'. *Apologetics,* on the other hand, is concerned with the principles and methods of commending or defending the Christian faith in relation to the wider field of culture in its articulate forms and expressions. No doubt particular misunderstandings or attacks against the Christian faith may arise from the context of a missionary encounter with culture and in answer to these an apology may have to be addressed. Christian apologetics, however, is not concerned with answering a specific charge. Rather, it seeks contact with the truth-claims of a culture in its various forms—scientific and technological, historical and sociological, philosophical and artistic, moral and religious—with a view to clarifying the truth-claims of Christian faith in relation to them, and of drawing out the implications of Christian faith for an understanding of the world and of human existence in it. Dogmatics or systematic theology unfolds, describes, and explains Christian doctrine as such, but apologetics shows the truth and relevance of Christian doctrine in relation to the various spheres of human knowledge. While its appeal is theoretical, its aim is pastoral and ultimately missionary. It addresses itself to honest seekers of truth and seeks to commend the Christian faith to them by expounding it as a rational and adequate system of truth for life, and by removing their doubts and prejudices against it. Thus, it strengthens faith or helps prepare the way for it.

EMERITO P. NACPIL

H. Richard Niebuhr: *Christ and Culture* (New York 1951); A. Richardson: *Christian Apologetics* (New York 1947); P. Tillich: *Systematic Theology* (3 vols., Chicago 1951, 1957, 1963); A. R. Vidler, *et al: Objections to Christian Belief* (London 1963); *NCE* I, 669–77.

APOSTASY (Greek *apo* from, and *stēnai* stand). Abandoning one's faith. Ancient A. took the form of return to Judaism, burning incense to the Roman emperor, or worshipping traditional pagan deities. A. is to be distinguished from heresy. An apostate gives up his faith, whereas a heretic continues to profess faith but adopts an interpretation contrary to the church's teaching. In practice, it has often been difficult to maintain the distinction. Many Gnostic and other ancient heresies led away, by almost imperceptible degrees, into beliefs and practices altogether alien to the NT. Understandably, then, in times of much persecution and harsh counter-measures, the church came to punish heresy and A. with equal severity, often with the extreme penalty. Such penalties were not uncommon throughout the Middle Ages. Today there are instances of A. as people abandon Christian faith for Marxian Communism, revived pagan religions or a naturalistic scepticism. Now, too, the exact designation is often difficult to apply. At what point does veneration of ancestors by a former Confucianist or African animist constitute apostasy? For that matter, when is racism, materialism, or sensual indulgence not the sin of a believer but rather evidence that in place of God false gods have been enthroned? We must distinguish, too, the A. of people under extreme persecution, the lapsing of professed Christians never deeply committed, and the deliberate, cold-blooded decision to forsake Christian profession for social, economic or political advantage.

L. HAROLD DEWOLF

ERE I, 623–25.

APOSTOLATE. The Greek word *apostolē* means simply 'mission', or 'being sent', just as the apostle is the 'messenger', the 'sent one'. In the NT, the word 'apostle' is used frequently, but the sense of it is not always easy to define. Thus Jesus Christ is himself referred to as apostle (Heb.3:1) very appropriately, since in the Fourth Gospel he himself constantly refers to himself as the 'sent one' of the Father. Further, the word is used often, but not exclusively, of the Twelve whom the Lord has called to himself and specifically sent out to be his messengers (as in Rev.21:14). The word is, however, used in a wider sense, e.g. of Barnabas (Acts 14:4), and apparently of the otherwise unknown Andronicus and Junias (Rom. 16:7); in those cases there is reason to think that the word is used in the special sense 'an eyewitness of the Resurrection of Jesus'. The word died out of general use at the end of the NT period, and though bishops have been regarded as 'successors of the apostles', the term apostle has not ordinarily been used of them.

There has been a tendency in recent theology, both Protestant and Roman Catholic, to revive the term *apostolate* in place of the more familiar 'mission', perhaps on the grounds that the term 'mission' has come to be so widely and loosely used as no longer to carry the special sense of the church being sent out into the world which does not know Christ. Thus, in RC circles, it is common to speak of the 'lay apostolate' the term being admirably suited to convey the ideas that the layman has his own special and personal vocation from Christ himself, and that this vocation is to be exercised by bearing effective Christian witness in non-Christian surroundings.

Among modern promoters of the idea of A. may be mentioned J. C. Hoekendijk, of Utrecht, now of Union Theological Seminary, New York. In his thinking the emphasis on A. seems to be associated with his intense dislike of the tendency, evident since 1938, to centralize everything in mission work in the church. The central task of the church is for him the joyful proclamation of the acts of God and the victory of Christ. This is certainly true. It does not alter the fact that there are other aspects of Christian life; when the proclamation of the message has been successful in gathering in

a number of believers, some measure of organization seems to be necessary, if they are to be held together, and some provision must be made for further care and nurture; the church is an inseparable part of the gospel.

STEPHEN NEILL

F. H. Rengstorff in Kittel's *Theological Dictionary of the New Testament*, Vol. I (Eng. Tr. Grand Rapids, Michigan 1964), pp. 398–447.

APPENZELLER, HENRY GERHART (1858–1902). Born in Souderton, Pennsylvania, USA, he graduated at Franklin and Marshall College, Lancaster, Pa., and at Drew Theological Seminary, Madison, NJ. Licensed as a Methodist preacher in 1882, he married Ella J. Dodge in 1884. A. was ordained in the Methodist Episcopal Church, 1885, and appointed to missionary service in *Korea. He and his wife arrived in Chemulpo on Easter Day, 6 April 1885.

The following year in Seoul A. founded Pai Chai School for Boys, which was approved and named by the king of Korea. As first president, and later principal of the theological department, A. erected the first two-storey brick school building in Korea, 1887. He also became first pastor of Chung Dong Methodist Church in Seoul, and built and dedicated a large brick church in the shadow of the royal palaces and the American embassy. A. became editor of the interdenominational *Korea Reporter*, established the first book bindery in Korea, translated Matthew, Mark and 1 and 2 Corinthians into Korean, and became librarian of the newly formed Asia Society, forerunner of the Royal Asiatic Society. He co-operated with the Presbyterians in establishing the Christian Hospital, later to become Severance Hospital, Medical College and Nurses' Training School, and today outstanding as a part of Yonsei University in Seoul. A. sponsored the erection of Independence Arch in the Capitol, commemorating Korea's freedom from imperial China, 1901. He lost his life while saving others after a collision of small steamers off the east coast of Korea. For many years afterwards some of A's children and grand-children continued to serve the church in Korea.

THOBURN T. BRUMBAUGH

ARABIAN PENINSULA, THE, bounded on the north by Iraq and Jordan, includes about 1,000,000 sq.m. Its population is about 7,000,000. In the 4th and 5th centuries there were Christian communities along its borders, but they disappeared completely after the spread of *Islam. Only rare penetration by individual Christians occurred from the 6th to the 18th centuries. Henry *Martyn worked briefly at Muscat in 1811; and Joseph *Wolff in 1836, and Henry A. *Stern in 1856, evangelized the Jews of San'ā'. But only in 1885 was the ongoing Protestant work begun in Aden by Ion *Keith-Falconer under the Free Church of Scotland. His youthful pioneering work, and his enthusiasm to enlist the churches of Scotland in missionary service to the Arabs, were cut short by his sudden death only two years after his first visit to the country, and after only five months of continuous missionary service. But on this beginning was built the Church of Scotland South Arabia Mission in Aden; and the Ion Keith-Falconer hospital in Sheikh Othman, suburb of Aden, carries on the medical work which he insisted would be important. Dr John Cameron Young who worked at the Sheikh Othman for 33 years, is perhaps the best known name among the doctors of the mission. In Aden also the Danish Church Mission in Arabia was begun by the Rev. Oluf Hoyer in 1903. The Scottish and Danish missions have worked closely together from the beginning, but the Scottish mission has centred its work largely in the hospital, and the Danish mission in its girls' school and its bookstore. Both missions have been interested in educational ventures and in medical dispensaries along the coast and in the interior. The Red Sea Mission Team also has a small work in Aden. The Church of Christ in South Arabia was formally established in 1961, a small group of sixteen converts from Islam. It is related to the Near East Council of Churches.

Protestant work in the Gulf was begun by the independent Arabia Mission, in 1889, the result of the efforts of three young men of the Reformed Church in America. Later it came under the responsiblity of the Board of Foreign Missions of the Reformed Church in America. James Cantine and Samuel M. *Zwemer explored the possibilities of the field, and settled first in Basrah, near the head of the Gulf. The mission later spread to Bahrain, then Muscat, then Kuwait. From the first, the emphasis was on medical work and educational work in support of the main task of evangelism. Schools and hospitals were established in each of the main stations. The hospitals in Muscat, Matrah, Bahrain and Kuwait have had long and outstanding histories. The schools have varied from the early school in Muscat for slave boys liberated by British official action and adopted by the mission, to the Basrah boys' boarding school, opened in 1912 and soon attaining important status in its educational contribution to prominent families of the city and of the whole area. From the first, there was determined effort to itinerate far beyond the stations themselves, with successful visitation in the Oman Peninsula and the Trucial Coast and penetration into the uplands of the Jabal Akhdar in Oman. Later came invitations to the doctors to come to central Arabia, and visits to Riadh itself became possible at the invitation of King Ibn Saud. In 1962 the work of Basrah station and southern Iraq was transferred from the Arabian Mission to the United Mission in Iraq. In 1967 the number of missionaries in the Arabian Mission was 54. Major work is carried on in Kuwait, Bahrain, Muscat, and Matrah. National churches in the first three cities are small but significant. In Muscat the church is entirely made up of Muslim converts. The churches are united in a loose fellowship (about 350 members altogether) which seeks to adopt a single discipline and form of government for a united church. They are represented in the Near East Council of Churches. The witness of these small Christian communities and of the Arabian

Mission is of crucial importance in areas that have been totally without Christian witness for centuries. The other significant Christian presence in Arabia is the communities of business and diplomatic people, especially the large settlements in Kuwait, Bahrain, and Dahran, where chaplains are in charge of the church communities of western Christians.

In 1960 at the invitation of the Sheikh of Abu Dhebi, a pioneer work in the interior of Oman at Buraimi was opened up by the Evangelical Alliance Mission. Their work centres in medical clinics and simple teaching.

Continuous RC work dates from 1875 when Mgr Lasserre settled in Aden. He brought there the *Capuchin order, which continues to be responsible for the mission, and a community of French *Franciscan sisters, to whom the British authorities entrusted Galla children rescued from slave ships. The mission has had little success in penetrating the interior of the country. The vicariate apostolic of Arabia was erected, with headquarters at Aden, in 1888, and that of Kuwait in 1954. The former numbers about 10,000 Catholics, the latter 5,000 (WCH 1968); in both the great majority are expatriates.

HARRY G. DORMAN, JR

K. S. Latourette: *A History of the Expansion of Christianity*, Vols. VI and VII (New York 1937–1945); A. D. Mason and F. J. Barny: *History of the Arabian Mission* (New York 1926); J. Robson: *Ion Keith-Falconer of Arabia* (London n.d.); S. Storm: *Whither Arabia?* (London 1938); BM II, 87–90; NCE I, 713–22.

ARCHITECTURE. In what style should Christian buildings be built in a non-Christian land? Missionaries have usually been inclined to build churches in the style familiar to them in their own country, RCs in debased Portuguese, British in imitation 19th century Gothic. There were reasons for this. A Hindu temple is a place where God lives, and is not intended for public worship, though all Hindus may be present at the temple ceremonies. A mosque is built for public worship, but only for men. There are no precedents in local architecture for a building intended for what Christians understand by public worship. Moreover, indigenous Christians for the most part wish their places of worship to look as different as possible from those of other religions. Attempts to use local traditions of architecture are usually the work of well-meaning missionaries who have become interested in questions of art, architecture and music. Under their influence, a number of very beautiful buildings have been erected, such as the Edwardes Memorial Church in Peshawar (Pakistan), the Anglican Church in Shiraz (Iran), the church of the Christukula Ashram, Tirupattur (South India); but such experiments are sometimes made against rather than according to the wishes of the local Christians. Interesting results have been obtained in such areas as the mountains of Taiwan, where the aboriginal Christians, who had never seen a Christian church and for years were left without any missionary, had to devise their own buildings in accordance with their own traditions. As the number of missionaries diminishes, and the younger churches are left more and more on their own, it is likely that genuinely indigenous styles of architecture will develop as the expression of their own understanding of the Christian faith.

STEPHEN NEILL

D. J. Fleming: *Heritage of Beauty* (New York 1937); A. Lehmann: *Die Kunst der jungen Kirchen* (Berlin 1957²).

ARCHIVES. Major depositories of missionary memorabilia and archival materials in North America are the Missionary Research Library, New York, the Day Missions Library at Yale University Divinity School (papers of *Mott, *Latourette, G. S. Eddy, *WSCF and *SVM), the Speer Library at Princeton Theological Seminary (papers of Sheldon *Jackson and R. E. *Speer), and the *YMCA Historical Library, New York. Virtually every mission board and society maintains archives. Some of these are found as follows: Methodist and United Presbyterian at the Interchurch

Center, New York; *ABCFM (now United Church Board for World Ministries) in the Andover-Harvard Library and the Treasure Room (Houghton) of the Harvard College Library; American Baptist at Colgate-Rochester Divinity School and the Headquarters Library at Valley Forge, Pa.; United Christian Missionary Society in the Disciples of Christ Historical Society, Nashville, Tenn., and the Headquarters Library at Indianapolis; and the Southern Baptist at Dargin Carver Library, Nashville, Tenn., and Jenkins Library, Richmond, Va.

There is no central depository for missionary archives in Britain. All the missionary societies, many of which (BMS, *CMS, *LMS, MMS, *USPG, etc.) have their headquarters in London, possess immense collections, not all of which are adequately arranged or catalogued. Much material of missionary interest is to be found in the Public Records Office, Chancery Lane, and in the library of the old India Office, Whitehall. There is a strong desire on the part of the younger nations and churches that documents relating to their past should be returned to their keeping.

In India a start has been made at the United Theological College, Bangalore, with the collection and proper storage of old documents and records. Many missions and churches still show unwillingness to part with their records, and it is to be feared that the ravages of flood, fire and termites will continue to promote the disappearance of irreplaceable material. RC material in considerable quantities has been collected at Kurseong near Darjiling.

In a number of African countries the public Archives have expressed their willingness to house missionary material under the best conditions, and with full rights of access for all accredited students (Rhodesia, Zambia, Tanzania, etc.).

The main centre for Roman Catholic material is naturally the Vatican at Rome. Access to documents is gradually being made possible, and doubtless there are many treasures awaiting discovery. Each RC order and missionary society has its own archives, and information about these must be sought at the headquarters of each. Masses of documents relating to the RC missions in the Spanish and Portuguese dominions are to be found in the public Archives in Madrid and Lisbon; these collections have only in part been sorted and catalogued.

A great deal of valuable material in the form of early diaries and letters is still in private hands. In many cases the owners do not realize the value of that which they possess, and have not recognized it as a duty to place this material where it can be kept safe from harm, and made available for students of missionary history and theology.

EDITORS

ARGENTINA is the second largest country in South America: 1,072,748 sq.m., 21,247,000 inhabitants. It has the highest per capita income, the lowest literacy rate (14%), the highest life expectancy in the continent. Originally inhabited mostly by nomad or little civilized Indian tribes, A. was discovered and settled by Spain in the first half of the 17th century. The emancipation movement broke out in 1810 and national independence was consummated in 1816. During the 19th and early 20th centuries British concerns and commerce played a large part in Argentine economic life. Strong waves of European (mostly Spanish and Italian) immigration entered the country between 1880 and 1914. Social unrest and political crises have characterized the 1950s and 1960s.

The first active missionary work among the Indians was begun by *Franciscans (1539); *Jesuits organized their 'missions' in the north-east (1586, expulsion of the Order in 1767). But only pockets of Indians are left today (300,000) served by Roman Catholic, Anglican, Methodist and Pentecostal missions. The first RC diocese was established in 1570. The time of the emancipation meant a crisis for the RC church because of the close relation of the hierarchy to Spain and of the penetration of the ideas of the French Revolution and Enlightenment and later of Positivism. Nevertheless, the National Constitution (1853), while it declares 'freedom of worship', grants to the RC church a special status pledging financial support of the state. The 'patronage' which reserved to the state the appointment of bishops was modified in 1966, recognizing that this is the right of the Vatican. In 1968 there were 50 dioceses, 12 archbishops and 55 bishops.

Protestant work dates from the 19th century. After the pioneer Baptist agent of the British Bible Society and educationist James *Thomson, who established primary schools and introduced the Bible (1818–1821), Protestant churches were permitted only among English-speaking immigrants: (Presbyterians, Brigham 1823); (Anglicans, Armstrong 1825) and (Methodists, Norris 1839). Only after the government of Rosas, which ended a period of internal conflict and anarchy, the Methodist John F. *Thomson was able to start missionary work in Spanish (1867). Italian Waldensian immigrants entered the country in 1859 and after some years began work in Spanish. Pentecostals, Assemblies of God, Evangelical Alliance and other groups entered A. in the early 20th century.

According to recent figures 93% of the population declares itself Roman Catholic, 2.5% Protestant, 1.8% non-Christian and the rest non-religious. The total Protestant community is estimated at 431,032, with 1,201 congregations and 850 full-time workers (half of them national). The largest Protestant churches are the German Evangelical community and the Baptist (Southern), Pentecostal (Church of God), Plymouth Brethren, Methodist (USA), United Lutheran and Waldensian churches.

Church growth is slow in A., a strongly European and secularized country, (RC statistics fix practice at 10% to 15%; Mass attendance as low as 7% in the cities). Protestants have developed centres of theological training (Union Theological Seminary, Lutheran Seminary, Baptist International Seminary) and journals (Theological Journal, Ekklesia) and one of the two large centres of publication in Latin America. Protestant co-operation finds ex-

pression in the *National Council of Churches, *theological education, the Argentine Bible Society and evangelistic work. Negotiations for union among Waldensians, Disciples of Christ and Methodists have been under way since 1964 (Lutheran and Anglican observers joined in 1966). A vigorous renewal is taking place in the RC church, expressing itself in biblical and liturgical studies, growing lay participation and a marked social concern. Protestant-RC relations are becoming much closer (united meetings of prayer for unity, theological symposia and discussion groups, joint public meetings of ecumenical diffusion and some social projects).

JOSÉ MÍGUEZ BONINO

A. Amato: *La Iglesia en Argentina* (Bogotá 1966); J. M. Davis: *The Evangelical Churches in the River Plate Republics* (New York 1943); T. R. Fillol: *Social Factors in Economic Development, The Argentine Case* (Cambridge, Mass. 1961); J. R. Scobie: *Argentina: a City and a Nation* (New York 1964); J. J. Zuretti: *Historia Eclesiástica Argentina* (Buenos Aires 1945).

ARMENIAN CHURCH. See EASTERN CHURCHES, LESSER OR SEPARATED.

ARNOT, FREDERICK STANLEY (1858–1914), was born in Glasgow, Scotland, the son of a shipper. As a child A. knew David Livingstone and played with his children. He left the Free Church of Scotland and joined the Plymouth Brethren. He wanted to follow in Livingstone's footsteps and became a missionary of the Brethren, sailed for Africa in 1881 and set out alone from Durban with the Zambesi as the goal. A. gained entry into Barotseland where he lived from 1882 to 1884, learned to know the people, language, and country, preached to chief Lewanika and his people, suffering through serious attacks of malaria and dysentery. He advised Lewanika to seek alliance with the Christian chief *Khama of the Ngwato rather than with Lobengula of the Ndebele, thereby influencing the course of African history. A. started work in

Angola in 1884, paving the way for the *American Board missionaries in Bihé district; went to Katanga, chief Msidi's territory, in 1886, whom he warned against signing papers submitted by Europeans. Other Brethren missionaries stabilized the work started by A. After a furlough in Britain in 1888 he opened another new work in north-western Zambia. A pioneer missionary and traveller rather than a pastor or an organizer, he was frequently ill. He died in Johannesburg.

PER HASSING

F. S. Arnot: *Missionary Travels in Central Africa* (London 1914).

ART, INDIGENOUS. The production of Christian A. can no longer be identified with the west, and with one particular culture. Just as in the so-called *younger churches faith in Christ manifests itself as a living reality in the manifold variety of tongues, so it does also in the manifold variety of the activities of painting, drama, music, the dance and architectural forms.

Artistic attainments outside the European world are conditioned by the circumstances of history, by the situation of the churches as minorities, as a *diaspora* (scattered people) and by the non-Christian world by which they are surrounded. The initial successes in the fields of *music, the dance, *architecture, and above all in painting and carving are astonishing and most creditable, both in regard to extent and to artistic capacity.

This A. of the worldwide church, the origin of which can be traced back to the period of the *Nestorian missions, but which has attained to wider expansion only in the last few decades, is inspired by the Bible. The artists wish to express their faith in their A.: they wish to proclaim: 'I paint for God'. Among the most popular subjects are the parables and the life of Jesus; on the RC side artists delight in representing the Madonna and the Holy Child.

This art has enriched artistic tradition in a number of ways. The tempter, for example, is represented in India as a beautiful young woman (the most powerful form of temptation); in the scene of Peter's denial, the shadow of Jesus is visible in the picture; the wise men from the East arrive at the cradle of Jesus travelling by canoe; the flight into Egypt is also carried out by boat: elsewhere, Joseph is carrying on his shoulder a Chinese yoke, and the Holy Child is in one of the two buckets. In the most ancient Indian church, that of the *Thomas Christians, we find the Holy Spirit depicted as a dove over the cross; and in our own time, quite independently, the same theme appears in New Guinea. The really important thing about this A. is that it turns away from western A. forms, and is, and desires to be, consciously Indian, Japanese, African, etc. Painting is carried out with the brush which is natural to this country or to that. Thus, behind the cross African round huts are visible, or an Indian house, or the Japanese way of doing the hair. Only very gradually did the artists overcome their hesitation over representing Jesus really as their fellow-countryman, truly as a Chinese, or as an African. Thus artistic activity is an attempt to 'translate' the sacred history. Precisely there lies its value—and its limitations. Here the line from the Incarnation is prolonged to its utmost point. We may think of the words of Luther's Christmas hymn—'the everlasting Good is disguised in *our* poor flesh and blood'.

Should it any longer be possible for Bibles to appear in Asia and Africa with western pictures? Hundreds of Protestant artists are today at work, in part in schools of A. and painting. The RC church, however, is far ahead of the other churches, both historically and in productivity; it promotes this indigenous A. by means of great exhibitions, and through commissions to artists. The Protestant churches have much to learn—in interest, in generosity, and in the commissioning of works of A.

ARNO LEHMANN

S. Costantini: *L'art chrétien dans les missions* (Paris 1949); D. J. Fleming: *Each with his own Brush* (New York 1935); E. A. Lehmann: *Die Kunst der Jungen Kirchen* (Berlin 1957²), *Afroasiatische Christliche Kunst* (with bibliography: Berlin 1966; Konstanz 1967; Eng. tr. London; St. Louis, Mo. 1969).

ARTHINGTON, ROBERT (1823–1900), was born in a well-to-do Quaker family in the north of England and studied at Cambridge. In about 1850 A. became deeply interested in Christian missions, and for 50 years the rapid propagation of the gospel among all the peoples of the world became his major interest, indeed the passion of his life. Although a wealthy man A. lived like the poorest of the poor, with the consequence that, although he had given generously to many Christian causes, his wealth was increasing all the time and far beyond his knowledge. A. had a strong prejudice against the institutionalization of missionary work; the primary task is proclamation—as soon as a small Christian fellowship has been gathered in one tribe, the missionaries should press on to the regions as yet unreached. A's one attempt to found and direct his own mission—the Arthington Aborigines Mission, for work among the unreached tribes in the north-east of India —was not successful, and the work soon passed to other hands. But the constant pressure of his ideas, expressed through an immense correspondence, understandably kept awake the idea of Christian witness 'on the frontiers', in a period during which there was a danger of the stagnation of the missionary enterprise within the frontiers of its own successes. When A. died, his fortune amounted to £943,130, and of this sum one half passed to the BMS, and two-fifths to the LMS. By the time that the distribution of this amount became possible, the capital had increased to £1,173,845, of which almost a million was available for missionary enterprises. Those responsible for the distribution bore in mind as far as possible A's principles, and tried to use the money for new work and new movements on the frontiers of the Christian mission. Though much of the money did go to hospitals and other institutions, no endowments were created, and such pieces of work were supported as were likely to be self-supporting at the time at which distribution was to cease. In 1936 the Trust was brought to an end. In 25 years the entire Protestant missionary enterprise had felt, directly or indirectly, the stimulus of 'Arthington's million', and the record of his generosity is written in lands as far apart as the Congo and the aboriginal areas of south-west China.

STEPHEN NEILL

A. M. Chirgwin: *Arthington's Million; the Romance of the Arthington Trust* (London n.d.).

ĀRYA SAMĀJ. A Hindu reforming religious society, founded by Dayānand Sarasvati (1824–1883) in 1875. The watchword of Dayānand was 'back to the Vedas'; he wished to cleanse Hinduism of everything which in terms of his own rather wilful interpretation did not belong to the pure Vedic tradition. Unlike most Hindu reformers, D. had a deep detestation of the Christian faith, and no respect or regard for Jesus Christ. In his principal work *The Light of Truth* (Eng. trans. 1946), he makes bitter attacks on the person and the understanding of Jesus; echoes of these attacks are still found in anti-Christian polemical works in India. One of the main purposes of the AS was to oppose Christian missionary work, and where possible to recover for the Hindu fold some of those who had been converted. In some areas considerable success has attended on these endeavours; where conversion of depressed class people has been hasty and superficial, and the inducements offered by Hindus for a return to Hinduism have been considerable, a number of converts have renounced their new faith and returned to the old. These efforts at reconversion still continue. STEPHEN NEILL

J. N. Farquhar: *Modern Religious Movements in India* (New York 1929[2]); O. Wolff: *Christus unter den Hindus* (Gütersloh 1965), pp. 106–125; *ERE* II, 57–62.

ASBURY, FRANCIS (1745–1816), was born near Birmingham, England, in an Anglican family. At twelve he left school and became an apprentice tradesman, but found fulfilment in his late teens as a travelling Methodist preacher. Under John *Wesley, he volunteered for America and landed there in 1771, believing that God was leading him in a special mission, that the American situation required itinerant, self-educated ministers, and that a man with an authority like Wesley's was needed to direct them. Of those Wesley had sent to America, only A. remained during the Revolution. He read the Bible in Greek and Hebrew, studied prodigiously, quietly recruited preachers, and by 1779 was American Methodism's acknowledged leader. Wesley appointed him in 1784 to be General Superintendent; but sensitive to realities, he accepted the post only after the American preachers had elected him. A devoted and paternal autocrat, he soon called himself 'bishop'. A. viewed American Methodism as a mission to a new land, remained purposely unmarried to fulfil this vast endeavour, and expected the same of the preachers whom he called 'missionaries'. Never robust, his saddle his only home, he travelled ceaselessly from Canada to Georgia, from the Atlantic coast to Kentucky, preaching, founding churches, creating new conferences. He was the chief figure in shaping American Methodism, and acknowledged before his death the need for missions to Indians and others; but he had given himself to one task—the mission among those who advanced the frontier.

W. RICHEY HOGG

E. T. Clark, ed.: *The Journal and Letters of Francis Asbury*, (3 vols., London and Nashville 1958); L. C. Rudolph: *Francis Asbury* (Nashville 1966); *DAB* I, 379–83; *DNB* II, 149.

ĀSHRAMS. In ancient *Hinduism these were forest dwellings where spiritual leaders or *gurus* lived a simple life of contemplation, discipline and instruction to disciples. Contemplation was based on the essential identity of the inner man (*ātman*) with that of the universe (*brahman*). Discipline was often rigorous, both mental and physical, and could follow the system of yoga. Instruction to disciples (*shishyar*) was as much through community life in the 'family of the *guru*' (*gurukula*) as by explicit teaching. The As made a significant contribution to the culture, religion and education of ancient India.

In modern times both Hindus and Christians have sought to recover the A. ideal and to adapt it to new conditions. Important Hindu examples are Santiniketan near Banaras, founded by the poet Tagore, the Pondicherry A. founded by Sri Aurobindo and numerous centres associated with the *Ramakrishna Mission. An outstanding Christian example is the Kristukula A. at Tirupattur in S. India where social, medical and evangelistic work is carried on by an inter-racial community. Other noted Christian examples include those connected with the *Mar Thoma and Jacobite Syrian churches in Kerala and that at Kodaikanal near Mathurai.

HENRY LEFEVER

P. Chenchiah: *Ashrams Past and Present* (Madras 1938); P. O. Philip: 'The Place of Ashrams in the Life of the Church in India' in *IRM* XXXV (1946), pp.265ff.; *WKL*, 95f.

ASIA CHRISTIAN COLLEGES ASSOCIATION, THE (1952), began in 1930 as the United Committee for Christian Universities of China, later known as the China Christian Universities Association, for the aid of the seven British-linked Christian colleges of that country. After the expropriation of those colleges attention was directed to the Chinese of Hong Kong and Malaya. Then in 1952 the CCUA in association with the Asia Committee of the *Conference of Missionary Societies, the Friends of *Vellore, the Ludhiana British Fellowship, and the Advisory Council for Christian Colleges in India, Pakistan and Ceylon formed the ACCA. Its objectives are to support the colleges 'through prayer, personnel, publicity, and financial support, and to co-ordinate the efforts of' the several agencies. Aid is given to 34 colleges in India, five in Pakistan, two in Taiwan, and one each in Singapore, Hong Kong, and Japan. The institutions concerned include arts and science colleges, agricultural institutes, medical schools, and theological colleges. Assistance is given to hostels and student centres in Bombay and Singapore.

Eleven missionary societies co-operate in the Association. Receipts and expenditures for the year 1965–1966 were £14,164. Periodical: *The ACCA Bulletin*. Headquarters: Annandale, North End Road, London, N.W.11.

R. PIERCE BEAVER

ASSEMBLIES, ECUMENICAL. The integration of the *IMC with the *WCC was effected only in 1961; but from the beginning the missionary movement had been regarded as an essential part of the *ecumenical movement. This brief article deals only with the missionary aspects of the four Assemblies of the WCC, which have so far taken place.

1. *Amsterdam*, 22 August to 4 September 1948. The Assembly and its programme were alike overwhelmingly western. The definition of an *'autonomous church' adopted by the Provisional Committee was such as to exclude a number of large churches in the lands of the *younger churches, especially in Africa; though the situation was improved, when it was agreed that large sending churches might give some of their places to 'minority churches' which had come into being as a result of their missionary work. Section II of the Assembly dealt with the theme 'The Church's Witness to God's Design'. The preparatory volume on this theme contained a great deal of valuable material; but the Section itself lacked direction and cohesion. It did not take as a basis for its studies the clear statements of the *Whitby Missionary Conference of 1947. The interests were too varied, and the definition of the theme too vague. Some members would have preferred not to use the word evangelism at all. The Orthodox were concerned only about the prevention of proselytism. Although the Report of the Section was rewritten three times, it can hardly be regarded as a memorable document. It did, however, contain one sentence which has left an impression on subsequent ecumenical thinking: 'The evident demand of God in this situation is that the whole Church should set itself to the total task of winning the world for Christ'. The existence of the younger churches was recognized in the choice of Dr T. C. Chao of China to be one of the six presidents of the WCC.

2. *Evanston*, 15–31 August 1954. At the second Assembly the representation of the younger churches had somewhat improved, but the millions of Christians in Africa were very weakly represented. The Assembly met under the frustration that the committee charged with preparing a document on the central theme, 'Christ the Hope of the World', had failed to produce a clear and unified statement as to the nature and content of the Christian hope. Section II was appointed to consider the theme: 'Evangelism: the Mission of the Church to those outside her life'. It had been hoped that the Report would go far beyond that of Amsterdam in presenting to the churches a clear understanding of what is meant by evangelism, and a ringing challenge to engage in it. But in fact this Report said very little that had not already been said at Amsterdam, except that it went a little more into detail at certain points. As one member remarked, it was not a report that would send people out as 'flaming evangelists'. It was decided to set up a Department of Missionary Studies to work closely with the Division of Studies of the IMC. Thirteen representatives of the younger churches were appointed to the Central Committee, and the Methodist Bishop Sante Barbieri of Buenos Aires was elected as president.

3. *New Delhi*, 19 November–5 December 1961. At this third Assembly the notable event was the integration of the IMC with the WCC. This had been carefully prepared for over a number of years, many difficulties had been eliminated; and when the proposal for integration was made, it passed so easily that few of those present realized the significance of what was happening. But, in point of fact, this decision was revolutionary. In the past, missionary work had been a special interest of individuals, groups or societies. Now for the first time in the history of the church, the Christian churches, through their representatives, declared that missionary work was their responsibility, and that they would undertake the evangelization of the world. It is not yet clear whether

the churches of the world are aware of the responsibilities solemnly undertaken on their behalf by their representatives. The claim of the younger churches to be heard in ecumenical affairs was recognized by the appointment of two of their number—the Rev. D. G. Moses of India and Dr Francis Ibiam of Nigeria to be presidents of the World Council.

The Assembly was addressed by Pandit Jawaharlal Nehru, the Prime Minister of India. Press coverage was fair, but the Assembly made far less impression on Indian public opinion than the later visit of the Pope to India for the Eucharistic Congress of 1963.

4. *Uppsala*, 4–20 July, 1968. The law of diminishing returns affects ecumenical assemblies as well as other matters. Voices were raised to suggest that the fourth Assembly should follow an entirely different pattern. These suggestions were disregarded. The fourth Assembly, with the general theme: 'Behold, I make all things new', was organized under six sections, and discussed a large variety of subjects, many of which had already come under ecumenical study in connection with the earlier assemblies.

The theme of missions was not disregarded; but the discussions were principally notable as revealing the profound cleavage in the Christian world between those who believe that the church is here to preach the gospel to every creature with a view to conversion and incorporation into the visible body of Jesus Christ, and those who so stress the idea of *dialogue as to suggest that the church has more to learn from the non-Christian religions and extra-ecclesiastical movements than it has to contribute to them. This will be one of the major areas of ecumenical debate in the ensuing period of ecumenical development.

STEPHEN NEILL

D. P. Gaines: *The World Council of Churches* (Peterborough, N.H. 1966); R. Rouse and S. C. Neill, eds.: *A History of the Ecumenical Movement 1517–1948* (London 1954); W. A. Visser't Hooft, ed.: *The First Assembly of the World Council of Churches* (New York 1949); *Evanston Speaks. Reports from the Second Assembly of the World Council of Churches* (London 1954); W. A. Visser't Hooft, ed.: *The New Delhi Report: The Third Assembly of the World Council of Churches* (London 1961); N. Goodall, ed.: *The Uppsala Report 1968* (Geneva 1968).

ASSEMBLIES OF GOD FOREIGN MISSIONS DEPARTMENT. The General Council of the Assemblies of God was organized in 1914. Though its experience of the baptism in the Holy Spirit was the main centre of doctrinal agreement, the immediate motive for organizing was the need to evangelize the world, so that since the very beginning foreign missions have been a vital concern.

In 1967 the Foreign Missions Department of the Assemblies of God had 920 missionaries working side by side with 13,000 national preachers in 72 foreign lands. The denomination leads all other religious groups in the number of foreign Bible Schools; there are 80 foreign schools for ministerial training, with a total of about 3,000 students. In all, the church has some 17,000 regular preaching points overseas with an attending constituency of about 1,600,000. None of these figures includes the USA, Canada, Britain, or Australia, which all have major enterprises of the AG but are not normally considered mission fields.

The international headquarters of the AG is at 1445 Boonville Avenue, Springfield, Missouri 65802 (USA). However, each country forms its own national organization; the international relationship is that of a fellowship rather than a tightly organized single body.

The AG does some institutional work, e.g. schools, orphanages, clinics, etc., but these are considered secondary to the main goal of evangelism. The AG believes that the only way to assist people in a permanent way is to change the nature of men through the gospel of Christ. The denomination has so emphasized the principle of the *indigenous church that today much of the work of evangelism, teaching and leadership overseas is being carried on by local, national ministers.

Missionaries are supported by pledged monthly offerings from churches and individuals. The average AG missionary spends four years out of every five on the mission field and one year itinerating among the churches in the USA.

The Foreign Missions Department publishes the bi-monthly *Global Conquest* and the monthly *Call to Prayer*. It is a member of *EFMA.

HAROLD LINDSELL

ASSOCIATED MISSIONS OF THE INTERNATIONAL COUNCIL OF CHRISTIAN CHURCHES, THE, was born out of the organization in Amsterdam in 1948 of the International Council of Christian Churches. The leading figure of the movement is Carl McIntire, a former United Presbyterian (USA) clergyman and editor of the *Christian Beacon*. Within the framework of the ICCC was a Missions Committee which, in 1952, 'resolved itself into the Associated Missions with seven mission agencies as charter members. The Associated Missions (TAM) is thus the official missionary arm of the ICCC reporting to each Plenary Congress.'

Practically all the regular member boards are from the USA, and more than two-thirds of the fewer than 1,200 missionaries are supported by two Baptist mission boards connected with the General Association of Regular Baptist Churches, the Association of Baptists for World Evangelism and Baptist Mid-Missions.

TAM is theologically fundamentalist; the leading Baptist agencies are generally in the *dispensationalist tradition. TAM separates itself from what it believes to be the 'great apostasy' of the *WCC. It stands in opposition to the National Association of Evangelicals and the *World Evangelical Fellowship, both of whom it accuses of fellowship with unbelief. A liberal estimate of TAM's total world constituency would be about one and a half million. TAM has its headquarters at 210 Kennedy Building, P.O. Box 188, Johnson City, New York 13790 (USA).

HAROLD LINDSELL

ASSOCIATION OF PROFESSORS OF MISSIONS (North America). In 1940 a group of Professors of Missions in the New England and Middle Atlantic states organized a 'Fellowship': 'to promote fellowship, spiritual life, and professional usefulness'. Meeting twice a year, they established a pattern of personal friendship and scholarly discussion which was to carry over to the larger, more formal body.

An expanded APM began in 1952 to meet biennially (although regional groups still gather more often). The constitution of 1954 (revised in 1962) specifies that membership is open to faculty in missions and related fields from member institutions of the American Association of Theological Schools—and other qualified persons invited by the executive committee. Current membership includes Roman Catholics and conservative Evangelicals, as well as others outside the AATS.

Papers delivered at the fifth biennial session in 1960 have been published as *Frontiers of the Christian World Mission, Essays in Honor of Kenneth Scott Latourette* (New York 1962). Reports from other meetings are reproduced in bound, mimeographed form.

CREIGHTON LACY

ASSOCIATION OF THEOLOGICAL SCHOOLS IN SOUTH-EAST ASIA, THE, was formally set up in Singapore in July 1959, after initial planning in 1956 and the approval of a draft constitution prepared by South-East Asian theological school principals in 1957.

Its aim is to up-grade theological education in South-East Asia, and to be an accrediting organization for theological schools in the area.

Dr John Fleming was Executive Director 1959–1968, and three Asian theological educators were appointed Associate Executive Directors in 1966. Dr Kosuke Koyama became Executive Director in 1968.

Financial support is provided by the *Foundation for Theological Education in South-East Asia, formerly the Nanking Theological Seminary Board of Founders.

The Association meets once in two years in full session, representing 21 theological schools. The Executive Committee meets in alternate years. The programme has included theological study institutes for theological teachers in East Asia, visiting specialists, exchange professorships in Asia, Theological Texts Translation Programme in Chinese, and consultations on various aspects of theological education. In 1966 the Association launched the South-East Asia Graduate School of Theology, offering a Master of Theology degree in certain disciplines.

JOHN FLEMING

The South-East Asia Journal of Theology. Quarterly. Singapore: 6 Mount Sophia, from 1959 onwards.

ASSYRIAN CHRISTIANS, a term incorrectly used of the surviving fragments of the ancient *Nestorian Church of Mesopotamia, more correctly known as the Church of the East. This small group has tenaciously held on, through centuries of Muslim rule and intermittent persecution, to its own traditions and its own ancient liturgy of Addai and Mari, regarding Nestorius as a saint and not as a heretic. From 1886 for 60 years the Archbishop of Canterbury maintained a mission of help among them, with a view to raising up a more educated generation of clergy and to strengthening the life of this small and very much isolated church. Renewed persecutions during and after the first world war greatly reduced the number of the faithful, who now for the most part live in Iraq. Their patriarch, Mar Shimun, lives in the United States. It may be taken as certain that this small church will not die out, but at present it can do little more than survive under affliction.

STEPHEN NEILL

A. J. Maclean and W. H. Browne: *The Catholicos of the East and his People* (London 1892); R. S. Stafford: *The Tragedy of the Assyrians* (London 1935); W. H. Wigram: *The Assyrians and their Neighbours* (London 1929).

ATHEISM implies unawareness of, or total denial of, the reality of God or of any spiritual principle outside the realm of the visible and the tangible. In the 19th century many ethnologists, believing that religion is a later development in the human consciousness, were eagerly on the look-out for some primitive race which had no religious sense at all. All such hopes have been disappointed; it is now known that even the simplest peoples have religious beliefs and systems, in many cases extremely complex; and that a number of them are aware of the existence of one supreme being. It appears that A. is not a primitive but a sophisticated attitude.

It will long be argued whether *Buddhism is or is not an atheistic system. It is clear that the Buddha himself was not at all interested in the question of God, believing that the one essential in religion is a message of deliverance, and that to this God, if he exists, can make no contribution. It is possible, however, to quote some texts in favour of the view that, behind this conditioned and changing world of illusion, there exists something that is unconditioned and unchanging. Marxism professes to be an entirely atheistic system, and to desire nothing more than the total disappearance of every form of religion. Marxism, however, does recognize the existence of certain values which it is hard to reduce to the terms of a purely materialistic system; and it is not certain that it will be able to keep its atheistic position permanently.

In the post-Christian west, a considerable number of intellectuals, among them a number of Christians, claim to be atheists. But the majority of these are caught occasionally making use of such terms as 'better' or 'worse', which can have no meaning in a genuinely atheistic system. It seems probable that they should rather be classed as agnostics, though this term itself is of recent origin, having been apparently created by T. H. Huxley, the exponent of the ideas of Charles Darwin.

STEPHEN NEILL

The entire controversy arising out of J. A. T. Robinson: *Honest to God* (London 1963) and the 'God is dead' controversy in the USA may be taken as relevant; especially T. J. J. Altizer: *The Gospel of Christian*

Atheism (Philadelphia 1966); S. P. Schilling: *God in an Age of Atheism* (Nashville 1969); *ERE* II, 173–90; *NCE* I, 1000–04; *WKL*, 101f.

ATLANTIC ISLANDS. Various islands in the Atlantic Ocean bordering Europe and Africa. They were mostly discovered and settled in the 15th century. The *Canary Islands* are a group 823 miles south-west of Spain that form two Spanish provinces (Tenerife and Las Palmas). Portugal laid claim to these islands in 1341 but a bull of Pope Clement VI gave them to Spain in 1344. They were established as a diocese in 1406 and were used to re-provision ships exploring the New World. They have a population of half a million, nearly all of whom are Roman Catholic. The *Azores* is an archipelago of nine volcanic islands. They were uninhabited before a visit by Gonzalo Cabral in 1432, after which they were settled from Portugal and Flanders. By 1457 Portugal had annexed the entire group. The islands were established as a diocese in 1534. The population today is over 300,000, practically all of whom are RCs. *Madeira* is a group of islands in the eastern Atlantic opposite Morocco. These islands were known to the Romans and then rediscovered in 1418. The capital, Funchal, was founded in 1421 by Portugal. Funchal has been an episcopal see since 1514. The population today is over 300,000, almost all RC. *São Tomé* is a volcanic island in the Gulf of Guinea which together with *Principe Island* forms a Portuguese province. The population is in excess of 50,000 and is RC. *St. Helena* is a British island 1,200 miles west of Africa. It was discovered in 1592 by Portugal and then abandoned. It was later occupied by the Dutch and British. The British also officially annexed *Ascension Island* in 1922 and *Tristan da Cunha* in 1939. The population of these islands is mainly Anglican, with some RC elements.

For *Fernando Po* see SPANISH EQUATORIAL AFRICA; SAKER, ALFRED.

ALBERT J. NEVINS, MM

ATLASES, MISSIONARY. Except for the *Atlas Missionum a Sacra Congregatione de Propaganda Fide Dependentium* (1958), which is limited to Roman Catholic missions, general missionary atlases for the modern missionary movement are conspicuous by their absence. In 1925 Harlan Beach and Charles Fahs, building upon two earlier works, edited the *World Missionary Atlas*, which contained not only maps but also an agency directory, statistical tables and descriptive materials. *Atlas du monde chrétien* (Paris 1959) edited by Anton Freitag, SVD, available also in German, Dutch and English editions, is an admirable RC study of the historical expansion of Christianity, with accompanying text and illustrations. In 1961 Clyde Taylor and Wade Coggins edited *Protestant Missions in Latin America; a Statistical Survey* (Evangelical Foreign Missions Association), accompanied by a box of outline maps locating the work of the various mission agencies. *Map of the World's Religions and Missions*, edited by Schlunk and Quiring (4th ed., Stuttgart 1966) gives statistics as well as location of Christian missionary work and major world religions. *C.S.M.C. World Mission Map* is an annual publication (Cincinnati) with the latest statistics on RC 'population' in all areas of the world.

Other publications at various times by denominations and non-church-related missionary organizations have helped further to compensate for the lack of general works, such as *The Churchman's Missionary Atlas* (several editions, SPCK), a mission atlas published in 1961 by the *WEC, and an atlas of the *CMA fields, revised in 1964 (Christian Publications, Inc.).

Atlases of church history (e.g. Meer's *Atlas of the Early Christian World*, Nelson) and of non-Christian religions (e.g. *Historical Atlas of the Muslim Peoples*, Djambatan) supplement the materials of a specifically missionary character. BURTON L. GODDARD

ATTITUDES TO NON-CHRISTIANS. For historical reasons Christianity in its early centuries was largely confined to the Roman empire (of which modern Europe is the heir), apart from the spread of Nestorianism into Asia and Monophysite

Christianity into Africa. In the main, what progress had been made in Asia and Africa was wiped out by the rise of *Islam in the 7th century, and it was only from the 16th century that the gospel was preached again in Asia, whilst much of African evangelization dates only from the 19th century. In the Roman empire the Christian church developed and grew *in spite of* and *against* the imperial power. In such a situation it was easy to emphasize the faith as the *ark of salvation*, into which the believer was saved from the oceans of dark sin and error. The religions and culture of the surrounding peoples were regarded as either evil or, at least, quite unrelated to the message of the gospel. Some writers (such as Origen and his master, Clement of Alexandria, who followed in the path of the Apologists) wished to affirm what they felt to be good in non-Christian thought and culture, and so looked for a 'Christianity' before Christ. Christ, as the Logos (the 'Word' of John 1), had illuminated all, and so any manifestation of 'reason' was attributed to him.

In Asia and Africa the situation was different. The Christian missionaries followed the great voyages of discovery and the imperialist ventures that succeeded them. Often there was a close link between the missionary and the colonizing powers. Because economic and military strength were linked with evangelization, conversion often meant not only the adoption of a new religion but also the adoption of a new and alien way of life. The convert would abandon the old cultures, and transfer his loyalties not only to the religion of the European, but also to his way of life. The missionary himself was often zealous to accuse the religions amongst which he worked of being initiated by the devil, whilst *'idol-worship' was rejected as being not only wrong, but primitive and inferior. This strongly antagonistic approach was succeeded in some missionaries by an anxiety to preserve what was good in the heritage and traditions of non-Christians. It was emphasized that Christ did not come 'to destroy, but to fulfil' and that there were insights into the nature of

divine truth, which God himself had scattered through the world.

In some cases a study of the religions of Asia and also a more sensitive approach to Africa's 'primal vision' of the divine led some writers to deny the ultimacy of Christianity itself, and to regard non-Christians as possessing a similar mingling of truth and error to that possessed by Christians themselves.

We may point, then, to three main attitudes: (1) *The identification approach*, which tries to discover a basic unity in all religions. According to this view, the common elements of all religions need to be brought together and a kind of 'super-religion' or 'world religion' established. This approach would claim to be the truly *tolerant* one, but it becomes dogmatic in its demand for complete flexibility from those who have strong convictions about their own religion. This approach also neglects the actual pattern of religious life and idealizes the situation in many non-Christian faiths. It is difficult for anyone who has a feeling of ultimate committal to Christ to follow this position.

(2) *The exclusivist approach*, which is so anxious to stress the crucial character of Christ for man's destiny and understanding of the world, that it denies the presence of God's light in other faiths. The other faiths are sometimes regarded simply as human products, as man's search for God, whilst Christianity is regarded as the one religion which (despite its imperfections) points to God's initiative. Christ is thus considered to be the judge of all religious faiths.

(3) *The mediating approach*, which is anxious to stress two fundamental truths, that are accepted in Christianity itself— the 'once-for-all' character of Christ's life, death and resurrection on the one hand, and the universality of God's grace and activity on the other. This approach would affirm that the commitment of the Christian to Christ does not prevent him from accepting what is authentic in his fellow-man, and that he must expect to find evidences of God's working in the traditions and religious beliefs of all men. This attitude leaves the

way open for a *dialogue between faiths, for dialogue demands both personal conviction and a waiting for the truth that may come through another's understanding and conviction.

RAYMOND J. HAMMER

E. C. Dewick: *The Christian Attitude to Other Religions* (Cambridge 1953); J. Neuner, ed.: *Christian Revelation and World Religions* (London 1967); H. R. Schlette: *Towards a Theology of Religions* (Freiburg 1966).

AUDIOVISUAL AIDS are materials and tools which assist one's perception through the senses of seeing and hearing.

AVs are not new to mankind, religion or the Christian church. The liturgies developed by Israel and described in Deuteronomy used sensory perception to dramatize the truth of the one God. The incarnation of God in Jesus the Christ is a divine example of audiovisuals. Baptism and Communion portray truth in sight and sound.

Although there are many theories of communication, almost all of them include three basic elements: the *message* (event or object), the receiver's *perception* (understanding) of the message, and the receiver's *response*.

Since the receiver's perception of the message is always influenced and distorted by his own emotions and experiences, the message is never perceived exactly as it is. It is the function of AVs, therefore, to reinforce the message itself by additional sensory data.

With the rise of Christian education for the masses during the 20th century, the use of AVs by the church has vastly expanded beyond the liturgy and the *sacraments. Although AVs are used in worship and evangelism, they are used most often and most effectively in Christian nurture.

In the widest sense of the term, AVs may be the very object or event to be perceived, such as experiences on a field trip. But the general use of the term AVs refers to reproductions (recordings, photographs), representations (drama, models, displays), or abstractions (maps, charts, graphs) of the message.

3

In general use around the world are: chalkboard, flat pictures, tackboard, flannelboard, displays, puppets, photographs, slides, filmstrips, motion pictures and recordings. Often two or more AVs are used together.

Ranging from simple non-projected aids to sophisticated multi-media presentations, the use of AVs is expanding more rapidly today than ever before. The development of electronic technology in recent years has produced many new AVs. Now commonly called 'instructional media', they include: educational and closed circuit television, video tape recorders, standardized tape cartridges, microfilm and 8 mm. movies. Instructional media permit each student to work at his own pace and free the teacher to work personally with each pupil.

The AVs which communicate the message best are those which are used in the same cultural setting in which they are produced. Many councils of churches have AV libraries for selling and renting AV materials and equipment. Some councils and denominations have production centres.

To train pastors and laymen to use AVs some councils employ communication consultants. These consultants conduct training workshops, develop communications curricula for universities and theological seminaries, select promising leaders for professional education, and co-ordinate the production of AVs for local churches.

See also RAVEMCCO.

HAROLD M. MARTIN

AUGUSTINIANS (OSA). The Order of St. Augustine, which traces its origin back to the great bishop of Hippo (354–430), was constituted in 1256 and in 1567 included among the mendicant orders. It consists today of 23 provinces, nine vice-provinces and some 5,000 religious, ruled by a Prior General who resides at S. Monica, Via S. Ufficio 25, Rome. The missionary history of the order dates from the 14th century, but its greatest period of expansion began in 1533 under St. Thomas of Villanova. The Spanish friars entered Mexico that year, and from there they established missions in the

Philippines (1565), Peru, Chile, Colombia, Brazil, Ecuador and Japan. The Portuguese friars entered India in 1572 and also founded missions in Guinea, Angola, Kenya, Arabia, Iraq, Persia, Georgia, Pakistan, Bengal, Siam, Indo-China and Macao. In the 17th and 18th centuries the Irish friars were working in Puerto Rico, Newfoundland and North America; they went to India in 1834 and to Australia in 1838. In 1879 the Spanish Augustinians opened missions in China and more recently the Anglo-Irish Province in 1938 entered Northern Nigeria, where they work in the dioceses of Yola and Maiduguri. At present the order has very large missions in S. America, the Philippines, Nigeria, Indonesia, Congo, Japan and Ethiopia.

M. B. HACKETT, OSA

D. J. Kavanagh: *The Augustinian Order* (New York 1937—a short account of the missionary history of the order down to 1937). The best guide to the present state of the missions is the official publication *Missionalia Augustiniana* (Rome 1962). See also *NCE* I, 1071–76.

AUSTRALIA. Area 2,974,581 sq.m. Population 11,544,691 (1966 census). The people are almost entirely of European origin. There are about 100,000 Aborigines of whom about 40,000 are full-bloods; 20,000 Chinese and 20,000 other non-Europeans. About 89% of the population claim membership of one of the four main churches, Anglican, Roman Catholic, Methodist and Presbyterian in that order, but probably only a third to a half are active members.

The Australian Aborigines are an *animistic people. They probably came to A. about 20,000 years ago, possibly much earlier. They dispersed themselves over the whole continent, dividing the area between their small tribal groups and living a nomadic, food-gathering life. About 680 groupings have been recorded. As they had no crops, they never settled in any one place. When white men first arrived, there were probably about 300,000. The arrival of an aggressive, agrarian and later industrial civilization resulted in the retreat of the Aborigines, either to remote areas or into spiritual hopelessness. The total dropped to a third, but is now increasing.

Today there are three main types of Aborigines—those who are assimilated in the white community and live in towns and cities, those who live as Aboriginal groups on the fringes of towns, and those who still preserve the remnants of tribal life in remoter areas in the central and northern parts of Australia. The churches have found it very difficult to exercise an adequate ministry or mission to the fringe-dwellers. Often this has been left to non-denominational missions such as the United Aborigines Mission and the Aborigines Inland Mission. In northern NSW, an *indigenous Aboriginal church has developed of a *Pentecostal type. In the remoter areas, Christian missions have been active and have a fine record of achievement. But for them, the Aborigines might have died out. They have established mission stations on Aboriginal reserves. These normally contain a school, a hospital, a shop, and a church, and have a basic industry, such as sheep, cattle, fishing, tropical agriculture or timber, together with training for that and also handicrafts. Some have also developed co-operatives. The chief missions are conducted by the Anglican, Lutheran, Methodist, Presbyterian and RC churches. The Anglican church works through its Australian Board of Missions which finds and supports chaplains for eight government Aboriginal communities; through the *CMS which has three missions in Arnhem Land and provides nursing staff and a chaplain at one government settlement and a chaplain at another; and through the Anglican Missionary Council of Western Australia. The Methodist Overseas Missions have five mission stations in Queensland, one in Western Australia and one in Central Australia. The RC church has 19 mission stations in the Northern Territory, Queensland, Western Australia and New South Wales, and institutions in seven urban centres. The Lutheran Church has two missions in Queensland and one in Central Australia. The Churches of Christ have three stations in Western Australia. They and the Baptists have missionaries on some government settlements. Most present-day missions were founded between 1914 and 1937. Important earlier missions were Yarrabah 1890, Mapoon 1891, and Mitchell River 1895. Recently, the missions of the Anglican Diocese of Carpentaria at Yarrabah, Mitchell, Edward and Lockhart Rivers and the Presbyterian missions at Mapoon and Weipa have been transferred to the Queensland government, with the church concerned providing a chaplain and maintaining a church. In the Northern Territory, there is some development of village or tribal councils which may accept responsibility for mission management.

Progress in building up congregations of baptized and confirmed Christians has been slow; there are very few ordained Aboriginal ministers. Notable are Pastor Doug Nicholls, a Church of Christ pastor in Melbourne, and the Rev. Lazarus Lami Lami of the Methodist Church in Arnhem Land. A generation ago there were the Rev. James Noble, an Anglican missionary in Queensland and David Unaipon, a well-known preacher in SA and Victoria. In recent years there has been stronger indigenous activity in worship, leadership, Christian education, and missionary witness. There is considerable difficulty in communicating the gospel to a dispossessed, animistic minority. Earlier policies were based on the assumption that the Aborigines were a dying race.

There are Chinese churches in Melbourne and Sydney which are related to the Presbyterian Church of Australia and the Anglican church respectively, and there is an independent church in Sydney.

The Australian Council of Churches has been active in the work of helping immigrants from Europe to settle in Australia and in helping Eastern Orthodox churches to establish effective ministries to their people. Several churches have also made buildings and other facilities available to migrant churches.

Negotiations are proceeding for church union between the Congregational, Methodist and Presbyterian Churches, and the Anglican Church has decided to seek entry to the negotiations.

FRANK G. ENGEL

Australian Encyclopaedia, 'Aborigines'; A. P. Elkin: *The Australian Aborigines* (London 1961), *The Australian Aborigines— How to Understand Them* (6th ed., Sydney 1964); *Encyclopaedia Britannica*, 'Australia'; F. G. Engel: *Turning Land into Hope* (Sydney 1968); W. M. Hilliard: *The People in Between* (London 1968); *Official Year Book of the Commonwealth of Australia* (Canberra); I. G. Sharp and C. M. Tatz: *Aborigines in the Economy* (Melbourne 966); *BM* II, 101–09; *NCE* I, 1083–92;1 *WKL*, 115–18.

AUTONOMOUS CHURCHES. The idea of autonomous churches as the goal of missionary work overseas came into being in the middle of the 19th century. As against the goal of individual conversion adopted by *pietism, and the *paternalistic manner in which foreign missionaries carried on their work, far-sighted strategists of missions recognized that only the formation of fully independent *indigenous churches could guard Christians in Asia and Africa against the perils of spiritual retardation, and the missionary societies against the stagnation of their impulse towards expansion. This idea found expression in the formula 'self-governing, self-supporting and self-propagating churches', put forward by Rufus *Anderson, Secretary of the *ABCFM, and Henry *Venn, Secretary of the (Anglican) *CMS, who also expounded in various memoranda strategic plans for the working out of their ideas. To Venn the way presented itself as an evolution through a series of steps; on the basis of self-supporting pastorates and districts, the independent diocese should finally be set up. As soon as this goal has been attained, the euthanasia of the mission should follow: the missionaries now leave the young church, and go on into the regions beyond, the as yet *unevangelized areas. In every case, self-support is the criterion by which the degree of independence actually attained is measured. Anderson, as a Congregationalist, naturally thought of the independent church principally in terms of the local church. After the pattern set by Paul, the church must from the beginning be organized on the basis of independence, in order that it may at once become the most significant instrument for the evangelization of the non-Christian world around it. Anderson's thoughts were taken up again in the writings of Roland *Allen and in the *World Dominion Movement. These ideas in their radical form have been put into practice in only a small number of mission fields; the *Nevius-method, adopted in the development of the Presbyterian church in Korea, comes nearest to them.

A clearly worked out strategy for the development of independent churches by the method of evolution or 'gradualism' is to be noted in some large churches in Africa and Asia, such as the Anglican Church in Uganda, and the Batak Church in Sumatra. But here gradualism, with its tendency to slow down the movement, came into conflict with the new movement of *nationalism among the coloured peoples, by which the *younger churches, especially those among them which were most highly developed, came to be strongly affected.

After the second world war, during which the majority of the Asian churches had attained to full independence, the new problem of the further co-operation of foreign missionaries in the work of the younger churches arose in connection with the unfinished missionary task. The *World Missionary Conference in Whitby in 1947 made use of the phrase 'Partners in Obedience'. In 1952 the Conference at Willingen recognized that the 'three-self' formulation cannot be accepted without question, since it can so easily introduce into the churches an inward-looking attitude which is not in keeping with ecumenical principles (cf. 'the three-self movement' in communist China). In the same year the Assembly of the Lutheran World Federation, meeting in Hanover, proposed to replace the expression 'autonomous churches' by 'Christonomous churches'. More important than a terminology which corresponds to the realities is a proper theological understanding of the 'autonomous', or better, of the 'responsible' church. The independence of a church consists in its power, readiness and freedom to fulfil the divine task committed to it in the area in which it lives. Today it is generally recognized that a legitimate independence of the church can exist only in the wider framework of the 'mutual interdependence' of all the members in the body of Christ.

PETER BEYERHAUS

P. Beyerhaus and H. Lefever: *The Responsible Church and the Foreign Mission* (London 1964).

AVIATION IN MISSIONS. Before the second world war there were several pioneer experiments in the use of mission-owned aircraft; a surge of interest followed the war. The chief development has been the short-range use of smaller planes, supplementing commercial airlines. Some missions attempted the specialized use of transport aircraft for inter-continental flights; but several such attempts were soon abandoned. Today the most commonly used are light aircraft capable of reaching remote places, particularly roadless areas, using minimum airstrips. The use of helicopters, however, is restricted by the high cost of purchase and maintenance, as well as by limitations of range and altitude.

Planes are used for the transport of evangelists, teachers, school children, doctors and nurses, for the distribution of supplies, for ambulance and humanitarian work and for evacuation. The largest operators are the *Missionary Aviation Fellowship, an inter-mission service agency, and Jungle Aviation and Radio Service, which serves the *Wycliffe Bible Translators. These groups emphasize professional standards and use specialists (predominantly dually-qualified pilot-mechanics). SIMAIR (serving the *SIM in W. Africa) and a number of other missions with one or more planes follow this operational policy. Numerous individual missionaries fly their own planes as airborne 'circuit riders'.

DONALD A. MCGAVRAN

AZARIAH, VEDANAIAKAM SAMUEL (1875–1945), was born, the son of a village pastor, at Vellalanvilai in the Tinnevelly District of South India. To four people he owed more than he could ever express—to his somewhat Spartan mother, from whom he acquired a deep love of the Bible and an unshakeable faith in Jesus Christ; to Sherwood Eddy, who drew him out from the limited background and narrow views of his early life into contact with the modern world; to the Bishop of Madras (H. *Whitehead) and his gifted wife who recognized his quality, believed in him, and prepared him for the great work he was to accomplish.

After some years of work in the *YMCA, A. accepted ordination, and went to work in the Nizam's dominions, in the area of the Indian Missionary Society which he had himself been instrumental in founding in 1903. Before long came the call to become the first Indian bishop of the Anglican church. There was much opposition to this step. Many missionaries believed that it was premature, and that no Indian was yet qualified to hold this high office. Some objected to A. personally because of his allegedly liberal views. Christians of high-caste origin looked askance at the Nādār *parvenu*. Nevertheless A. was consecrated Bishop of Dornakal in December 1912; as his experience grew, his area was enlarged until he was in charge of all Anglican work in the Telugu-speaking part of the Madras presidency.

A great *mass movement was in progress in the area. A. with his great gifts as pastor and teacher was just the right man to guide and direct the movement. An exceptionally gifted series of European archdeacons took from him nearly all the weight of administration, and left him free to travel, to supervise and to train. From an early date he began to ordain the best among his village workers, gradually building up to a well-educated ministry. In the course of 30 years, 100,000 people were added to the church.

A. represented the *younger churches at a great many international gatherings. As a young man he had delivered at the *Edinburgh Conference of 1910 a provocative address on the subject of missionaries and their relations to their indigenous colleagues. He was present at Lausanne 1927 and at Edinburgh 1937, and addressed the *Tambaram Missionary Conference of 1938. He had been present at the Tranquebar Conference of 1919 which launched the scheme for church union in South India; he was from its inception a member of the Joint Committee on Church Union, though he did not live to see the birth of the *CSI in 1947.

A. was not a great scholar, but he was an assiduous reader, especially of books dealing with the Bible. He himself produced a series of small books—on Baptism, on the Holy Communion, a simple commentary on the Book of Revelation and so forth. His book *Christian Giving*, originally written in Tamil, has been republished by World Christian Books (1955), and translated into 50 languages.

A. was the greatest leader yet produced by any younger church. It is to be regretted that no really adequate account of his life has yet been written.

STEPHEN NEILL

C. Graham: *Azariah of Dornakal* (London 1946); J. Z. Hodge: *Azariah of Dornakal* (Calcutta 1946); *RGG* I, 502f.

AZEVEDO, IGNACIO DE (1527–1570). Born at Porto in Portugal, he joined the Society of *Jesus in 1548. The third general of the society, Francis Borgia, appointed him in 1565 as visitor of the mission in Brazil. In order to meet the shortage in manpower, A. obtained permission to seek for volunteers for missionary work in Spain and Portugal. In 1570 he set to sea with two ships, and together with 39 companions reached the Canary Islands. Here his ships were attacked by Jacques de Sores with his fleet of privateers, which as one division of the 'sea-beggars' was hunting down the ships of the Iberian powers. The missionaries fell victims to the political and religious conflicts by which the Europe of the day was riven. A. was put to death, his com-

48   AZORES

panions ill-treated and then thrown into the sea. The other ship escaped the persecutors, but was driven back from Cuba to the Azores, where the same fate befell the survivors. Twelve of them died. A. and his companions soon came to be venerated as martyrs. In 1854 they were beatified by Pope Pius IX.

JOSEF GLAZIK

J. Brodrick: *The Progress of the Jesuits: 1546–1579* (London 1946); Petrus Jarricus (Du Jarric): *Thesaurus rerum Indicarum* II (Cologne 1615), pp.328–47; R. Ricard: *Revue d'Historie des Missions* (Paris 1937), pp.321–66, 435–70; *LTK* I, 1159; *NCE* I, 1144.

AZORES. See ATLANTIC ISLANDS.

B

BAHA'I RELIGION or BĀBISM is a form of the Muslim religion which developed in Iran out of the Shiah expectation that the Twelfth Imām, who disappeared in A.D. 940, would again manifest himself, or communicate with men, through the Bāb, or 'door'. On 23 May 1844 a young Persian named Mirza Ali Muhammad (1820–1850) claimed to be the Bāb, and later seems to have put forward Messianic claims. He was executed by the Iranian government on 9 July 1850, and his followers were subjected to most cruel persecution. After his death one of his followers, Husayn Ali (c. 1817–1892) took the name Baha'ullah, 'glory of God', and in 1863 succeeded in putting on one side the new head, Subh-i-Ezel, 'the dawn of eternity', appointed by the Bāb himself. The headquarters of the movement was moved to Acre in Syria, from which Baha'ullah sent out letters to many rulers, including Queen Victoria of England, in which he claimed to be Christ returned to earth, and demanded their allegiance. In 1892 Baha'ullah was succeeded by Abbas Effendi (Abdu'l Bahā, 'servant of the glory', 1844–1921), who headed the movement for the next 30 years. The year 1902 marked the beginning of missionary work in America and the development of Bahā'ism from a Middle Eastern movement to a worldwide religion.

Bahā'is claim that theirs is the final revelation of God to men, which does not contradict any previous revelation but takes up all earlier truth into itself. Thus, Baha'ullah is for Jews the descent of the Lord of Hosts, for Christians the return of Christ in the glory of the Father, for Shiahs the return of the Imām Husayn, for Sunnis the descent of the Spirit of God, for Hindus the reincarnation of Krishna, and for Buddhists the fifth Buddha.

The BR is optimistic, believing that sin is only negative and that all things are good in themselves. The Bahā'i temple is circular, as a house in which all can pray, with a dome in nine sections, representing the various religions of the world which find their unity in Bahā'ism. Bahā'is are expected to pray regularly, to abstain from alcohol, to maintain high ethical standards, and to devote all their efforts to peace and to the unity of the human race. They are convinced that their religion, as the final revelation, is destined to become the religion of the entire human race.

It is difficult to estimate the number of Bahā'i adherents in the world. There may be about half a million in Iran, and a million altogether in the world. Bahā'ism has made a number of converts from the Christian churches, perhaps as a result of its emphasis on peace, and its genuinely ecumenical spirit.

STEPHEN NEILL

Bahāi World Faith (2nd ed. 1966; official handbook); E. G. Browne: *A Year among the Persians* (1893; new ed. 1952), Art. 'Bābis, Bābī Religion' in *ERE* II, pp. 299–308); J. Ferraby: *All Things Made New* (London 1957); *NCE* II, 14f.

BAHAMA ISLANDS. See CARIBBEAN.

BAHREIN. See ARABIAN PENINSULA.

BAILEY, WELLESLEY COSBY (1846–1937). Born at Abbeyleix, Ireland. In 1869 he went as a lay missionary to teach in the American Presbyterian school at Ambala, Punjab, India, and began visiting the local 'leper asylum'. Together with the gospel he brought personal care and such material help as he could. In 1871 he married Alice Grahame who thenceforward shared in his work. Back in Dublin in 1874 he spoke and wrote about the needs of leprosy sufferers; as a result a fund was started; in 1878 this became the 'Mission to Lepers in India' (now the Leprosy Mission). Bailey travelled in India providing buildings and financial support for leprosy work, in co-operation with existing Protestant missions of many denominations. In 1882 he returned to Britain and from 1886 to 1917 was full-time secretary of the mission. Travelling in West and East Asia, North America and Australasia, speaking and writing, he gained widespread support for the work, which eventually extended far beyond India alone. When he retired the mission had an income of £44,133, with which it was helping 14,655 patients at 87 stations, in 12 countries, and in co-operation with 37 societies. B's compassion for a class of sufferers who were outcast and hopeless was united to exceptional gifts of leadership and administration. With limited financial resources he helped to bring physical relief and new spiritual life to many thousands.

See also LEPROSY MISSIONS.

JOHN GOODWIN

W. C. Bailey: *The Lepers of our Indian Empire* (London 1892); A. D. Miller: *An Inn Called Welcome: the Story of the Mission to Lepers 1874–1917* (London 1965).

BALI. See INDONESIA.

BANTU PEOPLES AND LANGUAGES. Africa is inhabited by Negroid and Caucasoid peoples, the former being the most numerous, generally having black or dark brown hair, skin, and eyes, curly hair and broad noses. They differ widely from one another. Bantu is a linguistic term referring to Negroid peoples living south of a line which may be drawn on a map from Calabar, Nigeria, to north of Lake Victoria, south into Tanzania, and northeast to Formosa Bay, Kenya. Nearly all peoples living south of this line are Bantu speaking, except the Bushmen and Hottentots in the extreme south. Bantu means people, singular, *muntu*, meaning man, from the root *-ntu*, e.g. Mu-ganda is one person and Ba-ganda are the people of the Ganda tribe, Bu-ganda is the country. The Bantu languages were formerly regarded as a distinct group from that of the west coast African languages, but are now regarded as part of the Niger-Congo family of the African languages, the other three being the Afro-Asiatic, the Sahara-Savannah, and the Macro-Khoisan families. The Bantu languages are closely related with important common structures, but are not mutually intelligible.

The people themselves differ considerably in physical features, culture, and religion, with marked differences in food, clothing, housing, and economic and political organization, which may be illustrated by comparing the Shona and their neighbours, the Ndebele, of Rhodesia. The Shona are small, loosely knit, tribal units with not very powerful chieftains; they are peaceful, pastoral, agricultural peoples. The Ndebele are warlike, with strong centralized chieftainships, interested in war and political pursuits rather than agriculture and peace.

Therefore it is possible to speak about the religion of the Bantu-speaking peoples only in broad outline. There are some common features. There is no prophetic founder, no sacred book, no creed, no systematic theology, in most parts no prominent temples of worship. All known tribes acknowledge a Supreme Being, accept the reality of the spiritual world, and give prominence to the departed ancestors in form of worship or veneration. There is no distinction between the secular and the sacred, and the line between the living and the dead is very thin. Bantu religion has been called *animism because of the belief that animate and inanimate objects have a soul; recently this has been called dynamism or vital force. There is widespread belief in *magic, sorcery, and *witchcraft. The Bible has been translated into about 200 of the Bantu languages.

PER HASSING

A. T. Bryant: *Bantu Origins, the People and their Language* (Cape Town 1963); *ERE* III, 356–67.

BAPTISM has always been the sacrament of initiation into Christ and his church. The baptismal rites of the mystery religions hardly influenced Christianity, if at all. Behind the Christian rites are various forms of Jewish baptism, such as John the Baptist's rite showing repentance for sin and proselyte baptism. The NT shows the church already practising the rite, and the *Great Commission (Matt.28:19f.) attributes its institution to Christ himself and links it with world mission. Paul, as in Romans, interprets it as a sharing in the death and resurrection of Jesus, the mark of forgiveness, the accompaniment of regeneration, and the beginning of the new life in Christ. Acts stresses the gift of the Holy Spirit for illumination and power in witness. As the liturgies developed, the 'sealing' of the Spirit was associated with the concluding act of confirmation in the Eastern churches, while in the west confirmation was made a separate rite, especially after infant baptism became common.

Infant baptism probably began in NT times and is clearly attested by the 2nd century (Origen). Immersion was probably the original mode, but the *Didache* (ch. 7) shows that by the beginning of the 2nd century affusion was permitted if abundant water was not available. The building of churches stimulated the trend to pouring and sprinkling, although for centuries some baptisteries were large enough for immersion. Very early the amount of water and the mode of application became secondary to the threefold application of water and the use of the Trinitarian formula. Exorcisms, anointings, and other acts were added to these essentials. The sponsors of adult converts eventually became the godparents of infants who were to ensure their Christian nurture along with the parents. The normal minister is the ordained priest or pastor, but baptism by laymen has always been recognized. As the result of the Donatist Controversy (4th–5th centuries) and the work of Augustine heretical baptism has been counted valid if the Trinitarian formula is used and the intention were that of the church. Neither infant baptism nor affusion were questioned until the age of the Reformation when the *Anabaptists insisted on believer's baptism by immersion. Various *Baptist churches have followed them. The *Friends dispensed with the sacrament.

Probably the earliest mission problem, apart from the mode, was the tendency of the socially élite to postpone baptism as long as possible because it was held to cancel

original and actual sin. Then when mission became the instrument of imperial power and the Carolingian monarchs imposed baptism on the conquered Saxons and Wends as the sign of submission, it lost its nature as a testimony of faith. Stress on both its power solely to open the gates of heaven and its indelible character led to its prostitution in forcible baptism of Jews during the Middle Ages. This resulted also in the questionable Roman Catholic mission practice of secretly and without consent of the individual baptizing hundreds of thousands of persons at the point of death. Protestant missionaries, emphasizing individual conversion, held that the real meaning of baptism became evident on the mission field, being clearly the beginning of radically new life in Christ. (Consequently *mass movements were accepted by many only with difficulty.) The *catechumenate has usually been linked with baptism by both RC and Protestant missions, involving both instruction and scrutiny of life. Protestants reproduced the modes, liturgies, doctrines, and requirements of the *sending churches, but the system of *comity implied that all who recognized it, with the exception of some of the stricter Baptist bodies, also recognized one another's baptism and accepted members by transfer.

R. PIERCE BEAVER

J. Baillie: *Baptism and Conversion* (London 1963); I. H. Enklaar: *De Scheiding der Sacramenten op het Zendingveld* (Amsterdam 1947); H. W. Gensichen: *Das Taufproblem in der Mission* (Gütersloh 1951); G. F. Vicedom: *Die Taufe unter den Heiden* (Munich 1960); WCC, Commission on Faith and Order: *One Lord, One Baptism* (London 1960).

BAPTIST MISSIONS. The BMS (English) was organized in 1792 to aid William *Carey in his mission to India. A Baptist Society was founded in the USA in 1814 by representatives of local missionary societies hastily formed when the news of Adoniram *Judson's decision for the Baptist belief was received. These two societies were the first of other similar organizations that have been

3*

created by Baptists in various parts of the world in later times: The Southern Baptist Foreign Mission Society (1885); the Swedish Baptist Foreign Mission Society (1881), and the New Zealand Baptist Foreign Mission Society (1885), are examples. By 1957 29 Baptist Foreign Mission Societies were reported to be at work. Baptist conventions and Baptist unions have acted through missionary committees of their own. And Baptist laymen, travelling overseas on business, have been self-appointed missionaries whose work has resulted in the formation of churches.

By these various means Baptists have shown their interest in missions. Carey went to India; Judson went to Burma. Since their day Baptist workers have entered practically all the lands of the earth; noteworthy have been the Baptist efforts in Burma, the Congo, North-east India, and Central America. Primary emphasis has been placed on evangelism, the winning of people to the Christian faith through the written and spoken word, and personal invitations. Supporting this evangelism have been *translation work and programmes for the training of indigenous leaders.

These efforts resulted in gathered groups of Christians wherever Baptists have gone and churches have been organized. Following western practice, churches in an area have joined in conventions or unions for their mutual help and united endeavours. Such local unions now exist in all parts of the world. These have created national conventions; in the Baptist World Alliance in 1965 there were 18 national organizations in Central and South America, six in Africa and 16 in the Near East and Asia.

Baptists have been active in higher education, in hospital and medical work, and in social service. In some of this they have acted alone, as in the Central Philippine University and the Moulmein Memorial Hospital, Burma, but more often they have joined with other Christian groups in the conduct of united work, as in the Chung Chi University, Hong Kong, and the *Vellore Hospital and Medical School, India. Baptists have also appointed and supported teachers in non-Baptist institutions of higher learning and doctors in hospitals and clinics conducted by non-Baptist organizations; they have established student centres and hostels at secular universities and chaplains at secular hospitals. Baptists, while having a primary concern for evangelism, have shared widely in maintaining other related enterprises.

Some noteworthy men are in Baptist history. The *Serampore Trio of Carey, Marshman and Ward; Judson of Burma; George *Boardman, who in a few short years established the church among the Karens of Burma; Timothy *Richard, who from his arrival in China to his death had an amazing influence on that nation through his varied activities which included a position as adviser to the government; George *Grenfell, who with the financial backing of Robert *Arthington explored the Congo area and established mission stations along its banks; and William Axling, who in 1908 began the development of a Baptist Centre in Tokyo, Japan, which in a variety of ways met the needs of the people there.

As the *ecumenical movement has developed and negotiations for *church unions in mission lands have begun, Baptists have had to decide on their participation or non-participation. Baptists have readily shared in co-operative non-evangelistic enterprises and in councils of churches, but have tended to draw back from joining in uniting churches. In some places they have suffered breaks in their ranks when the possibility of union has arisen, as in Japan. Baptists have held firmly to their own particular witness and have carried out their mission with that witness.

J. LESLIE DUNSTAN

W. B. Lipphard: *The Second Century of Baptist Foreign Missions* (Philadelphia 1926); R. C. Torbet: *Venture of Faith* (Philadelphia 1955); H. C. Vedder: *A Short History of Baptist Missions* (Philadelphia 1927).

BARBADOS. See CARIBBEAN.

BARBUDA. See CARIBBEAN.

BARCLAY, THOMAS (1849–1935), was one of a group of three friends who, after studying together at Glasgow University, Free Church Divinity School and Leipzig, all gave distinguished missionary service in Asia; the others being D. MacKichan and J. C. *Gibson. Hearing of the needs of S.E. China, B. offered his services to the Presbyterian Church of England and was appointed to Formosa, where missionary work had begun in 1865. He arrived in Tainan in 1875 and died there 60 years later. He devoted his long career to the spiritual needs of the growing church. Founder and principal of Tainan Theological College, his clear and reverent Bible teaching and broad general interests contributed much to the quality of the Formosan ministry. Greatly concerned that all should read and understand the Bible, and believing that this could not be done through literary Chinese, he was a lifelong advocate of romanized script and compiled a dictionary of romanized Amoy Chinese, the main language of Formosa. In 1884 he founded a monthly church magazine, the *Kau-hoe-po*, which has been published regularly ever since. But his greatest work was his translation of the NT (1915) and OT (1927–1930), which gave the Formosan church its first accurate colloquial Bible and is still standard.

BORIS ANDERSON

E. Band: *Barclay of Formosa* (Tokyo 1936).

BASEL MISSION, THE (*Evangelische Missionsgesellschaft in Basel*), was founded in 1815 by members of the *Deutsche Christentumsgesellschaft* (German Christian Fellowship). The first secretary was C. G. Blumhardt. In the mission seminary (1816–1955) men of all professions were trained (more than 2,500 of them). At first they worked for other societies, 88 for the *CMS, including Bishop S. *Gobat, J. L. *Krapf, J. Rebmann, S. W. Koelle. In 1822 Count Zaremba was sent to the Caucasus, but work in that area was made impossible by the Russian government. Subsequently missionaries were sent to the following countries: 1825 Ghana; 1834 India (S. *Hebich); 1846 Hong Kong and South China; 1886 Cameroon (taking over from the English Baptists); 1912 North Togo; 1921 Borneo (Kalimantan); 1952 North Borneo (Sabah) among the Rungus tribes; 1959 North Cameroon (now Nigeria) among the hill tribes. In 1914 the staff consisted of 450 missionaries in five countries. In all areas except China the first world war put an end to the work, as all the missionaries were interned or repatriated. In 1925 work was restarted in India, Ghana and Cameroon.

In 1949 the BM like all other missions was expelled from China. In 1954 a separate German branch was founded, with head office in Stuttgart. In 1955 it was decided that all missionaries should receive university training, and the old seminary ceased to function in its original form. In Kalimantan church and mission were completely fused in 1956 and in Ghana in 1963.

The BM has from the start been ecumenically-minded, drawing support from several countries (S. Germany, Switzerland, Austria, Alsace) and from churches of both Lutheran and Reformed Confession; and co-operating with other missionary societies and churches. (A Lutheran missionary of the BM became a bishop in the CSI). It has combined evangelistic and practical work (1849 weaving mills; 1870 production of tiles in India; 1857 introduction of cocoa in Ghana); hospitals, schools, training institutions. In 1968 the staff consisted of 360 missionaries from five countries; the budget was for £804,960.

WALTER ZUMBRUNNEN

W. Schlatter: *Geschichte der Basler Mission* (3 vols., Basel 1916); H. Witschi: *Geschichte der Basler Mission*, vol. 4 (Basel 1965).

BASHFORD, JAMES WHITFORD (1848–1919). Born in a pioneer home near Fayette, Wisconsin, USA. After studies at University of Wisconsin and Boston University School of Theology he served five pastorates and was president of Ohio Wesleyan University (1889–1904). At the age of 55 he was elected a bishop of the Methodist Episcopal Church and by his own request was assigned to China. There he laboured for 14 full years. Tireless traveller, eloquent preacher, wise administrator, advocate of capable indigenous leadership, active in many interchurch and union movements, he became one of the best known and most influential missionary statesmen and prophets of his time. Problems within the young Republic of China and its relations with foreign countries engaged his serious concern; for instance, he persuaded the US government to block Japan's 21 demands upon China in 1915 and to support China's national integrity. Through voluminous correspondence and numerous articles he presented the needs and hopes of the Chinese people to the west. Wide-ranging studies and observations bore fruit in a notable volume, *China: An Interpretation* (1916, revised and enlarged in 1919).

F. W. PRICE

G. R. Grose: *James W. Bashford, Pastor, Educator, Bishop* (New York 1922); Bashford Journals in MRL, New York; *DAB* II, 33f.

BASUTOLAND. See LESOTHO.

BATAILLON, PIERRE-MARIE (1810–1877), was born at Saint-Cyr-les-Vignes near Lyons, France, and died on Wallis Island. He joined the Marist Fathers and was ordained priest in 1835. In 1836 he was sent as one of the first Marists to Oceania under the leadership of Mgr. *Pompallier. Together with a lay-brother, Joseph Xavier, he was sent (1837) to the island of Wallis, which – as he reported to Mgr. Pompallier – he had completely converted by 1842. In that year he became first *Vicar Apostolic of Central Oceania. He remained at the island of Wallis and used it as a base for further missionary activities to the islands of Samoa, Rotuma and the Fijis until his death. He used a very special method in his conversion work: a number of people interested in Christianity were transferred from their surroundings to a centre already christianized. There they were trained and instructed. Once they were fully trained and baptized, they were brought back to their homes and a missionary was sent with them to provide for their spiritual needs and to continue the spreading of Christianity from the new centre.

ARTHUR MCCORMACK, MHM

Les Missions Catholiques LXXII (Lyon 1940); *LTK* II, 50; *NCE* II, 163.

BATAK CHURCH. See INDONESIA.

BECHUANALAND. See BOTSWANA.

BEIRUT, AMERICAN UNIVERSITY AT. See NEAR EAST COLLEGE ASSOCIATION.

BENEDICTINE MISSIONS. St. Benedict (480–543), the founder of the order, concerned himself with the conversion of the pagans and half-pagans in the neighbourhood of Monte Cassino. A great period of Benedictine mission history (7th-12th century) is marked by names like St. Augustine of Canterbury (+c.604), St. Wilfred (+709), St. Willibrord (+738), St. Boniface (+755), St. Ansgar (+865), St. Adalbert (+997), Vicelin B. of Oldenburg (+1154), who planted or consolidated Christianity in England, Central Europe and Scandinavia. In the early 19th century we find different Benedictine abbeys carrying on missionary activity in Australia, North America, South Africa and Ceylon. In the years 1884–87 a new approach to mission work in the order was made, when Dom Andreas Amrhein, a monk of Beuron, founded the Congregation of St. Ottilien (Bavaria) for monks, and the Congregation of Tutzing (Bavaria) for nuns, with the specific orientation to foreign missions. At present (1967) 600 clerical and 700 lay monks of six abbeys in Germany, Austria and USA and a priory in Switzerland, staff and maintain two dioceses in Tanzania (Peramiho and Ndanda), one diocese in South Africa (Eshowe, Zululand); the abbey and mission of Waegwan, S. Korea; an abbey in Venezuela, and a priory in Columbia. Before the partition of Korea, the Ottilien Benedictines had also charge of two dioceses north of the 48th parallel (Wonsan, Korea, and Yenki, Manchuria).

H. J. MÜLLER, OSB

C. Butler: *Benedictine Monasticism* (London

1919); Dom Ramanus Rio: *Benedictines of Today* (Stanbrook Abbey, 1946); *NCE* II, 288–303.

BENTLEY, WILLIAM HOLMAN (1855–1905),

was born in Sudbury, Suffolk, England. One of the first missionaries of the BMS to leave England for the Congo after the prospecting trip of George *Grenfell and Thomas Comber, he reached San Salvador in July 1879. The BMS aimed to press forward to the upper river and use the Congo as a highway into central Africa. B. was associated in attempts to reach Stanley Pool overland, eventually succeeding with Crudgington in February 1881. In 1884 he was present at the Berlin West Africa Conference to give evidence helpful to Leopold II in delimiting his lower Congo frontiers with France and Portugal. In 1887 B. arrived at Bolobo with his wife and baby, who made a great impression, but after Comber's death he returned to the lower river and took charge of the mission station of Wathen (Ngombe). Instruction at its school included telegraphy and printing. B's great work lay in the field of language study and translation. He produced a Kikongo dictionary and grammar, and translated the NT into Kikongo. B. wrote an account of his missionary activities entitled *Pioneering on the Congo* (2 vols., London 1900).

RUTH SLADE

H. M. Bentley: *W. Holman Bentley: The Life and Labours of a Congo Pioneer* (London 1907).

BERLIN MISSIONARY SOCIETY, THE,

was founded in 1824 by a group of Prussian government servants, professors and others who had been inspired by the neo-Pietistic awakening in Eastern Germany. Originally serving as a supporting agency for the *Basel Mission and other agencies, the Berlin M.S. founded a seminary in 1829, and began to function as a sending agency in its own right when in 1833 the first five missionaries were commissioned for work in South Africa, which has remained the principal field of work ever since. New fields were opened in China (Kwangtung and S.

Kiangsi) in 1882 and South Tanzania in 1891. Although based on the Prussian Union Church (Lutheran and Reformed), the Berlin M.S. developed a distinctively Lutheran character. With the division between Eastern and Western Germany the Berlin M.S. was faced with great difficulties. The headquarters of the mission remains in East Berlin. Since 1963 the Berlin M.S. has had very close relations with the Evangelical Church of the Union (as the Prussian Church is now known). The Berlin M.S. has succeeded in remaining one of the largest of German missionary societies. It strongly supports the three Evangelical Lutheran Churches which were founded in South Africa in respectively 1960, 1962 and 1963.

H.–W. GENSICHEN

J. Richter: *Geschichte der Berliner Missionsgesellschaft* (Berlin 1924).

BERMUDA. See CARIBBEAN.

BESCHI, CONSTANTINE JOSEPHUS

(1680–1746), an Italian *Jesuit, was in the service of the Madura mission from 1710 till 1746 when he died at Manapparai. He carried on the strict tradition of Robert de *Nobili, wearing Indian dress, and avoiding anything that could give offence to the high caste Hindus. From an early period of his career he devoted himself to the study of Indian languages, especially Tamil, and acquired a greater mastery of them than perhaps any other European in history. He composed in Latin excellent grammars, both of classical Tamil and of the common speech (1732). He was the author of a great many books in both classical Tamil poetry and in prose. His masterpiece, the epic *Tēmbarani*, in 3615 quatrains, is a history of the life of Joseph the husband of Mary, into which large sections of the Gospel story have been introduced. To western taste it is tedious, but Tamil scholars are agreed that it may be regarded as a minor classic of Tamil literature. No other work by a foreigner has ever attained to this distinction. The period of B's service overlapped with that of *Ziegenbalg and the first

Lutheran missionaries at Tranquebar. His attacks upon them did not lack vigour; in a somewhat elaborate tract he compares them to the locusts of Rev.9, which were let loose upon the earth when the shaft of the bottomless pit was opened. Yet his Tamil grammars were printed at the Lutheran press in Tranquebar. B. was the last great missionary of the original Madura tradition.

STEPHEN NEILL

L. Besse: *Father Beschi of the Society of Jesus: His Times and his Writings* (Trichinopoly 1918); *LTK* II, 290; *NCE* II, 364f.

BETHEL MISSION, THE, was founded in Berlin in 1886 as the Evangelical Missionary Society for German East Africa. In 1890 it was saved from collapse through the intervention of Friedrich von Bodelschwingh. In 1906 the direction was transferred to Bethel, Germany, and in 1920 the mission received its present name. It grew together with the 'Zion Congregation' of Bethel. In the process of integration, in 1965 representatives of the church joined the directing body of the mission. The first mission field was Zanzibar, with Dar es Salaam and its surroundings; these were handed over to the *Berlin Mission in 1903. In 1891 P. Wohlrab and E. Johannsen opened up work in Usambara; in 1907 E. Joahannsen in Ruanda. In 1910 the first station at Bukoba was founded. During the first world war the church in Usambara became independent. After the war work went forward in Usambara and Bukoba. During the second world war, American and Scandinavian missions took over these fields as trustees. After the war Lutheran work was developed on an international and co-operative basis, and to this the BM adhered. The churches which have grown out of the work of the BM belong to the North-West and North-East (Usambara-Digo) dioceses of the Evangelical Lutheran Church of Tanzania, the first with 80,000, the second with roughly 46,000 baptized members.

J. BUSSE

C. Hellberg: *Mission on a Colonial Frontier West of Lake Victoria* (Lund 1965); G.

Jasper: *Das Werden der Bethel-Mission* (Bethel 1936).

BHUTAN. Area 18,000 sq.m. Population c. 600,000. An independent state in the eastern Himalayas, between Tibet and India, B. is a picturesque country of lofty mountains and steep valleys. The dominant race are the Bhotias of Tibetan origin whose religion is a form of lamaistic *Buddhism with large monasteries.

Until the beginning of the 20th century the government of the country was feudalistic, but since 1907 there has been a hereditary monarchy, guided by the government of India with regard to external relations. Progress has been made both in education and communications, with the aid of Indian loans. Seventy new schools have been opened by the government since 1960.

Evangelistic work is not permitted in B. itself. Christian missions have been engaged in work among Bhutanese across the frontiers, especially in East Bengal. The Church of Scotland established a congregation and a dispensary on the western frontier and operates some village schools in B. itself. Its medical and educational work in Kalimpong is of special importance. The Scandinavian Alliance Mission began work in Baksa Duar, five miles from the frontier, in 1892, but though friendly relations have been established with Bhutanese there is no Christian community in Baksa itself. Since 1959 the Free Church of Finland has also been at work among Bhutanese, but outside the borders of the country.

HENRY LEFEVER

A. McLeish: *The Frontier People of India* (London 1931); *Christian Handbook of India* 1959 (Nagpur); *BM* II, 143f.; *ERE* II, 561.

BIBLE AS A MISSIONARY FORCE, THE. Christian evangelistic work and Christian Scriptures have normally gone hand in hand. The earliest work of the apostles was, of course, oral, but it was not long before the church built the written records of the life of Jesus and the letters of early leaders to a number of their churches into a NT that could be used with authority.

St. Cyril (A.D. 826–869), in his mission to Moravia, invented an alphabet and translated the Scriptures into Slavonic. Wycliffe and Tyndale began the British religious revival with their versions of Scripture. Luther's German Bible was one of the mainstays of the Reformation on the continent of Europe. In more recent times it was William *Carey's zeal for the spread of the Christian faith that inspired him to devote his life to translation.

Nearly all translators today are missionaries and nationals identified with the church or with pioneer evangelism in the countries where they live and work. Very few persons do Bible translation as an independent, purely academic task.

Translation work usually begins with a Gospel, which can be distributed to open-air crowds. When a church is formed, it must be supplied first with a NT and then with a complete Bible. From time to time this Bible will need revision, preferably by men and women who have the language as their mother-tongue, so that it may speak naturally to its readers.

There are many accounts of individuals who have been won for Christ simply by reading the Scriptures, before they have had any close personal links with Christians. Mahatma Gandhi knew the NT well, and often commended the Sermon on the Mount in particular to others, though he never had any intention of actually becoming a Christian. Scriptures have also been able to continue to find their way into closed countries such as Tibet, where direct missionary work is impossible.

The Bible has also sustained the church during persecution. In Madagascar, in the middle of the 19th century, there was a period when foreign missionaries were driven out and national Christians were put to death in considerable numbers. They had their Bibles, however, which they read secretly and kept buried in holes in the ground. When the persecution was over and communication with the outside world was restored, it was found that the church was larger and stronger than before. Christian schools throughout the world have taught the Bible in English or the local language, and have thus assisted in character formation, whether the teaching has led to *baptism or not. In 1964 the Ghana government ordered half a million NTs for use in its schools. County authorities in England, where the missionary need is as great as anywhere, order large supplies from the Bible Society for use in their schools.

The Bible makes its primary appeal through the sheer fact of translation. Readers at first have something that is intelligible. They go on to cherish the Book almost as though it had been written originally in their own mother tongue. Indeed a great many readers unconsciously assume that it was. That is perhaps the supreme missionary power of the Bible. It comes right home.

HAROLD K. MOULTON

BIBLE DISTRIBUTION. The combined circulation figures for the Bible Societies during 1968 were as follows: Bibles 4,801,653; New Testaments 9,227,854; Portions (mainly Gospels) 32,785,242; Selections (i.e. Christmas and Easter stories, etc.) 63,693,141. In addition there were commercial sales in many countries for which no figures are obtainable.

In most countries Bible Society Scriptures are sold at a loss, at prices which it is estimated that purchasers can reasonably afford. The balance is made up by monies raised in countries where incomes are higher. In such countries Scriptures are sold at a small profit, as also are leather-bound and other luxury editions everywhere.

The most recent BFBS figures show that 49% of the society's circulation is done direct through Bible Houses, Bible vans and *colporteurs, 33% through bookshops, religious and secular, 11% through churches and missions, and the remaining 7% in other ways. Bookshops, colporteurs and church agents are allowed discounts so that their selling prices may be the same as the standard Bible Society prices.

Colporteurs in many countries have sold

millions of Scriptures by their personal approach. Their travels have usually involved them in hardship and often in danger from the forces of nature or of persecution. Bible vans are increasingly using modern methods of transport to take larger loads over longer distances to more readers. Direct sales by the churches need particular encouragement. The Bible Societies are not a separate organisation, but the handmaids of the church, and the two must work always in the closest co-operation.

HAROLD K. MOULTON
The Bulletin of the United Bible Societies, quarterly from 101, Queen Victoria Street, London, E.C.4. 6s. or 75c. a year.

BIBLE SOCIETIES. See UNITED BIBLE SOCIETIES.

BIBLE TRANSLATIONS AND VERSIONS. The OT was originally written in Hebrew, with a small part in Aramaic. The NT was written in Greek, the most widely used language in the Mediterranean world.

The earliest translation work was done by Greek-speaking Jews in Alexandria. They began translating the OT into Greek some time in the middle of the 3rd century B.C., and completed it before the 2nd century ended. A tradition arose that it was done by 70 (or, more exactly, 72) translators who worked independently for 72 days and produced identical translations at the end! Hence the Greek version of the OT is known as the Septuagint, from the Latin word for 70 and is referred to by the Latin figure LXX. It contains a number of books not in the Hebrew Bible. In Protestant Bibles these are placed for the most part between the OT and NT and are called the Apocrypha. In the Latin Vulgate and in RC Bibles they are intermingled with the books of the OT and are known as Deutero-Canonical (i.e. Second Canon).

Translations of the NT began in three main languages: Syriac, Egyptian and Latin. Syriac translation was first undertaken about A.D. 170 with a Harmony (combined Gospel story) made by Tatian. The Syriac Bible reached its standard form in the Peshitta, or

Common, Version before A.D. 400. This version is still read where Syriac is used in church worship.

Two main Egyptian versions, the Sahidic in Southern Egypt and the Bohairic in the north, were made in the 4th and 5th centuries.

Translation into Latin began before the end of the 2nd century. Various early efforts were consolidated by St. Jerome. He began his work in A.D. 382 and completed the Vulgate Bible, which has remained the standard version of the RC church until very recent times, though this church is now paying increasing attention to the original languages.

Versions in Gothic, Armenian, Georgian, Ethiopic, Arabic, Anglo-Saxon and other languages played their part in the spread of Christianity, but progress in translation work during the Middle Ages was relatively slow. It quickened again during the Reformation and the period which led up to it, with translations in German (especially Martin Luther's Bible, 1534), Italian (1471), French (NT 1474), Dutch (OT 1477), Spanish (1478), and languages in Scandinavia and Eastern Europe. In English there were translations beginning with the Wycliffe period and culminating in the King James, or 'Authorised', Version of 1611.

During this time and in the next two centuries some pioneer translation work was done in other parts of the world also; for example, Persian (1546), Malay (1629) Mohican (1663), Tamil (1715), Sinhalese (1739), Urdu (1743), Ashanti (1764) and Bengali (1800). The last was the work of William *Carey, the astonishing Baptist who spent 40 years in India. He was responsible, directly or indirectly, for translations into over 30 Indian languages.

Up till 1804 only 72 languages had translations of the Scriptures in whole or part. The foundation of the BFBS in that year inaugurated a remarkable increase. By 1850 the number had grown to 223; in 1900 it was 567. The figure at the end of 1968 was 1,392. This figure includes 242 Bibles, 320 NTs, and 830 Portions.

The majority of these versions have been

stimulated and published by the BFBS. The Netherlands Bible Society has been responsible for a number of major translations, particularly in Indonesia. In recent years the American Bible Society has published in many languages, specializing in Gospels for new areas. This society has also been working on a number of 'common language' versions, with a simple vocabulary and idiom, adapted to the needs of ordinary folk.

It is impossible to say how many languages have so far no part of the Christian Scriptures. A mere count of languages is in any case misleading, as some are spoken by millions, others by only a few hundred. It is estimated that at least one Gospel is available for 97% of the world's population, and the whole Bible for 90%.

At the present time many Bibles are undergoing revision. Scholarship has developed since the first translations were made. The orthography and actual vocabulary and idiom of many languages have changed. Above all, first translations are inevitably made by missionaries who are translating into a foreign language. Many of these translations have been deservedly successful, but the ideal translation must be made into a man's own mother tongue. Translators with the requisite scholarship and feel for their own language are increasingly performing this essential task.

HAROLD K. MOULTON

S. L. Greenslade, ed.: *The Cambridge History of the Bible: The West from the Reformation to the Present Day* (Cambridge 1963); J. S. M. Hooper: *Bible Translation in India, Pakistan and Ceylon,* 2nd ed. revised by W. J. Culshaw (Bombay 1963); F. G. Kenyon: *The Story of the Bible, A Popular Account of How it Came to Us* (London 1949); H. W. Robinson, ed.: *The Bible in its Ancient and English Versions* (Oxford 1954); J. M. Roe: *History of the British and Foreign Bible Society, 1905–1954* (London 1965); *WKL,* 154–58.

BIBLICAL BASIS OF MISSIONS. See THEOLOGY OF MISSION.

BIBLIOGRAPHIES. Raymond Morris' *A Theological Book List* (Blackwell, Allenson)

contains a basic missions bibliography by subjects, and scores of books dealing with the missionary enterprise have helpful bibliographies. Sources for current listings include the *Cumulative Book Index; Subject Guide to Books in Print; Library of Congress Catalog, Books: Subjects;* the *International Review of Mission,* and the fourth quarterly issue each year of *Het Missiewerk* (Nijmegen).

The *Dictionary Catalog of the Missionary Research Library* (17 volumes, G. K. Hall) provides a vast amount of data, as do the 10 volumes of *The Shelf List of the Union Theological Seminary Library in New York City* (G. K. Hall). Robert Streit's *Bibliotheca Missionum* (20 volumes plus, Herder) and the annual *Bibliographia Missionaria* (Rome, Macioci and Pisani) present the missionary literature of the world by areas.

John Barrow's *A Bibliography of Bibliographies in Religion* and the *Bibliographic Index* list many bibliographical sources. Subject specialization is implemented by *The Encyclopedia of Modern Christian Missions: The Agencies* (Nelson) and by such publications of the Missionary Research Library as *Missionary Biography, An Initial Bibliography;* Gerald H. Anderson's *Bibliography of the Theology of Missions in the Twentieth Century,* and his *Christianity in Southeast Asia: A Bibliographical Guide.* In 1967 the Hispanic-American Institute in Austin, Texas, published John H. Sinclair's *Protestantism in Latin America: A Bibliographical Guide.* 'Bibliography of the Society for African Church History I', edited by A. F. Walls, appeared in *Journal of Religion in Africa* (Leiden 1967), I, No. 1. *Critical Bibliography of Missiology* by Livinus Vriens (Nijmegen) is valuable for RC literature.

The Scottish Institute of Missionary Studies (Dept. of Church History, King's College, University of Aberdeen, AB9 2UB) has undertaken 'a bibliographical programme which, if successful, will be the most comprehensive listing of current literature on Christian mission yet attempted'. It will compare with the *Bibliografia Missionaria.*

The *Index to Religious Periodical Litera-*

ture, the *Christian Periodical Index*, the *Guide to Religious Periodicals*, the *British Humanities Index*, and *The Catholic Periodical Index* are keys to the location of magazine articles, and *The Guide to Catholic Literature* supplies further indexing for Catholic missions. In 1969 the last two publications mentioned merged to form *The Catholic Periodical and Literature Index*.

See ARCHIVES; JOURNALS FOR MISSION STUDIES; MISSION LIBRARIES.

BURTON L. GODDARD

WKL, 159–61.

BICKERSTETH, EDWARD (1850–1897). Born at Banningham, Norfolk, England, he studied at Cambridge under B. F. Westcott and J. B. Lightfoot. In 1877 he went to India as first head of the Cambridge Mission to Delhi, where he worked as pastor, evangelist, educator and administrator, but was invalided home in 1882. Appointed missionary bishop of the Church of England in Japan, B. arrived there in 1886 and began to gather together the various Anglican elements – two missions from Britain (*CMS and *SPG), one from USA and one from Canada, as well as independent minded Japanese Christians. B. enlisted the co-operation of all in framing a constitution for the Nippon Sei Kokwai, the (Anglican) Church in Japan; the rules of the new church provided for a board of foreign missions. B. travelled widely as pastor and organizer. Amidst other duties he continued to study and was concerned that evangelism should have theological depth. He founded the St. Andrew's University Mission in Tokyo for men, and the St. Hilda's Community Mission for women, and himself began a Bible commentary in Japanese. In England for the Lambeth Conference of 1897, he died at Chisledon, Wiltshire. His biographer justly calls his work for the NSKK 'the first instance of the foundation of a fully organized and autonomous church in the near or far East in modern times'.

JOHN GOODWIN

S. Bickersteth: *Life and Letters of Edward Bickersteth, Bishop of South Tokyo* (London 1899); *DNB*, 1st Suppl., 194.

BIGANDET, PAUL AMBROSE (1813–1894), was born at Malans (Doubs), France. He joined the *MEP and began his missionary service in southern Burma at Mergui. From 1841 he served in Penang, and returned to Burma as bishop in 1856. Two years later he was nominated as *Vicar Apostolic for the area. B. rapidly made himself master of the Burmese language, and used this knowledge for profound researches into the *Buddhism of Burma. His great work, *The Life or Legend of Gaudama, the Buddha of the Burmese*, appeared first in periodical form between 1852 and 1855; first edition as a book 1858, second much enlarged edition 1866, fourth edition London 1911. This work is still accepted as the classic exposition of Buddhism in its Burmese form. Under his guidance the work of the RC church acquired new vigour; the Christian Brothers were brought in to develop schools, and various sisterhoods to start work among women and girls. By 1866 the work had grown so extensively that B. recommended to Rome the division of the country, and this was carried into effect by the creation of the Vicariates Apostolic of Eastern, South-Western and Central Burma. At the outset of his work B. had a force of no more than twelve European priests; during the course of his episcopate he was able to ordain ten Burmans to the priestly office.

STEPHEN NEILL

P. Bigandet: *An outline of the history of the Catholic Burmese mission from the year 1720 to 1887* (Rangoon 1887).

BINGHAM, HIRAM (1789–1869), was born at Bennington, Vermont, USA, and educated at Middlebury College and Andover Theological Seminary. He sailed in 1820 for the Sandwich (Hawaiian) Islands as a member of the first missionary company appointed for that area by the *ABCFM. By virtue of his own character and abilities B. became the unofficial leader of the mission. Located at Honolulu, he was pastor of Kawaiahao Church, the first church in the town. He worked with other missionaries in reducing the Hawaiian language to writing and in translating portions of the Bible and a number of books for use in the schools. With William *Ellis of the *LMS he prepared the Hawaiian Hymn Book. B. was confidant and trusted adviser to the royal family and some of the island governors; he helped them to prepare laws guiding the moral behaviour of the people and restricting the activities of visiting seamen and traders. Although opposed and threatened by persons of lax morals, he gave the Hawaiians a lead in establishing Christian standards. In 1841 B. returned to the USA owing to his wife's ill health. Of their seven children, two were active in the missionary enterprise – Hiram Bingham 2nd, for nearly 10 years in the Gilbert Islands, and Mrs. Lydia Bingham Coan, wife of a missionary who served for many years in Hilo, Hawaii.

J. LESLIE DUNSTAN

R. Anderson: *History of the Sandwich Islands Mission* (Boston 1870); H. Bingham: *Residence of Twenty-one Years in the Sandwich Islands* (Hartford 1848); *DAB* II, 276.

BINGHAM, ROLAND VICTOR (1872–1942), the founder of the *SIM, was born in East Grinstead, Sussex, England. B's father died when the lad was 13. Although his father was a Christian, B. was not converted until his teens in a *Salvation Army meeting. Because B. shared the SA's opposition to tobacco, he finally drew his savings from the bank and left for Canada, not wishing to impose his personal convictions on his mother, who sold tobacco in her store.

In Toronto B. was invited to the home of Mrs. Gowans whose son had gone to the Sudan (the area of Africa immediately south of the Sahara) to open it to the gospel. Through conversation with her he was convinced that God was calling him to the Sudan. He accompanied Walter Gowans and Tom Kent to Lagos in 1893, determined to open the Sudan, although a Methodist missionary leader told them it would never happen in their generation. B. was felled by malaria and remained at Bida while Gowans and Kent went on. Both of them died. B. returned to Canada, went to Cleveland,

USA, for medical training of a sort, and to Simpson's Bible College in New York. In 1898 he married Helen E. Blair and decided to start a missionary agency, although he had neither money nor workers. In 1901, after his third effort, a station was opened in Patigi in West Africa and the SIM was established.

The mission grew slowly but within 50 years of its beginning the staff numbered almost 1,300. Through B's broad vision the mission engaged in medical work, education, and Bible translation and printing. The Niger Press was established and from it poured out many thousands of pages of reading material. The *African Challenge*, begun as the *West African Christian* in 1948 and renamed in 1951, became a widely used instrument of the mission.

B. was directly or indirectly responsible for the establishment and propagation of many new ventures outside Africa. The *Evangelical Christian and Missionary Witness*, later called *The Evangelical Christian*, was his creation. The Gowans Home for Missionaries' Children was established in 1923. The Canadian Keswick Conference was another of B's dreams that was realized. Deeply concerned for the fighting men of the second world war, B. organized the Soldiers' and Airmen's Christian Association in Canada, really a branch of the Scripture Readers' Association in England.

B. was both a gifted writer and a fluent and effective public speaker. The SIM was the lengthened shadow of its founder, but he built well and established the mission on a firm foundation of evangelical faith and theology. Convinced that God would supply the needs of the workers, the mission was committed to a *faith platform from its beginning, looking only to God to provide. B. was followed in his leadership of the mission by Guy Playfair, then Albert D. Helser, and at present Raymond J. Davis. B. died in Toronto, 4 December 1942.

HAROLD LINDSELL

J. H. Hunter: *A Flame of Fire, The Life and work of R. V. Bingham* (Toronto 1961).

BIRKELI, OTTO EMIL (1877–1952), one

of the most distinguished missionaries of the Norwegian missionary society, was sent to Madagascar in 1903, where he opened up pioneer work among the primitive Schelawa people of the west coast. He took special pains with the study of the Malagasy language, and also with investigation of the ideas and traditions of the people among whom he worked. In 1919 B. returned to Norway, and became a teacher at the school for the preparation of missionaries in Stavanger, with special responsibility for history and theory of missions. He was principal of the school from 1937 till 1944, and also for a number of years editor of the missionary journal *Norsk Misjonstidende*. B's studies of *primitive religion in Madagascar had served as an excellent training ground for scientific research into the ancient pre-Christian traditions of Norway, and into the survival of primitive ideas in later times. He published important works on *ancestor-worship and kindred themes. B's son Fridtjov, also for some years a missionary in Madagscar, is at the time of writing bishop of Oslo.

STEPHEN NEILL

Norsk Misjonsleksikon, Vol. I (Stavanger 1965), pp.206f.

BLIND, MISSIONS TO THE. Before the coming of modern western civilization the blind in many countries followed traditional occupations, such as music, story-telling and begging. When some of these became obsolete in Europe monasteries and special charities for the blind helped those whose families could not meet their needs; some poor relief was organized by the state (first at Frankfurt-on-Main in 1437). The first school for educating and employing the blind was founded in Paris, France, in 1784 by V. Haüy. A school was started in England in 1791, followed by similar schools in most European countries. Christians sought to meet the spiritual, social and physical needs of the blind through such organizations as the interdenominational Indigent Blind Visiting Society, founded in London by Lords Shaftesbury and Ebury in 1834, and the Roman Catholic order of the Blind

Sisters of St. Paul, founded in Paris by Anne Bergunion in 1853. The first institutions in America were founded at Boston and New York in 1830, and the first in Australia at Sydney in 1880.

Most of the early work in Asia and Africa was done by Christian missionaries. M. Mott of the British Syrian Mission founded a blind school in Beirut in 1868; W. Hill Murray of the Bible Society of Scotland opened a school in Peking in 1875 and began to adapt Braille to the Chinese language; Miss Sharp of the CEZMS opened the first blind institution in India at Amritsar in 1887; W. Murray of the DRC opened the first institution in South Africa at Worcester in 1881. The first institution for the blind in tropical and equatorial Africa was started by the Salvation Army near Nairobi as recently as 1942. The John Milton Society, founded in New York in 1928 and supported by Protestant churches in USA and Canada, provides literature in Braille and financial aid to Christian institutions serving the blind in many countries. Today many of the larger missionary societies have some work specially for the blind, including the prevention and medical treatment of blindness. In most countries this is carrried out more and more in co-operation with the state.

JOHN GOODWIN

Report of the International Conference on the Blind, held at Westminster, 1914 (London 1914); *Report of the First African Conference on Work for the Blind, held at Lagos, 1966* (Lagos 1966).

BLISS, DANIEL (1823–1916), founder and first president of the American University of Beirut, was a pioneer in higher education in the Near East. He grew up on a Vermont farm, and very early had to support himself. He worked his way through Amherst College and Andover Theological Seminary, and was ordained a Congregational minister in 1855. That same year he married Abby Wood, and under appointment of the *ABCFM sailed from Boston to join the Syria Mission. From 1856 until his death in 1916 he made Syria and Lebanon his home, with only occasional visits to America. After only a few years on the field, he was charged by his colleagues in the mission with the task of founding a college or university of higher learning. He spent long months in the USA and Britain raising funds, returning to Beirut to open the Syrian Protestant College (now the American University of Beirut) and became its first president in 1866. The brilliance and wisdom of his leadership for the next 36 years guided the college in its formative period, until the inauguration of his son, Howard Sweetser Bliss, as president in 1902. The student body had grown from sixteen to 626, the schools of medicine and pharmacy being especially strong, and the early rented quarters had been replaced by a magnificent, spacious campus overlooking the Mediterranean. At the laying of the cornerstone of College Hall in 1871, B. gave expression to the Christian purpose of the institution. He said: 'This college is for all conditions and classes of men . . . Christian, Jew, Mohammedan or heathen may enter and enjoy all the advantages of this institution for three, four, or eight years; and go out believing in one God, in many gods, or in no God. But it will be impossible for anyone to continue with us long without knowing what we believe to be the truth and our reasons for that belief.'

HARRY G. DORMAN, JR

F. J. Bliss, ed.: *The Reminiscences of Daniel Bliss* (New York 1920); H. H. Jessup: *Fifty-three Years in Syria* (New York 1910).

BLUMHARDT, CHRISTIAN GOTTLIEB. See BASEL MISSION.

BOARDMAN, GEORGE DANA (1801–1831). Pioneer missionary to Burma; influential in opening work among the Karens. He was born in Maine, USA, and educated in Waterville, Maine and Andover Theological Seminary. Early he became interested in the work of Baptists in Burma. In 1825 he married Sarah Hall and they were appointed as Baptist missionaries to Burma, serving in both Moulmein and Tavoy. His chief emphases were village preaching and the opening of village schools. Along with the famous Karen evangelist, *Ko Tha Byu, he was responsible for opening work among Karens, a largely uncivilized, minority hill tribe of Burma. These have since become one of the most responsive peoples in Asia to the Christian message. He developed a plan for Christian schools as a beach-head for Christian missions in a new culture. This included strong central schools which would train teachers for nearby village schools. This strategy became formative in mission policy in Burma and elsewhere, though its value was seriously questioned by his colleague, Adoniram *Judson.

Mrs. Boardman was a brilliant linguist and active in founding girls' schools. After the death of B. in 1831 she married Judson and continued her fruitful ministry in Burma until her death at sea in 1845.

PAUL CLASPER

J. Robbins: *Boardman of Burma* (Philadelphia 1940); R. Torbert: *Venture of Faith* (Philadelphia 1955).

BOLIVIA, a South American republic, bounded on the west by Peru and Chile, on the south by Argentine and Paraguay, on the north and east by Brazil. Area 424,163 sq.m., estimated population 3,668,000. More than half are Indian, one-third *mestizo* (mixed race), the remainder Spanish with some from other European nations. Spanish is the official language, but more than half speak Quechua or Aymara. The western part of the country is mountainous, and the capital, La Paz, lies 15,000 feet above the sea. Having lost its Pacific sea-coast in a disastrous war with Peru, B. is now entirely land-locked. For centuries its main source of revenue was tin. Recent attempts to diversify and modernize the economy have met with only partial success; the standard of living is low, and 68.9% of the population is illiterate.

The RC faith arrived in the 16th century with the Spanish conquerors, the majority of the early missionaries being *Jesuits and *Franciscans. The first bishopric was erected at La Plata in 1552, followed in 1605 by La Paz and Santa Cruz. Almost the whole population came in course of time to accept the new faith, but christianization was very superficial; and though today 95% of the population professes the RC faith, much pagan practice is mixed up with Christian observance. B. obtained its independence from Spain on 6 August 1825. In spite of liberal influence, Roman Catholicism remains the official religion of the country, and subventions are paid by the government to that church. But the principle of religious *liberty is now fully accepted. In recent years the Vatican has taken steps to raise the level of Christian knowledge and practice in the country.

Lucas Matthews of the BFBS entered B. in 1827; he was the first of many *colporteurs to work there for short times throughout the 19th century. The first permanent Protestant work was established by a Canadian Baptist, Archibald Reekie, in 1898; a year later he opened the first Protestant school, in Oruro. A law that prescribed the death penalty for anyone who proclaimed any form of faith other than the RC was abolished in 1906 through the efforts of Francis Harrington, Methodist missionary and founder of the first Methodist church and school, the American Institute, in 1907. Mr. and Mrs. George Allen founded the Bolivian Indian Mission (now Andes Evangelical Mission—AEM) in 1907. Today there are approximately 35 Protestant groups with 100,000 believers in B. Among the largest denominations are: AEM with about 10,000 believers, Canadian Baptists with 2,500 baptized believers, Oregon Friends with about 5,000 believers; Assemblies of God with from 4,000 to 5,000 believers including 1,600 baptized members. These groups are all self-governing, self-supporting and independent; the missionaries act only as advisers. In 1968 one half of the Canadian Baptist churches were self-supporting, and it was expected that within four years all would be. The Methodist Church has 3,500 full and probationary members; it has two schools with more than 1,000 students each, many smaller schools, a hospital and other medical work. It started a 10-year plan in 1966 which will lead to self-support. United Protestant organizations with legal entity are: the United Evangelical Church with from six to eight groups with believers totalling 10,000; and the National Association of Evangelicals, a new group that includes about fifteen denominations. Protestants also unite in literacy and social action organizations, and worked together in the Evangelism in Depth effort in 1965.

NATALIE BARBER

N. H. Dabbs: *Dawn over the Bolivian Hills* (Toronto 1952); C. P. Wagner and J. S. McCullough: *The Condor of the Jungle* (New York 1966); *BM* II, 149–56; *NCE* II, 643–48; *WKL*, 172.

BOMPAS, WILLIAM CARPENTER (1834–1906), first Bishop of Athabasca, 1874–1884; of Mackenzie River, 1884–1891; of Selkirk (Yukon), 1891–1906. B. was born in London, England, into a Baptist family and at the age of 16 was baptized by immersion. He first turned to law as a career but in 1858 decided to enter the ministry of the Church of England and was confirmed. After two curacies in England, he volunteered, in 1862, for work under the *CMS, in what is now North-Western Canada, an area stretching from Great Bear and Great Slave Lakes to the Arctic Ocean. Here he began establishing churches and schools and learning the Indian dialects. The bitter cold of an Arctic winter, temporary snow-blindness, loneliness and isolation did not daunt him. In 1874 he was consecrated Bishop of Athabasca, and married Selina Cox. In 1884 the diocese was divided and B. took the more difficult northern area. In 1891 he moved to the diocese of Selkirk (Yukon) where he added work among the miners of the gold rush to that among the Indians. In 1906, just after retiring, he died at Carcross. B. published translations in no less than seven Indian dialects, including Slavi, Tukudh, Beaver and Chipewyan, of manuals, prayers, portions of the prayer book, the NT and other Scripture portions. He also completed an English translation of the NT from Syriac, and parts of the OT from Hebrew.

KATHARINE B. HOCKIN

H. A. Cody: *An Apostle of the North;*

memoirs of Bishop W. C. Bompas (Toronto 1908); *DNB* 2nd Suppl. i, 190f.

BOOKS FOR AFRICA. Discussions on literature at the Le Zoute Conference, 1926, led to the formation in 1929 of the International Committee on Christian Literature for Africa (ICCLA) with Miss Margaret Wrong of Canada as secretary. In January 1931 ICCLA published the first number of the quarterly bulletin *Books for Africa.* Widely distributed among church workers in Africa, BFA carried articles to stimulate the writing, publishing and distributing of Christian books, together with book lists to help teachers, pastors, village workers, theological tutors. Margaret Wrong also influenced Christian literature in Africa by constant travelling and through the periodical *Listen.* When she died in Uganda in April 1948, first Mrs. U. H. S. Snow and then the Rev. C. de Mestral continued to edit BFA. Its last issue was July 1963, its work of more than 30 years' inspiration to the churches in Africa then being continued within Africa by the *AACC through its Literature Clearing Houses and through the literature committees of the *National Christian Councils.

T. A. BEETHAM

BOONE, WILLIAM JAMES (1811–1864), was born in Walterborough, South Carolina, USA. Having graduated in law, theology and medicine before the age of 26, B. was ordained a priest in the PECUSA in 1837. In the same year he was appointed a missionary to China. After studying Chinese in Djakarta for two years, he moved to the mainland, becoming the first missionary of his church in China proper. He returned to the USA after the death of his wife and launched a vigorous campaign to arouse support for the mission, which culminated with his election in 1844 as the first missionary bishop sent by PECUSA to China. When he arrived back in China B. moved the centre of his work to Shanghai where he laboured for the next 20 years. During his ministry he initiated virtually every aspect of his church's work in China. As a contemporary wrote,

'Thus he was pre-eminently *a founder'*. A cultured, winning, deeply spiritual man, B. was noted especially for his unusual linguistic and literary powers. He first put the Book of Common Prayer into the colloquial dialect, and he played a leading role in the revision of the Chinese Bible.

A. THEODORE EASTMAN

W. S. Perry: *The Bishops of the American Church* (New York 1897), p.99; 'Death of Bishop Boone' in *Spirit of Missions* (January 1865), pp.21–25.

BORGHERO, FRANCESCO (1830–1892), a priest of the RC diocese of Genoa, joined the *Society of African Missions in 1858 at Lyons. In 1861 he founded a mission station at Whydah in Dahomey, three years after the death of all the first RC missionaries at Freetown. He journeyed inland to the capital Abomey, recording how he offered Mass daily, was exempt from the rule that white people must watch the public human sacrifices, and met the 'King'. B. toured the coast west and east, at Whydah he opened a school and dispensary, and welcomed orphans. Public preaching was not permitted to him; B. considered *animism and *polygamy to be the two principal bars to conversions. In 1861 he wrote: 'What gives us confidence is the certain hope of being able to establish, quite soon, an African clergy. . . . Quite a number of young men have the right disposition for it: we might have some priests in ten or twelve years.' Actually it was to be 58 years. B. burnt himself out (and some of his fellow missionaries) in four years. In 1865, ill and depressed, he resigned. A pioneer, he had done his job. Whydah was flourishing, Porto Novo mission was opened in 1864; Lagos followed in 1868. B. worked in Italy for the rest of his life, something of a hermit.

JOHN M. TODD

J. M. Todd: *African Mission* (London 1962).

BORNEO (KALIMANTAN). See INDONESIA.

BORNEO, NORTH. See MALAYSIA.

BOTSWANA is a republic of southern Africa within the Commonwealth. Area: 222,000 sq.m.; population (1966 est.): 576,000. There are eight principal Botswana tribes; the principal languages are Setswana and English. A survey in 1964 showed 22% of the population literate in Setswana and 15% in English. First contacts with Europe came through the *LMS missionaries, R. *Moffat in the 1820s, and D. *Livingstone in the 1840s. In 1885 as a result of an appeal by Botswana chiefs the country became the British Protectorate of Bechuanaland; it became independent in 1966. B. has a cattle-based subsistence economy supported by overseas aid; it is seeking to strengthen its position by developing mineral resources.

The indigenous religion is *animism, but 'about one in seven of the population is Christian' (govt. estimate, 1965). *Khama, chief of Bamangwato, was a notable Christian. The principal missions now at work include LMS (Congregational), Hermannsburg (Lutheran), DRM, Anglican, RC, SDA, Methodist and United Free Church of Scotland (UFCS). In the new capital of Gaberones Anglicans, Congregationalists, Friends, Methodists and Presbyterians co-operate in Trinity Church, opened in 1966. In May 1966 the B. Christian Council was formed, and now includes Anglicans, Apostolic Faith Mission, Congregationalists, DRM, Lutherans, Methodists and UFCS (observers: Assemblies of God, RCs and SDAs); the Council is a member of *AACC and thus of *WCC. Educational and medical work, pioneered by missions, have become increasingly the responsibility of government, but the churches continue to share in both.

A. J. HAILE

C. P. Groves: *The Planting of Christianity in Africa* (London 1948–58), Vol. II, pp.121, 159–63, 185–89, 275–82; Vol. III, pp.31f., 35, 104f.; *Republic of Botswana Fact Sheet* (30 September 1966); *BM* II, 123f.

BOWEN, THOMAS JEFFERSON (1814–1875), was born in Jackson County, Georgia, USA. In 1849 he was sent, by the Foreign Mission Board of the Southern Baptist Convention, to penetrate into the interior of West Africa. In 1850 he reached Abeokuta, where he had friendly relations with H. *Townsend, S. A. *Crowther, and D. *Hinderer. Unable to reach Fulani country owing to local wars, he preached in the Yoruba-speaking area and studied the language. In 1853 B., with his wife, founded the Baptist Yoruba mission at Ijaye, where his work began to bear fruit in conversions. He then moved 50 miles further inland to Ogbomosho, where he founded a station. A colleague, J. M. Harden, founded one at Lagos. B's aim was a line of missions from Lagos to Sokoto and Kano.

B. combined zeal with humanity and commonsense. He believed that civilization is necessary to the maintenance and growth of those who have been converted. In 1856 he left Africa and was prevented by ill-health from returning. After this the supply of Baptist missionaries was greatly diminished for several years. The foundation which B. had laid, however, did not entirely disappear. A flourishing mission and church have been built upon it.

JOHN GOODWIN

T. J. Bowen: *Central Africa: Adventures and Missionary Labors* (Charleston 1857), *A Grammar and Dictionary of the Yoruba Language* (Washington, DC 1858).

BOXER UPRISING IN CHINA. This uprising took its name from Chinese anti-foreign armed groups which practised gymnastic exercises. The uprising was a reaction against the pressure of the western world on China and especially against recent measures which were regarded as aggressive and disturbing the traditional Chinese way of life. It became acute in the spring and summer of 1900 and was especially violent in the north-east. At its height foreign diplomats and missionaries stood siege in the legation quarter and a Catholic church in Peking. An international force fought its way from Tientsin to Peking, relieved the besieged, and suppressed the Boxers in other centres. Missionaries, who by their occupation were more widely distributed than other foreigners, especially suffered. Chinese Christians were also attacked. About 225 missionaries were killed, most of them Protestants. More than 30,000 Chinese Christians perished, the large majority Catholics, for they were far more numerous than Protestants or Orthodox. Much mission property was destroyed. Some indemnity was obtained, partly through the pressure of western governments and partly from local sources; but some missionary societies, notably the *CIM, refused to accept any compensation, even when offered, either for loss of life or for property destroyed.

KENNETH SCOTT LATOURETTE

A. E. Glover: *A Thousand Miles of Miracles in China* (London 1904); K. S. Latourette: *A History of Christian Missions in China* (New York 1929).

BRĀHMO SAMĀJ (Society of the Worshippers of Brahman and God) was founded in 1828 by Rām Mohan Roy (1772–1833). It succeeded the Ātmīya-Sabhā which Roy had founded together with Tagore, Mitra, Bose and members of other leading families in Bengal in 1814. R. M. Roy, 'the father of modern India', belonged to an influential Brahman family, studied many languages and made contact with the Baptist missionaries at Serampore. Deeply impressed by the example given by Jesus (1820: *The Precepts of Jesus, the guide to peace and happiness*) and by Christian ethics in general, he became a strong critic of certain Hindu traditions (especially of the caste-system and of the burning of widows). The BS became the first movement by which those reforms were propagated. In their services on Saturdays they read from the Bible as well as from the Vedas and Upanishads. A sermon during the meeting reflects Protestant influences. The society believes in original monotheism underlying all Hindu traditions. This idea became the key for its universal concept of a fundamental unity in all religions corresponding to the ethical principles of the unity of all men. Under the leadership of Devendranath Tagore (1817–1905) the BS had its golden age; under the influence of Keshub Chunder Sen (1838–1884) it split as a result of the foundation of the Ādi-Samāj in 1865.

HORST BÜRKLE

H. v. Glasenapp: *Religiöse Reformbewegungen im heutigen Indien* (Leipzig 1928); G. S. Leonard: *A history of the Brahmo Samaj from its rise to 1878* (Calcutta 1936); D. S. Sarma: *Studies in the renaissance of Hinduism* (Benares 1944); K. C. Sen: *The Brahmo Samaj. Lectures in India* (London 1901); *ERE* II, 813–24.

BRAINERD, DAVID (1718–1747), born at Haddam, Conn., USA, entered Yale College in 1739 shortly after an experience of conversion; but was expelled in 1742 for attending a separatist meeting and making disparaging remarks about the rector of the college. Although he subsequently apologized and tried on a number of occasions to secure his college degree, he was unsuccessful. Pietistic, mystical, highly emotional, overly conscientious and deeply religious, he kept a dairy of his experiences with God and of his work for God, which after his death was widely read. In 1743 he decided to give himself to work among the Indians, and was appointed by the agents in the colonies of the Scottish *SPCK for work in Western Massachusetts. He began at Kaunaumeek, about 20 miles west of Stockbridge, Massachusetts, but after a short while convinced the Indians that it was to their advantage to move to Stockbridge. After ordination in 1744 he moved to Pennsylvania and afterward to New Jersey, continuing to work among the Indians in those places. He had early contracted tuberculosis, which under the hardships of frontier life rapidly grew worse. He died in Northampton at the home of Jonathan *Edwards, to whose daughter Jerusha he was engaged to be married.

B's diary was for more than a century a highly popular work among all schools of Evangelicals. For instance, the Anglican Henry *Martyn records in his diary that, as the date of his ordination drew near, he thought much of B., and longed to be like him in total devotion to the work of Christ.

J. LESLIE DUNSTAN

R. P. Beaver, ed.: *Pioneers in Mission* (Grand

Rapids 1967); J. Edwards (ed. P. E. Haward, Jr): *The Life and Diary of David Brainerd* (Chicago 1949); *DAB* II, 591f.

BRAY, THOMAS. See SOCIETY FOR PROMOTING CHRISTIAN KNOWLEDGE; UNITED SOCIETY FOR THE PROPAGATION OF THE GOSPEL.

BRAZIL represents almost one half of South America in both area and population. Land area comprises 3,288,240 sq.m., and the 1967 estimated population was 85,785,339.

The population is of heterogeneous historical and racial origin, of three principal sources, Indian tribes, African Negroes brought as slaves, and white European immigrants. While all three are represented throughout the country, proportions vary regionally. The Indian stock is found predominantly in the central and northern regions, Negroes along the tropical coastline, while the heaviest percentage of whites inhabits the more developed south. These population groups explain the great variety of religious behaviour, from the major Christian denominations to indigenous Indian and primitive African practices. The mixing of these strains has produced a peculiarly Brazilian type of popular religion called *macumba* or *candomblé*, practised throughout the country very extensively, but impossible to measure statistically.

Christian mission began with the Roman Catholic missionaries and chaplains who arrived with the first explorers and settlers sent in the 16th century by the Portuguese crown. Among various orders, the greatest influence was that of the *Jesuits. Fathers Manoel de Nobrega and José de Anchieta are the two most famous Jesuits, working with both the settlers and the Indian tribes, and often defending the latter from the former.

Protestant activity in colonial times was associated with foreign invasion. In 1555 a French expedition under Villegaignon established a colony in the bay of Guanabara. Some Calvinists held services and preached until the Portuguese regained control and founded the city of Rio de Janeiro in 1567. The Dutch under Prince Maurice of Nassau dominated Pernambuco from 1630 to 1654, but in this case also the victory of Portuguese arms meant the extinction of all Protestant traces.

Successful non-Roman missionary efforts awaited the 19th century. B. became an independent nation under an emperor in 1822, and a republic in 1889, when religious freedom was decreed. The traditional Protestant denominations are now represented in B., mostly as a result of work by missionaries from the USA.

Early pioneers in establishing permanent congregations were Justin Spaulding, Methodist, in 1836; Robert *Kalley, Congregational, in 1855; and Ashbel G. *Simonton, Presbyterian, in 1859. Baptist work began in 1881 under Bagby and Taylor, and that of the Episcopal Church with the arrival of *Kinsolving and Morris in 1890. Of different character, however, is the Evangelical Church of Lutheran Confession formed in the south by immigration from Germany. The contribution of these churches in education has been notable, not only in maintaining many schools, but also by encouraging literacy for personal knowledge of Scripture and participation in worship.

There are now a large number of Protestant denominations, and also several missionary societies at work with indigenous tribes, such as the *Wycliffe Bible Translators, with more than 150 missionaries active.

The *Pentecostal movement has been the most significant development in mission in the 20th century, both in numbers reached and in degree of *indigenization. Among the many churches are the Assemblies of God, started by Swedish missionaries in the Amazon basin, the Christian Congregation of B., an almost completely indigenous movement with a slight initial connection with Italian Pentecostals, and Brazil for Christ, a powerful movement in the 1960s

The best available estimate (1964) of communicant membership in Protestant churches shows Pentecostals 1,689,000;

Lutherans 300,000; Baptists 235,000; Presbyterians 167,000; Methodists 53,000; Congregationalists 25,000; Episcopalians 13,000; others 110,000; total 2,592,000. These figures support the generally held estimate of a total Protestant community of about four million.

The RC church is understaffed in the light of its responsibilities. Over 90% of the population is baptized in that church, yet the total number of priests is only 12,293 (1966). A great deal of the energy of the church is directed to the maintenance of schools, hospitals, and other social agencies. Although the church has been traditionally a conservative force, recently figures such as the Archbishop of Recife, Dom Helder Câmara, have taken progressive, even radical, positions.

The *ecumenical movement is weak. Only the Lutheran, Methodist and Episcopal churches are member churches of the *WCC. The Evangelical Confederation of Brazil, organized in 1934, still does not represent a majority of non-RC Christians. On the other hand the Bible Society of Brazil holds second place in the world in the distribution of Bibles and portions of Scripture. Recent Protestant-RC contacts have been encouraging but are sporadic. Future developments are difficult to predict, but it seems likely that ecumenical experimentation in such areas of mission as the universities, agricultural frontiers, and industry, will be more important than official negotiations.

EDMUND K. SHERRILL

Anuário Católico (C.E.R.I.S., Rio 1966); *Anuário Estatistico do Brasil 1967* and other publications of the Brazilian Institute of Geography and Statistics; P. Calmon: *História do Brasil* (Rio 1959); G. U. Krischke: *História da Igreja Episcopal Brasileira* (Rio 1949); W. R. Read: *New Patterns of Church Growth in Brazil* (Grand Rapids 1965); D. Ribeiro: *Origens do Evangelismo Brasileiro* (Rio 1937); *BM* II, 158–74; *NCE* II, 762–78; *WKL*, 178f.

BREBEUF, JEAN DE (1593–1649), was born near Condé-sur-Vire, Normandy, France. In 1617 he applied for admission into the Society of *Jesus; in 1622 he was ordained priest at Pointoise. From university days B. was caught in the bitter strife between Jesuits and Huguenots, the war between England and France, and tribal wars between Hurons and Iroquois. Departures were delayed and supplies held up by the first two; the third was a factor in his martyrdom. In 1625 B. landed at Quebec; in 1626 he penetrated the Huron country around the southern end of Georgian Bay. Compelled by the fortunes of war to leave New France, B. took his final vows in France in 1630. In 1634 he was back in the Huron country and until 1638 was superior of the mission. B. had an amazing gift of language, and between 1635 and 1637 produced a dictionary, a grammar, instructions and catechisms in the Huron language. He was martyred, after fiendish torture, at St. Ignace, 16 March 1649. On 20 June 1930, he was canonized by Pope Pius XI. Pius XII proclaimed B. and his martyred companions patron saints of Canada, 16 October 1940. His spiritual journal and his *Relations* together with his letters form an important part of our knowledge of Indian life in that period of Canadian history. His whole life was regulated by his idea of duty —the salvation of souls entrusted to him by Christ.

KATHARINE B. HOCKIN

F. X. Talbot: *Saint among the Hurons* (New York 1949); R. Latourelle: *Etude sur les écrits de Saint Jean de Brébeuf* (Montreal 1952–1953); *LTK* II, 663.

BRENT, CHARLES HENRY (1862–1929). First Protestant Episcopal bishop of the Philippine Islands, and a founding father of the *Faith and Order Movement. Born in Newcastle, Ontario, Canada, B. was ordained a priest in 1887 and engaged in pastoral work in Buffalo, NY, and Boston, Mass., until his consecration as bishop of the newly created missionary district of the Philippines in 1901. Avoiding the proselytizing of Filipino Catholics, B. concentrated on a ministry to the American, British and Chinese residents of the Manila area and on missions among the Igorots of Mountain

Province and the Moros of Mindanao. B. came to international prominence in his fight against the opium traffic in Asia. In 1909 he presided over the International Opium Conference in Shanghai and represented the USA on the League of Nations Advisory Committee on Narcotics in 1923. Ill-health obliged B. to leave the Philippines in 1917, but almost immediately he answered General Pershing's call to become Chief-of-Chaplains of the American Expeditionary Force in France. From February 1919 until his death he served as Bishop of Western New York, to which diocese he had been elected prior to his departure for France.

Fired by a vision of the oneness of the Church of Christ, which came to him at the International Missionary Conference at *Edinburgh in 1910, B. worked zealously for the ecumenical cause, particularly in the realm of the all-important faith and order concerns. 'God has used, beyond anything we had a right to expect, our divided Christendom,' he wrote, 'but now that we know the sin and disaster of sectarianism, we cannot hope that He will use it much longer.' B. attended and addressed the Universal Conference on *Life and Work at Stockholm in 1925, and was one of the organizers and then the president of the First World Conference on *Faith and Order in Lausanne in 1927. He died in Lausanne on 27 March 1929, leaving behind a life full of achievement in Christ's service.

PETER G. GOWING

A. C. Zabriskie: *Bishop Brent: Crusader for Christian Unity* (Philadelphia 1948); *DAB* XXI, 155–57, *RGG* I, 1397; *WKL* 179f.

BRESILLAC, MELCHIOR DE MARION (1813–1859), was born at Castelnaudary, France, and educated first at home then in Roman Catholic seminaries. After being a parish priest for two years, he went as a missionary to India in 1842. He noted down his desire to 'direct all my own work and thought towards training a native clergy'. In 1844 he became superior of the seminary at Pondicherry, and in 1845 bishop at Coimbatore. He was opposed by the other French missionaries because he wanted to ignore the *caste system and to ordain a native clergy. Opposition finally led him to resign in 1855. In 1856 on 8 December, at Lyons, he founded the *Society of African Missions to work in West Africa. He spoke at this time of the Africans, 'so despised, who have not even been recognized as children of Adam, who have been treated in a way contrary to all justice like beasts'. He was determined that the society should proceed to ordain a native clergy as soon as possible. In 1859 B. went to Freetown and immediately caught yellow fever and died, with all the other four missionaries of the society then in Africa. Rome looked on B. as a great missionary though somewhat possessed with a *furia francese*, (a wild enthusiasm supposedly characteristic of the French).

JOHN M. TODD

L. le Gallen: *Vie abrégé du noble prélat, Mgr. de Marion Brésillac, Evêque de Prusa, fondateur des Missions africaines de Lyon, 1813–1859* (Lyon 1927); J. M. Todd: *African Mission* (London 1962); (Anon.) *Marion de Brésillac* (Namur 1939); *LTK* II, 87.

BRITISH GUIANA. See GUYANA.

BRITISH HONDURAS. See CARIBBEAN.

BRITTO, JOHN DE (1647–1692), missionary and martyr in India, was born in Lisbon, Portugal, of an aristocratic family, and while a page in the royal court, joined the Society of *Jesus. Against the wishes of his family he succeeded in securing appointment to the Madura mission in India, and arriving in 1673, selected the vocation of *Pardareswami*, i.e. to work not among the Brahmans but among the lower castes. This was a time of great difficulty for the mission, through the gradual break-up of the ancient kingdoms, ceaseless wars and disorders and famines. B. worked with the utmost devotion, was several times imprisoned, beaten and tortured, and finally condemned to death. Reprieved by the Rājā of Marawa (the Ramnad area) on condition that he no longer preached, B. returned to Portugal in 1687; but in 1691 was again in India, and, having refused the Archbishopric of Cranganore, returned to the scene of his former labours. Here he again fell into trouble, since a minor ruler converted by B. dismissed all his wives except the first. The youngest wife was a niece of the Rājā, who inflamed her uncle's mind against the missionary, accusing him of the use of magic to turn her husband's mind against her. B. was again arrested and beheaded on 4 February 1693 outside the little town of Uraiyur. He is regarded as second only to Robert de *Nobili in the history of the church in South India.

JOSEF GLAZIK

A. Bessières: *Le nouveau François-Xavier, St. Jean de Britto* (Toulouse 1947); H. Doering: *Johannes de Brito* (Freiburg/Br. 1920; also Eng. and Port. translations); *LTK* II, 87.

BROADCASTING, CHRISTIAN. The use of radio by Christians for evangelism, Christian nurture and community service in Asia, Africa and Latin America dates back to the beginning of radio itself, but has greatly accelerated in the last two decades. It represents the extensive use of modern technology in the mission of the church.

Christian radio has taken two forms, placement of programmes on commercial or government stations and the use of Christian stations. In countries such as Brazil, Japan and Zambia, for instance, extensive use is made of government or commercial outlets. There are also over 50 Christian radio stations, some of the best known being HCJB (Voice of the Andes), the oldest, in Ecuador; ELWA in Liberia; FEBC in Okinawa and the Philippines; TWR in Morocco and the West Indies; ETLF (Voice of the Gospel) in Ethiopia; HLKY (Christian Broadcasting System with five stations) in South Korea and SEARV (South East Asia Radio Voice) in the Philippines.

Fully half the Christian stations are in Latin America, about a quarter in East Asia.

The larger ones operate chiefly on short-wave.

Organizationally independent stations (often called 'missionary' or 'gospel' radio) are mainly North American in origin, and theologically conservative. They are linked by the International Christian Broadcasters organization (ICB). Others, on the RC side, are linked in the organization UNDA (Latin, 'wave'). On the Protestant side, stations serviced by *RAVEMCCO (the overseas communications committee of the NCCUSA), together with Christian councils using national outlets for radio, are linked by the World Association for Christian Communication (WACC). This organization was formed in 1968 by the bringing together of the World Association for Christian Broadcasting (WACB) and the Co-ordinating Committee for Christian Broadcasting (CCCB). Another extremely vigorous group is the Lutheran World Federation Broadcasting Services (LWFBS). LWFBS and CCCB together were the organizers of the RVOG project in Ethiopia, though the station is owned and run by the LWFBS. In stations connected with WACC and LWFBS great stress is placed on church control of broadcasting, and studios are set up in the 'target areas' so that nearly all material originates locally, and reflects the theological attitudes of the indigenous Christian communities.

Training is available to Christian broadcasters in church centres, of which those in Nairobi, Kinshasa (RC), Hong Kong and Jabalpur are well-known. Much training is done also in colleges in America and in public corporation training schools both locally and in Europe. TV training is available in church centres in Britain at Hatch End (RC) and Bushey (Protestant), but again many students are trained in the national and commercial stations.

B. M. LUBEN AND JOHN POULTON

BROWN, EDITH (1864–1956), was born in England, qualified as a doctor and in 1891 sailed for India for service with the Baptist Zenana Mission at the Charlotte Hospital, Ludhiana. She was largely responsible for the calling of a conference of women medical workers in 1893 which urged the establishment of a Christian medical school for women. This school was begun at Ludhiana, as one of the oldest Zenana missionary centres, seven societies co-operating on an undenominational basis. The initial courses for hospital assistants, dispensers, nurses and midwives proved so successful that numbers of students rapidly increased and buildings and equipment were enlarged and improved. Men students joined the college (as it had become) in 1951, and in that year the first male missionary doctor was appointed to the staff. Since 1953 courses have been conducted for the degree of MB, BS.

A woman of rigid theological views, EB required assent to a basis of faith by every candidate. In 1949 the supporting bodies 'recognized the need for appointing only such men and women as were in complete sympathy with the faith held by the other members of the staff'.

EB was awarded the silver Kaiser-i-Hind medal in 1911 in recognition of her public services, and the gold medal in 1922. In 1931 she was made a Dame Commander of the British Empire. In 1941 she retired reluctantly to Kashmir, but returned to the hospital again for a time in 1947 to help with the treatment of refugees and others injured during the massacres which followed Independence.

HENRY LEFEVER

F. French: *Dr. Brown's Hospital* (London 1954).

BRUNEI. See MALAYSIA.

BUDDHISM. The religion or way of life which has deeply affected Asian life for 2,500 years, and is a perennial challenge to Christian faith.

Gotama, a prince, was born in 560 B.C. (date contested) north of Benares, India. His sheltered life was shattered by seeing an old man, a sick man, a dead man and a monk. At the age of 30 years he left home to become one of many restless seekers after the truth which would cure human misery. After six years of philosophic speculation and extreme asceticism he found 'The Middle Way' of enlightenment and so became 'The Buddha', or Enlightened One. He continued until the age of 80 as teacher of the truth (*Dhamma*) and director of the growing order of monks (*Sangha*).

The essence of his earliest preaching and basis of orthodox B. is the Four-Noble Truths and the Eight-fold Path. All existence is filled with frustration, or suffering (*Dukkha*), which is caused by insatiable desire (*Tannha*). This passion must be eradicated and the means is a moderate path of discipline consisting of basic morality (*Sila*), strengthened by techniques of contemplation (*Samādhi*), which lead to the wisdom (*Panna*) which is the enlightened state. The Path leads to bliss or freedom (*Nirvāna*).

This is a way of self-deliverance; the idea of gods or a God is considered an irrelevant distraction from the serious business of doing what is immediately possible. The Buddha's final words express the essential spirit: 'Be lamps unto yourself.... Betake yourself to no external refuge.... Decay is inherent in all component things.... Work out your own salvation with diligence.'

In time the religion virtually disappeared from India, but was carried to other parts of Asia. Through the efforts of King Asoka (3rd century B.C.) missionary work was begun in Ceylon and later in Burma, Thailand, Cambodia and Laos. This southern B. is based strictly on the original scriptures and prides itself on today following the exact teachings and customs of the Buddha. This is called Thēravāda Buddhism, the Way of the Elders. Here the ideal is the saint (*Arahat*) who leaves the world and dedicates himself to understanding the truth.

Very early a liberal tendency arose which claimed to follow the spirit rather than the letter, and adapted the teachings to various philosophies and national cultures. This Mahāyāna Buddhism (the large vehicle— capable of including all) spread to China, Tibet, Korea and Japan, developing numerous sects. Among these are the Pure Land sects, the meditation sects (Zen), the intellectual sects (T'ien T'ai) and the socio-political sects (Nichiren). Important in this tradition is the *Bodhisattva* ideal of the compassionate Buddha, who forgoes *Nirvāna* in order to devote himself to saving others.

B. is being renewed in many places in Asia as new *nationalisms encourage appreciation of the specifically Asian heritage. Efforts have been made to unite the different Buddhist traditions. Missionary societies have been formed to spread Thēravāda teachings in remote sections of Asia and in the west. Zen Buddhism has great appeal in the west today, especially among younger educated people.

Christian faith faces a perennial challenge in B. The gospel has made but small penetration among peoples who have been strongly influenced by B. In one sense this is the light by which millions have lived and continue to live. It points to the emptiness of a passing world; encourages a quest for the abiding; and lives from the inspiration of one of the world's greatest teachers. Christian faith both fulfils and challenges this by the Way which originates in God who is active in history, supremely revealed in Jesus Christ, and calling into being a reconciling community as a chief instrument in his creative purpose. The relationship between Jesus Christ, believed in as the 'light of the world', and the Buddha, called 'the light of Asia', continues to be one of the persistent challenges to the Christian mission.

PAUL CLASPER

K. Ch'en: *Buddhism in China* (Princeton 1964); H. Dumoulin: *A History of Zen Buddhism* (London 1963); W. King: *Buddhism and Christianity* (Philadelphia 1962), *A Thousand Lives Away* (Oxford 1964); K. Morgan: *The Path of the Buddha, Buddhism Interpreted by Buddhists* (New York 1956); *WKL*, 188–91.

BURMA, a country shaped like a kite with a long tail, and 261,700 sq.m. in area, occupies the north-western third of the Indo-Chinese peninsula. It is bounded by India and the Bay of Bengal on the west, and China, Laos and Thailand on the east.

The population in 1968 was about 25 million.

There are many tribal groups, the Burmese forming the majority. Other large tribal minorities are the Karens, Shans, Kachins, Chins, Lahus, etc. These tribes have migrated from western China into B. To a large degree separate cultures have been maintained. B. continues as a country of rich diversity, and the problem of any effective unification is perennial.

Early history reveals numerous small kingdoms and dynasties attempting to establish control over the country. In 1886 the British annexed the kingdom of B.; during the following decades they also annexed Upper B., a large mountainous area inhabited by non-Burmese tribes. Movements for independence became strong in the early 1930s and continued up to the Second World War. During the war B. was occupied by the Japanese. In 1948 the country achieved independence and became the Republic of the Union of B.

The dominant religion of the majority Burmese, the Shans and many of the Karens is *Buddhism. This is the conservative, southern, scriptural (Pali) tradition of Thēravāda Buddhism (the Way of the Elders). This is similar to that found in Ceylon, Thailand, Cambodia and Laos. B. prides itself on the purity and vigour of its Buddhism. A revived Buddhism has characterized the new *nationalism. The famous Sixth Buddhist Council was held in Rangoon from 1954 to 1956. The largest Buddhist pagoda, the Shwe-Dagon, occupies the centre of the capital city, Rangoon.

Christian missions may be said to begin with the coming of Adoniram and Ann *Judson, America's first missionaries to Asia, in 1813. This pioneer Baptist founded churches among the Burmese and translated the Bible and produced a dictionary, both of which are still in use today. The response has always been slow among the people of Buddhist background. In contrast, the Karens, who lived by the myth-hope of the white brother who would some day come with the golden book to teach them the way to God and life, responded in great numbers.

Today roughly half the Christian population is found among the Karens. Other tribal peoples, largely *animist rather than Buddhist, have responded to the work of missionaries, both foreign and national.

From the first the Baptists have been the strongest denomination. The Church of England has had work since 1853, working through both the *SPG and the BCMS. Methodists have been active, with the British in Upper B. and the Americans in Lower B. Roman Catholics have had numerous missionary groups since 1856, including the *MEP, the Irish Good Shepherd sisters and the American *Jesuits in recent years. The *Salvation Army, SDA and a few *Pentecostal groups have also worked in B. Since the second world war the government has not allowed new missions to operate which were not in B. prior to the war. This fact has much to do with the degree of unity and co-operation found in the church in B. *Sectarian Protestant groups have not been active here as in other places. Although no strong movement for church union has taken hold in B., a remarkably high degree of co-operation has resulted through the Burma Christian Council. The Christian community numbers about one million, or approximately 4% of the population.

The great strength of the church in B. is its trained leadership. Through a network of graded, regional and central Bible schools and seminaries and the former system of mission and government schools, a relatively high level of lay and pastoral leadership has been available and early began to assume responsibility for the life of the churches. Since foreigners are no longer allowed to live in B., and the last missionaries were asked to leave in 1966, this tradition of trained leadership can be especially appreciated.

Today some of the chief challenges to the church can be seen in: (1) the perennial challenge of a vigorous Buddhist tradition; (2) the new ways of life demanded in a military-socialist régime, where the mission schools and hospitals have been nationalized; (3) the need to weld into some effective working unity such wide diversity as is found in B., and so in the church; (4) the need to work out a pattern of Christian citizenship, where the sense of national unity is weak and where the Christian community is found largely in groups with strong revolutionary tendencies; (5) the need to keep in contact with other Asian Christians and the ecumenical church at a time when government greatly restricts opportunities for travel and outside contact.

PAUL CLASPER

C. Anderson: *To the Golden Shore, The Life of A. Judson* (Boston 1956); G. H. Anderson, ed.: *Christ and Crisis in Southeast Asia* (New York 1968); *Burma Baptist Chronicle* (Rangoon 1963); J. F. Cady: *A History of Modern Burma* (New York 1958); W. King: *A Thousand Lives Away, Buddhism in Contemporary Burma* (Oxford 1964); Mi Mi Kaing: *Burmese Family* (London 1946); D. Smith: *Religion and Politics in Burma* (Princeton 1965); *BM* II, 144–49; *NCE* II, 901f.; *WKL*, 198f.

BURNS, WILLIAM CHALMERS (1815–1868), a pioneer missionary of the Presbyterian Church of England, was born at Duns, Scotland. After remarkable experiences of revival in the British Isles and in Canada, B. reached China in 1847 and engaged in evangelistic and literary work, in Amoy, Canton, Swatow, and finally in Peking. For seven months in 1855 B. was closely associated with J. Hudson *Taylor, on whom he exercised a profound influence. Many years later Taylor wrote of him that 'his holy and reverential life and constant communings with God made fellowship with him satisfying to the deep cravings of my heart'. In August 1867 B. reached Newchwang in Manchuria, and died there nine months later, in a narrow room where he slept on a bench, possessed two chairs, two bookcases, a stove, and little else. A Chinese commented, 'This man's religion must be true, because all he got for coming here was a grave, and that he could have had anywhere'. Before his death, B. charged his colleague, Wang Hwang, to pray with the enquirers that missionaries should come.

He appealed to the Presbyterian Church in Ireland to carry on his work. In response, two Irish Presbyterians, the Rev. Hugh Waddell and Mr Joseph Hunter reached Newchwang in 1869. B. was not actually the first missionary to Manchuria; Karl *Gutzlaff appears to have paid a short visit, in the 1830s, and in 1866 M. Williamson of the National Bible Society of Scotland penetrated as far as Sanshing selling gospels. But B's short witness and death were the starting-point of permanent Protestant work in the country, and of the great Presbyterian enterprises over more than half a century.

AUSTIN FULTON

I. Burns: *Memoirs of the Rev. Wm. C. Burns* (London, new ed. 1885); A. Fulton: *Through Earthquake, Wind and Fire: Church and Mission in Manchuria 1867–1950*, ch.2 (Edinburgh 1967); *DNB* VII, 439.

BURUNDI, formerly a kingdom under Belgian trusteeship, is a mountainous East African territory south of Rwanda between Uganda and the Congo. It has an area of 10,747 sq.m. and a population (1967) of 3,340,000, including 3,500 Europeans and 2,000 Asians. It is one of the most Roman Catholic countries on the continent: its four dioceses had in 1965 a total of 1,602,950 Catholics (60%). Protestant missions began in a large way after the first world war, and by 1966 seven missions were at work with a total community estimated at 240,194. Of these the largest was that of the Pentecostal Churches (*Svenska Fria Missionen*) with over 150,000. The Anglican Church in B. (Ruanda General and Medical Mission, CMS) with 43,223 adherents is a diocese in the church of Uganda, Rwanda and Burundi. The *Balokole* (Saved Ones) or Ruanda Revival has largely spread through CMS work to other churches in East Africa, but since a majority of its members were Watutsi it suffered disastrously in the political strife at the time of independence in both Rwanda and Burundi. In 1963 an Anglican worker Eustace Kinama seceded with two-thirds of Anglican congregations in southern Burundi, and founded *Eglise de Dieu au Burundi*; although at one time some 20,000 strong, it was later accused of subversion and suppressed. Other Protestant missions are: *Union des Eglises Baptistes (Dansk Baptistamfunds Yere Mission)*, *Eglise Libre Méthodiste*, *SDA*, *Mission Evangélique des Amis*, and *Mission Evangélique Mondiale* (World Gospel Mission).

DAVID B. BARRETT

BM II, 179–83; *NCE* II, 906f.

BUTLER, FANNY JANE (1850–1889). Born in London, in 1874 she became the first enrolled student of the School of Medicine for Women in London; graduated at Dublin in 1880 and in the same year sailed to India under the CEZMS. She had been influenced by the appeal of a Dr Elmslie who wrote in 1872 before his death in Kashmir, 'that women medical missionaries must be the key that would open the door to Indian homes'. From 1883 to 1887 she ran crowded dispensaries for women and children in Bhagalpur. An excellent linguist, she gave simple NT teaching together with instruction for preventing disease, and won the affection of her many patients. In 1888 her society sent her to Srinagar, where she remained until her death. She hoped that from Kashmir doors would be opened into unreached Central Asia.

FB was the first qualified woman missionary doctor from Europe to work in India. Her early death drew attention to the need for such work and inspired many to offer themselves for it. In 1890 a Fanny Butler Scholarship was founded at the London School of Medicine for Women, for the training of missionary candidates.

JOHN GOODWIN

E. M. Tonge: *Fanny Jane Butler: pioneer medical missionary* (London 1930).

C

CABLE, MILDRED (1877–1952), was a pioneer in Central Asia, and writer, in association with two sisters, Evangeline (1869–1960) and Francesca (1873–1960) French. MC was born in Surrey, England, and qualified as a chemist. In 1901 she joined Evangeline French, who had been a missionary of the *CIM since 1893. Francesca French joined them in 1909. Serving in Shansi until 1923, the trio then became the first missionaries in a vast territory in the far north-west. They made six long itinerations of the Gobi desert oases, a dangerous area almost unknown to Europeans. They 'gossiped the gospel,' gave medical aid, wrote accurate observations of local life, topography and conditions. When due for leave they crossed the Gobi in a cart, reaching Europe via Sinkiang and Siberia. After their first return MC wrote, 'with Eva French', *Through Jade Gate and Central Asia* (1927) which ran through 12 editions and was the first of a series which gave their name, adventures and Christian purpose worldwide fame at a time when missionary literature was little regarded by the general public. Among their best known books are *Something Happened* (1934) and *The Gobi Desert* (1942). When foreigners were ordered to leave the north-west in 1936, the trio returned to England, spending their remaining years writing and in honorary but strenuous service for the Bible Society.

JOHN POLLOCK

W. J. Platt: *Three Women* (London 1964).

CAIRO, AMERICAN UNIVERSITY AT. See NEAR EAST COLLEGE ASSOCIATION.

CALL TO MISSIONARY SERVICE. See VOCATION, MISSIONARY.

CALVINISM AND MISSIONS. See REFORMERS' CONCEPT OF MISSIONS.

CAMBODIA, a country 69,884 sq.m. in area, with a population estimated to be six million, is a Thēravāda Buddhist kingdom of S.E. Asia, independent since 1949. Tribes and 100,000 Cham and Malay Muslims are religious minorities. *Dominican Gaspar da Cruz, coming from Malacca, first visited C. in 1555. About that time Silvester *Azevedo, OP, received permission from the king to preach the gospel. The first converts included a Buddhist priest. Spanish *Franciscans followed in 1719 to introduce Christianity permanently. P. Levavasseur translated the catechism into the Khmer language about 1770. The apostolic vicariate C. was established in 1850 (Phnom Penh) and assigned to the *MEP. The strength of the RC community lies with Vietnamese immigrants and Chinese. Numbers declined, owing to re-migration of Vietnamese and political instability from 109,000 (1950) to 52,632 (1959), places of worship from 268 to 82 respectively. But numbers had reached 54,237 with 64 clergy and 84 parishes by 1966. The *CMA started evangelism in 1923, growing into the Evangelical Church of Cambodia with 14 local churches, 7 pastors, 734 members. Owing to anti-American feeling all missionaries had to leave by mid-1965. But a CMA French couple was able to assist the Christians in their efforts to obtain government permission for the re-opening of their chapels, which had been closed in all but two provinces since mid-1965. Work has been carried on chiefly among Cambodians, Chinese, Vietnamese and lately among the Mnong Biet (north-east Cambodia) and Kuoy tribes. The Bible has been translated into Cambodian. The Bible school at Tha Khmau, run entirely by national staff since 1965, had among its 18 full-term students some of high academic calibre. Five men graduated for the ministry before the school was closed by local authorities. 27 titles of Christian literature are being distributed, 15 of which were produced in 1964 alone. By its successful stress on lay witness and training, stewardship and self-support, the CMA has from the beginning laid strong foundations for the Evangelical Church of Cambodia, which is under severe testing and not yet officially recognized. Freedom of worship, however, prevails, with meetings at Battembang and Phnom Penh being resumed. The church has no ecumenical connections. Other Protestant groups, entering after the second world war, include SDA and CMML (Plymouth Brethren). Christianity among Cambodian Buddhists is still at the beginning.

LOTHAR SCHREINER

B. P. Groslier: *Angkor et le Cambodge au XVIe Siècle d'après les sources Portugaises et Espagnoles* (Paris 1958)—(early missionary efforts); J. Pianet: '*Histoire de la Mission de Cambodge*' in *Bulletin de la Société des Missions Etrangères* (Hong Kong 1928–29); *Annual Reports of the CMA*; *Missionary Atlas: A Manual of the Foreign Work of the CMA* (Harrisburg, Pa. 1964); *BM* II, 183–85; *NCE* II, 1097f.

CAMEROON, THE FEDERAL REPUBLIC OF. A tropical African country, lying between Lat. 2 and 12N, bounded on the west by Nigeria and the Atlantic Ocean, on the south by Gabon and Congo Brazzaville, and on the east by Chad and the Central African Republic. Area, with Western Cameroon, about 183,381 sq.m. Population 5,210,000 (UN estimate 1968). Christians: RC 950,000, Protestant 700,000 (total 30%); Muslims, 18%; traditional 52% (est. 1968).

Christian penetration. From the time of their emancipation in 1833, Negroes in Jamaica had been interested in a mission to West Africa, serving through the British BMS. In 1840 John Clarke, an ordained missionary, and Dr G. K. Prince, a medical man and former slave-owner, travelled to Africa to explore possibilities. Their report being favourable, Prince, Joseph Merrick and Alexander Fuller in 1843 left Jamaica for service in Africa. Clarke, together with Alfred *Saker and his wife, who had been recruited in England, returned to Jamaica,

and raised a team of 39 persons, men, women and children, who were to be evangelists, teachers and settlers, first in Fernando Poo, and later in Africa. By 1845 land for two mission stations had been purchased on the Cameroon river, and the first missionaries had been settled on the mainland. The Jamaican missionaries served in the C. for a whole generation.

Political and missionary affairs. In the division of Africa, Britain agreed in 1884 to the German occupation of the Cameroon area. Baptist missionaries were accused of fomenting rebellion and three of their stations were destroyed by the Germans. The mission found it wiser to withdraw, and in 1886 its work was handed over to the *Basel Mission. Not all African Baptists, however, were willing to accept the exchange. Attempts by the Basel Mission to enforce a stricter discipline were resented, as was their alleged infringement of the independence of the congregations. Matters were not improved by the attempt of German Baptists to establish a mission in 1890. The African Baptists steadfastly maintained their independence of the new mission. In 1892 the Basel Mission was joined by the American Presbyterians, who developed an extensive work in the interior of the country. The RCs did not succeed in entering until 1890, when the Fathers of the Pious Society of Missions (Pallotine) obtained from Bismarck rather grudging permission to enter, on condition that they did not enter territory where Protestants were already working —a condition which, though accepted, was not faithfully observed. The RCs followed the practice, established elsewhere, of collecting and educating rescued slave children in Christian villages; in the early years their progress was rather slow. In 1914 the German province of the Priests of the Sacred Heart began to work in northern C.

The missions were affected by the revolution of 1918, when the Germans were driven out and the French and British began to rule under League of Nations mandate. The Basel Mission found it wise to hand over their work to the *PEMS, which carried it on with great effect. The German RC missionaries were replaced by missionaries of the *Holy Ghost society in French mandated territory; *Mill Hill missionaries took up the work in British mandated territory. American missions were unaffected. The period of French and British occupation was one of general progress, the RCs advancing more rapidly than the Protestants, in part through their concentration on higher education and development of excellent schools.

Many missions, besides those already mentioned, entered the country in this period, notably the Church of the Lutheran Brethren; the Brethren Church Mission, USA; American Baptist Mission; SDA; *SUM, and Norwegian Mission.

Independence and new Problems. The independence of C. was proclaimed on 1 January 1960. On 1 October 1961, the former British trusteeship territory of Southern Cameroons acceded to the Republic, which then adopted its present name, the Federal Republic of C. Independence in itself has made little difficulty for the churches. But in the northern part of the country *Islam is strong. The fact that the first President of the Republic is a Muslim has apparently encouraged a number of officials to behave as though Islam was the state religion, to oppose the work of the missions in every possible way, and to make life uncomfortable for everyone who is not a Muslim.

Political independence has been accompanied by a desire for independence on the part of the churches. The Presbyterian Church of the Cameroon has been fully self-governing since 1943. Seven *African Independent Churches are listed, but the membership of these is comparatively small. For a period, the churches were so heavily burdened by the work of reorganization after the second world war that little was possible in the way of new evangelistic outreach. This period seems to have passed, and extremely active evangelistic work has been carried out in recent years by the *Eglise Evangélique* (PEMS) among the Bamileke on the border between C. and Nigeria. Large increases in member-

ship have been reported by a number of churches in recent years.

A very important event was the founding by the *TEF of a theological faculty at Yaoundé, to serve the needs of all the francophone Protestant churches in Africa for higher theological training. In 1967 the students had been enrolled for a four-year course; but not all of these were nationals of the C. Republic. By degrees this work will have a great effect on African leadership in the French-speaking churches.

The RC church made rapid progress after the first world war, showing an increase from 60,000 Catholics in 1920 to 700,000 in 1960. In 1955 the hierarchy was established, with Yaoundé as the archdiocese and metropolitan see for the whole country; by 1964 it had seven suffragan dioceses. In 1935 the first African priests were ordained, and in 1955 the first African bishops consecrated. In 1961 Jean-Baptiste Zoa became the first African archbishop of Yaoundé. In 1963 there were 550 priests (of whom 166 were Africans), 178 lay brothers, 572 sisters (including 175 Africans), and 5,900 *catechists.

ROBERT T. PARSONS AND EDITORS
J. Schramm: *Kamerun* (Bonn 1964); *BM* II, 186–93.

CANADA (mainly Indians and Eskimo). When, in the 17th century, C. was settled by the white man, the Indian population was probably between 150,000 and 200,000, in five broad tribal divisions, with the main linguistic groupings. From the start, the French regarded it as their duty to evangelize the tribes; the two first *Jesuits arrived in Acadia (Nova Scotia) in 1611, and in 1615 three Récollet Fathers established themselves in the neighbourhood of Quebec to work among Hurons and Montaignais. By the middle of the century there were 70 Jesuits and six lay brothers in the mission. Most famous of the RC missions was that to the Hurons, a semi-agricultural people, in which the leading figure was Jean *Brébeuf. Here the plan of the Jesuits was to centralize their mission in one town to which converts could be brought in order to segregate them from the evils of Indian life. Though carried on with the utmost heroism, the progress of the work was slow. Disaster fell upon the mission through the attacks of the untamable Iroquois; Isaac Jogues was killed by the Mohawks in 1646; Brébeuf and his companions were cruelly tortured and put to death in 1649.

This, however, was only a temporary set-back. The RC missions spread with, and often ahead of, colonial expansion; by 1674 they had reached as far as Sault Ste. Marie to the west, and Hudson Bay to the north. In 1659 the first group of Ursuline sisters arrived in Quebec under *Marie de l'Incarn-ation, to begin the work of education for Indian girls.

Far more serious than attacks without were the endless quarrels between British, French and Dutch, in which the Indian was lured into confederation with the white man and corrupted by a liberal supply of fire-water. The capitulation of Quebec in 1759 and the consequent transference of C. from French to British sovereignty, were naturally most unwelcome to the French, and though the free exercise of the RC faith was guaranteed by the Treaty of Paris of 1763, there was a natural weakening of RC missionary effort.

In the 19th century, however, the work was resumed with notable vigour. Two priests were sent in 1818 to the Red River settlement (Winnipeg), with such effect that in 1843 rather more than half the inhabi-tants of the settlement were RCs. The work of winning the west was assigned primarily to the *OMI, whose most famous member, Albert *Lacombe, apostle to the Blackfeet, earned the tribute of the Indians to whom he was known as 'the man with the good heart'. The work was extended to the Pacific Ocean. In Labrador two tribes of Indians had become mainly RC. In general RC policy was not to educate the Indian or to separate him from the life to which he had been accustomed, but to visit him where he was, and to alter only those things in Indian custom which were felt to be completely incompatible with Christian faith. This meant endless journeys and great hardship;

and, as little was done to provide the Indians with a ministry of their own, the main burden of the work fell on the mis-sionaries, who were increasingly Canadian by birth.

In the early days of British occupation, the Protestant churches were so much occupied with building up a ministry to their own people that not much energy was available for work among the earlier inhabi-tants; but gradually all the main Protestant churches entered the field of Indian work. From 1820 onwards the Anglican *CMS took as its responsibility the evangelization of the west and north. Two heroic bishops, John Hordern (1828–1893) and W. C. *Bompas, are remembered as pioneers in the neighbourhood respectively of Hudson Bay and the Yukon. Work was also developed in what is now British Columbia. Just a hundred years after having started the work, in 1920, the CMS, concluding that the work of primary evangelization had now been completed, handed over the responsibility to the Church of England in C.

Methodists were in touch with Indians in Ontario as early as 1823. Their first extension eastwards came when in 1840 at the request of the Hudson's Bay Company they sent representatives to various ports established by that company. By far the best known of these missionaries was James *Evans who, living at Norway House, invented the syl-labic script for the language of the Cree Indians, and set in hand the translation of the Bible into that language.

Presbyterians followed rather later. In 1851 the Rev. John Black went reluctantly to Kildonan, hoping ere long to return to Montreal; in fact he stayed for 30 years, building up an important work among the Indians. In 1862 James Nisbet moved further to the west, and set up a mission at Prince Albert, to which a flourishing school was attached. Presbyterians joined also in the evangelization of the far north-west and of British Columbia.

A new beginning was made when a Canadian church itself became missionary. In 1858 four missionaries of the Canadian

Wesleyan Methodist Church were appointed to work in the west. Inspired by their example, a teacher Thomas Crosby went to British Columbia, preached to the Tsimshian Indians in their own language, and was the inaugurator of the Pacific Mission Fleet, an enterprise in which several churches now share as the only means of reaching the inhabitants scattered along the many rivers and inlets of that land.

By 1914 it was reckoned that at least three quarters of the Indians in C. (at that date about 150,000) had become Christians. In the Eastern Provinces, Quebec and Ontario, evangelization had been completed, and almost the entire Indian population was Christian.

The evangelization of the Eskimos presented even greater problems than that of the Indians. Cold, darkness, isolation, and the immense difficulties of travel over the vast distances needed to reach a minute population scattered over an enormous area, would have been enough to discourage all but the hardiest evangelists.

In Labrador, as in other inhospitable parts of the earth's surface, the Moravians were the pioneers. The first missionary, who came in 1752, was killed by the Eskimos. But in 1764 Jens Haven, who had learned the Eskimo language in Greenland, arrived as missionary and agent of the British government, succeeded in maintaining himself and winning the confidence of the people. They were encouraged to gather in central settlements, and to support themselves by selling the products of their art. By 1804 the greater part of two tribes had accepted the Christian faith.

In 1876 the CMS took up the work of evangelizing the Eskimos. The former sailor E. J. *Peck arrived at Little White River, an area never reached by the Moravians, but carrying with him two or three books in the Eskimo tongue prepared by the Moravians. Within six years he had baptized upwards of 100 Eskimo. Later Peck moved even further north to Blacklead Island in Cumberland Sound, where the missionaries might hope to be visited once a year by a ship; the annual visit was invariably followed by an epidemic of colds and coughs, afflictions to which the inhabitants were at other times immune in their germ-free climate.

At a considerably later date the RC missions entered the Arctic, in many cases unfortunately in small Eskimo settlements where the Anglican mission was already at work. Their success has been modest. At the present time all the Eskimo in C. are Christians, 80% Anglican, 20% RC. In 1933 the whole area was constituted an Anglican diocese, with, as its first bishop, the faithful missionary A. L. Fleming, 'Archibald the Arctic'. A number of Eskimo have been ordained to the ministry of the church.

C., with its many minority populations, is faced with all the problems of the clash between simpler and more complex forms of culture. One solution appeared to be to segregate the Indians in reservations, and to leave the Eskimo in the seclusion of the Arctic wastes. But the penetration of industrial civilization cannot be indefinitely postponed; nor is it always the wish of the simpler peoples to be kept in what appears to them as perpetual childhood. On the other hand, the complete integration into western society of peoples, whose racial characteristics and mental patterns are singularly persistent, presents grave difficulties. It seems that in this time of change the churches will have an even more important function to fulfil than before, providing the element of stability and security in a world the foundations of which appear to have been shaken.

KATHARINE B. HOCKIN AND EDITORS

A. L. Fleming: *Archibald the Arctic* (autobiography—London 1957); K. S. Latourette: *A History of the Expansion of Christianity* (New York 1937–45) III, pp.168–85;V, pp.3–45; VII, pp.157–61; E. Stock: *The History of the Church Missionary Society* (London 1899) I, pp.24, 245–46, 362–64; II, pp.313–32, 605–22; III, pp.238–53, 615–40; H. H. Walsh: *The Christian Church in Canada* (Toronto 1956); *BM* II, 193–205; *NCE* I, 402f., *WKL*, 650–52.

CANAL ZONE, US. See AMERICA, CENTRAL.

CANARY ISLANDS. See ATLANTIC ISLANDS.

CAPE VERDE ISLANDS. See ATLANTIC ISLANDS.

CAPUCHINS (OFM Cap.). Committed to a stricter interpretation of the Rule of St. Francis, the Order of Friars Minor Capuchin began as a reform initiated by Fr. Matthew of Bascio. With papal approval (1528) the Cs became an autonomous branch of the *Franciscan order. The friars number 15,722 members (December 1965) with a varied, flexible apostolate in 70 countries.

Continually stressing missionary activity, Cs were instrumental in founding (1622) Rome's Congregation of the *Propaganda whose first martyr was the C. St. Fidelis. One of the most remarkable of C. missions was that to Tibet, which was maintained under great difficulties from 1707 to 1745, in an area which has since become completely inaccessible to Christian missions. Cs also had a long record of service in West Africa, providing one of the links between the 16th century Christian kingdom of the Congo and the renewal of missionary activity in the 19th. Notable contributions were made to *missiology by Cardinal Massaia (1809–1889) in Ethiopia and Bishop Anastasius Hartman (d.1866) in India. The order now has 47 missionary bishops and approximately 20% of its priests in mission work.

SIMON CONRAD, OFM Cap
Analecta Ordinis Fratrum Minorum Capuccinorum Vol. LXXXII, No.1 (January-March 1966), pp.96f.; S. Conrad, OFM Cap.: *Brothers of the Sun* (Chicago 1956).

CAREY, WILLIAM (1761–1834), was born at Paulerspury, Northants, England. After an experience of personal conversion he was rebaptized, and settled down to the five-fold function of village cobbler, Baptist pastor, teacher, student of languages and botanist. In his first great work, *An Enquiry into the Obligations of Christians to Use Means for the Conversion of the Heathen* (1792) C. set himself to overcome the hyper-Calvinist view then prevalent that God in his own good time would provide for the conversion of the nations without human aid. This book, together with C's famous sermon on Isaiah 54:2-3 to the Northampton Baptist Association, in which he set forth the principle 'Expect great things from God; attempt great things for God', prepared the way for the foundation in 1792 of the 'Particular Baptist Society for Propagating the Gospel among the Heathen'. Almost inevitably C. himself was sent to India as the first missionary of the society.

The opposition of the East India Company caused endless difficulties. C. was able to remain in India only by accepting an obscure position as manager of an indigo plantation in the interior. The five years spent there laid the foundation of his incomparable knowledge of the Bengali language; but when the translation of the NT into Bengali which he had prepared during those years was examined, it was found that the whole work had to be done over again, since at that time the self-taught C. lacked the philological preparation necessary for such work.

The situation changed completely when C. moved to the tiny Danish settlement of Serampore, 16 miles from Calcutta. Here he was joined by Joshua Marshman (1768–1837) and William Ward (1764–1823), each of whom was almost as remarkable as C. himself. Marshman spent 15 years learning Chinese and producing a Chinese NT, an enterprise which perhaps should not have been attempted in India. Ward undertook entire responsibility for the work of printing, was reckoned by far the best preacher at Serampore, and was instrumental in leading more than one of C's sons to the knowledge of Christ. Work now proceeded along five converging lines: (1) Minute study of the Indian languages, of the Hindu religion, and of the customs of the people. Ward's book on the *History, Literature and Religion of the Hindoos* (3rd ed. 1817–1820) was one fruit of this part of the enterprise. (2) Widespread preaching of the gospel in the towns and villages of Bengal. (3) The translation and printing of the Scriptures in as many as possible of the languages of India. C. himself produced a complete Bible in Bengali, Sanskrit and Marathi. Altogether some part of the Scriptures was produced in 37 languages. Many of the versions were rough-hewn, and none of them is in use today. More would perhaps have been accomplished with greater concentration and less speed. (4) The formation of a church on Baptist principles; this preceded, and did not follow, the baptism of the first convert. (5) The foundation of *Serampore College (1819), for the higher education of Indian ministers and preachers for the service of the Indian church. This was found to be premature; only a century later was Serampore able to fulfil the purpose for which it had been founded.

C's appointment as Professor of Sanskrit and Bengali in the government college of Fort William at a salary of £1,000 a year (equal to £10,000 today) enabled him to render the mission largely self-supporting. In his spare time C. wrote Bengali Collo-quies, which are recognized by the experts to have laid the foundations of modern Bengali prose literature; built up a botanic garden which was the admiration of the whole of Asia; and took a leading part in the campaign for the abolition of *Sati*, the burning of Hindu widows on their husband's pyre. His later years were saddened by the eccentricities of his eldest son Felix, and by tragic and unnecessary dissension between the older and younger generations of missionaries, and between Serampore and its supporters in England. But, when he died, strong and enduring foundations had been laid in every part of missionary work for which he cared. In the whole history of the church no nobler man has ever given himself to the service of the Redeemer.

STEPHEN NEILL

S. P. Carey: *William Carey* (1923); J. C. Marshman: *The Life and Times of Carey, Marshman and Ward* (London 1859); E. D. Potts: *British Baptist Missionaries in India, 1793–1837* (Cambridge 1967); *DNB* IX, 77; *RGG* I, 1614f.

4*

CARGILL, DAVID (d.1843), a Scotsman, graduate of Aberdeen University, went to Tonga in 1833 under appointment by the Wesleyan Methodist Mission Board. A man of impressive scholarship, he was assigned to carry to completion the translation work then in hand. Shortly after his arrival in Tonga a religious awakening among the people led thousands to seek church membership. At that time a request came from Fiji that missionaries be sent, and although the missionary staff at Tonga was hard pressed to meet the demands of the new converts, the decision was taken to meet the request. C., with William Cross, their wives and families, went, taking up residence at Lakemba in a community of Tongans. After three years of work converts appeared and a church with Tongan and Fijian members was formed. In 1839 C. moved to Rewa, where the chief was favourable to Christianity. Fiji was then made a separate mission district and C. placed in charge. He organized the extension of the work. Mrs C. died in 1840, and he took their four children back to England. On his return he was located in Tonga where he remained until his death in 1843.

J. LESLIE DUNSTAN

J. Calvert (G. S. Rowe, ed.): *Missionary Labours among the Cannibals* (Boston 1871).

CARGO CULTS are apocalyptic movements which have occurred most strongly especially during and after the second world war on many islands in the South Pacific. The name is derived from the general expectation that on a particular day and after certain exercises, usually under a 'prophet', all goods desired would come magically to the 'natives' as and like 'cargo' had come across the sea to the apparently wealthy and happy whites. The cults were often denounced as simply materialistic, but one must not overlook the fact that the dream of a life in earthly abundance was quite frequently interwoven with the expectation of eternal life, resurrection of the dead, the end of all sickness, the return of Christ, etc. Christian elements in, or sometimes even a Christian motivation of, these syncretistic cults suggest an insufficient understanding of the gospel message. Churches and missions suffered heavily. The Evangelical Lutheran Church in New Guinea issued a Declaration of Faith in 1964 in which it is said: 'God commands that I must be concerned about and do the work which he has given me to do, and to earn my food with toil and sweat. May the Lord Christ help me to be strong and put down the confused thinking about obtaining wealth.'

HANS JOCHEN MARGULL

P. Lawrence: *Road Belong Cargo* (Manchester 1964); P. Worsley: *The Trumpet Shall Sound, A Study of 'Cargo' Cults in Melanesia* (London 1957, with bibliography).

CARIBBEAN. 1. *General Description.* The C. is a vast island world, stretching 1,500 miles from the Bahamas in the north to the Guyanas in the south. The mean distance between Central America to the west and Barbados in the east is 2,000 miles. There is immense variety in the size and character of the islands, from Cuba which with an area of 44,200 sq.m. is not much smaller than England without Wales, down to tiny uninhabited 'cays' and isolated rocks. The political diversity is equally perplexing. Originally the entire area was assigned by the pope to the king of Spain (1493). This decision was increasingly challenged by other powers, and at different times and places France, Britain, Denmark, the Netherlands and the USA have exercised sovereignty. At the present time Cuba, since the Castro takeover in 1959, is a revolutionary republic on Marxist principles. Haiti and the Dominican Republic have long been independent states. Puerto Rico is a commonwealth closely associated with the USA, but without statehood. After the failure of a British attempt to create a federation of the West Indies, Jamaica, Trinidad, the Bahamas and Barbados are fully self-governing entities within the British Commonwealth. Smaller islands are progressing in various stages towards independence. Guadeloupe is an overseas department of France. The Virgin Islands of the USA, purchased from Denmark in 1917, are an unincorporated territory of the USA, under the full jurisdiction of the US Department of the Interior. The Netherlands Antilles are self-governing, with the queen of the Netherlands as head of the government.

The total population of the area appears to be between 22 and 25 million, of whom the vast majority are Christians at least in name, the major exception being the large East Indian population in Trinidad, which has proved highly resistant to Christian missionary work. About a quarter of the population of Trinidad is registered as adhering to the Hindu or the Muslim faith. Over-population is a grave problem in many islands; and excessive reliance on a single crop, sugar in most cases, has produced economic perplexities for which no fully satisfactory solution is as yet in sight.

Provision for inter-island communication has always been inadequate, and political and linguistic barriers have added further difficulties. The result has been a rugged individualism and an 'island concept', which has had its effect on religious no less than on political life. There has been little regional contact even between churches of the same persuasion. It is possible for a Spanish-speaking Christian to be almost unaware of the existence of English-speaking Christians and vice versa; in consequence it is very difficult to make any single statement which is applicable to the area as a whole.

2. *The Spanish Period.* The first Christian mission came to the C. with Christopher Columbus on 12 October 1492, when he landed on Wattling Island. His journal records that as he stepped ashore he knelt to give God thanks and to claim the New World for 'God and the Queen'.

Roman Catholicism did not come into contact with a religionless people. The original inhabitants of the C. were themselves migrants from the South American mainland. Little is known of the earliest settlers, the Siboneys. They were ousted first by the Arawaks and then by the Caribs. Both

Arawak and Carib had a common set of religious beliefs. It was a form of *ancestor and nature worship combined, and it had a developed cultus.

When the pope assigned the western world to the king of Spain, he did so expressly with the intention that the king should send to those regions 'wise, competent, pious and virtuous men, who will be capable of instructing the indigenous peoples in good morals and in the Catholic religion'. Superficially at least this purpose was carried out. Large numbers of priests and monks migrated to the west. The authorities stringently impressed on all European colonists the duty of seeing to the religious instruction of those who came under their control. The first bishopric west of the Atlantic, Santo Domingo, was erected in 1511: by 1522 the ecclesiastical organization of the Antilles, with eight bishoprics, was complete.

There was, however, a fearful gap between intention and practice. Under the cruel conditions to which they were subjected the C. peoples were beginning to die out. The first known protest was made by the *Dominican Antonio de Montesinos in a sermon preached in December 1511, in which he spoke bitterly of the 'cruel and horrible servitude' in which the Indians were kept. This was followed up by the life-long crusade of Bartolomé de las *Casas and others on behalf of the rights of the Indians. In Central and South America this campaign was largely successful. It was already too late to save the less hardy peoples of the islands; they have died out leaving hardly a trace behind.

The great crisis of the Caribbean world came with the decision to import slaves from Africa to replace the vanishing indigenous peoples. The RC church never condemned *slavery in principle. The pope did, however, issue strict instructions, notably in 1537, that slaves were to be treated as human beings, and in particular that they were to be instructed in the Christian faith and baptized. It seems that the second injunction, though not the first, was obeyed, and that the majority of slaves were bap-

tized within six months of their arrival in the C. area.

Inevitably the oppression to which the surviving Amerindians and Negroes were subjected led to violent revolts and insurrections, which in most cases were suppressed with the utmost cruelty by the stronger white man. One of the most notable of these took place in Trinidad, where on 1 December 1699 the mission of San Francisco de los Avessales rose in revolt and murdered the *Capuchin friars in charge of the mission, desecrated it and destroyed it. The governor who hastened to its aid was ambushed and his party wiped out. The Indians fled the scene and were besieged on a rocky peninsula called Point Galera. Many committed suicide rather than surrender. The Spanish authorities ordered the captured to be hanged after being dragged in the streets and, as a warning to others, they exposed heads and hands on stakes at the place where the crime had been committed.

3. *Protestant Influences and Work.* Protestants on the whole were harsher than RCs in their treatment of their slaves. British authority began in the C. with the settlement of Bermuda in October 1619, followed by the occupation of Barbados in 1627, and the capture of Jamaica in 1655. In early days the colonists' need for labour was met largely by the transportation of criminals under a system which was little better than slavery. But in these islands also African slavery presented itself as the better solution, and before long the greater part of the population was of African descent. The colonists were almost to a man opposed to any kind of Christian work among slaves, fearing that baptism and still more education might set up in their minds ideas of liberty which were wholly incompatible with the best interests of their owners. In 1739 the great bishop, Joseph Butler, preaching the annual sermon on behalf of the *SPG, spoke of the slaves and affirmed that 'it is inexcusable to keep them in ignorance of the end for which they were made, and the means whereby they may become partakers of the general redemption'. But this was a lone voice; only at the

end of the 18th century did concern for the welfare of the slaves become general among English-speaking Christians.

The *Church of England* had almost unchallenged responsibility for church life in the British West Indies. The number of clergy was always woefully inadequate, but a number of the islands had an established church supported out of public funds, a system which in Barbados, where 70% of the inhabitants are Anglicans, lasted well into the 20th century. An ingenious plan put forward by the philosopher bishop George Berkeley (1725) for setting up a college in Bermuda, to increase the number of clergy 'in our Foreign Plantations and for converting the Savage Americans to Christianity', came to nothing. (See also CODRINGTON, CHRISTOPHER.) The first Anglican bishoprics (Jamaica and Barbados) were set up in 1824, to be followed by six others; in 1880 the Province of the West Indies came into being as an independent and self-governing province of the Anglican Communion. A large proportion of the white inhabitants in the British islands are Anglican; for a long time the care of the slaves was left to other bodies.

Credit for the beginning of Protestant missionary work in the Antilles must go to the *Moravians*. When *Zinzendorf was in Copenhagen in 1730 for the coronation of Charles VI, he met a Negro from the Danish West Indies who told him that missionaries would be welcome in that area. It was accordingly decided to start a mission. The first two missionaries *Dober and *Nitschmann arrived in the island of St. Thomas in 1732. In 1739 Zindendorf himself paid a visit to the island. The mission spread into the Greater Antilles and by 1754 George Caries, Thomas Skalcross and Gottlieb Haberecht carried 'the Brethren' to Jamaica. Here the mission foundered, because the missioners through the gift of a plantation from a friend themselves became slaveowners. They did however set a pattern of kindness. Their work formed the base for Baptist work in the western end of the island. Far greater success attended their work in Antigua, where it is recorded that by 1791 they had gathered more than 7,000 converts. This mission developed education, and between 1809 and 1823 many existing Moravian-sponsored institutes sprang up, including a teachers' training college. From 1735 to 1816 the Moravians maintained a mission in what is now Guyana with varying success. Their work struck far deeper roots in Surinam (Dutch Guiana); the gospel was preached to Negro slaves, 'Bush' Negroes (escaped slaves who had settled in the interior), Indians, Chinese and East Indians. The mission made itself self-supporting through successful business enterprises, from which the church has taken steps to free itself in the 20th century. The Moravian church today has 50,000 members, about 15% of the entire population of the territories.

Methodism reached the West Indies in 1760 through the work of Nathaniel Gilbert, at one time Speaker of the Assembly of Antigua, who when in England had heard John Wesley and had an experience of conversion. On his return Gilbert began to preach to the slaves, among whom he gathered a congregation. On his departure to England, it was sustained by Sophia Campbell and Mary Alley. When he died (1774) it numbered about 200. On 2 April 1778 John Baxter, a shipwright, took employment at the Royal Naval Dockyard and being an ordained man, pastored the little church. The church might have gone unaided had not a gale blown the ship in which Dr Thomas *Coke was travelling to the USA to Antigua. He strengthened the church. Methodism then spread throughout the Caribbean and by 1816 it was actively promoted by the Wesleyan Missionary Society from England.

George Lisle was the first *Baptist* missionary to the C. He was a slave, born in Virginia, USA, in 1751. He was converted under the preaching of Matthew Moore in 1774 in Brooke County, Georgia, USA, and was ordained on 20 May 1775 after a trial sermon. He came to Jamaica in January 1783 and obtained employment at the Custom House in Kingston. He started a church in his house and preached at the Kingston race course. By 1791, a church was established in downtown Kingston and it spearheaded the Baptist cause in Jamaica and later in the C. as a whole. The British Baptists were invited to take over the work in 1813; but the mission declared itself independent in 1842 and has sustained itself since.

At this point the tiny Dutch island of St. Eustatius, with an area of 21 sq.km. and a population of 1,103 (1963) enters history. Black Harry was an African slave, who had been sold to a plantation on St. Eustatius in the Virgin Islands. He was converted and became a Methodist. He preached regularly to his fellow slaves and even preached before the governor, whose general consent he had obtained. When his preaching became explicit the governor withdrew his consent. Dr Thomas Coke visited Eustatius in 1787 to see the work but his presence was regarded with suspicion. Before he could preach publicly he was obliged to preach before the Council of State. He managed to obtain permission and organized Harry's work into six classes. In 1788 Governor Runnels suspended all preaching by Methodists and Harry was flogged publicly and imprisoned in an airless cell called 'the Sweater'. On his release he was sold overseas and the work lapsed for a time.

Presbyterians have been active in the C. One of their most remarkable efforts has been the work among the East Indians in Trinidad, which was started more than 100 years ago, and later extended to British and Dutch Guiana. The majority of Presbyterians in Trinidad are of East Indian origin. This work was an effort of the Canadian Presbyterian Church. Other Presbyterian groups have worked in other islands; within recent years these groups have coalesced to the point of forming an Assembly of Reformed churches for the whole area.

With the end of Spanish domination at the end of the 19th century, Protestant work became possible in areas which had previously been closed to it. Many American groups have entered, and the *Pentecostal* churches are strongly represented in many islands. For Cuba no less than 26 Protestant groups are listed, with a total membership of 300,000 out of a population of seven million, between 4% and 5%. In Puerto Rico 17 groups account for nearly 10% of the population. Most American churches have missionary districts in the region but there is no direct link between them and the British orientated churches. For example, the American Episcopal Church has no direct link with the Anglican Province of the West Indies; the same is true of Methodism.

The mission to *Central America* from the C. Islands began as early as 1815. A Methodist woman named Mother Abel landed in Bocas-del-Toro and gathered some Colombian fishermen for worship. Very little is known of the work until Thomas Geddes arrived in 1884. He was followed by his son Alexander. Subsequently Mortimer Surgeon, a Jamaican, took over from A.G. in 1913, and he established Methodism on the Isthmus. Surgeon was eventually succeeded by Ephraim Alphonse, a Panamanian who spearheaded the translation of the Bible into Valiente. The work has now been established as a sub-district of the Caribbean Methodist Conference.

Baptist work was begun by a Methodist layman in Bocas-del-Toro in 1889. It was then led by Nottman, an Englishman sent there by the Jamaica Baptist Missionary Society. He was succeeded by a friend of Surgeon, Terence Duncansen, who established the work. The Baptist work is now under the auspices of the Southern Baptist Convention of America.

The Anglicans through the help of the *SPG supported a chaplain to the migrants in 1882. The arrangement was however interrupted in 1885 when Colon was destroyed by fire. In the same year the bishop of the Falkland Islands who had jurisdiction over Panama formally handed it over to the diocese of Jamaica; but in more recent times the responsibility has been taken over by the American missionary district of the Panama Canal Zone.

4. *Missionary Work from the Caribbean.* The impetus towards missions was felt by

the churches of the West Indies in the middle of the 19th century. In 1834, the Jamaica Missionary Presbytery was formed. It was an amalgam of the Church of Scotland, the Secession Church and the original Associate Synod. It unified the church in Jamaica and became the base for missionary work in Africa (Nigeria).

The Jamaica Baptist Missionary Society was founded in 1842, to unify the Baptist witness in the island and to send the gospel to Africa. It became the sponsor of Calabar Theological College for ministerial and teachers' training in 1843, and provided personnel for the mission venture to Fernando Po in 1844.

The Church of England in Barbados began to train missionaries for the Rio Pongas area in West Africa in 1854. The first missionaries arrived in 1855. By January 1861 the spirit was caught by the Jamaican Church which organized the Jamaica Home and Foreign Missions. Its purpose was to give aid to rural churches where pastoral oversight was lacking and the economic standard low. It also sent missionaries to the Pongas and to the Mosquito Indians in the British Honduras area.

5. *Recent Roman Catholic Work.* The incursions of the Protestants naturally disturbed the RC monopoly in the islands. But here again it is impossible to generalize. In the Dutch Antilles in the 17th century, and in Jamaica for a long period after the British conquest in 1655, the practice of the RC religion was forbidden. On the other hand, when Trinidad and Tobago were surrendered, it was agreed that no change should be made in the status of the RC church. Today 40% of the inhabitants of T. and T. are RCs, cared for mainly by Dominican priests and sisters; the capital Port of Spain has been a bishopric (later archbishopric) since 1820. Gradually in other areas restrictions have been withdrawn and complete religious freedom prevails.

In the 19th century Rome steadily increased the number of vicariates apostolic. One was created for Guyana in 1837, a second for Surinam in 1842. Three vicariates were created in 1837 for the British West Indies. Spanish *Jesuits arrived in Jamaica in 1837, to be followed in 1847 by priests of the English Province, one of whom later became the first bishop of Jamaica. In 1894 the English province, having increasing responsibilities in Africa, handed over Jamaica to the Maryland province of USA, from which a supply of priests has come to Jamaica. The work of the priests was strengthened in 1890 by the arrival of Sisters of Mercy, who have devoted themselves specially to the care of orphans. In 1968 the RCs claimed 130,000 adherents in Jamaica. This church is particularly strong in the southern C.

6. *Survivals from the Past and New Forces in the Present.* Where christianization has been so superficial as it has been in most areas of the C., it is to be expected that much will survive from a distant past. Haiti is famous for the *Voodoo rites which are extensively practised, many of the adherents being without doubt also nominal members of Christian churches. (See also SPIRITISM.) In Jamaica and many other islands the Obeah cult—described by the Jesuit J. J. Williams in *Voodoos and Obeahs* (New York 1933) and by H. J. Bell in *Obeah, Witchcraft in the West Indies* (London 1893)—held sway over the minds of many Christians. Nowhere have the churches been entirely successful in suppressing these survivals.

A new and startling movement, not unrelated to the movement of *Independent Churches in Africa is the Ras Tafarian movement, a Jamaican *Cargo cult. This began when the Emperor Hailé Selassie, King of Kings, Lord of Lords, was crowned as Emperor of Ethiopia in 1930. To some Jamaicans he became the epitome of their suppressed hopes.

The doctrine of his divinity was first preached by Seward P. Howels, who claimed to have fought against King Prempeh of Ashanti (1896). He was followed by James Nathaniel Hibbert who had preached Selassie's divinity in Panama, and both joined forces. They were joined subsequently by Archibald Dunkley who opened a mission in Kingston and preached that Ras Tafari was the Son of the Living God.

The movement developed into two streams, one distinctly religious and the other secular. It is now estimated to have a membership of several thousands. (See *The Ras Tafari Movement*—Institute of Social and Economic Research, University of the West Indies.)

7. *Ecumenical Approaches.* The difficulties attendant on any united action in this island world have already been mentioned. But here, as in other parts of the world the 20th century has been a century of ecumenical progress. We have already mentioned the existence of the Anglican Province of the West Indies, and the Assembly of Reformed Churches. Since 1907 the Methodists have had their Conference, the headquarters of which are in Antigua, the original home of Methodism in the C.

A great step forward was taken when in 1962 the Trinidad Presbyterians took the lead in the formation of the Ecumenical Committee on Missions to plan missionary strategy on a regional basis, in view of the resurgence of eastern religions. In 1963 this considered the approach to both *Hinduism and *Islam, and its findings have been published (*Great Things He hath done*— Berbice 1963).

Even more important in the ecumenical sense is the formation in 1965 of the United Theological College of the West Indies, situated at Kingston, Jamaica, in the neighbourhood of the university campus at Mona. Ten denominations joined to create this ecumenical venture. It has brought together the traditions of many older seats of learning. Calabar, a Baptist College, was founded in 1843. Caenwood (Methodist 1928, the successor of York Castle 1875) and St. Colmes (Presbyterian 1898) had joined in a common programme of teaching in 1912, and these came together as the Union Seminary in 1954. When Calabar, and St Peter's College, Anglican, were also ready to join, the way was prepared for the formation of the UTCWI, the aim of which is to provide ministerial training for students from the C. region and beyond.

8. *Conclusion.* Apart from the still continuing responsibility for Hindus and Muslims in Trinidad and the Guianas, the churches in the C. are no longer in a strictly missionary situation. They are, however, faced with a gigantic task of missionary consolidation. The primary and continuing problem is that of poverty, for which, combined as it is in many areas with over-population, no government has yet found an adequate remedy. To a considerable extent the churches are still dependent on subsidies from outside, and find almost insuperable difficulty in maintaining an adequately trained and competent indigenous ministry. In the bad times slaves were not permitted to contract regular marriages. A consequence is seen in the unusually high percentage of illegitimate births in almost all the islands. Much advance in education will be needed, if this survival from the past is to be eliminated; and education is always expensive. *Secularism is growing in the cities. Local feeling, and the difficulty of bringing the Christians of different areas together in the spirit of co-operation, are further impediments to progress. There are, however, many encouraging signs of the determination of Christians of the C. area to take their destiny into their own hands and to move forward into the ecumenical century.

H. O. RUSSELL AND EDITORS

E. Alphonse: *Among the Valiente* (London 1938), *God at the Helm* (London 1967); F. R. Augier and S. C. Gordon: *Sources of West Indian History* (2nd ed., London 1967); C. Black: *History of Jamaica* (London 1958); A. Burns: *History of the British West Indies* (2nd ed., London 1966); J. B. Ellis: *The Diocese of Jamaica* (London 1913); J. L. Gonzales, Jr: *The Development of Christianity in the Latin Caribbean* (Grand Rapids 1969); J. T. Hamilton: *A History of the Missions of the Moravian Church during the 18th and 19th centuries* (Bethlehem, Pa. 1901); R. A. L. Knight: *Liberty and Progress* (Jamaica 1938); J. MacPherson: *Caribbean Lands* (2nd ed., London 1967); S. C. Neill: *A History of Christian Missions* (Harmondsworth 1964), Ch.5; E. A. Payne: *Freedom in Jamaica* (rev. ed., London 1946); W. Scopes: *The Christian Ministry in Latin*

America and the Caribbean (New York 1962); E. Williams: *Documents of West Indian History* Vol. I (Trinidad 1963), *History of People of Trinidad and Tobago* (Trinidad 1962); S. Zavola: *Defence of Human Rights in Latin America in the 16th and 18th century* (UNESCO 1964); *Report on the Rastafari Movement in Kingston* (I.S.E.R., University of the West Indies 1960); *Sex, Love and Marriage in the Caribbean* (WCC Publications, Geneva 1965).

CARMICHAEL, AMY BEATRICE (1868–1951) was born in N. Ireland of well-to-do Presbyterian parents but spent her later girlhood in Cumberland in the family of the evangelical Quaker, Robert Wilson, a founder of the Keswick Convention. In 1892 she became the first Keswick missionary, serving briefly with the *CMS under Barclay Buxton in Japan until, after an illness, she went to Ceylon and then to South India, with the CEZMS, where she was greatly influenced by Walker of Tinnevelly. When she uncovered the appalling traffic in small girls sold to prostitution in Hindu temples, (see C's *Things as they are*, 1903) she found her life work, rescuing them and bringing them up as fervent Christians at Dohnavur, where she created the Dohnavur Fellowship, an important training centre for strongly evangelical Indian nurses, teachers, and evangelists. She added a boys' school, and formed a Sisterhood of the Common Life though without vows. She gathered round her a family of British and Indian helpers with a very high standard of consecration, and remained unquestioned leader though crippled and confined to her room for her last 20 years. Of great independence of mind and deep knowledge of the Scriptures and of Christian mysticism, she wrote devotional books and stories of the work, which had wide influence (*Raj, Brigand Chief*, 1927; *Gold Cord*, 1932, etc.).

JOHN POLLOCK

F. Houghton: *Amy Carmichael of Dohnavur* (London 1953).

CARVER, WILLIAM OWEN (1868–1954), minister, author, educator and missionary statesman, was educated at Richmond College, Virginia, USA, and Southern Baptist Theological Seminary. He served his first pastorate in Caroline County 1889–1891, then became pastor of his home church in Tennessee.

In 1893 C. became professor of philosophy and ancient languages at Boscobel College, Nashville, Tennessee. In 1896 he moved to the Southern Baptist Theological Seminary, where he taught NT, homiletics and theology. In 1900 he became head of the missions department, a position which he held until his retirement in 1943. He visited several mission fields and became an influential figure in mission circles.

C. founded the Woman's Missionary Union Training School in 1907 and taught there for many years. At his death the school became The Carver School of Missions and Social Work. He was a charter member and long-time president of the Southern Baptist Historical Society and one of the founders of the Historical Commission of the Southern Baptist Convention, besides holding membership in several other Baptist historical societies.

From 1920 to 1942 he edited the *Review and Expositor*. He was also contributing editor to the *Commission* and wrote frequently for other journals also. He wrote nineteen books, seven of which related to the Christian mission.

J. HERBERT KANE

W. O. Carver: *The Bible—a Missionary Message* (New York 1921), *The Course of Christian Missions* (New York 1932), *God and Man in Missions* (New York 1944).

CASALIS, EUGENE, (1812–1891), a missionary of the *Paris Evangelical Missionary Society, was the founder of the Lesotho Mission (1833–1855), and from 1856 to 1882 the director of the society at Paris.

After a first foundation at Morija (1833) C. founded a second station at Thaba-Bosiu (1835), the residence of *Moshoeshoe I, the chief of the Lesotho tribe. From 1835 to 1855, in addition to carrying out with exemplary piety his work as a missionary, and producing important linguistic and ethnographical works, including the translation of the Gospels, C. was the deeply trusted adviser of the paramount chief, in all the complex affairs resulting from the wars of the tribe with the Boers and the British. In consequence he played a diplomatic role which has won the admiration of the historians of South Africa.

In 1849–1850 C. undertook a journey to France to reawaken missionary zeal, which had been disturbed by the consequences of the revolution of 1848; his sermons and addresses produced a profound effect. In 1856 he was recalled to France to undertake the direction of the society and its training establishment.

Unwearied in his task of inspiring others, C. trained an entire generation of missionaries, and extended the activity of the society. New fields were opened in Tahiti and Senegal, both in 1862. Attempts to start missions in China (1860) and Mauritius proved unsuccessful.

C. retired in 1882 and died in 1891. He was the first Protestant missionary to be honoured by membership of the Légion d'Honneur.

ETIENNE KRUGER

E. Casalis: *The Basutos; or Twenty-three Years in South Africa* (Reprint, Cape Town 1965); H. Dieterlein: *Eugène Casalis* (Paris 1930).

CASTE AND THE CHRISTIAN CHURCHES. Caste is the masterpiece of Hindu society. Every Hindu knows to what caste he belongs; by this is determined, traditionally, the work which he does, the speech that he uses, the jewels that his wife wears, the gods whom he worships and everything else that he does. The caste creates a real feeling of brotherhood, and serves as a kind of insurance society for all its members. These advantages, however, have been dearly purchased at the cost of the fragmentation of society, of the suppression of personal initiative, and of the exclusion of about one fifth of the population from all social privilege or equality.

Naturally, caste has presented the

Christian churches with an intractable problem. Robert de *Nobili regarded it as implying purely social distinctions, and as in no way incompatible with the profession of Christian faith; since his time this has been the policy of the majority of the RC missions. In the 19th century, the Anglican Daniel Wilson (Bishop of Calcutta 1833–1859) took a very harsh line, regarding caste as the canker of the churches, and demanding that it be immediately given up. This led a number of Christians of higher caste to adhere to the *Leipzig Mission, which under the leadership of Karl *Graul was taking a much less radical view. The Thomas Christians in Kerala established themselves at an early date as practically one caste among many Hindu castes, and have maintained their special privileges through the centuries. In 1966 a schism took place in the Central Travancore diocese of the *CSI, the members who had come from formerly untouchable communities believing that they would find greater liberty in a church of their own than in one which was mainly directed by ex-Anglican *'Syrians'.

Where converts have come in individually, they have in a great many cases found it necessary to marry out of caste, and have formed a small highly-westernized minority, in which the old caste traditions have been almost completely forgotten. Where a village, or a group of villages, has come in together, the new Christians have naturally brought in with them much of their caste feeling, and their old caste traditions: it has been hard for them to exchange the certain fellowship of the traditional community for the new and untried fellowship of the Christian church.

Untouchability has been abolished by law. In the cities caste distinctions are much less observed than they were. But in the villages changes are hardly as yet to be observed. In the end it is likely that the system of caste will change, but this may well take a very long time. In the meantime, all the churches attempt to mitigate the rigours of caste-distinction, but with limited success. Attempts made in the RC church in this century to break down the barrier-walls of caste have led to rioting and violence.

STEPHEN NEILL

J. H. Hutton: *Caste in India* (3rd ed., Cambridge 1961); and all the works on the history of the church in India; *ERE* III, 230–39.

CASTRO, MATTHEW DE (c.1603–1668/9), first Indian bishop of the RC church, was born at Goa of a Brahman family converted by Theatine missionaries. Becoming convinced that his desire to enter the priesthood would not be fulfilled in India owing to the opposition of the Portuguese authorities, he made his way to Rome, and, after the completion of his theological studies, was ordained priest in 1630 and sent back to India as missionary to the Brahmans. The Archbishop of Goa refused to recognize him as a priest,because he had not come via Portugal and with the approval of the king of Portugal necessary under the rules of the *padroado*. C. found it necessary to return to Rome to plead his case. Just at this time Ingoli, the first great secretary of the *Propaganda, was maturing his plan for the appointment of *Vicars Apostolic for Asia and Africa, who would not be subject to the king of Portugal. C. was among the first to be consecrated (1637), with the intention that he should proceed to Japan. When this proved impossible, he was instructed to take charge of the Vicariate of Bijapur, in the territory of 'Idalcan' inland from Goa, and so independent of the jurisdiction of the Portuguese.

Already known as a vigorous opponent of Portuguese and 'Paulists', as he called the *Jesuits from their College of St. Paul in Goa, C. was unsparing in his criticisms, and before long was engaged in full-scale controversy with the objects of his attacks. The situation reached such a point of embitterment that in 1658 C. was recalled to Rome, and spent the last nine years of his life in retirement there. Although he took no further part in the public life of the church, he seems to have retained the good opinion of the Cardinals and of the Propaganda till the end of his days, and to have been consulted by them on Indian affairs.

The de Castro affair, however, had a generally unfortunate influence on the history of the RC church in India; the opinion was formed, and maintained for more than two centuries, that the time had not come for the elevation of Indians to the episcopate. We hear of two more rather shadowy Vicars Apostolic in the 17th century, and then the succession ceases. The consecration of the first bishop of the Latin rite in modern times did not take place until 1923.

ALBERT J. NEVINS, MM

T. Ghesquière: *Matthieu de Castro, premier Vicaire apostolique aux Indes* (Louvain 1937); E. D. Maclagan: *The Jesuits and the Great Mogul* (London 1932).

CATECHISTS, TRAINING AND EMPLOYMENT OF. The C. has been more widely and consistently employed by Roman Catholic missions than by Protestant agencies, although the *evangelist also performs some of the same functions. A small number of missionary priests often relied upon a large number of Cs for pioneer evangelism, elementary education—especially catechetics—and some pastoral care of the local community. The itinerant C. opened the way for the preaching of the missionary, and the station C. cared for the day-to-day nurture of converts and frequently conducted a primary school. Cs were first introduced by *Franciscan missionaries in Mexico early in the 16th century, and spread through Latin America. Francis *Xavier next stressed their use in India and the East. The 16th–17th century *Jesuit mission in Japan made large use of them. The most systematic development was in Tonkin, Cochin, and Annam, where Alexander de *Rhodes in 1627 founded a lay order of catechists called 'The House of God' and Bishop Lambert de la Motte in 1670 organized a similar institute for women, 'Lovers of the Cross'. Cardinal *Lavigerie and Fr. Liebermann, founders of the *White Fathers and *Holy Ghost Fathers respectively, introduced the C. into Africa in the 19th century. The increase in national clergy and religious is causing a decline in the corps of Cs. Figures for 1959 were 18,000 in Africa and 22,000 in Asia. Outstanding leadership in recent years has been given by Fr. Johannes Hofinger, SJ, in the East Asian Pastoral Institute at Ateneo de Manila University in Quezon City, Philippines. *Good Tidings*, a practical journal for Cs is issued. Major training centres are located at Mwanza, Tanzania; Windhoek, S.W. Africa; Batafogo, Brazil; Santiago, Chile; Lima, Peru; Mexico City; Taipei, Taiwan; Singapore; Nagoya, Japan; and Poona and Tindivanam in India.

The *SPG employed more than a dozen lay Cs in a mission to African slaves in the American colonies in the early 18th century, Elias Neau (New York, 1705–1722) being the best known. Protestant missions have made most general use of the national catechist in Africa, where, according to Bishop S. C. Neill, he has been 'the real hero of the Christian situation'. On the whole qualifications demanded were low, training at the most three years but often only some months, status nil, pay meagre, and advancement rare. But in some areas, as in the *CMS mission in Uganda, ordained clergy were recruited from Cs, who might advance through grades of junior and senior C. and lay reader through experience and progressive stages of training in a central school. The increase in ordained ministers, the advancement of general education, voluntary service by laymen, and the lure of secular jobs are now rapidly reducing the number of African Cs.

R. PIERCE BEAVER

J. Hofinger, SJ, ed.: *Teaching All Nations*, tr. by C. Howell (New York 1961) of *Katechetik Heute*, papers of the International Study Week on Missionary Catechetics, Eichstätt, 1960 (Freiburg 1961); B. Sundkler: *The Christian Ministry in Africa* (London 1960); J. V. Taylor: *The Growth of the Church in Buganda* (London 1958); *NCE* III, articles on 'Catechetical Centers', 'Catechist, Missionary'.

CATECHUMENATE. In the early church the catechumenate played a very important part. Those undergoing *catechesis*, oral instruction with a view to baptism, were clearly distinguished from the baptized; they were allowed, at public worship, only to attend the first part of the service, and were dismissed before the liturgy proper began. Baptism was usually administered with great solemnity shortly before Easter, and the newly baptized took part for the first time in the Communion of Easter Day. As whole populations became at least nominally Christian and infant baptism became the rule, the catechumenate fell out of use, though many orders of baptism service have in fact come to their present form through a conflation of the service for the admission of catechumens and of the baptismal liturgy in the proper sense of the term.

On the continent of Europe, in the Protestant churches, the word 'catechumen' has come to be used in an entirely different and unhistorical way, of those young people who are being prepared for confirmation, or for full membership of the church of Christ.

In many Protestant missions, the word 'catechumen' is not used at all; but a distinction is often made between 'enquirers', those who are interested in the Christian faith, and 'candidates for baptism', those who have expressed a definite desire to join the church by baptism. But no uniformity of practice at all exists; and, even within the RC church, differences of usage between one area and another are very wide. It would be of great advantage to the work, if some principles could be arrived at in common, and some attempts made to regulate practice according to them.

Where the catechumenate is taken seriously, it has been found of great benefit to hold a special service for the admission of catechumens. This, obviously, cannot demand a profession of Christian faith; that is to come later at baptism. What can be expected of the catechumen at this stage is (1) a repudiation of idolatry and of all practices inconsistent with the Christian faith in so far as he comes to understand it. (2) A declaration of his willingness to attend instruction, and to understand more fully the faith to which he has given his preliminary adhesion. (3) A promise to attend

Christian worship regularly. (4) A willingness to accept certain elementary rules of Christian morality. If these promises are sincerely given, the candidate is given one Christian name, to which another will be added at the time of his baptism, and some outward token, such as a small cross, to indicate his real, but as yet incomplete membership of the Christian fellowship. His name will be entered in a special section of the church register, and from that time on the local church will be regarded as specially responsible to pray for him, and to do everything possible to help him forward to the completion of his Christian allegiance.

It is to be regretted that there are so few areas in which admission of catechumens is taken with the seriousness which it deserves.

STEPHEN NEILL

NCE III, 237–40.

CATHOLIC MISSIONS. See MISSIONS, ROMAN CATHOLIC.

CAYMAN ISLANDS. See CARIBBEAN.

CELEBES. See INDONESIA.

CENTRAL AFRICAN REPUBLIC, formerly part of French Equatorial Africa, is a landlocked territory of 238,000 sq.m. situated in the heart of the continent. Population in 1967 was 1,459,000 including about 6,000 Europeans. Prevailing religion is traditional *animism, with only some 45,000 Muslims; a Roman Catholic prefecture apostolic begun in 1909 has grown into four dioceses with (1965) 189,795 Catholics. Protestant missions began in 1921, and by 1966 ten denominations were at work, with a total community of 145,472; the largest bodies were *Eglise Evangélique des Frères* (Brethren Church Mission) with 65,000; *Eglises Baptistes* (Baptist Mid-Missions) with 50,000; *Union des Eglises Baptistes* (*Orebro Missionsforening*) with 25,000, and *Eglise Evangélique Centrafricaine* (AIM) with 5,000. Separatist movements have effected missions among the major tribes (Baya, Banda, Mandja) since 1956; the largest such body is *Comité Baptiste* with 7,000 adherents

under an elderly white-bearded pastor Boymandja, whose organization has received government recognition and is expanding into Cameroon also.

DAVID B. BARRETT

NCE III, 399f.

CENTRES FOR THE STUDY OF OTHER RELIGIONS. Many universities and seminaries have departments or courses for the study of 'comparative religion' or of this or that particular faith. A few inter-faith study centres exist, which conduct their work on a religiously neutral basis. As part of the mission of the church, however, a number of specifically Christian institutes have also been set up to study the major religions in various parts of Asia and Africa. Some of these fruitfully combine with this programme a study of the inter-relationship of religion and society. (In Latin America there are similar centres concerned with church and society issues and Evangelical-Roman Catholic relations.)

Each of these small study centres has its own particular character, and even the oldest still shows pioneering characteristics. Whatever their other activities and services, such as holding lectures, seminars or conferences, or publishing pamphlets and books, at the heart of their work lies the research or other form of study which justifies their name.

Their basic task is seeking to discover what is in the minds and hearts of those to whom the church must communicate the gospel. The harder part of the problem of communication is not that of clearly proclaiming the message, but that of expressing it so that it effectively links with the interests and understanding of the person addressed. If he is someone of another faith and culture, what he really hears will certainly not be what the speaker says. Only study of what is in the hearer's mind can help to bridge the gap.

What is being studied through these centres, therefore, is not so much the classic religious systems of the past, as the faith by which Hindus, Muslims, Buddhists, Sikhs and others actually live today. And th fundamental method has to be *dialogue with people rather than reading of books.

Developments of transport and communications mean that in all countries Christians now find themselves encountering men and women of other faiths. But the church has not adequately prepared them for this, either in the east or in the west. Hence the importance of these 'watch-towers of thought', as the late Hendrik *Kraemer called them.

List of Centres for the Study of Other Religions.

ALGIERS, Christian Centre for North African Studies.

BANGALORE, Christian Institute for the Study of Religion and Society.

BATALA, Christian Institute for the Study of Sikh Religion and Culture.

COLOMBO, Christian Study Centre.

HONG KONG, Christian Study Centre on Chinese Religion and Culture, Tao Fong Shan.

IBADAN, Institute of Church and Society.

KYOTO, NCC Centre for the Study of Japanese Religions.

LUCKNOW, Henry Martyn Institute of Islamic Studies.

MANILA, Christian Institute for Ethnic Studies in Asia.

NEAR EAST, Council of Churches' Study Programme (Beirut).

RAJPUR, Christian Retreat and Study Centre.

RAWALPINDI, Christian Study Centre.

VICTOR E. W. HAYWARD

CEYLON. Area 25,332 sq.m. Population (1967) 11,701,000, of these approximately 7½ million are Sinhalese (mostly Buddhist) and 2½ million are Tamil (mostly Hindu). There are also small communities of Moors (Moslem) and Eurasians (mostly Christian). The total Christian community is about 8.5% of the total population, approximately 800,000 Roman Catholics and 100,000 non-RC. The first effective penetration by Christianity took place with the Portuguese occupation of the coastal plain early in the 16th century.

RC work began with the arrival of a group of *Franciscans in Ceylon in 1543.

These were followed by *Jesuits in 1602, and later by *Augustinians and *Dominicans. Considerable success was achieved, and the impress of the mission was particularly notable in such cities as Colombo. This work was all brought to an end when in 1658 the Dutch finally drove the Portuguese from the island. The DRC had recognition from the government. No RC priest was permitted to reside in the island, and every inducement of favour and advantage was held out to persuade RCs to become Protestants. A large number yielded to this persuasion. It was only with the utmost difficulty that the Oratorian Fr. Joseph *Vaz was able in 1707 to smuggle himself into C., and set to work to reorganize the life of the Catholic communities. Gradually the restrictions on the residence of priests came to be less strictly enforced, and a certain number of Oratorians were able to maintain themselves, always under considerable difficulties, with such success that, when the British drove out the Dutch in 1796, they reckoned that there were still 67,000 RCs in the island, and that they outnumbered the Protestants. Throughout this period of 140 years, there was no bishop, and no Ceylonese priest in the island.

With the British occupation religious *liberty was established. But the weakness of the RC church in Europe made difficult any immediate resumption of activity in C. In fact it was not till the creation of the *Vicariate Apostolic of C. in 1834 that progress began to be assured. Oratorians from Goa remained in the island, to be joined later by Italian Sylvestrines, Belgian Jesuits, the *Oblates (OMI, largely Irish) and others. In 1856 Leo XIII created the hierarchy with Colombo as archdiocese and Jaffna and Kandy as suffragan sees. The first Ceylonese bishop Mgr. Pieris was consecrated for Chilaw in 1940. There are now six dioceses, almost all under indigenous bishops, served by 356 (1959) indigenous priests. The number of RCs has grown rapidly; in 1901 there were about 300,000, today probably at least three quarters of a million; the RCs far outnumber all other Christian churches taken together.

In 1893 the great pontifical seminary for the whole of India and C. was located at Kandy and placed under the direction of Belgian Jesuits. In 1955 this seminary was removed to Poona in India; the buildings now serve as the regional seminary, directed by the OMI, for the training of all candidates for the priesthood in C.

Like all other churches the RCs have suffered under the policies followed by the government since independence in 1947. These have included the taking over of most of the RC schools. The bishops have advised the faithful to accept the inevitable without approving of it.

Under British rule and religious neutrality, the Reformed Church rapidly dwindled. Large numbers of nominal Christians reverted to their traditional faith. This period was marked by the beginning of Protestant missionary work under the Baptists (1812), the Methodists (1814), and the *CMS (1818). The *ABCFM also established work in the Jaffna peninsula during the same period. The Protestant missionary societies immediately embarked upon a vigorous educational programme, and during the 19th century hundreds of village schools were opened and, towards the end of the century, many larger schools in the big towns using English as the medium of instruction. In the last two decades of the century there began a great revival of *Buddhism, powerfully aided by Col. Olcott and other *Theosophists from America, which led to the rapid expansion of Buddhist education; but up to the 1920s the church held a dominant position in education. Since the second world war, the attainment of independence and the growing self-awareness of Buddhism have led to measures to curb the influence of the Christian church and to re-establish Buddhism as the dominant religious influence. In 1960 the government established a national system of education, taking over most of the educational work of the church. Today only a very few of the larger schools remain under church control. In 1966 Sunday ceased to be a public holiday, its place being taken by the Buddhist *poya* day, based on the four quarters of the moon.

In spite of these measures, the government has on the whole maintained its professed religious neutrality. The church is given time on the radio in proportion to its numbers, and in government-controlled schools the children of the minority religions receive instruction in their own religion. There are no legal restrictions on the evangelistic work of the church. The main non-RC churches co-operate in the *NCC and, with the exception of the small DRC, they are all engaged in negotiations for union. The completed Scheme for Church Union was in 1970 before the churches awaiting their assent. All the churches involved are fully *autonomous and largely self-supporting. The largest is the Anglican, with a Christian community of about 45,000, and the Methodist, with about 25,000. The others, all of less than 5,000 members, are the Baptist Sangamaya, the Presbytery of Lanka, and the Jaffna Diocese of the *CSI.

G. BASIL JACKSON AND STEPHEN NEILL

G. H. Anderson, ed.: *Christianity in Southeast Asia: A Bibliographical Guide*, art. 'Ceylon' (New York 1966); Jonquet: *Mgr. Bonjean . . . premier Archévêque de Colombo* (Nîmes, 2 vols. 1910); D. J. B. Kuruppu: *The Catholic Church in Ceylon* (Colombo 1923); *BM* II, 210–15; *NCE* III, 418f.

CHAD, a republic, formerly part of French Equatorial Africa, is a territory of 495,000 sq.m., to a large extent Saharan desert. Population in 1967 was 3,410,200, including 5,000 Europeans. Some 50% are Muslims, with a large proportion of animists in the south among whom the missions work. A RC prefecture apostolic was not erected until 1947, growing by 1966 into four dioceses with 109,627 Catholics. Protestant missions arrived in 1925, and numbered seven denominations served by ten foreign missions in 1966, with a total community of 94,000. Of these the largest were *Eglise Evangélique au Tchad* (*SUM, French Mennonites, *WEC) with 50,000, *Eglises Baptistes du Tchad* (Baptist Mid-Missions) with 20,000, *Assemblées Chrétiennes* (CMML) with 15,000; and *Eglises*

Evangéliques des Frères (Brethren Church Mission), *Eglise Fraternelle Luthérienne du Tchad* (American Lutheran Brethren), *Mission Evangélique du Guera* (*Assemblées de France, Mission Evangélique Belge*), and *Mission Evangélique du Plein Evangile* (*Coopération Evangélique Mondiale*). Since 1951 four separatist movements with 2,000 adherents have emerged, but under government pressure most adherents have rejoined the mission churches.

DAVID B. BARRETT

BM II, 833–36; *NCE* III, 420f.

CHALMERS, JAMES (1841–1901), was born at Ardrishaig, Scotland, and died at Goaribari Island, New Guinea. After training under the *LMS he was ordained in the Congregational church in 1865 to minister in the South Seas; he married Jane Hercus, who sailed with him in 1866 to Rarotonga. For 10 years C. was a district missionary, organizing the work of Polynesian teachers in their stations and helping to train teachers for the evangelization of New Guinea. In 1877 the Cs were themselves appointed to New Guinea, of which a great part was in a chronic state of inter-tribal war. Their first station was among the cannibals of Suau, from where C. prospected for new sites and visited his Rarotongan teachers; his aim was 'the whole coast divided into districts worked by missionaries and native teachers'.

To protect the New Guineans against increasing exploitation by Europeans, C. encouraged the annexation of New Guinea to the British Crown; he was the trusted mediator between chiefs and British officials. In 1888 he wrote: 'Already laws . . . have been passed, by which the land has been secured to the natives. . . . Deportation of natives has been made illegal, and the introduction of intoxicants, opium, firearms and explosives is prohibited'. He believed in indirect rule and in government initiative in educating the people.

C's first wife died in 1879; in 1888 he married a widow, Eliza Harrison, who shared his life as he worked westward along the coast. In 1892 he made his headquarters at Saguane, near the mouth of the Fly River. From here he led and supervised the Polynesian and New Guinean teachers in evangelizing the interior and the Torres Strait islands. C. and the young missionary Oliver Tomkins, with ten teachers and other assistants, were murdered by New Guinean cannibals on 2 January 1901.

C. was 'the pathfinder through the New Guinea wilderness'. A man of physical, intellectual and spiritual strength, of love and personal magnetism, he was ideally fitted for pioneer work. His evangelical fervour was combined with a practical appreciation of conditions. Thus he could say: 'We preach the gospel in many ways; one of our best at present is making peace between the tribes;' and, 'Do not expect too much. Forced work is unhealthy and manufactured converts do not last long. Let the work grow with our lives. . . .' His personal care and example formed a large part of the foundation on which the indigenous church in S.E. New Guinea has been built.

JOHN GOODWIN

J. Chalmers: *Work and Adventure in New Guinea* (London 1885), *Pioneering in New Guinea* (London 1887); R. Lovett: *James Chalmers. His Autobiography and Letters* (London 1902); *DNB*, 2nd Suppl. i, 343–45.

CHARLES, PIERRE (1883–1954), was a Belgian priest, one of the principal RC representatives of the science of missions, and founder of the so-called Louvain School. From 1914 to 1954, C. was professor of dogmatic theology at the preparatory institute of the *Jesuits in Louvain, from 1923 onwards intensely concerned both in theory and practice with missionary problems. From 1932 to 1938 he was also professor of missionary science at the Gregorian University in Rome, and played a considerable part in the secret preparations for a Council which was to have been held under Pope Pius XII. Taking his stand against a romantic and individualistic understanding of mission, C. identifies the goal of mission as the founding or 'planting' of the visible church in all lands and in all cultural groups. For this reason he laid stress on the development of an indigenous clergy, on the *adaptation of the message, and on the social and cultural activity of the mission. His thinking exercised a powerful influence, especially in the Latin countries. The Second *Vatican Council held firmly to the churchly character of the mission, yet with less emphasis on church-centredness, and with a wider ecumenical vision.

                                PETER WANKO

P. Charles: *Etudes Missiologiques* (Bruges 1956, with bibliography); J. Masson: *Nouvelle Revue Theologique*, LXXX (1958), pp. 1042–61, and LXXXI (1959), pp. 41–59.

CHEN SU-LAN (1888–1967) was born of a Christian family in Foochow, China. Educated at the Anglo-Chinese College, Foochow, he married Miss Kok Kim Fook before coming to Singapore, where he graduated from the King Edward College of Medicine. A staunch and lifelong lay-member of the Methodist Church, he became a pioneer of medical and social progress in Singapore and Malaya. In 1911–1912 he was President of the Singapore Chinese Library, the first socio-political association in Singapore, with 2,000 members. His life was notable for three campaigns. During 1929–1957 he led an anti-opium campaign, was president of the Singapore Anti-Opium Society and Director of the Anti-Opium Clinic; as a result opium smoking was eventually banned in the country. During 1931–1941 he campaigned against prostitution and effected the closing down of public brothels. During 1931–1957 he worked for the prevention and cure of tuberculosis, founding the Rotary TB Clinic and the Singapore Anti-Tuberculosis Association. After the second world war he was a member of the Advisory Council of the British Military Administration. C. held many high positions and honours, was Director of the Rotary Club for many years from 1931, founder and first president of the Chinese *YMCA (1946–1947), and president of the British Medical Association (1949–1950). In 1947 he founded the Chen Su-Lan

Trust and donated $500,000 to it for charitable purposes.

                                HOBART B. AMSTUTZ

CHENG CHING-YI (1881–1939), was born in Peking, China, of Manchu parentage. His father, a convert from Buddhism, was pastor of a church of the *LMS, and C. followed his father in that ministry. In 1903, as a student in England, he made a significant contribution to the translation of the Union Mandarin version of the NT. At the First *World Missionary Conference (Edinburgh 1910) he startled the west with his statement, 'Your denominationalism does not interest Chinese Christians'. This declaration was prophetic of the direction his life was to take: From 1913 to 1922 he was secretary of the China Continuation Committee, from 1924 to 1934 secretary of the *National Christian Council, and from 1934 on secretary of the Church of Christ in China. Thus his life was spent in drawing together into one unified fellowship the fragmented results of the past century of missionary work. In 1918 he helped to organize the interdenominational Chinese Home Missionary Society, and in 1919 he was one of the organizers of the *IMC, of which he was a vice-president from 1928 to 1938. He was the only Chinese to attend all three of the great World Missionary Conferences at Edinburgh, Jerusalem and Tambaram.

                                FRANCIS P. JONES

Memoir by Charles Boynton in the *Chinese Recorder* for December 1939.

CHI-OANG (1872–1946), was born in Ka-wan, a small town on the east coast of Taiwan. The Taroko tribe, to which she belonged, is one of the ten mountain tribes which came to Taiwan several centuries ago. They are of Polynesian-Malayan origin, and are all *animists. After being a peaceful mediator between the Japanese and her own tribe, a successful trader, and finally a lonely old woman of a broken family, she was baptized at the age of 52. She was the first Taroko Christian (1 June 1924). She was brought to the Tamsui Presbyterian

Women's Bible School in 1929. Upon graduation, she went back to work among her own people. Under Japanese rule, travel in the mountains was restricted and preaching to the tribes was prohibited. She disregarded these laws. Her own people came from far and near and heard her gladly. During the second world war, they gathered secretly at night in a cave to hear her preaching. To save her from the police, the young men carried her upon their backs, or hid her in the rice stacks. The tribal Christians were persecuted for their faith. They were beaten, thrown into prison and killed; yet their numbers increased. After the war, several thousand mountain Christians awaited baptism—the fruits of her labours. The church has continued to grow, until now (1968) there are 411 mountain churches with 77,563 members in the Presbyterian church alone.

LIEN-MIN CHENG

M. L. Copland: *Chi-Oang—Mother of the Taiwan Tribes Church* (Taipeh 1961); J. Dickson: *Stranger Than Fiction* (Toronto 1948).

CHILE. A republic on the west coast of South America, extending 2,650 miles along a narrow, mountainous strip of land. Total area 286,323 sq.m. Estimated population 8,000,000. Predominant language Spanish. Agriculture is important in the central zone. Mining predominates in the north, copper has replaced nitrate as the major export commodity. Rapid urban growth and industrialization are changing social structures. The original inhabitants, Araucanian Indians, were defeated by the Spanish in 1541. National independence was obtained in 1818. Apart from old, Spanish-descent families, and European immigrants, today's Chileans are largely a Mestizo (mixed) race. Since the election of Christian Democratic President Eduardo Frei Montalva in 1964 Chile has been hoping to achieve peaceful social revolution (land reform, partial nationalisation of mining operations, etc.). Roman Catholicism was implanted by the Spanish conquerors. Its absolute power was progressively limited after political inde-

pendence, until formal separation of church and state was enacted in 1925. During the 19th and first half of 20th century Roman Catholicism supported conservative political and social tendencies. After the second world war the church's thinking began to change profoundly, with the establishment of up-to-date departments of sociology and economics at the Catholic university, the creation of Centro Belarmino (for study, research and publications), the formation of Catholic Action and participation in the Christian Democratic party. This process has been accomplished by much theological and pastoral re-orientation. In the mid-19th century British (Anglican) merchants and German (Lutheran) settlers introduced Protestantism to C. Anglicans also evangelized in Tierra del Fuego and among the Araucanian Indians. In the 1870s and 1880s Methodist, Presbyterian and later Southern Baptist missionaries entered the country from the USA. Progress was slow, owing to much resistance and persecution. In 1909 the Pentecostal movement arose within the Methodist church. The old structures were unable to contain it, and the new movement spread rapidly among the hitherto neglected working classes. Pentecostalism's marks are: sense of participation and belonging, speaking with tongues, emotional release, faith healing, existence of strong father (pastor-caudillos) and mother (prophetesses) figures, etc. Its strength is estimated between 500,000 and one million. At this time certain weaknesses show themselves: Pentecostalism does not easily adapt itself to new social conditions; increased social maturity undermines father and mother figures; church leaders have poor theological education. Ecumenical understanding between Pentecostals and non-Pentecostals is still difficult because of sociological factors. New efforts, such as the creation of a Theological Community and Church and Society studies, may help to close the gap creatively.

THEO TSCHUY

C. L. d'Epinay: *Haven of the Masses* (London 1969); W. C. Hoover: *Historia del Avivamiento Pentecostal en Chile* (Valparaiso 1948); J. B. A. Kessler, Jr: *A Study of the Older Protestant Missions and Churches in Peru and Chile* (Goes 1967); I. Vergara: *El Protestantismo en Chile* (Santiago 1962); E. Willems: 'Protestantismus und Klassenstruktur in Chile' in *Kölner Zeitschrift für Soziologie und Sozialpsychologie* (Cologne 12, 1960), 'Protestantism and Cultural Change in Brazil and Chile' in W. D'Antonio and Fr. Pike, eds.: *Religion, Revolution and Reform* (London 1964); *BM* II, 215–23; *NCE* III, 583–87; *WKL*, 214–17.

CHINA. (1) The People's Republic of C. (Communist C., Mainland C.). Government established in 1949, capital at Peking. Area 3,691,602 sq.m. (including *Tibet). 1967 estimated population 750,000,000 (Tibet 1,500,000).

(2) The (National) Republic of C. *Taiwan (Formosa, Free C.). Government moved from mainland in 1949, capital at Taipei. Area 73,952 sq.m. 1967 estimated population 13,000,000.

At the time of Christ four great civilizations—Rome, Persia, India and C.—dominated the earth. Christianity spread through the Roman empire with its Roman-Greek-Hebrew culture, by commercial routes to the Parthian empire (Persia and Mesopotamia), also to India beginning in the 2nd or 3rd century A.D., and finally crossed the vast deserts of central Asia to the Chinese empire with its rich culture influencing all East Asia. No doubt some Christian believers in the early centuries of the Christian era made contacts with individual Chinese along the 'Silk Road' or on lanes of sea travel, but the first known record of Christian missionaries entering the Middle Kingdom was not until the 7th century A.D. Some Christian communities were born but after two centuries *Nestorian Christianity, the 'Luminous Religion' as it was called, seemed to disappear.

With the rise of the powerful non-Chinese Mongol Dynasty four centuries later, C. was opened to *Franciscan missionaries journeying afar from Europe. They won adherents and founded churches but these too vanished when a century of imperial Khan patronage came to an end.

Another 200 years passed before expanding ocean transportation brought the Portuguese (1552), and a little later Italian, *Jesuit missionaries to C. (1582). During the 400 years since then Christian communities have taken root in C. The story of these centuries, however, has been marked by retreat as well as advance, periods of growth and of decline, and the harsh impact of national and international crises upon the Christian faith.

Protestant Christianity sent its first representatives to C. in the opening decade of the 19th century and has maintained a foothold there, along with the older RC church, up to the present time.

For a little more than one-third of the 2,000 years since Christ's birth there has been a Christian missionary witness of some kind among the people of C. Following a period of vigorous expansion between 1860 and 1950, interrupted at times by disheartening events, the Christian enterprise on the Chinese mainland has now met with its most severe challenge and stands within the shadow, awaiting another dawn.

The religious history of C. embraces both native and imported faiths. Archaeological studies show evidences of divination, *ancestor worship, animal and human *sacrifices, and worship of a supreme ruler alongside superstitious and *animistic practices, in the 2nd millennium before Christ. Ancient Chinese philosophy, ethics and religion, flowered in the Chou Kingdom (1122–221 B.C.). Confucius (K'ung Fu-tze) and Lao-tze, the Old Master, presumed founder of *Taoism, were both born in the 6th century B.C. and their seminal teachings gave rise to varied and stimulating schools of thought. Confucius was primarily a political reformer in a time of feudal unrest, reverent in his attitude toward *T'ien*, Heaven. He believed profoundly in the moral order of the universe and moral law in human relations, but he was a humanist and humanitarian, not a religious prophet or leader. However, the *Confucian philosophy and way of life became the basis of C's political and social organization up to recent times. Philosophical Taoism with its emphasis on the law of nature, non-action and quietism, mystic calm, and the path to immortality, combined with free art and charming folk tales, appealed to certain minds. Religious Taoism, embodying centuries of accretions—*magic, alchemy, astrology, fortune-telling and exorcism—became one of several strands in C's colourful religion of the masses.

Although the Buddha was a contemporary of Confucius, he and his teachings were not known in China until after the beginning of the Christian era, introduced—it is generally believed—over land and sea trade routes from India. Within a few hundred years *Buddhism, chiefly the Māhayāna form, had become naturalized in Chinese soil. Its voluminous literature, translated into Chinese by hundreds of scholars and pilgrims, could appeal only to a select group; it was too profound for the multitude. Yet popular Buddhism filled an emotional and religious need in the lives of the people, and offered a simple, practical ethical code that the common man could appreciate.

Two other important religions, both monotheistic, have come to C. from outside, *Islam and Christianity. C. is thus the meeting ground of five major religions and one radical revolutionary movement—Marxian Communism. Islam entered C. more than a thousand years ago through Muslim traders and soldiers. Large Muslim communities arose under the Mongol (Yuan) Dynasty in the 13th and 14th centuries. At one time more than 20 million Muslim faithful were counted in C., the nation's largest and oldest alien cultural stock, now increasingly assimilated into Chinese society. Small groups of Jews and Russian Orthodox believers have also made their homes in C.

Christians in C. have never exceeded 1% of the total population. The course of missionary effort from abroad has been a sadly broken line. Erected at the capital of the powerful T'ang Dynasty in 781 the world-famous Nestorian monument tells the history and doctrines of Nestorian Christianity from its official introduction to C. in 635. This stone, excavated from ruins

in 1623, long outlasted the church of the Nestorians at Sian. Again, in spite of the phenomenal labours of Archbishop John of Montecorvino, first RC missionary to reach C. (about 1294), the new converts won under the Pax Mongolia were after a few decades scattered and lost. The next Christian witness came on the tide of European Renaissance, Catholic Counter-Reformation, and world exploration. When Matthew *Ricci and other Jesuit missionaries were admitted to C. during the period of the Ming and Manchu dynasties, they taught western science as well as the Christian religion and were enabled to stay on because of their willingness to accommodate the Christian faith and practice to Chinese traditions and customs (see ACCOMMODATION). Since the *Dominican and Franciscan missionaries disapproved and Pope Clement IX condemned the Jesuits' tolerance of Chinese *rites and religious terms, a crisis occurred. The imperial court was angered and persecutions increased, but the RC church in C. though shaken did not succumb. At the end of the 18th century there were about 200,000 baptized Catholics in all C.

The 19th century saw heavy pressures by European governments and commercial companies for regular diplomatic and trade relations with the Chinese empire. Unfortunately this came at a time when the Manchu rulers, isolationist and proud, wanted to keep out all foreign influences, especially the opium trade with India. The western powers responded, sad to relate, with colonial policies and military force. The result was two groups of treaties unfavourable to C's dignity and independence, the first in 1842–44 when Hong Kong was ceded to the British and five ports were opened, the next in 1858–60 when residence of foreigners in both port and inland cities was permitted and Christian missionaries with their converts were accorded official protection. It should be noted that some missionaries, because of their knowledge of the country and language, assisted in the negotiation and writing of what were later called the 'unequal treaties'. Other critical events which presented the Christian church with both opportunities and dangers were briefly: the T'ai-p'ing Rebellion against the decadent Manchu government (1850–65) under a visionary leader who had studied parts of the Bible, finally crushed after bringing devastation to much of the country; C's defeat by Japan in 1895 and loss of control over Formosa and Korea; and at the turn of the century the wild, anti-foreign *Boxer uprising which made martyrs of nearly 200 Protestant missionaries and missionary children, a smaller number of Catholic missionaries, and several thousand Chinese Christians. Critical happenings of the 20th century include: the Sun Yat-sen revolution and downfall of the Manchu régime (1910–11); the period of civil wars and rise of strong nationalism (1915–37); the Japanese invasion of C., beginning with the attack on Manchuria in 1930 and ending with the defeat of Japan by allied forces in 1945; civil war again, followed by the Communist victory over the mainland in 1949.

In spite of persecution and occasional martyrdom, the thread of RC witness in C. was never completely broken. In 1810 31 European missionaries and 80 Chinese priests were at work in the country. But RC missions only began their immense modern expansion after the signing of the first treaties between C. and the European powers in 1842. From that time on, almost all the RC orders and missionary societies, both for men and women, entered the country, and large organizations were built up in all the provinces. In 1842 there may have been a quarter of a million RC Christians in C.; by 1914 this had grown to about a million and a half. Successive French governments desired to be regarded in a special way as the patrons and protectors of RC missions in C. Every missionary, of whatever nationality, was required to have a French passport; French consular protection was at all times available, and this protection was held to extend also to converts who might be suffering injustice at the hands of their fellow-countrymen. This had the advantage of affording much security for the work of RC missions. It had

the grave drawback that RC missionaries were generally regarded by the Chinese as political agents of a foreign power, a view to which some substance was accorded by actions of the French diplomatic authorities in C. Dislike and suspicion of the Christian cause broke out from time to time in scenes of violence, such as the terrible 'bloodbath' of Tientsin on 21 June 1870, in which two French priests and 10 Sisters of Charity lost their lives.

RC missions paid much less attention than Protestants to education; though a considerable number of priests had been ordained, little independent responsibility was granted to them, and, apart from the one experiment of Gregory *Lo in the 18th century, no Chinese had been raised to the episcopate. The specious argument was put forward that a Chinese subject who had become a bishop would not be able to claim French consular protection in the same way as a foreigner. This situation was radically changed in the 20th century, largely through the work of one man, Fr. Vincent *Lebbe, through whose influence in Rome the pope became convinced that the time had come for the elevation of Chinese to the episcopate, and in 1926 took the dramatic step of himself consecrating the first six Chinese bishops in St. Peter's at Rome. Since then the number of Chinese bishops increased steadily, until the crisis of 1949, after which all foreign bishops were expelled. The first Chinese cardinal was the greatly revered Archbishop Tien of Peking.

The highest point of RC missionary activity in C. was reached probably in 1939, when the number of foreign workers was recorded at 5,800. In spite of the new stress laid on the training of Chinese priests and bishops, foreign priests still outnumbered Chinese by 2,979 to 2,026. The centralization of the RC church in Rome has made it more difficult for the RCs than for the Protestants to develop what the Chinese themselves would accept as a genuinely independent and Chinese Church. With the Communist take-over in 1949, the continuing close connection with the west made the RC missionary and Chinese Christian in a special way an object of dislike and suspicion. Every attempt has been made entirely to disrupt communication between Rome and the Chinese church, and to subvert the loyalty of Chinese Christians to the 'western' head of their church. Little news about conditions in China since the revolution has reached the west; but it seems certain that the RC church is carrying on heroically in its isolation, and, though weakened, will survive into the days of greater freedom which must some day arrive.

The first Protestant missionary to the people of China was the scholarly Robert *Morrison of the *LMS (Congregational) who reached Canton in 1807 and became engaged largely in Bible translation and literary work for 27 strenuous years. In 1814 he baptized his first convert, Ts'ai A-ko, 'away from human observation', and prayed, 'May he be the first fruits of a great harvest, one of millions who shall believe and be saved'. When Morrison died there was a tiny Chinese church of a dozen Christians and one ordained Chinese preacher. The next arrival was a German missionary, Karl *Gützlaff, followed by two missionaries of the *ABCFM. In 1833 came S. Wells *Williams, printer, linguist, author, diplomat, sent by the same missionary organization. Dr Peter *Parker was the first medical missionary. In the 1830s American Episcopal, Baptist and Presbyterian missionaries entered the country. By 1840 there were nearly 100 baptized Christians. Mission work was started at Shanghai in 1843 and gradually extended to the surrounding areas, followed by beginnings at Amoy and Foochow in south C. The first Protestant church at Ningpo was organized in 1845. In the next 15 years the *CMS and Methodists and Presbyterians from Britain entered the country. After the Tientsin Treaty of 1858 missionaries found a larger opportunity to preach the gospel and many pressed to the interior at their own risk. The first *Bible Societies (British and Foreign and American) started work in the 1860s. By 1864 20 Protestant missionary societies and 189 men missionaries were serving in C. The *CIM which became the largest single Protestant missionary agency, launched its adventurous, pioneer enterprise in 1865. Shortly before this missionaries had entered Formosa. The first all-China Missionary Conference, in 1877, was attended by 152 missionaries; at that time 6,000 Protestant Christians were reported. The second missionary conference was held in 1890, attended by 445 missionaries belonging to 36 societies. Between these dates were recorded publication of the first widely acceptable Mandarin Bible, the first medical woman missionary, the first Chinese anti-footbinding society, and a widespread famine in North C. (1878–1879) in which missionaries first administered relief on a large scale.

Missionaries of many denominations and nationalities began to penetrate all the provinces, with a measure of *comity in their plans and efforts. At the time of the 1890 conference there were over 40,000 Protestant Christians in C.; the delegates included two Chinese Christian leaders. Arousing anxiety were the intense anti-foreign feeling and resentment against western aggression reported from many parts of the country. A brief reform movement at the capital was followed by the stratagem of the Manchu Empress Dowager to protect her own position by encouraging the fanatical Boxers to exterminate white aliens and also Chinese believers in the new foreign religion. The intervention of western powers and enlightened public opinion in China checked the bloody persecutions. Indemnities imposed by foreign governments deeply wounded the feelings of the Chinese.

By the time of the Centenary Missionary Conference of 1907 winds of change were blowing strongly and reforms in government and society were taking place. Registration at the conference was 1,186 of whom seven were Chinese Christians. Baptized Protestants had reached a total of nearly 190,000, while over 4,000 foreign missionaries, men and women, were engaged in evangelistic, educational, medical and social work alongside a growing number of national workers. The Chinese Independent

Church, an *indigenous denomination, had been formed. The Christian Associations (*YMCA and *YWCA) were being started in several cities. In 1910 the Edinburgh *World Missionary Conference drew a large delegation from C. including five outstanding Chinese leaders. Overthrow of the Manchus and inauguration of a republic in 1911 gave impetus to many new forms of missionary activity, especially the founding of Christian colleges, high schools, theological seminaries and medical schools, often by merger of existing small institutions. Chinese church bodies of the same denominational family began to unite, for example the *Sheng Kung Hui* (Episcopal Church of C.) in 1912, the Presbyterian General Assembly of C. in 1919 and the Lutheran Church of all C. in 1929. The years 1915 to 1930 saw the rise of several indigenous Christian sects, such as the Jesus Family and the True Jesus Church, and the strengthening of certain ultra-conservative evangelical missions in C. The mainstream of Protestant Christianity was represented in the National Christian Conference which met at Shanghai in May 1922, attended by 486 missionaries and 664 Chinese delegates —testifying to the rapid development of the Chinese churches. Dr *Cheng Ching-yi was elected Chairman. Dr Timothy T. *Lew in his keynote address said, 'The great foundation of the Church has been laid by the devoted servants of God, both missionaries and Chinese Christian workers. We who are here today stand upon this foundation with awe and reverence'. He pictured the kind of church which Chinese Christians desired and added, 'She shall teach her members to agree to differ but resolve to love'. Following the conference the *National Christian Council was organized, with a Chinese majority. The Protestant community in C. now numbered nearly 400,000. The foreign missionary body reached its peak in 1925, with a list of 8,518 in active service. Thereafter the number gradually declined.

Political turmoil and the 1927 revolution were followed by the unification of C. under a modern government, and a period of constructive church activity, notwithstanding the Yangtze River flood disaster of 1931, the increasing threat of Japanese aggression, and Communist-inspired civil strife. Theological education received more attention, in relation to the training of ministers for C's 10,000 rural churches as well as for growing urban and industrial congregations. An All-C. Theological Education Conference met in 1935 to consider joint planning and programmes in the light of special funds bequeathed to Nanking Theological Seminary. Other fruits of interdenominational co-operation were a growing interest in Chinese Christian literature and publication of the excellent *Hymns of Universal Praise* containing both new translations of western hymns and many original Chinese hymns. At the International Missionary *Conference in India (1938) the strong Chinese delegation made a profound impression; 31 Chinese leaders and 18 missionaries came from war-torn C.

The Sino-Japanese conflict which began in 1937 brought much destruction to China's main cities and disruption of the national economy and educational programmes. The large migration to unoccupied free C. included a great many mission and church institutions and workers. Christian worship and actitivies continued on both sides of the fighting lines. The churches played a vital part in various kinds of wartime service and relief. After the Japanese attack on Pearl Harbour hundreds of missionaries were interned at Shanghai and other cities; some were repatriated during the war, others were held in camps until peace came. Church buildings in areas of war and bombing suffered heavy losses. Currency inflation was alarming. However, Christian faith and life were strengthened in many ways by years of trial and testing. New Christian enterprises were started, such as the Border Tribes Mission of the Church of Christ in C., and a Student Volunteer Movement for church vocations. The end of the war in 1945 brought widespread joy, mixed with deep anxiety. Refugees returned to their homes, the task of rehabilitation began in the midst of political uncertainty and social unrest. About 4,000 missionaries were at work, evangelistic opportunities multiplied, and in 1949 the Protestant churches reported about 800,000 members, a 50% increase over the pre-war year of 1936. The first General Assembly of the *WCC, meeting at Amsterdam, was attended by ten Chinese Christian leaders, and Dr T. C. Chao, theologian, was elected one of the six presidents of the Council; he resigned in 1951.

In 1949 the Communist party and army took over mainland C. and soon afterward organized the People's Republic of C., while the National government was forced to move to Taiwan Island, 100 miles from the Chinese coast. At this time Protestant Christianity on the mainland had 13 universities and colleges, 240 middle schools, 322 hospitals and medical centres, 15 theological seminaries, more than 30 Bible schools, and various kinds of social service institutions; these represented all the major denominations but were soon to be incorporated into the state system of education, medicine and welfare. Foreign missionaries began to evacuate in larger numbers when Chinese 'volunteer' troops entered the Korean war and Communist suspicion of missionary activities increased. Following the organization of the Christian Church *Three-Self Church Reform Movement Committee (later termed the Patriotic Movement Committee), Christian churches and other organizations had to break all their connections with western missions and become completely 'self-supporting, self-governing and self-propagating'. Accusations were launched against many missionaries and Chinese church leaders considered to be hostile to the new régime or guilty of subversion or aggression in the past under cloak of religion. The Three-Self Committee has been under direct control of the government, also the similar Catholic Patriotic Association. A small number of churches have been left open to conduct worship services, Bible study and preaching, but their activities are carefully watched. Registered Christians have decreased somewhat but this loss has been balanced by deepened spiritual experience and the witness of Christian life and service. Not many missionaries or Chinese Christians have lost their lives, though some were imprisoned. Most missionaries were given exit permits by the end of 1952 and all Protestant missionaries had left C. before 1957. In the present 'proletarian cultural revolution' many churches have been ransacked and individual Christians have suffered material losses and various indignities. Few facts about the church as a whole are available, but it is certainly in existence, and thousands of Christians are holding to their faith. Ties with the ecumenical church have been broken.

Protestant Christianity in Taiwan celebrated its hundredth anniversary in 1965. The Chinese *diaspora* in south-east Asia and other parts of the world is estimated at twelve million. Among these, as among the Taiwanese, are several hundred thousand Christian believers, enjoying freedom of religious worship and action.

See also HONG KONG; MACAO; MALAYSIA; SINGAPORE; TAIWAN.

F. W. PRICE

R. C. Bush: *Religion in Communist China* (Nashville 1970); C. Cary-Elwes: *China and the Cross: A Survey of Missionary History* (New York 1957); P. A. Cohen: *China and Christianity: The Missionary Movement and the Growth of Chinese Anti-Foreignism 1860–1870* (Cambridge, USA 1963); G. H. Dunne: *Generation of Giants: The Story of the Jesuits in China in the last decades of the Ming Dynasty* (Notre Dame 1962); W. C. Harr, ed.: *Frontiers of the Christian Mission Since 1938* (New York 1962) ch.1, pp.1–22; F. P. Jones: *The Church in Communist China; A Protestant Appraisal* (New York 1962); F. P. Jones, ed.: *Documents of the Three-Self Movement* (New York 1963); K. S. Latourette: *Christianity in a Revolutionary Age*, Vol. V (New York 1962), pp.371–411, *A History of Christian Missions in China* (New York 1929); J. R. Levenson: *Confucian China and its Modern Fate* (Berkeley 1958); J. G. Lutz, ed.: *Christian Missions in China: Evangelists of What?* (Boston 1965); L. T. Lyall: *Come Wind, Come Weather; The present experience of the Church in China* (Chicago 1960); A. C. Moule: *Christians in*

China Before the Year 1550 (London 1930); S. C. Neill: *A History of Christian Missions* (Baltimore 1964); F. W. Price: *The Rural Church in China* (New York 1948); F. C. M. Wei: *The Spirit of Chinese Culture* (New York 1947); Resource materials in missionary libraries; *BM* II, 223–40; *NCE* III 591–616; *WKL*, 214–17.

CHINA INLAND MISSION, THE, was founded in 1865 by J. Hudson *Taylor to evangelize the twelve vast inland provinces and territories which no Protestant missionary had entered. Despite opposition and some internal dissension it grew rapidly from 24 members, and in twelve years had entered most of the farthest provinces. Interdenominational and without powerful backing, CIM lived by Taylor's principle of faith, 'moving men through God by prayer alone', and formed the 'shock troops' of Protestantism in China. The sailing of the Cambridge Seven including C. T. *Studd (1885) made CIM better known in Britain, and recruits were soon drawn also from USA and the Continent. The *Boxer rising (1900) hit CIM hardest of all missions but when Taylor died in 1905 every province had been entered. In the first half of the 20th century it included settled stations and pioneer missions, e.g. those to the southwestern tribes under J. O. Fraser, and in the far north-west associated with George *Hunter and Mildred *Cable. In 1935 it numbered 1,368 westerners. In 1951, withdrawing from China with all other missions, CIM transferred to other Asian countries as the Overseas Missionary Fellowship.

Its sweep of vision, quality of personnel and range of achievement gave CIM worldwide influence, for in K. S. *Latourette's words it was 'in some ways unique in the entire history of the expansion of Christianity'.

JOHN POLLOCK

N. G. Guinness: *The Story of the China Inland Mission* (London 1894[3]); L. Lyall: *A Passion for the Impossible* (London 1965).

CHITAMBAR, JASHWANT RAO (1879–1940), was born in Allahabad, United Provinces, India. His father, a Methodist minister, was disinherited by his family on becoming a Christian. C. was educated at Lucknow Christian College, received his B.A. from Allahabad University, and graduated from the Methodist Theological Seminary, Bareilly. In 1901 he married Viola Singh. He became a tutor at the Theological Seminary, Bareilly, in 1903, professor at Lucknow Christian College, 1906, and later its principal; was ordained in the North India Conference in 1907 and served as pastor and district superintendent. C. was one of the founders of the National Missionary Society of India; a delegate to the World Christian Student Conference, Tokyo, 1907, the *Edinburgh Missionary Conference, 1910, four times to the Methodist General Conference in America, and in 1931 was the first Indian to be elected bishop of his church. C. was a member of the committee revising *The Standard Hindustani Dictionary*, editor of the Hindustani Methodist periodical, *Kaukab-I-Hind*, 'Star of India', translator of hymns and author of two books, *John Wesley*, and *Mahatma Gandhi*. He had a fine sense of humour, was a popular, inspiring preacher, and outstanding spokesman for India in America and Europe. He died in Jubbulpore.

PER HASSING

B. T. Badley: *The Making of a Bishop* (Lucknow 1943).

CHRISTIAN AND MISSIONARY ALLIANCE, THE, was founded in 1881 by B. A. Simpson, a Presbyterian minister in New York, who left his church in order to start not a new church, but an evangelistic and missionary movement, although in recent years it has taken on the marks of a separate church. It was first two societies, the Christian Alliance for home mission work, and the Evangelical Alliance for work outside North America. The two bodies merged in 1897 and became the CMA.

Theologically the CMA is conservative evangelical, stressing the inerrancy of the Bible, and Jesus Christ as the Saviour, Sanctifier, Healer, and coming Lord. There is a strong quest for personal holiness and a deep devotion to the cause of Christ. Recently the missionary purpose has been stated to be 'to bring men and women to a knowledge of Jesus Christ as their Saviour, then to train them and send them forth to work among their own people. In the final analysis it is the national who must evangelize his own country through the indigenous church.' In North America CMA in 1965 had a full membership of 75,308 with 1,201 ordained workers in 1,246 churches. The total income was $4,708,437 of which 86.2% was spent outside the country. CMA has work among Indians, Jews, and Spanish-speaking immigrants. It operates four training colleges in North America and in connection with the Nyack Missionary College there is a specialized Jaffray School of Missions. It has its own printing and publishing agency and *The Alliance Witness* has a weekly circulation of 65,000.

The CMA opened its first work outside North America in the Congo in 1885, and its latest in Brazil in 1962. It has work in five countries in Africa, eight in Asia, three in the Pacific, six in South America, and three in the Middle East, including Israel. In 1965 there was a total of 861 missionaries; two of them were in Lebanon, but 118 in Vietnam. The total membership outside North America is 161,074 in 2,601 organized churches. The largest membership, 40,214, is in Vietnam, and the smallest, seventeen, in Israel.

The work is mainly evangelistic with stress on preaching, Bible schools, literature, and radio. There are some educational and medical institutions, such as in the Congo and Vietnam. The CMA is a member of *EFMA.

PER HASSING

J. H. Hunter: *Beside All Waters* (Harrisburg Pa. 1964); *Missionary Atlas—A Manual of the Foreign Work of the CMA* (Harrisburg 1964).

CHRISTIAN CHURCH, THE (Disciples of Christ), functions through the United

Christian Missionary Society, a board of national and overseas ministries whose headquarters are at 222 S. Downey Avenue,

Indianapolis, Indiana 46219, USA. The society was founded in 1920 by the merging of three older boards, one of which had belonged to the *Foreign Missions Conference of North America from its establishment in 1893. The united society has men and women represented equally on its governing board. At first the united society was opposed by some members of its constituent bodies, who feared ecclesiastical control and regarded certain missionaries' views as heretical; the opponents eventually developed their own missions.

The society's Division of World Mission works through witness and service both as a denomination and in ecumenical cooperation. Its main fields are in Africa (where its largest work is in Congo [Kinshasa] with 57 expatriate missionaries and a church membership of 269,000), India, East Asia (where it co-operates with the work of various united churches) and Latin America. Its strategy aims at confronting radical change in a revolutionary world, sharing in partnership with *younger churches, and joining in ecumenical ventures; it aims equally at mobility and flexibility in extending its work. The Division is aligned with the corresponding divisions of the *WCC and of the *National Council of Churches in the USA.

J. EDWARD MOSELEY

J. M. Smith: *A Strategy of World Mission* (Reprint Th.D. dissertation by University Microfilms, Ann Arbor, Michigan 1961).

CHRISTIAN INSTITUTE FOR THE STUDY OF RELIGION AND SOCIETY, THE, was founded in 1956 on the initiative

of the *National Christian Council of India with the late Dr P. D. *Devanandan as first director. Concerned with the place of the Christian religion and church in the new freedom age of India, the Institute has built up a team of (mainly younger) thinkers and writers who follow bold and creative lines of development in programmes of thought, witness and the study of religions. Co-operating with representatives of other faiths in religious *dialogue and social service, they meet not to make academic comparisons of systems but in personal endeavour to apprehend the characteristic meaning of the main religious words, and their effects, when used by men of different faiths, and to seek reconciliation in commitment to service. The Institute has produced a dozen books and twice as many pamphlets. It edits a quarterly bulletin *Religion and Society* and has become responsible for *The Guardian*, a Christian weekly journal of public affairs having a tradition of over a century. There is a system of 'Friends' of CISRS and of annual subscription to publications. *Director:* Sri M. M. Thomas, 19 Miller's Road, Bangalore 6, South India.

MARCUS WARD

Publications, edited by P. D. Devanandan and M. M. Thomas, include: *India's Quest for Democracy; Religious Freedom; Human Person, Society and State; The Changing Pattern of Family in India.*

CHRISTIAN LITERATURE. See LITERATURE, CHRISTIAN AND MISSIONARY.

CHRISTIAN LITERATURE FUND. Between 1958 and 1962 a series of international conferences of experts in literacy and literature held in Hakone (Japan), Mindolo (Zambia) and Bethel (Germany) made clear the unprecedented opportunity in the field, and the need of immediate and massive assistance to the agencies. On the basis of information thus available, an Exploratory Committee presented a report to the *CWME meeting in Mexico, 1963. Here the CLF was established as a service of the CWME, analogous to the *Theological Education Fund, for five years 1965–1970, to act not as an operating agency but to dispense funds for schemes to be carried out by agencies of the churches in Asia, Africa, Latin America, Oceania and the Caribbean. A representative international committee of 20 experts was appointed by the *WCC to administer the fund, with Mr C. G. Richards as Director, having headquarters at 6 chemin de Primerose, 1007 Lausanne, Switzerland. Thus, for the first time in history, the Christian church has taken a global look at its use of the written word and the part to be played by *Christian literature. The aim of the fund is the advance of Christian literature in each area through the development of a thriving, well co-ordinated, indigenous Christian literature of high quality, largely self-sustaining and capable of spontaneous growth. Grants are made annually to assist projects, developed by local agencies, which give promise of achievement superior to what exists, which have a measure of local support and can eventually be maintained without further assistance. Special attention is given to the encouragement of original creative writing; to projects having greatest significance for the total Christian literature programme of the area; and to the training of personnel in all phases of a programme. The fund, expected to total approximately $3,000,000, is being raised over the five-year period by churches all over the world including those to whom assistance is being given.

MARCUS WARD

E. D. Terry, ed.: *The Bethel Consultation on Christian Literature* (London 1963).

CHRISTIAN RURAL FELLOWSHIPS. See AGRICULTURAL MISSIONS, INC.

CHRISTIAN STUDENTS LIBRARY, THE, (published for the Senate of Serampore College by the *CLS of India at Madras) is the result of a survey of the needs for text books of theological students in India. Written in English by authors familiar with the background, the books are designed to be the basis of versions in the languages of India (and elsewhere if desired) at approximately the LTh level, and eventually to cover the whole range of theological study as outlined in the Serampore syllabus. From 1954 to 1968, 41 volumes had been published, many going into several editions, and being translated into upwards of 20 languages. The evidence of the original survey and the content of the series have had considerable effect on the development of the *TEF textbooks programmes. General

Editors: c/o Serampore College, W. Bengal, India.

MARCUS WARD

CHRISTIE, DUGALD (1855–1936), CMG, FRCS, was born in Glencoe, Scotland, and pioneered western medicine in Manchuria. He graduated in medicine from Edinburgh University in July 1881. Appointed by the United Presbyterian Church of Scotland in the same year, C. retired under the United Free Church of Scotland in 1922. His dedication to mission had been connected with the work of D. L. *Moody in Glasgow. C's great contribution was the Moukden Medical College. Undeterred by his board's refusal to assume financial responsibility C. saw the college opened on 28 March 1912. The aim included the creation in students of 'sympathy with the tenets of Christianity, and in particular to inculcate among the Christian students the spirit of Evangelism'. Not one of the largest, the college quickly became one of the foremost in China. Courteous attention to Chinese etiquette, added to a gracious personality and outstanding ability, contributed to the success of C's work. Chinese staff were usually prominent in church life. From 1917 to 1948, when the People's Government closed it, the college graduated over 500 men and women. From 1941 to 1945 the college had no missionary or other outside aid. C's work was a major contribution to the church in China and to medical work in Manchuria.

AUSTIN FULTON

Mrs D. Christie: *Dugald Christie of Manchuria* (London 1932); A. Fulton: *Through Earthquake, Wind and Fire: Church and Mission in Manchuria* (Edinburgh 1967).

CHURCH, THE. The church is the body of Jesus Christ, that visible organism through which the life of Jesus Christ is to be made manifest and his gospel to be proclaimed to all the nations, until in the eternal world the C. itself is absorbed into the undiminished glory of the kingdom of God. So far most Christians would be able to agree. In this sense one of the simplest and most satisfactory definitions of the aim of Christian missions is the planting of the C. among all nations. (When objection is taken to this formulation, as it has been by a number of continental theologians, this is usually because the C. is understood rather as an organization than as the spiritual reality of the life of Christ in the world.)

But in point of fact it is not possible for any of us really to plant the C. of Christ among the nations. All we can do is to introduce them to our own limited and denominational form of the C., often in a lamentably vague and truncated form. The task is at its easiest for the RC, since anyone converted to the faith anywhere from China to Peru automatically comes under the jurisdiction of the bishop of Rome. But again and again RC missions have been left without that which is regarded as the most essential element in them, the episcopate. Protestant missionaries have gone out with the earnest desire to win souls for Christ, but with very little idea of what is to happen to the souls when they have been won.

It was this failure in a true understanding of the nature of the C. which led the missions so often to keep the churches which they had been privileged to bring into being in a state of lamentable dependence upon the west. The aim from the beginning should have been that at the earliest possible moment each new C. should be able to stand upon its own feet, equipped with all that is essential to the being of a C., and without dependence on any outside body. This state cannot be attained in a day: a C. to be truly independent must have at least the NT intelligibly available in its own language. But when, through the blast of war or some other untoward circumstances, churches have suddenly been left on their own, it has in most cases become apparent that their equipment was lamentably inadequate.

By reaction against this unhappy state of affairs, immense attention has been devoted in recent years to developing the independence of the *younger churches. But independence is not a theological concept and the trouble has been that one misunderstanding has been replaced by another. The unity of the C. is more important than its independence. All over the world independent churches have been brought into being in total isolation from the body of Christ as a whole, and have then had artificially to find a unity in some regional body, or worldwide confessional organization. The primary duty of the C. is to preach the gospel. It is the danger of an independent C. that it tends to become so preoccupied with the ordering of its own affairs as to forget that it exists not for itself, but for those who are outside its borders. The question has been put to the 3% of Indians who are Christian how they propose to evangelize the 97% who are not, and the question has not yet been clearly answered.

A bad theology can be driven out only by a good theology. No task at the present time is more important for the churches, both older and younger, than that they should set themselves to think out more exactly in the light of the NT what they really understand to be the nature of the C., and to ask themselves in what sense the 'notes' of the C., that it is one, holy, catholic and apostolic, are to be understood in the Christian world of today.

STEPHEN NEILL

S. C. Neill: *The Church and Christian Union* (London 1968); J. E. L. Newbigin: *The Household of God* (London 1953, New York 1954); H. Küng: *Structures of the Church* (Eng. tr., London 1965), *The Church* (Eng. tr., London 1967).

CHURCH AND MISSION. See MISSION-CHURCH RELATIONSHIPS.

CHURCH GROWTH. It is often stated that the success of Christian missions is not to be reckoned in numbers of converts or Christian adherents. This is certainly true, in that in certain areas, such as Muslim countries, the possibilities of conversion are few, and in that in every country the influence of the gospel has gone out far beyond the limits of the visible and organized church. Yet some correlation is likely to exist between the growth of the church and the intensity and effectiveness of evangelistic work, and also the methods adopted in order to make the church itself a living entity, growing by its own spontaneous vitality from within. In many areas missionaries by excessive concentration have produced devout and educated congregations, which have almost entirely failed to grow. Study of work in a wide variety of areas has suggested that the following are the principles on which a growing church can be established. (1) As far as possible converts must live among their own people, with as little segregation as possible. (2) It must be clearly understood by all that from the moment of *baptism every church member must be a witness for Christ. (3) Christian instruction must be continued for a long period after baptism, in order that witness may become steadily more intelligent and effective. (4) Witness should follow the natural lines of kinship, the joint family, the tribe, the clan, the *caste or whatever exactly the local organization may be. (5) It must be accepted as the fact that the Holy Spirit is able to use the witness of very ordinary people to do great things. (6) Isolated converts must be constantly visited, to make sure that they do not become discouraged and fall away. (7) *Evangelism is the primary responsibility of all Christians, though specialists and experts may be needed for special purposes. (8) Groups of converts must be encouraged from an early date to take a large share of responsibility for public worship in the place in which they live. (9) The habit of personal intercession for non-Christian friends and relations must be inculcated and encouraged. (10) The most important witness of all is the life of the redeemed community itself; nothing can compensate for the harm done by a low level of Christian endeavour and achievement on the part of Christians of long standing.

The best methods in the world will not necessarily produce a powerful Christian movement. History has shown that all the classical religions of the world have successfully set up very strong resistance to the gospel, and that the main numerical successes have been won among people on the *animistic level, where group decision is well understood, and is practised in many fields other than that of religion. A Christian *mass movement has never arisen, for instance, among the Japanese people, where individual decision in matters of religion is the rule. But, allowing for differences in situations and openings, it may be felt that the ten principles briefly noted above, are relevant to all situations, and can be used and adapted by missions of every complexion. It will not be found, however, that the adoption of these methods will lead to any diminution in the required number of highly competent guides and teachers, whether foreign or indigenous. Many promising movements have run down and stopped, because the work of after-care and further instruction of converts could not be attended to. This period of intensive after-care should in most cases last for 30 years after the foundation of a church.

Many of these leading ideas were persuasively put forward in the early years of the 20th century by Roland Allen: *Missionary Methods: St. Paul's or Ours?* (London 1912); *The Spontaneous Expansion of the Church* (London 1927), etc. In recent times they have been taken up and propagated by Dr D. A. McGavran: *Bridges of God* (New York 1955) and *How Churches Grow* (London 1959). An institute for the study of church growth exists at Pasadena, California, in connection with Fuller Seminary. The ideas of congregational responsibility and personal witness also underlie the study developed by the *WCC under the title 'The Missionary Structure of the Congregation'. A series of books, edited by Dr D. A. McGavran and published by Eerdmans, Grand Rapids, deals with church growth in a number of countries. Details are available from the Institute of Church Growth, Fuller Theological Seminary, 135 North Oakland Avenue, Pasadena, California 91101, USA.

STEPHEN NEILL

D. A. McGavran: *Understanding Church Growth* (Grand Rapids 1969).

CHURCH MISSIONARY SOCIETY, THE, was brought into being by the Evangelical movement in the Church of England, and reflects two of its abiding principles: that mission is mainly the task of the laity, and that voluntary, unofficial associations are essential for the vitality of the church. Since its foundation in 1799 CMS has provided on average 50 new missionaries every year. But the society has always been primarily a fellowship, rather than simply an agency of recruitment. Today it binds together 40,000 members, of different races, not only to support the church's worldwide mission, but also to engage in it themselves in their own localities.

About 900 missionaries, besides others in looser association with CMS, are to be found in 69 Anglican dioceses from West Africa to Japan. Some 600 come from Great Britain and Ireland, the rest from sister societies in Australia, New Zealand and South Africa. CMS places workers unreservedly at the disposal of the receiving church, but hopes that as often as possible they will be used in outreach work. But CMS missionaries are not all professional church-workers. A growing number make their witness under contract to governments and other secular institutions.

JOHN V. TAYLOR

E. Stock: *History of the Church Missionary Society* (3 vols., London 1899; Vol. IV, London 1916); *CMS Newsletter* (monthly from the society, 157 Waterloo Road, London, S.E.1.).

CHURCH OF CHRIST, SCIENTIST, commonly called Christian Science, stems from the work and writings of Mrs Mary Baker Eddy (1821–1919) in Massachusetts, USA. She was healed from a severe illness by spiritual insight, and the movement she started recognizes healing in its broadest sense as an integral and dynamic part of the Christian message; this healing purpose is central to all activities of the church, each of which has a missionary function. Besides the Bible, *Science and Health with Key to the Scriptures* by Mrs Eddy is authoritative. The first church was organized in 1879, reorganized in 1897 as The First Church of Christ, Scientist, in Boston, Massachusetts, also called the Mother Church. All other churches are branches of this one church. There is no ordained clergy, but 7,000 licensed practitioners, laymen, have spread the movement to nearly 60 countries, with about 3,000 branches in North America, several hundred in Europe, 60 in Asia and Africa, 40 in South America, 80 in Australia and New Zealand. It has spread by the interest created in spiritual healing, through public reading rooms, extensive publications (most widely known is the highly regarded *Christian Science Monitor*), radio broadcasts and a bureau of distinguished speakers.

PER HASSING

C. S. Braden: *Christian Science Today* (Dallas, Texas 1958); R. Peel: *Mary Baker Eddy: The Years of Discovery* (New York 1966); S. Wilbur: *Life of Mary Baker Eddy* (Boston 1938).

CHURCH OF GOD MISSIONS. See PENTECOSTAL MISSIONS.

CHURCH OF SOUTH INDIA. See INDIA, CHURCH OF SOUTH.

CHURCH-STATE RELATIONS. The Christian mission has been intimately involved with the state throughout the course of history. The modern phase of this story began with the discoveries and colonial expansion of the Roman Catholic powers in the 15th-16th centuries. Papal bulls in 1454 and 1456 awarded all heathen lands in Africa and the east to the crown of Portugal along with patronage over the church, but required also evangelization of the heathen. Discovery of America by Columbus led to decrees of Pope Alexander VI in 1493 dividing the world outside Europe between Spain and Portugal for conquest and evangelization by a line drawn in the Atlantic Ocean (fixed at 370 leagues west of the Azores in 1494), awarding all lands to the west to Spain and those eastward to Portugal. Spain actually colonized the Americas, civilized and evangelized the

Indians. Missions were a function of state, but largely had to maintain themselves. Portugal's colonies, excepting Brazil, were mostly small trading bases, and control of missions by the crown throughout the Orient prevented adequate deployment of missionaries. That bottleneck was broken by dispensing with diocesan bishops and despatching *vicars apostolic, personal representatives of the Pope, consecrated as bishops of defunct sees. The state use of missions, arrogant usurpation of authority over the *Syrian Christians, Portuguese cruelty and contempt of Asians, and the unedifying spectacle of the conflict in East Asia which resulted from the meeting there of missionaries authorized by Portugal with those sent by Spain via the Philippines all resulted in lasting identification of missions with European *imperialism.

French state use of missions against British interests in North America and in the establishment of power in Indo-China further added to this view of the missions in the 16th–18th centuries. But it was in the 19th and early 20th centuries that France (despite an anti-clerical government at home) especially used missions in the building of empire and influence in Africa, Madagascar, the Levant, East Asia, and the Pacific. 'Protection' was claimed over all RC missions in China. Purely out of colonial policy Protestant missions were excluded from Indo-China until 1911 and RC missions were favoured and aided in most RC colonies. Restrictions on Protestant work in Portuguese Angola and Mozambique, along with state exclusion of such agencies from 'mission areas' in certain Latin American lands, are the last vestiges of that old order.

Protestant missions likewise began with an alliance with the state. Missions in Ceylon, Indonesia, and Formosa in the 17th century were a function of the Dutch East Indies Company and carried out by its chaplains. The Commissioners of the United Colonies of New England were the managers locally for the New England Company (1649), and the colonial governments in New England and New York assisted missions. A church-state partnership in missions to the Indians in the USA lasted until about 1890. The first Protestant mission in India at Tranquebar in 1706 was a Danish crown project. However, this close involvement of church and state did not continue in the great era of Protestant expansion following 1792. The British East India Company severely restricted missions, but the constituency of the societies in Great Britain through pressure on Parliament secured progressive lightening of the limitations, and complete freedom accompanied the taking over of India by the crown in 1858. The British government followed a policy of 'religious neutrality' in the colonies; but in India the Church of England was established, and in other places the quasi-establishment or special recognition favoured the Anglican missions. For political reasons the British government prohibited missions to Muslims in Malaya (although there was never a formal decree) and for a considerable period in northern Nigeria also. The British ambassadors were the great protectors of all Protestant missions in the Turkish empire.

Missions powerfully contributed to British, German and French colonial expansion in East and West Central Africa and were intimately involved with government (Protestants and RCs in contrary ways) in the Belgian Congo. At the beginning of German intervention in the early 1880s one new missionary society was founded in Germany to assist in colonial objectives. German and Dutch governments in parts of Africa and Indonesia assigned spheres of occupation and separated Protestants and RCs. A Missions Consulate was established in Batavia (Djakarta) in 1906 to be the common organ of the missions in relation to government.

British, American and French missionaries served as interpreters to the legations which forced the 'unequal treaties' on China beginning in 1842, and were largely responsible for the clauses which opened that country to missions. Some missionaries became diplomats, such as S. Wells *Williams, USA minister to China. The right of protection over missionaries and converts granted by the treaties led to repeated armed intervention and exacting of indemnities for deaths and property damage. Colonial governments in India and Africa found it more convenient to subsidize mission schools and medical work than undertake such services directly. Such subsidy continues in many independent countries because of need.

All these connections with imperialist states identified missions with them in the eyes of Asians and Africans, but 'Protestant' governments seldom directly used or subsidized them. Protestant missionaries were staunch champions of the people with, and even against, the colonial governments and forces of exploitation. Some missionaries entered into close relationship with national rulers as advisers and ministers of state, especially in the Pacific. Other aspects of the church-state story are the conflicts with governments in China, Japan, etc., brought on by nationalists in the 20th century, resulting in registration of schools in China and in the shrine worship issue in Japan and Korea. No generalizations can be made about the influence of missionaries and mission societies on foreign and colonial policy, but such influence was far from negligible and varied from place to place and time to time. A new aspect of church-state relations came into being with the end of the second world war and the emergence of many new nations. The missions are being made to pay for their long association with imperialism and *colonialism. Missionaries have been excluded from China, Burma, and the southern Sudan. There has been discrimination against Christians and church institutions, for example in Ceylon.

R. PIERCE BEAVER

R. P. Beaver: *Church, State, and the American Indians* (St. Louis 1966); F. Birkeli: *Politikk og Misjon (Madagascar)*, (Oslo 1952); L. Hanke: *The Spanish Struggle for Justice in the Conquest of America* (Philadelphia 1959), *Aristotle and the American Indians* (Chicago 1959); International Missionary Council: *Treaties, Acts, and Regulations Relating to Missionary Freedom* (London 1923); S. Neill: *Colonialism and Christian Missions* (London 1966); R. Oliver: *The Missionary Factor in East Africa* (London 1952); K. M. Panikkar: *Asia and Western Dominance* (rev. ed., New York 1959); M. A. C. Warren: *The Missionary Movement from Britain in Modern History* (London 1965), *Social History and Christian Mission* (London 1967).

CHURCH UNION MOVEMENTS. See UNION MOVEMENTS.

CHURCH WORLD SERVICE, a relief, rehabilitation and resettlement agency of the American Protestant and Orthodox churches, was founded in 1946 by the Federal Council of Churches, the Foreign Missions Conference and the American Committee of the *WCC. When the National Council of Churches was formed in 1950, CWS became a department, and in 1965 joined with the council's Division of Foreign Missions to form the *Division of Overseas Ministries.

Since 1946, CWS has shipped four billion pounds of food, clothing, medicines, vitamins and other relief essentials to more than 50 countries, and resettled over 154,000 refugees in the USA. In addition to shipment of food supplied by the United States government, CWS helped to organize CROP (The Christian Rural Overseas Program) as a food-collection agency of American farmers, and maintains clothing centres in various parts of the USA for the gathering and processing of clothing.

CWS pioneered in the development of long-range programmes of rehabilitation designed to help people to help themselves. Whenever possible, it works through *National Christian Councils in host countries and in close co-operation with the Division of Inter-Church Aid, Refugee and World Service of the WCC.

See also INTER-CHURCH AID.

FLOYD HONEY

CHURCHES, INDIGENOUS OR YOUNGER. See INDIGENOUS, and YOUNGER CHURCHES.

CHURCHES OF CHRIST MISSIONS. During the last 75 years, Churches of Christ in the USA have sponsored more than 400 missionaries in other nations. One of the first was John Moody McCaleb (1861–1953) who went to Japan in 1892 and served there 50 years. In 1969 approximately 200 missionaries were abroad, supported by about 150 congregations, about 1% of 15,000 Churches of Christ in the USA. Persons identified with these congregations do not use instrumental music in worship and believe the NT does not authorize missionary societies. Since mission boards are considered unscriptural, the sponsoring churches are responding to the NT command to take the gospel to those individuals who have not heard it, especially in great centres of population, and even to Roman Catholics and Jews. Indeed, prospects for conversion are considered to exist everywhere, at home as well as abroad. The programme for conversions is essentially the same everywhere, traditionally preaching and teaching. Churches of Christ missionaries serve in numerous countries of Africa, Asia, South-east Asia, Latin America, Europe, North America, Australia and New Zealand.

J. EDWARD MOSELEY

H. L. Schug, and others, eds.: *The Harvest Field* (Athens, Alabama 1958).

CHURCHES OF GOD (HOLINESS) MISSIONS. See PENTECOSTAL MISSIONS.

CHURCHES OF THE NEW JERUSALEM grew out of the writings of Emanuel Swedenborg (1688–1772), a Swedish scientist who died in London. There are two branches of the church, divided on the interpretation of Swedenborg's writings, the General Convention and the General Church, the latter group giving divine authority to Swedenborg's writings. Both groups are found in England and North America. The church spreads by translating Swedenborg's writings and by bringing interested persons to one of its theological seminaries. A Swedenborg Foundation in New York is responsible for publishing. The church has spread to many parts of Europe, North and South America, Africa, Asia, and Australia. The two branches have about 8,100 adherents in the USA.

PER HASSING

E. Swedenborg: *The True Christian Religion* (New York 1952).

CLARK, WILLIAM SMITH (1826–1886), was born of Puritan parents at Ashfield, Massachusetts, USA. Educated at Amherst College and Göttingen University (PhD 1852), he attained an international reputation as botanist and educator. After a distinguished career as a Union soldier, he became the first president of the Massachusetts College of Agriculture. During a sabbatical year (1876–77), upon invitation of the Japanese government, he established a similar school, now Hokkaido University, at Sapporo. His consistent Christian life, loving interest in the students and wise leadership soon overcame official opposition to his evangelistic efforts. As a result, the entire first class of fifteen students was converted; these in turn influenced a like number of the second class; all received baptism and signed the 'Covenant of Believers in Jesus', drawn up by C. This group of young *samurai* (members of the warrior class) included men of high moral and scholarly calibre, who became outstanding Christian leaders. C's parting admonition, 'Boys, be ambitious!' inspires students to this day and the Clark Christian tradition is still influential at the university.

GORDON K. CHAPMAN

O. Cary: *History of Christianity in Japan*, Vol. II (New York 1909), pp.124ff.; Hideo Kishimoto: *Japanese Religion in the Meiji Era* (Tokyo 1956), pp.209ff., 300ff.; Kanzo Uchimura: *Diary of a Christian Convert* (New York n.d.), pp.12ff.; *DAB* IV, 146f.

CLAVER, PETER DE (1580–1654), was born in Verdú, Spain. He studied grammar and rhetoric in Barcelona, entered the novitiate in Tarragona in 1602, and joined the Society of *Jesus in 1604. He went to Nueva Granada, Central America, in 1610

5*

as a brother coadjutor and continued his theological studies in Tunja and Bogotá. In 1616 he was ordained to the priesthood in Cartagena where he carried out a ministry to lepers and Negro slaves. In addition to serving as chaplain of the city's leper hospital he met the slave ships arriving from Africa, attended to the needs of the slaves, and taught Catholic doctrine to them in the slave sheds. During his 40-year ministry it is estimated that he baptized some 300,000 slaves. He became known as the 'Apostle of the Negroes'. His remains rest in the Jesuit church named for him in Cartagena, Colombia. Pope Leo XIII canonized him on 15 January 1888.

Relations between the Jesuits and the Inquisition, which had been established in Cartagena in 1610, were friendly. The Process of Beatification and Canonization states that C. had a great esteem for the Inquisition. He was present at the *autos-da-fé* and requested the inquisitors to send heretics to the Jesuit College, where he lived, for instruction in the Catholic faith. He attended those sentenced by the Inquisition, including two who were executed.

JAMES B. GOFF

A. Valtierra, SJ: *Peter Claver: Saint of the Slaves* (translated from the Spanish by J. H. Perry and L. J. Woodward—London 1960); *NCE* III, 922f.

CLINICS. See HOSPITALS, MISSIONARY, and MEDICAL MISSIONS.

CLOUGH, JOHN EVERETT (1836–1910), was born near Frewsberg, New York, USA. Appointed by the ABFMS, he went to India in 1865 and began work among the Telugus at Ongole. His first convert was the low *caste leather worker, Bangarapu Thatiah: he had belonged to the Rajayogi sect, which he found had prepared him to receive the gospel: 'but nothing satisfied my soul till I heard of Jesus Christ'. By 1867 C's work had gained 3,269 converts, mainly from the same caste. While C. was committed to the work of winning individuals to Christian decision, he also saw the social implications of the gospel. He withstood pressure from upper caste men to restrict enrolment in the mission school to their sons and admitted low caste pupils. During the famine of 1876–78 he contracted to build four miles of the Buckingham Canal, a government relief project, using Christians as overseers of more than 6,000 workers While that work continued C. refused to baptize or receive new church members, lest any should come forward for ulterior motives. In July 1878, when he eventually agreed to accept converts, 2,222 were baptized on one day. Despite C's initial doubts the movement continued; by 1883 membership was 21,000. The church was well grounded and continued to grow.

J. LESLIE DUNSTAN

J. E. Clough: *Social Christianity in the Orient* (New York 1914); H. W. Hines: *Clough: Kingdom Builder in South India* (Philadelphia 1929); E. Rauschenbusch-Clough: *While Sewing Sandals* (London 1889); *DAB* IV, 232f.

COCHRANE, THOMAS (1866–1953), was born in Greenock, Scotland. He qualified in medicine at Glasgow and in 1897 sailed for Shanghai, subsequently travelling in N. China and Mongolia under the *LMS and then settling in Chaoyang. In 1901, after the *Boxer rising, he was sent to Peking. He obtained a generous gift from the Empress Dowager to help build a medical college, the Peking Union Medical College, the responsibility for which was later assumed by the Rockefeller Foundation. C's own views on missionary policy had developed, and in 1915 he joined with Sidney Clark in London and with Roland *Allen to found what later became the *World Dominion Press (Survey Application Trust). After the first world war the enterprise expanded quickly. A long series of statistical surveys, then almost an innovation, was published on the distribution of Church and Mission throughout the world. Roland Allen's books and Sidney Clark's pamphlets emphasizing 'self-support, self-propagation, and self-government' in the church were given wide circulation. In 1931 C. promoted the purchase of the old Mildmay Conference Centre in London as a base for his newly-founded Movement for World Evangelization.

KENNETH G. GRUBB

F. French: *Thomas Cochrane* (London 1956); *RGG* I, 1842.

CODRINGTON, CHRISTOPHER (1668–1710), was born in Barbados into a wealthy sugar-planting family. After a distinguished career as a fellow of All Souls College, Oxford, he was in 1698 appointed to succeed his father as Governor-General of the Leeward Islands. He did much for the reform of justice and for the condition of the slaves, but was replaced as Governor-General, and spent the last five years of his life in his home in Barbados. By his will he provided £10,000 for a library at All Souls, and bequeathed his plantations to the *SPG to maintain on them professors and scholars, 'all of them to be under the vows of Poverty, Chastity, and Obedience, who shall be obliged to Study and Practise Physic and Surgery as well as Divinity, that by the apparent usefulness of the former to all mankind, they may both endear themselves to the people, and have the better opportunities of doing good to men's souls whilst they are taking care of their bodies'. This college began to take shape as a school in 1745, and was reconstituted as a theological college in 1830. From 1955 to 1969 it was run by men 'under the vows' intended by C., namely members of the Community of the Resurrection. It continues to function as a theological college for the Anglican Province of the West Indies.

JOHN WILKINSON

N. Longley: *Christopher Codrington and his College* (London 1964); *DNB* XI, 203.

COILLARD, FRANÇOIS (1834–1904), was born at Asnières, France, of Huguenot stock. His widowed mother apprenticed him to an English clergyman in France, then sent him to a school in Glay where poor boys were trained for the ministry. He was deeply influenced by the South African missionaries, Robert *Moffat, Eugène

*Casalis, and Adolphe *Mabille. After ordination he offered himself to the *PEMS who sent him to Magny, Paris and Strasbourg for further training. He became an eloquent preacher, a gifted poet, singer, translator, and explorer. He was also a prophet.

In 1857 C. sailed for Cape Town. He was sent to Leribé in Lesotho which became his home for 20 years. He proposed by mail to Christina Mackintosh, a daughter of an Edinburgh minister, whom he had met in Paris, and married her in Cape Town in 1861. The marriage was childless. He gained an intimate knowledge of the Sotho language and customs, soon becoming an adviser to the tribal assembly. He wrote hymns and Christian songs for national and tribal occasions, introduced Aesop's fables, and translated the Book of Proverbs.

When the PEMS sought further fields of service C. tried in 1877 to reach the Banyai in Rhodesia, but was driven away by the people, barely escaping with his life, was then arrested and kept by Lobengula, chief of the Ndebele, for four months. While with Lobengula he learned about the Lozi people in Zambia. In 1878 he set out to reach them, but being refused entry by chief Lewanika, returned to Lesotho. In 1884 he made his second journey to Barotseland, but because of inter-tribal wars was unable to cross the Zambesi until a year later. It was 1886 before he reached chief Lewanika who gave him a place at Sefula. The turmoil of the country and his complete dependence on Lewanika made the existence of the mission precarious. On Lewanika's behalf C. wrote a letter inviting Queen Victoria's protection. This resulted in a treaty in 1890 which caused C. much anxiety because it did not become effective until 1895. C. was invited, but refused, to become the first British Resident. C's wife died in 1891, but he firmly established the evangelistic and educational work, and after a furlough in 1898, brought in 15 new missionaries. His first convert in 1891 was one of Lewanika's sons. Four days after the railway crossed the Zambesi, C. died.

PER HASSING

F. Coillard: *On the Threshold of Central Africa* (London 1897).

COKE, THOMAS (1747–1814), born at Brecon, Wales, was educated at Jesus College, Oxford (BA, MA, DCL) and after a brief period as Anglican priest joined the Wesleyan Movement (1777). Called by John Wesley his 'right hand', C. made nine trips to America and became the foremost spokesman for missions among Methodists in both England and the new world. He gave his entire fortune, which was substantial, to missionary work, in addition to monies he received from bequests and solicitations. His pamphlet, *An Address to the Pious and Benevolent proposing an Annual Subscription for the Support of Missionaries* (London 1786), was the first Methodist missionary tract, and for years he was the sole missionary executive of the British Conference and the Methodist Episcopal Church in America —from c. 1784 until the organization of the Wesleyan Missionary Society in 1813.

Wesley appointed C. as Superintendent for America. He was elected General Superintendent by the preachers, with Francis *Asbury, at the formative conference of the Methodist Episcopal Church (Baltimore 1784). Asbury and C. drew up the *Doctrines and Discipline* of that body. C. solicited missionaries and their support for the West Indies, for work among the Indians and Negroes, for Sierra Leone, Nova Scotia, Ireland and France. During the French Revolution, with the church under attack in that country, he established a base in Guernsey. He organized work among the 70,000 French prisoners of war held by England during the Napoleonic wars. He died en route to India, leading a missionary band for which he had wrung permission from the British Conference by a brilliant appeal and by contributing £6,000 of his own money to launch the venture.

A highly educated man, markedly British and passionately inspired by a world-vision, C. was frequently in tension with Asbury and the American preachers. He was unable to give himself solely to the Methodist Episcopal Church in America and, perhaps inspired by the Moravian example, attempted rather unsuccessfully to serve simultaneously as a Conference member in England and a bishop in America.

FRANKLIN H. LITTELL

W. C. Barclay: *History of Methodist Missions, I: Missionary Motivation and Expansion* (New York 1949), pp.108ff.; E. Bucke et al., eds.: *History of American Methodism* (3 vols., Nashville 1964); J. Vickers: *Thomas Coke: Apostle of Methodism* (London 1969); *DAB* IV, 279f.; *DNB* XI, 247; *RGG* I, 1847f.

COLENSO, JOHN WILLIAM (1814–1883), mathematician and theologian, born at St. Austell, Cornwall, UK, and educated at Cambridge. In 1853 he was appointed as first bishop of the new Anglican diocese of Natal. He quickly showed astonishing versatility and skill as a linguist. In 1859 he published a grammar of the Zulu language, in 1861 a Zulu-English dictionary, and in 1876 the entire New Testament in Zulu. Through the questions put to him by young Africans who were working with him on the translation of Genesis, C. was led to question belief in the literal verity of the Scriptures, which he had held up to that time. Between 1862 and 1879 he published seven parts of a critical examination of the Pentateuch, expressing advanced critical views as to the date and composition of the Mosaic books. His Commentary on the Epistle to the Romans (1861) also expressed views very different from the then prevailing orthodoxy. Bishop Gray of Cape Town claimed the right to try the Bishop of Natal for heresy. C. was deposed on 16 December (1863), and later excommunicated; but in a long series of trials in England all the actions of Bishop Gray were declared unconstitutional, and the sentences passed by him null and void. C. remained in possession of the bishopric of Natal until his death. The controversies called into being by those events have not finally died away.

C. was among the first Europeans to believe completely in the capacity of the African, given proper opportunity and training, to rise as high as the European in every field of knowledge and activity. He was a tireless defender of the rights of the African. He intervened in England on behalf of the Amahlubi chief Langalibalele, who had been unjustly sentenced to transportation for life; and bitterly condemned the war of 1879, in which the power of Cetshwayo the Zulu king was finally broken. He fully deserved the title *Sobantu*, 'the father of the people', by which he was known among the Zulus.

STEPHEN NEILL

G. W. Cox: *The Life of Bishop Colenso* (2 vols., London 1888); P. Hinchliff: *John William Colenso* (London 1964); *DNB* XI 290.

COLLEGES AND UNIVERSITIES, CHRISTIAN. The Christian mission has always and in various ways been associated with education. There have, however, been varying opinions and sharp controversies as to the extent to which the church should engage in higher education; there has been a tendency, especially in the RC church, to concentrate on the education of the ordained ministry, and to make the school the gateway to the seminary. Others, however, have taken a broader view of the relationship between education and the development of a full Christian personality for the service of God both in the church and in the world.

(1) In the modern world the first Christian college for higher education would seem to be that founded by *Zumarraga, the first bishop of Mexico, at Tlatelolco in 1536, an institution the high promise of which was not to be fulfilled. During the two following centuries similar beginnings were made elsewhere in America and in Asia.

(2) A new departure was taken by *Carey and his colleagues in the great foundation of *Serampore in 1819. This proved to be premature, as there was no adequate substructure of education on which such a college could rest. The work was taken up in a different fashion by Alexander *Duff (1830), and later by John *Wilson, Stephen *Hislop and others, in schools, which gradually grew into colleges, and, after the

foundation of Indian universities (1855), were integrated into the general plan of federating universities. These colleges were originally intended as instruments for the evangelization of the higher classes. As the number of converts dwindled a new apologetic was developed by William *Miller (1879) and others in terms of 'preparation for the gospel'. With the growth of the church, it became clear that one of the main functions of the Christian college is the training of a Christian élite able to take its place on equal terms with the best qualified representatives of the other religions.

The RCs came later into the field. From about 1870 onwards the *Jesuits in particular developed larger, mainly non-residential, colleges, with a large majority of non-Christian teachers and students, in such cities as Madras, Bombay, Trichinopoly, Palayamkottai, etc. These were regarded as having reached a very high level of efficiency though the number of conversions was always small.

With the growth of national feeling, the question could not but be raised whether the interests of the Indian church would be best served by segregating the great majority of Christian students in Christian institutions. The answer has been given, first, in terms of quality—Christian institutions should not exist, unless they are markedly better educationally than others; secondly, in a wider concept of education, as the development of the whole man, than is accepted in institutions in which emphasis is only on the intellectual side. General opinion in the Indian churches seems to favour the continuance of Christian college education. There are now considerably more than 100 such colleges in India and Pakistan, attended by 10% of all college students, with a special emphasis on the education of women, and apart from the specialized institutions for medical and agricultural training.

(3) In China, where a national system of education on modern lines was entirely lacking, the Christian university was the pioneer institution in modern and western education. In the last quarter of the 19th century missions began to dignify with the title of university what were in reality only schools. In 1914, 33 of these were listed (all Protestant), but numbers were small, and standards of less than university grade, except in a small number of institutions, among which St. John's University, Shanghai, was perhaps the most distinguished. On the other hand the medical schools at Peking and in Manchuria were regarded as among the best in the Far East. With the communist take-over in 1949, all these institutions were lost to the Christian church.

(4) In Japan, Christian university history began with Joseph Hardy *Neesima and his Doshisha University, in which it was his aim to combine all that was best in the *samurai* tradition with an uncompromisingly Christian witness. Doshisha has been followed by many similar institutions, of which St. Paul's University, Tokyo, may be mentioned. The International Christian University in Japan, with its emphasis on small numbers, high standards, and a particularly close relationship between teachers and students, represents a new and hopeful type of Christian co-operation.

(5) In the Near East American initiative produced two notable institutions on the university level—the American University in Beirut and the American University in Cairo. In both these cases it has been found impossible to maintain both the necessary academic standards and the somewhat narrow missionary base; the contribution of these two universities today is made rather in the wider field of general education than in that of specifically Christian witness.

(6) In the western world, the pioneer institute was Mackenzie College at São Paulo in Brazil, recognized as one of the best academic institutions in South America. The churches, on the whole, have found it undesirable to compete on a major scale with the government systems of education, though there is much in these secular systems of which Christians and especially RC Christians cannot approve. In Puerto Rico, with its special relationship to the USA it is perhaps natural to find an American University, related rather to

Anglo-Saxon traditions than to the Spanish-American tradition by which Puerto Rico had been ruled for four centuries.

(7) In the Philippines where the situation is rather similar, but not quite like anything else in the world, American Protestant forces have been able to create two universities—Silliman, which opened at the beginning of this century 'with 15 barefoot elementary pupils', and Central Philippine University (Baptist). The RC church looks with suspicion on the generally secular system of education developed on the American plan of the separation of church and state, and maintains important institutions, notably Santo Tomás University (*Dominican, f.1611) and Ateneo de Manila University (Jesuit).

(8) Enough has been said to show that in many areas of the world Christian missions have been pioneers in higher education both for men and women. It is doubtful whether it will be possible to maintain this contribution for any long future. It was easy to start a college when no more was necessary than teaching in English, Religion, History, Philosophy and Mathematics. With the enormously increasing cost and complexity of university education, the share of the churches is likely to diminish, though excellent service can still be rendered by co-operative projects in certain areas. Moreover, even in countries in which religious liberty is practised as well as professed, it seems certain that governments will increasingly take over the responsibility for all education from private hands. A new field for Christian witness is the department of religion in secular and government universities in the African scene. Increasing provision of hostels by the churches for both Christian and non-Christian students will be a field of endeavour for many years. But perhaps in the end the most effective witness will be rendered by Christian teachers and students, who take the secular university or college as the sphere in which they are called to glorify God.

EDITORS

There are many studies and reports on Christian education in various countries, of which one of the most outstanding is the report of the Lindsay Commission, *Christian Higher Education in India* (London 1931). Most valuable is one study by a government servant, A. I. Mayhew: *The Education of India* (London 1926).

COLOMBIA, the fourth largest country in South America, bounded on the north by the Caribbean Sea and Venezuela, on the east by Brazil, on the south by Peru and Ecuador, and on the west by the Pacific Ocean, has an area of 455,335 sq.m., and a population of nearly 20 million. Although situated on the equator, the country has a wide variety of climate; the greater part of the population lives in the highlands created by three Andean ranges in the north-west of the country, the remaining two-thirds of the area being sparsely populated. There are Amerindian and Negro elements in the population, but these are smaller than in some other Latin American countries, and the Colombian people appears to take a special pride in its inheritance of Iberian culture and RC faith.

The Christian religion entered with the Spanish conquest of 'New Granada' in 1536–38. It was alleged that within two years the entire population had become Christian, but naturally the evangelization was very superficial. Bogotá became the seat of an archbishopric in 1553. The most famous of the RC missionaries in C. was Peter *Claver (1581–1654), who found his special field of labour among the African slaves who were being imported in ever-increasing numbers. At the present time the country is divided into 35 dioceses, with an additional 18 apostolic prefects and vicars. The great majority of the population are at least nominal RCs, the church claiming 15 million adherents (this may be an underestimate) ministered to by rather less than 3,000 parochial clergy, together with 2,000 members of religious orders.

Colombia became independent of Spain in 1821. Though the RC church is no longer the state church, under a concordat with the Vatican of 1887–88, that church enjoys a position of special privilege in various ways;

but religious liberty has been in principle established, and Protestant missions have found access, though often under conditions of considerable difficulty.

The first Protestant missionary in C. appears to have been a representative of the American and Foreign Christian Union who arrived in 1853. American Presbyterians began work in 1856, and have continued it for over a century. At the present time no less than 32 organizations are listed. At first progress was very slow, but from 1900 onwards the curve of success has mounted ever more steeply. In the 1950s a short period of sharp persecution of Protestants resulted in a number of deaths and a temporary setback to the work; but this was followed by a great improvement in the relationships between RCs and Protestants, and progress in the last decade has been more rapid than ever before. In 1968 Protestants were counted at ⸢11,069 (WCH 1968), an increase of more than 20% in five years; the largest numbers being claimed by the SDA, Pentecostalists and Presbyterians. For a long period the Church of England had provided services in English for English residents, but without any attempt to establish work in Spanish. In 1964, by agreement, the PECUSA set up the missionary district of C. and Ecuador. The policy of the first bishop has been to develop a genuinely Colombian Episcopal Church, and in the ecumenical spirit to improve relationships between RC and non-Catholic Christians, and between Colombians and foreigners in the church. Almost all the Protestant churches are now under Colombian leadership. An ecumenical problem arises from the fact that almost all the churches represent an extreme conservative evangelical position, and do not find any kind of co-operation easy, either with RCs, or with Protestants of less rigidly orthodox persuasion. But the great improvement in relationships among Christians of all types is one of the most notable features of the Christian scene in C. today.   JAMES GOFF

DAVID REED AND WILLIAM FRANKLIN

J. H. Sinclair: *Protestantism in Latin America: A Bibliographical Guide* (Austin,

Texas 1967), pp.136–41; *BM* II, 248–59; *NCE* III, 1020–24; *WKL*, 753f.

COLONIALISM AND MISSIONS. The word 'colonialism' seems to be of recent origin, and to have largely replaced the earlier 'imperialism'. But the word is used loosely and without accurate definition, and more often as a vehicle of abuse than as an instrument of thought.

The expansion of one people at the expense of another has been a familiar phenomenon of human history since the beginning of time. Three forms of such colonial expansion can be clearly distinguished. (1) A remedy for excessive population through the occupation of large and for the most part uninhabited territories. Notable examples in modern times have been the occupation of North America by the white races at the expense of the Indian and the Eskimo, and of Australia at the expense of the Aborigines. (2) The establishment of a powerful aristocracy in the midst of a weaker population, which in course of time is reduced to total subservience. In this connection the Spanish and Portuguese occupation of the Caribbean and of Latin America may be mentioned. (3) The establishment of trading ports, by agreement, and without intention of conquest. The British, Dutch and Danish ports in India will serve as a good example of this type.

The word 'colonialism' is generally used of the expansion of the western powers into Africa and the East. But it is at least as appropriate to Islamic policies in many countries, and to the activities of the Chinese and Japanese outside their own borders.

The expansion of Europe was contemporary with the expansion of the Christian world through the success of Christian missions. There is a widespread opinion that the latter was entirely dependent on the former. A study of history shows that the situation was far too complex to be summed up in a single sentence. (1) In most cases, the missionaries penetrated into the unknown far ahead of governments. Francis *Xavier and his companions appear to have been the first European residents of Japan. Such missionaries neither claimed nor expected any help from their governments if trouble should arise. (2) Even when the tentacles of European power had spread far and wide, it was the generally accepted principle of Protestant missions that no retribution should be exacted for the death of a missionary in service; a missionary was a soldier in the front line of Christian service. Later, Hudson *Taylor, the founder of the *CIM, extended the principle that no *compensation was to be asked or accepted for any kind of injury whatsoever. (3) RC policy was rather different. The French set up a kind of protectorate over all RC missions in China. After such events as the 'bloodbath' of Tientsin in 1870, heavy compensation for all injuries was exacted, and the Chinese were gravely humiliated. This was not to the advantage of the missionary cause. (4) In certain cases, the alliance between the colonial power and the Christian mission was extremely close. In the 16th century it was taken for granted that the kings of Spain and Portugal would exercise a Christian 'Vicariate', would find and despatch bishops and missionaries to all parts of the earth, and support them in their work. Thus, when a bishop was appointed for Malacca, his salary of 1,000 ducats, a considerable sum for those days, was made a charge on the revenues of the city. As a result, the church tended to be far too closely associated with the ruling power. Yet, when any voice was raised on behalf of the subject population, it was almost certain to be that of a churchman, as is seen in the famous case of de *Las Casas. (5) In a number of cases missionaries did call in the help of the western powers, but in almost every case this was in what they believed to be the interests of the people among whom they worked, as in the South Seas, when the local rulers had become completely unable to control the increasing swarms of white men living in their islands; or in Africa, when it had become clear that Arab slave-trading could be brought to an end only through occupation of the terri-

tories by western countries. The drawbacks of such occupation were not at the time very clearly seen. (6) Once the colonial power was well established, missions tended to collaborate with it in educational and medical work, and to receive very substantial financial subsidies. This did not necessarily mean the end of the independence of the missions; but they came to appear to the inhabitants as part of the establishment. In many cases, the missionaries made the same mistake as that of the colonial powers—believing in their own permanence. (7) But, where colonialism has come to an end, the missionaries have continued their work in the newly independent countries, wherever it has been possible for them to do so, even when they have felt that independence was premature and harmful to the people among whom they worked.

It will be a long time before anything like a true balance can be drawn of the colonial period. Certain conclusions can, however, be already drawn. Colonialism has created the unified world in which we now live. Ancient civilizations have been raised out of a torpid existence into new life. Isolated peoples have been drawn into the main stream of the life of the world. We have all become dependent on one another. A worldwide church has come into being. If unification was part of God's plan for the world, then colonialism, for all its glaring faults, may have had its part to play in the mysterious providence through which he guides the destinies of men.

See also IMPERIALISM.

STEPHEN NEILL

R. Delavignette: *Christianity and Colonialism* (Eng. tr., London 1966); S. Neill: *Colonialism and Christian Missions* (London 1966); L. B. Wright: *Religion and Empire* (New York 1965); *NCE* III, 1024–27.

COLPORTAGE has been one of the most effective ways of getting the Scriptures into the hands of people who would never enter a religious bookshop or a church. Colporteurs have been for the most part simple-hearted, dedicated men, often leading a hard life of constant travel under poor conditions, with frequent persecution. They have preached a plain gospel message which has aroused the interest of their hearers and thus enabled them to sell their books.

The *Bible Societies have been the outstanding employers of colporteurs. The BFBS lists some 55 countries where it has worked by this means. The American Bible Society has used them largely in Latin America and the Middle East, the National Bible Society of Scotland in China and Malaya. *L'Action Biblique de Genève* has both trained and employed colporteurs in recent years. Free lances have also taken Bible Society books and done effective work.

The peak period of colportage was the decade before the first world war. In 1912, for instance, the BFBS employed 1,200 men, who sold 5,000,000 Scriptures, half the total circulation of the society. Gospels were sometimes exchanged for rabbits, eggs, or even a pail of water for the colporteur's horse.

Motor vans are now employed in many places. One trial tour sold more Scriptures in a day than an average colporteur sold in a month. The personal work, however, of the best old-time colporteurs cannot be too highly praised.

HAROLD K. MOULTON

COMITY as a term was made current by the Centenary Missionary Conference in London in 1888, but the practice was followed as early as the 1820s. The word came to be used loosely to cover all forms of agreement and co-operation among societies, but essentially it means the mutual division of territory into spheres of occupation, on the one hand, and non-interference in one another's affairs, on the other. It produced 'denominationalism by geography', but its purpose was to prevent wasteful duplication, competition, and presentation of variant forms of worship and polity which might confuse non-Christians and hinder communication of the gospel. C. on an international, global scale aimed at agreement among societies for the evangelization of all peoples so that none would be forgotten.

The first recorded comity agreement was made on Tonga in July 1830, between Wesleyan and *LMS missionaries by which Tonga and Fiji were to be Methodist spheres and Samoa the LMS field. The parent societies in London ratified the compact in February 1836. Societies and boards usually expressed their adherence to the principle but left actual agreements to the missions in the field. Often these were verbal and never recorded. Priority of occupation was always to be recognized, but it was understood that no mission might continue exclusive claim to any area which it could not attempt to evangelize within a reasonable period. Large cities were always considered to be 'open'. Dutch, German and Australian colonial governments sometimes assigned Protestant and Roman Catholic missions to separate areas in order to avoid conflict, but among Protestant agencies C. was entirely voluntary. The observance of this practice was so general that the several American boards agreed upon a division of the Philippines before the first missionaries were sent, and the missionaries at their first meeting at Manila in 1901 set up the Evangelical Union and assigned territories according to the previous consensus of the boards. John R. *Mott at *Jerusalem in 1928 reported that it was a rare exception when any agency (such as the Missouri Lutherans and SDA) failed to accept both the letter and spirit of C. Certain Baptist bodies also felt in conscience unable to accept the principle. C. required not only agreement on boundaries, but also on standards of membership and transfer, recognition of each other's discipline, wage scales, and conditions for employment of workers from other missions. Various means of arbitration of differences and claims were provided, notably the national Board of Arbitration created by the All-India 4th Decennial Missionary Conference in 1902.

R. PIERCE BEAVER

R. P. Beaver: *Ecumenical Beginnings in Protestant World Mission: A History of Comity* (New York 1962); *WKL*, 248.

COMMERCE AND MISSIONS have been closely associated in a number of areas. Traders have in some cases preceded missionaries and prepared the way for them. Thus in the 13th century the first RC missionary to China reached that country in the company of a merchant, a fellow Italian, who had been preceded by other Italian traders. The first missionaries in Hawaii, Protestants from New England, came to the islands in response to information brought by traders. The first Protestant missionary to China arrived on a merchant ship; he and his immediate successors had their residence in the 'factory', the trading establishment, at Canton.

There were often tensions between merchants and missionaries. The former usually looked with disdain on the latter. The East India Company long attempted to exclude all missionaries from the area under its control, fearing that their presence would be harmful to the progress of commerce.

In less developed areas missionaries have usually been first in the field, and their presence has undoubtedly stimulated trade, by creating new wants among the simple peoples, and by demonstrating to traders that settled existence was possible among them. A few missionaries deserted their mission, themselves to become traders; many members of missionary families have followed this avocation in the countries in which they grew up.

Occasionally missionary propagandists have incautiously used the development of commerce as an argument in favour of missions—'trade follows the missionaries: therefore support missions'. Such ill-advised advocacy has in later years been used by communist propagandists in support of their case that missionary activity has been simply one more form of western aggression in less-developed countries. It can, on the other hand, be argued that efficient commercial enterprises, such as Waso Ltd., organized by the Lutheran church—Missouri Synod in New Guinea, are notably helping simple peoples to develop in the direction of financial and political independence.

No book appears to have been devoted exclusively to the subject of this article.

KENNETH SCOTT LATOURETTE

K. S. Latourette: *A History of the Expansion of Christianity* (New York 1937–45), II, p.332; III, pp.278, 338f.; IV, p.248; VI, pp.105, 297.

COMMISSION OF THE CHURCHES ON INTERNATIONAL AFFAIRS, THE (CCIA). It was founded at a conference at Cambridge, England, in 1946, chaired by John Foster Dulles, and representing the *WCC (then in process of formation) and the *IMC. It is today an agency of the WCC supported from its general budget and from special appropriations by the *CWME and *DICARWS. It enjoys a semi-autonomy defined in its rules.

The Commission consists of 55 Commissioners from many countries and churches, a high proportion being laymen of distinction. It has stimulated the formation of national and regional commissions of the churches, but eschews any pretension to direct these, maintaining, however, communication with 26 such bodies. It also corresponds with some 400 selected persons in 70 countries. Its principal offices are in New York, London and Geneva; the Director, the Rev. Dr O. F. Nolde, and the Chairman, Sir Kenneth Grubb, served the Commission in these capacities since its foundation until 1968. Its Executive Committee meets annually, and the full Commission occasionally.

The aims of the CCIA include: calling the attention of churches to international issues and suggesting lines of action; exploring Christian principles on the relations of nations and their application; promoting organs for education in international affairs; study and appraisal of relevant materials from the churches; study of the requirements of world order; representation at the UN and other international bodies, particularly so as to further development of effective international law and institutions, observance of fundamental human rights (especially religious *liberty), regulation of armaments, economic co-operation and advancement of dependent peoples and their free political institutions.

Accordingly, the Commission maintains regular contact with the UN and the principal Specialized Agencies. It is constantly preoccupied with the general questions of disarmament in the nuclear and space age, and with local threats to peace. It has devoted much time to human rights, and religious liberty and, through its Director, exercised a major influence on certain provisions in the Declaration of Human Rights, in addition to helping to deal with local violations. It has followed closely the advancement of dependent peoples, and has pioneered the churches' study of economic and social development, including the population explosion. To handle the political and international problems associated with the movement of refugees and migration has long been its responsibility. In such matters it acts for the *ecumenical movement generally. The Hague Conference of 1968 considered the Commission's future, and a new constitution was approved by the Fourth Assembly of the WCC in 1968.

KENNETH G. GRUBB

Annual Reports of the Officers of the Commission of the Churches on International Affairs (297 Park Avenue South, New York 10; 150 route de Ferney, Geneva 20; 27 Marylebone Road, London, N.W.1.).

COMMISSION ON WORLD MISSION AND EVANGELISM. When the *IMC and the *WCC were integrated at the *New Delhi Assembly in 1961, this Commission was created to carry on, within the new World Council, the work of the former IMC. The aim of the Commission is 'to further the proclamation to the whole world of the Gospel of Jesus Christ, to the end that all men may believe in him and be saved'. Its functions are to remind the churches of the range and character of the unfinished evangelistic task, to deepen their sense of missionary obligation, and to stimulate prayer, study and united action for world evangelization.

The Commission meets ordinarily once every five years. It lays down general lines of policy and programme for the *DWME. Its first full meeting took place in Mexico in 1963, and developed the slogan 'Witness in Six Continents', indicating the oneness of the task in all parts of the world, and the ideal that all churches should become both sending and receiving churches in the missionary enterprise.

At the time of integration 37 member councils were affiliated to this new Commission. Since then five more have joined. The Commission also maintains contact with other *National Christian Councils which are not formally affiliated with it.

VICTOR E. W. HAYWARD

R. K. Orchard, ed.: *Witness in Six Continents* (London 1964).

COMMITTEE ON AGRICULTURAL MISSIONS, DIVISION OF OVERSEAS MINISTRIES, NATIONAL COUNCIL OF CHURCHES OF CHRIST IN THE USA. Formerly the Rural Missions Co-ordinating Committee of the Division of Foreign Missions of the National Churches of Christ in America. Since 1 January 1965 this committee has functioned as a policy-making body in the structure of the NCC. The same board of directors, the same staff serve this organization.

Purpose: The purpose of the programme is to give help to the churches and their agencies and other organizations in their efforts to provide a Christian witness and service among rural people around the world through improved food production, rural community development, home improvement and nutrition, and the strengthening of rural church life.

Function: (1) To help in the establishment and guidance of programmes designed to improve agriculture, home economics, co-operatives, credit, rural industry and rural life in any country. (2) To help select and train professional and volunteer leaders for the churches in the field of rural development. (3) To produce and disseminate literature of a technical, promotional, and programme-planning nature related to rural development. (4) To foster co-ordination of thought and action among the agencies engaged in the improvement of rural life. (5) To encourage overseas church bodies as well as informal Christian organizations in various countries to develop their own programmes of rural development. (6) To conduct projects of a pilot nature where necessary or desirable. (7) To aid in the training of indigenous rural church leadership. (8) To carry out such other programmes as may be necessary for the accomplishment of the purposes of the committee as set forth above.

RENÉ RYTER

COMMITTEE ON CO-OPERATION IN LATIN AMERICA. Inasmuch as the *World Missionary Conference at Edinburgh in 1910 excluded Latin America from its discussions, the North American mission boards, in 1913, requested the Committee of Reference and Counsel of the *Foreign Missions Conference of North America to appoint a committee to organize a conference on Christian work in Latin America. The conference met in Panama in 1916, and it established the CCLA. Dr Robert E. *Speer and Dr Samuel Guy Inman were the Chairman and Secretary, respectively, of the committee for over 20 years.

In its early years, in an attempt to avoid duplication of missionary effort by mission boards, the CCLA organized a series of conferences in Latin America to work out *comity arranegments. Over the years co-operative programmes were initiated in the fields of Christian literature (production and distribution), Christian education materials, theological education, religious broadcasting, and evangelism.

The Committee also sought to interpret missions to the churches in North America, and to present the gospel to the educated classes in Latin America. The latter ministry was through its magazine, *La Nueva Democracia*, and by means of a lectureship programme by Dr George P. Howard.

Important conferences were organized by the CCLA in Montevideo (1925) and Havana (1929), and these were followed by those of Buenos Aires (1949) and Lima,

Peru (1961), which were initiated by the national evangelical councils.

The CCLA undertook a number of surveys. The two most important ones resulted in the establishment of The Board for Christian Work in Santo Domingo in 1920, and the United Andean Indian Mission in 1945.

For many years the CCLA provided stimulation and counsel to the Latin American churches through the formation and support of national evangelical councils.

With the reorganization of the *National Council of Churches in the USA, the CCLA became the Latin America Department of the Council's *Division of Overseas Ministries in 1965, leaving a worthy legacy of half a century of leadership in the mission of the church in the western hemisphere.

W. STANLEY RYCROFT

COMMITTEE ON WORLD LITERACY AND CHRISTIAN LITERATURE, THE, was organized in 1942 by the union of Dr Frank C. Laubach's World Literacy Committee and the Committee for Christian Literature of the *Foreign Missions Conference of North America. Known informally as 'Lit-Lit', it is the co-operative agency of the North American churches in technical assistance and promotion of literacy campaigns and the production of Christian *literature by the churches of Africa, Asia, Latin America and the Pacific Islands. Its policies are determined, and its major support provided, by some 25 mission boards and church agencies. The Committee gives assistance to responsible national and local groups in more than 60 countries. In literacy this includes, where necessary, linguistic analysis, the preparation of teaching materials, the organization of teacher training programmes and the general administration of literacy work. In Christian literature this includes the promotion of many kinds of literature for all types of readers, with emphasis on literature for the new literate. Special attention is given to the training of personnel at all stages: for surveys and planning, writing, editing, publishing and distribution. The Committee is a unit of the NCCC of the USA; it is a major supporter of the *Christian Literature Fund, and co-operates closely with related supporting organizations in Europe.

See also LAUBACH-LITERACY, INC.

FLOYD SHACKLOCK

Lit-Lit Newsletter (quarterly).

COMMUNICATING THE GOSPEL. Because the gospel is essentially Good News about what God has done in certain great events of history, it has to be communicated. News requires reporting. The apostles felt a strong compulsion to tell men what they knew about Jesus Christ and the meaning of his life, death and resurrection (Acts 4:20;1 Cor.9:16). From the beginning the apostolic church believed that it had to bear witness to Jesus Christ locally, nationally, and universally (Acts 1:8). All four Gospels end with some form of dominical command to make Jesus Christ known throughout the world (Mat.28:19;Mk.16:15; Lk.24:47f.;Jn.20:21). The gospel's power is dependent upon its being communicated. If the church has due regard for the gospel it must therefore be missionary.

The normal means of communication are sight and sound reaching men through eye and ear. Jesus used both. He came 'preaching the gospel of God' (Mk.1:14) and gave it to men in the form of words, particularly stories. It was noticed that he spoke with an authority beyond that of other men (Mk.1: 22). But the gospel was also to be seen in the form of deeds, particularly acts of healing in the widest sense of that word and of the widest range of human ills. There was an authority about his deeds as well as his words; his gospel was visible as well as audible (Mk.1:27;11:28). The deeds were the signs authenticating the truth of the words (Jn. 2:11;Mk.16:17). In the apostolic church the gospel was communicated both by preaching and healing, and although the NT documents pay more attention to the preaching, healing deeds are recorded in Acts, and Paul insists on the importance of this means of communication (Rom.15:19; 2 Cor.12:12).

Supremely the gospel is God's communica-

tion of himself to men. In Jesus God became uniquely audible and uniquely visible (Jn.1:14; Col.1:15; Heb.1:1–3). Gradually the church came to see that Jesus not merely preached the gospel but he embodied it. Communicating the gospel means communicating Christ. He may still be heard in the words of Scripture. He may still be seen in the life of the church. The church is called to *proclaim* his gospel and to *be* his body. The church is to be the ultimate visual aid in the communication of the gospel.

Today the church has to discover the most effective means of communication by discovering contemporary ways of making Christ visible, contemporary 'signs of an apostle'. The NT teaches that communication is not primarily a matter of technique, for God's first and final agent of communication is the Holy Spirit, who alone can convince and interpret and make men understand (Jn.16:6–8; Acts 2:1–11;1 Cor. 2:6–16).

DOUGLAS WEBSTER

F. W. Dillistone: *Christianity and Communication* (London 1956); H. Kraemer: *The Communication of the Christian Faith* (London 1957); M. A. C. Warren: *The Christian Imperative* (London 1955); D. Webster: *What is Evangelism?* (London 1959).

COMMUNISM AND MISSIONS. The attitude of the Communist to Christian missions is determined by two factors: (a) the conviction that every form of religion is opposed to 'science', and must therefore in time wither away; any attempt to maintain or propagate it must therefore be condemned as foolish and harmful; (b) the unshakeable belief that the Christian mission cannot be anything other than an arm of the capitalist and imperialist aggression of the west. It is, therefore, necessary for every communist power to take every opportunity to overthrow and destroy the work of Christian *missions*, though a measure of tolerance may for tactical reasons be accorded to the *church. This may be illustrated from four areas. (1) It is widely believed in the Christian world that the church cannot be destroyed. This is true of the church as a whole; it is not true of local and partial churches. The church in Central Asia was brought into being through the devoted work of the Swedish Missionary Society (Yarkand 1895). With the arrival of the Bolsheviks in 1938, the church was completely destroyed; the missionaries expelled, the Christians either killed or driven out; the orphanages closed and the children scattered; it is doubtful whether any trace of Christian existence is to be found anywhere in the region today. (2) The missionary work of the Russian Church came to an end shortly after the revolution. Some fragments of the great work of Archbishop *Nicolai in Japan remained, and have been taken over by other Orthodox churches. The communist authorities appear to be prepared to make use of the church in certain situations, such as Korea; but this is naturally a part of political tactics rather than of religious interest. (3) In China the communists seem to have distinguished somewhat clearly between the Christian mission and a genuinely Chinese church. All missionaries were naturally identified as imperialist aggressors, and all have been compelled, or have found it desirable, to withdraw from China. In so far as the Chinese church has found it possible to adapt itself to the revolution, it has been allowed to continue in existence, though under severe restrictions. (4) Direct communist penetration in Africa has suffered a series of set-backs. The great opportunity lies with the many thousands of African students who are being educated in countries under communist domination; care is taken to impress upon their minds the identification of church and mission with colonial aggression and exploitation. Some have returned as disillusioned communists; but it seems that this propaganda has had some success, and that it is being disseminated in Africa by those who have come back convinced of its truth.

STEPHEN NEILL

COMMUNITIES, ANGLICAN, IN MISSION. Community life under the religious

vows of poverty, chastity, and obedience came to an abrupt end in England just before the Reformation, and did not make a definite start again until the 19th century. Its revival was closely linked with the overseas missionary work of the church. When C.*Codrington made his will in 1699 he left his estates in Barbados 'for the maintenance of monks and missionaries to be employed in the conversion of Negroes and Indians', as a contemporary put it. But at the time there were no monks available. In 1842 John Keble was anxious to have the religious life tried abroad, but then saw it primarily as a spur to its acceptance at home. Fr R. M. Benson who founded the Society of St. John the Evangelist, Cowley (1866), gained his interest in the religious life through his life-long enthusiasm for missionary work in India, seeing the need to identify himself with Indians and to 'surpass them' in asceticism, and in 1865 Fr S. W. O'Neill, one of the original members of SSJE, wrote of the missionary's need for preparation in retirement, faithful companionship, celibacy, and mortification. Benson himself never served overseas, but the members of SSJE were called mission priests, and while many exercised their mission at home, others went to India in 1877 at the request of the Bishop of Bombay to work at Poona. With them went Sisters of the Wantage Community (founded 1845).

Most Anglican religious communities, wherever they were founded, have undertaken work outside their countries of origin, and their members have in several cases been chosen to be bishops. Their pastoral and evangelistic work has often been centred on a community building, except in cases where they have been ready to detach individual members from community life. They have done much teaching and medical work, and have been specially valued as spiritual directors and retreat conductors. The Community of the Resurrection (founded 1892) and the Society of the Sacred Mission (1894) have taken an important share in training ordinands in Australia, South Africa, and the West Indies.

Besides those who live in community

under life vows there are also religious societies like the Oratory of the Good Shepherd which has many members working abroad but not living in community, or the Australian Bush Brotherhoods which have religious vows, but not for life. At the present time there seems generally to be less need for the kind of institutional 'mission work' which was necessary in the past, and the future role of the religious in overseas mission is changing. Its value as a witness to a deliberate form of Christian dedication continues to be great, and although the numbers of Anglicans who have lived under religious vows is still small, their influence has been profound.

JOHN WILKINSON

A. M. Allchin: *The Silent Rebellion* (London 1958); P. F. Anson: *The Call of the Cloister* (2nd ed., London 1964); CSMV: *A Hundred Years of Blessing* (London 1946).

COMPARATIVE STUDY OF RELI-GIONS. Every man finds it natural to compare his own religion with that of others, out of sheer curiosity, with a hostile sense of superiority, or with that openness and willingness to learn which may lead on to *syncretism. But a comparative study of religions on a scientific basis is rather a late-comer in the field of human studies.

With the recovery of the long lost litera-tures of Egypt and Babylon, it was inevitable that the early part of the Bible should be studied afresh in the light of the new knowledge. There was a tendency to take the rather naïve view that, where there was correspondence, the relationship must in every case be that of borrowing on the Jewish side; it was felt by many that the uniqueness of the Bible was undermined by this method of study.

The real starting point of comparative study was the publication in 1871 of E. B. Tylor's *Primitive Culture*, in which he brought together a great mass of material, and drew attention to the significance of the so-called *primitive religions, which had up to that time been generally neglected. Tylor's work was followed up by the immense collections of material set forth by

Sir J. G. Frazer in successive editions of *The Golden Bough* (1st ed. 1890), and in other works. It has become clear that much of the material used in these early works was unreliable, and that much more careful examination of religious beliefs and cus-toms is needed. The work of Spencer and Gillan (from 1896 onwards) among the Australian Aborigines was a model in its time; but even here it has been found that much of the work has to be done again in the light of fuller knowledge and under-standing.

A new impulse was given to the study by the work of Emile Durkheim, especially *Les formes élémentaires de la vie religieuse* (1912). Durkheim insisted that religion must always be studied in its social context, as one aspect of the total life of man in society. This has been followed up by the work of the cultural anthropologists (the title of the notable work of Ruth Benedict: *Patterns of Culture* is significant) who see religion as the mythological expression of a people's understanding of, or ideals for, its own existence. The question of the truth or false-hood of a religion can, on this under-standing, hardly be allowed to arise.

The latest period may be held to open with the work of E. Evans-Pritchard: *Nuer Religion* (1956), in which the writer empha-sizes that he takes the view that 'religion is a subject of study *sui generis*, just as are language and law'; religion cannot be under-stood or interpreted in terms of anything else. Not all students of the subject would take this view.

How far can Christians accept the view that the Christian faith can be brought into comparison with other forms of faith? The Barthian school, with its highly gifted expositor, H. *Kraemer, would maintain that no comparison is possible, since Christianity as the authentic utterance of God himself is incommensurable with any other religion. Not all Christians would take so rigid a view. The problem, however, is that of finding any generally accepted defi-nition of 'religion' as a general term under which many different forms of religion can be brought into relationship with one another. In a very real sense all religions are unique, each being the expression of a total understanding of the nature and meaning of human life. It may seem that, if this unique-ness is taken seriously, comparison becomes impossible, whereas, if comparison is insti-tuted, it becomes impossible to do justice to the element of uniqueness in each religion.

STEPHEN NEILL

U. Bianchi: *Problemi di Storia delle religioni* (Rome 1964; German tr., *Probleme der Religionsgeschichte*, Göttingen 1965); E. G. S. Parrinder: *Comparative Religion* (London 1962); H. Pinard de la Boullaye: *L'Etude Comparée des religions* (4th ed., Paris 1929); E. E. Pritchard: *Theories of Primitive Religion* (Oxford 1965).

COMPENSATION FOR INJURIES AND INDEMNITIES. Policy, as regards claiming from governments and other authorities compensation for loss of life or property, has varied very much from mission to mission and country to country. In early days, when communications were slow and diplomatic relations had in many cases not been established, there was no authority at hand to whom the missionary could turn, and no means of enforcing his claims other than the direct exercise of military power. Matters changed considerably in the 19th century, especially in China, where through anti-foreign sentiment the lives and posses-sions of missionaries were likely to be often in danger. It became the settled policy of the RC missions to make every possible use of consular protection, to demand reparation for every kind of injury, and to extend the principle from the foreign missionary to his Chinese converts. This proved intolerable to the Chinese, since so often there was no means of proving whether injury had been done to a Christian because of his Christian faith or for other reasons; many cases are on record in which Christians appear to have used the missionary to bolster up false claims or cases. Sentiment on the Protestant side steadily developed in the other direc-tion. At first missionaries had been inclined to follow the same line as the RCs. Later it became clear to them that, quite apart from

the danger of encouraging mixed motives in possible Christians, the missionary himself would be in a far stronger position, if he did not make use of outside, especially foreign, help to establish his rights in the face of injury. It is always possible to win your case and lose your man. After the *Boxer troubles in China in 1900 a heavy indemnity was imposed on China by the victorious powers. The USA drew the indemnity for a year, but devoted the whole of the sum received to educational purposes for the benefit of China. The Director of the *CIM, J. Hudson *Taylor, laid it down that no compensation was to be asked, for either life or property, and that, if offered, it was not to be accep-ted. This was a notable example, since the CIM had lost a far larger number of mis-sionaries than any other society. This policy would probably commend itself to almost all missionary leaders today.

With the disappearance of *colonialism, the missionary has ceased to be a privileged person, as in many areas he was in the 19th century. He and his flock are dependent on the goodwill of their neighbours, and can have recourse, like anyone else, to the law-courts of the land. But church leaders and Christians would do well to resort to this method only rarely. In South India it was noticeable that in villages where Christians with missionary help had carried through a successful legal case against Hindu neigh-bours, though peaceful co-existence had been secured, there had not been a single case of conversion in 60 years. Often the willingness to endure hardness and to trust in God alone is in the end the most effective way of vindicating human rights.

STEPHEN NEILL

S. Neill: *Colonialism and Christian Missions* (London 1966).

CONFERENCE OF MISSIONARY SOCIETIES IN GREAT BRITAIN AND IRELAND, THE, was established in 1912 following the *Edinburgh Conference of 1910. It was preceded by the London Secretaries Association (1819) in which the secretaries of foreign mission boards with headquarters in London met for 'mutual counsel and fellowship', and by the United Council for Missionary Education (1907) which later became the Edinburgh House Press.

It is, in the words of its constitution, 'an association of missionary societies for the more effective propagation of the gospel of Jesus Christ in other lands, which task they seek to discharge in partnership with churches overseas. Its primary purpose is to provide for consultation between its members, and for such co-operation and joint action at home and abroad as it may deem advisable'. It is affiliated to the *Commission on World Mission and Evangelism of the *WCC, and it is 'in association with' the British Council of Churches. 51 bodies are members. Its annual conference is constituted by their delegates, and it works through a Standing Committee and committees concerned with geographical areas and particular functions. The Conference publishes an annual handbook.

RONALD K. ORCHARD

W. R. Hogg: *Ecumenical Foundations* (New York 1952), pp.51–53, 157f.

CONFERENCES, MISSIONARY. Protestant missionary conferences in the period following 1855 provide a valuable index into the life, problems, thought, concerns and growth of mission and church. Merely to catalogue denominational conferences would require a thick volume. Here only some interdenominational gatherings of large significance can be noted.

Pre-Edinburgh, 1910. Three major kinds of conferences emerged in this period: those regarded as at the 'home base' (see CONFERENCES, WORLD MISSIONARY), continuing gatherings of mission specialists in the west (see CONTINENTAL EUROPEAN MISSIONS CONFERENCE; FOREIGN MISSIONS CONFERENCE OF NORTH AMERICA, etc.), and those assembling in Asia, Africa, and Latin America.

These last mentioned gatherings brought together missionaries 'on the field' to explore their common concerns. India had the longest tradition with three conferences in the north (1855–63), three in the south (1858–1900), and four in an All-India decennial series (1873–1902). Of these, Madras, 1900, and Madras, 1902, were most important. China had three, all in Shanghai, (1877–1907), of which the third was most important. Japan had four (1872–1900). Also, South Africa had three (1904–09) and Mexico City was the site for two in 1888 and 1897.

All were remarkably similar in problems covered and in a growing sense of unity. They pointed to a growing missionary thrust from the west and to the steady growth of churches in Asia, Africa, and Latin America. Yet nationals were scarcely represented. Each conference pointed to areas of competition, disagreement, and sometimes conflict among the societies. Thus, several continuing boards of arbitration were created. And across half a century, the same common concerns were dealt with —Bible translation, medical work, social work, production of literature in the local languages, education at all levels, the place, work, and training of women, the evangelization of new areas, relations between missionaries and nationals, *church growth, *comity, the development in the churches of self-support and self-government, and often relations with governments. Many conferences expressed need for a continuing national body that would be clearing-house and co-ordinator for much that confronted the missions in common. Indeed, Bombay, 1892, appointed a standing committee, and after Tokyo, 1900, a body was organized which in 1907 took the name 'Federated Missions in Japan'. Moreover, each conference experienced a deep sense of unity and expressed a desire for further co-operation. The major Asian conferences also pointed explicitly to the ideal of a national, unified church.

These conferences provided a structural and procedural evolution that shaped *Edinburgh, 1910. Noting the unwieldy and unofficial character of preceding gatherings those who planned Madras, 1900, persuaded societies to *elect official delegates* for a *representative* assembly. Dispensing with addresses, they appointed committees to deal intensively with the relevant subjects and then submit the results to plenary sessions for discussion and resolutions. Questions of *faith and order were barred. Madras, 1902, and Shanghai, 1907, followed these procedures, and in 1907 Edinburgh's planners adopted them.

Post-Edinburgh, 1910. Edinburgh, 1910, was an ecumenical watershed, and, with J. R. *Mott as chairman, its Continuation Committee in 1921 became the *IMC. In the years 1911–1941 Mott was involved in most of the major missionary assemblies. Between November 1912, and April 1913, Mott convened national conferences in Colombo, Ceylon; Calcutta, India; Rangoon, Burma; Singapore, Malaya; Shanghai, China; Moukden, Manchuria; Seoul, Korea; and Tokyo, Japan, and thirteen other related regional conferences. Asians averaged 35% of those attending. These follow-up conferences to Edinburgh used its syllabus, and all came to near unanimity of judgment. Their most notable result was the creation of *National Missionary Councils—the first nation-wide ecumenical bodies in these lands—soon to become *NCCs and member bodies of the IMC.

Edinburgh, 1910, had had to exclude Latin America from its purview; but two unofficial gatherings at Edinburgh and a conference in New York in 1913, which created the *Committee on Co-operation in Latin America (CCLA), led directly to the Congress on Christian Work in Latin America held in Panama in 1916. That gathering with Latin Americans constituting 50% of its membership, patterned itself on Edinburgh, 1910, made the CCLA its continuing agency, and then conducted seven regional conferences.

Post-World War I. In the 1920s National Missionary Councils were transformed into National Christian Councils (NCCs), often in conjunction with a major conference (e.g. Shanghai and Tokyo, 1922). They were more representative of the churches. A series of gatherings in Muslim lands culminated in a Jerusalem Conference in 1924, from which emerged what in 1929 became the Near East Christian Council. What became the Committee on the Christian

Approach to the Jews convened conferences in Budapest and Warsaw in 1927 and in Atlantic City in 1934, after which date its major attention focused on problems of Jewish refugees. The Congress on Christian Work in South America, Montevideo, 1925, surveyed the scene there. Conferences on Africa were held in Britain in 1924, in Belgium in 1926, and in South Africa and the Congo in 1934.

Mott's Pacific Basin Tour in 1925–26 resulted in conferences from Tokyo to Melbourne, and from the latter came Australia's National Missionary Council. Mott travelled from the IMC's *Jerusalem meeting to Bangkok where a 1929 conference resulted in Thailand's NCC, and to Manila where the Philippines' NCC emerged. During the depths of the depression in the early 1930s relatively few major conferences met. Then came Tambaram, Madras, in 1938 and in 1939 the outbreak of the second world war. The last of the missionary planning conferences in which Mott played a large role were held in Latin America in 1940–41.

Post-World War II. A trend already strongly evident in the 1920s and 1930s came to completion in the decades following the second world war. Conferences once designated 'missionary' in Asia, Africa, and Latin America were now simply 'Christian'. Missionaries were still present, and many of the same problems had to be explored, but an *indigenous church with its own leadership was taking, in most cases, considerable responsibility for the mission in its homeland. More conferences met than ever before. Many were highly specialized in such areas as medicine, communications, literacy, home and family life, theological education, urbanization, and faith and order. Some were convened by continent-wide regional councils. Some were sponsored by the *WCC (jointly WCC–IMC until the 1961 integration).

Among conservative evangelical Protestants the *IFMA (founded in 1917) convened its first Congress on World Missions in Chicago in 1960. Then with the *EFMA (founded in 1945) it held the Congress on the Church's Worldwide Mission at Wheaton, Illinois, in 1966. Both reflected strong conviction of the duty to evangelize the world in this generation; they symbolize the great importance of boards and societies outside the larger co-operating denominations of Protestantism.

With one exception, every conference listed above has a published report or findings. Full bibliographical data on each can be found in *Ecumenical Foundations.* Mott's volume contains data about and often findings from all the missionary conferences in which he participated from 1910 to 1941.

W. RICHEY HOGG

China Centenary Missionary Conference Records ... Shanghai ... 1907 (New York 1907); W. R. Hogg: *Ecumenical Foundations* (New York 1952); H. Lindsell, ed.: *The Church's Worldwide Mission* (Waco, Texas 1966); J. R. Mott: *Addresses and Papers of John R. Mott,* Vol. V, *The International Missionary Council* (New York 1947); *Report of the South Indian Missionary Conference ... Madras ... 1900* (Madras 1900).

CONFERENCES, REGIONAL MISSIONARY. See REGIONAL CONFERENCES.

CONFERENCES, WORLD MISSIONARY. Ten major world missionary conferences in the period 1860–1963 provide a useful measure of the church's self-understanding and methodology in mission and of its worldwide growth in a century of revolutionary change. The first three are predecessors of Edinburgh 1910, and the remainder follow in the *IMC–*WCC stream.

Liverpool 1860. The first met in Liverpool, 19–23 March 1860. Of the 126 present, 37 were missionaries, including Stephen Hislop of India, William Shaw of South Africa, and Hope *Waddell of Nigeria, and one, the Rev. B. Singh from India, represented the churches outside Britain. Most were members of the British mission societies. Private daytime meetings facilitated discussion and the drafting of policy resolutions. Growing crowds attended the public evening assemblies. Well organized, the conference produced a remarkably useful report, and its findings provided policy guidelines for several decades. It examined recruitment, education overseas, and the development of strong, self-supporting churches with national pastors. It called for a first-rate missions journal and the enlistment of more university graduates as missionaries. Although using their language and being close to the people, the missionary was viewed as one of 'superior social rank and ... of a dominant race'. Thus the conference reflected its day. See: *Conference on Missions Held in 1860 at Liverpool* (London 1860).

London 1888. Another conference was held in London in 1878. A decade later the great 'Centenary Conference'—an imprecise but appropriately expansive designation—assembled 9–19 June. First of the truly international gatherings, it had nearly 1,600 members, with 219 from North America and 41 from the European Continent. Although not listed, some Asian pastors and teachers were present. Except for three High Anglican societies and the Salvation Army, all the non-Roman, British societies were represented.

Closed section meetings, open plenary sessions, and great public assemblies provided variety. The massive two-volume *Report* includes all speeches and shows that the sections dealt with current concerns: methods, medical outreach, women's work, literature, education, national churches, and relations with governments. *Comity claimed considerable attention. Many proposed a permanent committee for arbitrating differences among missions, but prevailing opinion favoured informal arrangements. In a notable paper Gustav *Warneck proposed creating then what the *IMC was eventually to become; but his proposal was so advanced that in 1888 it was not even discussed by the Conference. See James Johnston, ed.: *Report of the Centenary Conference ... London 1888* (2 vols., London 1888).

New York 1900. The New York Ecumenical (because its proposed campaign covered 'the whole area of the inhabited globe') Missionary Conference met 21 April–1 May 1900, and daily crowded more than 4,000 persons into each session at Carnegie Hall. Although some 200,000 attended, only 2,500 were members, two-thirds of them North Americans. The *Foreign Missions Conference of North America designed this gathering to influence a vast audience, and the press coverage helped guarantee that result. Of 500 speakers, eight—of whom three were women from India—represented churches outside the west. Aimed to inspire and provide mass education, the conference examined every subject on the missionary agenda—and then provided, region by region, a complete territorial survey.

On 2 May some 200 delegates from Europe, Britain, and North America gathered unofficially, heard an American Presbyterian, Frank Ellinwood, urge the formation of an international missionary committee, and unanimously adopted his proposal—for discussion with home constituencies. Despite interest and much correspondence, the project died. See *Ecumenical Missionary Conference, New York, 1900* (2 vols., New York 1900).

Edinburgh 1910. The World Missionary Conference (WMC) held at Edinburgh 1910, looms steadily larger in significance, It came, on the eve of the first world war, at the transition from the 19th to 20th centuries and marked the beginning of the organized *Ecumenical Movement on the Protestant-Orthodox side.

Four major streams contributed to what the WMC became. The first of these was the emergence of co-operative missionary conferences (see CONFERENCES, MISSIONARY) chiefly in India, China, and Japan. The second consisted of those gatherings held in Liverpool, London, and New York (see above) which disclosed growing unity and expressed need for the international co-operation that issued from Edinburgh 1910.

The third emerged from such bodies as the *Continental European Missions Conference, the *Ausschuss*, or 'standing committee' in Germany, and the Foreign Missions Conference of North America. These developed an essentially *inter*denominational rather than a *non*denominational form of co-operation. The fourth, and most dynamic, respresented the entire international *Student Christian Movement—the *YMCA, the *YWCA, national SCMs, the *SVM(U), and the *WSCF. Here J. R. *Mott, J. H. *Oldham, and others prepared for Edinburgh 1910.

The WMC met 12–23 June 1910, broke new ground, and became the prototype for the worldwide, ecumenical conferences that followed. From 1907 on, intensive international co-operative planning had laid the groundwork. Officially appointed delegates made it representative, and they came having already studied the printed commission reports. Except for the Roman Catholics and Orthodox, most of the remainder of the Christian spectrum was present—from the High Church *SPG to the *Salvation Army. The WMC marked the Anglicans' full entrance into ecumenical affairs—a major accomplishment in denominational inclusiveness. This resulted from SCM conviction and experience.

The WMC's one great action, based upon several recommendations in the preceding year, was to create the Continuation Committee to carry out internationally what the WMC had begun. By 1921 that body had become the *International Missionary Council. Edinburgh's more than 1,200 delegates, of whom 17 were Asians, assessed the 'foreign mission' from a western vantage point, but the WMC involved much more than this.

The WMC's larger significance must be noted. First, it made a shaping impact on key figures, among them Mott, Oldham. Charles *Brent, V. S. *Azariah, C. Y, *Cheng, and among the stewards William Temple and John Baillie. Second, not only did it set the operating pattern for ecumenical conferences, but it also established a principle earlier enunciated by the *Ausschuss* and the FMC, namely, that a council is the creation of its member boards and societies (and thus, in principle, of the churches) which alone have the right to determine policy. Thus the sole authority of the co-operative agency is the wisdom of its counsel as this commends itself to the member bodies. This is the key to ecumenical authority. Third, the WMC contributed directly and indirectly to the rise of the major non-Roman ecumenical structures, among them the IMC and its worldwide network of *NCCs, *Faith and Order, *Life and Work, and to the WCC itself. Fourth, and contrary to much popular thinking, the WMC focused major attention on 'The Church in the Mission Field' (Vol. II), 'itself now the great mission to the non-Christian world'. Theologically the WMC had a larger vision than most commentators have suggested: 'The whole world is the mission field, and there is no church that is not a church in the mission field'. The WMC belonged to its era, but was pointing toward a new understanding of the church in Asia *and* in Europe. Finally, the WMC strongly encouraged (Vol. VIII) unity and church union in Asia and Africa and co-operation in the west. With the world physically one and the divine intention unmistakable, it argued that there could be no artificial geographic or theological separations: mission and unity are 'the concern of the whole Church of Christ'. Questions of faith and order were necessarily barred from discussion, but discerning minds realized that God's mission involves the unity of the whole church. Thus a Congregationalist declared that he looked forward to a gathering that would include Roman Catholics and Orthodox. Others echoed this theme. Brent, the Episcopal (Anglican) bishop from the Philippines, saw that the WMC pointed inevitably to the unity of all Christians: 'That is the task before us. Let us be satisfied with nothing less'. And so were born the shaping convictions for the *Faith and Order movement. Edinburgh 1910 was an ecumenical keystone and, with the Second *Vatican Council, may some day be judged one of the two most decisive church councils in the first seven decades of the 20th century. See W. H. T. Gairdner: *Echoes from Edinburgh, 1910* (New York

1910); W. R. Hogg: *Ecumenical Foundations* (New York 1952) and 'Edinburgh, 1910—Ecumenical Keystone', *Religion in Life* Vol. XXIX, No. 3, Summer 1960; J. H. Oldham: 'Reflections on Edinburgh, 1910', *Religion in Life* Vol. XXIX, No. 3, Summer 1960; *World Missionary Conference 1910* (9 vols., Edinburgh 1910).

The IMC, a direct outgrowth of Edinburgh 1910, was officially constituted in 1921. Since its integration in 1961 with the *WCC, it has been the *Commission on World Mission and Evangelism (CWME) of the WCC. All the conferences that follow were sponsored by the IMC or the CWME.

Jerusalem 1928. From around the world a small group gathered on the Mount of Olives at Easter time in 1928—a decade after the first world war—to re-examine the Christian mission. They constituted the first globally representative assembly of non-Roman Christians, and of the 231 members, nearly one-fourth represented in full equality the churches of Asia, Africa, and Latin America. Here was Jerusalem's most noticeable difference from Edinburgo 1910—a fact that uniquely symbolized the reality of world Christian community. The meaning of a worldwide church—the only distinction being that between *'younger' and 'older' churches—involved in common mission had dawned. *Secularism, Jerusalem declared, had become a universal religion and made further apparent the oneness of the mission.

Jerusalem's agenda has a contemporary ring—urbanization and industrialization in Asia and Africa, rural problems, race relations, war, medical work, religious education, and relations between younger and older churches. Yet, nine years after Barth's *Letter to the Romans* (1919) had shifted the theological tide, many from the Continent greatly feared that the agenda meant the triumph of the 'social gospel'. From such apprehension came some interpretative reports which could not then see that—however its theological adequacy or deficiency may be judged—Jerusalem pointed to the relevance of the gospel everywhere for the whole life of man

When Jerusalem met, growing numbers around the world held that all religions are relative and that Christianity's truth about God is also relative. Accordingly, it made the Christian and non-Christian encounter its first concern. Already apprehensive, most of those from the European continent feared that Jerusalem would make a syncretistic compromise.

William Temple drafted the unanimously accepted 'Message' and incorporated in it the statement on the Christian Message prepared in 1927 at Lausanne by Faith and Order. The gospel announces God's truth. 'Either it is true for all, or it is not true at all . . . Christ is our motive and Christ is our end. We must give nothing less, and we can give nothing more.' After acknowledging elements of truth in other major religions, Jerusalem issued a call to non-Christians to engagement—to join with Christians in a 'study of Jesus Christ . . . in the Scriptures. . . . But to come to Him is always self-surrender.' Jerusalem enunciated 35 years earlier essentially the same position taken by the Second Vatican Council in outreach to men of other faiths [cf. *On the Church* (*Lumen Gentium*), *Relationship of the Church to Non-Christian Religions* (*Nostra Aetate*), and *Decree on The Missionary Activity of The Church* (*Ad Gentes*)]. See *The Jerusalem Meeting of the IMC, 24 March-8 April 1928* (8 vols., New York and London 1928); *The World Mission of Christianity. Messages and Recommendations . . . Jerusalem . . . 1928* (New York and London 1928).

Tambaram, Madras, 1938. Between 1928 and 1938 mankind experienced global recession, wars that foreshadowed larger conflict, and the rise of new tyrannies. In the Christian world Faith and Order met at Edinburgh, *Life and Work met at Oxford in 1937, and from both at Utrecht in 1938 came a plan and constitution for the WCC. Such was the background when the IMC next met at Christmas time, 1938, on the campus of Madras Christian College in Tambaram, a suburb of Madras. Nearly 500 persons from 69 countries gathered in what may have been the most representative

global meeting convened up to that time. More than half of those present represented the churches of Asia, Africa, and Latin America. China's delegation was recognized as the ablest of them all.

As Oxford and Edinburgh, 1937, had done, Madras focused upon the church. The meaning for mankind of its mission was the central theme, and it explored this theologically and descriptively in relation to the remarkable growth of certain 'younger' churches. Moreover, the reality, breadth and vigour of the worldwide church were visible in microcosm. The churches of Asia, Africa, and Latin America contributed in major fashion and emphasized the need for unity and for organic union.

Continuing the Jerusalem discussion, Madras also examined the nature and authority of the faith. The *Laymen's Foreign Missions Inquiry with its unrelieved optimism and theological relativism, and the study of its chairman, William E. Hocking's *Rethinking Missions* (1932), had reflected much current thought, but provoked a storm of controversy. At the opposite pole, and commissioned by the IMC, Hendrik *Kraemer's *The Christian Message in a Non-Christian World* (1938) provided Madras grist for debate. Kraemer's 'biblical realism' maintained that the spiritual truth disclosed by God's revelation in Jesus Christ is different from and not continuous with the world of nature, reason, and history. With his Barthian orientation, Kraemer rejected all 'natural theologies' and emphasized the gospel's 'discontinuity' from all religions. Thus emerged the 'Kraemer-Hocking debate' on Christianity's encounter with other religions.

Madras produced a brief statement of faith, delineated three great new world religions (*Nationalism, *Communism, Scientific Scepticism), and stimulated new interest in the biblical basis for mission. Its larger agenda was highly productive, but the second world war immediately ended any implementation of it, although recommendations on theological education and literature did bear some later fruit. The great and immediate contribution of Madras came from its unifying power which during and after the second world war strengthened the world Christian community. See *'The Madras Series' Papers . . . of the IMC at Tambaram, Madras . . . 1938* (7 vols., New York 1939) and *The World Mission of the Church. Findings . . . of the IMC . . . Tambaram* (New York 1939).

Whitby 1947. Realizing in late 1946 that the times demanded a gathering long before the one they had then recently planned for 1950, the IMC's officers arranged (with only the briefest preparation) for the first IMC conference after the second world war the following summer. Thus 112 persons from 40 countries met at Whitby near Toronto in July 1947. They surveyed the state of the worldwide church emerging from the ashes of war.

Whitby's chief hallmark was its deeply experienced unity after the long separation of war. It also declared worldwide evangelism to be the central task of the church. In that task, belonging to each generation of Christians, the churches of Asia, Africa, and Latin America have the major responsibility in their areas. Whitby's vision and thrust were akin to those of Edinburgh 1910 (cf. Second Vatican Council's *De Ecclesia* or *Lumen Gentium*, para.33, the final words of which reconstruct the SVM watchword). Yet the burst of new nations, new nationalisms, the founding of the WCC in 1948, the closing of China in 1949 and the expulsion of the missionaries there seemed to divert attention from Whitby's 'Expectant Evangelism', and few churches responded. Whitby laid the foundations for what fifteen years later became *'Joint Action for Mission'. Its statement on *'Supranationality' —*primary* loyalty to Christ and his church ecumenical, rather than to nation or race, may yet be seen to have been prophetic. See C. W. Ranson, ed.: *Renewal and Advance: Christian Witness in a Revolutionary World* (London 1948) and K. S. Latourette and W. R. Hogg: *Tomorrow is Here* (New York 1948). The larger bibliography for all the preceding conferences will be found in W. R. Hogg: *Ecumenical Foundations.*

Willingen 1952. By 1950 the post-Christendom era and the new shape of the post-war world were evident. Christianity held minority status everywhere. Intense nationalism and new biblical and theological perspectives challenged much traditional thought about mission. Against this background, some 190 persons met at Willingen, Germany, 5–17 July 1952, to examine the theological foundation of mission and to reformulate missionary policy. Willingen reflected theological confusion. Some missionary thinking was still conditioned by 19th century presuppositions, but the environment for mission had become the post-Christendom, ecumenical era in church and society. Mission itself had become the problem. Willingen's basic theological concern, 'The Missionary Obligation of the Church', issued in an inconclusive statement that was 'received' but not adopted. Participants could not agree on the relation of mission and church, especially in the eschatological context. If God is at work in all history, what is the special task of the church in mission? Yet from the impasse came a brief but decisive statement that was adopted. Its central affirmation: 'mission has its source in the Triune God, and the closer the church in mission draws to Him, the nearer it draws to the world'. In raising more questions than it answered, Willingen launched the new discussion on the theology of mission and shifted its emphasis from the 'church-centric' (Madras) to the Trinitarian theocentric (Willingen). See W. Andersen: *Towards A Theology of Mission* (London 1955) and N. Goodall, ed.: *Missions Under the Cross* (London 1953).

Ghana 1958. At University College, Legon, Ghana, 28 December 1957 to 8 January 1958, some 215 persons met in the IMC's final world conference.

Ghana took one all-important action. Although some reservations were expressed from Africa, Latin America, and Europe, it agreed in principle to the integration of the IMC and WCC—an achievement consummated at the WCC's Third Assembly in New Delhi, 1961.

Ghana also gave major attention to theological education, one of the chief concerns Madras twenty years earlier had placed before the churches, It elected its secretary C. W. Ranson, to be director of the new four million dollar *TEF for seminaries in Asia, Africa, and Latin America.

Ghana's official report consists chiefly of addresses and preparatory papers, and reflects the earnest groping of mission experts amid vast and confusing transition in missions. See R. K. Orchard, ed.: *The Ghana Assembly of the IMC ... 1958* (London 1958).

Mexico City 1963. The WCC's Commission on World Mission and Evangelism (CWME—the IMC reborn) assembled for two days immediately after the New Delhi Assembly. But the CWME's first world conference met in Mexico City, 8–19 December 1963, with 200 attending. Mexico City had obvious links with its past, but several features marked its new orientation. For the first time RC observers and Orthodox members were present, and the latter participated vigorously. Thus was fulfilled a hope expressed at Edinburgh 1910. Moreover, the theological shift begun at Willingen shaped the session and determined its theme: 'God's Mission and Our Task'.

Mexico City developed two thrusts begun at New Delhi. First, the 'six continent view of mission' affirms in a post-Christendom age that the church, now planted everywhere, is everywhere in mission. Second, Joint Action for Mission, going beyond traditional interdenominational efforts, urges that in a given geographical area Christians together should explore their mission and respond to it as the one people of God (cf. New Delhi's 'all in each place'). Involved are abandonment of irrelevant forms, willingness to forgo denominational gain, and fundamental questions of denominational conscience and church union. Mexico City also faced the problems of congregational structures and witness to men of other faiths. See R. K. Orchard, ed.: *Witness in Six Continents: Records ... of the CWME of the WCC ... Mexico City ... 1963* (London 1964).

These conferences mirrored a century (1860–1963) of remarkable worldwide expansion and change in mission. The growing unity of the church was reflected in unions, e.g., the *Church of South India, the United Church of Christ in the Philippines, the *Kyodan* in Japan, and in many plans for union. Prophetic hopes expressed in 1910 were being realized in 1963 with Orthodox and Roman Catholic involvement. The 1961 IMC-WCC integration symbolized the theological oneness of mission and church. The view of mission had changed from 'two continents-eastward' to 'six continents—outward'. The dominant theological motif for mission had shifted from the *Great Commission, to the nature of the church, to the purpose of the Triune God. That all three are closely inter-related reflects the varied theological perceptions and emphases of each generation and underscores the fact that the forms of obedience to God's call in mission differed in each generation of the century.

W. RICHEY HOGG

WKL, 1592–1600.

CONFESSIONALISM. The Church of Jesus Christ is divided up into 'confessions', i.e. a number of different and in part rival denominations. This is a fact which can be neither gainsaid nor disregarded. Those who have tried, like the *Disciples of Christ, to introduce a non-confessional Christianity, have usually ended by creating a new confession. A number of missions have started out as 'non-confessional' or 'inter-confessional'; but Hudson *Taylor, the founder of the *CIM, found it desirable to separate geographically his missionaries who adhered to different confessions. The *SIM seems to have in the end accepted the Baptist position.

All this is regrettable; but in practice it has caused far less harm than is generally supposed. *Hinduism, *Buddhism and *Islam are all religions divided up into innumerable sects. Africans are quite familiar with the idea that the religion of one tribe will not be quite the same as the religion of another tribe. Loyalty to one's own confession turns into confessionalism, which is always and inevitably harmful, only under the following conditions: (a) when the particular mission or denomination is so stressed in teaching that the convert becomes aware too late, or possibly never at all, of the one great Church of Jesus Christ, of which all existing denominations, including the RC, are such pale and partial reflections; (b) when such care is taken to reproduce overseas all the characteristics of a western denomination that the church necessarily becomes a foreign body in the area in which it has been newly planted; (c) when the particular confessional documents are so stressed that, for instance, the Indian or African Anglican becomes more devoted to the Thirty-nine Articles of Religion than the majority of his English or Irish brethren; (d) when the new Christian is taught to distrust, to dislike, and to despise his fellow-Christians of other confessional allegiances.

All these four conditions have been fulfilled in a great many areas of the missionary work of the church, and some of the most devoted and successful missionaries have been the most guilty in this field. The final remedy is the recovery of the full and visible unity of the church of Christ. In the meantime, certain steps can be taken. (1) Far better training of missionaries, in order that they may know something of those whom they will meet overseas, and may be delivered from the stereotypes and caricatures by which our knowledge of one another is disfigured. (2) Far better training in theological seminaries in the *younger churches, based on direct knowledge of the other Christian groups in the areas in which the students will serve. (3) Far more opportunities for Christians of different confessions to meet, to get to know one another, and to engage in joint enterprises for the glory of God. (4) The recognition that we have something to learn from one another, and that, while we have the right to provoke one another to love and to good works, any other form of provocation is excluded by the teaching of the NT.

STEPHEN NEILL

CONFESSIONS OF FAITH IN YOUNGER CHURCHES can be spoken
6

of in three ways. (1) There are preambles to church constitutions indicating the doctrinal and confessional position of a church. Most younger churches have some such formulated basis referring to the Apostles' Creed, to a catechism, e.g. the Heidelberg or Luther's Small Catechism, or to entire historical confessions. The biblical basis is confirmed throughout. Often missionaries composed new statements for their congregations, like the confession of faith of the United Basel Mission Church in South India 1937. Sometimes statements which owe their existence to the theological patronage of western missionaries are accepted as formal confessions of faith, e.g. the Statement of Faith of the Federation of Evangelical Lutheran Churches in India 1947, which attempts a united Lutheran consensus for negotiations with the CSI. The emphasis is on scriptural exposition and on a reformulation of the historical Lutheran confessions of the 16th century in the light of the church in India today. (2) The first confession of faith drawn up in an autonomous younger church by a commission of its own theologians is the confession of faith of the Batak Church, Sumatra, 1951. Historically motivated by the church's intention to join the *LWF, the confession affirms the teaching of the Reformation over against Roman Catholic and sectarian errors as well as pagan and secularist beliefs. Referring to the three ecumenical creeds, its 18 chapters expound the doctrines of God, of man and sin, of the church, and ethics and eschatology. Some influence of the Augsburg Confession is traceable in its ethics and the polemical passages (*damnamus*, 'we condemn'). The teaching on the sacraments, moulded after Luther's Small Catechism, has been agreed to by Reformed churchmen in Indonesia. This confession of faith transcends the traditional confessional positions of western Protestantism for eastern churches. In Japan the outcome of doctrinal discussions in the United Church of Christ 1954 did not produce a full confession of faith, but an exposition of the Apostles' Creed acknowledging its validity for the present church. It promises to uphold the affirmed position, but makes no reference to the situation into which the faith has to be confessed. It aims at a minimum basis of consent among the 30 member denominations of the *Kyodan*. (3) Christianity in Africa being doctrinally linked to the respective mother churches and societies tries to advance towards an indigenous formulation of doctrine, that takes account of the characteristic challenges of African life and beliefs. Topics like God, Spirit and the spirit world, sacrifice, worship and priesthood are central to the effort to confess the Christian faith relevantly (Yaoundé consultation of the 'Life of the Church' commission of the *AACC, 1965). In Asia efforts since 1961 concentrate more on 'Confessing the Faith Today' (*EACC consultation, Hong Kong 1966) than on the formulation of credal statements.

LOTHAR SCHREINER

W. F. Dankbaar: 'De ontwikkeling van de belijdenis in de jonge kerken', in *Ned. Theol. Tijdschr*. II, (1947–48); G. C. Oosthuizen: *Theological Discussions and Confessional Developments in the Churches of Asia and Africa* (Franeker 1958); A. Sovik: 'Confessions and Churches—an Afro-Asian Symposium', *Lutheran World*, V (1958–59); L. Schreiner: *Das Bekenntnis der Batak-Kirche* (München 1966).

CONFUCIANISM (in relation to Christianity). Until the Communist triumph on the mainland, Confucianism had been dominant in China for most of the 2,000 years since the 2nd century B.C. It took its name from Confucius (c.551–c.479 B.C.) and while books attributed to him were standard, it underwent many and sometimes reciprocally contradictory emphases and intepretations. Whether it is a religion or not depends largely on the definition of religion. Certainly from the close of the 14th century to the substitution of the Republic for the historical imperial structure in 1912 it had the official support of the state. The highly competitive civil service examinations through which the bureaucracy was recruited were based on the Confucian classics. The scholars who set the standards for ethics were trained in

the Confucian ideals and regarded them as the foundation of Chinese civilization. Every town or city which was the centre of a subdivision of the administrative structure of the realm had what was called a Confucian 'temple', in which the scholars including officialdom had periodic rites in honour of Confucius and the leading historic exponents of the Confucian school. The family with its ceremonies in honour of parents and ancestors was based on Confucian precepts. Under the last dynasty the regular public reading of the so-called *Sacred Edict*, a set of Confucian precepts, was required wherever a hearing could be had. The *Sacred Edict* denounced as heresies all non-Confucian religions, including Christianity.

In the 17th and 18th centuries *Jesuit missionaries sought for their converts *accommodation to Confucian ceremonies and terms but, after prolonged controversy, Rome disapproved. In the 19th century RC and most Protestant missionaries required abstinence of Christians from Confucian ceremonies, including those in honour of ancestors. Confucian scholars regarded missionaries as destructive of Chinese culture and stirred up the masses to persecution which often became violent. With the disintegration of the Confucian social and political structure in the 20th century, opposition to Christianity took other forms.

KENNETH SCOTT LATOURETTE

K. S. Latourette: *The Chinese: Their History and Culture* (4th ed., New York 1964), pp. 520–40, 558–61; *ERE* IV, 12–19.

CONGO-BRAZZAVILLE, formerly French Congo, lies to the north of the Congo river and has an area of 132,046 sq.m., and a population (1967) of 860,000, including about 10,000 Europeans. Traditional religion is still the prevailing religion, there being very few Muslims. A RC *vicariate apostolic was formed in 1890, and in 1965 there were three dioceses with 350,933 Catholics. The first Protestant missions arrived soon after 1870, and by 1965 the Protestant community had grown to 148,422. The largest denominations are *Eglise Evangélique du Congo* (served by

Mission Covenant Church of Sweden and Norwegian Covenant Mission) with 110,000, and the *Armée du Salut* (*SA) with 27,422. Two missions work in the extreme north: United World Mission, and *Eglise Baptiste de la Sangha* (Orebro Mission Society). Unlike Congo-Kinshasa to the south, the various revivals in the past have largely remained within the churches without secession, and syncretistic movements though present remain small in number of adherents.

DAVID B. BARRETT

E. Andersson: *Churches at the Grass-Roots: a Study in Congo-Brazzaville* (London 1968); *BM* II, 261–64; *NCE* IV, 165f.

CONGO-KINSHASA. The Democratic Republic of Congo occupies the major part of the basin of the C. River and a small part of the basin of the Upper Nile. It has a total area of 905,063 sq.m. with a coast-line to the Atlantic ocean of 25 miles extending north from the mouth of the C. to the Portuguese enclave of Cabinda. The southern bank of the river is Angola, with which country the C. makes common boundary to the south and south-west. On the north-west and north it is bounded by the C. Republic (Brazzaville) and the Central African Republic; on the north-east by Sudan; on the east by Uganda and Tanzania and on the south-east by Zambia. North-east of Lake Tanganyika are the territories of Rwanda and Burundi.

The physcial configuration is like a basin, of which the bottom is formed by a vast plateau with a mean altitude of 1,300 feet above sea level. The north central part of the basin between 4°N and 4°S is covered by rain forest which extends to the western and eastern boundaries. Extensive forests also occur to the north and south of the main forest. A ring of savannas and steppes surrounds the equatorial forest.

The population of almost 16 million is divided into a great variety of well over 200 tribes. Most tribes speak various *Bantu languages but in the north there are Sudanic, Nilotic and Nilo-Hamitic speakers. Numerous Pygmies are dispersed throughout the central rain forest.

In 1484 a Portuguese mariner, Diego Cão or Cau, reached the mouth of the C. River which he called *Zaire* (Kikongo *nzadi* —big water).

As early as 1490 *Franciscan missionaries were in the C., and in the following year King Nzinga was baptized. There followed the remarkable episode of the Christian kingdom of the C., under King *Affonso, whose son Don Henrique, the first African to rise to the episcopate in modern times, was consecrated titular bishop of Utica in 1519. The headquarters of the mission and of the kingdom was at San Salvador, now in northern Angola. This was made the centre of the bishopric in 1594. In 1640 the prefecture apostolic of the C. was created, and Italian *Capuchins were sent in to take charge of it; but decline followed upon prosperity, and when the modern period of missions opened, hardly anything of the old was left.

In 1865 a new start was made, when the *Holy Ghost Fathers were sent to Boma in the Lower C.; but they made no attempt to advance into the interior, and the work of penetration from the Atlantic coast was left to the Protestant missionaries.

On 9 August 1877 Henry Morton Stanley reached Boma on the estuary after having followed the Congo River from its source. The following year Stanley agreed to return to C. in the service of King Leopold II of the Belgians, acting as president of the International African Association. During the Berlin Conference in 1885 the IAA was recognized by all major powers and on 1 July 1885 the founding of the C. Free State was proclaimed at Banana with Leopold II, in his personal capacity, as sovereign. It was not until 20 August 1908 that the C. Free State passed under the control of the Belgian parliament.

The first serious attempt to enter the C. region from the east was made by French *White Fathers. In view of the strong preference of Leopold II for Belgian missionaries in his territories, Cardinal *Lavigerie formed a Belgian wing of his order of White Fathers, and to these the vicariate of the Upper C. was entrusted on its formation in 1888. Immediately on taking over control of the territory Leopold had directed an appeal to the *CICM, with headquarters at Scheutveld, to send him missionaries for the C.; this order was able to send in its first representatives only in 1885, but the work increased so rapidly that in 1912 the Scheutists had in the C. a larger staff than all the other RC missions combined. Belgian *Jesuits came in 1890 and were given the prefecture apostolic of Kwango east of Kinshasa. They were followed by almost all the RC missionary orders and sisterhoods, until the C. showed greater variety in RC operations than any other area in the world.

The RC missions, especially those with headquarters in Belgium, were much favoured by the government, which had to tolerate but did not approve of the presence of Protestant missions. In spite of this progress in the early days was slow, and was naturally gravely hampered by the German occupation of Belgium from 1914 to 1918. The first ordination of a Congolese priest took place only in 1917. It was reckoned that in 1921 there were 350,000 RCs in the entire area. The first Congolese bishop was consecrated in 1956. The hierarchy, with six archbishoprics and 34 bishoprics, was set up, just on the eve of Congolese independence, in 1959; the majority of bishops are still foreigners, but the proportion is constantly changing to the advantage of the African.

Helped by the government, and by the fact that the great majority of its missionaries were of French language, the RC church was able to make greater progress than the Protestants. It is reckoned that two-thirds of all the school-going children in the country are in RC schools. In many missions it was the custom to baptize children in the fourth year of school attendance; but it was noticed that from 60% to 80% of the children thus baptized ceased to attend church within a matter of months; it is now not taken for granted that the schools can be used so directly as a means for the increase of the church. The crown of the RC educational system is the Lovanium University in the neighbourhood of Kinshasa, which after a long period of preparation received legal recognition in 1949. With more than 1,200 students from many nations, and a theological faculty, Lovanium is perhaps the leading academic institution in French-speaking Africa.

The first Protestant missionaries to enter the C. were George *Grenfell and Thomas J. Comber of the BMS. Their first visit in January 1878 lasted less than three weeks, but when they returned in July they laid the foundations of the extensive work of the BMS in both C. and Angola. In February 1878 Henry Craven of the Livingstone Inland Mission disembarked at Banana and a short time later founded the first mission station at Palabala. In 1885 the LIM handed over its work to the American Baptist Missionary Union (later the ABFMS) and the *Svenska Missionsförbundet* (Covenant Church). The former advanced into the interior, establishing work in the Kwango and on the C. River as well as in the Lower C., while the latter society limited its work to the area north of Matadi. Another mission to grow indirectly out of the LIM was the C. Balolo Mission which in 1888 selected for its sphere of work the six southern tributaries of the C. beyond Equatorville (Mbandaka), the most inland station of the LIM. In 1885 a party of men, women and children sent out by the Methodist Episcopal Church in the USA arrived in C. to establish work on a self-support basis. The experiment was not successful and all the missionaries of this society had left C. by 1898. The first six missions to enter the C. did so from the Atlantic coast. At the end of January 1886, however, Frederick Stanley *Arnot, a member of the Plymouth Brethren, entered the country from the south-east and began work in the Garenganze country (now known by its Arab name, Katanga). The International Missionary Alliance (later the *CMA) began work on the northern bank of the estuary in 1885 and the American Presbyterian Congo Mission (Presbyterian Church, US) in the Kasai in 1890. In 1897 the Disciples of Christ in the USA entered the region around Mbandaka and in 1910 the Methodist Episcopal Churches, both north and south, commenced work in the Katanga and among the Batetela tribe respectively. The American Mennonite Churches arrived in the Kasai in 1911, while the hitherto neglected region of north-east C. was entered by the *AIM in 1912 and by the Heart of Africa Mission in 1913. The British Pentecostalists (Congo Evangelistic Mission) began to evangelize the Upper Lualaba in 1915. In 1918 there were still large areas of the country not yet effectively occupied by Protestant missions. Into these regions came yet more societies, American, British and Scandinavian, so that in the two decades between the two world wars the number of Protestant missions more than doubled. The *Salvation Army started work in 1934. By 1960 there were almost 50 missionary societies at work.

In spite of the number and variety of missions a remarkable spirit of co-operation existed almost from the beginning and a spirit of *comity ruled inter-mission relationships. The First United Missionary Conference in the Congo was held on 18 January 1902, and attended by 34 missionaries; every missionary society was represented except one. Between 1902 and 1924 nine such conferences were held. These gatherings were meetings of missionaries, not of mission societies. At the 1924 conference, however, a constitution for a new body, the Congo Protestant Council, which missionary societies were to be invited to join, was adopted. On 14 May 1925 the CPC came into being with the two-fold object of carrying on the work of the missionary conferences and of encouraging unity and co-operation in the work of Protestant Evangelical Missions in the conventional basin of the C. In 1934, following a series of conferences in different parts of the country under the chairmanship of Dr John R. *Mott, it was resolved that all Protestant churches should adopt a common name, the Church of Christ in the Congo, the name of the mission with which the church was connected being added as a sub-title. In 1961 the CPC became a Council

of Churches with which missions are linked as associate members. The first Congolese General Secretary was appointed in 1962.

Since 1960 almost all the missions have given autonomy to the churches connected with them, while at the same time continuing to help with funds and the recruitment and support of missionary personnel. In many instances all mission property has been transferred to the church.

The obstacles to the spread of the gospel in C. have been considerable. The work of the pioneer missionaries was hampered by adverse climatic conditions, difficulty of transportation, the absence of a written language and, not infrequently, the hostility of the people. In spite of many initial setbacks the work flourished. School-chapels were built in thousands of villages, medical care was provided, and literature prepared and printed in scores of languages. Beginning in 1948 when government subsidies became available to missions other than those with their headquarters in Belgium the educational work of the missions expanded greatly. In 1964–65 there were 278,064 pupils in 1,774 Protestant primary schools subsidized by the government and 11,001 students in 90 aided secondary schools. Most of the rural primary schools, with a student population far greater than that of the aided schools, are financed entirely by the churches. A Protestant-inspired university was opened in Kisangani in 1963. Protestant missions have also made a significant contribution to the country's health services. Hospitals, in both rural and urban centres, an extensive network of rural dispensaries, training schools for nurses and midwives, leprosariums, research in sleeping sickness and other endemic diseases, public health programmes, have all helped to meet the physical needs of the people. More recently, and often in connection with aid programmes to help Angolan, Sudanese and other refugees, agricultural projects have been undertaken.

After the second world war the C. was caught up in the fever of nationalism which was sweeping across Africa. Attempts to create autonomy for the C. in association with Belgium came to nothing, and on 30 June 1960 the complete independence of C. was proclaimed. This was followed by five years of grave disorder, with rapid changes of government at the centre, rebellion and civil war in many areas, and almost complete economic stagnation. Destruction of property was on the largest scale. Twenty-four Protestant missionaries lost their lives, and probably about 160 RCs; a much larger number of Congolese church leaders and Christians perished, especially where the rebellion was under the direction of Chinese, who carried out their policy of the systematic extermination of all elements of leadership among the people. Thousands of missionaries had to leave their stations, and there was grave disruption of every aspect of the work.

In spite of all the difficulties the rate of Christian progress has appeared to accelerate rather than to decline.

The RCs now claim a membership of six million, with numerous catechumens, amounting to about 40% of the population. This appears to be exaggerated; but it is difficult to come by accurate statistics, and many claim the name Christian, who have only the most rudimentary connection with the church. The number of adherents is certainly very large. One weakness in the RC work is that there are only 3,000 priests for this immense territory, and that of these considerably less than a third are nationals.

Progress in the Protestant missions has also been very rapid. The WCH for 1968 gives the total Christian community as 2,105,000; this, however, is possibly an underestimate, since many of the Protestant missions list only full members; it is likely that the figure should be three million rather than two. In these churches ordained Congolese outnumber ordained foreigners by three to one; here again the proportion should probably be even higher, since the term 'ordination' is used in very varying senses in the different missions. At the Annual Assembly of the CPC in 1966 it was agreed to launch a two-year nation-wide 'evangelism in depth' campaign under the slogan 'Christ for all'. Converts continue to be won for the Protestant churches in very large numbers.

One of the happiest features of the new situation is the much improved relationship between Roman Catholics and Christians of other persuasions; in the past tensions have at times been very severe. In the time of the troubles Kisangani (Stanleyville) was in the hands of the rebels, and it was impossible for the new Protestant university to continue its work. The authorities of the Lovanium offered to provide a temporary home for the Protestant teachers and students.

*Islam is almost unknown in C., except in the north-east of the country. But the country has been prolific in the production of *African independent churches. The largest, the 'Church of Jesus Christ upon the earth through the prophet Simon *Kimbangu' claims close on a million adherents, and has applied for membership of the *WCC. Missionary opinion regarding these independent churches is very much divided. The leaders themselves claim that this is an authentic African form of Christianity, neither RC nor Protestant, arising out of a genuine African attempt to hear the Word of God as spoken through the Scriptures and through his prophet.

H. F. DRAKE AND EDITORS

C. P. Groves: *The Planting of Christianity in Africa* (London 1955), Vol. III; H. H. Johnston: *George Grenfell and the Congo* (London 1908); A. B. Keith: *The Belgian Congo and the Berlin Act* (London 1919); E. Laveille: *L'Evangile au centre de l'Afrique* (Louvain 1926); R. M. Slade: *English-Speaking Missions in the Congo Independent State* (Brussels 1959), *King Leopold's Congo: Aspects of the Development of Race-relations in the Congo* (London 1962); *BM* II, 264–79; *NCE* IV, 166–68; *WKL*, 143–45.

CONGREGATION FOR THE PROPAGATION OF THE FAITH. See PROPAGANDA, SACRED CONGREGATION OF.

CONGREGATION OF THE IMMACULATE HEART OF MARY, THE, (CICM)

was founded in Belgium in 1862 and has its central house in Scheut, near Brussels (hence the popular names 'Scheut' and 'Scheutists'). It is a religious congregation of priests and brothers, which has as its principal task to preach the gospel and to plant the church among non-Christian peoples, and also to serve the *younger churches, and even older churches, where the mission situation still exists. It depends directly on the Sacred *Congregation for the Propagation of the Faith in Rome.

The society was founded by Théophile Verbist, a priest from the archdiocese of Mechlin who died in N. China (1868). It has been active in evangelization and social work in China, mainly in Inner Mongolia. It was also among the first to be sent to what is now Congo-Kinshasa and, after 1900, to the Philippines. The CICM has now about 2,000 members, of whom some 1,400 are working in 12 countries all over the world; 742 in the Republic of Congo-Kinshasa alone. During the first decades, practically all the members were either Belgian or Dutch. Now the congregation has also novitiates in the USA, the Philippines and the Congo.

V. RONDELEZ, CICM

V. Rondelez, CICM: *Scheut, Congrégation Missionaire. Ses Origines—Ses Débuts* (Brussels 1960).

CONGREGATIONAL COUNCIL FOR WORLD MISSION. See LONDON MISSIONARY SOCIETY.

CONGREGATIONAL MISSIONS. The enthusiasm of Congregationalists for 'missions' stems directly from evangelical convictions, (a) that man needs redemption; (b) that Jesus Christ came that *all* men might be redeemed.

These convictions obviously have not been characteristic of Congregationalists only. They were shared in the earliest days of American history by other Christians, especially Baptists. Another conviction which Congregationalists and Baptists have had in common is that missions could best be promoted and conducted by societies organized for that purpose. The 'church' ecclesiastically speaking, as such, has not formed a vital part of their theory or practice of missions. Contrariwise, the 'churches', local, *autonomous churches, bound together potentially in fellowship by common aims and methods, through elected representatives, formed societies or boards charged with the conduct of missions overseas and at home.

Thus it came about that Thomas Mayhew (1621–1657) on Martha's Vineyard and John *Eliot (1604–1690) in Massachusetts cried aloud in the wilderness, preaching the gospel to American Indians within reach. Thus it came about that a small group of Spirit-led young men at Williams College gave expression to their smouldering meditations and discussions, inspired by the current revival in New England, by lighting a torch for 'missions' with the flaming words 'We can if we will'. They appealed to the Congregational ministers of Massachusetts, who followed their instincts and appealed through a group of 'Commissioners', not to the church, for they did not recognize a church, but to the members of the local, autonomous churches, to implement the new-born passion for evangelization of the heathen abroad.

The creative genius and influence of the Rev. Rufus *Anderson, DD (chief secretary of the *ABCFM, 1832–1866) set the pattern of the working relationship between the Congregational churches of America and the churches overseas. He originated the phrase (possibly in collaboration with the Rev. Henry *Venn of the *CMS) 'self-governing, self-supporting and self-propagating churches', not to be episcopally controlled. This policy of *indigenization on all levels has characterized Congregational missions throughout their history and operations. Many concrete examples could be cited (see R. Anderson: *Foreign Missions: Their Relations and Claims* New York 1869).

'Congregational missions', *home* missions, as well as *foreign* missions, followed the non-episcopal pattern of the American Board for the conduct of missions until

1913, when sufficient momentum for remote control of the growing number of their missionary societies, by the National Council of Congregational Churches, developed and took form at the 1913 Kansas City, Kansas, meeting. This registered the growing desire of Congregationalists as a national body to 'control' their agencies in evangelism and social action, especially for Negroes and Asians.

Since 1913, in spite of vigorous opposition in some quarters, the majority of Congregational ministers and interested laymen and laywomen have pressed for centralized control and operation of missionary enterprises. A climax was reached in 1959–1961 when all the missionary societies and social service agencies of the Congregational Christian Churches and of the *Evangelical and Reformed Church (Presbyterian in polity) were united and made constitutionally subject to the authority of the General Synod of the newly formed *United Church of Christ.

The verdict of history remains to be rendered as to whether the virtual surrender of the principle of free enterprise in 'missions' will impede or promote the cause of Congregational missions.

See also LONDON MISSIONARY SOCIETY.

FRED FIELD GOODSELL

G. G. Atkins and F. L. Fagley: *History of American Congregationalism* (Boston 1942); F. F. Goodsell: *You Shall be My Witnesses* (Boston 1959), *They Lived Their Faith, an Almanac of Faith, Hope and Love* (Boston 1961).

CONTINENTAL EUROPEAN MISSIONS CONFERENCE. The CEMC, the first large-scale effort towards missionary co-operation across international boundaries, had its origin in Dr F. Fabri's conviction, shared by some other 19th century mission leaders, that closer co-operation between non-Anglo-Saxon missions was desirable, and that experts had to point the way. The first meeting was held at Bremen in 1866. Eleven more meetings were to follow till 1909, all of them taking place at Bremen, seat of the *North German Mis-

sionary Society. After *Edinburgh 1910, continuation of the CEMC appeared unnecessary. While participation in the various meetings varied, the CEMC had proved itself as a remarkably useful platform for joint thinking and planning in European missions, even during and after the outbreak of German colonial enthusiasm in the 1880s. Lectures and minutes were published. They provide even now a valuable source for missiological research. The CEMC not only 'represented the most important development in home-base missionary co-operation that had been seen to that time' (W. R. Hogg) but also helped to pave the way for future co-operative efforts on a large scale.

H.-W. GENSICHEN

CONTINUITY AND DISCONTINUITY. There are two major traditions in the history of Christian thought concerning the relation between Christian revelation and the non-Christian religions, between Christian faith and other faiths.

One tradition, while recognizing the *uniqueness and universality of Jesus Christ, emphasizes the *continuity* of God's revealing and redeeming activity in Christ with his activity among all men everywhere. It views Christian faith as the climax of a divine revelation which began long before human history and has been available to everyone. Jesus Christ, in this view, is crucial, normative and definitive, but not exclusive. What is true of Jesus Christ in a focal way, is pervasively true of the whole cosmos. He is the key or clue to the rest of God's working. But the Word of God is not limited to the revelation in the historic person of Jesus.

There is much biblical and patristic testimony in support of this view. John's Gospel affirms that the same light which was in Jesus enlightens every man (Jn.1:1–9). Paul said that a thousand years before the birth of Jesus, 'Christ' was with the Israelites in their wanderings in Sinai (1 Cor.10:4). And Acts 14:17 assures us that 'God did not leave himself without witness' even among those who knew none of the biblical revelation. In this view, the *logos spermatikos* is active everywhere, sowing seeds of truth, and thus preparing the way for the gospel. Justin Martyr went so far as to say that before Jesus was born 'those who lived according to reason are Christians; even though they have been thought atheists; as among the Greeks, Socrates and Heraclitus and men like them' (I *Apology*, ch.46).

Recent contributions to this tradition would include Paul Tillich's concept of 'the *latent church' and the *Jesuit Karl Rahner's thought about 'the anonymous presence of God' in the non-Christian world.

The other tradition, quite to the contrary, believes there is a radical *discontinuity* between the realm of Christian revelation, which is absolutely unique, and the whole range of non-Christian religious experience. In this view the non-Christian religions are the various efforts of man to apprehend his existence, whereas Christianity is the result of the self-disclosure of God in Jesus Christ. God has spoken to mankind only in the person of Jesus Christ and 'there is salvation in no one else' (Acts 4:12). The most forceful exposition of this position in modern times came from the writings of Hendrik *Kraemer based on the theology of Karl Barth.

Many theologians today believe that the debate over continuity and discontinuity has come to an impasse, and that instead of starting with the concept of revelation and the doctrine of God, the real point of contact between Christian and non-Christian is in their common humanity.

See also LATENT CHURCH CONCEPT; REVELATION, CHRISTIAN AND NON-CHRISTIAN.

GERALD H. ANDERSON

The Authority of the Faith, Vol. I in the Tambaram Series (London 1939); A. C. Bouquet: *The Christian Faith and Non-Christian Religions* (London 1958); E. C. Dewick: *The Christian Attitude to Other Religions* (Cambridge 1953); H. Kraemer: *Religion and the Christian Faith* (London 1956).

CONVERSION. In a critical moment Paul defined his mission as: 'to bring you good news that you should turn from these vain
6*

things to serve a living God' (Acts 14:15). This conversion of men is the purpose of mission. It is also a point of acute controversy. Gandhi was typical of many, not only in India, in deploring all attempts to convert men to another faith. The fact that the work of C. has, at sundry times and places, been mixed up with political and cultural aggression, organizational rivalry, and the use of worldly means, has made the word itself suspect. Societies in which religion is a strong cultural bond see C. to another faith as a threat to the stability of society. In spite of the growth of the idea of the secular society, and of the provisions of the UN declaration on religious *liberty, there are still many obstacles to the free change of religious allegiance. There are also many Christians who deplore the desire to convert others to Christianity.

In the OT the call to return (be converted) is repeatedly sounded by the prophets. It is a call to return to the LORD, and to the obligations of his covenant. The same call is sounded by John the Baptist, but here it is in the context of the coming Messiah, and accompanied by the visible sign of C., namely baptism. Jesus accepted the baptism of John as the point of inauguration of his own ministry, and sounded a like call to repentance. This call was made concrete by his calling to himself of particular men whom he bound to himself in a close community. To this community he at once began to teach the kind of behaviour that was appropriate to the new relationship with God (Matt.5:7). The call to be turned to Jesus thus included (1) a personal relation to him; (2) a visible community; (3) a pattern of behaviour. The same three elements are to be seen in the earliest beginnings of the apostolic preaching.

The relation of the first to the other two elements is a complex one, and had been the occasion of controversy from the beginning. Thus there was controversy about whether the Gentile converts were to be totally incorporated into Judaic Christianity, being circumcised like Jewish proselytes. The decision not to do this was a drastic break with precedent; converts were not to be mere proselytes; C. was a new work of the Holy Spirit, breaking old patterns (Acts 11:15–18). Nevertheless the new converts were firmly attached to the visible fellowship through baptism. The question what pattern of behaviour was to be demanded of new converts was similarly complex. The decision taken at the so-called Council of Jerusalem (Acts 15:28f.) included food laws which have not remained binding on subsequent generations of Gentile Christians. The question whether missionaries have the right to demand of converts the renunciation of—for example—*caste, *polygamy, alcohol, dancing, traditional dress, has been debated in one form or another wherever missions have worked.

The inner turning of the heart and will to Christ must neither be separated from, nor identified with, membership in the visible community and commitment to the pattern of behaviour. Thus: (1a) C. in the NT is never a purely inward experience, but always leads immediately to commitment to the visible fellowship; but (1b) the existing community does not simply absorb the convert—on the contrary, that which the Holy Spirit has accomplished in the convert must be permitted to change the existing community. Similarly, (2a) the Bible knows of no C. which is an internal emotional experience apart from a turning round to behave in a different way; but, (2b) C. does not mean the imposition of a new law—on the contrary, the gift of the Holy Spirit is freedom from law to serve God as he directs.

In this complex relationship there is much room for controversy, the circumcision controversy of the 1st century, the *Rites controversy of the 17th, and the controversy over *Industrial Mission in the 20th are illustrations of the fact that good men will differ on these matters.

Perhaps much confusion about C. has arisen because the original meaning of the call to 'repent and believe' has been forgotten. This call was given in the context of the announcement of the coming of the kingdom of God. It is a call to turn round in order to participate in this new reality.

C. to Christ is being turned round, by the action of the Holy Spirit, so as to participate with him, in the fellowship of his people, in the work of his kingdom. In its very nature it involves a commitment to action. Where C. has been thought of as something directed only to the salvation of the individual soul, the true biblical perspective has been lost.

Christians have committed many sins in the name of C. of which they should repent. But where C. is no longer sought and expected, Christianity has ceased to be a living faith.

LESSLIE NEWBIGIN

R. Allen: *Missionary Methods, St. Paul's or Ours?* (London 1912); P. Beyerhaus and H. Lefever: *The Responsible Church and Foreign Mission* (London 1964); P. Löffler: 'Conversion' (Paper for the World Council of Churches, Geneva, n.d.); A. D. Nock: *Conversion* (London 1933); A. C. Underwood: *Conversion, Christian and Non-Christian* (London 1925); *ERE* IV, 104–10; *NCE* IV, 256–92.

CONVERTS, TRAINING OF. In no field is there greater difference between the practice of various churches and missions than in the methods adopted for the training of enquirers, and the length of time required as preparation for baptism. RC missions have generally followed a policy of rapid baptism, reckoning that the process of genuine christianization can take place after baptism within the church rather than outside it. But in certain areas the *White Fathers have insisted on a period of four years' probation before baptism can be administered. On the Protestant side, the Methodist Episcopal mission in India, faced with a widespread *mass movement among the 'untouchables', held that baptism cannot be refused to those who desire it, and that Christian instruction should follow rather than precede baptism. Most missions expect to see some evidences of a change of heart in the enquirer; but on what principles is it to be determined whether this has taken place or not? If baptism is too long delayed, the enquirer is likely to lose interest, and to be seen no more, or to go over to another mission which makes less exacting demands. And no human eye can see into the recesses of the human spirit.

In the Protestant world there is general agreement that instruction should be based on the Lord's Prayer, the Creed and the Ten Commandments, to which most would add some teaching on the life of Christ, and instruction as to the meaning of Christian marriage and as to the responsibility of the Christian for the support of the church. The RC missions tend to concentrate more on the catechism, and on the rules and ceremonies of the church.

In many areas it has been found convenient to divide the preparation into three stages: (1) preparation for the catechumenate; this involved at least rejection of the non-Christian past; (2) preparation for baptism, including instruction of the kind outlined above; (3) preparation for confirmation or for full membership of the church, with fuller instruction in Christian duties and in biblical truth. Others, however, feel that this is a mistake, and that baptism, as the sacrament of initiation, should immediately be followed by admission to Holy Communion, and to all the privileges of the believer. It is certain that uniformity will never be reached, and that there must be many exceptions to all rules.

There is need for deeper study of the theological principles involved. Closer agreement between various missions working in the same area is much to be desired. G. *Warneck devotes 46 pages to the subject in his *Evangelische Missionslehre*, Section III, Part II (1900) pp.232–77; but remarks sardonically that 'at the great missionary conferences mainly under English direction, this subject seems hardly ever mentioned in the literature on the theory of missions'. There has been some improvement in this century, but there is great need for systematic and comparative study of the subject.

See also CATECHUMENATE.

STEPHEN NEILL

COOK ISLANDS. See PACIFIC ISLANDS.

CO-OPERATION marks Protestant missions from the beginning. Thus the officers of the *SPCK in London early in the 18th century served as forwarding agents and helpers to the *Danish-Halle men at Tranquebar and later took over the support of those missionaries working outside Danish territory. Until the American Revolution the New England Company of London and the Society in Scotland for Propagating Christian Knowledge jointly supported some of the missions to American Indians. Individuals co-operated across denominational lines to form the *LMS in 1795; and in the USA Presbyterian, Reformed, and Associate Reformed denominations officially founded the United Foreign Missionary Society in 1817. Important auxiliary services were created by individual joint action, notably the Bible and Tract societies. Although the informal London Secretaries' Association was formed in 1819 and executives widely shared information and worked for a common policy, effective home base co-operation was slow in developing and had eventually to be stimulated from the field. A considerable amount of joint effort went into the great popular *conferences from 1854 (New York and London) to 1900 (Ecumenical Missionary Conference at New York).

Pioneer missionaries in port cities aided newcomers in many ways, including selection of sites. This led to *comity and comity required agreement about boundaries, standards of membership, transfer of workers, and many practical matters. Comity arbitration and the need to share knowledge led to regional and national conferences (see REGIONAL AGENCIES, and MISSION COUNCILS), and out of these came the continuing *National Missionary Councils and Conferences, such as India, 1912. Occasionally two or more missions fostered a single national church, e.g. the English Presbyterians and the Reformed Church in America at Amoy China, in the 1850s. Actual united missions are a late development: United Mission to Iraq (three USA boards, 1922), United Andean Indian Mission, Ecuador (four USA boards, 1946), and the United Mission to Nepal (broadly interdenominational and international, 1953). Union Bible translation committees were frequent from the outset, and co-operative organs for literature were founded, such as the Society for the Diffusion of Christian and General Knowledge (later CLS) in China, 1887. Co-operation in functional ministries brought union institutions, especially in education and medicine. Colleges were most numerous, there being 20 in 1934. They include *Madras (1876), Hislop at Nagpur (1884), Lignan at Canton (1886), Shantung (1904, later Cheloo). Early medical colleges include Peking (1906), Tsinan (1910), Mukden (1912), and *Vellore (1918). There were in 1934 at least 13 major union hospitals. Normal schools were frequently union institutions, such as St. Christopher's Training College, Madras (1923), and these numbered 11 in 1934. Union high schools were founded in almost every field. Professional societies for mutual strengthening of ministry were created, such as the China Christian Education Association (1890) with its nine regional associations and the Christian Medical Missionary Association of India.

The *Edinburgh Conference of 1910 greatly stimulated co-operation along all lines. At that time the only national missionary councils were the German *Ausschuss* ('Committee' 1885, reorganized 1897) and the *Foreign Missions Conference of North America (1893). The single attempt at an international ecumenical body before 1910 was the *World's Missionary Committee of Christian Women formed after the Centennial Conference, London, 1888. The Edinburgh Conference created a Continuation Committee, and primarily through the efforts of its chairman, John R. *Mott, numerous western National Missionary Conferences and National Continuation Committees or Missionary Conferences were founded (see MISSION COUNCILS). These in due course became *National Christian Councils. Out of the Edinburgh Continuation Committee there eventually came in 1921 the *IMC with the many National Missionary Conferences and National

Christian Councils as constituent members. The IMC in 1961 merged with the *WCC as the *Division of World Mission and Evangelism. A vast global system of co-operation in study, consultation, formation of common policy, and the financing of field programmes developed under the IMC-DWME and the inter-action of its member councils. The *Orphaned Missions Fund, the *TEF, and similar special programmes are among its achievements. At the New Delhi meeting in 1961 a call went forth for more thorough-going total regional action in the proposal for 'Joint Action for Mission'. Regional organs for co-operation are now developing, notably the *EACC and the *AACC (see REGIONAL AGENCIES FOR CO-OPERATION). Some other ecumenical functional bodies exist for co-operation, such as the *World Council of Christian Education (founded as the World's Sunday School Association in 1889).

See also CONFERENCES, MISSIONARY; CONFERENCES, WORLD MISSIONARY; ROMAN CATHOLIC-PROTESTANT MISSIONARY RELATIONSHIPS.

R. PIERCE BEAVER

R. P. Beaver: *Ecumenical Beginnings in Protestant World Mission: a History of Comity* (New York 1962); C. H. Fahs and H. E. Davis: *Conspectus of Co-operative Missionary Enterprises* (New York 1935); W. R. Hogg: *Ecumenical Foundations* (New York 1952); R. Rouse and S. C. Neill, eds.: *History of the Ecumenical Movement* (2nd ed., New York 1967); H. P. Van Dusen: *One Great Ground of Hope* (New York 1961).

COPTIC CHURCH. See EASTERN CHURCHES, LESSER OR SEPARATED.

CORRESPONDENCE COURSES (INDIA). Bible correspondence is a method of teaching through the mail. A Gospel portion containing a sheet of questions and answer blanks is sold or given. The recipient reads the portion, answers the questions, and mails the completed sheet to a correspondence office where it is corrected. The sheet, together with another set of lessons, is then returned to the student. This postal tuition continues until the student completes the Gospel and receives a certificate indicating he has passed the course.

Bible correspondence courses are based ordinarily on a particular book, whose basic theme guides the arrangement of lesson material. Course names which illustrate themes are: The Kingdom of Heaven—Matthew; The Kingdom of God—Mark; Good News—Luke; and Light of Life—John.

Advantages of Bible correspondence are: students are able to progress privately and at their own pace. The method is inexpensive—one office serves an entire language area. Follow-up is simple. One method is on-the-spot camps for correspondents in those areas where the office indicates a substantial index of interest.

Further information may be obtained from: Box 66, Vellore, N.A., South India; Light of Life, Chalisgaon, East Khandesh, India; The Voice of Prophecy, P.O. 55, L.A., California, USA; John H. Piet, Western Theological Seminary, Holland, Michigan, USA.

JOHN H. PIET

CORRESPONDENCE COURSES (JAPAN).
In countries where literacy is common, a method employed in the teaching of the Christian faith is the correspondence course.

Such courses generally are of two types. One consists of simple Bible instruction with notes on the portion set and a question, which the student is invited to answer and send in to his instructor. The other type is of a more ambitious character, and is designed especially for enquirers who by reason of distance are unable to share in the life of the Christian community, and who may have no previous knowledge of the Christian religion. This kind of course was first worked out in connection with the method of Newspaper Evangelism employed in Japan.

The course consists of five main sections covering 20 weeks. Each day's study consists of a prayer, a Bible portion, an exposition of the same and a question for meditation. At the end of each week comes a series of questions which the correspondent is invited to answer and send in to the instructor for comment, etc., after which the next week's portion is sent.

The first section consists of a discussion as to the nature of God. The second section is a series covering several weeks of the character of Jesus Christ, his joy, his sympathy, his courage, his love, etc., at the end of which is posed the question 'What think ye of Christ?' It is of interest to note that in every case a student who reached thus far gave an answer similar to that of Peter in Matt.16:16. The third section is concerned with the cross, redemption and the experience of conversion; while the fourth section deals with Christian life and witness. The final week's study is on baptism, the service and its significance; by which time an introduction has been effected to the nearest Christian minister regardless of distance.

W. H. MURRAY WALTON

COSMIC DIMENSION OF CHRISTIAN MISSIONS.
The Bible speaks of the cosmos in two ways: (1) the cosmos is the earth and human habitation, and (2) the cosmos is the universe or sum of all created beings. Both understandings are relevant to this topic.

(1) The concept of cosmic *redemption as related to the earth is one dimension of the OT and NT doctrine of divine redemption. The Hebrew writers did not offer a systematic account of the relationship of God to the world. This was unnecessary since a primary assumption of faith was that the transcendent God was pervasively present and active throughout the world. All created things were good since they came from a benevolent Creator. Through the disobedience of man the whole creation was affected. Therefore God's judgment was expressed through physical disaster as well as through moral consequences (Amos 4:6–13). Israel's faith was essentially a redemptive faith, and when the judgment of God was viewed as being directed to nature as well as to man, it was logical that the doctrine of redemption should be extended

to cover the physical processes also. This is seen in the apocalyptic literature where any naturalistic optimism is checked with the thorough-going judgment of God, and simultaneously this is balanced with the picture of the whole creation once more redeemed. The highest expression of cosmic redemption regarding the earth is found in Isaiah 11:6–9 where the prophet sees a reconciliation between animals (vv.6–7), between man and animals (v.8), and between all aspects of creation (v.9). Like the OT, the NT does not treat the doctrine of cosmic redemption systematically. The exorcisms of Jesus point to the presence of God's kingdom in power. Natural power is subservient to God's power in the kingdom. To Paul 'this world' was a nexus of powers which threatened the life of the natural order. In his missionary encounter with the Gentile world, Paul announced that in Christ the world had been reconciled to God (1 Cor.5:19). Implicit in the NT message is the conviction that God's redemptive love for man is also a concern for the cosmic or natural context in which man lives his life. The Christian proclamation to this world is that in Christ man has been set free from bondage to any powers of the natural order; the natural order itself is subservient to Christ. This is essential for the Christian witness to persons of animistic background. The Christian is freed to live in the natural order as God had intended, for the natural order is God's creation redeemed through Christ.

(2) Cosmos is also understood as the sum of all created things. It is impossible to give an integrated statement of NT cosmology, but under the threat of Gnosticism the early Christian writers had to give attention to a view of the world which was considerably expanded. The author of Colossians argues that Christ reigns supreme over all powers and in him God has reconciled 'all things to himself whether on earth or in heaven' (1:20). Supporting this is the conviction that the same redemptive Christ was the eternally pre-existent One who was the divine agent in creation and hence has power over all spheres of the creation. His

redeeming love therefore has no spatial limits.

In the 'space age' the question arises: If intelligent species should be discovered on other planets, what is the relation of the Christ-event to these beings? The cosmic dimension of redemption leads the Christian to the conclusion that even the furthest parts of the universe are within the scope of God's redeeming purpose. In a new 'space age' the whole cosmic expanse will still need faith in the Creator God who acted in Christ to set man free from the cosmic powers for a new relationship with him.

JAMES C. LOGAN

W. Andersen: *Jesus Christus und der Kosmos* (Bad Salzuflen 1963); A. B. Come: 'The Cosmic Dimension of the Mission of the Church', *Significant Papers*, No. 3, COEMAR (New York 1962); A. D. Galloway: *The Cosmic Christ* (New York 1951); H. Sasse: 'Kosmos' in G. Kittel, ed.: *Theological Dictionary of the New Testament*, Vol. III (Grand Rapids 1965); H. Schlier: *Principalities and Powers in the New Testament* (New York 1962); J. Sittler: 'Called to Unity', *Ecumenical Review*, XIV, 1962.

COSTA RICA. See AMERICA, CENTRAL.

COX, MELVILLE BEVERIDGE (1799–1833), was born in Hallowell, Maine, USA, of farmer parents. He served as a Methodist minister in Exeter, New Hampshire, and Raleigh, Virginia, contracted tuberculosis in 1825 and tried to support himself as manager of a book store and editor of a weekly paper, being too weak to preach. He married in 1828, but his wife died in 1830. Incredible as it may seem, the Methodist Episcopal Church accepted him, suffering from tuberculosis, as their first missionary to Africa. He arrived in Liberia on 8 March 1833, on 12 April he had the 'African fever' and on 21 July he died, after having made arrangements for his funeral.

Before he died he made wise and comprehensive plans for the future of the

Liberian church, including an academic-industrial school in Monrovia. The plans were followed for decades. He made a survey of the religious situation in the city, started a Sunday school and called a conference where he regularized the local ministry to conform with Methodist usage. His ministry paved the way for further missionary service by his church, which never forgot what he said to a friend: 'Let a thousand fall before Africa be given up'.

PER HASSING

G. F. Cox: *Remains of Melville B. Cox* (New York 1840).

CREEDS. See CONFESSIONS OF FAITH.

CRIPPS, ARTHUR SHEARLY (1869–1952), was born in Tunbridge Wells, Kent, England, son of W. C. and Catherine C. Cripps; educated at Trinity College, Oxford (BA 1891; MA 1897); was assistant curate of Icklesham, Sussex, 1892–1894; Vicar of Ford End, Essex, 1894–1900; Anglican missionary in Rhodesia from 1901; he accepted an appointment at Ford End, Essex, 1926, but returned to Rhodesia in 1930 to live in semi-retirement on his own mission farm *Maronda Mashanu* (The Five Wounds) near Enkeldoorn.

A sensitive poet, he was a member of the Poetry Society, England, and won the Oxford University Sacred Poem Prize in 1902 and 1926. He published a number of books, several of them poetry; one of them, *Africa Verses*, came out in 1939. C. was a great champion of the rights, especially the land rights, of the Rhodesian Africans. He saw them being deprived of their land by European settlers and advocated the setting aside of ample, unalienable land for them. He was a spokesman for their cause in government offices, in Rhodesian and London newspapers, in the Southern Rhodesia Missionary Conference, and in his book *An Africa for Africans*, 1927. He was a self-sacrificing, humble servant, greatly respected and loved by all.

PER HASSING

A. S. Cripps: *The Sabi Reserve. A Southern Rhodesian Native Problem* (Oxford 1920), *Lyra Evangelistica: Missionary Verses of Mashonaland* (Oxford 1911).

CROWTHER, SAMUEL ADJAI (c. 1806–1891). Born in Yoruba country (W. Nigeria), he was captured by slave raiders in 1821 but rescued from a slave ship by the British Navy in 1822. Landed at Freetown, Sierra Leone, he was educated by missionaries of the *CMS and married Susan Thompson, also a Yoruba ex-slave. In 1834 C. became a tutor at Fourah Bay College, and in 1841 accompanied the British expedition up the river Niger. Ordained in London in 1843, he was sent as a missionary to Yoruba land, where incidentally he rediscovered his mother and eventually baptized her. C. accompanied the Niger expeditions of 1854 and 1857, and during the latter founded the first CMS stations in Ibo land. He compiled a Yoruba dictionary and translated parts of the Bible and Prayer Book into both Yoruba and Ibo. In 1864 at Canterbury he was consecrated first Bishop of the Niger Territories: the first African to become a bishop in the Anglican Communion. For the rest of his life he did pioneer work, extending and building up the church amid difficulties and dangers. Able, devoted and humble, both a gracious and a heroic figure, he became a legend in his own life time.

During C's latter years scandals and divisions broke out in his diocese: partly because he was not sufficiently stern and systematic, but equally because CMS had not given him the support and resources needed for his great administrative responsibilities. Moreover some European missionaries believed that the time was not ripe for an African to hold a position superior to their own; their attitude caused some resentment among the younger African church leaders. After C's death his son, Archdeacon Dandeson Crowther, constituted the 'Niger Delta Pastorate' and severed all connection with CMS. It was to take a full generation before the Delta Pastorate and the rest of the diocese were reunited. Yet C's positive work bore fruit. He founded a church which has steadily become more and more numerous, indigenous and self-supporting.

JOHN GOODWIN

J. F. A. Ajayi: *Christian Missions in Nigeria, 1841–1891: The Making of a New Elite* (London 1965); P. Beyerhaus and H. Lefever: *The Responsible Church and the Foreign Mission,* ch.4 'The Anglican Church on the Niger' (London 1964): more detail is given in the original, P. Beyerhaus: *Die Selbständigkeit der jungen Kirchen als missionarisches Problem* (Barmen 1956); J. Page: *The Black Bishop. Samuel Adjai Crowther* (London 1908); *DNB* Suppl. ii, 93; *RGG* I, 1886.

CUBA. See CARIBBEAN.

CULTS, POST-CHRISTIAN AND QUASI-CHRISTIAN. It is a basic fact that today all the religions of the world, through their confrontation with the Christian faith, are moving into a post-Christian situation. It becomes their aim to present themselves as a substitute for Christianity, or to make it superfluous. Furthermore, there is to be found today in Asia, in Africa, and in Latin America, an immense number of religious movements which have come into being as a result of the clash of cultures. These take that which is Christian as the model, and strive to attain to this model by emphasizing some of the basic ideas of the ancient religion, and by taking over a number of Christian ideas.

The **Brahmo Samāj* (1828) incorporated into **Hinduism a large number of Christian ideas. The **Bahā-ī* religion (1844), which has its origin in **Islam, stressed piety without formal worship, and the service of humanity. The *Caodai* movement (Indo China 1919) aims at uniting all religions in one single common belief in God, attempts to help men through spirit-inspired prophecy, and in its organization follows closely the Roman Catholic model. In Indonesia 75 new religious movements have been registered by the government. In Japan the number is said to be more than 400; the largest of these movements is the *Soka Gakkei*, with 20 million adherents. Many of

these movements draw their origin from older **Buddhist and **Shinto sects. The majority of them proclaim a divinity, who has become incarnate in the founder of the sect. In this way the divinity comes near to men.

These new religions make it their aim to help men and to make them happy by inner cleansing, by collective pastoral care, by introducing them to a new life of piety. How happiness is to be understood is determined by the religion itself. Many of them practise healing in answer to prayer.

Similar movements are to be observed in the world of **primitive or tribal religions. Messianic cults in the Congo region aimed to prolong the life of their adherents by opposing the practice of witchcraft, and by taking over a number of Christian ideas. This was also the object of the *Alice Movement* in Zambia, and of the *Tigare Cult* in West Africa. In Latin America, the *Umbanda, Makumba* and *Quimbanda* cults have developed out of the Amerindian and African inheritance, retaining at the same time the RC reverence for the saints, and are generally constituting themselves the popular religions of Latin America. The aim of these new cults, which have arisen among the adherents of the old tribal religions, is to create for the man who has been uprooted by the clash of cultures, new possibilities of establishing a relationship with the power by which the world is ruled. Common to all these movements is a certain legalism in the ordering of life, and intense voluntary participation by the individual. In these movements also, faith healing stands at the very centre of the cult.

We must make a distinction between all these movements and a group of **syncretistic sects the origin of which is to be found in Christianity. Among early manifestations of this spirit we should reckon the Mormons (1830), who have extended their work to the non-Christian world. Also in the 19th century the Hauhau movement grew up among the Maoris of New Zealand, on the basis of national feeling. Almost all the islands of the South Pacific have been affected by the so-called **Cargo Cult*, the aim of which is to bring prosperity and happiness to its adherents.

The classic region of quasi-Christian cults is Africa. In South Africa two great groups of sects have come into being—the *Ethiopian*, which with their special stress on the OT, lay claim to be the chosen people of God, and the *Zionists*, who also lay great emphasis on the OT, and seek to develop a deep inward African piety. The former wish to enter into relationship to the Church of Ethiopia; the latter lay great stress on the gift of prophecy. There are similar sects in West Africa, such as the *Cherubim and Seraphim* churches in Nigeria. Common to all these groups is the rejection of the western forms of Christianity, the yearning for the manifestation of a black African Christ, the brilliantly coloured vestments and uniforms, the emphasis on faith healing, and the adoption in worship of the dance and the ancient African musical tradition. All these sects themselves provide the means for the ordering and for the maintenance of their life. Those sects which have emerged from within the Christian world also make it their aim to master the problems arising from the clash of cultures, and to help their adherents to find the way to a new unification of life and experience.

See also AFRICAN INDEPENDENT CHURCHES.

GEORG F. VICEDOM

E. Andersson: *Messianic Popular Movements in the Lower Congo* (Uppsala 1958); D. B. Barrett: *Schism and Renewal in Africa* (London 1968); J. N. Farquhar: *Modern Religious Movements in India* (London 1915); P. Lawrence: *Road belong Cargo* (Manchester 1964); C. B. Offner and H. van Straelen: *Modern Japanese Religions* (Leiden 1963); B. G. M. Sundkler: *Bantu Prophets in South Africa* (2nd ed., Oxford 1961).

CULTURE, PROBLEM OF. The word 'culture' is sometimes narrowly defined as the aesthetic (or emotional) and conceptual side of a people's life, but others would prefer to include anything in a nation's life, which points to its historical traditions or the expression of its particular ethos in the world. Whichever approach we take, C. points to man's life in the world, the corporate ideas and emotions which influence him, his links with the past, and his desire to express himself not only in abstract imagery, but also in material creations of his own.

C. speaks essentially of man's life in community; he does not live a life of isolation, but always remakes his environment, language and customs.

The 'problem of C.' emerges, when we think of the relationship between Christianity and the entire pattern of life which surrounds the church. The church would emphasize, at times, its supernatural origin, but it is not able to escape the fact that it exists *in the world* and is part of human history. Is the church to be a thing apart from life in the world? Is there to be an entire rejection of the traditions and customs of the non-Christian society? A complete denial of C. has been argued by many, and the church's distinctiveness and separateness emphasized. This view seems, however, to deny the truth of the church's present limitations and imperfections, and also to disregard the need to stress the principle of identification with mankind. Just as Christ's own mission involved his acceptance of the customs and traditions of 1st century Judaism, so the church's present mission demands a similar identification. There is, however, still the problem that a nation's art or customs may be linked with non-Christian traditions or have actually emerged from religious beliefs which seem opposed to those of the Christian faith. Is the church, in this situation, to take an exclusive attitude and have no link with society? The exponents of an exclusive approach point to the dangers of *syncretism (where religious ideas and beliefs become mingled), and assert that this would mean the ultimate disappearance of an historic Christianity. Is the Christian faith, they would say, to be so dominated by the local traditions of a country, as to lose its distinctive identity and message? Does not the acceptance of C. by Christianity mean the loss of its finality, the sacrifice of its gospel? To such an argument it could be replied that the church belongs to 'two worlds'—this world, with its different languages, traditions and artistic activities, and 'the other world', where limitations cease and the fundamental unity of all men in Christ is fully manifested.

It would seem advisable, in this world, to accept the basic 'neutrality' of human activities. Man's work can be *for* God; it can also be *against* God. Just as an individual's life and work can be converted to God, so a nation's customs and traditions are to be converted to the service of the gospel. This belief in the possibility of conversion in the cultural sphere lies behind all attempts to indigenize the life of the church. It is realized that there is no absolute form of Christian music, art or architecture. The differing patterns in church life and custom can be a symbol of the sacrifice of distinctiveness of each race to God. At the same time, it is understood that the activity of all men (Christian and non-Christian alike) is conducted in the presence of God, and that what is human can be offered to Him.

See also ACCOMMODATION; ACCULTURATION; CUSTOM AND HABIT.

RAYMOND J. HAMMER

C. N. Cochrane: *Christianity and Classical Culture* (London 1944); H. Richard Niebuhr: *Christ and Culture* (London 1952); *NCE* IV, 522–32.

CUSTOM AND HABIT. In general 'custom' refers to the standard patterns of behaviour of a society as a whole and 'habit' applies to the consistently repeated behaviour of an individual, though in certain types of contexts one may speak of an individual's customs and the habits of a group. What makes the problem of diverse customs and habits so complex when viewed from a cross-cultural standpoint is the fact that people are generally impressed or appalled by the 'strange' practices of foreign nations or societies, but they take their own distinctive patterns of behaviour largely for granted. As a result, they misinterpret and misjudge the behaviour of others.

From the standpoint of Christian missions the customary patterns of behaviour of any group are of utmost significance, for they largely determine the openness or closeness of the society to the communication of the gospel. Unfortunately, even in cases where indigenous customs might have been employed as possible bridges or stepping stones to comprehension of the Christian message, the negative attitudes of missionaries and early converts have often made these customs into dividing chasms.

Customs and habits must be recognized as bearing important values. First, they tend to preserve and validate tested experience, and as such are closely related to the value system of a people. Second, they provide a sense of order and reason to various types of behaviour; and third, they facilitate the behaviour of a group, for individuals do not need to waste time trying to determine precisely how they are to act under each seemingly new set of circumstances. Moreover, if traditions are carefully followed, people are not at a loss to interpret the behaviour of others, for everything is relatively well structured.

Customs and habits may, however, involve very significant liabilities, for their traditional functioning may be either efficient or inefficient, constructive or destructive. For example, custom may constitute such a strong inertia as to make important changes virtually impossible. Custom may also lend a sense of reasonableness to behaviour which is entirely deceptive, in that the original reasons for such behaviour may no longer be valid. Lastly, customs may become social idols; that is to say, they may acquire a kind of internalized sanctity and an inviolate character which makes 'the way of life' of a people sacrosanct—and hence a real barrier to meaningful change.

Missionaries and Christians should as far as possible take a positive attitude towards existing customs. The problem arises over customs, such as twin murder, which may seem perfectly reasonable when seen as part of a particular structure of ideas and beliefs, but are irreconcilable with any interpretation of the Christian gospel. But even here cautious advance is better than too rapid extermination. If converts themselves become aware of the clash between their new understanding of God and of life, and certain things in their traditional inheritance, they will themselves take the initiative in abandoning those elements in the old life which cannot be assimilated to the new, and in this way the shock of culture change can be minimized. But this is possible only on the basis of careful and continuous explanation of all that is involved in the acceptance of Jesus Christ as Lord.

EUGENE A. NIDA

R. Benedict: *Patterns of Culture* (New York 1946); E. T. Hall: *The Silent Language* (Greenwich, Conn. 1959); E. A. Nida: *Customs and Cultures* (New York 1954); W. D. Reyburn: 'The Missionary and Cultural Diffusion', *Practical Anthropology*, Vol. V (1958), pp.139–46, 185–90, 216–21.

CYPRUS, a Mediterranean island with an area of 3,548 sq.m. and a population of about 500,000, has one of the oldest independent churches in the world. Since the 5th century, the Archbishop of the island has been held to take precedence immediately after the patriarchs of the great sees. The island has had an eventful history, as part of the Byzantine empire, as a Crusader kingdom, under Venetian and then under Turkish rule, from 1878 as a British colony, and since 1959 as an independent sovereignty within the British Commonwealth, the Archbishop being the civil as well as the religious head. Two-thirds of the population belong to the Greek Orthodox church. No serious attempt has ever been made by this church, the educational and spiritual level of which is not very high, to christianize the Turkish minority; the two races live side by side in an uneasy co-existence, and conversion from one faith to the other is unknown. There are small Armenian, Maronite, Anglican and RC communities. Some educational work of value has been done by American Protestant missionaries. A promising Greek Orthodox youth movement was destroyed during the years of conflict which led up to the independence of the island. In 1967 steps were taken, mainly by devoted laymen, to bring this movement into renewed existence; the future of the church in the island will largely depend on the success of their efforts.

STEPHEN NEILL

BM II, 245–47; *NCE* IV, 566–70.

D

DAHOMEY is a French-speaking West African republic adjacent to Nigeria and Togo, with an area of 44,913 sq.m. and a population (1967) of 2,505,000, giving one of the highest population densities in West Africa. Muslims are estimated at 120,000; adherents of traditional religion are at 80% very strong, the largest concentration being among the Fon tribe (900,000). A RC prefecture apostolic was erected in 1883, growing by 1965 into five dioceses with 322,705 Catholics. Protestant missions have had small success: the Methodist Missionary Society was the first to enter, visiting the Fon capital of Abomey in 1842, but its work has developed almost entirely among the coastal Gun tribe; of its total community of 31,631, less than 100 are Fon. Two other small missions are the Evangelical Churches of West Africa (*SIM), and the *Assemblées de Dieu*. The Fon, a dynamic and progressive people with highly developed fetishistic religion, have shown little inclination towards *Islam. In view of the inability of existing missions to undertake the evangelization of the Fon, in 1965 an *Action Apostolique Commune* scheme was undertaken to equip an international team including an agriculturalist and a theologian, supported by French-speaking churches elsewhere in Africa, Madagascar, Europe and the Pacific. RC scholars also are assisting them with the production of the first Fon scriptures.

DAVID B. BARRETT

R. Cornevin: *Le Dahomey* (Paris 1965); *BM* II, 299–303; *NCE* IV, 612f.

DAMIEN, FATHER (Joseph de Veuster, 1840–1889). Born at Tremeloo, Belgium, into a peasant family, he entered the Congregation of the Sacred Hearts of Jesus and Mary at Louvain in 1859. D. went as a missionary to Hawaii in 1863 and worked as a rural parish priest, 1864–73. He then volunteered to live on Molokai, an island of which the northern peninsula was set apart for lepers. Eight hundred patients resided there without supervision; disorder, violence, drunkenness and sexual laxity prevailed. D's work included nearly 200 burials each year. He introduced elementary medical care and persuaded the Hawaiian government to send regular supplies of food and cloth; he organized an adequate water supply for the settlements and acquired materials for building houses. The patients stopped their illicit distilling of liquor and followed D's lead in working for themselves. A school, a dispensary and churches were built; D. instructed and baptized hundreds of converts. In 1885 it was confirmed that he himself had contracted leprosy. During his last years he had four monks and three nuns to assist him, and a resident physician. His work became internationally known; as a result of his death the Mission to Lepers and other work received a new impetus (see LEPROSY MISSIONS).

JOHN GOODWIN

P. de Veuster: *Life and Letters of Father Damien* (London 1889); S. Debroey: *Father Damien. The Priest of the Lepers* (Dublin 1966: translated from the Flemish, *Wij Melaatsen* [Kasterlee]); *NCE* IV, 626f.

DANISH-HALLE MISSION (or TRANQUEBAR MISSION). King Frederick IV of Denmark was unable to find in his own country any ministers prepared to undertake missionary work in his colony of Tranquebar in India. In consequence the founders of the mission were the Germans B. *Ziegenbalg and H. Plütschau, who landed 'on the coast of Coromandel' on 9 July 1706. They engaged the interest of their teacher A. H. Francke, for their work, and before long Halle, the home of Francke, became 'the heart of the mission'. 49 Germans, six Danes and one Swede entered the service of this mission, which was supported from England also with money, a printing press, and other gifts. This was the first 'ecumenical quadrilateral', in which the boundaries of the Christian confessions as well as national boundaries were trans-cended.

The Tranquebar Mission was the first mission of the German Lutherans and Pietists. We can speak of a number of 'firsts' in its history—schools, seminary for the training of teachers, the first girls' school in India, the first Protestant printing press, the first doctors in the service of a mission, and on 28 December 1733 the ordination of the first Tamil pastor, Aaron. The ordination took place in the *New Jerusalem Church which had been dedicated in 1718, and in which Ziegenbalg is buried. He was the founder of the church and its first provost, the student of religions and languages, the translator into Tamil and from Tamil into German. He and Fabricius were the trans-lators of the Bible and of many hymns. Another 'bright star' of the mission was C. F. *Schwartz (1726–1798), who became famous as the 'Sanyasi Padri'.

In the time of the Enlightenment the mission collapsed; the church in the west failed in its duty to support it. In 1841 H. Cordes, appointed by the Dresden (later *Leipzig) mission took over all that was left of it. There were then only 1,400 Christians at Tranquebar. The number baptized by the mission during its first century was 36,970.

ARNO LEHMANN

J. F. Feuger: *A History of the Tranquebar Mission* (Madras 1906²); W. Germann: *Ziegenbalg und Plütschau* (Erlangen 1868); E. A. Lehmann: *It Began at Tranquebar* (Madras 1956; Berlin 1956²), *Alte Briefe aus Indien* (Berlin 1957).

DAVIS, JOHN MERLE (1875–1960), was born in Kyoto, Japan, the son of Jerome Dean Davis, an American missionary. Educated in Oberlin and Hartford Theo-logical Seminary, with post-graduate work in Germany, from 1905 to 1922 he was a *YMCA secretary in Japan, first in Naga-saki and then in Tokyo. In 1923–25 he was director of a race relations survey on the west coast of the USA under the Institute of Social and Religious Research of New York City. From 1925 to 1930 he was the first General Secretary of the Insti-tute of Pacific Relations, an organization which had sprung from the YMCA but was independent of it. From 1930 to 1946 he was the first Director of the Department of Economic and Social Research and Counsel of the *IMC. In that position he made extensive surveys of labour conditions in the mines of Central Africa, of modern industry and the African, of economic and social conditions of churches in East Asia, Indonesia, Latin America, and the Carib-bean, of the effects of the European impact on African marriage and family life, and of the social, economic, and religious condi-tions of the Indians in the High Andes. The findings of several surveys were published in a succession of volumes.

KENNETH SCOTT LATOURETTE

J. M. Davis: *An Autobiography* (Tokyo 1960); *RGG* II, 52.

DEACONESSES. A deaconess is a trained, disciplined lay woman consecrated or com-missioned (ordained in the Greek Orthodox Church) to a special office for the church. She may be single or married, may or may not wear a garb. (These depend on church regulations.) Exact definition is difficult since the term 'deaconess' is interpreted according to the theological, historical and cultural background of each confessional group using it. Service is primarily in home mission areas.

The first known deaconess was Phoebe at Cenchreae (Rom.16:1,2).

Theodor Fliedner, a German Lutheran minister, in 1836 opened the first Mother House to train single women as deaconess nurses.

Deaconess associations have been orga-nized in many parts of the world to bring together deaconesses for fellowship, spiritual strengthening, consultation and planning.

As churches become more involved in church union plans a clearer definition of the term and better understanding of deaconess work will be needed. They are serving in a wide variety of tasks and being called and trained for many new patterns of mission.

The ecumenical dimension of the work is

found in *Diakonia*, the World Federation of Deaconess Associations. In 1966 35 associations from 21 countries, representing nine confessional bodies, were members of *Diakonia*.

GLORIA M. WYSNER

'The Deaconess', WCC Studies No. 4 (Geneva 1966).

DEAF, MISSIONS TO THE. For most of human history no one who was born deaf ever learned to speak or to understand the thoughts of other human beings. The first known teacher of the deaf was Pedro de Ponce de Leon (1520–1584), a monk of San Salvador, Spain. A very few Europeans followed his example in the two following centuries. In 1771 the Abbé C. M. de l'Epée (1712–1789) opened a residential school in Paris at which all deaf-mutes were welcomed. His aim was both to teach and to evangelize them. Other institutions were founded in Europe and North America, usually through Christian initiative. Various churches organized 'missions to the deaf and dumb' to bring religious ministrations and social and economic advance. The ex-pupils of deaf schools started many of these.

Work in Africa was begun by *Dominican nuns from Cabra, Ireland, in 1863 at Johannesburg. The Dutch Reformed Church opened a school in 1881. In 1878 the first school in Asia for blind and deaf children was started by the Japanese themselves at Kyoto. Monsignor de Haerne opened the first centre for the deaf in India at Bombay in 1884. Many missionary agencies today have some work specifically for the deaf. Even so the needs of most of the deaf in Asia and Africa have not yet been touched.

During the 19th and 20th centuries much progress has been made in manual sign language, lip-reading and teaching the deaf to speak. In corporate worship a combination of manual signs and lip-reading is the method of expression which best enables the deaf to participate.

JOHN GOODWIN

R. E. Bender: *The Conquest of Deafness* (Cleveland, Ohio 1960); K. W. Hodgson: *The Deaf and their Problems* (London 1953).

DEMONS, DEMONOLOGY. Almost every people in the world has a belief in demons or evil spirits, though there is immense variety of view as to the origins and method of working of these powers. It is clear that in the days of Jesus Christ the belief was very widely held among both Jews and Greeks; to many of the first Christians Jesus came first as the conqueror of the demons, and only later as the deliverer from sin and death.

Almost all Christians in the *younger churches, except those who have become very highly sophisticated, believe in the existence and operation of demons, and they have what (to them) is irrefragable evidence that they are not mistaken. At innumerable shrines throughout the world, devil-dancing is practised, the express aim of the dance being to become possessed by an alien and invisible power. When the spirit has entered, the dancer speaks in a voice quite other than his own, and shows remarkable gifts of clairvoyance. (David's servant is quite sure that Samuel the seer will be able to tell them where the missing asses are to be found: 1 Sam.9:5–10.) This process is to be observed at its clearest in Shamanism; but it is also to be found in a great many other parts of the world as well.

Many cases of demon possession are on record, mostly of women. The vast majority of them can be identified as one form or another of hysteria. Where the sufferer is a Christian (and even sometimes in the case of non-Christians) relief can be obtained by the laying-on of hands with prayer. But few missionaries who have lived in close contact with primitive and non-Christian peoples are satisfied that all cases are covered by this simple and rational explanation. They become aware of the existence of a dark, malevolent, watchful and intelligent power of evil, which is bitterly hostile to the gospel, and the destructive powers of which from time to time come under observation. This subject deserves much closer study from every point of view than seems yet to have been given to it. Not much is gained by telling simple Christians that evil spirits do not exist. They remain unconvinced. What is important is to stress the positive side of the Christian message. Whatever evil and rebellious powers there may be in the world, Christ has subdued them all. The Christian, who puts his whole trust in the Master, and walks humbly and consistently in his way, has nothing at all to fear. He may be called in this world to face temptation and suffering; but he cannot be touched by any external and hostile power.

STEPHEN NEILL

ERE IV, 565–68, by L. H. Gray, who states that 'there seems to be no special treatise on this subject, so that the material must be gleaned from the writings of missionaries and travellers'. *NCE* IV, 756f.

DENOMINATIONAL MISSIONS have predominated among sending agencies. In England and continental Europe they have usually been voluntary associations with a denominational constituency, whereas in Scotland, the USA and Canada they have taken the form of official church boards. By creating boards churches theologically and officially recognize mission as a basic function of the church and discharge their obligation. Actually until recently neither form of organization enlisted a larger percentage of the membership in personal participation, but owing to various factors in the present the society now seems better able than the church to sustain the interest of individuals.

Voluntary societies originated in Britain, the first being the New England Company of 1649. Dr Thomas Bray was the father of denominational societies, and organized three Anglican agencies: the *SPCK (1699), the *SPG (1701) and Dr Bray's Associates. Then came the (Presbyterian) Society in Scotland for Propagating Christian Knowledge, organized 1701, chartered 1709; it began American Indian missions in 1730. The society pattern was copied in America, but the crown disallowed the 1762 society organized by Massachusetts Congregationalists. The society was a necessity in New England because associations of Congregational churches lacked power to administer institutions and enterprises. This

model was then followed in the founding of the Society for Propagating the Gospel among the Indians and Others in North America in Boston in 1787. That same year the (Moravian) Society for the Furthering of the Gospel among the Heathen was founded in Pennsylvania. A large number of Congregational, Baptist and union societies for mission were organized between 1787 and 1810.

When the great overseas mission movement began at the end of the 18th century, evangelicals were a minority and there was generally either lack of interest or opposition to mission. Churches would not act denominationally. The society was a necessity. The BMS, inspired by William *Carey, was the first in 1792. Despite the example of the union *LMS, *Basel Mission and other similar agencies, the denominational society became the rule. Examples: *CMS (1799), Netherlands Missionary Society (1797), Danish Missionary Society (1821). Exceptions have been the Wesleyan Methodist Missionary Society of 1818, organized as an agency of Conference, and the Church of Scotland's Executive Committee of Foreign Missions in 1824. In more recent times the Church of Sweden adopted the Swedish Missionary Society, and after the second world war the many societies within the Reformed Church of the Netherlands became a board of the church.

The *ABCFM was organized as a Congregational society in 1810, quickly became interdenominational, but after others withdrew was again Congregational after 1870. When the Congregational churches got a national organ, the ABCFM, while continuing the society form, became actually a church board. The Baptists organized as the Triennial Convention of the Baptist Denomination for Foreign Missions in 1814, changed name and form several times, and eventually, keeping the name of society, became a board of the American Baptist Convention. After the organization of the (Old School) Presbyterian Board of Foreign Missions in 1837, other denominations consistently created boards.

R. PIERCE BEAVER

DENOMINATIONALISM. See CON-FESSIONALISM.

DEPRESSED CLASSES (now, more correctly, Scheduled Castes) is a term used of those groups in India, sometimes called the outcastes, which exist on the fringe of Hindu society, with to a large extent the typical Hindu organization of the groups as *castes, but without any of the social and economic privileges distributed among the castes which are firmly within the Hindu system. It is probable that these groups belong to the very early Dravidian or pre-Dravidian inhabitants of India; while others fled to the hills before the Aryan and other invaders and so were able to maintain their separate and largely independent existence, these remained and became the servants of the conquerors, doing the meanest and most servile tasks, and receiving the smallest rewards. It is not the case that these people had no rights at all; they have their slender rights, and there are certain rewards to which they are entitled. Some own plots of land in their own right. None has access to a Hindu temple, but they have their own temples at which their animistic rites are performed. Between one-sixth and one-fifth of the inhabitants of India belong to these depressed classes.

The British government began the uplift of the depressed classes by opening to them such professions as the police and the army. The independent Indian government has carried the process further by legally prohibiting 'untouchability'. Mahātma Gandhi endeavoured to revise their status by giving them the name 'Harijan', 'children of God', but did not advocate the abolition of the caste system. By far the greatest contribution has been made by the missions. The majority of Christians in India are of depressed class origin. Poverty and illiteracy have hindered their progress; but, given opportunity, they have shown themselves equal in intelligence and capacity to other Indians and to other Christians. The *Ārya Samāj has dedicated itself with some success to the reconversion to *Hinduism of those who have become Christians. Governments

have a tendency to discriminate against Christians of these classes on the ground that they are no longer depressed. No doubt in the end reasonable social equality will be reached; but this is likely to be a long and painful process.

STEPHEN NEILL

J. H. Hutton: *Caste in India* (3rd ed., Cambridge 1961); J. W. Pickett: *Christian Mass Movements in India* (Cincinnati 1933).

DEVANANDAN, PAUL DAVID (1901–1962), was born in Madras and died in Dehra Dun. He was educated in the University of Madras, the Pacific School of Religion and the Yale Divinity School. For 17 years D. was Professor of Philosophy and History of Religions in the United Theological College, Bangalore, South India. Later, for a few years, he worked as Literature Secretary of the National Council of YMCAs in India. From 1956 to 1962 he was Director of the *Christian Institute for the Study of Religion and Society, Bangalore. The most mature years of his life were given to strengthening this institute and to shaping its policy. He was called to be William *Paton lecturer to Cambridge University and also Henry Luce professor to the Union Theological Seminary, New York. He was invited to give one of the major addresses at the *WCC assembly held in *New Delhi, 1961.

D's major contribution was to develop a posture of *dialogue in the Christian confrontation with other religions, particularly *Hinduism. He emphasized that the task was not an academic comparison of systems of thought but meeting each other at a deeper religious level on the basis of sincere friendship, sound scholarship and a genuine concern for the problems of personal and social existence. Avoiding shallow friendliness and aggressive fanaticism he stressed both the universality of God's love in Christ and the exclusive claim of the gospel. In this work which called for both a re-assessment of Hinduism and a re-examination of Christian fundamentals one might look for elements of a post-*Kraemer theology of the relation between Christian faith and other faiths. With his larger conception of evangelistic work, he called the church in India to move away from its detached isolation to an active participation in nation-building. All this was based on a firm faith that the redeeming work of God in Christ is all-inclusive and that the activity of the contemporary Christ continues in history bringing healing and wholeness to broken humanity.

S. J. SAMARTHA

D's major works include: *The Concept of Maya* (London 1950); *The Gospel and Renascent Hinduism* (London 1959); *Christian Concern in Hinduism* (Bangalore 1961); *Christian Issues in Southern Asia* (New York 1963). A collection of his sermons and Bible studies under the title, *I Will Lift Up Mine Eyes Unto the Hills*, 1963, and a collection of his major articles under the title *Preparation for Dialogue*, 1964, are published by the CISRS, Bangalore.

DEVOLUTION, in discussions of Protestant missionary policy, has the specialized meaning of the transfer of responsibility from a foreign missionary organization to the church in the country concerned which has come into being as a result of the preaching of the gospel. The well-known statement of Henry *Venn (1851) may be taken as typical of much 19th century thinking on the subject: '. . . the "euthanasia of a mission" takes place when a missionary, surrounded by well-trained native congregations under native pastors, is able to resign all pastoral work into their hands, and gradually relax his superintendence over the pastors themselves, till it insensibly ceases; and so the mission passes into a settled Christian community. Then the missionary and all missionary agency should be transferred to the "regions beyond".' This process did not, however, proceed 'insensibly'. The early years of the 20th century saw churches in Asia and Africa attaining a size and capacity which foreign missions recognized as requiring that they be responsible for the conduct of their own life; but what was involved in this and how it was to be brought about

were matters of protracted debate reflected in the *Edinburgh Conference (1910), and at the *Jerusalem meeting of the *IMC (1928). Amongst the issues raised were: (1) Can one properly speak of devolving responsibility on to a church? If a church exists, is it not thereby responsible under God for its life? Can any external body *transfer* responsibility to it? (2) What is it that should be transferred—responsibility for pastoral work, including the support of the ministry, or also for schools, colleges, hospitals and other institutions begun and supported by the mission? Or would responsibility for the latter place too heavy an administrative and financial burden on the so-called 'young' church? (3) What are the criteria by which it is decided whether a church has reached the stage at which it is wise to transfer responsibility to it? and who decides?

Most churches resulting from 18th and 19th century missionary activity are now *autonomous, and the term 'D.' is no longer much heard. Recently the discussion has almost been inverted. The question now is how churches can so order their life that they can be effectively missionary—a question which faces all churches everywhere—and, in this context, questions about what sort of ministry is needed and how it should be supported, and of responsibility for institutions.

The problem of D. presents itself differently in the Roman Catholic world. With the centralization of the entire life of the church in Rome and in the hands of the Pope, and of the oversight of the greater part of missionary enterprise under the direction of the Congregation of *Propaganda, development of independent churches is not possible in the RC world as it is in the Protestant churches. Nevertheless, much progress has been made in recent years in recognizing that the church in Japan or Central Africa should not simply reflect the characteristics of the church in Italy.

From 1744 on, the tendency was to insist that everything should be done everywhere exactly in the Roman fashion. Bishops were appointed from Rome and directly related to the Pope. Many countries had bishops but no episcopate, in the sense that the bishops were *vicars apostolic, in many cases far more directly related to Rome than to their neighbouring bishops. Furthermore, many bishops were members of religious orders, in this sense also more directly related to Rome than to a neighbouring bishop who belonged to another religious order. From 1886 onwards, when the hierarchy was erected for India, Rome has proceeded to create territorial hierarchies in almost all countries of the world. Since 1923 the consecration of indigenous bishops has proceeded rapidly, and at the present time probably one-eighth of the RC bishops in the world are of non-European origin. Bishops in the different countries have begun to meet in local conferences and synods and to develop something of a regional consciousness.

A great step forward was taken by the Second *Vatican Council, which recognized more fully than any previous council that local developments are necessary, and that in many matters of practice regional churches must be given liberty to develop according to the genius and outlook of the different races that have been brought into the church. One sign of this new spirit is the widespread use of the vernacular, in areas where previously Latin only had been used.

RONALD K. ORCHARD AND STEPHEN NEILL

Report of World Missionary Conference 1910, Vol. II *The Church in the Mission Field*, pp.11–38, 267f.; *Report of the Jerusalem Meeting of the International Missionary Council*, Vol. III *Relations between the Younger and Older Churches* (London 1928), especially the paper by A. L. Warnshuis: 'Major Issues . . .' which surveys the state of the question at that date, and Appendix A: 'Some Official Statements on Devolution'; P. Beyerhaus: *Die Selbständigkeit der Jungen Kirchen als Missionarisches Problem* (Wuppertal-Barmen 1956). A revision and condensation of this work is: P. Beyerhaus and H. Lefever: *The Responsible Church and the Foreign Mission* (London 1964).

DIALOGUE AS METHOD OF ENCOUNTER. The approach of the Christian to the adherents of non-Christian religions has always been a problem. All too often the Christian has adopted the arrogant attitude of knowledge as opposed to mere ignorance. His duty is proclamation; he has the truth and the others have it not, he is right and they are wrong. This is what many Christians, and all Muslims, feel; but the matter could be more tactfully expressed. Moreover the missionary has usually been brought into contact first with the less admirable features of non-Christian religion —the exposure of female infants in China, twin-murder in West Africa, temple prostitution in India, paederasty on the largest scale in Buddhist monasteries in Japan. His natural reaction has been denunciation, sometimes in tones of regrettable shrillness, though usually less shrill than the tones of the denunciations of the west in which the citizens, and Christians, of Asian and African countries have indulged over the last hundred years. It was only by degrees that the nobler features of the ancient religions were discerned; and Christian apologists such as J. N. *Farquhar who tried sympathetically to set forth these nobler elements, were often criticized as having betrayed the duty of Christian proclamation. But new ideas will make their way; gradually it became clear to the more intelligent missionaries that they were under an obligation to listen as well as to proclaim, and that listening itself could be a form of proclamation.

Notable experiments along this line were made by E. Stanley Jones in India between the years 1925 and 1940, and recorded in his book *Christ at the Round Table* (1927). The method was to invite a group of Christians and non-Christians to meet to discuss, not theoretical or dogmatic questions, but the experience of religion itself—what it meant to the Hindu to be a Hindu, to the Muslim to be a Muslim. All who took part were impressed by the friendly atmosphere which by this method it was possible to create, in contrast to the often arid polemics of the rostrum. For the Christians present the desolating experience was the discovery of the extreme poverty of the non-Christian religions, in the strictly religious sense, in the experience of those who professed them. They were always ready to orate—and this was true also of many of the Christian participants—but of a direct experience of God there was little trace.

In later years, the idea of dialogue has been taken up seriously by other Christian evangelists, notable among whom is Bishop Kenneth Cragg, the expert on *Islam.

It is important to make clear what is implied by dialogue. It is sharply to be distinguished from discussion, a merely theoretical enterprise which may lead to no more than mutual entertainment. Dialogue has always within it an existential element. As in the famous Platonic dialogues, the one concern is the manifestation of the truth, but, if truth is manifest, it demands a personal decision, the issues of life and death are always present. Conditions for successful dialogue are: (1) Intense seriousness. (2) Profound respect for the interlocutor as a person. (3) Extreme courtesy in maintaining one's own point of view. (4) Willingness to believe that the other has something to teach as well as to learn. (5) Readiness to be convinced, if the arguments of the other party are genuinely convincing. (6) A readiness to expose oneself to attack and to wounding criticism. (7) A desire that the other may be convinced, but an absolute refusal to exert any pressure on him to be convinced against his will.

To many orthodox Christians this method seems to involve the surrender of the principle of proclamation. If we admit even the possibility that we may have something to learn from the other, and that he may help us to understand our own Christian faith better, we may seem to have denied the certainty of our own Christian conviction. But this is by no means necessarily the case. Apart from theoretical considerations, in many Muslim countries, if we wish to bear any Christian witness at all, it can only be on these lines; and the same is likely to become increasingly true in other countries, with the notable revival of the non-Christian

religions. In practice Bishop Cragg has had considerable success with this approach. A Christian, even one who is expert in Islamics, cannot be certain that he has understood the Arabic terms of the Islamic faith; if he comes as one desiring instruction, he is in the right attitude for creating confidence and communication. When the utmost limit of Muslim understanding has been reached, it may be possible for the Christian to make plain that there is a vast further perspective on the subject to which the Muslim has not yet been able to attain.

The problem is to find the adherent of another religion who is prepared to engage in dialogue; the readiness is far greater on the Christian than on the non-Christian side. The Hindu is prepared to discuss without limit, but is unwilling to reach the point at which an existential decision has to be made. The Buddhist is convinced that no Christian can understand even the most elementary of the terms in which the Buddhist faith is expressed, and that therefore intelligent discussion is impossible. For the Muslim the Christian faith is abrogated by the later revelation, and he has therefore everything to teach and nothing to learn. But it is at times possible to overcome these hindrances; and the experience of genuine discussion of the great issues of life and death is found to be profitable to the Christian and to the non-Christian partner alike.

STEPHEN NEILL

K. Cragg: *Sandals at the Mosque* (London 1962); S. C. Neill: *Christian Faith and Other Faiths* (London 1962).

DICTIONARIES OF MISSIONS. 19th century dictionaries of missions included H. Newcomb, ed.: *A Cyclopedia of Missions* and E. Bliss, ed.: *The Encyclopedia of Missions* (1891, revised in 1904 by E. Bliss, H. A. Tupper and H. Dwight). During 1965–1967 the first three, of a projected five, volumes of a Norwegian dictionary, *Norsk Misjonsleksikon*, were issued jointly by Nomi Forlag and Runa Forlag. In 1967, Thomas Nelson & Sons published *The Encyclopedia of Modern Christian Missions: The Agencies*, edited on behalf of the faculty of Gordon Divinity School by Burton Goddard and others. This volume gives the history and descriptive, statistical and bibliographical data for more than 1,400 Protestant foreign missionary and related agencies and has survey articles describing Catholic and Orthodox missions.

J. Gründler's *Lexicon der Christlichen Kirchen und Sekten* (Vienna 1961) treats many missionary organizations; and numbers of mission agencies are described in such works of reference as F. L. Cross, ed.: *The Oxford Dictionary of the Christian Church* (London 1957); H. Brunotte and O. Weber, eds.: *Evangelisches Kirchenlexikon*[2] (Göttingen 1961); *Die Religion in Geschichte und Gegenwart*[3] (Tübingen 1957), and especially F. H. Littell and H. H. Walz, eds.: *Weltkirchenlexikon* (Stuttgart 1960).

Similarly, for RC missions, much information can be found in J. Höfner and K. Rahner, eds.: *Lexikon für Theologie und Kirche*[2] (Freiburg 1957); Propaganda Fide: *Le Missioni Cattoliche* (Rome 1950); and the *New Catholic Encyclopedia* (New York 1966). To these may be added two volumes in the *Twentieth Century Encyclopedia of Catholicism:* R. P. Millot: *Missions in the World Today* (Eng. tr., New York 1961), B. de Vaulx: *History of the Missions* (Eng. tr., New York 1961).

BURTON L. GODDARD

DIRECTORIES FOR MISSIONS. Early 20th century directories included that in the *World Missionary Atlas*, 1925, and its predecessors, as well as Joseph Parker's *Directory of World Missions*. About mid-century, the Missionary Research Library in New York City began to produce a missions directory series, including a biennial directory of North American agencies, and World Dominion Press published the first edition (1949) of the *World Christian Handbook*, which, in its several editions, has contained much directory information. Supplementing these is Gründler's *Lexikon der Christlichen Kirchen und Sekten.*

In 1967 *The Encyclopedia of Modern Christian Missions: The Agencies* (Nelson)

appeared, listing more than 1,400 Protestant agencies related to the work of foreign missions. The *Official Catholic Directory* (Kenedy), published annually, includes missions listings. The *US Catholic Missionary Personnel Overseas* (Washington, D.C.) is also published annually. A vast amount of information is contained in *Bilan du Monde* (2nd ed., 2 vols., Tournai 1964). Many countries, such as India, Japan, the Philippines and Taiwan, have detailed directories.

For the most up-to-date information, students of missions rely upon new editions of directories, including the periodic publications mentioned, as well as general and religious handbooks of various countries, yearbooks and directories issued by denominations and non-church-related mission agencies, and the various publications of such research agencies as the *Egede Institute (Theresesgt. 51 B, Oslo 3), the *Missionary Research Library (3041 Broadway, New York, N.Y. 10027), and the Missions Advanced Research and Communications Center (919 W. Huntington Drive, Monrovia, California 91016).

BURTON L. GODDARD

DISCIPLES OF CHRIST MISSIONS. See CHRISTIAN CHURCH.

DISCIPLINE, CHURCH. In contrast to almost all the Protestant churches of the west, in which church discipline fell practically into disuse centuries ago, in the younger churches in Asia and Africa it is still extensively applied. Church discipline is a basic necessity, where the church exists as a minority in non-Christian surroundings, has itself emerged only recently from heathenism, and is therefore continually threatened in its religious and ethical existence. True church discipline has three aspects: (1) Spiritual care for the church member who has fallen. (2) The cleansing and protection of the Christian community. (3) The maintenance of the power of the Christian community to bear witness beyond itself. That the pioneer missionaries kept these three aspects clearly before their eyes is evident from the liturgical forms used at the exclusion of members from fellowship, and of their renewed reception into the fellowship. For instance, in the Book of Order of the Evangelical Lutheran Church in the Transvaal (Berlin Mission), we read: 'Beloved in our Lord Jesus Christ! It is sad that you have been overcome by the malice of the enemy, and that through lack of self-control, you have fallen into sin, and have thereby separated yourselves from the Lord, have grieved him, have injured your fellow-Christians, and have brought the Church of the Lord into disrepute.'

This theological understanding of church discipline rests in practice on three presuppositions: (a) the awakening of the individual conscience to the biblical understanding of sin, (b) the pastoral responsibility of the leaders of the congregation for the individual members, (c) an understanding on the part of the congregation as a whole of its responsibility in relation to its members and to the world.

(a) In the non-Christian religions there is nothing which really corresponds to the biblical understanding of sin, since they are not directed to the one, holy, personal God. In primitive societies, conscience is determined in relation to society. Guilt is a proved breach of the law of the tribe. For this reason, church discipline will always be understood in a purely legalistic sense, unless the introduction of the individual believer into a personal relationship with God takes precedence over all other relationships in society.

(b) In the non-Christian religions and in primitive societies there is no office which in its personal and inward responsibility for each single member of the community corresponds to the biblical office of overseer and shepherd. The chief is the head of the community taken as a whole; the *guru* is the teacher of the pupil who of his own free will has placed himself under his protection. An understanding of pastoral responsibility could grow up in the *younger churches only through observation of the way in which the missionary carried out his duties, and this was possible only when for a considerable time the sphere of his responsi-bilities did not extend beyond the local congregation.

(c) In the higher religions, community of feeling is more a chance coincidence of interests without any sense of permanent mutual responsibility. In the fellowship of the tribe, the transgression of the individual is felt rather as a threat to the social order of the tribe or to its harmony with the invisible powers. Here the attribution of guilt comes about not through voluntary confession, but either through a formal trial —in which the accused may try to defend himself against the accusation—or through divination. Here the right application of church discipline demands a right understanding on the part of the congregation of the nature of the body of Christ, in its three-fold relationship—of the members to the Head, of the members to one another, and of all to service in the world.

The *occasions* for the exercise of church discipline are grave and open sins committed by members of the church, the toleration or extension of which would lead to the destruction of the community. Such church discipline must deal frequently with lapses into heathenism, quarrels between members of the church, sexual irregularities and drunkenness. The *initiative* may be taken either by other members of the church, or by the pastor, but most frequently by the elders of the church. In Africa, church discipline is always an affair of the congregation; the pastor is in the first instance not present, in order later to take action as the executive officer. If it is not found possible to set aside the open scandal by purely spiritual means, or if—as in the case of sexual transgression—this possibility is excluded by the nature of the offence itself, the group of elders decides on the measures that have to be adopted.

In most cases the exercise of church discipline is carried out in three stages: (1) Public suspension from Holy Communion and from the other rights of a member of the church. (2) A time of admonition, of testing, and of opportunity for penitence, the so-called penitents' class. (3) Public absolution and restoration to the fellowship of the congregation. It is very interesting that this practice follows almost exactly the penitential system of the early church, where the three stages were recognized as *excommunicatio*, *exhomologesis* and *reconciliatio*.

Unfortunately, church discipline in the younger churches has for a long time fallen into such an unsatisfactory condition that radical criticism of it is coming to be ever more widely heard. The trouble starts on the deepest level in the absence of the three presuppositions which have been named above. Church discipline has in many cases become ossified into a formal institution which is no longer adequate to its spiritual functions. In many cases, the only occasion for it is in cases of unchastity; pregnant girls, because of the unmistakable character of the evidence, are taken under discipline. Only in rare cases are methods of pastoral care employed before recourse is had to methods of discipline. The examination before the church council all too closely resembles a trial before the chief's council. On occasion excommunication is used to magnify the power of the pastor or of an authoritarian church council. Attendance at the penitents' class is regarded as a kind of punishment, often it consists of nothing more than a formal recapitulation of catechism lessons, and the public reception of the sinner into fellowship appears rather as his final humiliation. It is questionable how far church discipline has really had any valuable spiritual effects on the few members who have been subjected to it. In the attitude of the church members it is possible to note indifference, or some pleasure in the misfortune of others, rather than a strong sense of pastoral responsibility.

To sum up: it must be said that church discipline in its original form has outlived its usefulness. Because of its capricious application it is ineffective. It leads to hypocrisy. It often fails to take account of the really serious offences. Now that the closely integrated life of the congregation has become a thing of the past as a result of the social changes that have taken place, the application of it in the old way is no longer practicable. The excommunication of a church member in many cases leads to his final falling away from Christianity. The causes for this collapse of church discipline are to be found in part in the inadequate provision of pastoral care, in part in the changes that have taken place in the situation of the church as a society.

Synods of the churches and ecumenical consultations have for years been trying to find a way out of this dilemma. Proposals have been made for the complete abolition of church discipline, or for its reformation, or for the substitution for it of a new form of responsible pastoral care. In view of the genuine concern which is represented by the tradition of church discipline, and of the spiritual weaknesses of the *older churches which have entirely lost this tradition, the total abandonment of it, with no attempt to put anything in its place would be much to be regretted. On the other hand, it can rightly be asked whether, under the changed conditions of the modern world, a mere restoration of church discipline in its original form is really possible. Even in the days of the ancient church, the old system could no longer be maintained when the mass conversions of the nations had taken place.

Nevertheless, it is important that the church, for the sake of its ministry in the world, should care for the health of its own organism, and of its individual members. This can come about only if the church is prepared to tackle realistically the spiritual, psychological and sociological problems that bring Christians again and again into conflict with the ethical and religious standards of their church. At the same time a restoration of confidence between members of the church and the authorities of the church is most necessary. It must be made convincingly plain to them that, when the church intervenes to deal with their misdoings, the aim really is that of the restoration of true life, and not a Pharisaic infliction of punishment. Spiritual advice and private confession must also to a very large extent take the place of the old corporate exercise of church discipline; this must come into action only as the last resort, when all the efforts of the church to reach a spiritual solution have failed. The presupposition for this transformation is the creation of an adequate supply of ministers for the church, adequately trained to meet these new pastoral responsibilities.

PETER BEYERHAUS

P. Croupie: 'The Problem of Discipline in the Church', *Ministry*, I (1962), pp.9–19; E. Steinborn: *Die Kirchenzucht in der Geschichte der deutschen evangelischen Mission* (Leipzig 1928); H. Wyder: '*Gesetz und Gnade in der Zuchtübung der Gemeinde in China*', *Evangelisches Missions-Magazin*, XCI (1947), pp.97–99.

DISCONTINUITY. See CONTINUITY.

DISPENSATIONALISM is a system of biblical interpretation which originated in England among the people known as the Plymouth Brethren; more particularly it is associated with the name of J. N. Darby and in the USA with the Scofield Reference Bible. A dispensation is a stage in God's revelation to man. Dispensations are regarded as being specially adapted to the needs of particular nations or periods of time, e.g. the patriarchal D., the Mosaic D., the Christian D. Dispensationalists seek to understand God's dealings with man in terms of them. Differing schools have developed, which have divided dispensationalists over questions such as water baptism, the Lord's Supper, and the idea that, while all Scripture is written *to* us, all Scripture is not *for* us in the present age of grace. (Cf. C. I. Scofield: 'Doubtless much which is designedly obscure to us will be clear to those for whom it was written as the time approaches.')

Dispensationalists have always held to the great doctrines of the Christian faith. All of them believe, too, that we now live in a time before the tribulation which will precede the end of this world and before the millennium (Christ's reign of 1,000 years); and that the 'rapture' of the church, when Christ will take all its members into heaven, will occur without warning and without the knowledge of the world. This viewpoint necessarily distinguishes between Israel and

the church; it holds to the consistent use of normal, plain or literal interpretation of Scripture; and it sees the basic purpose of God to be his own glory. Dispensationalists believe that salvation, through the death of Christ, is secured by faith on the part of the sinner, and God is the object of his faith. But the content of faith depends on the particular revelation that God was pleased to give at any certain time. In the USA the leading institution propagating this viewpoint is Dallas Theological Seminary (Dallas, Texas).

HAROLD LINDSELL

C. C. Ryrie: *Dispensationalism Today* (Chicago 1966).

DISPERSIONS OF CHRISTIANS. Christians have from the start been accustomed to live as a *diaspora*, as the scattered people of God in a non-Christian world. In this sense, all Christians living at any time as a minority in a largely non-Christian world constitute a dispersion. This article, however, deals with the movement of Christians from their homes, and the effect of such movement on the spread of the gospel and on missionary policy.

The causes of dispersion are mainly economic. Educated Christians cannot find employment near home; they go far afield in search of work. It has thus come about that there is hardly a town in India which has not its Christian minority, even though no church exists and no mission has ever worked there. Trade has scattered the Chinese all over the Far East. Many Chinese Christians have brought their faith with them to such great trading centres as Singapore, where the majority of Christians are Chinese. Harsh economic necessity has driven hardy Tamils to lands as far away as Fiji to do the hard work to which more leisurely races are not inclined. Some of these have been Christians, and their presence has led to the formation of many new churches. A political revolution led to the arrival of a million mainland Chinese in Taiwan (Formosa); among these were many highly educated Christians belonging to a great variety of churches.

When the migration has taken place to an area in which the church is already established, the missions have in a number of cases been willing to leave the care of their adherents to the local church, even though it might belong to a confession other than their own. But in many cases this has proved impossible for reasons of language. And churches have shown themselves unwilling to let go of anything that they have once held; they have tended to follow the wanderers, regardless of what other Christian provision might be available, and thus to multiply divisions and rivalries. Until 1949, Taiwan was an island in which only Presbyterians and Roman Catholics were at work; since the arrival of the mainland Chinese, numerous missions have come in (36 Protestant organizations were listed in 1968), in most cases without plan and without consultation with those who were already in the field. A similar situation prevails in Hong Kong. This was perhaps inevitable. But nothing could show more clearly the need for better strategic thinking and a more co-operative spirit among the churches of the Christian world.

STEPHEN NEILL

For one example of dispersion, see N. C. Sargant: *The Dispersion of the Tamil Church* (2nd ed., Madras 1961).

DIVISION OF FOREIGN MISSIONS NCCC-USA. See DIVISION OF OVERSEAS MINISTRIES.

DIVISION OF INTER-CHURCH AID, REFUGEE AND WORLD SERVICE. See INTER-CHURCH AID.

DIVISION OF OVERSEAS MINISTRIES, THE, as an integral part of the *National Council of Churches, USA, is responsible for the ecumenical involvement of 70 churches and agencies in areas outside the United States. The DOM was organized in 1965 to integrate the consultation, enquiry and action formerly carried on separately by the Division of Foreign Missions and *Church World Service. The co-operative efforts of foreign mission

7

boards of North American churches led in 1893 to the formation of the *Foreign Missions Conference which later became an integral part of the National Council of Churches at its organization. The DOM combines both the 'mission' and 'service' aspects of the USA member churches overseas through departments for Africa, Asia, Latin America and Middle East-Europe. The departments represent co-operative concerns in designated geographical areas. For instance, the Africa Department unites 40 boards and agencies for assistance through the *All-Africa Conference of Churches and sixteen *National Christian Councils. The DOM includes a department for material resources, immigration and refugee programmes; committees on evangelism and education; and a specialized ministries department responsible for developing and maintaining medical, agricultural, literacy, literature and lay service programmes overseas.

ROLAND W. SCOTT

W. R. Hogg: 'Foreign Missions Conference of North America' in *Ecumenical Foundations* (New York 1952); *Annual Report of the Division of Overseas Missions 1965* (New York); *The Handbook of the National Council of Churches of Christ in the USA 1967–68–69* (New York), pp.59–70.

DIVISION OF WORLD MISSION AND EVANGELISM. One of the four Divisions through which the *WCC conducts its administration and operations, the others being the Division of Studies, the Division of Ecumenical Action, and the Division of *Inter-Church Aid, Refugee and World Service. The staff of this Division, directed by a Divisional Committee of some 30 members, representing many confessions and all continents, carry out the policies and tasks of the *Commission on World Mission and Evangelism.

Through correspondence and travel, DWME staff keep in constant touch with *National Christian Councils, mission boards, and other organizations concerned with the world mission of the church. DWME thus aids in constant cross-fertilization of thinking, and in joint planning and action, for the sake of more effective missionary obedience in all parts of the world, both east and west. Illustrations of DWME operations are consultations on *dialogue with other faiths, on the evangelization of particular areas, and on independent church movements; studies on the meaning of *conversion, on the role of Christian *laymen overseas, and on the churches' healing ministry; and pilot projects on missionary orientation courses and on *urban evangelism. See also CHRISTIAN LITERATURE FUND; INTERNATIONAL REVIEW OF MISSIONS; JEWS, MISSIONS TO THE; and THEOLOGICAL EDUCATION FUND.

VICTOR E. W. HAYWARD

Major publications include: J. Blauw: *The Missionary Nature of the Church* (London 1962); D. T. Niles: *Upon the Earth* (London 1962); *World Studies of Churches in Mission* (London 1958–70).

DOBER, JOHANN LEONHARD (1706–1766), was born in Münchsroth (Württemberg), Germany. A potter before he joined the *Moravian Brethren at Herrnhut in 1730, he was sent out along with David *Nitschmann to St. Thomas, Danish West Indies, on 21 August 1732. Their commission by *Zinzendorf marked the beginning of the historic missionary enterprise of the Moravian Brethren. Within 28 years after 1732 no less than 28 'fields' were opened. D. worked as a lay preacher among the Negro slaves of the island up to 1734, when he became general elder of the community church at Herrnhut. He evangelized among the Jews of Amsterdam in 1738. During a synodical conference in London in 1741 the Moravian Brethren established their 'special covenant with the Saviour'. D. was at his own request relieved of his eldership, which was transferred to Christ himself after consultation of the 'verse of the day', Isaiah 45:11. D. was ordained bishop in Herrnhut in 1747. He was the most eminent among Zinzendorf's lay fellow-workers, of great spiritual and intellectual standing and independence—a bishop before he became one. Through untiring travelling D. knew

and maintained contact with the Brethren churches throughout Europe. His intimate knowledge of the communities' business and of their members made him one of the most influential Moravian leaders during his lifetime. He died in Herrnhut.

LOTHAR SCHREINER

A. J. Lewis: *Zinzendorf, the Ecumenical Pioneer* (London 1962), ch.5; L. Schneider: *Dober, der erste Missionar der Brüdergemeinde* (1906, 2nd ed. 1932); *RGG* II, 214.

DOMINICA. See CARIBBEAN.

DOMINICAN REPUBLIC. See CARIBBEAN.

DOMINICANS (Order of Preachers), founded in 1216 for the work of preaching, from the very start were actively concerned with missionary work. St. Dominic's interest in the Cuman Tartars developed into the work of the 13th and 14th century Ds (*Fratres Peregrinantes*), in the Crimea, Armenia and Persia; a work often associated with the trading activities of Genoese merchants, and still represented by the work of Italian Ds in Turkey and the French in Iraq. Ds played a major part in the great missionary movement associated with Spanish and Portuguese colonial expansion in the 16th century. In the Caribbean and Latin America they were known as protectors of the oppressed Indians. From 1587 the Philippines Province organized the work of Spanish missionaries in the Philippines, China, Japan and Indo-China. The Japanese mission was almost destroyed in the great persecutions of 1617. In China some early successes, particularly in the training of indigenous clergy, were checked by the sterile disputes over Chinese *Rites, in which Ds played a large part. The most successful work of this period was done in the Philippines and Indo-China, where the foundations were laid for the flourishing churches of today. Ds have worked for 400 years in the Caribbean and have recently taken over large areas in Latin America. In the 19th century the order shared in the popular foreign missionary movements, and within the last 50 years much new missionary work has developed, particularly the founding of a number of houses throughout Africa for training of native vocations and specialized work among university students and in higher education. In 1965 there were 1,022 D. priests and 138 brothers working in the missions.

I. HISLOP, OP

R. Loenertz, OP: *La Société des Frères Peregrinantes* (Rome 1937); A. Walz, OP: *Compendium Historiae Ordinis Praedicatorum* (Rome 1948); *NCE* IV, 974–92.

DUBOIS, JEAN ANTOINE (1765–1848), was born at Saint-Remèze (Ardèche), France. He served as a Roman Catholic missionary of the *MEP in the Tamil-speaking area of South India and in Mysore from 1792 to 1821. His fame is principally derived from his book *Hindu Manners, Customs and Ceremonies*, a comprehensive work based mainly on the author's own notes and observations. He had lived in close contact with Indians, knew the language well, and noted down what came under his own observation with sympathy and minute accuracy. Though the book was written and revised before D. left India, by a series of chances the full text of it was not published until 1897. Though much has changed in India since he wrote, D. is still a fascinating and reliable guide through the maze of Hindu life. In his *Letters on the State of Christianity in India* (1823), written shortly after his return to France, he set forth a gloomy picture of things as they were, and a somewhat hopeless estimate of possibilities for the future. In his later years he served at the headquarters of the MEP in Paris.

STEPHEN NEILL

J. A. Dubois: *Hindu Manners, Customs and Ceremonies* (reprint of 3rd ed., London 1959) Preface by H. K. Beauchamp, pp.iii–xxviii; J. Hough: *A Reply to the Letters of the Abbé Dubois on the State of Christianity in India* (London 1824).

DUFF, ALEXANDER (1806–1878), first overseas missionary of the Church of Scotland, was born at Moulin, Perthshire, Scotland. He sailed for Calcutta in October 1829, and arrived seven months later, after being twice shipwrecked. Finding that many young Hindus were eager to be introduced to western literature and science, D. resolved to offer such instruction in close connection with Christian teaching. The school which he opened in 1830 grew rapidly, despite occasional sharp opposition, and the present Scottish Church College is its descendant. It was also the model for similar institutions elsewhere, and deeply influenced the whole methodology of Christian mission. D. himself became a power in Calcutta. In the Anglicist-Orientalist debate which preceded the 1835 Resolution of Government to promote the teaching of European literature and science, his opinion carried great weight, and he was also a moving spirit in the introduction of modern medical studies. Within three years of his arrival, D's work had resulted in the baptism of four young Hindus who later became notable servants of the church; and many others followed. Driven home by illness in 1834, D. laboured to invigorate the missionary effort of the Church of Scotland. He returned to Calcutta in 1840 for a second period of service during which he not only presided over the Institution, but conducted classes for older men, edited *The Calcutta Review*, and organized a girls' school, a residence for Christian students, and a new mission station near Calcutta. During his second furlough, 1850–55, D. resumed his work in Scotland, where he was Moderator of the General Assembly of the Free Church in 1851, and, in tours of England, Ireland, Wales and the United States, made a remarkable impact on Christian thinking. He also took part in the discussions which led to the establishment of the first Indian universities and of the grant-in-aid system. Soon after returning to India D. was offered, but declined, the Vice-Chancellorship of Calcutta University. He continued his work in Bengal, however, until invalided home in 1863, and was thereafter the leading figure in the Foreign Mission Committee of the Free Church until his death.

D. was distinguished as teacher, preacher and statesman, but his special importance in the history of missions rests on his first bold decision to offer a general education of the modern western sort, in closest union with Christian teaching. He thus set a pattern which is not yet outmoded.

A. J. BOYD

A. Duff: *India and Indian Missions* (Edinburgh 1839); W. Paton: *Alexander Duff, Pioneer of Missionary Education* (London 1923); G. Smith: *Life of Alexander Duff* (2 vols., London 1879); *DNB* XVI, 125; *RGG* II, 281.

DUTCH GUIANA. See CARIBBEAN.

E

EAST ASIA CHRISTIAN CONFERENCE. Its formation as an organ of continuing fellowship and co-operation among the churches and Christian councils in East Asia was formally proposed first in 1957 at a conference at Prapat, Indonesia. By the end of 1968 EACC had 94 member bodies comprising fifteen *National Christian Councils and 79 churches in sixteen countries in the region extending from Korea to West Pakistan and including Australia and New Zealand. Some of its members such as the CSI, or the Batak church in Indonesia or the Philippine Independent church have, as single churches, membership estimated respectively at 1,140,000; 690,000 and 2,050,000.

The themes round which the churches and Christian councils in E. Asia had come together had always to do with 'mission' and 'unity'. The need to have such an organ in Asia for mission in unity was expressed as early as in 1938 at the world missionary conference held at *Tambaram near Madras, where the desirability of the *IMC taking concrete action to promote further co-operative Christian efforts in E. Asia was voiced. With the outbreak of the second world war the proposal could not be followed up immediately. In the meantime the *WCC came into being and the two ecumenical bodies together sponsored the first post-war E. Asia Christian Conference in December 1949 at Bangkok, Thailand. The discussion, initiated at Tambaram in 1938, culminated in the unanimous support given by the Bangkok conference to the proposal that the two ecumenical bodies appoint a joint secretary in Asia 'to serve as an ecumenical ambassador among the Asian churches, interpreting them to one another, fostering mutual service and effective witness and strengthening the bonds between the churches in Asia and the church universal'.

In July 1955 some of the churches, primarily in the eastern part of E. Asia, came together at Hong Kong to set up the Asia Council on Ecumenical Mission (ACEM). Among its purposes and responsibilities as stated then ACEM gave emphasis to exchange of personnel among the churches in Asia, and to the allocation of funds to projects 'on the basis of need and ecumenical relevance, rather than on the basis of the sources from which the funds have come'. The formation of ACEM underlined the need for co-ordinating such initiatives with the ongoing work of the joint E. Asia secretariat of the two ecumenical bodies. ACEM willingly decided to dissolve itself and support the EACC as it was formally inaugurated on 14 May 1959 with the sevenfold purpose of: (a) survey of the mission of the church in E. Asia to the end that the total available resources of personnel and funds may be directed to the fulfilment of this mission; (b) consultation on issues of *comity, missionary policy and other subjects of common concern among the churches in the area and the related missionary societies; (c) promotion of Asian participation in the programme and activities of the ecumenical bodies; (d) visitation of churches and councils in the area; (e) encouragement of closer contacts, mutual sharing and exchange among Asian churches; (f) exchange of personnel, and (g) assistance in interpreting and co-ordinating the programme of ecumenical inter-church aid in E. Asia. EACC Assemblies were held in 1959, Kuala Lumpur; 1964, Bangkok; and 1968, Bangkok.

U KYAW THAN

Witnesses Together. Inaugural Assembly of the EACC (Rangoon 1959); *The Decisive Hour for Christian Mission* (London 1959); *The Christian Community within the Human Community* (Bangalore 1964); *Confessing the Faith in Asia To-day* (Singapore 1966); *Ideas and Services* (Christchurch 1968); *WKL*, 1090f.

EAST INDIES, in opposition to West

175

Indies or central America, referred in 1600 to 'all countries lying beyond the Cape of Good Hope or the Straits of Magellan' (Charter of the British East India Company; similar definitions were given by E. India companies established in Amsterdam and other trading centres of Europe). Before Columbus discovered central America, assuming it to be India, 'Indies', the plural form of India, had been used for India (Hindustan), its adjacent islands and the islands further east. In geography 'India' is applied to the area from the south-east of Iran to the south-west provinces of China, with the ranges of Elburz and Himalaya up to Yunnan as northern limitation, Ceylon with the Sunda Islands as southern limitation. The comprehensiveness of this connotation influenced the loose use of 'EI' in politics and commerce of the colonial age. The competition between the British and the Dutch EI companies in the 17th century also led to differing interpretations of the name EI. In Dutch popular use *Indiê* referred to the Dutch EI or Netherlands Indies until 1945 and in distinct preference to the term Indonesia which was first used by James R. Logam in 1850 for 'the islands of the Malay archipelago', but which was suspected of subversive meaning. In its widest sense 'EI' is applied to India, Indo-China and the Malay archipelago, in its narrowest sense to the former Dutch possessions Netherlands Indies. With the end of the East India Company 100 years ago and the rise of independent nations after 1945, the name EI has lost its relevance. While of historic importance, its use has been superseded by the names of the countries Pakistan, India, Ceylon, Burma, Thailand, Cambodia, Laos, Vietnam, Malaysia, Indonesia and the Philippines.

LOTHAR SCHREINER

G. H. Anderson, ed.: *Christ and Crisis in Southeast Asia* (New York 1968).

EASTERN CHURCHES. See MISSIONS, ORTHODOX.

EASTERN CHURCHES, LESSER OR

SEPARATED. These terms are used of groups of Christians, who in the 5th century came to be separated from the rest of Christendom because they would not accept what appeared to them to be the new-fangled Christological definitions of Chalcedon (451). They fall into two quite distinct groups:

(1) Those classed as 'Monophysite', though they would themselves repudiate the term, claiming that they have simply maintained the ancient orthodoxy of the church.

(a) *The Coptic Church of Egypt.* This body which numbers between two and three million, has retained Coptic as its liturgical language, though its members speak Arabic, and lives under the headship of a patriarch who resides in Cairo. In recent centuries there has been no persecution by the Muslims, but the Copts have suffered the loss of many of their most promising young people, who have yielded to the lure of the better prospects that open out before the convert to Islam. RC efforts have brought into being a small Uniate church (82,000 members); Protestant work has detached from the ancient church a number of its more independent-minded members, and has thereby weakened it, and made the renewal of its life more difficult.

(b) *The Church of Ethiopia.* This church almost certainly came into existence in the 4th century. It may claim to be the most conservative church in the world, having retained many features which must be regarded as Jewish rather than Christian. Through the centuries the Ethiopian Church was directly dependent on Egypt, and always received its bishop from Alexandria. Quite recently (1959) this church has obtained the right to have a patriarch and bishops of its own, but the spiritual link with Egypt has not been broken. It is hard even to guess at the number of Christians in Ethiopia; the figure lies somewhere between three and six millions though a higher figure is often quoted. Baptism of non-Christians is widely practised, but is only rarely followed up by instruction. There is a very small Uniate church (60,000), mainly in the former Italian colony of Eritrea; Protestant work has had considerable success among the pagan peoples, and its influence is widely felt. The Ethiopian church is, however, resistant to change, and suspicious of outside influences.

(c) *The Armenian Church.* This is one of the oldest churches in the world, having come into existence in the 3rd century. The Armenians are a most remarkable example of a people which, through a unity of race, culture, language and religion, has succeeded in keeping itself in existence over many centuries of oppression and persecution. In 1894, and again in 1915, the Armenians fell victims to vicious and inhuman persecution at the hands of the Turks. The number of those who died was very large, and the whole of national existence was disrupted. Between two and three million Armenians now live in the Soviet Union, under the headship of the Catholicos of Etchmiadzin. The unity of the church is gravely threatened by the difficulty of communication between those who live within and those who live outside the Russian sphere. The Catholicos of Sis, who now lives in Beirut, and the Archbishop of Jerusalem are almost wholly independent. The Armenian community in America is large (130,000) and prosperous. There is a small group of Armenians (5,000) in communion with Rome; a rather larger Armenian evangelical church, the fruit of American Protestant missionary enterprise.

(d) *The Syrian Orthodox Church.* The Monophysite element in Syria is small, probably not more than 150,000; their head is the Patriarch of Homs (Emesa), who now resides mainly in Beirut.

By far the largest part of the church is to be found in India, where in the 17th century one part of the *Syrian Christians placed themselves under the jurisdiction of the patriarch. This Malabar church now has about half a million members. For many years the church was riven by disputes as to the exact rights of the patriarch in India. These have now been happily settled (1959) and the church lives in peace. Members of this highly educated community have spread

all over India in the search for work; their influence is felt in many directions. After many centuries in which no missionary work was undertaken, various evangelistic enterprises have been set on foot in recent years.

In the past these four churches have had little to do with one another. But in recent years a new sense of fellowship has been created among them. Much better relationships have been developed with the Orthodox churches, and especially with the Church of Greece. All are interested in the wider ecumenical movement, as this has taken shape in the *WCC.

(2) The *Nestorian Churches.

(a) The ancient Church of the East, the *'Assyrians', has been reduced by bitter persecution to a small fragment resident in Iraq, but still faithful to its ancient traditions.

(b) There is a small Nestorian church in Kerala, S.W. India, which receives its bishop from Mesopotamia; but this arose through a 19th century schism in the RC church, and has no historical connection with the period in which the Christians of Kerala were dependent on the 'Chaldean' Patriarch of Babylon.

STEPHEN NEILL

W. F. Adeney: *The Greek and Eastern Churches* (New York 1908); D. Attwater: *The Christian Churches of the East* (two vols., rev. ed., Milwaukee 1961–1962); L. E. Browne: *The Eclipse of Christianity in Asia* (Cambridge 1933); A. Fortescue: *The Lesser Eastern Churches* (London 1913); R. Janin: *Les Eglises orientales et les rites orientaux* (4th ed., Paris 1956); P. Meinhold: *Oekumenische Kirchenkunde* (Stuttgart 1962); E. Molland: *Christendom* (Eng. tr., London 1959).

ECLECTICISM. See SYNCRETISM.

ECONOMIC PROBLEMS AND CHRISTIAN MISSIONS. The major source of support for the Christian missionary enterprise has been the voluntary contributions of concerned Christians motivated to support the wide variety of efforts to spread the Christian gospel across the world. Occasionally governmental tax support of state churches, particularly in Europe, has also assisted with the missionary outreach, but the major missionary movements of the 19th century have relied principally on voluntary giving.

From the standpoint of the donors, and of the organizations that utilized the funds for mission purposes, these problems can be noted:

(1) Uncertainty and instability of giving. People gave as motivated, but this motivation varied considerably from year to year. International conflicts (such as the first world war) reduced interest in giving. World economic recessions or depressions (such as the great depression of the early 1930s) greatly affected the giving potential of donors, and missionary enterprises suffered accordingly. Some consistency to giving was achieved by permanent funds coming usually from large gifts and wills, but these generally were small in comparison to the total enterprise.

(2) Relationship between giving and missionary cultivation. Many churches have found that most money can be raised for missionary endeavours if the giving is cultivated by missionaries themselves either on home leave or on special fund-raising tours. The problem is that giving then too often depends on the fund-raising skills of a missionary. Also, support may develop for a particular missionary as distinct from the total church he serves in a mission land, thus creating an unhealthy relationship between the missionary and the church he serves.

From the standpoint of the receiving mission or overseas church, voluntary giving tends to create other problems:

(1) The problem of designation. Donors often tend to designate their giving quite specifically, wishing their gifts to be used for particular programmes or projects which may or may not be those most in need of support overseas. The result is a measure of programme-control by donors who live far from the receiving mission and who do not know the mission situation well.

(2) The problem of long-term budgeting. Since income from voluntary sources tends to be fluctuating, it is extremely difficult to budget rationally over any extended period of time. Resources cannot be counted on as certain if donors' whims are in control of the resources. How to plan a rational programme development becomes one of the real problems of overseas missions and churches.

(3) The problem of mission giving vis-à-vis the need for growing local support. Every mission knows that to survive and grow it must increasingly depend on the local giving of those it serves. Developing such local self-support is often difficult, and often it is best stimulated if contributions from overseas are kept strictly limited. How to develop local giving while encouraging mission giving by mission donors is a most perplexing problem.

See FINANCIAL SUPPORT FOR MISSIONS.

EUGENE L. STOCKWELL

J. M. Davis: *The Economic and Social Environment of the Younger Churches* (Calcutta 1938).

ECUADOR, a South American republic, bounded on the west by the Pacific Ocean, on the north by Colombia, on the east and south by Peru. The area is 111,168 sq.m., and the population estimated at five million. There is a great difference between the coastal plain, with its largest city Guayaquil, and the high mountain area, which contains some of the highest mountains in S. America.

Christian history in E. begins with the arrival of the Spanish conquerors. The first Mass was said in August 1534 in the neighbourhood of Quito, the first missionaries being *Franciscan friars. In 1545 Quito became the seat of a bishopric. In the next two centuries, Roman Catholicism became the official religion of the country, great churches and convents being built in every area. But the great diversity of languages has proved a serious hindrance to missionary work, and in many areas evangelization was only superficial. From the date at which E. obtained independence from Spain, 1822, there has been continuous tension between 'liberals' and the church, Presidents Eloy Alfaro and Garcia Moreno being considered prototypes of the respective tendencies. In 1904 all religions were placed on an equality before the law, and divorce and civil marriage were introduced. Religious liberty was re-affirmed in Article 168 of the 1946 constitution.

Roman Catholicism remains the nominal religion of the vast majority of the population (an estimated 90%). In recent years attempts have been made to raise the level of RC observance, especially through the efforts of bishops of German origin.

Protestant missions entered in 1895 during the administration of Eloy Alfaro. Fifteen organizations are listed, with a total Protestant community of 19,162 (WCH 1968), the strongest being the Gospel Missionary Union, the *CMA, the SDA and the Southern Baptists. The PECUSA entered officially in 1964, with the formation of the missionary district of Colombia and Ecuador. In 1931 the World Radio Missionary Fellowship opened a powerful radio station (HCJB), which broadcasts in ten languages, and has recently acquired a television station.

In 1956 five young American missionaries were assassinated by the Auca Indians in the Amazon jungle. Undeterred by this disaster the mission continued its work. A number of the assassins were converted; one of the children of one of the martyred missionaries was baptized by one of the Indians who had been concerned in the murders. In 1967 the first ecumenical library was inaugurated in Quito with the participation of several churches. The ecumenical dialogue has begun, though only on a small scale up to the present time.

ONELL SOTO

E. Elliott: *Through Gates of Splendor* (New York 1957); R. T. Hitt: *Jungle Pilot* (New York 1959); E. E. Wallis: *The Dayuma Story* (New York 1960); *BM* II, 312–18; *NCE* V, 89–95.

ECUMENICAL INSTITUTES have arisen with the founding of the *WCC (Amster-

dam 1948). The term is sometimes loosely used to apply to the large number of *Vormingscentren*, Evangelical *Academies, and Lay Institutes which have arisen as training centres of the lay apostolate, largely since the years of the church struggle and the second world war. Representative of these, which number several dozens across the Christian world, are Iona (Scotland), *Sigtuna* (Sweden), William Temple College (England), *Kerk en Wereld* (Netherlands), Loccum and Arnoldshain and Bad Boll (Germany), Boldern (Switzerland), Mindolo (Zambia), Nippon Christian Academy (Japan), Five Oaks Christian Centre (Canada), etc. More precisely, the term refers to such centres as the Ecumenical Institute at Château de Bossey (Switzerland), an agency of the WCC, and the Ecumenical Institute in Chicago, a division of the Church Federation of Greater Chicago (USA).

All of these centres, including a greater number not listed, have been engaged in rethinking and programming and carrying out new experiments in Christian mission. In the process, a significant turn has been taken in the *theology of missions: 'mission' is the preferred word, reflecting the recovery of a consciousness of the calling of the whole church to witness and the desire to break the connection between missionary organizations and white western culture. Whether in mission in the Inner City, where 'the world is now different' (Eberhard Mueller) or through the 'Three Love Movement' on the land (Hokkaido and Northern Hokkaido Christian Centres), the new approach reflects the theological and practical changes which have occurred as a result of movements of lay renewal in the church. The work of the congregation in the church's mission has been a subject of special study and writing under WCC auspices.

At Bossey, courses are held for students from Africa and Asia as well as America and Europe. At 'EI' (Chicago), a disciplined order carries on extensive work in North America and Latin America, as well as in the depressed area ('Fifth City') surrounding

7*

the institute. The world of the ecumenical and lay institutes was well explored at the World Conference on Church and Society held in Geneva, 12–26 July 1966. Beginning in the church struggle, mounted on lay renewal, reflecting rapid technological change and world revolution, the EIs and their partners are engaged in a comprehensive struggle to recover the Christian initiative in interpreting and leading the church's mission to heal, to give sight, to release captives, to declare the Lord's visitation.

FRANKLIN H. LITTELL

M. Frakes: *Bridges to Understanding* (Philadelphia 1960); J. B. Mosley: *Christians in the Technical and Social Revolutions of our Time* (Cincinnati 1966); G. W. Webber: *The Congregation in Mission* (Nashville 1964); H. R. Weber, ed.: *Signs of Renewal* (Geneva 1957); WCC: *Centres of Renewal* (Geneva 1964).

ECUMENICAL MISSION. This term came into use in international discussions in the second half of the 1950 decade. It attempted to sum up a number of different but related insights about the nature of the Christian mission which in that period were prominent in international meetings. These included: (1) the supranational character of mission (emphasized at the *Whitby (1947) meeting of the *IMC); (2) the growing realization that mission was not basically from one country to others, but from Christians in all countries into the whole world (expressed at the *Willingen [1952] meeting of the IMC); (3) the conviction that mission and unity belong together (embodied in a widely quoted document from the Central Committee of the *WCC, Rolle, 1951).

The term was given prominence through the formation in 1955 by some churches in Asia and their associated mission boards of an 'Asia Council on Ecumenical Mission'. This was one of the factors leading to the creation of the *EACC.

RONALD K. ORCHARD

V. E. W. Hayward: 'The Concept of Ecumenical Mission' in *Basileia, Fest-*

schrift für Walter Freytag (Stuttgart 1959), pp.467–73; J. W. Decker: *The Asia Council on Ecumenical Mission: An Historical Outline* (IMC-CWME mimeographed 1955).

ECUMENICAL MOVEMENT. The term does not refer to one particular organization, but to all the bodies and individuals which seek to realize the ecumenical idea. The word 'ecumenical' comes from the Greek *oikoumene* which meant originally 'the inhabited world', but came increasingly to mean the whole church or Christendom as a whole (an ecumenical council is a council representing the whole church). In the modern use of the word both connotations are included. A well-known definition (*WCC, Rolle 1951) states that ecumenical 'is properly used to describe anything that relates to the whole task of the whole church to bring the gospel to the whole world'. The EM is therefore concerned with the manifestation of the essential unity of the church, with the solidarity and cooperation of the churches, with their common witness and their common action in and for the world. During all periods of church history attempts have been made to restore the unity of the church. The originality of the modern EM consists in the insight that, even though there remain important differences in matters of faith and order between the different confessions, churches and Christians can enter into fraternal relations with each other, cooperate in many ways, learn from each other, and enter into conversation with each other in order to overcome their disagreements. Thus the EM provides opportunity to express that unity which is given in the common calling of all churches and Christians by the same Lord Jesus Christ and which, though it cannot yet find its fullest expression in the complete fellowship of which the NT speaks, is a dynamic spiritual force and an important part of the Christian witness to the world. The historical roots of the modern EM are to be found in various movements which were independent of the churches, notably the Christian youth organizations (*YMCA, *YWCA, *WSCF), the Evangelical Alliance and the missionary movement. Christians of many different churches came to know each other in these bodies and learned to co-operate in common tasks while respecting each other's doctrinal convictions. Many of the men and women who became the architects of the larger ecumenical movement had their first ecumenical experiences in those 'independent' bodies (John R. *Mott, J. H. *Oldham, Nathan Söderblom). It is also noteworthy that the concern for unity in the missionary approach to the peoples of Asia and Africa was one of the main motives in the creation of the movement. The first of the larger ecumenical conferences out of which the modern EM has grown was the *World Missionary Conference in Edinburgh 1910, and ecumenical co-operation on the national level was developed in Asia long before it was developed in Europe.

In the 1920s many churches became involved in the movement through *'Faith and Order' and *'Life and Work', the first concerned with unity in doctrine and structure, the second with co-operation in social and international affairs. In that early period ecumenism was still the concern of a relatively small number of specialists and, since few churches in Asia and Africa had become independent, almost wholly under western leadership. Eastern Orthodoxy had made an important contribution to the creation of the movement through the Encyclical of the Ecumenical Patriarchate (Constantinople) in 1920 proposing the founding of a league of churches. But owing to political conditions a very large part of Orthodoxy had remained outside the movement. This situation changed in 1961 and 1962 when the large Orthodox churches of Eastern Europe began to participate fully. When in Asia and Africa many churches became *autonomous, they became at the same time very active in ecumenical relationships. Without reducing their participation in the world-movement they founded regional ecumenical bodies for East Asia and Africa which have

become dynamic centres of inter-church activity.

The Roman Catholic church took at first a negative attitude to the EM (Encyclical *Mortalium Animos* of 1928). In the 1930s and 1940s a number of RC theologians began to pay close attention to ecumenical developments. This led to informal contacts which were greatly intensified during the common struggle against the national-socialist ideology. By the time of the pontificate of John XXIII the situation had become ripe for a positive response to the challenge which the EM presented. The Secretariat for Promoting Christian Unity was created by the Vatican and the second *Vatican Council adopted an important decree on Ecumenism which defined the specific RC conception of the ecumenical task, but opened up new possibilities for conversation and co-operation.

Thus the little ecumenical stream of the early days has now become a broad river. Ecumenism expresses itself in a great variety of ways. There is the ecumenical activity of the churches which is now largely concentrated in the WCC, in the confessional alliances and in the councils of churches on a regional or national basis which now exist in very many countries and regions. There is the continuing activity of the YMCA, YWCA, WSCF and *World Council of Christian Education. There is the work of the specialized agencies such as the *Bible societies or the associations of theological teachers (NT scholars, etc.). There are the *Ecumenical Institutes and centres in many countries. And there is the 'non-official' type of ecumenism where men and women of different churches form spontaneous groups with the purpose of dialogue and common action. For the health of the EM it is important that the more institutional form of ecumenism and the 'free' ecumenism recognize each other's *raison d'être*. Both are needed. Ecumenical history shows that groups of individuals fired by the vision of a renewed and united people of God can render great service as pioneers. But the vision will only become a substantial reality when it takes shape in and through the life of the historical church bodies.

Ecumenism is essentially the product of rediscovery of the basic calling of the church of Christ. It stands for unity, but not for unity as an aim in itself or a unity at all cost or for unity as institutional uniformity. The unity which it seeks was defined by the *Amsterdam Assembly as arising out of the love of God in Jesus Christ, which binding the churches to Him, binds them to one another. That is why unity cannot be achieved without the renewal of the life of the churches and of their members. And that is also why ecumenism must not be concerned only with ecclesiastical organization or even Christian doctrine, but with the whole life of the church: with its worship and its service and with its witness in word and action in the whole world.

W. A. VISSER'T HOOFT

S. M. Cavert: *On the Road to Christian Unity* (New York 1961); P. A. Crow, Jr: *The Ecumenical Movement in Bibliographical Outline* (New York 1965); H. E. Fey, ed.: *History of the Ecumenical Movement, 1948–1968* (London 1970); N. Goodall: *The Ecumenical Movement* (2nd ed., London 1964); W. A. Visser't Hooft: *The Meaning of Ecumenical* (London 1953), *The Pressure of our Common Calling* (London and New York 1959); J. A. Mackay: *Ecumenics* (Englewood-Cliffs 1964); R. Rouse and S. C. Neill, eds.: *A History of the Ecumenical Movement, 1517–1948* (2nd ed., London 1967).

EDINBURGH 1910. See CONFERENCES, WORLD MISSIONARY.

EDINBURGH MEDICAL MISSIONARY SOCIETY. A society founded in 1841 by a number of leading medical men in Edinburgh, Scotland. The foundation resulted from a visit by the Rev. Peter *Parker, MD, from America, who was at that time a medical missionary in China. Dr John Abercrombie became first president, and the Rev. T. *Chalmers a vice-president. Since its foundation the society has helped to train and send out over 400 missionary

doctors to serve with most of the British Protestant societies throughout the world.

In 1853 Dr P. D. Handyside, one of the directors, opened the first home medical mission in Britain at Edinburgh; this provided training in medical and evangelistic work for hundreds of missionary doctors. Since 1861 the EMMS has been doing medical work in Nazareth, Israel, where today there is a fine modern hospital of 120 beds; thousands of patients are treated every year, and the gospel is preached daily. The society also ran a hospital in Damascus for 70 years, but this was closed in 1956 owing to political tensions.

The EMMS gives bursaries to medical students who intend to become missionaries and also grants to missionary doctors on furlough who wish to pursue further studies.

E. L. FARROW AND EDITORS

EDUCATION AS MISSIONARY METHOD. All evangelism involves teaching. But, when education is distinguished as one missionary method among others, the reference is primarily to Christian colleges and schools which endeavour to serve a missionary purpose through the medium of general education. These are not theological colleges and Bible schools. The colleges may be constituent or affiliated units of a 'secular' university, or they may be constituent units of a Christian university, or they themselves may have independent university status; but in any case their work is mainly in the field of Arts and Science, and they are distinguished from other colleges of that type, not chiefly by differences of curriculum, but by their commitment to Christian purposes. Similarly the schools are usually part of the public educational system, or closely linked with it; their curriculum is like that of other schools, except that they give an important place to religious instruction; their distinguishing feature is that, within the conditions thus set, they aim at a style of education which shall be Christian in method and effect.

The extent of Christian participation in education varies so widely from country to country that summary statement is impossible. At primary school level, the figures for Africa are especially notable; it has been calculated that, in the early 1960s, about 85% of all the school-children in that continent were in mission schools. Missionaries there were pioneers in primary education, and their work rapidly expanded when government grants-in-aid became available. Many thoughtful observers argue, however, that the burden of educational responsibility which has thus been bequeathed to the *indigenous churches is too heavy. Elsewhere Christian participation is not in general so strikingly preponderant, but in many countries it is very massive.

Is it possible to define more exactly the missionary purpose of the Christian schools and colleges, and the methods by which they seek to achieve it? Among those responsible, there are in fact noticeable differences of emphasis. The majority might point in the first place to the opportunity such institutions provide of explicit religious teaching in which Christ can be presented to non-Christians, but few would be content to say that the creation of this opportunity is the one purpose for which they exist. Even those who do think mainly in terms of the 'opportunity' that the schools and colleges provide generally have in mind not only religious teaching in the classroom, but also Christian influence exerted in personal contact with individual pupils. Probably, however, a majority would wish to make the still wider claim that the whole life and work of a Christian school or college can and should bear testimony to Christ through the close connection between work and worship, through the manifestation of Christian fellowship, through Christ-inspired care for individuals, through the very tone and assumptions of all the classroom teaching. But to what end? Should Christian schools and colleges aim at winning converts and leading them to baptism? Many hold that the very opportunities open to Christian educators imply certain corresponding

limitations; and, especially in countries where baptism almost inevitably involves a break with home and family, most Christian teachers would feel bound to exercise great restraint. How, then, would they express their purpose as Christian educators? Some would say that their overriding purpose *is* to bring individual pupils to personal 'decision for Christ': but they might or might not consider baptism the immediate next step, and they would seek to distinguish between 'fair' and 'unfair' influence, between genuine teaching and mere indoctrination. Others would lay the emphasis on the nurture of character through the mediation of a knowledge of Christ which might at a later stage result in conscious acceptance of Christ as Lord. Others again think mainly in terms of a gradual penetration of the whole mind and thought of non-Christian society with Christian truth, serving as preparation for full acceptance of the gospel.

In the work of Christian education, government policies have to be taken into account, and there always lurks in the background the difficult question, Where lies the ultimate authority for the determination of educational ends and means? Totalitarian governments have a short answer for that question, but, even when governments claim something less than omnicompetence, there is necessarily some degree of regulation by the state; and that is not to be regretted. If, however, government requirements seem to prejudice the deeper questions underlying educational theory and practice, churches and Christian educators sometimes have to consider whether they can rightly co-operate. For the education of Christians the church has a special responsibility which it cannot yield; to the education of non-Christians it can make what it believes to be a valuable contribution, but only if the state system is reasonably flexible.

A. J. BOYD

Report of the Commission on Christian Higher Education in India (London 1931); *Tambaram-Madras Series*, Vol. IV (London 1939); J. W. C. Dougall: *Christians in the African Revolution* (Edinburgh 1963); S. C.

Neill: *A History of Christian Missions* (London 1964).

EDUCATION OF MISSIONARIES. See PREPARATION OF MISSIONARIES.

EDWARDS, JONATHAN (1703–1758), was the son of Timothy Edwards, pastor of the East Windsor, Connecticut, church for 64 years. E. graduated at Yale and was pastor of the church in Northampton, Massachusetts, from 1727 to 1750. As preacher, pastor, teacher and author, E. was a leader of the Great Awakening. He became America's great theologian, an apologist for the Calvinism called 'The New England Theology'. Receiving from friends in Scotland a proposal for a Concert of Prayer uniting church people on both sides of the Atlantic, E. adopted the idea, published a pamphlet to promote it, and saw in it a plan to induce a general revival of religion. In 1734 a group of church members, meeting with E. in Northampton, determined upon the founding of a mission to the Indians in the Housatonic valley. Dismissed from the Northampton church in 1749 because of his teachings, E. refused a number of invitations to go elsewhere and became pastor of the church he had helped to found in Stockbridge, and missionary to the Indian population. Responsible for two congregations, the white settlers and the Indians, for the Hollis Boarding School for Indian boys and subsequently a companion school for Indian girls, E. found his work thwarted by circumstances. The Commissioners for Indian Affairs in Boston, acting through a resident agent and using funds supplied by the *SPG in London, were the authorities for the church. Funds for the boys' school came from Isaac Hollis. Certain white families, however, misappropriated much of the money. E. showed keen administrative ability in reports to the Commissioners; he succeeded in stopping the exploitation of the Indians and the misuse of funds by those entrusted with them, and he effected the removal of those responsible for difficulties in the community. Never able to master the langu-

age of the Indians, he preached regularly, taught them the Bible and the catechism, tested applicants for church membership, admitting those he deemed worthy and encouraging others to strive more diligently. By patient pastoral work he built up an orderly, instructed congregation. In 1754, at the outbreak of war, E's home became a fort for the white settlers of the neighbourhood and quarters for the soldiers sent by government. After the war E. settled down to the peaceful continuance of his missionary labours and his writing. Called in 1758 to assume the presidency of New Jersey College (Princeton), he accepted somewhat reluctantly, thus bringing to an end a period of seven years when he was a missionary to the Indians. A month after leaving Stockbridge he died from vaccination for smallpox.

J. LESLIE DUNSTAN

G. D. Henderson: *The Burning Bush* (Edinburgh 1957); P. Miller: *Jonathan Edwards* (New York 1949); O. E. Winslow: *Jonathan Edwards* (New York 1940); *DAB* VI, 30–37; *RGG* II, 309f.

EGEDE, HANS (1686–1758), born at Harrested in northern Norway, became in 1722 a pioneer missionary to the Eskimos of Greenland. From the start he was faced with the gravest of problems. He had difficulty in mastering the Eskimo language, and found it very defective as an instrument for the communication of Christian truth. The power of the local *shāmans*, the *angakut*, was so great that the people seemed incapable of freeing themselves from their domination and of listening to the gospel. In the first ten years E. hardly ventured to baptize a single adult Greenlander. It was the services rendered by E. and his devoted wife during the terrible smallpox epidemic of 1733 that in the end really opened the hearts of the Greenlanders to the missionaries and to their message; having seen Christian love so strikingly manifested in practice, they realized that the love of God is something more than a form of words.

E's difficulties were increased when in

1733 the first Moravian missionaries arrived, and set up work on lines very different from those developed by E. A better time began when in 1734 E. was joined by his son Paul, who had grown up in Greenland and could speak the language of the people. Under the influence of his preaching something like a religious revival broke out among them. E. returned to Denmark in 1736, to engage in the training of missionaries for the Greenland work. The mission was carried on by Paul E., who in 1766 produced the whole of the NT in the Eskimo language as spoken in Greenland.

Virtually all the inhabitants of Greenland today are Christians.

STEPHEN NEILL

L. Boebe: *Hans Egede: Colonizer and Missionary of Greenland* (Copenhagen 1952); O. G. Myklebust, ed.: *Hans Egede, 1686–1758* (Oslo 1958), *RGG* II, 310f.

EGEDE INSTITUTE OF MISSIONARY STUDY AND RESEARCH, THE, was founded in 1946 to promote intelligent interest in Christian missionary work, and scientific research into its history and problems. The EI works in close collaboration with the churches, the missionary societies, and the two theological faculties in Oslo. It publishes the *Norsk Tidsskrift for Misjon,* the most authoritative missionary periodical in the Norwegian language. It has established a library, and supplies information on missionary subjects as desired to churches, schools and individuals. The director from the beginning has been Dr O. G. Myklebust, who is also Professor of Mission in the Free Faculty of Theology in Oslo.

EDITORS

EGYPT (UNITED ARAB REPUBLIC). A republic of N. Africa. Area 386,198 sq.m. Population 29,600,000 (UN estimate 1965) consisting of Arabs, the majority group, and minorities of Armenians, Turks, Assyrians and Europeans. Religious divisions: Muslims 91%, Christians 7.89%, Jews 0.34%.

Distinctive Egyptian civilization is 5,000 years old. Other ancient cultures—Assyrian, Greek, Roman, Byzantine, Armenian and Arab—left their mark, and have been followed by the diverse influences of modern Europe and America.

Christianity came early to E. St. Mark is said to have preached there, and the patriarchate of Alexandria to have been founded in A.D. 67. In the 5th century there was a schism, out of which came the Monophysites who insisted that, after the Incarnation, the divine Word had one nature only, divine rather than human. Not receiving satisfaction at the Council of Chalcedon, A.D. 451, the group broke off from the Orthodox church amid bitterness and bloodshed, and formed the Coptic (meaning Egyptian) church in E. Christianity survived the Muslim Arab invasion, which it failed to do in other N. African countries; the Coptic church has kept its identity through sixteen centuries, thirteen of them under Muslim rule, and is still the largest Christian group in the country.

*Franciscan missionaries began work in the 13th century. St. Francis is said to have preached to Muslims in Damietta in 1219. Intensive work among Copts was begun in the 16th century by *Jesuits, *Capuchins and Franciscans. After the conversion of the Coptic bishop of Jerusalem to Roman Catholicism in 1741, he was named bishop of the Uniate Church of E., consisting of converts from the Coptic church to Catholicism. The Uniate church maintains communion with Rome, recognizes the supremacy of the pope, concurring in all matters relating to faith, while differing from the RC church in certain practical ways: services have always been in the vernacular, and married men may be ordained to the priesthood.

The greatest growth of the RC church has occurred since the middle of the 19th century. Its present total membership is estimated at 162,000 (WCH 1968). Educational work has been developed on all levels, especially by French orders of monks and nuns. All religious and racial groups are found in the schools. There are several medical workers, and the Franciscans have done some social welfare work among Muslims. During the 20th century the Uniate churches have increased their rate of growth, with membership coming from all minority racial groups of Orthodox Christians. Very few Muslims have accepted Christianity.

Protestant missionaries from Britain and continental Europe entered E. in the 19th century. Among them were: *BFBS 1818; *CMS 1825; the Society for the Promotion of Female Education 1856, closing in 1889; *North Africa Mission 1892; Egypt General Mission 1898. Although all such groups on entering hoped to reach Muslims, they found a more ready response among the Copts. The strongest Protestant work was carried on through schools and hospitals. The CMS started a training programme for Coptic clergy in the hope that, if the Coptic churches became stronger, they would themselves be able to reach out to win Muslims. Many Copts, however, influenced by Bible study and stimulated by the warmth and zeal of the evangelical missionaries, left their own churches and became Protestants; thus some Protestant churches were formed at the expense of the Coptic church. At the same time certain missionaries worked intensively to reach Muslims; this was a special concern of CMS for more than 50 years from the end of the 19th century. A notable achievement in this connection was the bilingual magazine, *Orient and Occident*, founded by D. M. Thornton and Temple *Gairdner in 1904. Other Christian literature was produced and distributed by the *SPCK and the Nile Mission Press (which moved to Lebanon in 1957).

Two groups sent missionaries to the *Jews: the LSPCJ and the Church of Scotland Missions to the Jews. Much of this work was educational. It all had to be closed in 1948 when the State of Israel was formed.

The United Presbyterian Church (USA) opened work in 1854. It is known throughout E. as the American Mission. It grew rapidly and has maintained schools, hospitals, an agricultural college, a seminary and work for literacy and literature. Its American College for Girls in Cairo provides education from kindergarten up to Junior College. Students come from several Near Eastern countries and from differing religious backgrounds. (Government requires that all children be taught their own religion in all private and public schools.) Students from the college, both Christian and Muslim, work together in developing village welfare programmes, and in projects for the betterment of family and home life, for better government and for the rights of women. Such schools have had a greater impact upon the life of people and country than any other type of Christian witness. The American University in Cairo has played an increasingly important role in higher education, attracting students from many religious backgrounds and from various parts of the world. The entire school system developed by the American Mission was placed under Arab leadership in 1963.

There is an active *autonomous Coptic Evangelical Church, Synod of the Nile. It is the largest Protestant body in E. (total community 100,000: WCH 1968). Its Arab pastors are trained at the seminary in Cairo. The Coptic Evangelical Church supports an Arab missionary family in Kenya. The church is a member of the *WCC.

Other Protestant churches in E. include the Anglican and the Armenian Evangelical churches. Some degree of co-operation among Christian bodies has been maintained but the extent of participation has varied. An annual Fellowship of Unity service has been held in the Anglican cathedral in Cairo.

The WCC has been working to help the Coptic church. Youth camps sponsored by the WCC Youth Department have made a valuable contribution. Through the Near East Christian Council Committee on Arab Refugees, *DICARWS has been aiding refugees in E. by means of funds and personnel. Local co-operation involves a number of Christian bodies.

The first literacy house in the world was opened in mid-E. after the second world war under the auspices of the *Committee on World Literacy and Christian Literature (National Council of Churches of the USA) in close co-operation with the Coptic Evangelical Church and the American Mission. To do the follow-up necessary to make a literacy programme effective the Coptic Evangelical Organization for Social Services was formed; it works through programmes for literature, Bible teaching, the improvement of agriculture, home economics and home industries. These have led to co-operation among all Christian groups at village level.

GLORA WYSNER

H. Ziock: *Ägypten* (Bonn 1958); *BM* II, 724–32.

EL SALVADOR. See AMERICA, CENTRAL.

ELECTION (Hebrew *bahar* and Greek *eklogē*, meaning 'to choose'). The concept of divine choice or election is the central and unifying theme of the biblical history of salvation. In the OT God chooses the nation Israel to be the conveyor of his grace to the nations. This is seen first in the choice of Abraham and his descendants (Gen.21:1–2; 22:15–18) and in the election of the whole nation of Israel (Exod.3:7–10; Deut.6:21–23). While election carries with it certain privileges, implicit in the divine choice is a corresponding responsibility on the part of those chosen. It is always election for mission.

In the NT election focuses upon the figure of Jesus Christ who is the instrument of God's election of the human race as the race that is to be saved and upon the church as the 'chosen race' (1 Pet.2:9). Always the election of the church is dependent upon the Elect One, Jesus Christ. Again, election carries with it a specific responsibility, i.e. Christian witness. Of particular importance is the latter feature for the Christian mission. The Christian is elected not for special prerogative but for specific responsibility. The new believer accordingly understands his relationship with God as one of election, and he, therefore, must assume his responsibility to bear witness to Christ's electing

grace. The essential features of the doctrine are the sovereign freedom of God which, at the same time, does not annul the freedom of response on the part of man, the decisiveness of God's electing act in Jesus Christ, and the corporate nature of this election as a community summoned to mission.

JAMES C. LOGAN

H. H. Rowley: *The Biblical Doctrine of Election* (London 1953); G. Schrenk in G. Kittel, ed.: *Theologisches Wörterbuch zum Neuen Testament*, IV (Stuttgart 1942), pp. 181–97; *ERE* V, 256–61.

ELIOT, JOHN (1604–1690), was born at Widford, England, and graduated at Jesus College, Cambridge. Falling into disfavour with the established church, he migrated to Massachusetts Bay Colony in 1632. He was pastor and teacher at the church in Roxbury until his death. Becoming interested in the Indians living nearby he mastered their language; through his preaching, teaching, and visiting among them numbers embraced the Christian faith. He recognized that the converts had special educational needs and opportunities for practical living, which they could not get while remaining in contact with the non-Christian Indians, and conceived the plan of establishing independent communities for them. The Massachusetts General Court set aside land for the use of Christian Indians to implement the plan. Natick, Nonantum (Newton), Ponkapoag (Stoughton) and other towns were built. Each community had its church, school, homes, and land for sustenance farming; the inhabitants were organized in groups for their mutual welfare, and through the groups a representative government set up; life was structured around the devotional and ethical requirements of the Christian faith. Leaders for church and government received special training. For the use of the Indians, E. translated into the Algonquin language the Catechism (1653), the NT (1661), the OT (1663), and a Grammar (1666). News of this work reached England, and in 1649 Parliament passed an act incorporating 'The Society for the Propagation of the Gospel in New England'.

Funds were raised by that society in support of E.'s enterprises and of those of other men similarly engaged. E. visited the Indian communities regularly, acting as a kind of superintendent. In 1675 various Indian tribes united under King Philip, of the Wampoags, in a war to drive the white man out. The conflict lasted more than a year with heavy losses on both sides. The Indian towns were disrupted and gradually disappeared. E. also joined with Richard Mather and Thomas Wilder in editing the *Bay Psalm Book*, used in the colonies for nearly a century.

J. LESLIE DUNSTAN

C. Beals: *John Eliot* (New York 1957); W. Walker: *Ten New England Leaders* (Chicago 1901); O. E. Winslow: *John Eliot, 'Apostle to the Indians'* (Boston 1968); *DAB* VI, 79f.; *RGG* II, 428.

ELLIS, WILLIAM (1794–1872). Born at Wisbech, Cambridgeshire, England, he offered his services to the *LMS and was trained by Dr Bogue of Gosport. Appointed to Tahiti in 1815 he took the first printing press and laid the foundation of elementary education in the islands. For a year in the Sandwich Islands he helped the *American Board pioneer missionaries to reduce the language to writing, to translate Gospels and hymns, and he baptized the first convert, the Queen Mother.

In 1832 E. was appointed foreign secretary of the LMS. He wrote many books and was an authority on Polynesia and Madagascar. His health broke in 1841 and he resigned, yet his greatest work lay ahead. As foreign secretary one great concern was Madagascar where the young church was undergoing prolonged and bitter persecution. This ended in 1852 by which time E. had regained his health. He was sent to Madagascar to help to re-establish the liberated and vastly increased church. For three years he encouraged and organized local congregations, schools, the printing press and theological training, and was adviser and friend to a new generation of missionaries.

ROBERT O. LATHAM

W. Ellis: *Polynesian Researches* (2 vols., London 1828), *History of Madagascar* (2 vols., London 1838); *DNB* XVII, 296.

EMDE, JOHANNES (1774–1859), initiator of the mission amongst the Javanese. Born at Schmillinghausen—Waldeck, Germany, E., a skilled miller, came as a sailor of the Dutch East India Company to Indonesia. After years of obligatory war service he settled in Surabaja (1811), learning and practising the trade of a watchmaker. As a leading member of a pietistic group mainly of Eurasians, E. was stimulated by Josef *Kam (1815) to undertake missionary work among the Javanese people. Assisted by his Javanese-speaking Eurasian wife and daughter he distributed handwritten tracts and Bible texts which he obtained from his friend, the translator of the first Javanese NT, Gottlieb Brückner. A group of 'seeking' Javanese Muslims sought contact with him; these had been influenced by the Eurasian Coenraad Laurens Coolen (1770–1863) who was at that time evangelizing in East Java. Unlike the evangelization of Coolen which was carried out within the framework of Javanese culture, unrelated to Dutch colonial ecclesiasticism, E.'s attitude was narrowly pietistic, but also bound up within the forms of the colonial church. In course of time E. led a number of Javanese into the Protestant church to be baptized (the first baptism was in 1843, when there were 30 candidates; by 1845 already 220 Javanese had been baptized). In opposition to the 'Javanese Christianity' of Coolen he strictly required the Javanese catechumens to adopt a European attitude (expressed e.g. in style of hairdressing and clothes). This contradiction was overcome when organized Dutch missions entered (1851). Rightly the East Javanese church reckons E. as well as Coolen among her 'fathers'.

See also INDONESIA.

T. MÜLLER-KRÜGER

T. Müller-Krüger: *Der Protestantismus in Indonesien* (Stuttgart 1968).

EPISCOPACY. From very early times it

has been recognized that the Christian ministry includes the elements of oversight (*episkopē*), pastoral care (*oikodomē*) and practical service (*diakonia*). As to the origins of the episcopate as a separate order to fulfil the ministry of oversight, the lack of clear evidence makes it impossible to hold any view with confidence. What is clear is that in the 2nd century the episcopate had developed with a special responsibility to maintain the unity of the church, in doctrine through continuity with the apostolic voice, in the world through fellowship with all the other bishops in the world, and in liturgical order through loving care of the presbyters and all other ministers. Until the 16th century, all forms of the Christian church, whether orthodox, heretical or separated, maintained the episcopal succession and attached the greatest importance to it. At the time of the Reformation, many of the churches which accepted reformed principles rejected an episcopacy which seemed to them to lack apostolic authority or evangelical character.

In countries in which the church exists as a small minority in the midst of a very large non-Christian population, and where the conditions therefore are very much like those of the 2nd century, almost all the churches have in a remarkable way, and for the same reasons, developed a quasi-episcopate of superintendents, moderators or chairmen, whose functions are much like those of the bishop, though in most cases without any formal act of consecration, and sometimes only for a limited period of years.

In negotiations for union between churches which have, and churches which have not, an episcopate with historic succession linking it to the distant past, the question of E. has naturally presented itself as a major difficulty. When the starting point of the discussion has been theories or methods of succession, the result has invariably been mutual frustration, and in a number of cases the breaking off of the discussions. It has been found more profitable to ask, What is a bishop and what does he do? When the answer has been

given that the bishop is 'a partner of your labours, a sharer of your griefs, a lightener of your anxieties, a helper of your joy' (Samuel Wilberforce), many ministers who have never known a bishop have welcomed the idea gladly. Once this concept of the episcopate has taken hold, the problems of how to secure bishops who will be able to count on the widest acceptance and recognition in the church has not been found to cause any great difficulty. In the *CSI (1947) the greatest success has been that of the bishops in commending themselves to all sections of the church as shepherds of the flock under Christ who is the chief Shepherd, and servants of the people of God.

STEPHEN NEILL

H. van Campenhausen: *Kirchliches Amt und Christliche Vollmacht* (Tübingen 1953); K. E. Kirk, ed.: *The Apostolic Ministry* (London 1957[2]); G. Kittel, ed.: *Theologisches Wörterbuch zum Neuen Testament*, II (Stuttgart 1942), pp.604–19, art. '*Episkopos*'; E. Schweizer: *Church Order in the New Testament* (Naperville, Ill. 1961); G. Simon, ed.: *Bishops* (London 1961); H. B. Swete, ed.: *Early History of the Church and Ministry* (Cambridge 1918); W. Telfer: *The Office of a Bishop* (London 1963).

EPISCOPAL MISSIONS. See ANGLICAN MISSIONS.

EPISCOPATE, INDIGENOUS. It would seem obvious that, in churches which maintain the episcopal system, no church can be regarded as complete until it has a complete hierarchy drawn from its own indigenous resources. In point of fact, however, isolated churches have over long periods preferred to have foreign bishops, as a link with the church outside their own area, and perhaps as a safeguard against absorption by a multitude of non-Christians near at hand. Thus in the ancient church of the *Syrian Christians in South India, no local member of that church seems to have been raised to the episcopate until the 17th century; and the church in Russia had

Greek metropolitans until after the Council of Florence in 1438.

With the renewal of *RC missions at the end of the middle ages, experiments were made with the creation of indigenous episcopates. In 1518 a young prince from the Congo, Dom Henrique, was consecrated titular bishop of Utica; it is not quite certain that he ever returned to Africa. In 1637 a young Brahman from Goa, Matthew de *Castro, was consecrated in Rome as *Vicar Apostolic for India, and died also in Rome in 1677, not apparently having been a success. In 1674 Gregory *Lo was appointed as Vicar Apostolic for North China, and succeeded in obtaining consecration in 1685; he seems to have been highly respected by all. But none of these experiments was followed up. A new beginning was not made until 1896, when an Indian hierarchy was created for the RC section of the Syrian Christians. The first Indian bishop of the Latin rite was consecrated for Tuticorin in 1923. Plans for the consecration of Chinese bishops were carried out, in the face of strenuous opposition from the missions, through the express insistence of the pope. The first African bishop, Mgr. Kiwanuka for Uganda, was consecrated in 1938. Since then progress has been extremely rapid in all the RC missions. Cardinals have been created for Japan, China, India, Africa and other areas.

The Philippine Independent (Aglipayan) church, had an episcopate from the beginning, but this lacked any succession recognized by other churches. This technical defect was rectified when in 1948 bishops of PECUSA consecrated three of the bishops of the Philippine church according to the Anglican rite.

Before the end of the 18th century Anglicans had begun to discuss the necessity of Indian bishops for an Indian church; but the state connection of the English church was held to stand in the way and nothing was done. The first initiative came from the famous secretary of the *CMS, Henry *Venn, who arranged that S. A. *Crowther should be consecrated in 1864 as missionary bishop for the Niger area.

From that time on the Anglican church has always had African bishops, but not until 1952 was an African again put in full and independent charge of a diocese. In India the first consecration took place only in 1912 (*Azariah); in China in 1918, and in Japan in 1922. From this time on progress was rapid. The heads of the Anglican provinces of Japan, China, India, Uganda, West Africa and Brazil are now nationals of those countries. 1966 has seen the election of the first Australian archbishop.

The Methodist Episcopal church followed lines similar to the Anglican. The first Japanese bishop (*Honda) was appointed in 1907, the first Indian (*Chitambar) in 1930.

In the appointment of an indigenous bishop, two questions have to be considered. Is the man chosen to be chief pastor of a small flock in his own country? or is he to be such a man as can make his voice heard on such great occasions as the *Vatican Council or the Lambeth Conference of Anglican bishops? The younger churches themselves seem to attach more weight to the second consideration than do the missionaries.

STEPHEN NEILL

EQUATORIAL GUINEA, known as Spanish Guinea until independence in 1968, consists of the small mainland territory of Rio Muni (10,140 sq.m.), the island of Fernando Po (in the Bight of Biafra), and three small groups of islands. Population in 1967 was 277,000. Until 1968 the territories were governed as an Overseas Province of Spain. RC Spanish missions claim to have baptized almost the entire population. The Protestant community numbers 9,000, including 7,500 in *Iglesia Evangelica Presbiteriana en Rio Muni* (served by the United Presbyterian Church USA, which began work in 1850), 700 in *WEC, and (on Fernando Po) 800 in *Iglesia Metodista* (MMS). Early in the 20th century the Fang *syncretistic movement Bwiti entered from Gabon, and there are numerous adherents. The only separatist movement has been *Asamblea de los*

Hermanos, a small break-off which began in 1937 among the Kombe tribe from the Presbyterian mission.

DAVID B. BARRETT

BM II, 733.

ESCHATOLOGY AND MISSION. Thinking as to the relationship between E. and M. as this has developed on the continent of Europe, and especially in German missionary thinking since the first world war, is a part of the process of liberation from the system of missionary theology established by G. *Warneck, and from a way of thinking which had aroused anxiety as early as the *World Missionary Conference held at Edinburgh in 1910—an anxiety which spread throughout the Anglo-American world of missionary interest—since it seemed to set up a line of unbroken continuity between Christian civilization and the gospel.

In the history of theological thought, the roots of this reaction lay in the rediscovery, at the end of the 19th century, of the significance of eschatology for NT theology, and in the dialectical theology of Karl Barth, with the radical question mark which it set against everything that happens purely within the world of men. The direction of attention to the eschatological character of mission should seem to emphasize the provisional character, and the 'eschatological limitation' of all missionary effort through 'the God who himself is coming again' (Hartenstein).

At the third World Missionary Conference (Tambaram 1938), the eschatological aspect came clearly into view in a declaration of the German delegation, supported by H. *Kraemer—signs of the influence of Kraemer's book *The Christian Message in a Non-Christian World*, written in preparation for the conference, are clearly to be seen in the declaration. The church is to be guarded against secularization, and the idea of the kingdom of God against identification with goals which can be reached in the realm of space and time. The kingdom of God will be achieved 'by a creative act of God Himself', the church stands 'between the epochs which God has appointed'; Christians are 'citizens of two world orders'; it is not for them to bring into effect 'a social programme for a new ordering of the world, or to establish a Christian state'.

The revolution in the east had brought the Christian missionary enterprise into a situation of crisis. The events of the second world war naturally exercised a profound influence on German thinking, and favoured the tendency, already present in German missionary thinkers, to see missions ever more closely in the light of the eschatological dimension. The lead was taken by W. *Freytag and K. Hartenstein, who based their conclusions largely on the exegetical works of O. Cullmann. The experience of crisis laid fresh emphasis on the importance of 'looking to the end' (Freytag), and raised the question of the significance of the interim period, between the 'already' of the resurrection of Jesus Christ, and the 'not yet' of his return. 'The significance of this time lies in the gathering together of the community which awaits the coming of the Lord. This significance of the pause in the history of salvation finds its full expresssion in the missionary enterprise' (W. Freytag). Through this enterprise the death of the Lord is proclaimed until he comes; the obedience of faith is set up; the people of God is gathered out from among the peoples of the earth with a view to the end. So mission is an anticipatory sign of the end; a condition for its coming, and a preparation for it. In mission God makes effective his plan for the world.

With this eschatological understanding of mission, it becomes possible to regard the missionary enterprise as a 'continuous activity of God himself', in distinction from the missionary service rendered by men. And from this eschatological direction of missionary thinking arose the possibility of understanding mission as *Missio Dei*, an activity in which God himself is the principal actor. This has been increasingly stressed since the Willingen Conference of 1952.

This, however, led to a modification of the original eschatological interpretation, which had been worked out in closest association with the understanding in terms of salvation history. God's missionary activity was now seen in relation to the whole of human history, and not only in relation to a particular salvation-history within it. God's sovereignty is now seen not simply as the goal of history, but as his sovereign dealing in the present with the nearer future of mankind. This new outlook—this all-embracing kingdom of *Shalom* (peace, justice), serves as a basis for hope for this world. Mission is the 'injection of hope into the situation' (Hoekendijk); it is 'hope in action' (Margull); it is 'the advocate of the world'; but this function can only properly be fulfilled, when mission is the advocate of the future of the world, based on the promises of God.

See THEOLOGY OF MISSION.

ARTUR SCHORZMANN

O. Cullmann: 'Eschatology and Mission in the NT' in G. H. Anderson, ed.: *The Theology of the Christian Mission* (New York 1961), pp.42–54; W. Freytag: '*Mission im Blick aufs Ende*' in *Reden und Aufsätze* II (1961), 186ff.; K. Hartenstein: *Die Mission als theologisches Problem* (Stuttgart 1933); H. J. Margull: *Theologie der missionarischen Verkündigung* (Stuttgart 1959); M. A. C. Warren: *The Truth of Vision* (London 1948); L. Wiedenmann: *Mission and Eschatologie* (Paderborn 1965).

ETHICAL PROBLEMS IN MISSIONS.

A man whose life has been deeply influenced by Christian ideas and who goes into a culture which has not been so influenced faces one set of issues which present grave ethical problems. On the other hand the man who is a native of that culture may find nothing unethical in what horrifies the other. There is yet another difference which has to be noted. The Asian or African who has become a Christian as a result of his first contact with the Christian mission will probably face quite different ethical problems from those with which his son and grandson, brought up as Christians, are

confronted. There is no easy definition of ethical problems in missions.

Two illustrations will make this clear. In their first contact with tribal Africa, missionaries from the west found the universal practice of *polygamy. What was the Christian attitude? Traditionally Christian teaching has insisted on monogamy. For missionaries polygamy presented a very great ethical problem. The African, on the other hand, often saw things differently. In African culture the man is the warrior, the woman is the cultivator. Furthermore in African culture, for the most part, a child would not be weaned for two or even three years. Polygamy for the tribal African was an economic necessity. And in a society which made no provision for unmarried women it was a social necessity. Faced by the Christian demand for monogamy the African had real ethical problems, not the least of which was justice to the wives he was expected to jettison. And this in turn was complicated by the fact that marriage with all his wives was a contractual matter involving the inter-relationship of different family groups, and also involving a complicated system of dowry. The ethics of the missionary thus easily conflicted with the ethics of the African, neither understanding the other.

The problem changes for the African who is a second or third generation Christian. He has been brought up to accept monogamy. But what are his responsibilities for the wider family group of which he is traditionally a part? Is he to build his life exclusively round the 'nuclear' family on the western pattern? Or is he to accept a moral responsibility for nephews and nieces and cousins, responsibilities generally recognized in African society? Such an African may offer himself for the Christian ministry. Relative to other occupations it is very badly paid. Probably his family has paid for his education, expecting him to get a well-paid post and so be able to provide for the education of others in the family. What is his duty as a Christian? This is one of the ethical challenges facing many Africans today.

A quite different ethical issue can be illustrated from Asia. In the 17th century there was a great controversy among Roman Catholic missionaries in China, the *'rites' controversy, as to whether it was right or wrong to accept the Chinese custom of venerating ancestors. Matthew *Ricci, the great *Jesuit missionary, favoured treating this as an act of piety but not of worship. *Franciscans and *Dominicans took the opposite view. In the 20th century in Japan something similar divided Christian opinion. Were the reverences directed towards the Emperor acts of worship or were they really no more than the Japanese equivalent of the American school discipline of 'saluting the flag'? Some missionaries saw it as the equivalent of offering incense to Caesar as to God. Others saw it as no more than an act of patriotism.

Missionaries as the conscious or unconscious agents of *imperialism have also posed for the churches and others a whole range of other ethical problems.

MAX WARREN

C. Fujisawa: *Concrete Universality of the Japanese Way of Thinking* (Hokuseido Press, Japan 1958); W. Ingleheart: *A Century of Protestant Christianity in Japan* (Vermont 1959); R. C. Jenkins: *The Jesuits in China and the Legation of Cardinal De Tournon* (London 1894); A. Phillips, L. P. Mair and L. Harries: *Survey of African Marriage and Family Life* (London 1953); O. Manoni: *La Psychologie de la Colonisation* (Paris 1950—Eng. tr. *Prospero and Caliban*, London 1956); O. Manoni: 'The Decolonisation of Myself', (tr.) in *Race* VII (London April 1966); A. Southall, ed.: *Social Change in Modern Africa* (London 1961).

ETHIOPIA has for many centuries constituted a kingdom occupying the high ground north of Kenya and east of Sudan; its present extent, with former Eritrea, is 457,265 sq.m. Population has never been counted by census, but was estimated (1967) to be 23,667,000. Around the year A.D. 350, Christianity was adopted by King Ezana of Axum after it had been brought to E. by two shipwrecked Greek youths from Syria; one, Frumentius, was later consecrated bishop by the patriarch of Alexandria. This custom of a non-Ethiopian being appointed by Alexandria to head the Ethiopian church continued for sixteen centuries. In the 19th century the emperor Johannes attempted to break this Egyptian control by appealing to the Greek Orthodox church, but without avail. In 1929 a compromise was reached by Alexandria consecrating five Ethiopian bishops, but retaining the right to appoint the *abune* (archbishop). The Italian military occupation in 1936 broke the link with Egypt and encouraged the 1937 coup d'etat in which the Ethiopian church proclaimed itself autocephalous, exiled the Egyptian *abune* K'erlos, and elected in his place Bishop Abraham who then consecrated twelve bishops. The reaction from Alexandria was immediately to excommunicate and anathematise the new *abune* and his bishops. In 1941 the emperor Haile Selassie re-opened negotiations with Egypt, but the Coptic Orthodox church was adamant, invoking an apocryphal 7th century canon of Nicea placing E. under Alexandria for all time. The excommunication was finally lifted in 1942 and agreement was reached in 1948; in 1950 an Ethiopian archbishop Bassilios was consecrated in Cairo. No census has been taken of the church, but in 1966 it was estimated to number five or six million, largely Amhara and Tigrai peoples, but with missionary work being begun among several other tribes under two missionary societies formed for the purpose.

Religious affiliation in 1960 was estimated to be: Ethiopian Orthodox, 35% of the population; Muslim, 35%; pagan, 25%; Protestant and Roman Catholic, the remainder. RC missions have been singularly unfortunate in E.; *Jesuit missions entered the country in 1557, but their hopes of converting the entire Ethiopian church rapidly dimmed, and in consequence Bishop Oviedo pronounced a sentence of excommunication against the entire Ethiopian church. A long period of bitterness followed, and RC missions never fully recovered their early influence. By 1966 there was an archdiocese of Addis Ababa and two suffragan dioceses following the Coptic rite, and five jurisdictions following the Latin rite; the total number of Roman Catholics was 125,000, about two-thirds belonging to the Coptic rite.

Protestant missions began in the 19th century but did not establish themselves until early in the 20th. By 1966 there were 27 denominations at work, with a total Protestant community of 227,125. The largest missions and churches were: Fellowship of Evangelical Believers (*SIM) with 125,000 adherents stemming from a large revival among the southern Wallamo, Darasa and other tribes; Ethiopian Evangelical Church Mekane Yesus (served by Lutheran missions from the USA, Denmark, Sweden, Norway, Iceland and Germany) with 59,510; the Bethel Evangelical Church (served by United Presbyterian Church USA) with 15,170; and others. Several of the larger missions attempted at first to work within the Ethiopian church without trying to form a separate denomination; opposition soon forced them out, and only the BCMS (Anglican) still continues its work within.

Separatist movements from Protestant missions began in 1955 when a large part of the southern revival seceded to form the Kambatta Evangelical Church, now with 25,000 adherents; this body has negotiated for entry into the Mekane Yesus Church.

Ethiopia is a land of many languages. The ancient Ge'ez remains the sole liturgical language of the Ethiopian church, but is not understood by the people, and only imperfectly by many of the priests. The Bible has been translated into Amharic since 1840 (most recent revision completed in 1961), and also into the Galla (1899) and Tigrinya (1957) languages; and scripture portions exist in 13 other languages. The decision of the government to make Amharic the sole official language has proved a hindrance to the work among non-Amharic-speaking peoples; but there is no indication that the other languages are likely to disappear for some time to come.

See also EASTERN CHURCHES, LESSER OR SEPARATED; FLAD, JOHN MARTIN; STERN, HENRY AARON.

DAVID B. BARRETT

K. Ewert: *Äthiopien* (Bonn 1959); G. A. Lipsky: *Ethiopia* (New Haven 1962); *BM* II, 358–64; *NCE* V, 583–86; *WKL*, 103–05.

EUROPE. The conversion of E. to the Christian faith took a long time. The terminal point is generally taken to be the conversion of Jagiello, king of the Lithuanians, in 1386. But the eastward spread of Christianity in Russia continued throughout the 15th century, indeed long after, though perhaps the later stages may be considered to belong to the history of Asia rather than that of E. But this general christianization of the population did not mean that all the people were even in name Christian. The church has always had to reckon with three types of resistance to the spread of the faith.

Long after 1386 there were groups, separated from the rest of the population by difference of language or customs, which had been hardly, if at all, christianized. Typical of these were the gypsies (Romany) and the Lapps of the far north. Missionary work among the Lapps was encouraged by the Swedish king Gustavus Vasa as long ago as 1559; but the NT was first translated for them as late as 1755, and only at the end of the 18th century was the work of their conversion completed.

The presence of the Jew in the midst has always been a problem for the church. Oppressed, persecuted, expelled, the Jews have managed to maintain themselves in every European country. Every possible method of missionary work has been tried—coercion, bribery, favour, cultural assimilation, assistance in times of distress, and plain preaching of the word of God. The number of conversions has been considerably larger than is generally recognized either by Jews or by Christians; but the people as a whole remains, an unassimilable element in society, usually in peaceful or even friendly co-existence, making a notable contribution to the life of the various countries in many directions, but still separate and aloof. The number of Jews in E. has greatly diminshed since the massacre of Hitler's *Third Reich*. (See also JEWS, MISSIONS TO THE.)

For centuries parts of E. have been in Muslim hands. Granada, the last Muslim stronghold in Spain, was captured by the Christians as recently as 1492. At the other end of E., the point of deepest penetration was Vienna, which was reached in 1683. The liberation of the Christian population began with the Greek war of independence in 1821. But until 1923 there was a considerable Muslim minority in the Balkan countries. Now the only countries with a strong Muslim element are Turkey in E., Albania, and the parts of Yugoslavia previously known as Bosnia and Herzgovina. Attempts to evangelize the European Muslims have not been very successful. In the 16th century the pious nobleman Hans Ungnad von Sonneck interested himself in the project of publishing translations of Christian books in Turkish, in the hope that it might be possible so to bring the Turks to the true Christian faith; but the project seems never to have got beyond the stage of planning. The Czech Vaslav Budovec, who resided at the imperial embassy in Constantinople from 1577 to 1581, is reported to have published a refutation of the Qur'an and to have converted one Turk. In the days of Muslim domination it was hardly possible for the eastern churches to do anything for the evangelization of the European Muslims; and, since emancipation, they do not seem to have interested themselves very much in the matter, apparently taking the view that the conversion of a Muslim is impossible. In Russia various attempts were made in the 19th century to convert the Muslim peoples in the borderlands between European and Asiatic Russia, with more apparent than real success. American Protestants entered in with such notable schools as Robert College, Constantinople (1863); but, though the influence of this western education was wide and deep, conversions did not result.

Since the beginning of the 16th century by far the greater part of the Christian mission-ary work in the world has been carried on by Europeans. Spain and Portugal were the chief sources of supply in the 16th and 17th centuries, to be outrun by France in the 18th. In the 19th century, the missionary enterprise became fully international, every country taking part; but in 1970 the majority of all Christian missionaries in the world were from E. Among Protestant missionaries, however, those from America were more numerous than those of all other countries put together.

In the 20th century the question arises whether E. itself should not be regarded as a mission field. The answer to some extent depends on the definition of terms. The situation in E. in the 20th century is much less favourable to Christianity than it was in the 19th. In the communist-controlled countries attacks on Christianity as on every form of religion are continuous and vocal; the success has been less than expected, though time must pass before it becomes possible to estimate the extent to which the younger generation has been permanently turned away from the faith. Industrialization and the growth of great cities have overthrown the traditional structure of the church and parish. For some reason that is not yet clear the dweller in a large city easily becomes alienated from the visible practice of any religion. E. had to take the first shocks of the industrial revolution and of modern scientific discovery, and its churches have been the first to show the effects of what is becoming a universal phenomenon. Church attendance in all countries is at a low ebb, the rural areas of RC countries showing up rather better than the rest.

It is, however, confusing to speak of E. as a mission field in the same sense as India or Japan. There is a great deal of residual Christianity. Almost the whole population has been baptized. Enquiries in many countries have shown that the majority even among those who do not themselves go to church send their children and are in favour of religious instruction in the schools. European culture has been deeply impressed by a thousand years of Christian teaching; opponents of the faith do not always recognize how deeply they themselves are indebted to this tradition. Christian worship and Christian instruction are everywhere available to any who wish to take advantage of them. It may be said that all this makes the task of the Christian witness more difficult than in a non-Christian country; it does mean that the task is not exactly the same task.

There are reasons to think that the present state of E. marks the sleep and not the disappearance of Christianity. The European churches have shown notable capacity for producing revivals of religion in unexpected ways and places. Christian theological and philosophical thought continues to exist on a very high level of competence. There is still a strong nucleus of convinced and devoted Christians. Recent conversions of adults, many of them of high intellectual quality, suggest that weariness of the dryness and barrenness of the other remedies offered for men's needs and sicknesses may drive people back to the faith of Christ. The worst way in which to face the situation today is the development or propagation of a mood of Christian pessimism.

STEPHEN NEILL

WKL, 374–77.

EVANGELICAL ALLIANCE. See EVANGELICAL CHURCHES.

EVANGELICAL ALLIANCE MISSION, THE (TEAM), was founded in 1890 by Fredrik *Franson, a Swedish-born immigrant converted in the USA, who toured much of the world as a missionary preaching the imminent coming of Christ and the need for repentance. Scores of missionaries were sent out under his leadership, particularly to China. Originally TEAM was known as the Scandinavian Alliance Mission of North America. The mission expanded gradually until today it has almost 900 missionaries serving in more than a score of countries. It concentrates on evangelism, church planting, and the training of national workers. Specialized ministries of radio, the printed page, hospitals, and translation work are conducted. The annual budget exceeds four million dollars.

TEAM is a member of *IFMA, publishes a bimonthly, *The Missionary Broadcaster*, and is active in evangelical co-operation. Following the retirement of T. J. Bach, early friend of the founder and later general director of the mission, and then of David H. Johnson, Vernon Mortenson was appointed titular head. Along with Louis King of the *CMA, he was co-chairman of the Wheaton Congress on the Church's Worldwide Mission which convened in Wheaton, Illinois (USA), in April 1966. This congress brought together representatives from IFMA and *EFMA in a conciliar situation. Mortenson continues to give leadership to the expanding unity movement among evangelicals. TEAM has recently constructed a new headquarters at 2500 North Main Street, Wheaton, Illinois, 60187 USA.

HAROLD LINDSELL

D. Woodward: *Aflame for God*: Biography of Fredrik Franson (Chicago 1966).

EVANGELICAL AND REFORMED CHURCHES. The E. and R. Churches came into existence in 1934 as the result of a merger between the Reformed Church in the United States (German Reformed) and the Evangelical Synod of North America. These churches, both of German origin, had supported missionary work over a long period, the Reformed mainly through the *ABCFM, and the Ev. Synod mainly through the *Basel Mission. Independent work began for the Reformed in 1879, when missionaries were sent to Japan by the church in its own name, and a strong centre developed at Sendai. The Ev. Synod in 1883 agreed to take over the work in Central India which had been started by the German Ev. Mission Society of the USA. In 1934, after the merger, the Board of International Missions (E. and R.) was formed to carry on the work previously undertaken by the two churches in separation. When the E. and R. agreed to further merger with the Congregational Christian Churches to form the *United Church of

Christ, the Board of International Missions was fused with the ABCFM and other organizations to form (1961) the United Church Board for World Ministries, which now became responsible for all the missions and world service projects of the uniting churches.

EDITORS

D. Dunn and others: *A History of the Evangelical and Reformed Church* (Philadelphia 1961); F. F. Goodsell: *You Shall Be My Witnesses* (Boston 1959).

EVANGELICAL CHURCHES. On the continent of Europe and in Latin America, the term is synonymous with 'Protestant'. In the UK, Canada and the USA, 'evangelical' is more commonly applied to denominations having traditional association with the Evangelical Alliance, one of the chief 19th century forerunners of the contemporary *ecumenical movement, or with the National Association of Evangelicals.

The Alliance, begun in 1846, united in co-operation those Protestants professing the authority of the Bible, the Incarnation, the atonement, salvation by faith, and the work of the Holy Spirit. A powerful influence was the evangelical wing of the Church of England, that section with strong affinities to Wesleyanism and keen opposition to the Tractarians who founded, for example, the *CMS. The Alliance strongly accented co-operative missionary work, carried through several international missionary conferences, and enlisted the participation of great Christian statesmen like Alexander *Duff (1806–1878), Hudson *Taylor (1832–1905), and Philip Schaff (1819–1893). It laid foundations in *comity agreements and co-operative assemblies which later became major marks of the ecumenical movement.

The National Association of Evangelicals (USA, founded 1942), rejects the 'modernism' of the *National Council of Churches; among its affiliates is *EFMA. Closely associated is the *Inter-Varsity Christian Fellowship. Among the prominent leaders have been Harold J. Ockenga of the Park Street Congregational Church in Boston, a church whose annual giving for missions is renowned, Carl F. H. Henry, former editor of *Christianity Today* (1956–1967), and Edward J. Carnell of Fuller Theological Seminary, Pasadena. The most famous evangelist associated with the cause has been Billy Graham (b.1918). The National Association of Evangelicals was founded to 'represent all evangelical believers in all denominations and groups', and it has strongly espoused evangelism and missions. Although it has avoided the sectarian excesses of splinters such as the American Council of Churches, the NAE has had difficulty in recent years in finding firm ground in the polarization between the floodtide of interchurch dialogue and co-operation (greatly enhanced by the Second *Vatican Council) and the pseudo-fundamentalism of minor leagues formed to perpetuate racism and economic reaction amidst present social tensions in the USA.

FRANKLIN H. LITTELL

W. R. Hogg: *Ecumenical Foundations* (New York 1952) pp.36ff; J. D. Murch: *Co-operation without Compromise: A History of the National Association of Evangelicals* (Grand Rapids 1956); J. C. Thiessen: *A Survey of World Missions* (Chicago 1961).

EVANGELICAL FOREIGN MISSIONS ASSOCIATION, THE, is a voluntary association of denominational and non-denominational foreign mission agencies. In the 1940s American evangelicals sought to organize an agency to counter the theological liberalism in the old Federal Council of Churches (now the National Council of Churches in the USA). Failure of evangelicals to agree on a number of matters led to the organization of two conservative ecumenical agencies, the American Council of Christian Churches and the National Association of Evangelicals.

In 1945 the EFMA was founded under the aegis of the National Association of Evangelicals. By 1968 more than 7,000 missionaries and 74 agencies were members of the EFMA; one out of every four

American Protestant missionaries was serving under EFMA member organizations in 120 countries around the world. The stated purpose of EFMA is to 'develop wider fellowship and a greater spiritual unity among evangelical missions. It encourages consultation and co-operation among evangelicals in national and international projects.'

EFMA provides united representation before governments for securing visas, etc.; it operates a missionary purchasing service in New York City and a travel agency in Chicago, Illinois. In 1966 it sponsored jointly with *IFMA the Congress on the Church's Worldwide Mission in Wheaton, Illinois.

HAROLD LINDSELL

J. D. Murch: *Co-operation without Compromise* (Grand Rapids 1956), pp.97–108.

EVANGELICAL INSTITUTES AND ACADEMIES. See ACADEMIES, EVANGELICAL.

EVANGELICAL UNION OF SOUTH AMERICA. This missionary society was born as a result of the disappointment felt by several evangelical leaders in Britain that the *World Missionary Conference held in Edinburgh in 1910 had excluded South America from its consideration. These leaders formed a board in 1911 with the intent of uniting and of stimulating the missionary work already being done in South America. The work of the South American Evangelical Mission in the Argentine and of the *RBMU in Peru was taken over in 1911. That of the Help for Brazil Mission was incorporated two years later. At the same time the branches of these missions in Canada were united into a North American council. The work of the EUSA in Brazil was greatly strengthened in 1942 by the union with the group of churches that had grown up on a self-supporting basis as a result of the influence of Dr *Kalley, one of the earliest pioneers. The British council continues to support work in the Argentine (except Patagonia),

in Peru and Central Brazil, while the North American council which now operates independently of the British organization, is responsible for missions in north-east Brazil, in Colombia, in Bolivia and in Patagonia. Both councils support at present about 80 missionaries each and are interdenominational in character, although it would generally be true to say that Baptist ideas predominate.

J. B. A. KESSLER, JR

EVANGELICAL UNITED BRETHREN MISSIONS. The EUB church was formed in 1946 from two denominations which arose from the 18th century revivals among German-speaking people in the United States. The United Brethren Church was founded by Philip W. Otterbein, a missionary of the German Reformed Church, and by Martin Boehm, a Mennonite lay minister. These men were united by a common assurance of personal salvation in an evangelistic meeting in 1767. Jacob Albright, the founder of the Evangelical Church, had a similar experience under the Methodists.

Impelled by this faith their followers carried the gospel to the German-speaking people around them and followed the migrations westward and into Canada. Conference and denominational missionary societies were formed to support these efforts. As English replaced German, the needs of other neglected minorities were recognized. Missions were established at various time among Italians, Jews, Hungarians, Poles, Chinese, freed Negroes, Appalachians and Spanish Americans.

Concern for Germans in the homeland sent the first overseas representatives of both groups back to Europe. The evangelical efforts there led to the formation of four conferences and a strong deaconess society.

The United Brethren Church established its first continuing overseas mission in Sierra Leone in 1855. Work among Chinese in Oregon led to a mission in Kwangtung, China, in 1889. A Japanese student in a United Brethren College led to work in Japan in 1895. The opening of Puerto Rico and the Philippines to Protestants through the Spanish American war resulted in sending missionaries there in 1899 and 1901.

Success in Europe delayed the movement of Evangelicals to other areas, but missionaries were sent to Japan in 1876 and to central China in 1900. Evangelical missionaries serving under other boards led to denominational involvement in North Nigeria in 1926 and Brazil in 1950.

The importance of co-operation and union was accepted early. *Comity assignments determined locations in Puerto Rico and the Philippines. The missions in China, the Philippines and Japan assisted founding of the united churches there. The mission board joined with other boards in establishing both the Board of Christian Work in Santo Domingo and the United Andean Indian Mission.

Individual missionaries were at times assigned to co-operating institutions such as Sekolah Theologia in Indonesia, and increasing shares of budgets were allotted to ecumenically determined concerns. In April 1968 the EUB and the Methodist Church merged to form the United Methodist Church, and thus their missionary responsibilities were similarly joined.

CALVIN H. REBER, JR

A. W. Drury: *History of the Church of the United Brethren in Christ* (Dayton, Ohio 1924); Paul H. Eller: *History of Evangelical Missions* (Harrisburg, Pa. 1942), *These Evangelical United Brethren* (Dayton, Ohio 1957).

EVANGELISM. *Euangelion* in the Greek means the spoken rather than the written gospel; it is proclamation of the good news. Evangelism or evangelization is, therefore, a correct term for the proclamation of the gospel to those who are unfamiliar with it. This work has been carried on in every imaginable form in non-Christian countries.

(1) One of the earliest approaches has been that of the public disputation. Robert de *Nobili (1606–1656) held public debates with the Brahmans in Madura, Henry *Martyn (1781–1812) with learned Muslims

of Shiraz, Adoniram *Judson (1813–1850) with the Buddhists of Rangoon. Provided that tempers are kept on both sides, this is a most valuable method.

(2) Protestant missions have extensively used bazaar preaching and open-air preaching in village streets. This has proved very exhausting and not highly repaying in results. A special form of itinerant preaching was developed by T. G. Ragland (1845–1858) in South India; an area of 1,000 villages was selected; each village was to be systematically visited at least once every year by a group of evangelists who would live in tents in order to keep themselves mobile.

(3) Much work among women, especially in Muslim countries where the rule of *purdah* is observed, can be done only by visits to the women in their homes. An extensive ministry on these lines has been developed by the various 'Zenana' missions. In many cases converts cannot be baptized, owing to the difficulties that would arise in their families. The most remarkable women's movement known to missionary history was that which came into being through the work of the Misses Elwin at Sivakasi in South India, as a result of which many hundreds of women were baptized, with the knowledge of their husbands but without public display.

(4) The school has from the beginning been an accompaniment of all Protestant missions, and in certain areas has been a powerful instrument of conversion. This was specially so in China after the *Boxer troubles of 1901, when many schools were able to report that every single pupil had been baptized before leaving the school. In other countries, the school has served rather as a means for the penetration of society by Christian ideas, though it is still the case that in many African schools a large proportion of the pupils seek baptism.

(5) Christian *literature is an indispensable aid to E. Many cases are on record in which a reader who had never met a single Christian has been brought to faith in Christ simply by reading some part of the NT. *Bible translation and distribution have

been carried on effectively and vigorously. Christian literature, especially that intended for non-Christians, continues to be what the *Tambaram Conference of 1938 said it was —the most neglected area of Christian missionary work.

(6) An extension of literature work has been the *correspondence courses for enquirers carried on with great success in Japan by W. H. Murray Walton, and in South India by John H. Piet. The popularity of such courses has revealed a widespread and unsuspected interest in the gospel among those who would not be likely to make a direct approach to a Christian worker.

(7) In modern times public lectures in a western language have attracted large and friendly audiences. In Japan, just after the second world war, when the interest in all things western was intense, the Christian lecturers could be assured of close attention. At an earlier date, from 1920 onwards, E. Stanley Jones took advantage, with immense effect, of the new interest in the gospel created in India in part by the friendly attitude of Mahātma Gāndhi to it. This appears to be still a possible method of E.

(8) Even more valuable is the small group, in which the method of *dialogue recommended by Kenneth Cragg, can be pursued. Earlier experiments along this line by Stanley Jones are recorded in some detail in his moving book *Christ at the Round Table* (London and New York 1928).

(9) But best of all is the individual witness to the individual. *Mass movements have generally come into being when one man who has found Christ tells his friends and relations of this great discovery, and they in their turn pass on the news to others. This is the natural method of *church growth in a non-Christian country. All other methods may be forbidden by governments or made impossible by the force of public opinion; the seed growing secretly will continue to grow, whatever any earthly power may decree.

STEPHEN NEILL

NCE V, 650.

EVANGELISTS. The noun *euangelion* and the verb *euangelizomai* are common in the NT for the good news of God in Jesus Christ and for the proclamation of it by men. The term 'evangelist' is rare; it is, however, used in Eph.4:11, the E. apparently standing with apostles and prophets as part of that ministry which is not limited to the care of one single congregation of Christians, as perhaps pastors and teachers are understood to be. No definition of the work of an E. is given. We may think of the group of young men whom Paul kept with him (Titus, Epaphras and others), trained and sent out to be ministers of the gospel in places which he was unable himself to visit. After the NT period the word appears to have died out, partly because, with the growth of the church, its expansion came about by spontaneous growth on its own immediate frontiers, partly because other terms were used of the direct proclamation of the gospel to non-Christians.

In modern times there has been no uniformity in the use of the term. Three main traditions can be definitely distinguished: (1) The term E. is used of men who seem to be specially raised up by God to carry out a great work of proclamation in one area, and in a number of cases in relation to a special class of person (e.g. E. Stanley Jones in India, G. P. Howard in Latin America). (2) A number of missionary societies have employed paid agents known as E. to reside, or in many cases to itinerate, in areas in which the church has not yet taken root. This has been found to be a dangerous practice, since it suggests to the ordinary Christian that the proclamation of the gospel is a specialized work of paid persons, with which the ordinary lay Christian need not concern himself, rather than the responsibility of the whole people of Christ. (3) Some missions have used the term in the sense in which *'catechist' is elsewhere used, of a lay pastor entrusted with the care and oversight of an existing Christian congregation. This seems to be confusing.

Recent missionary thinking has concentrated on the congregation as the missionary instrument *par excellence*; the people of

God has been elected to 'show forth the praises' of him who has called them out of darkness into light. This is unquestionably good missionary theology. None the less it seems likely that in all ages God will call out some men, or the church will set them apart, in a special way to proclaim the gospel where the name of Christ has not been heard.

STEPHEN NEILL

G. Kittell, ed.: *Theologisches Wörterbuch zum Neuen Testament*, III (Stuttgart 1942), art. *'Evangelistēs'*.

EVANS, JAMES (1801–1846), Methodist missionary to the Canadian Indians, was born at Hull, England, and in 1823 moved to Canada. As a result of the renewal of an earlier religious experience, E. decided to devote his life to service to the Indians. After five years as a teacher at Rice Lake, Upper Canada, in 1833 E. was ordained as a minister of the Methodist church and sent to work among the Ojibwa Indians on the St. Clair River. In 1837 he published a grammar of the Ojibwa language and translated part of the Scriptures. His greatest service, however, came with the invention of the syllabic script for the language of the Cree Indians. E's *Cree Syllabic Hymnbook* (1841), which he printed with his own hands on a press of his own contriving, is believed to have been the first book printed in the Canadian North-west. The group of translators organized by E. completed, after his death, the translation of the Bible into Cree; this work was printed in 1861 by the BFBS.

EDITORS

E. R. Young: *The Apostle of the North* (New York 1899); *Encyclopedia Canadiana*, Vol. IV, p.52.

EVANSTON 1954: See ASSEMBLIES, ECUMENICAL.

EXPANSION OF CHRISTIANITY. The growth of the church of Jesus Christ has not followed one single line of unbroken advance. There have been setbacks as well as successes. But on the whole the movement has been forward, from a little company of Jews in Jerusalem to what is now a world-wide church. Seven periods can be distinguished.

(1) To A.D. 313. During these three centuries the progress of the church within the Roman empire was astonishingly rapid. Every province had been reached, and to the east there were Christian groups beyond the limits of the empire. But it is reckoned that when the Emperor Constantine by the Edict of Milan (313) extended full toleration to Christianity, not more than 15% of the inhabitants at most can have been Christian.

(2) To A.D. 600. By the end of this period paganism had almost ceased to exist in the Mediterranean region. Christianity was firmly established in Ireland, and was returning to Britain. By this time, it had certainly reached India, and was beginning to spread along the trade-routes in the direction of Central Asia. Ethiopia was in part a Christian country.

(3) A.D. 600 to 1000. This was the period of greatest loss and disaster to the church. Through the Muslim invasions all the heartlands of the gospel—Palestine, Syria, Egypt, North Africa, the greater part of Asia Minor and Persia—were lost to the church and have never been recovered. At the same time, however, advance in another direction was continuous. What are now Holland, Belgium and Germany had been added to the Christian countries. By the year 1000 Scandinavia had been entered, and Poland and Hungary had been converted. Russia had been approached from Constantinople and a great Christian centre established at Kiev. The *Nestorian church flourished in China, but was unable to make its hold permanent.

(4) A.D. 1000 to 1500. In these centuries the conversion of Europe was completed, the process being generally reckoned to have been ended with the baptism of Jagiello, king of the Lithuanians in 1386. Heroic missions of the *Franciscans and *Dominicans spread throughout central Asia and as far as China; but little permanent success was achieved. In 1500 Christianity was almost exclusively a European

religion. The 15th century has less to show in the way of Christian advance than any other.

(5) A.D. 1500 to 1800. The period of the Reformation and the Counter-Reformation let loose new streams of Christian energy on the world. The RC missions, especially those of the *Jesuits, penetrated almost every known country, and some such as Japan which were almost wholly unknown to the west. Protestant efforts by comparison were small, and added little new territory to the Christian world. In Asia and Africa, however, advance was in most cases followed by retreat. The church in Japan was stamped out by persecution. The hold of Christianity on China and India was weak and precarious. The great achievement of this period was the conversion of what are now the Latin American countries, and of the Philippines. This conversion was incomplete, many indigenous peoples remaining untouched. It was also very superficial, and the Christianity of these regions today is riddled with superstition and ignorance. Yet these countries are unmistakably part of the Christian world.

(6) A.D. 1800 to 1914. The century in which the dominance of Europe was established throughout almost the entire world was also the period of the most rapid expansion of the Christian churches. Missionaries entered almost every country. The unknown interior of Africa began to be opened up. The greatest successes were won among primitive peoples—in the South Seas, in Africa, among the aborigines and outcastes of India. But every known form of religion yielded some converts to the faith, and every social level from the highest to the lowest. Moreover, the progress made by the converts in knowledge and self-reliance gave reason to hope that the establishment of the churches would now be permanent, and could survive, if necessary, the disappearance of the missionary.

(7) A.D. 1914 to 1969. This was, once again, a period of major disaster. The success of the Bolshevik revolution meant that for 40 years Russia ceased to play an active part in the affairs of Christendom. Similar success in China has meant the expulsion of all foreign missionaries, though not the suppression of the Chinese church. Political difficulties in many countries have hindered Christian progress. Yet in spite of all setbacks, this has been the period of most rapid Christian advance. In 50 years the Christian missionary force has doubled itself; the increase in the indigenous ministries, both lay and ordained, has been even more rapid. Certain countries, hitherto closed to Christian work, such as Nepal, have now been opened. Almost every tribe in Africa has been reached. An approach has been made to the almost inaccessible peoples of the Amazon region. It is reckoned that 97% of the world's population, in so far as it is literate, has access to at least some part of the Scriptures.

In this sense, then, the Church of Christ today is a worldwide church. But its distribution is very uneven. The block of Muslim countries has yielded very few converts. The number of Christians in Asia is relatively small. Roughly one-third of the human race is now in some sense Christian; one-third is in some way within reach of the gospel; one-third has possibly not heard so much as the name of Jesus Christ. The task is, therefore, still the unfinished task. But the effects of the gospel are not limited to the visible church; it is clear that Christian influence streams out far beyond, and that countless people who would not call themselves Christians yield to Jesus Christ a respect and reverence such as they do not pay to any other figure of past or present history.

See also LATENT CHURCH CONCEPT.

STEPHEN NEILL

K. S. Latourette: *A History of the Expansion of Christianity* (7 vols., London and New York 1937–1945); A. Mulders: *Missionsgeschichte* (Ger. tr., Regensburg 1960); S. C. Neill: *A History of Christian Missions* (London 1964).

F

FAILURE IN MISSION. The true measure of success is known to God alone. But there has, almost inevitably, been a tendency in missionary writing to present the story as a success story. It is important to remember that this is a distortion, and that many missionary enterprises have ended in failure.

First, it should be recalled that apparent failure is not necessarily failure in the sight of God. Charles de *Foucauld did not convert a single Muslim; but the fruit of his life is still seen in the work of the Little Brothers and Sisters of Jesus, who carry on his work in his spirit of total self-identification with those who are in need.

Nor can the church be blamed for those cases in which an entire work has been swept away by violence. This was the fate of the church in Japan in the great persecution of the 17th century, though the obliteration was less complete than had been supposed; and of the Swedish Mission in Central Asia, the work of which appears to have been destroyed without trace by the Bolsheviks in the 1930s.

There have, however, been Christian enterprises which, as far as human eyes can judge, have ended in calamity that could have been avoided. For such failure, three main causes may be adduced:

(1) Lack of continuity. A good beginning had been made by the Portuguese on the west coast of Africa in the 15th century. But by the end of the 18th century hardly anything remained. The number of missionaries sent out was always small; losses through disease were always heavy. The stream of continuous activity was very thin, hardly enough to maintain anything like a living church in being.

(2) Foolhardiness. Some devoted Christians have taken the promises of Scripture in so literal a way as to believe that nothing more was needed than for faithful Christians to go out to non-Christian lands with no preparation and no provision, in the expectation that God would supply every need of body and spirit. Much heroism has been expended to no purpose. Some of the early ventures of the *Moravians would seem to fall under this judgment. In the 18th century an attempt was made to establish a mission on the Nicobar Islands. The climate proved to be deadly, and the missionaries, who had had little if any training, had no idea how to adapt themselves to the situation. Loss of life was very heavy, and the mission was completely abandoned by the beginning of the 19th century. There are pathetic records of one-man attempts by devoted individuals to convert Africa, as hopeless as the attempt made by one single lone climber to scale Mount Everest.

(3) Wrong methods, by which enterprises have been doomed to failure from the start. Perhaps the most notable example is the involvement of many missionaries in West Africa, and some in the West Indies, in the slave-trade or in the ownership of slaves. It is easy for a later generation to see the total incompatibility of such practices with the profession of the gospel, and also the impression made on the minds of the observers, who were little likely to accept a gospel commended in such ways.

Partial failure, or the loss of great opportunities, have in a great many cases been due to inflexibility of missionary policies directed from the west, and to the lack of vision of churches which might have been expected to do better. India has seen many *mass movements. Hardly one has been developed to the full extent of what it promised; in hardly a single case was an adequate supply of foreign personnel built up and maintained throughout the period of growth (not less than 30 years) when such help was most needed for the development of indigenous leadership, both ordained and lay. In Africa in the 20th century churches have grown far beyond the point at which existing missions are able to care for them, and to build up in time the

8

indigenous ministry on which the future growth of such churches must depend.

If these are the conditions of failure, what are the conditions of success, if the term may still be used? They would seem to be three—vision, perseverance and humility. Vision, a sensitive awareness of the possibilities of a situation, and of the direction in which the Spirit of God seems to be moving. Perseverance, a recognition that substantial results cannot be obtained overnight, that both the time of sowing and the time of tending may be long before the harvest can be reaped. Humility, to recognize that mission requires a constant process of self-criticism, and the willingness to understand that the methods of yesterday may be out of date today, and that what the Spirit said to the churches in the past may not be the same as what the unchanging Spirit is saying today.

For a graphic presentation of the dangers in Africa today, see A. Hastings: *The Church in Modern Africa* (London 1967); on 'the missionary débâcle in China', see D. M. Paton: *Christian Missions and the Judgement of God* (London 1953).

STEPHEN NEILL

FAITH in Jesus Christ, in the full biblical sense of the term, is never a matter simply of intellectual assent; it is the total self-commitment of a person to a Person, involving elements of trust, hope and obedience. The outward sign of faith is baptism, in which the nature of faith as dying with Christ and being raised again with him is made visible. If this is the nature of faith even among those who have been brought up in the Christian tradition, much more must it be so when faith involves also the act of passing from one religious tradition to another.

How does faith dawn in the mind of a non-Christian? The process is so extremely varied that any generalization is precarious, and any analysis is bound to be somewhat schematic; but attention can be drawn to some of the stages and elements which seem to be present in a great many cases.

The first stage is almost always awareness of Jesus Christ as a living reality. The great Bishop *Azariah used to say that now, as in the days of the early church, the starting point must be the resurrection: 'What they need to know is that there is a living Saviour, and that he is not far from them'.

This awareness is often followed by anxiety, and a disinclination to go further, since it brings with it some understanding of the claims to exclusive loyalty that are likely to be made. A further search can be activated by mere curiosity; but more often by some striking act of service performed by a Christian beyond the claims of duty, or by the experience of fellowship within a living Christian group.

At this point the dangers that the development of a true faith may be inhibited by a pseudo-faith are very great. Mere rejection of the practices of a non-Christian religion and the acceptance of the gospel as a new law may be taken to be all that is necessary. A course of purely intellectual instruction, in which elements of the Bible and of Christian tradition are absorbed and a kind of certificate of competence issued, may conceal the real nature of the Christian challenge. Adoption of the Christian ceremonies, including baptism, may be taken as the essential thing; especially is this the case when baptism is administered at a fairly early stage of Christian indoctrination. Then the challenge to total renewal is evaded rather than faced.

If these dangers have not been avoided, the renewal of the search for a true faith becomes very difficult. It comes about in the majority of cases, when the convert realizes that salvation is not a pleasure to be enjoyed, or membership in a society which can offer a number of advantages; but a task and a warfare. The name of Christ is to be honoured in service and in proclamation; and bearing witness to him will often result in hostility and suffering. It is usually at this stage, and not before (though there are exceptions) that the convert becomes deeply aware of helplessness and sinfulness; it is only in the light of Christ that human imperfection is fully discerned. When this stage has been reached, something like a second conversion may take place. Then the battle of faith has essentially been won.

But this is not the end of the story. A great many converts pass through a period of great depression and sorrow, after a fully honest confession of faith in Christ leading to baptism. This is sometimes due to persecution and the hostility of friends and neighbours; sometimes to anxious questioning as to whether what has been gained in Christianity has really been worth the price paid for it; but sometimes apparently to sheer weariness in well-doing. It is at this point that the doctrine of Christ needs to be supplemented by the doctrine of the Holy Spirit. Only through daily renewal by the Holy Spirit can faith be permanently safeguarded against the temptations and discouragements which in the extreme case may even lead to apostasy. It is never possible to say that the battle of faith has been finally and definitely won.

The fullest discussion of the birth and growth of faith is R. Allier: *La Psychologie de la Conversion chez les peuples primitifs*, (2 vols., Paris 1928). A great deal can, of course, be learnt from the autobiographies of converts, though in many cases they are not as precise and as self-critical as could be desired.

STEPHEN NEILL

FAITH AND ORDER is a phrase commonly used for more than 300 years to designate the doctrine, polity, organization and character of the church. In 1910 it was adopted as the name of what became the worldwide movement for the visible unity of the church. During the *World Missionary Conference at Edinburgh the issues of church division and unity were considered too delicate to be on the agenda. One man, especially convinced of the need for unity in world mission, decided that there should be other world conferences on the ways to overcome historic divisions. This was Charles H. *Brent, of the PECUSA, serving as bishop of the missionary district of the Philippines. Working with a layman, Robert H. Gardiner, Brent convened a planning meeting in Geneva, 1920, which

led to the first world conference at Lausanne, 1927. Bishops V. S. *Azariah and E. J. Palmer of India brought the urgent voice of Asian Christians to this mainly European and American conference. They showed that church union in South India was on the way already.

For another decade F. and O. was led by English churchmen: Archbishop William Temple, Professor A. E. Garvie and Canon Leonard Hodgson. Theological studies on authority, grace, ministry and sacraments continued to the second world conference at Edinburgh 1937. At this time it was agreed to unite F. and O. with the *Life and Work movement to become the *WCC. In 1948 the Commission on F. and O. was established within the WCC itself as its chief instrument for exploring and promoting church unity.

Ecumenical study projects on the nature of the church, worship and intercommunion led to the third world conference at Lund, Sweden, 1952. The *IMC meeting at *Willingen, Germany, was held the same summer. These conferences, as well as the WCC central committee, spoke vigorously of the inter-connection of unity and mission, in recognition of the church's urgent task in the modern world.

Archbishop Yngve Brilioth of Uppsala, Sweden, and Dr O. S. Tomkins (later Bishop of Bristol) now led F. and O. African and Asian participation increased. National F. and O. commissions were formed. Ecumenical studies on four subjects continued: church, worship, tradition, and church institutionalism. Consultations on church union were arranged, as the union movement accelerated. Staff secretaries after 1953 were Dr J. Robert Nelson, Dr K. R. Bridston, Professor Paul S. Minear, the Rev P. C. Rodger and Dr Lukas Vischer. Dr Douglas Horton was succeeded as chairman by Professor Minear, and he in turn by Bishop H. H. Harms. After 1961 the participation of Eastern Orthodox Christians was fully realized. Also, discussions on church unity with both Roman Catholics and conservative Evangelicals were promoted. At *Uppsala in 1968 nine

RC members were elected to the Commission.

In 1963 at Montreal the fourth world conference was held. The time was characterized by several factors: the sense of missionary crisis in a world of secular revolution; the strong influence of Christians from Latin America, Africa and Asia; the challenge of radical theologians; the involvement of RCs and Protestant conservatives; the much increased tempo of church union efforts in many lands; and the general acceptance of the *New Delhi Statement on unity, which emphasized visible church unity of all in each place who confess Jesus Christ and keep continuity with all ages and places of the church's life and witness. After nearly 60 years, F. and O. is recognized for two things: its greatly expanded range of probing studies on the church's nature, unity and task; and its intensified influence upon the negotiations for union between two or more churches in numerous countries. Through these years F. and O. workers have emphasized the truth that 'co-operation is not enough' for the manifestation of the unity of the church in every place.

See ECUMENICAL MOVEMENT; WORLD COUNCIL OF CHURCHES.

J. ROBERT NELSON

J. R. Nelson: *One Lord, One Church* (London 1958); P. C. Rodger: *The Fourth World Conference on Faith and Order* (London 1964); J. E. Skoglund and J. R. Nelson: *Fifty Years of Faith and Order* (St. Louis 1964); O. S. Tomkins: *The Third World Conference on Faith and Order* (London 1952); L. Vischer: *A Documentary History of the Faith and Order Movement* (St. Louis 1964).

FAITH MISSIONS is a term generally applied to non-denominational and inter-denominational foreign missionary agencies whose governing concept is to look to God alone for financial support.

Faith missionary societies have been in existence for about 100 years. One of the earliest such agencies and still the best known is the *CIM formed in 1865, now the OMF.

Gradually other missionary agencies with similar outlook came into being, until today they represent a sizable part of the overseas missionary personnel. While many of them started with the same financial principles made famous by the CIM (never ask for money, never tell anyone except God of your need, and look to God through prayer to supply your needs) most of the faith agencies now ask for money or make their needs known to Christians everywhere.

North America became the key bastion for faith agencies and most of them have had dynamic connections with *fundamentalism. They have always been theologically conservative, often separatist as far as their relationships to structured denominations are concerned, and almost inevitably opposed to the *ecumenical movement on the grounds that it is either apostate or theologically liberal, and more concerned with social action than with proclamation of the gospel of redemption.

Around the faith missionary societies there gathered a constellation of Bible institutes and later Bible colleges along with independent Bible churches. In North America the development of the Federal Council of the Churches of Christ in the USA (which later became the National Council of Churches) made the cleavage between the major denominations and the faith agencies more pronounced. Rarely did faith agencies enlist overseas personnel from among the graduates of old line denominational seminaries, since most of them were held to have capitulated, in one fashion or another, to the inroads of theological liberalism. Thus the faith societies attracted most of their new personnel from the rapidly growing Bible institutes. At the same time faith missions were helped in their growth and development by disenchanted members of old line denominations; when they had lost confidence in their own boards and when their young people enlisted for service in the faith work around the world, they channelled their missionary money through faith agencies.

FM experienced their greatest growth in

the period since 1938. In North America the number of missionaries supported by FM far exceeds that represented by the National Council of Churches. And the trend will probably continue. In 1917 a number of faith missions banded together to form the *IFMA. This agency, which is ecumenical, now includes in its membership nearly 50 mission boards. It is moving forward aggressively in its programme.

HAROLD LINDSELL

H. Lindsell: 'Faith Missions Since 1938' in *Frontiers of the Christian World Mission Since 1938* (New York 1962); H. Lindsell, ed.: *The Church's Worldwide Mission* (Waco, Texas 1966) in which are found the proceedings of the Wheaton Congress on the Church's Worldwide Mission.

FALKLAND ISLANDS. See SOUTH AMERICAN MISSIONARY SOCIETY.

FAR EAST BROADCASTING COMPANY, INC. See BROADCASTING, CHRISTIAN.

FAR EASTERN GOSPEL CRUSADE, THE. An evangelical, interdenominational missionary fellowship, organized in 1947 as a result of evangelistic work begun at the close of the second world war by American servicemen in the Philippines and Japan. It reported in 1965 an income of $632,329, and 151 missionaries serving in Japan, Philippines, Okinawa and Hong Kong. In the Philippines they sponsor the Far Eastern Bible Institute and Seminary (FEBIAS) near Manila, founded in 1948 for training Christian workers.

Headquarters are at 14625 Greenfield Road, Detroit, Michigan. FEGC publishes *Crusader* (quarterly), *Prayer Warrior* (monthly) and is a member of *IFMA and of *EFMA.

GERALD H. ANDERSON

FARQUHAR, JOHN NICOL (1861–1929), went to India as a missionary in the service of the *LMS in 1890 and was assigned to college work as Bhawanipur. He gradually became deeply dissatisfied with missionary

work as it was then being carried on. Transfer to the service of the *YMCA in 1902 set him free to concentrate his energies on an intensive study of Sanskrit and Indian religions such as few missionaries of his time had been able to engage in, and to consider the needs of India for Christian literature of many kinds. His works of a purely scientific character, *Modern Religious Movements in India* (1915), and *An Outline of the Religious Literature of India* (1920) are of the very highest quality and still indispensable to every student. Much more controversial, and therefore much more criticized, was his *The Crown of Hinduism* (1913). It seemed to conservatives that he had rashly surrendered the *uniqueness of Christianity. But in fact F. never accepted a naïve evolutionism, as though* Hinduism by some inner power of its own could evolve into Christianity. His aim was to show that every earnest desire after the truth which is manifest in Hinduism can be fulfilled only in the revelation of God in Jesus Christ. The best comment on the book is that of a thoughtful Hindu to a missionary: 'We dare not read it to the end'. In 1922, failing health compelled F. to leave India. He was appointed Professor of Comparative Religion in the University of Manchester, and held this appointment until his death in 1929.

STEPHEN NEILL

E. J. Sharpe: *J. N. Farquhar* (Calcutta 1962), *Not to Destroy but to Fulfil* (Lund 1965); *DNB* (1922–1930), 296; *RGG* II, 877.

FEDERATION AS A PRINCIPLE OF UNION assumes that denominational churches have sufficient in common to make it feasible for them to form a central agency to which they may officially delegate certain functions and tasks, but continue in sovereign independence and maintain their own separate polity, doctrines, worship, and traditions. It seeks unity with great diversity. The political structure of the USA is usually cited as an analogy, the separate states surrendering certain powers to the federal government. This analogy is false, however, since the USA is the sovereign power and the states are subsidiary and dominated by the federal government. A better analogy would be the Swiss federal union of sovereign cantons. Federation, in theory, could be a far step towards union, but in actual practice it has never been so. Rather, it has been a demonstration of unity and an effective means of co-operation. The most successful venture of this sort has been the Federal Council of Churches of Christ in America, 1908–1950, which in the latter year united with other agencies to form the National Council of Churches of Christ in the USA. Neither it nor any other federation of churches has claimed to be a church, although in the case of the Congo Protestant Council the name 'Church of Christ in Congo' was common to all churches of the member missions.

R. PIERCE BEAVER

World Missionary Conference, 1910 (Edinburgh 1910), Vol. VIII, ch.5.

FEDERATION OF GERMAN EVAN-GELICAL MISSIONARY SOCIETIES.
The Federation was founded in 1922 and reconstituted in 1933 as *Deutscher Evangelischer Missionstag* (DEMT). Its membership includes almost all German missionary societies and supporting or related agencies. The DEMT meets once a year for missiological study and discussion of matters of common concern. It is remarkable for its ecumenical composition, including virtually the whole range of *'faith missions', Free Church, and church related missions. Its executive body is the German Evangelical Missions Council (DEMR). While the period of Nazi rule found the DEMT almost without a dissenting voice behind the Confessing Church, the post-war division of Germany has proved to be seriously disruptive, as joint meetings of East and West German missions have been impossible since 1961.

H.-W. GENSICHEN

FEDERATIONS OF CHURCHES using
that title have been few, the great majority being known as *National Christian

Councils. The earliest is the Federation of Independent Churches in Madagascar, which in 1862 brought together the churches founded by the *LMS, and thus was actually a denomination. The churches of the Friends and of the Reformed Church of France joined in 1869 and 1895 respectively. The Federation of Evangelical Churches of Puerto Rico was established in 1905, embracing the churches of the missions which entered the *comity agreement. The Evangelical Alliance of Japan in 1911 became the Federation of Churches, but gave way to the NCC in 1923. The Presbyterian and Methodist churches in Korea in 1918 joined in the Korean Federal Council of Churches, and in 1924 this became the KNCC with wider membership.

See also FEDERATION AS A PRINCIPLE OF UNION; NATIONAL CHRISTIAN COUNCILS.

R. PIERCE BEAVER

C. H. Fahs and H. E. Davis: *Conspectus of Co-operative Missionary Enterprises* (New York 1935); index in W. R. Hogg: *Ecumenical Foundations* (New York 1952); directory in latest edition of *WCH* (London); and annual list with addresses in each January issue of the *IRM*.

FERNANDO PO. See EQUATORIAL GUINEA.

FETISHISM. See ANIMISM.

FIJI. See PACIFIC ISLANDS.

FILMS FOR MISSIONS. See AUDIO-VISUAL AIDS; RAVEMCCO.

FINALITY OF CHRIST. See ABSOLUTE-NESS OF CHRISTIANITY.

FINANCIAL SUPPORT FOR MISSIONS. Money for the prosecution of the Christian mission has been raised in a great many different ways. (1) When in the 15th century the popes created the *Patronato* of the Spanish and Portuguese kings in all the newly discovered and newly conquered lands, it was taken for granted that this included responsibility for the financial support of bishops, missionaries and their work. In Goa Hindu temples were closed and their revenues applied to Christian purposes. When the bishopric of Malacca was created, the income of the bishop was made a charge on the revenues of the city. In the Caribbean and Latin America large estates were made available for the support of the religious orders. (2) Much more commonly missions have depended on the voluntary contributions of faithful Christians, sometimes paid through the churches, in many cases collected by the missionary societies. The 19th century saw an immense increase in Christian generosity, both in the Roman Catholic and the non-RC world. This has proved a somewhat fluctuating and uncertain source of revenue. During the economic crisis in the west, 1929–1935, there was a heavy fall in the amounts received by the missionary societies, missionaries in some areas suffered severe hardships, and many important pieces of work had to be closed down. (3) During the colonial epoch, in some areas and especially in the territories controlled by Britain, under the grant-in-aid system missions received very large subsidies of government money, in consideration of services rendered in the educational, medical and social fields. This made possible a rapid expansion of missionary services in many areas, with the accompanying danger that the missions might come to be regarded as no more than an extension of government activity. (4) The idea that Christians in *younger churches ought to be self-supporting only gradually took hold. From an early date Christians had been encouraged to take up collections for charitable purposes and to meet special needs. The life of the church itself continued to be almost wholly dependent on foreign support. The pioneers in promoting a contrary doctrine were Henry *Venn (from 1851 onwards) and Rufus *Anderson. Great progress has been made in almost every area of the world. Those churches which concentrate almost wholly on evangelism and the life of the church, without the development of large institutions, naturally show the closest approximation to total self-

support. Where the life of the church is strengthened by large and expensive institutions such as theological seminaries, the measure of foreign help is proportionately higher. In some areas campaigns for self-support have been driven through with such vigour as to injure the life of the church. But everywhere the principle that self-support and spiritual maturity are closely linked would find acceptance. (5) In recent years churches as such have been inclined to take responsibility for the support of the overseas work of the churches. For example, in the PECUSA overseas missionary work is included in the general budget of the church, and the cost met by the contributions received from the dioceses. The great German organization 'Bread for the World', and the *Arbeitsgemeinschaft für Welt Mission* (Board for World Mission) represent the participation of German churches in the worldwide responsibility of the church. (6) A new sense of ecumenical solidarity was expressed in the work of *Orphaned Missions. The afflictions of the two world war periods in the 20th century have shown the churches that they cannot stand alone, and that, when one member suffers, all the members suffer with it. Means for the expression of this sense of joint responsibility of all for the work of the whole church, have not yet been fully worked out.

No complete study of the problem of missionary finance has ever yet been undertaken; but constant references to the subject can be found in every form of missionary literature. There are endless complaints of the inadequacy of the support provided; it could, however, be argued that in general the missions have suffered from having too much money rather than too little, and that this has tended to perpetuate the domination of the missionary, and to inhibit the development of genuine independence in the churches.

See ECONOMIC PROBLEMS AND CHRISTIAN MISSIONS.

EDITORS

FISK, PLINY (1792–1825), is accounted

the pioneer of American Protestant mission work in the Near East. He was ordained in 1818, and the next year he and Levi Parsons sailed from Boston as 'missionaries to Western Asia with reference to a permanent station at Jerusalem'. Their commission from the *ABCFM stated: 'The two grand inquiries ever present to your minds will be: What good can be done? and by what means? What can be done for Jews? What can be done for pagans? What for Mohammedans? What for Christians? What for the people in Palestine? What for those in Egypt, in Syria, in Persia, in Armenia, in other countries in which your inquiries may be extended?' F. settled in Smyrna for three years, (1820–1823), and from 1823 to 1825 lived in Beirut, where he was the founder of the American Mission in that city. He travelled to Alexandria, Jerusalem and Aleppo, but decided on Beirut rather than Jerusalem as the best place for mission headquarters. F. and Parsons were together on a trip to Alexandria in 1822 when the latter succumbed to the chronic ill-health from which he had been suffering, and died. F. continued the work they had begun together until his death from 'malignant fever' three years later. He was an energetic explorer, reporting in his letters the political, social, and religious conditions in the eastern Mediterranean lands. His constant distribution of the Bible and of tracts brought him into difficulties with both Muslim officials and RC priests. He had no plan for the formation of a national evangelical church, his whole assumption being that the work of mission was to bring new life to the eastern churches. At the time of his death three other missionary recruits had taken up residence in Beirut and formed the nucleus of the new mission.

HARRY G. DORMAN, JR

H. H. Jessup: *Fifty-three years in Syria* (New York 1910), pp.32–38; G. H. Scherer: *Mediterranean Missions 1808–1870* (Beirut, MS n.d.).

FJELLSTEDT, PETER (1802–1881), belonged to that group of European missionaries who during the 19th century worked under British missionary societies. Ordained in the Church of Sweden, F., who was inspired by Moravianism, came in touch with the *Basel Mission but was sent to South India by the *CMS. After some years of service in Tirunelvelli F., for health reasons, left India and devoted himself to Bible translation in Turkey. In 1843, when the Evangelical Revival had begun to change church-structures, he returned to Sweden to promote the increase of missionary concern. He joined the Lund Missionary Society which co-operated with the *Leipzig Evangelical Lutheran Mission in South India. In Lund he established a missionary college and trained candidates for India. His ecumenical concerns, however, did not altogether correspond with the Pan-Lutheran programme and F. moved to Stockholm where his missionary college was intended to become a uniting force. But the interdenominational Swedish Missionary Society could not authorize these plans, nor did F's version of pietism strike the same notes as that of Rosenius, the leader of the Evangelical Revival within the Church of Sweden. As a pietist preacher and through extensive writings F. greatly influenced the emerging Swedish missionary movement during significant decades of the 'great missionary century'.

CARL F. HALLENCREUTZ

FLAD, JOHANN MARTIN (1831–1915), was born at Undingen, Württemberg, Germany. He studied in Jerusalem under Bishop S. *Gobat, who sent him with three companions to Ethiopia in 1856. They worked as craftsmen, and circulated the Scriptures, finding most response among the Falashas (Ethiopian Jews). Returning to Jerusalem F. married Pauline Kneller, who accompanied him to Ethiopia in 1859. After the visit of H. A. *Stern in 1860 F. continued his work under the LSPCJ (see JEWS, MISSIONS TO THE). In 1863 King Theodore imprisoned several Europeans, including F's family, sending F. to England as ambassador. They were rescued by a British military expedition in 1868. After this F. was not allowed to stay permanently in

Ethiopia, but he frequently visited the frontier to train church leaders and confer with them. He made a new translation of the Bible and of other literature into Amharic. Despite the Dervish and Italian invasions the Falasha church leaders maintained the work. By 1908 some 1,500 Falashas, known as 'children of Flad', had been baptized. F. had the satisfaction of both pioneering the mission and fostering its growth over 50 years into a mature Christian community.   JOHN GOODWIN

J. M. Flad: *The Falashas (Jews) of Abyssinia* (translated from the German by S. P. Goodhart, London 1869); W. D. Veitch, ed.: *Notes from the Journal of J. M. Flad* (London 1860).

FLIERL, JOHANNES (1858–1947), was born in Bavaria in a peasant family. Through the influence of his pastor he became acquainted with the claims of missionary work. The same pastor secured his entry into the Missionary Institute at *Neuendettelsau, where he received his missionary training. In 1878 F. was sent to Australia, where, in association with Australian Lutherans, he undertook missionary work among the Aborigines at Bethesda. When N.E. New Guinea became a German colony, he urged the directors of his mission to send him to that area, in which there were indigenous peoples which had heard no word of the gospel. As he was delayed in the journey, he founded a mission-station in the neighbourhood of Cooktown. In 1886 he reached New Guinea, and settled in the neighbourhood of Finschhafen. F. was a true pioneer, who spent his life with courage and the utmost self-sacrifice in the midst of the wildest savages. By means of his journeys he made a contribution to the opening up of the country. He always combined evangelistic with physical labour, often to the advantage of the inhabitants. His basic principle was that the missionary must show how little he is able to do with. In order to provide the mission with a sound economic basis, and to induce the local people to work, he established a plantation. His missionary methods were those of the

8*

church at home, and did not appeal to peoples for whom the group and not the individual is the unit. F. was the leader of the work of the Neuendettelsau Mission in New Guinea until 1930. His greatness lay in the wide outlook, which enabled him always to do the right thing at the right time. He had the ability to put the right man in the right place. Each was free to develop his gifts in his own field of work. F. was able to let others surpass him, without feeling jealousy. And yet he kept all the threads in his own hands. On his journeys during periods of leave, he set himself more than anything else to develop ecumenical relationships between the Lutherans of Australia and those of North America. These helped to keep the work of the mission in being through two world wars.

GEORG F. VICEDOM

J. Flierl: *Christ in New Guinea* (Tanunda, S. Australia 1932); G. Pilhofer: *Johann Flierl, der Bahnbrecher des Evangeliums unter den Papua* (2nd ed., Neuendettelsau 1962).

FLYNN, JOHN (1880–1951), was born at Moliagul in Victoria, Australia. Ordained to the Presbyterian ministry in 1911, he devoted his life to the settlers in the Inland of Australia, a vast region covering two million square miles. From 1912, he was Superintendent of the Australian Inland Mission, founded as a result of his reports to the General Assembly of the Presbyterian Church. F. evolved a missionary strategy especially adapted to the physical, social, cultural and spiritual needs of the outback. Missionaries patrolled frontier areas by camel and horse in the early days, and later in motor vehicles. Eighteen hospitals and welfare homes were established. A special radio transceiver was invented and widely installed. In 1928, the world's first civilian flying doctor service was inaugurated by F. at Cloncurry, Queensland. Subsequently, he was the main organizer of the Royal Flying Doctor Service of Australia, currently with sixteen bases. F's mission won the support of the Australian government, and made him a national folk-hero. He received an honorary DD from McGill University, Montreal, Canada, in 1940, and was Moderator General of his church from 1939 to 1942.

W. S. MCPHEAT

W. S. McPheat: *John Flynn—Apostle to the Inland* (London 1963).

FONG FOO SEC (1869–1938). Widely respected publisher in modern China, one of the Christian founders of Commercial Press and chief editor of English textbooks, prominent and influential Protestant church-man, active in many educational and social welfare projects and associations for inter-national goodwill, *YMCA leader. F. (Kuang Fu-cho) was born in a poor farming family in Sunning District near Canton, was taken to the US as an immi-grant at the age of 13, studied English and worked as a household servant; under the influence of a Chinese pastor he embraced the Christian faith. For seven years he served in the *Salvation Army, travelling through many western states. Later he received formal education at college and graduate school, and returned to China at the age of 37. There he entered the rapidly growing publication field, preparing books on many subjects for China's school youth. In 1922 Pomona College, his first *alma mater*, honoured him with the degree of Doctor of Laws. He helped to initiate the first modern reform movement in China. Talented, industrious, modest, upright in character, he was an inspiring example to Chinese students. All his public service was motivated by a vital and contagious Christian experience.   FRANK W. PRICE

In memory of Dr Fong F. Sec (privately printed, Hong Kong 1966); H. L. Boorman: *Biographical Dictionary of Republican China* (New York 1967).

'FOREIGN' MISSIONS. The earliest use in the English language (1609) of the word 'mission' in a religious context, according to the *Shorter Oxford Dictionary*, denotes 'the sending of the Second or Third Person of the Trinity by the First, or of the Third by the Second, for the production of a temporal effect'—a reflection in linguistic history that mission begins in God's act, not in men's activities. It soon (1613) came to denote 'the action of sending men forth with authority to preach the faith and administer the sacraments', but without any specific reference to where this was to be done; and later instances show its use of activities within one's own country as well as in foreign parts.

The missionary societies which arose at the end of the 18th and the beginning of the 19th centuries had the aim of preaching the gospel throughout the world to those who had not heard it. Many of them had simply the word 'missionary' in their title; others, to distinguish their sphere of activity from mission in their home country, included the word 'foreign'. At least one combined both: 'The Domestic and Foreign Missionary Society of the Protestant Episcopal Church' (1821).

With the growth of churches in Asia, Africa and the Pacific, and the developing sense of partnership between them and the churches of western Europe and North America, the term 'foreign missions' tended to give place to 'the mission of the church', 'world mission'. The question then arose, if mission is the mission of the church, and if all churches are involved in one world mission, is there any reason for sending missionaries from one country to another? The question formulated after the *Willingen meeting of the *IMC as 'Are foreign missions a theological necessity or a historical contingency?' continues to be debated, and with the increasing realization of the clamant missionary task confronting the churches in Europe and North America, the debate is not academic. Something of a theological consensus seems to be emerging of which a statement (formulated in a report of a committee on the main theme at the *Evanston Assembly) may not be untypical: 'How necessary it is, then, that the church's obedience to the gospel should also involve a determination on the part of the church in every country to take this gospel to other lands. There are frontiers which the gospel must cross within each land, areas of life which must be brought into subjection to the mind of Jesus Christ. But it is of special significance when the gospel crosses geographical frontiers, for it is when a church takes the gospel to another people and another land that it bears witness to the fact that the new age has dawned for all the world.' (*The Christian Hope and the Task of the Church* [New York 1954], p.18). Part of the answer in action is given by the increasing number of Christians from Asia, Africa and the Pacific engaged in 'foreign' missions.

Though RC missions have differed considerably both in ideals and methods from Protestant, it is possible to discern a certain parallelism both in terminology and ideas. At the time of the great revival of RC missions in the 13th century the *Dominicans formed the *Societas Fratrum Peregrinantium propter Christum inter Gentes* 'the company of brethren *dwelling in foreign parts* among the heathen for the sake of Christ'. When the *Propaganda in Rome set itself to the task of breaking the Spanish and Portuguese monopoly in missions and to widen the scope by drawing the secular clergy into the task, the result was the formation of the *Société des Missions Etrangères*, the *Paris Foreign Missionary Society. But since the great majority of RC orders have a 'missionary' as well as a 'home' department, and some of them devote themselves especially to the holding of 'missions' in nominally Christian countries, the distinction between home and foreign has been less stressed than in the Protestant churches.

On the other hand, since areas have in a great many cases been committed to societies of which all the members belong to one country—the *Belgian* *Jesuits in Calcutta, the *German* missionaries of the *Society of the Divine Word in West Africa, the *Spanish* Carmelites in Kerala, RC missionaries no less than Protestants have been inclined to create a markedly 'foreign' enclave in an eastern or African situation.

One of the aims of the popes in their great series of *Mission Encyclicals has

been to fight against this unnecessary foreignness of the church. The great Encyclical of Pius XII bears simply the title *Evangelii Praecones*, 'the proclaimers of the gospel'. If the church is genuinely universal, no Christian should feel himself to be a 'foreigner' in any part of it. But, since we are constituted in diverse nations, the aim must be such adaption of the witness of the church as does not condemn but only purifies that which is good in the traditions of all men, to each situation, that any remaining sense of 'foreignness' may be lost.

Since, however, the universal character of the church has not been realized, and there are many areas which have been only in part or not at all christianized, the element of *peregrinantium*, 'serving as ambassadors abroad', is bound to remain part of the obligation of the church; and, as we have no assurance that the task of christianizing the world will ever be completed, the crossing of geographical and cultural frontiers is not a task from which the church is likely ever to be able to regard itself as exempt.

RONALD K. ORCHARD AND EDITORS

J. Blauw: *The Missionary Nature of the Church* (London 1962), pp.110–18, in which the post-Willingen discussion is summarized and discussed; N. Goodall, ed.: *Missions under the Cross, the Willingen Meeting of the IMC* (London 1953), pp.22, 208–12.

FOREIGN MISSIONS CONFERENCE OF NORTH AMERICA, THE. One of the oldest interdenominational fellowships, the FMCNA was organized on 12 January 1893 by 75 men representing 21 mission boards of the USA and Canada. Among the early leaders were John R. *Mott and Robert E. *Speer. Eventually a large number of North American missionary societies joined the conference which met annually for study and discussion and for co-operative planning and endeavours. In 1917 the organization was incorporated as the Committee of Reference and Counsel of FMC. In that year 287 delegates attended the annual meeting, representing nearly 100 agencies. Various regional and specialized committees became increasingly influential. The names of conference chairmen in succeeding years form a roster of outstanding mission leaders. In 1921 the conference became a member of the newly organized *IMC and in 1950 one of the eight constituent bodies of the National Council of Churches of Christ in the USA, changing its name to Division of Foreign Missions and in 1965 to *Division of Overseas Ministries, related now to the *CWME of the *WCC. The Canadian societies withdrew in 1950 to form the Department of Overseas Missions, Canadian Council of Churches.

F. W. PRICE

20th Century Encyclopedia of Religious Knowledge, Vol. I, p.434; Annual Reports in Missionary Research Library, New York.

FOREIGN MISSIONS OF PARIS. See PARIS FOREIGN MISSION SOCIETY.

FOREIGN STUDENTS. See STUDENTS, CHRISTIAN WORK AMONGST.

FORMAN, CHARLES WILLIAM (1821–1894), Presbyterian missionary in the Punjab, came from a landed family of northern Kentucky, USA. Reared without religious interests he experienced a conversion at the age of 20 and entered the service of the church. Immediately upon his ordination, in 1847, he left for India. In 1849 he was sent to Lahore which had just been taken by the British. He had long had an interest in educational work, and immediately began a small school there. In 1853 the school secured the old Rang Mahal palace and has borne the Rang Mahal name ever since. In it F. built up an unusual corps of teachers, primarily Bengali Christians, who became outstanding leaders in church and public life. In 1864 he decided to open a college section in connection with the school. This had to be closed in two years, but the college charter did not lapse and in 1886 it was re-opened as a separate institution with F. as its first principal. He withdrew in 1888 at the age of 67. F. continued to be held in high respect and affection by former pupils

of his who were scattered all over the Punjab, and by the people of the city of Lahore through which he had made it a practice to walk daily to and from his school for 40 years. At his death the college, as a memorial to him, changed its name from Mission College to Forman Christian College.

CHARLES W. FORMAN

E. M. Wherry: *Our Missions in India 1834–1924* (Boston 1926).

FORMOSA. See TAIWAN.

FORSYTH, CHRISTINA, née MOIR (1844–1918), was born in Glasgow, Scotland. She had a definite religious experience at the age of 14. She embarked on her missionary career in 1879 to South Africa, as unpaid worker representing the Mission Board of the United Presbyterian Church, at Paterson station. After three years' splendid work she went to Scotland but returned after marrying a Mr Forsyth, who was drowned a year after their marriage. She resumed her missionary work in 1886 but this time at Xolobe, a most isolated place among the Fingoes. She laboured with great devotion and determination, speaking their language fluently, visiting the huts, reading from the Scriptures and praying for them, visiting the sick carrying some simple medicines with her. She often found herself in danger of her life and had to fight against fear, superstitition, the opposition of the chief and the ill-treatment of converts, especially women, by their husbands. She was very much like Mary *Slessor but directed her interest more to individuals than the whole tribe, although she exercised a marvellous influence over the tribe as a whole. She taught them to contribute to their own school. She never took furlough but before she eventually left in failing health in 1916 a deputation of Fingo women urged her, their 'White Mother' to stay. Although not ordained, she was a truly apostolic figure.

GERHARDUS C. OOSTHUIZEN

W. P. Livingstone: *Christina Forsyth of*

Fingoland: The story of the loneliest woman in Africa (London 1919).

FOUCAULD, CHARLES EUGENE DE

(1858–1916). Born at Strasbourg, France, into a Roman Catholic family, F. entered the army, and afterwards, in 1883–1884, explored Morocco, disguised as a Jew. Converted in 1886, he became a Trappist monk in 1890. Feeling called to still greater solitude and service, he desired to found a community which should 'lead the life of our Lord as closely as possible, living solely by the work of their hands, without accepting any gift . . . giving to all who ask . . . adding to this work much prayer . . . forming small groups only . . . scattered, above all, through infidel and neglected lands'. In 1901 F. was ordained priest, to work among the Muslims of N. Africa; from 1904 he lived with the nomadic Tuaregs. He translated portions of Scripture into Tuareg and compiled a dictionary and grammar of the language. Living in great simplicity, doing elementary medical and social work, F. baptized a very small number of converts, but his influence extended throughout the Sahara. He was murdered by Tuareg tribesmen in disturbances caused by the first world war.

Although no disciple joined F. permanently during his life time, his plans were followed from 1933, when the first group of Little Brothers of Jesus was formed in the Sahara. They were recognized as a religious order by the RC church in 1936 and have fraternities in Africa, Asia, Europe and S. America. In 1939 the first group of Little Sisters of Jesus was founded among the nomads of the Sahara; by 1967 there were 180 groups in 120 dioceses. JOHN GOODWIN

R. Bazin: *Charles de Foucauld. Explorateur au Maroc, Ermite au Sahara* (Paris 1921. Eng. tr. London 1923); C. Voillaume: *Au Coeur des Masses: La Vie religieuse des Petits Frères du Père de Foucauld* (Paris 1952. Eng. tr.: *Seeds of the Desert. The Legacy of Charles de Foucauld*, London 1955); *Jesus Caritas. Quarterly of the Charles of Jesus Association* (London 1967—); *LTK* IV, 227; *NCE* V, 1040.

FOUNDATION FOR THEOLOGICAL EDUCATION IN SOUTH-EAST ASIA, THE (FTESEA),

since 1963 is successor organization to the Board of Founders, Nanking Theological Seminary, set up in 1937 to administer income of capital left in 1930 by the New York Swope-Wendel family for maintenance of 'The Nanking Theological Seminary at Nanking, China'. The Board of Foreign Missions of the Methodist Episcopal Church, the legal trustees of the capital, invited four other boards related to Nanking Theological Seminary to co-operate as charter members of the Board of Founders. On request of the Board of Governors in Nanking the Board of Founders became in 1938 a degree-granting corporation chartered according to the rules of the Regents of the University of the State of New York. The charter was amended in 1952 eliminating territorial limitation of Nanking, China, and the object of the corporation amended as 'to receive and disburse funds for any purpose contributing to Christian theological education in China or in areas of Asia and of the western Pacific beyond the confines of China, and for educational assistance to Chinese and other Far Eastern students preparing in these or other lands for the ministry or other service in the Christian church when the said corporation shall deem the same advisable because of conditions existing in China'. The name was changed to FTESEA in 1963 and the Constitution amended by adding an additional statement of purpose: 'The improvement of Christian theological education in the countries of South-east Asia, or in such other countries as the Foundation may from time to time determine'.

The constituent board membership is: American Baptist Foreign Missions Society; Commission on Ecumenical Mission and Relations of the United Presbyterian Church in the USA; Board of World Missions of the Presbyterian Church in the US; United Christian Missionary Society of the Disciples of Christ, and World Division of the Board of Missions of the Methodist Church. This has been enlarged

(1966) by the addition of seven more North American Boards of Missions having responsibility for theological education in South-east Asia.

Major projects supported by the Board of Founders and now by the Foundation have been: translation into Chinese of Christian classics since 1942 (30 volumes); writing and translation programme of contemporary theological texts in Chinese since 1962 (45 volumes); grants to South-east Asian theological schools for libraries, student scholarships, faculty fellowships, Asian faculty short-term support, visiting and exchange professorships, regional and national faculty study institutes, support of *Association of Theological Schools in South-East Asia (from 1959) and a scholarly journal the *South-East Asia Journal of Theology* (from 1959) and the South-East Asia Graduate School of Theology (1966). Executive Director (1968-), Dr Alan C. Thomson, 6 Mount Sophia, Singapore 9.

JOHN FLEMING

F. T. Cartwright: *A River of Living Water* (Singapore 1963); annual minutes of FTESEA.

FRANCISCANS (OFM). Francis of Assisi (1181-1226), founder of the Friars Minor, was the first to make the ideal of missionary service an integral part of the religious life, recommending it in his Rule and himself setting the example. Missionary activity has since remained a principal feature of the Franciscan vocation. Even during Francis' life-time five friars died for Christianity in Morocco. In the 13th century Franciscans penetrated deep into Asia. John of Monte Corvino, founder of the Catholic missions in China and first Archbishop of Peking (c.1246-1329), was given by the pope seven Franciscans as suffragans; of these, however, only three reached China, becoming in succession bishops of Zaitun (Ch'uan-chow). The order continued this work in China until the recent suppression of the missions there. Franciscans travelled with Columbus to America in 1493, with Cabral to India (1500), with Cartier to Canada (1535), were in Japan in 1593 and have

laboured in these countries ever since. The Franciscan apostolate is worldwide and friars have suffered for Christ in the Middle East, North Africa, India, China and Japan. Today, 4,388 Franciscans work in 115 missions throughout the world.

S. MCGOLDRICK, OFM

da Civezza, OFM: *Storia Universale delle Missioni Francescane* (Rome 1857); *Historia Ordinis Fratrum Minorum* (Freiburg 1909).

FRANSON, FREDRIK (1852-1908), evangelist and missionary leader, born in Sweden but resident in the USA, had come deeply under the revival influence of D. L. *Moody, and of the missionary principles of Hudson *Taylor and the *CIM. He was deeply concerned about the spiritual state of recent immigrants in the USA, many of them of Scandinavian origin, and about the lack of any missionary organizations through which the convinced Christians in these groups could make their own special missionary contribution. In 1890 F. organized a Bible and missionary training course for young people in Brooklyn, N.Y.; and a few weeks later in Chicago a mission board—he had himself been commissioned as an evangelist by Moody Church in that city. The first party of missionaries sent out by this new board arrived in Shanghai on 17 February 1891; they worked in close association with the missionaries of the CIM in Shansi and Kansu. Another early mission field was the frontier between India and Tibet, Sikkim and Bhutan (a work later handed over to the Free Finnish Mission). There is a moving account in *Hudson Taylor and the China Inland Mission* (London 1918), pp.500–02, of the arrival in Shanghai of the first contingent—the authorities of the CIM had not been warned to expect 35 guests.

The original name of the mission, The Scandinavian Alliance Mission of North America, was changed in 1949 to The *Evangelical Alliance Mission (TEAM). F. retained the position of General Director from the foundation of the mission until his death in 1908.

In 1967 the mission was reported as having 870 missionaries in active service in nineteen different fields. True to the wishes and the inspiration of its founder, TEAM has always made direct evangelism the central part of its work; but, like other missions has discovered that spiritual care of those converted involves the development of many activities other than that of the direct preaching of the gospel.

STEPHEN NEILL

D. Woodward: *Aflame for God. Biography of Fredrik Franson* (Chicago 1966).

FRASER, DONALD (1870–1933), was born at Lochgilphead, Argyll, Scotland. After studies at Glasgow University and Free Church College, he became secretary of the *SVMU and then of the Inter-Collegiate Christian Union, forerunner of the *SCM. He travelled extensively among the colleges of Britain, continental Europe, America and South Africa. In 1896 F. joined the Livingstonia (Nyasaland) Mission of the Free Church, and served there until, in 1920, he was impressed into service at home, being the most powerful exponent of the church's missionary task. He organized and led the Scottish Churches' Missionary Campaign from 1921 to 1923, and was Moderator of the General Assembly of the United Free Church in 1922. Within months of his return to Nyasaland in 1925, he was recalled to service in Scotland as a secretary of the Foreign Mission Committee. The culmination of his work in this period was his leadership of The Forward Movement in the Church of Scotland from 1931 till 1933, the year of his death. F. is memorable for his combination of flaming missionary zeal with humour and humility, his understanding love of the African people whom he served, his moving eloquence, dynamic leadership and infectious faith.

A. J. BOYD

A. R. Fraser: *Donald Fraser of Livingstonia* (London 1934); D. Fraser: *Winning a Primitive People* (London 1914), *The New Africa* (London 1927); *DNB* (1931–1940), 295f.

FRATERNAL WORKERS. This is a term used by a few missionary societies in recent years when referring to their missionaries as they came to realize that the *paternalism of the past was wrong. The missionaries and the Christian workers in the places of service overseas were now to be brotherly and sisterly in their relationships. Accompanying these new relationships was the dissolution of the 'mission' as an organization of a foreign body and the transfer of authority to the local churches of a given area. There was also the development of a partnership between the churches overseas and the sister churches with which they were affiliated.

ROBERT T. PARSONS

FREE CHURCH MISSIONS. The term 'Free Church' was originally applied to those English churches which dissented from the established Church of England—Baptists, Congregationalists, Methodists, etc. In England and America these churches have been pioneers in the rise of modern missions, as the names John *Wesley (1703–1791), George Whitefield (1714–1770), William *Carey (1761–1834), Samuel J. *Mills (1783–1818), Adoniram *Judson (1788–1850), Thomas *Coke (1747–1814) indicate.

Carey's *An Enquiry into the Obligations of Christians to Use Means for the Conversion of the Heathens* (1792) was the beginning of modern missions; and the Society of Brethren, at Williams and Andover, which counted Mills a member, launched the first agency in America: the *ABCFM (f.1810).

More recently, the term is used to apply to the 'third force' in Christendom—those churches which have come to flower in America and on the mission field, originating in protest against Catholic and Protestant establishments and embracing both 'Christendom' and areas not formally Christian in a common missionary theology and strategy. The Free Churches take the view that the primitive church is normative in their interpretation of church history, and in their attempted restitution of the life and spirit of the early church they lay heavy weight on the authority of the *Great

Commission over every baptized Christian. They also commonly emphasize the work of the Holy Spirit, preferring to refer to the divine initiative in human affairs in the language of the Third rather than the Second Person of the Holy Trinity. One concrete result of the literal acceptance of the missionary mandate is that they give a very high proportion of their resources to missions; and the presence of their representatives on the mission field, as revealed in such surveys as Parker's 1938 study for the *IMC or the 1960 *Weltkirchenlexikon*, is out of all proportion to the number of members in the home churches.

In recent years a number of old-line churches like the Evangelical Lutheran Church of Lower Saxony (acting in 1952), have officially adopted the position that support of missions is an obligation upon all Christians and not alone a matter for separate societies. This doctrine has been maintained consistently throughout the historical line which comes from the *Anabaptists through the radical Puritans, *Moravians and Wesleyans to the Free Churches of America and the *younger churches.

FRANKLIN H. LITTELL

F. H. Littell and H. H. Walz: *Weltkirchenlexikon: Handbuch der Oekumene* (Stuttgart 1960), articles on various lands; F. H. Littell: 'The Free Church View of Missions' in G. H. Anderson, ed.: *The Theology of the Christian Mission* (New York 1961), pp. 112–21.

FREEDOM, RELIGIOUS. See LIBERTY, RELIGIOUS.

FREEMAN, THOMAS BIRCH (1806–1890), was born at Twyford, near Winchester, England, his mother being English, his father African, a freed slave. He followed his father's occupation as a gardener, becoming head gardener to an Ipswich squire, a job he lost on becoming a Methodist. In 1837 F. offered his services to the Wesleyan Methodist Missionary Society in London for work in Africa and was sent to the Gold Coast where the first Methodist missionaries had died from fever. He and his wife arrived at Cape Coast Castle on 3 January 1838. She died two months later. Freeman himself only visited England twice in the next 52 years. At first he strengthened the Methodist societies round Cape Coast and then visited Kumasi in Ashanti in 1839, Badagry and Abeokuta in Nigeria in 1842, Whydah and Abomey in Dahomey in 1843. Helped by missionaries sent from England and by Ghanaian assistants he rapidly extended the number of towns where mission houses were built and occupied. The rate was faster than the committee in London could finance; they were constantly being faced with bills of exchange beyond the approved budget. After severe reprimands F. resigned from the ministry in 1857 and was appointed Civil Commandant to the Accra District. In 1873, at the age of 67, he returned to the ministry and served for 13 years in the circuits. As 'Father' Freeman he preached the official sermon at the Jubilee celebrations of Methodism in Wesley Church, Cape Coast, in 1885.

In contrast to colleagues whose service was often counted in months F. brought continuity of pastoral oversight to the church. With the continuity went the application of John *Wesley's 'Methodist' pattern. F. was wise in his appointment of colleagues, selecting the first generation of Ghanaian ministers and entrusting the care of the societies to them in far-away places like Whydah. He made plans for their training. F. patiently sought interviews with the great chiefs of West Africa, seeking permission for preachers to be allowed to live in their kingdoms. Among these were Kwaku Dua of Ashanti, Sodeke of Abeokuta, Gezo of Abomey. His early botanical training is revealed in many references to forest plants in his Journal. He set up a model farm at Dominasi, some 25 miles from Cape Coast, taking out with him in 1841 two ploughs from Britain.

T. A. BEETHAM

A. Birtwhistle: *Thomas Birch Freeman* (London 1950); T. B. Freeman: *Journal of*

Various Visits (London 1844); F. D. Walker: *Thomas Birch Freeman* (London 1929).

FRENCH, THOMAS VALPY (1825–1891), linguist, evangelist and bishop, was born at Burton-on-Trent, England, and went to India in the service of the *CMS in 1850. He quickly made himself master of Persian and Arabic in addition to a number of Indian languages. He was unwearied in the preaching of the gospel, especially to Muslims, in addition to his duties at St. John's College, Agra, and the Divinity School, Lahore. On 21 December 1877 he was consecrated as first bishop of the Anglican diocese of Lahore, which covered the whole of north-western India, including Kashmir. He was not wholly happy in this position, and resigned his see in 1887. In 1891, distressed by the failure of the churches to carry out any direct missionary work in Arabia, the cradle of *Islam, he decided to carry out a one-man mission to Muscat: his companion in the voyage to Arabia was S. M. *Zwemer. The burning climate was too much for the health of the bishop, and he died after a brief ministry of only three months. He is regarded by many as the most distinguished of all the missionaries who have served the CMS.

STEPHEN NEILL

H. Birks: *Life and Correspondence of T. V. French* (2 vols., London 1895); *DNB*, Suppl. ii, 253.

FRENCH GUIANA. See CARIBBEAN.

FRENCH POLYNESIA. See PACIFIC ISLANDS.

FRENCH SOMALILAND. See SOMALILAND, FRENCH.

FREYTAG, WALTER (1899–1959), German missiologist, was born in Neu-Dietendorf/Thuringia, Germany. Prevented from undertaking educational work in China, he became a highly stimulating missionary executive in Germany and eventually chairman of the German Missionary Council. From 1953 he held the chair of missiology and ecumenics at the University of Hamburg. He participated in all *world missionary conferences from Jerusalem to Ghana, became chairman of the *WCC Division of Studies in 1954 and an *IMC vice-president in 1958. A thoughtful observer of missionary processes he registered in a famous dictum the present 'lost directness' of traditional missions and in connection with this introduced in 1953 the term 'Mission of God'. To free the missionary enterprise from its ecclesiological, cultural and political misconceptions as to its nature was the aim of his scholarly work. F. was one of the leading theologians in the discussion of the eschatological motivation of mission. On the problem of mission and unity he stated, 'By virtue of the proclamation of the gospel . . . there always comes into being another and a different church', and 'only the churches which agree to go forth on mission progress towards the achievement of unity'.

HANS JOCHEN MARGULL

W. Freytag: *Reden und Aufsätze*, (2 vols., Munich 1961). For a full bibliography see *Basileia, Tribute to Walter Freytag* (Stuttgart 1959).

FRIENDLY ISLANDS. See PACIFIC ISLANDS.

FRIENDS' MISSIONS (QUAKERS). From its beginnings in England, in 1652, the Quaker movement has been a missionary movement in the widest sense of the word. Its founder George Fox and his followers travelled widely 'publishing Truth'. In the five continents there are now, as a result of these efforts, over 50 independent groups called Yearly Meetings, the one in Kenya with its 32,000 members being the largest in the world. The Yearly Meeting in Madagascar joined the United Church in that country in 1968. The organized Quaker movement is known as the Religious Society of Friends (Quakers).

For Quakers 'mission' and 'service' are one. While some put more stress on the proclamation of the message, others place more emphasis on work for peace, rehabilitation and reconciliation. Today the main missionary activity is carried out through the following agencies: The Board on Missions of the Friends United Meeting, with headquarters in Richmond, Indiana, and by member Yearly Meetings of the Alliance of Evangelical Friends. Several other Yearly Meetings have their own mission work. The main service organizations are the American Friends Service Committee and the Friends Service Council with headquarters in Philadelphia and London respectively. Addresses of all organizations can be obtained from the Friends World Committee for Consultation, Woodbrooke, 1046 Bristol Road, Selly Oak, Birmingham 29, England.

BLANCHE SHAFFER

FULFILMENT THEORY OF MISSIONS. A missionary must inevitably act on some assumption regarding the relation of Christian faith to the non-Christian religions. Although there are theories of wide variety in detail, regarding this relation, all fall basically into three types. At one extreme is the view that the non-Christian religions are simply human constructions or even satanic inventions evil or worthless before God. The Christian missionary, if this idea is accepted, has the task of eliminating every non-Christian religion and establishing in its stead the faith in Jesus Christ. This type of thought is therefore commonly called 'the displacement theory'. At the other extreme is religious relativism. The relativist believes that the Christian faith is simply one religion among many. All have their own values, more or less culturally conditioned. A professing Christian relativist may serve as a missionary in order to share in the exchange of religious insights and traditions with representatives of other religious cultures, for the mutual enrichment of all, but not to convert any.

Fulfilment theory stands between these two extremes. It takes its clue and name from Jesus' attitude towards Judaism, as recorded in Matthew 5:17, as follows: 'Think not that I have come to abolish the law and the prophets; I have come not to abolish them but to fulfil them'. Jesus did not accept all the teachings which had been given in the OT, as he makes clear by his contrasts, 'You have heard . . . But I say' (Matt.5:21–22,27–28,31–32,33–34,38–39,43–44). Yet he did carefully interpret his own ministry in terms of Jewish teaching. The primitive church continued in this tradition. Thus Paul, when speaking to Jews or to others instructed by them, grounded his evangelistic message in the OT; and when speaking to others he appealed to their own best thought or the best clues in their common human experience. Compare Acts 17:22–31, 14:15–17; Rom.1:18–23, 2:12–16; also Justin Martyr's *First Apology*.

To such argument, proponents of displacement reply that Judaism is a special case, being revealed as preparatory to Christ's coming. It will also be said that whatever the evangelistic appeal used, the effect, when people were won to Christian faith, was to displace the old religion altogether. While advocates of fulfilment may acknowledge, or even insist, that the central focus of loyalty is displaced, they may yet find so much of Jewish thought and practice in the Christian church as to lend strong support to the fulfilment theory. They point also to many deposits of pagan culture in the very heart of traditional Christian teaching and rejoice in modern signs, too, that God 'did not leave himself without witness' (Acts 14:17) among any people of the world. Finally, it is argued that a missionary cannot even communicate with people without starting where they are and seeking to draw out certain implications, suggestions, or symbols which point in the direction of Christ.

See CONTINUITY AND DISCONTINUITY.

L. HAROLD DeWOLF

G. H. Anderson, ed.: *The Theology of the Christian Mission* (New York 1961), pp. 168–78; 199–212 (by L. H. DeWolf); A. C. Bouquet: *The Christian Faith and Non-Christian Religions* (New York 1958); S. C. Neill: *Christian Faith and Other Faiths* (London 1961).

FUNDAMENTALISM. The word designates a theological and sociological movement generally American in background and strength but worldwide in its ramifications. F. was largely a protest movement designed to preserve the theological essentials of historic orthodoxy against modernism. It was transdenominational in that it represented all of the major Protestant groups whose roots lay in the Reformation.

Between 1910 and 1912 *The Fundamentals: A Testimony to the Truth* were published. From this series of volumes the movement obtained its name. The twelve books, written by some of America's ablest theologians, constituted an apologetic of those doctrines considered essential to historic orthodoxy. In its earliest days F. was more a theological movement than a sociological phenomenon. As the years passed it became both. Thus more recently F. has been a theological viewpoint wedded to a pietistic sociology characterized oftentimes by an extreme separationism from the world and from the old-line denominations. Independentist, there has grown up around it a cluster of Bible churches, educational institutions of the Bible school and Bible college variety, and a host of ancillary appendages.

F. generally has included within its theology: (1) the infallibility and inerrancy of the Scriptures; (2) the Trinity, including the virgin birth and deity of Jesus Christ; (3) the fall of Adam and the need for personal regeneration based on the substitutionary atonement of Christ; (4) the bodily resurrection of Christ and his ascension; (5) the personal and imminent return of Christ; (6) the everlasting bliss of the righteous dead after their resurrection, and the everlasting and conscious torment of the unbelieving following the final judgment. For many years there existed the World's Christian Fundamentals Association led by men like W. B. Riley and Paul W. Rood. In 1952 it merged with the Slavic Gospel Association.

Some men and groups, of whom J. Gresham Machen and Westminster Theological Seminary are examples, identified popularly with F., have vigorously denied kinship. Yet it is undeniable that many who deny kinship with F. hold similar theological viewpoints but are demarked by sociological differences, primarily concerning standards of Christian conduct.

In the last two decades there has sprung from fundamentalist sources a new movement identified variously as The New Evangelicalism or Neo-Fundamentalism. Unhappy with the negative stance of F. and the incipient legalism of its separationism, and supportive of a growing tendency to work within the old-line denominations from which F. so often dissociated itself, the new evangelicals have moved forward vigorously. Harold John Ockenga, first president of the National Association of Evangelicals, has often been credited as being the father of the new movement, and extreme right-wing fundamentalists have claimed that Billy Graham is its evangelistic arm, Fuller Theological Seminary its educational arm, and *Christianity Today* its journalistic arm. The new evangelicalism has itself been divided and it continues to be plagued by its younger generation of leaders educated in Europe and returning to America questioning the inerrancy of the Scriptures, a pivotal doctrinal concept that has always undergirded F. Whether this means that the new evangelicalism will ultimately cease to be fundamental in its theology remains to be seen.

HAROLD LINDSELL

S. G. Cole: *History of Fundamentalism* (Hamden, etc. 1963); N. F. Furniss: *The Fundamentalist Controversy, 1918–1931* (New Haven 1954), *The Fundamentalist Movement in America, 1870–1920* (Doctoral dissertation, University of California, Berkeley, 1959).

G

GABON, a republic, formerly part of French Equatorial Africa, is a rich and densely-forested territory south of Cameroon with an area of 102,317 sq.m. Its population in 1967 was 473,000, including about 5,000 Europeans. The largest religious group is Roman Catholic; a prefecture apostolic was erected in 1842, which has now grown to two dioceses with 232,765 Catholics. Muslims are very few in number, estimated at 2,000. Protestant work dates also from 1842, and has resulted in one large church, the Evangelical Church of Gabon (served by *PEMS) with 75,000 community, and the smaller Evangelical Church of South Gabon (*CMA) with 5,000. There is a third body, the Pentecostal Evangelical Church, with 1,000 adherents. There have been no clearcut separatist movements, but the syncretistic movement Religion of Eboga, or Bwiti, is estimated to have 60,000 adherents among the Fang tribe.

DAVID B. BARRETT

BM II, 398–401; *NCE* VI, 234.

GAIRDNER, WILLIAM HENRY TEMPLE (1873–1928), was born at Ardrossan, Scotland, and died at Cairo, Egypt. He graduated at Oxford, worked among British students with J. R. *Mott and J. H. *Oldham, and was ordained in the Anglican church. Sent by the *CMS in 1899 to Cairo, he worked as teacher, pastor and evangelist among Moslems. In 1902 he married Margaret Dundas Mitchell. With D. M. Thornton he founded the English and Arabic Christian magazine, *Orient and Occident,* in 1904. A master of Arabic, G. wrote textbooks of the colloquial language; an artist, he composed hymns, biblical dramas and versified gospel stories, and was recognized by Arabs as an original Arabic poet; a musician, he collected Near Eastern tunes for use in Christian worship; a student of Islamic thought, he wrote *The Reproach of Islam* (1909, revised ed. *The Rebuke of Islam,* 1920) and (with W. A. Eddy) *The Values of Christianity and Islam* (1927). Administrative burdens prevented the full expression of his gifts but did not affect his care for individual souls. During his last years at Boulac he 'created . . . a welded group of Egyptians, Syrians and Europeans in one church', helped to train indigenous leaders in the Arabic Anglican community, and worked for fellowship and unity between denominations. His writings and personal influence have had an enduring effect in equipping the whole Near Eastern church for its evangelistic task.

JOHN GOODWIN

C. E. Padwick: *Temple Gairdner of Cairo* (London 1929).

GAMBIA, THE. Area 4,000 sq.m.; population 316,000: Muslims 250,000; Traditional 50,000; Protestants 3,500; Roman Catholics 5,500. The first mission, the Methodist in 1821, was among Africans repatriated from America at Bathurst. *Islam was not then so widespread, but fever prevented continuity of witness among up-country tribespeople. An agriculturist died within a month; an Arabic scholar was invalided from McCarthy Island up-river in 1836 after only seven months. The 50 Methodist missionaries between 1821 and 1900 averaged 2½ years' service; fifteen of them died in the Gambia. The RC *Holy Ghost Fathers, who began in Bathurst in 1849, ascribed to fever among a constantly changing missionary personnel the absence, until very recent years, of any up-country mission. The Anglican mission of the *SPG, although based on West Indian enterprise from Barbados, fared no better. The churches have a good record of secondary education in Bathurst. In 1966, this small Christian community formed the most widely based Christian Council in Africa when the RC, Anglican and Methodist churches subscribed to a constitution based on worship of the Trinity, acceptance

223

of the Scriptures of the OT and NT, an established church organization, a teaching ministry and the exercise of Christian discipline.

T. A. BEETHAM

G. G. Findlay and W. W. Holdsworth: *The History of the Wesleyan Methodist Missionary Society*, Vol. IV (London 1922), pp.118–46; K. H. Pfeffer: *Sierra Leone und Gambia* (Bonn 1958); *BM* II, 401f.; *NCE* VI, 276.

GARDINER, ALLEN FRANCIS (1794–1851), was born of godly parents in Basildon, Berkshire, England. He chose the Navy as his profession in 1808 and enjoyed a successful, worldwide naval career. In 1822 a period of ill-health brought G. into a closer relationship with God. While serving in the ship *Dauntless* he was deeply moved by the plight of the South American Aborigines. Thenceforth he resolved to devote his life to missionary work among unevangelized tribes. After the death of his wife in 1834 he went to Africa and founded the first mission station at Port Natal. In 1836 he married again and returned to South America. G. spent the next fifteen years endeavouring to start missionary work among the South American Indians. The hostility of the indigenous peoples and the intolerance of prevailing RC laws made his task impossible. In 1843 he returned to England to gain support for his venture. In 1844 G. founded the Patagonian (later *South American) Missionary Society. He declared, 'I have made up my mind to return to South America and leave no stone unturned to establish a mission among the aboriginal tribes. While God gives me strength, failure shall not daunt me.' G. and his companions perished of starvation and exposure on the shores of Tierra del Fuego in 1851. A few days before his death he wrote in his diary: 'Poor and weak as we are, our boat is a very Bethel to our souls, for we feel and know that God is here. Asleep or awake, I am, beyond the power of expression, happy.'

HENRY SUTTON

J. Marsh: *Commander Allen Gardiner RN* (London 1874); *DNB* XX, 410.

GEDDIE, JOHN (1815–1872), was born at Banff, Scotland. The family migrated to Pictou, Nova Scotia, in 1816. G. studied at Pictou Academy and was noted for his diligence and continued interest in missions. Later he was described as a genius never equalled for understanding and entering into the psychology of the pagan mind. After graduation, he was ordained minister of Cavendish and New London, Prince Edward Island, in 1838; married Charlotte, daughter of Dr Alexander McDonald, 1839; sailed for New Hebrides 1846, and reached Aneityum 1848. The work began under the auspices of the *LMS, in conjunction with the Presbyterian Church of Nova Scotia. After the American Civil War, the New Hebridean Missions were carried on conjointly by the Australian and New Zealand Presbyterian churches. In 1864 the G. family visited the UK and Prince Edward Island. Queen's University, Kingston, conferred on him a doctorate in 1866. He returned to his work at Aneityum. In 1871 he went to Australia to organize the printing of the Bible in Aneityumese. He died on 14 December 1872 in his 58th year. Memorials were erected in the Geelong Public Cemetery, Victoria, Australia, and in the Aneityum church; an extract from the latter inscription is as follows: 'In memory of John Geddie, D.D., born 1815. When he landed in 1848 there were no Christians here, and when he left in 1872 there were no heathen.'

ESMOND NEW

G. Patterson: *Life of John Geddie, DD* (Toronto 1882).

GEOGRAPHICAL EXPANSION. See EXPANSION OF CHRISTIANITY.

GERMAN EAST ASIA MISSION (Deutsche Ostasien Mission). The GEAM was founded in 1884 as *Allgemeiner Ev.-prot. Missionsverein* (General Protestant Missionary Association). As the original name indicates, the society was meant to serve as an instrument of missionary concern and action for all those who did not feel at home with either the confessional societies or with the Neo-Pietist and *'faith missions'. The Swiss pastor E. Buss had as early as 1876 emphasized the need for a mission which would take due account of the findings of contemporary studies in *Comparative Religion and critical liberal theology. It was on that basis that the GEAM sent its messengers to China and Japan where they worked preferably among the educated and with special emphasis on medical and educational work. Owing to the change of climate in theology the mission changed its name and outlook in 1929. After the first world war the Swiss branch became independent, while the German branch, after the loss of the work in Shantung Province, continued part of the work in Japan, retaining its special concern for the theological and cultural impact of the Christian message in the setting of a rapidly changing Asian scene. Few missions of so comparatively small a size have produced so large a number of renowned scholars (e.g. Ernst Faber, Richard Wilhelm, Wilhelm Seufert, Gerhard Rosenkranz).

H.-W. GENSICHEN

GERMAN EVANGELICAL MISSIONS COUNCIL. The Council (DEMR), although technically the executive of the Federation of German Evangelical Missionary Societies established in 1922, goes back to the older Standing Committee of German Protestant Missions (*Ausschuss*), founded in 1885, which owed most of its inspiration to Gustav *Warneck and 'became normative for the standing committees of co-operative missionary agencies' in many sending countries (W. R. Hogg). Today the DEMR is mainly responsible for ecumenical relations of mission bodies, representation of common interests in relations with governments and other non-church agencies, and other matters which member bodies entrust to it and which are handled either by the council itself or by specially appointed commissions of experts. Traditionally the council carefully avoids interfering with internal concerns of missionary societies. But there has been a steady intensification of its integrating function, expressed most clearly in the setting up

of a permanent Joint Committee of the council and the Evangelical Church in Germany (1951). In recent years it was the chairmanship of the late Prof. W. *Freytag which more than any other single factor contributed to the confidence increasingly placed in the council.

H.-W. GENSICHEN

GERMAN SOCIETY FOR THE STUDY OF MISSIONS (Deutsche Gesellschaft für Missionswissenschaft). In 1918, shortly before the end of the first world war, a small group of German theologians and missiologists under the leadership of the church historian Carl Mirbt decided to set up a society of mission studies. Inopportune as the time seemed to be, the founders embarked on their project with the conviction that both their obligation to the development of mission studies in the past and their commitment to the future justified so daring a step. Until the second world war the society concentrated on publishing two series of missiological studies and on assisting in the establishment of chairs and lectureships in missions in German theological faculties. When work could be resumed after the second world war, the society tackled new tasks as well, e.g. a scheme of scholarships, assistance in research projects of various descriptions, missiological documentation, etc. The financial means are mainly provided by the Protestant churches in Germany. As the society is passing the half-century mark, its membership has become more international than ever (half of its 110 members being non-Germans). The society also took a leading part in the European Consultation on Mission Studies (Birmingham 1968), the first of its kind. Professors M. Schlunk (since Prof. Mirbt's death in 1929), G. Rosenkranz (1951–1965), and H.-W. Gensichen have served as chairmen.

H.-W. GENSICHEN

GHANA. Area 92,000 sq.m. Population 7.5 million. Religions (1960 census, over 15 years of age): Traditional 38%, Christian

43%, Muslim 12%, none stated 7%. Christians are subdivided as percentages of whole: Roman Catholic 13.4, Methodist 10.3, Presbyterian 9.9, Anglican 2.6, African Methodist Episcopal Zion 0.4, Seventh Day Adventists 0.7, Apostolic 2.4, African Christian 1.5, others 1.6.

The first Christian preaching was by the RC chaplains at Elmina Castle following 1482. Later there were Protestant chaplains at the larger fort settlements: Dutch, Danish, English. Jacobes Capitein, the first African Protestant to be ordained to the ministry, was schoolmaster at Elmina about 1742. Thomas *Thompson of the *SPG went outside Cape Coast Castle to Winneba and other towns in the 1750s. His pupil, Philip Quaque, was ordained in England and served as schoolmaster at Cape Coast from 1766 to 1816. German Moravians sought to establish a mission in the middle of the 18th century, but withdrew after a heavy death-roll. The first effective missions outside the fort areas were those of the *Basel Mission at Christiansborg (1828) and Akropong (1835), the Wesleyans round Cape Coast (1835) and the Bremen Mission at Peki (1847) and Keta (1853). All these efforts, maintained continuously throughout the century, were accompanied by heavy loss of life among the missionaries and their wives. The RCs returned in 1880 under the *Society for African Missions of Lyons, and at the turn of the century in the north under the *White Fathers. The SPG returned in 1904; there had been Anglican chaplains at Cape Coast and Accra in the interval but no organized mission. Later arrivals were the SDA (1894), African Methodist Episcopal (1896), Salvation Army (1920).

Christianity spread steadily during the 19th century among the Twi, Fante, Ewe and Ga people, with an acceleration in the early decades of this century. The same was true of Ashanti after 1896. This progress was very often the result of individual witness by church members as they moved about the country as traders or government servants. Something approaching *mass movements occurred through the work of two prophets, the Liberian William Wadé

*Harris in Appollonia to the west in 1914 and Samson Opon in Ashanti in 1919. It was from the preaching of Prophet Harris that the first major *African Independent Church in this region sprang, the Church of the Twelve Apostles. The largest Independent Church in Ghana is the Musama Disco Christo Church. Such churches form about 3.5% of the total Christian community.

The most significant impact made on the community by the missions was in the provision of formal education. The earliest schools were at the Castles. As the church moved out into the country, primary schools sprang up in towns and villages everywhere (cf. *Aggrey's schooling at Cape Coast and pupil teaching at Abura Dunkwa). Secondary schools and teacher colleges followed, the earliest begin Akropong, Mfantsipim, and Wesley Girls High School. The name most known outside Ghana, Achimota, was not mission-founded, but was the first independent school to seek the service of Christian teachers from Britain on direct appointment, a pattern developed later through the two organizations, the Overseas Appointments Bureau of the Christian Education Movement and Catholic Overseas Appointments, in London. Today, as the famous schools and colleges founded by missionaries continue to serve G., they offer education based on the Christian faith through a system of independent boards of governors which include strong, though not necessarily majority, church representation. The influence of the churches in education, in both management and training, is now increasingly exerted more through individuals whose faith is an integral part of their professional service than through the direct participation and direction of church synods and assemblies.

The missions have now become churches through a long process in which constitutional autonomy was sometimes the seal, sometimes the instigator of full and vigorous local action. The forced withdrawal of Basel and Bremen missionaries during the 1914–18 war led to the autonomy of the two Presbyterian churches. The Anglican church became part of the autonomous Province of West Africa in 1951. The Methodist church became an autonomous Conference in 1961. The RC vicariates apostolic were raised to the level of an Ecclesiastical Province in 1950.

The Christian Council of Ghana was founded in 1929. It provides a focus for consultation between the Protestant churches, leading to united action in certain spheres of service and witness. Under its auspices the churches share in Home and Family Weeks and a Family Planning Clinic, literature production, the planning of religious education syllabuses and syllabuses in sex education for primary and secondary schools, relief work in areas of need, and agricultural training. A united theological college—Trinity College—was begun in Kumasi in 1943 to serve the Presbyterian and Methodist churches; it moved to new buildings near Legon University in 1965, where Anglican students later joined it.

The Ghana church is still engaged in mission. The early spontaneous movement from village to village reached to the limit of the Akan peoples, but did not move over the cultural boundary which divided them from the peoples of the north. Since the second world war this boundary has been crossed; established congregations in the south send missionaries, Ghanaians and expatriates, with their financial support into the northern regions, Presbyterians in the east, Anglicans in the centre, Methodists in the west. Ministers have also been seconded to work in Gambia and the Ivory Coast, and others, including laymen, to the staff of the *AACC.

See also AGGREY, J.K.; FREEMAN, T.B.; RIIS,A.

T. A. BEETHAM

C. G. Baeta: 'Aspects of Religion' in *A Study of Contemporary Ghana*, Vol. II, (Neustadt, Omaboe, 1967); C. G. Baeta: *Prophetism in Ghana* (London 1962); F. L. Bartels: *The Roots of Ghana Methodism* (Cambridge 1965); H. W. Debrunner: *A History of Christianity in Ghana* (Accra 1967); R. T. Parsons: *The Churches and Ghana Society 1918–1955* (Leiden 1963); K. H. Pfeffer: *Ghana* (Bonn 1958); N. Smith: *The Presbyterian Church of Ghana, 1835–1960* (Ghana 1966); S. G. Williamson: *Akan Religion and the Christian Faith* (Ghana 1965); R. M. Wiltgen: *Gold Coast Mission History 1471–1880* (Techny, Illinois 1956); Various: *Christianity and African Culture* (Gold Coast 1955); *BM* II, 403–08; *NCE* VI, 460; *WKL*, 489f.

GHANA 1958. See CONFERENCES, WORLD MISSIONARY.

GIBSON, JOHN CAMPBELL (1849–1919), son of a Free Church of Scotland theologian and missionary of the Presbyterian Church of England in S.E. China. He was appointed in 1874 to Swatow, which he made the centre of his life's work. From the first G. was interested in education and literacy. He was a strong advocate of the Romanized Chinese script and established a printing press to supply Christian literature in the Swatow dialect. He worked on Bible translation in both vernacular and literary styles and was one of the authors of the Easy Wenli translation of the NT (1890–1892). G. was also increasingly concerned with the development and order of *indigenous churches. He was largely responsible for the production of the Swatow Church's Book of Church Order. By the end of the century G. was already seen to be one of the leading church statesmen in China. From 1901 he was deeply concerned in the union of Presbyterian churches in China, which he saw as a step towards a united Protestant church. He was British chairman of the Missionary Centenary Conference (Shanghai 1907) and chairman of the Commission on the Church in the Mission Field of the *Edinburgh Conference in 1910, in which capacity he wrote much of Vol. II of the report. This and his *Mission Problems and Mission Methods in South China* (1901) give the best idea of his thought.

BORIS ANDERSON

P. J. MacLagan: *J. Campbell Gibson* (London 1922).

GILBERT AND ELLICE ISLANDS. See PACIFIC ISLANDS.

GILMOUR, JAMES (1843–1891). 'The Apostle to the Mongols' was born at Cathkin near Glasgow, Scotland, in a devout Congregationalist family. After a brilliant record in university and theological college he was appointed by the *LMS to a pioneering mission in Mongolia. G. reached Peking in May 1870 and soon afterward started on a 54-day caravan journey by Kalgan and across sparsely settled, wind-swept grasslands of Outer Mongolia to Kyakhita on the border of Siberia (now USSR). Through fifteen years—except for periodic visits to other North China provinces—he made lonely, heroic efforts to share the rough life of nomadic Mongols that he might preach and teach the gospel to a people steeped in Lamaist forms of *Buddhism. Hardly any conversions resulted, yet G. won much esteem and affection. After his wife died in 1885 he combined evangelism and lay medical service among the agricultural Mongols of eastern Mongolia. Typhus took his life when he was directing a conference of missionaries and native workers at Tientsin. G's books with their vivid word pictures of Mongol life were widely read. 'We shall reap if we faint not' was his motto.

F. W. PRICE

H. F. Beach: *Princely Men in the Heavenly Kingdom* (New York 1903), pp.77–106; J. Gilmour: *Among the Mongols* (London 1884).

GOBAT, SAMUEL (1800–1879), Anglican bishop in Jerusalem, was born in the Jura region of Switzerland, and, after training at the Missionary Institution in Basel, in 1825 joined the service of the *CMS. He was sent to Egypt, where he spent five years, but later was successful in entering Ethiopia. Ill-health led to his withdrawal, but in the comparatively brief period of his service he had been able to acquire a great deal of accurate and valuable information on the state of Ethiopia and its church.

In 1840 the British government had taken steps to create, with the Prussian government, the curious experiment of the Anglo-Prussian bishopric in Jerusalem. After the early death of the first bishop M. S. Alexander, G. was nominated by the Prussian government to the see. In one week in 1845, G. was ordained as priest and consecrated as bishop, and sent out to take up his new duties. From the start his position was extremely difficult. He was in the anomalous position of being responsible for both Anglican and German Lutheran missions and congregations. At the same time he was exposed to violent criticism, based on the allegation that he had carried on an extensive campaign of proselytism from the ancient Eastern churches. G. explained that these churches were so conservative that even to read the Bible was regarded as an offence and that young people had been excommunicated from their churches on no other ground than this. What could he do but offer them a new Christian home? This explanation was unconditionally accepted by all the archbishops in Britain; nevertheless the attacks continued.

A man of profound personal piety, G. was also a highly gifted linguist, who had made himself master not only of Arabic but a number of other oriental languages. He carried on a variety of social and educational enterprises, beginning in 1847 with the first Christian elementary school to be opened in Palestine; the school which still bears his name is evidence of his concern for the well-being of people of all races and religions in the area under his care.

Two years after the death of G. the Anglo-Prussian agreement fell into abeyance and the bishopric in its original form ceased to exist. Later it was reconstituted as a purely Anglican office, the bishop being charged with the double task of supervising Anglican missions and congregations, and working for a good understanding among Christians of all the persuasions represented in the Holy Land.

STEPHEN NEILL

S. Gobat: *Journal of a Three Years' Residence*

in Abyssinia (London 1834), *Samuel Gobat, His Life and Work* (selected writings, London 1884).

GOD, TRANSLATION OF TERM. One of the most complex problems in Bible translating is the choice of a term for God. In general there have been four types of solution: (1) a generic term which may have an exclusive referent, (2) a proper name, which identifies a specific deity in an indigenous religious system, (3) a descriptive phrase based on some characteristic or function, e.g. 'the Creator', 'the Great Father', and (4) a transliteration from some dominant language in the area, e.g. the borrowing from Spanish of *Dios* in many Indian languages of Latin America.

The most widespread alternative is to select some generic term. This is what occurred in Greek, when *Theos* was used to translate the Hebrew *Elohim*. Latin *Deus* and Germanic *Gott* later served similar functions. Wherever a generic term can be used to specify a unique deity, this procedure is preferable, for it makes possible the radical distinction of the Scriptures, in which the God of Israel is put in contrast with the gods of the heathen. One cannot, however, adopt some unique term for God and then tack on a plural, as some translators have attempted to do after borrowing *Allah* for God.

The proper name of a specific deity in an indigenous pantheon may be a valid choice, but it is a dangerous one, for traditional associations with such a deity may be in utter contrast with the biblical revelation. Not infrequently, however, indigenous Christians have themselves made the identification and have often explained away any unfortunate aspects in the meaning of a term by insisting that their forefathers had been deceived.

Descriptive phrases, e.g. 'Father in heaven', 'heavenly ruler', 'the Creator', 'the Eternal One', 'the Great Father, are essentially titles, but they have often been employed, especially if they have had some pre-Christian usage. On the other hand, these phrases are often developed by new believers in attempting to explain the significance of their faith to unbelievers.

Borrowing a transliterated term is often thought to be the safest procedure but it is probably the most dangerous. In the first place, the borrowed name is often regarded merely as a 'proper name' and hence is thought to be either 'a foreign deity' or simply the foreigner's name for one of the local deities. As a 'zero' word it must be filled with meaning, and frequently the meaning selected is the least desirable one, for the procedure by which terms acquire meanings cannot be controlled to any significant degree.

EUGENE A. NIDA

E. A. Nida: *Bible Translating* (London 1947, 1961), pp.204–09; H. Rosin: 'Questionnaire Concerning the Divine Names', *The Bible Translator*, III (1952), pp.199–204; G. W. Sheppard: 'The Problem of Translating "God" into Chinese', *The Bible Translator*, VI (1955), pp.23–30.

GOES, BENTO DE (1562–1607), missionary and explorer, was born in the Azores and died in Suchow, China. While serving as a soldier in India, G. joined the Society of *Jesus as a lay brother, and for some years was active in Agra at the court of Akbar the Great Mogul. In 1601 he carried out in Akbar's name negotiations for peace with the Viceroy of Goa. In October 1602 G. undertook an expedition, to ascertain whether China is identical with the Cathay spoken of by the brothers Polo and the medieval missionaries. The journey of about 2,500 miles led him via Lahore to Kabul. There he crossed the Pamir range, and by way of Yarkland and Kashgar reached in 1605 the Chinese city of Suchow. Matthew *Ricci sent a Chinese Christian from Peking to meet him; but when he found G., the latter was already in a dying condition. He was able to pass on only a small amount of information to Ricci, since G's diary had been stolen by Chinese Muslims; it is possible that they had also poisoned him. Ricci published the information received from G. in his *Commentaries* (Fonti Ricciani II 391–445).

JOSEF GLAZIK

E. Maclagan: *The Jesuits and the Great Mogul* (London 1932); C. Wessels: *Early Jesuit Travellers in Central Asia 1603–1721* (The Hague 1924); H. Yule: *Cathay and the Way Thither* (London 1866); *LTK* IV, 1034.

GOFORTH, JONATHAN (1859–1936), pioneer missionary of the Presbyterian Church in Canada to China, was born in South Nissouri, Ontario, Canada. Reading the memoirs of Robert Murray McCheyne he experienced his 'call' to the Christian ministry. At Knox College, Toronto, he was one of 33 students who in 1887 offered for missionary service. He married Miss Rosalind Bell-Smith and they arrived in China in 1888. They lived first at Cheefoo in Shantung Province and later pioneered in N. Honan. By 1895 G. was working from his first permanent centre in Honan, Changtefu. Sharing in revival experience in the Korean church, and being seconded to the church in Manchuria for six months, he became a leader of the Great Revival in Manchuria of 1908. In 1925 the Gs returned to Manchuria after the newly formed United Church of Canada had taken over the Honan mission. Welcomed by Irish and Scottish missionaries in Manchuria, the Presbyterian Church in Canada opened a new field based on the railway town of Ssupingkai. By 1941 fifty organized congregations flourished. After 1946 this church was preparing to join the Manchurian synod of the Church of Christ in China which had been reconstituted after the war.

AUSTIN FULTON

J. McNab: *They Went Forth* (Toronto 1955), pp.168–87.

GOLD COAST. See GHANA.

GOREH, NEHEMIAH NILAKANTH (c. 1828–1895), was born of a Brahman family in Benares. Possessed throughout his life of a profoundly sceptical spirit, G. could not accept any truth until the reasons for it were made clear to his mind. After long hesitation he accepted baptism on 14 March 1848. For 20 years he supported himself by literary and translation work, at the same time rendering voluntary service as a Christian witness. In 1868 he sought ordination from Bishop Milman of Calcutta and was ordained deacon on 20 December of that year (priest 1870). Increasingly attracted by the catholic aspect of the church, he was admitted on 27 June 1876 as a novice of the SSJE (Cowley Fathers), the first Indian member of that society. Brought into touch with the Brahman widow *Ramabai, he was able to meet her intellectual difficulties regarding the Christian faith and to lead her to baptism in 1883. A man of great simplicity and humility, he bore witness to the Hindu world both by public preaching and by writing; the best known of his works is the *Shaddarshana Darpana, or Hindu Philosophy examined by a Benares Pundit.* G's only daughter Ellen Lakshmi became a deaconess of the Church of England; she wrote the well-known hymn, 'In the secret of his presence how my soul delights to hide'.

STEPHEN NEILL

C. E. Gardner: *Life of Father Goreh* (London 1900); R. D. Paul: *Chosen Vessels* (Madras 1961).

GOSPEL, THE. Gospel (evangel) in pre-Christian secular use meant news of victory. It took religious significance in connection with the worship of the emperor as divine saviour. So any event concerning him was good news. In the OT the reference is to the distinctive message of the salvation which God has in store for his people, and through them for the world. The related verb is to proclaim the beginning of the promised era of salvation and, indeed, to bring the new age into being. Thus, whereas for the pagan the good news looks back and reflects the happy event, in the OT the good news points forward as the messenger announces the beginning of salvation time and thereby effectively introduces it.

Jesus, himself the evangelist who brings good news to men (Eph.2:17), began his ministry by using G. in the prophetic sense, to define his message of salvation, (Mk.1:15, cf Matt.4:23; 9:35; 11:5; Lk.4:18,43; 7:22). He acts as gospel-herald declaring that the era to which the prophets looked forward has now arrived. He claims that in him and his works the kingdom of God is now present (Matt.12:28;Lk.11:20); the long years of unfulfilled longing have given way to the time of fulfilment (Matt.13:16f.;

During his ministry, Jesus appointed men to make proclamation, by word and deed, of the G. which he announced and made provision for its continuance (Mk.13:10; 14:9; 16:15; Matt.24:14, cf. Acts 15:7; Rom. 1:9, etc.). This 'word of the G.' concerning Jesus Christ as Lord and the salvation which had come in him takes the form of a complex of confident assertions about the love of God and the salvation of man based upon the words and works of Jesus. Its content can be traced in the preaching of the Apostles, e.g. Acts 10:36–43; in echoes in the letters, e.g.Rom.1:2–5 ;1Cor. 15:3–7, and at length in 'the Gospels' (the term being applied to the written record from the 2nd century). It is concerned not with what men ought to do but with what God has done. He has fulfilled the promises made in the Old Covenant. He has brought to focus and to climax his eternal purposes, already disclosed in part to his people, in the life, death and resurrection of Jesus of Nazareth, Son of God, who is Christ and Lord, alive and exalted as Judge and Saviour, and who will return to complete his work. Thus the G. is good news about God: that his character and purpose may be seen plain in Jesus Christ. His ministry and passion, with the glory to come at the second Advent, are the acts of God for the redemption of the world. His words and works reveal the nature of that redemption as it works itself out among men. With this theological insistence that the God of creation and redemption is one God the G. combines a plain invitation to respond to the love of God in Christ, challenging men everywhere to repent; to accept the forgiveness of sins offered in Christ; to receive the gift of the Holy Spirit; and so experience the new life of fellowship.

MARCUS WARD

GOSPEL MISSIONARY UNION, THE,

had its genesis in 1889 in a Bible school sponsored by the Kansas State *YMCA with H. Grattan *Guinness and James H. Brooks as leaders, during which the state secretary, George Fisher, dedicated himself to missions. Nine missionaries were sent to the Sudan in 1890 before organization, but five died en route and the mission was abandoned. A committee was organized in 1892, and a party of eight sent in 1893 in association with the *CMA. That connection was severed almost at once. The society took the name Gospel Union, later changed to GMU, and initiated direct sending in 1894 with Morocco as the first field. That difficult work continues. Fisher personally began the Ecuador mission in 1896, including work among the Jivaro and Quechua Indians. Pioneering in Colombia started in 1908 and the mission was organized in 1912. A well organized self-supporting church has grown. Bible translation and distribution have been emphasized in these fields. The GMU's other missions include Panama, northern Canada, British Honduras, Mali and Mexico. In 1966 it had 302 missionaries and 15 accepted candidates. Contributions were $897,719. The GMU is a member of *IFMA. It publishes the periodical, *Gospel Message*. Address: Smithville, Mo.64089, USA.

R. PIERCE BEAVER

GOSPEL RECORDINGS INC. See AUDIO VISUAL AIDS.

GOSSNER, JOHANNES EVANGELISTA (1773–1858), was born at Hausen in Swabia, Germany, educated at Augsburg, Dillingen and Ingolstadt, and ordained priest in the RC church in 1796. He belonged to the 'Awakened Brethren', a group of RC priests and lay people in S. Bavaria who had experienced the new birth through conversion; the group was suspended by the Inquisition in 1802. G. published the NT in German, with financial help from the BFBS, at Munich in 1815. Banished from Bavaria owing to his biblical and pietist activities, G. moved to St. Petersburg

(Leningrad) in 1820, but was expelled from Russia by the Czar, Alexander I, and went to Prussia in 1824. He joined the Lutheran Church 23 July, 1824, and was minister of the Bohemian (Moravian) Congregation of the Bethlehem Church, Berlin, 1829–46.

In 1836 G. founded his own association on faith principles (see FAITH MISSIONS) for training artisans as mission workers, intending that, like the Moravians, they should maintain themselves by their own skills and trades. He sent missionaries to Australia, New Zealand, New Guinea, Samoa, Indonesia, S. and W. Africa, N. America and India. After G's death a board of trustees reformed the association as a conventional missionary society. Today only the Gossner Evangelical Lutheran Church in Chota Nagpur and Assam retains associations with the society in Berlin (see GOSSNER MISSION SOCIETY).

G's pioneer work in social service is continued in Germany by the Gossner Industrial Mission under the direction of Horst Symanowski.

BERNARD H. MATHER

W. Holsten: *Johannes Evangelista Gossner: Glaube und Gemeinde* (Göttingen 1949); H. Lokies: *Johannes Gossner* (Giessen and Basel 1956); C. Sauer: *Fremdling und Bürger. Lebensbild des Johannes Evangelista Gossner* (Berlin 1965); *RGG* II, 1696f.

GOSSNER MISSION SOCIETY. J. E. *Gossner (1773–1858), a Roman Catholic priest who joined the Lutheran church in 1826 and participated in many activities of the Evangelical Awakening of his age, began to send out missionaries in 1836 while serving as a pastor in Berlin. Shortly before that he had started a mission magazine of his own. The mission remained a one-man affair until it became a chartered society in 1842, a step to which the individualist Gossner agreed with much hesitation only. Missionaries were sent out to various parts of the world. Many of them served with other societies till the Ganges valley, Chota Nagpur and Assam in northern India emerged as the main fields of the GMS. There was a further concentration when after

the first world war the Ganges valley work had to be abandoned. At the same time, the repatriation of the Gossner missionaries led to the Gossner church declaring itself *autonomous in 1919—one of the first and and largest *'younger churches' to do so. The GMS has since then assisted the Gossner church in various ways and, after the loss of its East German constituency, engaged increasingly in home mission and industrial evangelism in Germany.

H.-W. GENSICHEN

W. Holsten: *J. E. Gossner: Glaube und Gemeinde* (Göttingen 1949); *RGG* II, 1697.

GOVERNMENTS AND MISSIONS. Most governments have desired to have as little as possible to do with missions, western (especially Protestant) governments regarding them as a nuisance, and non-Christian governments as a menace. When government policies have been formed, this has usually been the result of pressure from the philanthropically-minded section of Christian populations, especially in connection with the abominations of the slave-trade. A turning point was the Berlin International Conference of 1884, at which it was agreed that it was the duty of governments to protect and favour Christian missions. The original draft read 'to favour and aid'; this was modified, owing to the presence of Turkey among the powers, and the desire to avoid placing Muslim emissaries on the same privileged level as Christian.

Many treaties with individual non-Christian countries have contained a special clause guaranteeing to missions the right of entry and the freedom to carry on their work. These clauses have in many cases been grudgingly accepted, but on the whole have been honestly carried out by the governments concerned.

Non-Christian governments such as that of Thailand have generally felt themselves bound to provide for missionaries the same measure of protection and facilities as are granted to other foreigners, but no more.

With the recovery of independence by the peoples formerly under colonial control, there has been a marked worsening in the situation of missions and missionaries. Naturally no missionaries are admitted to communist-controlled countries. It has been made clear that no foreign missionary will be allowed to work in Burma; the same is probably true of the southern Sudan, though one exception has recently been made (1968) in favour of an African RC priest from Tanzania, who desired to enter the country as a teacher of theology. It is increasingly difficult for missionaries to obtain entry visas and residence permits for India and Indonesia. Guinea has expelled all foreign Christian workers, and has refused to permit their replacement by nationals of other independent African countries. It is likely that similar difficulties will arise in the future in other newly independent countries. This change of situation may be regretted by Christians in countries such as Britain which grant unrestricted admission to the emissaries of the non-Christian religions. But it is wiser for the time being to make no protest, and to await the time when a change in political climate leads to a dissolution of the present close association between *nationalism and religious feeling, and a climate is created more favourable to international Christian operations.

STEPHEN NEILL

S. C. Neill: *Colonialism and Christian Missions* (London 1966).

GRACE. The idea of grace is not wholly lacking in the higher forms of non-Christian religion, and particularly in some sections of *Hinduism.

The word *prasāda* or *prasanna*, which occurs fourteen times in *Bhagavadgītā*, can in ten of these contexts rightly be translated 'grace'. It is through the grace of Krishna that the votary can be delivered. The twice-repeated 'thou art dear to me' of Krishna gives a beautiful picture of the way in which the relationship between the devotee and the god he worships is understood. A thousand years later in the philosophy of *Rāmānuja*, the idea of grace is so fully developed that it was possible for the scholar Rudolf Otto to write a book with the title *India's Religion of Grace*.

A similar tradition is found in the *Bhakti* religion of South India, where the native Tamil word *Aruḷ* seems to bear many of the shades of meaning that are associated with the Greek *charis*. The devotee was sunk in the mire of ignorance and sensuality. One day the Lord (Siva or Vishnu) in sheer grace revealed himself, dispelled illusion and made the singer his own. From that time on, the singer can do nothing but pour out in melting verse the transports of his heart and of his devotion to the god.

How far can this teaching be regarded as a direct preparation for the revelation of the grace of God in Jesus Christ? Is there a radical difference between the two, and, if so, where does it lie?

It may be noted, in passing, that in actual practice the *Bhakti* tradition has not been found to serve as a preparation of human spirits for the encounter with God in Jesus Christ, and few converts seem to have found in Christian faith the perfection of that which they had in embryo form in Hinduism.

The differences seem to be in two directions.

There is much talk of sin. But ultimately it seems that the sinner is injuring himself, since sin will hinder his chance of attaining to that final deliverance which is his goal. There is little recognition of sin as outrage against the majesty of God, still less as injury to his love.

From this follows a different concept of the relationship of God to his world. The existence of the universe is in itself indeed a sign of the grace of God, since he has brought it into being as the instrument through which fallen souls can escape their fallenness and return to unity. But there is no suggestion that the creation itself can be delivered from corruption into the glorious liberty of the children of God.

This being so, in an incarnation God appears in the world, but he does not take upon himself the very nature of man in his weakness and alienation. The incarnation is a temporary vesture, not a 'taking of the manhood into God'. There is not that total

2

34   GRACE, PREVENIENT

self-identification with the lost which is the picture of the Gospels; hence no road to Calvary, and no price to be paid for the redemption of the lost.

All this being so, the deity remains external to the devotee; there is no thought of that indwelling of the Redeemer in the redeemed, through which the baser substance of the earthly is progressively transformed after the image of the heavenly.

The devotee will remain in the neighbourhood of the temple where the illumination has been granted to him. It is not clear that he finds himself impelled to perform those simple works of charity in which the Christian attempts to make visible to others the grace which has sought him, and which has driven him out to seek others as undeserving as himself.

'The grace of the Lord' says Radhakrishnan 'is not arbitrary but is determined by the devotion of men' (*Brahma Sūtra* p.498). This is perhaps precisely the point of difference; in this sense the grace of the Lord in the Christian tradition is arbitrary; long before the sinner has made any movement of response, the free grace of God in Christ has gone out to seek and to find the helpless, the ungrateful and the lost.

STEPHEN NEILL

W. D. P. Hill: *The Bhagavad Gita* (London 1928); S. Kulandran: *Grace: A Comparative Study of the Doctrine in Christianity and Hinduism* (London 1964); Mānikkavāsagar: *Tiruvāsagam*, ed. and trans. by G. U. Pope (Oxford 1903).

GRACE, PREVENIENT. The idea of divine spiritual assistance freely given and prevenient to, that is, coming before, saving faith, is implicit in much Christian literature from the beginning (cf. Jn.1:9;6:44). The term and elaboration of the doctrine characterize the work of Jacobus Arminius (1560–1609) and the Methodists. Two kinds of PG may be distinguished, namely, the general benign influence of God's Spirit upon all persons, generating whatever aspiration towards good is to be found in them, and the specific grace given to an individual, enabling him truly to hear and

to respond to the *gospel with *faith. Such enabling power is not thought to overcome or limit free will, but to give free will the new liberty to receive Christ. The missionary who believes in PG sees non-Christian men not as people without any spiritual presence or work of God within them. Rather, he sees all that is best in them as evidence that God's love has already been at work within them seeking to draw them to himself. When such a missionary presents the gospel to men without faith he does so in the hope that the outward hearing of the Word may be accompanied by the inward working of the Holy Spirit so that the Word may be rightly understood, and accepted with faith.

L. HAROLD DeWOLF

GRAUL, KARL (1814–1864), was a German theologian, a member of the Lutheran church, and first director of the *Leipzig Mission (1844–1860). Born the son of a poor weaver, he raised himself to great heights in the kingdom of God and in the world of learning. He was the first German to qualify himself for higher academic teaching in the field of missionary science, but died before he was able to take up his appointment as the first German professor of this subject. He had a special gift for languages; he went to Italy as tutor to an English family, where he was required to teach the children French; he was acquainted with none of these languages, but soon acquired them and translated Dante's *Divina Commedia*.

As director of a mission, it was his wish to send to India every other year one missionary well qualified in theology; but owing to the lack of suitable candidates at that time, even this proved impossible. G. was the first German director of a missionary society (continuing the work of the Tranquebar Mission) to undertake a visit to India, which in his case lasted four years. He learned the Tamil language in its common, its high and its poetical forms, and by his series of translations *Bibliotheca Tamulica* (4 vols. 1854–65) and his *Outline of Tamil Grammar* (1855), took a leading position among the experts in the Dravidian languages. In the great controversy over *caste in the Christian church, which was raging at the time of his visit to India, G. took a less harsh view of caste than was common among British and American missionaries. He laid the foundations for a solid science of the missionary enterprise.

ARNO LEHMANN

K. Graul: *Reise nach Ost-Indien* (5 vols. 1854–56); G. Hermann: *Dr Karl Graul* (Halle 1867); S. Krügel: *100 Jahre Graul-Interpretation* (Berlin 1965, with bibliography); *RGG* II, 1832.

GREAT COMMISSION. The term 'Great Commission' is the name commonly given to the command of Christ found in Matt. 28:18–20 (cf. Mk. 16:15,16; Lk.24: 46–49; Acts 1:8). It has inspired countless missionaries to take up their task and has sustained them in it in trying times. The Great Commission is generally viewed as a command which Christ's followers are to obey. It is more properly viewed as a law of the life of the church. The coming of the Holy Spirit has so constituted the church that it is her nature, her being, her inmost character to be a witnessing community. The command given at the beginning of the old creation, 'Be fruitful and multiply and replenish the earth and subdue it' (Gen. 1:28), finds its counterpart at the beginning of the new creation in the words of the Great Commission. The former was the means of realizing man's purpose in the natural creation. The Great Commission is the law that governs the realization of the new order that has been created in Christ. The command was given to the apostles and through them to the entire church in all times, places and conditions of her existence.

HARRY R. BOER

R. Allen: *Essential Missionary Principles* (London 1913), ch.1; K. Barth: 'An Exegetical Study of Matt. 28:16–20,' in G. H. Anderson, ed.: *The Theology of the Christian Mission* (New York 1961), pp.55–71.

GREENLAND. The largest island in the
9

world. Area 840,000 sq.m. (but about 708,000 sq.m. is ice covered). Population 38,600 (1964). Politically, the area belongs to Denmark.

Through colonists from Iceland and Norway, Christianity came early to G. A bishopric was established in 1125; there were several churches and at least two monasteries. This population later gradually disappeared—and with it Christianity. The first Protestant missionary, Hans *Egede (Lutheran from Norway), arrived in 1721 on the west coast; the people he found were Eskimos and not, as he had expected, descendants of the northern colonists. Egede was appointed by the king, and the mission was closely connected with trade. In 1733, on the initiative of Count *Zinzendorf, a Moravian mission was started in Greenland, but in spite of the best intentions close co-operation between the two missions never proved easy. Egede left Greenland in 1736 for Copenhagen. The mission came under the supervision of the *Missionskollegium* in Copenhagen (abolished 1860) and later under a governmental department for Greenland.

By the end of the 19th century direct missionary work was in the main completed. In 1900 the Moravians handed over their work to the Danish church. The church in G. is now part of the church of Denmark and is under the supervision of the bishop of Copenhagen. There are at present 29 ministers in G. of whom four come from Denmark.

ERIK W. NIELSEN

S. C. Neill: *A History of Christian Missions* (London 1964), pp.235–38; H. Ostermann: *Den Grönlanske Missions of Kirkes Historie* (Copenhagen 1921); *BM* II, 416; *NCE* VI, 752–54.

GRENADA. See CARIBBEAN.

GRENFELL, GEORGE (1849–1906), was born at Sancreed, near Penzance, UK, and studied at Bristol Baptist College before working with the BMS in Cameroon for several years. Here he married his second wife, a West Indian lady. In January

1878 G. was sent with Thomas Comber on a prospecting trip to the lower Congo; Robert *Arthington had offered the BMS one thousand pounds if it would undertake mission work there, and push up the Congo to meet missionaries from the east coast in the region of the Great Lakes, so that a chain of Christian mission stations would stretch across central Africa. G. shared this vision, and it stimulated his extensive exploratory work and his mapping of the upper river and its tributaries. He brought out a steamer, the *Peace*, from England and assembled it at Stanley Pool in 1884, after the pieces had been carried round the lower river cataracts, and did the same with the *Goodwill* in 1893. Owing to his work the BMS was able to choose suitable sites for mission stations along the Congo river as far as Stanley Falls. G. tried to get a line of posts established through to the upper Nile, but failed because of the unwillingness of the Congo state authorities to grant new sites to Protestant missions in his later years, which were clouded by this failure and by worsening relations with the state authorities in the early period of the Congo reform campaign.

RUTH SLADE

G. Hawker: *The Life of George Grenfell, Congo Missionary and Explorer* (London 1909); H. H. Johnston: *George Grenfell and the Congo* (2 vols., London 1908); *DNB*, 2nd Suppl., ii, 164f.

GRENFELL, WILFRED THOMASON (1865–1940), was born at Parkgate, Cheshire, England. He grew up by the sea and among fishermen, studied medicine at the London Hospital, and was converted through D. L. *Moody. Qualifying in medicine in 1886, G. joined the National Mission to Deep Sea Fishermen, working first in the North Sea, and from 1892 in the N.W. Atlantic. Ministering to the men afloat he also visited the small, isolated and hitherto neglected communities living in N. Newfoundland and Labrador. Through his initiative doctors, nurses and ministers were established on the coast, hospitals, seamen's institutes, schools and orphanages built, and co-operative stores founded to free the people from the monopoly of traders who exploited them. G. began to introduce agriculture, lumbering, mining, cottage industries and tourism. He visited the USA, Canada and Britain, raising funds and attracting thousands of volunteers. In 1912 the International Grenfell Association was formed, and in 1926 this was finally separated from the parent mission. G. was knighted in 1927.

G. preached simple, evangelical Christianity and expressed it in care for the whole life of man. His autocratic individualism often tried his friends, and his tactlessness gave opportunity to enemies seeking to discredit him; but the resulting difficulties were always overcome. Fearlessly and imaginatively he followed every new path which he believed Christ was opening up. His example has inspired four generations in Britain and N. America with the ideals of social service in the name of Christ.

JOHN GOODWIN

W. T. Grenfell: *Forty Years for Labrador* (London 1933); J. L. Kerr: *Wilfred Grenfell: His Life and Work* (London 1959); *DNB* (1931–1940), 364f.

GROUP MINISTRIES. See TEAM MINISTRIES.

GROVES, ANTHONY NORRIS (1795–1853), born at Newton, Hampshire, England, became a successful dentist in Exeter, Devon, and was associated in Plymouth and Dublin with those who were afterwards called Plymouth Brethren. He offered his services to the *CMS but withdrew on learning that as a layman he would not be allowed to administer sacraments. In 1829 with his wife and young sons he went by Russia and the Caucasus to Baghdad and carried on successful missionary activity despite plague and war. In 1833 he moved to India and travelled widely conducting Bible teaching among missionaries. This was appreciated; but his urging them to break sectarian barriers and open their Communion table to all Christians was misunderstood. Rebuffed as a schismatic, he formed in 1836 a missionary colony near

Madras with thirteen recruits from England. They supported themselves by agriculture and sent out Indian evangelists. His emphasis on an indigenous ministry, and on the union, regardless of denominational labels, of believers to forward the cause of evangelism, was in advance of his time, and his direct influence was thus limited to creating the first of a long succession of 'Open Brethren' missions in India. He died while on a visit to England, at the home of George Müller.

JOHN POLLOCK

E. H. Broadbent: *The Pilgrim Church* (London 1931), pp.347–60; *Memoir of A. N. Groves*, compiled by his widow (London 1856); *DNB* XXIII, 299.

GRUBB, WILFRED BARBROOKE (1865–1930), was born at Liberton, Midlothian, Scotland, of a medical family. During boyhood he regularly studied the Bible and religious books. In 1881 he joined the *Edinburgh Medical Mission. After brief medical training he sought to join an expedition to Africa but was considered too young. Contact with *Moody and Sankey in 1884 led G. to devote his life to missionary enterprise. After acceptance by the *SAMS he departed for the Western Falklands in 1886. He soon volunteered as a pioneer missionary to the Indian tribes and in 1889 was appointed to take up pioneer work in the Paraguayan Chaco. He gradually won his way among the hostile Indians and was said to be the first white man ever to penetrate the interior of the Chaco and come out alive. In 1900 he initiated the Chaco Indian Association in an endeavour to provide work and industrial training for the neglected Indians. In 1914 he accompanied others to begin a similar mission in the Argentine Chaco. He suffered double pneumonia in 1921 and returned to England. He undertook deputation work on behalf of SAMS until his death. G. was acclaimed as one of the greater missionaries of his generation.

HENRY SUTTON

W. B. Grubb: *Church in the Wilds* (New York 1914); R. J. Hunt: *The Livingstone of South America* (London 1933).

GUADELOUPE. See CARIBBEAN.

GUAM. See PACIFIC ISLANDS.

GUATEMALA. See AMERICA, CENTRAL.

GUIANA, BRITISH. See GUYANA.

GUIANA. DUTCH. See CARIBBEAN.

GUIANA, FRENCH. See CARIBBEAN.

GUINEA, a republic, formerly part of French West Africa, is 95,935 sq.m. in area, with a population of 3,702,000 (1967), about 10,000 being non-Africans. The greater part of the population has for long been Muslim. A RC prefecture apostolic was erected in 1897; by 1965 there were three dioceses with 26,595 Catholics. A small Anglican work based on Conakry has for some time been part of the diocese of Gambia and the Rio Pongas (about 800 adherents in Guinea). Protestant missions were the *PEMS, Open Bible Standard Church, and the Evangelical Protestant Church of the *CMA (1,350 adult members); the total Protestant community including Anglicans is under 3,000. In 1967 as part of its programme for the indigenization of its institutions, the government expelled all foreign missionaries, Protestant and Catholic.

DAVID B. BARRETT

BM II, 425–29; *NCE* VI, 855f.

GUINEA, PORTUGUESE, is a low-lying coastal area of 13,944 sq.m. in West Africa, with a population of 600,000 including (1965) 7,000 Europeans; its status is that of Overseas Province of Portugal. The majority of the African population are Muslims. Roman Catholics in the prefecture apostolic of PG are largely foreigners. The only Protestant mission is the *WEC, with a total community of 1,320.

DAVID B. BARRETT

BM II, 429f.; *NCE* VI, 856.

GUINEA, SPANISH. See EQUATORIAL GUINEA.

GUINNESS, HENRY GRATTAN (1835–1910), was born in Dublin, Ireland. Converted at the age of 20, he began immediately to win others for Christ. He left New College, London, without completing his studies for the ministry and instead became an international itinerant evangelist. Burning with zeal, he lived in complete poverty and often faced violent persecution.

From 1855 to 1859 G. preached to many thousands in England, Ireland, Scotland and the USA during the great revival. He offered in 1865 to go to China, but was advised by Hudson *Taylor to continue in his present ministry. A visit to France in 1865 resulted in the founding of the McAll Mission. In 1873 G. opened the Missionary Training Institute at Harley House in East London, with Dr Barnardo as co-director; by 1875 there were 100 students evangelizing in the London slums. G. helped to found the Livingstone Inland Mission (1877), which started work in Congo and afterwards moved on to S. America and N. India, becoming in 1899 the *RBMU. The *NAM was formed on G's advice. In 1889 G. encouraged Drs A. J. Gordon and H. Mabie to start missionary training colleges in Boston and Minneapolis. By 1910 some 1,400 students, men and women, had gone from Harley House and Cliff College to serve abroad.

G's two daughters married leading missionaries and seven of his children and grandchildren have entered the Christian ministry. John R. *Mott said that it was to G. that he owed the original inspiration of his own worldwide missionary travels.

GORDON AND PAUL GUINNESS
Regions Beyond (periodical), January 1911.

GULICK, ORRAMEL H. (1830–1923), was born in Honolulu, his parents being pioneer missionaries to Hawaii. After a period of service in this area, he and his wife were assigned to the Japan mission of the *ABCFM in 1869. They were first located at Kobe, where their language teacher and his wife were arrested for aiding in Scripture translation and having a copy of *Hepburn's translation of Mark in their possession. The former died in prison, with a firm faith in Christ, in 1872, the first Protestant martyr. Disappointed in their inability to secure a residence permit for Kyoto, the Gs were assigned to Osaka, which became their permanent station in 1873. Two years later, G. started publication of the first Christian newspaper, the *Weekly Miscellany*, to meet the needs of Christian families and instruct enquirers. This became the journal of the Japan Evangelical Alliance in 1883, under the name *Gospel News*. Later it became the official organ of the Congregational church and in 1889 was named the *Christian News*, the ancestor of the present conciliar organ. In view of the increasing emigration of Japanese to the Hawaiian Islands, the Gs were re-assigned to this field in 1894, where he rounded out a total of 60 years of evangelistic service in the Islands and Japan.

GORDON K. CHAPMAN
O. Cary: *History of Christianity in Japan* (New York 1909), Vol. II, pp.73ff., 97, 105, 122, 202; W. T. Thomas: *Protestant Beginnings in Japan* (Tokyo 1959), pp.78, 111, 123.

GURNEY, SAMUEL (1860–1924), was born at Long Branch, New Jersey, USA, studied at New York Missionary Training School and Drew Theological Seminary, was ordained in 1891 in the New York East Conference of the Methodist Episcopal Church, serving pastorates in New York and Connecticut while at the same time attending Yale University, where he received his Doctor of Medicine degree in 1901. He left for Rhodesia in 1903 where, except for two years of furlough, he served till he died. G. pioneered in many parts of the work of the Methodist Conference, at first at Old Umtali and at Chief Mutasa's, then, when the work was expanded, at Mrewa, Mtoko and Nyadiri. Wherever he went his winsome personality, combined with medical skill and constant effort, broke down barriers of suspicion and resistance. One settler said when G. arrived: 'Everyone was against him'. One official told him: 'We have been spared two evils—cattle sickness and missionaries'. Chiefs Mangwende and Nyajina refused to deal with him. He won them all. He refused to share in interdenominational rivalries, and was chairman of the Southern Rhodesia Missionary Conference, 1922–1924. G. was buried in Salisbury, beloved by all.

PER HASSING

H. I. James: *Missions in Southern Rhodesia under the Methodist Episcopal Church, 1898–1934* (Old Umtali 1935).

GUTMANN, BRUNO (1876–1966), was born in Dresden, Germany. He served from 1902 to 1938 as a missionary of the *Leipzig Mission among the Chagga people of the Kilimanjaro (Moshi) region of Tanzania. He was among the most outstanding missionaries to Africa, and was distinguished alike in ethnology and in the scientific study of missions. Basing himself on the work of W. Wundt, philosopher and exponent of the ideas of tribal or racial psychology, G. laid down the basic principle of his doctrine of man—that man is to be understood not as an individual, but as a member of an organic whole. G's ethnology, his doctrine of the church and his missionary practice were determined by this principle.

In extensive scientific researches, in recognition of which he received an honorary doctorate of theology from Erlangen (1924) and of law from Würzburg (1926), G. developed the view that there are three primeval forms of human organization—the clan (blood), neighbourhood (soil and place), the age-group (age); these he regarded as unchanging forms of human relationships, and exalted to the status of the primeval links between man and man. Passing beyond the limits of the African context, he affirmed this to be the basic form of every human association. These 'primeval links' correspond to the will of the Creator for men, and have therefore absolute validity. From this analysis he deduced a programme for the education of a people, and for a strategy of mission.

In point of fact, even in G's day his analysis did not correspond to the structures of the life of the Chagga people. Through the development of civilization and the great society, the basic forms which G. assumed to be permanent had already been caught up in an inevitable process of dissolution. In order to judge this process as destructive, G. further affirmed that his basic forms belonged to the order of creation, which had not been broken by human sin.

Against the mortal foe of this structure—civilization and its consequences in the formation of a proletariat and the disintegration of a people—the only available weapon is the quickening of the original culture, i.e. the restoration or renewal of those cells of the original plasma of a people which are still in existence. The result of this attitude is a missionary method based on the idea of an organic approach to the whole life of a people. Here 'the understanding of mission as the organic approach to a people is definitively set up as the answer to civilization' (Hoekendijk). Church and the 'primeval links' are brought into the closest possible association with one another as parts of the divine ordinances of creation. The aim of mission is the incorporation of the organic structure of a people's life into the body of Christ. 'Mission' cannot therefore have within itself an idea of dispersion; its aim is not the gathering of a new community, but the perfecting of an order of society which is already present. So the task of the missionary is not the conversion of the individual, but the service of 'redirection', that is of the regeneration of the old forms of society; correspondingly the task of the leader in the congregation is 'concern for relationships'. G. put his own ideas into effect in the congregation at Moshi with astonishing consistency and notable effect.

The anthropological and ethnological ideas of G. were exposed to vigorous criticism. Theological criticism arose in connection with the dialectical theology of Karl Barth, and with the rediscovery of the eschatological dimension of missions. The starting-point of mission was held to be not so much the doctrine of creation as the doctrine of the Holy Spirit and the church

(W. Freytag, K. Hartenstein). The idea of creation, reflected in the laws of a people's life, was found unacceptable.

It remains, however, the contribution of G. that he meditated profoundly and theologically on the nature of the meeting between the gospel and African societies, and on the real scheme of relationships by which the existence of men is determined. In recent discussions of missionary theory questions of structure have again become important. It seems likely therefore that in the future the theology of mission will turn back, to its own advantage, to the work of G.

ROLF CHRISTIANSEN

There is no adequate study of Bruno Gutmann in English. See J. C. Hoekendijk: *Kirche und Volk in der deutschen Missionswissenschaft* (Ger. tr., München 1967), pp. 139ff.; Collected Essays, with bibliography (500 items) in E. Jäschke: *Bruno Gutmann, Afrikaner-Europäer in nächstenschaftlicher Entsprechung* (Stuttgart 1966); pp.215–31; P. P. A. Kamfer: *Die volksorganiese sendingmetode by Bruno Gutmann* (Amsterdam 1955). BG's most important works are *Gemeinde-Aufbau aus dem Evangelium* (Leipzig 1925); *Das Recht der Dschagga* (München 1926); *Die Stammeslehren der Dschagga I–III* (München 1932–1938). See also *RGG³* II, 1918f.

GÜTZLAFF, KARL FRIEDRICH AUGUSTUS (1803–1851), the first Lutheran missionary to China, was born in Pyritz, Pomerania, in a pietistic home. He received his training at Jänicke's Mission School in Berlin. Here he came into contact with not only Moravianism but also Evangelicalism and Romanticism. His final training took place at Nederlandsch Zendelinggenootschap, in Holland. On a visit to London he met Robert *Morrison. G's first missionary field was in Indonesia, where he met missionaries working among the Chinese 'dispersion'. He learnt Chinese and started to work among them. His society did not approve of this. In 1828 he became a free-lance but was still often supplied from it and in touch with his former friends. G. worked in Siam (Thai-

land), translating the Bible, etc. into Siamese. He took a Chinese name and wore Chinese clothes. During 1831–33 he made three journeys along the coast of China, and made it known in Europe and USA that China was not open for commerce but for the gospel. The people were friendly; he distributed publications and preached. His accounts of these journeys aroused great interest in the west as to the possibilities of missionary work in China. In 1833–39 G. visited several parts of the interior of southern China with some success, but soon the Chinese authorities forbade his works and his books. When Morrison died in 1834, G. became Chinese secretary to the British commercial authorities. He translated the Bible into Chinese. During the Opium War, 1839–43, G. was authorized to accompany the British navy. As he had not enough European missionaries, he trained Chinese Christians to follow up his missionary work. After the Peace of Nanking he lived in Hong Kong and devoted himself to training Chinese assistants and to sending them out as evangelists and tract-distributors. Six cities were now opened for missionary work. but G. still worked in the interior through his evangelists. His plan was to evangelize China in one generation. With this in view he founded the Chinese Union. The Chinese were to become Christian through indigenous evangelists. This sound idea was rendered ineffectual owing to bad training and leadership. In 1844 G. had 20 evangelists, three years later 300. He did not exercise enough control over their work. In 1847 he recruited a Swede, Th. Hamberg, and a German, R. Lechler, as helpers. They found the work of the evangelists very limited and superficial. To find more money and missionaries for all the provinces of China, G. went in 1849 to Europe—his only home visit—and began a triumphal progress through most European countries. After his return to China in 1851 he died, the Chinese Union being dissolved and his work taken over by other organizations such as the *Basel and *Berlin mission societies. G. has been called the grandfather of the *CIM. Through him

*Livingstone and Hudson *Taylor received their missionary call. G. was a member of different societies in Europe and USA and was awarded the honorary degree of DD (Groningen).

HERMAN SCHLYTER

H. Schlyter: *Karl Gützlaff als Missionar in China* (Lund 1946); *RGG* II, 1905f.

GUYANA is an Amerindian word meaning land of waters. The country (formerly British Guiana) lies on the north-east coast of south America, and covers an area of 83,000 sq.m. About 90% of the population live on a narrow plain along the coast-line which is mostly below high tide sea level. Population (1960) 560,620: Christian 317,850, Hindu 187,403, Muslim 49,290, other 6,077.

Amerindian tribes were the sole inhabitants of the country until Europeans arrived about A.D. 1500. The colony of Demerara and Essequibo finally came under British rule in 1814. The county of Berbice was added to the Colony of British Guiana in 1831. Guyana became an independent nation within the Commonwealth on 26 May 1966. Education is within reach of all. A university has been founded.

The date of Christian penetration is not precisely known. 'On the occasion of a visit by Gideon Bourse, the Commandeur of Berbice and the Predicant of that colony in 1683, Beekman (Commandeur and Governor of Kyk-over-al, situated in the river of Isekepe) was very glad to avail himself of the Reverend Gentleman's services to baptize two children and administer the Sacrament. In March 1688, a Predicant named Rudolph Heynens . . . arrived at Kyk-over-al.' (James Rodway: *History of British Guiana*, Vol. I, p.42.)

Churches represented in Guyana are: Anglican Province of the West Indies; Church of Scotland (Overseas Council); Moravian Church, USA; African Methodist Episcopal, USA; Methodist Church, Caribbean and American; Roman Catholic (*Society of Jesus).

A few churches are self-supporting and self-governing. Most churches receive 20% to 60% grant-in-aid from overseas. Ecumenical spirit is active in study groups, prayer cells for Christian unity, joint action in education, social problems, broadcasting and relief work of the Christian Social Council.

JAMES DAVISON

BM II, 431–33.

H

HAHN, CARL HUGO (1818–1895), was born in Latvia, eastern Europe. He experienced conversion as a young man and joined the *Rhenish Mission Society, which sent him to South West Africa in 1842 as a pioneer missionary. There he did research into the Herero language, for which he was the first to compile a grammar. After almost 20 years of missionary effort without result, he conceived the far-reaching idea of establishing and developing a mission colony at Otjimbingue, where African Christians would be integrated into a small community of lay workers (1863). He opened a theological seminary in the same place in 1866, to which the most talented young men of the country were sent (at first only the sons of chieftains were admitted) to be trained as evangelists and teachers even before actual Christian communities had come into being.

As the Rhenish Mission was unable to extend its work during those years, H. summoned the Finnish Lutheran Mission to the country to take up their work among the Ambo tribes in 1868. He himself had made arrangements to make this possible.

In South West Africa H. became more decidedly Lutheran and prevailed upon the Rhenish Mission, which included both Lutheran and Reformed elements, to establish and develop a church of Lutheran character. His Lutheran attitude, however, was not of an exclusive kind, but was intended to serve the stability of the work of the mission.

THEO SUNDERMEIER

T. Sundermeier: *Mission, Bekenntnis und Kirche* (Wuppertal-Barmen 1962); *RGG* III, 28f.

HAITI. See CARIBBEAN.

HANDBOOKS FOR MISSIONS. See BIBLIOGRAPHIES; DIRECTORIES FOR MISSIONS.

HARRIS, WILLIAM WADE (WADDY) (c. 1865–1929), was a Grebo, a member of a subdivision of the Kru peoples of Liberia. He was brought up as a Methodist but in 1885 he was confirmed by Bishop S. D. Ferguson in the Protestant Episcopal Church. As a teacher and catechist for this mission he preached against 'fetishes' and trial by ordeal or 'drinking sasswood', and at times he was in danger of undergoing this trial himself. In 1909 he became involved prematurely in a Grebo rebellion against the Liberian authorities, raising the British flag as a signal for revolt. He was put into prison and was freed only after the suppression of the Grebos in 1910. While in prison H. underwent a mystical experience during which he was convinced God had designated him a 'prophet' to convert West Africa. He dressed himself in a white turban and long white robe and wandered far from home, preaching as he went. In 1913 he crossed into French territory, the Ivory Coast, where he had a tremendous impact and discredited completely the traditional beliefs in a pantheon of varied spirits among many of the coastal peoples. In 1914 he also visited the Apollonia (Nzima) area of the Gold Coast where he was equally successful. Initially welcomed in Ivory Coast by the only missionaries, members of the *Société des Missions Africaines de Lyon*, H. soon proved too alarming on account of his charismatic influence over the Ivoirians. The French officials, who at first thought him a possible instrument of social reform, feared him, after the outbreak of war in Europe, for the same reason. He was therefore expelled early in 1915. His work lived on and developed under the guidance of a number of the Fanti and Sierra Leonean employees of the trading firms in the country, most of them Methodists. They preached and baptized extensively and were accepted as H's disciples delegated by him to use his powers of healing and exorcism. Usually it was the leaders of the traditional religious observances who undertook the leadership of the new churches, so that there was little rift in the social patterns of village solidarity. Everywhere little churches were built and used for services which, from the influence of the 'clerks', developed a strongly Methodist flavour. When after 1924 Methodist missionaries, led by W. J. Platt, began to work in the Ivory Coast, they were able to enrol immediately some 25,000 catechumens. For H. himself, the years after 1915 seem to have been an anti-climax, for though he travelled extensively inland and up the coast he never repeated his Ivory Coast triumph. Increasingly H. sought to defend polygamy as a legitimate African institution, and to criticize missionaries for condemning it. He had always advocated the reform of traditional customs, not abolition in favour of European ways. Today in Liberia, Ivory Coast and Ghana such groups as the Harrisites and the Church of the Twelve Apostles, who emphasize spiritual healing and are fiercely suspicious of European influences, claim to be his true followers.

G. M. HALIBURTON

J. Gorju: 'Un Prophète à la Côte d'Ivoire' in L'Echo des Missions Africaines de Lyon, XIV, 4, Sept.-Oct. 1915; J. E. Casely Hayford: William Waddy Harris, the West African Reformer: The Man and His Message (London 1915); G. Joseph: La Côte d'Ivoire, le Pays, les Habitants (Paris 1917); W. J. Platt: An African Prophet: The Ivory Coast Movement and what came of it (London 1934).

HAWAII, earlier known as the Sandwich Islands, is 6,454 sq.m. in area and had a population in 1960 of 632,772. It was settled by Polynesian people before 750. After Captain Cook's death there in 1779, European and American ships called frequently and induced cultural disintegration and population decline. Kamehameha I united the islands into a kingdom, and later tabu and idolatry were abolished. Thus the situation was favourable when the *ABCFM's first party of 15 American and three Hawaiian missionaries was sent in

1819. The chiefs were won, the royal family converted, and the people followed their leaders in large numbers. Some missionaries left the mission and served as ministers of state. Through the influence of the missionaries a new society was given legal form modelled on New England, despite the fierce opposition of foreign seamen and merchants. Churches and schools multiplied, the production of the Bible and literature in the vernacular was extensive, and a native ministry was raised up. Half the population had been won by 1836 when a remarkable revival resulted in mass conversion between 1838 and 1843. Few Hawaiians remained pagan, but the population of 100,000 was but a quarter of that at the time of discovery. A smallpox epidemic in 1858 followed by the introduction of leprosy took further toll. Since the church was mature, self-supporting, and conducting its own foreign missions to Micronesia and the Marquesas (begun 1852–1853), the Hawaiian Evangelical Association was formed in 1854, when the mission was terminated, all American Board support and connection ending in 1863. The HEA was then reorganized and the remaining evangelistic task undertaken as home mission work.

The Sacred Heart Fathers began the Roman Catholic mission in 1827 in connection with a French colonization scheme, were expelled in 1831 and 1837, and in 1839 were permanently established through French naval intervention. The most famous work of this mission was Father *Damien's mission to the lepers of Molokai begun in 1873. Filipino, Portuguese and mainland immigration brought large numbers of RCs. Other orders, including the Marianists, Marists, and *Maryknoll Mission, were introduced. The RC church now claims about one-third of the inhabitants of the islands, but few are the original Hawaiians.

American Episcopal chaplains to seamen ministered to British and American Anglicans in Honolulu, but no Anglican mission was established. Later, at the request of King Kamehameha IV, Bishop T. N.

Staley arrived in the islands, to set up a mission on high Anglican lines, which came to be called the Reformed Catholic Church. This was suspected by many Americans of being a British effort to thwart the growing American political influence. Staley's churchmanship was not acceptable to all Anglicans; and his patronizing attitude towards the American missionaries and the large Congregationalist populace gave offence. More peaceful relationships were established under the second bishop, Alfred Willis who served from 1872 till 1901. When the islands were annexed by the USA, Willis resigned, and H. B. Restarick was appointed as the first American bishop of what now became the missionary district of Honolulu.

*Mormon missionaries entered the islands in 1850 and drew off some of the Christians into churches they established.

In 1894 the monarchy in H. was replaced by a republic, and the USA annexed the islands in 1898. H. acquired statehood as the 50th State of the Union in 1959.

The decline of the Hawaiian people and their unwillingness to labour on the plantations led to the importation of large numbers of Chinese beginning in the 1860s and of Japanese in 1886. After American annexation of the Philippines Filipinos, too, came in large numbers. The Hawaiian Evangelical Association began evangelism among the Chinese and Japanese, but the church could not cope with the floodtide. *Buddhism and *Shinto came with these people. The population in 1950 divided: Hawaiians 17.2%; Caucasians 23%; Chinese 6.5%; Filipinos 12.2%; Japanese 36.9%; others 4.2%.

R. PIERCE BEAVER

R. Anderson: *A History of the Sandwich Islands Mission* (Boston 1870); B. Smith: *Yankees in Paradise, the New England Impact on Hawaii* (Philadelphia 1956); Sister A. M. Lemon, CSJ: *Hawaii, Lei of Islands, A History of Catholic Hawaii* (Honolulu 1956); H. B. Restarick: *Hawaii 1778–1920 from the Viewpoint of a Bishop* (Honolulu 1924); *NCE* VI, 952–54; *WKL*, 529f.

HAYSTACK MEETING. The call to preach the gospel to all nations came to Samuel J. *Mills while he was ploughing his fields in Connecticut in 1802. Four years later he entered Williams College, Williamstown, Massachusetts, to prepare for the Christian ministry. There he attracted a group of kindred spirits—James Richards, Francis Robbins, Harvey Loomis, Gordon Hall and Luther Rice. Deeply concerned for the salvation of the 'heathen', these young men, known as the Society of Brethren, met frequently in a grove of maples near the campus for discussion and prayer. One day on their way to prayer they were caught in a sudden thunderstorm. Taking refuge in the lee of a nearby haystack, they had their usual time of prayer, following which they stood to their feet and said, 'We can do it if we will'. They thereupon signed a pledge to devote their lives to missionary service.

After graduation several of them went to Andover Seminary, where they were joined by Adoniram *Judson from Brown, Samuel Newell from Harvard and Samuel Nott, Jr, from Union College. Under the leadership of Judson, the brilliant valedictorian, they formed the Society of Inquiry on the Subject of Missions. In June 1810 Judson, Mills, Nott and Newell presented a memorial to the General Assembly of the Congregational Churches, offering themselves for missionary service and soliciting their 'advice, direction, and prayers'. Not without some misgivings the 'reverend fathers' accepted the offer. Shortly thereafter they formed the *ABCFM. Two years later Judson, Newell and Nott, with their brides, and Gordon Hall and Luther Rice sailed for India.

J. HERBERT KANE

C. P. Shedd: *Two Centuries of Student Christian Movements* (New York 1934), pp. 48–60.

HEALTH OF MISSIONARIES. In his book *Tropical Climates* (1820), Dr Andrew Simpson writes: 'the nature and fountain of most if not all of the infectious complaints remain veiled in inscrutable obscuration'. Little wonder therefore that about 50% of early pioneers in Africa either died, or were invalided within two years. To the general ignorance was often added a particular hazard in a belief in immunity from venomous bites and poisonous potions, suggested in Mark 16:18, for those who would go into all the world to preach the gospel. That turned out to be a pious hope. So also healing of the sick by laying on of hands appeared as wishful thinking unless those hands were more chirurgical than spiritual. The development of medical missions provided a corrective to faith and a safeguard to health. Medical training for laymen was first started by Dr Charles Harford at Livingstone College in London, Sir Patrick Manson being the first lecturer in 1891. Modern preventive measures based on nature's own method of producing immunity, as in Jenner's vaccination, have led to potent preventive vaccines for yellow fever, poliomyelitis, tuberculosis, diphtheria, whooping cough, tetanus and measles, as well as less effective ones for typhus, typhoid, plague and cholera. *Chemoprophylaxis* by specially prepared drugs supplement this in sleeping sickness, malaria, meningitis, bilharzia, filariasis and dysentery. *Chemotherapy* by specific drugs is available for the cure of most of these diseases including tuberculosis and leprosy. All these are now generally recognized as part of the whole armour of God and accepted by all but a few objectors. But missionaries are still subject to the fiery darts of the wicked one in their occupational hazards. These are no longer the pot, since cannibals recognized that they could not keep a good man down. But the doctrine that 'missionaries are your worst enemies' has lately been fostered and resulted in the brutal mass murders of missionaries and indigenous Christians. More insidious however are the mental and spiritual stresses and strains exaggerated in small communities of men and women of strong convictions. It used to be said that if a colleague was difficult he should be given a dose of castor oil. But if one found all colleagues difficult one should take a dose oneself. The psychiatrists have made this more complicated with their complexes, conflicts, drives and urges which need more subtle catharsis. Moreover the glamour of missionary work has largely faded and it requires rare qualities to work with the *younger church colleagues who, although they admit that they need the expatriate and invite him, feel not unnaturally that they wish they did not. Thus this ambivalent 'call' is not so strong as the old missionary vocation and when combined with falling standards produces frustration and depression. But release and reward still come to those who are content to follow the Master and go, not to be ministered unto, but to minister.

CLEMENT C. CHESTERMAN

HEBICH, SAMUEL (1803–1868), was born of a pastor's family near Ulm, Württemberg. In 1834 he was sent out by the *Basel Mission as one of the first three pioneer missionaries to south-west India where he founded the mission stations at Mangalore and Cannanore, the latter becoming the base for a unique Christian community composed of Indians and British soldiers alike. He had exceptional success in the conversion of the young British officers of the regiments stationed in Cannanore. His autocratic inclinations made H. a difficult man to work with. Both his rather oversimplified revivalist preaching and his uncompromising fight against Hindu 'paganism' aroused considerable criticism. However, when he retired after 25 years of service a solid foundation had been laid on which an Indian church could be built.

H.-W. GENSICHEN

T. Schölly: *Samuel Hebich* (Basel 1911); G. S. Thomssen: *Samuel Hebich of India* (Cuttack 1905).

HENRY MARTYN INSTITUTE OF ISLAMIC STUDIES, THE, was founded in 1930 as 'The Henry *Martyn School' bearing the name of the first modern missionary to Muslims (1781–1812). It held 'the object of providing a centre for research, for the training of Christian workers, and for the preparation of Christian literature, with special reference to Islam in India'. The resident staff, seconded from various churches, moved from Lahore and Landour to Aligarh in 1940; the fine library and central activities were thus cut off from Pakistan at the time of Partition. Political considerations dictated the setting up of the HMI in East Pakistan as a separate body in 1966; the West Pakistan Christian Council has similar plans. In India a central staff, which travels widely, was first based on Jabalpur, but moved to a new, permanent home at Lucknow; a field staff, located in all regions of India, joins with them in residential courses, in summer schools, in teaching at theological colleges, in correspondence courses, in literature work, and in personal dialogue with some of the 50 million Muslims in India. The HMI fosters 'adequate and sympathetic understanding of Islam' among Christians to assist their 'evangelistic obligation to Muslims'.

JOHN B. TAYLOR

The Bulletin of Christian Institutes of Islamic Studies, succeeding *News and Notes* of the Missionaries to Muslims League, founded 1912, and still published quarterly.

HEPBURN, JAMES CURTIS (1815–1911), was born in Milton, Pennsylvania, USA, and graduated from Princeton and the Pennsylvania University Medical School. He went to Singapore in 1841 and two years later to Amoy, but returned to New York in 1846. In 1859 he left for Japan under the Presbyterian Board of Foreign Missions, and worked there till his retirement to America in 1892. Most of his work was in Yokohama (the city of Japan's first Protestant church), and he engaged not only in medical work, but also in the preparation of tracts (the first on 'The True Doctrine Made Plain or Easy' being printed in 1864), the translation of the Scriptures (begun in 1861) and in lexicography (the writing of Japanese-English dictionaries and grammars). In 1872 (when anti-Christian laws were still unrepealed) he presented the emperor with a copy of the English Bible and his Japanese-English dictionary. A much respected missionary,

he chaired the NT translation committee, which produced its first complete Japanese NT in 1880, and also the Osaka Missionary Conference (the first major ecumenical gathering) in 1883. His work in Japan was recognized by the state on his 90th birthday, when he was decorated by the emperor.

RAYMOND J. HAMMER

O. Cary: *A History of Christianity in Japan* (New York 1909); *DAB* VIII, 567f.

HERMOSILLA, HIERONYMUS, *OP (1800–1861), was born in Spain, became a *Dominican in Valencia in 1823, was sent to the Philippines in 1825, and in 1829 to Tongking. Highly distinguished as a missionary, in 1840 he was appointed *Vicar Apostolic of East Tongking and Bishop of Melitopolis. He lived for 32 years through a period of ceaseless persecutions under the kings Minh Menh, Thieu Tri and Tu Duc; he had to bear the execution of his predecessor Ignaz Delgado, of three other bishops, of many priests and lay believers, and was an observer of the heroic stand of the congregations, especially during the time of the war with the French. In spite of everything the number of Christians continued to grow. H. ordained many indigenous priests, and in periods of comparative calm attempted to rebuild churches, schools and monasteries. Though constantly sought by his enemies, he was able to escape every trap set for him, until through treachery on board a fishing boat, he was delivered up into the hands of the executioners. His execution was carried out with great pomp in Hai Duong (East Tongking) together with that of Valentin Berrio Ochoa, Vicar Apostolic of Central Tongking, and of the Spanish Dominican Petrus Almató. On 20 May 1906 the three martyrs, together with the catechist José Khang and six other Dominicans, were beatified by Pope Pius X.

P. BENNO M. BIERMANN, OP

Bibl. Miss.XI 89f; Marcos Gispert: *Historia de las Misiones Dominicanas en Tungkin* (Avila 1928); *LTK* V, 262.

HERRNHUT MISSIONARY SOCIETY. See MORAVIAN MISSIONS.

HIGGINBOTTOM, SAM (1874–1958), born in Manchester, England, journeyed in 1894 to the USA to attend D. L. *Moody's Mt. Hermon School. Graduated with a B.A. from Princeton in June 1903, he reached India that November. Missionary conviction, a chance encounter with Henry Forman from India, and correspondence with Robert E. *Speer had set his course. Assigned as a lay member of the Presbyterian (USA, Northern) Mission to what became Ewing Christian College in Allahabad, H. took his first economics students into the countryside for observation. Resulting studies on poverty led him to devote his life to improving the Indian villager's food production and way of living as evidence of the Christian concern for man. In 1904 he married Ethelind Cody. He gained a B.Sc. in agriculture at Ohio State University in 1911 and that year, as India's pioneering scientific agriculturalist, began at Ewing what was to become the Allahabad Agricultural Institute. This all-India institution (that land's educational prototype for scientific farming) improved strains of stock, poultry and grain, advocated fertilizing by trenching all organic wastes, and trained village workers. It associated with Allahabad University in 1932 and in 1934 graduated its first B.Sc. class. H. served India's rural needs everywhere. When many of his colleagues, regarding the Institute as non-evangelistic and inappropriate, voted it out of the misson for five years (1925–30), the board in New York continued it separately. H. always held the work to be an essential part of the Christian evangelical witness in India. Vindicated, he later served as Moderator of his church (1939–40) and retired from India in 1945.

W. RICHEY HOGG

S. Higginbottom: *Sam Higginbottom: Farmer* (New York 1949).

HILL, DAVID (1840–1896), was born in York, England. After theological study and ordination he was sent to the Central China field of the Wesleyan Methodist Missionary Society. Financially independent, he yet lived in simple Chinese style, putting the balance of his income into the work of the church. Celibate but not ascetic, he carried with him everywhere an infectious joy. Although stationed at Wuchang and other Hupeh cities he was like Paul 'in journeyings often' by land and water, preaching the gospel, planting new congregations in towns and villages, training western and Chinese lay workers, always pressing on. Shunning official positions he yet had to assume certain administrative responsibilities. At the Missionary Conference of 1890 at Shanghai he was chairman of the British section. H's social concern was manifested in two years of famine relief 1878–80, when he was instrumental in the conversion of Pastor *Hsi. He fought the infamous opium trade, started a hospital, founded homes for the aged, the blind, and orphan boys, laid foundations for later Christian secondary and college education, and helped to launch the Religious Tract Society. He was a saintly missionary pioneer with ecumenical vision. His untimely death at the age of 56 was mourned throughout the Christian world.

F. W. PRICE

H. B. Rattenbury: *David Hill, Friend of China; A Modern Portrait* (London 1949).

HINDERER, DAVID (1819–1890), born at Weisbach, near Schorndorf, Württemberg, Germany, was sent as an Anglican clergyman, by the *CMS, to West Africa in 1849. In 1851 he became the first European to enter Ibadan. On returning to England, he urged the CMS to start work there before the Moslems should influence the chiefs against Christianity. In 1853 he married Anna Martin (1827–1870) and with her founded the Ibadan mission. In 1855 the first converts were baptized; eventually 20 African children were living in the Hinderers' home and as many more were receiving continuous Christian teaching and practical education. From 1860 to 1865 Ibadan was at war with other towns and the Hinderers were virtually prisoners, suffering much privation and sickness. During this period H. translated Bunyan's *Pilgrim's*

Progress into Yoruba. In 1869 they retired to England, where Mrs Hinderer died. H. returned to Yorubaland in 1874 and founded the stations of Leke and Ode Ondo before retiring finally in 1877. His main work in Ibadan continued for several years under his former assistant, the Rev. Daniel Olubi, and grew into a large and flourishing church. Today this church has great opportunities, situated as it is at the political, commercial and educational centre of Western Nigeria.

JOHN GOODWIN

A. Hinderer: *Seventeen Years in the Yoruba Country* (London 1871).

HINDU MAHĀSABHĀ is the oldest and most orthodox party among the 'communal' parties in India today. Founded more than 30 years ago it found support among the Hindu-religious minded, non-westernized and largely non-English-speaking lower middle class in former princely states. Its membership is limited to Hindus only. All non-Hindus are regarded as aliens in India: 'A change in religion connotes change in nationality'. Part of the party programme is therefore the 'reconversion of those who have left Hinduism'. Consequently the *Sabhā* demands a ban on foreign missions and became the strongest speaker in public against Christian mission work in India. They reject any cultural influence from the west, promote the protection of cows and want to revive the 'glorious ideals of Aryan womanhood'. Hindi is regarded as the only official language in the nation. The government is expected to be 'a champion of Hindu causes', to make 'Hindudom military-minded', and to create an independent 'Pan-Hindu bloc' without Commonwealth relations. During the last general elections the *Sabhā* won 0.9% of the votes and four seats in the Parliament.

HORST BÜRKLE

J. R. Chandran and M. M. Thomas, eds.: *Political Outlook in India Today* (Bangalore 1956); M. Weiner: *Party Politics in India* (Princeton, N.J. 1957).

HINDUISM, CLASSICAL. Little from classical H. has survived in the conscious-ness of the average Hindu of the present day. The religion of the 80% of the population who live in the villages is rather to be described as *animism; among the educated many have retained H. as part of the social order rather than as religion which demands faith and obedience. The extremely complex story can be summarized under four heads, which roughly correspond to historical periods.

(1) The original tradition of the Vedas (1500–900 B.C.) has left little mark on later periods, though treated by all sects and groups in H. as canonical. The names of the Vedic gods are little known and the religious practice of later periods has retained little from this distant past.

(2) The ritual literature of the Brahmanas, etc. (1000–500 B.C.) has left a solid deposit in the formulae which are still used on many occasions of personal or family history. It is in this period that the organization of society in *castes begins to become apparent.

(3) The philosophical period, which begins with the early Upanisads (800–200 B.C.) still survives in the idea almost universally held by Hindus of the unreality of the visible and the reality of the invisible world. To this period belongs also the appearance and the first development of the doctrine of *Karma* (retribution) and reincarnation.

(4) The period of *Bhakti*, personal devotion to a deity (200 B.C.–A.D. 1000) of which the earliest classical manifestation is the *Bhagavad Gita*, and which came to a notable flowering in the Tamil devotional hymns from the 7th to the 10th century A.D. Here the non-Hindu encounters Hindu religion in the form in which he can best understand it. This *Bhakti* tradition still has immense influence. The *Bhagavad Gita* is the best loved of all Hindu classics and has been translated into many modern Indian languages. The Tamil hymns are sung daily in countless temples, and are known by heart by many Hindu worshippers.

To the question, who is a Hindu? it is not possible to give any clear answer. Some would reply that no more can be said than that a Hindu is a member of some recognized caste from which he has not separated himself, and the minimum obligations of which he has fulfilled. In almost every case, however, it is possible to add to the qualifications of a Hindu the belief in *transmigration and rebirth, and the belief that by the accumulation of merit the consequences of sin can be mitigated or wholly overcome. To this minimum, of course, many Hindus add a great many other beliefs and practices.

Much has been written in recent years about the revival of H.; it is not clear in what sense this is to be taken. Is there marked increase in devotion at the temples, or in the family? Has there been a marked revival of personal devotion along the traditional Hindu lines? Is there a more widespread acceptance of the fundamental principles of Hindu thought? To such questions it is difficult to give a clear answer. It is certain that H. still retains an enormous power as a social system, by which every part of human existence is touched, and that very few of those born as Hindus, even though sceptical in matters of religion, would wish to separate themselves from this system; it is perhaps this social cohesion rather than religious conviction which is the greatest obstacle to Christian progress In India.

STEPHEN NEILL

The best general account is certainly J. Gonda: *Die Religionen Indiens* (2 vols., Stuttgart 1961, in the series *Die Religionen der Menscheit*). For a short survey see also S. C. Neill: *Christian Faith and Other Faiths* (London 1961); and P. Devanandan: *The Gospel and Renascent Hinduism* (London 1959); *ERE* VI, 686–715; *NCE* VI, 1123-36; *WKL*, 557–5⁰.

HINDUISM, MODERN. The modern period in the history of H. extends roughly from Ram Mohun Roy (1772–1833) to Radhakrishnan (1888–). During this period seeds of a fruitful dialogue between H. and Christianity were sown. Many Hindu leaders, while being impatient with the dogmas of Christianity and critical of the church as an organization, were, nevertheless, greatly attracted by the person and ethical teachings of Jesus Christ. They were,

however, convinced of the self-sufficiency of H., and their interest in Christianity was primarily as an *additional* source of spiritual enrichment rather than as a serious alternative to H.

The years immediately following independence (1947) were marked by a sense of political achievement through non-violence, a recognition of the importance of India in the world community, a hope in planning to bring about rapid economic and social progress and a confidence in the cultural and religious foundations of the nation. The mood affected H. also. New shrines have been built, temples have been renovated, revival meetings organized, cultural renaissance encouraged and literary activity both in English and the regional languages greatly strengthened. In recent years, however, several factors have given rise to a more militant mood of criticism. There is an insistent demand that traditional beliefs should either be totally rejected or drastically reinterpreted. (1) The Chinese invasion of 1962 jolted the country from its complacency. In its wake Gandhian *ahimsa* (non-violence) has been seriously criticized. (2) The growing gap between promise and fulfilment in national planning has given rise to disappointment and anxiety and calls for a drastic re-examination of the foundations of national life. (3) The increasing influence of science and technology has drawn attention to *this* world and *this* life. Nehru called the newly built factories 'temples of modern India'. K. M. Panikkar, emphasizing the secular character of Hindu society, called for social change through legislation rather than through religious reformation. Tangible goals here and now are accepted as more important than the benefits of a distant *moksha*. Poverty is no longer accepted as fate. All this demands a radical revision of approach to the religious situation of today. Certain trends in this complex situation may be noted.

(a) A tendency to define the word 'Hindu' in *cultural* terms. N. C. Chaudhuri argues that the Hindu way of life is 'the most massive, powerful, determinate and active human phenomenon in India' and that it includes both religion and secularity. Others try to dissociate Hindu culture from various religious beliefs. This has obvious implications to the church's understanding of *'baptism', *'conversion' and *indigenization. Is it impossible for a person to *be* a Hindu culturally but become a Christian by conviction?

(b) A recognition of the possibility of *controlling* nature and of *participating* in history. Irrigation projects, health programmes and planned parenthood mean that man is no longer bound by natural necessity. Historical progress, with tangible goals, is more attractive than the benefits of a transcendent immateriality. This means that the Hindu conception of time and the whole structure of Hindu values are being reexamined.

(c) It is accepted that material values *do* contribute to human welfare, for personal and social fulfilment. The social dimension of H. expresses itself not only in its changing attitude towards *caste, but also in its service projects wherever human needs have to be met. This calls for a new understanding of what 'spirituality', a nebulous word, really means to the Hindu in the present context.

(d) In the struggle between tradition and modernity a more drastic re-interpretation of some of the classical Hindu doctrines is going on. Sometimes, even though the term is retained, the interpretation amounts to a rejection of the past. It is pointed out e.g. that *nishkāma karma* (action without attachment) is too individualistic and otherworldly. Without commitment to certain goals and without interest in the fruits of one's actions (*phalāsa*) there can be no responsible action. What is needed today is a 'goal-oriented', not a 'self-oriented' attitude.

(e) The presence of Christ in the heart and mind of India is significant. Men, who do not always join the visible church, still show genuine respect to Jesus Christ and try to follow his way. Acknowledging the universality of Christ, the church must be sensitive to 'The Hindu Response to the Unbound Christ' and seek to understand 'The Unknown Christ of Hinduism'.

(f) The mood of friendliness towards other religions in a climate of open secularism is a healthy sign. Hindus generally welcomed the election of Dr Z. Hussain, a Muslim, as President of India. One of his first acts, after becoming President, was to seek personally the blessings of a Hindu *jagadguru* and a Jain *muni*. The church has great possibilities in this mood of *dialogue which is opening what was hitherto a one way street to two way traffic. What is needed today is not an academic comparison of systems of thought, but a genuine sharing of convictions at deeper religious levels in an atmosphere of friendliness and understanding. It must, however, be pointed out that the recent mood of militant Hindu orthodoxy, expressing itself through legislation in certain states against conversion, is not in harmony with the spirit of tolerance. One hopes that this is a passing phase and that responsible Hindus would be more generous in their attitude towards other religions in the country.

S. J. SAMARTHA

W. T. de Bary, ed.: *Sources of Indian Tradition* (London and New York 1958); D. S. Sarma: *The Hindu Renaissance* (Banaras 1944).

HISTORY AND THE CHRISTIAN MISSION. Ever since the earliest days of Israel's involvement in the history of the surrounding peoples and empires, biblical faith has been interwoven with historical happenings. Apart from those happenings, in which a disclosure of God's purpose was discerned, theology could have been only a matter of abstract ideas. The coming of Jesus and his *church certainly affected men's thinking, but this was primarily because of their impact upon the course of historical development. For centuries this impact was relatively local; for a millennium after the rise of *Islam, Christian influence was almost entirely restricted to Europe, where the great Christian humanist and scientific revolution began. During the last two centuries or so, the renewal of the church's mission has begun to spread the blessings of Christian civilization throughout the world, whatever other forces or subsequent evils may have followed in its wake. However that may be, the significant new fact of our time is that the whole world is now beginning to participate in a single universal history. All the nations are today eager to enjoy the blessings of education, of modern scientific technology, medicine and agriculture, which are the secular blessings (unless they are misused) of the achievement of Christendom. The whole world is fast becoming Europeanized, all the more rapidly as *colonialism disappears. Millions of people, who until recently could hardly be said to have entered upon a truly historical existence, are now participating in history, and the history in which they are participating is universal history, a new phenomenon created by scientific and technological advances in our century. An event occurring, or a word spoken, in one corner of the world today, may tomorrow have an impact upon all the nations and their peoples. In this sense the Christian mission is confronted with an entirely new situation, which implies a new kind of involvement in and responsibility for universal history; and if the dangers which beset the world in this new form of history are very great, the opportunities which await the church will be limited only by the smallness of her vision and the inadequacy of her faith.

ALAN RICHARDSON

S. C. Neill: *The Church and Christian Union* (London 1968); A. Richardson: *History, Sacred and Profane* (London 1964).

HISTORY OF MISSIONS. The materials for writing missionary history are almost unlimited. A great many missionaries have kept diaries; and all have written lengthy reports to the societies which sent them out. The publication of these original sources can be of greatest value. In A. Lehmann's *Alte Briefe aus Indien* we can follow in *Ziegenbalg's letters every step in the development of the first Protestant mission in India. But often these sources are tendentious; the *Lettres Edifiantes et Curieuses* of the *Jesuit Fathers are often more curious than edifying, and can be used as sources for

history only after the most careful and critical sifting. Many of the early histories are mere compilations. Occasionally a historian stands out, as Pierre du Jarric stands out above all the other early historians of Christian work in India (3 vols. 1608–1614; also 1615 in Latin translation); but James Hough's *History of Christianity in India* (5 vols. 1839–1860) is marred by its lack of critical assessment, and its strongly anti-Roman bias. Much early missionary biography is purely hagiographical. The first modern and serious biography is the life of Bishop James Hannington by E. C. Dawson (1886); Fr G. Schurhammer's *Franz Xaver* (to be completed in three volumes) sets new standards of thoroughness and accuracy.

Many of the older histories deal only with the work of one society. The best of all is E. Stock's three-volume *History of the Church Missionary Society* (1899); on the RC side Launay's history of the *Missions Etrangères* may be mentioned. Most RC histories deal only with the work of RC missions. The pioneer was Fr J. Schmidlin: *Katholische Missionsgeschichte* (1924); this has been superseded by Mgr. A. Mulders: *Missiegeschiedenis* (1957; also in German); and by the more popular work in four volumes, edited by Mgr. Delacroix: *Histoire universelle des missions catholiques* (1956). Similarly on the Protestant side the massive work of J. Richter, *Allgemeine evangelische Missionsgeschichte* (1906–1932), pays hardly any attention to RC or Orthodox work.

A new epoch began with K. S. Latourette: *A History of the Expansion of Christianity* (7 vols. 1937–1945). For the first time the whole field was covered, with careful attention to sources and with complete impartiality as between races, confessions and missions. Latourette claims that his is a pioneer work, and points out that on many subjects no satisfactory book as yet exists. On a far smaller scale S. C. Neill in his *History of Christian Missions* (1964) has tried to supply an interesting narrative, conveying the sense of the movement of the gospel through the centuries and through the world.

Gaps are gradually being filled in. A notable feature is the appearance of excellent pieces of research into missionary affairs by historians who have no special interest in missionary work. Two admirable examples are Sir E. Maclagan: *The Jesuits and the Great Mogul* (1932) and C. R. Boxer: *The Christian Century in Japan 1549–1650* (1951). A great difficulty in the past has been the lack of evidence from the side of the *younger churches themselves. A notable exception is the diary of Andrew Ly (1693–1774) in China. The first outstanding history by a younger church writer in modern times is Judge P. Cheryan: *The Malabar Syrians and the Church Missionary Society 1816–1840* (1935). To this we can now add such works as Fr H. de la Costa's admirable study of *The Jesuits in the Philippines 1581–1765* (1961), and Professor Ajayi's work on the missions and the creation of Nigeria (1965). The new ecumenical spirit is making it possible for RC and non-Roman scholars to work together, as shown by *Studies in Philippine Church History*, edited by G. H. Anderson (1969). This in itself will correct many perspectives. In 30 years' time all existing text-books will have to be re-written or substantially modified.

EDITORS

HISTORY OF RELIGIONS. The scientific study of religions is a product of the modern scientific spirit, and has already gone through many phases. It is generally recognized that a turning point was the publication in 1871 of E. B. Tylor's *Primitive Culture*. Tylor was almost the first to make *primitive religion the object of serious and sympathetic study: his concept of *animism, the belief in spiritual presence in physical objects, though now outmoded, served to bring together a vast number of apparently unrelated phenomena. Rather later, Sir J. G. Frazer attempted to distinguish between *magic and religion; religion is the submission of man to a supposedly higher power, magic is man's attempt to use these higher powers to his own advantage. In this evolutionary period it was taken for granted that monotheism was a later stage in the development of the religious consciousness. This was challenged by Andrew Lang, and later by the Vienna school under its leader W. Schmidt, who discovered a primitive *monotheism in the ideas of many of the backward peoples of the world; magic, animism and *polytheism are here interpreted as a backsliding from an original revelation of truth.

Although these ideas have not won universal favour, the simple evolutionary theory is no longer held by any serious student. Other means of classification must be applied, and each form of religion must be seen in its own historical situation. Certain valid distinctions can be drawn.

One clear distinction is that between the religions of a book, notably *Judaism, Christianity and *Islam, and the religions which depend purely on oral tradition. The book religion has in general a clearer concept of revelation; it tends to the definition of doctrine as against the mere observance of traditional practice.

A second distinction is that between religions which have a known and historically identifiable founder—Christianity, Islam—and those which look back to an endless and impenetrable past, notably *Hinduism.

A third distinction is that, stressed by N. Söderblom, between the mystical and prophetic types. In the latter, God speaks from without and is to be obeyed; the emphasis is on the difference between the divine and the human. In the former, man is seen as wholly akin to the divine, and the aim is the full realization of that divinity which is apprehended as already present in man.

A fourth is the distinction between those religions which are of purely local significance (as all tribal religions) as against those, such as *Buddhism, Christianity and Islam, which have from the start made a claim to universal validity. In very recent times, such a claim has been made also by Hinduism, which traditionally has been no more than the religion of one area of Asia.

Much can be learned by the comparative

study of religions. In recent times, however, much more stress has been laid on the identification of each type of religion in its separate identity and in its wholeness. The history of religions does not deal with the question of the truth or validity of any religion; this belongs to a different department of study. Yet it is possible for the honest historian to reach certain conclusions as to the extent to which any religious system meets, or fails to meet, the age-long needs and strivings of the human spirit.

STEPHEN NEILL

C. J. Adams, ed.: *A Reader's Guide to the Great Religions* (New York 1965) contains very useful bibliographies. U. Bianchi: *Problemi di Storia delle Religioni* (Rome 1964; also in German: *Probleme der Religionsgeschichte*, Göttingen 1965).

HOCKING, WILLIAM ERNEST (1873–1966), was born in Cleveland, Ohio, USA, the son of a physician. He graduated from Harvard in 1901 and had his MA and PhD from the same university. After teaching philosophy in several institutions, including Yale (1908–1914), he returned to Harvard as professor of philosophy and remained there until because of age he became emeritus (1943). He wrote extensively on philosophy, and especially on religion and philosophy. An early major book was *The Meaning of God in Human Experience* (1912), followed (1918) by *Human Nature and Its Remaking*. As Chairman of the Commission of Appraisal of the *Laymen's Foreign Missions Inquiry which in 1931–1932 travelled in India, Burma, China and Japan to make a first hand study of a number of American Protestant Foreign Missions, he edited the findings of that commission in the volume *Re-Thinking Missions* (1932) and wrote the section on 'General Principles'. The chapter provoked controversy, for it seemed to many to undercut the motive for Christian missions. Somewhat later, in *Living Religions and a World Faith* (1940) and *The Coming World Civilization* (1956) H. made it clear that, while appreciative of other religions, he believed in the Incarnation of God in Jesus Christ,

the risen Christ, and the Trinity, and that Christianity was best fitted to be the world religion.

KENNETH SCOTT LATOURETTE

Who's Who in America, especially 1938–1939, p.1226, and 1966–1967, p.977.

HOLINESS MISSIONS. The emphasis in some smaller churches upon sanctification and/or upon such gifts of the Spirit as ecstatic utterance is largely a product of 19th century revivalism in America. Charles G. Finney (1792–1875), Congregational preacher and Arminian theologian, was one of the major popularizers of the doctrine of entire sanctification. Following the Civil War, the National Holiness Movement gained considerable following among the major churches (especially Methodist), and a number of small groups split off on Holiness grounds: *Pentecostal denominations, *Nazarenes, *CMA, International Church of the Four Square Gospel, Church of God and Saints of Christ, etc. In England the teaching of holiness was associated with the *Keswick Convention.

The gift of speaking with tongues has been especially attractive to mountain whites and rural Negroes in the USA, and it also has helped greatly to spread the movement in Latin America and West Africa. Holiness churches are characteristically restitutionist, believing that the early church is normative and that the church later 'fell' into corruption; they stress the recovery of the Spirit of inspiration which blessed the early church, and they are very vigorous in home and foreign missions. Some are premillennialists, a number practise divine healing; temperance and non-resistance are frequently stressed, and separation from the world is cultivated. The Nazarenes, among others of this bent, are noted for ranking near the top in annual per capita giving to Christian causes. In a number of mission fields Holiness groups account for the majority of workers.

Centres of the Holiness movement include colleges such as Asbury, Taylor, Alma, Olivet. Leaders of renown include Phinias F. Breeze, Martin W. Knapp, A. B. Simpson,

A. J. Tomlinson, Alma White, T. P. Ferguson and Aimie Semple McPherson.

FRANKLIN H. LITTELL

F. E. Mayer and A. C. Piepkorn: *The Religious Bodies of America* (4th ed., St. Louis 1961), pp.305ff., with bibliography; K. McDonnell: 'The Ecumenical Significance of the Pentecostal Movement' in *Worship*, XL (1966), pp.608–29; T. L. Smith: *Called Unto Holiness* (Kansas City 1962).

HOLLAND, HENRY TRISTRAM (1875–1965), was born in Durham, England. He became one of the best known and best loved missionaries in the great subcontinent of India-Pakistan. Some measure of his stature may be gathered from the fact that though he died at a moment of great crisis in the affairs of Pakistan the local radio gave time to an appreciation of a man 'greatly beloved'. In 1900 he went out to Quetta in Baluchistan, a qualified doctor in the service of the *CMS. There he established a reputation for surgical skill, particularly in the treatment of cataract, which brought him international fame. The friend of princes and distinguished soldiers, Sir Henry Holland was also the beloved physician of wild tribesmen and of the poorest men and women. So trusted and venerated did he become that he could travel without danger in areas where others could only venture in armed convoys. Above all he was a man of prayer. Asked the secret of his success as a surgeon he gave it in the words 'prayer and disinfectant'! Whenever possible he used both. If disinfectant was unavailable he never failed to use prayer. He performed his last cataract operation when he was 81 years old.

MAX WARREN

H. Holland: *Frontier Doctor* (London 1958).

HOLY GHOST FATHERS—*Congregatio Sancti Spiritus*—grown out of the *Séminaire du St. Esprit*, founded, assisted by the *Jesuits of the *Collège Clermont*, by the Breton clergyman Claude François Poullart des Places (1679–1709) for the training of

poor students for pastoral work in Paris, on Pentecost 1703. From its very beginning members of the congregation also worked as missionaries. Suppressed during the French Revolution, it was restored by Napoleon with the sole aim of educating the clergy for the colonies left to France in 1802. From this national restriction the congregation was freed by Francis Libermann (1802–1852), the converted son of the rabbi Lazarus Libermann of Zabern, Alsace. In 1848 he joined it with a small community, founded by him for the conversion of Negroes. He formed its present character and gave it an organization resembling that of a religious order, and worldwide aims in schools, social enterprises, and missions. In 1966, 46 bishops, 3,545 fathers, 915 novices and students of theology and 817 lay brothers belonged to the Congregation of the Holy Ghost. The congregation has seventeen provinces, and its members work among about six million Catholics in 48 dioceses of Africa and 23 dioceses in Latin America.

J. RATH, CSSp.

P. Blanchard: *Vénérable Libermann* (2 vols., Lyon 1960); H. J. Koren: *The Spiritans. A History of the Congregation of the Holy Ghost* (New York 1956); J. Michel: *Cl.Fr. Poullart des Places* (Paris 1962); *NCE* VI, 70f.

HOLY SPIRIT. The word 'Spirit' in the OT usually translates the Hebrew word *ruach*, which means breath or wind. The *Ruach* of God is the vital energy of God directed towards the creation or man. By it men are enabled to accomplish remarkable feats of strength (e.g. Samson), courage (e.g. Gideon), wisdom in leadership (e.g. Moses), skill in craftsmanship (e.g. Bezalel) and prophetic insight. In the prophetic books the gift of the Spirit is promised to the Messiah who will be the faithful Ruler (Isa.11:1–5), to the Servant of the LORD, who will bring justice to the nations (Isa. 42:1–4), to the people of Israel who are like old dry bones (Ezek.37:1–14) and to 'all flesh' (Joel 2:28).

The Gospels tell us that the birth of Jesus

was the work of the Spirit and that the Spirit anointed him for his mission and empowered his mighty works. The fact that the Spirit is thus at work in him is a sign of the presence of the kingdom of God (Matt. 12:28). Jesus also promises that the Spirit will be given to the disciples to teach them what to say in answer to their accusers (e.g. Matt.10:20), to witness to Jesus (Jn.15:26; cf. Acts 1:8;5:32), to convict the world (Jn. 16:8–10), to guide and teach them (Jn.14:26; 16:13) and to empower them to forgive sin (Jn.20:22f.).

In the Acts the Spirit is depicted as the activator and guide of the apostolic mission. At Pentecost the disciples, hitherto apparently an enclosed group, are given boldness and power to communicate the gospel effectively to men of all races. While Pentecost is the unique beginning of the mission, there is a 'little pentecost' at the critical moments of advance when the church breaks barriers—into Samaria (Acts 8:9–24), into the Gentile world (Acts 10:44ff.) and into Ephesus, the great centre of the mission in Asia (Acts 19:1–7). It is the Spirit also who directs the setting apart of Saul and Barnabas (13:2), and guides them on their missionary journeys (e.g. Acts 13:4;16:6ff.;19:21).

In the Epistles greater stress falls upon the work of the Spirit as the power of the new life of freedom, sonship and hope (Romans 8), as the giver of a new kind of life (Gal.5:22ff.), as the bestower of manifold gifts for the building up of the fellowship (1 Cor.12–14) and as the guarantee of final salvation (2 Cor.1:22; Eph.1:14). Co-partnership in the Spirit is listed along with the grace of Jesus Christ and the love of God as one of the fundamental blessings of the Christian life.

While there is no contradiction between the picture given in the Acts of the Spirit as the inspirer of mission, and the picture in the Epistles of the Spirit as the builder and sustainer of the church—for he is both—it is perhaps important to correct a prevalent tendency in the church to think only of the latter. The Holy Spirit of God cannot be domesticated within the church. This does not mean—as some have suggested—that we may acknowledge the presence of the Spirit wherever we see signs of creative energy. St. Paul and St. John both warn us that we have to test the spirits, for there are other spirits in the world, and that the criterion is the confession of Jesus Christ as Lord (1 Cor.12:1ff.) or 'Jesus Christ come in the flesh' (1 Jn.4:1ff.). But the Holy Spirit is the mighty power of God to convict the world, to bear witness to Christ, and to bring men to faith in him. He is Lord of the church and has not surrendered his freedom to its control.

J. LESSLIE NEWBIGIN

R. Allen: *The Ministry of the Spirit* (London 1960); H. Berkhof: *Doctrine of the Holy Spirit* (London 1965); H. R. Boer: *Pentecost and Missions* (London 1961); J. E. Fison: *Blessing of the Holy Spirit* (London 1950).

HOME BASE AND ADMINISTRATION at first referred to the location and character of the societies and boards by which missionaries were sent and supported overseas, and to which they were responsible for their work. These organizations were the basis and means of planning, directing and financially supporting the enterprise in other lands. The 'mission field' recognized the primary control exercised by the societies and boards, and accepted their final authority in forming policies and programmes. While the different missions at work in a field might consult together on the common objectives of evangelization, they nonetheless remained responsible to their respective 'home' authorities, and proceeded according to the decisions at the home base. The effects of geographical and cultural separateness were in part mitigated by consultation with the administrative and functional secretaries of the boards in their visits to the fields.

In relation to the overseas churches the societies and boards at home retained their ecclesiastical and confessional character both in membership and in supporting constituency. A few that were interdenominational in origin became primarily related to one of the supporting denominations, and proceeded in the same way as others at the home base. The selection of missionary personnel and the determination of questions of polity and doctrine at the home base directly influenced the character of the churches overseas. Mission boards and committees in many cases were originally constituted by the *'sending' churches which made them responsible to the general ecclesiastical councils. The home base in this case assumed a character reflected and transmitted in conformity with the doctrine, polity and practice of the 'home' church.

While home administration of necessity has included various functions of the missionary enterprise, these have mainly consisted of the recruitment, preparation, sending and support of missionaries. Mission institutions have also required a considerable share of administrative attention and financial support, and until recently have been dependent upon the home base in matters of major decision. From the beginning the establishing of growing churches on the 'field' was considered to be the main objective of the boards and societies, and assistance rendered to the churches has continued to be an important *aim of missions. With the emergence of the *indigenous churches and their assumption of responsibility for their own ministry and service a concern for the missionary nature of the church has found expression among them. The pattern of 'home' administration gradually changed. The first stage in *devolution was the formation of mission committees on the 'field' which were given increasing authority while they continued to recommend and report to the home base on matters still within the purview of the boards and societies. In many cases these committees were composed of national as well as missionary members. A second stage was soon reached whereby national churches and institutions exercised full responsibility for their affairs while they maintained relations with the societies and boards, and established more direct relations with the parent churches.

The growing ecumenical life of the *younger churches accelerated change in the form and responsibility of home administration. Society and board executives found it necessary to become more closely related to the churches and missions overseas in order to fulfil their own functions. The *World Missionary Conference at Edinburgh in 1910, which was organized and attended mainly by 'home base' representatives and foreign missionaries, recognized co-operation as essential to the boards and societies at home as well as to the missions overseas. Successive ecumenical conferences expressed more explicitly the missionary character of the whole church and therefore the responsibility for the initiation and execution of mission as belonging universally to the church. The home base of mission has come to be recognized as essentially everywhere, and consequently administration has become the responsibility of both the sending and the receiving churches wherever they may be situated.

ROLAND W. SCOTT

World Missionary Conference, 1910, The Home Base of Missions, Report of Commission VI (London 1910); Jerusalem Meeting of the International Missionary Council, 1928, Vol. III: *The Relation Between the Younger and Older Churches* (New York and London 1928); 'The Younger and Older Churches', *The World Mission of the Church: Findings and Recommendations*; *Madras, 1938* (London and New York 1939), pp.142–44.

HONDA, YOICHI (1848–1912), was born of high ranking *samurai* (warrior class) parents at Hirosaki and educated at the clan school. The reading of a Chinese Bible elicited his interest and while a student at Yokohama he was converted under the ministry of J. H. Ballagh and joined the Christian student group known as the Yokohama Band, which organized the first Protestant church in Japan (1872). With John Ing, a Methodist missionary teacher, H. returned to his native town. A Christian school was started, with converted students constituting the Hirosaki Band which became the nucleus of the first Methodist church, of which H. was pastor (1878).

Under his influence, over 200 went out from this church and the local Christian schools into full-time service. H. was active in politics and was first president of the Prefectural Assembly and a leader in reform movements. He also headed the Christian Wartime Service Associations during both the wars with China and Russia. After taking graduate work at Drew Seminary he served as president of the Methodist Aoyama College from 1890 to 1907, when he became the first bishop of the Japan Methodist church. He was also a leader in many interdenominational causes and represented the Protestant forces at a number of international gatherings, including the *World Missionary Conference at Edinburgh. He combined in an unusual degree the qualities of gentleness and strength which under God make a great leader.

GORDON K. CHAPMAN

F. Cary: *History of Christianity in Japan*, Vol. II (New York 1909), pp.122ff., 229, 317, 340, etc.; C. Iglehart: *Century of Protestant Christianity* (Tokyo 1959), pp. 53ff., 78, 99ff., 101, 118, 142ff., etc.

HONDURAS. See AMERICA, CENTRAL.

HONDURAS, BRITISH. See AMERICA, CENTRAL.

HONG KONG. A British Crown Colony on the south-east coast of China, comprising Hong Kong island (29 sq.m.), Kowloon Peninsula (3 sq.m.) across the magnificent harbour, and the New Territories (365 sq.m.) on the adjoining mainland. HK and Kowloon were acquired in 1842 and 1860; the New Territories are held on lease expiring 1997. Estimated population about four million (1966), 99% Chinese. Growth has been rapid, especially since 1949 owing to migrations from the nearby 'People's Republic' of China. Entrepot and tourist business has made HK a booming crossroads of free trade. Varied industries have developed. One out of five persons is in school. However, livelihood of the refugee multitude poses serious problems. Chinese religions are losing their hold while Marxism gains in influence among certain classes. Christianity (Protestant and Catholic) has a history coterminous with that of the colony. The Christian population is increasing at the rate of 11% a year. The HK Christian Council Survey in 1964 showed 344 Protestant congregations; nearly 100 own permanent buildings. Adult membership is 112,000; the Protestant 'community' is approximately 200,000 belonging to 23 different denominational families and several independent sects. The RC 'community' is about the same size: which means that about one-tenth of the population is avowedly Christian. Ministerial and lay leadership is of generally high quality. Protestant missionaries from western countries number more than 500, representing about 100 different missionary societies and agencies. RC foreign missionaries are fewer. The *Jesuit and *Dominican orders have founded seminaries. Protestants support four theological schools—*Lutheran, *CMA, Southern Baptist, and Chung Chi Seminary (union of seven church bodies). Openly Christian, Chung Chi College is one unit in the new federated Chinese University of HK. Many fine Christian secondary schools, such as the famous True Light Middle School for Girls, moved from Canton, supplement the government educational system. The Christian Study Centre on Chinese Religion and Culture and the Chinese Christian Literature Council are significant union endeavours. Welfare and relief programmes of HK missions and churches attract worldwide sympathy and aid. Ecumenical agencies such as *Church World Service, *WCC Service to Refugees, and Lutheran World Relief, work with local organizations. A union Christian hospital is planned. The HK churches support government efforts to provide low cost housing and to combat narcotics and other social evils. HK is a place of baffling contradictions —anxiety and hope, insecurity and also indomitable courage.

F. W. PRICE

A. T. Roy: *On Asia's Rim* (New York 1962), pp.122–52; *BM* II, 448–52; *NCE* VII, 120f.

HOOVER, JAMES MATTHEW (1872–1935), was born in Greenvillage, Pennsylvania, USA. He moved later to Chambersburg where he attended a local academy, then graduated from the State Teachers College in Shippensburg. H. taught for nine years in Franklin county schools. In March 1899 he expressed his willingness to go to Asia as a missionary of the Methodist Episcopal Church, leaving New York in July for service in the Anglo-Chinese school in Penang, Malaya. He was later transferred to a similar post in Sibu, Sarawak. In 1904 H. married Ethel Mary Young, the daughter of a British missionary. Using Foochow Chinese as teachers and evangelists, H. established more than 40 churches and schools in Borneo, especially along the Rajang River. He brought to Sarawak the bicycle, the motor launch, ice-making machinery, mechanical rice mills, electric lighting for churches and hospitals, new medical techniques and equipment, modern export-import procedures, improved agricultural facilities, and wireless telegraphy.

Though his work was largely among the Chinese, an effective approach was also made to the Malays and to the 'long-houses' of the Sea-Dayaks.

A noteworthy feature of all H's enterprises was the large degree of self-support accomplished, particularly through better methods of farming and marketing.

The British 'White Rajah' Sir Charles Vyner Brooke conferred on H. honours never before given to an American or a Christian missionary, and ordered Sarawak's flag to be flown at half-mast and all schools to be closed on the day of H's funeral. Known affectionately by the Malays as 'Tuan' (Lord) and by his Foochow friends as Ho (Ho-over) Sing-sang (Teacher), H. died of malignant malaria and was buried in the land he loved.

THOBURN T. BRUMBAUGH

F. T. Cartwright: *Tuan Hoover of Borneo* (New York 1938); and personnel materials in files of Methodist Board of Missions, New York; *DAB* XXI, 433.

HOSPITALS, MISSIONARY. In 1967 there was an estimated total of 1,238 medical institutions related to Anglican, Orthodox and Protestant churches in Asia, Africa, Latin America and the Near and Middle East with combined operating budgets in excess of US $100,000,000 per annum. With corresponding Roman Catholic ventures in these areas the total number of church-related medical institutions is about 2,500.

Most hospitals were established as part of the activities of missionary agencies (missionary societies and religious orders) in Europe and North America beginning towards the end of the 18th century but mainly during the last 100 years. Distribution of Christian medical institutions was largely determined by denominational factors and involvement, traditionally for the most part in the forms of curative medicine and training programmes for medical personnel. This pattern has generally been retained when national churches have taken over mission hospitals or founded new ones on their own.

The mission hospitals often acted as a spearhead for work of Christian missions and according to varying theological concepts they were used to support or supplement the spreading of the gospel. For a long time these hospitals represented the only available medical care in many countries, where they acted as models for health services later developed by governments.

The small hospital or clinic has tended to be more easily integrated into the church and its mission to the world, and to be understood as an expression of its healing ministry. Many institutions have, however, grown according to their own laws, becoming 'foreign bodies' to local Christians and a financial burden to supporting agencies. This becomes evident when, in the process of *devolution from mission to church control, hospitals and clinics are handed over to the management of ecclesiastical bodies which do not always possess the administrative expertise or resources to operate them. These complicated institutions require adequate planning and administration within the basic concept of the healing ministry of the church.

Recent development within (a) *theology of mission and (b) medical care, especially in developing countries, are influencing church-related medical work and the Christian hospitals. Consideration of regional health factors and joint planning with government health agencies are now also determining the church's involvement in medical care. This necessitates ecumenical co-ordination and co-operation between medical institutions of various Christian groups, both with regard to seeking the role of the church in health and socio-economic development and executing joint programmes. The traditional, denominationally isolated, mission hospital mainly involved in curative medicine is no longer a valid expression of Christian concern for man in health and disease. As part of a more comprehensive approach to medical care including also prevention, rehabilitation, family planning, general health education, training programmes, etc., a central institution has a new role to fulfil. In the future there will be fewer Christian hospitals, and the institutions maintained by the church will be an integrated part of a comprehensive attempt to 'make man whole'.

See also MEDICAL MISSIONS.

M. SCHEEL

Missionary Research Library: *Directory of Protestant Church-Related Hospitals Outside Europe and North America* (New York 1963).

HOSTE, DIXON EDWARD (1861–1946), was the son of a God-fearing British general and became a Royal Artillery officer. Converted under D. L. *Moody in 1882, he soon offered himself to Hudson *Taylor as a missionary with the *CIM. He thus became the earliest of the 'Cambridge Seven', the aristocratic, athletic group whose departure to China in 1885 deeply stirred British universities. After service in Shansi with the converted Confucian scholar, Pastor *Hsi,

H. was selected in 1901 by Hudson Taylor to succeed as General Director of the numerous, far-flung mission. H. was not yet 40. Some believed CIM would not survive its founder's retirement. Moreover it had been severely mauled in the *Boxer Rising. Based on Shanghai H. led it for 34 years of advance through crises: e.g. the revolution, the dangerous phase of excessive popularity, the period of civil strife, the Manchurian Incident. H. had a reserved, disciplined character, a strong sense of duty balanced by whimsical humour. His sound judgment, ministry of intercession and administrative skill did much to establish CIM's continued significance. He led it firmly towards indigenization. H. retired in 1935, was interned by the Japanese (1941–1945) and died in London.

JOHN POLLOCK

P. Thompson: *D. E. Hoste* (London 1947).

HSI, Pastor (c. 1830–1896), Confucian scholar and opium smoker, was brought to Christ through the ministry of a Methodist missionary, the Rev. David *Hill, in 1879. At the time the province of Shansi, in which H. lived, was almost without Protestant missionaries, and Christian work was in its very infancy. In consequence H. developed with very little help or guidance from foreign missionaries, and though later he greatly valued their help and co-operation, there was never any doubt as to who was in command of the situation. Having himself been delivered through his Christian faith from the chain of opium smoking, H. was led to open in a number of places refuges in which opium smokers could be cured of the habit. A man of simple faith, and with a profound experience of the reality of prayer, H. believed and expected to see results, and to a large extent his faith was justified. But mistakes were made; H. himself was far from perfect in Christian knowledge and character, and successes were matched by failures. It was part of his greatness that he was able to admit failures and to learn by them. In 1886 H. was ordained as the first Protestant pastor in Shansi, not to one congregation but in a supervisory capacity. At the same time D. E. *Hoste, later Director General of the *CIM, was sent to work with H. and to give him the benefit of western experience and advice. Hoste was often tried to the limit by the autocratic ways of his colleague who never completely lost the arrogance of the Confucian scholar; but the two men lived together in deep mutual respect which was a model of Christian co-operation. H. was an eloquent and vivid preacher, a loving shepherd of souls, though at the same time a stern disciplinarian. Hoste wrote of him that 'as years went by, his masterful character grew more and more mellowed and softened', and when he died in 1896, 'it is no exaggeration to say that hundreds wept for him as for a father or elder brother'.

STEPHEN NEILL

Mrs H. Taylor: *Pastor Hsi, one of China's Christians* (1st ed. 1903; many times reprinted).

HUC, EVARISTE REGIS (1813–1860), was born in Caylus, France. He joined the Vincentians as a young man and was sent to a Chinese mission some 300 miles north of Peking. Five years later, with Fr Gabet as companion, H. was directed to make a survey of Mongolia and Tibet. The two priests studied Tartar dialects, donned the secular dress of Tibetan lamas, bought camels, and set out with a Mongol cameleer, named Samdadchiemba, and Arsalan the faithful dog.

They left their mission in 1844 and arrived in Lhasa in 1846, having forded raging rivers, toiled over arid deserts and scaled ice-clad mountains. In Lhasa they were well treated by the Tibetan regent and the Grand Lama. The regent, curious about foreign ways, asked the Christian lamas to write something in their language. H. wrote: 'What does it profit a man if he conquers the whole world but loses his own soul?' This saying of Christ, translated into the Tibetan tongue, made a profound impression on the pious Buddhists. The two priests would gladly have remained in Lhasa, but the unfriendly Chinese ambassador had them expelled. H's book, *Travels in Tartary,*

Tibet and China (Eng. tr., 2 vols., London 1928), is one of the world's famous travel stories. H. had hoped to return to Tibet to stay, but it was not to be. He died in Paris in 1860.

SISTER M. JULIANA, MM

LTK V, 504f.; *NCE* VII, 184.

HUMANISM. In general, any view which stresses the importance of man and his fullest and freest development in this world. Renaissance H., stimulated by the rediscovery of the ancient classics, asserted the worth of man's life here and now, and sought a human culture liberated from otherworldliness and ecclesiastical control.

Among many varieties of contemporary H. the following deserve special mention:

(1) *Scientific* or *naturalistic* (Russell, Szczesny, Morris R. Cohen). According to this view, man finds truth only when he uses the experimental method: on the basis of objective observation he sets up hypotheses which must be tested for workability and held open to revision in the light of newly discovered facts. Such a method affords no basis for belief in God or a supernatural order, but emphasizes the significance of men's earthly activities. Man is totally and solely responsible for himself and his world. His goal is the fullest development of all his capacities.

(2) *Religious* (Julian Huxley, Lamont, Wyneken). Some humanists, while fully accepting scientific method and a naturalistic world view, recognize a genuinely religious aspect in human life. This non-theistic religion relates the realization of ethical and other values in men's day-by-day relations in the world to their sense of a sacredness in things, attitudes of reverence, awe, and wonder regarding their destiny, and their dependence on forces which are greater than their private selves.

(3) *Marxist* (Bloch, Lukács, Garaudy). Dialectical materialism holds that there is active in matter or nature, which is ultimate, a process which advances from stage to stage through the interplay of opposites. Man is the highest expression of nature, hence centrally important. He is responsible

for fulfilling or 'producing' himself through his own work.

(4) *Existentialist* (Sartre, Merleau-Ponty, Camus). In this view there is no central or enduring structure in nature or man. Each person is his own law-maker, who must make his decisions without principles to guide or determine him. He is what he chooses from moment to moment. The individual, responsible for his own existence, fulfils himself by seeking a goal outside himself in an inter-dependent human universe.

Such humanisms hold that theism interferes with man's freedom and responsibility by making him dependent on an all-powerful sovereign God. In dialogue with them, Christians (a) share the humanist rejection of a sharp separation between the sacred and the secular, the holy and the profane, and (b) agree that men should seek to realize their highest powers in a just earthly society. However, they (c) recognize the negative influence of self-interest, pride, and desire for power in all human endeavours, and (d) base the dignity, worth, and fulfilment of all men on the activity of the God revealed in Jesus Christ. *Christian* humanism assigns to man full responsibility for his acts, but asserts that without God he cannot be fully man.

S. PAUL SCHILLING

E. Fromm, ed.: *Socialist Humanism* (Garden City, N.Y., 1966); J. Huxley, ed.: *The Humanist Frame* (New York 1961); C. Lamont: *Humanism as a Philosophy* (New York 1949); J. P. van Praag: *Humanism* (Utrecht 1957); J.P. Sartre: *Existentialism* (Eng. tr., New York 1947).

HUMANITARIAN CONCERN. The NT clearly teaches the inseparable unity of word and deed in Christian witness. The message of him who came to serve has to take visible form in deeds of disinterested service. A deep humanitarian concern, nourished by the love of Christ and guided by his example, became one of the most impressive contributions of the early church to the development of European life. The 'gospel of love' (Harnack) manifested itself in deeds of charity towards the poor, the sick, the lonely and the oppressed and in this way became a dominant factor in the rapid spread of Christianity. In the Middle Ages the monastic orders especially carried on the tradition of Christian charity in connection with missionary work. A new interest for humanitarian concern in the context of the missionary task of the Christian world arose around 1800 in the circle of the 'evangelical revival' (cf. the work of the 'Clapham sect', the group of William Wilberforce and his friends). In the 19th century, the figure of David *Livingstone became the symbol of the integral unity between missionary and humanitarian interests. Humanitarian concern was seen in the light of Christian ideals; conversely in missionary work the direct preaching of the gospel was accompanied by humanitarian activities of various kinds (anti-slavery movement; work in the field of medicine and education). In the 20th century, humanitarian activities in the non-western world began to break away from their traditional Christian background. In the circle of missions we meet with a double development: while in some sectors of evangelical missionary activity there was a tendency to see humanitarian activities merely as a preparation for direct missionary work, in more liberal circles the humanitarian emphasis tended to become dominant. The idea of the 'comprehensive approach', which arose in the second quarter of this century, was an attempt to transcend the antithesis between both points of view by accentuating the fundamental unity between *kerygma* (proclamation) and *diakonia* (service). This relationship—exemplified in the relation between the words and the deeds of Christ—makes humanitarian concern an essential part of the missionary task. Today, a number of humanitarian activities (especially such as are rooted in the missionary tradition) still find their place in the context of direct missionary work, while other activities (especially those of a more accidental kind such as refugee-work, help in calamities, etc.) take place in the context of ecumenical work; western churches and missions also assist the churches in non-western countries in the fulfilment of their social tasks; lastly, the preaching of the gospel can help to pave the way for modern forms of aid to countries in *rapid social change by dissolving a mythical and magical world-view which is a hindrance to social development.

J. VAN DEN BERG

A. Harnack: *The Mission and Expansion of Christianity in the first three Centuries* (Eng. tr., 2nd ed., New York 1908); E. M. Howse: *Saints in Politics. The Clapham Sect and the Growth of Freedom* (London 1952); A. T. van Leeuwen: *Christianity in World History* (London 1964); M. A. C. Warren: *Social History and Christian Missions* (London 1967).

HUNT, JOHN (1812–1848). Son of a poor, God-fearing farmer in Lincolnshire, England, H. was put to work at the age of ten. Converted in a Wesleyan chapel in late adolescence, he developed into an effective preacher. In 1835 the superintending minister proposed him to the mission board for service. After some theological training, he was sent to Lakemba in the Fijis. The chief of Somosomo, a town on Taviuni Island, asked for missionaries, and H., with Richard Lyth, a young missionary physician, volunteered. The place was a notorious centre of cannibalism. The chief was completely unpredictable, and his son openly hostile to the missionaries. They were subjected to almost continuous harassment; on occasion their lives were threatened, and for a time they suffered from lack of food. Forced to witness the revolting practices of the people, they openly declared their judgment upon such evils. Few responded and no converts appeared. Eighteen months after their arrival the king's brother, an old man, fell ill. Lyth cured him, and he made open profession of the Christian faith. Others followed, although neither the cannibalism nor an occasional mistreatment of the missionaries ceased. In 1834 H. moved to Viwa where he became mission chairman. In that capacity he visited the churches and stations, teaching, preaching and superintending the work until his death.

J. LESLIE DUNSTAN

G. S. Rowe: *A Missionary among Cannibals* (New York n.d.); *DNB* XXVIII, 276.

HUNTER, GEORGE W. (1861–1946), was born in Scotland. After his fiancée's death he dedicated himself as a celibate pioneer. Joining the *CIM in 1889, H. served first in Kansu, the far north-west of China proper. Except for one return to Scotland after the *Boxer Rising H. thenceforth lived in Central Asia. In 1906 he penetrated to Urumchi, capital of Chinese Turkestan (Sinkiang) which became his base for long apostolic journeys. A 'loner', who for years had no western companion nor allowed close friendship with nationals, H. had the rigid outlook of the Scottish kirk of his early youth; humour and emotion lay deep beneath reserve. He was well read, highly respected by European travellers and savants, and was decorated by King George V. In 1914 Percy Mather, a young Lancashire man, joined him, and the close companionship of these contrasting men greatly enriched both. And whereas H. grudged time spent on building up local churches, Mather combined pioneering skill with pastoral ability.

In 1932 CIM sent six young men to Urumchi. Within six months disease killed them all, and Mather. H. remained. During Soviet occupation H. was tortured, imprisoned a year, and expelled from Sinkiang. He died on the border, hopefully awaiting return.

JOHN POLLOCK

M. Cable and F. French: *George Hunter, Apostle of Turkestan* (London 1948).

HYMNOLOGY. Christians have always wished to sing. In almost every country in the world, as soon as missionaries have learned a language, one of the first tasks they have set themselves has been to produce hymns in that language. Sometimes the success has been notable, as in the translation of German chorales into Tamil by Philip Fabricius (d. 1791). But on the whole the results have been poor and stilted, and the melodies to which they have been sung bore no relation at all to the melodic tradition of the language in which the words were written. The effects were specially disastrous, and sometimes ludicrous, in tonal languages, since the use of western melodies demands that the tones be disregarded. On the other hand, these western hymns, many of them of rich theological content, have become beloved and understood by the people; it is unlikely that they will ever become completely disused. One of the great achievements of the Protestant missions in China was the careful revision of the Chinese hymn book and its production in a form in which it was acceptable to almost all the churches.

The *younger churches have also a second and entirely different tradition of hymnology. It was the great good fortune of the Tamil church that a younger contemporary of Fabricius, Vedanayaga Sastriar, (born c. 1770), produced a large body of Christian lyrics in the classic metres and set to Indian melodies. These are still widely used, and he had many successors. In a great many areas, the major difficulty, largely overlooked by missionaries, in the use of indigenous forms and melodies arises from the pagan associations which in the minds of the Christians make impossible their use in a Christian context. By the third generation, this difficulty seems to be no longer felt so strongly. In many areas of Africa, over the last ten years, experiments have been begun in the use of traditional musical forms with appropriate words; but the writing of such hymns is for the most part in a pioneer stage, in which good intentions are not matched with achievement. In *Church and People in New Guinea* (London 1961), G. F. Vicedom gives some interesting examples of very simple songs of praise produced by Papuan Christians at a very early stage in the church's development. In 1964 the *EACC Hymnal*, edited by D. T. Niles, was published, containing contributions from numerous Asian traditions.

STEPHEN NEILL

IDENTIFICATION, MISSIONARY. The attempt by the missionary to enter as completely as possible into the life and circumstances of the people to whom he goes with the gospel, derives from the very heart of the gospel itself, from the Incarnation of Jesus Christ. 'The Word became flesh and dwelt among us and we beheld the glory . . .' That is the principle. Its application calls for dedicated imagination, and also some common sense. The two main areas of missionary activity in which identification presents a problem are *first*, language, and *second*, way of life.

(1) As to language, this is fundamentally a question of translation. How far can a word which, within a Christian culture, has over centuries come to have one meaning, be translated into the language of a culture which has had no Christian influence? This poses a very difficult problem for the translator, for the man who wants to identify all that a word means in Christian experience with some analogous experience in, for instance, a Hindu, Buddhist or Muslim culture. The very word **'God'* is not easily translatable. Enduring controversy, for instance, has surrounded the choice of the right Chinese word to render what Christians mean by God. Again in areas where the population is Muslim there is still controversy as to whether the name of our Lord shall be translated 'Isa' as in the Qur'an or 'Jesus', some missionaries believing that a Muslim will only give to 'Isa' the value given to our Lord in the Qur'an.

(2) The *second* question is that of a way of life, sharing the customs of the people, their dress, their food, the rhythm of their existence. One great pioneer in such identification was Robert de *Nobili, the *Jesuit missionary in South India. He tried as far as possible to become a Brahmin in order to win Brahmins. His dedication and devotion is beyond praise, though many would insist that in going as far as he did he compromised other essentials of the Christian faith, particularly in regard to fellowship with Christians of lower *castes.

In regard to this subject one thing only is essential and is universally applicable, and that is a humble loving concern for the people among whom the missionary lives. Provided that the love of Christ constrains him the wisdom of Christ will guide him as to what in any particular circumstances is the way of identification. The clothes he wears, the house he lives in, the food he eats, these only separate if the inner attitude is wrong.

MAX WARREN

V. Cronin: *A Pearl to India* (London 1959); M. Rogers: 'Immersion and Emergence: the way of the Foreign Missionary in the 1960's', *National Christian Council Review* (India): Vol. VIII (1961), pp.257–68; D. H. Smith, 'The Missionary's Problems in Religious Communication', *IRM*, Vol. LI (1962); M. Warren: 'The Meaning of Identification' in G. H. Anderson, ed.: *The Theology of the Christian Mission* (New York, Toronto, London 1961), pp.229–38.

IDOLS AND IDOLATRY. Though idols and idolatry are widespread, they are not universal religious phenomena. Perhaps what makes people regard them as more universal than they are is the tendency to confuse idols with images, for in popular parlance they are often thought to be the same. Images, however, are only symbolic representations of some supernatural spirit or power, while idols not only possess some formal resemblance to the spirit in question but also have within themselves some supernatural power. Theoretically the images in Roman Catholic churches are supposed to be merely representations but in the minds of many worshippers they have acquired distinctive powers. For example, the Virgin of one church is good for curing barrenness and the Virgin of another may be thought to have powers to cure epilepsy.

Whenever power is associated with a specific object, and not with the spirit for which the object stands, then that object has become an idol and is no longer merely an image. The practice in some regions of blindfolding an image to keep it from seeing what is going on or of turning its face to the wall if prayers are not answered, is evidence that the image has become in some measure an idol.

Idolatry is a very understandable phenomenon. All peoples believe in some types of supernatural personal powers, e.g. gods, spirits and demons, but these beings are generally very elusive and distant. Therefore it seems essential that one have some concrete representation of the spirit power. Gradually, however, in the minds and affections of the people the representation tends to supplant the spirit of which it is supposed to be a constant reminder.

In idolatry there are, however, other even more powerful psychological forces at work. In the first place, an idol is much easier to control than an unpredictable spirit. By being objectified as an idol the spirit is made manageable—and having been created by man it is symbolic of man's innate desire to be greater than the gods by demonstrating his power to make them.

As something which substitutes for and hence takes the place of God, 'idol' may be rightly used to speak of anything which usurps a position of highest value and loyalty. Thus for modern man, who generally does not feel obliged to make or worship idols of wood or stone, there are nevertheless a number of idols, e.g. status symbols, financial success, national destiny, and theological formulations (which hew God out to the measure of man's words).

EUGENE A. NIDA

R. H. Lowie: *Primitive Religion* (New York 1924); E. A. Nida and W. A. Smalley: *Introducing Animism* (New York 1959); *ERE* VI, 110–159.

IMPERIALISM AND MISSIONS. Imperialism is a word the sense of which has deteriorated with the passage of time. When it first came into wide currency about 1885,

it had deep roots in Virgil's splendid vision of what the Roman empire could mean to the subject peoples in terms of prosperity and peace. First among British statesmen Lord Rosebery realized that Britain, together with the great English-speaking dominions, Canada, Australia and New Zealand, with the USA somewhere in the background, was by far the strongest power in the world. But power can be used for good or for evil. Therefore the citizenry must be educated in the responsible use of power for peaceful ends. Liberal I. in its early days meant responsibility, peace, service, and mutual loyalty.

At that time South Africa did not exist as a single unit, and India belonged to a different order of existence. But there was no reason why the same principles of responsible co-operation should not have been extended to India. The Indian liberals had drunk deep at the sources of British democracy. The last of the great Indian liberals was Sri Rājagopalāchāri, who in 1948 became the first Indian Governor-General of India. If India had been ruled by liberal statesmen, and power had gradually passed from their hands into that of the Indian liberals, the history of the world would have been very different from what it has been. But the fact that in the era of independence all the countries of the Commonwealth, with the exception of Burma, Ireland and South Africa, have decided to remain within it, is an indication that there was a good, as well as a harmful, side to I.

Liberal imperialists were, as a whole, not interested in missions. They tended to be irritated by the missionaries' habit of getting into scrapes, through which public opinion was aroused to the point of compelling governments to take action which they would very much have preferred not to take. The more alert of them, however, realized that the ideals by which the missionaries were inspired were very largely the same as their own. Missionaries of the stamp of Dr W. Miller in Madras taught their pupils to read Burke and Milton and Mill *On Liberty*. They were consciously training them for independence of thought and action, and this could as readily be directed to the political sphere as to the areas of religion and education. The same was true of the American missionaries in China, Korea and Japan.

This hopeful situation was marred on the one side by growing arrogance, on the other by growing resentment. From 1900 on, the imperial link was increasingly understood in commercial terms, and by some at least was taken to guarantee the permanent right of the white races to rule over all others. The liberals in India and elsewhere were succeeded by another group, the aim of which was to use the weapons of the west to destroy the west. This attitude was seen in its extreme form in the violent Indian nationalist, Subash Chandra Bose, a graduate of the University of Cambridge.

The imperial age has receded permanently into history and it is certain that it will not recur in its old form. I. has come to be a term of reproach and not of honour. The idea of families of nations linked together by a common tradition and common ideals has been replaced by the loose and as yet precarious unity of the United Nations. The ideal of peace has receded, as the rivalry between the USA, Russia and China has increased to the point at which the peace of the world is continuously threatened. The ideal of mutual service has been replaced by the system under which the wealthier nations give to the less prosperous as little as they dare, and the less prosperous try to exact by a kind of blackmail as much as they would like to have. This is an entirely different situation; the extent to which the change can be regarded as progress is a matter of opinion.

In this changed situation the witness of the churches is even more important than in the past. The ideal of integrity and responsibility in the exercise of power seems unattainable apart from the Christian gospel. The church is the only genuinely international society, ruled by a common purpose and by the concept of spiritual equality. The instrument of the divine purpose in the 19th century was the mis-

sionary society; in the 20th it appears to be the *ecumenical movement.

See also COLONIALISM AND MISSIONS.

STEPHEN NEILL

NCE VII, 398–400.

INCARNATION, CHRISTIAN AND NON-CHRISTIAN. Incarnation is the act of a divine being in entering the phenomenal world in human form and continuing in that form throughout the life-time of a particular person. It is thus to be distinguished from a temporary manifestation (as in *Hinduism), from inspiration in which a human being is filled with divine force and wisdom (as in *Buddhism) and from emanation which does not involve a deliberate act of divine will (as in pantheism).

Christianity alone of the world's religions asserts that the divine has become incarnate in one Person only, and in Christianity alone is the doctrine of I. central and determinative. In the Christian doctrine, too, I. signifies the assumption of full humanity by full divinity, as was declared by the Council of Chalcedon in 451.

In modern times, the full divinity of Christ has been emphasized by the Barthian school, often at the expense of interest in the historic Jesus and so in the reality of the I. Others, emphasizing the full humanity of Jesus, have emptied him not only of divine prerogatives but also of his powers.

While serious scholars no longer speak of a 'Christ Myth', the demythologizing tendencies of the Bultmann school presuppose the existence in the Gospels of mythological or at least symbolic elements. While this presupposition does not necessarily deny the reality of the I. it does involve a reappraisal of the forms in which that doctrine has often been expressed. The debate continues.

The Sanskrit word *avatāra* (lit. 'descent') is often translated 'incarnation', but although it conveys a sense of divine concern it falls short of complete identification with the human lot. The Hindu gods are declared in the Rigveda to be but different names or forms of the one Reality; as such these gods do not lend themselves to the possibility of a true and individual I.

Orthodox *Islam has no room for incarnation though the heretical Shi'ites speak of Ali, the prophet's son-in-law, as divine. The stricter view, however, is that he is a divinely-appointed leader of the community. In *Zoroastrianism, too, there is a tendency to speak of those, like royalty, endowed with heavenly light, as divine. This view is peripheral, however, and strictly incompatible with the monotheism of the Avesta. Both these examples refer to a too general divine indwelling of human beings to be accurately termed I. The birthstories of Mahayana Buddhism are similarly too general in their ascription of divine indwelling.

HENRY LEFEVER

E. L. Mascall: *Christ, the Christian and the Church* (London 1955); J. M. Robinson: *A New Quest of the Historical Jesus* (London 1959); N. Söderblom: 'Incarnation', *ERE* VII, pp. 183f.; E. W. Thompson: *The Word of the Cross to the Hindus*, Part 2, ch.1 (London 1933).

INDEPENDENT ASSEMBLIES OF GOD MISSIONS. See PENTECOSTAL MISSIONS.

INDEPENDENT CHURCHES. See AFRICAN INDEPENDENT CHURCH MOVEMENT; CARGO CULTS; SPIRITISM.

INDIA. The Indian sub-continent, with an area of about 1,800,000 sq.m., and a climate varying from the sub-temperate to the tropical, has been for millennia the home of a great variety of peoples, speaking hundreds of languages and dialects. For all its variety, it does represent a single geographical unit. Its history has been marked by a continuous though not always conscious striving after unity. In the 3rd century B.C. the Buddhist emperor Asoka brought large parts of the peninsula under his dominion, and set up the southernmost of his rock-pillar inscriptions in the neighbourhood of Mysore. After 1,600

years of the rise and fall of local kingdoms and empires, the Mogul emperors of Delhi once again extended their dominion in all directions, though their influence never penetrated to the extreme south. With the collapse of the Mogul power in the middle of the 18th century, the British entered into the vacuum thus created, and after a century of struggle established for the first time over every part of the sub-continent political and economic unity. An era of unexampled peace followed; the ancient fortifications decayed, and a man could walk in untroubled security from Cape Comorin to the Khyber Pass. It seemed that India's destiny had now been determined for an unlimited future; the nationalist movement and the will of politicians decided otherwise. Obstinacy and a somewhat naïve optimism on the one hand, and obstinacy and unreasonableness on the other made peaceful settlement between Hindus and Muslims impossible, and in 1947 the fragile unity was broken by the creation of the resentful and hostile states of India and Pakistan. This article deals only with the history of Christianity in India until the fateful year of division.

(1) It is certain that Christianity has existed in India from a very early date. The acts of the Council of Nicea (A.D. 325) were signed by John, Bishop of Persia and Great India. This suggests Christian penetration of India by the north-western route from churches already existing in Persia. The *Acts of Thomas* (3rd century) tell how the Apostle Thomas was sent to India by Jesus Christ himself; this story is devoutly accepted by all the Thomas Christians of Kerala and by many Roman Catholic authorities. All that a sober historian can say is that, in view of the archaeological evidence of lively trade between the Roman empire and India in the 1st century A.D., the story is by no means incredible, but that actual confirmation is lacking. What is quite clear is that, from the 4th century at latest, a considerable Christian community existed in Kerala. The Christians seem to have been merchants from Mesopotamia, who in course of time acquired almost a monopoly

of the pepper trade, settled permanently in India, and were recognized as a prosperous and respectable part of society. They received their bishops and priests from Mesopotamia, and made little, if any, attempt to christianize their non-Christian neighbours. (See SYRIAN CHURCHES.)

(2) In about the 8th century the Muslims made themselves masters of the sea-routes between Europe and Asia, and the Christians in India were cut off from almost all communications with fellow-Christians elsewhere. Occasional travellers made the perilous journey to India, and have left in their letters some evidence of the continued existence of Christians. Most important of these was John of Monte Corvino, the first RC archbishop of Peking, who was in India in 1291–92, and a few of whose letters have been preserved. He found groups of Christians in South India, all of whom were Nestorian in faith and retained their allegiance to the patriarch of Babylon. There were also faint traces of Christianity in the neighbourhood of Bombay.

(3) A new period opens, both for India and for the west, with the arrival of the ships of Vasco de Gama in the neighbourhood of Calicut in A.D. 1498. With Portuguese dominion came the first serious attempt at the evangelization of India. The primary interest of the Portuguese was the conversion of the inhabitants of their own small colonies; the *Jesuits conceived evangelization on a much larger scale.

(a) Francis *Xavier, arriving in Goa in 1542, heard that the entire Parava (Bharatha) *caste in S.E. India had been converted, but that no provision had been made for spiritual care for the new Christians. For three years he made this a major interest; the foundations of Christian education and worship were laid, and by the end of the century the Paravas had been grouped in sixteen villages, each under the care and authority of a resident Jesuit.

(b) The emperor Akbar the Great, with his tolerant mind and ready interest in all religions, was prepared to welcome a Jesuit mission at his court. The first mission arrived in Agra in 1550, and the work was maintained, though fitfully, until 1803. Fr Jerome *Xavier, a great nephew of Francis, was resident in Agra from 1585 till 1605. Some conversions resulted, a few within the circle of the royal family itself. But the mission never fulfilled the great hopes which had been centred on it at its inception.

(c) The Portuguese and the Thomas Christians were delighted by their mutual discovery in the early years of the 16th century. On the whole relations were friendly. But in 1599 a new archbishop of Goa, Aleixo de Menezes, decided that the separate existence of the ancient church must end, and that all must be brought under the jurisdiction of the pope. By a combination of charm, flattery, force and fraud, a great Synod was held at Diamper (Udiyamperur), at which the entire position of the Counter-Reformation was accepted, and the ancient church as such ceased to exist. This situation continued till 1653, when at the Coonen Cross a number of priests declared their independence, and carried about a third of the church back with them into independent existence.

(d) In the mission of Madura Robert de *Nobili (in India 1606–56) carried out the great experiment of total self-identification with the higher castes of Indians, and of the method of adaptation of the gospel to the Indian situation (see ACCOMMODATION). Legend has greatly exaggerated the success of this method; the number of high-caste Hindu converts was never large, and many of those baptized later apostatized. The miracle was that there were any such converts at all. And a considerable movement among the lower castes was brought into being. De Nobili's methods were harshly criticized by others. During his lifetime he was fairly well able to defend himself; the long and tedious controversy dragged on after his death, until in 1744 Rome decided against any form of *'accommodation', thus condemning the RC missions to that policy of total Europeanization from which they have not yet been able to free themselves.

(4) By the end of the 17th century Portugal had faded out as a political power

in India, and was replaced by the Dutch. Some missionary activity by the Dutch is recorded, but it did not amount to very much. The Church of England, from 1612 on, had supplied a number of chaplains to its factories; but, in spite of pious adjurations from London, Anglican missionary work hardly existed at all. Much more important was the formation, on the initiative of the King of Denmark, of the first Protestant mission in India. *Ziegenbalg and Plütschau arrived in Tranquebar in 1706. The work was extended to British territories, and with financial support from the *SPCK by a number of missionaries, C. F. *Schwartz (in India 1750–98) being by far the most distinguished among them. A number of converts was won, the foundations for an Indian ministry were laid, the NT was translated into Tamil (1714); and just at the end of the century an unexpected *mass movement brought 5,000 people in the Tinnevelly district into the Christian church.

But the best days of both the RC and early Protestant missions were over before the end of the century. The dissolution of the Jesuit order in 1763 dealt the RC missions a heavy blow, and the secular priests of the Missions Etrangères (*MEP) were far from being able to supply all that was needed. The rationalism of the Enlightenment had sapped the missionary spirit in Protestant Europe. A new beginning needed to be made elsewhere.

(5) The new beginning was the fruit of the revival movement by which the dull religious life of the British Isles had been stirred in the 18th century. In 1793 William *Carey arrived in Bengal as the first missionary of the newly formed BMS. For the first time the English-speaking world was seriously engaged in the work of foreign missions. Carey, who with his colleagues Marshman and Ward in 1800 took up residence in the tiny Danish colony of Serampore, developed a vast and varied missionary programme, (a) for the widespread preaching of the gospel, (b) for the formation at the earliest possible date of Indian churches, (c) for the intensive study of Indian languages and ideas, (d) for the translation and circulation of the Scriptures in all the languages of the east and (e) for the formation of an intellectual élite by means of which the gospel could be far more widely preached than by the ministry of western missionaries alone. An astonishing measure of success was attained in all these five aspects of missionary work.

(6) The revision of the East India Company's Charter in 1813 opened the way to far more and better organized missionary work. The first great successes were achieved in the far south. In 1820, on behalf of the *CMS, C. T. E. *Rhenius settled in Palamcottah, and developed an immense movement, on the basis of the village school, the teacher of which was also the *catechist of a nascent Christian congregation. At the time of writing (1966) the primary schools in the diocese of Tinnevelly cater for 67,000 pupils, of whom 41,000 are non-Christians, and 26,000 are girls.

A mission of help sent by the CMS to the ancient church of the Thomas Christians in Kerala brought new life to that church by the circulation of the Scriptures and better training for the clergy. This led, unhappily, to schisms; but the initial impulse was never finally lost (see SYRIAN CHURCHES).

Many other societies entered the south, with varying measures of success. Especially notable was the work of W. T. *Ringeltaube of the *LMS (in Travancore 1809–15), whose work laid the foundations for the great church of South Travancore.

At the same time, Protestant societies were spreading out over the vast plains of northern India—Baptists, Methodists, British and American, Anglicans and many others. The rapidity of the advance is seen in the fact that the CMS founded its station in Amritsar in the Punjab in 1852, and in Peshawar on the North-West Frontier in 1855. Numerical success in these areas was far smaller than in the south, but churches were beginning to come into existence.

(7) A new note was given to Protestant missions in India by the work of Alexander *Duff (in India 1830–58) who founded in Calcutta a school, with the instruction in

the English language, the aim of which was an approach to the highest castes in the land. The success of the school as an educational instrument was immense. Even more remarkable was its success in the conversion of a number of young men from the leading families in Calcutta; nothing like it had been seen in India since the days of Robert de Nobili.

The example of Duff was followed by John *Wilson in Bombay, by Anderson and Johnston in Madras, by Stephen Hislop in Nagpur, and by Robert Noble in Masulipatam. In each case the results were the same. The number of converts was never large; but they were of the highest quality, and laid the foundations of most of the famous Indian Christian families.

(8) The year 1858 marked the beginning of a new epoch for the state as for the church in India. In that year the government of Britain took over from the East India Company responsibility for the administration of India. A number of Indian Christians, missionaries and chaplains had lost their lives in the Sepoy Rising of the year 1857, but there is no evidence that Christians as such were specially the object of the animosity of the mutineers. Queen Victoria's proclamation of religious neutrality came as a declaration of liberty for the Indian Christians, who from now on were free from the grave disabilities under which they had suffered in the days of the Company.

A natural result was a great extension of missionary work in the two following generations. All the old methods were followed, including new attention to the problems of *Bible translation and of Christian *literature. More remarkable was the increasing diversification of the work. Before 1858 unmarried women in the missions were almost unknown; from 1858 on their number steadily increased, until the unmarried women outnumbered the men and the married women together. This made possible an immense increase in work for women and girls, in school and hospital as well as in the patient work of visiting women in their homes. Medical work

increased rapidly, not merely as a means of contact with the population in specially difficult areas such as the North-West Frontier, but also as part of the service which Christian love is called to render to the needs of suffering humanity. Missions reached out into industrial and agricultural enterprises; the *Basel Mission in Malabar, famous for its tiles and its textiles, won special regard for the excellence of its products and the efficiency of its administration. There was hardly a single field of human need or human activity in which the missions were not to be found.

(9) As we have seen, the RC church in India started the 19th century in sad weakness and disarray. The *Letters from India* (1823) of the famous Abbé J. A. *Dubois record a mood of despondency and almost of hopelessness. Recovery was somewhat slow, but from about 1830 onwards the RC missions began to resume and expand their work. The Jesuit order was reconstituted, and many other orders now found their way to India. As with the Protestant missions the women came in course of time to outnumber the men.

During the greater part of the century the RC church in India was troubled by the ghost of an old controversy which refused to be laid. In the 15th century the pope had given the king of Portugal authority to create, man and support bishoprics throughout the east, including India. Clearly the task had grown far beyond the strength of Portugal; but the king was extremely unwilling to give up any of his privileges. The popes avoided the difficulty by appointing *Vicars Apostolic, bishops without territorial jurisdiction; but this led to rivalries and in Bombay to most unseemly rioting. In 1886 Pope Leo XIII decided that this situation must end, and set up a complete territorial hierarchy for India, while maintaining in a reduced form the ancient rights of Portugal. At that time none of the bishops was an Indian.

(10) Christian work between 1858 and 1914 saw notable extension, especially in two directions.

The efforts of the early missionaries had

been directed almost entirely to the Hindu and Muslim populations. About the middle of the century, they became aware of the possibilities of work among the aboriginal and animistic peoples of the hills. The Germans of the *Gossner Mission were led to work among the Kolarian peoples of Chota Nagpur, with such success that the wholly independent Lutheran church which they called into being now has more than 200,000 members. Later the RCs entered the same field, and the Belgian Fr Constant *Lievens, by posing as the champion of the Aborigines in their disputes with their Hindu landlords, was successful in sweeping very large numbers of them into the RC church. The Scandinavian Mission under the Norwegian L. O. *Skrefsrud had great success among the Santals. Less success attended work among Gonds and Bhils. The Baptists won converts from among the Khonds, well known to ethnologists because of their peculiar practices of human sacrifice. Even the tiny people of the Todas in the Nilgiris, who since their discovery by the Europeans 160 years ago have never numbered more than 1,000, have yielded about 160 of their number to the Anglican church.

About one-sixth of the population of India consists of the scheduled castes, previously known as the outcastes, who live on the fringe of the villages in great poverty and social deprivation, carrying out the meanest tasks and without hope of improvement. ('Untouchability' has now been made illegal by the independent Indian government, but the social problems remain.) Missionaries had on the whole avoided these people, holding that they should be the last rather than the first to be reached. But, about 1878, what proved to be an immense movement began in the Telugu area; through the efforts of Anglicans, Baptists, Methodists and Lutherans, a million people were brought into the church. Similar movements broke out in the United Provinces and the Punjab. This was much objected to by a number of missionaries and many leading Indian Christians, on the ground that the admission of so many of

these people would lower the already too low social and educational level of the church in India; those more directly in touch with the movement felt that it was a direct call from God himself, and that the work of the Holy Spirit among the poorest, the lowliest and the lost could not be gainsaid.

(11) All this did not take place without opposition from the Hindus and Muslims. There has never been anything like systematic persecution of Christians in India; but almost every new Christian group has been called to endure for a period hostility and hardship of a variety of degrees. Patience and gentleness have usually done more to restore fellowship than harsh measures taken by the authorities under the influence of missionaries.

The strongest form of organized opposition to the gospel was the *Ārya Samāj, founded by Swāmi Dayānand Sarasvati in 1875. This was a reformed Hinduism claiming to base itself entirely on a right understanding of the original Vedas, but was at the same time bitterly anti-Christian, one of its activities being the reconversion to Hinduism of outcastes who had been converted to Christianity.

More subtle were the various forms of syncretistic religion, which grew up as Christian influences penetrated among Hindus but failed to win their full allegiance to Jesus Christ. The *Brahmo Samāj, founded by the noble Rammohun Roy in 1828, never exercised wide influence, and even the passionate eloquence of the devoted but unstable Keshub Chunder Sen did not succeed in kindling it to any great vigour. But every restatement of Hinduism over the last century has shown how deeply the best minds in Hinduism have fallen under the spell of Jesus Christ. Mahātmā Gandhi was not alone in being able to say that his favourite hymn was 'When I survey the wondrous Cross'.

(12) The end of the century was marked by the rise of Indian *nationalism; the pace was quickened very much after the war of 1914–18. Most missionaries, and the great majority of Indian Christians, regarded the

movement with anxiety and disfavour. This attitude did not begin to change until the late 1920s. But, with the political movement, went also the urgent question as to the nature and character of the Indian church. Had not its dependence on the west and on missionary leadership gone on far too long? Had not the time come for the church to become genuinely Indian? A beginning had been made before the end of the 19th century with the formation of local church councils in which the voice of Indian Christians could genuinely be heard. But many of the ablest young men and women felt that they could not serve under the conditions of missionary dominance which still prevailed, and found their vocation in the YMCA or other organizations in which they were assured of greater freedom and initiative. The trouble was that few of the missions had given any serious thought to the nature and structure of the *Church; they were still bounded by the idea of the mission. The result could only be jealousy and friction; a great deal of energy was wasted between missionaries anxious to hold on to their own position, and ambitious young men anxious to replace the missionary in the best jobs.

The nature of the change which came about is easily seen by a glance at the development of the indigenous *episcopate. In the RC church a beginning was made with the creation of an Indian hierarchy for the ancient church of the Thomas Christians in 1896. The first Indian bishop of the Latin rite was consecrated only in 1923. After this for a number of years progress was very slow, and became rapid only after 1945. The seal was set on this process by the creation of the first Indian Cardinal, Valerian Gracias, Archbishop of Bombay, in 1952. The first Indian bishop of the Anglican church in India was V. S. *Azariah, consecrated in 1912. Here again progress was very slow, and not till 1952 did that church receive an Indian as Metropolitan and bishop of Calcutta. The Methodists appointed their first bishop, J. R. Chitambar, in 1930; at the time of writing all the Methodist bishops in India are Indians. In principle the

process is complete; but many Indian Christians complain that financial aid from the west is still used to secure that the last word on every subject is said by the representative of the western missionary society and not by the church.

(13) From an early date the Protestant missions became aware of the grave handicap of their divisions, and of the lack of any systematic planning of the work. In many areas, such as Bible translation, co-operation became the rule. The principle of *comity was used to help in the elimination of overlapping and rivalry. All-India conferences of missionaries and Christians led to increasing understanding and mutual help. But the decisive steps belong to the 20th century. In 1912, under the inspiration of Dr John R. *Mott, the *National Missionary Council of India was formed, to be transformed in 1922 into the *National Christian Council of India, with William *Paton as one of its secretaries, and with the salutary rule that at least half of the membership must be Indian.

Proposals for church union had been made by Bishop Reginald Heber of Calcutta (1823–26). More than 80 years were to pass before anything was accomplished. In 1908 Presbyterians and Congregationalists agreed to form the South Indian United Church. A similar body, the United Church of North India, came into being in 1929. The challenge issued by the Tranquebar Manifesto of 1919 led by slow degrees to the formation of the *Church of South India in 1947, from Anglican, Methodist, Presbyterian and Congregationalist bodies. Later negotiations between the CSI and the Lutherans have not led as yet to any decisive result; and the negotiations for a wider union in North India have also failed as yet to reach a conclusion.

Relations between the RCs and other missions have not in the past been cordial. The Second *Vatican Council has given the impulse to a more friendly attitude on both sides, and co-operation has been found possible in a number of cases.

(14) Under the Constitution of the new and independent India, religious *liberty is

fully guaranteed. As was to be expected, however, Christians in the republic have had to face a number of new difficulties. There has been sharp criticism of the inadequacies of missionary methods in the past. It is becoming increasingly difficult to secure visas for missionaries desiring to enter India. Many Hindus desire that India should take a stand as Hindustan, the national home of the Hindus. But on the whole Christians have little to complain of in their present situation. The number of Christians is still very small. The census of 1961 gives a figure of 2.6% of the population—this is likely to be too low rather than too high a figure. But the influence of Christians is not to be judged by their number. The gigantic educational effort of the 19th century has shown its effect not only in the fact that the Christian community stands ahead of almost every other in its standard of literacy, but in the existence of a large educated Christian middle-class, representatives of which are to be found in every town and city in the republic. The level of spiritual life and evangelistic zeal is not high. Political independence and ecclesiastical liberation have not produced the inner renewal of which the churches stand in need. Numbers continue to increase but very slowly. The next step is for the Indian churches to become aware of the great new opportunities that God has given in the changed situation in India, and to reach a deep conviction that all the resources of God are available to churches which are prepared to become humble, believing and resolute in life and witness.

STEPHEN NEILL

K. Baago: *A Bibliography of Indian Christian Theology* (Madras 1969); C. B. Firth: *An Introduction to Indian Church History* (Madras 1961); K. S. Latourette: *A History of the Expansion of Christianity*, Vol. VI (London and New York 1945); S. C. Neill: *A History of Christianity in India and Pakistan* (Grand Rapids 1970); J. W. Pickett: *Christian Mass Movements in India* (Nashville 1933); J. Richter: *A History of Protestant Missions in India* (Edinburgh 1910); B. G. M. Sundkler: *The Church of South India* (London 1954); *BM*

II, 461–76; *NCE* VII, 435–61; *WKL*, 578–83.

INDIA, THE CHURCH OF SOUTH, was inaugurated on 27 September 1947 by the union of the four southern dioceses of the (Anglican) Church of India, Pakistan, Burma and Ceylon, the larger part of the South India United Church (Congregational, Presbyterian and Reformed) and the (British) Methodist Church in South India. It was the consummation of what began in 1919 when Indian Christian leaders met at Tranquebar to consider co-operation with a view to more effective evangelism. They were led to see that if the church is to be the church and to do the church's proper work it must not only have unity of spirit but be seen by men to be one. This first successful attempt, since the Reformation, to unite episcopal and non-episcopal communions, had circumstances more favourable than those of the older churches, which are more conscious of the causes of separation and perhaps less conscious of the needs of mission. Yet the protracted negotiations are a sign of the difficulty. The eventual union was on the basis of Scripture, the creeds, the dominical sacraments, and the recognition that episcopal, presbyterial and congregational elements are all necessary to the life of the church. While it was agreed that all ministers after union should be episcopally ordained, any idea of integrating the ministries at union by some form of 're-ordination' was rejected. The solution, characteristic of CSI, was an agreement to wait 30 years before deciding the question of exceptions to the general principle of an episcopally ordained ministry, and a pledge not to override the conscience of the individual or to transgress long established traditions by imposing forms of worship or ministry to which any congregation might conscientiously object. The CSI is organized in 15 dioceses, under the authority of the synod of which the Moderator (presiding bishop) is elected biennially. The total baptized community is 1,200,000 of whom 100,000 are converts since 1947. CSI itself would be the first to agree that the high hopes at the inauguration have not all been fulfilled either in the life of the church itself or in the anticipation of union between the parent churches. Yet the important thing is that CSI exists and shows that a comprehensive union of this kind can happen. The most significant evidences of the fact and point of union are the enhanced sense of missionary obligation and the deepening of the worship of the church. *The Book of Common Worship*, and notably the Order for Holy Communion, show how the treasures of various traditions can come together into a greater whole.

MARCUS WARD

M. Hollis: *The Significance of South India* (London 1966); R. D. Paul: *The First Decade of the C.S.I.* (Madras 1958); B. Sundkler: *The Church of South India: The Movement towards Union 1900–1947* (London 1954); M. Ward: *The Pilgrim Church: An Account of the First Five Years in the Life of the C.S.I.* (London 1953); *NCE* XIII, 483f.

INDIANS OF AMERICA, MISSIONS TO. See CANADA; USA.

INDIGENIZATION. The idea of *indigenous churches has steadily gained ground. The western churches manifest considerable differences among themselves; these can be traced back to certain national peculiarities and to differences in historical process. If this is possible in the west, why should there be any anxiety if churches in the east should develop certain peculiarities, reflecting their psychological constitution, the manner in which the gospel has come to them, and their understanding of their own history?

It must be recognized that the word is used in two senses.

There is first the question of the emancipation of *younger churches, and their freedom to develop on their own lines without rigid control from the west. From about 1890 on, this principle has been fully accepted in the non-Roman Christian world, less fully and with more hesitation in the RC world; though in the implementation of the principle the Protestant missions have

10*

been much more hesitant than the younger churches would have desired.

The second question is more radical—what should be the relation of a Christian church to the non-Christian past which it has inherited? The heroic attempts of Robert de *Nobili and Matthew *Ricci to grapple with this problem are recorded elsewhere in this work. After the Roman condemnation of *'accommodation' in 1744, for 200 years the RC missions settled down to the idea that a missionary church must reflect in every detail the Roman custom of the moment. Protestant missions allowed a limited freedom, but in the main they worked for an exact reproduction of European models. In this they were not wholly to blame; the converts regarded difference as a sign of inferiority, and demanded exact assimilation to the European models. Only with the rise of nationalism at the very end of the 19th century did this westernization of the younger churches come to be questioned. Groups such as that which produced *Rethinking Christianity in India* in 1939 asked whether far greater use should not have been made of traditional Indian forms of art and language.

The demand for indigenization has more often been made by missionaries with a sentimental regard for the past or by emancipated Christians in reaction against the west, than as a genuine manifestation of the Spirit in the churches as a whole, and the results have at times been unfortunate. A well-known church in India was built on the model of a Hindu temple, and was generally objected to by the local Christians on the ground that a temple should look like a temple, a mosque like a mosque, and a church like a church. This view expressed more than mere prejudice; no Hindu temple is built for public worship, public worship is the very purpose of a Christian church; it is therefore natural that this essential difference of purpose should be reflected in architectural forms. A Christian service of allegedly Indian character was passionately rejected by Christians of Islamic origin on the ground that all the symbolism incorporated in it was Hindu and idolatrous in origin, and therefore wholly unacceptable to those whose background was Islamic. Asian and African music has been so closely associated with a non-Christian world of ideas and worship that the first generation of Christians in almost every country has found it impossible to make use of it for purposes of Christian praise; the melody cannot be detached from its associations. Only in the third generation have the associations been so far forgotten that a Christian use of ancient forms becomes possible.

The process of indigenization must go forward. But, to be creative and useful, it must arise from a deep response of the Christian spirit to the movement of the Spirit, and not derive from any romanticization of the past or from a merely national and sectarian expression of Christian truths.

STEPHEN NEILL

INDIGENOUS CHURCHES. The demand for the *indigenization of the churches in Asia and Africa which have come into being as the result of the modern missionary enterprise has three sources:

(1) The experience of western missionaries that not only they themselves as human individuals, but also the form of their proclamation and of the ecclesiastical inheritance that they had brought with them, had been strongly conditioned by the atmosphere of the country from which they came. This meant that both they and their ministry had a foreign character, which was bound to make it appear unassimilable in the eyes of the indigenous people among whom they worked. For this reason the missionaries who best understood the situation did their utmost to adapt themselves to the local manner of living, and to present their message in forms which would be intelligible in the mission field. Seen in this way, the striving for indigenization can be followed backwards through history— beyond the *accommodation practised by the *Jesuit missionaries to the instructions given by Gregory the Great, and so to Paul (1 Cor.9:20) and indeed to the incarnation of the Son of God himself.

(2) The second source of thinking about indigenization is to be found in German missionary thinking with its idea of the 'people's church' as the goal of the missionary endeavour. German theology in the 19th century from Schleiermacher on had affirmed an essential relationship between nationality and the kingdom of God on earth. Similarly, outstanding men such as Karl *Graul and Gustav *Warneck put forward the demand that missionary work should lead on to the creation of independent indigenous churches, which, from the point of view of social structure and culture, should be built up on the basis of the ethnic structure of the people among whom missionary work was being carried on, and in close relation to its inherited cultural values. In the work of Christian *Keysser and Bruno *Gutmann we can see this idea of the people's church most strongly based in theory and most logically carried out in practice.

Keysser, on the basis of his missionary experience in New Guinea, abandoned completely the idea of individual conversion, and worked successfully for the *'tribal conversion' of entire tribal groups among the Papuans; here decisions as to the rejection, retention, or modification of traditional customs in the church, were made by the tribal community itself, helped by advice from the missionary.

Bruno Gutmann, in his work among the Chagga people on Mount Kilimanjaro, developed his doctrine of the 'primordial ties'. In his missionary method, he did his utmost to christianize and incorporate into the church all the functions and offices as these existed in tribal society, and also the African principles of law as these had been revealed to him through his thorough researches.

(3) The third source in the movement for indigenization of Christianity is to be found in the wishes of the Afro-Asian Christians themselves, in many cases influenced by the anti-western reaction of coloured nationalism. As early as the second half of the 19th century clear signs could be observed both in West Africa and in Japan of resentment

awakened by a feeling of cultural estrangement as a result of missionary teaching. This in part determined Henry *Venn's idea of the necessity of independent indigenous churches. At the Conference of Chinese Churches held in Shanghai in 1922, sharp criticism was expressed of the western form of the missionary churches, their organization and their worship, and the demand for a national church was put forward.

Now that the churches in Africa and Asia have become independent, leading scholars have been trying to work out means by which indigenous thought-forms and values of religious experience in the traditional and pre-Christian religions can be employed to the enrichment of the theology and the worship of the church. They are concerned about the particular contribution that their churches should be making to the spiritual wealth of the universal church.

In this desire for indigenization we have to take account also of a five-fold concern:

(a) The concern that, in all missionary operation, account should be taken of the traditional sociological structure, in order to avoid both a religious individualism and inwardness in which little account is taken of social relationships, and also the isolation of the Christian community from the continuing life of its social environment.

(b) The adaptation of the ecclesiastical organization and the manner of its working to the economic standards of the indigenous community. The introduction of expensive ecclesiastical institutions on the western model makes it impossible for the local Christians to identify themselves with this structure, and creates a social barrier between the office-bearers of the church and their people. See the writings of J. Merle *Davis on the socio-economic conditions of the younger churches.

(c) The affirmation of the indigenous culture as a form for the proclamation of the Christian message. This involves the use of local architectural styles for church buildings, the creation of Christian art and sculpture in the traditional style, the adaptation of African or Asian tunes, rhythms and instruments for church music, the development of an indigenous tradition of Christian lyric poetry.

(d) The use of the mother-tongue and its idiomatic forms for preaching, cultural exchange, and instruction up to the level of *theological education.

(e) The relating of proclamation, teaching and confessional expression to the thought-forms, the questionings and experiences expressed in the traditional philosophy and religion of the area.

To put it briefly, the demand for the indigenization of the church really means simply the effort to set the proclamation of the church free from the traditional western form in which it seems repulsive to the hearers, and to present it, clothed afresh in Asian or African form, so as to appear intelligible and relevant to both Christian and non-Christian hearers.

When this does not take place the church which has grown out of the mission falls into cultural and social isolation; or it comes to be afflicted by retrogressive reactions, either in the form of the revival of old-time paganism among Christians, or of syncretistic movements like the prophetic-messianic movements which have been observed in many mission-fields.

On the other hand, grave dangers are involved in an uncritical acceptance of the demand for indigenization.

(1) In the demand that the foreign character of the church must be given up, it is easy to overlook the fact that the church, quite apart from its particular historic form at any given moment, is a pilgrim people which has no continuing city here upon earth. Too strong an insistence on the principle of indigenization may take from the church not only its quality of foreignness, but its Christian substance as well, and so subject it to a legalistic, political or even syncretistic captivity, 'The church must not be rooted in the soil, but be related to the soil' (*Willingen 1952).

(2) When the church is closely tied to the ethnic structure of its members, the result may be to make it powerless as far as concerns missionary work among peoples of

other ethnic structures and to isolate it from the worldwide church. Excessive emphasis on national or tribal characteristics can bring back to consciousness causes of opposition between different groups among the church's members, which had been forgotten, and so split the newly founded church.

(3) Too close identification of the church with a traditional and pre-existing culture may make it stiff and inflexible in face of historic change and ideological challenge. In this way the church may become a stronghold of cultural conservatism, and in consequence lose missionary opportunities, or lose its hold on whole sections of its own membership. For example, the intellectual élite in South Africa today detests the idea of 'development along their own lines', since this seems to debar them from that access to contemporary world civilization, which is the object of their desire.

These perils should serve as a warning against a parochial and regressive understanding of the nature of indigenization. A church, which has taken as its task the maintenance and practice at all costs of its traditional sociological forms and the cultural inheritance of the world around it is not genuinely indigenous (related to the soil). To be indigenous means that a church, in obedience to the apostolic message that has been entrusted to it and to the living guidance of the Holy Spirit, is able in its own particular historical situation, to make the gospel intelligible and relevant in word and deed to the eyes and ears of men.

PETER BEYERHAUS

R. Allen: 'The Use of the Term Indigenous' *IRM* XVI (1927), pp.262–70; P. Beyerhaus: *Die Selbständigkeit der jungen Kirchen als missionarisches Problem* (Wuppertal-Barmen 1959; Eng. ed., with H. Lefever: *The Responsible Church and the Foreign Mission*, London and Grand Rapids 1964); J. M. Davis: *New Buildings on Old Foundations* (New York 1947); J. C. Hoekendijk: *Kirche und Volk in der deutschen Missionswissenschaft* (Ger. tr., München 1967).

INDO-CHINA. See CAMBODIA; LAOS; VIETNAM.

INDONESIA (735,865 sq.m., population 112,000,000) contains the oldest Protestant community in Asia and one of the largest. It is the only country in South Asia in which Protestants outnumber Roman Catholics; and Christians proportionately form a larger group than in any East Asian state except the Philippines and South Korea. I. also represents the most extensive field dominated by continental European missions.

The evangelization of I. was begun by the Portuguese shortly after their establishment at Malacca, with *Franciscans celebrating mass in eastern Indonesia in 1522, but it was Francis *Xavier who laid the foundation of the church in the Indies. Great losses occurred to the work of the *Jesuits, Franciscans and *Dominicans through an anti-Portuguese reaction led by the Sultan of Ternate. According to some reports as much as four-fifths of the Christian community was lost, the remainder, some 30,000, largely becoming Protestant at the behest of their new Dutch masters after 1605.

The Dutch instituted a kind of 'Reformed *padroado' via the monopoly of their East India Company. In the renewed charter of the company in 1623 provision was made for 'the preservation of the common faith'. All employees of the company were to be members of an official church, whose pastors were sent out and supported by the company. Eventually nine congregations were established, some of which included Indonesian members, and New Testaments in Malay were published in 1668 and 1733. Growth throughout this period was slow, reaching a total of 55,000 baptized members in 1727. Visitation to preaching points beyond the handful of congregations was rare and a sharp discrimination was made between adult baptism and confirmation, so that in 1727 there were but 1,200 communicants.

During the British occupation (1811–16) the first missionaries of the *Nederlandsch Zendeling-Genootschap*, founded in 1797, were permitted to work under the auspices of the *LMS. In 1816 the Indies became a colony under the Dutch crown, and the Protestant Church of the Indies was established as an independent body, wholly distinct from the parent Netherlands Reformed Church. This body was intended as a 'unionist' church, without a definite credal basis, to serve Dutch Protestants of all persuasions, including Lutherans, Arminians and Mennonites. There was no internal church government, all congregations being wholly subject to a *Kerkbestuur* ('church committee') in Djakarta (Batavia), which was under the direct control of the Governor General of the Indies. This church was entirely supported by state funds, its pastors appointed and placed by the colonial administration, which, until 1935, forwarded—and examined —all correspondence with the Dutch church. Eventually this church—in agreements with mission agencies—took over all congregations in the areas of early European settlement, Ambon, Minahassa, and the island of Timor, as well as Dutch congregations in all other areas. A sharp line was drawn between university-trained men ordained by the Netherlands Reformed Church and missionaries, who came from special training schools. The latter were qualified to offer the sacraments only to non-Europeans. The church of Minahassa, for instance, just before becoming independent in 1934, had one minister, 11 'assistant pastors', i.e. missionaries, 89 evangelists— Indonesians with state salaries—and 374 'church-teachers'— laymen supported by their congregations and doing the normal pastoral work. The colonial administration permitted RC work, and in 1817 granted subsidies for it on the same basis as Protestant work, an arrangement which continued until 1950. By means of work-permits, the government strictly enforced *comity by assigning missions to specific regions. As a result the churches of Indonesia continue in remarkable degree to be regional or tribal churches, whatever their confessional colouring.

Between 1816 and 1914 the foundations of the church were laid in every major area of Indonesia. Among the first wave of NZG missionaries was Joseph *Kam, 'Apostle of the Moluccas'. Arriving in Ambon in 1816 to find the church building turned into a warehouse, he sailed throughout East Indonesia, establishing Ambon as a major church centre. After the restoration of Dutch control the NZG also opened important work in Timor and Minahassa, the latter becoming the first region to be completely christianized. A rebellion on Java in 1825 led the authorities to ban evangelism there and to confiscate the first edition of the Javanese NT. Nevertheless the gospel spread almost spontaneously in soil prepared by Javanese mystical groups. The efforts of a Dutch-Javanese planter (F. L. Coolen) and a German pietist watchmaker (J. *Emde) working separately in East Java resulted in the first of a series of Christian villages, founded in 1848, the form by which the church spread through East and Central Java resulting in the largest single group of converts from (a special kind of) *Islam in the world. Meanwhile the *Rhenish Mission had opened work in Kalimantan (Borneo), and Dutch Mennonites began work in North Central Java. In 1855 the first NZG missionaries arrived on the western end of Irian, beginning a forbiddingly difficult and disappointingly slow work there. In 1826 the *Propaganda created an apostolic prefecture in Indonesia, and shortly work began in what proved to be the chief area of RC strength, the island of Flores and the northern part of Timor. By the private efforts of several Dutch women, evangelism began also in the cities of Central Java, with their court traditions.

Required to leave Kalimantan on account of a rebellion, the Rhenish Mission left the field to the *Basel Mission, and turned to the Batak tribes of northern Sumatra in 1861. Under the leadership of Ludwig *Nommensen they deliberately set out to capture an entire region for the gospel, Nommensen becoming the *Ephorus* first of the Barmen work, then of the Batak *Volkskirche* ('people's church'), whose elders were the native princes. Work was extended to the island of Nias, again with great success.

In 1881 a national missionary conference was formed, holding periodic assemblies, and in 1906 a central missions bureau, the *Zendingsconsulaat*, handling all relations between missions and government, which continued to operate until 1953. Shortly before the first world war, the last major area of Christian work was opened in Central Sulawesi (Celebes) by a remarkable team of workers from the Netherlands Bible Society, who held off on conversions until the entire groundwork was laid for the up-building of an *indigenous church. Here as elsewhere a basis was laid for a great series of *mass movements, mainly developing between the wars. Note must be taken of the impressive record of patient, skilful evangelistic labours of a great group of Dutch, German and Swiss workers of whom Nommensen, *Adriani, *Kraemer and Bavinck are only the best-known. The first work of consequence not originating from the continent of Europe was that of American Methodists, first with Chinese in the Djakarta area, then increasingly in Sumatra.

After the first world war came the rapid growth which established the great Christian community of the present. In the Batak lands arose a Christian community of nearly a million, while a long-continued spiritual movement on nearby Nias led to the nearly complete christianization of that island. Quite as impressive and continuing to the present are mass movements among the Toradjas of Central Sulawesi, in the interior of Timor and in West Irian, the first in the face of sometimes bloody persecution. Recently the small Protestant church of Bali more than doubled its size in a decade on that strongly Hindu island. Elsewhere there is steady growth in the form of adult baptisms, often ahead of the general population increase. The RC church has also grown rapidly in a number of areas, and the same is reportedly true of Pentecostal groups. The member-churches of the Council of Churches of Indonesia represent a Christian community of perhaps six million, with 'non-co-operating' groups adding a half-million more. The latter includes Pentecostals (although three Pentecostal bodies are members of the Council), Adventists, Southern Baptists from the USA and a number of *faith missions, especially strong in Kalimantan and southern West Irian. The *CMA had an important part in opening Bali to missions, and had great influence among Chinese Protestants. The RC church, with a membership of 1,750,000, was granted an independent hierarchy in 1962, and some bishops were prominent in the deliberations of the Second *Vatican Council. The continental societies never emphasized Christian institutions on the scale of the British and American societies and although elementary schools of three grades were plentiful before 1940, the first Christian institution of higher education was opened only in 1953. There were a number of general hospitals and many small clinics opened by the missions.

The larger churches started receiving their independence from the missionary societies beginning with the Protestant Christian Church of the Bataks (HKBP) in 1930, but in most cases the tie with the mission remained a close one. The *ephorus* of the Bataks continued to be chosen in Barmen until 1940, and the Dutch minister in Menado was *ex officio* the moderator of the Christian Evangelical Church of Minahassa. The Protestant Church of the Indies was set free from its financial dependence on the Dutch government only after Indonesian independence. The second world war brought hardship and considerable suffering to the churches. The Japanese discriminated in favour of Islam, and often suspected church leaders of collaboration with the Dutch. Missionaries were interned, and many church leaders imprisoned, some being executed. At the same time it was during this period that the churches began to experience real independence and self-confidence. On the whole Indonesian Christians supported the nationalist and independence movements, although Christians in certain areas were involved in pro-Dutch or separatist movements in 1950 and 1957–61. The Evangelical Church of West Irian, including possibly half the entire population of the area, was involved in the struggle leading up to Indonesian sovereignty in 1963 and separatist tensions since. The Council of Churches itself, which is the effective national voice of the churches, has followed consistently a policy of discriminating support for the central government, and a number of Christians have figured prominently in high political office.

The Council was founded in 1950 with 30 (now 37) member-churches, organized with the express intention of creating 'the one Church of Christ in Indonesia'. It has proved to be the centre of all inter-church activities, but the goal of union remains remote. At present the Council is considering a plan for an 'ecumenical synod' or federation of churches. Fourteen churches are members of the *WCC, nine having been charter members; and the Council itself joined the *IMC at Willingen 1952. Although there are different confessional groupings within the Council (Hervormd, Gereformeerd, Lutheran-Unionist, Methodist, Mennonite, Pentecostal) *confessionalism itself has rarely been an issue. Most churches are content to call themselves 'Christian', 'Evangelical' or 'Protestant'. A special position is that of the Batak Church (HKBP), which adopted a very striking confession in 1951 and joined the *Lutheran World Federation. Working together has been facilitated by an active Christian Literature Society, by the Indonesian Bible Society, with a new translation of the whole Bible nearing completion, and by the existence of union theological schools in Djakarta, Makasar, and Jogjakarta. Most Protestants are members of the Christian political party, PARKINDO, which works closely with its Catholic counterpart. The Indonesian *SCM has a prominent place in church life. Shortage of church workers is a matter of concern, with the church of Minahassa, for instance, reporting 70 ordained pastors and 455 regular congregations. This problem became more pressing after the unsuccessful coup of October 1965 led to greatly increased prestige for religious groups and a flood of candidates for baptism. This political upheaval has, on the other hand, encouraged the aspirations for an Islamic state which have haunted the republic since independence.

ALAN C. THOMSON

The only church history, published first in Indonesian, and afterwards in German, is Th. Müller-Krüger: *Der Protestantismus in Indonesien* (Stuttgart 1968). Most other material is in Dutch and pre-1940. Major works include the following: H. D. J. Boissevain, ed.: *De Zending in Oost en West* (2 vols., The Hague 1945), discusses each mission working in the Dutch possessions; C. W. Th. Baron van Boetzelaer van Asperen en Dubbeldam: *De Protestansche Kerk in Nederlandsch-Indië, Haar Ontwikkeling van 1620–1939* (The Hague 1947), on the Protestant Church of the Indies; a RC history is that of Arn. J. H. Van der Velden, SJ: *De Roomsch-Katholieke Missie in Nederlandsch Oost-Indië* (Nijmegen 1908); in English, F. L. Cooley: *Indonesia: Church and Society* (New York 1968) is a reliable survey; H. Kraemer's field notes 1922–35 are contained in *From Missionfield to Independent Church* (London 1958); brief surveys are included in K. S. Latourette: *A History of the Expansion of Christianity* (New York 1939–1945), Vol. III, pp.300–06, Vol. V, pp.275–95, Vol. VII, pp.199–210, and *Christianity in a Revolutionary Age* (New York 1958–1962), Vol. III, pp.424–27, Vol. V, pp.353–60; also M. S. Bates and W. Pauck: *The Prospects of Christianity Throughout the World* (New York 1964), pp.247–58; in German, J. Richter: *Die Evangelische Mission in Niederländisch-Indien* (Gütersloh 1931) deals with the work of German missions; and L. Schreiner: *Das Bekenntnis der Batak-Kirche* (München 1966) is a thorough study of the Batak Confession. See also *BM* II, 476–84; *NCE* VII, 478–81; *WKL*, 584–86.

INDUSTRIAL MISSIONS were included in the Protestant mission programme from the beginning, and the teaching of crafts was deemed essential to achieving 'civilization'. This was a marked feature of the 17th century New England missions to the

Indians. The *Moravian mission enterprise of the 18th and 19th centuries was supported by communal industrial and commercial activities in centres such as Bethlehem, and crafts were introduced locally as part of the Herrnhut pattern as well as for evangelistic opportunity. The first company of missionaries sent to Tahiti by the *LMS in 1796 was made up largely of craftsmen, and for several decades spinning, weaving, sugar refining, dairying and coconut oil industries were attempted. A century later the LMS created Papuan Industries, Ltd., in New Guinea. The *Basel Missionary Society's industrial work is well known. Coffee and cocoa growing were introduced into the Gold Coast; the Basel Mission Trading Co. organized to facilitate trade without alcohol and firearms; and craftsmen were trained at Accra. Basel carpenters, masons, coopers, blacksmiths and engineers were found in every business house along 2,000 miles of coast. Basel (Mangalore) tile factories, weaving establishments (original source of khaki cloth), carpentry, and printing were famous in south-west India.

IMs became increasingly popular during the 19th and early 20th centuries. They were said to teach the dignity of work and foster reliability and frugality, to provide self-support for individuals and the Christian community, and to afford evangelistic opportunity. American Methodists (examples: Moradabad and Bareilly, 1868) and the United Free Church of Scotland were active in India, the latter forming the Scottish Missions Industry Co. There were special conferences on industrial missions in Bombay and Mahabeleshwar in 1901 and 1902. But interest waned, and all that remain in India today are about 45 printing houses and some three dozen miscellaneous industries, among which lacemaking and embroidery find a place. Such missions were numerous in Africa. Lovedale (1841) of the Free Church of Scotland, in Kaffraria, was the prime model for others. It taught masonry, carpentry, wagon-making, blacksmithing, printing and bookbinding. Similar stations of the Free Church were Blythswood in Transkei, and Blantyre in Malawi.

Other industrial centres in the same general area were Old Umtali of the American Methodists in Rhodesia, the Zambezi Industrial Mission (1892) and the Nyasa Industrial Mission. In Nigeria industrial work was carried on by the African Industrial Mission (Toronto), the Qua Iboe Mission and the *CMS at Onitsha. The United Brethren (USA) had industrial work in Sierra Leone; and the American Lutherans and Episcopalians at Muhlenburg and Cape Mount, Liberia. In East Africa the Scottish Industrial Mission, initiated by the Imperial British East Africa Company in 1891 under James *Stewart of Lovedale, was taken over by the Church of Scotland after a few years. The English Friends established a mission on Pemba Island in 1896 and the (American) Friends Africa Industrial Mission located in Kavirondo in 1901. CMS industries in Uganda were given over to the Uganda Co. The Industrial Missions Aid Society was founded in London in 1897 and set up industries at Ahmednagar, India (rug factory), Freretown, Kenya, and in the West Indies. One of its founders, Henry W. Fry, then established the Foreign Mission Industrial Association of America.

Many missions which did not create large industrial centres founded industrial schools with the same motivation, and small industries were introduced into orphanages. The last full census of such schools in 1925 (*World Missionary Atlas*) reported 297, of which 100 were in India and 87 in Africa south of the Sahara. IMs and schools fell out of favour some 50 or more years ago and rapidly declined. This seems to have been due to labour troubles, disruption due to political conditions, the difficulty of placing in profitable employment those who had been trained, and above all the desire of nationals for academic education and white collar jobs. Since the second world war, however, motor transport and the developing countries' interest in industrialization have led to new opportunities for IMs connected with engineering and kindred occupations, e.g. the Christian Industrial Training Centre, Pumwani, Kenya, and

Auto-skills Industrial Training Centre, Nasik, India.

R. PIERCE BEAVER

J. S. Dennis: *Christian Missions and Social Progress* (1906), Vol. II, pp.153–67 Vol. III, pp.95–127.

INITIATION RITES, ATTITUDE TO.
The classic reference is the letter of S. Gregory to S. Augustine of Canterbury giving instruction as to dealings with the heathen Anglo-Saxons, and telling Augustine not to despise heathen practices, but to 'baptize' them, e.g. to use heathen temples for Christian worship on the conversion of the worshippers. But many later missionaries, revolted by what seemed to them the indecent and sometimes cruel practices of the initiation rites of Africa, have felt obliged to demand a complete abandonment of heathen practice. In South Africa it was demanded that young men on conversion should refuse the rite of tribal initiation. Some converts nobly accepted this, and were all their lives regarded as children, and not adult members of the tribe. Later some missionaries realized that Christianity had come to mean separation from the tribe. In Kenya in 1929 the CSM and the AIM agreed that parents who allowed their daughters to pass through the tribal initiation rites, even in a modified form, must be subjected to church *discipline, and the girls forbidden to remain in a mission school. Many of the parents did not see that there was anything morally wrong in what was thus forbidden, and formed an independent church. The Anglican bishop of Mombasa (Heywood) did not feel able to concur with the two missions, and issued a pastoral letter setting forth as the Christian goal the abandonment of any custom or rite when it was realized to be contrary to Christian standards of purity. The great protagonist of such rites was Bishop W. V. *Lucas of Masasi (Southern Tanzania). For many years he refused to take disciplinary action against African Christians who in good conscience performed rites which others saw to be contrary to Christian morals or doctrine. Only when African

Christians came to ask what to do when they found themselves bound by tribal custom to do things which they had now come to realize were contrary to Christian faith or morals, did he set out his ideas of how, by cutting out what was immoral or un-Christian, leaving what was good or neutral (e.g. circumcision), and adding Christian prayer and teaching, the rites could be 'baptized'. He held that tribal life would be the right foundation for the national life of the new nations of Africa; that it was essential that that life should be fully Christian; and therefore the initiation to that tribal life must be christianized and not arbitrarily forbidden.

R. G. P. LAMBURN

A. Hastings: *Church and Mission in Modern Africa* (London 1967); R. G. P. Lamburn: *Die Yao von Tunduru* (privately published: 3 Hannover Kirchrode, Bünteweg 13); E. R. Morgan, ed.: *Essays Catholic and Missionary* (London 1926); D. Shropshire: *The Church and Primitive People* (London 1926); J. V. Taylor: *The Primal Vision* (London 1963).

INTELLECTUAL UPLIFT.
The missionary movement has made five significant contributions to the intellectual life of mankind. *First* it has made a sustained attack upon the vast problem provided by illiteracy. Even today there are many areas where the illiteracy rate is still over 80% of the population. Increasingly, however, governments are accepting responsibility for the task which Christian missions pioneered. The notable work of Dr Laubach, an American missionary to the Philippines, has been widely accepted by governments as well as churches as a means towards spreading literacy. In the *second* place Christian missionaries have been concerned to reduce languages to writing in order that the Bible might be translated into the common speech of the people. Today the Bible in whole or in part is to be found in some 1,100 languages, the great majority of these never having been reduced to writing before the advent of Christian missionaries. In the sequel it is a significant fact that for numerous races the Bible has proved to be

the basis of their literature and in this way a peculiarly formative influence on the thought, life and practice of many peoples. It was a missionary of the early church, Ulfilas, who first translated the Bible into the language of a people living outside the bounds of the Roman Empire. This remains a major responsibility of the Christian church in its missionary outreach. *Third* in the contribution of missions to intellectual uplift may be said to be the cross-fertilization of cultures. Through its campaign for literacy, through the translation of the Scriptures, and through the extensive work of Christian education, the missionary movement has broken down cultural isolation and made a considerable contribution towards making the world a neighbourhood, thus laying the foundations for an international order of justice and peace. *Fourth*, through the stimulus of these other activities there has begun to be the creation of an indigenous literature in many countries, and among many peoples, for whom previously only oral transmission had been available as a channel for the preservation of traditions and the recording of history. *Fifth*, missionaries, among other orientalists, have done much to make familiar to the western world the traditions and literatures of the great cultures of Asia, in this way making some small contribution towards reducing the intellectual arrogance of western man, thereby in turn making possible inter-faith *dialogue and the growth of mutual respect between the peoples of the world.

MAX WARREN

F. Laubach: *Teaching the World to Read* (London 1943); H. Richard Niebuhr: *Christ and Culture* (London 1952); E. E. Wallis and M. A. Bennett: *Two Thousand Tongues to Go—The Story of the Wycliffe Bible Translators* (London 1960); H. R. Weber: *The Communication of the Gospel to Illiterates* (London 1957).

INTERBOARD COMMITTEES. An IBC is a co-operative agency of mission boards related to a *united church overseas. Its purpose is to ensure active recognition and

support of the unity attained by the church as it seeks to continue the historic mission from which it is derived. Mission boards and societies have responded to requests from united churches in Japan, Philippines, south and north India, Indonesia (the *NCC), Zambia, Nigeria and Iraq for co-operative relationships that further the integration of the different units of the growing churches. The historic denominational ties become altered by the policies and relationships adopted by the mission agencies represented on an IBC. The functions of a committee depend on the extent to which the agencies agree to act in common through it instead of through the former denominational channels. While a direct financial relationship of the agencies with the united church ceases to exist, new possibilities of church-to-church relationships are opened.

The ability of an IBC to consult readily and adopt common forms of action is affected by two factors. One is the extent of the geographical separation of the mission agencies themselves, and the other is the diversity of missionary policy and ecclesiological understanding of the agencies related to the church overseas. Thus, the Church of South India Related Missions Committee for Common Action exists to provide opportunity for consultation so that agreed policies may be reached for taking part in the life and witness of the *CSI, but the committee in order to meet must secure representation of agencies in five countries and three continents.

An IBC may seek for an increasingly positive role in missionary action by not allowing itself to become merely a means of response to requests from the church, or an office for administration of new relationships. Its nature and functions after some time may need to be redefined as the united church becomes more firmly established and seeks for mature relationships with those churches with which it has had historic missionary ties. The IBC for the United Church of Christ in Japan, after being for many years a liaison for the church and supporting agencies, has begun to re-examine its purpose and functions in the light of the missionary understanding of the agencies. Questions are raised about the adequacy of the stated purpose of the committee for the continuing mission of the church, which is 'to act as the agent of those mission boards and societies desiring to co-operate and render assistance'. Instead the committee has made proposals in the direction of its own missionary understanding and in order that it may become an instrument by which the churches themselves can have effective relationships. A more complete ecumenical function thus becomes the advanced goal of interboard co-operation.

ROLAND W. SCOTT

C. H. Germany: 'The Ecumenical Significance of Japan's Interboard Committee and Council of Co-operation', *The Japan Missionary Bulletin* Vol. XVII, No. 1 (Tokyo 1963); N. Thurber: 'Statement on the Nature and Function of the Interboard Committee for Christian Work in Japan', a paper privately circulated by the Interboard Committee for Christian Work in Japan (New York 1966); 'The Church of South India Related Missions Committee for Common Action. Statement of Purpose' (London 1964).

INTERCESSION FOR MISSIONS. Protestant missions arose undergirded by intercession and have continued to be supported by prayer. The Concert of Prayer developed out of a call by Scottish ministers in 1744 and renewed in 1746. Jonathan *Edwards in New England in 1747 published his *Humble Attempt to Promote . . . Extraordinary Prayer for the Revival of Religion* and this gave power to the movement. The Baptists at Nottingham in 1784 made it the Monthly Concert and the *LMS in 1795 converted it into the union Monthly Concert of Prayer for Missions. It became general practice in mission circles in all English-speaking areas, and missionaries carried it around the world. Until well after the middle of the 19th century it was the chief means of promoting intercession, diffusing knowledge and stimulating financial support. Each

reprinting of Edwards' *Humble Attempt* further stimulated the movement; the last being an abridged edition edited by George Burder of the LMS in 1814. Burder states that the practice had by then also been adopted in Holland, Switzerland and Germany.

Intercessory prayer was an important part of each meeting of local, regional and national missionary associations and conferences as they developed, for example, in India: the Bombay Missionary Union, the North and South India Missionary Conferences, and the All-India Decennial Conferences. Each of the great popular Anglo-American conferences from New York and London 1854 to the Ecumenical Missionary Conference, New York, 1900, was preceded by special services of intercession in parish churches and mission stations. The co-operation of 60,000 pastors and influential laymen in promoting prayer was asked before the last. Dr John R. *Mott attributed much of the success of the *World Missionary Conference at Edinburgh in 1910 to worldwide intercession. 'Intercession Sheets' were distributed beginning in 1908, and churches observed 15 May 1910 as a day of prayer for the conference. It has been said: 'The heart of Edinburgh was not in its speeches but in its periods of prayer'. After its formation in 1921 the *IMC issued intercession sheets, and in 1927 requested fellowship of prayer for spiritual revival in preparation for the *Jerusalem Conference.

It has long been the custom for many societies and boards to request prayer for missionaries, nationals, churches, institutions and causes and to publish aids for this purpose, such as the *CMS Prayer Paper* and companion annual prayer calendar and the *Mission Yearbook of Prayer* published jointly by the Board of National Missions and the Commission on Ecumenical Mission of the United Presbyterian Church in the USA.

R. PIERCE BEAVER

On the Concert of Prayer see: R. P. Beaver: 'Concert of Prayer for Mission', *Ecumenical Review*, July 1958, pp.420–27.

INTER-CHURCH AID. The 20th century expression of the church's age-old concern to serve mankind in need has been marked by an increasing desire to give service ecumenically across denominational and geographical boundaries. A key instrument forged for this is the Division of Inter-Church Aid, Refugee, and World Service (DICARWS) of the *WCC. DICARWS has grown out of the decision of the Provisional Committee of the WCC at its first meeting in January 1939 to appoint Dr Adolf Freudenberg to organize help for refugees in Europe. Then at a meeting in Geneva in September 1942 it was agreed that the WCC when formed should have a Department of Reconstruction to ensure that needy churches in war-devastated lands had adequate help from, if need be, other denominations or confessions. This department was set up in December 1944 with Dr J. Hutchison Cockburn, Scotland, as Senior Secretary and embraced the European Central Bureau for Inter-Church Aid which Professor Adolf Keller had led since 1922. When the WCC was constituted at Amsterdam in August 1948 the Department was re-christened Inter-Church Aid and Service to Refugees, changed to DICARWS in 1961. Its function is to receive service projects from the churches, confirm that they meet agreed criteria, and then present them to WCC member churches or their related agencies for support. Except with refugee work DICARWS is not itself operational, but is essentially a central co-ordinating body and has no funds of its own to dispense; all money for service projects is given by the WCC member churches and their agencies, such as Christian Aid in Britain, *Church World Service in USA, and others in various countries. All money passed through DICARWS for projects and emergencies is forwarded without any deduction whatsoever. DICARWS publishes an annual project list of some 600 approved projects in every continent with requests totalling around $25 million. A major concern is with development in the 'Third World'.

DICARWS has area secretaries for Africa, Asia, Europe, Latin America, and the Near East; specialists for the refugee programme; and functional secretaries for migration, scholarships, literature, teams, material aid, development education, and information. To provide the whole WCC with advice on difficult projects, a committee with panels of experts in many fields was created in 1961 and re-formed as ACTS (Advisory Committee on Technical Services) in 1968. ACTS' secretariat is located outside DICARWS. Related to DICARWS are the Ecumenical Church Loan Fund (ECLOF) and Casa Locarno, a rest centre for church workers recovering from severe illness. Best known of the DICARWS activities is its worldwide refugee programme which by 1967 had helped 300,000 uprooted people to begin life afresh in new lands, and thousands more to integrate within the communities where they had found asylum. For DICARWS' role after disasters, see RELIEF WORK.

GEOFFREY MURRAY

L. E. Cooke: *Bread and Laughter* (Geneva 1968); G. Murray: *A Time of Compassion— the Churches and World Refugee Year* (Geneva 1961); DICARWS: *Annual Reports* (1950—).

INTER-CHURCH RELATIONS. See COMITY; ECUMENICAL MOVEMENT.

INTERDENOMINATIONAL AND NON-DENOMINATIONAL SENDING AGENCIES. Technically an interdenominational sending agency should be one established for joint commissioning and maintenance of missionaries by two or more denominational church judicatories. Actually no such organizations now exist. They have been most rare, and all instances occurred in the USA at an early period. The New York Missionary Society was such an agency (founded 1796), at least during the few years when the Baptists, by vote of their New York association, joined in it with Presbyterians and Reformed. The United Foreign Missionary Society was founded in 1817 by official action of the Reformed,

Presbyterian and Associate churches. When it merged with the *ABCFM (a Congregational organ founded in 1810 and admitting Presbyterians individually), the ABCFM then became such an interdenominational agency and remained so until 1870, when the last of the non-Congregational denominations withdrew. There have been many interdenominational agencies, but not for sending. (See MISSION BOARDS AND SOCIETIES, INTERDENOMINATIONAL.)

Actual interdenominational sending agencies have usually been voluntary associations not created by acts of ecclesiastical judicatories but rather incorporated by individuals for securing the co-operation of the constituencies of two or more denominations in a joint mission. The very first Protestant missionary society, the New England Company, was chartered as a Puritan independent agency in 1649 but was rechartered in 1660 as a society of Anglicans and dissenters. But it is the *LMS of 1795 which is the prototype of such agencies. It united evangelicals of Congregationalist, Presbyterian and Anglican churches, and proclaimed its fundamental principle to be: 'not to send Presbyterianism, Independency, Episcopacy or any other form of church order and government . . . but the glorious Gospel of the Blessed God to the Heathen'. Eventually because of the organization of denominational societies the LMS became virtually Congregational, but always remained ready to send members of other churches. It is significant that the churches founded by the LMS and the ABCFM have, with few exceptions, been more ready than others to enter into organic unions. The LMS example was influential in the organization of a number of union Reformed and Lutheran societies on the European continent: *Basel (1815), *PEMS (1822), *Berlin (1824), *Rhenish (1828), *North German (1836), and *Gossner (1836). There was during the early part of the 19th century among the constituents of both union and denominational societies a consensus that the differences among the Protestant churches were largely accidents of history which could have little meaning for people in Asia

and Africa, that the common message and heritage were to be transmitted, and that much liberty could be allowed the emerging churches on the fields. However, confessional pressures resulted in the Berlin and Gossner societies becoming Lutheran and the North German Society, Reformed.

A new type of society, non-denominational in organization, but considered by its founders and constituents to be thoroughly interdenominational, appeared in the middle of the 19th century, but having a slightly earlier origin. Members of such a society considered it to be an agent of the church in extension of the church, usually with some special objective. The earliest were three British organizations: the Society for Promoting Female Education in the East (1834), the short-lived Chinese Evangelization Association (c. 1850), and the Indian Female Normal School Association (1852), later called the Zenana Bible and Medical Mission. The Woman's Union Missionary Society of America was formed in 1861. To these may be added the *Morrison Educational Association in Canton, China, formed by resident Europeans in 1835 as a memorial to the pioneer Protestant missionary.

However, it was the *CIM, founded by J. Hudson *Taylor in 1866, primarily to reach the untouched interior provinces at a time when the older agencies were bogged down in the ports, which became the enduring inspiration and prototype for this kind of mission. The CIM, in Dr Taylor's strategy, was an exercise in mission and unity, thoroughly interdenominational in reality although non-denominational in organization. Evangelical missionaries and their support were received from many denominations, and an effort was made to group some of the personnel by denominational affiliation in proximity to a mission of that same denomination. Thus Anglicans were assigned to Szechuan where the churches fostered by the CIM and those by the *CMS were incorporated into one diocese. On the same principle Baptists were put into Shansi. In general, however, although stress was put on rapid diffusion of the gospel rather than planting churches,

churches naturally came into being and formed a 'CIM denomination'. After exclusion from China about 1950, the CIM evaluated its experience and resolved henceforth to stress church planting to a far greater degree. A cardinal principle was that there should be no guaranteed salaries or allowances and no personal solicitation of funds, but dependence was to be on God's providence in faith. Thus arose the concept of the *'faith mission. (The CIM now has the name Overseas Missionary Fellowship.)

The appeal of 'the regions beyond' and the 'faith' principle in combination stimulated an ever-growing company of such mission agencies patterned similarly after the CIM. By 1900 there were to be found in Great Britain the *North Africa Mission (1881), South America Evangelical Mission (1895), Egypt General Mission (1898), British branch of the *SAGM (1889), *RBMU (1899); in Ireland the Qua Iboe Mission (1887); in North America the Scandinavian Alliance Mission (1891, later the *Evangelical Alliance Mission), Gospel Union (1891), the South America Evangelical Mission (1892), the *SIM (1898) and the AIM (1895); in South Africa the SAGM (1894), and in Australia and New Zealand several branches of European societies. Branches of the CIM were by that time established in North America and elsewhere. The directors and missionaries of these societies generally co-operated with the denominational missions, and intersociety fellowship was warm until the Fundamentalist-Modernist controversy of the 20th century, when they began to draw apart. The development of the *ecumenical movement and of the *WCC, suspected by evangelicals of being modernist, universalist, and ambitious to establish a 'superchurch', has further divided the missions. It should be noted that British evangelicals have generally been 'churchmen', while North Americans have generally been far less interested in the church and more concerned about proclamation and individual conversions. However, the teaching of Dr R. Kenneth Strachan of the *Latin America Mission, Dr Billy Graham's insistence on co-operation with churches, and the OMF emphasis on church planting in mission have been stimulating a new concern for the church.

About 1940 and especially after the end of the second world war a vast number of non-denominational missions was organized in the United States and Canada especially. They are on the whole rather anti-church and do not consider themselves interdenominational in character. Many of them vigorously proselytize.

The stable conservative evangelical societies which consider themselves 'interdenominational' are in the USA members of the *IFMA formed in 1917, and they have a comparable fellowship in Great Britain. Forty-four mission societies are members of the IFMA. Half a dozen others hold membership in the *EFMA. The missionary force of these societies steadily increases in proportion to that of the ecumenically related denominational boards and societies which are now engaged largely in *interchurch aid in personnel and funds. As these societies raise up young churches on their fields they tend to form into local separate denominations.

R. PIERCE BEAVER

See articles on the individual mission agencies which provide references; *EMCM*; Missionary Research Library: *North American Protestant Ministries Overseas Directory* (8th ed., New York 1968); *World Christian Handbook*, latest current edition; Interdenominational Foreign Mission Association: *IFMA News* (bi-monthly except July-August); J. H. Kane: *Faith Mighty Faith, Handbook of the IFMA* (New York 1956).

INTERDENOMINATIONAL FOREIGN MISSION ASSOCIATION, THE, was organized on 13 March 1917 by leaders of several well known *faith missions (missions without denominational affiliation) for purposes of spiritual fellowship and co-operation. The IFMA has no superimposing administrative authority over member missions but does function on behalf of its members in accrediting them to the

Christian public as societies worthy of support. The Association's standards assure the public that its members are evangelical, financially responsible, committed to reliance upon God through prayer and faith, and controlled by a properly constituted board of trustees.

The IFMA also acts as an information centre on missionary societies and activities around the world. It assists pastors and churches in establishing a church-missionary programme and helps its member missions in internal administration and governmental matters.

From an original membership of four missions, IFMA has grown so that it currently represents 48 agencies who support more than 8,000 missionaries around the world. The IFMA has a strongly evangelical doctrinal platform and is generally regarded as being in the fundamentalist tradition. It publishes the bi-monthly *IFMA News* (except July-August) along with books and pamphlets on a variety of missionary concerns.

While the IFMA has generally been opposed to the 'tongues-movement', it has recently drawn closer to the *EFMA, which has in its membership a number of Pentecostal groups. In 1966 the Congress on the Church's Worldwide Mission convened in Wheaton, Illinois (USA), under the joint sponsorship of the IFMA and the EFMA. *The Church's Worldwide Mission*, edited by Harold Lindsell (Word Books) presents the Congress papers and proceedings along with a historic overview.

IFMA's headquarters are at 54 Bergen Avenue, Ridgefield Park, New Jersey 07660 (USA).

HAROLD LINDSELL

INTERNATIONAL MISSIONARY COUNCIL, THE (IMC), sprang from The *World Missionary Conference, Edinburgh, 1910, and had a continuous evolution through the first world war until its formal constitution in 1921. It joined in an international federation the *National Christian Councils and councils of churches in Asia, Africa and Latin America with the

mission councils of the west. In principle it was the first worldwide ecumenical council of churches. Its purview included most of the problems confronting the Protestant churches outside the west. Among its larger accomplishments were the creation of a strong global network of NCCs, the convening of major *world missionary conferences, the formulation (chiefly through its member bodies) of major policies for worldwide mission, stimulation of creative thought in the continuing development of a *theology of mission, support of *'orphaned missions' during two world wars, and a major contribution to the emergence of the *WCC. In 1961 it merged with that larger body and continued to function as the WCC's *Commission on World Mission and Evangelism (CWME).

Background: 1910–1920. *Edinburgh 1910, in its one major action, created a Continuation Committee. With John R. *Mott as its chairman and Joseph H. *Oldham as its secretary, the Continuation Committee was to carry out what had emerged from Edinburgh 1910, and to establish an agency for international missionary co-operation. Mott's conferences in Asia, 1912–1913, often overlooked, were really an extension of Edinburgh 1910, and its fulfilment on Asian soil. These resulted in *national missionary councils. The rise of similar agencies in Europe and Africa provided an international network of co-operative councils which looked to the Continuation Committee as their central link. The Continuation Committee's scholarly quarterly, the *International Review of Missions* (IRM, 1912 ff.), furthered the sense of unity.

The first world war ended the Continuation Committee as an organization, but Oldham, Kenneth Maclennan and Miss Betty Gibson worked through the *Conference of Missionary Societies in Great Britain and Ireland (CBMS) and Mott functioned through the *Foreign Missions Conference of North America (FMC) to continue its essential activities. German missions were a major concern. In 1918 the CBMS and FMC created the Emergency committee of Co-operating Missions (the Continuation Committee in a new form) with Mott as chairman and Oldham as secretary. Oldham's labours resulted in the Versailles Treaty's Article 438 which saved German missions from expropriation. The larger work associated with Mott and Oldham made clear the need for a permanent, international, co-operative agency.

1921-1927. Thus the IMC was constituted at Lake Mohonk, NY, in October 1921. Aggrieved by wartime developments, the Germans held back, but within six months had joined the IMC. In 1921 A. L. *Warnshuis, an American of Dutch descent and with China experience, opened the IMC's New York office, and in 1927 William *Paton, English and with service in India, joined the London secretariat at Edinburgh House. Among important IMC concerns in the 1920s were German missions and the securing of their rights, work among Jews and Muslims, work in Latin America and Africa, race, and the development of Christian literature. During this period some of the important Asian missionary councils became NCCs.

1928-1937. The first great ecumenical assembly called by the IMC met on the Mount of Olives at Eastertide 1928 (see CONFERENCES, WORLD MISSIONARY, Jerusalem 1928). One-fourth of those present represented the *younger churches. Jerusalem's 'church-centric' doctrine of mission focused on the *indigenous church in Asia, Africa and Latin America as the determining centre for mission. From Barthians and others came a storm of criticism on what was judged to be Jerusalem's naïve optimism and relativism in approaching the missionary 'message'. Jerusalem pointed to secularism as the new universal religion which involved all Christians in missionary encounter and destroyed the geographical notion of a 'non-Christian' over against a 'Christian' world. Through this and other insights Jerusalem shaped Oxford 1937, when Oldham became organizing secretary for the latter.

In the late 1920s, the IMC began its Department of Social and Economic Research, headed by J. Merle *Davis, and

its International Committee on Christian Literature for Africa. The IMC's work in the rural mission led to the Agricultural Missions Foundation and courses at Cornell University for rural missionaries. (See also ORPHANED MISSIONS for IMC efforts in the 1930s on behalf of German Missions.)

1938-1947. The *Tambaram Conference met at Christmastide 1938-1939 on the campus of Madras Christian College in Tambaram, a suburb of Madras, India. The most representative Christian assembly convened to that time (more than half its members were Asians, Africans and Latin Americans), Madras centred upon the church constituted by mission. A tremendous demonstration of worldwide Christian unity, Madras prepared the churches and missions for holding together through the tragic and disruptive period of the second world war. (See ORPHANED MISSIONS.) Major debate centred upon the authority of the faith. The American *Laymen's Foreign Missions Inquiry, among other results, issued in the relativistic *Re-thinking Missions* of its chairman, W. E. *Hocking. Commissioned by the IMC, Hendrik *Kraemer's Barthian and influential *Christian Message in a Non-Christian World* established the polar opposite for theological discussion.

The IMC forged close links with the *WCC. During the 1930s the IMC staff had actively aided *Life and Work and *Faith and Order. At Utrecht in 1938, Paton, with W. A. Visser't Hooft, became one of the two secretaries of the WCC (In Process of Formation). In that office and without surrendering his IMC post, he served in London until his death in 1943. Begun in 1939, the IMC-WCC Joint Committee functioned through the war and after Amsterdam 1948, grew in importance as the two bodies worked closely together and sponsored many enterprises jointly. Each officially designated itself as 'in association with' the other, and the widespread conviction mounted that the two should unite—a view seriously challenged in some quarters.

After the second world war, the IMC assembled in 1947 at *Whitby, near Toronto,

Canada. Whitby provided another remarkable demonstration of post-war Christian unity. Expectant evangelism was the motif, and 'partners in obedience' summarized the understanding of interdependence among *'older' and 'younger' churches in world mission.

1948–1957. This was a period of transition. Major staff changes had been and were to be extensive. Oldham had resigned in 1938 and Mott and Warnshuis had retired in 1942. In New York John W. Decker succeeded Warnshuis, directed the Orphaned Missions effort, retired in 1957, and was followed by George W. Carpenter. When Paton died, Norman Goodall took responsibility for the London Office until 1955 when, succeeded by Ronald K. Orchard, he became full-time secretary for the important Joint Committee of the IMC-WCC. As the IMC's full-time chairman, Mott also had been in fact general secretary. Those who succeeded Mott could not assume this additional role, and so at Whitby the IMC made Charles W. Ranson (its new Research Secretary and one with India experience) its first General Secretary. He was succeeded in 1958 by the Rt. Rev. J. E. Lesslie Newbigin of the Church of South India, who facilitated the integration of the IMC into the WCC and in 1965 returned to India as Bishop in Madras. The Rev. Philip Potter followed him as General Secretary of the CWME. But for the limits of space, many others such as Rajah Manikam, joint IMC-WCC East Asia Secretary from 1951, who had served notably in the IMC's secretariat should also be listed.

*Willingen 1952, the IMC's first assembly in Germany, marked an important stage in the theology of mission. Mission, it declared, is of the essence of the church and has its roots in the Triune God. Willingen's thrust influenced Faith and Order, as evidenced by Lund 1952, and Montreal 1963, and stimulated important further theological reflection on mission.

With its constituting assembly at *Amsterdam in 1948, the WCC became the prime symbol of worldwide non-Roman Christian co-operation. In a period of new nationhood and intense nationalism, the churches of Asia and Africa found in the WCC their chief agency for unity. Moreover, growing recognition that mission is basic to the life of the church made integration of the IMC (a council of councils) into the WCC (a council of churches) imperative: such integration would symbolize the true relation of mission and church.

After the WCC's 1954 *Evanston Assembly major attention centred upon IMC-WCC integration. The chief action of the IMC's assembly in Ghana 1958 (see CONFERENCES, WORLD MISSIONARY) was to proceed to that objective. The majority approved, yet the Orthodox equated mission with proselytism. Latin American Protestantism was uneasy about the WCC. The Norwegian Missionary Council feared that mission would be submerged in the WCC. The Congo Protestant Council determined to maintain local co-operation with conservative bodies which refused WCC membership. All these posed major problems. Yet, except for the withdrawals of these two councils, overwhelming approval came, and at *New Delhi in 1961 the IMC became the WCC's *Commission* on World Mission and Evangelism. The CWME's members (NCCs) meet every five years and establish policy. The WCC's *Division* of World Mission and Evangelism consists of the working secretariat administering CWME policy and is responsible to the CWME. This structural rebirth of the IMC as CWME has a profound theological significance. It demonstrates that world mission and mission to the world help constitute the essential life of the church.

W. RICHEY HOGG

W. Andersen: *Towards a Theology of Mission* (London 1955); W. R. Hogg: *Ecumenical Foundations* (New York 1952); K. S. Latourette: 'Ecumenical Bearings of the Missionary Movement and the IMC' in R. Rouse and S. C. Neill: *A History of the Ecumenical Movement, 1517–1948* (2nd ed., London and Philadelphia 1967); *WKL* 597–601.

INTERNATIONAL MISSIONS, INC., is

a *faith mission society founded in the USA by the Rev. Benjamin Davidson in 1930. There are now branches in Canada, England and Australia. The old Oriental Boat Mission to the junk families of south China merged with it in 1966. There is a wide variety of evangelistic work including radio in India. Fields are India, Pakistan, Iran, Japan, Kenya, Philippines, Surinam, and international students in America. The missionaries numbered 152 plus two retired in 1965, and income that year was $490,250. Publication: *Eastern Challenge.* The society is a member of *IFMA. Its headquarters: P.O. Box 323, Wayne, N.J. 07470.

R. PIERCE BEAVER

INTERNATIONAL REVIEW OF MISSION, THE, was founded in 1912 by the Continuation Committee of the Edinburgh *World Missionary Conference (1910). Under its first editor, Dr J. H. *Oldham, it at once took rank as the most valuable missionary periodical in the world. Its purpose was to convey information on all important topics, but also to serve as a forum for the discussion of all burning questions in church and state. Its annual surveys of the state of the Christian missions throughout the world (including the Roman) gave a balanced picture of Christian progress, and in certain areas regress. An international bibliography, remarkably complete, of all significant books and articles, supplemented by careful reviews of all the more important publications, make of it an indispensable instrument of research for anyone who wishes to trace any missionary theme over the last 60 years. When Belgian Roman Catholics wished to start a high-grade missionary journal, they cast their net widely, and found in the IRM their nearest model; the valuable journal *Eglise Vivante* was the result.

With the integration of the *WCC and the IMC in 1961, the IRM was faced with new problems. It has become increasingly difficult to see exactly where the line between 'missionary' and 'ecumenical' is to be drawn, especially since the idea of 'mis-sion in six continents' has become popular. In these years a tendency has become manifest for the IRM to become less full in respect of information and of research, and to find space for more discussion of ecumenical problems. Reflecting this emphasis, in 1969 the final 'S' was dropped from the original title, *The International Review of Missions.*

STEPHEN NEILL

INTERNATIONALITY OF MISSIONS. See SUPRANATIONALITY OF MISSIONS.

INTER-SEMINARY MISSIONARY ALLIANCE, THE, founded in 1880 and representing 32 seminaries, brought together 250 students in the USA to consider themes related to foreign and home missions The first national convocation was held at Rutgers University, New Brunswick, N.J. This first convention was the largest national student religious meeting held up to that time. It was also the first student missionary conference in the USA.

In three years it grew to be an organization representative of 50 schools to which were related 15 denominations.

The conventions were the forerunners of the quadrennial meetings of the future *SVM.

When the *WSCF was organized in 1895 the Alliance became the theological section of the American Intercollegiate YMCA and the Alliance as such was formally dissolved in 1898.

Throughout its life it pressed upon the churches, as well as upon seminaries and universities, a fresh consideration of the home and foreign missionary obligations of Christian groups and individuals.

EUGENE L. STOCKWELL

C. H. Hopkins: *History of the YMCA* (New York 1951); C. P. Shedd: *Two Centuries of Student Christian Movements* (New York 1934).

INTER-VARSITY FELLOWSHIP. See STUDENT FOREIGN MISSIONS FELLOWSHIP OF THE INTER-VARSITY CHRISTIAN FELLOWSHIP.

IRAN, a country in Western Asia, consisting for the most part of one vast plateau. Area: 636,000 sq.m. Estimated population in 1964: 22.4 million. The vast majority of the inhabitants are Shiah Muslims. Christians are estimated at 153,000, of whom two-thirds belong either to the Gregorian (Armenian) church, or to the ancient church of the *Assyrians. Christianity dates from the 3rd century A.D. From then on there has been an unbroken though very chequered witness in I., mainly through the *Nestorian Church which, in spite of serious but spasmodic persecution, survived the coming of *Islam (A.D. 651) and in the 8th century sent missionaries to Chinese Turkestan, India and Arabia and established branches of the church there. In I. the church over the centuries gradually declined, but even today traces of the aboriginal church remain especially in the north, in the so-called Assyrian church.

Relations between I. and the rest of Christendom were suspended somewhere in the 9th century until the time of the Mongols when a delegation of Mongolian Persians at the Council of Lyons (1274) sought the reunion of the Nestorian church with the church of Rome. In 1308 the Catholic archdiocese of Soltanieh was established. Soon after, with the Portuguese expansion in the Persian Gulf, *Franciscans, Carmelites and later *Dominicans and *Jesuits were active; the peak of their influence occurring during the reign of Shah Abbas the Great (1587–1629). It was at this time that the present day Armenian community was established in I., when Shah Abbas invited Armenian craftsmen to come and beautify his capital, Isfahan. After the Afghan invasion in 1719 all the Catholic missions were dispersed and not recommenced until the middle of the 19th century, when the Soeurs de la Charité and the Salesian Brothers began educational work in Tehran and Isfahan. Later they were joined by Dominican fathers, and Little Brothers and Sisters of Jesus run a leprosarium near Tabriz.

Protestant missionary work dates from 1811 when Henry *Martyn spent a period in Shiraz translating the Bible and conducting religious debates. In 1825 the Jewish convert Joseph *Wolff visited I. on an extended missionary journey. Permanent work started with the coming of Dwight and Smith, sent by the *ABCFM to work in Tabriz in 1830. In 1834 the American Presbyterian Church began work by sending Dr Perkins and Dr Grant to Tabriz. A year later they moved to Urumia (now Rezaieh) which had a predominantly Nestorian population. In 1872 Presbyterian work was begun in Tehran and later stations were opened in Tabriz, Resht, Hamadan and Meshed. In 1844 the LSPCJ sent the Rev. Aaron *Stern to I. where he stayed for some time. But the permanent Anglican work began with the coming of Dr Robert Bruce to Isfahan on a visit. Soon after he arrived there was a serious famine and he felt called to give up his mission work in India and stay in I., which he did at his own expense until finally the *CMS took over his work. Educational and medical work were begun and the famous Mary Bird was active for many years. In 1897 work started in Kerman, in 1898 in Yezd and in 1900 in Shiraz, all of which are still church centres. In 1886 the Archbishop of Canterbury sent a special mission of help to the Assyrian Church; the Sisters of Bethany helped in educational and women's work and the mission was not closed until the end of the first world war. In 1888 the Church Mission to Jews began work amongst the Jews of Isfahan, moving later to Tehran where their work continues under the diocese. Other societies which have worked at various times in Iran include the Lutheran Orient Mission, the Church of Scotland, the Swedish Church and the Bible Churchmen's Missionary Society.

Today the Anglican and Presbyterian churches are firmly established and largely indigenized. The diocese of Iran, founded in 1912, after three missionary bishops now has a Persian bishop from a Muslim background, and clergy with Jewish, Muslim and Zoroastrian backgrounds. Schools and hospitals are run by both churches and an important blind work in Isfahan is shared between the Anglicans and the German Christoffelblinden Mission; recently the

Dutch churches have given valuable help in this and other work. More recently missionary work has been started by Brethren, Pentecostalist and other sects; and an interdenominational *faith mission, the International Mission, has for some years been running an orphanage at Faraman and doing valuable evangelistic work by *correspondence courses. An interdenominational Christian hospital has been opened at Qorveh in Kurdestan.

H. B. DEHQANI-TAFTI
AND ROBIN WATERFIELD

B. Biggs: *The Four Gardens* (London 1959), a pamphlet on Anglican work; H. B. Dehqani-Tafti: *Design of My World*, autobiography (World Christian Books No. 28, London 1960, 'Special' London 1968); J. Elder: *History of the Presbyterian Mission in Iran* (Tehran 1960); C. Guzzetti: *Catholics of Persia*, pamphlet, (Tehran 1952); J. Labourt: *Le Christianisme dans l'Empire Perse* (Paris 1904); D. Lyko: *Gründung u. Wachstum der evangelischen Kirchen in Iran* (Leiden 1964); *BM* II, 490–95; *NCE* VII, 608–10; *WKL*, 603f.

IRAQ is a country of 169,284 sq.m., with a population of about 8,000,000 the great majority of whom are Muslims. Christian penetration of the area came very early in the Christian era, and grew stronger after the 4th century, especially through *Nestorian missions. The Nestorian church and its Catholic counterpart, the Chaldean church, remain the largest Christian communities. Roman Catholic missions have a history reaching as far back as the crusades. In recent years they have had success especially among the Nestorian or *'Assyrian' community, with corresponding growth of the Chaldean church. Two important institutions today are the Al-Hikmat University and Baghdad College for Boys, both *Jesuit projects in Baghdad.

Protestant missions in I. began in 1841 with the coming to Mosul of three missionary families under the *ABCFM. The work had to be abandoned in 1845, but it was resumed from 1850 to 1860, and again in the last decade of the century, finally closing in 1898. British *CMS missionaries were working in Baghdad from 1882 on, and in 1899 formed the Turkish Arabia Mission. Until 1914 they maintained a hospital, a boys' school and a girls' school. Soon after the war the CMS withdrew for various reasons.

Later several small missionary groups, Danish and American, made a beginning without being able to carry on long. The chief missionary work came to be the United Mission of Mesopotamia. Afterward renamed the United Mission in Iraq, it was formed in 1923, including missionaries of the Presbyterian Church in the USA and the Evangelical and Reformed Church (which became in 1961 the United Church of Christ). Later the Reformed Church of America and the Presbyterian Church in the US (southern) joined in the United Mission. Baghdad and Mosul were the chief stations. Kirkuk, Basheeqa, Dohuk, and Hillah also served as centres of residence and work. In 1962 the field of southern Iraq was transferred to the United Mission from the Arabian Mission. In 1967 all 20 missionaries were resident in only two centres, Baghdad and Basrah, their work centring primarily in the Baghdad School for Girls in Mansour and the School of High Hope for Boys in Basrah. The two schools in their long career have stood high in public respect and patronage. Both are effective influences in the national life. Government restrictions since 1958 have limited the mission work to the educational institutions, except as church work, literature, audio-visual activities, and ecumenical contracts are carried on by school personnel. The national Protestant churches in I. are six congregations, with smaller groups in scattered localities. A movement for union into a single synod or presbytery has not yet borne fruit. Co-operation between mission and church is cordial, but national feeling against western influence does not make the church eager for unification with the American mission. The churches are related to the Near East Council of Churches. Ecumenical co-operation in literature and radio matters has had encouraging support from the Orthodox (Armenian, Nestorian and Jacobite) and the Catholics as well as the Protestants. Christians in I. number about 300,000 of whom less than 2,000 are Protestant.

HARRY G. DORMAN, JR

K. S. Latourette: *A History of the Expansion of Christianity* (New York 1937–1945), Vols. VI and VII; J. W. Willoughby: *The United Mission in Iraq, 1924–1962* (New York 1962, MS); *BM* II, 484–90; *NCE* VII, 610; *WKL*, 602f.

IRIAN. See INDONESIA.

ISLAM (MUHAMMADANISM) is based upon the prophet Muhammad's claim to have experienced receipt of the Qur'ān as revelation from God. Muhammad (570–632) met initial opposition in Mecca, a centre of pagan idolatry; in 622 he emigrated to Medina where the Muslim community prospered. After his death the Muslims quickly displaced the Byzantines' hated rule over predominantly Nestorian Syria and strongly Monophysite Egypt; in Iraq and Iran the Muslims defeated the recently enfeebled Sasanian empire. Within a century the Umayyad dynasty's expansion had reached India and Spain. The 'Abbāsid caliphs were often merely religious figureheads over local independent rulers. The Muslim world resisted the abortive Crusades but succumbed to the Mongol invasions; Baghdad fell in 1256. After two and a half centuries of political fragmentation to which the mystical orders brought more cohesion than did the adventurer Tīmūr (Tamerlane), the Ottomans, who took Constantinople in 1453, the Safavids in Persia, and the Mughals in India brought back structures of Islamic law and government which survived until assailed by colonialist and modern pressures. The dissolution of the caliphate in 1924 removed a fiction of central theocracy. Recently Muslims' faith has proved increasingly confident as Islamic ideologies have supported local nationalisms and international Islamic

solidarity. (Cf. W. C. Smith: *Islam in Modern History* [London 1957].) See MUSLIM MISSIONS.

The five 'pillars' of Islam are as follows: (1) God's unity and Muhammad's prophethood are confessed; these are seen in the line of Semitic monotheism and prophecy, including the recognition of Jesus as a prophet (for a sensitive understanding of Islamic faith see K. Cragg: *The Call of the Minaret*, London and New York 1956). (2) Ritual prayer (*salāt*) is to be offered five times a day; congregational prayers and sermon are on Fridays (cf. C. Padwick: *Muslim Devotions*, London 1961). (3) The legal alms tax (*zakāt*) aims to provide social justice for all needy Muslims. (4) For one lunar month yearly (*Ramadān*) Muslims fast from dawn to sunset. (5) Once in a lifetime, if possible, Muslims should perform the pilgrimage to Mecca.

The text of the Qur'ān (best translated by A. J. Arberry: *The Koran Interpreted*, London 1955) had been settled by 651. The canonical texts of the *Hadīth* literature (traditions concerning the life of the prophet) were fixed later. Movements of scholastic theology, philosophy and mysticism (see SUFISM) within the orthodox (*Sunnī*) branch of Islam were to some extent synthesized by al-Ghazālī (d. 1111), but none displaced law as the most characteristic religious discipline of Islam. In the heterodox (*Shī'ī*) world, notably Persia, a more theosophical and individual tradition developed and included messianic tendencies.

Today the pressures of *secularism are strong, especially among young people in cities. Yet outspoken *atheism is rare. Organizations like the Muslim Brotherhood appeal to the claim that I. holds all the political, social and economic answers. I. is presented as an ideology rather than dogmatically. There is little theological questioning of basic premises, and there is often a marked defensiveness against western scholarship. Belief in God is still supported by mediaeval arguments on the rationality of I. Apart from the tensions over Israel, many Muslims are showing a rediscovered religious tolerance and a desire to stand with men of other religious traditions against *communism or materialism.

J. B. TAYLOR

NCE VII, 676–84; WKL, 603f.

ISRAEL is mentioned in the Bible for the first time in Gen.32:28, where the patriarch Jacob receives this name from God. We then find I. throughout the whole OT to signify the chosen people in such connections as the children of I., the house of I., the God of I., the land of I., the king of I., etc. From the death of Solomon (about 934 B.C.), when his kingdom was divided, the name was used only for the Northern Kingdom of the ten tribes (around Samaria), while the Southern Kingdom (around Jerusalem) of the two tribes Judah and Benjamin was called Judah. I. ceased to exist as a kingdom and as a people in the year 722 B.C., when it was captured and the Israelites were brought to Assyria and scattered over the Asian countries. There I. more or less disappeared, although some remnants have appeared in our days as immigrants (from China, India, Iraq, Iran, Kurdistan, etc.) to 'the land of the fathers', Israel, created on 14 May 1948. The two tribes in Judah were also taken captive in 586 B.C. to Babylonia, but after 50 years returned in part to Jerusalem. In the 5th century B.C. *'Judaism' was created under the leadership of Ezra and Nehemiah. From that time we speak of Judaism and *Jews, although I. still is used as a synonym to signify that the Jews, too, belong to the chosen people of God. In the NT I. is very often synonymous with the Jews, but appears mainly in connection with the ideas of Messiah and of salvation. The Christian church soon began to use I. to signify itself as the 'New Israel', the true heir of the 'Old Israel' as 'the people of God'. In the last 150 years of missionary enterprise among the Jews the name I. has often been used without any clear distinction.

I. means one who 'fights for (or with) God'. I. in the OT should be and was the witness of the One, Holy God. Jesus of Nazareth counted on the people of I. to be his witnesses to the end of the world. When the remnant of I. (the Jews) in Palestine as a whole failed, he turned to 'other folds', praying 'Father forgive them, for they know not what they do'. St. Paul made clear both the difference and the unity between the old and the new I. In common they have the promises, the law, the prophets and the holy Scriptures in the OT. But they differ in the belief in Messiah, in the way of salvation and in the kingdom of God. The old I. 'after the flesh' symbolizes through its history the way in which God deals with man, and the failure of man to be saved without acknowledging the grace of God. The fact that an I. still exists 'outside the church' is in itself a challenge to the church to activate its responsibility towards the salvation of the world because when 'the fulness of the Gentiles be come in, all Israel shall be saved'.

Since 14 May 1948 there has existed the State of *Israel in the Holy Land according to a decision by the United Nations in November 1947, where now (1970) more than two million Jews have become Israeli citizens. To the Jews and to many Christians this means a fulfilling of God's promises to his people. To others the state of Israel is just another secularized national creation.

GÖTE HEDENQUIST

G. Hedenquist, ed.: The Church and the Jewish People (London 1954); Freiburger Rundbrief (published annually in German by Caritasverband).

ISRAEL, THE STATE OF. A republic bounded by Lebanon, Syria, Jordan, the UAR and the Mediterranean Sea. Area: 8,000 sq.m. Population (1967 est.): 2,624,900.

On almost any showing the Christian situation in the modern state of Israel is unique. Here in the midst of a predominantly Jewish setting, Jesus was born, exercised his ministry, died and rose. From that time on, Christians and Jews have had to relate to each other in this land. Although throughout the centuries Christians have nearly always been in the minority, yet they have occasionally ruled the land and often achieved great political power and privilege.

The present dependent Christian role in an essentially Jewish context is an intriguing likeness to the primitive Christian situation.

The complex historical development of Christianity in the Holy Land is reflected here today. Amidst a total Jewish population (including all of Jerusalem but excluding the occupied territories of the West Bank and the Gaza Strip) of two and a half million Jews, there are a total of 72,000 Christians. The largest number of Christians are Arabs belonging to the Eastern Churches: 23,500 to the Greek Catholic and 21,000 to the Greek Orthodox. About two-thirds of the 12,000 Christians of the Roman obedience and the 3,000 Anglicans and Protestants are Arabs. There are about 400 Christians of Jewish origin in the RC community and as many in the various Anglican and Protestant churches and groups.

The Greek Orthodox Patriarchate of Jerusalem claims to be the direct successor of the first Christian church in Jerusalem, presided over by James the Apostle. This is only a historical possibility; it is equally probable that both early and later waves of Jewish Christians may well be some of the ethnic forbears of Israel's present Arab Christians.

Christianity spread speedily outside the Holy Land; yet early in the 4th century, under the impetus and patronage of Helena, mother of Constantine, pilgrimage back to the Holy Land was established as an enduring pattern that has now been intensified by modern facilities of travel and communication.

The unhappiest aspect of Christian comings to this land were the Crusades. The resentment built up from the 11th to the 13th centuries, both on the part of eastern Christians against western Christians and on the part of Muslims and Jews against Christians, still has its bad effect today.

The first RC mission dates after the Crusades with the establishment in Palestine in 1332 of the *Franciscan order, who took on the responsibility of guardians of the holy places. The renowned order of Ratisbonne, orientated particularly towards the Jews, was not established until 1875. Today there are no less than 30 RC orders and congregations. Protestant work began in the 1820s, and the first Anglican bishop in Jerusalem arrived in 1841. Today the United Christian Council in Israel comprises eighteen Anglican and Protestant churches and agencies. There are about 30 RC schools of all grades and five hospitals, and a dozen Anglican and Protestant schools plus three hospitals.

There is complete freedom of religion as guaranteed in Israel's declaration of independence. This freedom is in the context of the development of religion in the Middle East terms of community. The *Millet or Community system goes back to the decrees of Theodosius in A.D. 425, which were clarified by Sultan Abdul Mejid in A.D. 1852 and reiterated and extended by other international treaties at almost regular intervals. This means that marriage, divorce, and other aspects of personal status are the judicial province of the established religious communities. Anglicans and Protestants, on account of their late arrival, are not a legally recognized community. However, the complicated process for such recognition has now been initiated.

Mainly because of the tragic history of Christian treatment of Jews and misunderstanding of Judaism, there is an antipathy to Christians of Jewish origin. However, as relations improve and confidence increases, this prejudice can be overcome, though the essential ethnic character of Jewry cannot but take offence at any and every attempt to convert Jews. The most significant change has been in the Jewish attitude to Jesus, which in the present situation is once more evaluating him against the background of his people and land, though this must not be confused with Christian terms and insights.

The chief difficulty of Arab Christians is their ethnic involvement in the Arab-Israel deadlock. The absence of peace is bound to affect the welfare of the church. Despite the uncertainties of the political situation there is the beginning of a growth towards a genuinely multi-racial church in an ecumenical direction. It is imperative for Christians in I. to relate relevantly to the majority people and religion; this fact, and the unique links between the two religions, provide an impetus towards the development of a dialogue-relationship that involves such far-reaching questions as common origins and roots in this land and participation in the People of God.

PETER SCHNEIDER

S. Colbi: *Short History of Christianity in the Holy Land* (Tel Aviv 1966); J. Parkes: *A History of Palestine* (London 1969); P. Schneider: *Sweeter than Honey* (London 1966; paperback version, *The Dialogue of Christians and Jews*, New York 1967); H. Weiner: *The Wild Goats of Ein Gedi. A Journal of Religious Encounters in the Holy Land* (New York 1961); *Lutheran World*, X, No. 4 (Geneva 1963), XI, No. 3 (Geneva 1964); *BM* II 504–11; *NCE* VII, 712–14; *WKL*, 612f.

IVORY COAST, a republic, formerly part of French West Africa, is situated between Liberia, Ghana and Guinea and has an area of 124,550 sq.m. Its population of 4,010,000 in 1967 included 12,000 French. The prevailing religion is traditional *animism. There are about 709,000 Muslims. The first permanent RC mission was established in 1687, and a prefecture apostolic in 1895. There were by 1965 six dioceses with 402,655 Catholics. During the years 1913–1915 the IC was the scene of one of the most remarkable indigenous mass movements to Christianity anywhere in Africa. A Grebo from Liberia later known as Prophet William Wadé *Harris met with such a great response to his preaching that about 120,000 adults of the Ebrie, Avikam, Adjukru and other tribes were converted and baptized. Harris was deported by the French authorities in 1915, and for ten years his converts sought pastoral help from foreign missions before the MMS answered the appeal. Of his converts 20,000 are estimated to have joined the RC church and 35,000 the Protestant missions; but the rest were not satisfied with the help they received, and a large *Eglise Harriste* emerged as an independent body, with an estimated 70,000 adherents in 1965. There are some 40 other independent bodies in the nation including the syncretistic *Eglise Déimatiste* with 90,000 adherents (1958), making a total of about 200,000 independent adherents. There are nine Protestant denominations at work with a total community of 97,120; the largest are *Eglise Protestante Méthodiste en Côte d'Ivoire* (served by MMS) with 68,776; Evangelical Protestant Church of the Ivory Coast (CMA) with 12,000; *Mission Evangélique* (*Mission Biblique en Côte d'Ivoire*, Unevangelized Fields Mission) with 9,450; *WEC with 2,500; *Assemblées de Dieu*, Free-Will Baptists, Conservative Baptists and the Southern Baptist Convention. Government since 1965 has levied a head tax with which to build four cathedrals (Catholic, Protestant, Harrist and Muslim) in the capital, Abidjan.

DAVID B. BARRETT

F. Raynard: *Elfenbeinküste* (Bonn 1962); G. Rougerie: *La Côte d'Ivoire* (Paris 1964); *BM* II, 290–93; *NCE* VII, 788.

J

JABAVU, DAVIDSON DON TENGO (1885–1959), eldest son of John Tengo Jabavu, one of the two first Africans to pass the matriculation of the old Cape of Good Hope University. J. T. Jabavu was a famous journalist who in 1884 founded and edited the first African weekly newspaper in South Africa, *Imvo Zabantsundu* ('African Opinion'); he became a spokesman for African people and a stout fighter for their advanced education. He was co-founder, and member of the first governing council, of South African Native College (later Fort Hare University College).

DDTJ was educated at Lovedale, S. Africa, and Morija, Lesotho, completing his Junior Certificate. When he was refused admission to a white English medium school he went away to school in Colwyn Bay, N. Wales, and afterwards to London University, where he graduated BA with honours in English, 1912. He then gained a Diploma in Education at Birmingham, England, and also studied methods of education in USA.

He returned to S. Africa, and in 1915 the newly formed governing council of S. African Native College appointed him to the staff; thus he became the first university lecturer in Bantu studies in Africa. In 1942 he became professor, responsible for Bantu languages (Xhosa, Zulu, Sotho), History and Latin, but later concentrated on Bantu languages and social anthropology. A leading Methodist layman, J. had a decisive influence on the spiritual lives of many students.

As a pioneer of his people in general education he maintained the closest contact with them, utilizing weekends and holidays to instruct them in hygiene, nutrition, temperance and agriculture. From this work teachers' and farmers' associations developed. J. was for many years president of the Cape African Teachers' Association and the South African Federation of Native Teachers.

J. was author of several books and pamphlets, including *The Black Problem*; *The Segregation Fallacy*; and *Native Disabilities in South Africa*. A number appeared also in the Xhosa language. (His daughter, Noni, is author of *Drawn in Colour* and *The Ochre People*). Active in politics, J. chaired numerous conventions and conferences, became African spokesman before government and its commissions, and was untiring in the struggle against racial prejudice. A great lover of music, especially vocal music, he was an outstanding choir leader and founded Fort Hare choir. A cheerful and friendly man, rich in human qualities, he held a position of great influence among his people.

GERHARDUS C. OOSTHUIZEN

A. Kerr: *Fort Hare, 1915–1948: The Evolution of an African College* (London 1968); R. H. W. Shepherd: *Bantu Literature and Life* (Lovedale 1955).

JACKSON, SHELDON (1834–1909), Presbyterian home mission pioneer in the Rocky Mountains and Alaska, son of Samuel C. and Delia J., was born at Minaville, NY, USA. He married Mary Vorhees in 1858. Educated at Union College and Princeton Seminary, he was ordained by the presbytery of Albany in 1858. His missionary career included a Choctaw boys' school in Oklahoma, 1858–59; missionary, Minnesota, 1859–64; pastor at Rochester, Minnesota, 1864–70; superintendent of Home Missions for the entire region from Montana to Arizona, 1870–82. Against opposition but with co-operation of the women of the church, J. began in 1877 to establish missions in Alaska. In 1884 he became pastor in Sitka and superintendent of the missions. Appointed superintendent of education for the Territory in 1885, he held government and mission posts together until shortly before his death, developing a school system against intense political opposition and founding white, Indian and Eskimo missions. He introduced reindeer from Siberia to provide Eskimos with better food. J. edited the *North Star* of Sitka, 1887–97, published three books and many articles. The Presbyterian Church USA made him moderator in 1897.

R. PIERCE BEAVER

J. A. Lazell: *Alaskan Apostle, the Life Story of Sheldon Jackson* (New York 1960); Robert L. Steward: *Sheldon Jackson* (New York 1908); *DAB* IX, 555f.

JAESCHKE, HEINRICH AUGUSTUS (1817–1883), Moravian missionary to Tibet and distinguished linguist, was a descendant of George Jaeschke, one of the original Moravian refugees to settle on *Zinzendorf's estate, Herrnhut, in 1722.

J. early mastered Latin, Greek, Polish, Swedish and Hungarian and later acquired a working knowledge of Arabic, Sanskrit and Persian. He spent his first year as a missionary living with a simple Tibetan family at Stok in Ladak and then settled at Kyelang where he laid the foundations of his unrivalled knowledge of the Tibetan language.

After eleven years in Tibet J. returned in 1868 to his native Germany, owing to ill-health, and worked at Herrnhut on his Tibetan-English dictionary and his Tibetan-German dictionary, published in 1871. He was already the author of a *Short Practical Grammar of the Tibetan Language with reference to the Spoken Dialects* published at Kyelang in 1865, and an elaborate treatise on the phonetic laws of the Tibetan language, submitted to the Berlin Academy in 1866 and published in 1867. He also translated into Tibetan the NT except for the Epistle to the Hebrews and many hymns and other Christian writings.

J. laid the foundations on which all his successors have built and is regarded as the most distinguished linguist in the history of the Moravian church.

HENRY LEFEVER

J. E. Hutton: *History of Moravian Missions* (London 1922); C. R. Markham: *Mission and Journeys of Bogle and Manning* (London 1876); A. C. Thompson: *Moravian Missions* (London 1883); *Third Jublilee of Moravian Missions, Brief Historical Sketch* (London 1882); *Allgemeine Missionszeitschrift* (1884), pp.21–29.

JAINISM is an ancient religion of India. Mahavira (c. 600 B.C.), though not its founder, gave J. its organized form. The sacred texts of J, consist of the twelve Angas and other Sutra literature. A Jain believes that by following the requisites of right faith, knowledge and conduct he can realize the highest perfection of his original pure nature free from any bondages of life or death. Mahavira expresses this ideal of self-realization in the classic phrase: 'Man! thou art thine own friend; why wishest thou for a friend beyond thyself?' (*Akaranga Sutra*, I, 3, 4, *Sacred Books of the East*, Vol. XXII, p.33). The basic principle which guides the Jain on his path is *ahimsa* (non-violence). Non-violence embraces a wide spectrum of practices and attitudes, from vegetarianism (free from the stain of animal murder) and the building of rest houses for old and diseased animals, to outspoken criticism of international nuclear armament. J. is a non-proselytizing, non-competitive religion and asserts universal tolerance of all religions. Its followers number only 1,600,000. Christian influence upon J. is reflected in the Young Men's Jain Association, and western interest in J. is evidenced by the Jain Sacred Text Society.

JAMES W. BOYD

S. Dasgupta: *History of Indian Philosophy*, Vol. I (Cambridge 1922), pp.169ff.; M. Stevenson: *The Heart of Jainism* (Oxford 1915); *Jaina Sutras* in F. M. Müller, ed.: *Sacred Books of the East* (Oxford 1879–1910), Vol. XXII; *ERE* VI, 465–74; *NCE* VII, 801f.; *WKL*, 626f.

JAMAICA. See CARIBBEAN.

JANES, LEROY LANSING (1837–1909), was born in Ohio, USA. With a background of education and teaching at West Point, and the rank of captain, J. was confronted with an unusual opportunity at Kumamoto,

Japan, in 1871, immediately following the Imperial Restoration. The local Clan had not fared too well in the period of the revolution which overthrew the Shogunate and opened Japan to western influence. Thus the *Daimyo* (feudal lord) decided to start a new school to train promising young *samurai* in western learning, and asked *Verbeck to secure for him a teacher of military background; and J. who was an able teacher and earnest Christian was recommended. Upon J's arrival at Kumamoto in 1872, the Japanese faculty incensed at this selection resigned, thus giving him freedom to do as he pleased. For three years J. followed Arnold's Rugby school system and concentrated on practical matters. Then he emphasized the importance of Christianity as the basis of western culture and started a voluntary Bible class in his home; with the result that 35 students were converted and signed a 'Declaration of faith', which precipitated severe persecution. As a consequence, the school was closed in 1876 and J. entrusted the students to *Niijima at Doshisha. The first graduates in theology were of this Kumamoto Band and they became the most influential leaders of the Congregational church and of liberal Protestantism. J. later accepted the liberal trends in western thinking and in connection with a lecture visit to Doshisha University persuaded some of his former students to do likewise.

GORDON K. CHAPMAN

C. Iglehart: *A Century of Protestant Christianity* (Tokyo 1959), pp.50ff.; H. Kishimoto: *Japanese Religion in the Meiji Era* (Tokyo 1956), pp.206–09, 266ff.; M. Kōsaku: *Japanese Thought in the Meiji Era* (Tokyo 1958), pp.171–76.

JAPAN, or NIPPON. (1) *Geography.* J consists of a long chain of islands off the east coast of Asia, divided from the mainland of China, Korea and Siberia by the Japan Sea and washed by the Pacific Ocean on the eastern side. There are four main islands, Honshū ('Japan proper'), Hokkaidō ('the way of the northern sea'), Kyūshū ('the nine districts') and Shikoku ('the four

kingdoms')—with a total area of about 142,000 sq.m. and a population of about 100,000,000. Although sub-tropical in latitude, J's climate is affected by the cold current flowing down the east coast of Asia, and the half of J. which faces the land mass of Asia has severe winter weather. There are a number of active and dormant volcanoes, so that in most parts there are numerous hot spring resorts, and earthquakes are frequent, some of great severity. Despite a long coastline of 17,000 miles (much of it extremely beautiful), there are only a limited number of bays which permit modern, large-scale navigation. The country is very mountainous, and 70% of the land is wooded. As only 15% of the land is arable, a large proportion of the population is to be found in the areas around the large cities, of which seven have a population of more than one million—including Tokyo (nearly 11,000,000 and so the largest city in the world). Apart from these, more than 80 cities have a population of more than 100,000. There has been a great shift into urban centres since the war, and more than 70% of the population is reckoned to be urban—a striking difference from 1945, when 70% of the population was still reckoned to be largely rural.

Immediately after the war the population rose steeply, but the widespread use of abortion and birth control means that J. now has one of the lowest birth-rates in the world, and the increase in the population is scarcely one million a year. It is estimated that, if the present trend continues, the population would begin to drop after reaching its peak in 1990. With such a large population for so limited an area, J. depends largely on intensive agriculture and rice growing for her needs. Fish was at one time the chief protein, and J. still has one of the largest fishing fleets in the world, but meat consumption has increased considerably in the post-war period, and in 1966 was four times what it had been in 1955. There has also been some experimentation in crop production and dairy farming in the mountainous areas far above the rice-yielding areas, in which the Kiyosato educational experimental project, sponsored by the Anglican church, has played an important part.

(2) *Industries and Economy.* Since the Meiji era (beginning A.D. 1868) J. has been an industrialized nation, but the advance since the devastation of the war (1941–45) has been phenomenal. There has been an annual economic development of almost 12% since 1952. Before the war J. was already noted for her textile industries, but the more recent development has been in the area of heavy machinery and optical and electronic equipment. Mining and manufacturing production has more than doubled since 1960. J. now has the world's third largest merchant fleet, builds more than half the world's shipping each year, and has now taken the third place in the production of motor vehicles. Almost 90% of the homes have television sets, and in 1967 1¼ million colour TV sets were produced, of which a third were for export. With a largely affluent society, where 87% of the population regard themselves as middle-class (and 49% as being 'middle of the middle class'), J's position is unique in Asia. Whilst most Asian countries are 'developing' and have not yet reached economic and industrial maturity, J. is one of the 'helping' nations and is an active member of the Colombo Pact for the development of under-developed countries in South East Asia. Through the United Nations, J. also gives financial and technical aid to countries in Africa, Europe and South America. With growing prosperity has come wider concern for social security and the development of public health services, although there is much of a voluntary or haphazard nature. Labour organizations flourish, and there are 55,321 trade unions with 10,566,000 members.

(3) *History.* J's written history begins with the early 8th century A.D., when the country was consciously emphasizing its national heritage after the wide spread of Chinese culture from the 6th century A.D. According to the early writings, it is claimed that the Japanese imperial line had begun in 660 B.C. and continued without a break to the time of writing. (The pre-war and wartime nationalistic régime spoke of 2,600 years of unbroken rule.) Modern historians, however, would speak of successions of invaders both from Malayan and Altaic (i.e. Siberian) stock, and would reckon that the present imperial family is descended from the leaders of the Yamoto class which came into prominence nearly 2,000 years ago, but which only achieved national unity as late as A.D. 700. The Ainu (in Hokkaido) are the sole relic of pre-Japanese stock, and (apart from dialect differences) present-day Japanese share a common language and a common culture.

From the 5th century A.D. there has been almost continuous contact with China and Korea, but, apart from a threatened Mongol invasion in the 13th century, J. had no fear of losing her independence.

In early times the country was divided into small clan units, but Chinese influence led to the establishment of large estates. In each of these the people belonged to distinct social levels, and members of the imperial or other noble families, moving out from the capital (at Kyoto from A.D. 798), established local centres of authority. Gradually the rural military aristocracy, enjoying a large measure of local, feudal autonomy, asserted their dominance. It would be true to say that feudalism in J. continued until the 'restoration' of imperial power in 1868, when J. entered into relations with the outside world after Commodore Perry's black ships from the US navy had sailed into Shimoda in 1853. Under the Tokugawa Shogunate (from 1600) there had been strong central control, centred in Edo (later called Tokyo). It was with Meiji's reign (from 1868) that Tokyo became the capital city.

Having entered the modern world after 250 years of isolation, J. embarked upon a programme of intensive industrialization, and the demand for markets as well as reasons of self-protection led to the occupation of Taiwan (formerly called Formosa) and Korea, as well as the Russo-Japanese war of 1904–05, when J. gained her first foothold in Manchuria. The Anglo-Japanese Naval Treaty led to J's entry into the first world war on the allied side, but, after the war, renewed isolationist and nationalist policies led to the occupation of Manchuria in 1931–32, the China 'incident' of 1937 (which led to eight years of bitter war) and the Pacific war (1941–45). The post-war occupation had as its main aims the limitation of J. to her main islands and the 'democratization' of its life, to which the 1947 constitution bears witness. Since 1952 the country has been independent and has won a position of economic and political strength.

(4) *Culture and Education.* Japanese culture reflects the movements of her history. The principle has been one of absorption, and alien patterns have been successively Japanized. The impact of religion, too, has been very great, and art, sculpture, architecture and literature all reflect the influence either of *Shinto naturalism and simplicity or of the Buddhist sense of the absolute. During the past century the impact of the west has been strongly felt, and many visitors to J. comment first of all not on its oriental aspects, but on its apparent acceptance of the western mode of life. It is probably more correct to say simply that J. has become fully industrialized, for there is much in the west that has not been fully absorbed, although western music is now more popular than traditional modes and western dress has largely replaced the kimono apart from formal or leisure occasions.

J. claims to be more than 98% literate, although universal education only dates from the Imperial Rescript on Education in 1890, which made six years of primary education compulsory. University education had begun in the 1870s with the impact of the west, but the years since 1945 have seen a rapid increase in facilities for higher education. Earlier education patterns—with six years of primary education, followed by five years of middle (or normal) school, three years of high school, and three years at the university—had largely followed German and French patterns, but the post-war pattern was influenced from America. Six years of primary education and three

years in middle school form the compulsory section, but in the cities more than two-thirds pass on to high school (three years), whilst 16% attend university (four years). Most of the pre-war high schools have been up-graded to university status, and J's enrolment in the universities is the third highest in the world. In 1966–67 the enrolment in universities and junior colleges was more than 921,000, whilst 4½ million were enrolled in high schools (almost three times the figure in 1950–51!). An interesting feature is the group of 200,000 *rōnin* (a name once given to dispossessed *samurai*) or students seeking entrance to a university. The multiplication of universities, many of which are private, means tremendous competition to enter those of greater reputation and the *rōnin* may wait two or three years to pass the examination for the university of his choice.

(5) *Religions.* Some would say that J. has three religions—Shinto, *Buddhism and Christianity, but others, seeing an abundant crop of sects in all three, many of which claim to be 'religions', would speak of J's hundreds of religions. Shinto (the Way of the Kami gods) claims to be the indigenous faith, and is served by tens of thousands of shrines which are dedicated to one or other of the 'Eight Million Kami'. Many of the Kami were originally clan divinities, and the imperial shrine at Ise which enshrines the Sun goddess (the supposed ancestress of the imperial family) is the chief shrine, and had special significance when State Shinto (a nationalist form of the religion) was enforced from 1890 till 1945. By 1941 thirteen Shinto sects (newer groups founded from the middle of the 19th century onwards) were established, but the post-war toleration has led to many new groups that reflect largely Shinto ideas.

Buddhism entered J. from Korea and China in A.D. 539, and by *accommodation to older Shinto ideas and practices, gradually gained acceptance. From the 9th century there was a fusion of Shinto and Buddhism, which formed the popular faith, although a resurgence of Buddhism in the 13th century and the establishment of new sects won over the majority of the population, so that J. became basically a Buddhist country. The ruling class, however, was strongly influenced by Confucianist patterns of behaviour and the feudal ideal (Bushido) was largely Confucianist in its inspiration. At the popular level Taoist superstition (from China) had mingled with older Shinto mysteries, so that the particular religious strands could not be disentangled.

The Imperial Restitution in 1868 encouraged those who were concerned for a Pure Shinto (uninfluenced by Buddhist ideas), but 'Pure Shinto' could not free itself from Confucianist hierarchic ethics and Buddhistic philosophizing.

In the post-war period there have been so many new movements that it has been called 'The Rush Hour of the Gods'! Most are *syncretistic, and many seek to incorporate Christian notions and values into an older Shinto-Buddhistic heritage.

(6) *Missions and the Christian Church.* J's first contact with Christianity (if one discounts the possibility of Nestorian influence in the 9th century) was in 1549, when Francis *Xavier, the great *Jesuit missionary, arrived. At first Christianity was understood to be a new Buddhist sect, but the clash with the older faith soon occurred. Feudal rivalries favoured the growth of the church, and, although missionaries were few, within 30 years Christians totalled 130,000, and in 1614, when the anti-Christian laws (which expelled missionaries and forbade the practice of Christianity on pain of death) were passed, Christians numbered as many as 300,000 (more than 1% of the population). At first this legislation was not enforced, but, as Christianity became identified with sedition or foreign alliance, it was more strictly adhered to, and thousands died for their faith. The culmination of this first missionary era came with the Shimabun rebellion in 1637, when the rebel forces were largely Christian. After holding out till the following year, over 30,000 were massacred. The country was closed to the foreigner, and yet, despite persistent persecution and strict legislation (which continued till 1873),

there was a continuing Christian 'underground' movement.

Protestant missionary work began in 1859 with the arrival of American Episcopalian and Reformed Church missionaries, but 250 years of anti-Christian propaganda meant that the first fourteen years of combined Protestant missionary activity produced no more than twelve baptisms. Roman Catholics re-started work in 1863, and the missionaries were joined by a number of the 'underground' movement, which laid the basis of a strong RC church in the Nagasaki area.

The year 1873 marked not only the beginnings of a new freedom for Christian evangelism, but also J's new pattern of society, when the desire for western science and culture enabled the Protestant missionaries to lay the foundations of educational institutions which have now grown to enormous proportions. The following fifteen years was an era of rapid advance—with vigorous groups in Kumamoto and Kyoto (Congregational), Yokohama (Reformed) and Sapporo where *Uchimura, the founder of the *'Non-Church' movement, was a leading figure. Gradually, however, there was a hardening of denominational boundaries, although mission *comity continued in the first decades of the 20th century.

Reaction against the new faith came with the new constitution of 1889 and the Imperial Rescript on Education of 1890, which applied Confucian ethics to the national structure, of which the emperor was the figure-head. Although Christianity was reckoned as *a third* religion in J., and educational and social institutions flourished, it was a tolerated faith and was not able to exercise a prophetic ministry towards the nation. Christians like *Kagawa, however, won universal respect.

The war was a time of constraint, as many of the missionaries were interned and links with former sending-churches were broken. In 1942 the government had tried to control religious bodies by enforcing unions, and the United Church of Christ came into being. It was, however, largely a federation, and many bodies (including

Lutherans, Baptists, Anglicans and the Salvation Army) seceded after the war. It is still, however, the largest Protestant church with nearly 200,000 members. The RCs have more than trebled their membership in the post-war period, increasing from 97,000 to 340,000. They have intensified their work in the big cities and have entered more vigorously educational, social and cultural spheres, where formerly only Protestant Christianity was strong. Although Christians number less than 1% of the population, they exercise an influence far beyond their numerical strength. The first prime minister after the war, Katsuyama, was a Christian; more than 3% of the seats in the Diet are held by Christians, and social legislation has been furthered by Christian agitation.

In 1947 the *National Christian Council was formed, replacing the old mission-centred organization, and this now is being transformed into a Council of Churches. Since 1961 there has been close ecumenical interchange between Catholics and Protestants. The Japanese churches have also begun to use their leadership potential in overseas evangelistic projects, directed not only (as was once the case) towards expatriate Japanese.

RAYMOND J. HAMMER

T. Aikawa: *The Mind of Japan* (Valley Forge, Pa. 1967); R. Drummond: *A History of Christianity in Japan* (Grand Rapids 1970); C. H. Germany, ed.: *The Response of the Church in Changing Japan* (New York 1967); R. J. Hammer: *Japan's Religious Ferment* (London 1961); J. L. Van Hecken and J. Van Hoydonck: *The Catholic Church in Japan since 1859* (Tokyo 1963); R. Lee: *Stranger in the Land* (London 1967); J. J. Spae: *Christian Corridors to Japan* (2nd ed., Tokyo 1965); *BM* II, 531–40; *NCE* VII, 828–35; *WKL*, 620–23.

JAPAN INTERNATIONAL CHRISTIAN UNIVERSITY FOUNDATION. An inter-denominational agency established in New York State in 1949 'to aid in the founding and development of an institution of higher learning known as the International Christian University in Japan'. Its constitution states further that 'the purpose for which this Foundation is formed is for the advancement of the Japanese people through democratic education on Christian principles'.

Through the assistance of the Foundation, ICU opened its Tokyo campus in 1953 with an all-Christian faculty (full-time, permanent) and Board of Trustees. Since then, the Foundation has carried on its intended advisory and supporting relationship. It assists ICU in securing a modicum of competent teachers from other countries, in strengthening its spiritual and moral emphasis, in obtaining funds for its development, and in maintaining its excellent academic standards.

Whereas in Japan the university is a member of the Education Association of Christian Schools, and the *National Christian Council and United Church of Christ are represented on its board, in New York the Foundation relates to many inter-denominational and denominational mission boards and agencies which helped to give it birth and which continue financial and other assistance.

Represented on the Foundation's Board of Directors are members designated by the following agencies: American Baptist Convention; the Council of Community Churches; Christian Churches; the Episcopal Church; National Baptist Convention USA, Inc.; Presbyterian Church in the US; Reformed Church in America; Religious Society of Friends; United Church of Canada; United Church of Christ; the United Methodist Church; the United Presbyterian Church in the USA, and the National Council of the Churches of Christ in the USA.

The Foundation offices are in Room 1220 The Interchurch Center, 475 Riverside Drive, New York, N.Y. 10027, USA.

THOBURN T. BRUMBAUGH

C. W. Iglehart: *International Christian University: An Adventure in Christian Higher Education in Japan* (Tokyo 1964).

JAVA. See INDONESIA.

JEHOVAH'S WITNESSES. Although the JW in their early years rejected statistical reporting and the critical comparative method, their publications now use footnotes from other than biblical sources and their *Yearbook* now gives overt information on the expansion of the movement. In 1966 there were reported 1,118,665 members in 199 countries. All are counted as 'ministers of the gospel', and the local societies consider themselves a restitution of primitive Christianity. Adventists, they look for the coming triumph of the kingdom of Jehovah under Jesus Christ which will replace all earthly governments. They refuse to fight for any existing nation, and have been savagely persecuted in Germany's Third Reich, the Communist states, and in some of the new nations of Africa.

All JW are counted as preachers, missionaries and colporteurs, and many distribute literature or do evangelism from house to house during hours not on the job or during vacations and off seasons. Since their founding by Charles Taze Russell (1852–1916) and their re-organization by J. F. Rutherford (1869–1942), they have grown rapidly. Two world wars have given credibility to their proclamation that the last events are taking place (beginning with a secret return of Christ in 1914), that Armageddon is at hand and that 'millions now living will never die'. The rise of Communism and Nazism, under which JW have suffered greatly, and the recurring news of international conflict strengthen their conviction that the faithful remnant is being gathered in and prepared for the thousand years of the millennial age.

In 1921 a theocratic dictatorship was established as church order, and since 1922 all members have been enrolled for field service (evangelization, home and foreign). The JW message is bitterly anti-Roman Catholic, and this—as well as the refusal to identify with patriotic slogans and acts (such as saluting the flag, from which US courts now exempt them)—has frequently led to popular outcry and occasional violence against them in Canada and the USA. All existing churches are rejected as false: only the JW represent primitive Christianity. A vast publication work in many languages is carried on at the Brooklyn headquarters where those in residence follow a communal way of life modelled on the church at Jerusalem (Acts 4:32). Marriage is discouraged for the end is coming soon. Pressing close behind the imminent blood bath and time of trial is the glorious kingdom of Christ, to whose sovereignty all men must be called at once.

FRANKLIN H. LITTELL

K. Hutten: *Seher, Grübler/Enthusiasten* (6th ed., Stuttgart 1958), pp.82ff.; *NCE* VII, 864f.

JELLESMA, JELLE EELTJES (1816–1858), the 'apostle of Java', from Hintzum, Friesland, Holland, passed through East Java in 1848, saw an open door for Christ and immediately pleaded with the Netherlands Missionary Society for permission to remain. For fear of disturbances, the Muslim island of Java had been closed to missions by the Dutch colonial government, but through the witness of the German pietist, J. *Emde, a first Javanese Christian congregation had grown in Wijung, while another group had come into being through the teaching of a Russo-Javanese layman in Ngoro, C. L. Coolen. In Wijung baptized Javanese had become imitation westerners, while in Ngoro unbaptized Javanese Christians were immersed to the point of *syncretism in the local culture. J. brought the two together and laid the basis of an *indigenous church. He settled in 1851 in the village of Modjowarno, created by Christians from Ngoro who, against Coolen's advice, had received baptism. There he collaborated with the Javanese spiritual leader, Paulus Tosari, in the building up of a mature Christian congregation. J. also made wider missionary plans for Java, travelled extensively and trained and sent out Javanese evangelists. He was not spared the hardships of pioneer missionaries: a serious setback because of a case of church *discipline in Modjowarno, the loss of three children and an early death.

HANS-RUEDI WEBER

H. Kraemer: *From Missionfield to Independent Church* (The Hague 1958), pp.74–80; C. W. Nortier: *Van Zendingsarbeid tot zelfstandige Kerk in Oost-Java* (Hoenderloo 1939), pp.40–54.

JERUSALEM 1928. See CONFERENCES, WORLD MISSIONARY.

JESSUP, HENRY HARRIS (1823–1910), is one of the outstanding figures of Protestant missionary history in the Near East in the 19th century. A missionary of the *ABCFM and later of the Board of Foreign Missions of the Presbyterian Church in the USA, he lived and worked for more than half a century in Syria and Lebanon. He was born in Montrose, Pennsylvania, where his father was a lawyer. After being ordained in 1855, he sailed from Boston for Syria that same year, arriving in Beirut in February 1856. He worked in various mission stations, in Tripoli, in Abeih, and later in Beirut, as evangelist, writer and teacher of theology. To his efforts both in Syria and in America must be attributed a large part of the growth of interest in the mission of the church to the Near East during the latter half of the century. As speaker, church statesman and public figure, he was well known outside church circles. In 1882 he declined an unexpectedly announced appointment by President Arthur as the first minister of the United States to Persia. His two volumes entitled *Fifty-three Years in Syria* are not merely a biography, but a history of the Syria Mission from the time of its inception until 1910, the year of J's death. The drama, humour and vigour of the writing make this a significant contribution to the knowledge of church history as seen against the background of Near Eastern social and political life in the 19th century.

HARRY G. DORMAN, JR

H. H. Jessup: *Fifty-three Years in Syria* (New York 1910); *DAB* X, 61.

JESUITS. A popular title for members of the Society of Jesus, a religious order

founded in Paris in 1534 by Ignatius Loyola, a Basque and ex-captain in the Spanish army. Ignatius after being wounded in battle had come to the University of Paris to study. He gathered a few men for apostolic work and called the group the Company of Jesus. After their approval by Pope Paul III in 1540, the society dedicated themselves to the service of the papacy. The growth of the society was rapid and its work expanded broadly. Almost from the beginning, the Js engaged in foreign mission work and their progressive methods are models to this day. Those early missioners included such famous figures as Francis *Xavier, Apostle of the Indies; Robert de *Nobili, the Christian Brahmin; the Jesuit martyrs of North America; the Jesuits who smuggled themselves into England to care for Catholics there; Matteo *Ricci, who opened the door to China; the founders of the Reduction of Paraguay; Eusebius Kino, builder of missions in Mexico and the American Southwest. The society has developed many of the RC church's leading scientists and theologians. The society has always met with extraordinary opposition from powerful individuals and groups both within and without the RC church. One of the main reasons is that in seeking the broad interests of the church they often come into conflict with particularized interests. In 1964 there were 6,993 Jesuit overseas missionaries, of whom 4,937 were at work in Asia and 1,338 in Africa.

ALBERT J. NEVINS, MM

J. Brodrick: *The Origins of the Jesuits* (New York 1940), *The Progress of the Jesuits* (New York 1947); M. Harney: *The Jesuits in History* (New York 1941). For full bibliography see M. J. Heimbucher: *Die Ordnen und Kongregationen der katholischen Kirche* (3rd ed., Paderborn 1933, 1934), Vol. II; *NCE* VII, 898–909.

JESUS CHRIST is repeatedly spoken of in the 4th Gospel as the one sent by God. The Christian mission has its origin in the sending of the Son by the Father, and is the continuation of this sending (Jn.20:21). He is also the substance of the missionary

11*

message; the missionary is sent to 'preach Christ'. This place of Jesus in Christianity is not paralleled in any other religious system. Moses, Buddha, Muhammed are prophets and teachers. The names invoked in some forms of Hindu worship (Rāma, Krishna) have no crucial place in the system. The Christian message is not merely a message taught by Jesus, but a message of which Jesus is the central substance. In a remarkable degree Jesus is honoured and even worshipped by millions who have no visible connection with the Christian church.

The double name Jesus Christ indicates a distinction which has sometimes been expressed as 'The Jesus of history' and 'The Christ of faith'. The name Jesus, his own proper name, draws attention to the fact that he was a man living in Palestine during the reign of Herod; the title Christ or anointed one, indicates that he is honoured as much more than a figure of history—in fact as eternal Lord. In the tension between these two the whole truth of the Christian faith is involved.

The facts about Jesus are a matter of historical record. With the rise of critical historical study in Europe, the records were subjected to a scrutiny which acknowledged no right of believers to limit it. The effort was made to get 'behind' the traditional believers' picture of Jesus and to discover, by critical research, the real 'Jesus of history'. A stream of 'Lives of Jesus' poured from the presses. The famous work of A. *Schweitzer, *The Quest of the Historical Jesus* critically reviewed this vast effort, concluded that a 'Life of Jesus' could not be thus constructed, and spoke of him as one 'who comes to us as one unknown, without a name . . .' Schweitzer's own reconstruction in terms of 'thoroughgoing eschatology' was in turn criticized, but it had become clear that the only record we have is a record made by those who believed in Jesus as Lord, the primitive Christian church.

Interest shifted to the study of the way in which this primitive community might be thought to have shaped the traditions of the words and deeds of Jesus before they were committed to writing. The 'Form-Criticism'

school was able to show that much of what stands written in the record reflects the experience and faith of the primitive church. This movement went so far (in the work of R. Bultmann for example) as to suggest that almost nothing can be known about Jesus as a historical figure of the past. What is available to us, it was argued, is not material for any historical portrait, but the proclamation of the gospel. 'It is not the historic Christ who is Lord, but Jesus Christ as he is encountered in the proclamation' (*Glauben und Verstehen*, i [2nd ed. 1954] p.208, quoted in S. C. Neill: *The Interpretation of the New Testament*, p.271). In this reconstruction the name of Jesus becomes little more than the symbol for a personal experience interpreted in terms of existentialist philosophy. As could be expected, a reaction has set in and the attempt to state what can be stated with certainty about Jesus as a historical figure is now being undertaken afresh by German scholars deeply influenced by the 'Form-Critical' movement.

We must expect this kind of oscillation between emphasis upon the 'Jesus of history' and upon the 'Christ of faith' to continue. It arises from the tension already spoken of. It is the Christian faith that this man whose name is Jesus is also Lord of all, Alpha and Omega. There is, therefore, a provisional tension between the claims of historical research and the claim of faith. This tension may not be cut by (for example) allowing the word 'Christ' to be severed from the name Jesus, and given a sort of independent existence uncontrolled by the historic facts (cf. the 'Unbound Christ' of Hocking: *The Coming World Civilization*). The bearing of this tension is part of the working out of Christ's mission, for it will only be resolved when it is seen that Jesus is indeed the clue to cosmic history, and that therefore the most rigorous historical research and criticism leads to a deepening and enlargement of the Christian faith concerning him. Towards this resolution there is therefore needed, not only the scientific work of scholars on the NT records, but also the boldness of the church as a whole in seeking to interpret and act in contemporary history in the light of the revelation of God in Jesus Christ.

LESSLIE NEWBIGIN

X. Léon-Dufour: *The Gospel and the Jesus of History* (Eng. tr., London 1965); N. Perrin: *Rediscovering the Teaching of Jesus* (London 1967); H. Zahner: *The Historical Jesus* (London 1963).

JESUS, SOCIETY OF. See JESUITS.

JEWS, MISSIONS TO THE. (1) *History*. The first Christian mission goes out to 'the lost sheep of the house of Israel', but the *'great commission' of the risen Christ also includes the Gentiles. Through the medieval church, however, there is a long parenthesis as to the mission to the Jews (see ANTISEMITISM). The Reformation to some extent changed this attitude, especially through the declaration of Martin Luther in his book *Dass Jesus ein geborener Jude gewesen* ('That Jesus was born a Jew'), 1523. But only the *Pietism of the 18th century started organized missions to the Jews by Francke, Spener, *Zinzendorf, Stephan Schultz, and others. Francke founded an *Institutum Judaicum* in Halle, 1728, and Stephan Schultz, leader of the same Institute, travelled during 14 years all over Europe, to Palestine and Egypt to create interest in Jewish mission. The first organized mission to the Jews on the continent of Europe was the Berlin *Israelmission*, 1822, the most famous participant in which was Prof. H. L. Strack (d. 1922), who started an *Institutum Judaicum* in Berlin 1883. During the 19th century several organizations for mission to Jews appeared in Germany, and in 1869 Prof. Franz Delitzsch gathered them all into the *Evangel. Luth. Zentralverein für Mission unter Israel* with headquarters in Leipzig, where he also in the following year created the *Institutum Judaicum Delitzschianum* (now in Münster, Westphalia). He became the leading Christian in Jewish-Christian relations until our days, equally respected by Jews as by Christians. His life work for the Jews cul-minated in the translation of the NT into Hebrew, 1877, on which he laboured for 51 years. This is the best available translation and is still in use.

(2) *Present situation*. Outside Germany organized missions to Jews first started in England, 1809, with the interdenominational LSPCJ, which afterwards became an Anglican society and continues today under the name of the Church's Ministry among the Jews (CMJ), with workers in England, Morocco, Tunisia, Egypt, Israel and Iran. Another organization is the International Society for the Evangelization of the Jews, with mainly Baptist background, 1842, now working in England, Israel, South Africa, South America and Australia. In Holland, Scotland and Switzerland there are mission societies, connected with the churches of those countries, as well as in Norway (since 1844), Sweden (1875) and Denmark (1885). The Norwegian *Israelsmission* has mission work in Israel, the Swedish *Israelsmission* in Casablanca, Marseille, Paris, Vienna, and a Theological Institute for studies and dialogue in Jerusalem, Israel. The Danish *Israelsmission* has a representative in Nice, France, and one in Jaffa, Israel. Today most Jews are living in the USA and Canada (almost six million). Several churches have mission work among the Jews and a number are represented in the American Committee on the Christian Approach to the Jews of the *NCC. Some mission societies are independent, the largest being the American Board of Missions to the Jews, of mainly Baptist background.

(3) *World Church and Jewish Missions*. The RC church has had no organized mission to Jews during recent centuries, but individual Catholics have taken an interest in them and borne a faithful witness. The Second *Vatican Council (1962–65) made considerable progress in bringing the church's official attitude to the Jews up to date. The *Freiburger Rundbrief*, an annual RC publication, is an excellent source of information on the Christian-Jewish encounter.

Since 1932 most Protestant work among the Jews has been co-ordinated in the

IMC's Committee on the Christian Approach to the Jews, from 1961 integrated in the WCC as its Committee on the Church and the Jewish People. Thanks to the efforts of that committee the *WCC Assembly in *Amsterdam 1948 received a report on the Church and the Jews, and recommended to its member churches to consider their attitude towards Jews along lines of *dialogue, Christian love and responsibility, and to emphasize studies of Judaism in order to find out what we have in common and where we differ. For such studies several 'Jewish Institutes' have been rebuilt in Germany after the second world war, the largest being *Institutum Judaicum Delitschzianum*, now in Münster, Westphalia. For the same purpose the Swedish Theological Institute in Jerusalem, Israel, was created in 1951. International study courses have been arranged by the WCC committee every second year (1966 in Sweden). Periodicals are produced by several churches and mission societies in America, England, Scotland, Holland, the Scandinavian countries and others, as *Judaica* (Zürich), *VAV* (*Mission Suédoise*, Paris), *Christusbote* (Swedish Mission, Vienna), *Friede über Israel* (Münster), *Messiasbote* (Berlin) and *ASTI* (Swedish Theological Institute in Jerusalem).

GÖTE HEDENQUIST

R. de Corneille: *Christians and Jews* (New York 1966); J. F. A. de la Roi: *Die evangelische Christenheit und die Juden* (3 vols., Berlin 1884–92); W. T. Gidney: *History of the LSPCJ* (London 1908); G. Hedenquist: *The Church and the Jews* (London 1961); A. Thompson: *A Century of Jewish Missions* (London 1902); *WKL*, 630f.

JOHN, GRIFFITH (1831–1912), pioneer Protestant missionary to Central China. Born at Swansea, Wales, he trained for the Congregational ministry at Brecon College, was ordained 1855, and sailed in the same year for China under *LMS. At this date there were few settled 'mission stations' in China, and J. spent many years in exploratory journeys, often at great personal hazard. His was the first Protestant missionary undertaking in the Szechuan Province, and he was amongst the first westerners in modern times to visit the cities of Hupeh and Hunan and to travel through the Yangtze gorges. His unfulfilled ambitions included plans for missionary pioneering in Korea and Japan. J. brought a Welshman's native gift of oratory to preaching in Chinese and was most at home in the public proclamation and discussion of the gospel. Crowds attended his preaching, whether in the open air or in the city preaching halls which became a feature of the period. An explorer by nature and in constant travel (one inland journey covered 3,000 miles), his name became chiefly identified with Hankow where he initiated settled work in 1861 and where for many years after his death a flourishing high school continued to be known as Griffith John College. His mastery of Chinese found expression not only in powerful vernacular preaching but in much literary work. He became Chairman of the Central China Tract Society and produced single-handed a Mandarin version of the NT and a translation of the Psalms, Proverbs and the NT in Wen-li. Between 1855 and his death soon after retiring to England in 1912 he paid but few visits to Britain ('To leave China is to leave home', he said) but continued to be held in honoured remembrance by the churches in Britain. In 1888 he was elected Chairman of the Congregational Union of England and Wales but declined to serve because of more pressing needs in China. In 1889 he was awarded an honorary DD by the University of Edinburgh.

NORMAN GOODALL

G. John: *Sowing and Reaping* (London 1897) *A Voice from China* (London 1907); R. W. Thompson: *Griffith John; The Story of Fifty Years in China* (London 1908).

JOINT ACTION FOR MISSION is a method designed to secure the fullest possible united action by all churches and mission agencies in the whole of their work in a specified area. The aim is to engage all available resources for a total plan of mission, but without necessarily using the already established denominational relationships in the area. JAM is understood as a more complete form of unity in mission than can be attained by co-operation in institutions and specific programmes. The emphasis is placed on the fullest possible action by the greatest number of Christian groups and agencies. The plan is employed where the object and the method are accepted by all concerned, and an organization is designed to meet the need of the particular situation. Three steps are considered essential: (1) A survey of the needs, the opportunities and the available resources; (2) Consultation and decision on the goals, and the deployment of both existing and anticipated new resources to reach them; (3) Implementation of the plan by the churches and the mission agencies acting together through such organization as is essential to its operation.

JAM was conceived by the *IMC and formulated in its meeting in 1961. It was subsequently adopted as a plan of ecumenical mission and recommended by the *Commission on World Mission and Evangelism of the *WCC to be followed in all six continents.

ROLAND W. SCOTT

L. Newbigin: *Joint Action for Mission* (Geneva 1962); R. K. Orchard: 'Joint Action for Mission' in *IRM*, Vol. LIV (1965), pp.81–94; *Reports of Situation Conferences* (New York, Geneva, London 1963).

JONES, DAVID (1797–1841). Pioneer Protestant missionary and first of a long line of Welsh missionaries to Madagascar. Born in Neuaddlwyd, South Wales, he was educated at famous 'Dissenting Academies' in Neuaddlwyd and Gosport. Ordained 1817 in the Congregational ministry, he sailed in 1818 under the *LMS with a fellow student Thomas Bevan. The two young missionaries with their wives and two children reached Tamatave but within a few weeks J. was the sole survivor of this company of six. The fever which killed the others left J. with weaknesses which handicapped him for the rest of his short life.

Having won the confidence of King Radama I—a Hova chief under whom some semblance of inter-tribal unity had been achieved—J. established schools and began to reduce the Hova language to writing. The Malagasy people proved quickly responsive to the gospel, but Radama's death in 1828 was the prelude to a violent anti-foreign and anti-Christian régime under the notorious Queen Ranavalona. Christianity was proscribed and there followed a long period of savage persecution in which great numbers of Malagasy converts sealed their fidelity in martyrdom. In 1830 J. was compelled to leave the island; but in the meantime he and later colleagues had so used their opportunities that, in addition to schools and churches, they left behind a complete translation of the Bible, the prototype of the famous 'buried Bibles' which survived the massacres and nourished the persecuted *younger church. J's short life and shorter period of active service thus laid the biblical foundation for one of the most heroic and remarkable Christian movements in the whole story of the expansion of Christianity.

See MADAGASCAR.

NORMAN GOODALL

R. Lovett: *History of the LMS* (London 1899), Vol. I, pp.673–710; *DNB* XXX, 95.

JORDAN, THE HASHEMITE KINGDOM OF, was constituted as Transjordania on 22 March 1946, enlarged on 24 April 1950 by the incorporation of the Arab parts of Palestine which were not included, on the termination of the British mandate, in the state of Israel. Area 36,715 sq.m. Population rather more than two million, of whom 550,000 are refugees from Israel. Since the 'Six-Day War' of 1967, large parts of the territory of Jordan, including the whole of the territory to the west of the Jordan river, are in Israeli occupation, and it is impossible as yet to predict what the future of this area will be. A large number of missionary societies has worked in the area, many of them with headquarters in Jerusalem; but it is difficult to separate the work carried on in the area which is now

Jordan from that which is now Israel. RC missions have largely been concerned with shepherding resident Christians of the Latin rite (*Franciscans), and the small Uniate communities (Armenian and others) of the Eastern Churches in communion with Rome. In 1878 the *White Fathers set up a seminary for the training of Melkite clergy. On the Protestant side the first in the field were the *ABCFM and the LSPCJ (1820), followed by the *CMS (1851), Lutherans, Baptists and many others. There was a rapid development in evangelistic, pastoral, educational and medical work, among both Jews and Muslims. Most of this was carried on west of the Jordan; but the old land of Moab was not forgotten. It was a CMS missionary, F. A. Klein, who travelling in that region discovered in 1868 at Dhiban, the Dibon of the Bible, the famous Moabite stone (c. 850 B.C.). Several missions established work in Amman, the capital; and the CMS set up a hospital at Kerak in 1894.

The most recent figures show a Christian population of about 30,000 of whom roughly two-thirds are RCs. The strongest Protestant group is The Evangelical Episcopal Community associated with the Anglican communion, with 5,323 members (1968); next in order are the Lutherans, the Church of the Nazarene and the Southern Baptists. The great majority of the Christians of all groups live in the old city of Jerusalem, or in the area west of the Jordan now occupied by Israel. Christians, like others, have suffered in the disturbances consequent on the war; but there is no reason to think that the Israelis will be less tolerant than the Arab rulers whom, at least for the time being, they have replaced.

EDITORS

BM II, 540–45; NCE VII, 1101f.; WKL, 627f.

JOURNALS FOR MISSION STUDIES.
Missionary literature is to a large extent periodical literature. The Missionary Research Library, New York, for instance, receives about 750 current periodicals.

The premier English language mission journal is the *International Review of Mission (Geneva), published since 1912, first by the *IMC and now by the *Division of World Mission and Evangelism of the WCC. It is noted for its scholarship, ecumenical scope and valuable bibliographies. Frontier (London) is published quarterly by the Christian Frontier Council, World Dominion Press and the Friends of Reunion. Evangelical Missions Quarterly (Washington, D.C.), a conservative evangelical journal, began publication in 1964. A selection of Protestant missionary society journals in English would include: Alliance Witness (CMA, NYC), The Commission (Southern Baptist, Richmond, Va.), East Asia Millions (OMF, Philadelphia), East and West Review (Anglican, London), Mission (American Baptist, Valley Forge, Pa.), The Missionary (American Lutheran, Minneapolis), Overseas Mission Review (Episcopal, Washington, D.C.), World Call (UCMS, Indianapolis), and World Outlook (Methodist, NYC). Outstanding European Protestant journals are: Evangelische Missions-Zeitschrift (Hamburg), Evangelisches Missions-Magazin (Basel), De Heerbaan (Amsterdam), Nordisk Missions Tidsskrift (Aarhus), Norsk Tidsskrift for Mi.jon (Oslo), and Svensk Missionstidskrift (Uppsala).

Among the numerous notable Roman Catholic journals are: Christ to the World (Rome), Eglise Vivante (Louvain), Misiones Extranjeres (Burgos), Het Missiewerk (Nijmegen), Neue Zeitschrift für Missionswissenschaft (Beckenried), Rythmes du Monde (Bruges), Spiritus (Paris), Teaching all Nations (Manila), Worldmission (NYC), and Zeitschrift für Missionswissenschaft und Religionswissenschaft (Münster).

Go Ye, a quarterly magazine, is the organ of the Inter-Orthodox Missionary Centre Porefthendes in Athens.

Some specialized journals related to mission studies are: Anthropos (St. Augustin/ Bonn), The Bible Translator (London), Bulletin of the Society for African Church History (Aberdeen), Ecumenical Review (Geneva), Indian Church History Review

(Serampore), *Japan Christian Quarterly* (Tokyo), *Le Monde non Chrétien* (Paris), *Muslim World* (Hartford), *Practical Anthropology* (Tarrytown, N.Y.), *Religion and Society* (Bangalore), *South East Asia Journal of Theology* (Singapore), and *Student World* (Geneva). Important also are: *Occasional Bulletin* from the MRL (NYC), *Church Growth Bulletin* (Pasadena), *Bulletin of the Scottish Institute of Missionary Studies* (Aberdeen), and *Bulletin of Christian Institutes of Islamic* Studies (Lucknow).

GERALD H. ANDERSON

J. T. Ma: *Current Periodicals in the Missionary Research Library* (2nd ed., New York 1961).

JUDAISM has had a long and eventful history through the many centuries since the separation between church and synagogue became absolute at the end of the first century. Distrusted, despised, ostracized, exploited, persecuted, the Jews have yet managed to hold together, to maintain the faith in one form or another, to spread themselves out over almost the entire world, and to keep themselves in the main free from the influence of the non-Jewish world around them.

By far the most important event in Jewish history in recent years has been the formation of the state of *Israel. Not all Jews were Zionists, and not all welcomed the rash intrusion of the political upon the religious. Nor has Israel found a neat answer to the question of what it means to be a Jew. In this small country it is possible to find every conceivable expression of the idea of Jewishness—the extreme Talmudic conservatism which wishes to maintain every iota of the law; the mysticism of the Kabbalah; the deep personal piety of the Hasidim; various forms of reformed Judaism which desire an *accommodation with the modern world; the scepticism which is prepared to accept the OT as an important element in the Jewish cultural heritage but not as divine revelation. All these are deposits from different strata in the history of Judaism.

The first great figure in modern Jewish history was Moses Mendelssohn (1729–1786), who in his book *Jerusalem* (1783) put forward the idea that the Jews had been given a law and customs which distinguished them from other peoples; but that the distinctiveness was not so absolute that Jews could not feel themselves fully at home in the life and culture of a Christian people. This was put persuasively, so persuasively that many young Jews began to ask themselves whether the distinctiveness was in point of fact worth preserving; many of them did actually become Christians.

A very different position was maintained by Franz Rosenzweig (1886–1929), who very nearly became a Christian, but in the end found his home in his own Jewishness. He developed the doctrine of the fire and the rays; of the two covenants: Jesus is the covenant of God for the Gentiles to bring them to the place where the Jew already is; the task of the Jew is to abide where he is—with God. This attitude has been taken up by many thoughtful Jews, as making possible a deep loyalty to their own faith, and at the same time an understanding appreciation of the Christian faith.

Relations between Jews and Christians are probably as good today as they have been at any time through the centuries. Many Jews, such as Martin Buber and Sholem ben Chorin, have eagerly studied the Gospels, and are prepared to speak of Jesus as the 'elder brother' who walks with them in the way. This is excellent, but it, of course, repudiates violently the idea that the Jew can be in any need of a 'mission', and excludes from the start the possibility of conversion. But, however humbly, the Christian is bound to raise the question: Jesus either is the Messiah of the Jews or he is not; every Christian must pray earnestly for his Jewish brethren; the most heartfelt prayer of all is that they may come to see that Jesus of Nazareth is their own Messiah, whom they once mistakenly rejected.

See ISRAEL.

STEPHEN NEILL

I. Epstein: *Judaism: a Historical Presentation* (Harmondsworth 1959); G. Hedenquist, ed.: *The Church and the Jewish People*

(London 1954); S. C. Neill: *Christian Faith and Other Faiths* (London 1961), pp.20–39; *ERE* VI, 581–609; *WKL*, 631–34.

JUDGMENT, DIVINE. God's condemnation of sinners and approval of the righteous. Much missionary work has been motivated by desire to rescue people from the judgment and subsequent eternal suffering believed to await all excepting faithful Christians. Such motivation is still evident in some missions. However, the predominant and increasing motive is the positive desire to share with others blessings received from God, especially the blessings of Christian faith, without reference to judgment or hell. One reason for the change is the growing recognition that the NT, while consistently teaching that God irrevocably draws the line between good and evil, describes in various ways the basis of the judgment, the manner and time of its occurrence, and the consequences. In Matthew 25:31–46, the basis is active loving-kindness or lack of it; in John 3:18, it is believing or not believing in Christ. In Matthew 19:28, the apostles will judge 'in the new world'; in John 3:19, the judgment has already occurred in men's own choices. In Revelation the condemned suffer fiery torment forever; in all the letters of Paul there is no mention of hell or torment, but the contrast between 'life' and 'death'. The NT affords little basis for a detailed dogma on the subject, but declares in various figures the profound and lasting seriousness of good or evil conduct, and of faith or faithlessness.

L. HAROLD DeWOLF

E. Brunner: *Eternal Hope* (London 1954); L. H. DeWolf: *A Theology of the Living Church* (revised ed., New York 1960), pp. 280–86; A. Richardson: *An Introduction to the Theology of the New Testament* (London 1958).

JUDSON, ADONIRAM (1788–1850), pioneer Baptist missionary to Burma, was born at Malden, Mass., USA, the son of a Congregational minister. He graduated from Brown University, and though sceptical of the meaning of Christianity he went to Andover Seminary as a seeker for the truth. During seminary days he became a convinced Christian and caught the early interest in missions to the orient which began to develop in New England at that time. He went to England and received appointment by the *LMS to India. Then he returned to USA and challenged the newly formed *ABCFM to appoint him. He married Ann Hasseltine and sailed for India in 1812.

On ship, while preparing to confront William *Carey in Calcutta on the scriptural basis of baptism, he became convinced of the Baptist position, and was baptized in Calcutta by the Rev. William Ward. This change in doctrinal position necessitated writing to American Baptists to see if they would undertake his support. This led to the unification of Baptists in the cause of foreign missions through the Triennial Convention. After many difficulties in finding a place to settle the Js arrived in Rangoon, Burma, on 13 July 1813. This was to mark the beginning of modern missions in Burma and a new denominational life for Baptists in America.

J. was a brilliant linguist who mastered the Burmese language and eventually translated the Bible and produced a large dictionary, both still in use in Burma today. He considered these to be necessary tools for future work, but public preaching and leisurely conversation with Buddhists were always the highest priorities in his idea of missionary service.

After difficulties in Rangoon he and Ann moved to Ava, the capital of the Burmese kingdom. Here J. was imprisoned and passed through a time of great suffering. Following the treaty which ended the Anglo-Burmese war J. moved to Amherst, then Moulmein, where he could work more safely in the areas protected by the British. Ann died in 1826 and J. knew many periods of depression, but nothing daunted his evangelistic and literary labours. Although rejoicing in the growing response to the gospel among the Karen hill people, he kept persistently at his work among the Buddhist-background Burmese.

In 1834 he was married to Sarah Boardman, whose husband had died in missionary service in Burma. Together they continued their literary work. Following her death in 1845 J. made his first visit to USA in 32 years. There he did much to unify Baptists in the cause of foreign missions. When asked about the prospects of the gospel in Asia his famous answer was: 'The future is as bright as the promises of God'. He returned to Burma after marrying the novelist Fanny Forester. His last years were spent largely in Rangoon and Moulmein giving direction to the mission work among the Burmese. He died in 1850 on a sea voyage taken in the interests of his health.

J. was a man of intensity and purpose, with pronounced ideas of mission work which he described in his many letters and treatises. The articulation of the gospel in clear and thoughtful form was his dominant passion. He rebelled against becoming a school teacher, and had no patience for teaching the culture of western civilization as a means to break down the cosmology of the Buddhist religion. He trained his national workers informally and had a gift for inspiring youth to become teachers and preachers. He was suspicious of transferring to Burma the western idea of a seminary education. He knew the great difficulties of a Buddhist becoming a Christian, but lived in the hope that 'the hills of Burma, now dotted with the spires of pagodas, will some day be dotted with the spires of Christian churches'.

J. stands out as one of the great pioneers of the modern missionary movement: a hero to Asian Christians, and also a deep influence on American church life.

PAUL D. CLASPER

C. Anderson: *To the Golden Shore* (Boston 1956); R. Torbet: *Venture of Faith* (Philadelphia 1955); S. Warburton: *Eastward: The Story of Adoniram Judson* (New York 1937); F. Wayland: *A Memoir of the Life and Labors of the Rev. Adoniram Judson* (Boston 1853); *DAB* X, 234–36.

JUNOD, HENRI ALEXANDRE (1863–1934), was born at Saint Martin, Neuchâtel, Switzerland, where his father, a staunch freechurch man, had founded the Independent Protestant Church. J. studied in Neuchâtel, Basel and Berlin, was ordained in 1885 and served for two years as a pastor. After an inner struggle he decided to become a missionary to Africa, for which purpose he went to Scotland to study. In 1889 he married Emilie Biolley of Couvet, sailing shortly afterwards for Mozambique where Paul Berthoud, a relative of his wife, was head of the Swiss Romande Mission. J. was stationed at Ricatla, near the city of Lourenço Marques, where one of his earliest experiences was the Ronga-Portuguese war of 1894–95 when Ricatla was burned. J. served also as principal of the Bible School at Shiluwane, Transvaal.

J. used his free time to collect butterflies, one of which had never been classified and was given his name *Papilio Junodi*. His butterfly collections may be seen in museums in Switzerland and South Africa. J. studied the Bantu languages, publishing a Ronga grammar in 1896, and, with Eli Chatelain, a Shangane dictionary and grammar in 1909. In 1897 he published *Chants et Contes des Ba Ronga*, a missionary novel in 1910, and in 1933 the story of the founding of the mission. A chance remark by Lord Bryce in 1895 turned him to the study of ethnography, which led to the publishing in 1912 of his *The Life of a South African Tribe*. The book made him famous, came out in three editions, the last one in 1962, and has been called 'the finest monograph written on an African tribe'. In his research for the book he was guided by questions raised by Sir James Frazer in *The Golden Bough*. Because of his early arrival in Mozambique J. was able to isolate those elements of African life which were traditional and relatively untouched by western influence.

J's second wife died in 1917, and he retired to Geneva in 1921, where he helped to bring African pastors to Switzerland for study, served as president of the International Bureau for the Defence of Native Interests and was consultant to the Mandates Commission of the League of Nations. The University of Lausanne conferred on him an honorary doctorate.

PER HASSING

H. P. Junod: *Henri Alexandre Junod, Missionaire et Savant, 1863–1934* (Lausanne 1934).

K

KAGAWA, TOYOHIKO (1888–1960), one of the most outstanding Christian witnesses in Asia in modern times, was born in Kobe as the son of a wealthy business man and his *geisha* wife. Baptized in 1903, K. was disowned by his family and not long after went to live in the slums of Kobe. While others theorized, K. experienced himself the desolation of the poor in the cruel age of Japan's rapid change from the conditions of a medieval state to those of a modern industrial country. Always a convinced evangelist, believing that in Jesus Christ alone is the ultimate source of man's redemption, K. became convinced that Christian witness must at the same time find expression in every form of social service and regeneration. Hence his life-long belief in co-operatives, a number of which he himself was instrumental in starting. From 1915 to 1917 K. was a student at Princeton, N.J., and from that time on became increasingly well-known in the west. K's personal experience is reflected in his novels, especially in *Across the Death Line* (Eng. tr. *Before the Dawn*), which were something new in Japanese literature, and sold in enormous numbers both in the original Japanese and in the English and other versions. The best of his poems represent, with singular sweetness and purity, real depths of Christian experience.

Naturally K's strong views on social and political matters made him an object of suspicion to reactionary and military elements in Japan. He was arrested in 1940 and again in 1943, but in view of his popularity with the masses the government felt it wiser not to keep him in prison. When peace came, K. was invited to enter politics and to help in the rebuilding of Japan; he refused the invitation, believing that it was his vocation to preach, and to attend to rebuilding on a level deeper than that of politics.

The influence of K. was certainly greater in the west than it was in his own country,

Japan. Other Japanese Christians tended to be critical of him as a man who started many more things than he was able to finish, and who did not always keep his feet firmly on the stable ground of reality. But he has had very few rivals indeed in the difficult art of making the authentic voice of Asian Christianity heard outside the Asian lands.

STEPHEN NEILL

W. Axling: *Kagawa* (London 1932); T. Kagawa: *Before the Dawn* (London 1925), *Songs from the Slums* (London 1935); J. M. Trout: *Kagawa, Japanese Prophet* (World Christian Books No. 30, London 1959); *RGG* III, 1088; *WKL*, 647–49.

KALIMANTAN. See INDONESIA.

KALLEY, ROBERT REID (1809–1888), 'missionary to the Portuguese of three continents', was born near Glasgow, Scotland. He graduated from the university of Glasgow and practised medicine. He was accepted by the *LMS as a missionary to China; but upon his marriage to Margaret Crawford K. was released from his contract, since her health barred appointment to overseas work. The couple initiated an independent missionary career in the Madeira Islands, arriving in Funchal on 12 October 1838, and the following year were in Lisbon for language study. K. was licensed there 'to practice medicine in Portugal and adjacent islands'. Also in 1839 K. was ordained a minister by the LMS Board of Examiners. In 1840 K. opened a twelve-bed hospital in Funchal which served the poor, who reciprocated by calling K. 'the good English doctor'. Between the years 1839 and 1845 more than 2,000 persons, mostly adults, were taught a programme of literacy and Bible study, in the seventeen elementary schools opened by the Kalleys. K. also composed the first evangelical hymns in Portuguese. Workers everywhere sang these popular hymns and two hymn books, *Louvemos todos ao Pai do Céu* and

Meu fiel Pastor, were published. In 1842 violent persecutions were launched against the Protestants. For six months (July 1843–January 1844) K. was imprisoned. More than a thousand converts were forced to flee from Madeira. As the fury of the persecution mounted K. was finally forced to listen to his counsellors and to escape from the island. His house was burnt, along with all the furniture, medical equipment and supplies, and his priceless library. Later the British government exacted an indemnity of £7,000 from Portugal to cover a part of K's losses. After visiting Madeira refugees in the British West Indies and Illinois, K. served brief terms as a missionary to Malta and to Palestine. Early in 1852 Mrs K. died in Beirut and in December of that year, K. married Sarah Poulton, a talented writer, musician and poet. K. then went to Brazil, arriving in Rio de Janeiro, 10 May 1855, beginning another fruitful term of service that was to endure 22 years until retirement in England in 1876. K. founded the *Igreja Evangelica Fluminense* on the congregational system, 11 July 1858, and the following year was licensed to practice medicine in Brazil. K. and his wife made a notable contribution to the cultural life of Brazil, gaining converts at the imperial court, and composing a hymnbook that has been the standard for church singing until the present time. Dr A. Bonar in the General Assembly of the Free Church of Scotland termed the work of K. 'the greatest achievement of modern mission'.

ROBERT L. MCINTIRE

W. M. Blackburn: *The Exiles of Madeira* (Philadelphia 1860); Michael P. Testa: *O Apostolo da Madeira* (Lisbon 1963). The English extract of Testa's work appeared in the *Journal of Presbyterian History*, December 1964.

KAM, JOSEPH (1769–1833), was born at 's-Hertogenbosch in the Netherlands and died at Ambon, Netherlands Indies. He has been called 'the apostle of the Moluccas'. Born and brought up in the DRC, K. nonetheless was strongly influenced by the Moravian Brethren centre at Zeist. Desirous

from his youth to commit himself to the cause of foreign missions, it was only in 1808 that he was able to offer his services to the newly founded (1797) Netherlands Missionary Society. After several years of preparation, at Rotterdam and Zeist, K. with two other candidates succeeded in reaching London in spite of Napoleon's Continental System (1812). After further training at Gosport, England, K. and his friends were sent out in December 1813 by the *LMS to Java as the first missionaries for the Netherlands Indies in the 19th century.

At Batavia K. accepted the appointment by the colonial government as pastor of the large *indigenous church in the Moluccas, the result of two centuries of Dutch East India Company missionary work. On his way to Ambon, his future residence, he spent several months at Surabaya to minister to the long neglected congregations in and around that town. Here he influenced the beginnings of evangelistic work among the local population.

During the last eighteen years of his life K. laboured at the spiritual renewal and development of the church in the eastern archipelago, at the same time devoting his full energy to its missionary expansion. K. defended the Calvinistic character of the church against Baptist influences introduced by William *Carey's youngest son Jabez. In addition to his preoccupation with church order and discipline, preaching, administration of the sacraments and education, both religious and secular, he devoted much attention to the training of preacher-teachers, the printing and distribution of Bibles, hymnbooks and Christian literature, the erection of church buildings, the promotion of church music, and most of all to an unceasing evangelistic endeavour.

K's main field of work was formed by the scores of congregations at Ambon and adjacent islands, but he also travelled extensively, covering thousands of miles by sea, partly in his self-built schooner, to the remotest islands of Eastern Indonesia, from far in the north (Sangir and North-Celebes) to deep in the south (Kisar to Aru). At his urgent request the NMS sent out a large number of new missionaries, whom he placed and supervised. Though his methods were doubtless rather superficial, he deserves his legendary fame at Ambon as the great promoter of modern missions in the Moluccas.

I. H. ENKLAAR

I. H. Enklaar: *Joseph Kam, 'Apostel der Molukken'* (The Hague 1963).

KASATKIN, NICOLAI IVAN (d. 1912), Russian Orthodox missionary to Japan, began his activity in Japan as chaplain to the Russian diplomatic mission in Hakodate (1861) 'with definite and well-considered plans for missionary work'. As Christianity was still a prohibited religion, K. at first devoted himself to the study of the Japanese and Chinese languages. In 1868 he secretly baptized three Japanese, one of them being a *Shinto priest and another a doctor. When in 1871 the Russian Orthodox Mission to Japan was officially brought into being, the small community already consisted of twelve baptized Christians and 25 catechumens. The instructions for missions, which K. himself had drawn up, provided for intensive study of the language, preaching in houses but not in public, no polemical utterances against other religions or confessions, participation of Japanese Christians in the work of evangelization, rejection of all tendencies to the imposition of Russian ways and Russian culture. When, in 1873, the penal laws against Christianity were abrogated, K. moved to Tokyo. There he opened a seminar for priests and catechists, and set up a translators' committee of nine persons, who were to be responsible for the preparation of Christian literature. From that time on he celebrated the liturgy only in Japanese. His congregations had lay representatives, who came together in a Great Synod once every two years, while in the alternate years the clergy met in the Minor Synod. By 1875 K. had a thousand Christians under his care; the Shinto priest and the doctor referred to above had by now been ordained priests. In 1878, K. had between Hakodate and Osaka 100 congre-gations with 5,000 believers. His success was recognized in his consecration as bishop, and the mission to Japan was placed under the direct supervision of the Holy Synod. It is remarkable that K. attached very little importance to educational activity on the part of the mission. In 1904, when he had 28,000 Christians in 260 congregations, he had only four schools, and these were for the most part attended by the children of priests. K. did maintain Sunday schools and Catechism schools, as a counterpart to the *Buddhist schools, in which the teachings of Gautama and Buddhist songs were imparted to children. In 1891 K. was able to conse-crate 'the largest and most beautiful church in Japan' (Ohm). The beauty of its dome and the solemnity of its liturgy attracted many Japanese. K. also created his own press; he published an official organ of the mission, and two monthly periodicals (1900). K. had integrated his work with such sensitivity into the Japanese soul that the Russo-Japanese War of 1904–05, though it hindered the work, did not bring it to the point of collapse. In 1906 K. was promoted to be Archbishop of Tokyo. He saw the jubilee of his mission (1911), and died in the following year, mourned by more than 33,000 Christians.

His work is the best evidence for his apostolic zeal, and his skill as a shepherd of souls.

JOSEF GLAZIK

S. Bolshakoff: *The Foreign Missions of the Russian Orthodox Church* (London 1943), pp.25–78; O. Cary: *A History of Christianity in Japan* (2 vols., New York 1909); J. Glazik: *Die russ.-orth. Heidenmission* (Münster 1954), pp.178–94; K. S. Latourette: *A History of the Expansion of Christianity* (New York 1937–1945), Vol. VI, pp.379f.; C. F. Sweet: 'Archbishop Nicolai and the Russian Ecclesiastical Mission to Japan' in IRM II (1913), pp. 126–47.

KASHMIR (Jammu and Kashmir). Area 92,000 sq.m., population 4,500,000. A state in the Indian sub-continent including much Himalayan country, bounded on the north-west by Afghanistan, north-east by the Sinkiang Province of China and east by Tibet. It is important politically as one of the main north-western approaches to India and as a source of friction between India and Pakistan.

The population comprises three million Muslims, one million Hindus and half a million Buddhists and others, including about 5,000 Christians.

The *CMS (Anglican) began work in 1863 following an appeal by British officers and civilians. The Rev. C. E. Tyndale-Biscoe established a notable Boys' School at Srinagar but there have been few converts as a result of its work. Recently the Moravian Christians of Ladakh asked to come under the care of the Amritsar diocese of the Anglican church.

The (Anglican) CIPBC carries on medical, educational and evangelistic work in the North K. district, especially at Srinagar and Anantnag. The United Church of North India (Presbyterian and Congregational) works principally in Udampur and Bhadarwah. The Roman Catholic church has educational work at Srinagar, Baramulla, Udhampur and Jammu, and a hospital at Baramulla.

The political tensions since 1947 have led India to keep large armed forces in the state, and the K. valley is a dangerous flashpoint both politically and in the Hindu-Muslim communal setting. Since 1962 China also has become involved in the K. conflict. The entry of further overseas missionaries is restricted, but evangelistic work is being carried on by itinerant groups, mainly from South India. A proportion of the Indian military forces are Christian.

HENRY LEFEVER

A. Neve: *Medical Missions* (Calcutta 1891); *Christian Handbook of India* (Nagpur 1959); E. Stock: *History of the CMS* (London 1899); C. E. Tyndale-Biscoe: *Tyndale-Biscoe of Kashmir* (London 1951); E. D. Tyndale-Biscoe: *Fifty Years against the Stream* (Mysore 1930); *WKL*, 655f.

KEITH-FALCONER, ION GRANT NEVILLE (1856–1887), third son of the ninth earl of Kintore, Arabic scholar and

pioneer missionary, was born at Edinburgh, Scotland. He qualified himself in theology and oriental languages at the universities of Cambridge and Leipzig. At the same time he became the champion bicyclist of Great Britain, and made himself one of the leading experts in the history and practice of shorthand. Always a man of profound and practical piety, he gradually became convinced that he ought to devote himself to missionary work in some part of the world in which his profound knowledge of Arabic could be useful. During a four-months' visit to Arabia in 1885–86 he fixed on Sheikh Othman, nine miles from Aden, as the site for the medical mission which is still carried on by the Church of Scotland. In 1886 he was appointed Lord Almoner's Professor of Arabic at Cambridge, and lectured on the pilgrimage to Mecca. At the end of the same year he returned to Arabia and set to work to build the mission at Sheikh Othman. But insufficient account had been taken of the rigours of the climate; K-F's strength was undermined by repeated attacks of fever, and he died five months after his arrival.

STEPHEN NEILL

R. Sinker: *Memorials of the Hon. Keith-Falconer* (2nd ed., London 1888); *DNB* XXX, 336.

KENNEDY SCHOOL OF MISSIONS, THE, Hartford, Connecticut, USA, was founded in January 1911, in response to the *World Missionary Conference at Edinburgh, 1910, which called for special preparation of missionaries. Originally called the Hartford School of Missions, it was endowed generously shortly after its founding by Mrs Emma Baker Kennedy, of New York City, in memory of her husband John Stewart Kennedy.

The basic purpose was to train missionary candidates and missionaries on furlough in the theory and practice of missions. Much emphasis was given to area studies, cultural backgrounds and strategy of churches in all parts of the world.

In 1939 it had more missionaries in preparation or on furlough than any other theological school in the USA, and a larger missions teaching staff than any other Protestant school. During its first 25 years it had 810 students.

It no longer exists as a separate institution, for it merged with the Hartford School of Religious Education and the Hartford Theological Seminary into one institution under the Hartford Seminary Foundation.

EUGENE L. STOCKWELL

E. W. Capen and L. Hodous: *The Kennedy School of Missions, 1911–1936* (Hartford 1936).

KENYA is an East African republic, 224,960 sq.m. in area, bounded by Somalia, Ethiopia, Sudan, Uganda and Tanzania. Population (1967 estimate) was 9,928,000, including 183,000 Asians, 49,000 Europeans and 36,000 Arabs and others. Religious affiliation is estimated (1966) as 10% Muslim, 9% Protestant, 11% Roman Catholic, 8% African Independent, with the remainder adherents of traditional religion; there is also a number of Indian religions among the Asian population, largest of which is *Hinduism, followed by *Sikhism and *Jainism. Hindu missionary work among Africans was begun in 1966, and the first African converts were received into the *Arya Samaj Churches of E. Africa (also called the Vedic Church) in 1968. A 1965 census of *Islam revealed that it was far stronger than had previously been realized, with 900,000 adherents; in addition to Ismailis (Khojas of Indian origin) and coastal Arabs, concentrations of Muslims exist in Nyanza around Lake Victoria and in the Northern Province. The Ahmadiyya Muslim Mission has a strong work and edits a national newspaper, and has translated the Qur'an into Swahili. As elsewhere throughout the continent, the African Muslims are almost without exception Sunni, whilst the immigrant communities from Asia are Shi'ite.

The Roman Catholic mission was founded in 1862 as the prefecture of Zanzibar; by 1965 this had become the ecclesiastical province of Kenya with nine dioceses and 1,027,614 Catholics (1963 figures). The major missionary orders are the *Holy Ghost Fathers, *Mill Hill Fathers, Consolata Fathers and Kiltegan Fathers; but there is a large number of missionaries from other orders.

Protestant missions began with the arrival of Johann *Krapf of the *CMS at Mombasa in 1844, followed by Rebmann the discoverer of Mount Kilimanjaro. In the early days of work among the coastal tribes, settlements for freed slaves were begun, the most famous being at Rabai and Freretown near Mombasa. Around the year 1900 a number of other missions began work, and such was their success that all soon had large and flourishing communities. By 1966 22 distinct denominations of European or American origin had come into being, with a total community of 788,070. Of these the largest was the Anglican church with 136,294 adherents in five of the thirteen dioceses of the Church of the Province of East Africa created in 1960. The Africa Inland Church (served by the AIM) had 130,000 adherents, with very strong work among the Akamba tribe east of Nairobi. The *SA, with well-developed work in the cities, had a total of 107,418 persons. Other large missions and churches include the SDA (81,264), East Africa Yearly Meeting of *Friends (the world's largest Friends mission, with 76,000), Presbyterian Church of East Africa (56,975), Methodist Church in Kenya (17,554), Africa Gospel Church (World Gospel Mission; 15,000), Lutheran Church in Kenya (7,234), Baptist Churches of Kenya, Church of God in East Africa, Gospel Furthering Fellowship, etc. *Pentecostal missions are among the most rapidly growing of all: there are four separate groups, Pentecostal Assemblies of God (served by Pentecostal Assemblies of Canada: about 100,000 adherents), Full Gospel Churches of Kenya (Norwegian and Finnish Free Missions: about 10,000), Pentecostal Evangelistic Fellowship of Africa (Elim Missionary Assemblies: 700 adherents), and Swedish Free Missions (Svenska Fria Missionen: 2,076). Anglican dioceses and a majority of Protestant denominations co-operate in the *National

Christian Council of Kenya, which also has close links with the Kenya Catholic Secretariat.

Kenya must be ranked with South Africa and Nigeria for the early growth of its *separatist churches and for their enormous proliferation. The first body was the Nomiya ('God has given me a revelation') Luo Mission which left the CMS in 1914 and in 1966 claimed 51,806 adherents; others followed in profusion until by 1966 some 160 distinct *African Independent Churches existed in Kenya, with an estimated 700,000 adherents. Of these, 70 had registered with the Kenya government by 1967. The two largest have been the Church of Christ in Africa (ex-Anglican church: 75,000), and the Legion of Mary Church (ex-RC church: 90,000 at origin, including a large number of lapsed Catholics). The NCC has extended a sympathetic hand to these bodies, and seven of the largest are members of it.

Church union discussions and schemes have gradually gathered momentum since the *Kikuyu Conference of 1913, and in 1970 Anglican, Methodist and Presbyterian churches were expected eventually to merge into a single ecclesiastical province of Kenya. Several smaller bodies including African Independent Churches have also participated in talks. The level of co-operation in bodies such as the NCC and the Bible Society in East Africa is so advanced that numerous successful co-operative ventures in religious journalism, broadcasting, scripture distribution, urban mission and training have come into being.

DAVID B. BARRETT

E. Weigt: *Kenya und Uganda* (Bonn 1958); M. Whisson: *Change and Challenge* (Nairobi 1964); *BM* II, 545–51; *NCE* VIII, 160f.; *WKL*, 673f.

KESWICK CONVENTION, the annual meeting 'for the promotion of Scriptural holiness', which was founded in 1875 in the English Lake District, has profoundly influenced missions. The first twelve Ks made no official provision for missionary representation, though sympathetic. Since 1888, however, the last morning has been set apart for a meeting at which ten or twelve missionaries or overseas nationals are each invited to set out briefly 'the claim of Christ to his people's willing service in the cause of the evangelization of the world'. These meetings have been a vital factor in the call of multitudes of recruits. Since 1889 a hospitality fund has enabled any missionary on furlough to attend K., which thus has aided spiritual renewal after arduous service, while in recent years many overseas nationals have also attended. In 1892 Amy *Carmichael, adopted daughter of a K. founder, was the first 'K. missionary' (those serving with societies overseas and receiving support from K. funds). In 1889 K. sent its first 'mission to missionaries', and conventions on K. lines began in India, North America and elsewhere. K. speakers have toured regularly in most parts of the world. The annual report, *K. Week*, the broadcast service, and a tape library of addresses have also contributed to the strengthening of national churches. The K. motto is 'All one in Christ Jesus'.

JOHN POLLOCK

J. C. Pollock: *The Keswick Story* (London 1964), pp.80–94, 169–72, 177f.

KEYSSER, CHRISTIAN (1877–1961), was born in Bavaria as the son of a forester, and grew up under strict Christian discipline. He attended a high school in Nuremberg, and while there came under the influence of the *YMCA. He received his training for missionary service at the Missionary Institute in *Neuendettelsau. In 1899 he was sent to New Guinea, and located in the mission station at Sattelberg, which continued to be his home throughout his entire time of service in New Guinea. K. was a highly cultivated and many-sided man. He took an interest in everything which fell within the concern of a *pioneer missionary. He made a name for himself through collections of botanical and zoological specimens, and also as ethnographer and geographer. In order to open up the still closed island of New Guinea for missionary work, he made repeated and perilous journeys of discovery into lands that had not as yet been penetrated. He climbed the mountain Saruwaged in the Finisterre range, which is 13,400 feet in height. Through close association with the people, he learnt quickly and thoroughly the Kate language, for which he published the *Dictionary of the Kate Language* in 1925.

K. started by working along the traditional lines of missionary effort; but he soon came to realize that the inhabitants of New Guinea are so tightly bound to the community to which they belong that it is hardly possible to win them as individuals. As a result of his acquaintance with the indigenous peoples, he changed over to the method of *tribal conversions. K. was averse to all traditional and western ways. He founded his church on NT principles and in accordance with the sociological structures which he found already in existence. The congregation as a whole was responsible for each individual member. The members took an active part in the planning of the life of worship of the congregation. A considerable treasury of hymns written by members of the church came into being. K. handed over to the church responsibility for the proclamation of the gospel. From 1906 onwards, evangelists were sent into the still non-Christian territories; for these and for their support the congregation was responsible. His basic principle was that every congregation must have its own missionfield. He thus inspired the New Guinea church with a great vision.

In 1920, as a result of difficulties with the government K. was compelled to leave New Guinea. In 1920 he was appointed Inspector of Missions, and teacher at the Missionary Institute in Neuendettelsau, where he exercised a profound influence on the preparation of missionaries. He was one of the most influential writers on missionary subjects of our time, and one of the most acceptable speakers. He was thus able to bring his influence to bear on the churches as well as on the missions.

GEORG F. VICEDOM

C. Keysser: *Anutu im Papualande* (Nüremberg 1925), *Eine Papua-Gemeinde* (Neuendettelsau 1929), *Das bin bloss ich* (Neuendettelsau 1966); G. F. Vicedom: *Church and People in New Guinea* (London 1961); *RGG* III, 1263.

KHAMA (c. 1828–1923). Chief of the Bamangwato Tribe in Bechuanaland and one of the greatest Africans of his day; for 60 years a dominating figure in both Christian and secular affairs. His first Christian teachers were missionaries of the Hermannsburg Mission by whom he was baptized in 1862; but from 1863 the fortunes of K. and the Bamangwato people were closely allied to the work of the *LMS. In 1872, after much internal strife in the tribe, K. succeeded to the chieftainship and asserted his leadership in a powerful reforming movement which—amongst much else—included the strict prohibition of alcohol. In effect, K. was the leader of a *mass movement or community movement through which the Christian church became the folk-church of the tribe. In 1895 K. took the lead in a deputation of three chiefs who were received in London by Queen Victoria. This marked the acceptance by the Crown of the chiefs' plea for 'protection', largely in defence against feared encroachments by the British South Africa Company, a commercial enterprise. For many decades a deep and affectionate relationship between K. and the LMS missionaries (a relationship sometimes strained but never broken) made possible the great progress of the tribe through education as well as through the life and worship of the church. K's monument is now to be seen in a strong *indigenous church and in the independent country of Botswana whose prime minister—Sir Seretse Khama—is K's grandson.

NORMAN GOODALL

Histories of the London Missionary Society —R. H. Lovett (London 1899), Vol. I, pp. 633–44; N. Goodall (Oxford 1954), pp. 245–63; J. Mockford: *Khama: King of the Bamangwato* (London 1931).

KIKUYU CONFERENCES. A series of conferences was held at Kikuyu in Kenya, East Africa, in 1913 and following years, with a view to working out closer co-operation, and eventually the formation of a united church. Most unexpectedly, these simple meetings of Christian workers produced a storm that raged round the Christian world. At the end of the conference held in August 1913, the non-Anglican representatives were invited to receive Holy Communion at an Anglican Communion service. Bishop Frank *Weston of Zanzibar was deeply disturbed, and, convinced that a betrayal of all Anglican principles was being planned, delated the Bishops of Mombasa and Uganda to the Archbishop of Canterbury (Davidson) for heresy. Sides were quickly taken, and an immense literature on both sides of the question sprang into being. The Archbishop's very careful *Answer* did not appear till Easter 1915, when the whole world was occupied with the tragedies of the first world war. In all essential points the *Answer* declared the Kikuyu proposals to be in line with the opinions expressed by three Lambeth Conferences in succession, but, because of the misunderstanding that might arise, recommended great caution in the matter of united Communion services.

In later years the attention of the missions and churches in Kenya was rather in the direction of planned co-operation than in that of church union. The Christian Council of Kenya is one of the most successful in the whole world, including within itself most of the Protestant missions in Kenya. But no union of churches has as yet taken place in East Africa.

STEPHEN NEILL

J. W. Arthur and J. J. Willis in *Towards a United Church* (London 1947), pp.17–74; G. K. A. Bell: *Randall Davidson* (3rd ed., London 1952), pp.690–708.

KIMBANGU, SIMON (1889–1951), was born at NKamba in Central Congo, lost his parents early and was brought up by his grandmother Kinzembo. He attended the Baptist Primary School for four years, and worked for some time as a catechist at the Baptist Mission, where he was married to Mwilu Marie, the leader of the movement after Simon's imprisonment.

One night, in 1918, he heard the voice of Christ sending him to convert his brethren.

He refused and, to escape the recurrent call, went to Kinshasa. On 6 April 1921, when he was back at NKamba and went to the market, he felt constrained, against his will, to enter the house of a sick woman. He laid his hands upon her in the Name of Jesus and she was healed. First accused of magic and avoided, Simon became suddenly after further healings the centre of a tremendous revival movement. With the Bible in his hand he preached repentance: trust in Christ, separation from idolatry (fetishism), monogamy and obedience to God's commandments. Thousands left their work and came to Simon. Blind people were sent to the spring at NKamba, which after Simon's arrest and up to this day is the holy spring in which the faithful bathe and pray silently for spiritual blessing or healing.

Protestant and Catholic churches emptied, the movement spread across the river Congo. Missionaries and colonial administration became suspicious and wrongly accused Simon and his followers of political subversion and hostility to Europeans. The colonial administration sent a commission of enquiry. Simon escaped arrest accompanied by five *bansadisi* (helpers) and twelve apostles whom he taught. On 24 September 1921, only six months after his first healing, he returned to NKamba to be arrested and offered no resistance. A military court sentenced him to 120 lashes and death, but King Albert commuted this sentence to one of life imprisonment. K. was taken to Lubumbashi and died in October 1951 after 30 years in prison.

The movement initiated by him was persecuted from 1921 to 1957 and had to go underground. Many sects and politico-messianic groups sprang up all over the Congos claiming wrongly the name of Simon Kimbangu. Since 1957 the genuine movement established itself as the *Eglise de Jésus-Christ sur la terre par le Prophète Simon Kimbangu* (The Church of Jesus Christ on earth through the prophet SK), a church that was officially recognized in December 1959 and had already then one million members. It reaches out today to ten different countries and seeks ecumenical contacts. It is hierarchically organized, led by K's three sons and by councils. The youngest son Joseph Diangienda is the spiritual head. NKamba-Jerusalem is the holy place and administrative centre. It is a truly evangelical church for which Christ has become relevant through the life and suffering of its prophet. It rejects all tribalism, racialism and violence, has a strict code of conduct and has built up a large network of social and educational activities.

MARIE-LOUISE MARTIN

E. Andersson: *Messianic Popular Movements in the Lower Congo* (Uppsala 1958); J. E. Bertsche: 'Kimbanguism, a Challenge to Missionary Statesmen', *Practical Anthropology*, Vol. XIII, 1966, No. 1; 'The Kimbanguist Church in the Congo', *The Ecumenical Review*, Vol. XIX, 1967, No. 1 (no author indicated); M.-L. Martin: *Prophetic Christianity in the Congo* (Johannesburg 1968).

KINSOLVING, LUCIEN LEE (1862–1929), was born in Middleburg, Virginia, USA. When health prevented two fellow theological students from going to found a mission in Brazil, K. and his classmate James W. *Morris replaced them. Sponsored by the unofficial American Church Missionary Society (Episcopal) and supported largely by funds they raised themselves, the two young clergymen sailed for Brazil in 1889. They selected Porto Alegre, capital of the southernmost state of Rio Grande do Sul, as the site of their work, mainly because of sparse RC and Protestant efforts there. Farsighted, daring and eloquent, K. quickly became a respected leader among the Brazilians. In 1898 the tiny, independent *Egreja Episcopal Brasileira* elected him its bishop and he was consecrated in New York the following year. K's strategy, as viewed by an admiring contemporary bishop, was to set up reformed apostolic Christianity, to enter great centres of population, to start with simple but relevant worship, to train qualified and capable Brazilian clergy, and to be fully prepared to expand northward. When the ACMS disbanded in 1907, the Brazilian church was forced to take a back-ward step and become a missionary district of the American church. K. was retitled Bishop of Southern Brazil. Fifty-seven years later K's original design was restored when the *Egreja Episcopal Brasileira* gained autonomy as the 19th member church within the Anglican Communion.

A. THEODORE EASTMAN

A. B. Kinsolving: *Lucien Lee Kinsolving* (Baltimore 1947); A. P. Stokes: *Lucien Lee Kinsolving of Brazil* (New York 1956).

KIVEBULAYA, APOLO (c. 1864–1933), was the son of Baganda peasants who had come under Muslim influence. As a young man he fought in the religio-political wars in Uganda, and in 1894 joined the expedition sent to pacify the Kingdom of Toro in western Uganda. Returning to Kampala, he was baptized in 1895 by a *CMS missionary, taking the name of Apolo. By this name and the nickname Kivebulaya he was always known. In 1895 he returned to Toro as a church teacher, and in that area spent the rest of his life. He was ordained deacon in the Anglican church in 1900, and priest in 1903. From 1897 to 1899 he worked at Mboga, on the edge of the Ituri forest over the border in Congo, and there underwent considerable persecution. In 1916 he returned to build up the weak church there, and from Mboga he began the evangelization of the pygmy peoples of the forest. Never married, yet never touched by scandal, he was deeply loved by all who knew him. In 1922 Bishop Willis appointed him a canon in the Church of Uganda in honour of his long and faithful service. A. represents *par excellence* the many devoted Baganda evangelists who pioneered the preaching of the gospel in every corner of Uganda, and beyond.

DAVID B. BARRETT

A. Luck: *African Saint: The Story of Apolo Kivebulaya* (London 1963).

KO THA BYU (1778–1814), was the first convert to Christianity among the Karen people of Burma and became known as 'the Karen apostle'. K. was born in a jungle village near Bassein; as a young man he became a notorious criminal and was guilty of some 30 murders. He was bought out of slavery by a Burmese Christian and later, under the influence of Adoniram *Judson, was radically converted. The small church in Moulmein hesitated to accept him owing to his past reputation, and also because he belonged to the Karen tribe who were considered crude and inferior. In 1828 he was sent with G. D. *Boardman to help open a mission in Tavoy, S. Burma; there Boardman baptized him. Some Karens witnessing his baptism urged him to visit and preach in neighbouring Karen villages. For the remaining twelve years of his life K. preached and witnessed with very great effect among his own people, the largest minority group in Burma. They were *animists, unlike the Buddhist majority who despised them, but were in many ways 'ripe for the gospel'. Following on K's work, one of the strongest self-supporting churches in Asia has arisen among them. About one half of the Christians in Burma today are Karens.

A large Christian high school in Bassein is named after K., and a special day in the Karen church calendar celebrates his memory. The story of his conversion and evangelistic work is frequently acted out in church and village dramas, making his memory a living force among Karen Christians.

PAUL CLASPER

J. Robbins: *Boardman of Burma* (Philadelphia 1940); R. Tobert: *Venture of Faith* (Philadelphia 1955).

KOREA (REPUBLIC OF KOREA). K. is a peninsula set between Japan and China and Siberia. The Japan Sea is on the east, the Korean Straits on the south (separating K. from Japan), and the Yellow Sea on the west. On the north, it is separated from Manchuria by the Yalu river and the Tumen river, both of which flow from the top of Paik Tu mountain. The people of K. are justly proud of their ancient tradition which goes back to 2333 B.C., though the recorded history begins at about the time

of Christ. The country is now divided in two (about some 25 miles north of Seoul), the line of division between Russian and American zones of influence having been fixed, at the end of the second world war, at the 38th parallel of latitude. The area of K. including North K. is 85,256 sq.m. This is about the area of Kansas or of Great Britain.

Recent population. The present population of South K. (October 1966 census) is 29,382,504. The population of North K. is not known publicly, though 20,000,000 is an estimated figure.

Religious statistics. As at June 1964, when the population of South K. was 28,000,000, the number of believers in some religion was given as 3,571,438, that is approximately 12.75% of the total population: a breakdown according to their faith is: Christians 1,566,725 (Protestants 812,254, Catholics 754,471—5.6%); Buddhists 962,625 (3.4%); adherents of Chondokyo 623,397 (2.2%); Confucianists 62,821 (0.2%); other religions 955,890 (3.4%) The census seems to have taken account only of full members of Protestant churches: the total Protestant community was given by these churches themselves in 1969 as 2,104,748. According to these statistics, there are 24,430,000 who have no religious faith. It is a safe guess that these people are adherents of Shamanism. (See ANIMISM.)

*Buddhism came to K. in 372 A.D. and later was passed on to Japan in 552. *Confucianism, properly speaking, is not a religion but a system of moral teaching and behaviour, based on 'O-kang'—The Five Relations: king-subject, parent-child, husband-wife, elder and younger brother, and friend and friend. Shamanism comprises a vast number of gods, demons and demi-gods, the legacy of centuries of nature worship.

Date of first Christian penetration: There are traces to indicate that some contact was made with Christians as early as 1592, when Korea was invaded by Japan. During the seven years of warfare it is reported that some Korean converts were made by the Japanese soldiers.

The first missionary work was begun not

by foreigners, but by Koreans. Those who made official visits to Peking had opportunities to contact Catholic priests and to read Christian literature. Among these persons, it is said that Lee Sung Hoon was the first convert who truly made an effort to evangelize his people. In 1794, the first missionary priest, a Chinese, James Choo (Choo Moon Mo) succeeded in entering the country. For several decades, the Korean Catholics were severely persecuted by the government and no foreigner was given permission to enter. Three foreign priests were put to death in 1839. It is reckoned that there were at least 100 martyrs in the persecutions of 1839, 1846 and 1866–69. In 1882, a treaty was made between K. and the USA. In 1884, the first resident missionary, Dr Horace N. Allen and his family arrived in K. and the next year the Rev. Horace G. *Underwood, a Presbyterian, and the Rev. H. D. *Appenzeller, a Methodist, came to K. as the first evangelical missionaries.

In 1966 22 Protestant missions or churches were recorded as being at work in K., most of them being of North American origin. By far the strongest bodies are the Presbyterians, mainly American, but receiving support also from Australia. Second are the Methodists. The Oriental Missionary Society, which entered the country in 1907, has been successful in bringing into existence a large self-governing church, the Korean Holiness Church. There is a considerable work of the Salvation Army, as of the Seventh Day Adventists and the Baptists. Special mention may be made of the Anglican Mission, founded and supported from England; this stands a little aside from the Protestant missions, and has been marked from the beginning by its special concern for and interest in Korean literature and culture. Lutherans, Pentecostalists, the Church of the Nazarene, and others have smaller causes. All the Korean churches have from the start emphasized autonomy and self-support; at the present time ordained Korean pastors outnumber ordained foreign missionaries by ten to one. Presbyterians, divided into four separate

groups, numbered, in 1969, 1,434,377, served by more than 6,000 workers; Methodists 268,165; Holiness 144,422, SDA 122,451. The other twelve groups together accounted for about 150,000, in a combined total for all non-Roman churches of 2,104,748.

The RCs never gave up their hope of maintaining their work in K.; but they were later than the Protestants in establishing a strong and permanent mission, and their progress has in consequence been slower. Two missionaries of the *MEP managed to enter K. in 1876; they were followed in 1877 by Felix Clars Ridel, who had escaped from the persecution of 1866, and now returned as Vicar Apostolic. He was arrested, but released as a result of French and Japanese pressure. The RC mission, later the others, profited from the new and more open relations between K. and the western world from 1882 onwards. The hierarchy was established in 1962. In 1964 there were 11 dioceses, six of the bishops being Koreans. The faithful numbered (1964) 754,471, ministered to by 593 priests, of whom the majority were Koreans.

The Korean Protestant churches are shamefully divided. For the last fifteen years the strength and pride of the Korean churches has been sapped by internal problems; splits and schisms have exhausted their energy and dimmed their light. The Presbyterians have split into more than ten different groups; there are three Methodist groups, two Holiness groups, and five Baptist groups, etc. No actual plan for church union has appeared within our present church history, though it is now being discussed. With many organizations such as *YMCA, *YWCA, the Christian Literature Society, the *National Council of Churches, the Council of Christian Education, the Korean Association of Accredited Theological Schools, co-operation exists; also in the United Graduate School of Theology, established by the major grant of the *TEF in 1964 at Yonsei University in Seoul. Here four major theological schools joined to train theological students at the post-graduate level, and to make available to ordained ministers refresher courses for short-term periods in the spirit of the *ecumenical movement.

Special difficulties. The Korean churches have the same difficulties as other countries with regard to non-Christian tradition and culture. In addition, the major problems are *syncretism, subjectivism and escapism. A prominent type of syncretism is nature worship combined with Christian teachings, in which emphasis is placed on healing and ecstatic experience. Here sound theological thinking and effort are despised or ignored. Subjectivism: many churches are composed of religious fanatics and emotion-ridden leaders who have a strong sense of egotism and dogmatic subjectivism. The Bible is interpreted individually, not historically or theologically. This subjectivism has caused some of the splits in the churches. Escapism: some Korean Christians try to escape from the realities of life, placing their hopes on the life after death; because of this their sense of participation in history and their social consciousness are very weak; thus the church has lost her leadership in society.

Recognizing these difficulties, the Korean churches have also recently felt a necessity for the indigenization of Christianity. Since 1963 a special effort has been placed on this by the theologians and Christian leaders. The purpose of this indigenization movement is well expressed in Dr Brunner's dictum: 'All of Christ for Korea; all of Korea for Christ'.

NORTH KOREA (COMMUNIST KOREA). Since 1945, Korea has been divided into South Korea and North Korea; no adequate information or material on North Korea is available within the Republic of Korea. It is reported that no Christian churches and activities are allowed within the communist controlled area. Since 1953 refugees continually reaffirm this.

KIM CHUNG CHOON

A. Choc: L'Erection du premier vicariat apostolique et les origines du Catholicisme en Korée (Schneck-Beckenried 1961), The Catholic Church in Korea (Hong Kong 1924); S. C. Chung: Schism and Unity in the Protestant Churches of Korea (New Haven, Conn. 1955); C. A. Clark: The Korean Church and the Nevius Method (New York 1930); S. K. Cooper: Evangelism in Korea (Nashville 1930); C. Dallet: Histoire de l'Eglise de Corée (2 vols., Paris 1784); H. S. Hong et al.: Korea Struggles for Christ (Seoul 1966); G. H. Jones: Korea, the Land, People and Customs (Cincinnati 1907); Y. S. Kim: History of the Korean Church in the ten years since Liberation 1945–1955 (Seoul 1956); L. G. Paik: The History of Protestant Missions in Korea; 1832–1920 (Pyeng Yang 1929); S. J. Palmer: Korea and Christianity (Seoul 1967); R. E. Shearer: Wildfire: Church Growth in Korea (Grand Rapids 1966); C. D. Stokes: History of Methodist Missions in Korea (Doctoral thesis 1947, New Haven, Conn.); K. Tilmann: Todesverächter, ein Tatsachenbericht aus der Geschichte der Kirche in Korea (Freiburg 1955); BM II, 280–87; NCE VIII, 254–57.

KRAEMER, HENDRIK (1888–1965).
During the period 1930–1960 K., who was a layman, probably exercised a greater influence on missionary thinking than any other single man in the Protestant world. After brilliant studies in oriental languages, he went to Indonesia in 1922 in the service of the Netherlands Bible Society. In the next fifteen years he acquired an expert knowledge of Indonesian *Islam, and pondered deeply the relation of Christianity to other faiths. At the same time he became deeply disturbed over the state of the *younger churches and the failure of the missionaries to grant them that freedom without which they could not develop as churches.

K. was not well known outside Indonesia, when in 1936 he was asked to write a book in preparation for the third (Tambaram) *World Missionary Conference. He produced what is certainly the greatest of his books, The Christian Message in a non-Christian World (1938). In this he sharply distinguished 'biblical realism' from all other forms of faith. His forceful expression of these views naturally provoked opposition in liberal circles, and controversy was sharp both at the conference and after it; but the second world war intervened to make international discussion of these themes impossible. K. returned to the question in later books (*Religion and the Christian Faith*, 1956) but did not very much modify his earlier position; he was prepared to admit that God may have spoken in and through the other religions, but never came to the point of saying when and how this may have taken place.

From 1937 onwards K. was Professor of the Phenomenology of Religion at Leyden. Towards the end of the war period, K. was placed by the Germans in a concentration camp. After the war he played a leading part in the working out of the new constitution of the DRC, in which for the first time mission was recognized as an integral part of the life and work of the church. In 1947 he was invited to become the first director of the Ecumenical Institute at the Château de Bossey. No better choice could have been made. In spite of the ill-health by which he was increasingly troubled, K. by his gift for languages, his very extensive knowledge of theology, and his genuinely ecumenical outlook, contributed greatly to establishing the institute on a sound foundation, and to adding distinction to its work. Even after his retirement, he continued to write and lecture till within a few weeks of his death.

STEPHEN NEILL

C. F. Hallencreutz: *Kraemer towards Tambaram: A Study in Hendrik Kraemer's Missionary Approach* (Uppsala 1966); H. Kraemer: *From Missionfield to Independent Church* (London 1958. Extracts from K's own reports from Indonesia); A. T. van Leeuwen: *Hendrik Kraemer als Dienaar der Wereldkerk* (Amsterdam 1959—German translation *Hendrik Kraemer Pionier der Oekumene*, Basel 1962).

KRAPF, JOHANN LUDWIG (1810–1881), was born near Tübingen, Germany, son of a well-to-do farmer. He studied at the *Basel Missionary Training Institute, and in 1836 was sent by the *CMS to Ethiopia to evangelize the Galla. Frustrated in this work, he moved to Mombasa in 1844. There he commenced the study of Kiswahili, and there within a few months his wife and infant daughter were buried. Joined in 1846 by a fellow-German, Johann Rebmann, he established a station at Rabai, near Mombasa. From Rabai K. and Rebmann penetrated inland, and in 1849 K. reached Ukambani and became the first white man to see Mount Kenya. K. saw the coast mission as 'the first link of a mission chain between East and West Africa', but he did not see his vision realized. His next journey to Ukambani ended tragically, and in 1853, broken in health, he returned to Europe. His *Travels and Missionary Labours in East Africa* was published in 1860. In 1862 he returned briefly to Mombasa to help the Methodists establish a mission. K's greatest achievements were probably linguistic. As well as his pioneer work in Kiswahili he published a *Vocabulary of Six Languages* and translated Mark's Gospel into Kikamba.

DAVID B. BARRETT

J. L. Krapf: *Travels, Researches and Missionary Labours* (London 1860); *RGG* IV, 40.

KRISHNA PILLAI, H. A. (1827–1900), was born in a high-caste family in the Tirunelvēli district of South India. From early years he had been deeply interested in the classics of Tamil literature and acquired a wide acquaintance with them in all their branches. In 1853 he was appointed Tamil teacher in the Christian school at Sawyerpuram, but at that time he was strongly opposed to the Christian faith. He was gravely disturbed by the conversion of a number of his friends, but still maintained his opposition, until in 1858 he became convinced of the truth of the gospel. He was baptized in Madras on 18 April of that year, and given the Christian names Henry Alfred, which, however, he never used, retaining all his life his original Hindu name. For 40 years the one idea of KP was to make Christ known, and especially to use for this purpose his remarkable knowledge of Tamil and his skill in the writing of Tamil verse. His most famous work, the *Rakshanya Yātrikam* ('the journey of salvation') is based on the *Pilgrim's Progress:* but this is a thoroughly Tamil work, in which the original material has been completely re-thought and re-expressed. It was published in 1894. The style is too difficult for the ordinary reader, but the work has been highly praised by both Hindus and Christians. KP was not learned outside the Tamil sphere, and never mastered English; his strength was in the simplicity and completeness of his devotion. He was instrumental in the conversion of the doyen of all South Indian Christians, Dewan Bahadur Appasamy Pillai, whose son Bishop A. J. Appasamy has written his life.

STEPHEN NEILL

A. J. Appasamy: *Tamil Christian Poet* (World Christian Books, No. 56, London 1966).

KUMM, HERMANN KARL WILHELM (1874–1930), was born at Osterode, Hanover, Germany. He sailed from England in 1898, under the *North Africa Mission, to Egypt, where he married Lucy E. Guinness in 1900. In the same year he founded the German 'Sudan Pioneer Mission', but his colleagues decided not to start work south of Egypt; K. therefore left them. In 1904, after beginning the study of Hausa in Tripoli, he helped to found the *Sudan United Mission and led its first party of four missionaries to

N. Nigeria. In 1906 he visited the USA, and in 1907 South Africa: branches of SUM were established in both countries and missionaries were sent from them to the Sudan. In 1909 K. crossed Africa from the Niger to the Nile, prospecting for the mission, and in 1911 visited Australia and New Zealand, where branches were soon afterwards formed. During the first world war he had to give up the direction of the British branch owing to prejudice due to his German origin. Henceforth he worked mainly from the USA.

K. was an able leader, organizer and evangelist. At the moment when the opportunity was presented to evangelize the tribes south of the Sahara, he was ready to lead, and in large measure to recruit, an international and interdenominational agency of evangelical Christians. The indigenous Evangelical Church, which was planted by it, numbers 122,125 members at the time of writing (1968) and is still growing.

JOHN GOODWIN

I. V. Cleverdon: *Pools on the Glowing Sand. The Story of Karl Kumm* (Melbourne 1936); J. L. Maxwell: *Half a Century of Grace* (London 1954).

KUWAIT. See ARABIAN PENINSULA.

L

LABRADOR. See CANADA.

LACOMBE, ALBERT (1827–1916), of the Oblate order, one of the greatest of RC missionaries in Canada, was born at St. Sulpice, Lower Canada, and, after ordination as priest in 1849, was sent to the Canadian north-west. In 1852 he moved to Edmonton, at that time the furthest outpost of civilization to the west, and later to St. Anne. Never the pastor of a settled parish, L. covered immense distances, ministering to scattered groups of Indians and people of mixed race. He founded a number of the first schools in the area. He had so completely won the confidence of the Indian peoples, that he was able to serve as a mediator between these warring tribes, and on a number of occasions to help the Canadian government in its complex negotiations with these peoples, who felt their whole way of life threatened by the arrival of the settlers and the disturbing influences of western civilization. L's name is still held in veneration, and not only by RCs, throughout Western Canada.

EDITORS

K. Hughes: *Father Lacombe, the Black-robe Voyageur* (Toronto 1911); J. Phelan: *The Bold Heart: the Story of Father Lacombe* (Toronto 1956); *Encyclopedia Canadiana*, Vol. VI, p.42.

LAITY. 'Laymen are the spearhead of the church in the world; the true 20th century evangelist is the instructed and witnessing layman.' This description came out of the preparation for the *WCC Assembly at *Evanston in 1954. In fact, laymen and very especially lay women have played a crucial missionary role ever since the first centuries. Not only have laymen in all generations helped to build up the inner life of the church through their prayers, their obedience to God's will, their material gifts, and their gifts of service, theological reflection and leadership, but the quality of their Christian lives and their spontaneous 'gossiping the gospel' to neighbours and colleagues have been decisive in the missionary outreach of the church. This is increasingly being recognized in all confessions and continents. Consideration of the history, the present state and the future of Christian missions can therefore no longer be limited to the work of professional missionaries (ordained and unordained) and the activities of missionary societies and institutions, but must include the total witness of a missionary church in which the L. immediately comes to the forefront.

In the different periods of development of modern missions the following major lay contributions can be discerned: (1) Laymen were instrumental in the creation of Protestant missionary societies and of Bible societies. Outstanding among them were Baron J. von *Welz (1621–1668), Count N. L. von *Zinzendorf (1700–1760), the members of the 'Clapham Sect' in Great Britain and above all J. R. *Mott (1865–1955) and his colleagues in the *YMCA, *YWCA and *WSCF. Similarly members of Orthodox Christian youth organizations are now behind the present missionary awakening of the Orthodox churches. In the RC church also, where missions were mainly run by monastic orders, a marked shift towards the lay apostolate is noticeable. (2) In the initial period of many younger churches both in the non-western world and in the secularized industrial-urban society of the west, the spontaneous witness of the L. plays a decisive role. It is amazing how often this witness has preceded the work of pioneer missionaries and thus laid the foundation of a church. A new awareness of this fact has led to the present-day emphasis on the missionary significance of 'laymen working abroad', i.e. Christians who in their daily work as civil servants, teachers, employees of commercial enterprises advisers in governmental and inter-governmental development projects witness to their faith in areas where no church exists. (3) In the period of missionary guidance, characterized by clerical *paternalism, laymen made their greatest contribution through their devoted service in missionary institutions as teachers, nurses, artisans, etc. In this period, which in many places still persists, the 'church-employed' laymen helping or opposing the missionaries and the laymen involved in church organizations and activities came to the forefront. Lay training is then mainly conceived as training for church work. (4) More recently the layman's collaboration with men of other religious and secular faiths, his responsible participation in the political, social and economic struggles of our time, his *being* the church in and for the world have been emphasized. Lay training thus means in the first place the discovery of God's will for concrete life-and-work situations in the modern world, the learning of Christian joy and the gaining of a spiritual discipline enabling the L. to be present as Christians where men suffer and face crucial decisions.

An ecumenical consensus is growing about the definition of the L. Formerly emphasis was laid on the fact that laymen are not ordained like ministers or priests, that they have not committed their whole life to church work like monks, nuns and professional church workers, or that they have not studied theology. Today it is increasingly seen that baptism is the 'ordination' into the L., committing laymen to a lifelong ministry of consecrating the world to God in their secular jobs, a ministry for which much theological discernment is needed.

HANS-RUEDI WEBER

P. Löffler: 'Laymen abroad in World Mission', a select bibliography in *Occasional Bulletin* of MRL, 1966/1; S. C. Neill and H. R. Weber, eds.: *The Layman in Christian History* (London 1963); *The Documents of Vatican II*, Dogmatic Constitution on the Church, chs.2, 4; Decree on the Apostolate of the Laity; Decree on the Church's Missionary Activity; *NCE* VIII, 328–30.

LANGUAGE BARRIERS. Two principal functions of language are (1) effective interpersonal activity and understanding and (2) group identification: the language habits of a speech community are its most distinctive feature in that they are the most difficult to imitate successfully. The combination of these functions presents to the missionary a number of serious barriers.

First, the mastery of any foreign tongue is difficult, for even though the sound and grammatical structures of the language may seem relatively simple, the semantic structure of the language requires almost a lifetime for a foreigner to master fully. Moreover, in many instances, a missionary is required to learn a language which has not been reduced to writing; or if it is written, the facilities for learning it may be pitifully inadequate. Furthermore, he sometimes encounters opposition from local Christian leaders, who may see in his mastery of the local language some threat to their own controls.

When there are a number of relatively small tribes in a given area, missionaries have not infrequently tried to manufacture a 'union dialect', but these have been singularly unsuccessful, for the reactions of the people are simply that 'no one speaks that way'. The more common response in areas of many tribal tongues is not to learn any language, the reason being given that if the missionary learned any one language, the other people would be jealous. This problem becomes even more acute in situations in which the local people are far more interested in acquiring the missionary's language than in his learning to speak theirs.

When there are two competing language groups in the same area, it is often the case that the one with lower socio-economic prestige and status is more likely to accept the missionary's benevolence and message. The result may be that a church is formed of people speaking the less prestigeful language; then persons from the more prestigeful language may refuse to become associated with the church, even though there is considerable bilingualism within the two groups.

In densely populated multi-language communities there is a tendency for the first generation of converts to have distinct churches for each language group. But if there is a unifying language of education, there is often a serious rupture in church life as young people refuse to use the language of their parents.

EUGENE A. NIDA

J. Bram: *Language and Society* (New York 1955); J. A. Loewen: 'Language: Vernacular, Trade, or National?', *Practical Anthropology*, Vol. XII (1965), pp. 97–106; W. A. Smalley: 'Culture Shock, Language Shock, and the Shock of Self-Discovery', *Practical Anthropology*, Vol. X (1963), pp.49–56.

LANGUAGE STUDY AND LANGUAGE SCHOOLS. There are three principal types of situations in which missionaries are involved in language study: (1) major languages in which there are usually some schools on the field, (2) minor languages, which are generally reduced to writing and have some rudimentary but usually inadequate grammatical and dictionary materials, and for which the missionary must depend upon some other missionary or inadequately trained local tutor for help, and (3) primitive languages, which must be learned directly from native speakers and reduced to writing (for this type of work some orientation in linguistics is essential).

The study of language by missionaries may be divided conveniently into (1) pre-field preparation and (2) field study. In the pre-field preparation there are three major types of programmes: (a) short courses on how to learn a foreign language, e.g. the courses given each summer at Victoria College (Toronto, Canada), and at Drew University (Madison, New Jersey), and a number of more elementary programmes taught in various Bible schools and training colleges, (b) special courses in *linguistics, designed primarily to help a person reduce a language to writing and prepare to translate the Scriptures into it (these courses are conducted primarily by the Summer Institute of Linguistics in the USA, UK, Germany and Australia), and (c) intensive

programmes in the learning of specific languages, as sponsored by a number of universities in the USA and Europe, usually with significantly good results, since the languages are taught with the aid of good texts and native speakers of such languages.

Language schools for missionaries abroad include a wide variety of approaches to language learning. Some of these schools, e.g. Spanish (San José, Costa Rica), Portuguese (Campinas, Brazil), Thai (Bangkok, Thailand), and Tagalog, Ilocano, and Cebuano (Manila, Philippines), are well organized and employ effectively modern methods. A number of other schools are attempting to introduce modern methods under adequately trained personnel, but for the most part the level of language instruction in missionary language schools is low.

The major liabilities which missionaries face in language study are (1) the inadequacy of many language schools, (2) insufficient time to give to language study (the fault of the sending boards), (3) over-emphasis upon grammar rather than speaking, (4) insufficient study of the written form of the language in the case of Japanese and Chinese, (5) lack of follow-up instruction and guidance, and (6) failure of the leadership to demand an adequate level of language competence.

EUGENE A. NIDA

E. A. Nida: *Learning a Foreign Language* (New York 1957); W. D. Reyburn: 'Don't Learn That Language!', *Practical Anthropology*, Vol. V (1958), pp.151–78; W. A. Smalley: 'Missionary Language Learning', *Practical Anthropology*, Vol. III (1956), pp. 5–12.

LAOS. A Thēravāda Buddhist kingdom of South-east Asia, in area 88,780 sq.m., and with a population estimated in 1967 at 3,000,000: of these over 30% adhere to tribal religions. *Jesuits from Tongking reached L. in 1630 and the RC *Paris Foreign Missions (MEP) a century later. Permanent RC work has been in progress only since 1876; an apostolic vicariate was set up in 1899. In 1935 the *Oblates of Mary Immaculate (OMI) were assigned to North

L. (apostolic vicariate at Vientiane and Luang Prabang), the MEP to South L. (their headquarters are now at Savannakhet, where an apostolic vicariate was established in 1958). The first priest of the Lao people was ordained in 1963. RC membership, mainly found among Vietnamese immigrants, numbers about 27,000 (WCH 1968), with eight national and 80 expatriate priests.

The Evangelical Mission to L. of the Swiss Open Brethren started work in South L. in 1902 among the lowland Buddhists and finished translating the Lao Bible in 1932. They were joined in 1957 by the *OMF. Their united mission has established 20 local churches with 500 baptized members and an estimated 1,500 adherents. The *CMA began work among the tribes of North L. in 1929; their indigenous Gospel Church of L. has 82 local churches with 3,086 members (WCH 1968). The three Protestant groups co-operate in literature and radio evangelism. In the late 1960s religious freedom was maintained and there were great opportunities among the tribes with very little competition from Buddhism; but access to many mountain areas was hindered by the Vietnamese war.

LOTHAR SCHREINER

G. H. Anderson, ed.: *Christ and Crisis in Southeast Asia* (New York 1968); C. Corthay: *Le Laos, découverte d'un champ missionaire* (Yverdon 1953); J. B. de George: *A la Conquête du Laos* (Hong Kong 1926); *BM* II, 553–55; *NCE* VIII, 381f.

LARSEN, LARS PETER (1862–1940), was born on the island of Zealand in Denmark. In 1888 he obtained his theological degree at Copenhagen University and in 1889 went to India (Madras) as a missionary of the Danish Missionary Society (Lutheran). Mainly because of theological differences L. left the DMS in 1899, and after some years with Madras *YMCA in student work he became professor (1910) at the new United Theological College, Bangalore, and from 1911 Principal. His main subjects were OT and history of religions. In 1918 L. was given an honorary DD by Lund University,

Sweden. From 1924 he worked for the BFBS on the revision of the Tamil Bible.

L. was soon recognized as an outstanding linguist and theologian; he was constantly wrestling with the Bible and its message and relationship to Hinduism and the Hindu (*Christ's Way and Ours*, Calcutta 1923, rev. ed. 1930; *The redemption of man according to Hinduism and Christianity*, Madras 1905). He had close friendship with many Hindus and tried 'to be one with them in their search'; 'our task is not to refute or combat or conquer the others' but 'to understand, not in order to describe but to help'. L. had an extraordinary capacity for friendship—was a 'great listener'. He was widely used by the various churches and was convinced 'that for us out here, Lutheranism cannot be the main question'. In 1932 L. returned to Denmark where he died.

ERIK W. NIELSEN

C. Bindslev: *L. P. Larsen* (Bangalore and Calcutta 1962).

LAS CASAS, BARTHOLOMEW DE (1474–1566), went to the New World in 1502, and accepted without question the leisured life of a well-to-do cleric. But in 1514 he underwent a kind of conversion, declared that everything done by the Spaniards since they came to the western world had been wrong and cruel, and constituted himself a lifelong champion of the rights of the indigenous races. Undoubtedly he idealized and romanticized them; undoubtedly, also, he stood on the side of the gospel in declaring that the Indians were men, and to be treated as such, and that they were perfectly capable of understanding and accepting the gospel. The high point of his activities came with a great public debate, held at Valladolid in 1550–51 between LC and Juan Ginés de Sepúlveda, a learned scholastic theologian, who maintained the contrary view, that the Indians are among those races which Aristotle had declared to be naturally destined for *slavery. The dispute was carried on with great learning by both the disputants; but the question proved to be so thorny that the judges did not venture to pronounce a judgment as to which had proved his case. From 1544 to 1547 LC was bishop of Chiapa in Mexico; but he resigned this office in order to return to Spain and to carry on for another 20 years his battles on behalf of the Indians.

Not all the enterprises of LC were successful. An attempt at missionary work in Guatemala, on what he believed to be the correct lines, was frustrated by the violence of the local inhabitants. For a short time LC himself was an advocate of Negro slavery in the western world, as the only means by which the weaker inhabitants of the Caribbean could be saved from extermination. He soon changed his mind, when he saw what the realities of that slavery were. His real monument lies in the humane and civilized legislation brought into force, largely under his influence, by the king of Spain. By the New Laws of 1542 the *encomienda* system, under which the Indians were left helpless at the mercy of their masters, was brought to an end. Those laws could not be put into force with the fulness that was intended, and did not put an end to the brutality of the white man towards the brown and the black. But at least the voice of Christianity and civilization was heard. LC is to be remembered as one of the founders of the modern world.

STEPHEN NEILL

L. Hanke: *Aristotle and the American Indians* (London 1959), *Bartolomé de Las Casas* (The Hague 1951); *LTK* VI, 802f; *NCE* VIII, 394f.

LATENT CHURCH CONCEPT. The idea of the 'hidden church' has been familiar in all epochs of Christian theology. No man may presume to define exactly the limits of the *church; we know exactly where its centre is—in the risen Jesus Christ: the location of its circumference is known to God alone. But special attention has in recent years been drawn to the concept in three separate ways: (1) The church in the west is faced with the phenomenon of a calamitous decline in church attendance, and in an apparent diminution of the Chris-

tian substance, which had been built up over the centuries. But, apart from a not inconsiderable number of atheists and militant anti-clericals, people in general seem to regard themselves as still being in some way related to the church. They arrange for their children to be baptized; in most cases they desire that they should have religious instruction; they are offended if they are bluntly told that they are not Christians; they understand extremely well Christian ethical demands, though in the majority of cases they do not intend to accept them as the rule for their own lives. Clearly in a great many cases what remains of the Christian substance is extremely little; but would the church be justified in treating these people simply as heathen, as though no sound of the gospel had ever reached them? (2) In many countries it is clear that the *rayonnement*, the spiritual outreach of the church, is far greater than would be suggested by its actual membership. Countless pupils in missionary schools have retained something of what they learned. Reverence for the person of Jesus Christ in non-Christian countries is astonishingly widely diffused. Some sincere believers are held back from baptism by family circumstances which seem to make open confession of faith almost impossible. Sales of Bibles in Japan, which make of it a perennial best-seller in that country, suggest that allegiance to Jesus Christ, though in many cases far less than complete, is a reality in the lives of a great many Japanese whose names are not to be found in any church register. (3) The view has been spreading among theologians that the effects of the death and resurrection of Jesus Christ are universal for the human race and cannot be limited to 'the elect' alone. He died for all; it is impossible for his death to be wholly ineffective in relation to any of them. Since Easter it is impossible for any human being to be born into the world and to be totally unrelated to the risen Christ. What is the nature of this relationship? The question has been discussed at length in a number of works by the *Jesuit theologian Karl Rahner, who is perhaps prepared to go rather further than the majority of his fellow-theologians. The new status of the human race, he says, must become sacramentally evident, and this can take place within the church through baptism; but any genuine seeking after God, even outside the church, may have quasi-sacramental validity. Others would not be prepared to go so far. Certainly Christ died for all; but what difference does this actually make to the inhabitants of Tibet, who have never so much as heard the name of Christ? It seems that much careful theological thought on this issue is still required.

STEPHEN NEILL

S. C. Neill: *The Church and Christian Union* (Oxford 1968), pp.26–27, referring to K. Rahner: *Schriften zur Theologie*, Vol. II (1960), pp.7–94.

LATIN AMERICA. See AMERICA, LATIN.

LATIN AMERICA MISSION. The LAM is a service mission with headquarters in San José, Costa Rica. It was founded in 1921 as the Latin America Evangelization Campaign by the Rev. and Mrs Harry Strachan and continues to give priority to evangelism. Under its auspices 'Evangelism in Depth' campaigns (with emphasis on evangelism by a mobilized church) were held in seven republics, 1960 to 1967.

LAM expanded into leadership training in 1923 with the founding of Seminario Bíblico which in 1966 had 59 students representing fifteen countries and 23 evangelical groups. Social concern was early revealed in the founding of a hospital in 1929 and an orphanage in 1932. Further interest in youth produced *Escuadrón de Servicio Christiano* in 1947, camp grounds in 1948, primary and secondary schools in Costa Rica and Colombia, and university work patterned in part after the *Inter-varsity Christian Fellowship.

A literature division was organized in 1948 which publishes among its titles the Spanish Bible *Concordancia* and *Diccionario*, and has book stores in four countries. Also in 1948 LAM established TIFC ('Light-

house of the Caribbean'), the second missionary radio station in history, initiating a broad communications ministry.

In 1937 LAM began an extensive missionary work in northern Colombia. Church work in Costa Rica has produced *Asociación de Iglesias Bíblicas Costarricences*.

WILTON M. NELSON

Latin America Mission: *Evangelism in Depth* (Chicago 1961).

LATOURETTE, KENNETH SCOTT (1884–1968), American historian of missions, was born in Oregon City, USA, where his grandfather had come as one of the early settlers of that area. He was educated in McMinnville College (later Linfield College), Oregon, and at Yale University and was ordained as a Baptist minister. While at McMinnville he joined the *SVM, and throughout his life he continued to play an active part in that organization. After completing doctoral studies at Yale he spent two years (1910–12) as a teacher at Yale-in-China at Changsha. Illness forced his return to America. He then taught in Reed College, Oregon, and Denison University, Ohio, before assuming the professorship of missions at Yale University in 1921, where he continued to labour until his retirement in 1953.

L's major interest was in the education of successive generations of students, especially in matters related to the world mission of the church, and in writing on East Asian history and Christian missions. He was one of the pioneers among American scholars in the study of East Asia. His first widely known books were *The Development of China* (1917) and *The Development of Japan* (1918). These were followed by *A History of Christian Missions in China* (1929), a work which has remained unrivalled in its field, and *The Chinese: Their History and Culture* (1934), a two-volume standard work. From this emphasis on China his studies soon expanded to a global coverage. The work for which he is most famous and which has become the major work on the history of missions is his seven-volume study of *The History of the Expansion of Chris-*

tianity (1937–1945). In this he covered six continents, 20 centuries and all branches of the church. Numerous other books came from his pen. The major ones were a general *History of Christianity* (1953) and the five-volume *Christianity in a Revolutionary Age. A History of Christianity in the Nineteenth and Twentieth Centuries* (1958–1962).

L's greatest contribution lies in the comprehensiveness of his grasp and presentation. Not only did he cover all periods and all parts of the church in his studies but he branched out beyond the organized church to deal with the movements springing from it and its influence upon its environment. In addition to his writing and teaching he played an active role in the central councils of the missionary movement. He was a member of the board of the ABFMS for over 20 years and was at one time president of the American Baptist Convention. He was actively involved in the *IMC, the International *YMCA and the Yale-in-China board, and was president of the Far Eastern Association and the Japan International Christian University Foundation. He was long active in the *WCC and played a part in drafting its constitution. He was elected president of the American Society of Church History and of the American Historical Association.

CHARLES W. FORMAN

E. T. Bachmann: 'Kenneth Scott Latourette: Historian and Friend' in W. C. Harr, ed.: *Frontiers of the Christian World Mission since 1938. Essays in Honor of Kenneth Scott Latourette* (New York and London 1962); K. S. Latourette: *Beyond the Ranges. An Autobiography* (Grand Rapids 1967).

LATTER-DAY SAINTS MISSIONS. See MORMON MISSIONS.

LAUBACH LITERACY, INC., is a non-profit educational organization founded in 1955 by Dr Frank C. Laubach (1884–1970), originator of the 'Each One Teach One' concept of adult literacy instruction. Beginning in 1930, Laubach developed his unique methods as a missionary among the Lanao Moros of the Philippines; from there he and his associates have gone on to work with government leaders, educators, missionaries and other concerned citizens in more than 100 countries. Adult literacy charts, primers, graded books and other materials have been prepared in 312 languages and it is estimated that over 100 million people have been taught to read by the Laubach methods. With headquarters in Syracuse, NY, but with branch offices and centres in many parts of the globe, LL. conceives of its main function as showing others how to combat illiteracy for themselves by (1) training workers and (2) providing materials for their use. Nonsectarian, the organization retains its original missionary inspiration. In the words of its founder, it is 'an organization of volunteers motivated to Christian compassionate service to the helpless half of the world'.

PETER G. GOWING

F. C. Laubach: *Thirty Years with the Silent Billion* (Westwood, N.J. 1960).

LAVIGERIE, CHARLES MARTIAL ALLEMAND, CARDINAL (1825–1892), the most outstanding leader of the RC missionary enterprise in Africa, was born at Bayonne, France, became bishop of Nancy in 1863, archbishop of Algiers in 1872, archbishop of Carthage and primate of Africa in 1884. From the start of his work in Africa, L. was marked both by breadth of vision, and by vigour and skill in execution. He saw it as his task first to make of Algeria a Christian country, and from that as base to extend the sway of the Christian church throughout Africa, much as the French government was spreading French authority and the influence of French culture. L's greatest achievement was the foundation in 1868 of the *'White Fathers', the society the members of which were to carry out his ideals for the spread of the Christian faith throughout Africa. The Missionary Sisters of our Lady of Africa followed in 1869. L. steadfastly refused to consider any partition of areas as between RC and Protestant—the whole of Africa was his business, and the presence of the *CMS in Uganda could not stand in the way of his plans to enter that field with his French missionaries.

L. played an important part in the history of the French church through his tolerant attitude towards the Third Republic. When the majority of bishops were still committed to the uncompromising hostility proclaimed by Pius IX, L. was prepared to accept the more positive attitude of Leo XIII, and was one of the mouthpieces through which that pope declared his new policy of 'rallying' to the Republic (12 November 1890).

A pitiless foe of *slavery, L. carried on in the RC world an anti-slavery campaign which recalls the similar campaign carried on by Wilberforce and his friends in the Protestant world nearly a century earlier. It was a personal triumph for him, when in 1890 the General Act of the Brussels Conference for the Abolition of the Slave Trade was signed, and for the first time the great powers officially accepted it as their responsibility to see to it that the slave trade should disappear from Africa.

STEPHEN NEILL

J. de Artèche: *The Cardinal of Africa: Charles Lavigerie* (Eng. tr., London 1964); G. D. Kittler: *The White Fathers* (London 1957); A. Pons: *La nouvelle Eglise d'Afrique* (Tunis n.d.); J. Tournier: *Le Cardinal Lavigerie et son action politique, 1863–1892* (Paris 1913); *LTK* VI, 841f.; *NCE* VIII, 541f.

LAWES, WILLIAM GEORGE (1839–1907), made outstanding contributions to the development of the Christian mission in two Pacific areas, particularly in New Guinea. He was born in Berkshire, England, and in 1860 was appointed by the *LMS as the first resident missionary at Niue (Savage Island). An enthusiastic teacher and painstaking student of language and culture, L. began training evangelists and translating the NT. By 1870 this work was both completed and revised. When the LMS began operations in New Guinea in 1871, L. was transferred from Niue and settled at Port Moresby in 1874, bringing with him a party of Niuean evangelists. He made many journeys along the coast and inland to the ranges, but his principal contribution lay in

language study, translation and simple ministerial training. L's *Grammar of the Motu Language*, several times revised, is still the basic text for the study of this vernacular. The Motu NT used today is a revision of L's translation first printed in 1891. Glasgow University honoured him with a DD in 1895. Lawes College in Papua is named after him. In 1906 L. retired and made his home in Sydney, New South Wales, where he died.

NORMAN COCKS

J. King: *W. G. Lawes of Savage Island and New Guinea* (London 1909); W. G. Lawes: *The Four Gospels in Motu* (Sydney 1885), *Grammar of the Motu Language* (Sydney 1885); *DNB*, 2nd suppl. ii, 424–26.

LAWS, ROBERT (1851–1934), was born at Mannofield, Aberdeen, Scotland. He studied while working in his father's cabinetmaker's workshop. A delicate but determined boy, a born organizer, he developed a tough physique suited to his later arduous life. Ordained in 1875, he departed for Malawi to establish a large mission at Livingstonia in memory of *Livingstone, as a centre of commerce, civilization and Christianity. Assisted by devoted colleagues, clerical, medical, educational and industrial, he planted the gospel among the warlike Abangoni. He trained promising youths as teachers and artisans, established and directed a hospital and printing press. L. was the first Moderator of the Church of Central Africa Presbyterian, with which the DRC (South Africa) later joined. His own work, sponsored both by the Free Church of Scotland and by the Established Church, was a unified effort. L. emphasized indigenous responsibility and unity. Three African ministers were ordained before the first world war. By 1925 Livingstonia was a flourishing community with 19,000 communicants and 1,100 office bearers and 43,000 children attending mission schools taught by 1,500 African teachers. Where Livingstone wandered 50 years earlier as a solitary Christian, this Christian community developed. Highly appreciative of his sound judgment the government appointed him to the Legislative Council in 1912. He obtained many square miles of land for the Africans. He resembled Livingstone in many ways; in aim and character he was a sort of living sequel to Livingstone—a real pioneer.

GERHARDUS C. OOSTHUIZEN

W. P. Livingstone: *Laws of Livingstonia* (London 1921); *DNB* (1931–1940), 532f.

LAY MISSIONERS (RC). In a sense LM are as old as the church. During its earliest years the *laity played a crucial role in spreading the teachings of Christ. And it was a layman, Peter Ri, who introduced Christianity in his native Korea in the 18th century, after he had studied and been baptized in China.

Today's organized structure for lay mission work is, however, relatively new in the RC world. It goes back to 1922, when an institute was founded in Germany to send doctors to mission lands.

In the USA the movement started growing in an organized way only after the second world war. Since then more than 20 different lay mission groups have been formed. Some specialize in serving particular areas of the world, others in providing special types of vocational skills. Among the largest are Papal Volunteers for Latin America, founded at the request of the Holy See in 1960, and the Extension Society Volunteers, which recruits lay personnel for home mission work. Laymen's Overseas Service (LAOS), another such agency, was initiated in 1962, with headquarters in Jackson, Miss., USA.

The role of LM is threefold. They give an example of Christianity lived fully in daily life to unbelievers at every level of society. They dedicate their professional and technical skills to the welfare of the people among whom they work. And they inspire or train local leaders to join in the effort to build a Christian social order.

RAYMOND M. BOYLE

P. Jacquemart: chapter (pp. 317–28) in J. Hofinger, ed.: *Teaching all Nations* (Freiburg 1961); G. Nische: chapter (pp.34–41) in M. Bates, ed.: *The Lay Apostle in Latin America Today* (Washington, DC 1960).

12*

LAYMEN IN MISSIONS. See LAITY.

LAYMEN'S FOREIGN MISSIONS INQUIRY. On 17 January 1930 a number of Baptist laymen were called together in New York City by Mr John D. Rockefeller Jr to discuss with Dr John R. *Mott, who had just returned from a trip around the world, some of the difficulties that the world missionary enterprise was going through. They determined rather spontaneously that night to see what they could do about the situation. A committee was formed and other denominations were invited to join until eventually the LFMI came into existence with membership drawn from seven denominations: Baptist (Northern), Congregational, Methodist Episcopal, Presbyterian Church in USA, Protestant Episcopal, Reformed Church in America and United Presbyterian. The seven denominations were each unofficially represented by a group of five men and women who constituted the 35 Directors of the Inquiry.

The first stage of the Inquiry was carried on by the Institute of Social and Religious Research which was engaged to get the facts upon which the Inquiry might be based. In the fall of 1930 the Institute sent out three teams of fact-finders, about 10 each to the three fields with which the Inquiry had decided to deal: India-Burma, China and Japan. Their work took nearly a year and was 'the most careful, objective study of a large cross-section of Protestant missions ever made'.

The second stage of the Inquiry was carried out by a distinguished 15-member Commission of Appraisal, of which Harvard Professor William Ernest *Hocking was chairman. Its purpose was 'To aid laymen to determine their attitude toward Foreign Missions, by reconsidering the functions of such Missions in the world of today'. This Commission, with the material collected by the fact-finders in their possession, sailed from New York in September 1931, and spent nearly a whole year together visiting the three fields of inquiry in Asia and drawing up their report. The report, entitled *Re-Thinking Missions*, was published and formally presented by the Directors and Sponsors of the Inquiry to representatives of foreign mission boards at a two-day meeting in the Hotel Roosevelt, New York City, on Friday and Saturday, 18–19 November 1932.

The three parts of the report dealt with the principles of missions, aspects of mission work, and mission administration. It suggested that the aim of missions is 'to seek with people of other lands a true knowledge and love of God, expressing in life and word what we have learned through Jesus Christ'; that 'the Christian will regard himself as a co-worker with the forces which are making for righteousness within every religious system'; that 'the relation between religions must take increasingly hereafter the form of a common search for truth'; and that the missionary 'will look forward, not to the destruction of these (non-Christian) religions, but to their continued co-existence with Christianity, each stimulating the other in growth toward the ultimate goal, unity in the completest religious truth'. This approach departed sharply from the more traditionally held concept of missions, the role of the missionary, and the relation of Christianity to other religions. As such, the report stimulated recognition of the missionary problem as a theological problem and provoked basic re-thinking of the issues involved, but was itself widely criticized for its tone of optimism and relativism.

Unfortunately, the controversy surrounding theological aspects of the report diverted attention from the great wealth of information and material presented elsewhere in the Report, and also in the *Supplementary Series* of seven volumes published in 1933 which contained selected material from the 'Fact-Finders' Reports' and the 'Regional Reports' of the Commission of Appraisal.

GERALD H. ANDERSON

K. S. Latourette: 'The Laymen's Foreign Missions Inquiry', *IRM*, XXII (1933), 153ff.; K. S. Latourette: 'Re-Thinking Missions After Twenty-Five Years', *IRM*, XLVI (1957), 164–70; J. A. Mackay: 'The Theology of the Laymen's Foreign Missions Inquiry', *IRM*, XXII (1933), 174–88; *Re-Thinking Missions* (New York 1932); R. E. Speer: '*Re-Thinking Missions' Examined* (New York 1933); *Laymen's Foreign Missions Inquiry, Supplementary Series* (7 vols., New York 1933).

LEBANON. A republic of west Asia, bounded on the west by the Mediterranean sea, on the north and east by Syria, and on the south by Israel. Area 4,015 sq.m. (10,400 sq.km.); population (estimated in 1963) 1,750,000, of whom rather more than half are Christian and somewhat less than half are Muslim. Christianity has had a continuous history in L. from the 1st century. The largest Christian community is Maronite, the only eastern church which is wholly in communion with Rome. Second in size among the Christian groups is the Greek Orthodox church.

RC missions have existed since crusading times and are strong today. Among the uniate churches, (i.e. eastern rite churches under the authority of Rome), the Maronite church is by far the largest, making up about 30% of the population of the country. A movement to come under Rome began during the crusades, and culminated in official confirmation in 1516, since which time the whole of the Maronite church has been catholic. The *Jesuit University of St. Joseph in Beirut (founded 1881) is the best known of the RC institutions.

Protestant work was begun in 1823 by P. *Fisk and E. Parsons, sent by the *ABCFM. In 1870 the mission was handed over to the American Presbyterians, and in 1959 it was integrated into the *indigenous church which had come into being through its work, the Evangelical Synod of Syria and Lebanon. It engages in evangelism, education and medical work, as do other Protestant groups; these include the Union of Armenian Evangelical Churches, the Lebanon Evangelical Mission (formerly British Syrian Mission), Southern US Baptists, Friends Service Council, SDA, Church of God, Swiss Friends of Armenia, *Oeuvres Protestantes Françaises*, the Danish Birds' Nest, Schneller's Orphanage, and others.

The total Protestant community numbers about 23,000.

The Near East Council of Churches, with membership from 14 countries, has its headquarters in Beirut. Ecumenical relations between RC, Orthodox and Protestant have made important advances in L. in recent years.

HARRY G. DORMAN, JR

F. J. Bliss, ed.: *The Reminiscences of Daniel Bliss* (New York 1920); H. H. Jessup: *Fifty-Three Years in Syria* (New York 1910); G. H. Scherer: *Mediterranean Missions* (Beirut n.d.); *The News Bulletin of the Near East Christian Council*, quarterly (Cairo, Beirut, 1926); *BM* II, 555–62; *NCE* VIII, 594; *WKL*, 841f.

LEBBE, VINCENT (1877–1940), was born at Ghent in Belgium, and in 1895 entered the Congregation for Missions at Paris. Here he adopted modern ideas of historical criticism, biblical renewal, the liturgical movement, Christian democracy. In 1901 he was sent to China, where the traces of the *Boxer rising were still evident, and later in the same year was ordained priest. L. set himself, especially during his activity at Tientsin from 1906 to 1916, to make links between the Christian faith and the Chinese national renewal. He set himself to free the church from the ties which bound it all too closely to the politics and the culture of the west. He was met with misunderstanding and opposition, was removed from Tientsin and sent to work in South China. In 1917 he addressed a remarkable letter to his bishop, Mgr. Reynaud, in which he stressed the duty of patriotism on the part of Chinese Christians, the urgency of freeing the church from the foreign protectorate, the need for an indigenous clergy, eligible for admission to all levels of ecclesiastical responsibility, including the episcopate. The bull of Pope Benedict XV, *Maximum Illud* of 1919, confirmed him in his views, but exasperated his opponents. In 1920 he was sent to Europe as chaplain to Chinese students, a work for which he carried out the preliminary organization. In the same year he was summoned for consultation by Cardinal Van Rossum,

was received by the pope, and indicated the names of Chinese priests suitable for elevation to the episcopate. Several of those named by him were among the first six Chinese bishops consecrated by Pius XI on 28 October 1926. On the authority of one of these L. returned to China in 1927. Following his example a number of European secular priests placed themselves at the disposal of Chinese bishops; this was the origin of the Missionary Auxiliaries who take their place in the ranks of the indigenous clergy, entirely under the authority of Asian and African bishops.

In 1927 L. founded at An-kwo the 'Little Brothers of St. John the Baptist' and the 'Theresian Sisters', to combine monastic life with missionary and social activity. During the conflict with Japan, L. put himself at the disposal of the Chinese army, with a corps of voluntary stretcher bearers organized by the Little Brothers. In 1938 the government asked him to accept responsibility for calling into being a patriotic and cultural movement for the whole of China. Completely worn out L. died at Chung King in June 1940. He was proclaimed a national hero, and his Chinese name *Lei Ming-yuan* is inscribed in the official annals of China.

J. BRULS

J. Leclercq: *Thunder in the Distance: the Life of P. Lebbe* (Eng. tr., New York 1964); A. Sohier, ed.: *Lettres du P. Lebbe* (Tournai 1960); *Eglise Vivante* XVII (1965)—special number devoted to the work of P. Lebbe; *LTK* VI, 847; *NCE* VIII, 595.

LEGGE, JAMES (1815–1897), was born at Huntly, Aberdeenshire, Scotland. Educated at King's College, Aberdeen University (M.A. 1835), he thought of teaching Latin, but offered himself to the *LMS, and after theological training at Highbury Theological College, London (a Congregationalist foundation, opened in 1826 and now incorporated in New College, London), he was ordained a Congregational minister, appointed to the Ultra Ganges Mission and sailed for Malacca in 1839. Arriving in 1840 he took charge of the Anglo-Chinese College, founded by William *Milne. When

Hong Kong became a British possession in 1842 the LMS decided to move its missionaries from Malaya and the East Indies to Hong Kong and the Treaty Ports in China. L. moved the ACC to Hong Kong in 1843. He was the first minister of Union Church, Hong Kong (1843–73), and concurrently head of the Anglo-Chinese College which he developed as a theological college and boys' school. The publication of his famous translation of the Chinese classics began in 1861 and the five volumes were completed in 1886. L. retired from Hong Kong in 1873 and was made a fellow of Corpus Christi College, Oxford, in 1875. He became the first professor of Chinese at Oxford in 1876, a post he held till his death.

His great contribution was his translation of the Confucian classics and of the texts of Taoism. His was the first full translation into English and it opened up a vast new field of study. From the time of his arrival in Malacca in 1840 until his death he was a diligent student of Chinese classical literature. The contents of his five volumes of translation are: Vol. 1, The Prolegomena, Confucian Analects, the Great Learning and the Doctrine of the Mean; Vol. 2, The Works of Mencius; Vol. 3, The Shoo King or Book of Historical Documents; Vol. 4, The She King or Book of Poetry, and Vol. 5, The Chun Tsew (Spring and Autumn Annals) with the Tso Chuen (Tso's Commentary). Each volume contains the Chinese text, an English translation and extensive notes, mostly translated from Chinese commentators. In addition L. translated the Hsiao King or Book of Filial Piety and the Taoist texts including the Tao Teh King and selections from Chuang Tzu and other writings. Also besides reproducing some of his translations in The Sacred Books of the East he added translations of the Yi King (the Book of Changes) and the Li Ki (the Record of Rites). Editions of the English translation and notes of the Confucian Classics were also published and to these L. prefaced introductory essays and lives of Confucius and Mencius.

FRANK K. BALCHIN

H. E. Legge: *James Legge* (London 1905); *DNB*, Suppl. iii, 87.

LEIBNIZ, GOTTFRIED WILHELM VON, AND MISSIONS. In 1689, in the course of a sojourn in Rome, L. (1646–1716) came in close contact with *Jesuit missionaries from China (notably Grimaldi) who thereafter supplied him with copious information about China. The active interest which he thereafter took in that country was especially focused in the emperor Kong-hi, who in his eyes represented the ideal ruler. So he desired to promote the foundation of Protestant missionary work in China. As a challenge to this task, for which he regarded Russia as the most suitable jumping-off place, he published in 1697 *Novissima Sinica* ('Latest News from China'), a work which exercised a deep influence on A. H. Francke, the founder of the *Danish mission to South India, and on the formation of the Anglican *SPG. When L. was successful in bringing into existence the 'Society' (the Academy of Sciences in Berlin), he set before it as a project the opening up of China and the effecting of an exchange between its culture and that of China. As the chief result of such a mission he hoped to see the promotion of science on all levels, especially the study of languages, and the spread of civilization; he defined the principal goal of the mission as being 'the propagation of the faith by means of the sciences'. Whereas the *pietistic school of the time (Spener, Francke) saw as the basis for mission only the biblical and religious factors, L. brought to the fore the motives of culture and civilization as the direction of all missionary activity towards the common well-being.

That which was specifically new in the thought of L., in contrast to the missions of the *Jesuits and the colonial mission of the Dutch, is to be found in his demand for a purely scientific foundation for missionary work. The presupposition for this is a purely philosophical knowledge of God, which is to be used as a criterion of the truth of religion in general. L. is concerned to bring into prominence the analogies between Chinese religion and the Christian faith, which are to be referred back to the substantial unity of the human spirit. The mind of L. tended towards the reconciliation of all contradictions. In consequence he hoped that a mission, conceived as an inter-confessional enterprise, would serve greatly to promote his efforts in the cause of Christian unity. On his view, the confessional differences of Europe should not be carried over to the mission field. He was thus concerned to go behind the various manifestations of religion to central truths, and hoped that the progress of science and learning would lead to an approximation of the religions to one another. As a missionary method, he approved of the collection of the so-called *logoi spermatikoi* (seeds of truth in the religions), as points of contact between them.

L's ideas exercised an inspiring influence on many of his contemporaries (A. H. Francke, Conrad Mel, Gilbert Burnet, La Croze) but in his lifetime were not put into effect, and least of all by the Berlin Academy. For the immediately following period the pietistic understanding of mission prevailed. Only at the end of the 19th century were L's ideas taken up again, and some of his plans carried out in practice.

ROLF CHRISTIANSEN

F. R. Merkel: *G. W. von Leibniz und die China-Mission* (Leipzig 1920), *Leibniz und China* (1952), 'The Missionary Attitude of the Philosopher G. W. von Leibniz, *IRM* IX (1920), 399–410.

LEIPZIG MISSIONARY SOCIETY, THE, was founded in 1836 in Dresden, Saxony, as the missionary arm of the new awakening of European Lutherans. Under the able leadership of Dr Karl *Graul it found its field of work in South India where it revived the heritage of the *Danish Halle Mission, centred in Tranquebar, with special emphasis on high professional and linguistic qualifications of mission workers. Graul's intention to make the Leipzig MS the one central Lutheran mission enterprise failed. Co-operation with the Church of Sweden Mission resulted in the establishment of the Tamil Evangelical Lutheran Church. A new field was opened among the Chagga people in British East Africa (1893) which became the basis of the Lutheran church in Northern

Tanganyika. In 1955 the Leipzig MS joined in existing Lutheran work in New Guinea and began training Lutheran ministers for Brazil. Disruption and restrictions after the second world war hit the society specially hard. While headquarters remained in Leipzig, East Germany, most of the work is now based in West Germany.

H.-W. GENSICHEN

P. Fleisch: *Hundert Jahre lutherischer Mission* (Leipzig 1936).

LEPROSY MISSIONS. During the Middle Ages leper houses were founded in all parts of Europe as acts of Christian charity. The Order of St. Lazarus ministered to lepers from the 4th century until 1490; the *Franciscans continued to serve them as occasion offered in their missions to each continent. It was only in the 19th century, however, that systematic missionary work among leprosy sufferers began on any large scale. Often it took the form of co-operation between missions, or between mission and government. In 1811 W. *Carey helped to found a leper asylum in Calcutta; in 1817 the *Moravian Mission in South Africa began work in the new government segregation centre at Hemel-en-Aarde. Eventually the governments of many countries established such centres, in which both RC and Protestant missionaries were allowed to work. Among the former the Franciscan nuns were particularly numerous and effective. In 1874 W. C. *Bailey founded in Ireland the Mission to Lepers in India, known since 1965 as the Leprosy Mission. He and his colleagues travelled in India gathering leprosy sufferers into homes, where they found security, medical treatment, opportunities of education and work to help maintain themselves, and an introduction to the Christian gospel. Most of these homes were staffed by existing Protestant agencies with financial help from the mission. In 1888 the mission opened the first of its own stations at Purulia, Chota Nagpur. The work spread from India to other parts of Asia and to Africa. Support grew in Great Britain, Canada, Australasia and the USA, where the American Mission to Lepers (now American Leprosy Missions Inc.) was founded. In the mid-20th century missionary doctors, with others, discovered that sulphone drugs may be used to cure leprosy. Owing to the discharge of large numbers of former patients symptom-free, the population of most leprosy settlements has decreased. Missionary welfare work is directed to rehabilitating former patients for life and work in their home community. See also BAILEY, WELLESLEY COSBY; DAMIEN, FATHER.

JOHN GOODWIN

A. D Miller: *An Inn Called Welcome: the Story of the Mission to Lepers, 1874–1917* (London 1965).

LESOTHO, up to independence in October 1966 called Basutoland, is surrounded on all sides by the Republic of South Africa; area 11,720 sq.m. Population: present in L. 883,000; absent on migratory-labour and studies 117,000; total 1,000,000. King *Moshoeshoe I, founder of the Basotho nation, gathered between 1820 and 1830 the broken tribes of the mountainous Drakensberg region into a homogeneous nation and defended them against hostile tribes and the Boers of the Orange Free State from his fortress Thaba Bosiu. The first missionary penetration was made in 1833 by the French Protestants E. *Casalis, Arbousset and Gosselin of the *PEMS, invited by Moshoeshoe and stationed at Morija. In 1862 the French RC missionaries Bishop Allard and Fr Gerard arrived and were placed in the Roma-valley. French Canadians continued the work. After L. had become a British Protectorate in 1868, the Anglican church began to work in Leribe, in 1872. Later the Methodists, the Assemblies of God, the SDA and a number of independent African churches began working in L.

In 1886 after a victory of the Free State Boers the French missionaries were expelled for a short time. The first national (Protestant) synod was formed in 1872. Full autonomy was granted to the Lesotho Evangelical Church, which had grown out of the work of the PEMS, in April 1964.

70% of the Basotho are estimated to be Christians, 44% of whom are RC, and the great majority of the remaining 26% are Protestants. In August 1965 the L. Christian Council was formed with RC participation. A fully ecumenical department of theology (RC, Protestant and Anglican lecturers) is operating at the new university of Botswana, Lesotho and Swaziland at Roma, Lesotho.

MARIE-LOUISE MARTIN

E. Casalis: *The Basutos* (Cape Town 1965); L. Damane: *Peace* (Morija 1947); U. Ellenberger: *A Century of Mission Work in Basutoland* (Morija 1938); R. C. Germond: *Chronicles of Basutoland* (Morija 1967); *BM* II, 120–23.

LESZCZINSKI, FILOFEI (1650–1727), a Russian Orthodox missionary in Siberia, was originally a monk of the cave-monastery at Kiev. In 1702 he was appointed by Peter the Great as bishop of Tobolsk, and charged with the organization of the mission to Siberia and the founding of a mission to China. In 1705 he sent a missionary to Kamchatka. In 1707 he founded the suffragan bishopric of Irkutsk, and a mission to the Ostiaks. In 1711 he resigned from his position as Metropolitan of Siberia and devoted himself entirely to the work of the mission. He travelled in all directions in Siberia, from the Arctic to Dauria, and from the Ural Mountains to the River Lena. In 1715 he succeeded in founding the Orthodox Mission in Peking.

The number of those baptized by L. is given as 40,000. He increased the number of churches from 160 to 448; of these 37 were mission churches. His success is to be explained in part by the fact that he was able to win for his new converts exemption from taxes, and that he gave them presents at the time of baptism. The adoption of Christianity had been merely external, and many lapsed to paganism as soon as L. was out of sight. Only where the converts remained in contact with Russian settlers did they in course of time come to adopt a Christian manner of living. In spite of the defects of his missionary methods, L. has not unjustly been called 'the Enlightener of the Siberian peoples'.

JOSEF GLAZIK

J. Glazik: *Die russ.-orth. Heidenmission*, pp.42–47 (Münster 1954); K. S. Latourette: *A History of the Expansion of Christianity* (New York 1937–1945), Vol. III, pp.368f.

LEW, TIMOTHY TINGFANG ('T. T. LEW', 1890–1947), scholarly, versatile, articulate Chinese Protestant leader. Born in Wenchow, Chekiang, he studied at St. John's University, Shanghai, University of Georgia, Yale University (BD) and Columbia University (PhD in educational psychology). Returning to China in 1920 at the beginning of the Literary Renaissance he taught in government universities and joined the faculty of Yenching School of Religion. Ordained minister of the Congregational Church of North China, L. played an important role at the National Christian Conference in 1922 ('agree to differ but resolve to love') and the subsequent inter-denominational council. Lectures and conferences in China and abroad engaged much of his time. He founded and edited three Christian journals of theology and literature, and was chairman of the Religious Education Fellowship. His most notable contribution was as chairman of the Union Committee that produced *Chinese Hymns of Universal Praise* (Shanghai 1936). Intensely patriotic, he urged Christian schools to register with the national government. His frail body housed a scintillating mind and indomitable energy but he was forced by war conditions to spend his last years in the USA where he died of tuberculosis. He was a symbol of the vigour and promise of *'younger church' leadership.

F. W. PRICE

H. L. Boorman, ed.: *Biographical Dictionary of Republican China* (New York 1967).

LIANG FA (1789–1855) was born in a village about 30 miles south-west of Canton, South China. After four years at school, he was apprenticed to a Canton printer, and learned to chip away the wood around Chinese characters on boards—the 'block' printing which Europe abandoned with the invention of movable type in 1454. This printer secretly worked for Robert *Morrison. Thus in 1815 L. was engaged by Morrison's colleague William *Milne and taken to Malacca, where he helped to print Morrison's Chinese version of the Bible. He was baptized by Milne in 1816, returned to Canton to assist Morrison, and was ordained by him in 1823, the first Chinese Protestant minister. He wrote *Good Words Exhorting the Age* (Bible extracts with comments), and in 1834 handed copies to candidates for the civil service as they came out of the Canton examination halls, till stopped by police. This book, received by Hung Hsiu-ch'uan, influenced his 'visions', which led him to proclaim *T'ai-p'ing T'ien-kuo*, 'the Kingdom of Heaven of Great Peace', with himself as first Emperor of this new dynasty. The Taiping rebellion was thus a revolutionary movement of Christian origin, though far from orthodox Christian expression. The rebels overran all South China before the defeat and suicide of Hung at Nanking in 1864. Modern Chinese are taught to regard this as forerunner of the Communist revolution. L. spent his last years as chaplain to China's first Christian hospital, opened in Canton by the American Dr Peter *Parker.

JOHN FOSTER

J. Foster: 'Christian Origins of the Taiping Rebellion' in *IRM* XL, pp.156–167; G. H. McNeur: *Liang A-fa* (Shanghai 1934); McNeur's *Liang A-fa* and Liang's *Good Words Exhorting the Age* are published in Chinese (2nd ed., Hong Kong 1959).

LIBERIA, Africa's oldest republic, situated on the west coast of the continent, comprises an area of 43,000 sq.m. and has a population of 1,250,000 persons.

Since 1822 the Christian church has played a very important role in this country. The first church, Baptist, was founded aboard the ship bringing the first Negro immigrant settlers from America in 1822. In 1823 the first missionary from the Methodist church in the USA came to L., and in 1830 missionary activity of the

PECUSA began. The Presbyterian church initiated its work in 1833, the Lutherans in 1860, the African Methodist Episcopal Zion church in 1876, the Roman Catholics in 1884, and the African Methodist Episcopal church in 1891. Many other missions followed in the early part of the 20th century.

All the groups above have had a continuous history. The Liberian Baptists developed as an independent church. A Liberian Native Baptist Church also grew independently. Since 1890, when the Presbyterians, USA, (now the United Presbyterian Church), withdrew from the country, the Presbyterian Church in L. has been an independent church. In 1964 the Lutheran Church in L. became an independent church and elected its first Liberian president of the church. In 1965 the Methodist Church in L. attained autonomous status and elected its first Liberian bishop. The Episcopal church had a Liberian suffragan bishop until 1941. The foreign mission societies continue to co-operate with the independent churches and to send personnel under the direction of the national church. Recently also mutual programmes have been worked out with the Baptists and a mission group (Southern Baptist) in the US, and the Presbyterians and a similar group in the States (United Presbyterian Church).

From the early pioneer days, the religious and educational activities of foreign boards, especially American, have been very closely related to L's spiritual, educational, economic and social development. Practically all the present leadership in government, religion and education is the product of mission schools. There are at least 28 different mission groups in L., many with only one or two persons operating them, and very meagre support from the groups in America which they represent. In spite of the proliferation, the missions have done a very effective job in the field of education and health. As to numbers of members, the best figures indicate that there are about 110,000 persons on church rolls. There are many more people who are involved in and have come under the influence of the activities of the churches and missions in L., but who are not communicants. The subtle influences cannot be reflected in statistics.

DAVID N. HOWELL

C. H. Huberich: *Political and Legislative History of Liberia* (New York 1947); F. A. Querengässen: *Liberia* (Bonn 1965); N. Richardson: *Liberia's Past and Present* (London 1959); *Liberian Year Book*; *BM* II, 562–65; *NCE* VIII, 113f.; *WKL*, 843f.

LIBERTY, RELIGIOUS. The most widely recognized definition of RL is in Article 18 of the Universal Declaration of Human Rights proclaimed by the UN General Assembly, 10 December 1948: 'Everyone has the right to freedom of thought, conscience and religion; this includes freedom to change his religion or belief, and freedom either alone or in community with others and in public or private, to manifest his religion or belief in teaching, practice, worship and observance.'

Modern ecumenical thought on the subject includes the following emphases:

(1) That this freedom is not something confined to acts of worship or religious teaching, but includes the 'right to proclaim the implications of belief for relationships in a social and political community' (cf. the 'Declaration on Religious Liberty' adopted by both the *WCC and the *IMC in 1948). This right to bear witness in public and political affairs is justified theologically by Christians by reference to the lordship of Christ over all life. This element of RL is not easily recognized by secular states, and not widely exercised by the churches.

(2) That RL is a right of all men, not only or particularly of Christian minorities. 'We do not ask for any privilege for Christians that is denied to others' ('Declaration' of WCC and IMC). On the contrary, Christians have a duty to secure for atheists their right to maintain their convictions, but on condition that neither party secures a peculiar advantage in putting forward its convictions publicly (see action of the WCC Executive Committee, Odessa, USSR, 1964).

(3) That RL is not an isolated right, but is both the guarantee of many other human rights, and in turn cannot itself be secured in a society where human rights in general are denied. The two are inseparable, and both involve rights of assembly, free speech, publication, travel, etc.

(4) That there now exists a possibility of establishing recognized international standards of behaviour in this field. The Universal Declaration of Human Rights, Article 18, is a beginning. It 'proclaims' an acceptable standard of RL, but this proclamation is not legally binding in any way on governments. To make it possible for a complainant to bring his case before a court, first it is necessary to draft and agree specific legal covenants; then national governments must formally ratify them in accordance with their domestic constitution, and finally they would have to conform their own domestic legislation and practice to the agreed standard. A beginning in this process has been made; and an international covenant, for instance, has been completed on 'Civil and Political Rights' in which provisions for RL are included. It awaits ratification by governments. Greater progress has been achieved regionally in Western Europe (under the European Convention for the protection of Human Rights and Fundamental Freedoms, 1950), where individuals in several countries can arraign their own governments before an international court. Similar regional schemes in areas of generally common cultural tradition may be the next hopeful steps. Meanwhile Article 18 of the Universal Declaration has provided a model in the drafting of provisions for RL in the constitutions of many newly emerging states.

Legislation alone, however, cannot secure those patterns of social behaviour on which real RL depends. The development of common ethical convictions in this matter depends not least on the unremitting task of education and persuasion whereby men accept inwardly as well as obey outwardly the duty to respect each other's conscience.

The Declaration on Religious Liberty made by the Second *Vatican Council has been welcomed by the WCC as indicating 'a large measure of agreement among all the churches in these matters' (action of Central Committee of WCC, February 1966), thus opening a new chapter in Christian history. No similar rapprochement regarding RL is in sight with Islam.

ALAN R. BOOTH

A. F. Carrillo de Albornoz: *The Basis of Religious Liberty* (London 1963); G. Miegge: *Religious Liberty* (London 1957); 'Declaration on Religious Liberty' in the *Official Report of the Assembly of the WCC, New Delhi, 1961*; 'Declaration on Religious Liberty' in W. M. Abbott: *The Documents of Vatican II* (New York 1966).

LIBRARIES. See MISSION LIBRARIES.

LIBYA. A kingdom of N. Africa, bounded on the north by the Mediterranean, east by Egypt, west by Algeria and Tunisia. Area 679,338 sq.m.; population 1,617,000 (UN estimate 1965); the majority are Arab Muslims with minority groups of Oriental Jews and Italians.

Christianity, brought in by Italian settlers, has never taken root. Conrad of Ascoli, a *Franciscan monk, is reported to have won 6,400 Muslims to Christianity in the 13th century, but there is no evidence that these remained faithful or helped to spread Christianity. Franciscans are mentioned at work in the 17th century. Europeans have continued to be nominally RC, but there have been extremely few converts from the Muslim community.

Protestant work began in 1829 when the LSPCJ distributed Bibles in Tripoli. Visits for the same purpose were repeated in 1870 and 1890. The *North Africa Mission opened a centre in Tripoli in 1890. The Italian Baptists began work among Italians in Tripoli in 1913.

The country, largely desert, is making tremendous economic gains since the discovery of oil in 1957. Government has been able to open schools and hospitals, build roads and establish welfare work. Between 1946 and 1966 school enrolment increased from 40,000 to 250,000. Private Koranic,

Greek, Italian and Jewish schools continue, and literacy is 40%.

Christianity has made little progress among Muslims and Jews. The law forbids direct missionary work, and the 40,000 RCs and 2,651 Protestants are virtually all expatriates (WCH 1968).

GLORA M. WYSNER

H. Schiffens: *Libyen* (Bonn 1958); *BM* II, 566–69; *NCE* VIII, 729f.; *WKL*, 843f.

LIEVENS, CONSTANT (1856–1893), was born at Moorslede, Belgium, and died at Louvain. In 1878 L. joined the Society of *Jesus, and in 1880 was sent to join the mission to Bengal, where he completed his theological studies and was ordained priest in 1883. From the beginning of 1885 onwards, he worked in the mission of Chota Nagpur, which had been taken over by the Belgian Province of the Jesuits as their field of work. He studied the local languages and the customs of the various tribes (Oraons, Mundas, Kharias, Santals, etc.), who in their religious outlook were *animists, and had no temples, *idols or *caste distinctions. But almost the entire area where they lived had in the course of the 17th and 18th centuries fallen into the hands of Hindu Rajahs and large land-owners, who were in process of depriving the small landholder of his land and livelihood by means of heavy taxes and exorbitant rates of interest. The Lutheran *Gossner Mission had worked among the Kols since 1845, and had baptized several thousands of them. Faced with the exploitation of their people, the missionaries had supported freedom movements among the Kols, and had thereby brought upon themselves considerable difficulties, not least with the British authorities. Profiting by this experience, L. avoided all involvement in political activity. He received instruction from a friendly employee of the government as to the peculiar situation in his area. Relying on the incorruptible character of the British administration of justice, he did not hesitate to bring legal complaints against the landlords (Zamindars) and money-lenders before the British law courts, and so to help the

Aborigines to their rights. This let loose a storm of opposition against the mission in the ranks of the higher Hindu castes, but at the same time won crowds of converts for Christianity. As a result of these methods, the Christian community had already reached in 1888 the figure of 11,000 baptized and 40,000 catechumens, scattered in 800 villages. Crowds, including adherents of other missions, came streaming in, in order to make sure of securing for themselves the missionary's help. Here the problem of mass conversions with material aims was posed in its sharpest possible form. There can be no doubt that L. advanced much too rapidly; he relied on his Indian co-workers, and on the effects of religious instruction, for which he produced a number of books and pamphlets. In 1889 he extended his activities to the highlands, and was successful in christianizing almost the entire territory. In one month he baptized 12,000 people. Excessive labour had so reduced L's strength that when he fell ill of tuberculosis, he was hardly able to oppose any resistance to the disease. He died in his home country aged only 37. The work of L. encountered setbacks but was not finally destroyed. His work on behalf of the Aborigines received legal recognition in the Chota Nagpur Tenancy Act of 1908.

JOSEF GLAZIK

F. J. Bowen: *The Apostle of Chota Nagpur* (St. Louis 1936); Josson: *La Mission de Bengale Occidental* (2 vols., Bruges 1921); P. Marlier: *P. Constant Lievens* (Louvain 1929); *LTK* VI, 1050.

LIFE AND WORK MOVEMENT, THE, reconstituted in 1930 as the Universal Christian Council for Life and Work, was one of the main branches of the *ecumenical movement in the period between the two world wars. The first world war had made many church leaders painfully aware of the failure of the divided churches to act as a reconciling community across the battle fronts and in planning for peace. One of these leaders was Nathan Söderblom, Archbishop of Uppsala, Sweden, who in 1919 proposed an Ecumenical Council of

Churches which would serve as the voice of Christendom in matters of social and international concern. Söderblom became the principal architect of the Universal Christian Conference on Life and Work in Stockholm in 1925, composed of Church delegates from all confessional traditions except Rome, but including only six nationals from the *younger churches. Advocating inter-church co-operation irrespective of doctrinal differences, the conference was a remarkable affirmation of Christian fellowship and social responsibility. 'The nearer we draw to the Crucified', its message stated, 'the nearer we come to one another, in however varied colours the Light of the World may be reflected in our faith. Under the Cross of Jesus Christ we reach out hands to one another'. The appeal to the churches 'to apply the Gospel in all realms of human life' was developed in an expanding programme of social study and action, youth work, aid to churches and refugees, theological co-operation, ecumenical information and education, prefiguring many of the later activities of the *WCC.

While western in outlook and operations, the council was not unmindful of the term 'universal' in its title and sought, with limited success, to engage the younger churches in its work. An agreement was reached by which the *National Christian Councils in Asia and Africa were recognized as representing the council in these areas. Its staff in Geneva established close relations with the Department of Social and Economic Research of the *IMC and with such IMC leaders as J. H. *Oldham and W. *Paton.

The deteriorating world situation in the early 1930s, and especially the rise to power of national socialism with its totalitarian ideology and the ensuing life-and-death struggle of the German churches, presented the movement with a formidable challenge that gave sharper focus to its activities and thrust it into a leadership position in marshalling Christian forces in the battle for religious freedom and human dignity. Under the guidance of its chairman, the bishop of Chichester, G. K. A. Bell, the council gave active support to the so-called Confessing Church in Germany. Realizing that the issues at stake transcended the internal church-state relations of particular countries, and in fact involved the worldwide threat posed by the emergence of post-Christian totalitarian societies, the council decided, in 1934, to launch a vast programme of study and consultation leading up to a world conference on Church, Community and State in Oxford in 1937. J. H. Oldham became the directing genius of the enterprise. The Oxford conference, chaired by John R. *Mott, was the culminating point in the history of Life and Work. Its watchword, 'Let the Church be the Church!', reflected a maturing conviction of the integrity and universality of the Christian church, attested in the solidarity with suffering sister-churches and in a common stand against social and ideological idolatries. Its statements on religious *freedom, the criteria for a responsible economic order, and the Christian attitude to war, laid the groundwork for an ecumenical social ethics. The younger churches were represented by only 29 out of 425 delegates, but these included men of outstanding stature such as Bishop V. S. *Azariah and S. Devanesan of India, Y. Ichimura of Japan, Francis Wei and Timothy Tingfang *Lew of China. The growing community of interest with the missionary movement became apparent also in the fact that the *IMC conference at Tambaram largely built on the results of Oxford.

Following the decision to integrate the Life and Work and *Faith and Order movements in a WCC, Life and Work transferred its concerns and responsibilities in 1938 to the latter body in process of formation.

NILS EHRENSTRÖM

N. Ehrenström: 'Movements for International Friendship and Life and Work, 1925–1948' in R. Rouse and S. C. Neill, eds.: *A History of the Ecumenical Movement, 1517–1948* (London 1954), pp.545–96.

LINGUISTICS. Though L. goes back to Pānini in the 4th century B.C. in India, the application of linguistic science to mission problems of language learning and communication is largely post-second world war. This does not mean that missionary work on language was previously inadequate, but it does mean that it was generally not on the same type of scientific basis.

Since 19th century L. was concerned primarily with historical and comparative problems, it is understandable that this did not greatly concern missionary work. However, with the 20th century concern for structural L., resulting in important discoveries of new principles and techniques for the analysis of all types of languages, it was soon evident that a number of these techniques had important implications for many phases of missionary work, where the practical needs of an aural-oral approach and the requirements of effective translations have been all-important.

From the distinctive standpoint of missions themselves, the Summer Institute of Linguistics has had by far the most important influence, having trained more than 10,000 persons in their summer programmes and having sent to the field more than 1,800 persons under the auspices of their own organization, now working in more than 400 languages. The American Bible Society has also had considerable influence on the application of L. to mission principles and procedures through a number of technical and popular publications and by means of a highly trained team of translation consultants. Another important influence of L. upon missions is to be found in the summer programmes in Victoria College (Toronto, Canada) and Drew University (Madison, New Jersey). A number of language schools in other countries have also been influenced in considerable measure by modern L. methods.

But perhaps more important than the influence of L. upon specific practical phases of missionary activity has been the extent to which this science of language has made people aware of a number of vital propositions: (1) all languages are amazingly complex in structure and fully capable of expressing anything that one wants to say

within that culture (that is to say, there are no 'primitive languages'), (2) there is no such thing as a 'primitive mentality', in the sense that primitive man possesses a different type of mental apparatus from that of so-called civilized man, and (3) language is an indispensable tool for understanding culture, for it is not only an integral part of culture, but a mirror of it as well.

EUGENE A. NIDA

H. A. Gleason, Jr.: *An Introduction to Descriptive Linguistics* (Revised Edition, New York 1961); 'Linguistics in the Service of the Church', *Practical Anthropology*, Vol. IX (1962), pp.205–19; R. H. Robins: *General Linguistics: An Introductory Survey* (London 1964); E. Sapir: *Language* (New York 1921, 1949).

LIQUOR TRAFFIC AND MISSIONS. This article deals only with the problem of the importation of alcoholic liquors from developed into less developed countries.

A great many races have discovered the use of alcohol, and in many areas missionaries were faced with the problem of the manufacture of native beer in large quantities, and in certain areas of spirits. Missionaries have differed considerably in their attitude to the use of alcohol. Roman Catholics have not in general forbidden it, and most RC missionaries drink wine on occasion, if not frequently. The early Protestant missionaries accepted the view that some absorption of alcohol is necessary to health in the tropics; but their successors from about 1830 were for the most part teetotallers, and not merely refrained from the use of alcohol themselves but tried with greater or less success to suppress the use of it by those whom they had converted to the faith.

A different situation arose when trade began to bring strong liquors into areas in which they had been previously unknown. It is generally agreed that one of the many causes for the degeneration of the American Indian was the lavish scale on which 'fire water' was supplied him by British, French and Dutch with undistinguishing regard. Missionaries in the South Seas noted with pain the evil effects, on the simple races under their care, of western spirits to which they were entirely unaccustomed. But it was West Africa in which the traffic in liquor reached the level of an international scandal. Payment for slaves destined for the western world had always been made at least in part by way of barter, and one of the trade articles most highly valued by West African potentates was rum. From about 1860 'trade spirits' often referred to as 'gin', but more probably in reality 'schnapps' or 'aquavit', began to enter in enormous quantity. Endless protests were made by both German and British missions. But international action proved impossible since the Germans maintained that their economy could not stand any limitation of the traffic. Large areas of north Germany were being reclaimed by the planting of potatoes; the only way to dispose of this production was to turn these potatoes into 'schnapps' and to export the spirit to other countries. The main ports engaged in the traffic were Bremen and Hamburg; the quantities involved were immense and the profits proportionate.

In 1894 an 'International Federation for the Protection of Native Races against Alcoholism' was formed, and various representations were made to the British government. In 1909 a Committee of Enquiry into the Liquor Trade in Southern Nigeria was appointed. Its report found that some of the charges made by missionaries were unfounded and that there was no sign of racial deterioration among these people, in spite of the large quantities of liquor consumed. But the general policy of governments has been to exclude 'trade spirits' of the old type, and by steadily increasing the duty on better types of liquor to reduce both the amount imported and the amount consumed. In this they have had the support of almost all missions and churches. Alcoholism is no longer a major problem in the majority of African territories.

STEPHEN NEILL

C. P. Groves: *The Planting of Christianity in Africa* (4 vols., 1948–1958), see references throughout. No comprehensive study of the problem appears to have been written.

LITERATURE: CHRISTIAN AND MISSIONARY. The Christian missionary is a man of the book. This is in the first place the Bible, the translation of which has always been a primary concern in the preaching of the gospel and in the establishment of the church. Hardly less important is literature wherewith to understand and apply the Bible message. Pioneers in this field were John *Murdoch and Timothy *Richard, in India and China respectively. The traditional triangle used to symbolize the totality of mission—at the apex evangelism, supported either side by the school and the hospital—is not strictly accurate in that all these activities rest upon and require literature. At *Tambaram, in 1938, renewed understanding of the part played by literature was matched only by the recognition that what was being done, both by the 'sending' churches and on the field, was wholly inadequate to the need.

In the present age certain factors in the total missionary situation have added to that need. On the one hand, in the new freedom age of the old missionary lands, the traditional ways of mission are being challenged or superseded. Freedom of public proclamation is being curtailed. The work of education and healing, often pioneered by missions, is rightly becoming the responsibility of the governments. But the highway of literature remains open. It may soon be the only way in which the *older churches can help the new. On the other hand, the present literacy explosion has created millions of new readers who cannot be fed by existing resources and institutions. Recent international conferences have shown what must be done, both by Christian literature societies and committees on the spot and by supporting agencies, e.g. The *Committee on World Literacy and Christian Literature, the *SPCK, the *USCL, etc. in the older Christian lands. From this has developed the *Christian Literature Fund and attempts to enable local literature agencies to increase production. A feature of present strategy is a shift from the older method of providing literature from overseas to the recognition that each area must be free to provide its own, and help given accordingly, especially in training of personnel for writing, publishing and distribution. The short answer, therefore, to the question: What is Christian literature? runs: anything in print which responsible men in each place deem necessary to enable the church to be the church and to do the church's proper work. It is literature of many kinds and forms, which serves the church in its life and witness. It presents the gospel of Jesus Christ to all men that they may turn to him and be saved. It is directed to building the believers into responsible members of the witnessing community and of secular society. It provides a means by which Christians contribute to the life and thought of community and nation. Christian literature finds its inspiration in Christ and it commends Christ to men. It is literature in any form, from tract to novel, that expresses the concern of the Christian writer for man —his needs and problems; his joys and his destiny. In the current scene there are elements of encouragement. Campaigns like 'Feed the Minds' in Britain and 'Bread for the Heart' in the Netherlands have opened the minds of many to a new dimension of mission and the recognition that Christian aid must do more than meet merely bodily needs. There is an increasing willingness in the specialist literature societies in each country to take joint action and, as between countries, regularly to take counsel together. This is being matched overseas by similar long-term planning and co-operation. Thus, in many countries, the church is being helped to meet and deal with obstacles to a growing literature which in all its variety builds up the church and speaks to the nations.

MARCUS WARD

H. F. Huff, ed.: *Hakoné Communique* (Tokyo 1959)—Report of East Asia Christian Literature Conference, 1958; B. Simonsson: *The Way of the Word* (London 1965); *The Bethel Consultation on Christian Literature* (London 1963); *Literature for the Anglican Communion* (London 1960)— SPCK survey, applicable to all, of the needs and opportunities for the printed word in

the world mission of the church; J. G. Williams: *Hungry World* (London 1961)— a review of the situation as disclosed in the above.

LITERATURE ON MISSIONS. See BIBLIOGRAPHIES; JOURNALS FOR MISSION STUDIES; MISSION LIBRARIES.

LIT-LIT. See COMMITTEE ON WORLD LITERACY AND CHRISTIAN LITERATURE.

LITURGY. From the beginning Christian life has expressed itself in worship. Much was taken over from the Jewish tradition; much that was specifically Christian developed very gradually, and in different forms in different churches. Something of the process can be discerned, but the classical Ls are all anonymous. A living church will find the appropriate liturgical form for the expression of its life, but the process may take a very long time.

Almost all missions have introduced their converts to the forms of worship with which they themselves are familiar. It could not be otherwise. The people have watched the missionaries at worship for years before the first converts come in; they know exactly how Christians should behave, and wish themselves to do everything in the proper fashion. Even on the island of Bali, where the utmost care has been taken to shield the people from missionary control, the services took on the form of the worship of the Dutch Reformed Church.

No *younger church worships exactly in the same way as the church from which it has sprung. But liturgy is sacrosanct and invariable; and signs of independence are likely to be seen first in quasi-liturgical or para-liturgical areas, such as the lyrical preaching of South India, the dances of Christian Todas also in South India, songs set to the ancient Balinese melodies, religious plays used by the Roman Catholics since the 18th century in Paraguay. Such developments tend to spring up spontaneously, and require little control or direction on the part of the church.

Of actual liturgical development there is as yet very little to report from the lands of the younger churches. The liturgy of the *CSI has been highly praised, but there is hardly anything about it that is specifically Indian; it is made up for the most part of western elements, with certain features from the Eastern Orthodox liturgies which from the Indian point of view are also western. No one as yet has any idea of what a genuinely Indian liturgy would be like, and certainly the differences will be great according to the background, Hindu, Muslim, or animistic, from which the Christians have come. When the inner spirit begins to express itself, it is likely to do so in forms that will shock or shake the observer. A distinguished RC theologian has said that, when the African Christian obtains his liberty, he will certainly want to 'dance the Mass' (Cardinal Daniélou).

But this is unlikely to happen for a considerable time. The younger churches are still very conservative, and unsure of themselves when they move out of familiar paths. This inner freedom will come, and their contribution will be rich; but this is not a thing of today or to-morrow.

See SYMBOLISM; WORSHIP.

STEPHEN NEILL

T. S. Garrett: *The Liturgy of the Church of South India* (2nd ed., Madras 1954).

LIVERPOOL 1860. See CONFERENCES, WORLD MISSIONARY.

LIVING STANDARDS, MISSIONARY. As a matter both of missionary strategy and of missionary finance the prevalent pattern has been for the 'foreign missionary' to be paid a subsistence allowance related to the cost of living of the country in which he is living.

In the case of Protestant missions supplementary allowances, as in the case of married persons, have been related to the initial subsistence allowance of a single man. It has not been assumed that such allowances made possible any form of saving: they were strictly subsistence. Provision for old age or for incapacity for work through illness has varied, but has never been substantial. While, for a short period in the first half of the 19th century, it may have been the case for some missionaries, drawn from the artisan section of the community, that becoming a missionary meant a rise in social status and material advantages, this was never general.

In the missions of the Roman Catholic church members of the religious orders have been dedicated to 'holy poverty' and have been maintained as to material things by their respective orders. Secular priests and lay workers have commonly shared much the same pattern as their opposite numbers among Protestant missionaries. Living standards have, of course, been concerned to insure that the missionary should remain alive! This has in most places, dictated his diet, and, until modern prophylactics against disease were discovered, has often dictated the kind of house in which he lived. The large 'mission bungalow' of India for instance, was intended for health not prestige, though today it appears as a prestige factor and is a grave embarrassment to many missionaries.

There is no easy resolution of the problems posed by 'living standards'. A missionary from Europe or America working in Asia or Africa or Latin America will be, in comparison with his compatriots working in the same country, a 'poor white'. But in relation to many of the people of the country concerned he will appear to be a person of immense wealth, particularly if the people are either primitive or desperately poor. A factor, however, which must not be ignored is that the way in which a missionary lives, and this applies in many subtle ways to his standard of living, may significantly contribute to raising the living standards of the people in the midst of whom he lives.

MAX WARREN

J. J. Considine, MM, ed.: *The Missionary's Role in Socio-Economic Betterment* (Glen Rock, NJ, 1960); D. J. Fleming: *Living as Comrades* (New York 1950); W. H. Scott:

'Some Contrasts in Missionary Patterns', in *IRM* LIV (July 1965), 315–24.

LIVINGSTONE, DAVID (1813–1873). The son of poor Scottish parents, L. worked for 13 years in a cotton mill in his native town of Blantyre. Under the influence of the Independent Chapel at Hamilton he decided to be a foreign missionary and, after two years at the Charing Cross hospital, London, he was accepted by the *LMS. A man of middle height, L. had a dour, determined look with an immense capacity for independent action.

His life falls into five periods. (1) *The African Apprenticeship* (1841–52). From *Moffat's pioneer settlement at Kuruman —where L. married Mary Moffat—he began to take in the size of Africa with journeys into the Transvaal, through Bechuanaland, into the Kalahari Desert where he discovered Lake Ngami (1849) and caught his first sight of the Zambesi (1851). The fascination of Africa gripped him and at his mission stations of Mabotsa, Chonuane and Kolobeng he conceived his grand design of a coast to coast trek to open up the heart of Africa to Christianity and civilization. (2) *Master Traveller* (1852–56). To accomplish this journey, L. sent his family home to Britain. It was a cruel parting for this very tender-hearted man. 'Take the children all round you, and kiss them for me' he wrote to his wife, 'tell them I have left them for the love of Jesus'. From the Cape he went northwards to the Zambesi, canoed on the great river with his Makololo men, struck westwards through Portuguese Angola to the coast at Loanda, and then turned eastwards for the transcontinental journey coming out on the east coast at Quilimane, at the mouth of the Zambesi, on 20 May 1856. It was a peerless one-man adventure, and after sixteen years in Africa, L. arrived in Britain a popular hero. (3) *Expedition Leader* (1858–63). His transcontinental journey convinced L. that the heart of Africa could be made a habitable place for whites as well as blacks and that the Zambesi was 'God's highway into the interior'. To put this to the test he took the rank of consul and led an official expedition. He failed in his main objective owing to the Kebrabasa Rapids in the lower Zambesi defeating his navigation plans— and he also failed personally as an expedition leader. Baulked on the Zambesi he turned into Nyasaland (Malawi), blazed the trail for the coming of the Church of Scotland and the Universities' Mission, and saw the miseries of inland slave trading. He crowned his venture by sailing his ship *Lady Nyasa* across the Indian Ocean, practically single handed, to sell her in Bombay. (4) *The Liberator* (1866–71). In this period L. was again acting independently, largely financed by his own resources. His two books *Missionary Travels* (1857) and *Zambesi Narrative* (1865) had been very successful and the sale of the ship brought him further help. Still faithful to his 'missionary calling' L. determined to 'open Africa to civilizing influences' being convinced that slave trading could only be stamped out by other forms of trade and commerce. On this venture he was again alone with African carriers and attendants, and struck across Tanganyika (Tanzania) and Nyasaland to Lake Tanganyika encountering widespread evidence of slave trading. He got as far as Manyuema in Congo worn down physically largely owing to the disastrous loss by theft of his medicine chest. He was without medicines for four years until H. M. Stanley met him at Ujiji (1871). Reduced to a skeleton, he refused to admit any thought of retreat from Africa while the 'open sore' of slave trading remained. (5) *The Lonely Pilgrim* (1871–73). Nothing that H. M. Stanley could do in his four months' association shook L's resolve to stay on in Africa 'to finish my work'. He turned southwards into the swamps of the Lake Bangweolo region of Zambia racked with dysentery, losing pints of blood, carried on a litter but with all the old passion for exact observation and comment undimmed. On the morning of 1 May 1873 his attendants found him dead on his knees by his bedside at Ilala in Northern Zambia. They buried his heart in the soil of Africa, and carried his emaciated body to the coast.

He was buried in Westminster Abbey, London (18 April 1874).

The Africa L. knew was an immense white space on the map. But his multiform accomplishments as missionary, geographer, explorer and ethnographer, filled in the blank spaces, lifted the veil of mystery and displayed an Africa of wonder and possibilities. He directed the attention of the world to Africa and in his wake followed the great missionary expansion of the late 19th century.

CECIL NORTHCOTT

G. Seaver: *David Livingstone, His Life and Letters* (London 1957) is the best modern biography. See also *DNB* xxxiii, 384.

LO, GREGORY (LO WEN-TSAO, 1616–1691), first Chinese priest, first Chinese bishop. L. was born in a village in Fukien Province of pagan parents. At the age of 17 he heard a *Franciscan missioner preach and asked to be received among his catechumens. He was baptized in 1634 and shortly thereafter brought his elder brother and other members of his family into the church. He offered his services to the Franciscans as a catechist. When persecution exiled the Franciscans to Macao, Gregory followed. He was sent to Manila where he worked at the *Dominican College of Santo Tomas. He became a Dominican in 1650 and four years later was ordained priest. L. was sent back to China to work. When in 1665 persecution forced European missioners to retreat from China, Father L. remained alone at his post. He travelled through ten Chinese provinces during this period, ministering to the faithful. Despite the persecution, he converted and baptized over 5,000 adults. Father L. was consecrated a bishop in Canton on 8 April 1685. He continued his missionary work until his death in 1691. After him, no other Chinese was raised to the episcopate until Pope Pius XI consecrated six Chinese bishops in Rome in 1926.

ALBERT J. NEVINS, MM

Scriptores Ordinis Predicatorum, Vol. II (1721).

LOGOS SPERMATIKOS. The history of the *Logos* idea begins with the Greek philosopher Heraclitus of Ephesus (c. 535–475 B.C.), who emphasizes one divine principle in the world, to which he gave the name *Logos* (= reason). This *Logos* is present in the world as reason. In Stoic philosophy, the *Logos* is thought of as *Spermatikos* (i.e. the seed of reason within the world). All the phenomena of nature manifest this same *reason,* and the plural form is used to express the widespread permeation of this divine principle.

Christian writers, like Justin Martyr (c. 100–165), used this doctrine to link Greek philosophy with Christianity. Every man, he says, from his birth shares in the universal reason (*Spermatikos Logos*) and this is identified with the Johannine Logos which 'lights every man'. As a result, he can argue the salvation of pre-Christians like Heraclitus and Socrates, because they lived by the *Logos.* The seminal *Logos* is sometimes thought of as God himself as the principle of the cosmic process, which he directs to a rational and moral end. This concept is used by some modern writers to emphasize the validity of non-Christian religions, for, whilst Christ is regarded as ultimate, his presence, as the universal *Logos,* is looked for in non-Biblical sources as well as in the Christian revelation.

See also CONTINUITY AND DISCONTINUITY; LATENT CHURCH CONCEPT.

RAYMOND HAMMER

H. Chadwick: *Early Christian Thought and the Classical Tradition* (Oxford 1966).

LONDON 1888. See CONFERENCES, WORLD MISSIONARY.

LONDON MISSIONARY SOCIETY, THE, was founded in 1795 by evangelical churchmen of many denominations to spread the knowledge of Christ among the heathen, and not to propagate Episcopacy, Presbyterianism or Independency, or any particular form of church government about which they had serious differences. They agreed to leave the persons converted 'to assume for themselves such form of church government as to them shall appear most agreeable to the Word of God'. This was the Fundamental Principle.

The society claims a distinguished list of pioneer missionaries: William *Ellis, John *Williams of the Pacific; *Moffat and *Livingstone of Africa; *Morrison of China; *Lawes and *Chalmers of New Guinea. The majority of the churches founded are now part of united churches. Some have taken the name Congregational. The main support has come from Congregational churches in both missionaries and money.

In 1966 the society revised its constitution and became the Congregational Council for World Mission, of which the members are the seven Congregational Unions of the British Isles and Commonwealth countries. The Fundamental Principle has been retained in all essentials. The CCWM shares in the mission of united churches in Zambia, South Africa (including Rhodesia and Botswana), Madagascar, North and South India, and Papua; also in churches in Malaya, Singapore, the Pacific Islands, the Caribbean and Hong Kong. The number of full-time missionaries serving in 1968, not counting wives, was 149; the number of associates was 83.

Address: Livingstone House, 11 Carteret Street, London, S.W.1.

ROBERT O. LATHAM

R. Lovett: *The History of the London Missionary Society, 1795–1895* (2 vols., London 1899); N. Goodall: *A History of the London Missionary Society, 1895–1945* (Oxford 1954).

LOUW, ANDRIES ADRIAAN (1862–1956), was born at Fauresmith, Orange Free State, South Africa, where his father was a minister of the Dutch Reformed Church, his mother being the daughter of Andrew *Murray. A graduate of the Theological Seminary at Stellenbosch, although suffering from ill-health, he was accepted by his church as the pioneer for their new field in Rhodesia. He reached it in 1891, calling the first station *Morgenster*, the Morning Star, near the famous Zimbabwe ruins among the Karanga people. He was ordained

at Stellenbosch in 1894. L. soon learned the vernacular, published the translation of St. Mark's Gospel in Cicaranga in 1897; by 1904 the four Gospels, Acts, and some of the Epistles had appeared, and by 1919 the whole of the NT was published. He also completed the whole of the OT, but never published it. The translation of the whole Bible into Union Shona was completed by his son, A. A. Louw, Jr, in 1950. L. was president of the Southern Rhodesia Missionary Conference in 1906–08, 1930–32, and superintendent of the DRM till retirement in 1937. He was awarded the OBE, Officer of the Order of the British Empire, in 1954. He was greatly beloved and honoured by all sections of Rhodesian society.

PER HASSING

A. A. Louw, Jr: *Andrew Louw van Morgenster* (Cape Town 1965); W. J. van der Merwe: *The Day Star Arises in Mashonaland* (Lovedale 1953).

LOVEDALE. See INDUSTRIAL MISSIONS.

LUCAS, WILLIAM VINCENT (1883–1945), first bishop of Masasi, was educated at Oxford and ordained in the Anglican church in 1906; he joined the *UMCA in 1909 and did educational work in Zanzibar, 1909–12, then went to Masasi (Southern Tanzania). Invalided in 1913, he returned as Chaplain to forces, 1917. From 1917 till his consecration as bishop in 1926 he worked at Masasi. His great work was the christianization of tribal rites. The tribes at Masasi performed certain rites at adolescence, puberty, marriage and childbirth. Some of the practices were contrary to Christian morals and doctrine, e.g. indecent songs, *ancestor worship; but also there was much of value, e.g. excellent manners taught. L's plan was to wait till African Christians awoke to the fact that some practices of the rites were incompatible with their Christian profession; then only, and at *their* request, did he show how the rites could become a valuable part of the African Christian life.

All indecency was cut out, prayer to God replaced prayer to ancestors, etc. The rite of circumcision, held by the tribes concerned to be essential, he held to be a neutral thing to which no objection need be taken.

R. G. P. LAMBURN

W. V. Lucas: 'The Christian Approach to Non-Christian Customs' in E. R. Morgan, ed.: *Essays Catholic and Missionary* (London 1926), *Christianity and Native Rites* (a reprint of the above with memoir of L. by W. G. de L. Wilson: London 1948).

LUTHERAN MISSIONS. After sporadic attempts in the age of the Reformation and in the 17th century, hampered by the rigid orthodox emphasis on regular vocation to the ministry and on territorialism, continuous Lutheran mission work was inaugurated only under *pietist influence, with royal backing, in the *Danish Halle Mission at Tranquebar, South India, in 1706. As support from Lutheran rulers waned and the established churches continued to be suspicious of what appeared to be the work of fringe groups, the pattern was set for a mission relying on *ecclesiolae* (small church groups) rather than on the whole *ecclesia*, with the exception of the *Moravians where, at least ideally, the church was to be the mission. The society pattern was carried over into the missionary awakening of the early 19th century when the Revival, which provided the inspiration for the new societies in Britain and America, invaded continental Lutheranism as well. Both in Germany and in Scandinavia several new Lutheran missionary societies were founded, most of them in more or less close contact with churches in their area, yet none of them succeeding in becoming an instrument of the church as a whole. North American Lutheran churches, however, constituted from the outset as free churches, consistently made missions a concern of the church and were thus enabled to develop a relatively stronger missionary potential than their European parent bodies. But for their generous assistance during and after the two world wars many continental Lutheran mission enterprises would have been *'orphaned' for a long time to come. As new *indigenous Lutheran churches came into being in the former mission fields, new patterns of Lutheran co-operation in mission had to be developed in which the Commission on World Mission of the Lutheran World Federation is playing a prominent part. At the same time, the growth of the *ecumenical movement, the integration of the *WCC and the *IMC, increasing uneasiness with regard to the continuation of confessional church structures in Asia and Africa, and the fact that, in proportion to their size, Lutheran churches in general have done less than their share in world missions, confront LM with new questions which may call for a drastic reappraisal of the Lutheran heritage in an age of ecumenical mission.

H.-W. GENSICHEN

LUTHERAN WORLD FEDERATION. The most highly organized of the world confessional groups, the LWF was formed in 1947 because Lutherans saw the need to co-operate in the *ecumenical movement, in service to refugees and the needy and in Christian witness around the world. The LWF is a free association of about 70 autonomous churches with 50 million members, and acts 'as their agent in such matters as they assign to it' (Constitution). A staff at headquarters in the Ecumenical Centre, Geneva, administers both study and practical work under direction of several specialized commissions. The most important are the commissions on Theology (faith and order and other theological study, theological education), World Service (refugee and welfare services, inter-church aid in Europe), Latin America (assistance and co-operation in Latin America) and World Mission (missionary concerns in general and assistance to churches in Asia, Africa and the Pacific).

Originating from co-operation in helping Lutheran missions and churches cut off from support during and after the second world war, the LWF Department of World Mission has become the focus of common planning as well as of mutual assistance. It works in three ways: (1) By gathering and distributing information, holding conferences, doing study and research it has become a centre for consultation and counsel. The annual Commission meeting assembles over 100 church and mission leaders to discuss work in Asia and Africa. (2) Through distribution of limited grants-in-aid to churches (less than 5 % of the total Lutheran expenditures in overseas work) it helps to match resources with opportunities and meet emergency needs. (3) It administers on behalf of member churches certain activities which can best be done internationally. The most important of these is Radio Voice of the Gospel, Addis Ababa, LWF owned and operated but serving and supported by many Christian councils as well as Lutheran churches. A specialist consultant in religious education curricula is available to churches needing help, and in the Far East consultant services in mass media evangelism are offered.

The LWF also operates a Community Development Service, which helps churches to plan and to find funds for welfare and economic development projects. It helps to recruit expatriate workers for the churches, especially specialist and short-term personnel. It operates an extensive scholarship and exchange programme, with emphasis on the training of servants for the *younger churches. Without any authority that would infringe the autonomy of its members, but simply because it has been able to provide in increasing measure the assistance needed, the LWF has become an essential instrument of Lutheran churches in their missionary effort.

Headquarters: 150 route de Ferney Geneva, Switzerland.

ARNE SOVIK

S. Grundmann: *Der Lutherische Weltbund. Grundlagen—Herkunft—Aufbau* (Cologne 1957); *Lutheran Churches of the World* (Minneapolis 1957); *Lutheran Directory*, Parts I and II (Geneva 1963, 1966); *Lutheran World/Lutherische Rundschau*, quarterly journal published by the LWF in identical German and English editions; *RGG*[3] IV, 527–30.

M

MABILLE, ADOLPHE (1836–1894), a missionary of the *PEMS to the Basotho (1859–94), was born in Switzerland and died at Morija in Lesotho. The son of a teacher, who was an active member of the Free Church of the Canton of Vaud, M. greatly distinguished himself in his studies first at Yverdon and then at Basel. In 1854 he became a teacher of French at the Hague, and later at Kendal, England. It was here that he underwent the experience of conversion and decided to become a missionary.

From 1856 to 1859 he studied in Paris. Just before setting out for Lesotho, he married Adèle Casalis (1840–1923) who had been born in Lesotho, and was the daughter of E. *Casalis, founder of the mission, and later director of the society. With his wife for teacher, he learned the Sesotho language during the voyage.

From 1860 to 1894 he carried out a great variety of tasks. Primarily he was an evangelist; but he was the first to use the help of catechists whom he trained in a Bible school which he had himself brought into being. He directed a printing press, a publishing house, and a school for the training of teachers. He was occupied with the translation and printing of the Bible, with a dictionary of Sesotho, a book of hymns and numerous tracts. As adviser to the paramount chief *Moshoeshoe, he played a part in the war between the Boers and the Basotho, and was for a time exiled. A new crisis arose with the 'Gun War' of which he saw only the beginning and the end, having paid a visit to Europe, in order to see through the press in London the second edition of his Sesotho Bible. On his return to Morija, he was in full harness till the moment of his death, which was brought about by overwork.

ETIENNE KRUGER

H. Dieterlen: *Adolphe Mabille, Missionaire* (Paris 1898); E. W. Smith: *The Mabilles of Basutoland* (London 1939).

MACAO. A small, hilly peninsula and city, 6 sq.m. in area, attached to mainland China and 35 m. by sea west of Hong Kong. The population is estimated to be over 200,000, of whom 95% are Chinese and Eurasian. Chinese religions predominate, but there are about 36,000 Roman Catholics and a diminishing community of two or three thousand Protestants, chiefly Baptists and small indigenous sects. M. has been a Portuguese overseas territory since 1557. The only foreign foothold for three centuries, and a helper in the introduction of China to the western world, it was often a stepping-stone for missionaries wishing to enter China, including the famous M. *Ricci and other *Jesuits; the RC bishopric of M. was created in 1580. During periods of anti-foreign activity M. was a point of deportation. R. *Morrison and other Protestant missionaries of the early 19th century, limited to a narrow strip on the Canton waterfront, often visited the Portuguese colony. In the greater freedom of M., Morrison did some of his important literary work; here too he baptized near a secluded spring the first Protestant convert, Tsae A-ko, and saw in a vision 'millions who shall believe'. M. has been better known for its gambling and opium than for its ornate churches and temples; but it has been also a fishing town, an attraction for tourists, and a haven for small numbers of refugees escaping mainland China. Up until recently the RC church has been educating about one-half (25,000) of M's school children, but Communist forces have in repeated confrontation won more and more over the nationalistic teachers and pupils and Catholic authorities. The future is very uncertain. Protestant societies which have worked in M. until recently include the Southern Baptist Convention, the Swedish Alliance Mission and the Christian Nationals Evangelism Commission.

F. W. PRICE

BM II 573f.; *NCE* IX, 2f.

McDOUGALL, FRANCIS THOMAS
(1817–1886), medical doctor and priest,
was sent in 1847 to open up pioneer work
in the then almost unknown area of North
Borneo. In that inhospitable climate the
work was carried on with the greatest
difficulty, the Ms losing through death no
less than five of their children. Progress
among the Chinese was very slow, but M.
found a readier response among both Land
and Sea Dayaks and a church began to
come into existence among this extremely
primitive people. The baptism of the first
five converts took place in 1851; in that
same year, Bishop Daniel Wilson of
Calcutta, after a visit to Kuching, wrote,
'there is no mission field on the face of the
earth to be compared with Borneo'. M.
became friendly with Sir James Brooke, the
white Rajah of Sarawak, some of whose
adventures he shared and recorded with
greater gusto than was thought suitable in
missionary circles in England. On Brooke's
request, M. was in 1855 appointed as
bishop of Labuan and Sarawak, and
consecrated in Calcutta, the first Anglican
consecration in Asia. In 1868 he resigned
his office, and returned to England, where
he served with distinction in various
positions in the Church of England.

STEPHEN NEILL

C. J. Bunyon: *Memoirs of Francis Thomas
McDougall, D.C.L., F.R.C.S., sometime
Bishop of Labuan and Sarawak, and of
Harriette his Wife* (London 1889); *DNB*
XXXV, 62.

MACFARLANE, SAMUEL (1837–1911),
aided two significant Christian developments in the Pacific: the growth of the
church in the Loyalty Islands, near New
Caledonia, and the inauguration of the
*LMS's New Guinea work. Born in
Scotland, M. was appointed by the LMS
to the South Seas in 1858. He was stationed
at Lifu, where in 1966 the Pacific Conference of Churches held its first assembly.
M's work was hindered by disagreements
with the French government, which in 1871
demanded his withdrawal. During these
years he set up a pastors' school and
completed a translation of the NT.

The LMS then authorized M. and the
Rev. A. W. Murray to explore the possibility
of a mission in New Guinea. With them
went eight Loyalty Islands evangelists who
settled on the mainland and nearby
islands. After M. visited LMS headquarters
in Britain, three additional European
missionaries were appointed, assisted by
evangelists from Samoa, Cook Islands and
Niue. By 1883 several Papuan teachers,
trained by M., were settled among the Fly
River tribesmen. In 1887 M. was made
LLD (St. Andrews). From this year until
his retirement in 1896 he was a member of
the LMS staff in Britain.

NORMAN F. COCKS

S. MacFarlane: *The Story of Lifu Mission*
(London 1873), *Among the Cannibals*
(London 1888).

MACHRAY, ROBERT (1831–1904), was
born at Aberdeen, Scotland, and from 1855
to 1865 was fellow and later dean of
Sidney Sussex College, Cambridge. In 1865
he was consecrated as the second bishop of
Rupert's Land. Conditions were still
primitive in the area of the 'Red River
Settlement', the land of the Indians and
the *métis* (people of mixed race); the railway
reached Winnipeg only in 1881. In 1885
there were only eighteen Anglican clergy in
the whole area; when M. died in 1904 there
were nine episcopal sees and more than 200
clergy. M. cared for all classes of the
population under his jurisdiction, promoted
education on all levels, in 1866 refounded
St. John's College, and became in 1877
first chancellor of the University of
Manitoba, a position he held until the time
of his death. In 1887 M. became the first
archbishop of the Province of Rupert's
Land. When in 1893 the Church of England
in Canada was organized in full independence of the Church in England, M. became
the first Primate of all Canada. 'Unselfish,
moved by a high sense of duty, indomitable,
hard working, and hating cant' is the
characterization of M. given by K. S.
*Latourette.

EDITORS

R. Machray: *Life of Robert Machray*, *D.D.*, *LL.D.* *D.C.L.* (London 1909); *Encyclopedia Canadiana*, Vol. VI, p.268; *DNB*, 2nd Suppl. ii, 522f.

MACKAY, ALEXANDER (1849–1890), was born in Rhymie, Aberdeenshire, Scotland, the son of a Free Church minister. He trained as teacher and engineer. In 1875, reading of the *Church Missionary Society's proposed party for Uganda, to be sent in response to H. M. Stanley's appeal, M., though not an Anglican, immediately volunteered. In 1876 he sailed with seven others, and finally reached Kampala, in 1878, the only one of the party who was to serve long in Africa. He quickly showed himself to be the 'practical missionary' Stanley had hoped for. Blacksmith, road-builder, printer, carpenter, boatbuilder, as well as teacher and evangelist, he soon gained the respect of the Baganda. Other missionaries joined him, enquirers came, and in 1882 the first converts were baptized. After Bishop Hannington's murder in 1885 the young church went through a time of sharp persecution, followed by civil war. M. remained at his post, for eleven months the only missionary in Uganda. When reinforcements arrived in 1887 he went to Usambiro, south of Lake Victoria, and continued the translation of John's Gospel into Luganda (having previously completed Matthew). He died of fever at Usambiro early in 1890.

DAVID B. BARRETT

C. E. Padwick: *Mackay of the Great Lakes* (London 1917); *DNB* XXXV, 118; *RGG* IV, 572.

MACKAY, GEORGE LESLIE (1844–1901), was born in Zorra, Oxford County, Ontario, Canada. After receiving education both in Princeton and Edinburgh, he was appointed by the Canada Presbyterian Church in 1871 as its first missionary to China. Arriving at Tamsui in 1872, he became the first missionary to bring the gospel to the northern half of Taiwan (Formosa). By the time of his death at Tamsui (1901), there were 60 churches with 3,000 members in north Taiwan. By 30 years' labour, through the political turmoils of French-Chinese and Chinese-Japanese wars, he built up this church almost single-handed. Beside this great evangelistic achievement, he opened a mission hospital in Tamsui. He became an expert in pulling teeth, altogether he pulled more than 30,000 teeth. For the training of national preachers, in 1882 he opened a theological school, which has expanded to become the present Taiwan Theological College located near Taipei. In 1884 he opened a girls' school in Tamsui, which was the first educational school for women in Taiwan. He received the degree of DD from Queen's University, and in 1894 was elected to be the moderator of the Pres-byterian Church in Canada. M. wrote a book describing his own work in Taiwan, entitled: *From Far Formosa* (4th ed., New York 1896). He was married to a Taiwan-ese lady in 1878; they had two daughters and a son.

LIEN-MIN CHENG

M. Keith: *The Black Bearded Barbarian* (Toronto 1912); D. MacLeod: *The Island Beautiful* (Toronto 1923), pp.50–92.

MACKENZIE, CHARLES FREDERICK (1825–1862), was born in Scotland and graduated in mathematics at Cambridge in 1851, when he was ordained and elected fellow of Caius College. In 1854 he was appointed Archdeacon of Natal, where he ministered to scattered congregations of Europeans and Africans. In 1858 at the church conference at Maritzburg he advocated the right of African congrega-tions to an equal voice with white con-gregations in the proposed church synod. Severely ill in 1859 he returned to England, where he was invited to lead the *UMCA, newly formed in response to Dr *Living-stone's appeal for 'commerce and Christianity' to eradicate the slave trade. Consecrated in Cape Town to be 'bishop of the mission to the tribes dwelling in the neighbourhood of Lake Nyasa and the River Shiré', he joined Livingstone on the Zambesi in January 1861, and eventually landed on the Lower Shiré in July. Despite disagreements and difficulties, the two men came to trust and admire each other. Under Livingstone's guidance M's party made for the highlands, where they intercepted slaves of the Nyanja tribe and released them from their Yao masters. With these they began to build a fortified village at Magomero, and soon they became deeply involved in defending their Nyanja neighbours from Yao invaders. M. died of fever on 31 January 1862 on the Lower Shiré on his way to meet Livingstone, and the work of the mission was eventually withdrawn to Zanzibar. The UMCA returned to the region of Lake Nyasa in 1886.

JOHN LEAKE

O. Chadwick: *Mackenzie's Grave* (London 1959).

MADAGASCAR. Area 228,000 sq.m. Population (1966 estimate): 6,500,000 including besides the Malagasy about 40,000 Europeans, 20,000 Indians and Chinese, and a few thousand others. Traditional religion includes belief in a rather distant 'High God' (Andriamanitra, Andriananahary, Zanahary); destiny (*vintana*) and the 'science' of *fanandroana* needed to understand it; divination (*sikidy*); an emphasis on ancestors (*razana*), especially family continuity and the family tomb; and the system of beliefs, tabus, major ceremonies and individual practices which is described by those who approve of it in its entirety as 'the customs of the ancestors' (*fomban-drazana*) and by Christians as (literally) 'the service of idols' (*fanompoan-tsampy*), although Christians retain as 'good' many old ways.

Europeans first saw the island in 1500; the first Christian contacts were through Portuguese officials and sailors. 'Official' missionary work can be divided into two main periods.

(*a*) *Spasmodic Activity* (1587–1818). The first missionary (a Portuguese, perhaps a *Dominican) was killed after brief service in 1587. Several Portuguese *Jesuits worked near Fort Dauphin and on the west coast

(1613–30); followed by the French (chiefly Lazarists) at Fort Dauphin (1642–74). No lasting results were produced, largely because, by force of circumstances, the missions were too closely linked with the plans of their governments. Despite numerous plans and a few short visits, the 18th century was even less successful. In this period several missionaries paid with their lives (because of ill-health or through violence) for their zeal. Protestant influence in M. was exercised almost entirely through laymen; there was no official mission.

(*b*) *Continuous Work* (1818 to present day).

(1) *Protestant missions* date from 1818 (arrival of missionaries D. *Jones and T. Bevan of the *LMS). The church founded in the pioneer period (1818–35) was not overwhelmed in the persecution lasting from 1835 to 1861, led by the xenophobic Queen Ranavalona and her advisers. The number of Malagasy Christians deliberately put to death (by burning, stoning and in other ways) was small—under 50; but hundreds suffered and even died from the effects of the punishment meted out to them. Acceptance of Christianity by a new ruler and prime minister and the burning of the royal 'idols' in 1869 led to a mass movement, resulting in a wide, though often superficial spread of Christianity, especially in the central provinces. Missions engaged also in extensive education, founded hospitals and a 'Medical Academy' to train Malagasy doctors. In general, Protestantism was the form of Christianity most favoured by the rulers of the country—and by their subjects, who tended to follow their lead. But in 1896 M. became a French colony and religious conditions were immediately, and powerfully, affected by the influence of the connection with France. Political differences between Britain and France made life more difficult for Protestants in M.; the Roman Catholics, on the other hand, were able to take full advantage of the new situation. A few years later French anticlericalism and anti-religious prejudice

severely restricted the work of the churches. Matters were improved when, after strong protests had been made by the missions to the government in Paris, a law on the churches was promulgated in 1913; this included detailed rules about the authorization of meetings and church buildings; the churches (of all denominations) were less subject to the arbitrary whims of administrators. Besides the LMS, the other major Protestant missions (with their dates of arrival) are: Norwegian Lutheran, 1866; British Friends, 1867; Lutheran Church of America, 1888; French Protestant,1896; American Lutheran Board of Missions, 1897. *Comity arrangements have ensured that for the most part these missions have worked in different areas. Number of missionaries (European and American) for all types of work, about 100; Malagasy ministers (1963) 1,190.

(2) *Anglican.* *SPG began work in 1864; it has given birth to the Malagasy Episcopal Church; it has stood outside the Protestant territorial arrangements, but has worked mainly on the east coast. It claims to be a sort of bridge between the Protestants and RCs. European missionary staff, under five; Anglican (Malagasy) priests, 60.

(3) *Roman Catholic.* Continuous work by the *Holy Ghost Fathers and the *Jesuits dates from the 1830s, but during the reign of the persecuting Queen Ranavalona remained in outlying coastal areas. Other congregations (Lazarists, Monfortains and very many others) have joined the above. The European personnel has always been very numerous and very varied in its skills; the church has made good use of this wealth of talent not only for parochial work, but also notably in education. On the other hand, less effort was made (as compared with the Protestant approach) to train Malagasy personnel for church-work, until more recent years. There are approximately 1,000 workers of all kinds from overseas; and about 200 Malagasy priests, 500 Malagasy sisters and 5,000 catechists.

Recent figures suggest that rather under

half the population (about 2,500,000) regard themselves as 'Christians' (members and adherents), though that description covers varying degrees of commitment. The most far-reaching effects of Christianity are to be found in the centre among the populous and progressive Merina and Betsileo groups. The church today contains both Christians of the third generation (often with the familiar problems) and those who have only just been converted from the traditional religion. The oldest and most important 'revival movement' was founded in the 1890s (Soatanana) and for years worked closely with the main churches; recently one section (only) of this movement has formed itself into an independent revivalist church. There are a few other such groups, of recent origin.

A new atmosphere has been created by the formation of the Malagasy Republic (1958) and the declaration of independence (1960). The church therefore now finds itself within one of the developing nations of the Third World. But in recent years great improvements have been made in the church as an instrument of witness. This is seen in almost all groups. The RC organization is headed by Malagasy archbishops, and some bishops are Malagasy. The Malagasy Episcopal Church (Anglican) has three Malagasy bishops and is forming links with neighbouring dioceses. The churches developed out of Protestant missions have for several years been churches (synods) in their own right, who may invite missionaries to work with them. These main synods, since 1968, have been only two in number, namely the Lutheran, and the united Church of Jesus Christ in Madagascar.

The Protestant synods work together in a Protestant Council (originally formed as a result of the *Edinburgh Conference of 1910). This tries to co-ordinate by common discussion, and by certain joint projects, the activities of the Protestant churches in their witness to the nation, and in the varied forms of practical service. (Though formerly within this organization, the Anglicans have been outside it since the 1920s; the Advent-

13

ists also are not members.) There are two or three Pentecostalist groups and Jehovah's Witnesses. The Orthodox church is represented by the few hundreds of the Greek community; but their local church has virtually no contact with other churches.

The organized aspect of church life within society is regulated by the new law promulgated by the Malagasy government. While the constitution states a belief in God, this law emphasizes the separation of church and state (the intention being to assert impartiality and reciprocal non-interference).

Over the last 100 years Christianity has held, and still holds, a most important place in the life of the Malagasy people, not only for the faith it has engendered, but also for its influence on social and moral life and for its cultural benefits, e.g. pioneering in education. It now faces 'attack' from two main directions. On the one hand, the 'traditional religion' has never, of course, been entirely eliminated; it regained impetus during the independence uprising in 1947–48; and full independence has encouraged it among some. On the other hand, there are all the problems arising out of modern conditions, though not all of these are by any means hostile. But it is not always easy for a church which has inherited a certain outlook and manner of doing things suitable in former days to see just how it should carry out its witness today.

J. T. HARDYMAN

F. Birkeli, etc.: *Det Norske Misjonsselskaps Historie: Madagaskar* (Stavanger 1949); A Boudou: *Les Jésuites à Madagascar au XIXe Siècle* (Paris 1942); A. Burgess: *Zanahary in South Madagascar* (Minneapolis 1932); F. Ditmanson: *In Foreign Fields* (Minneapolis 1927); W. Ellis: *The Martyr Church of Madagascar* (London 1870); C. W. Forman: 'A Study in the Self-Propagating Church: Madagascar', in W. C. Harr, ed.: *Frontiers of the Christian World Mission* (New York 1962), pp.115–40; K. Hämel: *Madagaskar* (Bonn 1958); J. T. Hardyman: *Madagascar on the Move* (London 1950); G. Mondain: *Un Siècle de Mission Protestante à Mada-*

gascar (Paris 1920); R. S. M. O'Ferrall: *One Hundred Years in Madagascar* (London 1964); W. White: *Friends in Madagascar* (London 1967); *Rythmes du Monde* (Bruges, special issue 1966 No.1–2); *BM* II, 574–81; *NCE* IX, 102f.; *WKL*, 871f.

MADRAS CHRISTIAN COLLEGE. See COLLEGES AND UNIVERSITIES, CHRISTIAN; MILLER, WILLIAM.

MADRAS, TAMBARAM, 1938. See CONFERENCES, WORLD MISSIONARY.

MAGIC, a word which is everywhere known and generally understood, has successfully defied all attempts to define it exactly. The view of Sir J. G. Frazer that magic chronologically preceded religion, and that it is in some way akin to science, though a bastard science, has now been generally abandoned. In broad outline it may be said that, in magic, man believes that the world is governed by unseen powers, knowledge of which can be obtained by those who possess the necessary secrets, and which can then be controlled in the interests of the operator; whereas in religion man places himself at the disposal of the unseen powers in order to carry out their purposes. But it is clear that there is a large overlap between magic and religion, and that in religions of self-realization such as classical *Hinduism, there can be no talk of carrying out the will of the higher power.

Magical practices are so widespread as to be practically universal. Among the majority of peoples a quite clear distinction is made between magic which is used for good purposes, and that which is used to hurt or to destroy. Sympathetic magic, based on the idea of correspondences, may play a large part in both types.

(1) A good example of magic used for the common welfare is the ritual human sacrifice carried out until recently by the Khonds of South India. The *meriah*, the chosen victim, was treated kindly until the appointed day, and then killed without cruelty. Immediately after death the

body was hacked to pieces and carried to the fields to ensure fertility. Here the magical power is expected to act directly without the intervention of any other power. It was unfortunate that one man had to die, but he was dying literally for the people.

(2) To the primitive mind no happening is 'normal'. If anyone has fallen sick or died, that can only be because someone has directed magical power against him. This may have been done deliberately; but there are men and women who spread around them harmful power without being aware that they are doing so. There are innumerable methods of smelling out witches; and, when the wizard is found, most primitive peoples agree with the law of Moses that 'thou shalt not suffer a witch to live'.

The verdict of Scripture is plain: magic belongs to the world of darkness, and no member of the chosen people may have anything to do with it. This is clearly laid down in the OT, and reiterated in the NT. But it is equally clear that magical practices of all kinds continue on a very large scale even among Christians. Sometimes these take the comparatively harmless form of the possession of amulets or charms; but darker deeds are not unknown. The forbidding of such practices is never by itself effective; the whole attitude to life has to be changed. This can be achieved partly by the teaching of simple science; though experience shows that the scientific and the magical views of the world can most strangely co-exist in the same mind. On the Christian side, there must be plain teaching on the doctrine of creation, and an awareness of the living God as the sole source of all true power, and as the one who can care for and protect the Christian in all conceivable situations, and against all real or imaginary foes.

STEPHEN NEILL

The literature is immense. R. R. Marett's article in Hastings *ERE*, Vol. VIII, pp.245–52 is still most valuable. Bishop C. G. Diehl's *Instrument and Purpose* (Lund 1956), and the many writings of Mircea Eliade can be recommended as illuminating.

MAIGROT, CHARLES (1652–1730), RC

bishop in China, born in Paris, died in Rome. A member of the *Paris Foreign Mission Society and Doctor of Theology of Sorbonne University, he went with Bishop *Pallu to the Far East, was in Siam, 1681–83, then in China. After Pallu's death in 1684 M. succeeded him as papal administrator of all Catholic missions in China and tried to exact from all missionaries an oath of exclusive fidelity to the pope which many *Padroado missionaries were unable to swear. In 1687 he was named *Vicar Apostolic of Fukien and in 1696 titular bishop of Conon. He held severe views on the Chinese *Rites and prohibited them for his subjects in a mandate of 26 March 1693. Meeting with contradiction he pressed Rome for an authoritative decision and procured through Nicolas Charmot a condemnation of some of these rites by the theological faculty of the Sorbonne (1700). In 1705 he conferred with the papal legate *Tournon at Canton and received a laudatory *Breve* for his zeal. Considered an expert on the rites by Tournon, he was called before Emperor Kanghsi in 1706 to justify his views, but was found so poor a Sinologist that he was officially censured. Because of his unyielding attitude he was formally expelled from China. He returned to Europe and, invited by Pope Clement XI, lived in Rome as consultor in matters of Chinese rites and missions.

BERNWARD H. WILLEKE

A. Launay: *Mémorial de la Société des Missions Etrangères*, Vol. II (Paris 1916) pp.417–23; L. Pastor: *History of the Popes*, Vol. XXXII, pp.648–50, XXXIII, 408–28, 935–40 (Eng. 1940, 1941); *Enciclopedia Cattolica*, Vol. VII (1951) p.1854; *LTK* VI, 1292.

MALAGASY REPUBLIC. See MADAGASCAR.

MALAWI, formerly Nyasaland, is a central African, landlocked republic, 45,725 sq.m. in extent, bounded on the west by Zambia, on the north-east by Tanzania, on the east, south and west by Mozambique. The estimated population (1966) is 4,042,412, of whom 16,000 are Asians and people of mixed race, and 12,000 Europeans. The Bantu-speaking Africans are divided into many tribes, of which the Nyanja, the the original inhabitants of the country, the Ngoni, invaders from the south, and Yao, Muslim invaders from the north, are the most important. English is the official language, but Chinyanja is understood widely. The country is largely agricultural and about 160,000 men are away annually, attracted to Zambia, Rhodesia and South Africa by higher wages.

Portuguese travellers reached the country in the 17th century. Arab and Yao slave raiders made the conditions terrible in the 19th century, the slave trade not coming to an end until the beginning of the 20th century. Great Britain declared a protectorate over the country in 1889 and ruled it until it became part of the Federation of Rhodesia and Nyasaland, 1953-63. Malawi gained independence in 1964 with Hastings Banda as prime minister; later, under a republican constitution, Banda became president.

David *Livingstone explored the country in 1858-64. *UMCA under Livingstone's guidance came in 1861, but the first attempt ended in disaster and temporary withdrawal. In 1875 the Free Church of Scotland founded Livingstonia mission, made famous by Robert *Laws, and the Church of Scotland started work at Blantyre, so named after Livingstone's birthplace, in 1876. The UMCA re-entered M. in 1879 and made Likoma Island its headquarters, while the Dutch Reformed Church of South Africa started in 1888, making Nkoma its central station. The *White Fathers came in 1889 and the Zambesi Industrial Mission in 1902. Also at work in M. are the Africa Evangelical Fellowship, Assemblies of God and Baptists. The United Free Church of Scotland, the Church of Scotland, and the DRC have formed the Church of Central Africa, Presbyterian, the largest completely autonomous Protestant church in M.; its theological college is at Nkoma. Proposals are being made for further church union negotiations. There are now about 750,000 Protestants, 500,000 Roman Catholics, and 1,000,000 Muslims in M.

The churches pioneered in education and medical services. A Christian Council has been organized and the Bible has been translated into two languages with the NT in at least three more.

PER HASSING

A. J. Hanna: *Beginnings of Nyasaland and North-Eastern Rhodesia, 1859-1895* (Oxford 1956); G. Jones: *Britain and Nyasaland* (London 1964); E. Schimmelfennig: *Malawi* (Bonn 1965); *NCE* IX 108.

MALAYSIA since 1963 consists of West M., formerly the Federation of Malaya (50,960 sq.m.), and East M., formerly the crown colonies of Sarawak and British North Borneo, renamed Sabah, (together 79,500 sq.m.). Population of West M. around ten million, Sarawak 700,000 and Sabah 500,000. In West M. 49% are Malays, 40% Chinese and the rest Indians, Pakistanis, Eurasians and Europeans. Malays are Muslims; Chinese religion is an amalgam of *animism, Mahāyāna *Buddhism, Confucian ancestor worship and its moral and social values. In Sarawak 32% are Sea Dayaks or Ibans, 31% Chinese, 17% Malays. Tribal religion is animistic and the Ibans were formerly head-hunters. In Sabah the rural Kadazans are the largest group, then Chinese and Malays.

Christianity came first to Malacca, West M., with the Portuguese in 1511. Francis Light annexed Penang for the British in 1786 and Roman Catholics moved there. The East India Company appointed a Church of England chaplain in 1809. The earliest mission was the *LMS which appointed William *Milne to Malacca in 1813. A Presbyterian chaplaincy in Penang for Europeans was established in 1851, leading to the development of the M. Presbytery of the Presbyterian Church of England. The English Presbyterian Mission among Chinese began in 1881, which led to the Singapore-M. Synod of the Chinese Christian Church. American Methodism spread from Singapore in 1885 and has been fastest growing.

Today in West M. the RC archbishopric of Malacca has a Christian community of about 100,000 (including Singapore); the Methodist church about 30,000; Anglican church 20,000; Singapore-M. Chinese Christian church 18,000; Presbyterian Church of England 1,000; Evangelical Lutheran Church of M. 1,500; Mar Thoma Syrian and Syrian Orthodox churches 2,000; Lutheran Church of M. 1,200; Baptist Church in M. 3,000; the Bible Presbyterian Church, a breakaway from the Chinese Christian Church 1,500; several congregations of Brethren (Christian Missions in Many Lands) 2,500; Salvation Army 2,000. The work of the Overseas Missionary Fellowship (*CIM) has resulted in a few independent congregations in M., but the mission works with churches of other denominations at local level.

In Sarawak and Sabah, East M., the Anglican mission began in 1848 (*SPG) with chaplaincy work among Europeans and mission among Chinese and Ibans, now over 20,000. Since 1962, Sabah has been a separate see with a Chinese bishop and about 6,000 Christian community, mainly Chinese. The RC mission of the *Mill Hill Fathers began in 1881 and now has over 100,000 Christian community. The Methodist church, centred in Sibu, Sarawak, grew from migration from South China, and has resulted in Chinese and Iban conferences of some 14,000 and 18,000 Christian community.

An earlier migration (1886) of Chinese Hakkas led to the Basel Christian Church in Sabah about 8,000.

The Borneo Evangelical Mission founded in 1928 has led to the formation of the Evangelical Church of Borneo, now over 30,000.

In West M. and Singapore there has been inter-church co-operation since 1948 through the Malayan Christian Council (now Council of Churches of M. and Singapore) and the union Trinity Theological College. A new start in church union negotiations was made in 1967.

In West M. mission among the Malays has been made almost impossible. *Islam is the official religion of M. but East M. has constitutional safeguards to conserve its greater religious freedom. In 1966 the M. government announced new regulations forbidding foreign missionaries to reside longer than ten years in the country.

The lack of a Malay church is a serious weakness.

JOHN FLEMING

J. R. Fleming: 'Singapore, Malaysia and Brunei: The Church in a Racial Melting Pot' in G. H. Anderson, ed.: *Christ and Crisis in Southeast Asia* (New York 1968), pp.81–106; 'Bibliography on Malaysia', MRL *Occasional Bulletin* XV, 3 (March 1964), 31pp., 363 items on Singapore, West and East Malaysia; *BM* II, 581–86; *NCE* IX, 108f.; *WKL* 873f.

MALI, 464,873 sq.m. in area with a population of 4,697,000 (1967 estimate), is a landlocked West African republic, a large part of which is Saharan desert. For several centuries most of the population has been Muslim. In 1965 there were 36,632 Roman Catholics in six dioceses. Five Protestant missions have been at work in recent years, with an estimated 3,000 communicants and 7,000 total community; they are the Evangelical Baptist Mission; Evangelical Christian Church of Mali and Upper Volta (served by the *CMA); Gospel Missionary Union; *PEMS and United World Mission. Of particular interest has been the CMA's work among the 130,000-strong Dogon tribe, a largely animistic people with strong traditional customs; their response to the gospel has been such that a large Christian community, with its own ministry, has resulted.

DAVID B. BARRETT

BM II, 587–90; *NCE* IX, 113.

MALTA, a Mediterranean island, has with neighbouring islets, an area of about 125 sq.m., and a population of about 350,000. Christianity is supposed to have existed in the islands since the visit of St. Paul recorded in Acts 27 and 28. In 1530 M. was handed over to the Knights of St. John, who had recently been expelled from Rhodes, and by them was made one of the principal barriers against the further westward advance of the Turks. In 1565 the knights, under their Grand Master La Vallette, successfully endured a tremendous siege, and thereafter maintained themselves in the islands till 1798, when they were driven out by Napoleon. In 1814, the Maltese by their own desire were incorporated into the British Commonwealth, to which they still adhere with greatly increased powers of self-government. Almost the entire population is Roman Catholic, and Roman Catholicism is the recognized religion of the islands, though Christians of many other denominations have come in in the service of the British naval base. M. makes a brief appearance in Protestant missionary history. From 1815 to 1831 the *CMS maintained there the printing press, which was part of its plan for developing Christian work in the Muslim countries of the Middle East. After the withdrawal of the CMS, Anglican Evangelicals, under the leadership of Lord Shaftesbury, maintained for a short time a Protestant college in the island.

STEPHEN NEILL

BM II, 590–93; *NCE*, 118–20.

MANCHURIA is a non-Chinese name for the 'Three Eastern Provinces' of China: Heilungchiang, Kirin and Fengtien. The country of the Manchus who ruled China from 1644 to 1911, it is bounded on the north and east by Siberia, on the west by the Mongolias, and on the south by Korea and the sea. With an area of 382,000 sq.m. there is a central fertile plain surrounded by hill masses. Summers are hot, winters bitterly cold, and rainfall is monsoonal. Manchuria possesses the most advanced heavy industry complex in China, first developed by the Japanese. The 1953 census showed a population of 43 million of whom about three million are in the capital city, Moukden.

Roman Catholic work may have begun by 1838. It was carried on by workers from France and *Maryknoll missionaries from N. America. The RC mission did not undertake much educational or medical work but developed considerable ecclesiastical establishments in the cities and larger towns. From the *Boxer persecutions onwards relations between RC and Protestant missionaries personally and socially were very good.

*Gützlaff visited Manchuria sometime in the 1830s; a Dr Williamson of the Scottish National Bible Society sold Scriptures there in 1866, and the Rev. William *Burns worked in the port of Newchwang for nine months in 1867–68. Interest aroused by Burns' death brought the first Irish and Scottish Presbyterian missionaries to Manchuria in 1869 and 1872. Others followed, notably the Danish Lutherans in 1896, and the Canadian Presbyterians in 1927. The Irish and Scots worked as one mission and built up a church which soon proved the most independent Synod of the Church of Christ in China. In 1940 it had 247 congregations, one hundred ordained ministers entirely supported by the Chinese congregations, and over 30,000 communicant members, Other denominations together probably numbered another 20,000. The church endured heavy oppression during the Manchukuo period and survived severe persecution. With no missionary help during the war years 1940–45, the Synod kept up the work of the Moukden Medical College (see CHRISTIE, DUGALD) and ran thirteen hospitals. Contacts with Ireland and Scotland were resumed in 1946, but missionaries had all withdrawn again by 1950. *Tien Feng*, the periodical of the *Three-Self Movement, reported a meeting of the Executive Committee of the Synod in 1957.

AUSTIN FULTON

A. A. Fulton: *Through Earthquake, Wind and Fire: Church and Mission in Manchuria* (Edinburgh 1967).

MAR THOMA SYRIAN CHURCH, an independent Indian church in Kerala, belonging to the group generally known as Thomas or *Syrian Christians. Under the influence of the mission of help sent by the *CMS to the ancient church in 1816, many young Syrians began to read the Bible and to become critical of the ancient institutions of their church. The mission of the CMS came to an end in 1836, but the evangelical leaven continued to work, especially under the influence of Abraham Malpān, and received support from the Metropolitan Matthew Athanasius, who had been consecrated in 1843. Relations between the conservative and reforming parties became increasingly difficult, and in 1889 a rupture took place, the majority remaining with the conservative wing. The reforming party lost almost all its property in a series of painful and expensive lawsuits; but organized itself as an independent eastern church, the MTSC, under Bishop Thomas Athanasius. This church, which now has about 250,000 members under four bishops, has retained many eastern usages, but in its theology and outlook reflects the Anglican and evangelical influences under which it came into separate existence. Under the outstanding leader Bishop *Abraham Mar Thoma (1880–1947), the church developed a strong missionary and ecumenical activity. It is a member church of the *WCC, and has set itself to develop good relationships both with the *CSI, and with the Malankara (unreformed) section of the Thomas Christians.

STEPHEN NEILL

C. B. Firth: *An Introduction to Indian Church History* (Madras 1961); F. E. Keay: *History of the Syrian Church in India* (2nd ed., London 1951); C. P. Matthew and M. M. Thomas: *The Indian Christians of St. Thomas* (New Delhi 1967).

MARIE DE L'INCARNATION (MARIE GUYARD 1599–1672) was born at Tours, France, and died at Quebec. After two years of married life she lost her husband and was left with a son, Claude Martin, who later published her two autobiographies, *Letters* and *Méditations et Retraites*. As soon as her son was able to take care of himself, she entered a convent of Ursuline Sisters (1631) to follow a way of life she had always found attractive. At the urgent appeal of Père Paul Le Jeune, a French *Jesuit in Canada, she went to Quebec in 1639 and took charge of some Indian girls in a school at Quebec. She possessed an unusual capacity for both leadership and the mastery of the Indian tongue; and so her institutions expanded greatly. She became the first Mother Superior of the Ursuline Sisters in Canada. Bossuet called her 'the Teresa of our days and of the New World'.

ARTHUR MCCORMACK, MHM

H. Bremond: *Histoire littéraire du sentiment religieux en France depuis la fin des guerres de religion jusqu'à nos jours* (11 vols., Paris 1916–1933), Vol. VI, pp.1ff., *NCE* IX, 219f.

MARKS, JOHN EBENEZER (1832–1915), Anglican missionary to Burma, gave 38 years service to that country, and left his impression on it as one of the greatest educational missionaries. Born in London, England, he started his work in 1860 in a small way in Moulmein, but in 1864 was moved to Rangoon, recently established as the capital of Lower Burma. A further move took place in 1868 to Mandalay, the capital of Upper Burma. Here M's school was attended by nine princes, sons of King Mindon Min—'it was more like a procession of Sanger's Circus through the streets than that of pupils coming to school'. When the king's favour was withdrawn, M. had to leave, but, after furlough in England, returned to continue his educational work in Rangoon. His methods were uncompromisingly British; his ideal was Thomas Arnold, of Rugby fame, and he was sure that there could be nothing better for Burmese boys than to be moulded after the best pattern of the English public school boy. His schools were open to all of every race, the only difference being that European boys were taught Burmese and Asians English. A stern and somewhat narrow Anglican, M. perhaps did not fully appreciate the value of the labours of other missions. In character he was authoritarian; but he secured the lasting affection of his pupils, some of whom under his influence became Christians and leaders in the church in Burma. M. returned to England in broken health in 1898.

STEPHEN NEILL

J. E. Marks: *Forty Years in Burma* (London 1917).

MARRIAGE PROBLEMS OF CONVERTS.

Among the social changes which follow upon the conversion of non-Christians, the change in the understanding of marriage and family life is perhaps the most revolutionary of all.

Christian marriage is founded on three factors, to none of which the conditions in non-Christian societies fully correspond.

(1) The recognition of Christian marriage as a partnership in mutual love, which draws its strength and its standards from the recognition of marriage as a divine ordinance.

(2) The full recognition of the human personality of the wife, as a partner whose rights are equal to those of the husband.

(3) The ideal, and the realization, of genuine self-mastery on the part of the Christian, which corresponds to the sanctity of marriage.

The great difficulty in the way of the acceptance of the Christian understanding of marriage is the subordinate role played by the women in all pre-Christian and non-Christian societies. Neither Europe in the early days, nor the cultures of China, India, Indonesia, the Near East or Africa, recognize the wife as possessing social or religious equality with her husband. She is a creature of lower rights and religious inferiority.

In consequence, she is in effect, in non-Christian marriage, charged with three functions: she secures the preservation of the clan into its own future; she lifts part of the burden of work from her husband, from her mother-in-law or from other senior wives; she is the object of her husband's sexual desires. To speak generally, in non-Christian and especially in *polygamous marriage, there is no opportunity for the full development of the personality of the woman, or for the exchange in full measure of giving and receiving. This is the general rule, even if in the history of culture it is possible to point to a number of famous exceptions.

The difficulty by which the introduction of Christian marriage among non-Christians is faced, is that non-Christian ideas of marriage based on the inferiority of women are deeply rooted in the tribal laws governing marriage and family life; and from these it is not possible for the new convert as an individual to withdraw himself. Even when an ethnic community has been so far christianized that new communities with a Christian character come into being, the replacement of the old order by the new constitutes a task of no small difficulty, since the old types of relationship are so deeply rooted. A change in the understanding of marriage presupposes a change in the ordering of society, and in its axioms.

We may take as an example problems arising in certain parts of Africa. In the African tradition, marriage is not primarily an agreement between bride and groom, but between the two clans to which the parents belong. Marriage is often arranged for the children by the parents. The loss of the life-force involved in the departure of a daughter is in part compensated for by the payment of the *lobola*, the bride-price of cattle. This payment ensures the right of the husband, or of his family, to the possession of the offspring of the wife, without strict regard to the actual biological paternity of the children. The *lobola* was also a protection for the wife, in that in the case of serious ill-treatment by the husband she was entitled to return to the house of her parents, without obligation for the repayment of the *lobola* being incurred. The social value which was traditional in the *lobola* has been radically called in question by the introduction of a money economy. The parents-in-law are tempted to make excessive demands on the suitor; this often leads to pre-marital sexual intercourse or to the total breakdown of the proposal for marriage later. The *lobola* reduces a widow to the position of a slave in the house of the parents-in-law. She is either compelled to enter on a levirate marriage with her husband's brother, or by generally approved unchastity to produce more children for the family into which she has married. A second marriage is either wholly impossible, or possible only on condition of the surrender of the children to the family of the first husband.

The threefold misunderstanding of the function of the wife in marriage mentioned above was the basis for the polygamy which is so widely recognized in Africa—in an agricultural society it is the economic factor which carries the greatest weight. Today, as a result of the system under which men work far away from their homes, the polygamy which was regarded as legitimate has been replaced by the secret polygamy or promiscuity of both partners.

The churches have carried on a long and often unsuccessful campaign against bride-price and polygamy. The method most widely used was that of the legalistic application of church *discipline; but this either led to hypocrisy, or made it impossible for a polygamist to become a Christian, since the dismissal of his excessive wives would have led to their social ruin. Today all the *indigenous churches are in process of re-thinking their traditional approaches to the problems of social change. The introduction of a system of preparation for Christian marriage, and of marriage counselling seems to be specially important and full of promise for the future.

PETER BEYERHAUS

Report of the All-Africa Seminar on the Christian Home and Family Life (WCC 1963).

MARSDEN, SAMUEL (1764–1838), pioneer in Australia and New Zealand, was born at Farsley, Yorkshire, England; after education at Cambridge he was sent to New South Wales in 1794, as chaplain with special responsibility for the spiritual welfare of the convicts in the penal settlements. He worked with great devotion, but appears to have been somewhat insensitive to the extreme harshness of the penal system, and has been sharply criticized by later generations for his share of responsibility, as a magistrate, for the cruelties to which

the convicts were subjected. In 1807, after a visit to England, M. changed the entire history of Australia by introducing into it five fine Spanish merino sheep, the gift of King George III. M's most memorable work was done in New Zealand, though this never formed part of his official duties. He had been deeply impressed by the quality of Maoris he had met in Australia. Having been unsuccessful in the attempt to persuade the *CMS to take up work in the islands, he purchased the brig *Active*, in 1814 made the voyage to New Zealand, and on Christmas Day of that year conducted the first Christian service ever to be held in New Zealand. This was the first of seven voyages; the last took place in 1837. M. was highly successful in winning the confidence of the Maoris; they seem to have been always willing to listen to him, and his efforts as a peacemaker among the tribes were notable. His ideas of missionary work were, however, questionable. Although a man of strong evangelical views, imbibed under Charles Simeon in his Cambridge days, he felt that civilization and conversion should go forward together, and to this end sent in as his first missionaries artisans who were to live among the people, and teach them handicrafts as well as the gospel. But the system did not work well, and little progress was made until the CMS did take over the mission, and appointed ordained and competent missionaries. The Maori people, who today are all Christians, still think of M. with gratitude as the apostle who first brought them the gospel. His faults, which were many, are outweighed by his merits, which were great.

STEPHEN NEILL

J. R. Elder: *The Letters and Journals of Samuel Marsden, 1765-1838* (Dunedin 1932); S. M. Johnstone: *Samuel Marsden, A Pioneer of Civilization in the South Seas* (Sydney 1932); J. B. Marsden: *Memoirs of S. Marsden* (London 1859); *DNB* XXXVI, 205.

MARTIN, WILLIAM ALEXANDER PARSONS ('WAP MARTIN', 1827–1916), brilliant missionary scholar and educator, did much to interpret Christianity in

Chinese terms, and also oriented Chinese leaders to western learning and ways of thought and practice. Born in the USA in a devout Pennsylvanian family, he early felt the call to China and was appointed a Presbyterian missionary in 1850. His first Chinese book, *Evidences of Christianity*, was widely read. Other books helped China in establishing relations with foreign powers and in inaugurating a modern school system. M's abilities as a translator were recognized in various diplomatic negotiations. His talents in many fields and his devotion to the awakening China were appreciated when he was appointed president and teacher in the new T'ung Men Kuan (School of Combined Learning) designed to train modern diplomatic and civil staff officers. After the reform movement, and the reactionary *Boxer uprising, M. was appointed president of the Imperial University, later the Peking National University. All this time he continued his evangelistic labours, translating the Scriptures, managing the Presbyterian Mission Press and its literature production, and building up the influential Peking mission station. M. died in his 90th year, honoured in China and abroad, and revered by many as a sage.

F. W. PRICE

W. A. P. Martin: *A Cycle of Cathay, or China South and North with Personal Reminiscences* (New York 1906), *The Awakening of China* (New York 1907).

MARTINIQUE. See CARIBBEAN.

MARTYN, HENRY (1781–1812), born at Truro, Cornwall, UK, studied with great distinction at Cambridge, and became a fellow of St. John's College. At Cambridge he came under the influence of Charles Simeon, absorbed intense evangelical principles, and was ordained priest in 1805. In the same year he left for India as a chaplain in the service of the East India Company. In Calcutta he made the acquaintance of *Carey and his colleagues, and took great interest in their work of translation. It is clear that, though mutual

respect was deep, there were tensions; the Baptists were self-taught men, whereas M. had received the best philological training that the west offered; he quickly became aware of the defects in their equipment, and of the amateurish quality of a good deal of their work. Carey and his colleagues had worked mainly in Sanskrit and cognate languages. M. concentrated on Arabic, Persian and Urdu, the three great languages of the Muslim world. He was posted respectively to Dinapur and Kanpur as chaplain. In those places translation work went relentlessly forward. He proved to have, in addition to knowledge and unwearied diligence, a remarkable sense of the niceties of language. The Urdu NT has undergone many revisions, but the basis of that which is in use today is still M's translation. He next engaged on Persian and Arabic versions. His health, never strong, had been seriously undermined by the climate and by excess of work. He decided to seek health in Persia. and at the same time to complete his Persian version where alone it could be satisfactorily brought to a conclusion. He spent an idyllic year in Shiraz, completing the translation, disputing with the Muslim Moulvies, and baptizing one single convert. Then, in a desperate attempt to reach England, he set out to ride across Asia Minor to Constantinople; but his strength was exhausted, and he died at Tokat on 10 October 1812; he was buried by the Armenian clergy of the place. Sensitive, introspective and devout, M. committed his thoughts to a *Journal*, which was published after his death by his friend John Sargent; it remains a priceless classic of Anglican devotion.

STEPHEN NEILL

C. E. Padwick: *Henry Martyn, Confessor of the Faith* (London 1922); J. Sargent: *A Memoir of the Rev. Henry Martyn* (London 1819); S. Wilberforce, ed.: *Letters and Journals of the Rev. Henry Martyn, B.D.* (London 1837); *DNB* XXXVI, 315.

MARTYRDOM AND MARTYRS. The Greek word *martus*, from which 'martyr' is derived, was in its original Christian use a term descriptive of one who was a witness to the life of Christ and to his resurrection. With the spread of persecution it came to be reserved for those who suffered hardship for the faith, and finally was restricted to those whose witness led to their death. As such they were properly venerated by their fellow-Christians. Indeed 'baptism by blood' was accepted as the equivalent of 'baptism by water' in the case of those who died for their faith in Christ before they had the opportunity of being baptized. The anniversary of the martyr's death came to be observed as his 'birthday'. This tradition and this usage of the word martyr has followed the church in its expansion throughout the world, and there are probably few churches anywhere existing which cannot claim an honoured list of names of those who have died for their loyalty to Jesus Christ. It remains true nevertheless that the composition of martyrologies needs to be undertaken with care and a frank recognition that many a Christian man and woman has been killed not because of their witness by word to Jesus Christ, but for quite different reasons, reasons in no way concerned with such witness. An illustration from contemporary history can make this clear. In the course of the tragic events in the Congo since 1961 a number of white missionaries have been butchered in conditions of great horror. Very understandably they are considered to be martyrs. They were, however, not killed because they were Christians. They were killed because they were white. It was their colour not their creed which led to their death. What we can and must add about these gallant men and women is that had they not been Christian missionaries they would not have been in the Congo to be killed. Their presence there made them witnesses to Christ rather than any testimony given by their lips. On the other hand the Kikuyu Christian who, during the Mau Mau period in Kenya, was dragged out of his hut at night and offered the choice of denying Christ or being hacked to death if he chose Christ, and

died stood in the classic tradition of martyrdom. Meanwhile we do well to remember that to live may be a greater martyrdom than to die.

MAX WARREN

MARYKNOLL FATHERS is the popular name of the Catholic Foreign Mission Society of America, Inc., a society of secular priests and brothers that was established by the archbishops of the USA in 1911 and authorized by Pope St. Pius X on 29 June 1911. The Congregation of Maryknoll Sisters is an order whose aims and work are parallel to those of the MF. After the departure of the first four missioners to China in 1918, the work grew rapidly, spreading to Japan, Korea, Manchuria and the Philippines. The second world war saw work begin in Latin America and then in Africa. The MF now staff missions in Tanzania, Kenya, Mexico, Guatemala, El Salvador, Venezuela, Colombia, Peru, Bolivia, Chile, Hawaii, Japan, Korea, Formosa, Hong Kong and the Philippines. The chief work is apostolic, conversion and the building of the Christian community; however, the society's missioners go out well prepared for the works of mercy. In different areas, according to need, they engage in social service work, medical work, educational institutions, student hostels and seminaries; they also operate co-operatives, credit unions, radio schools, housing projects, better-farming movements, co-operative factories and leprosaria. Strong emphasis is placed on the use of social communications in the apostolate. The society accepts members only from the USA and seeks to build an indigenous clergy to whom its work can be transferred. Headquarters are at Maryknoll, NY, USA. Training houses are maintained in various regions of the United States.

ALBERT NEVINS, MM

G. D. Kittler: *The Maryknoll Fathers* (Cleveland 1961); A. Nevins: *The Meaning of Maryknoll* (New York 1954).

MASS MOVEMENTS. See PEOPLE MOVEMENTS.

MATEER, CALVIN WILSON (1836–1908), American Presbyterian from a strong Scots-Irish heritage, was appointed to missionary service at Tengchow, Shantung, China, in 1862. Because of his educational gifts he was assigned the task of building up a primary and middle school, then a college, which some years after his death became the Shantung Christian University (Cheeloo). In his teaching and administration he set high standards and inspired faculty and student body with ideals of excellence, in the departments of arts and sciences and also in the training of a professionally competent Chinese ministry. At the 1870 Missionary Conference and on many other occasions he defended the need for a high quality of education in the missionary enterprise, and the preparation of adequate textbooks. M. was an eminent, modest scholar in both spoken and written Chinese; one of his most appreciated contributions was the publication of *Mandarin Lessons*, so widely used by new missionaries. In addition to his school and literary responsibilities he showed a deep interest in village evangelism and the nurture of Chinese churches. He disagreed with Dr John *Nevius on certain methods, believing that careful supervision and a number of well trained pastors were essential to a system of local, unpaid lay leaders. M. was a missionary genius in many ways, scholarly, skilful, resolute, creative, admired and loved by a large circle of students, colleagues and Chinese of all classes.

F. W. PRICE

D. W. Fisher: *Calvin Wilson Mateer, Forty-five Years a Missionary in Shantung, China* (London 1911); also articles in March, April, May *Chinese Recorder* (Shanghai 1900); *DAB* XII, 385f.

MATHER, COTTON (1663–1728), was born at Boston, Massachusetts, USA, graduated from Harvard College and entered the Congregational ministry. As assistant pastor, then pastor of the Second Church, Boston, he was deeply involved in the affairs, societies and organizations of the colony. He wrote extensively, publishing more than four hundred works. He was one of the Commissioners for Indian Affairs, the agents responsible for dispensing funds provided by the Society for Propagating the Gospel among the Indians, and supervising the work done with those funds. He took this responsibility seriously, was convinced that the commissioners were lax in their duty and unconcerned for the Indians' welfare, and with some frequency presented plans for the greater benefit of the Indians. He wrote about the Indians and for them, saw to the sending of a missionary to the Mohegans in Connecticut, arranged for the ordination of a man to assist the Indian pastor on Martha's Vineyard, proposed a scheme for educating Indians for the Christian ministry, and in various other ways was, for nearly a quarter of a century, the gad-fly of the commission. In 1724 he resigned, stating that he could no longer be party to the endless procrastination and disinterest of the commissioners, and urging the employment of an agent who would be concerned for the condition of the Indians. He was in this, as in other of his activities, the 'Keeper of the Puritan Conscience'.

J. LESLIE DUNSTAN

P. Miller: *The New England Mind* (New York 1939); S. H. Rooy: *The Theology of Missions in the Puritan Tradition* (Delft 1965), pp. 242–85; *DAB* XII, 386–89; *RGG* IV, 807f.

MAURITANIA, THE ISLAMIC REPUBLIC OF, in north-west Africa is a large territory of 419,230 sq.m., mostly arid desert, supporting a population of 1,100,000 (1967 est.), mostly Arab and Berber nomads who are 100% Muslim. Various attempts have been made to begin Protestant work, but the latest achieved nothing and missionaries were withdrawn in 1965. Most of the 5,500 Roman Catholics in the diocese of Nouakchott (formed 1965) are expatriates from France and French-speaking West Africa.

DAVID B. BARRETT

BM II, 605–07; *NCE* IX, 509.

MAURITIUS (Ile de France) is an island in the Indian Ocean, with an area of 759 sq.m. including dependencies, and a population (1968 est.) of 787,400. Having been discovered by the Portuguese, abandoned by the Dutch and ruled by the French (1715–1810), M. became a British colony, and in 1967 a fully independent and self-governing dominion within the British Commonwealth.

The original inhabitants of M. were the giant turtles and the dodoes. When the French discovered that M. has the ideal climate for the cultivation of sugar, African slaves were imported in large numbers; their descendants now make up about a quarter of the population. With the emancipation of the slaves, and their strong unwillingness to work for their former masters, Indian labourers were brought over in such numbers that Indians now make up about two-thirds of the population. There is a small Chinese minority, and some inhabitants of European origin. The language generally in use is a local form of French.

Almost all of the 'general population' are RCs. The most famous RC missionary in the island was Jacques Désiré Laval (d.1864) who is said to have converted 67,000 Mauritians of African descent. The RC diocese of Port Louis was constituted in 1847.

There is an Anglican diocese of M., constituted 1855, which ministers to English-speaking residents, and has had some success among the Indians, of whom less than 5% have become Christians. In 1867 Archdeacon Buswell (1839–1940) founded St. Paul's Theological College, and trained the first Mauritians for the priesthood. Anglicans number 7,800.

The Church of Scotland has a small cause, dating back to 1814 when the *LMS sent to M. the Rev. Jean le Brun, who founded the French-speaking Independent Church, now united with the C. of S. The SDA are credited (WCH 1968) with 3,742 adherents.

The chief problems of M. are over-population and excessive economic dependence on one crop, sugar. Work among the Indian and Chinese populations is difficult, and no church has won dazzling success among them; but this is the area in which there are some hopeful opportunities for the expansion of the church.

ALAN C. J. ROGERS

P. J. Barnwell and A. Toussaint: *A Short History of Mauritius* (London 1949); K. S. Latourette: *A History of the Expansion of Christianity* (New York 1937–1945) Vol. V, pp.314f.; *BM* II, 603–05; *NCE* IX, 509f.

MEDICAL MISSIONS. The work of Christian missions was from the beginning closely linked to charitable service to man in his need. Just as Christ made himself available to men in their need and suffering, so must those who make it their aim to follow him direct their attention to those whom he has characterized as our neighbours. In consequence, very soon after the beginning of Protestant missions, as early as 1730 Dr Schlegelmilch was sent to India as a missionary doctor. When, in the 20th century, the triumphal progress of scientific medicine began, missionary doctors were often found in the ranks of the pioneers of tropical medicine.

Since the medical aid provided by colonial governments was in many areas insufficient, and the measures taken by independent governments failed to meet the need, medical missions in many areas took over representatively responsibility for social service in the form of care for the sick. Exactly on the lines of the development that had taken place in the west, this was carried out mainly through the establishment of institutions such as hospitals and clinics. Doctors and nurses were sent out from Europe and America, and carried out their service in these missionary institutions. In the first half of the 20th century this service attained to considerable proportions. In the year 1925 the Protestant missions in Europe and America alone had in their service overseas 1,157 doctors and 1,007 nurses. From an early date efforts were made to train indigenous helpers. An ever increasing number of locally-trained nurses work side by side with missionary colleagues from the west in mission hospitals. The work of training indigenous doctors and securing their services has gone forward much more slowly, and even now the proportion of those who have found a vocation in the service of the church is comparatively small.

As independent states have taken in hand with success the development of their own programmes of health and healing, the services of the missions, begun as emergency service, have become increasingly superfluous. So the focus of the work has shifted from that of pioneer service to that of service in the cause of medical education.

During the period of representative service to man in his need and sickness, of necessity the aim of many doctors and nurses could not be other than that of bringing help to the largest possible number of human beings. The result was the enlargement of existing institutions or the extension of the work. In the second phase, when education was seen as the decisive contribution of missionary medical work, special stress was laid on the quality of the work.

If it is no longer necessary for medical missions to work in a representative capacity, the question arises whether medical missions are really anything more than help rendered in an emergency situation. When *younger churches, which had become independent, were faced with the question of their responsibility in the field of practical service, deep reflection as to the significance of Christian medical activity became inescapable. Developments in the field of medicine made medical work increasingly costly; in view of the restricted means available, it became impossible for the missions to carry on more than a restricted activity.

For these and other reasons, reflection on the essential character of Christian healing activity and Christian medical work in missions and in younger churches became inescapably necessary. These considerations have led to a series of consultations over the last ten years. The Tübingen consultation of 1964 exercised a worldwide and inspiring influence on this process of reflection.

It is quite impossible to separate the question of the significance of Christian medical service from the deeper question as to what the Christian mission itself is really all about. If we understand mission as setting before itself extensively the aim of conversion and proclamation through the word, medical work cannot have more than a secondary role as an aid to the primary purpose. This would involve a devaluation of Christian medical service. Moreover it would mean that the man who enters into contact with the mission is not taken seriously in the totality of his human existence. For Christ, acts of healing were signs of that coming kingdom of God, which in Christ himself has clearly broken in upon the world. Christian healing is the overcoming of the powers of evil. Among these powers of evil are to be reckoned death, anxiety, and the sense of meaninglessness; in consequence, alongside the problem of physical meaning, man's spiritual meaning must also be taken seriously into account.

So the task of healing, as this has been committed to Christians, has to do with more than the restoration of a man's capacity to work, or of his sense of physical well-being. What it means is that with Christ, and under the power of his cross, we can live filled with hope in situations in which physically there is no hope, and face to face with death. This means that for Christian doctors there is no hopeless situation, even when no healing, in the medical sense of the term, is possible.

Moreover healing in the name of Christ means that man, in the event of sickness and healing, encounters the living God. Christians know no healing which does not come from God himself. But encounter with the living God leads on to a willingness to be at God's disposal for his service. So healing is not simply a gift given to the one who is healed; it is also a call to service to the neighbour. This service can be rendered also by those who are chronically ill, or by those who are commonly called incurable, according to the gifts that have been given to them—through words, conduct, intercession, and the small services they can render to others.

So understood, the activity of healing is no longer to be considered as a question directed to the specially qualified doctors and nurses. Every Christian is called to participate in the work of healing.

This understanding of the situation produces questions as to the form in which the work of medical missions is to be carried on today. Not only should a question mark be placed against institutions in the maintenance of which the Christian community has no share, and which are in consequence isolated. Each congregation in each particular place must ask how it can best carry out its healing vocation in that particular place which has been assigned to it. The new understanding of medical service in developing countries lays stress on the need for medical practice directed to the community, in which medical assistants may be of much greater importance than highly specialised personnel. Great possibilities open out here before Christians who are aware of their responsibilities. The primary task of medical missions will then be to help Christians to fulfil that service in the realm of healing which is open to them. Only on condition that this has been achieved is it possible to think of the carrying on of specialized services in specialized institutions.

Service in institutions may actually hinder the development of genuinely Christian communities with a right understanding of service, since the community may be led to delegate to specialists something that really belongs to every Christian by the fact of his being a Christian. All this has led, as can be seen, to a radical rethinking of the place of the medical mission. But, since the radical rethinking is a necessity not only for the so-called younger churches, the results attained by these new insights pose a question to congregations and churches everywhere in the world. From this it is evident that participation in the *Missio Dei is not due to mere luck or circumstance, but is a gift from the Lord himself, who as Lord sends us out to the ends of the earth and calls us to his service. In relation to a great many things which we seek to accomplish, the decisive question is whether it corresponds to the plan of God that this should be accomplished (in other words, whether its *kairos*, its appointed time, has come). We are of the opinion that, from all that has happened in the sphere of medical missions in the last few years, we may learn that precisely in the time in which we live God has been giving us new insights, and new possibilities of service.

M. SCHEEL

E. M. Dodd: *The Gift of the Healer* (New York 1964); M. Scheel: *Ärztlicher Dienst im Umbruch der Zeit* (Stuttgart 1967); *Directory of Protestant Church-Related Hospitals Outside Europe and North America* (New York 1963); 'The Healing Ministry', special issue of *IRM*, LVII, No. 226 (April 1968); *The Healing Church* (WCC Studies, No. 3, Geneva 1965).

MELANESIA. See PACIFIC ISLANDS.

MENNONITE MISSIONS are widespread today, although for three centuries following the suppression of the early *Anabaptists the remnants of the movement survived primarily by following the frontier. In Transylvania, Danzig, Russia, North America and Latin America they existed until the early 20th century as enclaves, using a foreign language, avoiding outside social and political contacts, conducting little evangelism and no missions. Within the last forty years, in Canada and the USA, Mennonites have begun to use English and to work energetically in home and foreign missions. Although there were 19th century beginnings, the time of their late blooming began with the founding of the Mennonite

Central Committee (1923), a relief and service agency of worldwide significance, and *The Mennonite Quarterly Review* (by Harold S. Bender in 1926), a major journal of theological and church historical dialogue.

The initial impetus of MM (1525–70) came from Anabaptist-Mennonite understanding of the nature of the true church: (1) they rejected the territorial principle of Christendom and gathered on Pauline principles of preaching and letter-writing; (2) they applied the *Great Commission to all believers; (3) laymen were very active in the movement; (4) their theology of suffering authenticated the imprisonments and martyrdoms which accompanied their missionary work throughout Christendom.

After an interim of nearly three centuries, during which most energies were devoted to simple survival, missions again sprang up among Mennonites during the 19th century. The recovered emphasis reflected *Pietism and Wesleyan influence to a marked degree, and was paralleled by revival meetings and other modern methods of evangelism. In 1847 a Dutch Mennonite Missionary Association was founded. M. colonies in Russia raised money and sent missionaries in co-operation with the Moravians. By 1855 Canadian and US Ms were recognizing 'the high duty to support missions for heathen' in their conferences: work was begun among the American Indians and in India (1900), China (1901), Japan (1950), Taiwan (1954), Africa (1901), Colombia (1954), Argentine (1943), Ethiopia (1948), etc.

American Ms now spend over $1,000,000 annually on foreign missions, and the various branches of the movement had the following numbers on the field in 1957: General Conference Ms—127 missionaries, with 25,295 members; Old Ms—266 missionaries, with 4,103 members; M. Brethren—196 missionaries, with 30,904 members. They also participated in strength in the Congo Inland Mission. Special phases of work today include city missions, Negro missions, rural missions, and Jewish missions.

FRANKLIN H. LITTELL

A. F. Pannabecker: 'Missions, Foreign Mennonite' in H. S. Bender, ed.: *The Mennonite Encyclopedia* (Scottdale, Penna. 1957), Vol. III, pp.712–17.

MESSAGE OF THE MISSIONARY. The NT presents the picture of a community convinced that it had been entrusted with a message, which it must at all costs proclaim, centred in convictions about Jesus Christ, the living Lord, which they knew to be central to God's purposes for mankind. It is as bearer of this message that the church is truly called apostolic: sent, to the ends of the earth and to the end of time, to preach, teach, heal, baptize and love. To those who have false or inadequate ideas about God the message is the good news about what God in Christ has done, is doing, and is going to do; to those with no idea of God, that there is a God and that the news is good. The mode of expression of the message, in the varied circumstances of those to whom it must be communicated, has ever been a problem to the missionary. He knows that it is not his word but the given Word of God, yet there is no communication unless it be expressed in such a way that the hearer will understand. This means finding the way whereby the life in Christ so penetrates into the life of men in the world that the message is encountered at every level and in the midst of daily experience.

The complexity of the problem can be illustrated from the series of international missionary *conferences from Edinburgh 1910 to Ghana 1958. At Edinburgh under the question *How Mission*? the concern was strategic. It was assumed that it was simply a matter of obedience to the command of Christ to go into all the world. In Jerusalem 1928 *Wherefore Mission*? was considered in relation to other religions. Ten years later at Tambaram *Whence Mission*? involved research into the meaning of revelation. At Whitby 1947 *Whither Mission*? centred on evangelism in reference to which the whole church, including the 'young churches', was under obedience. This led to the *Why Mission*? of Willingen

1952 and the ultimate *What is the Christian Mission?* of Ghana. Today ongoing discussions recognize that there can be no adequate *theology of mission without full understanding of the nature of the message and that this final question lies beneath all the others.

The fullest and most generally accepted formulation is that of the World Conference on Faith and Order, Lausanne 1927, endorsed a year later at Jerusalem:

The message of the church to the world is and must always remain the *gospel of Jesus Christ. The gospel is the joyful message of redemption both here and hereafter, the gift of God to sinful man in Jesus Christ. The world was prepared for the coming of Christ through the activities of God's spirit in all humanity, but especially in his revelation as given in the Old Testament; and in the fulness of time the eternal Word of God became incarnate and was made man, Jesus Christ, the Son of God and the Son of Man, full of grace and truth. Through his life and teaching, his call to repentance, his proclamation of the coming of the kingdom of God and of judgment, his suffering and death, his resurrection and exaltation to the right hand of the Father, and by the mission of the Holy Spirit, he has brought to us forgiveness of sins, and has revealed the fulness of the living God and his boundless love toward us. By the appeal of that love, shown in its completeness on the cross, he summons us to the new life of faith, self-sacrifice, and devotion to his service and the service of men. Jesus Christ, as the crucified and living One, as Saviour and Lord, is also the centre of the worldwide gospel of the apostles and the church. Because he himself is the gospel, the gospel is the message of the church to the world. It is more than a philosophical theory; more than a theological system; more than a programme for material betterment. The gospel is rather the gift of a new world from God to this old world of sin and death; still more, it is the victory over sin and death, the revelation of eternal life in him who has knit together the whole family in heaven and on earth in the communion of saints, united in the fellowship of service, of prayer, and of praise. The gospel is the prophetic call to sinful man to turn to God, the joyful tidings of justification and of sanctification to those who believe in Christ. It is the comfort of those who suffer; to those who are bound it is the assurance of the glorious liberty of the sons of God. The gospel brings peace and joy to the heart, and produces in men self-denial, readiness for brotherly service and compassionate love. It offers the supreme goal for the aspirations of youth, strength to the toiler, rest to the weary, and the crown of life to the martyr. The gospel is the sure source of power for social regeneration. It proclaims the only way by which humanity can escape from those class and race hatreds which devastate society at present into the enjoyment of national well-being and international friendship and peace. It is also a gracious invitation to the non-Christian world, east and west, to enter into the joy of the living Lord. Sympathizing with the anguish of our generation, with its longing for intellectual sincerity, social justice and spiritual inspiration, the church in the eternal gospel meets the needs and fulfils the God-given aspirations of the modern world. Consequently, as in the past so also in the present, the gospel is the only way of salvation. Thus, through his church, the living Christ still says to men, 'Come unto me! . . . He that followeth me shall not walk in darkness, but shall have the light of life.'

That such an understanding has informed the message of the missionary down the years, whether in the word of preaching or in the deeds of teaching, healing and the like, cannot be doubted. The question today is whether the changing circumstances of the 20th century, both within the church and outside, require radical changes in the message. It has become the more acute since the second world war with the involvement of mission in various forms of

Christian aid, often so close as to suggest virtual identification. There are those who would argue that Christian *presence* is sufficient. Others, however, are still of the opinion that for all the new factors implicit in the emergence of the world church and the new attitudes to resurgent religions, the traditional understanding of the message as expressed above remains largely and essentially true.

MARCUS WARD

METHODIST MISSIONS were shaped initially by John *Wesley, Thomas *Coke and Francis *Asbury and then by the distinctively different forms of British and American Methodism. Wesley understood the mission of his societies to be the revival of true Christianity in England. This revival would spread to all Christendom, and then the faith would commend itself to all men (cf. Sermon No. 68). Asbury saw Methodism's mission in America to be winning to the gospel a new land in which most of the settlers were little influenced by their supposedly Christian background in Europe. His conception of Methodism as a mission to the frontier greatly shaped that body's early self-understanding. Late in life Asbury recognized the need for missions also to Negroes and Indians and pre-figured the later Methodist 'settled church' view of national missions in the USA as outreach to the under-privileged and non-Anglo-Saxons.

Coke saw the need to take the gospel to the whole world, and led the Methodists in this larger dimension of mission. Eight years before *Carey's *Enquiry*, Wesley scuttled Coke's 1784 Plan (for a) Mission Among the Heathen, but undaunted, Coke later encouraged work in Canada and launched MM in the West Indies and Sierra Leone. He died at sea in 1814 leading a group of volunteers who began work in Ceylon and India. One outcome of Coke's leading was the founding in London of the Methodist Missionary Society in 1819. That same year in New York, a group convinced that American Methodism had larger and then unmet responsibilities, founded—as an integral part of the denomination—what was later known as the Board of Missions.

British Methodism launched missions in Canada, the USA, the West Indies, and the Caribbean world; in West Africa, South Africa and Kenya; in Australia, New Zealand, Samoa, Tonga, Fiji—and the resulting churches moved to other Pacific islands; in Europe, notably Germany and Italy; in Ceylon, India and China. Most of the churches issuing from these missions, while maintaining spiritual kinship with British Methodism, were not bound to it by strong organizational ties and quickly found considerable or complete autonomy.

The outreach of American Methodism—with its strong episcopacy and General Conference and with its distinctive self-understanding as one of the two largest Protestant bodies in America—was quite different. With Japan, Korea, Mexico and Brazil as notable exceptions, most of the churches resulting from it retained membership in the General Conference in the USA. Thus, the Methodist Church in Korea belongs to the *WCC; but the 800,000-member Methodist Church in India—six times larger—or that in the Congo are only indirectly represented in the WCC through American Methodism. In addition to having churches in those lands indicated above, American Methodism spread in Germany and Scandinavia; to China, Hong Kong, Taiwan, the Philippines, Burma, Malaysia and Indonesia; to Liberia, Mozambique, Angola, Rhodesia and Johannesburg, and throughout most of Latin America. Many problems arose from the relation of all these bodies to the General Conference in the USA and gave rise during the 1960s to major reciprocal efforts toward autonomy.

Methodists are loosely united in the World Methodist Council, but the pattern of Methodism around the world is changing rapidly as many bodies have already entered *united churches and others are in process of doing so. Methodist missions have emphasized lay evangelism, printing and publishing, education and medical work.

W. RICHEY HOGG

W. C. Barclay: *History of Methodist Missions* (New York—Vols. I-III, 1949–1957, Vols. IV-VI to be published); G. C. Findlay and W. W. Holdsworth: *History of the Wesleyan Methodist Missionary Society* (5 vols., London 1921-1924); I. L. Holt and E. T. Clark: *The World Methodist Movement* (Nashville 1956); J. Wilkins, ed.: *The Christian Mission Today* (New York 1960).

METHODS, MISSIONARY. In principle, all missions have only one method, the preaching of the *gospel. There are, however, many possibilities of variation in the manner in which the message is presented; and even those bodies which set out with the most purely evangelistic aim—to preach the gospel untrammelled by any other consideration—have found themselves driven by the force of circumstances to recognize that proclamation by word is very far from being the only method by which Jesus Christ may be set before men as challenge and opportunity. In fact there is hardly any limit to the variety of means which have been used—*education on all levels, *medical work, schools for *blind children and for the *deaf and dumb, orphanages, *literature and the distribution of tracts, *correspondence courses for enquirers; in days of less developed techniques the magic lantern, later, cinema, *radio as in the famous 'Voice of the Andes' in Ecuador, the Far East Broadcasting Co., and the Lutheran broadcasting station in Addis Ababa; *agricultural and *industrial centres, the monastery, the sisterhood, the *āshram.

More significant than the variation of outward form have been the inner differences in the understanding of the nature of missionary work which have led to the wide variation in practice which can be observed in the course of missionary history. These can be conveniently set out in the form of a number of pairs of opposites: (1) Non-Christian religions are to be treated as wholly false, and wherever possible to be destroyed—all non-Christian religions have in them much of truth, and the transition from the old to the new is to be made as easy as possible for the convert. (2) Christian faith and western culture go together, and the convert is as far as possible to be Europeanized—culture and religion have nothing to do with one another; old customs are not to be disturbed unless they are clearly irreconcilable with the Christian gospel. (3) Education is to be supplied without discrimination to all who are desirous of receiving it—education is to be reserved for Christians; its aim is not evangelization but the production of a Christian élite. (4) When political circumstances permit, a measure of pressure may be exercised on non-Christians to become Christians—decision to follow Christ must be left entirely to the individual conscience, the liberty of which must be in no way infringed. (5) Everything must be directed to the baptism of those who are willing to receive it—faith in Christ is far more important than baptism; it is likely that many true believers should continue to live as unbaptized Christians in their own original surroundings. (6) When dealing with poor and oppressed people, an improvement in social conditions must precede the preaching of the gospel—the direct preaching of the gospel must come first, since this is the only power through which an improvement in social conditions can be secured. (7) The whole faith, as understood in the *older churches, must be transmitted to the peoples which have not yet received it—it suffices to communicate the essentials of the gospel, and to leave the converts to make their own discoveries as to the full meaning of the faith. (8) From the start the aim must be the establishment of living churches—the church is a secondary matter; the essential is the gathering out of believers; the form in which they express their new fellowship is a matter that can safely be left to them. (9) Conversion, or decision for Christ, is the aim of all Christian preaching—the idea of conversion should be excluded from the start; the aim is the creation of a climate of mutual understanding and fellowship, in which adherents of different faiths can work with one another, and mutually enrich their various religious traditions. (10) The aim is the formation of living Christian cells within a non-Christian culture—the aim is such a penetration of a non-Christian culture by Christian ideas that in the end that culture will be transformed from within into the Christian likeness. (11) Christians must be a 'garden enclosed', as far as possible separated from the corrupting influences of the world—Christians must be fully in the world, and influencing it on every level by their presence within it. (12) Christians should have nothing to do with politics— Christians should be prepared to play a leading part in the social and political revolutions of our time.

It will be noted that adherence, in an extreme form, to any one of the positions noted above, is likely to lead to a weakening of the force of the gospel. In many cases, the true position is one of tension, in which each of the positions is held in a creative relationship to the other. But in every case the criterion is the extent to which the word of Jesus Christ is being effectively proclaimed, in such a way that he is glorified and human life is transformed through his power. In so far as the term 'success' can be used in this connection, all missionary history goes to show that the work is 'successful', in so far as the exaltation of Jesus Christ is central, a steady but unsentimental call to decision for Jesus Christ is maintained, and the work is carried out in the calm assurance that there is no limit to what may be effected by the Holy Spirit in our day.

See also STRATEGY FOR MISSION.

STEPHEN NEILL

MEXICO. A republic of North and Central America, 761,600 sq.m. in area. Population (1965 estimate) 40, 913,000, of whom approximately 70% are *mestizo* (of mixed race), 28% American Indian, 1% European and 1% Negro. The language is Spanish, and the prevailing religion Roman Catholic.

RC missions began at the time of the Spanish conquest, 1519–21. Organization of the work began with the nominal creation of the bishopric of Yucatan in 1519, and was fostered by J. de *Zumárraga, first bishop of Mexico City from 1528. Three *Franciscans arrived in 1522; thereafter the religious orders, including *Augustinians, *Dominicans, *Jesuits and others, began to take a large share in pioneering, educational and pastoral work. Co-operating closely with the state, the church acquired great power and wealth. In education it concentrated on institutions of higher learning; the University of Mexico was founded in 1553. During the colonial period, however, the general standard of education was low and literacy was confined to a small minority. The methods used in converting, protecting and civilizing the Indians were on the whole *paternalistic. In 1805 there were in M. an archbishop, eight bishops, 1,703 parishes and 254 religious houses.

The Protestant constituency (1966 estimate) is about 800,000. The first Protestant penetration was made in 1827, by James *Thomson, agent of the BFBS, distributing Scriptures. No religious freedom existed at that time, and he was compelled to withdraw in 1830. Under a new constitution granting freedom of worship, full missionary work, started by Baptists and Presbyterians, began about 1860. The Church of Jesus, an indigenous movement launched by former RC priests, began in 1861, which developed into the Mexican Episcopal Church. Friends, Methodists and Congregationalists entered between 1870 and 1880. Other groups followed.

In 1910, at the end of 30 years of a dictatorship that fostered modernization of the country, with little improvement of conditions for the mass of the people, a revolution broke out. This resulted in profound political, social and economic changes. A new constitution was issued, of a liberal democratic and socialistic trend. An agrarian reform was set on foot, based on the distribution of lands and the breaking up of the old large private estates. Legal rights and privileges for the working class were established. Literacy and education received special impulse. Illiteracy dropped from 72% to about 30%, and only the demographic explosion has kept it at almost the same level. The largest proportion in the national budget is going to education. Social security now extends to practically all salaried persons. At present the army plays no political role at all. The last four presidents have been civilians. Transfer of power has been peaceful since 1952. The one-party (government) system has been evolving towards a moderate pluri-party rule. Opposition parties now automatically get a number of seats in Congress, apart from result of elections. Economic development has been energetically fostered, but a measure of economic inequality still exists.

Religious freedom, limited by law to private practices and public worship only in churches, is not curtailed in practice. The RC church is opening more and more to the ecumenical dialogue, and several instances of co-operation with non-Catholics are occurring. There is a noticeable Catholic biblical renewal. Most Protestant churches are self-governing; these include Methodists, Congregationalists, Episcopalians, Presbyterians, Baptists, Disciples of Christ, almost 29 Pentecostal movements, and others. Most of them belong to the Evangelical Council (of churches). A Union Seminary is supported by three demoninations, and a Union Publishing House by five. Plans are under way for a Theological Community formed by at least four denominational seminaries. There are pioneer experiments in Catholic-Protestant dialogue. A Mexican Bible Society was founded in March 1966.

GONZALO BAEZ-CAMARGO AND EDITORS

C. Bennett: *Tinder in Tabasco* (Grand Rapids 1968); D. A. McGavran: *Church Growth in Mexico* (Grand Rapids 1963); *BM* II, 607–17; *NCE* IX, 762–85; *WKL*, 914f.

MEXICO CITY 1963. See CONFERENCES, WORLD MISSIONARY.

MEZZABARBA, CARLO AMBROGIO (c.1685–1741), papal legate to the court of Peking, was born at Pavia, Italy. After graduating in civil and ecclesiastical law he entered papal service and successively was governor of Todi and Sabina. On 18 September 1719 Pope Clement XI appointed him legate to China, made him Visitor General of all missions of the empire with comprehensive powers, and archbishop with the title of Patriarch of Alexandria. Travelling by way of Lisbon he arrived at Macao on 23 September 1720 and at Peking by Christmas. He was to ask the ageing Emperor Kanghsi to recognize him superior of all missionaries in China and to permit Chinese Christians to follow the papal decisions on the Chinese *Rites. Meeting with the Emperor's displeasure he added to the constitution *Ex illa die* (13 March 1715) eight modifications permitting a purified cult of ancestors and Confucius, the use of tablets, prostrations, oblations and incense in so far as these were mere signs of respect and void of any superstition. Nevertheless the legation ended in failure and M. left Peking on 3 March 1721. In Macao he issued a secret pastoral instruction stating that the eight permissions allowed nothing that Rome had forbidden. Yet these only prolonged the dissensions and were nullified in the bull *Ex quo singulari* (1742). M. returned to Rome via Brazil and Portugal and died as bishop of Todi.

BERNWARD H. WILLEKE

Enciclopedia Cattolica VIII (1952), 924f.; L. Pastor: *History of the Popes* (Eng. tr., London 1941), pp.468–84; A. S. Rosso: *Apostolic Legations* (South Pasadena 1948); *NCE* IX, 791.

MICRONESIA. See PACIFIC ISLANDS.

MILL HILL MISSIONARIES (MHM). St. Joseph's Society for Foreign Missions was founded by the Rev. Herbert Vaughan (1832–1903) at Holcombe House, Mill Hill, in the north-west of London, and the college was officially opened by Archbishop Manning of Westminister on 19 March 1866. His first intention was to found a college for the training of missionaries to evangelize the many peoples of other lands, particularly in the British empire. He considered this a primary duty of English Catholics, challenged as they were by the great missionary zeal of the English Protestants. But he soon realized that he would have to form a missionary society, the constitutions of which were approved by its first General Chapter in 1875. He also realized that from Catholic England alone he could not get sufficient members, and he began recruiting from Holland, Germany and Austria. The society was finally approved by Rome in 1908. It is a society of secular priests and brothers who bind themselves by an oath to work for the missions. The society has some twenty training houses in Britain, Ireland, Holland, Austria, Italy and the USA. Its members work in Asia (India, Kashmir, Pakistan, Borneo, Philippines); in Africa (Uganda, Kenya, Congo-Kinshasa, West Cameroon and, until 1964, the Sudan); in New Zealand, the Falkland Islands and Chile. On 1 January 1967 there were 1,051 priests and 146 brothers. The Superior General resides at the society's Mother House, St. Joseph's College, Mill Hill, London.

ARTHUR MCCORMACK, MHM

A. McCormack, MHM: *Cardinal Vaughan* (London 1966), *Emigrants for God* (London 1962).

MILLER, WILLIAM (1838–1923), born at Thurso, Caithness, was sent to Madras in 1862 by the Free Church of Scotland. Madras University had recently been established, and M. resolved that the Free Church School should prepare pupils for matriculation and thereafter have a College Department affiliated to the university. By 1867 the college was in being, and for 40 years M. was its principal. In 1877, two more missionary societies having meanwhile joined in its support, it was re-named Madras Christian College. The college, and its principal, soon won high esteem. By 1878 the number of students had risen from six to 700. M. was for a period

Vice-Chancellor of the university, and was its first LL.D. The Free Church of Scotland elected him as Moderator of its General Assembly in 1896. M. is renowned for his outstanding qualities of leadership, and for his affectionate personal interest in his students. From another angle, he stands out as a pioneer of inter-mission co-operation. His attitude to *Hinduism and *Islam was, for his time, unusually liberal. Some Christians thought it too accommodating. But he was firm in his resolve to leave criticism of other religions to those who professed them, and to present Christ as judge of all religion, Christianity included. In various notable discussions of the functions of a Christian college, M. observed that it might contribute usefully to the training of Christians, and might also lead to the conversion of individual non-Christians. But such results were in his view 'side-products' of its main work. This was to *prepare* for the gospel by helping to create a climate of thought favourable to its reception. And the end-result that he chiefly hoped for was not so much the winning of individuals from Hinduism as the permeation of Hindu society by the mind of Christ.

A. J. BOYD

O. K. Chetty: *Dr William Miller* (Madras 1924); W. Miller: *Educational Agencies in India* (Madras 1893).

MILLET SYSTEM, the method by which the Muslim, especially Turkish, authorities dealt with non-Muslim religious minorities in their midst. The religious head of each community was recognized also as its civil head, and as the point of contact between that community and the government. Each community was allowed to live under its own personal laws in such matters as marriage, and to settle disputes relating to such matters in its own courts. The system had certain advantages, in that it secured to Christians and other minorities certain essential rights, and guarded those minorities against the danger of being wholly absorbed by the Muslim majority around them. On the other hand,

Christians became enclosed communities, with little opportunity or desire to bear a Christian witness before their non-Christian neighbours; and, in a very undesirable way, ecclesiastics became engaged in legal and political affairs, to the detriment of their spiritual care for their people. The MS was abolished by the Treaty of Lausanne between Turkey and the Allied Powers after the end of the first world war (1923). Separate Christian courts have recently been abolished in Egypt by the revolutionary government.

STEPHEN NEILL

MILLS, SAMUEL JOHN, Jr (1783–1819), was born in Torrington, Connecticut, USA, and died at sea on the return trip from his journey of exploration of the west coast of Africa. His father being a minister, he had come under deep religious influences and determined at the age of 18, while he was still at Morris Academy in Connecticut, to be a missionary. During his years at Williams College, he and a few friends formed the Society of Brethren, the first foreign missionary society in America. After graduation he studied theology at Yale University for a few months and then went to Andover Seminary. He became one of the founders of the *ABCFM, but his early missionary efforts were in the southern and south-western part of the USA. M. conceived an idea to help Africans educationally, and the establishment of the African school at Parsippani, New Jersey, in 1816 was largely due to him. In this school, young men of colour were trained as preachers and teachers not only for the US but for the West Indies and Africa.

In 1817 M. volunteered his services to the American Colonization Society to visit Africa as the agent of the society. His responsibility was to explore the west coast for the best possible site for location of a colony of 'the free people of colour of the United States', and to secure the same if possible. His efforts, and those of Ebenezer Burgess who came with him, were directed at securing land on Sherbro Island near Sierra Leone as a home for the oppressed

Negroes of America. As things worked out, this was not to be the home but another point further south on the coast, and yet M's work is commemorated in Liberia by the name of one of the settlements, Millsburg. As a matter of fact, Liberia itself is a tribute to the vision and humanity of M., who wrote at the end of his exploration 'that it was particularly proper for the American government to commisson an armed ship to this coast, to capture slave-trading vessels as two thirds of them are or have been American: that the free people of colour would be better situated in Africa than they are, or can soon expect to be, in America. I am everyday more convinced of the practicability and expedience of establishing American colonies on this coast'.

DAVID N. HOWELL

K. S. Latourette: *A History of the Expansion of Christianity* (New York 1937–1945), Vol. IV, pp.79ff.; T. C. Richards: *Samuel J. Mills* (Boston 1906); *DAB* XIII, 15f.

MILNE, WILLIAM (1785–1822). He described himself as born of humble parents 'in the parish of Henethmont in Aberdeenshire. My father died when I was six, and my mother gave me the education common to others in the same condition of life'. At the age of sixteen he was strongly influenced by a home where he was a welcome visitor and shared in family prayers. He lived on the farm where he worked. 'The only place where I could be quiet and unnoticed was a sheep-cote. Here, surrounded by my fleecy companions, I often bent the knee.' He left the Church of Scotland for the 'more evangelical' Congregational church at Huntly, a small town forty miles north-west of Aberdeen. This congregation a generation later produced James *Legge. M. was accepted by the *LMS in 1810, trained at its college at Gosport, ordained in 1812, and sailed for China in 1813. He began language study with *Morrison in Canton, spent some months distributing tracts among Chinese of the East Indies, and then settled in Malacca. He started a school and a printing press, employing *Liang Fa who became his first convert. In 1820 Morrison provided him with funds for an 'Anglo-Chinese College', never more than a small class training for the work of the mission. M. acted as chaplain to both English and Dutch. He translated the books Deuteronomy to Job for Morrison's Chinese Bible. Morrison lists, also in Chinese, 'numerous short essays, a catechism, village sermons, a discourse on the soul, and a commentary on Ephesians'. M. received an Hon. DD from Glasgow in 1818. Morrison writes, 'A man so intent on great objects, . . . so severe with himself, might not always attend to the convenience of others, and might jostle some in passing onward to gain his end'. Selections from his writings in Morrison's *Memoirs* reveal him as sombre, humourless, and never entirely freed from the narrowness of his upbringing.

JOHN FOSTER

R. Morrison: *Memoirs of the Rev. William Milne, D.D.* (Malacca 1824—rare); article in Dwight, Tupper and Bliss, eds.: *Encyclopedia of Missions* (revised ed., New York 1904); *DNB* XXXVIII, 9.

MINISTRY IN YOUNGER CHURCHES. All the *sending churches have from the beginning recognized that sooner or later the *younger churches would have to have ministries of their own; but the steps taken to provide for these have been haphazard and in many cases unduly delayed.

(1) The Roman Catholic church took two very different lines. The *Jesuits demanded such high standards that in their great mission in South India, and in Paraguay which they controlled for a century and a half, they never put forward a single candidate for the priesthood. Others had no such inhibitions, and in Goa, for example, a large number of Indians was ordained to the secular priesthood. Celibacy presented grave difficulties in a land in which it is unknown; and reports of the period suggest that the experiment was less than wholly successful. For the same reason, very slow progress was made with the development of the priesthood in

Africa. The pace has greatly increased in the last few years; but voices have been heard in the RC church suggesting that the recent developments have been too rapid, and that quality and quantity have not kept pace.

(2) In the 18th century, the Danish Mission in India ordained a small number of experienced catechists as pastors. One Ghanaian, Philip Quaque, was ordained to the ministry of the Anglican church. The Dutch in Indonesia developed quite a large indigenous ministry; but the Indonesians could not rise higher than the level of an assistant minister, and had always to work under the direction of a missionary.

(3) Revolution came when the Anglican missions in South India began to train men for the village ministry in their own language. It was recognized that all ordained men would be spiritually equal, but that the tasks to which they would be assigned would not necessarily be the same for all. The first ordination of this class of men took place in 1849. The experiment was so successful that the example was generally followed, and this is still the practice in the less advanced churches.

(4) It had long been recognized that a higher level of theological training was needed, if the younger churches were ever to have trained leadership which could in course of time replace the missionaries. But little was done until the 20th century. In 1917, the centenary of the foundation of *Serampore College in Bengal, the college was completely reorganized, the old charter of the king of Denmark under which the degree of BD could be given was revived, and Serampore took the lead in providing theological training in English and as an examining centre for the whole of India. Bishop's College, Calcutta, was at the same time put on the BD footing, as also the United Theological College, Bangalore, founded in 1910. In all these cases, the language of instruction was English, both as the only common language and as the key to the riches of western theology. The aim was to provide teaching up to the level of an English or American university or seminary.

Seminaries on this level were soon in existence in China, Japan, Korea, the Philippines, South Africa and the Argentine (in 1966 about fifty).

(5) But the Third World Missionary Conference (Tambaram 1938) in its 8th report, declared that 'it is our conviction that the present condition of theological education is one of the greatest weaknesses in the whole Christian enterprise'. As a result of this report, a number of studies were made and reports issued, one of the results being the merging of small and expensive denominational schools into large interdenominational units. In 1958 the *Theological Education Fund of the *IMC came into being with a view to strengthening the work throughout the world. One of its achievements has been the founding of a higher school of theological studies for French-speaking Africans at Yaoundé, Cameroon. In some parts of the world the situation has been eased by the establishment of departments of religion in government and secular universities. A steadily increasing number of students is sent annually for higher theological study in the western world. But the situation is not as yet one that can be viewed with complacency; it appears that in some areas standards are falling rather than rising.

(6) Improvement in training has resulted everywhere in transfer of authority. At the beginning of the century, the missionary controlled almost everything, with the indigenous minister practically though not always in name as his servant. Today in almost every younger church there is a fully developed ordained ministry, acting independently and taking the initiative into its own hands. This process is described in the articles DEVOLUTION; YOUNGER CHURCHES, etc.

(7) Many forms of the unordained ministry exist in the younger churches. Information on these should be sought in the separate articles on CATECHISTS; LAITY; LAY MISSIONERS.

STEPHEN NEILL

Tambaram Report Vol. IV (London 1939) pp.199–250; Y. Allen, Jr.: *A Seminary Survey*

(New York 1960); C. W. Ranson: *The Christian Minister in India* (London 1945–1946); B. G. M. Sundkler: *The Christian Ministry in Africa* (London 1959); Theological Education Fund: *Directory, Theological Schools in Africa, Asia, etc.* (New York 1966).

MISSIO DEI is a concept used in RC dogmatic theology to describe those activities within the divine Trinity itself by which the way for mission is prepared. The Father sends the Son; the Father and the Son together send the Spirit for the redemption of mankind. The phrase was taken over by the Conference held at Willingen in 1952, in order to find a basis for missionary activity of the Protestant Christian world in the activity of the Triune God himself. The term *Missio Dei* defines mission as an activity of God himself, which he has begun in the sending of his Son, and which he continues through his Holy Spirit in the church until the end of time. The missionary activity of the church is thus brought into the closest relationship to the missionary activity of God himself. Thus the church takes its place in the service of God for the proclamation of his gospel. The church cannot really be the church of God, unless it takes its share in the mission of his Son. Mission thus comes to be seen as the basic function of the church. It would, however, be too narrow an interpretation of the term *Missio Dei*, if the idea were limited solely to that of missionary activity. To it belongs everything that needs to be done, everything that God actually does, for the communication of salvation. Vocation, preparation, the sending out of workers, and the carrying out of their manifold forms of service, are ways in which the love of God, defined by the *Missio*, finds visible expression.

See THEOLOGY OF MISSION.

GEORG F. VICEDOM

G. F. Vicedom: *The Mission of God* (St. Louis 1965).

MISSIOLOGY (the science of missions), Roman Catholic and Protestant. The church has at all times been conscious of its duty to be missionary; but 'mission' as a complex whole had not been systematically and comprehensively treated as a theological subject. Of course studies of particular problems of missionary work and its methods appeared from time to time. The first theories of mission in the modern understanding of the term were the work of José de Acosta, SJ: *On procuring the Salvation of the Indians* (1588), and of the Carmelite Thomas à Jesu: *On procuring the Salvation of all men* (1613). In the world of the Protestant churches, similar approaches are to be found in Holland (Gisbert Voetius, 1589–1676). But it was not until the 19th century that the claim was made that mission should be accorded its own proper place in the system of theology. On the Protestant side the pioneer was F. Schleiermacher (1768–1834), on the Catholic side J. B. Hirscher (1788–1865): both these men attached mission to the section on pastoral or practical theology. Not much later an attempt was made in the Russian Orthodox Church to work out a scientific basis for missionary work (N. I. Ilminsky 1821–1891).

Efforts to establish an independent 'doctrine of missions' were made almost contemporaneously in England and Germany. The foundation for the scientific study of missions was laid by K. *Graul (1814–1864) in his academic lecture 'On the place and significance of the Christian mission in the scientific studies of a university considered as a whole' (Erlangen 1864). A. *Duff (1806–1878) held in Edinburgh and Glasgow from 1867 onwards the first professorial chair of evangelism. However, G. *Warneck (1834–1910) can be regarded as the real founder of Protestant missionary science. In 1874 he brought into being the *Allgemeine Missions-Zeitschrift* (AMZ), and made of it the rallying point for efforts in the direction of missionary science. His 'Protestant doctrine of missions' (*Ev. Missionslehre* 1892², 1897–1903) brought him the reward of an honorary professorship in Halle. On the RC side there are only individual efforts to be recorded. The

decisive step forward was taken by Josef Schmidlin (1876–1944), who gathered up the existing impulses, founded in 1911 the *Zeitschrift f. Missionswissenschaft* (ZM), and as first full Professor of Missions in the University of Münster set out the new discipline in systematic form. In his understanding of the situation, he was to a large extent dependent on G. Warneck. In consequence, the criticisms of Warneck are also the criticisms of Schmidlin, and the corrections which have to be made are much the same. The cause for this is to be found in their common approach to the problems of missionary activity. The differences are to be found rather in the use of terms than objectively in the way in which the questions are framed.

In the Protestant missionary world, understanding of the problems was deepened by the various World Missionary *Conferences. The church, as the bearer of missionary responsibility, came in consequence into the foreground; proclamation as a missionary method was understood in terms of the comprehensive approach, and the idea of individual conversion was replaced by that of the Christian community, the young church.

In the RC world, it was recognized that missions must be freed from their European clothing; and this led to the much discussed, but often one-sidedly presented method of *'accommodation'. This led further to the theory of missions as the 'plantation of the church' (P. *Charles), which was to culminate in the formation of an indigenous clergy, and in the setting up of the regular ecclesiastical hierarchy. Münster was supposed to represent the theory of evangelization, and Louvain that of the planting of the church. During the Second *Vatican Council it was found possible to define the matter more correctly. Through the understanding of the church at which we have newly arrived, it has become possible to understand missionary work *both* as the proclamation of the gospel and the gathering together of the people of God. So 'accommodation' has been transferred from the sphere of method to that of theology (the incarnation of Christianity), and the final universality of the church is regarded as an eschatological event.

Our present situation in a unified world has compelled missionary science to take up the problem of missionary activity in 'all six continents'. Under this new concept, mission is understood as being addressed no longer merely to the world which is 'not yet Christian', but to the whole secularized world community. This would mean the end of missions as previously understood, and would demand of the church and of theology that they should become missionary, and identify the church with its mission. If the mission of the church came to be regarded as a fully integral part of theology, it would no longer be possible to justifiy the existence of missionary science as a separate discipline. It would have accomplished its own mission.

JOSEF GLAZIK

G. H. Anderson: *Bibliography of the Theology of Missions in the Twentieth Century* (New York[3] 1966); J. Blauw: *The Missionary Nature of the Church* (New York 1962); P. Charles: *Etudes missiologiques* (Bruges 1956); A. Freitag: *Mission und Missionswissenschaft* (Kaldenkirchen 1962); J. Glazik, ed.: *50 Jahre Katholische Missionswissenschaft in Münster* (Münster 1961); O. G. Myklebust: *The Study of Missions in Theological Education* (2 vols., Oslo 1955–1957); T. Ohm: *Machet zu Jüngern alle Völker* (Freiburg 1962); J. Schmidlin: *Katholische Missionslehre* (Münster[2] 1923); *NCE* IX, 900–04; *RGG* IV, 1011–16.

MISSION BOARDS AND SOCIETIES: ASIA.

All living churches are to some extent missionary, but for the most part their missionary activity is exercised in their own immediate neighbourhood, and along the lines of kinship or racial association. The planning of missionary work on a larger scale and at a greater range is usually a later development, coming at a time at which a church has developed a considerable measure of stability and self-consciousness.

India. (1) The first missionary effort of this second kind in India seems to date from the year 1903, when V. S. (later Bishop) *Azariah persuaded like-minded friends to form the Indian Missionary Society of Tinnevelly. Work was started in a pioneer area of the Telugu country 600 miles to the north, which later developed into the diocese of Dornakal; and among the Palia people of the S. Ghauts. The work continues, and a new station was opened in 1967 in Orissa, among a mountain people still entirely untouched by the gospel. (2) At a slightly later date, the National Missionary Society of India was formed under the Presidency of Mr K. T. *Paul. This society took charge of a considerable variety of unrelated pieces of work in different areas of India. (3) Under the impulse of Bishop *Abraham, the *Mar Thoma church of Kerala started *āshrams* in Hardwar, North Kanara district, and other places. At the same time a certain beginning of missionary interest was manifest also in the Malankara church.

China. (1) In 1936 the Anglican Church (*Chung Hua Sheng Kung Hui*) in China decided to start its own mission field, staffed and supported by the gifts and efforts of the Chinese church alone. Shensi was selected as the sphere of operations and T. K. Shen was consecrated as the first bishop. (2) At about the same time the Church of Christ in China formed its missionary society to work among the aboriginal peoples in western China (Miao, No-su, etc.). It is not known whether it has been found possible to carry on this work since the communist take-over.

General. In 1956, on an invitation coming from the Philippines, the Asia Council on Ecumenical Mission came into being, with the aim of co-ordinating the efforts which were being made by a number of Asian churches to help one another in missionary work. A number of exchanges was carried out, but these belong rather to the area of *inter-church aid than to that of missionary effort in the narrower sense of the term. Through the Manila Conference of 1948 the *IMC and the *WCC encouraged and supported steps which led in due course to the Prapat Conference in 1957, and to the formation of the *East Asia Christian Conference; whereupon the ACEM ceased to function. The EACC regards itself as responsible for the survey and planning of Christian witness throughout the whole of East Asia.

STEPHEN NEILL

MISSION BOARDS AND SOCIETIES: AUSTRALIA.

The number of Australian missionaries in 1965 was 4,416. Of these 972 were working amongst Australian Aborigines and 3,444 overseas. The total was made up of 1,330 Roman Catholics working in 36 fields; 1,607 denominational missions from other main churches working in 74 fields; 895 sent by non-denominational societies to 86 fields, and 584 representatives of sects working in 47 fields. A total of 76 overseas countries was involved.

The geographic distribution of the total missionary force is: 47% in the Pacific including 35% in Papua-New Guinea, 22% amongst Australian Aborigines, 20% in Asia, 6% in Africa, 2% in Latin America and the Caribbean.

Figures for the main non-Roman churches were Anglican 482, Methodist 335, Presbyterian 137, Baptist 133, Churches of Christ 108, Lutheran 267, Salvation Army 101, and Congregational 37.

FRANK G. ENGEL

Australian Missions: A Statistical Survey (Sydney 1967).

MISSION BOARDS AND SOCIETIES: CANADA.

Roman Catholic. Many French-speaking Canadians serve in missionary orders, notably the *White Fathers in Africa (founded 1868). Their share in overseas work increased considerably during the 20th century. In 1921 the Society of Foreign Missions of the Province of Quebec was founded; it has trained and sent abroad thousands of secular priests, especially to China, Japan and South Africa. The English-speaking Scarboro Foreign Mission Society has working

parallel to it the women's group Our Lady's Missionaries.

Anglican Canadians have served abroad in the 19th and 20th centuries with *USPG, *CMS and other British societies. Overseas missionary outreach is now administered through the Missionary Society of the Anglican Church of Canada. There are workers in all continents, many of them in association with members of the Anglican societies.

Baptist missionaries worked with the American ABMU in Burma from 1845 and eventually in India and China. In 1873 the first Canadian Baptist mission board was founded. In 1898 Canadian Baptists began the first continuing Protestant mission in Bolivia. In 1912 the overseas work of the Baptist churches was co-ordinated under the Canadian Baptist Foreign Mission Board.

Congregationalists founded the Canadian Foreign Missionary Society in 1854. Their workers joined the American *ABCFM in Angola in 1886. Canadians continued to share in this work after the Canadian Congregational Union joined the United Church of Canada (1925).

The *Lutherans* formed their own Canada Conference in 1853. Their missionary expansion has taken place mainly within Canada itself.

The *Methodist* Canada Conference on its formation in 1824 immediately set up a missionary society, primarily for the evangelization of the Indian tribes. In the late 19th century it began work in Japan and West China. In 1925 the Methodist Church of Canada joined the United Church of Canada.

Presbyterians from Canada were working with Scottish missions in India from the 1850s. In 1876 the Presbyterian Church in Canada sent its own first missionaries to India. After 1925, when about half of the Presbyterian Church joined the United Church of Canada, the continuing Presbyterian Church retained a portion of the overseas programme. Today its Board of World Missions has work in Formosa, Japan, India, Guyana, Jamaica and Nigeria, and also contributes personnel to ecumenical projects in other places, e.g. Italy.

The *United Church of Canada*, formed in 1925 by a union of the Congregational and Methodist churches with about half the membership of the Presbyterian Church, is the largest non-RC body in the country. Its Board of World Mission supplies workers to sister churches in other parts of the world in areas where there has been historic connection and also responds to new appeals from indigenous church bodies, as well as making appointments to ecumenical programmes for the *WCC or the *WSCF. Personnel are serving in Japan, Korea, Hong Kong, Central India, Nepal, Angola, Congo, Zambia, Kenya, Trinidad, Jamaica and Brazil, etc.

Interdenominational Missions. Canadians have supported and shared in the work of *OMF, *SIM, *CMA, the *Grenfell mission in Labrador and other societies.

KATHARINE B. HOCKIN

WKL, 936f.

MISSION BOARDS AND SOCIETIES: DENMARK.

Total population is about 4,500,000. The National Church of Denmark (Lutheran) includes about 95% of the people. Other churches are small, for instance, Roman Catholics about 26,000; Baptists about 7,300 (adults); Methodists about 3,500 (adults).

There are 24 mission boards and societies. Seventeen are Lutheran working as independent societies not formally connected with the official church; in the Free Churches missionary work is mostly integrated with the church. The total number of missionaries is at present about 315 of whom about 240 come from Lutheran societies. Two societies have between 50 and 75 missionaries; seven have between ten and twenty-five; the rest less than ten. Organizations with more than ten missionaries are (figures 1 January 1966): Danish Missionary Society (Lutheran, established 1821, 75: missionary work Tanzania, Aden, India, Taiwan, Japan); Danish United Sudan Mission (Lutheran, established 1911, 66: missionary work Nigeria); Moravian Mission (Lutheran, established 1843, 22: missionary work mainly Tanzania); Pentecostal Movement (established 1912, 22: missionary work Africa, India); Baptist Church (established 1912, 17: missionary work Rwanda-Burundi); Lutheran Missionary Association (established 1868, 17: missionary work Tanzania, Surinam); Danish Santhal Mission (Lutheran, established 1867, 16: missionary work North India, East Pakistan); Salvation Army (established 1887, 13: missionary work Africa, Indonesia, India, South America); Apostolic Church (Pentecostal, established 1924, 12: missionary work mainly South Africa).

ERIK W. NEILSEN

P. Hartling, ed.: *The Danish Church, Det Danske Selskab* (Copenhagen 1964).

MISSION BOARDS AND SOCIETIES: FINLAND.

The oldest and largest missionary organization in Finland, the Finnish Missionary Society (FMS, in Finnish *Suomen Lähetysseura*), was founded in 1859 as the missionary organ of the Evangelical Lutheran Church. In 1868 the first missionaries were sent to S.W. Africa, where the Evangelical Lutheran Ovambo-Kavango Church with 180,000 members is a fruit of the work of this society. Another field was opened in China, N. W. Hunan, in 1902. At present the FMS is working in S.W. Africa, Tanzania, Ethiopia, Taiwan, Hong Kong, W. Pakistan, and among the Jews in Jerusalem. The missionary staff (including wives) in the fields amounts to 175.

In 1900 the Lutheran Evangelical Association of Finland (*Suomen Luterilainen Evankeliumiyhdistys*), which had been founded in 1873 by one branch of the great 19th century revival movement within the church, started a mission of their own in Japan. The association has at present fourteen missionaries in Japan where they are making their contribution to the Evangelical Lutheran Church of Japan. The Swedish-speaking section of the association, called *Svenska Lutherska Evangeliföreningen* (Swedish Lutheran Evangelical Association) started mission work in Kenya in 1963 in co-operation with the *Bibeltrogna Vänner* (Bible-true Friends) from Sweden.

The question of integration of the church and missionary organizations is under discussion in Finland.

In the smaller churches in Finland, of which the Free Church, the Methodists and the Baptists have missionaries of their own, the church and mission are integrated. The Free Church (with primarily Congregational tradition) sent its first missionaries to China in 1891, in co-operation with the *CIM, and to N. India (Himalaya) in 1895, in co-operation with the Scandinavian Alliance Mission. Since 1922 the Free Church has been divided into the Finnish-speaking section *Suomen Vapaakirkko* and the Swedish-speaking *Fria Missionsförbundet*. The former has at present missionaries in N. India, in Nepal and in the Congo (Brazzaville); the total number is thirteen. The latter has three missionaries in Taiwan. The Methodists and the Baptists are also divided into Finnish and Swedish-speaking organizations and have each one or two missionaries working in larger denominational co-operation. The same is the case with the Salvation Army who have at the present nineteen workers in the various mission fields.

The *YWCA of Finland has taken responsibility for a few women missionaries in the fields of the FMS.

A very conspicuous feature in the picture of the Finnish missions today is the activity of the Pentecostal Movement. The Pentecostal congregations with an active membership estimated at 25,000–40,000 have sent a very large number of missionaries, today about 180, to many different parts of the world, especially Asia.

MATTI PELTOLA

K. A. Paasio: *Finlands insats i världsmissionen* (Helsinki 1928); M. Peltola, T. Saarilahti, P. Savolainen: *Mestarin käskystä* (Helsinki 1959); M. Peltola: *Finnish Lutheran Missions* (Helsinki 1963).

MISSION BOARDS AND SOCIETIES: FRANCE. This article deals with French Protestant missionary efforts other than the *PEMS.

The *Mission biblique en Côte d'Ivoire*, founded in 1927 by the Church of the Tabernacle (Baptist) in Paris, is engaged in the evangelization of the south-west portion of the Republic of the Ivory Coast. The churches which have sprung from this work have been independent since 1960 and are known as the Union of Protestant Churches of the South-West. In 1968 these churches were served by 48 French and Swiss missionaries, including the wives of missionaries, and the British missionaries of the Unevangelized Fields Mission. There were 20 churches, 39 pastors or evangelists, 150 lay preachers, 156 places of worship, 2,047 baptized members; 3,400 pupils in schools receive instruction, all of whom are indigenous.

L'Action chrétienne en Orient, founded at Strasbourg in 1922 by Pastor Berron, works among the Armenians both in France and in the Near East. More recently it has undertaken the evangelization of Algerians resident in France. It is actively supported by Protestant Churches in French-speaking Switzerland.

The *Mission Rolland*, founded in 1902 by Pastor Emile Rolland and now carried on by his son, has three stations in the mountains of Kabylia (Algeria).

The Lutheran churches of France have a *Commission for Relations with the Churches overseas*, which occupies itself with finding French-speaking teachers for Lutheran colleges and schools in Madagascar and Cameroon, founded respectively by the Norwegian mission (Stavanger) and the American Lutheran Mission (Minneapolis).

See also PARIS FOREIGN MISSION SOCIETY.

ETIENNE KRUGER

MISSION BOARDS AND SOCIETIES: GERMANY. In Germany there are 63 missionary societies and organizations for service. The older among them are connected with revival movements, and with the awakening of missionary interest in England: these include the *Basel Mission (1815), which has its greatest field of support in

Germany, the *Berlin Mission (1824), the *Rhenish Mission (1828), the *Gossner Mission (1836). In many areas of Germany the *pietistic awakening was paralleled by a churchly and confessional movement of renewal. From this second movement arose: the *Leipzig Lutheran Mission (1836), the Lutheran Mission of *Neuendettelsau (1849), the Schleswig-Holstein Missionary Society (1876), the Mission of the Lutheran Free Churches (1892). The *German East Asia Mission was at first the mission of the liberal wing in theology. Only one new mission came into being in the colonial era—the *Bethel Mission (1886). The following may be classed as belonging to the group of the *'faith missions': The Institute for Orphans and for Mission, Neukirchen (1878); the Alliance Mission, Barmen (1889); the Hildesheim Mission to the Blind (1890); the Free Church Missionary Fellowship (1890); the Liebenzell Mission (1892); the Wiedenest Bible School (1905); the Christoffel Mission to the Blind (1908); the Mission of the Bible Study Groups for Girls (1925); the Marburg Mission (1929); the *WEC (1931); the Velbert Mission (1954). Missions to Muslims include the following: the Jerusalem Fellowship (1852); the Syrian Orphanage (1860); the German Fellowship of Service (Hilfsbund – 1896); the Protestant Mission in Upper Egypt (1900); the Protestant Carmel Mission (1904). Missions to Jews are undertaken by the Central Lutheran Union for Missions to Israel (1869); the Service of the Gospel (Evangeliumsdienst – 1947); the Fellowship of Service to Israel (1952). Medical missions are represented by the German Institute for Medical Missions (1906).

Since 1885 the German missions have been working together in a committee. The German Missionary Council has been in existence since 1922. In 1933, the German Missionary Assembly, to which all the Protestant missions adhere, was founded.

The majority of the German missionary societies came into existence as a counterpart to the organized church. Their work was supported by voluntary circles, which were gathered in the congregations with the help of the pastors. The confessional missions, however, from the beginning regarded themselves as representatives of their churches. The more the work increased, the greater the efforts the missions were compelled to make to secure the inward support of the churches for their work. Gradually the churches began to raise collections for missions. Since the end of the war the churches have taken the field with very large financial contributions to the missions. The faith missions have behind them serried ranks of convinced supporters; out of these, in some cases, a Free Church has come into existence.

As the missionary societies regarded themselves as a parallel organization to the church, only in rare cases did they send out ordained pastors of the church for missionary work. They themselves trained their own candidates in their own seminaries or Bible schools. As the candidates were not authorized to enter the service of the church, the missionary societies had to take entire responsibility for them. Missionary service was reckoned to be a lifelong vocation. Support of missionaries in old age proved to be in many cases a heavy burden for these societies to carry. With few exceptions the directorate of the mission regarded itself as constituting also a directorate for the *younger churches.

Through the independence of the younger churches, and through 'integration', many things have changed. All the larger missions are engaged in close and harmonious cooperation with their churches, and regard themselves as the mission of these churches. In most cases there has been as yet no legal determination of this relationship. In 1963 the churches and missions co-operated in setting up the Protestant Fellowship of Work (Arbeitsgemeinschaft) for World Mission, which carries out tasks in the field of *inter-church aid, which the missionary societies alone would not be able to undertake.

See also MISSIONS, ROMAN CATHOLIC.

GEORG F. VICEDOM

W. Oehler: *Geschichte der deutschen evangelischen Mission* (2 vols., Baden-Baden 1951); *WKL*, 932–41.

MISSION BOARDS AND SOCIETIES: GREAT BRITAIN. The revival of Christian faith and practice in Britain in the 18th century, known as the Evangelical Revival and focused in the Wesleys and George Whitefield, led to a great increase of activity amongst Christians both for the proclamation of the gospel and for service to the socially dispossessed. The characteristic form of organization through which the resulting activities were carried on was the voluntary society, through which Christians banded themselves together for the carrying out of a specific purpose. In the latter part of the 18th and the earlier part of the 19th centuries, particularly in the years from 1795 to 1815, an astonishing number of societies was formed for an extraordinary range of purposes, not only for the propagation of Christianity, but also for the abolition of slavery, the promotion of education, the provision of literature, and many other concerns for human welfare. Many were closely linked, and the same men were involved in the formation and work of several. A prominent part in them was taken by laymen.

The reasons why this outburst of activity amongst Christians was carried out through the formation of voluntary societies were complex, but include the desire of Christians who shared a common experience and concern to work together with others who shared that experience and concern; impatience with the slowness, reluctance and in some cases opposition of official church bodies; and the fact that the atmosphere and conditions in society favoured the voluntary society as an instrument for carrying out a specific purpose.

The earliest of the British societies concerned with the proclamation of the gospel amongst non-Christians antedates this great upsurge by nearly a century. The Society for the Propagation of the Gospel in Foreign Parts was founded in 1701, chiefly through the efforts of Thomas Bray, Rector of Sheldon and Commissary in Maryland for the Bishop of London. Its original purpose was the support of Anglican clergy in British colonies and the winning to the Christian faith of the Aborigines and the Negro slaves in these possessions. In 1965 it and the Universities' Mission to Central Africa, founded in 1859 as a result of David *Livingstone's addresses at Cambridge and Oxford, combined to form the *United Society for the Propagation of the Gospel.

The first society exclusively directed towards the evangelization of non-Christians throughout the world was the Baptist Missionary Society founded in 1792 through the faith, vision and determination of William *Carey. It provided the stimulus for the formation of many others.

In the second half of the 19th century, the explorations of Speke, Burton and Livingstone in Africa, the ending of the privileged rule of the East India Company in India, and the opening of doors to evangelistic work in China and Japan led to a new outburst of misionary energy and the formation of further societies, many of them, like the *China Inland Mission (now the Overseas Missionary Fellowship) undenominational and international.

Missionary societies, based as they were on popular support and not on the action of either church or state authorities, were the instruments through which the Christian mission became an enterprise of the rank and file of church members. As engagement in the world mission became more widespread and was increasingly acknowledged as an integral part of church life and responsibility, many missionary societies became in various ways more and more closely linked with the official bodies of churches.

Today the large number of missionary bodies in Britain vary greatly in size, methods of organization and ethos. They include societies of individuals, of which some have as their purpose evangelistic work in a particular country or area (e.g. the Japan Evangelistic Band, or the Oxford Mission to Calcutta), or in unevangelized areas (e.g. the *RBMU); some of them are international (e.g. the AIM, *SUM); some serve a particular function (e.g. the BFBS, the Leprosy Mission) or a particular section of the community (e.g. the Missions to Seamen, the British Sailors' Society). Some autonomous societies serve a particular denomination and have close links with its official bodies (e.g. the BMS and the *CMS). Other missionary bodies are in varying ways constitutionally part of the structure of their denomination (e.g. the Overseas Council of the Church of Scotland, the MMS), the latest of these being the Congregational Council for World Mission, continuing the work of the former *LMS and the former Commonwealth Missionary Society.

Roman Catholics in England have always been a small minority of the population (at present about 8%), suffering, until Catholic Emancipation in 1829, under considerable civil disabilities. England was, and to some extent still is, regarded by them as a mission field, a receiving rather than a sending country. Individual English RCs have served as missionaries, notably Thomas *Stephens, the *Jesuit who worked in India from 1579 to 1619. The only major missionary society with headquarters in England is St. Joseph's Society for Foreign Missions, commonly called the *Mill Hill Fathers. This was founded by (Cardinal) H. Vaughan in 1866 and received full papal approval in 1908. The society now has more than 1,000 priests in service, in seventeen mission fields in different parts of the world, notably Uganda. But a number of the members are Dutch, and it is not possible to say how many of them are English.

The situation in Ireland is, naturally, entirely different. The great majority of the population is RC, and for its size Ireland has contributed as large a number of missionaries as any other country. It is reckoned that about 2,000 Irish priests are living abroad (179 in the specially Irish foundation of the missionaries of St. Patrick); to these must be added the Christian Brothers, with educational work in many parts of the

14

world, and an immense number of sisters, especially Sisters of Mercy, who carry out most extensive work in both the Christian and non-Christian worlds.

RONALD K. ORCHARD AND STEPHEN NEILL

There are histories of the larger and older missionary societies. The movement of which they are the expression is described in K. S. Latourette: *A History of the Expansion of Christianity*, Vol. IV (London 1941). A brief account is given in E. A. Payne: *The Growth of the World Church*; the *Story of the Modern Missionary Movement* (London 1955). See also *WKL*, 937f.

MISSION BOARDS AND SOCIETIES: HOLLAND. In 1797 the *Nederlandsch Zendeling Genootschap*, Netherlands Missionary Society (NZG) was founded as a sister society of the *LMS. In the course of the 19th century the society extended its labours to various parts of the Indonesian archipelago: the Moluccas, Timor, Celebes and the eastern part of Java. Objections against more or less liberal tendencies led to the formation of three new societies: the *Nederlandsche Zendingsvereeniging*, Netherlands Missionary Union (NZV — 1858), the *Utrechtsche Zendingsvereeniging*, Utrecht Missionary Union (UZV—1859) and the *Nederlandsche Gereformeerde Zendingsvereeniging*, Netherlands Reformed Missionary Union (NGZV—1859). The NZV (evangelical, with no specific church connection) found its field of labour on Java (western part) and Celebes (south-eastern part), the UZV (evangelical, with a stronger orientation towards the Netherlands Reformed Church) on New Guinea, Halmaheira and Buru, the NGZV (Calvinistic) in the southern part of Middle-Java. In 1905, the NZG and the UZV founded a mission school at Rotterdam, which moved to Oegstgeest in 1917; the NZV joined in 1919; the name is since 1951 *Zendingshogeschool der Nederlandse Hervormde Kerk*, Missionary College of the Netherlands Reformed Church. A number of missionary societies (e.g. the NZG, the UZV and the NZV) joined hands in the *Samenwerkende Zendingscorporaties*, Co-operating Missionary Corporations (from 1907 onward). In 1946 six of the co-operating societies united to form the *Verenigde Nederlandse Zendingscorpora-ties*, United Netherlands Missionary Corporations, which handed over their work to the Netherlands Reformed Church in 1951; the executive agency became the *Raad voor de Zending*, Board of Foreign Missions. One missionary society within the NRC remained intact as a separate society: the right-wing calvinist *Gereformeerde Zendingsbond*, Reformed Missionary Alliance (founded in 1901); it closely co-operates, however, with the Board of Foreign Missions. Nowadays, the NRC has a missionary responsibility in Indonesia, where it supports some general ecumenical projects and co-operates with a number of Indonesian churches, and in West Africa: Cameroon (where it supports, e.g. the centre for literature at Yaoundé and the theological seminary at Ndoungué), Nigeria (e.g. support to the Islam-in-Africa project), Ghana and Senegal; the GZB works in Indonesia (Celebes) and in Kenya.

In 1894, the NGZV handed over its work to the *Gereformeerde Kerken in Nederland*, Reformed Churches in the Netherlands, formed in 1892 as a result of a union between two churches which had separated from the NRC in the course of the 19th century. Until 1958, the only mission-fields were in Indonesia (Middle Java and Sumba); nowadays, the *Gere-formeerde Kerken* also work in West Pakistan (where they co-operate with the United Presbyterian Church in the USA, the Associate Reformed Presbyterian Church and the Church of Scotland), in Central Africa (Rwanda, in co-operation with the Protestant Churches in Belgium) and in South America (Brazil and Argen-tina), while they give support to the work of the Moravian church in Surinam. They have their missionary centre and seminary at Baarn. In 1969 the general synods of the NRC and the Reformed Churches decided to unite the seminaries of Oestgeest and Baarn.

Other Dutch Protestant missions are:

the *Zendingsgenootschap der Evangelische Broedergemeente*, Missionary Society of the Moravian Church (founded at Zeist in 1793 as an auxiliary missionary society; mission-field, Surinam); the *Doopsgezinde Zen-dingsraad*, Mennonite Missionary Board (the continuation of the work of a Menno-nite missionary society founded in 1847; missionary work in northern Java, Irian Barat, Ghana and Chad); the *Zendingsraad der Evangelisch Lutherse Kerk*, Missionary Board of the Lutheran Church (the con-tinuation of the work of a Lutheran missionary society, founded in 1852; it supports Lutheran missionary work in Tanganyika and India); the *Zendings-commissie der Unie van Baptisten Gemeenten in Nederland*, Committee for Missions of the Union of Baptist Congregations (it supports the work of the Baptist Missionary Society in the Congo); the *Vereniging van Gemeen-schappelijke Zending van de Vrije Evan-gelische Gemeenten in Nederland*, Common Mission Union of the Free Evangelical Congregations (mission field: Samosir on Sumatra); the Dutch branch of the *Morgen-landzending*, Missions in the Near East, the *Vereniging tot Uitbreiding van het Evangelie in Egypte*, Union for the Propagation of the Gospel in Egypt, and the *Stichting voor Werelddiaconaat en Zending van de Remon-strantse Broederschap*, Foundation for World-Diaconate and Missions of the Arminian Churches (co-operates with the NRC in Ghana). All these mission boards co-operate in the *Nederlandse Zendingsraad*, Netherlands Mission Council (founded in 1929; reorganized in 1946; general offices at Amsterdam). Outside this council remained the mission of the *Christelijke Gereformeerde Kerken*, Christian Reformed Churches, the mission of the *Vrijgemaakte Gereformeerde Kerken*, Liberated Reformed Churches and the mission of the *Gerefor-meerde Gemeenten*, Reformed Congrega-tions (these missions have their fields in Indonesia and in Africa); furthermore, there exist some daughter-organizations of foreign agencies which belong to the group of the *'faith missions'.

In the 19th century, Dutch Roman

Catholicism took a relatively small part in the mission work of the RC church. The 20th century, however, saw a rapid increase of the participation in missionary activity. A great number of missionaries was sent to various parts of the world; support was given to papal missionary societies and to the work of a number of religious orders. In 1967, the *Nederlandse Missieraad* was founded as an overall organization; it has good contacts with its Protestant sister organization. An inter-academic institute for the study of *missiology and ecumenics, in which Protestants and Catholics participate, came into being in 1969 (*Interuniversitair Instituut voor Missiologie en Oecumenica*, Leiden and Utrecht).

J. VAN DEN BERG

S. Coolsma: *De Zendingseeuw voor Nederlandsch Oost-Indië* (Utrecht 1901); I. H. Enklaar (in co-operation with J. Verkuyl: *Onze blijvende opdracht* (Kampen 1968); E. F. Kruyf: *Geschiedenis van het Nederlandsche Zendelinggenootschap en zijne zendingsposten* (Groningen 1894); C. W. Nortier: *Anderhalve eeuw zending 1797-1947* (Oegstgeest 1947); *WKL*, 945f.

MISSION BOARDS AND SOCIETIES, INTERDENOMINATIONAL. The Protestant world mission has been distinguished by a strong sense of unity from the beginning, and union societies were early evidence of it. They were generally inspired by the example of the *LMS, founded in 1795 for united action by evangelicals in Independent, Presbyterian and Anglican churches. Across the Atlantic the New York Missionary Society was established the next year, 1796, by pastors and laymen of the Reformed Dutch, Presbyterian and other churches, and the Baptists held membership for a few years. The Northern Missionary Society in the state of New York was founded in 1797 in the Schenectady-Albany region. The Congregational General Association of Massachusetts in 1810 founded the *ABCFM as the overseas sending agency of all New England Congregationalists, but at once admitted Presbyterians by request. The

formation of the ABCFM inspired the synod of the Reformed Dutch Church, the General Assembly of the Presbyterian Church, and the synod of the Associate Church to organize in 1817 the United Foreign Missionary Society, centring in New York. Its field was to be the world, but it engaged only in Indian work, also taking over the missions of the two earlier New York societies. Financial difficulties led to its merger with the ABCFM in 1826. That brought Presbyterians and Dutch Reformed into the American Board, and soon the German Reformed Church also affiliated. However, the Presbyterians split in 1836, and the 'Old School' set up its own mission board. The Reformed Church in America began independent sending in 1857, and the German Reformed Church withdrew in 1862. The Presbyterian reunion of 1870 took the remaining Presbyterians out of the ABCFM and left it a Congregational organ. Only one other society was formed for union action, the 1865 German Evangelical Missionary Society or 'New York Society', which served German language churches in several denominations. After a few years it was taken over by the Evangelical Synod of North Amerca.

The example of the LMS also had profound effect on the continent of Europe. Although a denominational Reformed organ, the Netherlands Missionary Society, was founded in 1797 to co-operate with the LMS, early societies were mostly joint Lutheran and Reformed organizations. These union societies included the *Basel Evangelical Missionary Society 1815; the *Berlin Missionary Society, 1824; the *Rhenish Missionary Society of Barmen, 1828; the *North German Missionary Society of Bremen, 1836, and the *Gossner Missionary Society. Confessional strains and stresses, however, resulted in the Berlin and Gossner societies becoming Lutheran, and the Bremen Reformed. The *PEMS, founded in 1828, has continued to serve both Reformed and Lutheran churches. A specialized British agency modelled after the LMS should be noted, especially for the aid it gave pioneer missionaries of other societies in the Near East. This was the LSPCJ, or London Jews Society, 1808; but in 1815 it became Anglican. A union society of non-established churches was then founded.

Auxiliary services clearly called for joint action, and Bible and literature societies were the first attempts at co-operation. These societies were non-denominational in form, but interdenominational in intent, and national denominational bodies contributed to many. The BFBS was founded in 1804, the American Bible Society in 1816 (uniting many local societies), and soon others were established far and wide. Union Bible translation committees co-operated with them on the fields. The societies themselves inter-acted co-operatively and eventually formed the *United Bible Societies (1946). The Religious Tract Society of London was organized in 1799, and the American Tract Society in 1825. Union organizations for literature were established on the fields with representation from the several missions, such as the East China Religious Tract Society (1844), the China Tract Society, and the Society for the Diffusion of Christian and General Knowledge (1887), which became the Christian Literature Society. The Mission to Lepers (1874) and the John Milton Society (1928) for work with the blind represent the later development of union societies for specialized ministries, supported by denominations as well as by individuals.

Some intra-confessional union societies were organized for special objects. Two Scandinavian missions are examples. The Santal Mission of the Northern Churches (1867; reorganized 1910) for work with aboriginals in Bihar and Orissa has been supported by the various Scandinavian Lutheran churches and by a number of the American ones. Dr Karl A. *Reichelt's Northern Mission to Buddhists in China (now also Japan) has a similar relation to Scandinavian churches.

Inadequate provision for work for women and children led to the formation of special union societies, intended by the women to be inter-denominational, although non-denominational in form. The Society for Promoting Female Education in the East was founded in 1834, and the Indian Female Normal School Society (later Zenana Bible and Medical Mission) in 1852. The Woman's Union Missionary Society of America was organized in 1861, but most of its leaders withdrew under pressure to found denominational societies; and it continues as a non-denominational *faith mission.

Co-operation in major union institutions in the several fields required interdenominational promotion, technical assistance and support. Incorporated boards were created, especially in the UK and USA (including Canadian participation). Thus there were interdenominational boards in the USA for each of the China Christian colleges. These were eventually brought together in the United Board for Christian Colleges in China (1932; 1945) now the *United Board for Christian Higher Education in Asia (1955), and in Britain there is a counterpart *Asia Christian Colleges Association (1952). Others are the boards of *Vellore and Ludhiana Medical Colleges, St. Christopher's Training College (Madras) Women's Christian College (Madras) and Tokyo Women's Christian College. The Board of Founders of Nanking Theological Seminary with five member boards has become the *Foundation for Theological Education in South East Asia (1963) with twelve participating boards.

Finally, there are to be noted some interdenominational boards which administer united missions. Three are American: the Board for Christian Work in Santo Domingo, the United Mission in Iraq, and the United Andean Indian Mission. One is broadly interdenominational and international with headquarters in India, the United Mission to Nepal (1953).

R. PIERCE BEAVER

Refer to articles on the various societies, and consult the indices to Vols. III–VII of K. S. Latourette: *A History of the Expansion of Christianity* (New York 1937–1945).

MISSION BOARDS AND SOCIETIES: NEW ZEALAND.

Mission boards and societies based in New Zealand and associated in the *National Council of Churches maintain missionaries in Melanesia, Polynesia, West Pakistan, India, Malaysia, New Guinea, Indonesia, Hong Kong, Rhodesia, East Pakistan, Madagascar, South Africa, South America, West Indies, Korea and Jordan, totalling 305, of whom 122 are in Melanesia and 60 in India. Denominationally the largest groupings are Anglican 98, Presbyterian 75, Methodist 42 and Salvation Army 39. Many other New Zealanders are missionaries under the aegis of societies outside the NCC.

DAVID M. TAYLOR

MISSION BOARDS AND SOCIETIES: NORWAY.

In the Church of Norway (Lutheran), to which 96% of the population belong, missionary activities are the concern, not of the church as such, but of voluntary associations: the Norwegian Missionary Society, the Santal Mission, and the Norwegian Lutheran Mission, founded respectively 1842, 1867 and 1891 (these three alone account for more than 80% of the total income for foreign missions and for about 60% of the total number of missionaries) as well as a number of other societies, including specialized agencies for work among Jews, Muslims and Buddhists. The small but active free churches, namely the Lutheran Free Church and the Methodist, the Baptist, and the Pentecostal groups, carry out their missionary obligation as part of their regular activities. Among the interdenominational bodies, the Norwegian Orient Mission, the Norwegian Missionary Union, and the Norwegian Missionary Alliance, are particularly prominent. In 1966 there were 23 societies and boards for foreign missions, including five auxiliary organizations. Contributions in Norway totalled Kroner 35,360,000. Norwegian missionaries, 1,014 in all, are at work in 31 countries (662 in Africa, 283 in Asia, and 69 in Latin America). The *indigenous churches, associated with Norwegian missions, have a total membership of more than 450,000. By far the largest church is in Madagascar (240,000 baptized Christians).

O. G. MYKLEBUST

Norsk Misjonsleksikon (3 vols., Stavanger 1965–1966); *WKL*, 947.

MISSION BOARDS AND SOCIETIES: RUSSIA.

Bodies of this kind, responsible for the carrying on of missionary work, have never existed in Russia, except for one or two monasteries, which on occasion have sent out monks for missionary work, e.g. Valamo to Alaska and the Aleutian Islands in the 18th century. There were, however, missionary unions which supported the work of the missionaries, e.g. the Society for the Restoration of Orthodox Christianity in the Caucasus (1860), the Missionary Society for the Promotion of Christianity among the Heathen (1865), which later was absorbed into the Orthodox Missionary Society founded by Innokenti *Veniaminoff (1870). In 1900 this society had only 16,358 members but its achievements were considerable. Above all it financed the translations commission of the brotherhood of St. Gurij in Kazan, which in 25 years circulated more than a million and a half copies of Christian writings in the languages of the peoples of the Volga basin. The greatest service rendered by the missionary societies was that they disseminated the sense of missionary responsibility among the Orthodox believers (Missionary Sunday, Missionary Festivals, etc.).

JOSEF GLAZIK

J. Glazik: *Die russ.-orth. Heidenmission seit Peter d. Gr.* (Münster 1954), *Die Islammission der russ.-orth. Kirche* (Münster 1959).

MISSION BOARDS AND SOCIETIES: SOUTH AFRICA.

From the earliest period of European occupation of the Cape (1652), spontaneous missionary work among the non-Christian slaves was carried out by the settler families. Systematic activity on the part of missionary societies began with the arrival of the Moravian missionary George *Schmidt, who from 1737 to 1744 gathered Hottentots together round his station at Baviaanskloof in the neighbourhood of Cape Town. As a result of legal and ecclesiastical difficulties, the Moravian mission could not be resumed till 1792, when it found its new centre in Genadendaal. The result of this work is seen in independent churches formed in the western (Coloured) and Eastern (Xhosa) Provinces. The *LMS entered in 1799 with considerably stronger forces, and commenced work among the Hottentots, the Xhosa (1816) and the Bechuanas (Moffat in Kuruman in 1817). The LMS played a very important part in the history of SA, through the courageous interventions of its pioneer missionaries J. T. *Van der Kemp and Dr John *Philip on behalf of the human and political rights of the indigenous population. The liberation of the slaves in 1833 led to the great trek of the Boers, and this in its turn led other missionary forces to undertake work in as yet unreached areas of SA.

Three types can be distinguished among the many churches which undertake missionary work in SA and South West Africa: (1) Overseas churches which through their missionary societies carry on work among the Coloured, the Bantu and the Indians. These are, apart from those already mentioned, mainly the Lutheran missions, which are to be found everywhere in SA (*Rhenish 1829, *Berlin 1834, Norwegian 1844, Hermannsburg 1854, Finnish among the Ovambos 1870, Swedish 1876, American 1928); the *Paris Mission (Basutoland [Lesotho] 1829); the *ABCFM (Natal 1835); the Swiss Mission (North Transvaal 1875). Besides these there is a large number of Free Church and Alliance Missions. Today the overseas missions work as aids to the missionary work of the independent national churches. (2) Churches which use their white settler congregations as the starting-point for interracial *indigenous churches—the Wesleyans (from 1816 in Cape Province, later throughout SA); the Anglicans (1847 foundation of the bishopric of Cape Town, with R. Gray, a strong friend of missions as the first bishop,

followed by other dioceses over the whole extent of SA); the Scottish Presbyterians (from 1821; 1841 educational missions with Lovedale as the strongest centre); the RCs. In 1802 the RCs obtained permission to found their church in SA. In the course of their missionary work *vicariates apostolic were created (1837 in the Cape, 1892 in Natal, Orange Free State and Transvaal). Numerical growth was particularly remarkable in Natal and Basutoland. Between 1914 and 1931 the number of vicariates and prefectures apostolic increased from eight to nineteen. In 1951 Pope Pius XII by his bull *Suprema Nobis* erected the hierarchy of the church in Southern Africa and transformed the vicariates apostolic into four ecclesiastical provinces. These incorporate 'white' parishes as well as 'black' but continue to be served by the *Propaganda. The work of the Anglican and RC churches is strengthened by the presence of a number of religious orders and congregations, both for men and women (the Community of the Resurrection, *Jesuits, etc.).

(3) European churches with their base in SA, which as a result of separate evangelization have brought into being separate churches for non-European Christians. This is especially the case with the Dutch Reformed churches—the motto of their missionary work is 'unity in diversity'. Their missionary efforts were unified as early as 1824, and eagerly promoted by Andrew *Murray. The South African Baptist Mission Society founded in 1927 the Bantu Baptist Church. The *South Africa General Mission (1894) and the Dorothea Mission form a cross between the first and the third types.

PETER BEYERHAUS

L. Cawood: *The Churches and Race Relations in South Africa* (Johannesburg 1964); J. du Plessis: *A History of Christian Missions in South Africa* (London 1911); *WKL*, 951f.

MISSION BOARDS AND SOCIETIES: SWEDEN. During the 11th century Sweden was drawn into the Christian fellowship and the Swedish church started missionary work among the Laplanders. The Reformation brought Luther's teaching to Sweden and the Swedish church continued its mission in the north. Later on *Pietism began to widen the horizons and the 19th century saw the outburst of Swedish missionary interest.

The Evangelical Revival brought many Swedish Free Churches into being, some of which were related to British and American churches. The Mission Covenant Church grew in criticism of the *confessionalism within the Evangelical National Missionary Society, the so-called *Fosterlands-Stiftelsen*, established in 1856 as a lay movement within the Church of Sweden. At the end of the century American influences awoke a second evangelical revival which created many interdenominational missionary societies, which later became conservative evangelical Free Churches. In the early 20th century Pentecostalism began to filter into Sweden.

The Free Churches were aware of their missionary calling and integrated their missionary agencies into the church structure. As a confessional missionary society the *Fosterlands-Stiftelsen* launched the first autonomous Swedish mission. Challenged by the Evangelical Revival, the Church of Sweden faced its missionary responsibility and established in 1874 a church-mission, the Church of Sweden Mission.

German interests influenced the *Fosterlands-Stiftelsen* and the CSM to start work in Ethiopia and South India. The CSM became involved in Lutheran co-operation in South Africa as well. During the 1880s the Mission Covenant Church established an independent mission in the Lower Congo and managed in 1909 to expand into the French Congo. E. V. Sjöblom joined the American Baptists and became a renowned critic of Leopold's colonial régime in the Congo area. China was another sphere of interest of the Free Church Missions. Some of them joined the *CIM. After the gold rush some conservative evangelical missions became involved in South Africa. In 1907 the Swedish Methodist Church was called to Mozambique. Latin America became a field for Salvationists and Pentecostalists. In Brazil Swedish Pentecostalists contributed to the development of *Assembleias de Deus*.

The 20th century has seen the *devolution from mission to *indigenous church. In areas such as the Congo Republic and Ethiopia flourishing churches have developed. The missionary integration into the indigenous churches is a present task of the Swedish missions.

Twentieth century developments have also opened new fields. Swedish Pentecostalists apply a worldwide missionary strategy. In Tanzania the *Fosterlands-Stiftelsen* and the CSM faced new tasks during the second world war. Developments in China forced the Swedish missions to start anew in Japan and South East Asia.

There are, perhaps, two characteristics of the Swedish missionary contribution. One is its variety, due to the 19th century growth of Swedish Free Churches. The other is its interest in Bible translation, literature, and studies in the conditions of the indigenous Christians.

CARL F. HALLENCREUTZ

C. F. Hallencreutz: *Swedish Missions* (Stockholm 1968); *WKL*, 949f.

MISSION BOARDS AND SOCIETIES: SWITZERLAND. For so small a country, S. has produced an unusually large number of missionaries, and societies to support them. Some of these are small, and avoid co-operation with any other Christians; the larger societies are linked to one of three co-operative bodies: the Swiss Mission Council (SEMR), the Co-operative Association of Protestant Churches and Missionary Societies in German speaking Switzerland (KEM), or the Missionary Department of the Protestant Churches of French-speaking Switzerland. The main societies fall into the following three groups. (1) *Societies supported only in Switzerland*: Here by far the largest society is the Swiss Mission in South Africa, which works in Mozambique (see JUNOD, H.A.), Transvaal and Natal. There are small societies for work among Jews and gypsies, and a Protestant society for work in the Kwango area of the Congo. (2) *Societies of Swiss origin, but supported also in other countries.* Here pride of place must be given to the *Basel Mission (365 missionaries). But mention should also be made of the Swiss Alliance mission, which works in Angola, Japan and Brazil; the Nileland Mission working in Egypt, Sudan and Ethiopia; the *Mission Biblique*, which has work on the Ivory Coast; and the Swiss Mission to the Indians, which has work among the Amerindians of the Andean region of Peru. To this should be added a mission of recent origin, the Swiss Evang. Brotherhood Mission (1950), which supports 53 missionaries in Australia and New Guinea. (3) Finally there are *Societies of Foreign Origin, with a Swiss Branch.* Here a special place of honour must be given to the *Moravian Mission, with its great work in the Transkei, in Tanzania and other areas. The *Paris Mission, with its special responsibilities in Africa (see COILLARD, S.), Tahiti and New Caledonia, has drawn largely on Swiss aid in personnel and finance. The *SA, *OMF, *SIM, *SUM and *WEC all have Swiss contingents. Mention may also be made of smaller societies such as the Protestant Mission to French Guiana, and the Dorothea Mission in South Africa.

Individual Swiss have served in a number of non-Swiss societies, such as the Dohnavur Fellowship in South India. The Old Catholic Church in S. does not maintain a missionary society of its own, but supports the work of the Anglican Province of South Africa, by means of an annual missionary collection, transmitted through the St. Paul's Mission in Hilversum, Holland.

WALTER ZUMBRUNNEN

WKL, 950f.

MISSION BOARDS AND SOCIETIES: THE UNITED STATES OF AMERICA.

Partly because of its religious pluralism, the USA has more mission boards and societies than any other country. They have progressively multiplied. Soon after political independence from Great Britain, societies began to appear, chiefly for the spread of the faith on the expanding frontier and among the Indians. The earliest major organization was the *ABCFM, organized in 1810 by the Congregationalists of New England. At the outset it was not narrowly denominational, but sought to include all evangelicals who sympathized with its purpose. Many Presbyterians and a few from other denominations co-operated with it. Some other societies adopted the name American and sought support from evangelicals regardless of denominational affiliation. Prominent among them were the American Bible Society (1816) which, like the BFBS that inspired it, had the entire world in its purview, the American Home Missionary Society (1826), and the American Tract Society (1825).

Early in the 19th century denominational societies arose. One of the first was the General Missionary Convention of the Baptist Denomination in the United States of America for Foreign Missions (1814). In 1819 the Missionary and Bible Society of the Methodist Episcopal Church was formed and the following year it obtained the endorsement of the Methodist General Conference. In pursuance of action (1820) by its General Convention, in 1821 the PECUSA initiated its Domestic and Foreign Mission Society. In 1837 the Presbyterian Foreign Missionary Society came into being, the outgrowth of the (Presbyterian) Western Foreign Missionary Society. Large numbers of women's 'auxiliaries' were formed to supplement what was being done by societies controlled by men.

As suggested by their names, some societies were for both 'home' and 'foreign' missions, but, like the American Home Missionary Society, others were organized purely for reaching the non-Christian elements, white, Indian and Negro, in the USA. Thus in 1832 the American Baptist Home Mission Society came into being. It regarded as its field not merely the USA but all North America.

While bearing denominational names some of these societies were independent of control by the central structure of the denomination. Their funds and personnel were obtained from members of the denomination, but either because the denomination had no central organization or because of only loose connection with that organization, they developed their own constituencies within the denomination. Others were officially adopted by their denominations. Some denominations declared that as a whole they were missionary societies and for functional purposes operated through societies or boards for specific purposes. Several denominations, such as the Baptists of the northern states, who only in 1907 formed the Northern Baptist Convention (later renamed the American Baptist Convention), were late in developing a comprehensive structure; while others, such as the Baptists of the southern states, who in 1845, differing over slavery from their northern brethren, formed the Southern Baptist Convention, had a centralized organization which operated through boards.

In the course of time undenominational organizations for missions developed. Thus the *YMCAs of the USA and Canada co-operated in assisting the formation and growth of similar associations in other lands. At the outset they called that programme 'Foreign Work' and later 'World Service'. The *Near East College Association (1927) supported some of the Protestant colleges in the Near East. The *CIM, with headquarters in London, had an office and contributors in the USA.

Co-operation developed among the various societies and boards. Thus in 1893 the *Foreign Missions Conference of North America was organized. Later it became the Department of Foreign Missions of the National Council of Churches in the USA, and then, after being integrated with *Church World Service, the *Division of Overseas Ministries of the National Council (DOM).

Not all mission boards and societies co-operated with the DOM and its predecessors. The largest to hold aloof was the Foreign Mission Board of the Southern

14*

Baptist Convention. For some years that Convention had a larger church membership than any other Protestant denomination in the United States. The Southern Baptist Convention believed an obligation rested upon it to encourage the formation of churches affiliated with it in every state in the nation and in every land in the world. By 1966 it had begun missions in more than sixty countries. In 1942 the National Association of Evangelicals was formed 'to represent all Evangelical believers in all denominations and groups'. It had as members not only denominations but also several hundred individual congregations and colleges, and eight conferences of other churches. Affiliated with it was the *Evangelical Foreign Missions Association of North America. The undenominational societies were in the *Interdenominational Foreign Mission Association of North America. There was also the smaller Associated Missions of the International Council of Christian Churches. The members of the four bodies which did not co-operate with the DOM were more conservative theologically than the latter. In the 1960s they had more missionaries but a smaller income than it had. Most of the societies affiliated with them were younger and more nearly in the pioneer stage than those in the DOM and therefore as a whole had not built up equally extensive educational and medical institutions and were not aiding as large daughter churches as they were.

The Roman Catholics of the USA were later in engaging in foreign missions than were Protestants. That was because they had developed chiefly from extensive immigration in the 19th and 20th centuries. When they arrived the overwhelming majority of the immigrants were poverty-stricken and had come to better their economic status. Their church, accordingly, had its resources absorbed in erecting church buildings, and schools and providing personnel for its constituency. Until 1908 the RC church in the USA was under the *Propaganda, the body to which has been entrusted the supervision of the foreign missions of the RC church; before that year the USA was regarded as a mission field. Not until 1911 was the first indigenous organization for sending missionaries founded. In that year the Catholic Foreign Mission Society of America was inaugurated. Only in 1916 did its first missionaries embark. Thereafter, from its headquarters at *Maryknoll, north of New York City, several hundred priests and sisters—'Maryknollers'—went abroad, at first to China and eventually to many countries in Asia, Africa and Latin America. Other agencies, chiefly orders and congregations with European headquarters, from their branches in the USA eventually recruited hundreds of men and women to go as missionaries. In the 1960s the total was much less than that from Europe. However, the Society for the Propagation of the Faith, the largest fund-raising body for Catholic missions, and with headquarters at Rome, in the 1960s obtained more money from the faithful in the USA than from any other country.

KENNETH SCOTT LATOURETTE

K. S. Latourette: 'Missionaries Abroad' in *The Annals of the American Academy of Political and Social Science* (Philadelphia, Nov. 1966), pp.21–30; MRL: *North American Protestant Ministries Overseas, Directory* (8th ed., Waco, Texas 1968); *U.S. Catholic Missionary Personnel Overseas, 1967* (Washington, DC 1967).

MISSION-CHURCH RELATIONSHIPS.

From the 16th century, that is from the start of the modern period of the church's missionary activity, the missionary movement has been until very recently a movement depending on the initiative of Christians from the west. That this is beginning to change today does not affect the record of the past or the legacy of problems created by that record.

It is commonly forgotten that when the missionary from the west first came either to Asia or Africa, to the Americas or to the islands of the Pacific, he brought with him an idea of religion which was completely new. The very idea of a church as a community of people transcending all other divisions in society was *new*. The forms of worship, as well as the object of worship, were *new*. The idea of the religious leader as a pastor was *new*. The ethical demands of the Christian religion were *new*. The organization of the Christian community was *new*. And in the nature of things only the missionary could expound this *newness*. No doubt he also brought with him many other new things, a new and strange manner of dress, a new and strange culture, and often was involved, consciously or unconsciously, in the establishment of a new political dominion. But it was the newness of all that was involved in the preaching of the good news of the gospel, which determined that for a very long time the initiative in regard to matters Christian remained with the missionary. This was true whatever ecclesiastical tradition the missionary represented.

Further, it was also true that in all essentials the missionary movement was carried out until well into the 20th century almost entirely by volunteers and by voluntary organizations. The orders of the Roman Catholic church, that church's main instrument of missions, and the missionary societies of the other churches, were for all practical purposes independent organizations. The organization of the de *Propaganda Fide* in Rome might keep a watching eye on developments. Popes might encourage this initiative or that. But, in days where communication was difficult, effective control was vested in the hands of the organizations concerned with missions. Whatever the formal relationship of the Protestant missionary societies with their several churches might be, the same obtained with them.

Very slowly, within the 'scaffolding' set up by the missionary organization, local churches came into being. However, only with the 20th century, with the emergence of new nations in Asia and Africa, and with the retreat of *imperialism, did it become generally recognized that a local church, whatever its affiliations with other churches might be, must be *autonomous. It is only realistic to acknowledge that the strains and stresses arising from this new and proper development are likely to be with us for a long time to come.

A very large part of the continuing strain and stress lies in two factors in the present situation. For the most part the churches which have been born out of the missionary movement are found in countries which are economically underdeveloped. Again, these churches are composed, for the most part, of small minority groups, often suspect because of their relations with former imperial powers. Both these factors spell a degree of continuing dependence on finance and even leadership from the west which continue to create friction long after constitutional authority is fully vested in the local church.

Missionary statesmanship both in the parent and daughter churches is today preoccupied with finding ways and means of demonstrating that the church is one and its task missionary—a mutuality of responsibility in the body of Christ.

MAX WARREN

P. Beyerhaus and H. Lefever: *The Responsible Church and the Foreign Mission* (London 1964); D. McGavran: *How Churches Grow* (London 1959); S. C. Neill: *Creative Tension* (London 1959), *The Unfinished Task* (London 1957); H.-R. Weber: *Asia and the Ecumenical Movement 1895-1961* (London 1966); D. Webster: *Local Church and World Mission* (London 1962).

MISSION COUNCILS (FEDERATIONS) are of two kinds, 'home base' and 'foreign' in the language of the past. The *Ausschuss der deutschen evangelischen Missionen* (Committee of the German Protestant Missions) was formed in 1885 to represent the societies before the German colonial office; in 1922 this became the standing committee of a larger *Missionsbund* (Missions Fellowship), which has been renamed the *deutscher evangelischer Missions-Tag* (Missions Assembly). Its executive organ is the *Missions-Rat* (Missions Council). An annual conference of North American mission boards was created in 1893 and became the *Foreign Missions Conference of North America. In 1914 it got a permanent secretariat and developed into the largest and most active of the councils. The *World Missionary Conference, 1910, stimulated in 1913 the formation of the *Conference of Missionary Societies in Great Britain and Ireland and the *Dansk Missionsraad* (Danish MC). Thereafter action was slow. In the Netherlands the *Commissie van Advies* Advisory Committee (1915) to the Missions Consulate in Batavia served as liaison agent in international relations until the founding of the *Nederlandsche Zendingsraad* (Netherlands MC) in 1929. The *Svenska Missionsrådet* (Swedish MC) was created in 1920, when the Norwegian General Missions Committee also became the *Norsk Misjonråd* (Norwegian MC). The National Joint Missionary Committee of Finland (1918) was eventually transformed into the Finnish Missionary Council. The National Missionary Council of Australia dates from 1920, and that of New Zealand resulted from Dr *Mott's visit in 1926. The Delegation of Swiss Missions for International Relations (1923) was reorganized in 1944 as the Swiss Evang. Missionary Council. The Australian, New Zealand and North American bodies have in recent years become Divisions of *National Councils of Churches. Consequent upon the formation of the NCCCUSA in 1950, the Canadian societies organized the Overseas Department of the Canadian Council of Churches, but retain membership in the committees of the *Division of Overseas Ministries.

Previous to 1910 there were a few national field organs mostly concerned with *comity: the Board of Arbitration in India (1902), the General Council of Evangelical Missions in Korea (1905, changed in 1911 to Federal Council of Evangelical Protestant Missions), and the Standing Committee of the Co-operating Christian Missions in Japan (1900, changed to the Federated Missions, 1910). Dr John R. Mott, as chairman of the Edinburgh Continuation Committee, held a series of conferences in Asia in 1912–13, which brought into being the National Missionary Council of India, the China Continuation Committee, the Korea Field Advisory Committee and the Japan Continuation Committee. They all published journals and yearbooks—*The Harvest Field* (India), *The Korea Mission Field, The Christian Movement in Japan, The China Mission Yearbook*—and provided useful common services for the missions and churches. During the 1920s they became *National Christian Councils.

Councils developed slowly in Africa. A Standing Joint Consultative Committee was set up in Madagascar in 1913. The biennial Congo General Missionary Conferences did not produce a continuing committee until 1911, and the Protestant Council was not formed until 1924. An Alliance of Missionary Societies in British E. Africa was formed in 1918. By 1935 there were south of the Sahara 28 mission councils of various sorts. Arab north Africa belongs with the Near East, and for that vast area the Near East Christian Council for Missionary Co-operation was founded in 1927. It took under its care the Egypt Inter-Mission Council (1921) and United Missionary Conference of Syria and Palestine (1919), and fostered organization of councils in Sudan, Algeria and Iran. Latin America was thorny ground for the growth of councils. Much was achieved from outside through a USA body, the *Committee on Co-operation in Latin America in literature, evangelism, etc. It brought into being a Committee on Co-operation in Brazil and another in Mexico (1917). These two respectively entered a Confederation (1933) and a National Council (1929). Regional committees were organized in Cuba and elsewhere. Major councils were members of the *IMC. Nearly all became National Christian Councils, and few missionary councils now exist except in Europe.

See also NATIONAL MISSIONARY COUNCILS.

R. PIERCE BEAVER

C. H. Fahs and H. E. Davis: *Conspectus of Coöperative Missionary Enterprises* (New York 1935); W. R. Hogg: *Ecumenical Foundations* (New York 1952); *The Continuation Committee Conferences in Asia, 1912–1913* (New York 1913).

MISSION ENCYCLICALS OF THE POPES are circular letters dealing with missionary affairs, sent by the pope to all bishops in communion with the apostolic see. Thus, long before the Second *Vatican Council, it was made clear that the missionary vocation was not something which belonged to the pope alone (see Canon Law, canon 1350), but was communicated by way of the bishops to the whole church. All papal circulars dealing with missionary themes are classed as Encyclicals, whatever their exact title may be, provided that they are directed to the entire episcopate. Thus the Bull of Honorius III, *Ne si secus*, dated 25 February 1221 to the thirteen Metropolitans of the Church as it then existed, asking them to send missionaries, may correctly be taken as the first of the ME. On the other hand, the messages sent to the Chinese people by Pope Pius XII in 1955 and 1958 are not in the full sense of the term ME, though they are described as Encyclical letters.

The following utterances of popes in recent times are recognized as ME: Leo XIII: *Sancta Dei Civitas* (1880), on help to missions from the home churches; Benedict XV: the Apostolic Letter *Maximum Illud* (1919) on the founding of *younger churches; Pius XI: *Rerum Ecclesiae* (1926) on the creation of an indigenous clergy; Pius XII: *Evangelii Praecones* (1951) to recall *Rerum Ecclesiae* after twenty-five years; Pius XII: *Fidei Donum* (1957) on the urgent needs of the mission to Africa; John XXIII: *Princeps Pastorum* (1959) to celebrate the fortieth anniversary of the *Maximum Illud*.

The ME in part reflect the outlook on missions of the period in which they appeared, but they also present many new aspects which have proved fruitful in the *theology of missions. Unfortunately the ME have never attracted the attention due to them, and in consequence many demands which are rightly made in them have never been carried into effect.

The ME are officially published in the *Acta Sanctae Sedis*, later *Acta Apostolicae Sedis*. The references for the Encyclicals quoted above are: ASS 13 (1880) 241–248; AAS 11 (1919) 440–455; 18 (1926) 65–83; 43 (1951) 497–528; 49 (1957) 225–248; 51 (1959) 833–864. A summary of the doctrine contained in the ME is given by M. Balzarini and A. Zanotto: *Le missioni nel pensiero degli Pontefici* (Milan-Bologna 1960); T. J. M. Burke, ed.: *Catholic Missions. Four Great Encyclicals* (New York 1957); F. X. Clark: *The Purpose of Missions* (New York 1948); J. Glazik: *Päpstliche Rundschreiben über die Mission von Leo XIII bis Johannes XXIII* (Münster-schwarzach 1961); A. Rétif: *Introduction à la doctrine pontificale des missions* (Paris 1953). See also *WKL*, 933–35.

JOSEF GLAZIK

MISSION LIBRARIES. Two outstanding Catholic mission libraries are in Rome: the library of the Congregation for the Propagation of the Faith (*Pontificia Bibliotheca delle Missioni*), and the library at the *Pontificia Universitá Gregoriana*. The Maryknoll Seminary Library of the Catholic Foreign Missionary Society of America has a good collection, though limited. Other notable Catholic mission collections are found at Münster, Louvain, Lisbon and Madrid.

The two leading Protestant mission libraries are the Missionary Research Library at Union Theological Seminary, New York, and the Day Missions Library at Yale University Divinity School. Other specialized Protestant mission collections in North America are the Case Memorial Library at Hartford Seminary Foundation, and the Speer Library at Princeton Theological Seminary. Some Protestant theological libraries in the United States with strong sections on missions are: University of Chicago Divinity School, Duke University Divinity School, Fuller Theological Seminary, Garrett Theological Seminary, Harvard University Divinity School, Pacific School of Religion, Perkins School of Theology at Southern Methodist University,

and Southern Baptist Theological Seminary at Louisville. The two largest mission board libraries in the USA are: the United Presbyterian Mission Library, and the Library of the Board of Missions of the United Methodist Church, both in the Interchurch Center, New York.

In Europe the Vahls Missions Library (*Statsbiblioteket i Aarhus*, Denmark) is famous. Other collections of varying size and value are found at the Egede Instituttet in Oslo, Uppsala University in Sweden, Hamburg University, University of Tübingen, Hackmannsche Bibliothek at Marburg, the libraries of the Norddeutsche Mission at Bremen, the Rhenish Missionary Society in Wuppertal Barmen, and the Paris Evangelical Missionary Society.

In London the CMS and the USPG have large libraries. Selly Oak Colleges at Birmingham, and New College, University of Edinburgh, possess library collections that are rich in missionary material. A new Missionary Studies Library at Christ's College, Aberdeen, opened in 1968.

Specialized libraries related to missions are: the YMCA Historical Library of the National Council of the YMCAs of the USA, and the American Bible Society Library, both in New York; the World's Alliance of YMCAs Library, and the World Council of Churches Library, both in Geneva, and the neighbouring Library of the Ecumenical Institute at Bossey. Two unique historical libraries in Asia are: the Morrison Library on China, now in Tokyo, and the library of Serampore University, India, which preserves records of early missionary work in India. The library of the United Theological College, Bangalore, contains much valuable material on 19th century missions in India.

The 'copyright' libraries—the British Museum, the Bodleian Library at Oxford, and the Cambridge University Library—have copies of all books on missionary subjects published in Great Britain. The British Museum is especially rich in periodical material.

See also ARCHIVES.

EDITORS

G. H. Anderson: 'Research Libraries in New York City Specializing in Christian Missions', *Journal of Asian Studies*, XXV, 4 (1966), 733–36; F. W. Price: 'Specialized Research Libraries in Missions', *Library Trends*, IX, 2 (1960), 175–85.

MISSION RESEARCH. See ARCHIVES; MISSION LIBRARIES.

MISSION STUDIES IN THEO-LOGICAL EDUCATION. PROFESSOR-SHIPS OF MISSIONS. The belief that the church is missionary by nature and that all Christians share responsibility for the conversion of mankind requires that the missionary cause holds an undisputed place in the general scheme of the church's life and work, even though only a minority is active. In practice, the attitude of a church to the missionary cause tends to follow that of its ministry, and this in turn depends on their training. In theory, the church through its theological institutions will provide the education required for effective missionary understanding, criticism and leadership. Mission Studies ('Missions', 'Missiology') understood as the scholarly treatment, historical and doctrinal, of the expansion of Christianity among non-Christians (and including or related to History of Missions, Contemporary Missions, Theology and Practice of Mission, Comparative Study of Religions, Ecumenics) have for long had at least some academic standing. They have helped the theologians to a fuller understanding of their task by enlarging the field of knowledge and providing needed correctives and perspective to their thinking. Yet still most universities make little or no provision for the teaching of the subject. Those that do tend to make it an optional extra for those interested or, when a required subject, to put it in a subordinate place in the curriculum. Even in the seminaries the need for general instruction in *Missions* is by no means universally recognized.

The story of the place of *Missions* in theological education goes back to the attempt of Ramon Lull in the 14th century to establish, in the great centres of learning, colleges for the preparation of missionaries in the full academic sense. His hopes were unrealized until the College of *Propaganda* was set up in Rome, 1627, five years after the Protestant Seminary at Leiden undertook the training of missionaries for India. Only in the 19th century do we see the institution of academic lectures and the emergence of a scholarly and extensive missionary literature. This coincided with the reorganization of theological studies through Schleiermacher. He saw the need to combine the science of theology and the practice of missions. From his insistence that it is all 'Practical Theology' came the endeavour to win for missions a worthy place in the system of theological education. At first interest was limited to the continent of Europe, especially Germany. In the USA Princeton Seminary made an organized attempt to confront students with the world task of the church, but in the USA, as in the UK, it was generally agreed that the ordinary preparation for the ministry is the best training for the missionary.

The real pioneer of the modern concern is the great missionary statesman Alexander *Duff. Himself a missionary, his work in missionary education, in east and west, by means of scholarly missionary literature, quickened the mind of the church in Scotland to recognize the force of the missionary imperative. This led to the idea of a missionary professorship and to the setting up at New College, Edinburgh, on 6 November 1867, the Chair of Evangelistic Theology, with Duff as the first holder. It was a great experiment but it did not lead to the recognition of missions as a full subject in the curriculum. After Duff's death, amid confusion as to the content of the Chair, it was reduced to a lectureship and finally abolished. Some, however, claim that the present Chair of Apologetics, Natural Science, Homiletics, Pastoral Theology and Missions stands in historic succession to that of Duff. If Scotland had the honour of instituting the first professorship it fell to Germany to develop the

Science of Missions. Gustav *Warneck (1839–1910) is the real founder of scientific study leading to the wide recognition of the subject as a separate branch and the establishment of many professorships and lectureships, especially on the continent and in the USA where many decisive contributions have been made, including the establishment of the Missionary Research Library in New York in 1914.

In the present ecumenical age there has been increased recognition of the significance of missions for theology, yet it cannot be said that the rediscovery of the missionary nature of the gospel has been adequately matched by measures to secure the place of missions as a subject in ministerial training. This is especially true of the UK where, apart from Selly Oak Colleges (non-university), there is still no Chair of Missions. Missions has a place in most curricula, usually as an option under Church History or Practical Theology, and closely related to the Comparative Study of Religions, but rarely as a separate subject. Pride of place goes, as the list below makes clear, to USA, followed by Germany.

Recently, under the lead of Dr H. J. Margull, Professor of Missions at Hamburg, courses on missions have begun in two major theological schools in Tokyo. Similar developments at Manila, Bangalore, Serampore, Buenos Aires, etc. point to the recognition of the subject in the churches of the developing countries.

Professorships of Missions (Protestant). In the first five groups, all the Chairs are established in universities. In the USA they are in various Divinity or Theological Schools, Seminaries, and other institutions of post-graduate status.
**with Comparative Study of Religions.
***with Comparative Study of Religions and/or other subjects.
Germany (9): Erlangen***; Halle-Wittenberg**; Hamburg; Kiel; Leipzig; Mainz***; Marburg***; Münster (Protestant Faculty)***; Tübingen.
Holland (4): Amsterdam**; Groningen***; Leiden***; Utrecht***.

Denmark: Copenhagen.
Norway: Oslo (Free Faculty).
Sweden: Uppsala**.
North America: Andover Newton; Andrews Univ.; Asbury; Ashland; Bangor; Berkeley Baptist; Bethany Lutheran; Bethel; Boston Univ.; California Baptist; Calvin; Capital Univ.; Central Baptist; Chicago Theol. Sem.; Christian Theol. Sem.; Claremont; Colgate Rochester; Columbia (Decatur); Concordia (St. Louis); Concordia (Springfield); Conservative Baptist; Crozer; Drew; Dubuque; Duke; Eastern Baptist; Eastern Mennonite; Ec. Institute of Canada (Toronto); Emory; Erskine; Evangelical Congregational; Evangelical Seminary of Puerto Rico (San Juan); Evangelical (Naperville); Fuller; Garrett; Golden Gate Baptist; Gordon; Goshen; Hamma; Hartford; Howard; Iliff; Interdenominational Center (Atlanta); Johnson Smith Univ.; Kenyon; Lancaster; Lexington; Louisville Presbyterian; Luther (St. Paul); Lutheran (Maywood); Lutheran (Rock Island); Lutheran (Gettysburg); Lutheran (Philadelphia); Lutheran Southern (Columbia); McMaster Univ. (Hamilton, Ont.); Memphis; Mennonite Biblical; Methodist (Delaware, Ohio); Midwestern Baptist; Montreal Diocesan-McGill Univ.; Moravian; Nashotah House; Nazarene; New Brunswick; New Orleans Baptist; New York Theological; North American Baptist; North Park; Northern Baptist; Northwestern Lutheran; Nyack; Pacific Lutheran; Pacific School of Religion; Payne, Phillips; Pittsburgh; Presbyterian (Richmond); Princeton; Saint Paul; Scarritt; Seabury-Western; Southeastern Baptist; Southern Baptist; Southern Methodist-Perkins; Southwestern Baptist; Texas Christian; Trinity Evangelical; Union-New York; Union-Richmond; United-Dayton; United-Twin Cities; Univ. of Chicago; Wartburg; Wesley; Western Conservative Baptist; Western (Holland, Mich.); Westminster; Yale.

MARCUS WARD AND EDITORS

O. G. Myklebust: *The Study of Missions in Theological Education* (2 vols. Oslo 1955)— the pioneer survey of the history of the

Study of Missions as a theological subject and a factor in ministerial training.

MISSION STUDIES (PROTESTANT) go back to the *Seminarium Indicum* at Leiden (1622) and the work of theologians such as Gisbert Voetius (1589–1676) at Utrecht. The first major work in English was Robert Millar's *History of the Propagation of Christianity* (1723). Continental European works on theory and history were more numerous than English during the 19th century, such as Christian Kalkar's histories of Evangelical and RC missions (1857, 1863). Karl *Graul (1818–1864) of Leipzig fostered study, and the academic study of missions was established by Gustav *Warneck (1834–1910), professor at Halle and editor of *Allgemeine Missionszeitschrift*. The first great international programme of survey and study was undertaken for the *World Missionary Conference at Edinburgh 1910. Publication of the *IRM (1912–) stimulated studies. Study was a major function of the *IMC in 1921, and that responsibility now rests on the *WCC's Department of Missionary Studies. English and European societies trained their missionaries in their own seminaries, while Scottish and American agencies relied on universities and denominational seminaries. The pioneer professorship was that of Alexander *Duff at Edinburgh (1867), and numerous chairs were later established in German and American universities and seminaries. Scholarly societies include the *Deutsche Gesellschaft für Missionswissenschaft* and the US *Association of Professors of Missions.

R. PIERCE BEAVER

O. G. Myklebust: *The Study of Missions in Theological Education* (Oslo 1955).

MISSIONARY, THE. This word came into the English language as late as the 17th century. It refers to one engaged on a mission. Until recently its use was almost entirely confined to the Christian religion. Now it is increasingly found in secular contexts. Other religions are also using it of their agents working in foreign countries with a view to making converts.

'Mission' and 'missionary' are in origin the Latin forms of the Greek 'apostleship' and 'apostle', but the meanings have in the course of time been subtly changed. Both sets of words are intended to emphasize that the *church has been *sent* out into all the world to continue the work and ministry of Jesus Christ and to proclaim the everlasting *gospel. Since its foundation the Christian church has always had missionaries, but they have not always been so described. Anyone who takes part in spreading the knowledge of Christ is to that extent being a missionary. In the first days this was done by apostles and evangelists, called and probably commissioned by the church; but it was also done by countless ordinary Christians who earned their living and gave their witness in secular occupations. There was no class of people called 'missionaries', but all the people of God were expected to be participating in his mission.

As the church developed its organization and its hierarchical structure, missionary work was usually done by clergy or monks and sometimes by bishops (e.g. Augustine of Canterbury). They were still not a distinctive category; rather they were discharging their Christian function in the regions beyond, where the church was not as yet organized. With the great explorations and discoveries of the 15th and 16th centuries and the opening up of the new world and the rise of the Spanish and Portuguese empires the church was faced with a new situation. It now sent missionaries to preach the gospel and build the church in continents that had known neither. Protestants were somewhat later in the field. It is among them chiefly that the concept of the M. as a distinctive type of person arose, for many of the early Protestant Ms were laymen and (later) women, sent not by a church but by a missionary society or board.

Subsequently the role of the M. has changed. This was inevitable once an *indigenous church came into being. The missionary began as pioneer and founder; later he became leader and manager, bishop and moderator and chairman, superintendent and principal, taking charge of the church, the hospital, the institution, which he or his predecessors had built up. The M. therefore became a figure of power, and 'the mission' a power structure over against the church.

Since the end of the second world war and the passing of the colonial era, most churches have become *autonomous if not wholly independent. This has radically altered the status of the M. Far less often is he (or she) required to be a leader or in charge of anything, except at the invitation of the church to which he goes. Today the M. is usually expected to be at the disposal of the receiving church rather than the sending board or society. In many countries he is warmly welcomed on these conditions if he is prepared to be a servant, even if he is an expert and specialist and required for that reason. Often he is wanted for life service, but the M. is no longer entitled to assume this and he may not be in a position to give it.

The foreign M. remains a symbol and representative. He is a gift from one church to another. He represents what Christ has done in another church or culture. He symbolizes the mutual caring of different parts of the body of Christ.

The M. is not necessarily white nor western. Asian and African churches are sending Ms outside their own countries.

Some countries will not accept professional Ms. This is leading to a return to the earlier pattern of *non-professional Ms, serving Christ and his church, in secular vocations. No country has yet excluded Christians.

DOUGLAS WEBSTER

R. Allen: *The Spontaneous Expansion of the Church* (London 1927); S. C. Neill: *Colonialism and Christian Missions* (London 1966), *Creative Tension* (London 1959); D. T. Niles: *Upon the Earth*, Part 2 (London 1962); M. A. C. Warren: *Challenge and Response* (London 1959), chap.4.

MISSIONARY AVIATION FELLOWSHIP. A service agency which exists to help evangelical missions with air transport and communications. The MAF consists of three autonomous but co-ordinated organizations (American, Australian and British); there are 140 families operating 67 aircraft in the service of more than 80 societies in nineteen countries.

The MAF deals with problems affecting personnel, equipment, logistics and professional standards. Its aircraft are used for the transport of evangelists, teachers and school children, for administration, supplies, the distribution of literature, and for ambulance work, medical and humanitarian projects and evacuation. It aims always at supplementing existing facilities and minimizing duplication. Its work in communications includes the development of equipment, control of manufacture, distribution at subsidized cost, and maintenance.

Qualifications of MAF personnel include undergraduate education and Bible training; (for airmen) demonstrated proficiency in addition to commercial pilot and mechanic ratings; (for radio technicians) extensive servicing experience plus two years' formal training, and a first class commercial licence. Preparation includes a two months' residential course followed by two months' specialized orientation.

The American MAF, founded in 1944, now (1970) operates 44 aircraft in Mexico, Honduras, Venezuela, Ecuador, Guyana, Surinam, Brazil, Congo, Rhodesia, Indonesia, the Philippines and Laos. The British MAF, founded in 1945, served at first in the Southern Sudan but was expelled with other missions in 1964; today it operates ten aircraft in Ethiopia, Kenya, Uganda, Chad and Central African Republic. The Australian MAF, founded in 1948, operates thirteen aircraft in New Guinea and the Solomon Islands. The American MAF is a member of *IFMA. The communication services of Missionary Engineering, Inc., were integrated with MAF in 1961.

CHARLES J. MELLIS

MISSIONARY RECRUITMENT AND SELECTION (The process by which mission boards find and choose new missionaries). Nineteenth century appointments were made in response to the pressure of the candidates' missionary calling. Today many appointments are made in response to requests from overseas churches for specific professional qualifications not necessarily found in available volunteers. Therefore recruiting is increasingly important.

Many opportunities for short-term secular employment overseas now provide channels for service as *non-professional missionaries. Since many potential recruits have serious questions about church structures, the role of the missionary, and the nature of the church's mission in a world of rapid change, guidance from a recruiter is very important.

Recruiting activities may include campus and church visitation, publicity, conferences, distribution of literature and cultivation of *SCMs or the *IVCF. Teaching on Christian vocation and church occupational guidance can provide the base for later recruiting by candidate secretaries of mission boards. Most applicants have had personal contact with missionaries or with some other inspiring Christian worker. Many have had some first-hand overseas experience, as in a work camp or Junior Year Abroad. Unofficial recruiters, who continually search for potential missionaries, are among the best sources of recruits.

Qualifications for missionary appointment vary somewhat from one society to another. In general, however, the selection process seeks to identify candidates who have a personal knowledge of Jesus Christ, capacity to interpret the gospel, an awareness of the kind of world in which we live, a readiness to make the universal church a reality. They must be physically sound, emotionally stable, intellectually alert, socially sensitive, professionally competent and adaptable.

A small society with a well-known and limited constituency may use relatively informal arrangements in selecting its missionaries: a few simple factual statements, medical examinations and group interviews with a personnel committee or the board itself.

Large boards, who work with as many as 1,500 new enquirers a year, and make one appointment for every eight to twelve enquiries, must use more complex processes involving sizeable staff and expenditure of funds.

The most extensive personnel selection processes are found among North American boards, making use of detailed applications including summaries of personal and professional background, a statement of faith, life sketch, comprehensive references, interviews, rigorous medical examinations, psychological tests and psychiatric evaluations. Some boards include successful participation in an extended orientation programme as final confirmation of the selection process.

DONALD P. SMITH

Committee on Missionary Personnel, DFM, NCCC: *Recruiting, Selection and Training of Missionaries in North America* (New York 1957); E. K. Higdon: *New Missionaries for New Days* (St. Louis 1956); A. T. Houghton: *Preparing to be a Missionary* (London 1956); K. E. Moyer: 'The Selection and Training of the Overseas Personnel of the Christian Church', Occasional Bulletin from the MRL, Vol. VIII, No. 8, 15 August 1957.

MISSIONARY RESEARCH LIBRARY. See MISSION LIBRARIES.

MISSIONARY STRUCTURE OF THE CONGREGATION was the programmatic title of an ecumenical study carried out by the *WCC Department on Studies in Evangelism between the WCC Assemblies of New Delhi 1961 and Uppsala 1968. The theme grew out of more than a decade of evangelism discussion the findings of which found expression in *A Theological Reflection on the Work of Evangelism* (WCC Geneva 1959). In it was stated that (1) the average local congregation poses a major problem for the accomplishment of present evangelistic tasks and that (2) the quest for the

renewal of the church is intimately connected not only with spiritual regeneration but
also with structural (organizational)
changes. The study was launched at the
time of the integration of the *IMC and
WCC for dealing scrupulously with matters
of church and mission, and it was conducted, by various regional working groups,
in an attempt at laying out the terms for
the re-shaping of churches in new missionary situations. The findings can presently be
summed up in the following theses: (1) Not
only in its missionary activities but also in
its entire life the church participates in the
mission of God and therefore mission is
given to every congregation. (2) The
churches' structures must be as flexible as is
demanded by the ways and actions of
God's mission. A congregation seeking an
actual presence within the changes of the
present world will be a congregation in
mission. (3) As history shows, all organizational structures of the churches are
temporary. In their very essence, missionary
congregations exist in different forms in
order to meet different situations. (4) In
a time when traditional local parish
congregations are found not being able to
shoulder adequately present missionary
tasks, new forms of missionary presence are
emerging. Industrial missions, ecumenical
teams, small task forces, house-churches,
academies, Christian coffee shops, etc., are
pointing to the possibility of various new
forms of congregational life and witness.
(5) Churches must be ready to recognize
officially new congregational structures.
(6) Particularly in areas of rapid industrialization and urbanization churches find
themselves living in new localities. Social
changes have enlarged widely the traditional parish or the field for mission of a
local congregation. The greatest possible
diversity and mobility must therefore be
attained by future local churches. (7)
Biblically as well as in the light of recent
insights about the witness of the 'laity', the
local parish congregation ought to be seen
as a community of ministries rather than a
collectivity of individuals.

HANS JOCHEN MARGULL

G. Casalis, W. J. Hollenweger, P. Keller,
eds.: *Vers une église pour les autres* (Geneva
1966); H. J. Margull, ed.: *Mission als
Strukturprinzip* (Geneva 1965); T. Wieser,
ed.: *Planning for Mission* (New York and
London 1966); *The Church for Others and
The Church for the World* (Geneva 1967).

MISSIONS, ORTHODOX. As is to be
expected from Orthodox Christianity's
own characterization of itself, and its
historical development, variations in the
doctrine and the national character of the
individual churches play only a small part in
the delineation of Orthodox missions.
The propagation of faith is regarded as a
common contribution to the universal
missionary task of the church. The area
to which faith in Christ spread in early
days is indicated in the narrative of the day
of Pentecost (Acts 2:9–11); it extended
beyond the limits of the Roman empire.
From a very early date we have evidence of
the existence of churches in Persia, Armenia,
India (the *'Thomas-Christians'), Georgia
and Ethiopia, and these in turn carried the
gospel further by witness and proclamation.
Special activity was manifested by the
church in Persia, monks from which pressed
forward as far as India and Turkestan. The
so-called *Nestorian monument at Hsian-Fu
is evidence of their activity in China in the
seventh or eight centuries; the manuscripts and other literary finds at Turfan
provide evidence of a similar activity in
Central Asia. On the northern frontiers of
the eastern Roman empire Christianity
gained influence over Germans and
Slavonic peoples. The translation of the
Bible into Gothic by Bishop Ulfilas, and the
mission of the brothers Cyril and Methodius
to the Khazars about A.D. 860 are evidence
of the wide extent of that influence. This
influence was strengthened by the baptism
of Vladimir of Kiev in 989 and brought the
peoples of what was later to be called
Russia into the fold of the Byzantine
church. After 1054 the church of Byzantium
did not carry on any further missionary
work. The fall of Constantinople in 1453
condemned it decisively to a defensive

position. Only the missionary work of the Nestorian church in Persia saw a second spring in the Mongol period. In the period during which the Uighur Turk Yabalaha was Catholicos (1283–1317) there were in all parts of Asia about 30 Metropolitans, and in all some 250 dioceses. But, as a result of forced conversion to *Islam under the rule of Timur or Tamerlane (1336–1405), nothing but small fragments of the Nestorian church remain today. Since that period the church of Russia has carried on missionary work, and with the greatest success, where the work has been done indirectly, through settlers, traders and monks. Colonization was understood to involve also christianization, and this came later to be understood as involving also Russification. But this co-ordination of different elements was always recognized to be dangerous.

St. Stephen of Perm (1340–1396) is regarded as an example for missionaries of all times. As apostle of the Zyrjan people he translated the Bible and the liturgical books into the local language, and thus formed their traditional way of living into a Christian order.

After the fall of Kazan the last Tartar Khanate in 1552, Siberia became the great field of missionary activity. Peter the Great lent the support of the state to the Christian mission, and extended it as far as China (1715). In the 19th century the peoples of Siberia with the exception of some tens of thousands were won for Orthodoxy, after M. Glukhareff had directed the mission into new ways under pietistic influences and on the model of the London Bible Society. The highest success was attained by the work of I. *Veniaminoff in the Russian Far East, and by N. *Kasatkin in Japan. In 1897 a mission was started also in Korea.

The Russian revolution of 1917 brought missionary work to a standstill. Nevertheless the churches which have come into being as a result of the missions have maintained themselves and have been organized into new Eparchies. The China mission placed itself under the Exarchate of Karlowitz, whereas the Japan mission

recognized Moscow. Since 1945 the Japanese Orthodox church has been placed under the jurisdiction of the Metropolitan of the USA, whereas the Chinese church since 1959 has been recognized as autonomous.

From the Orthodox believers, who are scattered far and wide in the diaspora, the idea of mission has taken on new life in the Orthodox churches. The Orthodox Student Fellowship Syndesmós has adopted missionary work as part of its project and publishes the periodical *Porefthendes* (Matt. 28:19, Greek – 'Go ye'). This has proved the rallying point for the International Orthodox Missionary Centre (Athens 1961). The special interest of this group is directed to the Orthodox church in Uganda, Kenya and Tanzania, which in 1957 claimed a membership of 20,000.

JOSEF GLAZIK

S. Bolshakoff: 'Orthodox Missions Today' in *IRM* XLII (1953), pp.275–84; H.-W. Gensichen: in *Die Kirche in ihrer Geschichte*, IV (Göttingen 1961); J. Glazik: *Die russ.-orth. Heidenmission seit Peter d. Gr.* (Münster 1954), *Die Islammission der russ.-orth. Kirche* (1959); A. Schmemann 'The Missionary Imperative in the Orthodox Tradition' in G. H. Anderson, ed.: *The Theology of the Christian Mission* (New York 1961), pp.250–57; G. Stökl in *Die Kirche in ihrer Geschichte* II (Göttingen 1961); *WKL*, 921–24.

MISSIONS, ROMAN CATHOLIC. The start made in the second half of the 15th century was carried on in the 16th century, only more intensively: the discoveries and conquests of new territories by the Spanish and Portuguese were accompanied by zealous efforts at evangelization. Mission activity was therefore almost exclusively carried out under the patronage (*Patronato*) of these two Catholic maritime nations who were given extensive powers in ecclesiastical matters. In order to avoid a clash of interests between them the pope had drawn a demarcation line between their spheres of influence: Spain obtained Central and South America and took also the Philippines, while Portugal received Africa, Asia and also Brazil. While Spain tried to evangelize the whole territory, Portugal limited herself generally to the coastal areas. Amazing results were obtained, on the surface at least; depth, however, was absent due to lack of adaptation, neglect in the formation of a native clergy, and other factors resulting from too close a bond between church and state. Both the success and failure of this system of *patronato* can be seen, even today, in the condition of the church in these countries. The outstanding missionary of this period was the trail-blazing St. *Xavier.

In the 17th century this *patronato*-dominated activity continued. But there emerged a totally new force, the Congregation of the Propagation of the Faith (*Propaganda), established in 1622. Its origin was due to a desire to withdraw missionary control from Spain and Portugal and to centralize it in Rome, thus giving it a more international character. Initial difficulties were immense. Propaganda had to rely mainly on French missionaries, especially those of the Foreign Missions of Paris (*MEP, founded 1662). The attempt by Propaganda to make its authority felt led to struggles between *patronato* and Propaganda, residential bishops and *Vicars Apostolic, regular and secular missionaries, Spanish-Portuguese and French missionaries. Meanwhile, mission work had been taken up among the Indians of North America, and in new territories in South-east Asia. In what is now called Vietnam French missionaries made a successful effort to train native priests and catechists, while the *Jesuits in both China and India (*Ricci, S. J., de *Nobili, S. J.) were embarking on a far-reaching programme of *adaptation, crystallized in the *Rites-question, which owing to small-minded rivalries was eventually to lead to a condemnation of this form of Chinese and Indian adaptation. This had grave repercussions on the whole missionary activity of the next centuries. The church of Japan, so auspiciously begun by St. Francis Xavier, was forced underground by cruel persecutions in the first half of the 17th century,

until its remnants re-emerged two centuries later.

The beginning of the 18th century looked quite promising: Propaganda was now better organized, new mission institutes were founded, activity abounded everywhere. Yet by the end of this century mission work had practically come to utter ruin. The causes for this disastrous development are to be found both in Europe and in the missions. In Europe new trends in theology, philosophy and politics (Jansenism, the atheism of the Enlightenment, the French Revolution) killed religious fervour and consequently vocations for the mission. The hostility between Catholic and Protestant powers created confusion and rivalry in the missions. The suppression of the Jesuit order by various countries (Portugal, France, Spain) and finally by Rome (1773) forced the return of 3,500 missionaries who could not be replaced. Around the year 1800 Propaganda had only 300 missionaries, and Propaganda itself ceased to function when Napoleon seized the Papal States. In the missions the continued rivalry between the various institutes, between Christian nations, between the *patronato* and Propaganda, led to a serious decline of efficiency, a decline aggravated by the effects of the slave trade and by the absence of firm direction by Propaganda, due to poor communications, unreliable information, changeable policies and lack of funds.

The 19th century witnessed a gradual recovery of the missionary enterprise, now firmly supervised by Propaganda and zealously promoted by the popes. New mission institutes arose, a spirit of romanticism created enthusiasm, the opening up of Africa stirred the imagination for new spiritual conquests, so that from the middle of this century a new period of unheard-of growth began which was to last for over a century, almost to our own days. Now also religious sisters began to play their part in ever growing numbers, so that in little over a century their total number grew from a few to the present 50,000. Mission work achieved a universal character, not only in as far as almost every country was being evangelized but also because there was a more general participation on the part of the Christian countries of Europe and America. A few statistics indicate the extent of growth: in 1969, the number of foreign missionaries (priests, sisters, brothers, lay people) approached 100,000; local personnel from the missions themselves: 350 bishops, 15,000 priests, 50,000 sisters; number of Catholics: in Africa 30 million, in Asia 46 million, in Oceania 4 million.

At the beginning of this century *missiology began to receive attention and is now recognized as an important field of studies in several universities and institutes.

New tendencies have appeared since the last world war. Their influence has been positive as well as negative. Among the positive gains can be mentioned: the acceleration of the process of adaptation as a result of a better mission theology; increasing erection of local hierarchies; growing ecumenical co-operation between Christian denominations in the mission field; participation of the whole church in the mission effort; the growth of *lay missionaries; socio-economic and educational responsibility in developing countries. Among the disturbing factors should be reckoned: a decrease in the number of missionary vocations due to a general vocational crisis; the adverse effect on missionary zeal by new insights into the value of non-Christian religions and their role as instruments of salvation; the expulsion of missionaries from some newly independent countries, or a restriction of their activities; the problematic position of the church in the educational and socio-economic field, in which on the one hand the church had taken the initiative in the past and still feels it her duty to co-operate often at the expense of the direct apostolate—which is appreciated by many governments—while on the other hand certain governments are anxious to exercise in this field total control, barely tolerating activities sponsored by the church and restricting her to the purely religious field.

The missions' past connection with the colonial powers is also a serious handicap.

On the whole, one can speak at present of a crisis in missionary activity, or at least of confusion. Easily won converts are largely a matter of the past; new policies and methods are called for; the personnel shortage demands new approaches. The Decree on the Missionary Activity of the Second *Vatican Council, though it deals with these problems, needs still more study and especially urgent implementation. It may be another decade or more before a clearer picture will emerge of the future of Catholic missions.

PETER J. DIRVEN

T. J. M. Burke, ed.: *The Popes and the Missions: Four Encyclical Letters* (New York 1957); G. Goyau: *Missions and Missionaries* (London 1932); R. P. Millot: *Missions in the World Today* (London 1961); S. C. Neill: *A History of Christian Missions* (London 1964); W. J. Richardson, ed.: *The Modern Mission Apostolate* (Maryknoll, New York 1965), *Revolution in Missionary Thinking* (Maryknoll, N.Y. 1966); J. Schmidlin: *Catholic Mission History* (Techny, USA 1933); B. de Vaulx: *History of the Missions* (London 1961); *Decree on the Missionary Activity of the Church* (Washington D.C. 1966; also London 1966); *WKL*, 943–45.

MOFFAT, ROBERT (1795–1883), pioneer missionary in southern Africa, Bible translator and traveller, was born at Ormiston, Scotland, of a humble family and was apprenticed as a gardener. His mother's enthusiasm for foreign missions and his own conversion led him to offer his services to the *LMS. After the most meagre preparation he arrived in Africa (1817) at the age of 22 and stayed there for 50 years. He was the pioneer of Christian missions north of the Orange River, and his mission station at Kuruman (1821) became the bridge-head for expansion northwards towards the Zambesi and a model missionary settlement. He early saw the importance of being literate in the local language, Sechuana, and through his printing press printed the first books in

Sechuana. His complete translation of the Bible in Sechuana (1857) was the first Bible in an African tongue not previously reduced to writing. In 1829 he paid his first visit to the great Matabele Chief Mzilikazi, then established near modern Pretoria, and followed him on four other journeys (1835–1859) finally establishing the first white settlement at Inyati in Rhodesia (1859). M's friendship with the fierce Matabele chief is one of the strangest episodes in southern African history and gave M. an ascendancy in Matabeleland which traders and hunters had to recognize. In Bechuanaland the pressure of Boer farmers compelled M. to be the guardian of the 'missionary road' to the north which he saw threatened by the land-hunger of the Boers and their demands for native labour. He strongly opposed the withdrawal of British influence north of the Orange River. As the 'apostle of Bechuanaland' M. established the Christian church in Botswana, winning the esteem of the tribal chiefs and preparing the way for other missionaries including his son-in-law David *Livingstone. The great stone church he built at Kuruman (1838) became the 'cathedral' for Sechuana-speaking Christians over a vast area of the Northern Cape. With his patriarchal beard and handsome presence M. was the exemplar of the 19th century missionary; his book *Missionary Labours* (1842) went into many editions; his descendants in South and Central Africa have sought to maintain the concern for Africa and her peoples which Robert and Mary Moffat so nobly began.

CECIL NORTHCOTT

R. Moffat: *Missionary Labours* (reprinted, New York 1966); C. Northcott: *Robert Moffat, Pioneer in Africa* (London 1961), based on the original Moffat papers in the Central African archives at Salisbury; E. W. Smith: *Robert Moffat* (London 1925); *DNB*, XXXVIII, 97; *RGG* IV, 1085.

MOFFETT, SAMUEL AUSTIN (1864–1939), Presbyterian missionary to Korea, was born in Madison, Indiana, finished at Hanover College (1884), and McCormick

Seminary (1888); he reached Korea in 1890, barely five years after its opening to Protestant work. He has been called the major architect of Korean Presbyterianism, the nation's largest Christian body. He shared in his mission's crucial, early choice of the Korea Plan (modified *Nevius method) stressing lay evangelism, unsubsidized worship groups and leaders' training in Bible conferences. In 1893 he was assigned all of north Korea as his field and as first resident Protestant missionary there resolutely put the Plan into action. Pyongyang became the centre of spectacular church growth. In 1901 he founded Korea's oldest theological school, now Presbyterian Theological Seminary. Around its first graduating class (1907) was formed the first presbytery of the autonomous Presbyterian church in Korea. It elected M. its first moderator, and again moderator of the seventh General Assembly (1919). He represented Korea at *Edinburgh 1910, and was president of Soongsil College (1918–1928). For opposing compulsory attendance at Shinto shrines he was forced from Korea in 1936. He was posthumously decorated by the Republic of Korea (1963).

SAMUEL H. MOFFETT

R. E. Shearer: *Wildfire: Church Growth in Korea* (Grand Rapids 1966), pp.103–51.

MOHAMMEDANISM: See ISLAM.

MONASTICISM AND MISSIONS. Of the monastic orders properly so called the *Benedictine monks and nuns and the Cistercian monks and nuns are engaged in missionary activity. Their foundations are for the most part contemplative communities. Only the Benedictines in Lumumbasha, Congo, in Tanzania, in Transvaal, S.A., and in Tokyo, Japan, work as pastoral missionaries.

In Africa there are 18 *Benedictine monasteries*: Vila Luso, Angola (15 expatriate monks – 1 national); Yaoundé, Cameroon (5–5); La Bouenza, Congo (7–9); Lumumbasha, Congo (4–14); Bouake, Ghana (8–7); Zagnando, Dahomey (6 e.); Koubri, Upper Volta (5–12); Toumliline,

Morocco (14 e.); Eleme, Nigeria (6 e.); Mahitsy, Madagascar (8–17); Butare, Rwanda (7 e.); Keur Moussa, Senegal (9–4); Eshowe and Pietersburg, S. Africa; Hanga, Tanzania (8–56); Peramiho and Ndanda, Tanzania; Dzobegan, Togo (8–8). There are 17 *Benedictine convents*: Medea, Algeria; Vila Lusa, Angola; Inkamana, S. Africa; Otele, Cameroon (6 expatriate nuns–5 national); Lumumbasha, Congo (7 e.); Lubudi, Congo (7–48); Bouake, Ghana (7–2); Koubri, Upper Volta (7–15); Toffo, Dahomey (5 e.); Tororo, Uganda (8–7); Mananjari, Madagascar (4–5); Peramiho, Tanzania. There are 10 *Cistercian monasteries*: Medea, Algeria (15 e.); Bela Vista, Angola (31–25); Obout, Cameroon (6–12); Kasanzas, Congo (18–10); Goma, Congo (8–18); Asmara, Ethiopia; Lumbwa, Kenya (13–19); Vohipeno, Madagascar; Maromby, Madagascar (9–7); Bamenda, Cameroon (8–10); and three *Cistercian convents*: Bukavu, Congo (12–9); Parakou, Dahomey (12–2); Masaka, Uganda (12–5). The members of these orders, while retaining the independence of each monastic house, organize themselves in a Monastic Africa Conference (CMA), after the pattern of regional episcopal conferences.

Benedictine monasteries in the Middle East are situated at Kobbe, Lebanon; Jerusalem, Israel; Tabgha, Israel; *Benedictine convents* at Jerusalem and at Bethlehem, Jordan; a *Cistercian monastery* at Latroun, Jordan.

In Asia there are *Benedictine monasteries* at Asirnavam, India (3 expatriate – 28 national); Kep, Cambodia (10–20); Manila, Philippines (12–28); Thien-An, S. Vietnam (4–75); Thien-Hoa, S. Vietnam (14 n.); Taipei, Taiwan; Waegwan, S.Korea; Tokyo, Japan; *Benedictine convents* at Ban-Me Thout, S. Vietnam (8–13); Taegu, S. Korea; a *Cistercian monastery* at Mitsuishi, Japan; *Cistercian convents* at Hong Kong, and at Tananggung, Java (5–25).

Contemplatives are not exempt from the apostolic duty of every Christian, which was emphasized at the Second *Vatican Council. Their contribution to mission consists largely in the multiplication of small settlements which identify themselves in their own way with the local population. A deep interpenetration has to take place between the country and the monastery in matters of culture, style and problems to be faced. Monks who 'achieve' nothing in a visible way can have a serving function as a pure 'Christian presence'. In many countries this is one of the few forms in which the preaching of the gospel is permitted. To assist the propagation of the monastic life Benedictines in the *younger churches have established a secretariat, named *Aide à l'Implantation Monastique* ('Help for the planting of the monastic life') or AIM, with headquarters at 7 Rue d'Issy, 92 Vanves, Paris, France.

See also ROMAN CATHOLIC RELIGIOUS ORDERS AND CONGREGATIONS.

CORN. PROSP. THOLENS, OSB
WKL, 943–45.

MONGOLIA. Although no one can pinpoint a precise date for the arrival of Christians in M., it may be assumed that the Nestorian penetration to China in the 7th century at least touched the barren, sparsely populated area which lies in Central Asia between China and Russia and includes the Gobi Desert. Introduced largely by traders, nomadic tribesman, and a few missionaries from the west, Christianity seems to have disappeared from M. by the 10th century, with the general decline of Nestorianism.

The phenomenal, and terrifying, spread of Mongol power to the threshold of Europe at the end of the 12th century, under the leadership of Genghiz Khan, brought new contacts with Christianity and stimulated not only the travels of Marco Polo but courageous adventures by *Dominican and *Franciscan missionaries. Most famous of these were Wilhelm de Ruysbroeck (c.1250) and John of Montecorvino (whose arrival in China is variously dated from 1289 to 1294). The latter, from the Chinese capital, translated the NT and Psalms into a Mongolian dialect and celebrated Mass for the Mongol overlords. Under the favour of a foreign court, there may have been 30,000 Christians in the empire by 1350, but most of these were Mongols, and there is little evidence of lasting influence in Chinese society.

In 1798 two Chinese priests were sent from Peking to M., to be followed in the 1830s by Joseph Martial Mouly, a Lazarist who became the first *Vicar Apostolic of M. In the first of many modern persecutions against the church in that area, Mgr. Mouly surrendered to the authorities in 1853 and accepted deportation to Shanghai in order to protect his flock. Most active of 19th century Catholic orders were the Scheutist Fathers from Belgium, beginning with Theophile Verbist, who sailed in 1865 and laboured to reconcile Chinese and Mongols, farmers and nomads, in Inner M. until his death from typhus three years later. The expanding order concentrated on establishing Christian settlements, famine relief and orphan care. Later came the *Congregation of the Immaculate Heart of Mary, the Franciscan Sisters of Mary, the Congregation of the Daughters of Mary and Joseph, the (Chinese) Brethren of the Sacred Heart, and others, significantly attempting to encourage an agricultural base for a precarious nomadic economy.

Despite earlier concern by *Gützlaff and other China missionaries, few Protestant groups penetrated to M. until late in the 19th century. James *Gilmour, of the *LMS, as inexperienced in horsemanship as at the Mongolian language, became a beloved 'Christian lama' but won not a single baptism in two heroic decades (1870-1891). A few *CIM families settled in Inner M., followed by the Scandinavian Missionary Alliance, the Scandinavian Alliance Mission, the *CMA, the Krimmer Mennonite Brethren, Irish Presbyterians and some *Pentecostalists. In proportional terms the martyrdom of missionaries and Chinese Christians during the *Boxer Rebellion of 1900 was as severe in Inner M. as anywhere in the country. Yet the numbers of both Protestants and Catholics continued to grow, despite a serious plague in 1910-11 and withdrawals during the first world war. In 1924 Outer M. was incorporated as the

Mongolian People's Republic within the Soviet Union, and all missionary activity there ceased. Even the Russian Orthodox Church had been virtually non-existent in the area since the turn of the century. A very few missionaries continued to work in the Inner Mongolian Autonomous Region until it fell under Chinese communist control soon after the second world war.

CREIGHTON LACY

D. G. Broughton: *Mongolian Plains and Japanese Prisons* (London 1947); C. H. Dawson: *The Mongol Mission. Narratives and Letters of the Franciscan Missionaries in Mongolia in the 13th century* (New York 1955); K. S. Latourette: *A History of Christian Missions in China* (New York 1929), *A History of the Expansion of Christianity* (New York 1937-1945), Vols. II, III, VI, VII; C. Lhotte: *Dame Pauvreté chez les Mongols; l'epopée franciscaine de Plan Carpin et de Guillaume de Rubrouck au XIIIe siècle* (Paris 1947); W. P. Nairne: *Gilmour of the Mongols* (London 1924); M. Polo: *Adventures of Marco Polo* (ed. R. J. Walsh: New York 1948); *ERE* VIII, 806-08; *NCE* IX, 1058f.

MONOTHEISM, PRIMITIVE. In almost all primitive religions, the idea of a supreme Being (the 'High God') is found. In many cases he is regarded as the Creator. He has laid down rules for the relationships between man and man. He sees and knows everything. Death, both as a general phenomenon and as an individual event, is often attributed to him. In many cases he is regarded as having withdrawn from the world, and so is not particularly interested in men. He is generally regarded as kindly; little or no direct worship is paid to him. In some cases the High God is nameless. If he has a name, this will tell us nothing as to the nature of the High God, and as in the case of the *Modimo* of the Sotho, may well go back to what was originally a purely local conception.

PM is nowhere encountered as the sole form of a people's religion; it is always mixed with ideas of *magic, belief in spirits, *ancestor-worship, totemism or *polytheism. It can exist in detachment from these other forms of religion, or can be brought into close contact with them in a single system. By itself PM is colourless and lacking in religious power. In this respect it is a little like the deism of Europe.

No scientifically satisfactory answer can be given to the question as to the origin of PM. Some scholars place it at the very beginning of man's religious development; and some such as Pater W. Schmidt associate it with the idea of a primitive revelation (*Uroffenbarung*), of which all other forms of religious belief are a corruption. Others, especially evolutionists, see in PM the high point of a long religious development. In any case, this belief falls within the rational area of man's being.

When primitive peoples become Christian, the name of the High God is often used to serve as the name of the God revealed in the Bible. Just because of its indefiniteness, this name is very well suited to be filled with specifically Christian content by means of instruction, preaching and pastoral care.

ERNST DAMMANN

W. Schmidt: *Der Ursprung der Gottesidee* (12 vols., Münster 1926–1955); *ERE* VII, 817–21; *NCE* IX, 1066f.

MONTSERRAT. See CARIBBEAN.

MOODY, CAMPBELL NAISMITH (1866–1940), was born in Scotland and ordained as a minister of the Free Church after a distinguished academic career. Home mission work was followed by appointment in 1895 to Formosa as a missionary of the Presbyterian Church of England. Arriving in Tainan he was transferred to Changhoa (Shoka) in 1896 and it was there, in the centre of the island, that his most notable work was done. Troubled by ill health which resulted largely from his austere and self-sacrificing way of life, he spent several periods away from Formosa but it was not until 1924 that he finally retired.

M. was a rare combination of fervent, itinerant evangelist and Christian scholar.

Most villages in central Formosa heard his summoning trumpet and were moved by his preaching. In many of them he left churches. As occasion demanded he took responsibility for the theological college and turned his talents to ministerial training. Both during his years abroad and after retirement he found time and energy to write, two of his works becoming minor classics: *The Heathen Heart* (London 1907) and *The Mind of the Early Converts* (London 1920).

H. D. BEEBY

E. Band: *Working His Purpose Out: The History of the English Presbyterian Mission*, Vol. II (London 1947).

MOODY, DWIGHT LYMAN (1837–1899), was born at Northfield, Massachusetts, USA. With Ira D. Sankey as singer he became famous during his first British campaign, 1873–75, and stands unrivalled as the 19th century's greatest evangelist in USA and Britain. His influence on world missions was profound. Countless British and American missionaries were products of his campaigns, among the best known being Sir Wilfred *Grenfell and (indirectly) C. T. *Studd. The Cambridge Seven, whose sailing to China (1885) was a major missionary stimulus in Britain, resulted from M's Cambridge mission, 1882. In their wake strong missionary interest emerged at the sixth of the annual *Northfield Conferences which M. had founded on the campus of his schools. M. and the delegates issued in August 1885 an Appeal to Disciples Everywhere, urging that if all churches took the missionary call seriously, the entire earth could be evangelized by 1900. ('Evangelized' did not mean 'converted' but that all people would have heard the Christian gospel clearly enough to be in a position to respond.) Although this hope was not fulfilled, the appeal did much to enhance missionary zeal, enterprise and co-operation, especially through the Centenary Conference, London 1888, to which it led.

In 1886 M. held his first students' conference at Northfield. Through Robert

*Wilder and John R. *Mott, with M's encouragement, it became intensely missionary minded; 100 students signed a declaration of willingness to serve overseas, and thus began the *Student Volunteer Movement, which was the foremost factor in missionary recruiting from universities and colleges in most parts of the world over the next 25 years. Many outstanding leaders were originally SVs. It was also one of the earlier sources of the *IMC and the *ecumenical movement.

Though M's health twice prevented evangelistic tours in India (1888, 1891) he was unstinting in enlisting support for missionary societies and denominational boards, but speedily suppressed an attempt by his friends to form an independent missionary scheme under his leadership. He also founded in Chicago the M. Bible Institute to train non-graduates for home and foreign missions; since the last years of M's life it has had a very lengthy roll of missionary alumni, mostly American, and was the prototype of Bible Institutes in other countries. M. also founded a Colportage Association (now Moody Press) which published and distributed evangelical literature in many languages. M's own sermons were enormously influential on mission fields. As Mott said, three years after M's death, 'Next to the words of the Bible, and possibly those of Bunyan, M's words have been translated into more tongues than those of any other man'.

JOHN POLLOCK

J. F. Findlay, Jr.: *Dwight L. Moody: American Evangelist* (Chicago 1969); W. R. Moody: *Life of Dwight L. Moody* (New York and London 1900); J. Pollock: *Moody without Sankey* (London 1963), pp.216–20, 224–29, 251; W. M. Smith: *An Annotated Bibliography of D. L. Moody* (Chicago 1948); *DAB* XIII, 103–06; *NCE* IX, 1102f.; *RGG* IV, 1125.

MORAL PROBLEMS. See ETHICAL PROBLEMS IN MISSIONS.

MORAL REARMAMENT, the movement brought into being by Frank Nathan Daniel Buchman (1878–1961), earlier under the name 'the Oxford Group', to bring about changes in the world by faithfulness to the four absolutes—honesty, purity, unselfishness and love. In its early days the movement was unmistakably Christian in origin and intent. In more recent times, in the light of such declarations as that of B. himself (1948) that in this way 'Catholics, Jews and Protestants, Hindus, Mohammedans, Buddhists and Confucianists' can find themselves at one, friendly as well as hostile critics have wondered whether depth has not been sacrificed in the desire for breadth. MRA does not itself undertake missionary work, but sends teams to various areas of conflict, to undertake particular works of renewal and reconciliation. It may be thought that MRA is inclined at times to over-estimate the significance of its interventions, and the permanence of their effects.

STEPHEN NEILL

F. Buchman: *Remaking the World* (New York 1949). For a carefully critical estimate, see H. H. Wolf in *EKL* II coll.1447f., art. '*Moralische Aufrüstung*'. See also *NCE* IX, 1108f.; *WKL*, 978f.

MORAVIAN MISSIONS are carried on by the *Brüdergemeinde* and related societies in Europe and by the Moravian church in the USA. The former groups, in direct descent from one of the major streams which merged in *Pietism, have functioned chiefly as societies or orders within the European state churches. In North America and on other mission fields, they have founded churches. In the USA they now number 172 churches and 60,643 members governed in two 'provinces'. Since the reorganization of their movement in 1722, in co-operation with Count Nicholas von *Zinzendorf (1700–1760) at Herrnhut, the Moravians have been very active in foreign missions and have also greatly inspired and influenced the commitment of other persons and churches to the conversion of the nations. One of the most inspiring symbols of modern missions is the painting 'The First Fruits' (Rev.14:4) on the wall of the Great Hall at Zeist (Netherlands) and Herrnhut (the latter destroyed in the last days of the second world war).

The Moravians go back to the work of John Huss (c.1369–1415) and Jerome of Prague (c.1370–1416), both of whom suffered martyrdom at the hands of the Council of Constance as 'reformers before the Reformation'. Their followers, known as the *Unitas Fratrum*, were decimated during the Counter-Reformation. A small band re-grouped on Count Zinzendorf's estates, considering themselves a leaven in nations Christian in name only and developing a vigorous missionary work in America and elsewhere. David *Nitschmann (1679–1772), who influenced John *Wesley, was their first bishop in the reorganization, and Zinzendorf was the second.

In Pennsylvania they founded Christian communities at Bethlehem and Nazareth and Lititz and from this base worked energetically to evangelize the Indians. Their Christian Indian colonies, *Gnaden-hütten*, were successful in christianizing the Indians, but they were harrassed and destroyed by the whites. Moravian work among the Eskimos of Greenland, Labrador and Newfoundland, among the slaves of the Danish and British West Indies, in Central America, and Africa, was more abiding. At the opening of the first world war they had 15 stations, 28 missionaries, and 1,780 baptized Christians in Central Africa.

The initial goal of the Moravians was to set before 'Christendom' (a concept which they repudiated) the model of a 'pure church'. In Europe they followed the pietist instruction to found *ecclesiola in ecclesia* (a church within the church). Their passion for missions was a result of their commitment to the style of preaching and letter writing which marked the spread of the early church. They condemned mass conversions and worked for personal decision in each individual. Their respect for the integrity of every human person, however lowly his tribe, slowed their growth but improved the quality of their product. As primitive Christians they have stressed style of life, including lay share in the ministry, more than confessional or liturgical order. The *Losungen*, a yearly manual with a daily schedule of personal and family prayer and meditation, has been translated into many languages and is still the most frequently used handbook of private devotions among German-speaking Evangelicals.

FRANKLIN H. LITTELL

E. Benz and H. Renkewitz, eds.: *Zinzendorf-Gedenkbuch* (Stuttgart 1951); E. Langton: *History of the Moravian Church: The Story of the First International Protestant Church* (London 1956).

MORMON MISSIONS. Believing themselves to be the only true Church of Jesus Christ in the world, the Latter Day Saints have naturally been from the start a missionary body. Among their first concerns was the evangelization of the Indians, the fallen people of America, who must be brought back to the true way. As early as 1837 the M. emissaries had reached England, and had considerable success. It was reckoned in 1850 that in 13 years 17,000 converts had crossed the Atlantic to seek a new life in America; 'to English poor, hungry with the poverty and squalor of the hungry forties, Nauvoo towered dreamlike among meadows flowing with milk and honey' (Chadwick, p.437). The M. arrangements for the emigrants were admirable at every stage of the journey and contrasted most favourably with the mean and squalid arrangements made by others.

At the present time a large proportion of the young men of the community spend two years on missions in foreign countries at the charge of their families. These missionaries are extremely well prepared, taught to know the kind of questions they may expect to meet and the correct M. answer to give on every occasion. They meet with a good deal of success, and the M. community is growing in many countries. Notable in recent years has been progress in Africa, especially in Nigeria, but the ambiguous attitude of the church on questions of race and colour causes difficulty in a number of areas.

STEPHEN NEILL

O. Chadwick: *The Victorian Church* (London 1966), pp.436–39; R. Mullen: *The Mormons* (London 1967); *The Book of Mormon* (originally published 1830); *ERE* XI, 82–90.

MOROCCO. A monarchy of N. Africa, bounded on the north by the Mediterranean, west by the Atlantic ocean, south by the Spanish Sahara, and east by Algeria. Area 172,164 sq.m.; population 13,323,000 (UN estimate 1965). The original inhabitants, the Berbers, are divided into numerous tribes, of whom the Riffs, a strong, independent people in the high Atlas mountains, are the best known. The literacy rate is low.

There was a considerable Christian population before the eighth and ninth centuries when Muslim Arabs conquered the country, wiping out the churches, and made M. a stronghold of *Islam. A considerable Jewish minority, dating back several centuries, has been diminishing since the second world war through migration to Israel. The small European minority, Spanish and French, is in large measure nominally Christian.

The RC church brought the gospel again to M. in the early part of the 13th century. Pope Honorius III sent *Dominican and *Franciscan missionaries in 1225; five friars sent by St. Francis were martyred. A Franciscan bishop was appointed to Fez in 1233, and Spanish Franciscans had a measure of success among Muslims and Jews. At the end of the 19th century reinforcements were sent, including the Franciscan Missionaries of Mary (sisters); workers were urged to study Arabic, and schools and hospitals were opened.

Protestant work began when the BFBS (founded 1804) entered early in the 19th century. The *North Africa Mission began work in Tangier in 1885. The Southern Morocco Mission (from Scotland) came in 1888, followed by the Central Morocco Mission (English Presbyterian), the Gospel Union (USA) and the Brethren (British).

Societies entering to work among Jews were the LSPCJ (from 1844) and the Mildmay Missions to Jews. Work among all groups, Arabs, Berbers, Jews and Europeans, included schools, dispensaries, and the translation, publication and distribution of the Bible.

The constitution adopted by M. in 1963 makes practically all missionary work illegal. Converts from Islam are very few. Recent statistics (WCH 1968) list a RC community of 400,000 and six Protestant groups (the North Africa Mission and the Southern Morocco Mission united in 1958), with 27 places of worship, 1,458 communicant members and a Christian community of 6,056. Clergy and full-time lay workers, both RC and Protestant, are predominantly foreign, and Protestants have no organized indigenous church. The Christian community is not represented in ecumenical organizations, but some of the Protestant missions co-operate among themselves, particularly in the promotion of Christian literature.

GLORA M. WYSNER

R. Feiland: *Marokko* (Bonn 1958); *BM* II, 594–600; *NCE* IX, 1148–50; *WKL*, 889f.

MORRIS, WILLIAM CASE (1864–1932), was born at Soham, near Ely, Cambridgeshire, England. As a boy he went to South America with his widowed father. M. pursued a successful business career for some years but his attention was constantly arrested by the plight of the ragged orphans who roamed the streets of Buenos Aires. He opened his home to some of these children and soon found himself overwhelmed with the demand. He gave up his job to devote himself fully to the children's welfare. In 1897 he returned to England to gain financial support for his enterprise. He was accepted by the *SAMS who undertook to pay his personal stipend. M. raised a sufficient sum whilst in England to purchase land for a school for destitute children at Palermo, Buenos Aires. This was the beginning of the Argentine Philanthropic Schools and Institutes which, by the time of M's death in 1932, operated from four centres and consisted of 22 schools, libraries, laboratories, museums and sports fields.

M. was ordained in 1898 and was a powerful preacher and missionary. He was responsible for the production of Christian magazines and the translation into Spanish of books on Anglican theology, hymns, sermons and pamphlets.

HENRY SUTTON

'The Story of William C. Morris' in *Angle*, I No. 3 (January 1966), pp.7f.

MORRISON, ROBERT (1782–1834). When the British and Foreign Bible Society was founded in 1804, there was much talk about Bible translation, and about Chinese as the language of the greatest number of non-Christians. So the *LMS looked for a missionary for China, and found RM. He was born at Morpeth and brought up at Newcastle, Northumberland. He was apprenticed to his father's trade of making lasts, i.e. wooden 'feet' to keep boots in shape. He believed he was called to the ministry, was helped by his Presbyterian minister to improve his scanty education, and in 1802 entered the Dissenting Academy (Congregationalist Theological College) at Hoxton, London. When designated for China, he added to his theological studies elementary instruction in medicine, astronomy, and Chinese. He copied in the British Museum a RC Chinese version of most of the NT, and a Latin-Chinese dictionary. In 1807 he was ordained and sent to China.

Every kind of difficulty beset him. The British East India Company's ships would not convey an intending China missionary, because he had little chance of being permitted to land. The Chinese government allowed foreigners only at 'The Thirteen Factories' (merchant houses), a narrow strip of river bank outside the one city of Canton, and they allowed only merchants there. They forbade Chinese to teach their language to a foreigner. However, M. sailed via (i.e. *round*) America, taking seven months to reach China. He was introduced to a pious American merchant who gave him lodging in the 'Factories'.

And he found two RC Chinese who risked their lives to teach him Chinese. In 1809 the East India Company appointed him their translator. This secured his right to remain, without interfering with his mission work.

He completed his Chinese Bible by 1818, helped in the NT by the RC version mentioned above, and in the OT by William *Milne who translated from Deuteronomy to Job. The translation was too literal, lacked Chinese idiom, and was in some parts unintelligible, but it was a beginning, to be revised and improved upon, a remarkable achievement, considering the limitations of Morrison's training, and of his situation in Canton. He produced a large Chinese dictionary by 1821, and rightly claimed that this set English readers foremost in the chance to learn Chinese.

In his own cramped conditions, he was able to foresee a future of wide opportunity. He produced other language aids for future missionaries, appealed for women as well as men, and Americans as well as Europeans. He also advocated a cultural two-way traffic with Chinese language and literature studied in the west. He received an honorary DD from Glasgow in 1817, and was made Fellow of the Royal Society in 1824.

After 25 years the China mission could record only ten baptisms. M. said that it might take a hundred years to win a thousand Chinese. He died in China in 1834, and was buried in Macao. By 1934 the Chinese Protestant Christianity community numbered more than five hundred times as many as he had dared to hope.

JOHN FOSTER

M. Broomhall: *Robert Morrison* (London 1924); E. Morrison: *Memoirs of the Life and Labours of Robert Morrison . . . with critical notices of his Chinese works by S. Kidd* (2 vols., London 1839); *DNB* XXXIX, 111; *RGG* IV, 1141f.

MOSHOESHOE I (Moshesh), Paramount Chief of the Lesotho, was born in 1786, and died at Thaba-Bosiu on 3 February 1870.

Remarkable by reason both of his character and of his intelligence, M. was successful in uniting into a single nation the Basotho clans which had been scattered by the successive blows of the conquest of Chaka and the Zulus. Understanding that peace is more powerful than war, his constant policy was to establish his power on the basis of conciliation and diplomacy rather than by means of war.

In 1833 he received Eugene *Casalis, a missionary of the *PEMS, and gave him permission to preach the gospel in his country. A lasting friendship grew up between the two men, and Casalis became in consequence the adviser and the secretary of M.

From 1842 to 1869, almost without a break, M. had to fight and to negotiate in the course of the successive crises provoked by the infiltration of the Boer farmers into the territory of the tribe. On several occasions (the battle of Viervoet, 1851, the battle of Thaba-Bosiu, 1852), he believed himself to have overcome the invaders; but the truces subsequently negotiated did no more than to legalize the aggressions of the colonists. It was not long before M. came to see that Britain alone could protect him, and on several occasions asked for the protection of the Queen. This was finally granted by the proclamation of the governor, Sir Philip Wodehouse, on 12 March 1868, and confirmed by the second treaty of Aliwal North (12 February 1869). M. did not live to enjoy the peace that had thus been established.

Throughout his life he had supported and encouraged the missionaries; at the very end of his life he asked for baptism, but died before the ceremony had been performed.

ETIENNE KRUGER

MOTIVES, MISSIONARY. During the history of the church several motives have, each in its own way, contributed to the awakening of missionary concern. In the earliest period, as it is reflected in the NT, the missionary outlook was seen to spring directly out of Christian faith. Obedience to the command of Christ to make all men disciples (Matt.28:19) combined with the compelling force of

Christian love; the words of Paul, 'the love of Christ leaves us no choice' (2 Cor.5:14, NEB), apply to the whole of his missionary activity, which was marked by love for men founded on the love of Christ (in both senses: love for Christ, and love springing from Christ). There was also an *eschatological expectation, that the worldwide preaching of the gospel would bring in the end of the present age (e.g. Matt.24:14). In accordance with all this, the NT sees it as belonging to the nature of the church to proclaim the gospel (1 Pet.2:9); at the same time an essential part of missionary work is the planting and expansion of the church: through the act of baptism men were incorporated into the church as the 'body of Christ'. These four motives, the motive of obedience, the motive of love, the eschatological motive and the church motive, find their centre in Jesus Christ, God's missionary to mankind.

As a result of these motives the church spread rapidly during the early centuries. In the Middle Ages the love of Christ was often combined with ascetic motives, especially in monastic circles. The church motive broadened into what may be called the 'Christendom' motive: missionary work became part of the expansion of the socio-political pattern of Christian civilization as it had taken shape in the christianized part of the world. This motive was strong in the missionary activity of the early Middle Ages; it was perhaps dominant in Portuguese and Spanish missionary work in the 15th and 16th centuries; it was also present in the missionary expansion of the Protestant seafaring nations in the 17th century, where it combined with the theocratic ideals of Dutch and British Calvinism. In the 18th century the motive of love became a strong stimulus in the circles of *Pietism and *Methodism; it received a special form in the community of the *Moravians. Eschatological expectations played a large part in the 'missionary awakening' around 1800. In the context of African missions in the 19th century the motive of debt (arising from a feeling of guilt because of western participation in the system of slavery) was an important factor. In some evangelical circles the motive of love received a one-sided and individualistic accent (concentration on the 'salvation of souls'), while in liberal circles the social aspect of that motive was more strongly marked. Other motives also played their part: romantic motives (especially in the missions to the South Sea islands), cultural (the spreading of the 'blessings' of western culture), economic (with the missionary as a precursor of western trade), political (particularly in relation to colonization: see COLONIALISM). The breaking up of 'Christendom' in the present century has led to a return to the simplicity and self-evidence of the central biblical motives.

J. VAN DEN BERG

R. P. Beaver: 'American Missionary Motivation before the Revolution', *Church History* XXXI (1962), 216–26; R. P. Beaver: 'Missionary Motivation through Three Centuries' in J. C. Brauer, ed.: *Reinterpretation in American Church History* (Chicago 1968), pp.113–51; J. Dürr: '*Die Reinigung der Missions-Motive*', *Evangelisches Missions Magazin* XCV (1951), 2–10; R. Rouse: 'The Missionary Motive', *IRM* XXV (1936), 250–58; J. van den Berg: *Constrained by Jesus' Love* (Kampen 1956); P. A. Varg: 'Motives in Protestant Missions 1890–1917', *Church History* XXIII (1954), 68–82; M. A. C. Warren: *The Missionary Movement from Britain in Modern History* (London 1965).

MOTT, JOHN RALEIGH (1865–1955), was born at Postville, Iowa, USA, the son of a prosperous timber-merchant. Christian home influence led to membership of the Methodist church. An outstanding student at Upper Iowa and Cornell Universities, he planned a career in public life. But in 1886, while a member of the Student *YMCA at Cornell, he was challenged by J. E. K. Studd of Cambridge, England, to make a 'life-investment decision'. At the *Mount Hermon Student Conference, under D. L. *Moody's inspiration, he signed, with the first hundred, the Student Volunteer declaration for missionary service.

In 1888 M. became a national intercollegiate secretary of the YMCA and served that organization in many capacities for 60 years. In 1895 he founded the *WSCF and became general secretary, later chairman until 1929. In 1910 he chaired the Edinburgh *World Missionary Conference, and became chairman of its Continuation Committee, later the *IMC, including its conferences at Jerusalem (1928) and Tambaram (1938). In 1937 he was business chairman of the Oxford Conference on Church, Community and State, became vice-chairman of the Provisional Committee of the *WCC, Honorary President after Amsterdam (1948), attending Evanston (1954).

M. was a notable evangelist. To a fine presence he added a powerful, aphoristic way of speaking which convinced his hearers of the urgency of the Christian message. He developed world-wide evangelization amongst students in view of their key importance in the community. He had a remarkable gift for finding the right men for the right jobs in Christian mission, ensuring their support and keeping personal contact. He was the most widely travelled Christian leader of his time, and his range of personal influence and friendship created and strengthened ecumenical relationships.

M's distinctive contribution to mission was structural. His WSCF experience led to his insistence on Christian co-operation as the key objective of Edinburgh 1910. He worked tirelessly to form national Christian, or missionary, councils and to hold them together internationally in the sole interest of united Christian witness. He promoted national, regional and world conferences and, through organized intercession, detailed preparation, superb chairmanship and imaginative follow-up, he made them a powerful instrument for missionary advance.

ROBERT MACKIE

B. Mathews: *John R. Mott: World Citizen* (London 1934); *Addresses and Papers of J. R. Mott* (6 vols., New York 1946);

R. C. Mackie and others: *Layman Extraordinary* (London 1965); *NCE* X, 43; *RGG* IV, 1163, *WKL*, 985f.

MOUNT HERMON MISSIONARY AWAKENING. See NORTHFIELD CONFERENCES.

MOZAMBIQUE is an east African territory, 302,328 sq.m. in extent, bounded on the south and west by the Republic of South Africa and Swaziland, on the west by Rhodesia, on the north west by Zambia and Malawi, on the north by Tanzania, on the east by the Indian Ocean. The population is estimated (1963) at 6,789,000 of whom 100,000 are Europeans, 45,000 Asians. The largest Bantu-speaking tribes are the Ronga, Senga, Tonga, Tswa and Yao. Portuguese, the official language, and the only one permitted in education, is being increasingly understood by Africans. M. is officially an overseas province of Portugal with a governor responsible to Lisbon. Africans are regarded as citizens of Portugal. Portuguese rule became effective at the end of the 19th century with rapid economic development after 1945. There is a growing African opposition with support from outside Mozambique. The religion is the traditional Bantu with belief in a Supreme Being, the veneration of ancestors, practice of *magic and *witchcraft. There are about 800,000 Muslims in the north.

For the Portuguese, colonization and christianization are identical. The first missionaries arrived in 1506 with the *Dominicans leading the RC effort through the centuries. There are 228,000 RCs, with 212,428 children in Catholic primary schools. Catholicism is the official religion, state supported and preferred, with almost monopoly in education. About 100 Africans have secondary education, some have technical education. About 95% of the people are illiterate.

The Protestant efforts began in 1879 with the *ABCFM which in 1888 turned its work over to the Methodist Episcopal Church. The Suisse Romande Missions started near Lourenzo Marques in 1881. The Free

Methodists came in 1886, the Wesleyan Methodists and the Anglicans in 1893. Among the other churches are the International Holiness Mission (1921), the Church of the *Nazarene (1922) and the Africa Evangelical Fellowship (1922). Protestant churches work under severe handicaps: restriction on entry and free travel of missionaries, on building of schools and churches, on free assembly. About 6,000 pupils are in Protestant primary schools, some hospital and health services are allowed. There are about 100,000 Protestant Christians. The Christian Council of Mozambique was organized in 1944. It has now started publishing a paper. The whole Bible has been translated into three languages and the NT into two more. Of the six Protestant theological training centres, the ecumenical Union Seminary at Ricatla is the largest and most advanced.

PER HASSING

J. E. Duffy: *Portuguese Africa* (Cambridge, Mass. 1959), *Portugal in Africa* (Cambridge, Mass. 1962); R. von Gersdorff: *Mocambique* (Bonn 1958); *BM* II, 619–22; *NCE* X, 57.

MRA. See MORAL REARMAMENT.

MU KYO KAI. See NON-CHURCH MOVEMENT.

MURDOCH, JOHN (1819–1904), was born in Glasgow, Scotland. He went to Ceylon in 1844 as head of a government training school for teachers, but resigned in 1849 to free himself for evangelism and education through books and pamphlets. Sponsored by the United Presbyterian Church in Scotland, but with no assured income save an annual grant of £56 from his old congregation in Glasgow, he founded the Sinhalese Tract Society, collected funds, borrowed a small printing-press, and in one year produced 100,000 tracts, 10,000 books and a monthly magazine. Visiting India in 1854, he noted there also the lack of books suitable for Christian schools, and urged missions to joint action. In 1858 he became the first secretary of what was ultimately the Christian Literature Society of India, now incorporated in the *USCL. For 50 years M. travelled strenuously all over India, working for united Christian participation in all-India planning. He himself was a prolific writer of books and pamphlets directed to the needs of teachers and pupils, and the problems of village people. His *Manual for Missionaries* is perhaps the best commentary on his own faith and life.

A. J. BOYD

A. W. McClymont: *The Travelling Bookman, John Murdoch of Madras* (London 1947).

MURRAY, ANDREW (1828–1917), was born in Cape Town, South Africa. His father, a Scottish clergyman, had come to serve the *DRC of South Africa, and his mother was of Huguenot and Lutheran ancestry. M. was educated at Aberdeen and Utrecht universities. At Utrecht M. and his brother helped to form a student missionary society. He was ordained in 1848. He served pastorates at Bloemfontein, Worcester, Cape Town and Wellington; was interpreter between the Dutch and the British at the Sand River Convention, 1852; helped to found the Grey College, now the University College of Orange Free State, 1856, and was its first rector; he further helped to found the Stellenbosch Theological Seminary, 1857; the Huguenot Seminary, 1874, and the Wellington Missionary Training Institute, 1877. He was moderator of the Cape synod of his church, 1862, president of the *YMCA, Cape Town, 1865, and president of the *South Africa General Mission from 1888 till his death. He received honorary doctorates from the universities of Aberdeen, 1898, and of the Cape of Good Hope in 1907. M's was an ecumenical spirit, and he was one of the main promoters of the missionary awakening in South Africa. Mission was to him 'the chief end of the church'. A frequent devotional speaker in Britain and Africa, he wrote 240 books and pamphlets. His *Abide in Christ* is a devotional classic.

PER HASSING

J. Du Plessis: *The Life of Andrew Murray of South Africa* (London 1919); W. J. van der Merwe: *The Development of Missionary Attitudes in the Dutch Reformed Church in South Africa* (Cape Town 1936).

MUSCAT AND OMAN. See ARABIAN PENINSULA.

MUSIC IN EVANGELISM AND WORSHIP. Traditionally missionaries have taken western church music to the mission field, adapting the tunes to fit vernacular words. It is now realized that only indigenous music can be a satisfying spiritual vehicle for most people. Sporadic examples of the use of native musics date from at least the beginning of this century, but only within the last 30 years has a serious attempt been made in this matter. Until 1955 most of the progress towards the use of indigenous music lay with non-Roman churches: but in that year the papal encyclical *Musicae Sacrae disciplina* initiated much effort in RC missions.

The All-Africa Church Music Association (Salisbury, Rhodesia) is a fully interdenominational attempt to foster the movement. Note also the Rev Ola Olude's Yoruba hymns (Methodist) and the Catechism *Watoto wa Munga* issued by the Benedictines at Ndanda, Peramiho, East Africa, which abounds in Swahili tunes.

The composing of hymns set to indigenous music is much easier than the setting of liturgical prose texts such as the *Gloria* in the Eucharist. Such extended and non-rhythmical texts are foreign to much native idiom. One solution—to give the text to a solo singer, with the congregation breaking in at intervals with an invariable refrain—has the disadvantage that the latter never sing the full text.

The whole move to a vernacular music in Christian worship must, in the end, depend on musical indigenous Christians. Their conservatism and the feeling of many that their own music is secular and 'non-Christian' poses a problem. But they are correct in feeling that merely to set Christian words to a secular tune is not good enough.

The European missionary can help by encouraging national musicians to compose new tunes in their own idiom: what is needed is a Christian music born of deep Christian experience composed by indigenous Christian musicians.

A. M. JONES

A. M. Jones: 'Hymns for the African', in *Books for Africa* (London 1957–1958); *Rythmes du Monde* (Le Bulletin des Missions), nouvelle série, 32ᵐᵉ année, VI, No. 1 (Bruges 1958).

MUSLIM MISSIONS have been organized largely by heterodox movements such as the *Ismāʻīliyah* from mediaeval times, and by the modern *Ahmadīyah*, who have been repudiated by orthodox *Islām not least because of their polemical disparagement of Jesus. *Ahmadī* missions are concentrated in East and West Africa; there are signs of indigenization after long dependence upon Pakistani leadership. As part of its ideological impact upon Africa, Egypt is offering missionary training in the modernized al-Azhar University. Yet the most effective Muslim missionaries are still the saints (see SUFISM), traders and local Muslim communities whose solidarity and piety are so attractive to ex-*animists.

JOHN B. TAYLOR

H. J. Fisher: *Ahmadiyyah* (Oxford 1963).

MUTHIAH, NARAYANA (1872–1959), was born at Pālayamkōttai, Madras, of high-caste Hindu parents. As a youth he was actively antagonistic to Christianity, but after listening to the challenging witness of an Indian *Salvation Army officer in an open-air meeting, he made his decision for Christ in the presence of his colleagues. On becoming a Christian he had to sign away all his property. While training to be a SA officer he was imprisoned for holding an open-air meeting. All this strengthened his faith and for seventy years he preached Christ to his fellow countrymen, in 1924 becoming Salvationist leader in Madras, and later in Lahore. He was the first Indian to become a Commissioner, the Army's highest rank.

THOS. H. LEWIS

R. M. Wheaton: *Indian Pilgrim* (London 1960).

NANKING THEOLOGICAL SEMINARY, BOARD OF FOUNDERS. See FOUNDATION FOR THEOLOGICAL EDUCATION IN SOUTH-EAST ASIA.

NATAL. See SOUTH AFRICA, REPUBLIC OF.

NATIONAL CHRISTIAN COUNCILS. In the period between 1910 and 1921 great progress was made in the development of indigenous leadership in the *younger churches and in the sense of independence and church responsibility in those churches. The age of the missionary was clearly at an end, though the age of the independent church had not yet fully come. The formation of the *IMC in 1921 placed Christian co-operation on a permanent footing in a manner never known before: it was fitting that permanent national bodies should come into existence in the countries in which the Christian churches still existed only as small minorities.

India was the first country to take action in the matter. In January 1922 the *National Missionary Council met and drafted a constitution for a National Christian Council. An important change was the new rule that at least half of the membership of the Council was to be Indian. It was noted that, though the membership of the new council was individually less able than the older, the council as a whole was a far stronger council. William *Paton was summoned from England to be the first secretary of the council.

Japan took action in May 1922, with a National Christian Conference, at which the majority of the members, including the chairman, Dr S. Motoda, were Japanese. This conference drew up the plans for the NCC of Japan, which was inaugurated on 13 November 1923, 'to foster unity within the church in Japan and to link it with the rest of the world Christian community'. One of the two secretaries, Dr W. Axling, was a

foreigner. Immediately on the formation of the council, the Japanese *Federation of Churches merged itself with it. The Federated Missions continued in existence, but having little to do faded from importance.

China also moved forward, with its National Christian Conference of May 1922. Here for the first time the majority of the delegates were nationals; the main achievement of the meeting was the creation of the NCC of China, 'to foster and express the fellowship and unity of the Christian church in China'. This was a time of great tension in China between more liberal and more conservative forces; the ecumenical spirit of the council was expressed by T. T. *Lew in the words: 'The Chinese church shall teach her members to agree to differ and to resolve to love'. One of the three secretaries, Dr H. T. Hodgkin, a Quaker, was a foreigner; his contribution to the development of the work of the council was notable.

Korea, which had started with a Federal Council of Protestant Evangelical Missions in Korea (1911), advanced by way of a Korean Federal Council of Churches (1918) to a Korean NCC (1924). In spite of the name, this council was not fully representative until 1927. All its officers have from the start been Koreans.

Africa, where missions are of such recent origin, was naturally slower to develop organs of Christian co-operation. The first country to take action in this direction appears to have been the (Belgian) Congo, where in 1924 the Congo Missionary Conference accepted a constitution for a Congo Protestant Council. This body was one of the few councils which withdrew from international co-operation in 1961, because of the integration of the IMC with the *WCC.

Almost all National Councils are linked to the central ecumenical organization, but there are exceptions. The Christian Council of Kenya which in 1943 succeeded the Kenya Missionary Council (1924) has been able to draw into fellowship all the Protestant missionary bodies in the country; but, as some of these bodies are conservative and highly suspicious of ecumenical co-operation, this happy result has been attained only by sacrificing international relationships in favour of local unity.

The WCC today has relations with NCCs (or other bodies differently named but fulfilling the same functions) in several countries in each continent; but at the time of writing continual new additions and reorganizations make it impossible to give a precise list.

There are naturally many variations of form and type. But the general pattern of the councils tends to be the same all over the world. (1) All such councils are advisory, and have no authority beyond that committed to them by their constituent bodies. (2) Almost all include, beside churches, such bodies as the Bible society, and other missionary organizations. (3) All were founded on a Protestant basis. Some have managed to include Orthodox or Eastern Christian bodies; but, in spite of the great improvement in relationships with the Roman Catholics, RC membership of the great majority of councils is not as yet a fact. (4) All the councils occupy themselves with subjects of common interest, such as education. (5) A number of councils are recognized by governments as the agency with which they will deal in matters affecting the interests of Protestant Christians. (6) No council is directly responsible for promoting corporate unity of churches; but all of them serve as a centre in which the spirit of unity is developed, and can prove helpful to bodies actually engaged in negotiations with a view to unity. (7) In all councils there is a marked tendency for the missionary element to decrease, and for the centre of gravity to shift to the churches. (8) Membership, and especially office-bearing, in such councils has been found to be an excellent training ground for participation in wider ecumenical efforts.

STEPHEN NEILL

R. P. Beaver: *Ecumenical Beginnings in Protestant World Mission* (New York 1962); W. R. Hogg: *Ecumenical Foundations* (New York 1952); R. Rouse and S. C. Neill, eds.: *A History of the Ecumenical Movement 1517-1948* (London 1954).

NATIONAL COUNCILS OF CHURCHES have come into being only in the 20th century, and are one of the most impressive forms of modern ecumenical co-operation. Councils of this kind have come into existence mainly in the nominally Christian countries. They differ from NCs in mainly non-Christian countries in that they tend to be made up of member-*churches* only, and not to include such other bodies as missions and voluntary societies. What is new is the fact that all these bodies have a continuous existence, and a permanent staff; they are at all times available for the service of the churches.

The first council of this kind to come into existence was the Federal Council of the Churches of Christ in America (1908). The man who did more than any other to work for it and to bring it into existence, Elias B. Sanford (1843–1922), a Congregationalist, deliberately planned that it should be a rival form of ecumenism to corporate union, which according to his opinion, 'aside from the impossibility of its achievement is by no means desirable'. The main aims of the Federal Council were to express the fellowship and catholic unity of the Christian church, to bring the Christian bodies of America into united service, to encourage devotional fellowship and mutual counsel, and to secure a larger combined influence for the Churches of Christ in all matters affecting the moral and social condition of the people. In 1950 the Federal Council was reorganized as the NC of the Churches of Christ in the USA. It represents a larger number of Christians than any other similar council elsewhere, and has served as the model for a large number of other councils.

A few further councils may be briefly mentioned.

The British Council of Churches was

formed in 1942 by the action of sixteen denominations. This had been preceded in 1941 by the formation of the NC of Churches in New Zealand; this is probably the most representative of all councils in the sense that 90% of New Zealanders belong to the eight churches of which it is made up. Canada followed in 1944, with the Canadian Council of Churches, the first secretary of which, Dr J. W. Gallagher, held office for twenty years, 1944-64.

On the continent of Europe, France heads the list with the Protestant Federation of France, which was formed in 1905, but which, in view of the small number of Protestants in France, does not assume the name of National Council. The federation of Protestant Churches in Switzerland followed in 1920. An Ecumenical Council had existed in Holland since 1935. This was reorganized in 1946, to bring it more closely into line with the principles of the *WCC.

What is the theological status of councils of this kind? This is an ecumenical problem to which less thought has been given than it deserves by reason of its importance. Such a council is not a church, but in many ways it acts as a church. All its concerns are church concerns; its officers and members are there because each of them belongs to a church which has agreed to work with other churches in the spirit of ecumenical fellowship. To many Christians it appears that conciliar unity—Christian unity in the shape of a myriad of local, regional and national councils, with the WCC at the head—is the right form of Christian unity for the 20th century. It can be quickly brought into being without the endless delays attendant on corporate unity. It provides fellowship, means for common action and witness, and those preliminaries of mutual understanding which are essential if corporate unity is ever to come. This is all the unity which the church can stand today. This can be persuasively argued. It seems, likely, however, that the main flow of ecumenical thought will be in the other direction, and will not be content with anything less than full visible and corporate union.

STEPHEN NEILL

S. M. Cavert: *The American Churches in the Ecumenical Movement 1900–1968* (New York 1968); H. P. Van Dusen: *One Great Ground of Hope* (New York and London 1961), especially Part III.

NATIONAL MISSIONARY COUNCILS. The trend in the direction of missionary co-operation in the field received great stimulus from the first World Missionary *Conference (Edinburgh 1910), and still more from John R. *Mott's great journey during 1911-13, in which he held 'Continuation Committee' conferences in a large number of places in Asia. In almost every area the result was the formation of a national body, to serve as the local 'Continuation Committee', and to prepare the way for further co-operation in the future. The actual term NMC seems to have been used only in India, but it might well have been found applicable elsewhere as well. It was a great advance that at the National Conference held at Shanghai in 1913 nearly one-third of the membership was Chinese; but the missionary element was still large, and direction tended to be in foreign hands. The functions of such conferences and committees were clearly defined in the instructions issued to the Indian Council; they were to assist the local bodies, to deal with problems national in scope, and to maintain communication with the Continuation Committee. Like the latter, they embodied no legislative authority, but were to be consultative and advisory only. The situation in Japan was peculiar, in that prior to Dr Mott's visit, two Federations had come into existence, the 'Federated Missions', and in 1911 the 'Federated Churches of Japan' with exclusively Japanese leadership. The Continuation Committee of Japan, formed after Dr Mott's visit, had a membership of thirty, divided equally between the two federations. These bodies were of great importance in their time, but it was clear that they could be of only transitory and provisional significance. The formation of the *IMC in 1921 carried Christian co-operation a step further, on a basis of permanence; in course of time it came to be related to similar permanent bodies, the *NCCs in many parts of the world.

STEPHEN NEILL

R. P. Beaver: *Ecumenical Beginnings in Protestant World Mission* (New York 1962); W. R. Hogg: *Ecumenical Foundations* (New York 1952).

NATIONAL STUDENT CHRISTIAN FEDERATION, COMMISSION ON WORLD MISSION. The CWM was formed by the integration of the *Student Volunteer Movement in the USA with several national Christian student organizations in the NSCF. From 1959 the CWM provided a strong emphasis on mission, generally interpreted on college campuses as the dynamic thrust of the Christian into the world. The organized missionary structures of the churches were not essentially related to this reformulated objective of mission, but the concerns of university students developed an ecumenical character which influenced international Christian student conferences in the USA, and was evident in the outlook of the CWM. When the University Christian Movement was formed in 1966 by reconstituting the NSCF, the contribution of the CWM to the statement of purpose was 'to encourage members of academic communities to respond to God's world in ways that will lead to fuller humanity for all men, to work for unity among those who are separated, and to reflect theologically upon what they are doing'. The CWM, among the first to act on the formation of a movement fully representative of the churches, agreed that the sense of mission was sufficiently embodied in the student movement for the Commission to cease a separate existence.

ROLAND W. SCOTT

NATIONALISM. The term 'nation' is a difficult one to define. It may be said that any large body of human beings which decides to share a common life, some common traditions, a common ideal of human life lived in society, with at least some central organs of government, is

already a nation. Once national sentiment is aroused it becomes a very powerful force. It usually emerges at an early date in countries which have clearly marked national boundaries; it is clearly present in England at the time of Agincourt in 1415. But no country has stronger national feeling than Poland, which has no natural boundaries at all. The power of N. has generally been stronger than that of religion. Though the *Corpus Christianum* was a reality in the Europe of the Middle Ages, the unity of the Christian faith was not strong enough to prevent the incessant dynastic wars by which progress of civilization was so often held up.

Just at a time at which the European nations were discovering that uncontrolled N. is an ever-present danger, the nations of Asia and Africa were beginning to arise to claim their national inheritance. The sense of N. first grew strong in an Asian island kingdom, Japan. In India, Indonesia and other countries which have no natural unity, N. may be said to have been created by opposition to the dominance of a colonial power; it is none the less for that a very thriving plant. In Africa, boundaries were constantly drawn by the colonial powers without any regard for ethnic or tribal frontiers; in a number of cases (Nigeria, the Congo), tribal feelings have shown themselves so strong as to threaten national existence.

Many Christians, in the light of the biblical revelation, would be prepared to recognize the nation as one of the orders appointed, or at least permitted, by God for the good ordering of the life of men in society. Few would regard as anything but dangerous the total identification of the interests of the church with those of a particular nation. The church must stand for a supra-national unity, and for the fellowship of all the children of God. In the past the work of the church has been hindered where the impression has been given of too close an identification of the interests of the missions with the policies of the colonial powers. But the situation would be no better if the new nation states were able to make good the claim, which some of them are prepared to put forward, that the churches should be entirely at their disposal for the work of nation-building as they understand it. In the 'revolutionary' period, churches and missions were tempted to identify themselves with what proved to be one political party. But a church which is the church of one party cannot ever be the church of a nation, let alone the representative of ecumenical Christianity. In calmer times it has come to be recognized that Christians must be free to belong to any political party of their choice or to none. Christian witness must be maintained within the framework of the new national organization, but not in such a way as to involve surrender of the essential liberty of the church.

Similarly, where a strong national tradition has been developed, Christians are right in demanding that the church in their area should take account of their national traditions. The church is enriched as the nations and languages learn to bring their special treasures into the city of God. But in this respect too the independence of the church must be safeguarded; the controlling power at all times must be the gospel of Jesus Christ himself. In a real sense there can be no national churches; or only national churches such as are prepared to make their contribution to that international fellowship of all believing Christians which they are prepared to regard as the greater reality.

STEPHEN NEILL

S. W. Baron: *Modern Nationalism and Religion* (New York 1947); H. Kohn: *Nationalism: Its Meaning and History* (Princeton 1955); *NCE* X, 240–44.

NAURU. See PACIFIC ISLANDS.

NAZARENE, CHURCH OF THE, MISSIONS. When the church was founded in 1908, the uniting US bodies had missions in India (begun in 1898), Cape Verde, Japan, South Africa and Mexico. By 1966, domestic districts (US, Britain and Canada) had also entered Alaska, Argentina,

15*

Australia, Barbados, Bermuda, Bolivia, Brazil, British Honduras, Chile, Costa Rica, El Salvador, Guatemala, Guyana, Haiti, Hawaii, Israel, Jamaica, Jordan, Korea, Lebanon, Malawi, Mozambique, New Guinea, Nicaragua, Okinawa, Panama, Peru, Philippines, Puerto Rico, Rhodesia, Samoa, Swaziland, Syria, Taiwan, Trinidad, Virgin Islands and Zambia. There were 613 missionaries in 1966, 2,479 churches and preaching points, 78,291 members and probationers, 37 Bible colleges and seminaries with 845 enrolled, 160 primary and secondary schools with 15,584 enrolled, three nurses' training schools (India, South Africa and Swaziland), one junior college (Japan), one teacher training school (Swaziland), 91 special schools (adult education), 47 dispensaries, and four hospitals (India, New Guinea, South Africa and Swaziland). The Spanish Department produces eleven periodicals, plus books and hymnals, and a Spanish radio programme aired on 391 stations.

P. R. ORJALA

M. Taylor and R. DeLong: *Fifty Years of Nazarene Missions* (3 vols., Kansas City 1952, 1955 and 1958).

NEAR EAST COUNCIL OF CHURCHES. See REGIONAL AGENCIES FOR CO-OPERATION.

NEAR EAST COLLEGE ASSOCIATION, INC., is a service organization for American sponsored non-profit institutions overseas, established in 1919 and governed by a Board of Directors composed of representatives of member institutions. Basic services include finance and accounting, purchasing and shipping, personnel services.

Members: Athens College, Athens, Greece; Anatolia College, Thessaloniki, Greece; American University of Beirut, Lebanon; International College, Beirut, Lebanon; Robert College of Istanbul, Turkey; Sofia American Schools, Bulgaria (not operating).

Associated non-members: American Hospital of Istanbul; American University in Cairo;

American Community School of Beirut; American Farm School, Thessaloniki, Greece.

The American address of NECA is 548, Fifth Avenue, New York 10036.

WILLIAM H. FOX

NEAR EAST SCHOOL OF THEOLOGY. See THEOLOGICAL EDUCATION.

NEESHIMA, J. H. See NIIJIMA, JO.

NEPAL. Area 55,000 sq.m. Population (1968 estimate) 13,107,000. An independent state on the southern flanks of the Himalayas. Since the 18th century the Gurkhas have been the dominant tribe, though the ruling family is of Indian (Rajput) descent. Kathmandu is the only large town. The Nepalese are Hindu or Buddhist or a mixture of both. Buddha himself was born in the low-lying southern region. Christianity was introduced into the country by *Jesuit missionaries at the end of the 17th century, but missionaries and Nepalese Christians were expelled in 1767, settling in Bettiah in North Bihar where there is still a flourishing community.

N. remains closed to direct evangelistic work by foreigners, but medical work was established, chiefly in and around Kathmandu, at the end of the 19th century by the Church of Scotland mission and by the Methodist Church of Southern Asia. Later, work was begun by the Seventh Day Adventist Mission, the Mission to Lepers, the Mar Thoma Evangelistic Association (from Kerala in South India) and the Roman Catholics who opened a hospital in Kathmandu in 1953. Since 1954, the United Mission to Nepal has operated under the auspices of the *National Christian Council of India. Since 1950 freedom of worship and association has been granted to Nepali Christians and to members of the staffs of Christian institutions. A vigorous literacy campaign is being conducted through the *Committee on World Literacy and Christian Literature.

The latest statistics show a total

Protestant community of 500 with 112 ordained workers, local and expatriate, and 29 lay workers.

HENRY LEFEVER

A. McLeish: *The Frontier People of India* (London 1931); *Christian Handbook of India* (Nagpur 1959); E. W. Oliver: 'Nepal' in *IRM* XLIV (1955), pp.408–17; *BM* II, 622f.; *ERE* VIII, 321–23; *NCE* X, 338; *WKL*, 1000f.

NESTORIAN CHURCHES, THE, refused in the 5th century to accept the decrees of the Council of Chalcedon (451) which seemed to them inadequately to safeguard the distinction between the divine and the human natures in Christ. Their headquarters were in Mesopotamia, where they received a measure of protection from the Persian kings, and even after the incursions of the Muslims continued to obtain for themselves rather favourable terms. From the 8th century onwards the NC carried out an immense missionary extension through Central Asia as far as China. It is reported that at one time they had 250 bishoprics in Central Asia, where a number of Turkish peoples had been converted. Conclusive evidence of the presence of the NC in China is afforded by the stone erected at Sian-Fu in North West China in 781, and discovered in 1625. But changes in the political situation proved unfavourable to this widely extended work; it gradually collapsed, and today hardly a fragment is left.

The remaining fragment of the NC lived in Mesopotamia, always exposed to oppression or violence on the part of the Turks and the Kurds. During the first world war, under suspicion of disloyalty, the N. were cruelly driven from their homes by the Turks, and it is reckoned that in this period of expulsion half of them died. The survivors were gradually settled in North Iraq, in Cyprus and in the USA. Since 1940 their patriarch has resided in Chicago. It is believed that 'the Church of the East' now numbers about 75,000 members. There is a rather larger Uniat section, the 'Chaldeans', the first union with Rome having taken place in 1551. A few have joined Protestant churches. It is notable that the N. have survived, but they are able to exercise little if any Christian influence on their Muslim neighbours. See also ASSYRIAN CHRISTIANS; EASTERN CHURCHES.

STEPHEN NEILL

L. E. Browne: *The Eclipse of Christianity in Asia* (Cambridge 1933); J. Joseph: *The Nestorians and their Muslim Neighbors* (Princeton 1961); P. Kawerau: *Amerika und die orientalischen Kirchen* (Berlin 1958); *NCE* X, 343–48; *WKL*, 1001–05.

NETHERLANDS. See HOLLAND.

NETHERLANDS ANTILLES. See CARIBBEAN.

NEUENDETTELSAU MISSIONARY SOCIETY. 'A society for home and foreign missions according to the principles of the Lutheran Church' was founded in 1849 by Pastor Wilhelm Löhe at N. in Germany. In it he gathered together those who had been awakened by his preaching. The mission regarded it as its principal task to provide church ministrations for German Protestant emigrants who had settled in America (1841), Australia (1872) and Brazil (1897). A missionary college was founded in 1853 for the training of pastors. In connection with the work in North America a mission to the Indians came into being, but this was dropped in 1860 as a result of disturbances among the Indians. In Australia a mission to the Aborigines was founded, and this was further developed by the Lutherans in Australia. New Guinea is the principal field of the mission. Missionary work is in process of development in Brazil. Pastors have been trained to serve Protestant communities in Ukraine, and Arabs of evangelical confession. Since mission can be carried on only by a living church, the society has carried on a variety of activities in the home church. Its character is that of a confessional Lutheran society, and it feels itself specially respon-

sible for the maintenance of the Lutheran tradition.

GEORG F. VICEDOM

F. Eppelein: *Das Neuendettelsauer Missionswerk* (Neuendettelsau 1933); G. Pilhofer: *Die Geschichte der Neuendettelsauer Mission in Neuguinea* (3 vols., Neuendettelsau 1961–1965); *RGG* IV, 1410.

NEVIUS PLAN. John Livingstone Nevius (1829–1893) arrived in China in 1856 as a missionary of the American Presbyterian board, and served both in the Yangtse Valley and in Shantung. He became dissatisfied with the usual method of missionary work, under which *evangelists were paid by the missions to preach the gospel to their fellow-countrymen. A visit to Korea in 1890 gave Nevius the opportunity to formulate his famous plan, and to encourage the Presbyterian missions in Korea to put it into effect. The first principles of the plan are:

(1) *Bible Study*. The Bible to be thoroughly and systematically taught to all Christians.
(2) *Self-propagation*. Every Christian to be a missionary, and to feel the reponsibility for passing on the message, while at the same time carrying on his ordinary avocations.
(3) *Self-government*. Groups of believers should select from among themselves their own unpaid leaders; such groups should be organized in circuits, which would be served by paid helpers, not necessarily paid by the Korean Christians themselves.
(4) *Self-support*. Each group should be prepared to build its own church, and to call and support its own pastor. Only such church buildings should be put up as the Korean Christians were really able to maintain.
(5) *Missionary Itineration*. Missionaries should itinerate widely, always accompanied by a Korean 'helper'; but missionaries should not accept appointment as ministers of Korean congregations.

The plan has been criticized by some as laying too much stress on self-support, and by others as laying too little stress on self-government from the beginning. In the main, however, the plan commends itself to the modern Christian conscience. Presbyterians in Korea hold that the rapid increase in the numbers of Christians which began not long after N's visit was due at least in some measure to the implementation of the NP.

See MOFFETT, SAMUEL AUSTIN.

STEPHEN NEILL

C. A. Clark: *The Korean Church and the Nevius Methods* (New York 1930); S. H. Moffett: *The Christians of Korea* (New York 1962); H. S. C. Nevius: *The Life of John Livingstone Nevius* (Chicago 1895); *DAB* XIII, 449.

NEW CALEDONIA. See PACIFIC ISLANDS.

NEW DELHI 1961. See ASSEMBLIES, ECUMENICAL.

NEW GUINEA, discovered by Antonio d'Abreu in 1512, is the second largest island in the world. Its area is 341,424 sq.m. The landscape is very mountainous and broken; the highest summits reach over 16,000 feet, the rivers are not navigable. The island is volcanic, its climate tropical and unhealthy. The western half of the island was under Dutch control, but now under the name West Irian belongs to Indonesia. Since 1918 the whole of the rest of the island has been governed by Australia. The population of the island is probably about two and a half million. Until very recent times these people belonged to the culture of the stone age. The population is very much broken up by the mountain ranges, and only in the highlands are large tribes to be found. It is said that there are 700 languages—this has placed grave difficulties in the way of missionary work. In the centre of the island are to be found the Papuans, a primitive people resembling Pygmies. The coastal region and the river valleys in the east are inhabited by Melanesians; in the west there are traces of Indonesian influence. The basis of society is totemism. Religion is akin to that of most *primitive peoples. Belief in a creator God is present, but a strong belief in spirits and demons is widespread among them. The ancestor-cult is the focal point of religion. Many tribes practised cannibalism and head-hunting.

As early as 1546 the western part of NG was visited by Francis *Xavier. Roman Catholic work was given up in 1666. In 1890 it was taken up again on the southern coast of West Irian by Fathers of the Sacred Heart. This mission has about 80,000 Christians. In 1862 the Utrecht Missionary Society set to work on the north coast, and through the conversion of entire tribes was able to bring into being a rapidly growing church. This church became independent in 1956, and now has a membership of 150,000. The Protestant Church of Indonesia has a small work in the south. In 1960 the *Rhenish Mission started a pioneer work in the Central Range.

Eastern NG is divided between Papua and the Mandated Territory of NG. Since 1901 Papua has been an Australian colony, in which an area was assigned to each of the missions by the government. The Sacred Heart Fathers have been working in the Makeo district, with missionaries from the Philippines and from France. The first Papuan priest was ordained in 1946. The mission has altogether 50,000 adherents. On the south-east coast the *LMS came in in 1872 with Samuel *MacFarlane as its first missionary. To this mission belonged also James *Chalmers, who was killed and eaten by cannibals in 1901. The work was developed with the help of pastors from Tonga. In 1890 the Methodist Mission took up work on the adjacent islands. In 1891 the Anglicans, with the co-operation of the *CMS, *SPG and *SPCK, began work on the south-east coast. Before long they also set to work to train an indigenous clergy, and now have their first Papuan assistant bishop. The Seventh Day Adventist Mission started school work in 1914. The Kwato Mission, which had its origin in the LMS, but has also been deeply influenced by the *Oxford Group Movement, built up an *industrial mission, and made it one of its primary aims to develop the area economically. In 1932 the Unevangelized Fields Mission opened up work in the Fly River district. The Protestant missions together have about 200,000 Christians. Their congregations for the most part manage their own affairs, but the missions have not in all cases granted them independence.

In the Mandated Territory, of which the former Kaiser Wilhelmsland is only a part, RC work has been carried on since 1895 by the *Society of the Divine Word in the area between Madang and the boundary of West Irian. But since the end of the war they have set up their hierarchy in the whole of NG, and in particular have begun work in all the towns. They are supported in their work by the Marian Society, by the missionaries of the Heart of Jesus, and by the *Franciscans. Whereas the Protestant missions have mostly carried on their work in the local Papuan languages, the RCs have used Pidgin-English (neo-Melanesian) as the means of communication. The total number of RCs in the whole eastern part is given as 380,000.

Since 1886–87 the Protestant missionary cause has been represented in the Mandated Territory by the *Neuendettelsau and the *Rhenish missions. The former started work in Finschhafen, the latter in Madang. In 1929 this field was handed over to the American Lutherans. The Neuendettelsau Mission had from the beginning excellent relations with the Australian Lutherans; in 1918, under pressure of the crisis created by the first world war, the American Lutherans also came to the rescue. Since the beginning of the second world war, these have been in entire charge of the field.

In 1951 the already mentioned societies and the *Leipzig Mission joined to form the Lutheran Mission, NG, as an independent corporation. From now on churches and missions in the western countries were to have only a supporting function. The direction of the mission is located in NG. This amalgamation gave the mission an immense power to advance. The work had received its character from the solid pioneer work of its founder Johannes *Flierl, and from the method of tribal conversion introduced by Christian *Keysser. Under this system, the congregations themselves were made responsible for the carrying of the gospel from tribe to tribe. The first ordination of Papuan pastors took place in 1939. In 1956 the Evangelical Lutheran Church of NG, which now had a membership of 320,000, became fully independent. Since 1934, Lutherans from Australia, and since 1951, Missouri Synod Lutherans from America, have been working in NG. After the end of the second world war a multitude of missions, among them the Anglicans and the Baptists, came in and settled principally in the highlands. Not all of these recognize the work of the Lutheran Church of NG. Steps are being taken to unite all the Lutheran forces. Conversations are being held with a view to bringing into existence one single Melanesian church as a home for all the Protestants in NG.

All the missions in NG had immense difficulties at the start, until the power of the old savage heathendom was broken. Usually ten to fifteen years passed before the first converts could be baptized. After this, however, religious revivals set in, and these, if wisely handled, could lead to the conversion of whole tribes, and to a continuous process of expansion. The new converts were everywhere marked by eagerness to carry out missionary work, unless this was discouraged from above. Many volunteered for service as evangelists, and were prepared to risk their very lives among the wild heathen.

All the missions developed an elaborate school system, in order to make available to the indigenous Christians the literature of which they stood in need, and to make possible for the Papuan as such the step forward into the modern world. Professional schools have been founded. Medical missions have taken care of the worst sicknesses. Since the end of the war the Australian government has taken over responsibility for the school system, though it is possible for the missions to co-operate. In view of the immense variety of languages, it has been decided to make English the common language of instruction; this introduction of English has led to a large extent to the collapse of the old mission schools in the villages. By way of instruction in English the Papuans now have access to all the professions.

Relations between the missions and government have always been good. Only in West Irian has the taking over of the area by the Indonesian government caused some difficulties for the missions. The gravest difficulty in NG is the complete collapse of the old social order. Under pressure from the United Nations, the Australian government is setting itself to bring the Papuans out into the modern world as fast as they are able to adjust themselves to this development. There is a clash between the culture of the Stone Age and the most modern technical developments. The simple Papuan is incorporated into the modern system of work. He is so obsessed with the idea of progress that the tasks of the church appear to be of secondary importance. The old social organization is breaking up. The congregations have hardly an idea as to how they are to find a solution for their problems.

The clash of cultures has provoked, in NG as everywhere else in the South Seas, a syncretistic movement called the *Cargo cult. With their pagan outlook on the world, the Papuans expected to reap from the gospel advantages for their daily life. They are under the impression that the whites have failed to make known to them that secret of the gospel, through which the way to prosperity and riches on the basis of religion is made known. They tend to turn back to ancestor worship and to magical practices. Together with this movement, a certain messianism and *nationalism, which are anti-white in character, are coming to be diffused.

NG belongs to the regions in which the Christian mission is still in process of winning great success.

GEORG F. VICEDOM

J. W. Burton: *Modern Missions in the South Pacific* (London 1949); J. W. Dovey:

The Gospel in the South Pacific (London 1950); I. Shevill: *Pacific Conquest* (Sydney 1949); G. F. Vicedom: *Church and People in New Guinea* (London 1961); *BM* II, 645–48; *NCE* X 372f.

NEW HEBRIDES. See PACIFIC ISLANDS.

NEW JERUSALEM. See CHURCHES OF THE NEW JERUSALEM.

NEW RELIGIONS OF JAPAN. The term *Shinko Shukyo*, translated 'New Religions', is applied to the popular religious movements or sects which have risen sporadically in Japan in times of stress during the past century and more, especially following the second world war. As far as their tenets are concerned the roots are to be found in *Shinto and *Buddhism, and in a few cases even in Christianity. The innovations have chiefly to do with interpretations, rites, architecture, organization, propaganda, ministry and activities; these are calculated to appeal to the average man. The post-war mushrooming of new sects may be attributed to the new religious freedom, the discrediting of old faiths with resultant estrangement and religious vacuity, and the uncertainty and discontent following military defeat; with the crisis intensified by an intrusive culture. Because the Japanese attitude towards a religion is largely functional, and plural religious affiliation is tolerated, no serious break with traditional religious institutions is required by the NR. A possible exception to this rule is the largest sect, the *Soka Gakkai*. There are at least 170 of these sects, with about one-third each registered under Shinto and Buddhism, respectively, a few under Christianity and the rest under 'miscellaneous', with most affiliated with the 'Union of New Religious Organizations'. It is estimated that the total number of adherents does not exceed twenty millions, with several claiming a total membership in the millions. The popular following of some is witnessed to by great mass gatherings, numerous costly building projects and extensive use of mass communication media.

Certain distinctive elements characterize most of the NR. Each has its founder or his successor who often claims to be the recipient of divine revelations which give sanction to authority. Frequently the leader is endowed with a charismatic personality and is a master of human psychology. Some are of a shamanic type, whose ecstatic behaviour is little short of a paranoiac megalomania, equating themselves with the gods or the great spiritual leaders of the past. Though the relationship between believers is horizontal, that with the leader is vertical, based on the hierarchical principle of father over son. Such leaders may be regarded as *ikigami* (living gods), this not to be interpreted in strict theistic terms. They often claim miraculous powers of healing, and this plays an important role in their ministry. The most successful groups maintain very imposing headquarters and temple buildings, to which devotees are wont to resort, thereby imbibing a sense of pride and dignity and of being a part of something big. The local churches or meeting places are easy of access and open every day, with counselling service always available. In accordance with the eclectic genius of the Japanese, the central teachings of the NR are quite syncretic, though simple and closely related to everyday life. Indeed, much of the doctrine and ritual is still fluid and open to innovations. The NR are usually easy to enter and follow and monthly fees nominal, calling for little sacrifice except in the case of special appeals for the giant building funds. Much of the appeal is pragmatic, with the primary emphasis upon worldly benefits—meeting physical and material needs, with the promise of freedom from various evils such as ill-health, poverty and unhappiness in marriage; with the affluence of the leaders symbolic of what may be expected. Thus the aims are quite likely to be hedonistic, with a very optimistic view of man's ability to be happy here and now and to achieve world peace. At the local level believers gather in community groups of ten to twenty persons, where the benefits of group dynamics and therapy are available for lonely and troubled souls, with joint participation in recreational and social activities. Based on individual faith and experience, each believer is expected to become an enthusiastic witness. However, many of the activities of these sects are carried out *en masse*, with gatherings of the largest NR running into the tens of thousands at national conclaves. Though the NR are clearly rooted in Japanese folk religion and have been superficial in their initial approach, they are steadily becoming more institutionalized and sophisticated, with increasing appeal to the more intellectual middle and upper classes. Though generally regarded by Christians as a hindrance to the gospel cause, under God they may be a part of the process of preparing the soil for the growth and harvest which will inevitably follow the unprecedented sowing of the seed of the word in Japan.

GORDON K. CHAPMAN

N. S. Brannen: *Sōka Gakkai* (Richmond, Va 1968); H. N. McFarland: *The Rush Hour of the Gods—A Study of New Religious Movements in Japan* (New York 1967); H. Nakamura: *Ways of Thinking of Eastern Peoples* (Tokyo 1960); C. B. Offner and H. Van Straelen: *Modern Japanese Religions* (New York 1963); H. Thomsen: *The New Religions of Japan* (Tokyo 1963).

NEW TRIBES MISSION, THE, was founded in 1942 by Paul Fleming and several others who were burdened to take the gospel to unreached tribes around the world. Fleming was killed in a plane crash in November 1950. From the beginning this non-denominational, independent *faith mission emphasized *linguistics and indigenous NT missionary principles in its candidate training courses. In recent years the training course has been extended to two, and even to three and one-half years, depending on the background of the candidate. The founders believed God could use any Christian, regardless of his education or lack of it, if his heart was right and he was willing to give his life for tribal evangelism. This principle is still practised.

By October 1968 more than 500 missionaries were working among 65 tribes in twelve fields. More than 350 prospective missionaries were in training in the USA with additional training centres located in New Zealand, Australia, the Philippines and Brazil. Occupied fields include Panama, Venezuela, Colombia, Brazil, Bolivia, Paraguay, Japan, Philippines, Thailand, New Guinea, India and Senegal.

A result of the strong emphasis on indigenous NT churches is the establishment of several hundred mission churches with national leadership. Five complete New Testaments have been translated and printed along with individual NT books in other languages. The mission publishes *Brown Gold* (monthly), has headquarters at Woodworth, Wisconsin, USA, and is unrelated to any larger missionary association.

HAROLD LINDSELL

NEW YORK 1900. See CONFERENCES, WORLD MISSIONARY.

NEW ZEALAND. Area 103,736 sq.m. Population 2,676,919 (1966 census). Over 90% of the population is of British stock. The Maori people numbered 198,188, or 7.4% of the population in 1966. There are also some 20,000 Polynesians of recent arrival.

The Maori people are the most southerly representatives of the Malayo-Polynesian speaking race, having migrated over a period of at least 600 years prior to white settlement in the 19th century.

The Rev. Samuel *Marsden, Anglican chaplain to New South Wales, established the first mission, on Christmas Day 1814, at Rangihoua in the Bay of Islands, preaching from the text, 'Behold, I bring you glad tidings of great joy which shall be to all people'. His interpreter was his Maori friend, Ruatara. He left behind a party consisting of a carpenter, a shoemaker and a teacher, Thomas Kendall.

In 1819 the first ordained missionary, John Butler arrived at Kerikeri, and in the 1820s Henry and William Williams began work at Paihia. In 1831 a mission farm established at Waimate North, and the work extended in the north and southwards to the Waikato and Poverty Bay. The years 1840–56 saw widespread development throughout many areas of the North Island. Bishop G. A. *Selwyn became the leader and missionary statesman. By 1900, there were 69 Maori clergy.

In 1822 the first Wesleyan missionary, Samuel Leigh, arrived and opened a station at Whangaroa in 1823. This station was destroyed in intertribal conflict in January 1827 and, after a brief withdrawal to Sydney, John Hobbs and James Stack recommenced at Hokianga Harbour. The work extended rapidly along the west coast to Raglan 1834, Kawhia 1834, Kaipara 1836, Pakanae (Newark) 1837. By the 1860s nine other stations had been opened in the North Island.

In 1840, the first Christian missions in the South Island were opened by Wesleyan missionaries: James Watkin at Waikouaiti and Samuel Ironside at Port Underwood.

Roman Catholic missions commenced under Bishop *Pompallier in 1838. The first RC service was conducted at Totara Point in the Hokianga. The intense sectarian controversy in Europe was reflected in unhappy conflict in New Zealand. Bishop Pompallier travelled extensively and a considerable number of converts were made. As with the other missions, the work had a great setback in the Land Wars of the 1860s, and all priests were transferred to European parishes. Father James McDonald kept up the work after the Wars, until in the 1880s the *Mill Hill Fathers opened work in Northland, Bay of Plenty, Waikato and the King Country.

The Presbyterian Church commenced work in the Manawatu in 1844 under James Duncan, and this continued until 1894 there and in the Rangitikei. In 1895 work was opened at Taupo. It extended to Taumarunui, Nuhaka and the Urewera country, and the Bay of Plenty, with the current extensive programme. J. G. Laughton is a distinguished recent name.

All these missions trained Maori teachers and catechists, and ordained Maori ministers; and developed schools for general and technical education.

The Maori wars of the 1860s left a heritage of confusion. Maori religious and political movements drew numbers from the churches, and such movements still hold the loyalty of many. Of these the Ratana Church and Ringatu Movement numbering 21,954 and 5,275 respectively, are the largest. The major Maori churches are Anglican (51,148), Roman Catholic (28,656), Methodist (12,611), Mormon (12,179) and Presbyterian (3,947); but 21,814 refused to state their religion (1961 census).

The outlook today is brighter than for some decades, in spite of the large movement of people from rural areas to urban centres (from 10% to 50.5% in 30 years), with the resulting upset and stresses. There are some helpful educational and social service developments.

GEORGE I. LAURENSON

An Encyclopaedia of New Zealand (1966, article 'Missions', Vol. II pp.569–74 and articles on individual missionaries); L. Keys: *The Life and Times of Bishop Pompallier* (Christchurch 1957); W. Morley: *History of Methodism in New Zealand* (Wellington 1900); *Proceedings of Wesley Historical Society* (London); *N.Z. Official Year Book 1967* and *Population Census* reports (Department of Statistics, Wellington); E. Stock: *History of the Church Missionary Society in New Zealand* (Wellington 1935); H. M. Wright: *New Zealand 1769–1840* (London 1960); *BM* II, 651–55; *NCE* X, 406–08; *WKL*, 1007–09.

NEWSPAPER EVANGELISM. See CORRESPONDENCE COURSES (JAPAN).

NGWANE. See SWAZILAND.

NICARAGUA. See AMERICA, CENTRAL.

NICOLAI, ARCHBISHOP. See KASATKIN, NICOLAI IVAN.

NIGER, formerly in French West Africa, is a landlocked semi-desert republic of 459,180 sq.m. with a population (1967) of 3,546,000, including 3,500 Europeans. As with other Saharan territories, the population is almost entirely Muslim. A RC prefecture apostolic was erected in 1942; this is now the diocese of Niamey with 11,000 Catholics. Protestant missions arrived from 1927 onwards, but have met with small success; the *Mission Chrétienne d'Afrique*, or Evangelical Baptist Church, works among the Djerma tribe; *SIM congregations number twelve, and there is a small *Eglise Méthodiste* catering for African expatriates from the coastal territories. Nationals who are Protestants number under 500.

DAVID B. BARRETT

BM II, 627–29; *NCE* X, 465f.

NIGERIA. A West African republic, 356,700 sq.m. in area, bounded on the west by Dahomey, on the south by the Atlantic Ocean, on the east by Cameroon, and on the north by the territories of Chad and Niger. It is difficult to estimate the population; the most recent census gave a figure of 56 millions, but it is believed that this has been inflated by the rivalry between the various regions, and that 44 millions probably corresponds more nearly to the reality. This vast area is inhabited by more than 200 tribes, speaking a great variety of languages; it has never had any other unity than that imposed upon it by the colonial powers. The area does, however, fall into three fairly clearly defined regions—the north, running up towards the Sahara, where Islamic penetration has been powerful over many centuries, and where authority was concentrated in the hands of the great Muslim Emirs; the west, where the dominant people are the Yorubas, city-dwellers (Ibadan is the largest purely African city in the world), with a tradition of African art of unusually high development; the east, where the Ibos, hardy, thrifty and commercially-minded people, have never developed states or kingdoms on a major scale.

Contact with Europeans began in the 15th century with the coming of the Portuguese. But such contacts were intermittent, and were associated mainly with the slave-trade, Bonny, on one of the effluents of the Niger, being one of the great entrepots at which African rulers made themselves wealthy by selling their fellow-Africans to the white traders. British interest in this area developed through the 19th century, and a considerable trade in palm-oil kernels grew up. It was left to Sir George Goldie, one of the really passionate British imperialists of the 19th century, with his United Africa Company (1879) to aim at the annexation of the whole area to the British Empire. But the progress of *colonialism was very slow. In 1851 Lagos was occupied as a British colony. In 1885 a British protectorate was proclaimed over the entire coast from Lagos to the Cameroon. Only when, at the very end of the 19th century, it became clear that if Britain did not annex the territory France would do so, was the British Government stirred to declare in 1900 a protectorate over Northern N. The whole country was unified on 1 January 1914 under the British Crown. In 1960 Nigeria became an independent country within the British Commonwealth, considerable independence being reserved to the three regions. For a short period progress in the direction of democratic self-rule seemed to be extremely promising; but troubles grew, until the unity of the country was threatened by the disastrous civil war between Biafra in the east, and the federal government, the full consequences of which it is too early to estimate.

Roman Catholicism was introduced by the Portuguese in the 15th century, and there are traces of *Capuchin missions in the 17th. But all this had disappeared, and everything had to be begun again in the 19th century.

Anglican missions began when freed slaves from Sierra Leone began to return to their homeland in West N. and invited the *CMS to follow them. Henry *Townsend arrived in Abeokuta in 1842, to be followed in 1853 by David *Hinderer, who established the work at Ibadan. The British government's expedition up the Niger was accompanied by the Yoruba S. A. *Crowther, who in 1857 was sent by the CMS to open up a pioneer mission in the Niger area. In 1864 he was consecrated as the first African bishop of the Anglican Communion and held office till his death in 1891. His episcopate is still a subject of major controversy; the appointment of a European Herbert Tugwell to succeed him led to a schism, and to the formation of the first great *African independent church in the area. In 1900 the CMS advanced into northern N. The Bible was translated into Hausa (completed 1932; an earlier version of the NT 1880), one of the leaders in the enterprise being Dr W. R. S. Miller, who lived in N. for fifty years. But converts were few, and the northern missions tended to become chaplaincies to Ibo and other Christians from the south, rather than vigorous evangelistic agencies.

The British Wesleyan Methodists came in almost at the same time and for the same reason. In 1842 T. B. *Freeman was sent to organize the work, which took as its two centres Badagry and Abeokuta. This mission developed on solid rather than extensive lines. At the other end of N., the Primitive Methodists, who had worked for many years in Fernando Po, crossed over to the mainland in 1893, and set up a highly successful work on the borders of Calabar. Calabar was the main field of the Church of Scotland mission. In 1846 Hope *Waddell, who had worked for a number of years in the West Indies arrived at the mouth of the Calabar River. One of the distinguishing features of this mission, first among the Efik people and then further inland, was the participation of West Indians in the work.

The *SIM entering in 1893 was successful in penetrating northern N. by means of concentration on medical work (a notable eye hospital at Kano). The Southern

Baptists, who had first entered in 1849 and after many misfortunes returned in 1875, noted that, though it was customary to speak of 'the Muslim north', such a description did not apply to the whole area. Although this region, because of the British method of indirect rule through the Muslim chiefs and consequent discouragement of Christian missions among Muslims, was regarded as unfavourable for the development of missionary work, there were in the southern belt of the northern region pagan tribes numbering at least four million, which had never been reached by any mission. The Southern Baptists set themselves systematically, and with exemplary zeal, to open up this area. In later times other Protestant missions, too numerous to list separately, have entered the country.

From an early date Christian co-operation was well developed. As early as 1926 a Christian Council was formed for northern N. In 1950 a Christian Council for the whole of N. came into being.

RC enterprise was resumed at about the same time as the entry of the Protestant missions, the area being committed to the *Society of African Missions, The first missionaries arrived in Lagos in 1865. Beginnings were slow, this mission, like others, being decimated by the ravages of tropical disease. Notable progress came about during the episcopate of Bishop *Shanahan in the Ibo region, when converts came in in large numbers, and school work was on a major scale to match that of the Protestants. In about 1900 the *Holy Ghost Fathers spread over the border from Gabon and established themselves in the eastern region, to be strengthened in 1932 by the St. Patrick's Society for Foreign Mission.

In 1870 a Vicariate for Benin and Dahomey was established to be followed by other Vicariates. In 1950 the full hierarchy was established. In 1964 the three archbishoprics of Lagos, Onitsha and Kaduna had under them 14 other dioceses: six of the diocesan bishops in 1964 were Nigerians.

It is difficult to assess the number of Christians in N. In 1967 the RC figure is given as two millions with about 800,000 catechumens. The WCH for 1968 gives the Protestant figure as 2,523,647. These together represent about 10% of the population. But a much larger number of Nigerians return themselves as Christians, even though they have had little contact with the Christian faith and have never actually joined any church. In some areas it is said that as many as 70% of the population claim to be Christian. Progress is at present most rapid in the area of the Twi people in the north-east of the country.

N. has been prolific in the production of sects and independent churches. Reference has been made to the African Church in the Yoruba country. During the first world war Garrick Sokeni Braid proclaimed himself to be the prophet Elijah, and attracted a large following, which was not immediately dispersed on the imprisonment of the prophet. The Aladura Church of the Lord is strong in certain areas. The Cherubim and Seraphim Church has many followers in Lagos and the adjoining regions. There are a great many others, some of which have followed their adherents to distant parts of N., and even beyond its borders to other territories. The numbers belonging to these groups may stand as high as a million.

In 1965 N. had five universities. In four of these departments of religion had been set up, in which Christians of various allegiances were at work, provision being made also for the study of other religions. In most cases 80% of the students are registered as Christians. A notable piece of co-operative work was the Port Harcourt project, in which a number of Protestant groups joined together to meet the needs of the rapidly growing population of Port Harcourt, the city founded as recently as 1905, but in which, after the discovery of oil in the region, the population increased extremely rapidly. The aim of the project was to help the inhabitants on every level of personal and social existence.

A project for church union had been developed between Anglicans, Methodists and Presbyterians, more or less on the lines of the union successfully brought into being in South India in 1947. Terms of union had been agreed on, and the date fixed, 10 December 1965. But at the last moment strong objection was raised by a group of Methodist laymen in Lagos; it became clear that the Methodist rank and file were less convinced of the need of union than had been supposed. Other churches, too, may have been insufficiently aware of the meaning of union. It was agreed to postpone the union until these unexpected difficulties had been overcome.

A bitter civil war between the Ibos and the rest of N. ended in January 1970. At the time of writing it is impossible to assess fully the damage caused to the life of the nation; it is certain that it is disastrously large; clearly Christians and churches have shared to the full in the affliction of their people. The period of reconstruction will be long and exacting.

STEPHEN NEILL

J. F. A. Ajayi: *Christian Missions in Nigeria, 1841–1891: The Making of a New Elite* (London 1965); E. A. Ayandele: *The Missionary Impact on Modern Nigeria, 1842–1944* (London 1966); A. Burns: *History of Nigeria* (5th ed., London 1955); S. Crowther and J. C. Taylor: *The Gospel on the Banks of the Niger* (London 1859); J. B. Grimley and G. E. Robinson: *Church Growth in Central and Southern Nigeria* (Grand Rapids 1966); C. P. Groves: *The Planting of Christianity in Africa* (4 vols., London 1948–1958), Vol. II; H. Kaufmann: *Nigeria* (Bonn 1958); K. S. Latourette: *A History of the Expansion of Christianity* (New York 1937–1945), Vol. V, pp.435–43; Vol. VII, pp.244–46; H. W. Turner: *African Independent Church* (2 vols., London 1967); J. B. Webster: *The African Churches among the Yoruba, 1888–1922* (Oxford 1964); *BM* II, 630–38; *NCE* X, 466; *WKL*, 1023–25.

NIIJIMA, JO (1843–1890, also called NEESHIMA, JOSEPH HARDY), was born in Yedo (Tokyo), Japan, to a *samurai*, a retainer of the feudal lord of the Annaka Clan. Reared in a devout but idolatrous household, he was trained in the martial arts and Chinese classics, and studied English and Dutch. N. was intrigued by new western ideas, especially the revelation of God the Creator and Heavenly Father, of whom he read surreptitiously in a Chinese Bible. This served to free him from the bonds of Confucian filial piety and encouraged him to defy the law and escape to America, arriving at Boston in 1864. Here he was befriended by the ship's owner, Alpheus Hardy, a Christian merchant and member of the *ABCFM, who underwrote his education at Amherst College and Andover Seminary. During this period N's purpose to establish in Japan a Christian college after the New England pattern became fixed. When the Iwakura embassy visited the US and Europe in 1871, N. consented to serve as interpreter, subject to official pardon and permission to teach Christianity upon his return. This afforded him an opportunity to observe many colleges, and won the esteem and co-operation of political leaders for the achievement of his purpose. When he returned to Japan in 1874 he had the assurance of support for the college project from ABCFM and the status of a missionary. A visit to his aged parents at Annaka afforded a chance to preach the gospel and here was born the first church in the interior. Through the backing of influential friends, N. secured an excellent site for the college in Kyoto, across from the palace grounds. Official permission was given to open Doshisha ('One Purpose') College in association with the missionary, J. D. Davis; Christianity to be taught as Moral Science and Bible exegesis to be extra-curricular. In spite of opposition from local *Buddhists, college sessions began with eight students in 1875, with the later addition of 31 young *samurai* of the Kumamoto Band (see JANES, LANSING LEROY). It was organized as a Japanese institution and in time became the largest Christian college and the only one to attain university status by 1890, the year of N's death. His spirit is best revealed by his paradoxical saying, 'we must stand on our own feet but advance on our knees'. Although N's primacy was at Doshisha, his influence was the decisive factor in the formation of the Congregational Church of Japan, which had most of its ministers trained at Doshisha. N. was one of the chief instruments of the Spirit in the revivals which triggered the rapid growth of the churches in the 1880s, with Doshisha swept by the movement in 1884, characterized by many student conversions and Christian witness in the home communities. Though repeatedly offered high government positions, N. held fast to his 'one purpose', to found a Christian university which would nurture leaders for the christianizing of his people.

GORDON K. CHAPMAN

O. Cary: *History of Christianity in Japan* (New York 1909) Vol. II, pp.114–18, 137–39, 168–70, 203–04, 225, etc.; J. D. Davis: *A Sketch of the Life of Joseph Hardy Neeshima* (New York 1894); A. S. Hardy: *Life and Letters of Joseph Hardy Neeshima* (Boston 1891); W. T. Thomas: *Protestant Beginnings in Japan, 1859–1889* (Tokyo 1959), pp.48, 73–75, 94, 101–06, 114f., 131f., 146, 151–56, 168–70, 175.

NITSCHMANN, DAVID (1696–1772), born in Zauchtental, Moravia, is called 'DN, the bishop', in distinction from three other DN contemporary *Moravians. The N. family joined *Zinzendorf's Herrnhut, Saxony, in 1724. Leaving wife and children behind, DN was sent out along with J. L. *Dober to St. Thomas, Danish West Indies, where he worked as a lay preacher among the Negro slaves for just five months. Their commissioning by Zinzendorf on 21 August 1732 marked the beginning of the missionary enterprise of the Moravian Brethren, a venture with no ecclesiastical authorization or financial backing. Within 28 years from 1732 no less than 28 'fields' were opened. Overseas missions grew to become the most distinguished and most successful feature of the Herrnhut Moravians. N's consecration as the first bishop of the Brethren in

Germany by the Polish Brethren Bishop Jablonski of Berlin in 1735 linked the Herrnhut community to the historical Moravian tradition, delivered the apostolic succession to the Brethren and established the order of ministers in the Brethren church. His office was not connected with Herrnhut and indicated no jurisdiction. But on the basis of it the English parliament recognized the Moravians as a legitimate episcopal church in 1749. N. was licensed to ordain Brethren missionaries in the Moravian settlements and missions to enable them to administer baptism to non-Christians. N. travelled widely serving the Moravian cause. When in 1735–36 he led the second group of 26 Moravians sailing for America to settle in Pennsylvania, they met on board ship with John and Charles *Wesley. A significant spiritual encounter took place. N. visited St. Thomas again in 1740 and negotiated successfully for the progress of the Brethren mission on the neighbouring island of St. Croix. He died in Bethlehem (Pa.), USA.

LOTHAR SCHREINER

A. J. Lewis: *Zinzendorf, The Ecumenical Pioneer* (London 1962), ch.5; *RGG* IV, 1499.

NOBILI, ROBERT DE (1577–1656) was born in Montepulciano (province of Siena, Italy) and died at Mylapore, Madras. Together with St. Francis *Xavier, Matthew *Ricci and Alexander de *Rhodes he may well be called the ablest and most original missionary of his time. In 1597 he joined the *Jesuits despite opposition from his rich and influential family. Having finished his studies, he was sent, at his request, to India in 1605; after a short period at the Fisher Coast he went to Madura in 1606. When he found that at Madura and practically everywhere else in India outside the Portuguese influence, few converts were being made, because Christians were regarded as Portuguese and despised, he initiated a new method. He applied himself to the study of Tamil, Sanskrit and Telugu, of Indian philosophy and religious literature. He identified himself completely with the *sannyāsīs*—holy men of India—and even went as far as adopting their dress, diet and some of their customs. To do this effectively, he separated himself from his companion, although keeping in contact with him, and built a dwelling in the Brahmin quarter where he received all those who wished to talk to him. He would explain the Christian message, debate with them, and discuss certain errors he had found in Indian writings. He devoted most of his time to finding points of agreement between Christianity and *Hinduism. In the *caste system, as he found it, he saw two elements: one superstitious, therefore to be eliminated, the other social-psychological, which could be retained by Christians. In this way he received several high-caste Indians into the Catholic church. His whole method, however, led to an attack on him and his converts by some of his own companions and the hierarchy of India. They accused him of watering down Christianity, because he was afraid of opposition if he preached the full Christian message. But he defended himself very ably, and his new method was allowed by Pope Gregory XV in the Apostolic Constitution *Romanae Sedis antistes* (31 January 1623), which settled the matter temporarily. The number of his converts has often been exaggerated. In reality he baptized about 600 high-caste Indians. But he did not neglect the lower castes. For them he introduced the Pandārasvāmi missionaries who devoted themselves completely to work among the depressed classes. He was an active writer. His main works are: *Gnanopadesam* (Spiritual Teaching); *Attuma Nirunayam* (Disquisition on the Soul); *Agnāna Nivāranam* (Dispelling of Ignorance) and *Tivviya Mādirigai* (The Divine Model). His motto was: To open the door of India to Christ. After working 38 years in Madura he was ordered to leave by his Portuguese Superior, and went to Jaffna. In 1646 he went to Mylapore, spending his last years almost blind and in great poverty.

ARTHUR MCCORMACK, MHM

V. Cronin: *A Pearl to India* (London 1959); *LTK* VII, 1015f.; *NCE* X, 477–79.

NOMMENSEN, LUDWIG INGWER

(1834–1918), 'apostle of the Bataks' in Sumatra, was born in the island of Nordstrand in Schleswig, at that time under the Danish crown. After a fundamental faith experience he joined the *Rhenish Missionary Society of Barmen and arrived at Barus, north-west coast, in 1862 to stay in the island for a lifetime. When N. was not permitted to settle in that area, he worked with earlier missionaries in Angkola. Under protection of his later friend, the chief Pontas Lumbantobing, champion of the new Christian era, he settled in the independent Silindung valley in 1864. Further main events concur with the rise of the Batak church. After the first group of families was baptized, N. composed a church order and was joined in 1866 by P. H. Johannsen, teacher, writer and linguist. When after years of severest contest with the tribal religion and the *datu*-priests, church membership reached 2,000 in 1876, N. felt convinced that the mission was able to survive further opposition. He drafted a more *indigenous church order, used until 1930, and was appointed Ephorus of the Rhenish Batak mission in 1881. After the first three pastors were ordained in 1885, N. moved north to take up *pioneer work in the Lake Toba plain. He directed the *mass movement into the growing 'people's church' and extended evangelism northward again in 1903, anxious to have the Simelungun-Batak area penetrated before it turned to *Islam. N. lost his wife and four children, married again in 1892, but by the death of his second wife in 1909 was left with the care of three motherless children. He was made honorary Dr Theol. of Bonn in 1904, officer of the Dutch order of Orange-Nassau in 1911.

N's character stands out for his steadfast singleness of purpose and immovable trust in God. His indomitable resolution to advance made him a leader as much as his humility showed his spiritual power. N. wanted missionaries 'who take God at his word, who count with God as they would count with numbers, and who in joining battle already look forward to victory'—a self-portrait. N's work shows a rare unity of strategy, organization and pioneering in Christian mission, founded on faith as deep as it was simple. In his vision he seized the unique opportunity of leading the whole people, surrounded by advancing Islam, from heathenism to the gospel 'now'. In the beginning individual baptism was the rule, as was clanwise baptism in the later period. He encountered the people with untiring patience free from any polemics. From the outset he instructed and commissioned elders in order to root the church into the closely woven village community, preserving their social structure (*adat*). For the growth and self-support of the local churches and their schools he introduced a teacher-preacher 'order'—which numbered 637 men in 1910. He used the pivotal influence of the tribal chiefs for the expansion and upbuilding of the church. N. translated Luther's *Small Catechism* (1874) and the NT (1878). He wrote countless letters, a few of which are extant. When he died, the Batak church had 34 pastors, 788 teacher-preachers, 180,000 members in more than 500 local churches. His name lives on in the Batak church's Nommensen University, established in 1954.

LOTHAR SCHREINER

N. de Waard: *Pioneer in Sumatra* (London 1962); J. Warneck: *Ludwig Ingwer Nommensen, ein Lebensbild* (Barmen 1934[4]). *RGG* IV, 1508.

NON-CHRISTIAN RELIGIONS. See HISTORY OF RELIGIONS; COMPARATIVE STUDY OF RELIGIONS, and each religion by name.

NON-CHURCH MOVEMENT is the name popularly given to a group of Japanese Christians who look on themselves as disciples of Kanzo *Uchimura (1861–1930) and his followers. The movement rejects the historic developments in the life of the church, and seeks to affirm the church of the NT. It includes a large number of scholars and university teachers, and two presidents of Tokyo university were amongst its leaders. There is no definite membership, and the Christian sacraments are not observed, although many associated with the movement have been baptized in regular churches. It reflects in part the highly individualistic character of 19th century Protestant Christianity, and in its forms of prayer and worship displays a simple Protestant piety. The chief emphasis is on biblical study and exposition, and some of Japan's best biblical scholars belong to the movement. As the Bible lecture is central, the meetings are more like university lectures than church gatherings, and the ancient Chinese and Japanese reverence for the teacher is very marked—with a respected teacher drawing to himself a large group of disciples. It is estimated that members number about 50,000—but the influence of the movement through its lectures and literature is very wide. Members are sometimes called the 'cross-legged Christians' because they sit and act in a traditional Japanese way, and the founder was a strong opponent of a vague 'universal' Christianity. His aim, and that of his followers, was not the creation of a church, but the christianization of Japan.

RAYMOND J. HAMMER

R. P. Jennings: *Jesus, Japan and Kanzo Uchimura* (Tokyo 1958).

NON-DENOMINATIONAL MISSIONS. See INTERDENOMINATIONAL AND NON-DENOMINATIONAL SENDING AGENCIES.

NON-PROFESSIONAL MISSIONARY. The professional missionary is the man or woman who goes to some other country with a view to devoting all his time and energy to proclaiming the gospel by word and action. That is the traditional understanding of the word 'missionary'. The labourer being worthy of his hire, the support of such missionaries is generally accepted as the responsibility of the church or society which 'sends' them. In the past these 'sending' churches or societies have been 'western' and the

missionaries have, in the first instance, generally been westerners. Today two developments have taken place or are taking place. Western *imperialism, as earlier centuries knew it, is in retreat. Political independence is the goal of every nation. This means that in many places the western missionary is either suspect for his association with a past imperialism and resides on sufferance, or he is not allowed in the country at all. In the second place, the local church is itself beginning to accept responsibility for many of the tasks originally accepted as the duty of the foreign missionary. For these two reasons, and also because of a growing recognition by Christians that a true witness to Christ must be given in all human occupations, the idea of the N-PM is being explored. Such a man or woman will work under the conditions imposed by his contract with a business or commercial firm, with a university or welfare agency. But at the same time the N-PM will seek by example, and where possible by word as well, to show the meaning and relevance of the Christian faith. And he will make a point of identifying himself with the local church if there is one. This is a development which may prove to be of very great importance indeed. In some places it may be the only form which Christian witness can take. It may be the only way in which a 'foreigner' can help the local church to remember that the Christian community is truly international. Meanwhile it remains to be seen if such an idea can be expressed in any form of organized effort or if in its very nature it must remain wholly spontaneous. Perhaps the greatest difficulty is to discover how those so engaged can secure the wealth of prayer support which lies behind the organized missionary movement.

MAX WARREN

Y. Congar, OP: *Lay People in the Church* (London 1959); W. A. Visser't Hooft, ed.: *The New Delhi Report* (London 1961), see Appendix pp.258f., 'The role of the Christian Layman abroad in the Mission of the Church'; C. Mackie and C. C. West, eds.: *The Sufficiency of God* (London 1963),

see essay by H.–R. Weber, 'The Laity— its Gifts and Ministry', pp.187–96; S. C. Neill and H.–R. Weber, eds.: *The Layman in Christian History* (Philadelphia 1963).

NORFOLK ISLAND: See PACIFIC ISLANDS.

NORTH AFRICA MISSION. An international, interdenominational and evangelical mission, with a total missionary personnel (in 1968) of 130. Its work lies in the so-called Barbary States (Morocco, Algeria, Tunisia and Libya), which have a total population of approximately 25,000,000. The population is almost entirely Muslim and the governments of these countries are committed to the Muslim faith. North-west Africa was Christian until the Muslim invasion swept across the country in the 7th century. Protestant missions began in 1881 with the founding of the Mission to the Kabyles. This quickly expanded into the NAM which now incorporates also the Algiers Mission Band and the Southern Morocco Mission. There is a small hospital in Tangier and there are nurses and midwives in other places. A growing radio and correspondence work is centred in Marseilles, which broadcasts the gospel, publishes a news-sheet in Arabic, and carries on Bible correspondence courses. The work faces two main difficulties: (a) the prejudice of all Muslim people against the preaching of the cross and the deity of Christ; (b) the close-knit social structure which makes it difficult for a Muslim to confess Christ without becoming a social outcast. There are, nevertheless, believers in ones and two's all over the country, and some groups which function as local churches.

The mission holds membership in the *IFMA.

The secretary-general's office is at Bâtiment Y, Loubassane, 13 Aix-en-Provence, France.

A. DOUGLAS PILCHER

NORTH AMERICAN INDIANS. See AMERICA, NORTH; CANADA; UNITED STATES OF AMERICA.

NORTH BORNEO. See MALAYSIA.

NORTH, FRANK MASON (1850–1935), author of the hymn 'Where cross the crowded ways of life', occupied a central position in world missions and the *ecumenical movement in America during the first quarter of the 20th century. After nineteen years in pastorates of the Methodist Episcopal Church in or near New York, he became corresponding secretary of the New York City Church Extension and Missionary Society. Here, for two decades, he directed a network of metropolitan missions and challenged the church to its urban responsibility. From 1912 to 1924 he held the same office in the Methodist Board of Foreign Missions, serving with Bishop William F. *Oldham and S. Earl Taylor.

Meanwhile, N. had helped to organize the Methodist Federation for Social Service and the Federal Council of the Churches of Christ in America. To the latter, at its founding session in 1908, he presented a report on the Church and Modern Industry which became the historic 'Social Creed of the Churches'. After chairing the commission on the Church and Social Service (with such colleagues as Rauschenbusch, Shailer Mathews, Josiah Strong and Herbert Welch), N. was elected chairman of the Executive Committee of the Federal Council in 1912, and president of the council during the critical war years of 1916–20. He attended the *Edinburgh Missionary Conference of 1910, served on the Continuation Comittee, and chaired the drafting committee for the Constitution of the *IMC, adopted in 1921.

N. published no books, but scores of sermons, speeches, and editorials, especially in *The Christian City*, and a significant series of four articles on Socialism and Christianity in *Zion's Herald* (14 January to 4 February, 1891).

CREIGHTON LACY

C. Lacy: *Frank Mason North: His Social and Ecumenical Mission* (New York 1967).

NORTH GERMAN MISSIONARY SOCIETY, THE, owes its existence to several small circles of friends of the 19th century Awakening and of the *Basel Mission, in Bremen and other North German towns, who in 1836 in Hamburg constituted a mission society which was to have its roots 'neither in Wittenberg nor in Geneva nor in Rome but in Jerusalem and on the Mount of Olives'. As this principle was in contrast to the growing confessional revival, the mission almost foundered on the rocks of Lutheran opposition. In 1851 it was reconstituted in Bremen and has since then retained its non-denominational character. Of its earlier fields only West Africa remained, where after many hardships—27 missionaries had died by 1880—a solid foundation was laid for a Protestant church among the Ewe people. While the NGMS always remained comparatively small, it has produced one of the most remarkable 19th century missiologists (F. M. Zahn) and two renowned Africanists (J. Spieth, D. Westermann). In 1953 the mission joined a co-operative German missionary effort in Japan and has more recently entered into a joint church and mission pioneer scheme in Togo. In 1967 it was supporting seven missionaries.

H.-W. GENSICHEN

NORTHERN RHODESIA. See ZAMBIA.

NORTHFIELD CONFERENCES. Northfield, a small town in rolling country of northern Massachusetts, USA, was the birthplace and lifetime home of Dwight L. *Moody, America's premier evangelist of the 19th century. Moody believed strongly in Christian education; he founded at Northfield in 1879 a seminary for girls and at Mt. Hermon, four miles south, a school for boys. The buildings and the beautiful grounds were used for conferences in vacation periods. The first Northfield Christian Workers' Conference, often called the Northfield Bible Conference, was opened by Moody in 1880 with 300 in attendance. Student conferences met at Mt. Hermon and here during a month-long gathering in 1886, under the inspiration of Moody, the *Student Volunteer Movement for Foreign Missions was born. One hundred of the 251 college students present dedicated themselves to missionary service abroad. The number of volunteers grew rapidly in response to the watchword, 'the evangelization of the world in this generation', and the movement spread to other lands. John R. *Mott served as chairman of the continuing organization until 1920. In 1891 the first Quadrennial Convention of the SVM was held. Since Moody's death in 1899 Bible and missionary conferences have continued to meet at the Northfield schools.

F. W. PRICE

J. F. Findlay, Jr.: *Dwight L. Moody: American Evangelist* (Chicago 1969); W. R. Moody: *D. L. Moody* (New York 1939).

NYASALAND. See MALAWI.

O

OBJECTIVES OF MISSIONARY WORK. See AIM OF MISSIONS; THEOLOGY OF MISSION.

OBLATES OF MARY IMMACULATE (OMI) were founded at Aix (France) in 1816 by Père Charles-Joseph-Eugène de Mazenod (born 1782, Bishop of Marseilles 1837, died 1861).

The first aim of the Congregation, called Missionaires de Provence, was to repair the spiritual havoc caused by the French Revolution. So they worked for the revival of the faith among the rural and industrial populations, giving missions and retreats. In 1826 the Congregation received papal recognition and its name was changed to its present form. In 1841 the Congregation was asked to take its share in the world mission and sent its first missionaries to Canada. In 1847 the Oblates went to Ceylon and in 1850 to South Africa (Natal). At present they are working in all five continents. One of their main tasks is also the direction of seminaries and universities (e.g. Ottawa and Roma, Lesotho), and they have been, and still are, prominent in the field of *missiology (e.g. the *Bibliotheca Missionum* was founded and is continued by the OMI—so far twenty-one volumes have been published). In 1966 they had nearly 8,000 members of whom some 3,000 are working in the world missions.

B. CORLEY, OMI

F. Veuillot: *Les Oblates de Marie Immaculée* (Paris 1946); *NCE* X, 611f.

OLDER CHURCHES. This term hardly admits of exact definition. It came into use only after the term *'younger churches' had come into currency after the *Jerusalem Missionary Conference. Clearly the reference is to the strong and wealthy churches of the west, in countries where the greater part of the population is Christian in name at least, and the prevailing culture has undergone profound Christian influences over a long period of time. But this is not a matter of age; the ancient churches of the east are far older than those of the greater part of Europe, and owe their present weakness only to the accident of having been subjected for many centuries to Muslim domination. A more accurate term would be 'sending churches', but now that so many of the younger churches are themselves sending out their own missionaries, this term also seems to be already out of date. But some term is needed to express the difference between those churches which have come into existence as a result of the modern missionary enterprise, and those which were engaged in that enterprise. As long as this distinction is needed, it is likely that the terms 'older' and 'younger' churches will continue to be used, though with increasing irritation on the part of the younger churches.

STEPHEN NEILL

OLDHAM, JOSEPH HOULDSWORTH (1874–1969), one of the greatest pioneers of the contemporary *ecumenical movement, was born in Bombay, India, and died in England. After studies at Oxford and Edinburgh, O. spent three years as secretary of the *YMCA in Lahore, India. His first major task was the organization of the first *World Missionary Conference held at Edinburgh in 1910, a task he carried through with such brilliance that it seemed self-evident that he should become the first secretary of the Continuation Committee of the conference (1910–21), and of the *IMC when it came into being (1921–38). O. was also for many years editor of the *International Review of Missions, which soon came to be recognized as the most distinguished missionary periodical in the world. During the years following the first world war O. took the lead in persuading the British government to permit the return of German missionaries to the territories from which they had been ex- pelled. He devoted much attention to the problems of Africa, and became a trusted adviser of the Colonial Office, particularly in matters of African education. He was one of the first in England to judge rightly the menace of the rise of Nazi power in Germany. It was he who organized the Oxford Conference on Church, Community and State (1937) which was specially concerned with this problem. O. had a remarkable gift for seeing the direction in which Christian thought was moving, and for spotting in advance the young men and women who were likely to become leaders in Christian thought and action. This side of his work found expression in the *Christian Newsletters*, which he published from 1938 onwards, and in the Christian Frontier Council of which he was chairman from 1942 to 1947. O. was hindered by the deaf- ness from which he suffered for more than fifty years from becoming a great public figure like John R. *Mott; in the last thirty years of his life he was not known personally to many of the younger genera- tion of ecumenical enthusiasts. It is, however, certain that no man has made a greater contribution to the development of the modern ecumenical movement. A deep, inner, devotional life, never obtruded, was the power behind everything that he did.

Among the many books which he wrote, *Christianity and the Race Problem* (1924), *The Church and its Function in Society* (with W. A. Visser't Hooft, 1937), and *Life is Commitment* (1953) may be mentioned.

STEPHEN NEILL

A biography is in preparation; see also *RGG* IV, 1624f.; *WKL*, 1075.

OLDHAM, WILLIAM F. (1854–1937), was born in Bangalore, India, on 13 December 1854, the son of a British army officer, and educated at Madras Christian College. He served for a time as a govern- ment engineer and surveyor. Following his conversion and call to the ministry at Poona, O. proceeded to the USA to complete college and theological training and then returned to India for missionary

service. Appointed to found the Methodist mission in Singapore, 1885, he was to become one of the best known 'inter- national Methodist circuit riders serving his church in Asia, USA and Latin America'. On three continents and in four major capacities, O. helped mould the missionary service of the Methodist church—as a pioneer missionary in Malaysia, as a missionary bishop in India, Malaysia and the Philippines, as a corresponding secretary of the Board of Foreign Missions, and finally for 12 years as episcopal leader of all Methodist work in Latin America. In India, Malaysia and several Latin American countries there are churches and schools named in his honour.

O. founded the chair of missions and comparative religions at Ohio Wesleyan University. He was the author of *Thoburn— Called of God* (New York 1918); *India, Malaysia and the Philippines* (New York 1914); and *Malaysia—Nature's Wonderland* (New York 1907).

J. HARRY HAINES

DAB XXII, 449f.

ORDINATION. From the earliest times it has been the custom in the church of Christ that certain believers should be set apart in the congregation for special ministries of oversight, edification and service. Originally the call to such ministries came from the Christian fellowship, acting, as was believed, under the guidance of the Holy Spirit; the response of the one so called was obedience, without regard to any special inward feeling of vocation. Introduction to each form of ministry was by the biblical sign of the laying on of hands. Until the Reformation of the 16th century, no other essential form of O. was known.

This article deals only with the problem of O. in the so-called *'younger churches'.

In the ancient Indian church of the *Thomas Christians, priests were ordained by the bishop to serve in a particular parish; this union was lifelong, and transfer of a priest from one parish to another was unknown. Priests were married men; but, if the wife died, a priest could not marry again. Modifications in these ancient customs began to come in only as the result of influences from the west from the 16th century on.

Great variety is to be observed in Roman Catholic practice. A seminary for the training of secular priests was founded in Goa shortly after the Portuguese occupation in 1510, and a large number of young men were ordained. But the insistence on celibacy caused serious difficulties, and the gravest objections were raised to the moral character of a number of the men thus ordained. By reaction, the *Jesuits maintained the most rigid opposition to premature ordinations in Asia and elsewhere. In the 170 years of the existence of the Madura mission, not one single Indian was raised to the priesthood. The same was true in the great Jesuit missions in Paraguay, the 'Guarani republic'. This prejudice lingered very long. It led to the resignation of the young *Vicar Apostolic of Coimbatore, de Marion *Brésillac, in 1854, when he had failed in ten years to shake the prejudices of his French colleagues. A change in attitude was brought about only by very firm action on the part of successive popes; the *Missionary Encyclicals of Gregory XV, Pius XI and Pius XII compelled the RC missions to take in hand the creation of an indigenous ministry, and eventually hierarchy.

In the world of Protestant missions even greater confusion has naturally reigned.

The first Protestant missionary in India, *Ziegenbalg, saw that an Indian church could not come into being without an Indian clergy, and therefore from 1709 onwards pleaded that a member of the mission in India should be given power to ordain. From 1733 onwards the Tranquebar missionaries ordained a small number of Indian pastors, always men of considerable experience in the work though without much special training, and always by the laying on of hands.

The British missions seem to have started out with the view that any 'native' minister must have received the same training as a missionary. The African, Philip Quaque, had been ordained in the 18th century, but only after many years' residence in England. The revolutionary change came with the Tinnevelly proposal that candidates for the ministry should be thoroughly trained in their own language, and then fully ordained. The success of this method was so great (1850 onwards) that an Indian ordained ministry was rapidly created. The example was followed by other missions in India and in other parts of the world, and is still in vogue in many areas today. In Uganda Bishop A. R. *Tucker ordained a number of men on the basis not of wide theological knowledge, but of tried Christian virtue and status in the community.

Anglicans, Lutherans and Presbyterians have held much the same view of ordination as the introduction to permanent and whole-time service in the church. Methodists, Baptists and others have held a rather different view, with correspondingly diverse practices. In India, faced with the problems of a mass movement, the British Methodists, rather than lower their standards of ordination, annually licensed a number of village 'pastors' to minister the Lord's Supper, without any act of ordination. Some missions in Africa give the title 'pastor' to those who in other churches would be called 'catechists' or 'evangelists'; in some cases this title carries with it the right to minister the sacraments, in others not.

No adequate survey has yet been made of these diversities of practice or of the diverse theologies that underlie them. Clearly, the question of ministry and of the nature of ordination plays a highly significant part in all plans for Christian reunion. Frequently dispute centres on the question of episcopal ordination and 'succession' in the ministry. This is unfortunate. Differences about ministry and ordination arise from radically different understandings of the nature of the church. Only when the doctrine of the church has been settled is it possible usefully to discuss the question of ordination, and of the status and authority of the ordained minister in the church.

STEPHEN NEILL

Y. Allen: *A Seminary Survey* (New York 1960); J. Beckmann, OSB, ed.: *Der einheimische Klerus in Geschichte und Gegenwart* (Schoneck-Beckenried 1950); A. Huonder: *Der einheimische Klerus* (Freiburg 1909); The Tambaram Series, Vol. IV, *The Life of the Church* (Oxford 1939).

ORIENT CRUSADES. See OVERSEAS CRUSADES, INC.

ORIENTAL MISSIONARY SOCIETY (The Inter-American Missionary Society in Latin America) is an evangelical, international, interdenominational society with fields in Japan, Korea, Formosa, Hong Kong, India, Greece, Brazil, Colombia, Ecuador and Haiti. Founded in 1901 by Charles Cowman, it emphasizes extensive and intensive evangelism, Bible training institutions and the establishment of *indigenous churches. It was the first society systematically to reach every home in an entire nation (Japan's 10,300,000 homes in 1912–17). Its 222 missionaries, over 1,000 national workers, and 140,771 members of organized churches seek to maintain a passion for winning men to Christ, total dependence on the Holy Spirit, and a hunger for revival. It has twelve Bible schools and seminaries, 72 orphanages with 11,567 children, four beggar homes with 729 children, one boys' town with 486 boys, four schools for blind and deaf mutes, ten widows' homes, twelve baby homes, three leper colonies with 1,030 inmates, 54 day nurseries with 3,790 children, five medical centres, one international radio station; and 197 feeding stations care for 74,500 people daily.

Its worldwide prayer movement, with over 2,000 prayer groups, is called World Intercessors. Its international lay movement is Men for Missions. Its world headquarters is at 1200 Fry Road, Greenwood, Indiana 46142, USA. It has offices in Australia, Britain, Canada, New Zealand and South Africa. It is a member of *EFMA.

HAROLD LINDSELL

ORIENTATION FOR MISSIONARIES. See PREPARATION OF MISSIONARIES.

ORINOCO RIVER MISSION, THE, was founded in 1920 by Dan V. Eddings as a non-denominational *faith mission operating in Venezuela, South America. It was incorporated in 1924 in California, USA. Its work is largely evangelism and church planting, and includes the operation of a Bible institute and a book store. The mission maintains a motor launch on the Orinoco River for evangelism and works among several Indian tribes of southern Venezuela. The mission supports more than fifty missionaries, has an annual income of more than $200,000, and publishes the *Orinoco Outlook, News* and *Prayer and Praise Letter*. It is a member of *IFMA and maintains headquarters, c/o P.O. Box 611, South Pasadena, California 91030, USA.

HAROLD LINDSELL

ORPHANED MISSIONS. The term OM designates those missions and missionaries cut off from their home base of support during the two world wars and who became, figuratively, orphans.

During the first world war, German missionaries in many parts of Africa, in India, and in the Pacific Islands were removed from their work. Some were interned, but most were repatriated. Funds from British and American churches were channelled, through the structures that were to become the *IMC, to the missionary councils in China and India which sustained, or provided alternative coverage for German work there. Also, Lutheran societies in Scandinavia and the USA provided funds and additional workers to maintain what the Germans had begun. The most seriously affected missions were those in Africa. Here was the first example of international, interdenominational support across warring lines to maintain the missions of those from enemy nations.

Much more vast were the similar efforts undertaken during the second world war, chiefly by the IMC and the *Lutheran World Federation. During the 1930s the IMC and certain member-bodies already had aided German missions when for some months they could transmit no German funds overseas. But with the outbreak of the second world war in 1939, some 1700 German missionaries were completely cut off from home support. The majority were in British territories. Interned, they were quickly released to resume their work, yet all were penniless. French Protestant missions also were severly affected. Then, with Russia's invasion of Finland, Finnish missionaries in Asia and Africa were 'orphaned'. Plans made by the IMC and its members in July 1939 immediately went into operation. From around the world support came for the stranded missions and missionaries.

With the German *Blitzkrieg* (invasion of Holland, Belgium and France) in 1940, all continental European Protestant missions, except those from Switzerland and Sweden, became orphaned. Their missionaries numbered 3,500, and their churches included 22% of Protestant Christians in Asia and Africa. The US committee of the LWF took reponsibility for Europe's 54 Lutheran missions, and the IMC cared for the other 114 missions. Both bodies administered their funds separately, but the LWF always reported its money for inclusion in the Orphaned Missions Fund totals. This noteworthy operation continued throughout the war and managed to maintain most of those missions that had been functioning in 1939 on a total annual budget of $4.5 million. Yet Orphaned MF contributions never quite reached $1 million annually.

Sustaining this work could never have been achieved without the enlarged contributions of the Asian and African churches, the heroic self-denial of the missionaries, and several government grants, most notably that of China which

from 1943 provided a doubled allowance on currency exchange for missions.

So vast were war's dislocations and so extensive the rehabilitation required by the missions involved, that the Orphaned MF had to continue until 1952. In the thirteen years of the Orphaned MF, well over $10 million was collected and distributed, of which 90% came from North American churches. Of the latter more than 50% came from Lutheran sources.

In concept and achievement the Orphaned MF was unique in the history of the church and provided visible evidence of the reality of a growing world Christian community.

W. RICHEY HOGG

W. R. Hogg: *Ecumenical Foundations* (New York 1952), pp.167–72, 269f., 304–18; K. S. Latourette and W. R. Hogg: *World Christian Community in Action: World War II and Orphaned Missions* (New York 1949); *WKL*, 1588f.

ORTHODOX MISSIONS. See MISSIONS, ORTHODOX.

OVERSEAS CRUSADES, INC. (formerly known as Orient Crusades), rose out of the missionary ministry of its founder Dick Hillis. He first went to China in 1933 under the *CIM (OMF), spending most of his seventeen years there in the Province of Honan in Central China.

In 1950 Hillis led a team of missionaries to Formosa to preach to the Chinese Nationalist troops. This small beginning led to the formation of a missionary service organization first known as Orient Crusades and then OC, Inc. The purpose of the mission is to awaken, train and mobilize the national church for effective growth and continuous witness. The motto of the mission is 'Every heart without Christ a mission field, and every heart with Christ a missionary'.

Methods used include radio, literature, personal evangelism, city-wide crusades, village training evangelism, Bible correspondence courses, sports evangelism and pastors' conferences.

OC now has missionaries in the Philippines, Vietnam, Formosa, Mexico, Argentina, Columbia, Brazil and Greece. Dr Dick Hillis is the General Director and the international headquarters are at 265 Lytton Avenue, Palo Alto, California, USA. The mission is a member of *EFMA. The official USA publication is the *Cable* (bi-monthly).

HAROLD LINDSELL

OVERSEAS MISSIONARY FELLOW-SHIP. See CHINA INLAND MISSION.

OWEN, WALTER EDWIN (1878–1945), son of an army warrant-officer, was brought up in Northern Ireland. After leaving school O. worked in a library, continuing his education through night-classes, and in 1903 offered his services to the *CMS. After a year's training he was ordained deacon, and sailed for Uganda. From 1904 to 1918 he gained wide experience working in different parts of Uganda. Appointed Archdeacon of Kavirondo (western Kenya) in 1918, O. found himself responsible for organizing a new, still weak but rapidly growing church. He learned the two languages of the area, and threw himself into evangelistic and social work. Never a conventional missionary, he became from the 1920s a controversial figure in Kenya because of his outspoken opposition to legislation which he regarded as unjust to Africans, such as the hut-tax and forced labour. He asserted the right of the missionary as a citizen to take part in politics, and was misunderstood by his colleagues as well as by government officials and settlers. But he was just as outspoken in denouncing wrongs he saw in African customs. When war broke out in 1939 O. offered to stay on, though past retiring age, and was engaged on revision of the Luo Prayer Book when he died at Limuru in 1945.

DAVID B. BARRETT

C. G. Richards: *Archdeacon Owen of Kavirondo* (Nairobi n.d.).

OXFORD   GROUP   MOVEMENT. See MORAL REARMAMENT.

P

PACIFIC CONFERENCE OF CHURCHES. See REGIONAL AGENCIES FOR CO-OPERATION; REGIONAL CONFERENCES.

PACIFIC ISLANDS (excluding Hawaii and New Guinea). Oceania consists of three groups of islands, as indicated in general by their location and the ethnic origin of their inhabitants: Polynesia in the east, Melanesia in the west, and Micronesia north of the equator. Portuguese ships touched at some of the islands in the 16th century and Dutch ships in the 17th, but not until the 18th was exploration of the area seriously undertaken. Wallis, Bougainville, Cook, La Perouse, Kotzebue and others visited islands and reported their experiences and findings to their homelands.

The explorers were soon followed by traders, sealers, whalers and ships sailing to Asiatic ports. These used the islands as places for refreshment and supplies. They left behind them a trail of shipwrecked or deserting seamen, many of whom were low riff-raff or criminals, and the diseases, fire-arms and customs of the west. Among the men who survived to live on the islands were a few who, because of their knowledge of native languages and ways were of help to the missionaries when they arrived.

Moved by reports about the islands, the *LMS in 1796 sent out a company of missionaries, consisting of 30 men, some with wives and children; four were ordained ministers, the others artisans. The plan was to establish a self-sustaining community and convert the inhabitants to the ways of that community. The majority of the group landed at Tahiti in the Society Islands, a number went to Tongatabu in the Tongas, and one man went to the Marquesas. The situation the group faced was so different from the plan that had been envisioned that discouragement set in. Some of those on Tahiti left for

Australia, three on Tongatabu were killed and the man in the Marquesas escaped to England. Those who remained persisted, learned the language, and through the favour and support of a chief won converts to the church, the power of that chief over neighbouring chiefs being enhanced by his acceptance of the new religion.

Among the reinforcements the LMS sent out in 1817 was John *Williams. He began work on the island of Raiatea. From there he moved westward, launching Christian enterprises on a number of nearby islands both by his own efforts and by those of Christian islanders whom he took with him. Native teachers proved to be the most effective missionaries throughout the entire area, carrying the gospel during the course of the years to Rurutu in the Australs, Aitutaki in the Cook Islands, Samoa, Wallis Island, Niue and the Penrhyn group. By 1839 Williams had reached the New Hebrides, where, on the island of Erromanga, he was killed. He had dreamed of carrying the Christian message to all of Oceania through the agency of native leaders and a small mission staff.

In 1882 the Wesleyan Methodist Church, urged by the Methodists in New South Wales, sent missionaries to the Tonga Islands. Some years later men from that mission staff went to the Fiji Islands at the request of a chief, lived in a community of Tongans there and started work among the Fijians.

When the missionaries arrived they found the islanders living in small tribal groups, each with its own chief or head man. Warfare was endemic as· one chief tried to extend his power over others. While a tribe gave a measure of unity and support to its members, life was brutal and uncertain. Cannibalism was practised. Infanticide, abortion, theft and murder were common. The work habits of the people were unorganized and dilatory. The motives of fear, suspicion and self-interest were strong factors in behaviour. The undependability of the people made dealing with them difficult. And their earlier experiences with white men made them distrustful of all approaches except as such might be of advantage to them.

The missionaries set out to transform the life of the people, to eradicate the evils which they saw and to establish as far as possible the kind of orderly existence which they knew. To them their ways were right, God-given, and the means by which men might receive God's favour. They worked through their powers of persuasion and the example of their own lives. They set up in the islands the manner of life to which they were accustomed and urged the inhabitants to copy their ways. They learned the native languages, reduced them to writing, printed books, started schools and taught as many of the people as would submit to instruction. They set up churches and conducted worship among themselves; they preached to the people and urged them to give up their native gods and turn to the one true God. They publicly condemned behaviour that was repugnant to them and on occasion tried to stop by personal interposition actions they abhorred. And they suffered with patience indignities, persecution and death at the hands of the islanders. Through the relationships they established with tribal chiefs they were able to effect changes in island life, for when they won a chief to the church he brought his people with him. They became involved in the political affairs of the people; taught chiefs about law, wrote legal codes and planned enforcement procedures. They were on occasion involved in inter-tribal warfare, advising a chief who had embraced Christianity. Inevitably they became implicated in trade both between themselves and the islanders and that which took place between the islanders and the visiting ships.

The missionaries broke into the social and political structure of island life and worked a transformation in it through their own western moral and religious ways. They could not and did not turn the people into copies of themselves but they did succeed in bringing about a more orderly, person-regarding society than had previously existed. On some of the islands the tribes which were converted became small Christian kingdoms with rulers who defended the faith: Pomare in Tahiti, Thakombau in Fiji and *Taufaahau in Tonga. There was nothing ideal about any of this, for there were many relapses and always present the setting of earlier life.

There was continual intrusion into the work the missionaries were doing by ships from the west; the sailors and many of the ship captains had little use for the aims of the missionaries or for their achievements, and the two were often at odds with each other. On occasion the ship masters rescued missionaries when their circumstances got out of hand, but more often the missionaries, working through the native chiefs, opposed the actions of the sailors and tried to make them conform to the laws: efforts which usually failed.

After the close of the Napoleonic era, during which the Roman Catholic church had sustained serious losses in public interest, territory and personnel, there was a revival of religion in France. One aspect of this was the formation of new missionary orders. The congregation of the Picpus Fathers was confirmed by the pope in 1817, and in 1825 was given responsibility for work in Oceania by the congregation of the *Propaganda. In 1815 the Society of Mary, or Marists, was formed, primarily for service in the Pacific. In 1835 the area was divided between the two orders, the Vicariate of East Oceania assigned to the Picpusians and the Vicariate of West Oceania to the Marists.

In 1834 priests of the Picpus Fathers landed on the Gambier Islands. Within a short while they had converted the islanders and had organized native life around the church. In 1836 priests went to Tahiti. The reigning queen, advised by Protestant missionaries, refused them permission to land. They returned later on a French naval vessel and secured, under threat, the right to teach their religion unhindered. Thus began a conflict which continued during the following years. Neither Protestant nor Catholic recognized the validity of the other's faith and the presence of both in the islands created an unending struggle between them for native allegiance. Moreover, RC missions tended to operate under the protection and support of French naval power, for the missions were part of the national policy. This put Protestant missions at a disadvantage since the British government disclaimed any direct interest in the islands except as their citizens needed protection.

From their base in the Society Islands the RC missionaries moved into the Marquesas, and then westward to Wallis and Fortuna Islands (1837) where they worked without Protestant opposition, to Tonga (1842) where their arrival, through the alliance they made with a native ruler, accentuated the civil war which Taufaahau's attempt to unify the islands under his authority had precipitated, and Fiji (1844) where a similar inter-tribal struggle resulted. In each case a French show of force helped the RC missionaries to establish themselves. The missionaries built the church wherever they went, started schools and inculcated their moral principles. They wrought changes in island life, although their teachings were not as strict as those of the Protestants. And through their work tribe and church developed a unity through which the mission had a direct influence on the lives of the people. On some islands the RC church came to have a majority of the natives as members, while on other islands the church was a minority. Throughout Polynesia, with few exceptions both missions worked on all the islands.

Melanesia presented a much more difficult problem for missions. The inhabitants were more primitive than the Polynesians and much less open to friendly approaches. Their tribal groups were relatively small and in general each tribe had its own language. This greatly lessened the possibility of using native teachers in

moving from one tribe to another. Through a number of unfortunate experiences with westerners the people were extremely suspicious of any new arrivals. Because of their fear and basic instability there was danger to those who attempted to land among them. Attempts were made to establish missionaries on various islands, but again and again they failed. All too often the missionaries were killed. Williams had taken Samoan teachers with him when he reached Erromanga, and although he lost his life the teachers survived by moving to another island. The LMS reinforced their number, but it was not until 1848, with the coming of Presbyterian missionaries from Nova Scotia and Scotland, that the work could be considered established.

Bishop George *Selwyn of the Anglican church in New Zealand, because of the way his assigment had been made, assumed responsibility for work in the area. He made a number of journeys through the islands to acquaint himself with the situation. On occasion he took back to New Zealand with him native young men to train them for mission work, planning to return them to their homes in due time. That plan, although continued for some time, did not prove to be as effective as was expected. In 1850 the bishop formed the Melanesian Mission, with representatives of the Anglican Church in New Zealand and Australia. In 1861 John *Patteson was consecrated bishop of Melanesia working through the Melanesian Mission.

RC priests, Marists, landed in the Solomons in 1844, but after suffering losses they retreated; they returned in 1898. In 1843 Marists went to New Caledonia. The naval officer in command of the gun boat that took them negotiated with the natives for the transfer of sovereignty of the island to France, an act which was interpreted as giving France possession. At that time the priests were driven out. They returned in 1851 and with government support were able to establish their work. From 1864 for a period of 30 years the French used the island as a place for the deportation of convicts. The same methods were used by the missions in Melanesia as in Polynesia. Languages were reduced to writing, translations made, schools opened, churches set up, and every effort made to win the inhabitants to the Christian faith. But the response was slow. By 1870 only a few of the islands could be considered to have accepted Christianity, and on those islands only some tribal groups.

The Marshall, Caroline and Mariana Islands north of the equator, with the Gilberts lying across the line, are mainly small, low, coral islands, widely scattered. There are a few high islands, probably of volcanic origin, which are large enough to support commercial agriculture. These islands were known to the west through the work of the explorers, but appeared to be of little consequence. Spain laid claim to the Marianas in the 17th century and missionaries of the RC church converted the inhabitants to the faith. In 1852 the *ABCFM sent a group of American and Hawaiian Christians to the island of Ponape and Kusaie in the Carolines; five years later other workers went to Ebon in the Marshalls and Abiang in the Gilberts. Those enterprises spread to other islands in Micronesia. The same pattern of work was followed as in the other island groups. The native political structures were used to effect changes in native ways, the tribal groups adopting Christianity as their religion and implementing that choice by legal codes, moral behaviour and worship. The RC church had missions in the Carolines in the 18th century conducted by Spanish priests. They made little effort to expand their work beyond that single island group.

In the meanwhile another development had begun. After the middle of the 19th century, as knowledge of the area increased men learned that opportunities for economic exploitation existed and western entrepreneurs took advantage of them. Sugar was first produced in 1857; within twenty years this had become a large scale enterprise. Guano deposits were found on some of the smaller islands; western companies began the process of extraction. Soap manufacturers increased their demand for coconut oil, and when a scheme was devised for the extraction of the oil from copra the industry grew rapidly. Nickel was discovered on New Caledonia and phosphate on Nauru and Ocean Islands. Companies such as the Pacific Phosphate Company, the Colonial Sugar Refining Company and Lever Brothers began to conduct mining, plantations and shipping throughout the area. In 1857 German traders came, Godeffray and Sons of Hamburg established headquarters at Apia in Samoa and worked at many points in the neighbouring islands. Subsequently the firm merged with the Jaluit Gesellschaft which had started operations in the Marshall Islands.

The companies needed land; they purchased some from inhabitants who claimed ownership and simply commandeered more. They needed labour; finding the population poorly distributed for their purposes they began a system of transporting men from one island to another. This grew into a substantial business carried on by traders who were paid for each labourer delivered to mine or plantation and who did not scruple to use any means to take the men they wanted. When the supply of islanders proved insufficient and their work of poor quality the companies looked elsewhere. Beginning in 1879 workers were brought from India under an indenture plan. Groups of Chinese, Malayans and Japanese were also imported although in much smaller numbers. Moreover the companies needed a stable society, patterned to their needs and responsive to their demands. The existing tribal groups could not serve their ends, negotiations with chiefs were unsatisfactory, and native laws were irrelevant. The companies did not intend to let the pattern of native life interfere with their purposes. They appealed to their own governments, which responded by taking control of the islands. By the end of the 19th century France held the Society Islands, New Caledonia, and under a Convention with the British, the New Hebrides; Germany held Western Samoa, Bougainville and Buka Islands in the Solomons, and all the islands of Micronesia except Guam; the USA held Eastern Samoa and Guam; and Britain held all the rest, but transferred responsibility for the Cook Islands and Niue to New Zealand. The western powers administered these possessions in various ways ranging from direct and complete control to a control allowing some recognition to a native ruler. Whichever was the case, the administration was for the purpose of safeguarding western economic interests with as much regard for native life as was possible.

In this development missionaries were directly involved. In many cases they stood between the westerners and the islanders to act in negotiations or to help in disputes. In other cases they spoke for the native interests when those were being disregarded by the companies. Wherever they could they took the part of the islanders, although they well understood some of the values that could accrue to island life through the coming of an effective economy.

More important, however, were the effects this development had on the churches and the lives of the people. The native society was disrupted as men moved from island to island; churches lost touch with their members. The towns which were built at the plantations and mining centres broke the ties binding individuals to their tribes and thus to the churches. The introduction of a money economy freed the people from dependence upon native relationships. And as the people participated in the new enterprises or were affected by them they gained a different outlook on life and a different set of values. Churches began to lose members and the interest of their people.

Missions continued to carry the main responsibility for general education and for other activities contributing to the health and welfare of the people. Both Protestants and Catholics added to the number of schools they conducted; hospitals were built and clinics opened on some of the islands. Additional arrangements were made for the training of native pastors and teachers: a school was opened at Rewa Bay in Fiji and another at Malua in Samoa by the Protestants, and a school in New Caledonia by the Catholics. Tobou College was opened in Tongatabu in 1866 for the preparation of islanders for government service. The churches continued their regular activities, reaching out to the non-Christians, entering the new communities, and making approaches to the alien labour brought to the islands. In the Society Islands the LMS withdrew in 1886, turning over its work to the *PEMS, a change dictated when the French government took control there.

During the 20th century Oceania has been involved, as has the rest of the world, in two wars. The first war caused hardship to the German missionaries at work in the area, especially those in Micronesia who were forcibly removed by the Japanese when they entered the islands; otherwise the war had little effect. The economic depression between the wars caused serious financial stringency to missions and churches. Support by mission boards and island people was greatly reduced; the churches on some islands were forced to return to subsistence support. Concern deepened over the condition of the Indian labourers on Fiji. The churches addressed the British government on the matter; the Rev C. F. *Andrews, a close friend of Mahatma Gandhi, made a visit of investigation and published an unfavourable report. In 1920 the government ordered the end of the indenture system and the granting of the right of repatriation to those workers who chose to return home. The missions made expanded efforts to reach the Indian workers, most of whom were Hindus or Moslems; the response was slight.

During the second war the islands were directly involved in the conflict. Islands in Melanesia were battle grounds; Samoa, Fiji and Tonga were staging areas for troops and supplies; the Marshalls were stepping stones to battle areas; the Marianas and Guam were scenes of heavy fighting. Church lands were confiscated or commandeered, congregations were disrupted or dispersed, missionaries were killed, imprisoned or called to other duties, native pastors lost their lives, schools were closed or schedules changed. In the midst of this native Christians met Christian men in the armed forces and thus discovered the universal character of the faith they held.

After the war the responsible western governments began to see that their concern had to be for more than keeping order and making possible western enterprises, that they had to consider the welfare and development of the people. While the war was going on governments began to provide public education; this has become general practice throughout the islands. Native leaders, having learned the meaning of freedom, began openly to press for more participation in government; on occasion the pressure erupted into overt action. Governments have responded by making possible an increased measure of local autonomy. Hospitals have been opened by governments and training provided for native practitioners to serve throughout the area. In 1947 the South Pacific Commission, consisting of representatives of Great Britain, France, the USA, Australia and New Zealand, was formed and given responsibility for the co-ordination of research, health and welfare in the islands. Mission representatives are invited to the Commission meetings and on occasion mission advice is sought.

The churches have faced the same problems as the governments. With the increasing introduction of western artefacts and the growing relationship between islanders and secular western leaders, a spirit of secularism has grown and church members are coming to be a minority among the population. It has become clear that the churches stand at the line between the old culture which is fast losing its hold and the new world into which the islands have been drawn and in which the people must live. The churches have paid special attention to the transfer of leadership to nationals and the training of those leaders. Numbers of ministerial candidates have

been sent out of the area for further education. Native ordinations have increased and men have been raised to positions of leadership in the hierarchy of the RC church. Lay participation in the work of the churches has increased: the Pauline Association of the Lay Missionary Secretariat has sent men to the Solomon Islands; and the Melanesian Brotherhood, a native organization of the Anglican church, has assumed much responsibility.

Churches have become more autonomous. Vicariates Apostolic are formed throughout the area. Protestant churches have organized local associations: the Church Association of Malaitea in the Solomons and the General Synod of the Evangelical Church in New Caledonia are examples. The Methodist churches of Fiji and Samoa now have conference status. A House of the Laity has been formed in the diocese of Melanesia. In 1943 the Pacific Christian Literature Society was organized, a joint enterprise of churches and missions for the preparation and publication of needed materials. The Melanesia Council of Churches was formed in 1946.

The effectiveness of the churches in presenting the gospel to the people and in working for peace and harmony continues to be weakened by the divisions in the Protestant ranks. Relationships between Catholics and Protestants have grown increasingly better. Joint meetings for prayer and Bible study are held and necessary printed materials prepared under joint auspices. But the existence of small sects which proselytize and are polemical remains a disturbing element in religious life.

In 1961 a Pacific Conference of Churches and Missions was held at Malua in Samoa for a discussion of island problems and the work needing to be done. Among the subjects considered: the more than a million non-Christians in the islands; the Asian communities; the changes taking place in island life; and the significance of the Christians who are becoming the political leaders. At the close of the meeting a continuation committee was appointed to arrange for a possible permanent organization. A visiting secretary was secured to travel throughout the islands explaining the proposed plan and enlisting the participation of the churches. The inaugural meeting of the Assembly of the Pacific Conference of Churches was held in the Loyalty Islands in 1966. At the close of the meeting the delegates went to Suva for the dedication of the newly established United Theological College.

J. LESLIE DUNSTAN

J. W. Burton: *Missionary Survey of the Pacific Islands* (London 1930), *Modern Missions in the South Pacific* (London 1949); W. E. B. Dubois: *Les Missions Maristes d'Océanie* (Paris 1926); G. C. Findlay and W. W. Holdsworth: *The History of the Wesleyan Methodist Missionary Society* (London 1921–1924); C. H. Grattan: *The Southwest Pacific to 1900* (Ann Arbor, Michigan 1963), *The Southwest Pacific since 1900* (Ann Arbor, Michigan 1963); J. B. Piolet: *Les Missions Catholiques au XIXe Siècle* (Paris 1902); J. Schmidlin: *Catholic Mission History* (Techny, Illinois 1933); A. R. Tippett: *Solomon Islands Christianity* (London 1968); J. Williams: *A Narrative of Missionary Enterprises in the South Sea Islands* (New York 1837); *The Pacific Journal of Theology* (Suva, Fiji) quarterly.

PADROADO. See PATRONATO REAL.

PADWICK, CONSTANCE EVELYN (1886–1968), was born at West Thorney, Sussex, England. She served in Egypt and Palestine from 1916 to 1947, and afterwards in Sudan and Turkey until 1957. CP may be said to have provided a bridge from Henry *Martyn (d.1812) to Hendrik *Kraemer (d.1965) and beyond, across the long reach from NT translation to dialogue with *Islam in the 1970s. She wrote a kindling popular biography of Martyn and was an eager consultant of Kraemer. CP was reared in the godly succession of the *CMS to which Martyn belonged in heart, and from its impetus she produced a definitive

study of Muslim devotion which will remain central for the open Christian mind towards Islam. This work, *Muslim Devotions* (London 1961), documented the main themes, phrases and emphases of Muslim personal religion, absorbed through more than twenty years of careful friendships, travel and imaginative skill, into a single compendium for the western reader. The pocket manuals of praise and prayer were gathered from mosques and markets from Morocco to Singapore.

Her other most influential work was the biography *Temple *Gairdner of Cairo* (London 1929), giving to a wider sphere the inspiration of a personality warmly loved in Egypt. Her literary gifts were evident in her initiatives in the Central Literature Committee for Muslims in the 1930s, and in the preparation of school texts during her time in the Nuba Mountains of the Sudan.

KENNETH CRAGG

The Muslim World, LXI (1969), pp.29–39.

PAGANISM, PAGANS. This word has a long history, but it is little used today. The *pagani* in the Roman empire were the villagers among whom the old religion lingered long, when most of the inhabitants of the cities were already Christians. The word came, thus, to have the significance of 'idolators, worshippers of the old gods'. Later, the word came to have the extended sense of 'those who do not worship the true God'; and so in the Middle Ages Christians unhesitatingly used the term of their Muslim enemies, and thus, as Gibbon truly remarks, 'the purest *Unitarians* were branded with the unjust reproach of idolatry and paganism' (*Decline and Fall*, chap.21, note 176). Since the term 'heathen' has come to be regarded as contemptuous and unseemly, it has been found difficult to know what term to use of those who do not adhere either to the Christian faith or to one of the great classical religions. Since the term 'non-Christian' is too general, as including for instance the Jews, some have found it convenient to use the terms 'pagan, paganism' of the adherents of the simple religions, who like the *pagani* of old are mostly village dwellers, and as yet untouched by the civilization or the ideas of the cities. But this term, too, seems to have certain overtones of superiority; it is not likely to be well received by those of whom it is used; and perhaps it would be well that these terms too should be abandoned in circles interested in the propagation of the Christian faith.

STEPHEN NEILL

NCE X, 862.

PAKISTAN. Area 365,000 sq.m. (West P. 310,000, East P. 55,000). Estimated population in 1967—115 million (West 53 million, East 62 million). Annual increase is about $2\frac{1}{2}$ million. 88% of the population are Muslims; less than 1% are Christians, of whom more than half are Protestant. The literacy level for West P. is 12.7%, and for East P. 17.6%. P. was founded in 1947 when the British handed over power in India. It is a sovereign Muslim state and comprises the areas in which Muslims formed a majority of the population.

It is possible that the gospel was preached in the Indus valley in the first Christian centuries; Roman Catholic missionaries worked in Sind and in Lahore in the 16th century; but no trace of these early efforts remains. In 1833 American Presbyterians came into the Punjab. The British annexation of Sind in 1842, and of the Punjab and Frontier areas in 1849, was followed by the establishment of missionary work there by the *CMS, the United Presbyterian Church of North America, the Church of Scotland and American Methodists. RC chaplains were appointed in the same period. Since then, year by year, a steady trickle of converts has been baptized— Hindus, Sikhs and Muslims—among them men of outstanding character. Through the ministry of these converts and their missionary colleagues, *mass movements began in the Punjab in the last quarter of the century and continued until 1915. During this period, thousands of casteless, *aboriginal people were baptized. The movements took place mainly in the rural areas north of Lahore, between Gujranwala and Sialkot, and the proportion of Christians to the rest of the population is still higher there than in the rest of the country. From these seedbeds, Punjabi Christians have migrated to all other parts of West P., providing a witness in areas where evangelism has not yet borne fruit. Through education, many of the descendants of these mass movement converts have moved into middle-class professions, so providing a Christian witness in the various strata of society.

The Sialkot Convention was founded by Presbyterian missionaries in 1905 for the spiritual nurture primarily of the large numbers who had joined the church in the mass movements. It has continued as an annual gathering of Christians of all denominations from the Punjab and far beyond, and has been used for the revival and upbuilding of the church. Since partition in 1947, annual conventions after the same pattern have come to be held in many cities of Pakistan. Both in these conventions, and in evangelistic campaigns, Christians of many denominations have worked well together. A wide range of joint activities has been carried on under the auspices of the Christian councils, formed in West P. in 1949 and in East P. in 1954.

In East P., RC missionaries were appointed to trading posts in the 16th century. Early in the 19th century, *Carey established missionary work in East Bengal: today Baptists are by far the largest Protestant denomination in East P. Mass conversions began in Mymensingh in the latter half of the 19th century. Today growth is mainly among the tribal peoples of the Chittagong Hill Tracts. One of the missionary groups which have started work in East P. since partition is Japanese. There are about half a million Protestant Christians in P., the great majority in the western section of the country.

While P. is constitutionally an 'Islamic Republic', the constitution provides that 'no law should prevent the members of a religious community or denomination from professing, practising or propagating, or from providing instruction in, their religion'. The only position reserved to Muslims is that of president. While the rights of minorities are safeguarded by the public authorities, Christians in P. have a sense of insecurity because of the popular antipathy to them, frequently expressed in agitation and propaganda against 'missionary institutions'. There is widespread suspicion about the activities of foreign missionaries, whose numbers have in fact increased since partition. Several undenominational societies, finding their work in India restricted, have started work in P., and under *comity agreements have been allotted areas which were not being effectively evangelized. In all the major denominations of the church, leadership and administrative responsibility have very largely passed from missionaries to Pakistanis. There is still considerable dependence on financial aid from overseas churches, but local giving is increasing. Despite financial difficulties, the five Protestant and eight RC colleges still play a significant part in the educational life of the country. The theological seminary at Gujranwala trains Presbyterians, Anglicans, Methodists, some Lutherans and (from East P.) some Baptists.

Partition did not interrupt the movement towards church unity in the north, (involving Anglicans, Baptists, Brethren, Disciples, Methodists, and the bodies already united in the Church of North India), but political developments since then have made the church in P. conscious of the danger of appearing to be under any kind of control from India. When union is achieved, there will be two united churches in full communion with one another, one in North India and one in P.

Roman Catholic missions in P. have suffered under the same difficulties as Protestant—a minority situation in an overwhelmingly Muslim population. Many orders have been at work—notably Holy Cross Fathers from Canada and the USA in East P. since 1850, *Mill Hill Fathers at Rawalpindi since 1887, Dutch *Franciscans at Karachi, taking over in 1935 work which

had been started by the *Jesuits in 1852; on the women's side Franciscan Missionary Sisters, and the Medical Mission Sisters, USA. It is noteworthy that there are five religious orders for Pakistani Sisters, with a membership of more than 200. Education is well cared for, there being more than 60,000 pupils of various grades, of whom roughly two-thirds are RCs.

In 1950 Dacca, which had been the seat of a bishopric since 1856, was raised to an archbishopric, with the suffragan sees of Chittagong, Dinajpur and Khulna; in the same year Karachi became an archbishopric, with Lahore, Multan, Rawalpindi, to which later Lyallpur and Hyderabad were added making up the ecclesiastical province. The first Pakistani bishop was consecrated in 1958. There are 341,000 Roman Catholics, ministered to by about 400 priests, of whom the great majority are still foreigners; but progress towards *indigenization is being made. P. does not present the same difficulties as India to the entry and residence of foreign missionaries.

D. M. DUNCAN AND STEPHEN NEILL

L. T. Lyall, ed.: *Missionary Opportunity Today* (London 1963); V. Stacey: *The Islamic Republic* (London 1962); I. Stephens: *Pakistan: Old Country/New Nation* (Harmondsworth 1964); R. V. Weekes: *Pakistan: Birth and Growth of a Muslim Nation* (Princeton, NJ 1964); *Plan of Church Union for North India and Pakistan* (4th ed., Madras 1965); *BM* II, 662–67; *NCE* X, 869; *WKL*, 1095f.

PAL, KRISHNA (c.1770–1822), a carpenter converted by the Baptist pioneers at Serampore, Bengal.

John Thomas, one of William *Carey's colleagues, was called to set P's arm and spoke to him of the gospel. After daily intercourse with the missionaries, especially with Carey and his son Felix, P. with his wife and daughter offered himself for baptism. P. and his brother Goluk, who had been in touch with the missionaries earlier, renounced *caste by eating with the missionaries on 22 December 1800. 'Thus' wrote Carey's colleague

Ward, 'the door of faith is open to the Hindus, the chain of caste broken',

This event was the occasion of much disorder in Serampore, and the missionaries and their converts were given military protection. Goluk and the women, however, in the end declined baptism because it entailed severing family and other social ties, but P. stood firm. He was baptized on 28 December 1800 together with Felix Carey, in the presence of a large company including the Governor. His sister-in-law was baptized the following year, the first Hindu woman convert at Serampore.

P. was ordained by the Baptist missionaries in 1806. He died of cholera in 1822 after more than twenty years of Christian witness as a pioneer evangelist, often in circumstances of much personal hardship and even peril.

HENRY LEFEVER

J. C. Marshman: Life and Times of Carey, Marshman and Ward, Vol. I (London 1859); S. Pearce-Carey: William Carey (4th ed., London 1924).

PALESTINE. See ISRAEL; JORDAN.

PALLU, FRANÇOIS (1626–1684), was born at Tours, France. In 1649 Alexander de *Rhodes, the great *Jesuit missionary, went to Rome to propose to the congregation of *Propaganda a new plan for the missions: the setting up of *Vicars Apostolic, depending directly on the pope, and not the kings of Portugal and Spain with their rights of the *Padroado. Their task would be the training of an indigenous clergy and hierarchy. Although Rome favoured the plan, it was only with the help of missionary-minded men from France that it materialized. In 1659 Alexander VII nominated two outstanding priests—Pallu and Lambert de la Motte—first Vicars Apostolic of Tongking and West China and of Cochin China and South China respectively. P. soon realized he would need helpers and asked Propaganda to set up a seminary for the training of future apostles for Asia. Propaganda agreed and so the first Missionary Institute

of secular priests was founded in Paris. In 1664 it was approved by Rome as the Société des Missions Etrangères de Paris (*MEP). In 1662 P. left for his mission in Tongking, but was unable to enter it. He stayed in Siam where he founded the first seminary for indigenous clergy to be the society's general seminary in the Far East. (In 1769 it was moved to Virampatnam near Pondicherry, India, and in 1807 to Penang.) In 1669 P. went to Rome to defend the rights of the Vicars Apostolic against the Portuguese and their representative, the Archbishop of Braga. In 1674 he again tried to reach Tongking, but was stranded at Manila where the Spaniards imprisoned him and brought him to Europe (1674–77). In 1680 he was made Administrator of the whole of China and Vicar Apostolic of Fukien, but died nine months after his arrival at Mo Yang.

ARTHUR MCCORMACK, MHM

J. Guennou: Les Missions Etrangères (Paris 1963); LTK VIII, 11; NCE X, 932f.

PANAMA. See AMERICA, CENTRAL.

PAPUA. See NEW GUINEA.

PARA-CHURCHES, in the strict meaning of the word, are formations like the *Non-Church' (mu-kyokai) groups in Japan or other various gatherings of people who believe in Christ but are not willing or able to form or join a church. Lacking the notae ecclesiae ('marks of the church') or eschewing the sacraments and therefore not being churches in the ecumenical sense, they exist 'alongside' (Greek: para) a church. However, the word has hardly been used in reference to such groups. It was primarily used in the post-war European discussion on evangelism in an attempt both to identify and to map out forms of churches which would exist half-way (hence also 'half-way churches') between the world and the church, such as discussion groups, neighbourhood meetings, community centres, evangelical *academies and the like. They were thought of as being or becoming a device by which the deep gulf, new in Europe, old in other situations, between the people and the church could be bridged. Yet the word was never generally accepted and it disappeared when it became clear that it could not be defended in the light of a theological doctrine of the church, and that it was coined under the wrong presupposition of the unchangeability or the historical perfection of the existing churches. In a later stage of the discussion, notably in the WCC's study on 'The *Missionary Structure of the Congregation', the traditional churches were called to become present in those situations where 'half-way churches' once were envisaged to be the solution. Herein was included the call for drastic changes in outlook and in function so that churches which were or had become detached from contemporary man would become 'churches for others', in service and dialogue. A classic example of such a 'church in Christian presence' is a coffee shop, called 'The Potter's House', of the Church of the Saviour in Washington, D.C. Giving the lead to the current Christian coffee shop movement especially in America (cf. John D. Perry: *The Coffee House Ministry*, Richmond, Virginia 1966) and signalizing the necessity and possibility of a new indigenization of the church in a world of change, the work in Washington started with a team of committed Christians, serving people in a metropolitan situation on behalf of a traditional congregation, and led to the formation of 'The Church of the Potter's House' to which people are invited for worship in a fashion congenial to secular man: the service happens at the tables of a coffee shop.

HANS JOCHEN MARGULL

E. O'Connor: *Call to Commitment* (New York 1963).

PARAGUAY, an inland republic of South America, extends over an area of 157,000 sq.m. and has a population of approximately two million. The majority of people live in the fertile area east of the River Paraguay which includes the capital city, Asunción. The west consists of the Gran Chaco, an extensive area of scrub and forest, swamp and prairie, uninhabited but for primitive Indian tribes and cattle ranchers. Ninety per cent of the population is Indian or has Indian blood. Recent generations have suffered a heavy toll of lives lost in warfare, particularly the Triple Alliance War (1865–70) and the Bolivian War (1932–35). European immigrants have a considerable influence on the economic, political and social life of the country.

The Spaniards discovered P. in 1536. The year 1556 marked the official establishment of the Paraguayan church when Father Pedro Fernandez de la Torre reached his diocesan capital of Asunción. In 1558 the first *Jesuits arrived seeking to christianize, civilize and protect the Indian. Before their expulsion in 1767 they had established 32 missions, not all of which, however, were on the soil of what is now called P. The Roman Catholic church remained but was long subservient to civil authority. In 1870 a new constitution insisted that the head of the RC hierarchy in P. must be a Paraguayan. Toleration was granted to other religions. A nominal allegiance to the RC church still prevails in P. today, although Protestant witness is increasing.

The first Protestant contacts were made by the American Bible Society in 1856. Today the ABS has been joined by the BFBS and the Norwegian Bible Society, to form the *United BS. They have a depot in Asunción. In 1886 an aggressive missionary enterprise was begun by Juan Villanueva of the American Methodist Episcopal Church. The Disciples of Christ entered P. in 1916 and enabled the Methodist mission to withdraw. They have a large college in Asunción, one of the finest schools in the country. In 1889 W. B. *Grubb of the *SAMS penetrated the interior to reach the Indian tribes. Today the SAMS has a pastoral, educational and radio outreach in the cities and suburbs of Asunción and Concepción, and an evangelistic, educational and agricultural ministry to the Indians. There is a team of ordained Lengua

Indians, evangelists licensed lay-readers and teachers.

In 1918 the Salvation Army established an orphanage in Asunción. In 1921 a Mennonite colony was founded, whose law-abiding and disciplined life gives testimony to the social results of the gospel. In 1945 the Southern Baptists of the USA started work in P. and now have an important hospital in Asunción. The New Testament Missionary Union, the *New Tribes Mission, the Free Brethren and the Free Methodists (American) are also active; and the *CMA commenced work in the late 1960s. The Pentecostal church, represented by groups from USA, Scandinavia and Chile, is expanding. The total number of Protestants in P. was estimated in 1968 (WCH) as 19,369.

Most of the population is at least nominally RC. Following the Second *Vatican Council the mass is said in Spanish and Bible reading is being encouraged in RC churches. There has been a general lessening of tension between RCs and Protestants where previously the latter had been persecuted. At the time of writing the RC church in P. is still conservative in outlook.

HENRY SUTTON

The South American Handbook (published annually by Trade and Travel Publications, Ltd., London—section on *Paraguay*); *BM* II, 671–76; *NCE* X, 992–94; *WKL*, 1107f.

PARIS EVANGELICAL MISSIONARY SOCIETY (Société des Missions Evangéliques de Paris). In 1819, in circles which had been touched by the revival, groups for prayer and for collection of funds for missions had come into being spontaneously in various provinces of France. Under the influence of C. G. Blumhardt and the Rev. Mark Wilks (Pastor of the English Free Church Congregation in Paris) a number of leading Protestants in Paris founded in 1822 an association which was intended to unite all these sporadic groups. The PEMS was from the beginning interdenominational and international. In 1824, the 'House of Missions' was opened to provide training for missionary candidates. From 1826 onwards appeared the *Journal des Missions Evangéliques*.

On the advice of Dr John *Philip (*LMS, Cape Town), the first missionaries were sent to Bechuanaland, not far from Robert *Moffat and his station of Kuruman; but the station of Mosiga was destroyed by the Matabele. In 1833, on the invitation of *Moshoeshoe, chief of the Basotho, Eugène *Casalis (director of the society 1856–82), and Thomas Arbousset (in Tahiti from 1863) founded among the Lesotho the first mission of the PEMS.

In 1878 François *Coillard founded in Barotseland (Zambia) a mission which, according to his plan, should have been that of the church of Lesotho; but the society had to step in and take the place of the church, when it was found that Barotseland was inaccessible to Sotho evangelists.

These are the only mission fields which the PEMS has founded of its own choice. All the others have been forced on it by political circumstances; the task was to replace foreign missions which the French colonial administration (which came under strong RC influences towards the end of the century) was no longer prepared to tolerate. The first of these to be taken over were the LMS missions in Tahiti (founded 1797) in 1863; Madagascar (founded 1820) in 1896; the Loyalty Islands (founded 1841) and New Caledonia in 1897.

In 1888 the society inherited the work in Gabon from the American Presbyterians. One of its stations served as the base from which in 1912 Albert *Schweitzer founded his independent hospital. In 1917 the society took over part of Cameroon, from which the German missionaries (*Basel Mission, Berlin Baptists) had been expelled; and in 1929 Togo (Bremen Mission), which had been left without missionaries since 1917.

All the churches founded by the society have now become *autonomous, and (with the exception of the church of Lesotho) are members of the *WCC. Christians in these churches number about 1,300,000, with 200,000 communicants. In 1966.

187,000 pupils in their schools were looked after by 3,191 teachers. The missionaries (including missionary wives) numbered 248 in 1966. One-third of the missionaries are Swiss, and part of the budget is raised in Switzerland.

ETIENNE KRUGER

J. Bianquis: *Les origines de la Société des Missions Evangéliques de Paris, 1822 à 1829* (3 vols., Paris 1930–35).

PARIS FOREIGN MISSION SOCIETY (Société des missions étrangères de Paris: MEP) came into existence in the 17th century as a result of the desire of *Propaganda Fide* in Rome to exercise much closer supervision of the missions than had earlier been possible, and also to open to secular priests a career of missionary service, which had been almost a closed preserve of the members of the religious orders. The seminary founded in Paris for the training of missionary candidates received papal approval in 1664. Between 1660 and 1700 a hundred missionaries were sent out, many of them to the Far East. The 18th century was a time of diminished zeal, but in the 19th work was resumed again with renewed power. Following the plans of *Propaganda Fide* for the formation of an indigenous priesthood in all countries, the society gave itself to the foundation of seminaries in the mission fields. In 1665 it founded the notable seminary of Ayuthia in Thailand (later transferred to Penang in Malaya) which for a long period trained priests for the whole of the Far East and South-east Asia. In 1963 the society was reported as having 800 members, with 24 bishops among them. The members do not take religious vows, but are pledged to spend their lives in the service of missions. Indigenous priests do not become members of the society, but are at once integrated in the ranks of the diocesan clergy.

One result of the foundation of the society was the predominance of French missionaries for two centuries; numbers are still large, but RC missions have in the 20th century become fully international.

EDITORS

J. Guennou: *Les Missions Etrangères* (Paris 1965); *NCE* X, 1016f.

PARIS MISSION. See PARIS EVAN-GELICAL MISSIONARY SOCIETY.

PARKER, PETER (1805–1888), pioneer prototype of medical missions overseas, was born in the USA on a Massachusetts farm and attended both medical and theological schools. He went to China in 1834 under the *ABCFM. P. disarmed much opposition and suspicion by his remarkable medical cures and surgical operations, especially removal of cataracts, in the ophthalmic hospital which he founded and where he trained Chinese assistants to work with him. Later, when the new anaesthesias were available, his work was even more effective. It was said of him that he opened the gates of China with a lancet. On furlough in 1842 he married a niece of Daniel Webster. Proficiency in the use of the Chinese language led to service as an interpreter in Sino-American treaty discussions and, again, in being appointed *chargé d'affaires* in Peking. P. urged mediation in the Opium War and strove earnestly for better international relations. But his major interest was always in medical missions and in the well-known Medical Missionary Society of Canton, organized to attract support from Chinese sources. After a long and fascinating missionary career he was forced by ill health to retire in the USA (1857) where he received numerous honours for his scientific and humanitarian endeavours.

F. W. PRICE

H. Balme: *China and Modern Medicine* (London 1921); E. M. Dodd: *Gift of the Healer* (New York 1964); G. B. Stevens: *The Life, Letters and Journals of the Rev. and Hon. Peter Parker, M.D.* (Boston 1896); *DAB* XIII, 234f.; *RGG* V, 115.

PARLIAMENT OF RELIGIONS 1893. See WORLD'S PARLIAMENT OF RE-LIGIONS.

PARRISH, SARAH REBECCA (1869–1952), was the pioneer Protestant woman missionary doctor in the Philippines. Born at Bowers, Indiana, USA, she was early orphaned and learned to face the adversities of life. After medical training RP sailed for the Philippines in 1906 under the Methodist Episcopal Woman's Foreign Missionary Society. Challenged upon arrival by the great poverty and unsanitary conditions in Manila, she saw the need for medical care of all kinds. The furnishings in her first one-room 'Bethany Dispensary' were 'one chair with a crooked front leg, a desk, a blue enamel basin, and a pitcher'. Within a year, another room with ten bamboo cots was added, and this became the 'hospital'. In 1908, with a gift of $12,500 from Mr D. S. B. Johnston of Minneapolis, Minnesota, RP founded the Mary Johnston Hospital and School of Nursing in Tondo, a slum district on the Manila waterfront. Through the early history of the hospital RP was the central figure and guiding light, combining her duties as doctor with evangelistic work and social service. In 1933, after 27 years of almost unremitting labour, RP returned to the USA where she lived for the rest of her life. In retirement she lectured extensively and wrote her memoirs entitled *Orient Seas and Lands Afar* (New York 1936). In 1950, a medal of honour from the Civic Assembly of Women was presented to RP by President Quirino of the Republic of the Philippines. The citation read: 'The blessings of health and of social welfare which the Philippines enjoys today have been inspired by the pioneering effort of this sincere and determined American missionary doctor, who came a long way across the sea, bringing Christian love, healing, and enlightenment, and a better way of life'.

GERALD H. ANDERSON

PARSIS. See ZOROASTRIANISM.

PATERNALISM. A term used to express the view that in many cases missionaries have held on too long to positions of authority and control in the *younger churches, trying to maintain the relationship of parents to children, instead of allowing such a relationship to develop naturally into one of colleagues to colleagues and friends to friends. It cannot be denied that there is truth in this view; but the situation has, in fact, been far more complicated than is generally recognized by those who make use of the term.

In the earliest stages of a mission the missionary was naturally everything. He was the only man who knew what the Christian faith was. Among primitive peoples he was the only man who could read. He inevitably assumed a position of authority, even of dictatorship. At this stage of development both Christians and non-Christians tended to accept this situation as right and proper. At a creditably early time in most areas the missionaries attempted to share responsibility by planning for the development of an ordained indigenous ministry. But these well-laid plans did not always work out well. Many of the Christians belonged to the less prosperous classes of society; they proved, when ordained, wholly unable to stand up to the more wealthy and influential among the non-Christians, and needed the backing of the missionary. Under the influence of the views of Henry *Venn, three attempts were made—in Sierra Leone, in Tinnevelly in South India, in Nigeria—to create wholly independent younger churches in which the missionary would no longer have any control. Each experiment proved to be a major disaster. The failure of such premature attempts to bring P. to an end led to a prolonged renewal of missionary control, and to widespread scepticism as to the capacity of younger churches to manage their own affairs. Exactly similar results followed upon the ill-success of the Roman Catholic attempt to create an Indian episcopate in the 17th century.

Inevitably, missionary control led in the end to resentment. It was hard to keep promising young men in the service of the church, and these tended to find their sphere either in the *YMCA or in entirely secular fields. It must, however, be borne in mind that very few of these well qualified young men were prepared to work for the salary that the church could afford to pay them, or to accept the harsh and gruelling task that was being carried out by the district missionary in remote and lonely areas. If the missionary had not been there to do the work, it would not have been done at all.

The situation has changed very much in the last 30 years. All over the world, and in missions of every confession, authority has been taken out of the hands of the foreigner, and placed solidly in the hands of the indigenous Christian, except in some cases in which the *indigenous church has made good its right to have the man of its choice who may happen to be a foreigner (Bishop J. E. L. Newbigin to Madras in 1965; Bishop C. G. Diehl to Tranquebar in 1967). Many younger churchmen, however, complain that the epoch of paternalism is as yet very far from having come to an end. One of the most annoying forms in which it can be perpetuated is financial control from abroad; if a mission board in London or New York decides in detail how the money it contributes is to be spent, no real transference of control has taken place. But has a mission board the right to abdicate completely responsibility for the use of money which has been contributed by church members, often at the cost of great personal sacrifice?

No simple answer can be given to any of these questions. The solution will be found as more complete participation and mutual confidence become possible, on every level of the church's life and work, in the new ecumenical spirit, which is gradually taking hold in all the confessions of the Christian world.

STEPHEN NEILL

PATON, JOHN GIBSON (1824–1907), was born at Kirkmahoe, Dumfriesshire, Scotland. He was reared in a humble but devoutly Christian home at Torthorwald,

Dumfriesshire. He left school early, but thereafter devoted his spare time to study. During ten years as a Glasgow city missionary (1847–56) he studied at the university in theology and medicine. He then volunteered to join the Presbyterian missionary work in the New Hebrides.

In 1858 he was ordained, and with his young wife proceeded to Port Resolution, Tanna, New Hebrides. In March 1859, Mrs. Paton and an infant son died. P. stayed on, endeavouring to convert the warlike Tannese. His life was often threatened, and he was repeatedly prostrated by fever. In February 1862 he was forced to escape from the island, taking only his Bible and some translations.

In the following years he travelled widely in Australia and Scotland, and was remarkably successful in gaining the support of Presbyterians for the New Hebrides mission. Money was raised for a mission vessel, the *Dayspring*, and for general purposes. In 1864, in Scotland, he was elected Moderator of the Reformed Presbyterian Church. He re-married, returned to the New Hebrides, and from 1866 to 1881 laboured successfully in christianizing the small island of Aniwa.

In later years, P. undertook many long and strenuous deputation tours in Australasia, North America and Britain. During his life-time he personally raised an estimated £83,000 for the mission. His autobiography, edited by his brother James, appeared in 1889. An immediate best-seller, it was republished in various editions and languages, and made its author famous. In 1890, the John G. Paton Mission Fund was established to support New Hebrides missionaries. In 1891 the University of Cambridge conferred on him the degree of DD.

Apart from his purely missionary work he was a notable public figure. He campaigned vigorously against the evils of the 'blackbirding' trade (the recruitment and transportation of Pacific Islanders as labourers) the sale of liquor and firearms in the islands, and the growth of French influence in the New Hebrides. He thus incurred the hostility of those whose interests he opposed.

P's last years were spent mainly in Melbourne, where he died on 28 January 1907. He was pre-deceased by his gifted and dedicated second wife, Margaret Whitecross Paton. Three of their children became missionaries in the New Hebrides, and a number of other descendants have continued the tradition there and elsewhere.

ROBERT R. PATON

A. K. Langridge and F. H. L. Paton: *John G. Paton*; *Later Years and Farewell . . .* (London 1910); J. G. Paton: *John G. Paton, Missionary to the New Hebrides*; *an Autobiography edited by his brother James Paton* (2 vols., London 1889); M. W. Paton: *Letters and Sketches from the New Hebrides* (London 1894); *DNB*, 2nd Suppl. iii, 77f.

PATON, WILLIAM (1886–1943), was born in Croydon, England, of Scottish parentage, and educated at Oxford University (1904–08) and Westminster College. Cambridge (1908–11). He was missionary secretary of the *SCM of Great Britain and Ireland (1911–21). After brief service in India with the *YMCA, he became the first general secretary of the *National Christian Council of India, Burma and Ceylon (1922–27). He was recalled to Britain, in 1927, to be joint secretary, in London, of the *IMC and editor of the *IRM, positions which he held for the rest of his life. He travelled widely for consultations in preparation for the world meetings of the IMC in Jerusalem (1928) and Madras (1938). An ordained minister of the Presbyterian Church of England, he spent his whole career in the ecumenical sphere, seeking to promote *co-operation and *comity among churches and missions, working for the foundation and strengthening of *National Christian Councils under national leadership, supporting further development in some more specialized fields, such as the Christian approach to the Jews. Regarding 'church' and 'mission' as synonymous terms, he looked towards the ultimate amalgamation of the IMC with

the *WCC and became joint general secretary of the Provisional Committee (1938) of the WCC, while retaining his IMC office. Edinburgh University conferred an honorary DD upon him in 1939. He shared indefatigably during the second world war in IMC emergency action, such as its *'Orphaned Missions' initiative. As broadcaster and writer, he did much to promote ecumenical understanding in wartime Britain and to maintain world Christian fellowship across political barriers.

MARGARET SINCLAIR

IRM VIII–XXXII (1919–1943); J. R. Mott: 'William Paton', *IRM* XXXIII (1944), pp.3–9; M. Sinclair: *William Paton* (London 1949); *The NCC Review of India*; *The Student Movement*.

PATRONATO REAL (Spanish: royal patronage). In general, concessions granted to monarchs by popes for service to the Roman Catholic church. The term is usually used in reference to the New World (*Patronato Real de Indias*) but is also extended to Spanish and Portuguese (*padroado*) colonies in Asia. There were precedents for royal patronage before the discovery of America. A quarrel over the appointment of the bishop of Cuenca, Spain, was settled in 1482 when Sixtus IV allowed the Spanish crown to propose nominees for vacant sees. The same pope at the time of the Granada Crusade gave the Spanish crown the right of patronage over all benefices reconquered, plus a third of all titles collected. The bull *Inter Caetera*, issued in 1493 by Alexander VI, empowered Ferdinand and Isabella to send missioners to the New World and be responsible for the christianization of the Indies. Alexander issued another bull, *Eximiae Devotionis*, in 1501 which allowed the monarchs to collect tithes in the colonies and to use the money to defray the cost of christianization. In 1508 Julius II published the bull *Universalis Ecclesiae* which allowed the Spanish crown to name the candidates for all ecclesiastical offices (from archbishops to curates) in the Indies, plus the right to define the territories of bishops. On the whole the Spanish monarchs used the *patronato* for the advancement of the church, but one adverse effect was that it handicapped the establishment of an *indigenous church. As a result when Spain was driven from its American colonies in the early 19th century the church there was left without leaders, a loss that is felt to this day. Portugal, on the other hand, came into violent conflict with Rome over its use of the *padroado*. Unlike Spain, Portugal did not have civil control over all the areas it claimed but the Portuguese presence was confined to a few small enclaves, such as Goa. Rome recognized the rights of *padroado* in those areas under the civil control of Portugal but in order to develop the missions in India insisted on appointing bishops and sending missionary personnel. The Portuguese resisted, going so far as to imprison missioners sent out by Rome.

While the *padroado* was never a serious hindrance to the mission effort in Brazil and Africa, it continued to plague apostolic work in Asia through the 19th century, Eventually in 1950 Portugal renounced the *padroado* in newly independent India except for a few enclaves such as Goa. A final agreement between Portugal and the Holy See in 1953 put an end to the system.

The Spanish *patronato* also died with difficulty. When independence came to Spanish America the new republics insisted on the same privileges of *patronato* that had been exercised by Spain. Gradually by negotiations up into the 20th century the matter was resolved and *patronato* no longer exists.

ALBERT J. NEVINS, MM

Da Silva Rego: *Le Patronage Portugais de l'Orient* (Lisbon 1937); De Leteria: *Relaciones entre la Sancta Sede e Hispanoamerica* (Anal. Greg. 101–103); S. M. Just: *Immortal Fire* (St. Louis, Mo. 1951); K. S. Latourette: *A History of Christian Missions in China* (New York 1929); W. E. Shiels: *King and Church. The Rise and Fall of the Patronato Real* (Chicago 1961); *NCE* X, 1113–16.

PATTESON, JOHN COLERIDGE (1827–

1871), was born in London, England, and, after education at Eton and Oxford, went in 1853 to join Bishop *Selwyn in the New Zealand mission. He was placed in charge of the Melanesian area of the mission, and in 1861 was consecrated first bishop of Melanesia. P. had two special gifts for missionary work, an unusual capacity for learning languages—he mastered no less than 20 forms of Melanesian speech—and a great capacity for friendship. He was far ahead of his time in his belief in the Melanesians, in his desire that as Christians they should continue to be Melanesians, untrammelled by western clothes and habits, and in the excellence of his relationships with the non-Anglican missions. In 1865 P. was given a large tract of land on Norfolk Island. He founded a school to which boys from many islands were brought together; and this became his home during the brief intervals between his journeys in the islands. His period of service was that in which were perpetrated the worst abominations of the blackbirders, who kidnapped islanders and either killed them or carried them off to the plantations in Fiji or Queensland. On 20 September 1871 P. landed at the island of Nukapu, not knowing that shortly before five boys had been kidnapped from the island. He was almost immediately killed, and the body allowed to drift back to the ship in a canoe; five wounds had been made in the body, and on the breast a palm with five fronds knotted. P's undoubted saintliness was the fruit of patience, self-discipline, humour and humble trust in his Redeemer.

STEPHEN NEILL

C. E. Fox: *Lord of the Southern Isles* (London 1958); C. M. Yonge: *The Life of John Coleridge Patteson* (2 vols., London ²1888); *DNB* XLVII (1895), 53–56.

PAUL, KANAKARAYAN TIRUSELVAM (1876–1931), was born at Salem, South India, on 24 March 1876. A graduate of the Madras Christian College, he became secretary of the National Missionary Society, an indigenous missionary organization, in 1907. In 1913 he was appointed national secretary of the Indian *YMCA and became the national general secretary in 1916. In the YMCA one of his earliest concerns was Christian rural reconstruction. During the first world war, however, he also directed YMCA work among Indian troops, for which he was awarded the Order of the British Empire in 1919. Immediately after the war he was largely responsible for the foundation of the Indian Students' Hostel in London.

A fervent patriot, he was also a staunch believer in the value of the British connection with India, the subject of his book published in 1927. He pleaded not for the severance of this connection but for a reformulation of it and urged such a plan at the First Round Table Conference held in London in 1930.

He was President of the South India United (Presbyterian and Congregational) Church in 1925 and represented India at various ecumenical conferences, notably at Stockholm in 1925 and Jerusalem in 1928.

HENRY LEFEVER

K. T. Paul: *The British Connection with India* (London 1927); H. A. Popley: *K. T. Paul, Christian Leader* (Calcutta 1938).

PAUL'S MISSIONARY METHODS. A study of the methods used by St. Paul in the expansion of the gospel was made by Roland *Allen in his book *Missionary Methods: St. Paul's or Ours* (London 1912). The main aspects of St. Paul's methods as he saw them (relying heavily on W. Ramsay's book *St. Paul the Traveller*, London 1908) were:

(1) *Conditions for Mission*. Paul preached in the focal centres of a region and to those people who could preach the gospel to others. He also related his preaching to the life of the people.

(2) *Presentation of the Gospel*. Paul used every opportunity, including miracles, but preached on the basis of common ground. He preached the historical facts of the gospel with a call to faith and moral decision. The response which Paul expected was one of local initiative in establishing a Christian community and furthering the gospel. He did not normally receive financial aid and as he was self-supporting he expected the local congregations to be so as well.

(3) *Training of Converts*. A minimum of instruction was given prior to baptism. Instruction and the sacramental life within the local community would build up the church. Men acceptable to the community with acknowledged gifts of leadership were appointed elders. All members of the community were to be given the opportunity to exercise and develop their own gifts (*charismata*) for the benefit of all.

(4) *Organization*. Faith in the power of the Holy Spirit led St. Paul to allow the local churches great independence in developing their own life and mission. Only fear tries to stop churches taking independent action. Any organization must be such that it is acceptable to the local community.

Roland Allen used these principles to criticize what he regarded as the excessive *paternalism and *colonialism of much missionary activity. Subsequent events in some areas have proved that he was right, and more experiments are now being made along the lines which he suggested. His understanding of Paul's activity has not been seriously questioned in recent Pauline studies though it may need to be qualified and verified. The techniques of Paul's preaching in Acts as he describes them will need qualification in the light of the debate about the nature of the apostolic preaching. Some may think that he does not sufficiently draw out the importance of prayer as an instrument of mission (see *A World to Win* by J. A. Grassi, Maryknoll 1965). Recent studies of the Collection for the Church in Jerusalem (see *The Collection* by F. Nickle, London 1966) require that more emphasis should be given to the care of Christian churches for each other. A more serious criticism may be that Allen does not allow sufficiently for the effect of persecution on the Christian communities. Allen also quotes A. Harnack's *Expansion of Christianity* (London 1904). Another detailed analysis of St. Paul's work is in *The History of Primitive Christianity* by

J. Weiss (New York 1937). An important critique of the assumptions behind the Tübingen school's thought about St. Paul is available in J. Munck's *Paul and the Salvation of Mankind* (London 1961)— we should not assume that the methods of the other apostles were very different.

R. M. C. JEFFERY

PECK, EDMUND JAMES (1850–1924). Born at Manchester, England, he lost both parents and had limited formal education. As a sailor in the British Navy from 1865 to 1875 he began to show spiritual leadership. In 1876 the *CMS sent him to the Eskimos on the shores of Hudson's Bay. He lived eight years at Little Whale River, North Quebec, evangelizing the Eskimos, composing a grammar of their dialect and translating the Gospels. Ordained in 1878 by Bishop Hordern of Moosonee, he baptized his first converts in 1879. By living in close personal contact with the people, and teaching them to read, he gave the young church a firm foundation. In 1885 he married Sarah Ann Coleman, who accompanied him to Fort George; from there he travelled widely among the Eskimos. By 1892 there were 140 adults under instruction and five Eskimo teachers had been trained. After his wife's ill health obliged her to stay in England, P. with J.C. Parker settled in 1894 at a trading post on Blacklead Island in Cumberland Sound; this is north of Quebec and Labrador and on the edge of the Arctic Circle. The first converts there were baptized in 1901. P. may be called the apostle of the Eskimos of Canada. From 1908 to 1924 he worked in other parts of the country, including Nova Scotia and Newfoundland, and died in Ottowa.

JOHN GOODWIN

A. Lewis: *The Life and Work of the Rev. E. J. Peck among the Eskimos* (London 1904).

PENTECOST AND MISSIONS. The event that launched the church of Christ on her missionary career is known as Pentecost. It is described in Acts 2:1–13. Pentecost is the fulfilment of OT prophecies, and particularly of the promise of Christ that he would send another Comforter after his departure. The descent of the Spirit on the disciples was accompanied by three distinct signs: the rushing as of a mighty wind, tongues like fire that settled on their heads, and speaking in tongues or languages. The first two are mentioned and not again referred to. Doubtless they point to the irresistible power, the light, and purity of the Spirit. The remainder of the account is devoted to the speaking in tongues. Here the deepest meaning of Pentecost and the nature of the church are indicated. The church is a speaking, a witnessing, a proclaiming community. It is its nature to speak forth the word of life. The preaching of the gospel is the mysterious reproductive act of the church whereby sons and daughters continue to be born into the kingdom of God. From this proclamation issues the new birth, the new creation, and out of the new life so given arise the many activities of the church— worship, teaching, fellowship, study of the Scriptures, service. The emphasis in the Pentecost account is on the speaking in tongues because the universal proclamation of the gospel is the unalterable condition for the founding and growth of the church. Pentecost is therefore both the beginning and the foundation stone of all evangelistic endeavour.

At Pentecost the people of God were radically reconstituted to fit them for their new task of universal witness. The church replaced Israel, the Christian replaced the Jew, the preacher took the place of the priest, the pulpit that of the altar, the sermon and the sacrament that of sacrifice, the gospel that of the law, and the universalism of the NT replaced the particularism of the OT. Pentecost marked the end of Israel's temporary service that stretched from Abraham to Christ and marked the beginning of the new age which irrupted openly into the life of the people of God in the coming of the Spirit.

Yet neither Pentecost nor the Spirit has

ever fully captured the imagination of the church. Perhaps this is because it is the nature of the Spirit to serve without being observed, to give without receiving. The Son points us to the Father, the Spirit points to the Son, but the reticent Spirit is content to be glorified in the Father and in the Son from whom he proceeds.

HARRY R. BOER

R. Allen: *The Spontaneous Expansion of the Church and the Causes which Hinder it* (London³ 1956); H. R. Boer: *Pentecost and Missions* (London 1961); D. M. Paton, ed.: *The Ministry of the Spirit, selected writings of Roland Allen* (London 1960).

PENTECOSTAL MISSIONS as they are known today are the direct outgrowth of a spontaneous spiritual movement beginning in the early 1900s. Missionary work carried on by P. groups in the first two decades of this century was largely sponsored by individual churches or groups of churches in local areas. The result was that when P. denominations as such began to form, P. missionary work was already well developed. For example, the largest P. missionary body operating from North America is the General Council of the Assemblies of God which at the time of its organization in 1914 had 11 mission fields, each with an established missionary body. The Assemblies of God in 1967 reported 880 foreign missionaries under appointment in 76 countries of the world with adult adherents numbering 1,560,000, two-thirds of whom are active members of mission-planted churches.

'By 1958 the number of adherents to P. churches throughout the world totalled approximately 8½ million in 105 countries. This included statistics from about 40 P. organizations. The largest P. constituency in the world is in the USA' (*Our World Witness*, p.22), with Latin America very close. It is estimated that a large part of the constituency so reported was the result of the missionary outreach of the P. organizations involved.

Four factors are important in P. missionary advance:

(1) The spiritual consequences of the P. experience (*glossolalia*).

(2) The large number of missionaries.

(3) The practice of indigenous principles on the mission fields.

(4) The hunger for knowledge around the world.

Under the first related factor should be listed the Pentecostals' literal belief that every believer is directly responsible for the fulfilment of Christ's *great commission, 'Ye shall be witnesses unto me'. The result is that new converts without theological training open their homes and conduct local services in order to communicate to others what they have received. In their simplicity and intense optimism Pentecostals successfully use methods which others have decided are unworkable.

Missionary work by Pentecostals in the Latin American countries has largely originated from North America. There are major exceptions, however, for much P. missionary work today in Brazil originates from Scandinavia. P. organizations within South America have in recent years begun sending missionaries of their own to adjacent countries. P. missions in Africa originally had a number of missionaries from Europe, particularly from Germany and Scandinavia. Today most missionary work is carried out from North America, with a few missionaries from France, England, Scandinavia or other countries. Europe has indigenous P. organizations in every country. Most of these did not result from missionary work, although the Scandinavian countries and Great Britain made major initial contributions. Since the second war a number of missionaries have gone to Europe in a teaching and advisory capacity. Most of these are from America, England and Sweden. In Asia and the Far East P. missionary work has been carried out from both the Americas and from European countries. For example, Laos and Thailand have been chiefly evangelized by P. missionaries from Finland. Italian populations in Australia are being evangelized by missionaries from Italy. Free China and Japan are being reached by missionaries of P. faith from many nations. Korea is being reached largely from the USA. Oceania is being reached from the USA and Europe. Included in the list should be Indonesia, initially reached by missionaries from Holland and USA, but now reached largely by indigenous organizations as well as by missionaries, from America.

From North America the principal P. organizations sending missionaries abroad are the Assemblies of God, Pentecostal Assemblies of Canada, International Church of the Foursquare Gospel, Open Bible Standard Churches, Elim Missionary Assemblies and the Church of God, Cleveland, Tennessee. Other P. groups also have missionary programmes.

R. T. MCGLASSON

G. F. Atter: *The Third Force* (Peterborough, Ontario 1962); N. Perkin and J. Garlock: *Our World Witness* (Springfield, Missouri 1961).

PENZOTTI, FRANCISCO G. (1851–1925). This name is important to the early history of Protestant missions in Peru. Born in Italy, P. emigrated to Uruguay in 1864. He was converted through the preaching of Dr. J. F. *Thomson, a Metho-dist missionary. A few years later he became a pastor of a Waldensian congregation in Uruguay. As an agent of the American Bible Society, he did colportage work in Argentina, Bolivia and Chile, entering Peru in 1888. To avoid trouble, his meetings were conducted according to the law, behind closed doors, but he found the work very difficult. In 1890 he was arrested and imprisoned in filthy, semi-subterranean quarters, on the charge that his preaching violated the constitution. He was imprisoned for eight months while fanatical crowds demanded his death and threatened the Peruvian believers. However, the national Protestant Christians loyally stood by him and continued to meet. An American mining engineer, hearing of P's plight, gave the story to the *New York Herald*. As a result, public opinion became so aroused that

several influential people intervened on his behalf and accomplished his release. He continued to work in Peru for a time afterwards, until he was transferred to Central America. His name is now associated with the Penzotti Institutes, whose object is to make more efficient use of regular Bible Society Scripture distributors and also to involve the churches and missions by offering training for their members in techniques of Scripture distribution and use. The first Penzotti Institute in 1962 drew students from many countries to Mexico City for a course lasting nine months. Later a series of mobile institutes was formed, and evening classes were organized. One class in Puerto Rico enrolled 200 evening students.

IRENE M. BAMPTON

F. G. Penzotti: *Spiritual Victories in Latin America* (New York 1916); W. J. Townsend, H. B. Workman and G. Eayrs: *A New History of Methodism* (London 1909); United Bible Societies *News and Views*, No. 44, March 1964.

PEOPLE MOVEMENTS are a major mode of church growth. At least two-thirds of all converts from non-Christian religions have come to Christ through PMs. The PM is the way in which most non-Christians are now turning and in the future will turn to the Christian faith.

PMs also convey a quality to the Christian church which individual conversion out of a hostile non-Christian population seldom does. Men become Christian without social dislocation so that the resulting churches have leaders and loyalties intact. Churches are therefore likely to be more stable and self-supporting, and to bear up better under persecution. Conviction is buttressed by social cohesion.

A PM is the joint decision of a number of individuals comprising some section of society (perhaps five families and perhaps 50) which enables them to become Christian without social dislocation, while remaining in full contact with their non-Christian relatives, thus enabling other groups of that people (tribe, caste or section of society) across the years, after suitable instruction, to confess Christ and be formed into sound churches. What really takes place is *multi-individual mutually-interdependent* conversion. Each member of the group becoming Christian participates in the decision to follow Christ, while observing others of his kin making similar decisions at the same time.

Obviously a PM is not large numbers of unrelated individuals becoming Christian at the same time, as in an evangelistic meeting in a western city. It is not to be equated with careless baptizing. It should never be called a mass movement—large masses are not involved. Usually only a small group of well-instructed converts is baptized at any one time.

God has given the beginnings of thousands of PMs to the church; but most of them have neither been recognized nor developed into mature churches. Many have died. Many have become static Christian enclaves. A few have swept through an entire population leaving congregations everywhere, as among the Hebrews, Celts, Karens, Bataks, Madigas, Koreans in the Pyongan provinces, Lushais, Lisu, Tzeltals, Kikuyus, Wallamos, Chilean and Brazilian masses, and hundreds of other pieces of the human mosaic known as mankind.

The nurture of PMs is a greatly neglected branch of missionary knowledge. The vast experience of the church in dealing with them is locked up in many geographic, linguistic and denominational pockets. Better things, however, lie ahead.

DONALD A. MCGAVRAN

D. A. McGavran: *Bridges of God* (New York ²1963), *Understanding Church Growth* (Grand Rapids 1969); J. W. Pickett and D. A. McGavran: *Church Growth and Group Conversion* (Fuller Seminary, Pasadena 1962); J. W. Pickett: *Christ's Way to India's Heart* (Fuller Seminary ²1960); J. Sunda: *Church Growth in West New Guinea* (Fuller Seminary 1963); G. Vicedom: *Church and People in New Guinea* (London 1961); J. Wold: *God's Impatience in Liberia* (Grand Rapids 1965).

PERIODICALS FOR MISSIONARY STUDY. See JOURNALS FOR MISSION STUDIES.

PERU. After the conquest in the 16th century, the Spanish king entrusted the evangelism of the Peruvian Indians largely to the new landowners. Coercion was often used and the results were very superficial. The work done by the missionary friars was on a much higher level but it was swamped by the general tide in which the Indians learned to express their old beliefs and superstitions in forms which were apparently Christian. After the declaration of independence in 1821 James *Thomson found that there were great opportunities for education and Bible circulation, but these soon passed as a result of a conservative reaction led by the landowners.

After several abortive attempts, Protestantism finally gained a foothold in Peru when Francisco G. *Penzotti, an agent of the American Bible Society, established a congregation in Callao in 1888, which became the basis of the Methodist church in P. Penzotti was imprisoned for supposedly having contravened the constitution, but the Supreme Court of P. finally declared him innocent because he had held his meetings in private. Only in 1915 did public non-RC worship become possible. In 1894 Charles H. Bright, a Plymouth Brother, established the Calle Negreiros congregation in Lima, which later under John Ritchie's leadership became the basis of the Peruvian Evangelical church. Permanent evangelistic work among the Quechua Indians of southern P. was started in 1898. In 1911 this work was taken over by the Evangelical Union of South America, but up to the present this field has remained difficult.

In 1910 Frederick Stahl of the SDA was asked to help the Aymará Indians living on the southern shores of Lake Titicaca. As a result of a largely self-supporting educational programme great progress was made in this field. In 1919 *Pentecostal missionaries established themselves in the

Callejon de Huaylas region and shortly afterwards they started to expand into other regions. In the 1920s various missions started to work in the jungle area to the east of the Andes. Since 1943, the arrival of the *Wycliffe Bible Translators has given a considerable impulse to this work and today one half of the 540 Protestant missionaries in P. are at work in this region.

At present Protestants represent about $1\frac{1}{4}\%$ of the population. Approximately half of them are Adventists, one quarter are Pentecostals and the remaining quarter includes all the other bodies. Protestantism is hindered by unnecessary divisions, in many cases of foreign origin, and by the fact that those churches which have excelled in lay ministry have largely failed to establish full-time pastors, while those churches which have established a strong professional ministry have been unable to maintain an enthusiastic lay participation. Recently the *Maryknoll Fathers from the USA have been making dedicated efforts to improve the content of Peruvian Roman Catholicism, but so far the renewal movement initiated by the Second *Vatican Council has had little obvious effect in P.

J. B. A. KESSLER, JR

J. B. A. Kessler, Jr: *A Study of the Older Protestant Missions and Churches in Peru and Chile* (Goes, Holland 1967); *BM* II, 687–94; *NCE* XI, 184–93; *WKL*, 1128f.

PETITJEAN, BERNARD (1829–1884), was born at Blanzy-sur-Bourbince (Saône-et-Loire), France. He was ordained priest on 21 May 1853 and worked in his home diocese, until in 1859 he entered the Seminary of the *MEP in Paris. He went to Japan in 1860. He built a church at Nagasaki, inaugurated on 19 February 1865. At this time he was approached by some women who questioned him seemingly on the Virgin Mary and the great 'king of doctrine', the pope. He soon discovered that these were descendants of the ancient church founded by St. Francis *Xavier. They had maintained the faith throughout the years of persecution and although their knowledge of the faith was somewhat

obscure, they had kept its essentials. The organization of the secret community was almost the same in all villages: there were two principal men, one of whom was leader of prayers on Sunday and ministered consolation to the dying, the other being the baptizer. There was considerable variation in the administration of baptism. (Recently, Fr J. van Hecken has made known that there are still 30,000 of the crypto-Christians on the islands to the west of Kyushu, who maintain their quasi-Christian faith and practices in total separation from the general life of the Christian church.) In 1866 P. was made first *Vicar Apostolic of Japan by Pius IX. In 1873 he conferred the tonsure on the first Japanese clerics, who were ordained priests in 1883. At his suggestion, Japan was divided into two Apostolic Vicariates by Rome in 1876: one being North Japan with Mgr. Ozouf resident at Tokyo, the other South Japan with Mgr. Petitjean, whose centre was first at Osaka and later at Nagasaki, where he died.

ARTHUR MCCORMACK, MHM

J. Guennou: *Les Missions Etrangères* (Paris 1963); *NCE*, art., 'Paris Foreign Missions Society'.

PFANDER, KARL GOTTLIEB (1803–1865), exerted great influence over the pattern of Christian missions to Muslims. He was born in Waiblingen, Württemberg, Germany, and for eleven years worked for the *Basel Mission in S. Russia and Persia, where he wrote his famous polemic *Mīzān al-Haqq*, (*The Balance of Truth*); first published in Persian in 1835, it was translated into many languages, including English in 1867 (Revised ed., tr. by W. St. C. Tisdall, London 1910). He vindicated Christian and Jewish Scriptures and went on to discredit the Qur'ān and Muhammad. From 1841 he worked for the *CMS among Muslims in Agra and Peshawar. His books and public debates with Muslims provoked reciprocal polemic against Christianity, especially in Iran. One of his most famous debates with four Muslims at

Agra may have sown the seed of the eventual conversion of one of his opponents, Imād ud-dīn. Despite the essentially apologetic argumentation with which he supports Christian morality, the doctrine of the atonement etc., P. does not depend entirely on human reason, and may seal an argument by insisting on divine discretion. From 1858 to 1865 he lived in Constantinople.

JOHN B. TAYLOR

PHILANTHROPIC MINISTRIES form a very minor part of Protestant work compared with Roman Catholic. This is due to the traditional devotion of orders of nuns to such service and to RC strategy in building the Christian community by marrying orphans to each other, while Protestants treated orphanages as rescue work. These ministries continue to expand in RC work and decline in Protestant missions. The first complete census of Protestant work, 1901, shows 247 orphanages with 16,916 children plus fourteen homes for uncontaminated children of lepers. There were 100 leper institutions of all kinds, with 7,523 inmates. Thirty schools and homes for the blind and deaf had 533 pupils. Rescue centres, opium refuges, homes for widows and for converts, and asylums for the insane, totalled 156, with 6,866 inmates. Eventually progress in the cure of leprosy shifted leprosaria from philanthropic to medical work. The last complete census, 1938, revealed only 171 orphanages with 7,981 children and 24 homes for aged, rescue homes and shelters with 1,515 inmates. In contrast, RCs in 1950 had 1,720 orphanages with 93,835 children and 260 homes for aged with 13,356 inmates. Protestants responded to specific needs; thus all but three opium refuges were in China.

See also BLIND, MISSIONS TO THE; DEAF, MISSIONS TO THE; HUMANITARIAN CONCERN; LEPROSY MISSIONS.

R. PIERCE BEAVER

See the standard occasional surveys, from J. S. Dennis: *Centennial Survey of Foreign Missions* (New York 1902), to J. I. Parker: *Interpretative Statistical Survey of the World Mission of the Christian Church* (New York 1937); *Le Missioni Cattoliche* (Rome 1950).

PHILIP, JOHN (1775–1851), was born at Kirkcaldy, Scotland, where his father was a weaver. As the manager of a power mill in Dundee P. resigned in protest over the conditions of the child labourers and set up his own business. In 1802 he completed his training as a Congregational minister, serving first at Newbury and then for fourteen years in Aberdeen. He married Jane Ross in 1809, became a resident director of the *LMS, and in 1819 received honorary doctor's degrees from Columbia and Princeton universities in USA.

When the LMS sent him to South Africa in 1819 to visit the society's work, he remained there as superintendent of the mission, having the responsibility of financing, staffing and planning the policy of more than thirty stations. He travelled extensively in S. Africa and probably knew the over-all situation better than any of his contemporaries. At the same time he was the minister of the Union Congregational Church in Cape Town. He is best known for his struggle on behalf of the Hottentots which basically resulted in alleviating their conditions but alienating white settlers and some government officials from the work of the LMS. He gathered extensive evidence regarding the Hottentot forced service, disabilities in land holdings and civil liberties. He believed the colonists to be the oppressors and presented evidence to British parliamentarians like William Wilberforce. His efforts led to a visit to South Africa of a British Government Commission of Enquiry and an Ordinance in 1828 giving the Hottentots equality with others in the Cape Colony. P. then turned to the reform of justice in the colony, which later was modelled on his plans. He fought for a free press in S. Africa and opposed much of the official native policy. He was not against the extension of the colonial frontier, but wanted to have the African assured of land. To protect the Africans on the land he proposed a policy of segregation where African land holdings would be out of reach of the settlers. He saw the frontier problems to be land and social disorder. He courageously called attention to the social problems of his time but was not always understood by his contemporaries. He helped the *ABCFM, the *Rhenish Missionary Society and the *PEMS to select their respective fields of service.

PER HASSING

W. M. Macmillan: *Bantu, Boer and Briton* (London 1928); J. Philip: *Researches in South Africa, Illustrating the Civil, Moral and Religious Condition of the Native Tribes* (London 1828); R. Philip: *The Elijah of South Africa: or the Character and Spirit of the late Rev John Philip, DD, Unveiled and Vindicated* (London 1851); *DNB* XLV, 156.

PHILIPPINE   INDEPENDENT CHURCH. See PHILIPPINES; AGLIPAY, GREGORIO; REYES, ISABELO DE LOS.

PHILIPPINES, 115,830 sq.m., 35 million population (1968 est.), 82% Roman Catholic. More than 7,000 islands form the archipelago, 90% of which are uninhabited, 60% unnamed. Two-thirds of the population live on the two largest islands, Luzon and Mindanao. Fully independent since 4 July 1946, the capital is Quezon City near Manila. Pilipino (based on Tagalog) is the national language; English is spoken by 40%, Spanish by 2%, and there are about 90 local dialects.

In the 14th century Arab traders and missionaries brought *Islam to the Sulu and other southern islands. Christianity was introduced by Ferdinand Magellan who claimed the islands for Spain in 1521. The RC church was permanently established by the expedition of Miguel López de Legazpi and Fr. Andrés de Urdaneta, OSA, in 1565, which also halted the spread of Islam.

The *Augustinians were aided by the arrival of the *Franciscans (1577), the *Jesuits (1581) and the *Dominicans

(1587). Within one hundred years the Spanish missionary orders, working hand in hand with the *conquistadores*, succeeded in converting the vast majority of the population and thereby establishing the only Christian nation in Asia. They founded the Colegio de San Ildefonso and Colegio de San Ignacio, 1595; University of Santo Tomás, 1611, and Colegio de San Juan de Letran, 1620.

Two perennial problems of the RC church in the P. are nominalism within its membership and an abnormally slow development of the native clergy. One Catholic scholar wrote in 1966 that 'at most 3% of all Filipino families are regularly practising Catholic families'. The first Filipino bishop was not appointed until 1905, the first Filipino cardinal in 1960, and in 1965 only 2,285 of the 4,175 priests were Filipinos. While there is an average of one priest for every 5,600 Catholics, it is estimated that there is only one priest engaged in the parish ministry for every 12,000 Catholics.

The desire for reform and nationalization of the Catholic church led to a split and the formation of the Philippine Independent Church (*Iglesia Filipina Independiente*) in 1902 under the leadership of Isabelo de los *Reyes, Sr., an eminent Filipino labour leader and journalist, and Gregorio *Aglipay, a Filipino priest who was elected *Obispo Maximo* (Supreme Bishop) of the new church. After a period of unitarian theological tendencies and schism within its own ranks, the PIC adopted a trinitarian Declaration of Faith and Articles of Religion, under the leadership of Isabelo de los Reyes, Jr., who was elected *Obispo Maximo* in 1946. In 1948 the PECUSA conferred the historic episcopate through re-consecration of three PIC bishops, and in 1961 these two churches entered into a Concordat of Full Communion; they jointly sponsor St. Andrew's Theological Seminary in Quezon City. The PIC has approximately two million members (5.2% of the population), and is a member of the NCCP, *EACC and *WCC.

The first regular Protestant missionaries

(James B. *Rodgers) arrived in Manila shortly after the *Bible Societies and *YMCA in 1899, in the wake of the Spanish-American war with the advent of the American régime. Prior to that time freedom of worship and circulation of the Bible were prohibited by the Spanish colonial government under pressure of the RC church. The American government guaranteed religious freedom and separation of church and state.

In 1901 the Evangelical Union was founded and a *comity arrangement agreed upon by the *Methodists, *Presbyterians, *United Brethren and American *Baptists. The *Disciples of Christ (arrived in 1901) and the *Congregationalists (1902) soon joined the Union. The Protestant Episcopal Church (1900), *CMA (1902) and SDA (1905) did not join the Union, but maintained friendly relations. Silliman University was founded by Presbyterians in Dumaguete City, 1901; Central Philippine University was started in 1905 by American Baptists. In 1907 the Union Theological Seminary was founded in Manila by the Methodists and Presbyterians. In 1908 the Methodists started Mary Johnston Hospital in Manila (see PARRISH, SARAH REBECCA).

The United Brethren, Presbyterian and Congregational churches united in 1929 to form the United Evangelical Church. In 1932 six smaller independent and indigenous denominations merged to form the *Iglesia Evangelica Unida de Cristo*. In 1943 a new and larger united church, the Evangelical Church in the P., was formed with the encouragement of the Japanese occupation forces. This merger dissolved at the end of the war, and in 1948 a larger and more inclusive church was formed with the organization of the United Church of Christ in the P. (UCCP). It was a merger of the United Evangelical Church, the remnant Evangelical Church, Philippine Methodist Church, part of the Disciples of Christ and some congregations of the IEMELIF and the *Unida de Cristo*.

Some of the larger Protestant churches, such as the Methodist and American Baptist, chose not to participate in any of these organic unions. But they have co-operated through membership in the *National Christian Council (1929), the P. Federation of Evangelical Churches (1938), P. Federation of Christian Churches (1949); and in 1963 seven churches formed the *National Council of Churches (NCCP): UCCP, Methodist, Baptist, Episcopal, PIC, IEMELIF and *Unida de Cristo*. The total Protestant community is approximately 3% of the population. In 1962, the UCCP had 135,467 full communicant members and Methodists had 71,973. Both these churches are members of the EACC and have been sending out Filipino missionaries since the 1950s. There is a nationwide ratio of one full-time minister per 350 Protestants. All bishops in UCCP, Methodist, PIC and Episcopal churches are Filipinos. The Bible is translated and published, in part at least, in 45 of the dialects. There are sixteen Protestant hospitals (1,700 beds) and 44 clinics.

Schism and proliferation have also marked the Protestant churches. The Methodist church was split in 1909 (Nicolas *Zamora) and 1933 (P. Methodist Church formed, later joined UCCP). Presbyterians, Disciples, Baptists and others also suffered splits. After the second world war, and especially with expulsion of missionaries from China, many new mission societies began work in the P., several of which are non-co-operating.

The *Iglesia ni Cristo*, an indigenous Christian sect of Protestant orientation founded in 1914 by Felix Manalo (1886–1963), has approximately 350,000 members (1% of the population) and is the fastest growing religious group in the nation.

Five per cent of the population are Muslim, concentrated in the southern islands; 2% are primitive animist, and 1% Buddhist, primarily among Chinese.

GERALD H. ANDERSON

P. S. Achútegui and M. A. Bernad: *Religious Revolution in the Philippines* (3 vols., Manila 1960 ff.); G. H. Anderson, ed.: *Studies in Philippine Church*

History (Ithaca, New York 1969); H. de la Costa: *The Jesuits in the Philippines, 1581–1768* (Cambridge, Mass. 1961); R. L. Deats: *The Story of Methodism in the Philippines* (Manila 1964), *Nationalism and Christianity in the Philippines* (Dallas 1967); D. J. Elwood: *Churches and Sects in the Philippines* (Manila 1968); P. G. Gowing: *Islands under the Cross* (Manila 1967); J. L. Phelan: *The Hispanization of the Philippines* (Madison, Wisconsin 1959); J. B. Rodgers: *Forty Years in the Philippines* (New York 1940); E. C. Sobrepeña: *That They May Be One* (rev. ed., Manila 1964); L. B. Whittemore: *Struggle For Freedom* (New York 1961); *BM* II, 694–703; *NCE* XI, 280–84.

PHILOSOPHY OF MISSIONS. See THEOLOGY OF MISSION.

PIETISM AND MISSIONS. P. began as a movement to recover the 'first love', the primary religious experience of the early Christians. Its abiding institutional effects today may be found in the *Moravians, the Church of the Brethren, and the Amana Colonies in Iowa. Its view of church history stands forth in Gottfried Arnold's *Kirchen- und Ketzer-Historie* (Frankfurt/M 1700), J. L. Mosheim's *Anderweitiger Versuch einer vollständiger und unpartheyischen Ketzergeschichte* (Helmstedt 1748–1750) and J. K. Füsslin's *Neue und unpartheyische Kirchen und Ketzerhistorie der mittlern Zeit* (Frankfurt/M and Leipzig 1770–1774). The Church of the Brethren, with *Mennonites and *Quakers one of the 'historic peace churches' in the USA, is noted for its international relief work through the Brethren Service Commission. The Amana Colonies, modelled for generations on the communism of the church at Jerusalem, have conducted no missions or other outreach and have recently declined to the status of a joint stock company.

Early leaders of P., with strong emphasis upon personal conversion, purity of life, lay initiative, non-resistance and the claims of the *Great Commission, include Philipp Jakob Spener (1635–1705), generally considered the founder of the movement (*Pia Desideria* 1675), August Hermann Francke (1663–1727), leader in the *Danish-Halle Mission and in the newly founded University of Halle (f. 1694 under Spener's influence). and Count N. von *Zinzendorf (1700–1760), leader in the reorganization of the Moravians and in early ecumenics and missions. The movement spread throughout Christendom, however, and profoundly affected the spiritual life, social service and missionary work of a number of persons and societies which remained within Calvinist, Lutheran and Anglican communions. Arising after the tragedy of the Thirty Years' War, in reaction to the dead orthodoxy of most of the Protestant establishments, P. spread in three generations to be an enlivening force in Europe and an ecumenical influence toward inter-church co-operation in America.

Although he finally decided to follow another theological and disciplinary line, John *Wesley (1703–1791), founder of Methodism, owed his conversion and his vision of a restitution of apostolic Christianity in good part to the Moravians. He issued von Mosheim's *History* as a basic reader for his preachers, adopted the 'Love Feast' and 'class meetings', and kept a Journal of spiritual progress and urged literate believers to do likewise. Charles Wesley (1707–1788) was also converted under the influence of the Moravian Peter Böhler, and like his brother wrote hundreds of devotional hymns of marked personal piety. By the time of the Evangelical Awakening, Pietist influences were also being filtered through the English Puritan strain. In both England and America the interaction of P. and Puritanism was very great— as documented by the correspondence of Francke and the American Cotton *Mather, and by the Wittgenstein Collection in the *Westdeutsche Bibliothek* (Marburg). John Wesley's vision of the world parish was made up of one part study of the Apostolic Fathers, one part Moravian influence, and one part recognition of the historic moment in the expansion of English culture and civilization across the world map.

Another major fruit of P. was the founding of missionary societies and works through established channels. The Tranquebar Mission (f.1706), authorized and financed by King Frederick IV of Denmark and staffed by men from the Halle Mission, is a prime example of this penetration. B. *Ziegenbalg and H. Plütschau, although resented by the garrison chaplains and harrassed by the commandant, learned the languages and converted some Portuguese and Tamils and enlisted support from Danish, German and English (*SPCK) sources. Among those who came to assist the work at Tranquebar none had a wider influence throughout India than C. F. *Schwartz (1726–1798). Educated in Halle, his active life was spent in missions and education of great impact throughout South India.

P. was revived in the 19th century in reaction to Rationalism, and profoundly affected cultural and national developments through men like the German F. D. E. Schleiermacher (1768–1834) and the Dane S. Kierkegaard (1813–1855) and church life through A. W. Neander (1789–1850) and A. G. Tholuck (1799–1877). Among major missionary societies founded at this time were the Evangelical Mission in *Basel (1815), the *Berliner Mission (1824) and the *Gossner Mission (1828). The *revival movements in Germany and Scandinavia, the Great Awakening and subsequent revivals in North America, and even the *Innere Mission* (closely identified with national churches though it was) were heavily influenced by the revival of P. in the great century of home and foreign missions, as were also the Evangelical Alliance and like organs of the early ecumenical movement.

FRANKLIN H. LITTELL

E. Benz: 'Pietist and Puritan Sources of Early Protestant World Missions (Cotton Mather and A. H. Francke)', *Church History*, XX (1951), pp.28–55; D. F. Durnbaugh: *European Origins of the Brethren* (Elgin, Illinois 1958); K. S.

Latourette: *A History of the Expansion of Christianity, III: Three Centuries of Advance* (New York and London 1939), pp.277–82; M. Schmidt: '*Pietismus*', RGG^3 (1961), cols. 470–81 (with extensive bibliography); B. M. H. Shambaugh: *Amana that was and Amana that is* (Iowa City 1932); *ERE* IX, 6–9; *NCE* XI, 354–56.

PIGNEAU DE BEHAINE, PIERRE JOSEPH GEORGES (1741–1799), was born at Origny-en-Thiérache (Aisne), France. In 1765 he became a member of the *MEP, and was sent to Cochin China, where he taught for a period in the General Seminary. P. de B. acquired an excellent knowledge of the language, and prepared among other works a dictionary of the Annamite language. He was made titular Bishop of Adran in 1770 and *Vicar Apostolic of Cochin China in 1771. Later he became active in local politics, and set himself to secure the restoration to power of Nguyen-Hanh, the last legitimate survivor of the dethroned dynasty, who took refuge with the bishop. P. de B. undertook to obtain the help of France, and for this purpose undertook a journey to Paris accompanied by the heir to the throne Prince Canh. On 25 November 1787 the treaty of Versailles was solemnly signed; but secret instructions were sent to the east that it was not to be put into effect. Undeterred P. de B. raised at Pondicherry a force of volunteers, through whose efforts Nguyen-Hanh, who later took the regnal name of Gialong, became master of the entire country. In spite of his sincere regard for the bishop he never became a Christian; indeed it is doubtful whether he ever had any intention of doing so. When P. de B. died at Quinhon on 9 October 1799, he was given something like a national funeral; but his grandiose schemes for linking political activity to the progress of the gospel came to nothing. Persecution of the RC church continued until the establishment of the French dominion between 1859 and 1885.

ARTHUR MCCORMACK, MHM

S. Delacroix: *H. U. des Missions Catho-*

liques, Vol. II (Paris 1957), pp.222–26; J. Guennou: *Les Missions Etrangères* (Paris 1963); E. Louvet: *Monseigneur d'Adran* (Saigon 1896); *LTK* IX, 503.

PIONEER WORK. The term may be held to cover all the stages in missionary work between the first making of contact with a previously unknown and non-Christian people, and the coming into being of a convinced and orderly, though perhaps very small, Christian community. In the extreme cases, the messenger of the gospel starts with no knowledge whatever of the language or the customs of the people. Everything must be toilfully learnt by endless trial and error; and even after many years of labour it can be taken as certain that the missionaries will have failed to understand fully the culture of the people in the midst of whom they work. The following stages are likely to be passed through, on the purely natural level, in the intercourse between the missionary and the non-Christian: (1) *Fear.* Often the white man has been taken for a god or a ghost; and the extraordinary things that he is able to do, such as to produce fire with a burning-glass, are taken as evidence of divine nature and power. (2) *Curiosity.* As time passes, and the white man is recognized to be at least in the main human, he becomes the object of ceaseless and watchful attention; in particular his religious activities catch the attention of those to whom they are completely unfamiliar. (3) *Interest.* It begins to dawn on the observers that they can learn from the white man; the message will penetrate, and the non-Christian discovers that it may be possible for him too to learn to read and to master the white man's magic. (4) *Boredom.* Familiarity begins to play its part. The missionary seems to be always talking about the same things. Learning to read is a very wearisome business. The missionary has exhausted his usefulness as a good milking-cow; he has learned to be more cautious in giving, and very likely has nothing more to give. (5) *Resentment.* The white man is clearly there to stay. He is beginning to interfere with the local way of life, and is trying to get things changed to suit his own ideas and convenience.

The period during which these experiences are being passed through is likely to be one of not less than twenty years. But during this period something else is also happening. A great deal depends on the patience and integrity of the missionary. If what he is corresponds to what he says, one and another will be awakened to enquire why the Christian life is so different from any other life that he has ever known. In this first period, enquirers and converts are likely to be very few; the time of rapid ingathering comes in the second generation. But when the missionary has gathered round him a flock of six persons, with whom he is able freely to converse, and who show signs of having really accepted the message, the pioneer stage of the work is at an end.

The great period of pioneer work was the 19th century. The Christian mission is now so widely extended that far less pioneer work in the strict sense of the term is needed. If the term is taken in a rather wider sense, a great part of the responsibility of the church is for missionary work in its pioneer stage. The areas in which pioneer work is urgently needed today appear to be:

Japan: almost the entire village population (20 million).

The mountain peoples on the borders of *Thailand, Laos* and *Cambodia.*

Indonesia: many of the smaller islands.

India and Pakistan: at least 100 million people, many of them living in what until 1947 were the 'Indian Native States'.

Iran: almost the entire village population (18 million).

Africa: about 50 million *animists, belonging to perhaps 300 tribes, which have remained wholly or almost wholly untouched by the gospel.

Latin America: many of the remote Indian peoples, as yet unreached by either Protestant or Roman Catholic missions.

Development of pioneer work has been gravely hindered by the theory held for about 60 years, according to which all evangelistic and pastoral work should be handed over to the *indigenous church. But in a great many cases the indigenous church has neither the men nor the money to engage in extensive work beyond its own borders; and experience has shown that the western Christian, with a longer Christian tradition behind him, with greater patience and resourcefulness, makes a better pioneer than the indigenous Christian. In view of these facts, a number of missionary societies (such as the picturesquely named *Regions Beyond and the *Worldwide Evangelization Crusade) have been formed expressly to go where no one else has ever gone before. Their work in reaching hitherto unreached regions is beyond praise.

So far we have considered the geographical aspect of missions. But in recent years areas have developed with wholly new problems, and in these it is legitimate to speak of pioneer work. We may mention as examples the great new cities of Africa; the world of industry and of the trade unions, in many countries largely under communist influence; and the new *dialogue with non-Christian religions and understandings of men (Marxist, etc.), which are now self-conscious, self-confident and missionary in their outlook.

Conditions for pioneer work today are far more favourable than those of a century and a half ago. Health in tropical regions is hardly any more a problem. The sciences of ethnology and philology can save the pioneer from many of the errors made by his predecessors in the past. The records of earlier missions offer guidance as to good and bad methods of carrying on the work. But no method has as yet been found of speeding up the slow and laborious processes described in this article. Faith and patience in no small measure are still demanded of the pioneer.

There is no recent survey of 'unoccupied fields', such as that prepared after the *Edinburgh conference of 1910 by Samuel M. *Zwemer: *Unoccupied Mission Fields of Africa and Asia* (1911). Much can be gathered from the RC publication *Bilan du*

Monde (latest edition 2 vols. 1965); and a study of the articles in this dictionary, country by country, will also serve as an indication of needs and opportunities.

STEPHEN NEILL

PITCAIRN ISLAND. See PACIFIC ISLANDS.

PLURALISM, RELIGIOUS. In the west it has been customary to think of one religion in one country. This kind of thinking was due to the spread of Christianity through Europe until the whole continent was nominally Christian. There were religious minorities (in particular, the Jewish communities), but the minorities were either scarcely tolerated or even persecuted.

In the east, however, religions have often coexisted. In India radically different ideas were embraced within the one *'Hinduism', whilst *Parsee, *Jain, *Muslim, *Sikh and Christian minorities existed. In China, *Confucianism, *Taoism and *Buddhism coexisted, and mutually influenced one another, whilst Japan's religious tradition was based upon both *Shinto and Buddhism, together with a large admixture of Confucianist and Taoist beliefs and practices.

This multiple-religious situation is referred to as 'religious pluralism', and, in the modern world, it has become a worldwide phenomenon. Where many religions are to be found in the same country, questions of their inter-relationship obviously arise. Is the faith, which is numerically dominant, to exercise authority over the rest, and seek to suppress other faiths and ideologies? Is one religion to be tolerant towards replies to fundamental questions, which are different from its own; and is it to go on to accept the validity of the different solutions? Here Christianity finds itself in difficulties. If the church, true to its mission, seeks to evangelize, and, in so doing, wins converts from other faiths, is this to be understood as an attitude of intolerance and superiority? Many religions claim to be tolerant, and attack what they regard as 'intolerance' on the part of Christians. There is obviously no place for arrogance on the part of Christians, but 'conviction' should not be misunderstood as 'intolerance'. The fact of religious pluralism must be accepted, and the situation demands that inter-religious dialogue take place. The Christian, in such dialogue, will respect the integrity and sincerity of the adherents of other faiths, and will accept the necessary link between religious pluralism and religious toleration. The same freedom for worship and belief that the Christian expects for himself must be granted to others—within the Christian institutions as well as in society as a whole.

RAYMOND J. HAMMER

A. T. Van Leeuwen: *Christianity in World History* (London 1964).

POLLARD, SAMUEL (1864–1915) was, born at Camelford, Cornwall, UK. Son of a Bible Christian (Methodist) minister, he became one of the first missionaries of that church, arriving in Yunnan Province, China, in 1887. He pioneered in Chaotung and Kunming, 1887–1904. He was visited by four Miao tribesmen in 1904 who asked him to bring the gospel to the mountain villages. This began his most significant work, and the rest of his life was devoted to *pioneer work amongst the Miao and No-su tribespeople of S.W. China. Large *mass-movement baptisms resulted; schools were begun, together with elementary medical work; moral and family life were transformed. Within ten years the Christian community numbered ten thousand. P. died of typhoid at Stone Gateway, a few weeks after completing the translation of the NT into Miao.

CYRIL J. DAVEY

E. Kendall: *Beyond the Clouds* (London 1949); E. Kendall, ed.: *Eyes of the Earth*; *The Diary of Samuel Pollard* (London 1954).

POLYANDRY is the term used of a regular and recognized marriage, in which one woman lives as the wife of more than one man; it is to be distinguished from cicisbeism, in which a number of men can for a limited period lay claim to a woman, who is, however, actually the wife of only one among them. There are isolated cases of P. in Africa, in North America and in the Marquesas Islands; but more frequently is it found in Ceylon and the Himalayas. The causes of the appearance of this custom seem to be complex, and affected by historic, demographic, sociological, economic and personal factors. The chief expert on the subject, Prince Peter of Greece, supported the anthropological view. The centres of the practice of P. lie within the sphere of the Buddhist religion. In India the British government forbade P. as early as the 19th century. Naturally it is irreconcilable with the Christian view of marriage. In the ancient Indian epic the Mahābhārata, 4th century B.C., Draupadī is the wife of the five Pāndava princes; this is thought by many scholars to be evidence of the antiquity of this practice in India.

ERNST DAMMANN

H.R.H. Prince Peter of Greece and Denmark: *A Study of Polyandry* (The Hague 1963).

POLYGAMY, POLYGYNY is that form of marriage in which a man is legitimately joined to a number of women. It is principally found in the *primitive religions and in *Islam, but is not unknown in other religious systems (e.g. *Hinduism). It is determined by sociological factors (a natural right to marry), and by economic considerations (help to the man, especially among peoples where agriculture is carried on). A woman gains protection through marriage, which in most cases is regarded as a relationship of possession. Among primitive peoples, polygamous life follows a set of prescribed rules. In most cases each wife has her own dwelling, and the wives are visited by their husband in turn. This relationship is not felt to be degrading. In Islam, where a man is not allowed to have more than four wives simultaneously, the wife is less completely protected. Abuses of P., in which the wife becomes no more than an instrument to satisfy the lust or the caprice of the husband, are not unknown. There are occasional manifestations of P. as a part of religious observance (Hinduism).

Movements for the emancipation of women have led to the widespread abandonment of P., at least in theory. The Ahmadiyya Muslims attempt to show that monogamy is in fact commanded in the Qur'ān.

In many *younger churches P. is one of the gravest problems that have to be faced. Almost everywhere the baptism of polygamists has been, and is, made dependent on willingness to put away all the wives except the first. To many Christians this practice does not seem to be reasonable, especially because in the OT they do not find the institution of P. condemned, and in the NT monogamy is not expressly enjoined. The question cannot be evaded whether the rigid practice so far followed has not involved the introduction of law into the life of the church, and whether it is really right to break up marriages which were legitimate when they were entered into.

It is possible that P. might be accepted as a temporary solution; but the goal to be aimed at must always be monogamy, in the light of which alone it is possible to interpret the NT picture of the relationship between Christ and his church.

ERNST DAMMANN

R. H. Lowie: *Primitive Society* (New York 1947); E. G. Parrinder: *The Bible and Polygamy* (London 1950); W. E. Peukert: *Ehe* (Hamburg 1955); T. Price: *African Marriage* (London 1954).

POLYNESIA. See PACIFIC ISLANDS.

POLYTHEISM, the worship of many gods, is found in almost every part of the world, and on many different levels of religious experience. It seems to reflect man's experience of the great natural forces around him, which he cannot control, and in fear of which he must live. The *Rig Veda* of India seems to stand at that very interesting point at which these natural forces are turning themselves into divine beings with individual existence and personal characteristics. Are the *Ushas*, the dawns, simply the bright days as they appear, or are they goddesses, of whom the dawn is the visible manifestation? In Homer the transition has clearly been made; the Olympian gods are already persons, all too human in their loves, their quarrels and their prejudices. The moment this stage has been reached, the polytheistic system runs the risk of being killed by mockery; we can see this developing through the Greek writers, Homer, Euripides and Lucian.

The view has been widely held that the gods were originally human beings who were conspicuous for strength, or had rendered great services to their people, and then after death in gratitude were raised to divine estate. But for this there seems little evidence. The Greeks recognized heroes and demigods, but these were not the same as gods. Almost all over Africa the distinguished dead become ancestors; these play an extremely important part in the life of the tribe, and have some divine attributes, but are not strictly speaking gods. The deification of the Roman emperors after death was artificial; reverence was paid rather to the *genius* of the emperor, that mysterious, numinous quality by which the fabric of the empire was held together.

Many religions distinguish between the Uranian gods of the world above and the Chthonic gods of the underworld. It would be too simple to say that the gods of light are good, and the gods of the dark are evil; yet naturally there is a tendency to identify light with life and hope, and the darkness with death and sorrow.

In some strictly monotheistic religions, such as *Islam, belief in spirits, good and evil, plays a very important part in the life of the simple worshipper. But these animistic survivals, though confusing to simple people, are not allowed to dim the reality of the one God, who alone is to be worshipped.

Many observers hold the view that even

the polytheist is a man in search of unity. The mind of man seems naturally to seek for unity of experience and understanding. It may be that he can express what he feels only in shadows and in many forms; he is still conscious of the underlying unity which he seeks. The thoughtful Hindu feels no sharp conflict between the monism of philosophy and the polytheistic practices which may be part of his daily life. But there is a long road to be travelled from this naïve awareness of, or search for, oneness, and the knowledge of the one God, Creator and Saviour of men.

STEPHEN NEILL

ERE X, 112–14.

POMPALLIER, JEAN-BAPTISTE-FRANÇOIS (1801–1871), was born at Lyon, France. In 1829 he was ordained a secular priest and in 1836 was nominated first *Vicar Apostolic of Western Oceania. In 1838 he arrived with some Marist Fathers in New Zealand and began his work of conversion among the Maoris. In 1842 New Zealand was made a separate Apostolic Vicariate with P. as its head. In 1848 he became Apostolic Administrator of the newly erected diocese of Auckland. Unfortunately, friction arose between the Roman Catholics and the Protestants. But much graver conflicts arose between the Maoris and the white immigrants. Wars broke out, first in the 1840s and then more extensively, in 1860. By 1871 the last of the scattered Maori forces were subdued. P. resigned in 1869 and returned to France where he died two years later.

ARTHUR MCCORMACK, MHM

J. J. Wilson: *The Church in New Zealand* (Dunedin 1910); *LTK* VIII, 603; *NCE* XI, 545.

POPES. See MISSION ENCYCLICALS.

POPULATION, GROWTH OF. It is estimated that it took from history's beginning to 1830 for world population to reach 1,000 million. By 1930, a century later, it reached 2,000 million, and in 1965

it passed 3,000 million. If the present rate of increase is maintained, present numbers will double so that by the year 2000 there will be over 6,000 million. The implications of these figures are startling: (a) Half of all the people ever born are alive today. (b) A century from now the population of the earth could be 24 billion. (c) 80% of the population expected for the year 2000 will live in the poorly nourished developing countries. (d) 60% of the world's population are young people under 30 years of age, and 40% of these are between the ages of 15 and 29. (e) Half the world's population is in five countries: China, India, Soviet Union, United States and Pakistan. (f) Famine of epidemic proportions is predicted as early as 1975 for nations of large population growth, notably China, India, Pakistan, Indonesia, Egypt and possibly Brazil.

The two major responses of the world to this growth are (1) the attempt to expand and cultivate arable land. The US Department of Agriculture estimates that the world's crop-land might be expanded 50% in time; and (2) family planning programmes to control population growth, which are increasing in magnitude but still remain quite unco-ordinated and weak.

The world Christian community has increasingly sensed a responsibility to face the implications of this vast demographic change. Many church leaders view rational family planning as essential, ethically and practically, to world stability and to the reduction of world poverty. The Christian community is divided as to the proper means to achieve such family planning. Protestant leaders and organizations in growing numbers favour the use of artificial contraception as one means of limiting family growth. Pope Paul VI, on the other hand, in his encyclical *Humanae Vitae* (Of Human Life), reaffirmed on 29 July 1968 the traditional RC teaching on contraception, stressing that the only acceptable method of avoiding births is temporary abstinence during the woman's fertile period, the so-called rhythm method.

EUGENE L. STOCKWELL

J. M. Jones: *Does Overpopulation Mean Poverty?* (Center for Economic Growth, 1962); Pamphlet, *The Churches Speak Up on Birth Control* (Planned Parenthood Federation of America, 1968); Pope Paul VI: *Humanae Vitae* (29 July 1968); *NCE* XI, 579–92.

PORTUGUESE GUINEA. See GUINEA, PORTUGUESE.

POSNETT, CHARLES WALKER (1870–1950). Born at Sheffield, England, he entered the Methodist ministry in 1895 and was appointed to the Hyderabad district where he served till 1939, seeing the Christian community grow from less than 4,000 to nearly 120,000. No scholar but a great teacher and with the qualities of the successful business man, he used the ample funds at his command to develop a few acres at Medak into a vast compound, the microcosm of the Christian mission in the *paternalistic era, with dwellings, schools, training centres and hospital, around a large and beautiful church which became the cathedral of the *CSI diocese in 1947. More than any, he used the opportunities of a *mass movement to Christianity, growing out of famine conditions, to build up the church. Concerned that baptism should be based on conviction and that philanthropy should not lead to pauperism, he laid great stress on training with a view to self-support. In every village opened to the gospel, he established a school-church with teacher-evangelist, and often a medical centre. Suitable young people from village boarding schools were trained as evangelists and Bible women. Summer schools were held for enquirers, especially from the higher castes. From this, he became a pioneer in many fields including adult literacy, leprosy treatment, agricultural training, and the beginnings of indigenous missionary work. Skilled in relating the duty of today to the hope of to-morrow, he was the greatest Methodist missionary of his day.

MARCUS WARD

F. C. Sackett: *Posnett of Medak* (London 1951).

PRAYER FOR MISSIONS. See INTERCESSION FOR MISSIONS.

PREACHING FOR MISSIONS. There have been interesting variations in the form of appeal on behalf of Christian missions. The chief emphases can be arranged roughly in chronological order, though of course most forms of appeal have existed in all the periods. (1) The sense of Christian obligation: 'Christ has a kingdom, and this kingdom must everywhere be proclaimed'. (2) The sentimental appeal: 'the poor heathen perishing in his darkness'; emphasis on poverty and sickness in the non-Christian lands. (3) The eschatological emphasis: we are called to 'hasten the coming of the day of God' (2 Pet.3:12); by the conversion of the heathen the date of the second coming of Christ can actually be chronologically advanced. (4) The utilitarian: 'missions are good for trade, therefore support missions'. (5) 'The evangelization of the world in this generation'; not 'the conversion of the world'; this was never expected. The renewal of the sense of obligation in the light of the greatly increased opportunities at the end of the 19th century. (6) Ecumenical fellowship—co-operation with the younger churches in the task of nation and church building. (7) Self-identification of the church with the world, since it is the world which God loves. The last formulation seems the most satisfactory, provided that the warning of the Whitby Conference of 1947 is borne in mind—that the church must be wholly identified with the world in its needs, and totally independent of it in its desires.

STEPHEN NEILL

M. Linz: *Anwalt der Welt* (Stuttgart 1964).

PREACHING TO MEN OF OTHER FAITHS is of central importance to the Christian mission, following the example and instruction of Jesus (Lk.4:18–19;

Matt.9:35; Mk.3:14,16:15; Acts 10:42), and the practice and teaching of the Apostles (Acts 2:14ff., 13:16ff., 17:22ff.; Rom.10:17; 1 Cor.1:21). In the NT, preaching is always concerned with the proclamation of the 'good tidings of God' to the non-Christian world; all preaching was missionary declaration of what God has done in Jesus Christ (cf. Alan Richardson, 'Preach' in *Theological Word Book of the Bible*, London 1950).

Preaching to men of other faiths should always proceed with an up-to-date understanding of the faith (or non-faith) of those to whom the gospel will be proclaimed. The preacher's attitude should be that of humility concerning his own inadequacy, and confidence in God as already at work among those to whom he will preach. This confidence in God's prevenient *grace gives incentive to the preacher and a point of contact for the gospel message. Genuine Christian preaching will combine loyalty to the apostolic faith with 'boldness to examine and faith to trust all truth'. Preaching is not the end, but the beginning of discussion and exchange. It may well be followed by listening that is sensitive and sympathetic to the questions and criticisms of the non-Christian.

The traditional sermon is an important, but by no means the only, form of preaching the gospel. Missionary witness is increasingly concerned with a more 'comprehensive approach' of extensive encounter with the whole man in the whole context of his life. This approach recognizes a very close relationship between proclamation, witness and service. Opportunities for preaching sermons to gatherings of non-Christians are severely restricted and limited in many parts of the world today. Therefore, other forms and structures for proclaiming the gospel must be found to supplement the traditional patterns. These would include, for instance, drama, radio *broadcasting, films, *ashrams, *literature and literacy programmes.

The preacher must take great care that the message he proclaims is not propaganda for a particular cultural (western!) ex-pression or even for a particular church or confession. The ultimate aim of preaching is to bring all men to decision and conversion, through saving knowledge and personal faith in Jesus Christ as Lord and Saviour, that they may be baptized and belong to the church.

GERALD H. ANDERSON

G. H. Anderson, ed.: *Sermons to Men of Other Faiths and Traditions* (Nashville 1966); H. J. Margull: *Theologie der missionarischen Verkündigung* (Stuttgart 1959, Eng. tr. *Hope in Action*, Philadelphia 1962); S. C. Neill: *Christian Faith and Other Faiths* (London 1961); E. A. Nida: *Message and Mission* (New York 1960); D. T. Niles: *The Preacher's Task and the Stone of Stumbling* (New York 1958); '*Heidenpredigt*', *RGG³* V, 538f.

PREDESTINATION. A doctrine derived from the OT emphasis upon Israel as an elect people and the NT conviction that through Jesus Christ the church continues as the 'chosen race' predestined as God's instrument of mission. Implicit within this concept of salvation history is the idea of an omniscient and omnipotent Creator who predetermines all things.

The doctrine has received two major expressions in the history of Christian thought. Supralapsarianism is the position which claims that before the creation and fall God predestined certain figures for salvation without consideration of merit. Infralapsarianism is the position which holds that after the fall God elected certain men in order to sustain his saving purpose in history. Augustine of Hippo was the first theologian to give P. full attention. John Calvin joined Augustine in continuing the emphasis upon double P. It was Calvin's conviction that the doctrine engendered humility and a desire to show forth the fruits of righteousness.

The doctrine has received significant attention in the 20th century in the work of Karl Barth who insists on approaching the doctrine from an undivided Christological perspective. Jesus Christ is both the Electing One and the Elect One showing that God wills unconditionally to be God for all men. The doctrine has value for the Christian mission in that through proclamation and witness there is made evident God's plan from the beginning of time that man should encounter salvation through Jesus Christ.

JAMES C. LOGAN

J. Calvin: *Institutes of the Christian Religion*, III, xxi, 5; K. Barth: *Church Dogmatics*, II, 2.

PREPARATION OF MISSIONARIES. In most churches it is agreed that missionaries need special training. They have to work in a country and a culture different from their own and to serve in a church which, while probably within the same confession or communion, is nevertheless different in many respects. The missionary has to be ready for a considerable culture shock. This applies equally in reverse to those coming from younger churches to the west, but for them training facilities are almost non-existent.

The length of training may vary from a few weeks to a number of years. In continental Europe this period of preparation is usually longer and more academic than in Britain or North America. Australia and New Zealand also have missionary training colleges.

The basic preparation of missionaries is a spiritual one, for the missionary vocation has strains and temptations of its own. The period of training is often regarded as a time of testing this vocation, almost a novitiate. Preparation will normally include a good grounding in Biblical knowledge and Christian doctrine. This may perhaps be assumed in the case of ordained ministers but it is often lacking among lay people who form the majority of today's missionaries. An understanding of what mission is, some introduction to the life and problems of younger churches, some experience in evangelism and doing a similar job at home, will all form part of a missionary's preparation. There will also be opportunities for some preliminary study of the country where he will serve and

of its religion(s) and social anthropology. An appreciation of its culture is also imperative.

Most missionaries work in some kind of community. The ability to live responsibly in a community may have to be acquired in training. Moreover, in many situations missionaries have to co-operate with those of other churches, and in some enterprises to work in an ecumenical team. For this reason missionary training is increasingly being carried out ecumenically, as in the Selly Oak Colleges, Birmingham, England; Stony Point outside New York, USA; and the Asian Missionary Orientation Program (*EACC sponsored) near Manila, Philippines.

There is a sense in which no missionary is ever fully trained; it is a life-long process. But it is customary to think of training in three stages. (1) Pre-service, either in a missionary training college of the sending church or in some college belonging to the receiving church. A period at a language school—probably on the field—would form part of this. (2) In-service, the missionary's first tour, which is often regarded as a time of probation with some degree of pastoral care and supervision. (3) First furlough: ideally this should be spent not on deputation tours but as a period for re-assessment and rehabilitation, learning from the various experiences in the field in a sympathetic and stimulating atmosphere.

It is being realized increasingly that the receiving church must take a larger share in the training of missionaries, either in its own milieu or by making available some of its more gifted members to serve for a time on the staffs of training colleges in the west.

DOUGLAS WEBSTER

H. L. Bailey and H. C. Jackson: *A Study of Missionary Motivation, Training and Withdrawal (1953–1962)* (New York 1965); D. Bonhoeffer: *Life Together* (London 1954); H. Morgan: *Who'd Be a Missionary?* (London 1967); J. H. Oldham: *Florence Allshorn and the Story of St. Julian's* (London 1951); D. N. Sargent: *The Making of a Missionary* (London 1960); *Statement from a Consultation on the Preparation of*

Missionaries, Toronto, August 1963 (WCC, Geneva).

PRESBYTERIAN MISSIONS. More than most other Protestant groups, the Presbyterian or Reformed Churches have been conscious from the start of the international character of their fellowship; in the 16th century France, Holland, Scotland and Hungary were aware of a common destiny. Nevertheless, each church tended to develop special characteristics of its own, a process which continued when Presbyterianism spread across the seas to America and other continents. This makes it difficult to give any general characterization of PM. This group of churches came rather late to the missionary enterprise; one reason no doubt was the prevalence of a strong Calvinist tradition, which held that God himself would take what action was necessary for the salvation of the heathen and that action by men was neither necessary nor seemly. Some earlier efforts can be quoted, particularly by Dutch churches; the Presbyterian churches as a whole took up missionary work only in the 19th century. Their share in the enterprise is now worldwide.

There is no part of the enterprise to which Presbyterians have not contributed. But three points may be stressed as common to the work of almost all Presbyterian churches, and appearing in many different fields. (1) The tradition of solid, careful, biblical preaching, finding one of its expressions in careful preparation of candidates for baptism, and in most areas a rejection of all short-cuts to the building up of churches. (2) A belief in the value of education for its own sake, but also as a means for the entering in of the gospel. The most famous enterprise of all was that of Alexander *Duff in Calcutta; parallels can be thought of in many other countries. (3) A strong church sense. In the 19th century the work of the Presbyterian churches, like that of most Protestant churches, was mission-centred, and in Indonesia far too closely related to state organization. The Presbyterian

churches were among the first to respond to the demand for independent younger churches, and to undertake the work of *'devolution'. They have been particularly successful in bringing into existence fully independent churches. In certain cases, the unit chosen has been rather small, and the church identified with the life of one tribe or people (Ambonese, Halmahera, etc. in Indonesia; Ewe in Togo) and this has not always been balanced by a sense of the wider unity of the church. This has in recent years been corrected by the participation of many independent Presbyterian churches in all the work of the *ecumenical movement. The ecumenical aspect of PM finds expression in the *World Alliance of Churches holding the Presbyterian form of government (founded 1875).

EDITORS

PREVENIENT GRACE. See GRACE, PREVENIENT.

PRIMITIVE RELIGIONS. This term describes what are also known as 'nature religions'. It is not to be understood as implying an unfavourable judgement. It means simply that we are here dealing with religions, which as far as our present understanding of religion goes, stand in a near relationship to the origins of religion. PR know no founder, no canonical book to serve as their basis, and in consequence no fixed form of doctrine. PR find outward expression in belief in powers (often associated with magical views), totemism (a special relationship, generally with an animal, which may be carried to the point of a feeling of identity), belief in souls (and especially in *ancestor-worship), a concept of spirits and divinities (daemonism) and belief in a supreme God. The greater number of these manifestations stand in a complex relationship to one another. To these powers men may take up an attitude of rejection (avoidance, exorcisms, amulets), or an attitude of craving (talisman, sacrifice, cult, prayer). Centres of the religious life are the medicine-man, the witch-doctor, the 'lord of the land', the *shaman*, the priest, the prophet. In PR sacred powers are thought to be concentrated also in certain places, e.g. the initiation camp, the place of sacrifice, the altar; but the whole of life is in any case penetrated by awareness of their existence. Hunting, agriculture and stock-farming reflect a variety of religious ideas; so also do social life (transition-ceremonies, religious and sacred authority) and the world of art (rock-paintings, masks, popular poetry).

The PR continue to exist as a sub-structure in the higher religions; but often break out into the open, and produce new forms of religion (Lāmaism, Mahāyāna-Buddhism). In *Islam attempts are made to legalise these survivals.

Where Christian faith has been accepted, the PR have in many cases only been superficially overcome. Secretly or openly they continue to be practised (e.g. consultation of the medicine-men, ordeals, circumcision, the use of magical operations). Many post-Christian movements manifest a close union of Christian elements with the PR, sometimes as a result of emotional tensions, but in some cases deliberately brought about.

See also ANIMISM; MONOTHEISM, PRIMITIVE.

ERNST DAMMANN

F. M. Bergounioux and J. Goetz: *Pre-historic and Primitive Religions* (London 1965); W. J. Goode: *Religion among the Primitives* (London 1964); M. Nilsson: *Primitive Religion* (Tübingen 1927); *WKL*, 1180–82.

PROBLEMS OF MISSIONARIES. To be a minister of the gospel is always difficult; the difficulty is enormously increased when the work is to be carried out in a distant land, and in surroundings marked by an alien and prevailingly non-Christian culture. The new missionary is faced with deep adjustments in three directions. (1) First, there is adaptation to the people and the culture of the area in which he has been called to work. Everything, including the elementary rules of courtesy, is strange and has to be enquired about. All this has to be done in an unknown tongue; only rarely have adequate arrangements been made for instruction in the local language, and in consequence the missionary tends to feel himself an alien in the land which he is to make his own. (2) The nature and quality of a *younger church has to be understood. Most missionaries come out with rosy expectations of that which they will find. As the weaknesses of the local church come into view, it is hard to resist the temptation to cynicism or even despair. (3) Nowhere is the clash between generations more acutely felt than in the mission field. The younger can see very clearly the weaknesses of their elders and the mistakes that have been made, often with a frustrating feeling that nothing can be changed.

Problems are different, but do not grow less, as time goes on. There is, first, the ever present problem of *health. There is less likelihood today of the decimation of missions by violence or by tropical disease; but few missionaries manage to maintain the same level of efficiency as in their own country. Limited financial resources make it difficult to keep up interests outside work. Bringing up children in a strange land is never easy. The missionary tends to be so conscious of his vocation as to find it difficult to relax and to be first of all a human being. As time goes on, he becomes so rooted in the land of his adoption as to be a stranger among his own people. As the number of missionaries is reduced, those who remain may suffer from an increasing sense of isolation. For many it is hard to know where to turn in times of depression and spiritual weakness.

The changed situation of the 20th century has brought with it new problems. (1) Few missionaries have found themselves wholly in sympathy with the national movements which have led to the establishment of so many new nations. Few, if any, have left their work because of changed political situations; a great many have had to endure cruel and often baseless accusations of *imperialism. (2) Missionaries have on the whole held on to control too long; they are in part responsible for the sense of rivalry between foreigners and nationals in the younger churches. But at times it has been their task to resist, at very great cost to themselves, the unscrupulous and the worldly. (3) Many who have accepted with joy the position of working under national leadership, have found themselves welcomed—and left with nothing to do. It is very serious that so many missionaries have served for one term only and no more; careful research is needed into the causes of this phenomenon.

A number of steps can and should be taken to ease this situation. (1) *Training of missionaries in the sending country and in the field needs to be far more thorough than it is. (2) Sending societies need to concern themselves very much more than they do with the spiritual care of those who have been sent out in their name. (3) The younger churches must recognize that it is now their responsibility to care for the well-being of the foreigner who has come to serve them. He must be treated as an honoured guest, initiated into the ways of his new home, welcomed into the homes and families of Christians, criticised to his face and not behind his back, appointed to a post in which he can work with pleasure, effectiveness and dignity, and helped by sympathy and understanding in the difficult periods which he is bound to pass through. There is as yet hardly any sign that the younger churches have begun to understand or accept their responsibility in the matter.

STEPHEN NEILL

Renewal and Advance: the Report of the Whitby Missionary Conference 1947 (London and New York 1948); D. Webster: *Yes to Mission* (London 1966).

PROPAGANDA, MISSIONARY, is a term which may be used honourably only until about the beginning of the 20th century, because thereafter it has a bad odour and is used only by adverse critics of missions. Until that time it means all forms of missionary promotion normally employed. P. began in the Protestant world with the publication of *New England First Fruits* and the other 'Eliot Tracts' published in London from 1643 to 1671, intended to stimulate support for the New England Indian missions. All missionary societies, following the example of the *SPCK (1699) and the *SPG (1701), published the annual sermon, usually with a report appended, and these tracts were supplemented by ordination and local society sermons. Sermons remained important instruments of P. until the mid-19th century, but by 1815 were displaced from first importance by magazines, annual reports and books. Magazines ranked first in effect throughout the 19th century. The *LMS *Chronicle*, the *ABCFM *Missionary Herald*, and the *CMS succession of *Church Missionary Record, Church Missionary Intelligencer, Church Missionary Review* and *CMS Outlook* are typical. The influence of reports and private letters from the fields was demonstrated by the Eliot Tracts and letters of the Lutheran missionaries at Tranquebar (beginning 1705), which were transcribed in London before transmission to Halle and Copenhagen, translated and published. Letters made up a large part of the contents of the magazines. Missionaries were prolific writers and their books were read avidly. They were also favourite subjects of biography, and the books were of such a nature as to constitute a 19th century collection of Protestant hagiography. As the custom of furlough became accepted, deputation visits by missionaries proved exceedingly effective.

The societies employed itinerating agents to collect funds, and these persons made addresses, but boards and societies paid little attention to promotional propaganda other than magazines and annual reports until the end of the 19th century. The one great P. device sponsored or encouraged by the societies was successful because it was combined with intercession. This was the Concert of Prayer for Missions. It began as a quarterly prayer meeting in Scotland in 1744; Jonathan *Edwards in New England gave it power; the English

Baptists made it a monthly meeting in 1784; and the LMS converted it into a monthly concert for missionary intercession in 1795. The practice was adopted in all English-speaking countries and spread to some extent in Europe. All the above mentioned material was used in the educational portion of the meeting. These were often union meetings in cities. P. reached its climax in the USA in the cultivation of the local churches by the women's missionary societies formed on a denominational basis beginning in 1867, and on both sides of the Atlantic in the activities of the *Student Volunteer Movement, especially the quadrennial assemblies. The SVM and the women's societies were responsible for the establishment of interdenominational union missionary study, and after 1900 societies and boards began to develop educational and promotional programmes as essential aspects of their work and responsibility. The several interdenominational programmes were united in the Missionary Education Movement of the USA and Canada, which through its publishing house, Friendship Press, produced annual home and foreign mission study books and related material. Merged with other ecumenical agencies in 1950 to form the National Council of the Churches of Christ in the USA, this agency continues to function as the Department of Education for Mission. The British societies undertook a similar programme together and published under the imprint of the Edinburgh House Press.

Roman Catholic mission P. runs parallel to Protestant in time and types, but on the whole appears less in extent and far less of a co-operative nature. The letters, reports and journals of the 16th–18th century missionaries were intended primarily for the information of their superiors rather than as popular fund-raising efforts. However, the *avvisi* and annual letters of the *Jesuits in the Far East especially were full of new information avidly sought by the intelligentsia of Europe and were made available. Substantial reports, such as Trigault's work on the mission in China

(published Augsburg 1615) got a wide reading. Such material was converted into popular P. when in 1707 the Jesuit writings were drastically selected and edited for edification and entertainment and published in French as *Lettres édifiantes et curieuses*, continuing through 1758, with a complete edition in 1780–83. Selections were translated, such as *Travels of the Jesuits* (London 1743). Comprehensive P. material was provided by *The Annals for the Propagation of the Faith* (Rome) and beginning in 1868 *Missions Catholiques*, a joint publication of the *Propaganda and Society for the Propagation of the Faith, with national editions in other languages. The romanticizing of missions in the 19th century led to the outpouring of missionary 'hagiographical' books similar in nature to biographies of Protestant missionaries. P. was primarily undertaken by the individual missionary orders, congregations, and institutes, chiefly in the form of magazines which brought in funds through subscription payments. By the end of the 19th century they numbered 467. Such magazines still continue to be the primary P. resource. Current information and statistics are disseminated through Fides News Service and private news agencies.

R. PIERCE BEAVER

J. Schmidlin: *Catholic Mission History*, tr. M. Braun (Techny, Ill. 1933); on the Concert of Prayer see R. P. Beaver, art. in *Ecumenical Review*, July 1958, pp.420–27; on sermons, Beaver: *Pioneers in Mission* (Grand Rapids 1966); on the women's role, Beaver: *All Loves Excelling* (Grand Rapids 1968).

PROPAGANDA, SACRED CONGREGATION OF. Although the idea of an authoritative missionary body in the Roman Catholic church goes back to Raymond Lull (d.1315), P. was not created until 1622 by Pope Gregory XV. In addition to requests for the founding of a congregation of cardinals in the interests of missions, there was desired an organization to procure finances for the missions, a publishing house to print Christian literature for distribution among non-Christians, and a seminary for the training of missionaries. The two chief factors which made a mission congregation necessary were the excessive control which Spain and Portugal were then exercising over the missions and the problems and deficiencies resulting from this state of control. P. set to work energetically to institute needed reforms and to promote the missions. It is constituted of cardinals chosen by the pope, one of whom is named Prefect and upon whom rests the daily administration of its affairs, along with a secretary, subsecretary, other minor officials and consultors. In general, this body handles all matters connected with the missions, which have been regarded as those regions of the world where the hierarchy is not yet established or where, if established, the church is still in its initial stage of development. Originally granted sweeping authority over all things missionary, its competence was modified in 1908. It now has ordinary administrative and executive power, but no longer judicial or legislative authority. Its chief accomplishment in this century has been the development of indigenous hierarchy and clergy. Indigenous leadership in the missions was stressed after the first world war when Benedict XV assigned to the P. as its special task that of building up as soon as practicable an indigenous clergy and hierarchy, to whom the government of the church in the mission lands should be turned over without delay. Its efforts in this have been on the whole quite successful, and the trend is for an increasingly greater role in church administration by local hierarchies rather than by P.

Headquarters: Palazzo di Propaganda Fide, Piazza di Spagna, Roma 106, Italy.

RONAN HOFFMAN

R. Song: *The Sacred Congregation for the Propagation of the Faith* (Washington 1961); *NCE* XI, 840–46.

PROPERTY, MISSION AND CHURCH, PROBLEMS OF. No church in the world manages to exist entirely without property,

17*

but the moment that it acquires property of any kind, it is landed in a variety of problems that have nothing to do directly with the spiritual sphere.

In the early days missionaries existed only by sufferance of the local authorities, and it was doubtful in what sense, if any, they could acquire property. Among primitive peoples the general view is that the land belongs to the ancestors, and cannot be alienated, though the use of it by others may be permitted. In many cases the missionaries seem to have thought that they had acquired much greater rights over P. than were recognized by the local peoples. One of the causes of the Herero war of 1904 (South West Africa) seems to have been the suspicion of the Africans that the *Rhenish missionaries had sold to the new German government land to which their title was not recognized by the local people.

As things became more settled, especially under colonial governments, the acquisition and tenure of property became much simpler. In a number of cases, missionaries acquired and held P. in their own name; but this was found to be undesirable, since complex questions of inheritance were likely to arise. In the great majority of cases P. acquired by the now growing churches was held by the local church, on whatever terms prevailed in each area; whereas P. acquired by the missionary society was held by it in trusteeship for its proper use for the benefit of the growing church. This arrangement worked well for many years. But new questions arose with the formation of independent *younger churches. To whom was the P. now to belong? In the 1930s, one great missionary society, finding that it had much property in India which it could no longer use, sold the property and brought the money back to England to be added to its general fund. There was no question as to its legal competence to act in this way, but intense bitterness was aroused, the Indian members of the church maintaining that the P. had been bought for the benefit of the Indian church, and that the money should have remained in India to its advantage. In many cases, societies hesitated to hand over valuable P. to small and inexperienced churches, for fear that the P. would not continue to be used for the purposes for which it had been acquired. In countries where there is legal provision for the incorporation of companies, and for the exercise of trusteeship, no difficulty arises. For instance, the Indian Church Trustees were created to hold Anglican property in India; the Trustees do not directly control any P.; but they are there to see that the use of the P. is not diverted from the original aims, and that no P. is sold without the necessary legal conditions having been fulfilled.

In a great many areas in which conditions of regular and orderly government exist, the process of transfer is complete, and an independent church has become heir to all the P. which once belonged to the missionary societies, except in so far as certain properties are still held for direct use by missionaries.

No more than any other kind of P. can missionary P. be safeguarded against arbitrary and unjust actions by governments in time of war or revolution. During the first world war the British government in India and Ghana secularized the very extensive textile and other operations of the *Basel Missionary Society and formed in their place the Commonwealth Trust. No communist government recognizes the claim of any mission or church to the possession of P., though temporary permission for the use of churches and other buildings may be granted. There is always a danger that churches may tend to overestimate the importance of wealth and security; it is perhaps good that they should from time to time be reminded that the kingdom of heaven does not subsist in such things.

STEPHEN NEILL

PROPHETISM refers to religious movements which arise in times of stress through an individual endowed with spiritual gifts, the prophet claiming a supernatural call, power and revelation, in order to reform or revitalize his people and deliver them from their ills or oppressors. Especially in Africa and Indonesia, Islamic influence has produced *mahdis* and other messianic prophets; but most prophetisms have arisen in recent centuries where western culture and Christian missions have disturbed the traditional society and religion of the so-called primitive peoples, notably in the Americas, Africa and the Pacific, and especially under colonial occupation.

These prophet movements range from earlier neo-pagan or nativistic forms, seeking to revive traditional religion, perhaps with borrowings from Christianity, through various degrees of syncretist movements, to the later independent prophet-healing churches. Most later prophets have had some Christian training, and some have begun their apocalyptic preaching and healing within their local church or mission, until the size of their following or their distinctive practices force them to found their own separate churches or to lead a *mass movement.

The main activities of the prophet (or prophetess, for many are women) may be spiritual healing, the giving of revelations in the form of messages, advice, or predictions, the disciplining of members, and the carrying of his message to other areas. Traditional practices such as the use of *magic, fetishes, *sacrifices or divination are usually condemned, and reliance placed on the true God and the power of the Spirit, with much prayer, and probably fasting, holy water, and certain moral requirements. The prophet as a herald or preacher sent by God should be distinguished from the traditional healer, diviner or seer who uses ecstatic states and magic techniques, although some leaders may belong to both groups, as Samuel (1 Sam.9), or as those in South African Zionist churches. Sometimes the prophet is regarded as a new Moses or Elijah, and less often as a native messiah replacing Jesus Christ. Many have promised a millennium, with the whites expelled and their powers given to the local people, who then enjoy peace and prosperity. The disturbance caused by a prophet movement, and the appearance of false prophets, either mercenary charlatans or deranged persons, have misled some governments to regard even the genuinely religious forms as mainly political and subversive, so that many prophets have suffered punishment and been suppressed.

The more Christian forms of prophetism, however, have made a considerable contribution as indigenous movements meeting local needs.

HAROLD W. TURNER

C. G. Baëta: *Prophetism in Ghana* (London 1962); V. Lanternari: *Religions of the Oppressed* (London 1963, New York 1965)—world survey; M.-L. Martin: *The Biblical Concept of Messianism and Messianism in Southern Africa* (Morija, Lesotho 1964), part III; B. G. M. Sundkler: *Bantu Prophets in South Africa* (London, rev. edn. 1961). The second and third concentrate on the messianic aspect.

PROSELYTISM originally referred to the attempt made by the Jews to spread their faith among the Gentiles. In the OT we have mention of the 'stranger' or 'client' (Heb. *ger*) who lived in the midst of Israel and had special privileges. The Hebrew word is translated into *proselutos* in the Septuagint, and so the 'proselyte' was a stranger accepted into the Israelite community. It seems that there were different classes, but only a circumcised proselyte (i.e. one who had fully accepted the Jewish faith) could enter the temple. The practice of making proselytes flourished in the Hellenistic period, when many Gentiles fled from the moral laxity and superstitions of the age. The Talmud speaks of three requirements made of a proselyte: circumcision, baptism and a sacrificial offering (which fell into disuse after the destruction of the temple in A.D. 70). The Pharisees were especially zealous in seeking out Gentile converts (see Matt.23:15), thus attempting to fulfil the prophetic vision of Jerusalem as the centre of the world's religious observances. P. ended in Judaism about the

beginning of the 2nd century, when Roman law forbade the Jews the right to make converts.

Because Pharisees were involved in P., the word has now come to express any form of missionary activity which enforces conversion on the other person instead of permitting a free response to the gospel.

Wherever the church presents itself as something foreign—not because its message comes from God, but because the message is clothed in a foreign dress and is allied with an alien culture or an alien politic—evangelism will seem to be little more than proselytizing. It is as the church becomes *indigenous and 'baptizes' the local culture 'into Christ', that conversion will appear not as sedition or the rejection of one's own culture, but a surrender to the power of the God who can make *all* things new.

See also LIBERTY, RELIGIOUS.

RAYMOND J. HAMMER

ERE IX, 400–03; *RGG* V, 640; *WKL*, 1190–92.

PROTESTANT MISSIONS, HISTORY OF. Not until the 1790s did Protestants engage extensively in foreign missions. Before that decade some beginnings were seen, partly by Pietists from the continent of Europe (notably the *Moravians), partly by minorities in Norway and the Netherlands, and by Anglicans through the *SPCK (1699) and the *SPG (1701).

In 1792 the BMS, initiated by William *Carey, followed by the *LMS (1795), the *CMS (1799) and the BFBS (1804) contributed to a new era. On the continent of Europe the Netherlands Missionary Society (1797), and schools in Berlin (1800) and Basel (1815) which trained missionaries came into being. In 1810 the *ABCFM was organized. In the 19th century other missionary societies arose in Great Britain, the continent of Europe, the USA, Canada, Australia and New Zealand. During most of the 19th century the major share of the Protestant missionary effort was from the British Isles. Much was from the continent of Europe. Most of the missions were by Evangelicals and Pietists, although high Anglicans also had an important share. Toward the end of the 19th century an increasing proportion of Protestant foreign missions was from the USA.

The spread of Protestant missions was greatly facilitated by the rapid expansion of European *commerce, *imperialism, and *colonialism in the 19th century in Asia, Africa and the islands of the Pacific. Missions were challenged by the opportunities afforded by the expansion.

Co-operation among Protestant missions grew, notably through the *World Missionary Conference in Edinburgh (1910) and the *IMC which arose from it.

The two world wars of the 20th century curtailed the resources of the missionary societies of the British Isles and Europe and by the mid-20th century the Protestants of the USA were carrying the major share of the burden for Protestant missions, both financially and in personnel. By that time about half the personnel from the USA was contributed by societies which did not co-operate with the IMC and its successor, the *Division of World Mission and Evangelism of the *WCC.

The rising tide of revolt against western imperialism and colonialism was accompanied by greater self-reliance of the churches which had arisen from Protestant missions and their mounting share in the Protestant missionary movement. The capture of the mainland of China and North Korea proved a major handicap to missions, including those of Protestants, but elsewhere in Asia, Africa south of the Sahara, and the fringing islands Protestants were growing in numbers and in indigenous leadership.

KENNETH SCOTT LATOURETTE

S. C. Neill: *A History of Christian Missions* (Harmondsworth 1964), pp.220–557.

Q

QATAR. See ARABIAN PENINSULA.

QUAKER MISSIONS. See FRIENDS' MISSIONS.

QUALIFICATIONS FOR MISSION-ARIES. The chief qualification required by any missionary is such a deep devotion to Jesus Christ that the desire to make his love known to others is almost irresistible. This devotion will be expressed in a life of dedication, the practice of prayer and spiritual discipline, a willingness to re-nounce some of the securities which most men take for granted, and to make financial sacrifices. The desire to make Christ known will require both sensitivity to the needs and feelings of others and courage to bear witness to the Way, the Truth and the Life.

For some *'faith missions' these spiritual qualifications would be enough, but the historic churches generally expect a mini-mum educational standard and some professional or technical skill to offer by way of service. Much depends on whether the missionary is being sent to a pioneering area where as yet there is no *indigenous church of any size or to be at the disposal of a church which is already *autonomous and has some years of history behind it. In the latter case the missionary will normally be wanted for educational, medical, agricultural, social, administrative, pastoral or evangelistic work. If he is to serve in an institution receiving government grants his professional qualifications will have to meet those demanded by the state. The number of countries which permit the entry of mission-aries with no such qualifications to be used for the general good and development is rapidly decreasing. It is advisable for anyone contemplating missionary service to complete his professional or technical training and to have some experience of using it in his own country before making a definite offer to serve overseas. But mission-ary societies have associations for those hoping to become missionaries and can give valuable advice and fellowship during this period of attaining necessary qualifi-cations.

Missionaries do not normally have all the amenities taken for granted in the west; it is therefore desirable that they should be practical and be prepared at times to endure physical hardship. A clean bill of health is essential for tropical countries. No one will get far without a capacity for making friends, taking initiative in a humble manner, and mixing well in personal relationships at all social levels.

The missionary is a servant of God and of humanity. He must be without any sense of racial superiority. Unless he is prepared to live 'in the form of a servant' like Jesus, his other gifts and qualifications will prove insufficient.

DOUGLAS WEBSTER

W. J. Lederer and E. Burdick: *The Ugly American* (New York 1960); R. Voillaume: *Seeds of the Desert* (London 1955); D. Webster: *Yes to Mission* (London 1965), chapters I and IV.

R

RACIAL PROBLEMS IN MISSIONS.
Race in itself should never have been a problem in Christian doctrine but has always complicated the human relationships in missions, i.e. between the missionary, his family, and the mission-sending churches on the one side and the peoples to whom the missionary was sent. This has been humanly inevitable, for historically the missionary movement has *ipso facto* been a movement from the old Christendom by its constituents for the conversion to Christianity of a variety of peoples elsewhere. The old Christendom happened to be what is now the west (or the North Atlantic community of nations), with its inhabitants almost entirely Caucasian (or white) by race, and categorically Christian by religion, whereas peoples elsewhere were pagans by definition, regardless of their religions, who happened to belong to a variety of coloured races. Furthermore, at the inception of the modern missionary movement western nations were immensely more advanced in science, technology and economics, and incomparably stronger, both militarily and politically, than the rest of the world. Hence missions invariably came to be conceived chiefly in terms of Christians enlightening the pagans, civilizing the primitive, helping the helpless, teaching the ignorant, and correcting errors. In the course of time an assumption came to be widely held among the mission-sending people, though seldom explicitly articulated, to the effect that the mission-receiving peoples were somehow racially inferior. Such an underlying assumption is bound to condition the behaviour pattern of mission-sending Christians in the west as well as that of the missionary himself towards mission-receiving peoples. The Indian Anglican, who was later to become Bishop *Azariah of Dornakal, spoke openly on the racial problem in missions at the *Jerusalem Conference of 1928. Earlier the *IMC secretary, Dr J. H. *Oldham, had made an extensive study of the problem (see his

Christianity and the Race Problem, London 1926). The *Life and Work Conference, Oxford 1937; the IMC Conference, *Tambaram 1938; the World Conference of Christian Youth, Amsterdam 1939, all grappled with the racial issue under the dark cloud of the Hitlerian racism. The Second Assembly of the *WCC meeting in the USA (*Evanston 1954) within a few months following the US Supreme Court decision declaring that racial segregation in public schools was unconstitutional, adopted the policy statement, which was later reaffirmed at the Third Assembly (*New Delhi 1961). In 1960, on the eve of the ultimate merger with IMC, the WCC established the Secretariat on Racial and Ethnic Relations in order to deal with the racial problem which had by then proved to be growing increasingly acute in the wake of decolonization in the very areas where Christian missions were seriously preoccupied with the issue of *indigenization. Historically Christianity had been so closely identified with the west, at least in the eyes of peoples among whom it was represented by the missionary movement, that their earnest effort to assert their newly gained national identity is apt to take on a note of anti-westernism. This tendency is unavoidable at this stage of history and necessarily makes race relations a vital issue for missions.

DAISUKE KITAGAWA

Ecumenical Statements on Race Relations (WCC, Geneva 1965); D. Kitagawa: *Race Relations and Christian Mission* (New York 1964); *WKL*, 1209–12.

RADIO. See AUDIOVISUAL AIDS; BROADCASTING, CHRISTIAN.

RAMABAI, PANDITA (1858–1922), was born the daughter of Brahman parents, and, contrary to the custom of the country, was instructed by her learned father in Sanskrit and in all the wisdom of the Hindus. After the death of her parents in the famine of 1877–78, R. made her way to Calcutta, and married a Bengali lawyer. His death after nineteen months of happy married life left her a young widow with one daughter. Deeply concerned about the unsatisfactory condition of India's women, R. could find no adequate power of renewal in *Hinduism. Fr Nehemiah *Goreh removed her doubts as to the intellectual validity of the Christian faith. During a visit to England she was brought into contact with the Wantage Sisters and was baptized in 1883. Later, in contact with Christians of a deeply evangelical character in India, she entered into a much deeper experience of the Christian realities.

Her first concern was for young widows who according to Hindu tradition could never marry again. A school was started in Bombay, later moved to Kedgaon near Poona. With the help of friends in the west, Mukti (Deliverance) grew to a great institution, with twenty foreign helpers, caring for increasing numbers of widows, for girls left orphans in the successive famines of the period, and for girls of lower *caste in need of help. No pressure to become Christian was brought to bear on the girls, but in fact many hundreds of them did so, especially during a 'revival' in the year 1901.

R. was much concerned for the better presentation of the gospel to educated Hindus. To this end she undertook herself a translation of the whole Bible into Marathi, in which much attention was paid to the use of words of Sanskrit origin and of those which would readily be intelligible to Hindus. There was a division of opinion among Marathi scholars as to the value of this work, on which so much labour had been expended.

R. was unique. The learned men of her country conferred on her the title 'Pandita', 'the learned one', which had never been accorded to a woman before. Never in history had any Indian woman, Hindu, Muslim or Christian, displayed such single and unconditional devotion to one aim, and such outstanding powers of leadership.

STEPHEN NEILL

N. McNicol: *Pandita Ramabai* (Calcutta 1926); R. K. Dongre: *Pandita Ramabai* (Madras 1963); *RGG* V, 772.

RAMAKRISHNA MISSION, THE, is one aspect of the Rāmakrishna Movement, founded in 1897 by Swāmi Vivekānanda the disciple of Swāmi Rāmakrishna Paramahamsa. Rāmakrishna taught the essential unity of all religions, but Vivekānanda emphasized also the superiority of *Hinduism, especially as meeting best the spiritual needs of men of all classes and stages of religious development.

The mission has over a hundred centres in India and elsewhere, all affiliated to the headquarters at Belur, near Calcutta. In these centres members of the mission engage in educational, medical, social and religious work.

The educational work of the mission includes university and teacher training colleges (including the noted Vivekānanda College in Madras), technical high and junior schools and a school for training nurses and midwives. The chief centres are at Calcutta, Madras and Coimbatore.

Medical work is carried on in thirteen hospitals and 67 wayside dispensaries. Social work takes principally the form of relief in areas and times of famine, epidemics, floods, etc., as well as among refugees.

Religious and cultural activities include the giving of lectures and publication work, aiming at contacting people of all religions and emphasizing that all religions are manifestations of one ultimate religion. The mission has adopted many Christian ideas and activities.

HENRY LEFEVER

G. B. Cooke: *A Neo-Hindu Ashram in S. India* (Bangalore 1966); V. C. Samuel: *The Rāmakrishna Movement* (Bangalore 1959).

RAPID SOCIAL CHANGE. All human societies exist in a condition of perpetual change. The idea that 'primitive' societies can be classed as static, while more developed societies are regarded as 'progressive' would not be accepted today by any sociologist. It is true that in some situations change is more readily observable than in others, though those who live in the midst of change are often less conscious of it than outside observers or their own posterity. Thus no society in history has changed more rapidly than that of Great Britain between 1900 and 1970, but, because there have been few violent accompaniments, the majority of the people who have lived in or through that period have been largely unaware of the magnitude and the rapidity of the changes that have taken place. The term RSC is often limited, inaccurately but usefully, to those societies in which change has for a long time gone on slowly but is then suddenly accelerated by the operation of some force external to the society itself. By far the most powerful forces operating for RSC are war and conquest, with their sudden alternations of freedom and slavery, and the intricate interchange of influences between conquerors and conquered. But this is not usually what is meant by those who use the term; they are generally referring to the impact of a *technically* more advanced on a *technically* less advanced society. This impact can be analysed, though not completely, under four heads.

(1) *Speed of communication.* Until this century the greater part of Africa was unacquainted with the wheel. Travel on foot was the only known form of locomotion, and for transport nothing was available other than the heads of human beings. Recent research has shown that, in that epoch, Africans travelled more widely than had been generally supposed. But such slow and difficult communications tend to produce isolated communities, and isolation is one of the situations unfavourable to rapid change. The first break in the old isolation was made by the steamship on the great rivers and lakes; the second by the 'Iron Snake', the railway. Then followed roads, and in course of time the aeroplane. Even today many people have never travelled more than ten miles from their homes, and the great majority of human beings has never seen the sea. But mobility is affecting a larger number every year. (2) *Industrializa-*

tion. No machine-made object can equal the beauty of the things that are produced by the human hand. Great cultures have been built up with the minimum of artifice. But generally cheapness and durability compensate for the loss of beauty, and the machine replaces the human hand and brain, sometimes to the great impoverishment of society, as in the near-destruction of the Indian hand-weaving industry by the introduction of mill-made cloth. It is the art of the trader to create new wants. Experience has shown that man is insatiable, and that however much he has he still wants more. The toll taken of human worth and dignity by covetousness is immeasurable. At the same time industrialization may bring to many an escape from grinding labour and a widening of experience. (3) *Urbanization.* The machine calls for ever greater concentration of labour forces in a restricted area. The city replaces the village. Except in Switzerland, where the decentralization of the watch-making industry in villages represents a triumph of intelligent organization, the city tends to have it all its own way. This is not wholly loss (Harvey Cox: *The Secular City*, New York 1965). But generally the less technically competent who stream into the cities find themselves homes in shanty-towns and slums, with all the problems of disease, unemployment and juvenile prostitution. (4) *Nationalism.* Increasing wealth breeds a spirit of independence. In the past individuals felt themselves to be poor; now whole peoples are claiming a larger share of the total world-product. A situation appears to have arisen, in which the richer nations are becoming steadily richer, and the poor becoming steadily poorer, since the price of primary products tends to fall, and the price of manufactured articles is rising all the time. Just as the older nations are trying to move out of the period of unbridled nationalism, the younger nations seem to be moving into it with irrepressible zeal.

Churches and religions always find it hard to keep up with the times. They tend to be conservative bodies, and rightly, since each of them believes that it has a treasure from the past to conserve, and the churches have in fact been among the greatest transmitters of culture from one generation to another. There is a danger, in a revolutionary epoch, that the churches may fail to detect the direction in which history is moving, and so fall out of step not so much with the spirit of the age as with the self-unfolding purpose of God.

What is the duty of the Christian church in an area of RSC? (1) The church must endeavour, with the best available help of the experts, to discern the signs of the times, not mistaking eddies for currents, and recognizing that in human affairs progress is much more often sporadic than continuous. (2) The church must continuously rethink its message in the light of changing situations. (3) The church must co-operate, but should not identify itself, with such groups and parties as appear to be directing change in the direction of the general well-being of the race. (4) The church must train an élite of intelligent and responsible Christians for service in politics, administration, industry and other related fields. (5) The church must care tenderly for the victims of change, for those who have not been able to adapt themselves to the demands of a new world. (6) The church must exercise its vigilant and critical function in relation to all parties in power. (7) The church must help young Christians to combine their national zeal with a sense of interdependence in the one worldwide family of Christ.

It cannot be said that any church, *older or *younger, in the world is fully meeting all these obligations. Much thought is being directed to the problems by such institutions as FERES (International Federations of Institutions for Socio–Religious and Social Research (RC), Louvain), and the *WCC, and practical experiments are being made at ecumenical centres such as that located at Mindolo, Kitwe, Zambia. But, as always, what is being done is far less than what needs to be done, and the revolutionary forces in the world move faster than the church which ought to be the chief instrument in working out the divine revolution.

STEPHEN NEILL

P. Abrecht: *The Churches and Rapid Social Change* (London 1961); R. Dickinson: *Line and Plummet: The Churches and Development* (Geneva 1968); W. Schweitzer: *Christians in Changing Societies* (WCB No. 58, London 1967); E. de Vries, ed.: *Man in Community* (London 1966), Report of the WCC Conference on Church and Society, held at Geneva in July, 1966.

RAVEMCCO, the Radio, Visual Education and Mass Communication Committee of the Specialized Ministries Department of the Division of Overseas Ministries of the National Council of Churches of Christ in the USA, was established in 1948. At the fifteenth anniversary it was stated: 'It is still the only organization in the world whose purpose is to encourage national Christians to develop their responsibility for the co-operative use of the mass media and to counsel and assist them in the effort'. It has worked largely through *National Christian Councils and national counterpart agencies similar to RAVEMCCO. Through it North American agencies pool personnel, funds, and other resources. The range of concern is from simple film strips to radio and television. The member boards provided $571,246 for the work in 1964. Major radio broadcasting agencies assisted by RAVEMCCO include stations DYSR and DZCH in the Philippines, HLKY in Korea, and the Radio Voice of the Gospel in Ethiopia, along with the Christian Audio-Visual Centre (CAVE) in Mexico and in Brazil. Aid is given to agencies in Japan, Thailand and Latin America in production of programmes to be transmitted over government and commercial stations. The training of nationals for administration, technical operation and programming is stressed. The Committee stimulated the formation of the World Association for Christian Broadcasting (now World Association for Christian Communication).

R. PIERCE BEAVER

RECRUITMENT OF MISSIONARIES, in the sense of active enlistment by societies, dates only from the 1920s. During the 19th century candidates were expected voluntarily to present themselves for selection and commissioning. Students largely recruited one another with help from teachers, missionary addresses and literature. Some tracts, such as Rufus *Anderson's *On Deciding Early to Become a Missionary to the Heathen* (1834) and *Ought I to Become a Missionary to the Heathen?* (1851) were exceedingly influential. Students created the major recruiting agency, the *Student Volunteer Movement for Foreign Missions (begun 1886, org. 1888), which rapidly spread from the USA to the UK and Europe. Aiming generally at enlisting students in support of missions, its specific major purpose was 'to enrol a sufficient number of 'volunteers' to meet the successive demands of the Missionary Boards'. It is estimated that by 1945 some 20,500 volunteers had reached the fields. American and British societies especially relied on the SVM. However, the movement declined rapidly in the 1920s and 1930s. From 2,783 new volunteers enrolled in the USA in 1920 the figure plunged to 465 in 1930 and to only 25 in 1938. Boards then had to do their own recruiting.

Training of new missionaries had become a continuing concern after the *Edinburgh Conference of 1910, and now the boards appointed candidate or personnel secretaries charged with recruitment and training. The *Foreign Missions Conference of North America established a Board of Missionary Preparation at that time, and it was succeeded by a Committee on Missionary Personnel (now Department of Missionary Personnel of the Division of Overseas Ministries, National Council of Churches), through which candidate secretaries consulted together, established policy and undertook joint projects in recruiting and training. Psychological testing and screening became standard procedure in the 1950s. The great expansion of mission personnel since the second world war has been in the non-denominational societies and some conservative evangelical church boards. The *IVF and more especially its Missionary Department, in relationship with these boards and societies plays a role in recruiting similar to that which was earlier exercised by the SVM.

Roman Catholic missionaries still continue to be largely recruited into special missionary congregations, institutes and orders at an early age, but, in the USA at least, a fair number are being sent abroad by the dioceses upon volunteering or accepting assignment by the bishop. The need for co-operation and the drastic decline in vocations along with drop-outs in the seminaries has led fifteen missionary institutes and congregations in 1969 to move through a study made by CARA to the creation of a union mission study institute and to some co-ordination in recruitment.

See also MISSIONARY RECRUITMENT AND SELECTION.

R. PIERCE BEAVER

REDEMPTION. On one level of religious experience man thinks of R. in external and this-worldly terms. He wants the gods to deliver him from disease, death, defeat and humiliation, and to grant him prosperity in this life. The oldest Hindu hymns, like many of the prayers of the OT, ask for these things, and they seek them both for the community and for the individual.

When the characteristic ideas of God held by each people become clear, ideas of R. become correspondingly distinct. Thus in the OT 'the LORD saves' in accordance with certain moral truths; these are expressed in his law and in the covenant he makes with his people. God intervenes in human affairs, and those who love and obey him can be sure of his mercy and help. Later Judaism looked also beyond the grave, and applied the same principles: in his own time God will judge all men, living and dead, and bring in his perfect kingdom.

The great Hindu thinkers came to other conclusions. By meditation on the mystery of the universe they decided that man could hope for 'deliverance' from the bondage of temporal existence. The goal to be reached is the knowledge that one's self is one with the impersonal, divine being, Brahman. The way to this goal is mental discipline, to be extended for most men through many incarnations. The reward is deliverance, not only from suffering and death, but also from life as ordinarily understood. The hope of the Buddha, too, was similar to this. Such an idea of R. is necessarily individualistic as well as life-denying.

Other religions, including popular forms of *Hinduism and *Buddhism, think of a personal God, or gods, who will reward men hereafter for the good and bad deeds of this life. The ethical principles by which this is to be done vary from one religion to another.

Christianity takes up the heritage of the OT and the early rabbis. Its teaching about R., however, arises out of a response to the person and work of Jesus Christ. Through his life, death and resurrection those who become believers are redeemed from sin, which has separated them from God; and they are made members of his family. R. is corporate, for the community of believers, but is also concerned with the individual, and is intended for the whole world. It affirms all that is good in this life but subordinates it to God's eternal and spiritual kingdom.

Christianity is a missionary religion because of its beliefs about R. Buddhism became missionary because the Buddha had compassion on his fellow men, even though to bring them his message hindered his own pursuit of individual R. There is no such contradiction in Christianity. Islam's idea of R., though it differs at many points from the Christian view, resembles it in being concerned with both community and individual and in having worldwide scope. Thus Islam, too, is essentially a missionary religion.

See also SALVATION.

JOHN GOODWIN

REFERENCE WORKS ON MISSIONS. See BIBLIOGRAPHIES; DIRECTORIES.

REFORMED CHURCH IN AMERICA

missions have as their task 'to present the gospel effectively in obedience to Christ'. They are at work in India, Japan, Hong Kong, Philippines, Taiwan, Singapore, Arabia, Iraq, South Sudan, Ethiopia and Pakistan.

In India they participate with funds and personnel in the work of evangelism, in several educational institutions, in an Industrial and Agricultural Institute, in a Bible Correspondence Course, in the United Theological College of Bangalore and in Rural Life centres.

The work in Japan consists of assistance in seven educational institutions of the United Church of Christ and in newspaper evangelism.

Thirteen missionaries work in the Philippines in the United Church of Christ in evangelism and in educational institutions.

The mission in Taiwan is one of evangelism, agriculture, religious education, medical work in one hospital and in two day schools.

Two missionaries in Singapore work among the overseas Chinese.

Fifty-one missionaries serve in the Arabian mission in four hospitals, in evangelism, two schools, an orphanage, in agriculture and in building.

Seven missionaries are assigned to the United Mission in Iraq.

The evangelistic and educational work of nine missionaries has come to an end through expulsion by the Islamic government of the Sudan. But some of the work of the church in evangelism, education and medicine is being carried forward by the local people.

The American Mission in Ethiopia has the assistance of four missionaries of this church.

Literacy work in Pakistan is carried on by two missionaries.

The RCIA takes part in the work of the Radio Voice of the Gospel as it reaches out to South Asia, the Middle East and Africa.

The headquarters of the Board of World Missions are at 475 Riverside Drive, New York, N.Y.10027.

ROBERT T. PARSONS

REFORMED CHURCHES. See PRESBY-
TERIAN MISSIONS; WORLD AL-
LIANCE OF REFORMED CHURCHES.

REFORMERS' CONCEPT OF MISSION.
With most scholars of church and mission
history it has long been a kind of dogma
that the Reformers of the 16th century
were incapable of both missionary thought
and action. This could hardly be otherwise
as long as the 19th century pattern of
foreign missions was the only standard by
which the Reformation was measured. With
the development of modern Reformation
research on the one hand, and the reconsideration of the mission of the church on
the other, a more balanced view has emerged
which may be summarized in the following
points, omitting minor differences of
emphasis among the Reformers.

(1) As it is not the Christian religion that
is to be propagated but the *gospel of Jesus
Christ, the mission is God's not ours.
The living Word itself moves out into the
world, beginning from Jerusalem and on to
the ends of the earth.

(2) The precedence of God's own initiative, far from paralysing human action,
even stimulates the witness of God's
people to God's saving grace which is
operative in and through faith.

(3) The missionary dimension of the
church as a whole must not be narrowed
into one special department of Christian
action among others. 'Nobody should hear
the gospel for himself only, but *everyone*
should tell those who do not know it'
(Luther).

If the Reformers did 'exceedingly little'
(S. Neill) to put such insight into practice,
this was at least partly due to unfavourable
circumstances: a desperate shortage of
preachers even at home, no Protestant
monastic orders, preoccupation with the
struggle for existence in Europe, lack of
contact with non-Christian nations, no
colonial expansion of Protestant powers
before the 17th century. Still, the Swedish
efforts to win the Lapps in Northern
Scandinavia, Lutheran endeavours to begin
a literature mission in the Balkans and the

ill-fated Calvinist attempt at colonial
mission in Brazil (N.D. de Villegagnon)
should at least be mentioned. Compared
with the achievements of contemporary
Roman Catholic missions, the record is not
impressive. Nor is there anything more
substantial to report about marginal groups
off the main stream of the Reformation. Yet
if pioneers of Protestant missions at a later
stage had to fight inertia and indifference in
their own ranks, the blame does not fall on
the Reformers but rather on the domestica-
tion of their original message in an intro-
verted theology and 'churchism'.

H.-W. GENSICHEN

H.-W. Gensichen: 'Were the Reformers
Indifferent to Missions?' in *The Student
World*, Vol. LII (1960, pp. 119–27
W. Holsten: '*Reformation und Mission*',
Archiv für Reformationsgeschichte (1953),
pp. 1–32.

**REGIONAL AGENCIES FOR CO-
OPERATION.** The *Foreign Missions
Conference of North America, including the
mission boards of both Canada and the
USA (1893–1950), was the only effective
regional agency of co-operation among the
older sending societies. When it became the
Division of Foreign Missions of the National
Council of Churches of Christ in the USA,
the Canadian boards withdrew and formed
their own Department of Overseas Missions
of the Canadian Council of Churches, but
individually continue membership in the
*Division of Overseas Ministries, as it is now
called. The *Continental European Missions
Conference and the Northern Missions
Council were organs for study, information,
consultation and inspiration rather than
co-operation. RAFC are institutions of the
younger churches.

The *Committee on Co-operation in Latin
America was actually a department of the
Foreign Missions Conference of North
America and administered co-operative
work from outside the region. The exclusion
of Latin America from the programme of
the *Edinburgh Conference in 1910 was the
immediate cause of its formation. It was
founded at a meeting called by the FMC in

New York in 1913. The CCLA called the Panama Conference of 1916, the first regional meeting of nationals and missionaries anywhere. That conference made the CCLA its continuation committee. Under its auspices a Conference on Christian Work in South America was held at Montevideo in 1925, national conferences and councils were created, a large literature programme was developed, evangelism was stressed, and many joint projects undertaken. The CCLA was a member council of the *IMC, but eventually surrendered that status when sufficient *national missionary councils came into existence. It was hoped that a genuine indigenous regional agency would result from the Lima Conference in 1961, but that effort failed, and such a body is still in the future.

The Conference on Work among Muslims at Cairo, 1906, and Lucknow, 1911, and IMC sponsored conferences in 1924 led to the formation of the Council for Western Asia and North Africa in 1927; and two years later this became the Near East Christian Council for Missionary Co-operation. The autonomy and maturity of the churches brought about its transformation into the Near East Council of Churches in 1964 with headquarters in Beirut.

The IMC and *WCC in 1950 made Dr Rajah B. Manikam joint secretary for East Asia, following the Eastern Asia Christian Conference at Bangkok in 1949. His ministry and the personnel exchange programme of the Asia Council on Ecumenical Mission resulted in a consultation at Bangkok in 1956, which prepared plans for an *East Asia Christian Conference. These were adopted at a conference under that name at Prapat, Indonesia, in March 1957. The EACC was formally inaugurated at Kuala Lumpur, Malaya, in 1959, and the next assemblies were held at Bangkok in 1964 and 1968. The EACC is an autonomous body serving its member churches, but co-operates closely with the WCC and its units. Office: 14 Pramuan Road, Bangkok, Thailand.

A younger agency is the *All Africa Conference of Churches. A preliminary conference at Ibadan, Nigeria, elected a provisional committee and appointed Dr Donald M'Timkulu roving secretary. Even during the preparatory period important conferences were held: Higher Education (Salisbury); Urban Consultation (Limuru); Home and Family Life (Mindolo), and Christian Literature (Mindolo). The inaugural assembly was held at Kampala, Uganda in April 1963. Office: P.O. Box 20301, Nairobi, Kenya.

The first Pacific Conference of Churches was held at Malua, Western Samoa, in 1961. A continuation committee working through five commissions leads the churches of the region towards a more permanent organization and an effective programme of mutual service.

See also REGIONAL CONFERENCES.

R. PIERCE BEAVER

I. All Africa Churches Conference: *The Church in Changing Africa, Report of the AACC, Ibadan* 1958; *Drumbeats from Kampala, Report of the First Assembly of the AACC*, 1963; *Christian Education in Africa, Report of the (Salisbury) Conference*, 1963; II. East Asia Christian Conference: *The Common Evangelistic Task, Papers and Minutes, Prapat*, 1957; *Witnesses Together, Report of . . . Inaugural Assembly . . . Kuala Lumpur, 1959; Assembly of the EACC, Bangkok, 1964, Minutes Parts I and II*; III. Committee on Co-operation in Latin America: Reports in *Annual Report* of Foreign Missions Conference of North America and Division of Foreign Missions (World Missions, Overseas Ministries), National Council of Churches of Christ in the USA, and *Latin America Newsletter* (NY); IV. Near East Council of Churches: *News Bulletin of the N.E. Christian Council*, and successors; for Muslim-Christian dialogue project, *Operation Reach* and *Emmaus Furlongs*.

REGIONAL CONFERENCES. Regionalism—thinking, planning and operating in relation to an entire region, e.g. S.E. Asia, Africa south of the Sahara, Europe, the Caribbean world—by the mid-20th century was well established. It took political

(Organization for African Unity), economic (European Common Market), religious (*East Asia Christian Conference), and other forms. Huge industrial firms were operating throughout the globe on the basis of vast regional divisions. Because technology has made the world's oneness—its inter-relatedness—apparent and has made obsolete almost all strategic planning limited to national boundaries, regionalism has emerged. The most viable units of today's world are entire, trans-national, human communities.

The need for regional structures within the church is apparent and found apt illustration in the Second *Vatican Council's first session. There, when Africa's RC bishops for the first time were all together, they discovered the need to face unitedly their common regional problems and to act accordingly. They formed the Pan-African Episcopacy, a body whose essential purpose is akin to that of the *All Africa Conference of Churches.

When the *WCC emerged in 1948, a network of *National Christian Councils already spanned the globe; but by the mid-1950s many of these NCCs recognized need for regional co-ordination and co-operation —for an intermediate agency serving a region as neither the WCC nor any NCC could do. This was the background from which the *EACC emerged in 1957.

East Asia Christian Conference (EACC) Two points require noting. Although 'conference' implies more informal structures than 'council', many view the EACC's functions as basically those of a council. Moreover, the EACC's 'East Asia' includes those lands within the vast triangle formed by Pakistan, New Zealand and Japan. There live the bulk of the world's people, and among them Christians are few in number— a bare 2% of the population. Yet evidencing their own mature selfhood, the Asian churches through the EACC have undertaken together primary responsibility for mission among two-thirds of mankind.

The EACC has a noteworthy history. Responding to Asian requests, *Madras 1938 had recommended an *IMC Far Eastern Office. After the war, steps were taken (at the Manila Conference, 1948), which led to the Eastern Asia Christian Conference, Bangkok 1949. Subsequently in 1951 the IMC and WCC jointly appointed Dr (later Bishop) Rajah B. Manikam of India's NCC as East Asia Secretary. His liaison work as roving ambassador fostered regional unity. In 1955 several East Asian churches created an Asia Council on Ecumenical Mission, and there followed at Bangkok in 1956 an Asia-wide IMC–WCC consultation. From it came the First Assembly (Preparatory) of the EACC at Prapat, Sumatra, Indonesia in 1957. Prapat's theme, 'The Common Evangelistic Task of the Churches in East Asia', appropriately launched the EACC's work. The Second Assembly (Inaugural) at Kuala Lumpur, Malaya, 1959, under the theme, 'Witnesses Together' gave the EACC its notable constitution. In 1963 the EACC convened in India, Japan and Singapore 'situation conferences' to explore the meaning of *Joint Action for Mission in Asia. Then its Third Assembly at Bangkok, 1964, launched the four-year study 'The Christian Community Within the Human Community'.

The Fourth Assembly met in Bangkok in January 1968. Representing nearly 40 million Anglican, Protestant and Orthodox church members, it proposed new thrusts in mission, a meeting with conservative Evangelicals and dialogue with Roman Catholics.

All Africa Conference of Churches
In Africa many factors similar to those in Asia pointed to need for an agency providing continent-wide Christian co-operation. The IMC undertook the initiative. A few days after its 1958 Ghana Assembly had ended, the first All Africa Church Conference met at Ibadan, with the Christian Council of Nigeria serving as host. It was a decisive moment. In Africa south of the Sahara only Ethiopia, Liberia, Ghana and South Africa were then independent.

Yet in the next five years with the birth of Africa's new nations, that continent's map was radically changed. Those at Ibadan for the first time saw the *African* church, heard its confident voice, and determined to achieve· wide co-operation. They voted to create a continuing agency and made Dr Francis Akanu Ibiam its chairman.

The AACC Provisional Committee in January 1960 began its active life with Dr Donald G. S. M'Timkulu as its General Secretary. His residence at the Mindolo Ecumenical Centre, Kitwe, Zambia, became its headquarters. Its six conferences, focusing on Christian Women, Youth, Urban Problems, Literature and Communications, Education, and Family Life made it known throughout Africa. These and a widely circulated provisional constitution led to the Inaugural Assembly of the All Africa Conference of Churches (AACC).

At Kampala, Uganda, 1963, the AACC was formally initiated. Its Constitution, similar to that of the EACC, provides for a quadrennial Assembly, an annual committee, and a General Secretary (since 1965, Dr. Samuel Amissah of Ghana) with associates and commissions dealing with areas of concern for African churches. AACC headquarters in 1965 were transferred from Mindolo to Nairobi. Relationships—organizational and financial—with the WCC are similar to those of the EACC.

Pacific Conference of Churches

Responding to a 1959 request from churches and missions in the Pacific, the IMC convened a conference at Malua, Samoa, in 1961. From it came a Continuation Committee, the annual meetings of which were strengthened by the wide travel of its secretary, the Rev. Vavae Toma. The increasing co-operation of the churches strengthened their outreach in mission and encouraged the opening in 1966 of the Pacific Theological College at Suva, Fiji, to serve the entire region. In 1966 at Chapanehe, Loyalty Islands, the Constituting Assembly of the Pacific Conference of Churches met. The PCC's Assembly meets every five years and its Continuation Committee meets annually.

Provisional Committee for Latin American Evangelical Units (UNELAM)

For historic, cultural, geographic and theological reasons wide co-operation among Latin America's rapidly growing Evangelical (Protestant) churches has been difficult. These bodies met in the First Latin American Evangelical Conference at Buenos Aires in 1949. Many hoped that the Second Conference at Lima in 1961 would result in a regional organization. It did not, but eventually, from efforts made there, the Provisional Committee for Latin American Evangelical Unity emerged in 1965. Its final shape remains to be determined.

Other Bodies. Efforts have been made for a Caribbean regional body. The Conference of Churches in Latin Europe has met for some years, and the more recently formed Conference of European Churches brings together bodies from 21 countries.

Although doctoral dissertations are in process on the EACC and the AACC, no one source in English provides a survey of these regional conferences. Each large assembly usually publishes a report, and some of these are available from the WCC.

See also REGIONAL AGENCIES FOR CO-OPERATION.

W. RICHEY HOGG

EACC: The most recent minutes were printed in two parts: *Assembly of the EACC . . . Bangkok . . . 1964* (Available from U Kyaw Than, 14 Pramuan Road, Bangkok, Thailand) and *The Christian Community Within the Human Community* (Available from Mr M. M. Thomas, 19 Miller's Road, Bangalore 6, India); AACC: *The Church in Changing Africa: Report of the All Africa Church Conference* (New York 1958), and *Drumbeats From Kampala: Report of the First Assembly of the All Africa Conference of Churches* (London 1963); PCC: *Beyond the Reef: Records of the Conference of Churches and Missions in the Pacific, Samoa, 1961* (London 1961).

REGIONS BEYOND MISSIONARY UNION developed from the interdenominational East London Institute for Home and Foreign Missions (Harley College) founded (1872) by the Irish evangelist Grattan *Guinness (1835–1910) in association with Dr Barnardo and Hudson *Taylor.

Most of the students went to established societies but Guinness being concerned for 'regions beyond', where no missions operated, sent a small group to the newly explored Congo in 1878; after five years the oversight was handed to the American Baptists. In 1888 he began another Congo mission, 96 missionaries going out during the first thirteen years. In Peru a mission begun in 1893 by three ex-students was adopted, and in 1899, following a journey by Guinness, an untouched area of Bihar, India, was entered. In 1927 Dr Cecil Duncan joined, later founding the important hospital at Raxaul on the India-Nepal border. After the second world war RBMU adopted or initiated missionary operations in Indonesian Borneo and West New Guinea, and was a founder-member of the United Mission to Nepal (1954). Councils were formed in North America. Numerically a smaller society, RBMU has specially emphasized aggressive evangelism, loyalty to a biblical gospel, a high level in personal consecration and devotional life, and prayer-partnership as a force in missionary strategy.

JOHN POLLOCK

Kenneth Holmes: *The Cloud Moves* (London, n.d.).

REICHELT, KARL LUDVIG (1877–1952), a missionary of the Norwegian Missionary Society in Hunan, China, from 1903 on, was led in 1922 to form a special organization, which came to be known as the Christian Mission to Buddhists, in order to approach Buddhist and Taoist monks in a manner more congenial to them than that provided by the general run of Christian missions. The first public statement affirmed that 'we will approach these religious people in a sympathetic way . . . showing them that their highest aspirations may be fulfilled in Jesus Christ, the all-embracing word of God'. In 1929, owing to the troubled state of China, the work was transferred from Nanking to the new territories of Hong Kong, where, in the calmer latitude of a British colony, the institution called *Tao Fong Shan*, 'the mountain from which the

Christ-Spirit blows', came into being. R.'s work was sharply criticized by some, on the ground that his sympathy with the Asian religions had led him so far in the direction of *syncretism that essential Christian values had been surrendered. In 1937 R. was able to show that such criticisms rested mainly on misunderstanding. In fifteen years about 80 monks had been baptized; and friends of *Tao Fong Shan* were scattered all over the Far East, even in such areas as Eastern Tibet and Mongolia.

Support for the work of R. came from many sources, especially Scandinavia. After his death the work was carried on by others, and has now become fully ecumenical, being recognized by both Lutheran and non-Lutheran churches in Hong Kong as a part of their joint responsibilities, though the difficulties in communication between Hong Kong and mainland China have limited the scope of operations, and have given a different character to the enterprise.

STEPHEN NEILL

S. Holth: 'Karl Ludvig Reichelt 1877–1952', *IRM* XLI (1952), pp. 444–51; L. E. Noren: 'The Life and Work of Karl Ludvig Reichelt', in *Ching Feng* (Hong Kong) X, 3 (1967), 6–33; K. L. Reichelt: *Truth and Tradition in Chinese Buddhism* (Shanghai 1930), 'Buddhism in China at the Present Time and the new Challenge to the Christian Church', *IRM* XXVI (1937), pp. 153–66; N. N. Thelle: *Karl Ludvig Reichelt* (Oslo 1959).

REINCARNATION. See TRANSMIGRATION AND REINCARNATION.

RELATIVITY, RELIGIOUS. Broadly speaking, the problem of understanding and evaluating the relations or comparative worth of various religious faiths.

More narrowly, the belief, better known as religious relativism, that the different religions are all culturally conditioned and that all alike offer partial views of truth.

Any attempt to establish the relative value of one religion, over against another, must include the scientific, the philosophical and the existential dimensions.

(1) The *scientific* study is descriptive. It uses the skills and methods of historians, linguists, sociologists and anthropologists to record, describe and analyse the various beliefs and practices of different religions, to see their similarities and differences ('comparative religions') and to trace their own inner historical development. The ideal of this approach is 'scientific' and 'objective' description, refraining from value judgments.

(2) The *philosophical* study of religion seeks to systematize and evaluate the data provided by the scientific approach, fitting the facts brought to light into a system of thought, sometimes attempting to classify religions on an 'objective' scale (example, Troeltsch).

(3) The *existential*. While both the above approaches to the study of any religion are indispensable, nevertheless their value to decide the question of the truth-claim of a particular religion remains limited, without taking into consideration this third dimension of the problem of RR. Since all men view life in the light of their beliefs, and personal beliefs may also be presupposed by the investigations of the scientists and the philosophers, the problem of deciding on purely intellectual grounds the relative value of different religions will remain an endless task. No one stands outside or above the culture and the historically existing religions of the world in such a way that he can achieve complete objectivity. Hence, with all possible comparative study, a person is still left with the question to what or to whom he will commit his own faith.

While religious relativism may have a certain theoretical persuasiveness and offers the practical attractiveness of a formula for broad tolerance, it can hardly be accepted as the final word. If one takes seriously the claims of any religious belief to be *true*, then either that belief or else beliefs which are contrary to it must be false.

The relationship of Christianity to other religions may best be recognized to include both **'continuity'* and 'discontinuity'. This tension is inherent in the very nature of the Christian revelation, which embraces both the universal and the exclusive points of view. The Christian missionary's dialogue with other religions must embrace this tension in the spirit of understanding love.

ROLAND E. KIRCHER

W. A. Visser 't Hooft: *No Other Name: the Choice Between Syncretism and Christian Universalism* (Philadelphia 1963); H. Kraemer: *World Cultures and World Religions: the Coming Dialogue* (Philadelphia 1960); S. C. Neill: *Christian Faith and Other Faiths, the Christian Dialogue with Other Religions* (London 1961); G. F. Vicedom: *The Challenge of the World Religions* (Philadelphia 1963).

RELIEF WORK AND REHABILITATION. When churches and their agencies desire ecumenically to offer aid after earthquakes, typhoons, floods, volcanic eruptions, the devastation of war, or similar disasters, the centralized international Christian organization they turn to is DICARWS (see INTER-CHURCH AID). DICARWS can usually arrange for help to be on its way within 48 hours of receiving news of a disaster and often much sooner. Although the immediate call may be for blankets, clothing, medicines and food, as well as cash, DICARWS tries always to ensure that help encourages permanent rehabilitation. DICARWS does not maintain depots of goods but it can call on church-collected resources in many countries and arrange to have these shipped or air-freighted. DICARWS co-operates with various voluntary, governmental and UN agencies. It has helped the churches to co-ordinate their work with the Freedom From Hunger Campaign, notably in Iran, Tunisia and Botswana. Where necessary it has created local agencies such as the Bengal Refugee Service, wound up in 1965 after resettling 8,000 persons, and the Christian Committee for Service in Algeria which *inter alia* planted 22,000,000 trees after training Algerians. DICARWS has raised $3m to attack famine conditions in India, and has sought $10m to support an Ecumenical

Programme for Emergency Action in Africa.

See also CHURCH WORLD SERVICE.

GEOFFREY MURRAY

RELIGION. It has never been found possible to give an exact definition of the word 'R'. E. B. Tylor (1871) proposed as a 'minimum definition' 'belief in spiritual beings'; but this would seem to exclude *Buddhism, which has at least many of the marks of a R. Sir J. G. Frazer suggests 'a propitiation or conciliation of powers superior to men, which are believed to direct and control the course of nature and of human life'; but there are many elements in R. besides those of propitiation. It is possible that a wider understanding of the word should be sought, such as 'awareness of the sacred, and belief that men can enter into relation with it'; or even more widely, 'that which is regarded by men as being of supreme importance'.

Over a considerable period ethnologists lived in hope of discovering some race or people among whom religion was unknown. Every claim to have discovered such a people has been proved by subsequent investigation to have been mistaken. Among the most primitive peoples, such as the Aborigines in Australia, an astonishing part of the waking hours of a tribe is spent in liturgical activity, which is regarded as essential to the being and the survival of the tribe. On this level the distinction between the religious and the secular has not been made; there is still a primal unity in the understanding of life.

In modern times various attempts have been made to abolish R. or to treat it as insignificant. (1) The Marxist regards R. as merely an ideology, the rationalization by a possessing class of its own dominant position in society, and therefore as incompatible with a scientific understanding of the being of man. (2) Many Freudians treat R. as illusion, as the projection of man's own hopes and fears on to the external world, but no more. (3) The cultural anthropologists regard R. as relative to a particular cultural situation;

any claim to objective truth is therefore nugatory and irrelevant. (4) Some regard R. as positively harmful—the cause of division, hatred and persecution, and therefore as a relic to be left behind by a world advancing in the direction of a common civilization. (5) Humanists would admit R. only as regard for the highest values that man has developed out of his own consciousness; the ideas of God and revelation belong to the childhood of the race, and must be abandoned.

In spite of these efforts, it seems unlikely that R. will cease to play a leading part in the life of men. As is very clear in the case of Marxism, when formal R. is excluded, a pseudo-R. very often takes its place.

Many attempts, none entirely satisfactory, at a classification of religions have been made. Two distinctions seem to be genuinely of value: (a) that between local and universal religions. From the beginning, Buddhism, Christianity and *Islam have claimed universality and have therefore been missionary religions. In recent times some Hindu leaders have made a similar claim. (b) That between prophetic and mystical religions. In the prophetic religions, God speaks to man, and R. enters in from a world outside man's own being. For the mystic, R. is the development of that divine spark in man which has never been extinguished, and through which he is alive to all else that is divine in the universe, whether this be understood as 'God' or in some much more general way. These two are not necessarily mutually exclusive; both are to be found, in various combinations, in the experience of Christian people.

It may be said that R. on its highest level is concerned with understanding, deliverance and hope. (1) Man desires to understand the universe in which he lives, and therefore to be able in a measure to master it. (2) That from which man desires to be delivered varies as between the different religions. The Greek longed above all for deliverance from corruptibility; the Hindu for release from the chain and the illusion of separate existence; the Christian longs for freedom from the power of sin and death. (3) Man desires assurance that existence is not meaningless, and that the daily struggle to be, and to be himself, is not in vain.

Christians who believe that the revelation of God in Jesus Christ is God's final word to men would maintain that the gospel offers (a) a clear understanding of man's place in the world, which can only be enriched and clarified by the process of scientific discovery; (b) complete deliverance from every kind of bondage into the glorious liberty of the children of God; (c) hope in the fulfilment of all good desires in unending fellowship with Christ and with all his people.

STEPHEN NEILL

S. A. Cook: 'Religion', *ERE* X, 662–93; *NCE* XII, 240–46; *WKL*, 1230–34.

RELIGION, COMPARATIVE. See COMPARATIVE STUDY OF RELIGIONS.

RELIGIOUS EDUCATION. See EDUCATION AS MISSIONARY METHOD.

RELIGIOUS LIBERTY. See LIBERTY, RELIGIOUS.

RELIGIOUS PLURALISM. See PLURALISM, RELIGIOUS.

RELIGIOUS TERMS, VOCABULARY. The RT in the vocabulary of any language may be divided into eight major classes: (1) supernatural beings, e.g. God, Lord, spirit, devil, demons, (2) personages, e.g. priest, apostle, deacon, (3) objects, e.g. altar, temple, image, (4) events, e.g. Passover, day of atonement, (5) revelation, e.g. sign, parable, vision, (6) ethically defined behaviour, e.g. good, bad, righteous, sin, (7) religious acts, e.g. justify, sanctify, expiate, and (8) eschatology, e.g. eternal, heaven and hell.

The alternatives which one faces in communicating the Christian message in another language are of three types: (1) the use of an indigenous term, even though certain modifications in the meaning may need to be suggested by the context, (2) descriptive equivalents, e.g. phylacteries may be as in Navajo 'little leather bundles with holy words in them', and (3) borrowed terms, which may be quite acceptable for easily described or picturable objects, but which should not be used for major features, e.g. spirit, sin, forgiveness, salvation and grace.

One of the basic difficulties with many persons is that they expect some sort of word-to-word conformity in a semantic structure. Thus they feel that for each term such as *redeem*, *forgive* and *believe*, they must have a single word in some other language. As a matter of fact, these concepts can always be expressed, but it is frequently necessary to use phrases, not individual words. For example, *redeem* in Bambara (West Africa) is 'to take the head out' (a reference to release during slave days), *forgiveness* in Shilluk (the Sudan) is 'to spit on the ground before' (a reference to the act of showing forgiveness by plaintiff and defendant after a trial in Shilluk courts), and *faith* (or to believe) in Tzeltal (a language of southern Mexico) is 'to hang on to God with the heart'.

The Scriptures must not be translated in a cultural vacuum; they must reflect the life of the growing Christian community. This means that the ways in which people describe their newly found faith will have a profound influence upon the religious vocabulary used by the translator. Conversely, of course, the form of the Scriptures will contextually condition the development of meaning of many religious terms.

The tendency to idolatry of words, i.e. reading into words more meaning than was intended, is a common failing, both for the naïve reader and for the theologically more sophisticated, who feels constrained to hang all his learning on some verbal pegs. Accordingly, religious vocabulary tends to become sacrosanct and revision is viewed as 'tampering' with the Word of God.

See also GOD, TRANSLATION OF TERM.

EUGENE A. NIDA

Anon.: 'Biblical Terms', *The Bible Translator*, Vol. III (1952), pp.225–33; J. Barr: *The Semantics of Biblical Language* (London

1961); E. A. Nida: *Bible Translating* (London 1961), pp.203–40.

RE-THINKING MISSIONS. See LAY-MEN'S FOREIGN MISSIONS INQUIRY.

REVELATION, CHRISTIAN AND NON-CHRISTIAN. R. is a universal phenomenon of religions. It is the characteristic function of every religion to unveil to humans what it understands to be the transcendent ultimate, i.e. the Truth which lies beyond man's experience of this world. It is this function of unveiling the transcendent ultimate that gives religion its autonomy and distinguishes it from other forms of human enquiry and creativity such as science, morality and art.

Religions differ in what they understand to be the transcendent ultimate. They do not differ in their claim to reveal, through the forms of their own religion, what is otherwise an unknown transcendent ultimate.

The religions are not satisfied to leave the transcendent ultimate concealed in an abstract idea, or 'before' or 'after' time, or beneath or behind the sense world. Religious experience in any of the traditions of religion is experience of the disclosure of the transcendent ultimate as the content of particular, humanly perceived phenomena or experiences.

R. is indispensable to everything that may properly be called religion. In every religion R. of its transcendent ultimate serves (1) to expose the unsatisfactoriness of man's finite and historical world, (2) to require a 'way' of overcoming the unsatisfactoriness of life, and (3) to provide the incentive and the 'environment', to provide the *milieu* conducive to faithful pursuit of or communion with the revealed transcendent ultimate.

While all religions are religions of R., formed and informed by what is believed to be a transcendent ultimate, not all religions are or claim to be *revealed* religions. Revealed religions are those which understand the transcendent ultimate to have taken the initiative or at least co-operated in making that ultimate known to man.

Theravāda *Buddhism, for example, does not claim to be a revealed religion in this sense. It understands the transcendent ultimate to be *Nibbāna*, the state of absolute perfection, which man can reach by following the correct path. Theravāda Buddhism categorically denies that *Nibbāna* extends any help to man in experiencing *Nibbāna*. Man has, from the Theravāda understanding, all the powers he needs to liberate himself from all bondages and unsatisfactory conditions whatsoever, and these powers do not come to him as gifts from Another but in the very nature of the existence. *Judaism, on the other hand, is a '*revealed* religion'. In Judaism the transcendent ultimate is 'the people of the LORD'; the LORD's dealings with his people throughout their history are the content of revelation. Although 'the LORD' of Judaism is not known apart from his involvement with his people, he is himself other than this involvement, for he came to them ('visited them'), found them, and made them a peculiar people. This movement toward men initiated by the ultimate transcendent itself is the distinguishing characteristic of 'revealed' religions. One way of classifying religions is according to the manner and means by which the transcendent became known. However, to be able to distinguish 'realization' religions from 'revealed' religions is not to be able to demonstrate the validity or worth of either. Our appraisal of the religions depends to a definitive degree upon personal convictions the validity of which is not scientifically demonstrable.

Christian R. is 'the *coming* of Jesus Christ'. Christianity is a 'revealed' religion since Christians understand their transcendent ultimate to be Jesus Christ who, though coming as a human, 'came' from *beyond* the world of space-time-history to help man to transcend his historical (spatio-temporal) existence. Jesus Christ is the ultimate transcendent (i.e. 'God' in the Scriptures, liturgy and language of Christian tradition) in its penetration of creation and history. Whatever else the transcendent ultimate may be 'beyond' man's possibilities of experiencing in his mortal existence is a matter of inference and unnecessary speculation. For the Christian, the transcendent ultimate has transcended itself ultimately in Jesus Christ. He is both the transcendent ultimate and the ultimate transcendence: 'In him the complete being of God came to dwell' (Col.1:19), 'My Father and I are one . . . If I am not acting as my Father would act, do not believe me. But if I am, accept the evidence of my deeds, even if you do not believe me, so that you may recognize and know that the Father is in me and I in the Father' (Jn.10:30, 37f., etc.). Further reference to, and even the use of the word, 'God' merely illuminates the full orb of the transcendent ultimacy of Jesus Christ.

It is not only play with language but the language of Christian faith to say that Jesus Christ is the one who 'put himself out' (Phil. 2:6–7, 'From the first he was what God was . . . but *put himself out* . . . and was born what men are, humbled his human self, and accepted death, even crucifixion. Therefore God raised him . . . and bestowed upon him the name above all names . . . "Jesus Christ is Lord",' cf. John's Christology: 'I came from the Father . . . I go to the Father'). As the transcendent ultimate—'what God was'—he put himself out for man; as the ultimate transcendent—'born what men are'—he put himself out for God. Jesus Christ is both the end of God and the end of man, the self-transcendence of both. By 'incarnation' Christians mean the meeting in Jesus Christ of this two-way and two-fold transcendence, each with the other for the other, the two made one. As the self-transcendence of humanity, Jesus Christ is both the judgment and the possibility of every man. In their humanity, all self-centred men are under the judgment of his selflessness; in his fulfilment of their humanity, Jesus Christ is already a part of, yet apart from, every man. Participating in the environment of their lives, Jesus Christ is the challenge to every man's self-defensiveness. Alive with his life, all men have the power to live in Jesus Christ and let their bearing towards one another arise out of the power of this life in Jesus Christ. The fulfilment of this possibility cannot be confined to the cult and culture of the Christian religion, although a Christian religion is an inevitable consequence of life in Jesus Christ. Yet, because of its pretentious rivalry with Jesus Christ, the Christian religion will always stand under his condemnation of self-defensiveness. Christians may properly celebrate together their life in Christ, but never with the approval of Jesus Christ may they celebrate without remembering gratefully those others whose life is in Christ but not in the Christian cultus.

EDMUND F. PERRY

REVIVAL IN MISSIONARY HISTORY. At strategic junctures in the history of the church and at unexpected times revival has come. By no means has R. been limited to the western world; while it is natural to recount the glories of European and American revivals, perhaps some of the greatest awakenings have occurred on the so-called mission fields of the world. At times there have been movements of the Holy Spirit that brought thousands of new converts into the church and at other times there have been reawakenings of a cold, lethargic or sleeping church.

The first awakening of the Gospel era occurred at Pentecost under the dynamic preaching of the apostle Peter. Three thousand people are reported to have confessed Christ and thousands more were added to the church later.

In the early centuries there were mass conversions attributed to the ministry of leading Christian missionaries. Gregory Thaumaturgus (c.213–270) evangelized Pontus and his ministry was summed up by the observation that there were only seventeen Christians when he came and only seventeen pagans when he died. Gregory the Illuminator (c.240–332) saw Armenia turn to God through the conversion of the king, Tradt (Tiridates). During the middle ages men like Anthony of Padua often preached to as many as 20,000 people.

Following the Reformation a succession

of revivals broke out in Europe and the USA. Ireland experienced revival in 1628 under Blair and Livingstone. Spener and Francke sparked the Pietistic Awakening that swept over large parts of Europe. Eighteenth century England was moved by the Wesleyan revival. Scotland experienced quickenings in the 18th century at Cambuslang, Kilsyth, Campsie, Calder and Lundie. Whitefield lighted revival fires in England and America. Under Freylinghuysen in New Jersey in the 1720s, Jonathan *Edwards in New England in the 1730s, and in Virginia in the forties, there were great movements of God's Spirit. Revival began in the Vosges mountains in 1765 under John Frederic Oberlin. In 1796 a revival commenced in Norway under Hans Nielsen Hauge. Scotland was moved by the Haldane brothers in 1800, and Canada, too, experienced an awakening.

In the USA in the 19th century college revivals swept Yale and Hampden Sydney. In 1816 Methodist camp meetings brought tens of thousands of converts into the church. There were also revivals in Germany, Geneva, Sweden, Hawaii and Scotland by 1840. In the middle of the century the great Fijian revival was in progress, and of John *Geddie in Aneityum it was said that 'when he landed in 1848 there were no Christians here; when he left in 1872 there were no heathen'. In the second half of the 19th century important revivals erupted in the USA, Ulster (Ireland), Scotland, Wales, Bechuanaland, Madagascar and among the Barotse in Africa. Names of evangelists like *Moody, Finney, Booth and François stand out.

In the early 20th century revivals occurred in Wales, Madagascar, Scandinavia, Korea, Chile, Manchuria, Ireland and the USA. There has been special and continuing revival in East Africa since 1932. Perhaps there has been no greater name in revivalism in the 20th century or any century than that of Billy Graham who has travelled more widely and spoken to more people—via mass meetings, radio and television—than any other evangelist in the history of the church.

HAROLD LINDSELL

K. S. Latourette: *A History of the Expansion of Christianity* (7 vols., New York 1937–1945).

REVOLUTION AND MISSIONS. The Christian mission, as is being increasingly recognized by secular historians, is one of the great revolutionary forces in world history, though the operation of this law is in many cases unconscious, and the missionaries themselves have often been unaware of the consequences of what they were doing. (1) Missionaries working under colonial régimes have frequently prepared the way for the disappearance of *colonialism by introducing the students in their colleges and schools to advanced western political ideas. Missionaries living in the midst of primitive and animistic societies have invariably undermined the stability of such societies by teaching younger people to criticize ancestral traditions, and, where the dissolution of the old order has been hastened by the action of traders and governments, have in many cases exercised a genuinely creative function in helping the younger generation to reconstruct in the revolutionary situation which they themselves have been in part responsible for producing. (2) Nevertheless churches and missions have rarely been eager to welcome revolution when it has come. Churches and their missionaries tend to be conservative, being more aware of the deposit of faith which must at all costs be preserved than of the explosive effects of that faith when applied to human situations. In many cases there has been good reason for the hesitation of the missions. Revolution is a destructive force; the ancient good which it sweeps away may be of greater value than the modern good which it attempts to introduce. Many missionaries and Chinese Christians were prepared to welcome the communist takeover in 1949; only in the light of long-term history will it be possible to judge whether they were right in their estimate that the takeover would in the long run be of advantage to the cause of Christ in the world. (3) In certain circles the doctrine is being forcefully proclaimed that Christians, just because they are Christians, must everywhere be on the side of the revolution. This is especially the case in Latin America, where the injustice of the status quo, with its immense gap between the few haves and the many have-nots, intimately linked to the power of the church, expressed in dictatorial régimes supported by the power of North American capital, is so deeply entrenched that it cannot be dislodged except by revolutionary action. Christians, it is argued, both RC and Protestant, should take the lead in the revolutionary movement. This is a position which other Christians, equally sincere, would not feel it possible to adopt without considerable reservations. (4) Interest in the progress of revolution does not mean that the church should ever identify itself wholly with a single revolutionary party. The church must be the church of all men, not of one group, even though the politics and policies of that group may seem to be more compatible with the Christian gospel. This is a difficult position to maintain, and younger Christians are inclined to maintain exactly the opposite thesis—that the church should uncompromisingly identify itself with what they are inclined to call the party of freedom. The problem can be well illustrated by the recent history of Ghana. Two parties were working for Ghanaian independence—the more moderate under the leadership of Dr Danquah, the more extreme under the guidance of Dr Kwame Nkrumah. If the party of Dr Danquah had prevailed, it is possible that the independence of Ghana would have been delayed by a number of years; but in the light of history it is possible to argue that the churches in that country were wise in maintaining a certain detachment in these political affairs. Perhaps the correct attitude was rightly defined by the Whitby Conference of 1947— that the church should be wholly identified with the world in its needs, and wholly detached from it in its desires.

STEPHEN NEILL

S. C. Neill: Colonialism and Christian Missions (London 1966); C. W. Ranson: Renewal and Advance: the Whitby Missionary Conference 1947 (London and New York 1948); M. M. Thomas: The Christian Response to the Asian Revolution (London 1966); Report of the Conference on Church and Society (Geneva 1966).

REYES, ISABELO DE LOS (1864–1938). Co-founder (with Gregorio *Aglipay) of the *Philippine Independent Church (PIC). Born in Vigan, Ilocos, Philippines, R. studied law at the University of Santo Tomás and enjoyed a distinguished career as an author and journalist in Manila. His criticism of the friars and Spanish colonial administration caused his imprisonment and transfer to Spain at the outbreak of the Philippine revolution in 1896. Back in Manila five years later, he organized the Unión Obrera Democrática—the first labour union in the Philippines. Responsive to the deteriorating relationship between many Filipino Catholics and the Church of Rome (which seemed determined to keep Catholicism in the Islands subject to foreign priests), R. proclaimed the formation of the PIC under the auspices of his labour union in August 1902. Later Fr Aglipay became supreme bishop of the new church. Author of the Oficio Divino (1906), R. constructed a liturgy for the church around some of his own peculiar rationalist, humanist and unitarian beliefs. Active in Philippine politics, he founded with Aglipay the short-lived Republican Party in 1904. He was elected to one term in the Philippine Senate in 1922. He died in 1938 reconciled to the RC church. His son, Isabelo Jr., became supreme bishop of the PIC in 1946.

PETER G. GOWING

P. S. de Achútegui and M. A. Bernad: Religious Revolution in the Philippines, Vol. I (Manila 1960).

RHENISH MISSIONARY SOCIETY. Not unlike other contemporary societies, the RMS grew out of an alliance of small local groups inspired by the example of British societies and the *Basel Mission. Founded in 1828 in Barmen, it represented the joint missionary endeavour of highly diversified circles, including Lutherans, Calvinists and non-confessional neo-Pietists. As a mission seminary had already been established in Barmen in 1825, the first trained workers could be sent out in 1829 to South Africa. Other areas of work included Borneo, China (as early as 1847) and New Guinea. But the most important field was to be the Batak country in Sumatra, opened up by L. I. *Nommensen from 1861, with successive extensions into the islands of Nias and Mentawei. Renowned mission leaders, such as F. Fabri, A. Schreiber and J. *Warneck, served as general secretaries of the RMS. After the second world war, only the work in Indonesia and South West Africa was continued, with the addition of a new pioneer effort in West New Guinea (Irian) since 1960. With a seminary of its own and remarkably close co-operation with regional churches in West Germany, the RMS continues to be one of the major German societies. In 1967 it had 178 missionaries.

H.-W. GENSICHEN

A. Bonn: *Hundert Jahre Rhein. Mission* (Barmen 1928); *RGG* V, 1082f.

RHENIUS, CHARLES THEOPHILUS EWALD (1790–1838), was born, converted and ordained in Prussia, but in 1814 arrived in India in the service of the Anglican *CMS. In 1820 he was sent to Palamcottah to open up the Tinnevelly mission. Here he showed exceptional gifts as linguist, evangelist and pastor. More than any other man he was responsible for the development of the system under which the school, the teacher of which was also the village catechist, became the centre of Christian expansion. Converts and congregations multiplied under his benign care. Always a man of independent mind, R. was frequently in controversy with the society which employed him. In 1830 he wrote to say that a number of catechists put forward for ordination could not conscientiously assent to the terms laid down in the Anglican Prayer Book, and asked permission to continue the older practice, by which the missionaries had themselves ordained Indian pastors; this was naturally refused, since episcopal ordination was by that time

18

available in India. Matters came to a head in 1835, when R. published a series of pamphlets sharply critical of Anglican rules and usages. The CMS declared his connection with the society at an end, and sent George Pettitt to replace him. R. left Tinnevelly, but later accepted an invitation from his friends to return, and brought about a lamentable schism in the church which he himself had so largely called into being. With the death of R. in 1838, the situation was eased, and all the dissidents gradually returned to the Anglican fellowship. The CMS, to its eternal honour, voted to Mrs. R. the pension to which she would have been entitled had the schism never occurred. The Tinnevelly church today honours R. as its second founder, after C. F. *Schwartz.

STEPHEN NEILL

G. Pettitt: *The Tinnevelly Mission of the C.M.S.* (London 1851); C. T. E. Rhenius: *Memoir, comprising extracts from his journal, etc.* (London 1841); *RGG* V, 1088f.

RHODES, ALEXANDER DE (1591–1660), missionary in Asia, was born in Avignon, France, and died at Isfahan, Iran. In 1612 he became a *Jesuit, and in 1618 was sent to the Far East for missionary work in Japan. Persecution of Christians in Japan made it impossible for him to attain this goal, so he settled down in Macao to intensive study of oriental languages. In 1626 he was sent to Cochin China, where he worked with unusual success. Like his colleagues *Ricci in China and de *Nobili in India, he devoted special attention to the higher classes of society, and developed friendly relations to the royal court. By these methods he was successful in bringing into being an almost completely independent *younger church, which not merely maintained itself financially, but was active in the propagation of its faith. Even when R. was banished and sanguinary persecutions broke out (1630–40) the Christians courageously held on. This was especially due to the work of the *catechists, who had been gathered by R. into a religious community under vows. These happy experiences led him, after his final expulsion from Vietnam (1646) to return to Europe, and to plead at Rome for the development of an indigenous clergy, and the setting up of a regular hierarchy. He had a measure of success, in that the congregation of the *Propaganda charged him with the mission of finding secular priests qualified to be raised to the episcopate. On many journeys through France and Italy he lectured and developed interest in the work of the mission in Indochina. At this time he made the acquaintance of the *Compagnie des bons amis* (fellowship of good friends), out of which the *Paris Foreign Mission Society (1658–63) was to be developed. From this group emerged the first of the *Vicars Apostolic, who were sent out to maintain the claims of the church against the *Padroado* powers (Spain and Portugal). In 1654 R. went to Persia, since Vietnam remained closed to him. His aim was to use this as a base for the formation of missions to Georgia and Mongolia, with a view to opening up and securing the land route to Indochina and the Far East. Through his Annamite Dictionary (1651), his grammar and his catechism, R. became the originator of the written Vietnamese language, and of the transliteration of it into Roman letters, which is still in use. His accounts of his missionary work and of his journeys are an admirable source for the missionary history of Indochina at that time.

JOSEF GLAZIK

H. Bernard-Maître in *Histoire universelle des Missions catholiques* (ed. S. Delacroix, Paris 1957), Vol. II, pp.53–70; C. Larre-A. Marillier: Introduction to the *Catechismus pro iis qui volunt suscipere baptismum* (Saigon 1961); *Rhodes of Viet Nam: Travels and Missions of Fr Alexander de Rhodes*, tr. by S. Hertz (Westminster, Maryland, 1966); *LTK* VIII, 1279; *NCE* XII, 461f.

RHODESIA (formerly Southern Rhodesia) is a landlocked country, 150,333 sq.m. in extent, between the Republic of South Africa on the south, Mozambique on the east, Zambia on the north and Botswana on the west, with a population of 4,580,000, of whom 215,000 are Europeans, and 10,000 Asians and people of mixed race. Salisbury, the capital, has 186,000 inhabitants. The principal African tribes are the Shona and Ndebele. English is the official language. The Kariba dam on the Zambesi river has produced the largest man-made lake in the world. The railway connects R. to South Africa, Mozambique and Zambia. R. is rich in mineral and agricultural products.

The peaceful Shona people, the oldest inhabitants, were conquered by the warlike Ndebele who settled near Bulawayo around 1837 under chief Mziligazi. His son, Lobengula, gave a mineral concession in 1888 to emissaries from Cecil Rhodes, a wealthy British mining magnate after whom the country is named, who organized the British South Africa Company, obtained a Royal Charter, and occupied the eastern part of the country in 1890. A war in 1893 broke the Ndebele power, and rebellions of the Ndebele and Shona in 1896–1897 were suppressed. The land was divided about equally between the Africans and Europeans. The company ruled the country till 1923 when it became a self-governing British colony; from 1953 to 1963 it was part of the Federation of Rhodesia and Nyasaland. In 1965 the Prime Minister, Ian Smith, declared the country independent from Britain. The franchise is open to all, but the qualifications are so stringent that few Africans qualify. In 1970 the tension between Africans and Europeans was high, with many Africans in detention camps, and with censorship of press and mail. A number of missionaries have been deported. Africans demand unqualified adult franchise ('one man, one vote') which the Europeans refuse.

The African people are Bantu-speaking and share the common Bantu religious beliefs and practices, which include belief in a Supreme Being, *Mwari*, reverence for ancestors, a spiritualized conception of nature, practice of *magic and *witchcraft. There is almost no Muslim influence. The first Christian approach was made by a Portuguese *Jesuit, Gonzalo da Silveira, in 1561, with some follow-up efforts in the following century. The modern penetration started with Robert *Moffat of the *LMS who received Mziligazi's permission to settle a party of missionaries at Inyati in 1859. The Dutch Reformed Church of South Africa, the Roman Catholics and the Anglicans made sporadic efforts in the seventies and eighties, but there was no visible result as long as the Ndebele rule lasted. The christianization of the country did not really develop until after 1890, with setbacks in 1893 and 1896–97. The LMS had been working without a break, then followed in rapid succession the Anglicans and RCs, 1890; the DRC of South Africa and the Wesleyan Methodist Church from England, 1891; the Salvation Army, 1892; the *ABCFM, 1893; the Seventh Day Adventists, 1894; the *South Africa General Mission (now the Africa Evangelical Fellowship), 1897; the Methodist Episcopal Church from USA, 1898; the Church of Sweden, 1903. In addition there are at least nine more churches and societies at work with a Protestant membership of 170,000 and 130,000 RCs, with a total Christian community of at least 1,000,000, with 2,576 churches and nearly 400 ordained African clergy. The Southern Rhodesia Missionary (now Christian) Conference was organized in 1903, and had 24 member bodies and four affiliated bodies in 1964. These bodies have given a united Christian voice to the country on a large number of issues important to the African people. There are six theological training centres of which Epworth Theological College, ecumenical in character, is the most important, with the Central Africa Diploma in Theology granted by an ecumenical body. There are no serious church union negotiations, but a few exploratory discussions are being held. The whole Bible was translated into Union Shona in 1950.

The churches have made magnificent contributions to African education, with the government playing an increasingly important role and now paying most of the cost. Ninety per cent of all African students are in government-aided church schools. In 1965 there were 3,099 primary schools with 627,806 students, and 75 secondary schools, 61 of them church schools, with 11,495 students. There are six schools for deaf and blind Africans, four of them church schools. The University College of Rhodesia is affiliated to London University and is multi-racial. The African literacy rate is estimated at 65%.

The churches pioneered hospital and medical services, the training of African nurses, and general social welfare. The major portions of the cost of these services are now borne by the government. The churches face the challenge of political and racial tension, and of keeping the allegiance of the growing, educated, African élite.

PER HASSING

P. Mason: *The Birth of a Dilemma* (Oxford 1958); N. Sithole: *African Nationalism* (Cape Town 1959); *NCE* XII, 463.

RICCI, MATTHEW (1552–1610), prototype of the great *Jesuit missioners to China. He was born the year St. Francis *Xavier died, of patrician parents, in the Italian hill town of Macerata. The world seemed to be exploding in all directions. Martin Luther had recently died, and among R's contemporaries were Ignatius Loyola, Galileo and Kepler, Shakespeare, Hakluyt, Henry Hudson and Captain John Smith. R., having joined the Society of Jesus, entered China via Macao, a Portuguese colony near the coast. Medieval attempts at setting up missions in China had perished without trace. R. had the vast empire before him, and he arrived on the mainland with a trunk full of clocks, astronomical and musical instruments, prisms, European paintings and prints, books richly bound and illustrated, and most astounding of all to the Chinese, a map of the world. China was indeed a vast land of culture and learning, but its scholars believed it to be the centre of the world, with a sprinkling of barbarians around its perimeter. R. mastered Mandarin, the language of scholars and royalty, and made a study of the Chinese classics. He frankly showed himself to be a Christian priest, while adopting the dress of Chinese scholars and meeting them as an equal. He made his way in official circles by his affability and his learning, and by making discreet gifts—of clocks, usually—to the Mandarins. Attracted at first by R's scientific learning, many were drawn further by the wondrous teachings of Christianity. In 1601 the Emperor Wan Li invited the Christian sage to Peking. This was R's chance. He brought along the biggest and best of his clocks, and the results were excellent. The Jesuit was not only asked to remain and teach science at the court, but was granted great liberty in the preaching of Christ. He translated Euclid and other European works into Mandarin and wrote several excellent books on Christian beliefs in that language. It was one of these—*The True Knowledge of God*, written in 1603—that led to the first conversions in Korea in the 1780s. R., the Emperor's official astronomer and mathematician, died in Peking, leaving some 2,500 converts to Christianity. He also, unintentionally, left the makings of a controversy that raged for centuries. The Jesuit, knowing the Chinese and their culture, had declared the honours which they paid to Confucius and to their ancestors to be merely expressions of loyalty and gratitude, not at all contrary to the Christian faith. Others, not so broadminded nor so sympathetic to the Chinese, contradicted this conclusion, much to the harm of Christianity in China.

See also RITES CONTROVERSY.

SISTER M. JULIANA, MM

V. Cronin: *The Wise Man from the West* (London 1955); *MSS of Father Ricci* (Eng. tr., Augsburg 1915); *LTK* VIII, 1255f.; *NCE* XII, 470; *RGG* V, 1090f.

RICHARD, TIMOTHY (1845–1919). Strange as it may seem to put a Welsh *Baptist beside a *Jesuit, a Roman Catholic historian has described the missionary policy of R. as 'akin to the technique' of Matthew *Ricci (C. Carey-Elwes: *China and the Cross*, p.219).

He was born in a village in Carmarthenshire, Wales; after a few years as a teacher, he entered a theological college at Haverfordwest; was sent to China in 1870, and became the real founder of the North China mission of the BMS. After famine relief, 1876–79, he was convinced that he must try to give China's leaders a Christian introduction to modern civilization. 'It was the worst famine in history . . . fifteen to twenty millions perished. Most could have been saved, if the officials had not thought that . . . they had nothing to learn from the Barbarians of the West.' He advocated a Christian college for every province, and missionaries 'competent to guide the *thinking* classes; when they are won for Christ the whole nation will follow'. Meanwhile at Tai Yuan he gave lectures and scientific demonstrations, attended by crowds of officials and students. In 1889 he edited a Chinese newspaper, *The Times*, writing on railways, telegraphs, education, reforms. This was read by viceroys and governors, discussed in the Foreign Office and even in the Imperial Palace. In 1891 he became secretary of the Christian Literature Society. 'Instead of writing goody-goody tracts . . . we decided to enlighten China on the world's progress and put her in a fair way of saving herself'. Defeat of China by Japan in 1895 roused urgent interest. R. translated a *History of the Nineteenth Century*. Six pirated editions appeared, and a million copies were sold. Ten thousand Chinese of the student class, as 'The Reform Society', petitioned the throne. 'I was astounded to find almost all the suggestions I have made condensed into marvellously small compass'. In 1896 the prime minister himself called on the missionary to discuss reforms. In 1898 R. was invited to become one of the emperor's advisers. Had he been appointed earlier he would have put a brake on the young emperor's enthusiasm, and so have lessened the alarm among conservatives. He did meet the emperor's tutor, but on the day of his audience with the emperor the empress dowager seized power, executed reform leaders, and began the reaction which ended in the *Boxer troubles of 1900.

R. got a punitive fine on the Province of Shansi devoted to establishing a university in Tai Yuan—returning good for evil, and making a repetition of the evil impossible. Soon modern style education spread throughout China, Christian schools, colleges and universities playing an ever-increasing part. The many Christian and pro-Christian Chinese who were leaders in the 1911 revolution, and in the resultant republic, were the fruits of R's own work and of the growing acceptance of his policies.

R. received honorary doctorates from the University of Wales and two in the USA, and two of the highest honours of the Chinese empire. Illness took him to England in 1916. He died in London in 1919, little known except in missionary circles and in Far Eastern embassies. In China the greatest of the land would have been present at his funeral.

JOHN FOSTER

B. Reeve: *Timothy Richard* (London 1912); T. Richard: *Forty-five Years in China* (London and New York 1916); W. E. Soothill: *Timothy Richard of China* (London 1924).

RIIS, ANDREAS (1804–1854), was born at Lygumcloster, Denmark, son of a glazier. After studies at the Mission Seminary, Basel, he was ordained in 1831 and sent by the *Basel Mission to the then Danish Gold Coast. With two colleagues he arrived at Christiansborg on 13 March 1832. All **four** predecessors had died of fever; within five months his two companions suffered the same fate. R. worked for two years as pastor to the Danish colony at Christiansborg, then in March 1835 he started work in Akropong, on a ridge of hills 30 miles inland from Accra. There he was joined in 1836 by two missionaries and his fiancée Anna Wolter. Within two years he had lost his daughter and the two co-workers, faced a civil war and the enmity of the Danish Governor, made an exploratory trip to Kumasi and left for Europe. Thence in 1842 R. and his wife sailed to the West Indies to select Christians of African descent to start a small Christian colony in Ghana. This company of 24

West Indians landed at Christiansborg in 1843. Akropong station was rebuilt and the new settlement scheme started. Owing to failing strength R. left Ghana in 1845; his wife died at sea. He worked in Stavanger, Norway, as pastor of the Norwegian Missionary Society and died on 20 January 1854.

R. was outstanding for his perseverance in the face of heavy odds. He created the first foothold for the church in the interior of Ghana; Ghanaians called him *Osiadan* (Housebuilder).

WALTER ZUMBRUNNEN

W. Oelschner: *Landung in Osu* (Wuppertal 1959); W. Schlatter: *Geschichte der Basler Mission*, Vol. III (Basel 1916).

RINGELTAUBE, WILHELM TOBIAS (1770–1816), was born at Schiedelwitz in Silesia, the son of a Lutheran pastor. After leaving Halle University he came under Moravian influence. He wished to join the *Danish–Halle Mission. They, having no place for him, recommended him to the *SPCK, who sent him to Calcutta (1797) after Lutheran ordination. Dissatisfied with conditions of service there, he soon resigned (1798) and returned to England. In 1803 he applied to the *LMS and they appointed him to South India. At Tranquebar, where he landed in December 1804 and stayed a year, his attention was drawn to Travancore by a convert, Vedamānikam, who told him that many in his village, Mayilādi, near Cape Comorin, wished to become Christians. At the request of J. C. Kohlhoff, SPCK missionary in Tanjore, he went in February 1806 to take temporary charge of the Tinnevelly mission, which had already a large Christian community but no missionary. He spent a couple of years in Tinnevelly District, ministering to the Christians in many villages and to the Europeans in Palamcottah. From there he got permission through the British Resident to enter Travancore, and made his first visit to Mayilādi (April 1806). More visits followed. He baptized 40 people there in 1807. When his Tinnevelly appointment ended, he went to live in Travancore; but almost immediately political disturbances caused him to retire to Palamcottah and the Christians to take to the jungle. After peace was restored (1809), South Travancore was the scene of his labours for the next six years. Impulsive and generous by nature, careless of appearances and personal comfort, he toured the district assiduously, baptizing many people of the Nadar caste, organizing congregations and elementary schools in six centres, with catechists and teachers chosen from among the converts. Now and then he visited Quilon, Palamcottah and other places, where European friends gave him help for his personal needs and his work. By 1813 he had a community of 600 who looked to him for their spiritual and temporal welfare. But from 1812 his health began to fail. He became so depressed and discouraged that he resigned and left India (1816), hoping that a voyage to the Cape of Good Hope might restore him. After waiting in vain at Colombo for a passage, he sailed instead eastwards. From Malacca (27 September 1816) he wrote that he was going to Batavia (Djakarta); but thereafter nothing more was heard of him. His fate remains unknown. His memory is treasured in the Kanyākumāri diocese of the *CSI as the pioneer Protestant missionary in that part of India.

CYRIL B. FIRTH

I. H. Hacker: *A Hundred Years in Travancore 1806-1906* (London 1908), pp.18–30; J. Hough: *The History of Christianity in India*, Vol. IV (London 1845), pp.62–67 and 277–85; R. Lovett: *The History of the London Missionary Society 1795–1895*, Vol. II (London 1899), pp.21–31; W. Robinson: *Ringeltaube the Rishi* (Sheffield 1902); *RGG* V, 1110.

RIO MUNI. See GUINEA, SPANISH.

RITES CONTROVERSY. Disputes in China and India among Christian missioners over the interpretation of customs had a retarding effect on Christianity. In China the controversy broke out following the death of Matthew *Ricci. He had held that the rites of *Confucianism and *ancestor worship were purely social and political in nature and could be practised by converts. When other religious orders, particularly the *Dominicans, arrived in China, they took sharp exception to the *Jesuit methods. A Dominican carried the case to Rome, where because of lack of knowledge the case dragged on. The Jesuits appealed to the Chinese emperor, who stated that Ricci's interpretation was the true one. When Rome appeared to question his opinion, he ordered that all missioners must obtain an imperial permit which would be granted upon a declaration of adherence to the Ricci interpretation. Some missioners refused and had to leave China. Two papal envoys—the first in 1715 and the second in 1730—failed to settle the dispute. Finally in 1742 Rome ruled against Father Ricci's viewpoint and ordered an oath of submission to the new decree which had to be taken by all missioners; also forbidden was any further discussion of the issue. It was not until 1938 that this oath was repealed. The 1938 decree also permitted the presence of Catholics at ceremonies honouring Confucius; the use in schoolrooms of a picture or tablet dedicated to him; the performance of acts of respect to the sage and ancestors.

In India another Jesuit, Robert de *Nobili had adopted the life and dress of a Brahman. He allowed his converts to continue many of the distinguishing marks of the Brahman caste. He allowed the marking of the forehead with santal and ceremonial ablutions, since he believed they did not have any pagan or superstitious meaning. This practice was also followed by other Jesuits. In the second half of the 16th century, *Capuchins made protest to Rome over the Jesuit methods. In 1704 a papal envoy ruled against the Jesuits, and his decree met violent opposition. Rome after long consideration issued a decree in 1739 and again in 1744 which ruled against the Jesuits. The controversy over rites both in China and India was complicated by national competition and the question of Portuguese royal patronage.

See also ACCOMMODATION.

ALBERT J. NEVINS, MM

S. M. Just: *Immortal Fire* (St. Louis 1951); K. S. Latourette: *A History of Christian Missions in China* (New York 1929); D. Navarette: *The Travels and Controversies of Friar Domingo Navarrette* (Cambridge 1962); A. S. Rosso: *Apostolic Legations to China* (South Pasadena 1948); *LTK* VIII, 1322–24.

RITES, RITUAL. All forms of religion find expression in ritual acts or words, which in many cases are believed to have actual power for good or evil in themselves, and are so secret that they may not be revealed to the uninitiated. Contrary to what is often believed, the apparently simpler peoples, such as the Aborigines of north-east Australia, have the most complicated rituals, on the performance of which the whole life of the tribe is held to depend. Everything depends on the ritual being carried out in exactly the right way, without the smallest variation of phrase or gesture. The Christian church also has in the course of centuries developed its own rituals, varying greatly in complexity from area to area. Even those churches in which the least use is made of visible objects, and in which liberty of prophesying (extempore prayer, etc.), is unrestricted, develop over a period of time particular patterns; things come to be done in one way and not in any other way, and certain formulations come to be regularly adopted and acceptable.

Ritual plays so large and important a part in the life, especially of simpler peoples, that a derangement of ritual tends to have gravely harmful consequences. It has been noted that where a vitally important ritual such as head-hunting has been put down by a western government, whole tribes become threatened by the disappearance of the will to live. It is at this point that the impact of Christianity is felt as menacing, and that the anthropologists find justification for their constant complaint that missionaries are the destroyers of ancient and beautiful forms of life. (Head-hunting is not experienced as beautiful by those who are the victims of it.) What is the missionary to do? It is clear that many of the ancient rituals in every part of the world have implications which are irreconcilable with the gospel. Can everything be simply jettisoned? The problem is felt even more acutely by the convert than by the missionary; it cannot be too often stressed that religion is experienced as a whole; to the convert every part of every ritual act is penetrated by the spirit of the whole; for him it is impossible to pick and choose, and he tends to cast away the whole of the old life and all its ways. Thus, for instance, the first Toda converts in South India decided that they would not continue to wear the old picturesque Toda dress—the associations would prove too strong for their new-found faith. Missionaries have tended to fall in too readily with the views of converts in the matter.

This abandonment of the old can cause serious psychic disturbance and a sense of impoverishment. Church-going is very dull compared to the old tribal dance. Preparation for confirmation is a poor substitute for the circumcision school, in which a boy is trained to become a man. If female circumcision is forbidden, as it usually is by the churches, what sign has the African girl that she has really come of age, and that she is fully identified with her people? Various methods have been used to fill the gap.

Some adventurous missionaries (*Ricci in China, de *Nobili in India) permitted the retention of a number of ceremonies, which they believed to be social rather than religious in character. But is it so easy to distinguish? Is Chinese *ancestor worship simply respectful commemoration of the ancestors, or does a religious element enter in? Were the non-*Jesuit missionaries in China right in saying that Ricci had added Confucius as a new saint to the Christian calendar? Efforts at *accommodation of this kind have usually let loose floods of controversy in the church; the disputes about the Chinese and the 'Malabaric' rites are famous in church history. It is perhaps good that the experiments have been tried, perhaps not too bad that in the end they were not found acceptable by the church.

A number of somewhat half-hearted

attempts have been made (see LUCAS, W. V.) to retain or adapt certain ancient practices to the service of the church. This has generally been found artificial and unsatisfactory. A hybrid does not always flourish. The strength of rites lies in their spontaneous growth in relation to a particular situation; a rite which is transposed from one world into another is hardly likely to flourish.

The only satisfactory solution is that the gospel should be so deeply absorbed by a people, should so take hold of their mind and their imagination that they begin to exercise creatively that kind of identification with the Christian faith out of which living, new and genuinely Christian patterns can emerge, but with the particular quality in which that people's experiences are reflected. To some extent this is happening in all the *younger churches, but often in small and not very observable ways. Living in an Indian or Japanese church is not like living in a western church, though it is not always easy to say in what exactly the difference exists. But these little developments are clearly the beginning of that freedom which must be developed to the full, if all the peoples are to bring their riches into the city of God.

See also INDIGENOUS CHURCHES; SYMBOLISM.

STEPHEN NEILL

ROBERT COLLEGE, CONSTANTINOPLE. See NEAR EAST COLLEGE ASSOCIATION.

RODGERS, JAMES BURTON (1865–1944), was born in Albany, New York, USA, and graduated from Hamilton College and Auburn Theological Seminary. Following ordination in the Presbyterian church and marriage to Anna Van Vechten Bigelow, R. was appointed in 1889 to service in the Brazil mission of the Presbyterian church. After returning to Brazil for a second term in June 1898, he was transferred to the Philippines because of his familiarity with work in RC countries and his ability to learn Spanish easily through his knowledge of

Portuguese. R. was the first regularly appointed and permanent Protestant missionary to the Philippines. He arrived in Manila on 21 April 1899, and pioneered for 36 years in evangelistic, educational and ecumenical work. He was instrumental in the founding of the Evangelical Union and the *comity arrangement in 1901; Union Theological Seminary, Manila, 1907 (where he taught theology, 1908–32), and the United Evangelical Church in 1929. R. was a member of the Presbyterian deputation to Mexico in 1922, the China Evaluation Conference, 1926, and the deputation to Korea, 1936. He had three children, and received the honorary DD degree from Union University in Jackson, Tennessee, 1905. R. retired in the Philippines in 1935, and died in Baguio City in April 1944, during the Japanese occupation.

GERALD H. ANDERSON

J. B. Rodgers: *Forty Years in the Philippines* (New York 1940).

ROMAN CATHOLIC MISSIONS. See MISSIONS, ROMAN CATHOLIC.

ROMAN CATHOLIC - PROTESTANT MISSIONARY RELATIONSHIPS. It is significant that it was Protestant missionaries who first acted on the scandal that a divided Christianity presented to the non-Christian world and that in the missionary conference of *Edinburgh in 1910 the foundations for modern ecumenism and the *WCC were set in place. For Roman Catholics, co-operation with Protestants was given great impetus by the Second *Vatican Council. In the Conciliar Decree on Ecumenism, Catholics were instructed to recognize 'the signs of the times and to take an active and intelligent part in the work of ecumenism'. The Council went on to add that this co-operation should 'be developed more and more, particularly in regions where a social and technical revolution is taking place'. The Council Fathers pointed out such areas as illiteracy, poverty, natural disasters, lack of housing, and the unequal distribution of wealth as prime subjects for co-operation.

In the past missionaries were not particularly interested in ecumenism. This was partly due to the amount of work which faced the missionary and which left little time for the 'luxury' of ecumenical conversation, but even more due to a competitive spirit for souls which sometimes resulted in open conflict. Today the *ecumenical movement makes rapid progress in the *younger churches because missionary activity is seen not so much as a conquest of souls but rather as a witness and service to human society.

There are many examples of modern inter-faith co-operation. Near Arusha, Tanzania, a new church was built for the use of the RC, Anglican and Lutheran congregations there. Also in Tanzania, Catholics and Protestants have approved a common prayer to be recited in all Christian schools. In Japan, as elsewhere, Catholics and Protestants hold joint prayer services. In a statement issued in 1966 by representatives of the relief services of the WCC and the RC church a five-point plan was put forward for co-operative action. At Toumliline, Morocco, there is a monastery for *dialogue, not only between Christians but also between Christianity and *Islam.

Conditions in the missionary world will spur even closer relationships between RCs and Protestants in the years to come. Former colonial nations look upon the division of churches as an European import. In their search for national unity they are impatient with all divisions, whether they be religious, cultural or tribal. They are concerned with practical and immediate problems, and in this area the Christian churches will find many opportunities for co-operation and collaboration.

ALBERT J. NEVINS, MM

J. P. Cotter, ed.: *The Word in the Third World* (Washington, D.C., 1968).

ROMAN CATHOLIC RELIGIOUS ORDERS, CONGREGATIONS AND SOCIETIES of *priests* (often also including lay brothers) to whom 75% of the mission territories are entrusted (25% to the local

clergy) numbered 62 in 1964. The following selection indicates: initials, popular name, country of the Founder: AA, Assumptionists, France; CICM, Scheutists, Belgium; CM, Vincentians or Lazarists, France; CMM, Marianhill, South Africa; CP, Passionists, Italy; CSC, Holy Cross Fathers, France; CSSp, *Holy Ghost Fathers, France; CSsR, Redemptorists, Italy; FSCJ, Verona Fathers, Italy; IMC, Consolata Fathers, Italy; IEME, Burgos Foreign Missions, Spain; MEP, *Paris Foreign Missions, France; MEQ, Quebec Foreign Missions, Canada; MHM, *Mill Hill Missionaries, England; MM, *Maryknoll Foreign Missions, USA; MS, La Salette Missionaries, France; MSC, Missionaries of the Sacred Heart, France; MXY, Yarumal Foreign Missions, Colombia; OC, Carmelites, Italy; OESA, *Augustinians, Italy; OFM, *Franciscans, Italy; OFMCap, *Capuchins, Italy; OFMConv, Conventuals, Italy; OMI, *Oblates of Mary Immaculate, France; OP, *Dominicans, France; OSB, *Benedictines, Italy; PIME, Milan Foreign Missions, Italy; SCJ, Priests of the Sacred Heart, France; SDB, Salesians of Don Bosco, Italy; SFM, Scarboro Foreign Missions, Canada; SJ, *Jesuits, Spain; SM, Marists, France; SMA, *Society of African Missions, France; SMB, Bethlehem Foreign Missions, Switzerland; SMM, Montfort Fathers, France; SPS, Kiltegans, Ireland; SSC, Columban Fathers, Ireland; SSCC, Picpus Fathers, France; SVD, *Society of the Divine Word, Germany; SX, Parma Foreign Missionaries, Italy; WF, *White Fathers, France.

Most of them now have their headquarters in Rome and are international; some are national (IEME, MEP, MM, MXY, SFM, PIME, SFM, SMB, etc.). Many, especially those of more recent origin, are exclusively missionary, others partially; yet the latter are, historically and numerically, more important, e.g. the Jesuits have 6,600 missionaries. From the list the false impression may arise that France and Italy are supplying most missionaries. France, indeed, is still leading although there has only been a relatively small increase in the last 30

18*

years. Small countries, like Ireland, Holland and Belgium, are providing more priests than Italy or Germany, and proportionately even England is doing more. The USA is rapidly making up for past arrears. Also contemplative orders (Trappists, Cistercians, etc.) and diocesan clergy (for a limited period) are stepping up their contributions.

Half of the 100,000 foreign missionaries are Sisters. Their Congregations are too numerous to be listed. Outstanding are the Franciscan Missionaries of Mary, who have more than 8,000 members.

Special Congregations of Religious Lay Brothers, especially for education, provide 13,000 personnel. Among them the Christian Brothers occupy an important place, but there are numerous others. Of late, a number of Missionary Institutes for Laypeople have been erected. Their contribution, though recent, is rapidly growing year by year.

PETER J. DIRVEN

No literature is mentioned, as the sources are too scanty and varied, and not available to the general public. A Latin source would be *Fides*, Statistical Appendices (Rome, 1964), pp.3–5.

ROOTS, LOGAN HERBERT (1870–1945), was born near Tamaroa, Illinois, USA. His first experience in world affairs came as a travelling secretary for the International Committee of the *YMCA between graduation from Harvard (BA 1891) and enrolment in the Episcopal Theological School (BD 1896). After being made a deacon in 1896, he departed for China. Two years of language study at Wuchang culminated in his ordination to the priesthood and his assignment to general missionary work in Hankow. In 1904 he was consecrated the second Bishop of Hankow, a post he held for 33 years. Along with other Anglican bishops, R. took part in the formation in 1915 of the Chung Hua Sheng Kung Hui (Chinese Holy Catholic Church). He served as Chairman of its House of Bishops from 1926 to 1930. Ecumenically he was active in drawing a majority of non-Roman churches into the *National Christian Council, which

was inaugurated in 1922. A year later he was elected its secretary, and from 1924 onward he served as honorary secretary. Though his accomplishments were often muted, R's influence is certified by one historian's observation that he was 'perhaps the most beloved and widely known American Christian in China'.

A. THEODORE EASTMAN

J. T. Addison: *The Episcopal Church in the United States* (New York 1951), p.353; *Who Was Who in America*, Vol. II (Chicago 1950), p.458.

ROSS, JOHN (1841–1915), Scottish pioneer in Manchuria and first translator of the NT into Korean, was born in Ross-shire, Scotland, educated at Glasgow University (1865–69) and went to China in 1872 under the United Presbyterian (later United Free) Church. His wife soon died and R. left Shantung in October for unreached parts of Manchuria, first in Newchang (Yinkow), then in Mukden (1874). His policy was to concentrate on city centres of population. His first baptism was of Wang Ying-Ming, soon to be outstanding as leader of Manchurian Protestantism. As early as 1873 R. became interested in the then closed country of Korea. In 1874 he persuaded a Korean pedlar, Yi Eung-Chan, to help him complete the first English-Korean primer. With the Rev. John McIntyre, his brother-in-law, and Korean teachers he began to translate Luke in 1875. Four of the helpers were baptized in Newchang the next year, the first Koreans to receive Protestant baptism. In 1882 Luke and John were published, and the Ross version NT in 1887, the first in the Korean language. In 1883 R. sent his helper *Suh Sang-Yoon as a Bible *colporteur into Korea, a full year before Protestant foreign missionaries could penetrate that land. At last in 1887 R. himself visited Korea and witnessed the organization of the first Presbyterian church in Seoul.

SAMUEL H. MOFFETT

J. Ross: *History of Corea: Ancient and Modern* (Paisley 1879), *Mission Methods in*

Manchuria (New York n.d.); Y. S. Kim: *The Ross Version and Korean Protestantism* (Eng. tr. by A. Clark, MS, Seoul).

RUGGERI, MICHAEL (1543–1607), *Jesuit pioneer in China, associate of *Ricci. In 1579 R. arrived in Macao from India. At this time Portuguese traders were allowed to make two annual trips to Canton. In 1581 R. accompanied the traders on both trips and used the opportunities to make contacts in Canton. The following year a Portuguese embassy was permitted in Canton and R. was assigned as adviser and interpreter. Through the gift of a watch, the first timepiece seen in China, R. won the friendship of the Chinese viceroy and was given permission to preach Christianity in Kwangtung Province. R. was joined by Francis Pasio and the two missioners set about winning the good will of the scholars and upper class. When the friendly viceroy was transferred, the two Jesuits were forced to return to Macao. However, influential Chinese petitioned the new viceroy that the missioners might be allowed to reside in the province. The viceroy sent an invitation and R. and Ricci set up a residence where Ricci matured his plans for his famous Peking apostolate. In 1588 R. returned to Europe to persuade King Philip II and the pope to appoint an ambassador to the imperial court of China. He became ill before he could succeed and died at the Jesuit College in Salerno. It was then left to Ricci to open the door to China.

ALBERT J. NEVINS, MM

G. H. Dunne: *Generation of Giants* (London 1962); S. M. Just: *Immortal Fire* (St. Louis, Mo. 1951).

RURAL MISSIONS. See AGRICULTUR-AL MISSIONS, INC.

RUSSIA. See EUROPE; UNION OF SOVIET SOCIALIST REPUBLICS.

RWANDA, formerly a kingdom under Belgian trusteeship, is an East African territory between Uganda and the Congo; its 10,166 sq.m. are the most densely populated in Africa south of the Sahara, supporting a population (1967) of 3,306,000 which includes 1,200 Europeans and 750 Asians. The Roman Catholic church has four dioceses with 909,351 Catholics (1966). There are few Muslims. Protestant missions have been at work over 50 years and have a total community of 170,645. Of these the largest are *Eglise Anglicane du Rwanda* (Ruanda General and Medical Mission, CMS) with 85,260, SDA with 60,000, *Eglises de Pentecôte* (*Svenska Fria Missionen*) with 9,201, *Eglise Presbytérienne de Rwanda* (*Société Belge des Missions Protestantes*) with 8,756 and *Union des Eglises Baptistes* (*Dansk Baptistsamfunds Yere Mission*) and *Eglise Libre Méthodiste*. The widespread and influential East African Revival (*Balokole*, or Saved Ones) originated at Gahini in Rwanda in 1927, and has since profoundly influenced Protestant churches throughout East Africa and more recently parts of the RC church. Unlike other territories adjoining it, revival in Rwanda has not become separatist at any stage but has remained within the churches; there are no *African independent churches at all (1967).

DAVID B. BARRETT

BM II, 767–71; *NCE* XII, 765.

RYUKYU ISLANDS. An archipelago stretching for 750 miles between the southern extremity of Japan proper and the northern shores of Taiwan. Total area is 1,850 sq.m. in about 140 islands, of which no more than 25 are inhabited. Present population is about 1,000,000, of whom 75% live on the main island of Okinawa.

Legendary history goes back to the second century B.C. Cultural, economic and political influences began coming in quite early, first from China and then from Japan. Local authorities paid tribute to both the Chinese and the Japanese until the middle of the 15th century. When the Japanese formally attached the Islands to their empire in the 17th century, the Okinawan monarchy was effectively eclipsed. With some political disturbances, the Ryukyus remained subservient to Japan until American occupation in 1945. 'Okinawa' is still recognized as residually a prefecture of Japan.

Religious traditions in the Islands are many and varied, including *animism, *ancestor worship, *Taoism, *Confucianism, *Buddhism, *Shinto, and of late Christianity. The first RC missionaries were French, arriving in 1844, departing soon thereafter, but returning in numbers in 1847. In 1846 Dr B. J. Bettelheim, a Calvinist convert from Judaism, arrived in the port city of Naha, and caused consternation by his aggressive evangelism until withdrawn; yet he is well known today for his early translations into Japanese of the Gospels of Luke and John, Acts and Romans.

American Methodist missionaries began work in Okinawa in 1887, followed shortly by Baptists from Scotland and the USA. Prior to the war in the Pacific there were about a dozen churches, with not more than a thousand active Okinawan members. Japanese Protestant and Catholic clergymen assumed leadership during the period of their nation's militant nationalism.

After the war, missionaries from many lands converged on the Ryukyus. In 1946 *Methodist, *Presbyterian, *Holiness and other bodies merged to form the United Church of Christ in Okinawa, now integrated within the United Church in Japan. Other groups now functioning in the Islands include the Episcopalians, *Baptists, *Lutherans, *SA, SDA, and a variety of *Pentecostals. A recently organized Council of Churches embraces some of those not otherwise affiliated including the Episcopalians, the Baptists, the *Bible Societies, the *YMCA and the *YWCA, and certain Protestant relief agencies.

It is estimated that the Protestant church membership numbers something under 5,000, RCs not over 2,500. Approximately 40 churches and preaching places are to be found, largely on the island of Okinawa. There are few Christian schools; candidates for the ministry follow their cultural affinity in going to Japan to study, as do many other students. Well established church bodies are led largely by native Ryukyuans. Younger and smaller groups are still for the most part directed by missionaries. Financial dependence on American and European mission agencies is still general. Communists, though not well organized, are quite articulate and take advantage of all evidences of *colonialism—whether religious, social, economic or political—to expound their revolutionary doctrines and procedures.

THOBURN T. BRUMBAUGH

E. R. Bull: *Okinawa or Ryukyu: The Floating Dragon* (published privately in Newark, Ohio 1958—to be found in many missionary libraries); G. H. Kerr: *Okinawa, The History of an Island People* (Tokyo 1958); W. P. Lebra: *Okinawan Religion* (Honolulu 1966); A. T. Roy: *On Asia's Rim* (New York 1962); *BM* II, 771f.

S

SABAH (BORNEO). See MALAYSIA.

SACRAMENTS as 'outward and visible signs of an inward and spiritual grace' have been universally accepted among Christians from the first days of the church. Even their apparent absence in traditional form as with the *Quakers and the *Salvation Army is more by way of a protest against the sacramental principle than its denial. The silent worship of the Quaker and its very simplicity is in fact highly sacramental in the profoundest sense. It would be difficult to deny that the uniform of the SA is intended as an outward or visible mark of an inward or spiritual experience. In the more strictly traditional sense the two great Ss of the gospel are recognized as being Baptism and the Lord's Supper. However various the attendant rites Baptism is in the triune name, and the Lord's Supper is celebrated in accordance with what is understood to be the intention of the Lord in instituting it. In addition some of the largest Christian communions would add as Ss the rites of Confirmation, Penance, Extreme Unction, Ordination and Matrimony. In some churches the rite of feet-washing, on the analogy of our Lord's action in the upper room on the night of his betrayal, is given sacramental significance. And there is a growing tendency to treat certain rites connected with Christian healing as being sacramental in character. There is considerable variety between the different churches, and within them, as to the frequency with which the S. of Holy Communion is partaken. In some churches presence at the S. is a prescribed duty while actual communion is rare. In other churches occasions of celebration of the Holy Communion are rare but the occasions themselves are attended with long preparation and great solemnity. Under whatever guise, obedience to the will of Christ, as that is understood, is intended. In the missionary outreach of the church the greatest problem has been the provision of a ministry duly authorized to celebrate the Ss when, as has often been the case, the rapid growth in the number of Christians, often scattered over great areas, has far outstripped the numbers of the ministry. In the sequel it has to be admitted that in many parts of the world even those churches which lay greatest store by the celebration of Holy Communion can only make this S. available to their people at infrequent intervals. A merely nominal Christianity can very easily be the result.

Other religions besides Christianity have their own sacramental expressions. Forms of prayer in *Islam, for instance, are 'outward and visible signs' of an inward attitude. Images may also serve as being sacramental in this wide sense. Gestures of reverence in all religions may partake of a sacramental character, as may architectural styles. The Christian has to be sensitively aware of the possibilities of *adaptation into Christian worship of this universal sense of the sacramental.

MAX WARREN

SACRED CONGREGATION FOR THE PROPAGATION OF THE FAITH. See PROPAGANDA, SACRED CONGREGATION OF.

SACRIFICE is a gift which is offered by men to a higher power in connection with some act of worship. Some scholars believe that S. antedates the development of clear ideas of God, and that it belonged originally in the sphere of magic. The offering of S. in worship is based on the idea that the higher power (an ancestor, a divinity, the lord of the animals) is either the true owner of everything that is upon the earth, or that he has a right to the ownership of part of it (offering of first fruits, propitiatory offerings), or that the maintenance of the order of the world is dependent on the S. (Aztec). In some cases the higher power is believed to be in some measure dependent on the S.

535

(this is often true in the case of ancestors). On the side of the giver the idea can easily arise that by means of S. the divinity can be encouraged, or even compelled, to give in return (*do ut des*—'I give that thou mayest give'). Originally, human sacrifice was very widespread, but in most cases it has been replaced by the S. of animals, plants or other objects. S. may be offered regularly (on fixed days, the beginning and end of the working year, etc.) or on special occasions (special need, or on the orders of the higher power).

Deeper religious understanding finds expression in the propitiatory offering, with which is associated the sense of guilt. A further development is the offering of praise and thanksgiving. In Christianity, the highest level has been reached, inasmuch as the self-offering of Jesus Christ makes any further offering unnecessary. Nevertheless the concern which in earlier times underlay the practice of S. must be maintained. Man is not his own master; he must at all times be aware of the claims which God has on him. In consequence, he may be asked to practise renunciation (asceticism). But this becomes a S. only when man experiences a felt loss in some area of his life which he feels to belong to him as of right (e.g. marriage). The Christian understanding of S. cannot include the aim of securing happiness or well-being for oneself. Its aim is the glory of God, or the well-being of other men.

ERNST DAMMANN

B. Goetz: *Die Bedeutung des Opfers bei den Völkern* (Leipzig 1933); E. O. James: *Origins of Sacrifice* (London 1937); H. Ringgren: *Sacrifice in the Bible* (World Christian Books No. 42, London 1962); *ERE* XI, 1–39.

SAHARA is the name given to the area north of the Sudan, which stretches from the Atlantic to the Nile, and south of the North African coastal territories; the Sahara Desert forms part of several nations including Mauritania, Mali, Algeria, Libya, Niger, Chad and Sudan. There is considerable evidence that in the first few centuries A.D. numerous Christian communities existed in the Sahara of which no trace now remains except the symbol of the cross in ornamentation, as for example among the Tuareg tribes. In recent times the most noted missionary effort has been that of Charles de *Foucauld (b. 1858), a Trappist monk who became ordained and lived as a hermit in Tamanrasset from 1906 till his murder there in 1916 at the hands of a raiding band of Senussi. As a result of his work the orders of *Petits Frères* (1933) and *Petites Soeurs* (1939) were formed, which continue his work. Protestant work in the Sahara is very sparse; Gospel portions only have been translated, into Tamahaq (Tuareg) in 1934, and Tamachek (Timbuktu) in 1953: each of these uses a distinctive non-Latin script.

DAVID B. BARRETT

NCE XII, 850.

ST. HELENA. See ATLANTIC ISLANDS.

ST. KITTS, NEVIS. See CARIBBEAN.

ST. LUCIA. See CARIBBEAN.

ST. VINCENT. See CARIBBEAN.

SAKER, ALFRED (1814–1880), was born at Borough Green, Kent, England. He worked as an engineer and in 1840 married Helen Jessup; they joined the *Baptist mission which left Jamaica for Fernando Po in 1843. In 1845 S. settled in Cameroon, and founded a station, Bethel, in Douala country. In loneliness, privation, illness and threats of violence he worked at preaching, teaching and translation. The first Douala convert was baptized in 1849, the first African minister ordained in 1859. S. was at Fernando Po in 1858 when the Spanish authorities forbade Protestant worship. He founded a settlement, Victoria, on the Cameroon mainland, which was occupied by 90 African families from Fernando Po. S. introduced the crafts needed for house-building, printing, boat-building and steamer traffic; in 1872 he completed the Douala translation of the Bible. He retired to England in failing health in 1876 and during his last years encouraged the founding of the BMS Congo mission.

A practical and mobile missionary, S. established work that was to flourish despite changes in place and circumstance. After Germany annexed Cameroon in 1885 the *indigenous churches continued their work, with help for a time from the *Basel Mission and American Baptist missionaries.

JOHN GOODWIN

E. M. Saker: *Alfred Saker of the Cameroons* (2nd ed., London 1929); E. B. Underhill: *Biography of Alfred Saker* (London 1882).

SALAZAR, DOMINGO DE (1512–1594), first RC bishop of Manila, Philippines. Born in Spain, he became a *Dominican friar and was sent to the Mexican mission, where he distinguished himself as a missionary to the Indians and was made vice-provincial of his order. King Philip II nominated him in 1579 for the newly created see of Manila. Arriving in the Philippines in 1581, S. ordered the affairs of his diocese, erected a cathedral, opened a college, established a hospital and in many ways sought to provide for the welfare of the Filipinos. History has justly called him 'the *Las Casas of the Philippines' for he at once made the cause of the oppressed Filipinos his own. A synod of his diocese, convened soon after his arrival in the Islands, roundly condemned the cruel abuses of the Spanish *conquistadores*.

S. was the first to deal with what was to be a serious and continuing obstacle to orderly ecclesiastical administration right down to the 20th century: the tendency of the missionary orders to exempt themselves from the jurisdiction of the bishop on the strength of their apostolic privileges— especially the *omnimodo* faculties granted by Adrian VI. On S's petition, Pope Gregory XIV in 1591 confirmed the bishop's authority over all the clergy of his diocese, including those in the missionary orders; but the matter was far from settled.

In 1592, at the age of 80, S. returned to Spain to plead in person the cause of the maltreated natives, and the king ordered the introduction of many of the reforms he advocated. At the same time, three new dioceses were created for the Islands and Manila was elevated to be a metropolitan see; but S. died in Madrid on 4 December 1594 before receiving the bull of his appointment as archbishop.

PETER G. GOWING

J. Ferrando: *Historia de los PP. Dominicos en las Islas Filipinas*, Vol. I (Madrid 1870); *LTK* IX, 980f.; *NCE* XII, 259.

SALVADOR, EL. See AMERICA, CENTRAL.

SALVATION. A clear understanding of S. is indispensable for all missionary work. The *gospel has been understood from the beginning as the 'message of salvation' (Acts 13:26) and as the 'power of God unto salvation' (Rom.1:16). However, it is widely said that the word 'salvation' has little meaning to modern man, who is not aware of any need to be 'saved'. On the other hand much of the biblical idea of S. is today embodied in secular myths. The 'Four Freedoms' of F. D. Roosevelt, for example, are very close to what is termed 'S' in some parts of the OT.

S. in the Bible is, first of all, deliverance from the powers that oppress men—from enemies, pestilence, storms and disease (cf. Ps. 107). The deliverance of Israel from Egypt and from the Babylonian captivity are supreme examples of God's saving power at work. But the perspective is not limited to what we would call secular deliverances. The dominant factor is the personal relation to the Lord who is Israel's Saviour (Ps.106:21). The words 'save', 'salvation' occur far more frequently in the Psalms than in any other books, and while the 'secular' reference is usually close at hand, the *dominant* is always the personal relation between the believers and the Lord, not the particular deliverance which is the subject of the Psalm.

In the NT also there is no sharp distinction between 'secular' and 'religious' interpretations of S. The phrase 'to be saved' can be said of the curing of an illness (James 5:15), deliverance from a storm

(Acts 27:20), from drowning (Matt.14:30), or from blindness (Lk.18:42). The word is constantly used to describe the healing acts of Jesus. And yet S. as offered by Jesus is not merely secular deliverance—either from Roman *colonialism or from hunger (Jn. 6:25-35) or from disease. It is more than these things. In the saying: 'Whoever would save his life will lose it, and whoever loses his life for my sake will find it' (Matt.16:25), it is obvious that we have passed beyond a purely 'secular' idea of S. Here S. is something centred in a personal commitment to Jesus, and its horizon goes beyond death and therefore beyond all 'secular' good.

The NT speaks of this S. both as future and as present. St. Paul is sure that we *shall be* saved (Rom.5:9-10), and that S. is nearer now than when we first believed (13:11). S. is therefore a matter of hope (1 Thess.5:8;Rom.8:18-25); it is 'ready to be revealed in the last time' (1 Pet.1:5); its coming is one aspect of the coming of the kingdom (Rev.12:10). And yet—like the kingdom—it is also present. 'Now is the day of salvation' for Zacchaeus (Lk.19:9), for the Gentiles (Rom.11:11), for all who will hear (2 Cor.6:2). The primary reference of the word is eschatological; it refers to the final healing of all things, the deliverance of the creation, and of the children of God, from all the powers of evil. But we are enabled now by faith (Eph.2:8) and in hope (Rom.8:24) to share in the blessings of S.—namely peace with God, the forgiveness of our sins, joy even in sufferings, patience in tribulation; and the gift of the Holy Spirit who is the 'earnest'—the guarantee—of the full inheritance to which we look forward (Eph.1:13-14).

The missionary church bears the message of God's S. This S. is not purely 'other worldly', nor purely 'this worldly'. It includes the completing of God's purpose for his whole creation, the healing of all that is broken, and the destruction of all that enslaves and exploits. We do not fully understand how God's purpose in this world is related to that which lies beyond death, but the cross and resurrection of Jesus are our assurance that 'Salvation belongs to our God who sits on the throne and to the Lamb' (Rev.7:10).

See also REDEMPTION.

LESSLIE NEWBIGIN

A. G. Hogg: *Redemption from this World* (Edinburgh 1922); L. Newbigin: *Sin and Salvation* (London 1956).

SALVATION ARMY, THE, is an embodiment of Christian world mission and is in the main stream of Christian tradition. From the moment in 1865 when, on Mile End Waste in London's East End, William Booth commenced his work, the organization has held an ever-expanding world view. 'There is no Salvation Army missionary society', states the official history; 'it is The Salvation Army on all its missionary fields as in the land of its birth. It is everywhere one, not only in organization but in the purpose so succinctly put into words by William Booth when he besought his soldiers everywhere to "go for souls and go for the worst".' This principle applies independently of language, colour, creed, culture, sex or political affiliation.

Today the one SA operates in 70 countries under the leadership of one General, with International Headquarters in London, England, but with delegation of all necessary responsibilities to local administration. The basic element in this unity in diversity is the maintenance of the original spirit and purpose of William Booth's own obedience to God in the world of his day based on true missionary motive.

Salvationists respond to human need by means of evangelism and practical concern for the welfare of the people, this two-fold response being combined in a unique way in the philosophy and practice of Salvationism. This is so, whether in the USA or India, in Australia or Congo, France, Germany, the Netherlands, Indonesia or Hong Kong. Their mission, in the name of Christ, is for the salvation of mankind.

The full implications of missionary work have been accepted—evangelism, and medical, educational and social approaches. Outstanding examples of initiative include work among the 'criminal tribes' of India;

the pioneering of specialized hospital work in the same land; the successful attack on prostitution in Japan; care of the blind in the Caribbean, East Africa and India; a ministry among leprosy sufferers in Indonesia and Zambia and among victims of tuberculosis in Japan; and educational work in Rhodesia, Congo and Hong Kong.

The SA accepts national leadership in an international community. It recognizes the social obligation of the Christian church to the needs of mankind. Over 2,000,000 people are fed annually at food distribution centres, while hospitals and clinics give medical care to another 900,000. Nearly 7,000 missing persons are traced every year.

Youth can receive instruction in Christian discipleship and service under the Army's guidance, and the basic beliefs and practice of Christianity are taught through its literature (129 evangelical periodicals are published with a circulation of almost 2,000,000). Alcoholics and drug-addicts in the UK and the USA, and the multitudes affected by poverty in Asia, are all a part of the Army's field. 'Where there's need, there's The Salvation Army'.

In the SA the soldiers (laity) accept the basic concept of Christian warfare on being 'sworn-in' by signing the Articles of War, which cover a profession of faith and commitment to active Christian service and pursuit of personal holiness.

Other distinguishing features of the SA include equality of women in matters of leadership. Of the more than 25,000 commissioned officers (trained and 'ordained') a large proportion are women. Over 700 officers serve away from their homelands in missionary situations.

It is the SA's firm conviction that certain ceremonies known as *'sacraments' are not necessary to salvation nor essential to spiritual progress; therefore they are not observed in the SA.

The use of music in propagation and interpretation of the gospel by over 170,000 unpaid Salvationist music-makers has become an established part of the world's life.

THOS. H. LEWIS

S. Chesham: *Born to Battle* (Chicago 1965);

R. Collier: *The General Next to God* (London 1965); R. Gout: *William Booth et le monde ouvrier* (Geneva and Paris 1955); R. Sandall and A. R. Wiggins: *The History of The Salvation Army* (5 vols., London 1947–1968); B. Watson: *A Hundred Years' War* (London 1964); *The Year Book of The Salvation Army* (London); *The Salvation Army: its Origin and Development* (London 1966); *The Sacraments—the Salvationist's Viewpoint* (London 1960).

SAMOA. See PACIFIC ISLANDS.

SAO THOME AND PRINCIPE. See ATLANTIC ISLANDS.

SARAWAK. See MALAYSIA.

SAUDI ARABIA. See ARABIAN PENINSULA.

SCANDINAVIAN MISSIONARY COUNCIL (*Nordisk Missionsråd*). Contact between missionary work from the Scandinavian countries began about the middle of the 19th century; the first Scandinavian missionary conference was held in 1863.

Formal organizational relationship between the Scandinavian missionary societies developed largely as a result of the *Edinburgh Conference 1910. National missionary councils were formed: in Denmark 1912, in Sweden 1912, in Finland 1919 and in Norway 1921.

The SMC was formed in May 1922, its constitution being accepted in February 1923 and two representatives appointed from each of the four Scandinavian councils. The council is a consultative body with no authority over its member councils. Its purpose is to further co-operation between member bodies, to arrange conferences (a Scandinavian missionary conference is normally held every three or four years), and—according to the original constitution—to try, when necessary, to develop and represent common Scandinavian interests and emphases in relation to the *IMC.

Apart from organizing regular Scandinavian missionary conferences, the SMC has had, and still has, rather limited importance; national and individual society interests were too strong to allow the SMC ever to play any really significant role, and relationship with international bodies (DWME/WCC, LWF, etc.) takes place through the national councils and not through the SMC.

ERIK W. NIELSEN

SCHALL VON BELL, ADAM (1591–1666), was born in Cologne, Germany. He studied in Rome and in 1611 entered the Society of *Jesus. He asked to be assigned to China and sailed to the orient from Lisbon in 1618. After the death of Matthew *Ricci (1610), court intrigues caused the banishment of the Jesuits; but when it was discovered that the imperial astronomers incorrectly predicted the hour of an eclipse and thus cast doubt on the whole imperial calendar, the Jesuits were invited to staff the Imperial Board of Astronomy in Peking. Because of his scholarship and outstanding knowledge of astronomy, S. was named head of the board in 1629. He soon became the most important foreigner in China. The emperor consulted him on state decisions and appointed him a mandarin of the first class. In 1661 the young emperor died and the regents who succeeded were hostile to the Jesuits. The Chinese scholars who had been displaced by S. and his companions launched a violent campaign of revenge. The Jesuits were arrested, chained and thrown in prison. Their trial dragged on for two years, ending with a sentence of death for S. and banishment of the other three Jesuits. Just at that time, Peking was shaken by earthquakes in which 300,000 people perished. The superstitious regents freed the Jesuits but S. did not long survive his sufferings. He died on 15 August 1666. During his apostolate, the number of Catholics in China had increased from 13,000 to over 250,000.

ALBERT J. NEVINS, MM

R. Attwater: *Adam Schall, A Jesuit at the Court of China* (New York 1963); G. H. Dunne: *Generation of Giants* (Notre Dame, Ind. 1962); S. M. Just: *Immortal Fire* (St. Louis, Mo. 1951); A. Schall: *Lettres et mémoires d'Adam Schall* (Tientsin 1942); *LTK* IX, 363; *NCE* XII, 1119f.

SCHERESCHEWSKY (pronounced Sher-e-scheff-skie), SAMUEL ISAAC JOSEPH (1831–1906), was born a Russian Jew. After an orthodox education in Lithuania and Germany he emigrated to the USA where he was converted by Christian Jewish friends; he then attended the Presbyterian seminary at Allegheny and graduated from General Theological Seminary (Episcopal) in New York. The opening of inland China to foreigners turned his eyes to missionary service there (1859). Remarkable mastery of the Chinese language inspired Bible translation into beautiful classical (Wenli) and colloquial (Mandarin and dialect) styles. S. also translated the Church of England Prayer Book and part of the Apocrypha. In 1877 he was elected bishop of the Shanghai Diocese and founded St. John's College, later university. In 1881 he was almost completely paralysed by a sunstroke. Following a period of special treatment in the west he returned to the orient, mind keen as ever, revised his translations and prepared them for the press. For two decades he was a 'mighty invalid', operating a typewriter with one finger and leaving a precious literary heritage to the church in China. His wife was devoted nurse, secretary and companion until his death in Japan.

F. W. PRICE

J. A. Miller: *Apostle of China, S.I.J. Schereschewsky* (Milwaukee 1937).

SCHMIDT, GEORG (1709–1775), was born in Kunewalde, Moravia. After conversion he emigrated to Herrnhut. He first witnessed in Moravia, where he was imprisoned by the RC authorities for six years. He was sent to the Cape of Good Hope by *Zinzendorf in 1739 as the first Protestant missionary to Africa. He gathered a number of Hottentots at Baviaanskloof, taught them reading, writing and singing in Dutch, and instructed them in the Christian faith. S. encouraged industry, agriculture and trade. He maintained himself through farming. Zealously he urged slaves, Hottentots, colonists and soldiers alike to be converted. In 1742 he received a letter of ordination from Zinzendorf and baptized five Hottentots. As the state church the DRC considered this to be their prerogative. S. eventually left for Holland in 1744 to clarify the situation but was unable to return. His flock waited for his return, teaching their children to read the Bible and pray. The Moravian missionaries who resumed the work nearly 50 years later were able to build on the foundations he laid so well. During this interim period Magdalena Vehettge, the last survivor of S's baptized first fruits, had continued to instruct others from her Dutch NT. S. proved what was thought to be impossible, namely to gather a Christian congregation from among the Hottentots, working on the basis of a closed settlement or mission station, which later became characteristic of work in Africa.

GERHARDUS C. OOSTHUIZEN

Diary of Georg Schmidt (Genadendal Archives); B. Krüger: *The Peartree Blossoms: The history of the Moravian Church in South Africa 1737–1869* (Genadendal 1966); *RGG* V, 1457.

SCHOOLS. See EDUCATION.

SCHREUDER, HANS PALUDAN SMITH (1817–1882), was born in Sogndal, Norway, where his father was a solicitor. He studied theology in the university of Oslo and passed his final examinations with highest distinction. In 1842 he published a treatise, addressed to the church of Norway, on the Christian's duty to be concerned about the salvation of his non-Christian fellow men. It aroused considerable interest and led to the formation of the first 'independent' agency for foreign missions. However, when the Norwegian Missionary Society was founded, S. became its pioneer. As such he laboured among the Zulu people in South Africa for almost four decades. Progress was very slow, and he had to wait for fourteen years until the first Zulu was baptized. S. was an able linguist and pub-

lished a scholarly grammar of Zulu, a pioneer venture described by experts as a remarkable achievement. The year 1866 saw S. in Norway where he was consecrated bishop. His diocese also included Madagascar where under his direction a new mission was established. Because of a dispute over new administrative measures he in 1873 severed his relations with the society. A new mission, 'The Church of Norway Mission established by S', was formed to enable him to carry on the work in South Africa. S's efforts as the first permanent resident missionary among the Zulus north of the Tugela River, and his introduction of other missions besides his own in that area, have won for him the title of 'the apostle of Zululand'.

O. G. MYKLEBUST

RGG V 1513.

SCHWARTZ, CHRISTIAN FRIEDRICH (1726–1798), probably the most able and influential worker in the Tranquebar Mission after the founder *Ziegenbalg, was born in East Germany and trained at Halle under the younger Francke. He arrived in India in 1750 and worked for ten years in Tranquebar. In 1762 he went to Trichinopoly, in 1772 to Tanjore. Thus he spent almost half a century in uninterrupted mission service in South India, although his health was often poor.

It was in the tradition of the Tranquebar Mission that he soon acquired a mastery of the Tamil language (to which he added Portuguese, English, Persian and Hindustani) and a remarkable knowledge of *Hinduism. Nor was S. unique in his untiring zeal as an evangelist and in his deep understanding of the Indian character. It is more likely that his saintly disposition and his integrity account for his extraordinary influence. 'Men who met S. knew that they had seen a man of God' (S. Neill). Yet in order to evaluate his specific contribution to Indian mission and church history, other factors must be mentioned as well. There was, first, his ecumenical spirit which made him agree to an appointment as a chaplain to the British community in

Trichinopoly, even against initial opposition on the part of the mission. While his influence on British soldiers was profound and, as has rightly been said, 'he retrieved the character of Europeans from imputations of general depravity', he never neglected his duties as a missionary to non-Christians or abandoned his loyalty as a Lutheran. Toward the end of his life he did not hesitate to reply affirmatively to an enquiry from Dr Thomas *Coke about openings for Methodist work in India.

Another unique aspect of his ministry was his involvement in politics. In Tanjore he quickly gained the confidence of the Hindu rajah, who on his deathbed appointed S. guardian and trustee of his young heir Saraboji. Although S. declined, he later had ample opportunity to assist the young prince when his right to the throne was disputed. He also tried to be of use to the British who on one occasion sent him as a special envoy of peace to the despot of Mysore, Haider Ali. S. returned with respect for the Muslim ruler but complained of the insincerity and avarice of the British.

Finally, S. contributed significantly to the strengthening of an *indigenous church in India. He not only made every effort to find and train young Indians for the ministry and as *catechists, whom he often supported from his own pocket, but also encouraged the spontaneous expansion of small groups of Christians whom he discovered during a visit in 1778 in and near Palamcottah—the nucleus of the large and vigorous Tinnevelly church. S. was also responsible for the education of Vedanāyagam, son of a catechist trained by S., who was to become one of the greatest poets and hymn composers of the Tamil tongue.

S. himself would have cared little for the two marble monuments erected in his honour after his death, yet the fact that one was set up by the Hindu prince Saraboji, the other one by the directors of the British East India Company indicates something of the unique measure of a man whose life was totally devoted to the cause of Christ in India.

H.-W. GENSICHEN

W. Germann: *Missionar C. F. Schwartz* (Erlangen 1870), still the most reliable account; H. Pearson: *Memoirs of the Life and Correspondence of the Reverend Christian Frederick Swartz* (2 vols., London 1835), the only adequate work on the subject in English; *RGG* V, 1589.

SCHWEITZER, ALBERT (1875–1965), was born at Kayserburg, Alsace, France, and studied at the universities of Strasbourg, Paris and Berlin. He had established a high reputation as philosopher, theologian and musician before deciding in 1906 to become a missionary doctor. Qualifying MD in 1913 he immediately sailed with his wife to Gabon, Equatorial Africa, where he founded a hospital at Lambarene in association with the *Paris Mission (PEMS). Interned as a German citizen during the first world war, he was brought back to Europe, but returned in 1924 to rebuild the hospital. He spent the greater part of his remaining years at Lambarene, where he died.

Although S. was not an orthodox Christian in the usual sense, he was devoted to Jesus as a person and as a living spiritual presence. His missionary work was based on this devotion, together with sympathy for suffering, reverence for life (the key to his ethical thought), and a desire to atone for the wrongs which the west had done to Africa. He maintained his vision by continuing to think and write in the midst of varied practical work. Many voluntary helpers from western countries joined him at Lambarene. In later years the hospital, dominated by his sometimes inflexible personality, was criticized as being medically and socially out of date. S's example, however, has been outstanding as an inspiration to missionary service among western-educated men of the 20th century.

JOHN GOODWIN

A. Schweitzer: *On the Edge of the Primeval Forest; More from the Primeval Forest* (Eng. tr. of *Zwischen Wasser und Urwald* and *Mitteilung aus Lambarene*—London 1948); *My Life and Thought* (Eng. tr. of *Aus meinem Leben und Denken*—London 1933); *EKL* III, 881ff., *RGG* V, 160f.

SCIENCE, CONTRIBUTION OF MIS-SIONS TO. So numerous and varied have been the contributions of missions to science that a very large volume would be required even to enumerate them. We must content ourselves with three examples. From his boyhood William *Carey had been interested in plants. After arriving in India he made botany a major recreation. In Serampore he developed a large herbarium and corresponded with European specialists on botany, introducing them to many varieties of which they had been unaware. In his translation of the Scriptures into several of the Indian languages, Carey pioneered in some phases of linguistics. In his journeys in the interior of Africa, David *Livingstone not only enlarged European knowledge of the geography of that continent, but also through his carefully kept journals he increased western knowledge of other aspects of Central Africa. A much earlier contribution of missions to science was that of the Catholic missionaries in China in the 17th and 18th centuries. A notable succession, mostly of *Jesuits, brought to China an enlarged knowledge of global geography, mathematics and astronomy. They also acquainted Europe with Chinese culture, especially philosophy.

KENNETH SCOTT LATOURETTE

K. S. Latourette: *A History of the Expansion of Christianity* (New York 1937–1945), Vol. III pp. 340–56, 364; Vol. V pp.345–49; Vol. VI pp.104–07.

SCOTT, PETER CAMERON (1867–1896), was born near Glasgow, Scotland, of pious Evangelical parents. In 1879 the family emigrated to Philadelphia, USA, where S. eventually underwent part-time college training. He was sent by the Missionary Alliance to Banana, Congo, where he began work in 1891. After some months his brother John joined him, but soon died; and S. himself returned sick to America. While recovering his health he felt a call to start work in the highlands of east and central Africa, where Europeans could better tolerate the climate and where no mission had yet been established. With A. T. Pierson

and others he founded the Africa Inland Mission as a non-denominational venture of faith in 1895, without any public appeal for funds (see FAITH MISSIONS). In the same year S. with seven companions sailed to Mombasa and proceeded 250 miles inland to Nzawi, where they established their first station. Their methods were preaching, teaching and elementary medical work. In 1896 S. founded three new stations and was joined by eight more missionaries; but in December 1896 he died of blackwater fever. At first it seemed that the mission would not long survive S's death, but it recovered and began to make progress under the guidance of C. E. Hurlburt in Kijabe from 1901. It eventually spread from Kenya to Tanganyika, Uganda, Congo (Kinshasa), Chad and Sudan.

JOHN GOODWIN

C. S. Miller: *Peter Cameron Scott. The Unlocked Door* (London 1955).

SCOTTISH INSTITUTE OF MISSION-ARY STUDIES. A body founded in 1967 'To encourage and provide means for the study of Christian missions; to locate and encourage the preservation of the materials for such study, particularly in Scotland; and to facilitate co-operation among institutions and individuals interested in such study.' The Institute has a corporate membership of institutions which are (for different reasons, and from different points of view) involved in or concerned for the study of the nature, history or effects of Christian missions, or in Christianity in the non-western world: these include churches, mission councils, colleges, university departments (divinity, history, social studies and area studies) and libraries. There are also associated institutions in over 30 countries.

The Institute has been especially concerned to encourage the preservation and accessibility of missionary archives, and the collection and safe custody of the personal papers of missionaries and others; to provide resources in Scotland for studying the missionary movement past and present (promoting co-operation between institutions to this end); and with the construction of bibliographical aids and other *instrumenta studiorum*. A *Bulletin* provides a twice yearly survey of current missionary literature, international and polylingual in scope, as well as an annual review of developments in archives and other resources. There is also an annual report and other occasional publications. The secretarial address is Scottish Institute of Missionary Studies, Department of Church History, University of Aberdeen, 25 High Street, Old Aberdeen, AB2 3EE.

A. F. WALLS

SCUDDER, IDA S. (1870–1959), the granddaughter of the first of the famous Scudder family to enter missionary service in India, returned from education in America to India in 1890, critical, and determined to have nothing to do with missionary work. Driven by sharp contacts with the misery of India's women to a reconsideration of Christian responsibility, IS went back to America, and returned to India a qualified doctor and a fully committed missionary. After years of exhausting and self-sacrificing labour in medical service and in the successful training of nurses, IS was driven to the conclusion that the needs of India could be met only by the training of a large number of women doctors; at that time it was unlikely that any candidates other than Christians would be forthcoming. There was strong opposition to the plan, which by many was regarded as wholly premature. But IS persisted; in 1918 the Christian Medical School came into existence; when in the first year all IS's pupils passed the examination and thereby put Vellore at the head of all the medical training institutions in South India, all criticism was stayed. Vellore offered only the qualification LMP, an excellent and useful medical degree, but not of university standing and not registrable in other countries. When Indian national pride demanded the abolition of this qualification, Vellore had to rise to university status. This was successfully achieved in 1942. The next step was to open the facilities to men as well; to this there was,

unhappily, again much opposition in the USA; but common sense triumphed, and in 1947 the Medical College opened for men as well as for women. Dr S. would have been the first to agree that all this would have been impossible without the help of countless friends in India, in Britain and in the USA; but the inspiration, the vision and the drive were hers. Decision, vision, precision, modesty and humour, based on a deep and unchanging Christian faith, made IS one of the most remarkable Christians of the 20th century. When she died, old and full of honours, she had a host of friends in every corner of the globe and not a single enemy.

STEPHEN NEILL

D. C. Wilson: *Dr Ida* (3rd ed., New York and London 1964).

SECTS, SECTARIANISM. (1) The English word 'sect' means simply a division or party and in itself conveys no stigma or disapproval. It occurs twice in the Acts of the Apostles in the AV, of 'the sect of the Sadducees' and 'the most straitest sect of our religion . . . a Pharisee' (5:17, 26:5; RSV 'party', in each case); here, though the Greek word so translated is *hairesis*, from which is derived the English 'heresy', there is no pejorative tone—the word simply means 'one group or division' among the people. (2) Nevertheless, the word has acquired overtones of contempt or disapproval. In the Roman *Canon Law*, non-RC groups and bodies are referred to as '*sectae acatholicae*', and from § 1099 it is clear that not only Christian bodies but such groups as the Freemasons are also included. In England in the 17th century the Presbyterians called the Independents, whom they disliked, 'the Sectarian party'. Anglicans have tended to refer to Protestant dissenters as 'Sectarians'. It is unlikely that anyone speaking the English language today will refer to himself, except humorously or ironically, as belonging to a sect, or as a sectarian. (3) The nature of the Christian sect-type as against the church-type was subjected to careful examination by E. Troeltsch. The difference is seen by him to lie essentially in the point that the church aims at the conquest of society, which involves penetration of society at all levels, and a certain modification of the provocativeness of the church by compromise with standards other than its own; whereas the sect-type, concerned more with purity in life and doctrine than with anything else, tends to withdraw from the world, having given up any hope of the total christianization of society. Up to a point this is illuminating, but the thesis of Troeltsch has come under a good deal of criticism. Is the distinction as clear as he imagined? It is certainly the case that Christian faith includes both world-affirming and world-renouncing elements, and tends to oscillate between extremes; but is it the case that even so extreme a movement of asceticism as the Trappist order has ever completely despaired of the world; or that the church, even in the most flourishing periods of its friendship with the world, as in the Caesaropapism of Byzantium, has ever completely abandoned its function as the judge and critic of the world? (4) It is possible to identify in Christian history a number of movements which correspond rather closely to Troeltsch's sect-type. This view may be taken, for example, of the Primitive Methodists in their early days. To their lasting honour, the *Pentecostalist churches have mostly begun as small assemblies of humble and obscure people, exercising no influence at all on society as a whole, cared for by shepherds who had themselves received no theological training, but radiant with the sense of the presence of the Holy Spirit in their midst. But in every such case the historian notes the tendency of a 'sect' to transform itself into a church. Many of the Pentecostal assemblies now have sumptuous buildings, orderly services, a trained and ordained ministry, and are conscious of belonging, albeit somewhat loosely, to a worldwide fellowship. A further characteristic of the 'sect-type' is the tendency to stress one tenet, or one aspect of Christian faith, to such an extent that the balance of truth is disturbed. If this tendency is carried beyond a certain

limit, the distortion reaches the point of heresy, and the 'sect' slips over the line and becomes the 'heretical sect'. Another article in this dictionary deals with the notable phenomenon of many African movements away from the established churches and missions. Many of these movements manifest many of the characteristics of the 'sect'—spontaneity, lack of organization, untrained leadership, an exaggerated puritanism, a withdrawal from the world. Many unfriendly observers would unhesitatingly use the term 'sect', or 'sectarian churches' of these movements. Some would add that, in some of them at least, the Christian substance has been so diminished that the term 'heretical' can rightly be used of them. No doubt many of these movements are unstable, tending to disappear, either through reabsorption into the churches from which they had separated, or through dissolution on the death of the original leader. In other cases, however, the tendency of the sect to become a church is very apparent—in size, in developing organization, in the desire for educated leadership, in a growing sense of mission to a whole people or country. It is for these reasons that there is a growing consensus that the correct term to use of these bodies is that which they themselves prefer— African Independent Churches.

See also AFRICAN INDEPENDENT CHURCHES; CULTS, POST-CHRISTIAN AND QUASI-CHRISTIAN.

STEPHEN NEILL

E. Troeltsch: *The Social Teaching of the Christian Churches* (German 1912; Eng. tr. 1931), esp. pp.331–43, *WKL*, 1327–31.

SECULAR, SECULARISM, SECULARIZATION.

These words are all derived from the Latin *saeculum*, which means 'century, age, or epoch', but in later Latin came to mean 'world', and was used in as many different senses as the Greek words *kosmos* and *aiōn* in the NT. That which was secular was not necessarily bad. 'Secular' priests lived 'in the world' and looked after parishes, but this did not mean that they were regarded as traitors to the cause. Until the Reformation, all worlds were regarded as God's worlds; church and state were simply different aspects of the one people of God. That which was 'worldly' in the sense of refusing to accept, or setting itself up against, the sovereignty of God would probably have been called 'pagan' or 'heathen' rather than secular. With the Enlightenment of the 18th century came in the separation, which has now become familiar to us, between the sacred and the secular; religion has become one separate and partial activity of man, and not the whole of man's life as seen in relationship to God. Other areas, such as politics, have declared their own autonomy. In such secular areas, if the existence of God is not denied, it is not taken seriously, and allegiance to his law is not regarded as binding. Marxism is only more logical than the rest in carrying to its extreme the 'secularization' of all things.

This sense of the word 'secularization' is generally accepted and familiar. Thus it is possible to speak of: (1) A secularized world, i.e. a world which is not interested in God, which does not seek to know or to do his will, and does not recognize any standards or values other than those which are immanent in its own structure. (2) A secularized church, when a church has gone so far in adapting itself to a surrounding world, and has adopted so many of the methods and weapons of that world as to have lost its own identity as a dwelling-place of God through the Spirit. (3) A secularized idea. When ideas or concepts which have their origin in religion have become so far separated from it that their origin is forgotten, then such an idea is said to have become secularized. Thus there is much in Marxism which seems to have its origin in the NT; but, as developed by Marx and his disciples, such ideas have become secularized caricatures of what they originally were. In all these cases the use of the word is intelligible and self-consistent.

In recent years a number of continental theologians, notably F. Gogarten, have introduced the use of the word 'secularization' in an entirely different sense, and propagation of their ideas in the English-speaking world has led to a great deal of confusion. According to Gogarten the increasing secularization of the world is not something to be deplored, but something in which the Christian should rejoice, as being in a real sense a product of the gospel which he proclaims. This secularization is dependent on the spread of scientific knowledge, and scientific knowledge is a fruit of the freedom which is given to men in the gospel. Earlier, men had regarded nature with superstitious awe, and believed it to be the home of mysterious entities in the grip and under the domination of which man is compelled to live, and from which he has no power to free himself. The Christian, on the other hand, regards nature with awe not because of any magical power which it may itself possess, but because he sees in it the handiwork of his heavenly Father. He is now a free man, with power to understand nature, to rule over it, and to adapt it to his purposes. Secularism is the denial of God, secularization is the assertion of the freedom which God has given to man in the world. The doctrine is in part true; the choice of words is most unfortunate, in German as in English. The correct English term for the process that Gogarten is describing is *desacralization* and, clumsy as this word is, it would be far better to use it in this context, and to use 'secularization' only in its classical and ordinary sense. The doctrine is only partly true: (1) It enormously underestimates the contribution of the Greeks, both in their understanding of history, and in their development of a scientific knowledge of the world. (2) It underestimates the extent to which the magical and the scientific approaches to nature can co-exist in the same person. Belief in astrology, magic, witchcraft, amulets and charms, are not unknown in the west, and are exceedingly common in the *younger churches, even among those who have received a western education. (3) It is nowhere the case that 'secularization' has made easier the entry of the gospel of redemption in Jesus Christ. In most cases the destruction of the old world-view leads on to secularism, to disbelief in any transcendent dimension of the world, which in many cases is combined with a passionate refusal to abandon a social system based on religious ideas which are no longer held. This is no argument against western education or against the duty of missions to make available throughout the world the best results of western scientific thinking; it is a warning against the drawing of any unduly optimistic conclusions as to the results which will follow on such dissemination of scientific knowledge.

STEPHEN NEILL

F. Gogarten: *Verhängnis und Hoffnung der Neuzeit: die Säkularisierung als theologisches Problem* (Stuttgart 1953); A. T. van Leeuwen: *Christianity in World History* (London, 2nd impr. 1965); L. Shiner: *The Secularization of History* (Nashville 1966); *ERE* XI, 347–50; *NCE* XIII, 36–38; *WKL*, 1289–92.

SELLY OAK COLLEGES, Birmingham, England. A centre of research and training in the world mission of the church and in community service. Nine separate colleges are federated in a central council which maintains a specialist library and provides teaching by a central staff. There are endowed professorial chairs in biblical and theological studies, in missionary studies and Islamics, and a department of social studies. Two one-year teaching fellowships are offered to members of the Afro-Asian churches. Students come from many countries and church traditions including the Lutheran churches of Europe. Special provision is made for missionaries on leave.

The colleges owe much to the initiative and continuing interest of the Society of Friends who founded the first college, Woodbroke, in 1903 as a centre of Quaker life and study. Later colleges were Kingsmead (1905), Methodist Missionary Society; Westhill College of Education (1907), training teachers and youth leaders; Fircroft (1909), adult education; St. Andrews including Carey Hall (1912), world service with Baptist, Presbyterian and Congregational churches; Overdale

(1920), a theological college of the Churches of Christ; College of the Ascension (1923), USPG (Anglican); Avoncroft (1925), agricultural and social studies; and Crowther Hall (1969), CMS (Anglican). A course is also conducted for housemasters of approved schools in Great Britain.

HENRY LEFEVER

SELWYN, GEORGE AUGUSTUS (1809–1878), was born at Hampstead, London, England. After ordination in the Church of England in 1833 S. taught at Eton and ministered pastorally in Windsor. In 1839 he married Sarah Richardson. Consecrated Bishop of New Zealand in 1841, S. made his headquarters among the Maori people. He appreciated and built upon the foundation laid by the *CMS, but sometimes disagreed with it since he expected missionaries to obey him as bishop without interference from the society which had sent them. He applied among Anglicans stricter rules than they had been observing in regard to communion with other Christians. This led to some early conflict with Methodist missionaries. In general S. had good relations with other churches and did not send Anglican teachers where other work had been established.

S's strenuous pastoral visiting among the Maoris won him their affection and respect. He founded St. John's College, Auckland, where Europeans, Maoris and Pacific Islanders were educated together. He frequently acted as peacemaker between European settlers and Maoris. Despite his warnings, the government did not control sufficiently the way immigrants acquired land, and in 1855 the Maori war broke out; this continued until 1865. S. ministered impartially to both sides; but each suspected him of favouring the other, and the war undid much of his work among the Maori people.

In 1857 S's constitution for the New Zealand church was adopted This provided for the laity to take a full share in its councils together with the clergy. The church as a voluntary organization was entirely independent of the state. From 1848

548 SEMINARIES

S. had travelled widely among the Pacific
Islands, founding the Melanesian Mission
and bringing young people from the islands
to be educated at Auckland. In 1861 he
consecrated J. C. *Patteson Bishop of
Melanesia. In 1867 S. took a leading part
in the first Lambeth Conference. In 1868 he
became Bishop of Lichfield, where he made
a notable contribution to progress in the
Church of England.

S. sought always to submit his great
powers of mind and body to the proper
authority: first to Christ, secondly to the
church, thirdly to the secular government.
His example led the church in England and
elsewhere to undertake more fully its
missionary responsibility. His organization
of the church in New Zealand and Melanesia provided models which others copied.
He was a man of decision, whose decisions
were generally right; nearly a century after
his death their effects can still be seen
throughout the whole Anglican Communion.

JOHN GOODWIN

G. H. Curteis: *Bishop Selwyn of New
Zealand and of Lichfield* (London 1889);
J. H. Evans: *Churchman Militant. George
Augustus Selwyn, Bishop of New Zealand
and Lichfield* (London and Wellington
1964); H. W. Tucker: *Memoir of the Life
and Episcopate of George Augustus Selwyn,
D.D.* (London 1879); *DNB* LI, 232.

SEMINARIES. See THEOLOGICAL
EDUCATION: SEMINARIES AND
BIBLE SCHOOLS.

SENDING AGENCIES. See MISSION
BOARDS AND SOCIETIES.

SENDING CHURCHES. See OLDER
CHURCHES.

SENEGAL is a French-speaking West
African republic 76,084 sq.m. in area, with
a population (1967) of 3,670,000 including
about 47,000 Europeans. S. was converted
to *Islam in the year 1040, and the vast
majority are Muslims to this day. A RC
*vicariate apostolic was formed in 1863;

Catholics in 1965 numbered 106,857. Seven
Protestant missions are at work, the largest
being *Assemblées de Dieu*, and *Mission
Evangélique de l'Afrique Occidentale*
(*WEC); the total Protestant community
is 2,000, together with a fluctuating number
of expatriates from France and French-
speaking West Africa.

DAVID B. BARRETT

H. Ernst: *Senegal* (Bonn 1965); *BM* II,
783–88; *NCE* XIII, 81.

SEPARATIST CHURCHES. See AFRI-
CAN INDEPENDENT CHURCH
MOVEMENT.

SERAMPORE COLLEGE (1818–1918).
Founded by *Carey, Marshman and Ward,
primarily to educate Indian Christian
leadership, the college in 1827 received a
Royal Danish Charter conferring university powers on its council. From 1883
work was restricted to training preachers,
but in 1910 a Higher Theological Department was opened 'available to students of
all denominations', and the BD degree
was first conferred in 1915, while arts and
science teaching were resumed. After consultation with missionary societies, the
council secured changes under the Serampore College Act (Bengal No. IV) of 1918,
whereby it was enlarged from five members
(of whom one might not be Baptist) to a
maximum of 16 (at least one third Baptist)
and a fully interdenominational senate was
constituted to administer the degrees.

The college council returned from
London to India in 1949 and, in 1959,
initiated a building programme to improve
facilities for all departments and rehouse
the 'Carey Library' of old and rare volumes.
The 1918 Act made possible affiliation of
other theological institutions (26 in 1966)
and, with these, the senate has been able
to maintain standards and promote consultation on theological education. The
BD degree is for graduates, but an LTh
diploma, taught through Indian languages,
is widely sought. Advanced degrees include
the MTh and the DTh (by thesis) while the
college honours distinguished scholars and

churchmen with the degree of DD (*honoris causa*).

WILLIAM STEWART

E. D. Potts: *British Baptist Missionaries in India, 1793–1837* (Cambridge 1967); W. S. Stewart, ed.: *The Story of Serampore and its College* (Serampore 1961).

SEVENTH DAY ADVENTISTS. See ADVENTIST MISSIONS.

SEYCHELLES. A group of 92 islands in the Indian Ocean of which only very few are inhabited. It is four degrees south of the equator and about a thousand miles from Arabia, Africa and India. The population of the whole group is about 45,000. In 1770 the French sent colonists from Mauritius who imported more slaves from Africa. Later freed slaves were brought by the British Navy, who had rescued them from Arab slavers. Much miscegenation has taken place since then. This has produced a handsome and charming Creole race who speak the French patois and some English. It is estimated that 43% are illegitimate as formal marriage presents difficulties not easily overcome. The majority are Christians 90% of whom are Roman Catholic. The *Capuchins have a large establishment, a bishop, a cathedral and many churches, eleven schools in Mahé, which is the main island, and two in Praslin. The Christian Brothers have a very good grammar school for boys, and the nuns of St. Joseph de Cluny one for girls. There is an orphanage staffed by the Sisters of St. Elizabeth. The Anglican church work, assisted by *SPG, began in 1843 and has an archdeacon and three or four priests, nine churches, six schools and a church membership of about 5,000. On the island of Praslin—21 miles away—out of a population of 3,000 one third are Anglicans who have two churches and three schools. In the town of Victoria Mahé there is a Seventh Day Adventist church with a small, keen congregation.

DONALD F. STOWELL

BM II, 788f.; *NCE* XIII, 152.

SHANAHAN, JOSEPH (1871–1942), Roman Catholic bishop in Eastern Nigeria, was born in Ireland in 1871, and in 1902 joined the RC mission among the Ibos, which at that time had shown few signs of success. In 1905 S. was appointed prefect apostolic, and in 1920 *vicar apostolic of what had by the later date grown to a flourishing work. From 1906 to 1932 the average number of baptisms annually appears to have been about 4,000. It was always the policy of S. to see the best in the people around him, to observe patiently, 'spiritualizing what I observed', and to submit the raw material to a 'spiritual sublimation'. He was convinced that the man who would treat the Ibo with courtesy and respect would find in him 'a treasure of goodness'.

During the same period the Anglican mission in the area was enjoying an even more rapid expansion than the RC; S. realized that in part this success was due to the wide-flung educational network of the Anglicans, and set himself to remedy what he saw to be a grave defect of his own mission. This policy met with little sympathy in higher quarters, and it was only in the face of considerable opposition that S. was able to supply his mission with schools and an increasing number of qualified teachers to serve 'the most attractive, the most docile and the most interesting (children) on the face of the earth'.

In 1932 S. resigned his post in Nigeria; but, after some years of rest in Ireland, he was sent in 1938 to East Africa where he died at Christmas-time 1942.

STEPHEN NEILL

J. P. Jordan: *Bishop Shanahan of Southern Nigeria* (Dublin 1949).

SHELEKOV, GRIGORI (1747–1796), was a Russian merchant, who in 1787 moved the Holy Synod to found an Orthodox mission to the Aleutian Isles, the expenses to be met by the Russian-American Trading Company. Eight monks of the Valamo monastery were sent out as missionaries, and reached the Aleutians in 1794. S., who was a devoted member of the church, and in high repute for his sense of justice, supported the mission to the utmost of his power, and was successful in having the mission raised in 1796 to the status of a suffragan bishopric of Irkutsk. But the first missionary bishop suffered shipwreck and disappeared. The bishopric was suppressed in 1799, and the Aleutian Christians were left to themselves, until the mission took on new life in the days of I. *Veniaminov.

JOSEF GLAZIK

J. Glazik: *Die russ.-orth. Heidenmission* (Münster 1954), pp.104–08.

SHINTO. The name *Shinto* ('Way of the *Kami* = gods') was coined in the 8th century to distinguish the native Japanese religion from *Buddhism which had been introduced into Japan from China and Korea in the 6th century A.D. The word *Kami* is often translated by 'God', but the idea conveyed is very different from the Christian view of God. The word can denote a whole variety of objects, both animate and inanimate—the mountain peak, a rough stone, the mysterious fox who appears at harvest season and was thought to be responsible for fertility, the flash of lightning, the brooding spirits of the departed, etc. The *Kami* is not an *absolute* being, but the whole universe is regarded as full of *Kami*, as the phrase *yaoyorozu no kami* ('eight million Kami') suggests. It is as if the whole world were alive with spirituality. What is of great value here is the rejection of any rigid distinction between the sacred and the secular. The holy can be found anywhere, and national affairs, such as politics, can be regarded as *matsurigoto* ('ceremonial affairs'—that is, 'religious affairs').

S. is regarded as Japan's religion from 'time immemorial', and it certainly embraces characteristics of the Japanese approach to life, that have resisted the impact of Buddhism and other foreign faiths. For example, S. is held to be responsible for the energy in Japanese character and for the positive approach to the material things of life. But S. itself was influenced from abroad, whilst, in addition, there was a tendency to make nationwide a whole variety of localized cults and unify them somehow or other into one system.

Originally the rites at the shrines were very simple, but gradually priestly families took over the more elaborate ceremonial, whilst the *miko* (female dancers) took the place of the older *shamans* (similar to witch doctors). Oneness with nature is a continuing ideal, and the shrines (approached through a series of *torii*, the distinctive poles and crossbeam which mark every shrine) are commonly erected far away from the rush and clamour of daily life, but the shrine is also responsible for maintaining the unity of the community (thought of as *ujiko*—children of the clan—under the guardianship of the *ujigami*—'Clan Kami'). Even in the large cities the shrine and its annual festival (when a portable shrine will be carried ecstatically through the streets by the young men of the neighbourhood) serve as a focal point of communal activity. The doctrinal teaching is extremely vague, but many enjoy the vigour and the tumult of the festival, whilst an inner sense of awe responds to the quietude and mystery of the shrine precincts.

Just as each community had its own *Kami*, so the Imperial family had its own particular cult—with the shrine of Ise as its centre, and the sun goddess (*Amaterasu-O-Mikami*) as the chief *Kami*. The emperor was regarded as the descendant of this *Kami*, but it should be noted that the so-called 'divinity' of the emperor did not mean that he was different in essence from anyone else. All were expected to become *Kami* at death; the emperor had anticipated this and was regarded till 1945 as a 'living *Kami*'. Because shrine S. was closely linked with the imperial cult, a number of separate S. sects were organized, which looked back to the particular teaching of the founders. In the post-war period the 82,000 shrines are independent of government control, and are organized into an association of S. shrines, being served by about 27,000 priests. In addition, the former thirteen S. Sects have full autonomy, and are now joined by a large group of *'New Religions' or 'New Sects', which reflect a mingling of S. and Buddhist teaching—the kind of syncretistic approach which has marked Japan's religious history.

Apart from a strong emphasis on thanksgiving for the bounty of the *Kami*, S. stresses the importance of *makoto* ('sincerity'), which involves man's openness to nature or the fulfilment of his basic humanity.

Because man, too, becomes a *Kami* in Shinto thought, the Japanese find it difficult to grasp the distinction in essence between the Creator and the creature, which Christianity seeks to make, although, under the influence of Buddhist thought, some S. scholars introduce the idea of an 'absolute' or an 'ultimate'.

RAYMOND J. HAMMER

R. J. Hammer: *Japan's Religious Ferment* (London 1961); D. C. Holtom: *The National Faith of Japan* (London 1938); G. Kato: *What is Shinto*? (Tokyo 1935); S. Ono: *The Kami Way* (Tokyo 1960); *NCE* XIII, 178; *WKL* 1334f.

SHORT TERM MISSIONARIES. Missionaries appointed for three to five years or less (recently used by some even for several months' service). Short termers are usually single (occasionally married, rarely with children), frequently teach or perform other specific tasks to which they often bring a fresh approach. However, they rarely learn language or culture well enough to work at depth. Later many enter long-term service.

USA boards began short term appointments as early as 1907 and one board had 31 in service by 1914. Such appointments increased markedly after the second world war, influenced by transportation, communication, international interest, a changing *theology of mission and need for specialized and service personnel. Of 55 US boards surveyed in 1958, 31 had used them. Short termers have become even more widespread since then. European agencies use them principally for service projects. Asian churches generally appoint missionaries for specific terms. One USA board has sent out over 1,000 since 1946 and two boards reported that 50% of 1966 appointees were in that category. Of boards

affiliated with *EFMA and *IFMA, 22 out of 51 answering a questionnaire in 1965 were using short termers. Several independent agencies now promote short term and volunteer service on behalf of other boards.

DONALD P. SMITH

Annual Reports of various USA mission boards; F. W. Price, K. E. Moyer: 'Mission Board Policies with Relation to Missionary Personnel', *Occasional Bulletin* from the MRL, IX, No. 7 (25 July 1958); W. T. Coggins: 'Whither the Short-Termer?', *Evangelical Missions Quarterly*, III, No. 3 (Spring 1967).

SIAM. See THAILAND.

SIERRA LEONE is a parliamentary state belonging to the Commonwealth and lying between Guinea and Liberia, with an area of 27,925 sq.m. and a population (1967) of 2,439,000. The most distinctive and influential element are the Creoles of Freetown and neighbourhood, descendants of West Coast slaves settled there between 1787 and 1870. Early Protestant mission work began with these efforts to settle repatriated slaves, and the *CMS built up a strong work, although some of its early evangelistic work (that among the Susu) met with no response and had to be abandoned. Sixteen denominations were established by 1966, with a total Protestant community of 77,251; the largest of these were the Anglican diocese of Sierra Leone (CMS) with 25,000; Methodist Church with 17,592; Evangelical United Brethren Church with 14,182 and the Assemblies of God with 2,968. A number of these co-operate in the United Christian Council. Roman Catholic missions have not spread extensively, and in 1965 there were 26,602 Catholics in two dioceses. Muslims are estimated to number 588,000, and there are still large areas where traditional religion is practised. Since the year 1819 there has been a number of ecclesiastical schisms led at first by ex-slaves in protest against alleged discrimination. The Nigerian independent church, Church of the Lord Aladura, began missionary work in Freetown in

1947 and has since expanded its work upcountry, especially among the Mende and Kono tribes. One independent body, the God is Our Light Church, has a larger Christian community among the Kono tribe than either the Protestant or RC missions there.

DAVID B. BARRETT

C. H. Fyfe: *A History of Sierra Leone* (London 1962); K. H. Pfeffer: *Sierra Leone und Gambia* (Bonn 1958); *BM* II, 790–92; *NCE* XIII, 203; *WKL* 1335f.

SIKHS, SIKHISM. The people of the Sikhs owe their existence to the Reformer Nānak (1469–1539). Nānak was a *Hindu Kshatriya; but, perhaps under *Muslim influence, he passionately adopted the doctrine of the unity of God, was the first Hindu reformer to reject *idolatry, and regarded *caste differences as a late perversion of Hindu truth. He gave his disciples the name *sikhs* (disciples); and, holding that they would always have much to learn, he arranged that at the head of his community there should always be a *guru* (teacher).

The fifth *guru*, Arjun (d.1606), realized that the Ss needed closer organization and a written Scripture. He therefore collected a large variety of writings as the *Ādi-granth*, (original treatise). This is an untidy collection of poetry and prose; scattered through it are to be found many of the sayings of *Nānak*. The original text of *Ādi-granth* in the Gurmukhi script, is kept in the Golden Temple in Amritsar, the sacred city of the Ss, in the Punjab. Although idolatry is strictly forbidden, something like idolatrous reverence is paid daily to the *Ādi-granth*. The tenth *guru*, Govind (d.1708), organized the Ss as a quasi-military body, the *Khālsā*, 'the community of the pure', ordered that all members of the body should add to their names the title *Singh* (lion) to express their martial quality; and that they should always bear with them five objects, the names of all of which begin with the letter K: *kes*=long hair and beard; *kangha*=a comb; *kripan*=a sword or dagger; *kaccha*= shorts reaching to the knee; *kara*=a steel armband.

The martial quality of the Ss has made them acceptable as soldiers, and they have served with distinction in the Indian army, both in the British period and afterwards.

It is reckoned that there are now about seven million Ss, the great majority of whom live in the Punjab, many having fled from Pakistan in the year of Independence. The Ss have long desired to have a state of their own, with the official use of their own language. After years of agitation, partly violent, increasing pressure led the government of India in 1966 largely to yield to their requests, to the partial satisfaction of the Ss, but not to the advantage of the unity of India.

The number of Ss who have become Christians is small. The best known among them was Sādhu *Sundar Singh.

STEPHEN NEILL

Classic is M. A. Macauliffe: *The Religion of the Sikhs* (6 vols., Oxford 1909). The *Ādi-granth* was translated into English (obscurely) by Prof. E. Trumpp, with valuable introduction, in 1877. See also Krishwant Singh: *The Sikhs* (London 1953); *ERE* XI, 507–11; *NCE* XIII, 211f.

SIKKIM. Area 2,800 sq.m. Population 162,000. A princely state in the eastern Himalayas and a protectorate of the Republic of India. The original inhabitants are Lepchas, but these now number only about 8,000, while Nepalese immigrants now account for 65% of the population. *Hinduism is accordingly gaining ground at the expense of lamaistic (Tibetan) *Buddhism which, however, remains the official religion of the state and of its ruling house. Both Hinduism and Buddhism, however, are present in highly *syncretistic forms.

The Church of Scotland Mission began work in S. in 1886 and started the first elementary schools in the state as well as a high school for girls in Gangtok, the capital. Now the government also takes an active part in education.

The Church of Scotland community numbers about 500 and is part of the United Church of North India. The Free Church of Finland Mission which started work in 1891 has a community of about 300. The entry of westerners for missionary work is still much restricted, but Indian nationals are allowed in freely. The chief centres of Christian work in the state are Gangtok, Tenni (UCNI); Lachung, Luchen and Mangen (FCFM). There are twelve schools and ten dispensaries with seven foreign and 30 indigenous workers.

HENRY LEFEVER

A. McLeish: *The Frontier People of India* (London 1931); *Christian Handbook of India* 1959 (Nagpur); *ERE* XI, 511f.

SILLIMAN UNIVERSITY. See COLLEGES AND UNIVERSITIES, CHRISTIAN.

SIMONTON, ASHBEL GREEN (1833–1867), was born in West Hanover, Pennsylvania, USA, not far from Harrisburg. Named for the illustrious educator and churchman, Ashbel Green, S. more than fulfilled the expectations denoted by his name. Educated at the College of New Jersey (later to be named Princeton University) and at the Princeton Seminary, this pioneer of the modern missionary movement in Brazil was awakened to mission by the preaching of Charles Hodge. Appointed by the Presbyterian Board of Foreign Missions, then undivided by the Civil War issue, S. arrived in Rio de Janeiro on 12 August 1859, the date accepted by the Presbyterian Church of Brazil for its founding and beginning. Convinced of the intensive method of evangelism and church growth, S. founded his work solidly in Rio de Janeiro, although he included several extensive evangelistic trips in his programme. He was joined in 1860 by his sister and her husband, the Rev. A. L. Blackford, who was a valuable co-labourer in initiating a broad campaign of evangelistic itineration. In 1862 S. returned to the USA and while there married Helen Murdoch, who died shortly after giving birth to a daughter, 28 June 1864. She was buried in Rio de Janeiro.

Three years later, S. also was taken, probably by yellow fever, then the scourge of Brazil, while visiting the Blackfords in São Paulo, 9 December 1867. S. was the founder of the first Presbyterian church in Brazil, the first Protestant seminary, the first evangelical newspaper, and was instrumental in the forming of the first Presbyterian presbytery. He nurtured into full faith Jose Manuel da Conceição, the first Brazilian Presbyterian minister, whose life as *O Padre Protestante* (Protestant priest) has inspired numerous other Brazilians. S. left a booklet of sermons *Sermões Escolhidos*, as well as his *Journal* (mss) which are still widely quoted. On his deathbed S. made a prophetic observation: 'God will raise up someone to fill my place. He will do his own work with his own instruments'. The strong Protestant community of Brazil stands as witness to the accuracy of that prophecy.

ROBERT L. MCINTIRE

P. S. Landes: *Ashbel Green Simonton* (Ft. Worth 1956); R. L. McIntire: *Portrait of Half a Century* (doctoral dissertation, Princeton Seminary, 1959), pp.67–147.

SINGAPORE is an island republic, in area 217 sq.m., at the southernmost tip of the Malay peninsula. Population: 2,000,000, of whom 80% are Chinese. The rest are Malays, Indians, Sikhs, Pakistanis, Persians, Arabs, Eurasians and Europeans. Chinese religion is an amalgam of *animism, magical *Taoism, Mahāyāna *Buddhism, Confucian ancestor reverence and moralism. The S. constitution provides for a secular state. Churches work on a Malaysia-S. basis.

S. was obtained for the British in 1819 by Stamford Raffles. In the same year a *LMS station was opened, and Roman Catholic converts from Malaysia moved in. RC progress was slow until Jean Marie Beurel (1813–1872) of the *MEP brought six Christian brothers and five sisters of St. Maur (Paris) to S. in 1852. He built a cathedral and two schools, and made S. a centre of evangelization. In the late 1960s the archdiocese of Malacca-Singapore, with the two suffragan sees of Kuala-Lumpur and Penang, claimed 258,000 Catholics in Malaysia-S. (separate figures for S. alone were not available).

The first Church of England chaplain was appointed to S. by the East India Company in 1826. When China opened up in 1843, the LMS closed down their work. The small Presbyterian church, developed mainly among Europeans, started in 1856. The English Presbyterian Mission among Chinese began through local efforts of this congregation, but from 1881 Chinese work developed largely through immigration of Chinese Christians from South China, now the Malaysia-S. Synod of the Chinese Christian Church, with a Christian community around 9,000 (EP and LMS co-operate).

The Anglican church developed through European chaplaincies and grew slowly among Chinese and Indians up till the time of the Japanese occupation (1942–45). Since then emphasis has been on autonomy, indigenous priesthood and national responsibility. The Anglican Christian community in S. is around 8,000 or 9,000 (*USPG, *CMS, Australian CMS and *OMF co-operate).

The US Methodist Episcopal Mission, started in 1885 with the Englishman William *Oldham, is now the largest Protestant church in Malaysia and S., with about 10,000 community in S. alone.

Churches among Indians have grown through association with South Indian churches. The Lutheran Church of America Mission, started in 1953 for work in Malayan Chinese New Villages, assists the Lutheran church there.

The Southern Baptist Mission since 1951 has been assisting Chinese Baptist congregations formed by Baptist Christians from South China. Others include the Salvation Army, the Bible Presbyterian Church, Pentecostalists, Brethren, the SDA church and the OMF with its world headquarters in S.

The Malayan Christian Council founded in 1948 had many joint programmes and encouraged member churches to enter into new church union negotiations in 1967.

It is now the Council of Churches of Malaysia and S.

Major difficulties are in separations of churches due to language and race, weak stewardship, dependency, misunderstanding between so-called 'evangelical' Christians and others, and a narrow individualistic understanding of the gospel.

JOHN FLEMING

'Bibliography on Malaysia', *Occasional Bulletin* from the MRL, XV, 3 (March 1964), 31 pp., 363 items on Singapore, West and East Malaysia; J. R. Fleming: 'Singapore, Malaysia and Brunei' in G. H. Anderson, ed.: *Christ and Crisis in Southeast Asia* (New York 1968), pp.81–106; *BM* II, 792f.

SKREFSRUD, LARS OLSEN (1840–1910), was born at Gudbrandsdal, Norway, and died at Benagaria, Santal Parganas, India. He grew up in poverty and received little formal education. Influenced by bad companions, S. spent three years in prison. During this period he became convinced of his missionary vocation and began to study languages. Discharged from prison in 1861, he went in the following year to Berlin for six months of study, after which he was sent to India by the *Gossner Missionary Society. S., with the Dane H. P. Børresen and his wife, left the GMS in 1865; they joined the Baptist E. C. Johnson in taking up work among the Santals in 1867. S. worked with the Indian Home Mission to the Santals until 1877, when support for his work was taken over by Norwegian and Danish committees (known from 1911 as the Santal Mission of the Northern Churches).

S. was an able pioneer missionary and the leader of the small mission staff in Santal Parganas. After 23 years of missionary activity the number of Christians in the area was 8,500, and at the time of S's death 16,000. In many respects S. was ahead of his time. Although he was himself somewhat autocratic he aimed at *indigenization: 'We came to the Santals to bring them Christianity and not to take away their nationality'. He used folk music for the Santal hymn book and was the first European to master the Santali language. An effective social reformer, he took an active part in the work which resulted in Sir George Campbell's 'Regulation for the peace and the good government of the Santal Parganas' of 1872. He helped to raise the Santals' standard of living and in 1880 organized a Santal colony in Assam. S. translated the four Gospels and other books and produced a valuable *Grammar of the Santhal Language* (1873) and an ethnographic study, *The Traditions and Institutions of the Santals* (1942; in Santali 1887).

NILS BLOCH-HOELL

O. Hodne: *L. O. Skrefsrud, Missionary and Social Reformer among the Santals of Santal Parganas* (Oslo 1966).

SLAVERY has existed since the earliest recorded date of human history. It is recognized in the OT, and not directly forbidden in the NT, though the harshness of it is mitigated by the reminder that masters and slaves alike are servants of a common Master. The Qur'ān permits slavery, which has always existed on a very large scale in Islamic lands.

The problem took on a new dimension with the European voyages of discovery from the 15th century onwards. Slaves were needed in large numbers for the Spanish and Portuguese dominions in the New World. The institution was defended on the ground that, according to the doctrine of Aristotle, some men are slaves by nature, and that for them the best destiny is to become the slaves of those who are naturally masters. To this was sometimes added the absurd biblical argument that Negroes are of the race of Ham, and that the curse pronounced on Hamites in Genesis 9:25–26 is naturally passed on to all members of this race.

S. existed in Africa long before the coming of the white man. The first great slave raiders were the Arabs. The oldest slave route seems to have been that from Senegambia across the Sahara to the cities of Algeria and Tunisia. The second moved steadily up the Nile; for centuries the Christian kingdoms of Nubia and Dongola

19

opposed the progress of the slavers, but by the 19th century they had nearly reached the great lakes. From the 15th century on, the Portuguese developed the slave trade from what is now Ghana, until, with the growing power of Britain and Holland, they were driven to develop a fourth route with its terminal point in Angola. The fifth route, shared by Arabs and Portuguese, spread steadily inland in the Zambesi region. The sixth, based on Zanzibar, in the second half of the 19th century reached the head waters of the Congo. Finally, there was, and perhaps still is, the overland route from Northern Nigeria via the Sudan to the Red Sea and Arabia. There has been a tendency to exaggerate the number of slaves actually deported from Africa, but it must have been very large; and, as the methods employed by the raiders were completely ruthless, the numbers of those who died in the raids and on the way to the coast, to which must be added those who died in confinement at the coast or on shipboard, was doubtless immense. As one region after another came to be depopulated, raiders moved ever further inland, and the routes seemed to be about to meet at some central point.

The first Christian body to take a really firm stand against slavery in all its forms were the *Quakers; the cause was taken up, on a large scale and with ultimate success, by the Anglican Evangelicals headed by William Wilberforce. The first success was the judgment of Lord Mansfield in 1773 that S. is incompatible with the laws of England and that a slave who sets foot on English soil is automatically free; the second was the abolition of the slave trade in 1807; the third, the abolition of S. throughout the British dominions in 1833. S. was abolished in the USA only in 1862, and in Brazil as late as 1873. For the greater part of a century British gunboats patrolled the west, and later the east, coast of Africa, to check the trade and to free those who had been taken as slaves. Men are still living who were kidnapped into slavery by the Arabs, and set free by the British.

The journeys of David *Livingstone drew fresh attention to the evils of the trade in

Africa itself. By 1882 the Christian world had become convinced that the danger of an Arab dominion in Central Africa based on S. was so great that the only remedy against it was occupation by the European powers. The Berlin Congress of 1884 expressed in part the imperialistic ambitions of the politicians, but in part also the genuinely humanitarian aims of the western world. The gradual abolition of S. was an inevitable consequence of European occupation; it was put down in Nigeria after the British occupation in 1900, and finally in Tanzania in 1922. It is probable that S. still exists in Ethiopia, certain that it exists in Arabia, and probable that it is still fed by organized kidnapping in Africa.

There is no other subject on which the mind of the western world has been so completely changed in modern times. What was generally accepted without comment five centuries ago is now the object of universal condemnation and detestation. It is to be hoped that the same change may come about in other parts of the world. But it is unlikely that progress will be maintained unless the minds of men go back constantly to the Scriptures, in which alone the true nature and dignity of man as the child of God are revealed.

STEPHEN NEILL

R. Coupland: *Wilberforce* (2nd ed., London 1945); *Encyclopaedia Britannica:* art. 'Slavery'; S. C. Neill: *Colonialism and Christian Missions* (London 1966); *ERE* XI, 595–631; *NCE* XIII, 281–87.

SLESSOR, MARY MITCHELL (1848–1915). Born at Gilcomston, Aberdeen, Scotland; died at Use, Calabar, E. Nigeria. In 1876 she was sent by the Foreign Mission Board of the United Presbyterian Church of Scotland to the mission at Calabar. First she taught at the schools in Duke Town and Creek Town. Although the slave trade had been suppressed, it had left the tribes of the Calabar area deeply demoralised. The unrestricted sale of trade gin and rum helped to keep them in this condition. Away from Calabar itself warfare between towns, twin-murder and human sacrifice

were universally practised. MS approached these problems as a pioneer, meeting people unaccompanied on their own ground and living among them 'native fashion'.

From 1888 to 1902 she worked inland among the Okoyong tribe. She started a school and preached as she had opportunity; but she was always ready to anticipate and settle quarrels and in other ways prevent bloodshed. She adopted many of the twins she had rescued and brought them up in her household. Eventually she persuaded the Okoyong people to overcome their mistrust of others and to trade with Calabar. In 1891 she was appointed the first consular agent of Okoyong under the Niger Coast Protectorate. Afterwards she moved further inland to the Enyong Creek and beyond. Here too, she combined missionary work with the administration of justice.

MS saw her work as preparing for the settled ministry which should care for congregations and build Christian communities. By her own character and personality she had persuaded a whole people to revolutionize its way of life, so as to make it accord with the Christian revelation.

JOHN GOODWIN

W. P. Livingstone: *Mary Slessor of Calabar* (London 1916).

SMITH, EDWIN WILLIAMS (1876–1957), was born at Aliwal North, Cape Colony, South Africa, where his parents were missionaries. He studied at Enfield College, England, entered the Primitive Methodist ministry in 1897, in 1898 went as a missionary to Africa serving in Lesotho, Cape Colony, and from 1902 among the Ba-ila of Zambia. S. joined the BFBS in 1916, first as secretary for Italy, then for western Europe; literary superintendent from 1932 till retirement in 1939. During 1939–43 S. lectured on African anthropology and history at Kennedy School of Missions and Fisk University in USA. He was president of the Royal Anthropological Institute, 1934–35, founding member of the International African Institute, editor of *Africa* and the *Journal of the Royal African Society*, recipient of Rivers Memorial Medal of the Royal Anthropological Society, 1939, and of an honorary DD degree from the University of Toronto, 1942. This great missionary and Africanist wrote sixteen and edited three books on African anthropology, languages, biography and history. Among them were: *The Golden Stool* (1927), *The Life and Times of Daniel Lindley* (1949), *African Ideas of God* (1950), and (with A. M. Dale) *The Ila-speaking Peoples of Northern Rhodesia* (1920).

PER HASSING

SOCIAL CHANGE. See RAPID SOCIAL CHANGE.

SOCIETIES FOR MISSIONS. See MISSION BOARDS AND SOCIETIES.

SOCIETY FOR PROMOTING CHRISTIAN KNOWLEDGE, THE (SPCK), was founded in 1698–99, for the purposes inherent in its name, by Dr Thomas Bray, a Church of England priest, and four laymen. As its founders intended, its mission has been primarily concerned with literature and education. First as pioneer of free schools and local libraries, then in publishing, distributing, and promoting the use of Christian literature on a worldwide scale, it sought in each generation to serve the church's needs, which have included some 200 Prayer Book translations. From 1710 till 1825 it supported the *Danish-Halle Mission, staffed by German Lutherans, in South India, and in the 19th century gave substantial financial aid to nearly 100 new Anglican dioceses.

Its chief overseas objective in these days is to help Anglican or united churches, particularly in Africa, Asia, the West Indies and the South Pacific, to develop their own complete systems of Christian communication through all mass media. This it now does in partnership with the interdenominational *USCL through an organization combining both, Joint Action for Christian Literature Overseas, which is linked also, through the Christian Literature Council of the Conference of Missionary

Societies in Great Britain and Ireland, with the general missionary societies. Vast as this shared overseas undertaking is, the SPCK is still dedicated equally to its home mission, of promoting Christian knowledge among persons of all kinds and ages. For this it has a publishing house, a growing chain of bookshops (as also overseas), a film theatre and audio-visual aids centre, and a service for church bookstalls.

F. N. DAVEY

W. O. B. Allen and E. McClure: *Two Hundred Years: the History of the Society for Promoting Christian Knowledge, 1698–1898* (London 1898); W. K. Lowther Clarke: *A History of the S.P.C.K.*, with an Epilogue by F. N. Davey (London 1959).

SOCIETY FOR THE PROPAGATION OF THE GOSPEL IN FOREIGN PARTS. See UNITED SOCIETY FOR THE PROPAGATION OF THE GOSPEL.

SOCIETY OF AFRICAN MISSIONS, THE, a body of RC missionary priests, was founded at Lyons, France, in 1856 by Mgr Marion de *Brésillac. Its first mission station to survive was founded by Fr *Borghero in Dahomey. The missionaries spread east and west from there along the African coast, until finally they worked in Liberia, the Ivory Coast, Ghana, Togoland, Dahomey and Nigeria, north and west. They also founded missions in Egypt. They still work in all these countries and number about 2,000 priests and brothers. Their founder had one aim, to found a native church on a native priesthood. Today the African priests and bishops in these areas are numerous.

The climate was the major factor till within living memory; perhaps it still is. Tropical diseases continually threatened achievement and prevented expansion. A missionary who had time and survived long enough to learn and to use the local language and dialect was a rare exception. Though the wish not to produce Europeanized Africans, as distinct from African Christians, was voiced by superiors, the possibility of avoiding this outcome hardly existed. *Missiology had not been thought of. The European traders were spreading throughout the country. The Africans were hungry for books and for medicine. Bricks and malaria stood high on the list of daily concerns. Fr Carlo Zappa an Italian at Lokoja and then at Asaba, both on the Niger, 1884–1915, tried to do something more, writing a French-Ibo dictionary, building up African Christian families, and African Christian communities. Later Fr François Aupiais in Dahomey studied the natural religious disposition of the African and looked forward to a radically African Christian society. This was in the 1930s and 40s; in 1945 Fr Aupiais was voted a representative of Dahomey to the French Constituent Assembly. More recently in Nigeria Fr Kevin Carroll has founded a school of African and Christian wood carvers. But for the most part the missionaries had not been trained with any special foresight, until after 1945. Irish, French and Dutch, they inevitably often cultivated their own national dispositions (Eastern Nigeria, where the *Holy Ghost Fathers worked, is sometimes called Little Ireland).

These missionaries still contribute a network of parishes and schools, and appear to be indispensable both to the newly independent states and to the church in them. They now serve a plural society. Perhaps a time will come when they are no longer needed. It is hardly in sight. Perhaps the future West African society will be multi-racial.

JOHN M. TODD

J. M. Todd: *African Mission* (London 1962).

SOCIETY OF JESUS. See JESUITS.

SOCIETY OF MISSIONARIES OF AFRICA. See WHITE FATHERS.

SOCIETY OF THE DIVINE WORD (Latin abbreviation SVD), better known as Divine Word Missionaries, is a Catholic missionary congregation founded in Steyl, Netherlands, on 8 September 1875, by the Rev. Arnold Janssen (1837–1909), of Goch, Germany. Members take the vows of pover-

ty, chastity and obedience, and are generally assigned to their posts for life. The policy of accepting men of all nations into its ranks quickly made the society international and inter-racial; today it has numerous Asians and Africans among its members. It also pioneered in training American Negroes for the priesthood. Although engaged in all the usual types of missionary work, the society early stressed a scientific approach and in 1906 founded the internationally known anthropological and linguistic review called *Anthropos*. Today there is an Anthropos Institute with members strategically placed around the world. Some twenty members of the society also hold degrees in *missiology. In 1966 the society had 26 bishops, 2,977 priests and 1,410 brothers at work in 34 countries. An additional 7,415 candidates were preparing for the priesthood and brotherhood.

RALPH M. WILTGEN, SVD

Word in the World 1966 (Techny, Illinois 1966); E. J. Edwards: *Herald of the Word: Life of Arnold Janssen* (Techny 1951); *RGG* VI, 370.

SOCIOLOGY AND MISSIONS. Sociology is the study of human society, its institutions, and the interaction of human beings in group relationships. During the 20th century it has become a part of the curriculum in many colleges and seminaries where ministers, missionaries and lay Christians have been educated. Sociologists do their work through field research, theoretical analysis of social conditions and problems, and application of resulting facts, generalizations and principles to life situations.

Social thought has a long history, but the term S. was first used by Auguste Comte in 1837 when the industrial revolutions were bringing changes and disorganization within old institutions which called for social amelioration and reform. S., as a social science, has been secular, humanistic, humanitarian and positivistic. Some have considered it as offering alternative or better ways for the improvement of society and facing of social problems than has the church. On the other hand, Christians have found its methods and techniques valuable in implementing religious motivation and purpose. For some, an undergraduate degree in S. has preceded professional and graduate study in religion.

S. deals with the social structures and processes in family, economic, political, religious and educational systems as well as in aesthetics, language, group co-operation and conflict, and with areas of specialization such as rural life, urbanization, population, poverty, crime, suicide, mass communication, social control, problems of children, youth and age, and others.

For many decades, S. was limited to European countries and the USA, but since the second world war it has been developing in other places, notably Latin America, Japan, China and India. Missionaries have had a part in introducing it, and in supporting its use in community development, village and minority group studies, and in understanding and helping to direct social change.

The various church bodies, including agencies for missions, have utilized sociological material and method in preparing resolutions, pronouncements, and programmes on the social order, in involving local churches in community work and social action, and in encouraging research to discover human needs and the impact of the Christian community on social relationships and behaviour.

HARRIET R. REYNOLDS

H. Becker and H. E. Barnes: *Social Thought from Lore to Science* (3 vols., 3rd ed. 1961); P. L. Berger: *Invitation to Sociology* (Garden City, New York 1963); R. K. Merton, L. Broom and L. S. Cottrell, Jr: *Sociology Today: Problems and Prospects* (New York 1959); J. M. Yinger: *Religion, Society and the Individual* (New York 1957).

SOLOMON ISLANDS. See PACIFIC ISLANDS.

SOMALIA, a republic, formerly the two territories of British Somaliland and Italian Somaliland, is a sparsely populated area of 270,135 sq.m. occupying the extreme eastern horn of Africa. Its population of 2,660,000 (1967) are Somalis of the Esa, Ishaak, Mijertein, Hawiya and Sab tribes, ethnically related to the Ogaden and West Somali tribes who fall largely in Ethiopia and Kenya respectively. Virtually the entire population is Muslim. Roman Catholic work dates from the erection of a prefecture apostolic in 1904, and in 1965 there were 3,500 RCs, mostly foreigners. Anglican work attached to the Episcopal church in the Sudan has been limited to chaplaincy work; the only two Protestant missions are the *SIM (29 missionaries in 1966) and the Somalia Mennonite Mission (28 missionaries in 1966), with only a handful of adherents. Political pressure against evangelism has restricted all aspects of the work.

DAVID B. BARRETT

BM II, 793–95; *NCE* XIII, 424.

SOMALILAND, FRENCH, renamed TERRITORY OF THE AFARS AND ISSAS in 1967 to distinguish it from Somali territories, is a French Overseas Territory situated on the Gulf of Aden at the entrance to the Red Sea; its 8,492 sq.m. of elevated arid plains support a population of 81,000 (1967), over half of whom live in the capital Djibouti. A RC prefecture was begun in 1914, and Catholics in 1965 numbered 5,500, mostly among the 7,000 Europeans. There are no Protestant missions although attempts have been considered.

DAVID B. BARRETT

BM II, 795f.; *NCE* XIII, 424.

SONG, JOHN. See SUNG, JOHN SHANG-CHIEH.

SOUL. The term S. is used in a number of different senses. In the nature-religions, it is often understood as the vital force, which is linked to particular parts of the body (e.g. heart, throat, kidneys) or with their functions (breath, pulse, etc.). This is the 'physical S.', which passes away with its bodily associates. Alongside this exists an imperishable factor, the free or detachable

S. which, while a man is still alive, can temporarily absent itself from him (e.g. in sleep), and at his death permanently severs itself from him. This S. is also conceived of as the shadow, or as a fiery spark, etc. After death, it may enter into an animal (snake, bird or butterfly) or continue in human form (as ancestor or ghost). Some form of existence after death is generally assumed. In so far as the S. exists in human form, it is dependent on the conduct of the survivors (mentioning of the name, offerings). In course of time the souls come together in a collective S., or pass away completely. Among many races the souls are thought to be gathered together in a home of the souls, from which they are sent out to be reincarnated upon earth. In the light of this it is easy to understand how belief in the pre-existence of souls comes into being. In this dualistic understanding of S., physical and non-physical ideas are held together.

In the higher religions a monistic understanding of the S. prevails. So in *Hinduism the *ātman* (originally 'breath') is the individual indestructible factor, which after death will be reborn in other existences. In early *Buddhism the S. is a bundle of ever-varying 'elements of being' which have no metaphysical significance.

The aim of these religions varies. In the nature-religions, the aim is to preserve the life-force and to increase it. The detachable S. which has been set free by death, in so far as it can exercise an influence on the living, is either feared or honoured, or rendered favourable by the offering of worship. Hinduism strives for the cessation of separate existence, and the return of the S. to the Absolute (Brahman). In Buddhism the S. is regarded as irrelevant, and is judged unfavourably, in so far as it serves as a hindrance to men in the quest of illumination.

In missionary theology, care must be taken to note that the idea of the S. can easily lead to a Platonic understanding of man's situation; for this reason stress must always be laid on the new creation of man in his entirety.

ERNST DAMMANN

A. Hultkrantz: *Conceptions of the Soul among North American Indians* (Dissertation, Stockholm 1953); A. E. Jensen: *Mythos und Kult bei Naturvölkern* (Wiesbaden 1960²); H. Fischer: *Studien über Seelenvorstellungen in Ozeanien* (München 1965); *ERE* XI, 725–31.

SOUTH AFRICA, THE REPUBLIC OF,

has an area of 471,455 sq.m. and an officially estimated population (1966) of 18,298,000 (12,465,000 Africans; 3,481,000 whites; 1,805,000 Coloureds and 547,000 Asians). The majority religion is Protestant Christianity.

The Dutch settlement was established in 1652 and soon afterwards a Hottentot girl was baptized and married a European. The sole bar to intermarriage, to which the colonists were a century later diametrically opposed, was only the question of religion. The Dutch Reformed Church (DRC) began work among imported slaves in 1658, but their baptism was not favoured by the general public since baptized slaves were set free.

The first missionary was the *Moravian, Georg *Schmidt (1737–44), after whose departure missionary work was abandoned until the Moravians returned in 1793. At about the same time a missionary spirit was awakened among the colonists by the Rev. H. P. van Lier and especially the Rev. M. C. Vos (DRC) whose activities led to more serious work among the Hottentots after 1794.

The first missionary of the *LMS, Dr J. T. *Van der Kemp, arrived in 1799 and co-operated with the colonists in the S.A. Missionary Society until differences of policy forced a separation. Thereafter the LMS established stations on and beyond the eastern and northern borders of Cape Colony. The work was supervised by the famous Dr J. *Philip, who also assisted the American Zulu Mission of the *ABCFM (1835) and the *PEMS (1829). Wesleyan Methodist missions were initiated by Barnabas Shaw (Namaqualand 1816) and William Shaw (Kaffraria 1823) and later spread to all parts of SA. The Glasgow

Missionary Society entered the Ciskei in 1821 and the Scottish Presbyterian mission at Lovedale played a significant role in African education. Anglican missions began in earnest only after the arrival of Bishop R. Gray in 1848. Other major Protestant societies included the *Rhenish Mission (1829), *Berlin Mission (1834), Norwegian Society (1850), the Hermannsburg Mission (1854), Swiss Mission (1875), Church of Sweden (1885) and *Salvation Army (1890). Roman Catholic mission work was commenced in the last quarter of the 19th century and has made tremendous strides. The 1911 census shows only 37,242 Catholics out of a non-white population of 4,697,152 of whom 1,438,075 were Protestants. In 1881 a separate DR daughter church was established among the Coloureds. DRC started mission work in earnest among the Africans after 1860. Its activities extend over fourteen different areas in Africa (including RSA) and make use of seventeen different languages. The Reformed Church (*Gereformeerde Kerk*) started missionary work in 1913.

The main characteristic of the work in the 20th century is the transition from mission projects to churches. The rapid growth of Christianity was assisted by the advent of many overseas missionaries and by the disintegration of African tribal life and traditional religion as a result of contact with western civilization. The clash of ideologies and policies often affected the young church. A feature of the 20th century has been the proliferation of *African independent churches and sects which numbered 320 in 1913 and nearly 3,000 in 1966. There are 78 churches officially recognized by the state. The attraction of the independent churches is such that they accounted for 20.1% of the total African population in 1960. In 1946 they constituted only 9.6% of the total African population. Their attraction is due to their use of indigenous methods of communication, the magical personality of the leader or prophet, ancestor worship, baptism as a repeatable purification rite in which sin is ceremonially washed or taken away, and

'holy' places. Factors which have brought them into being include the foreignness of Christianity, denominational divisiveness, the racial issue, social and economic upheaval, visions, dreams, and injunctions of 'the spirit'. There have been several attempts to co-ordinate these bodies, the latest being the African Independent Churches Association.

It is impossible in modern RSA sharply to distinguish the 'mission' from the church in general. The DRC has given autonomy to its African and Coloured daughter churches which, in principle at least, are free from missionary control. Some major denominations are independent of overseas finance and control but have a racially mixed membership. Local congregations are generally segregated but in the higher levels of church administration the non-whites have no separate ecclesiastical existence. Africans are also assuming increasing responsibilities within certain denominations: the Rev. S. M. Mokitimi was President of the Methodist Conference in 1964 and the Rt. Rev. A. H. Zulu became Anglican Bishop of Zululand in 1966.

Ecumenism is making gradual progress. The Inter-Denomination African Ministers Association of SA aims to co-ordinate African forces for evangelistic work. The Christian Institute, founded in 1963, is an inter-racial and undenominational body which promotes inter-racial contact and the study of the racial situation in the light of Scripture. It is giving special attention to improved theological training for independent church leaders. In 1965 the Student Christian Association of SA adjusted itself to government policy and dissolved into four separate movements for Afrikaners, Coloureds, Africans and English. In 1966 the English group adopted the basis of faith of the International Fellowship of Evangelical Students, whereupon more ecumenically-minded students established the Universities Christian Movement with the official support of five denominations. This became politically involved.

At the end of 1967 four denominations

(Anglican, Congregational, Methodist, Presbyterian) were engaged in church union conversations, while the Anglicans and RCs are also having discussions. A union was consummated in 1967 of the Congregational Union of SA, LMS and the Bantu Congregational Church (formerly American Board). Negotiations are also proceeding for the amalgamation of the Presbyterian Church of SA (mainly European), the Bantu Presbyterian Church (formerly CSM) and the Tsonga Presbyterian Church (formerly Swiss Mission). The African daughter churches of the DRC have united and train their ministers and evangelists in five ethnic seminaries. The Federal Theological Seminary of SA, near Alice, provides a common training for African students of the Anglican, Congregational, Methodist and Presbyterian Churches, who reside in denominational colleges on a single campus. The Lutheran Theological Seminary at Umpumulo is an ecumenical effort on denominational lines. The RCs train African priests at St. Peter's, Hammanskraal, and the African Methodist Episcopal Church at the Wilberforce Institution, Evaton. There is only one faculty of divinity for non-whites, namely that of the University College of Fort Hare. An Association of Southern African Theological Institutions has been formed, largely on the initiative of the *TEF.

Two government measures have vitally affected the Christian mission. The *Group Areas Act*, which attempts to separate residential areas racially, has necessitated vast church-rebuilding projects. The *Bantu Education Act* (1953) relieved the churches of the control of African schools. This extension of state control is analogous to developments elsewhere in Africa but provoked opposition because of its association with *apartheid*. Although the percentage of school-going children has been raised considerably, the government is accused of not having given adequate attention to the development of secondary school education, in spite of the more extensive facilities at university level (which however is ethnically oriented). One of the major problems is the lack of sufficient and adequately trained teachers for the secondary schools.

GERHARDUS C. OOSTHUIZEN

J. C. du Plessis: *A History of Christian Missions in South Africa* (London 1911, reprint Cape Town 1965); G. B. A. Gerdener: *Recent developments in the South African Field* (Cape Town, Pretoria 1958); C. P. Groves: *The Planting of Christianity in Africa* (4 vols., London 1948–1958); K. S. Latourette: *A History of the Expansion of Christianity*, Vol. V (New York and London 1943); G. C. Oosthuizen: *Post-Christianity in Africa* (London 1968); W. Schmidt: *Süd-Afrika* (Bonn 1958); B. G. M. Sundkler: *Bantu Prophets in South Africa* (London, rev. ed. 1961); H. J. Becken, ed.: *Our Approach to the Independent Church Movement in South Africa* (Mimeographed Lectures, Johannesburg, Christian Institute, 1965); Periodical: *South African Outlook* (formerly *Christian Express*); *BM* II, 25–36; *NCE* XIII, 477–79; *WKL*, 1402–04.

SOUTH AFRICA GENERAL MISSION, since 1965 renamed 'Africa Evangelical Fellowship (SAGM)', was founded in London in 1889 by Spencer Walton, Mr. and Mrs. George Osborn-Howe and the Scottish - South African leader Andrew Murray the younger, for evangelism and the strengthening of spiritual life in Southern Africa. Interdenominational (in Murray's words, 'the child of no denomination but the ally of all') and a *'faith' mission, not appealing for funds, its missionaries at first worked among all races: British troops, African tribes and mineworkers, Indian plantation and factory labourers. In the early 20th century it entered Northern and Southern Rhodesia (Zambia and Rhodesia), Nyasaland (Malawi) and Angola, but relinquished its work among whites to other bodies. In 1906 an American council was formed. By the mid-1960s SAGM had 265 missionaries, from South Africa, Britain, Canada, USA, Australia and New Zealand, serving in all countries of Southern Africa except Mozambique (entered 1936, missionaries excluded 1959). Activities include assistance to mission-founded churches now independent; medical work (five hospitals, leprosaria); the Johannesburg Bible Institute; a Christian press, radio programmes and evangelistic missions. From earliest days it has been closely connected with the *Keswick Convention, and the emphasis on the deepening of spiritual life has extended its influence far beyond its direct activities.

JOHN POLLOCK

SOUTH AMERICA INDIAN MISSION, THE, was founded in 1914 by Joseph A. Davis, with a view to reaching some of the many Amerindian tribes which had remained entirely untouched by the gospel. From 1919 to 1939 the mission was known as the Inland South America Missionary Union; from 1939 by its present title. With about 100 foreign workers, the mission now reaches 30 little-known tribes in Peru, Brazil, Bolivia and Colombia, and maintains two Bible schools, with a view to training converts to carry the gospel to their own people. Two missionaries were killed in 1930 by the Nhambiquara Indians. The aim of the mission remains that of pioneering in as yet unreached and unevangelized regions. Headquarters: P.O. Box 769, Lake Worth, Florida 33460, USA.

EDITORS

SOUTH AMERICAN MISSIONARY SOCIETY, THE, a society of the Church of England, was founded in 1844 by Captain Allen *Gardiner, RN, with the aim of making known the gospel of Jesus Christ among Indian tribes and other inhabitants of South America and to train national Christians for spiritual leadership. The first mission station was established at Keppel, one of the Falkland Islands, in 1854. In 1869 Waite Stirling, who later became first Anglican bishop in South America, extended the work to a station at Ushuwia, Tierra del Fuego. The Rev. Allen Gardiner, son of the founder, began chaplaincy work in 1860 in Lota, Chile. The SAMS eventually established over 30 chaplaincies throughout the continent. Barbrooke *Grubb pioneered in the Paraguayan Chaco in 1889 and

19*

established a mission station in the Argentine Chaco in 1914. Work among the Araucanian Indians of Chile began in 1894. Over 100 SAMS missionaries work today in the Republics of Chile, Paraguay and Argentina. There is an evangelistic, educational, medical and agricultural ministry to the Indians of Araucania and the Paraguayan and Argentine Chaco, and a pastoral, educational and radio outreach in some of the cities and towns. In 1915 the first Araucanian was ordained into the Anglican ministry; in 1964 the first Lenguas of Paraguay, and in 1966 the first Matacos of Argentina, in addition to national evangelists, licensed lay-readers and teachers. SAMS headquarters are at 157 Waterloo Road, London, S.E.1.

HENRY SUTTON

W. Mann: *An Unquenched Flame* (London 1968).

SOUTH INDIA, CHURCH OF. See INDIA, CHURCH OF SOUTH.

SOUTH WEST AFRICA covers an area of 381,261 sq.m., and stretches from the Orange River in the south to the Okavango and Kunene Rivers in the north. The Atlantic Ocean in the west and the Kalahari desert in the east are the other natural boundaries. The population is only 560,000 people (census 1966), of whom 11,762 are Bushmen, 44,350 Dama, 34,800 Nama, all of them Khoisan-speaking, 35,350 Herero, 239,360 Ovambo, 43,710 Okavango clusters, all of them Bantu-speaking, 23,960 Basters-Coloureds, who are Afrikaans-speaking, and 73,460 Whites.

In the year 1485 the Portuguese discovered the country. It was only during the 17th and 18th centuries, however that the land was populated by the various tribes, some having entered from the north, others from the south. In 1884 Bismarck extended the protection of the German Reich over the possessions of the German merchant, Lüderitz; the colony called 'South West Africa' came into being. After the first world war (1919), the country was transferred as C-Mandate (Art.22) to South

Africa by the League of Nations, a mandate no longer recognized by the UN as legally valid.

The first missionaries temporarily entering the region were of the *LMS, one of whom was H. Schmelen, who founded Bethanien in 1814 and who had asked the *Rhenish Missionary Society to work there. In 1842 the first RMS missionaries arrived (C. H. *Hahn) and commenced working among the Herero and Nama. Whereas their work among the Nama soon proved to be successful, they encountered many difficulties in the beginning in their work among the Herero.

Various tribal wars, particularly those of 1863 and those from 1880 to 1890, and later the massive Herero-insurrection as well as the first and second world wars, prevented the RMS from rendering steady and progressive work. Hence it was only in 1957 that the Evangelical Lutheran Church in South West Africa (Rhenish Mission Church) could be constituted, which today has 102,422 members from five different races with 32 national pastors (WCH 1968).

In the year 1870, the pioneer missionary, C. H. Hahn, called the Finnish Mission to the country, which, especially under the great missionary M. Rautanen, started admirable work among the Ambo tribes. In 1957 the Evangelical Lutheran Ovambokavango Church was constituted; it has a membership of 156,204, which is served by 83 national pastors (WCH 1968).

The Roman Catholic mission began its work in the year 1896 (*OMI and Oblates of St. Francis of Sales). And finally, in 1924, the Anglican church began its missionary work among the Okavango tribes.

Large separatist movements were experienced by the RMS only. In 1946 approximately 4,000 Nama joined the African Methodist Episcopal Church (AMEC), partly because they were dissatisfied with the slow advances made in training African pastors. In 1955 the Herero founded a national church, the Oruuano, which has, however, split once more, as the tension between the main tribes was too great. The Mbanderu founded the 'Church of Africa' without actually being able to consolidate themselves up till now. (Precise figures not available: the Oruuano has between 3,000 and 5,000 members).

When in 1957 the Evangelical Lutheran Church in South West Africa was constituted, the Basters of Rehoboth founded a 'Rhenish Church' (approximately 3,000–4,000 members), as they did not wish to become part of a Bantu church. The Rhenish Church afterwards split again into two groups. In 1968 all these splinter groups again requested the co-operation of the RMS for the training of their future pastors.

The latest statistics (WCH 1968) reveal the following church membership in SWA: Lutherans 258,626; Dutch Reformed 42,688; Anglican 38,000; Roman Catholic 76,000; Others 28,892.

THEO SUNDERMEIER

J. P. van S. Bruwer: *South West Africa: The Disputed Land* (Cape Town, etc. 1966); *BM* II, 801–03.

SOUTHERN RHODESIA. See RHODESIA.

SOVIET UNION. See UNION OF SOVIET SOCIALIST REPUBLICS.

SPANGENBERG, AUGUST GOTTLIEB (1704–1792), was born as the son of a Lutheran pastor in Klettenberg, Harz, in central Germany. Originally it was his intention to study law; but after his conversion in 1722 he changed over to theology. Through his meeting with Count *Zinzendorf in 1727 he was won over permanently to the church of the Moravian Brethren, and before long was an outstanding disciple and trusted colleague of the Count. In 1732 S. accepted a call to serve as Junior Lecturer in the University of Halle, but in the following year was dismissed, by order of the royal cabinet, because of the brotherly fellowship which he maintained with dissenters. This marked the beginning of his 60 years of service with the church of the Brethren. In Holland, England and Denmark, he obtained charters for the establishment of Moravian colonies in Surinam, Georgia and Ste. Croix. In 1735–39, 1744 and 1751–62 he was himself in America, and undertook the founding and supervision of these colonies. He adopted the manner of life of a farmer and a hunter, and thus came into close contact with many dissenters who had become exiled from Europe by reason of their faith—mainly Schwenckfeldians, Menonites, Quakers and Dunkers. Supported by Zinzendorf he set himself to the task of uniting all these groups, and thus became the pioneer of the *ecumenical movement in America. Of decisive importance was his meeting in Georgia in 1737 with John *Wesley who owed to him his insights into evangelical truth. Equally great was his significance for missions among non-Christians. In 1736 he baptized the first three converts in the island of St. Thomas. In 1739 he secured the sending out of C. H. Rauch as the first missionary among the Indians in Pennsylvania. His book on missionary theory, *Instructions for the Brethren and Sisters who serve the Gospel among the Heathen* (1784), is important. As bishop (1744) he contributed in decisive fashion to the final organization of the Moravian churches in the English-speaking countries. After Zinzendorf's death in 1762, S. returned finally to Europe as his successor.

The organization of the church of the Brethren had been 'monarchical', with all authority concentrated in the hands of a single person. By transforming this into a collegial system, and by setting the movement free from certain tendencies to uncontrolled 'enthusiasm' by which it was threatened, S. gave the community the inward and outward character which it has preserved until the present day. On his deathbed his last testament was the challenge, 'Do not forget Africa'.

PETER BEYERHAUS

Th. Bechler: *A. G. Spangenberg und die Mission* (Herrnhut 1933); *RGG* VI, 222f.

SPANISH EQUATORIAL AFRICA. See EQUATORIAL GUINEA.

SPANISH SAHARA (or, including the small territory of Ifni, Spanish West Africa) is a territory of 115,780 sq.m. on the northwest African coast sandwiched between Mauritania and Morocco, both of which claim the area as their own, and Algeria; it contains the world's richest and largest untapped deposits of phosphates. Estimated population (1967) is 101,000. Major tribal groups are the Imragen, Delim, Regeibat and Tekna, 100% Muslim. About 5,400 Spaniards live here, almost all Roman Catholics. There is no organized Protestant missionary work.

DAVID B. BARRETT

SPEER, ROBERT E. (1867–1947), was born of Scottish and Scots-Irish ancestry in Huntington, Pennsylvania, USA. His father was a lawyer and a member of Congress. The home was Presbyterian and deeply religious. S. graduated from Princeton in 1889. While there he became a member of the youthful *SVM. He entered Princeton Theological Seminary but, before he finished the course, to fulfil his missionary purpose he joined the staff of the Board of Foreign Missions of the Presbyterian Church in the USA. With it he continued, in later years as its senior secretary, until 1937, when, because of age, he retired. He not only helped shape the policies of his board, but as well was prominent in the entire Protestant foreign missionary movement. From 1916 to 1937 he was chairman of the *Committee on Cooperation in Latin America. For a term he was Moderator of his church. S. was a favourite speaker at student missionary conferences and preached in many preparatory schools, colleges and universities. A prodigious reader, he wrote many books, chiefly on topics and biographies related to foreign missions and on the life and teachings of Christ. Vigorous physically and mentally, stalwart in his loyalty to Christ, he was outstanding in the world Christian leadership of his generation.

KENNETH SCOTT LATOURETTE

R. E. Speer: *What Constitutes a Missionary Call?* (New York 1918), *The Finality of*

Jesus Christ (New York 1933); W. R. Wheeler: *A Man Sent from God: A Biography of Robert E. Speer* (Westwood, New Jersey 1956).

SPIRITISM, though met with extensively in various parts of the world, is specially strongly represented in Brazil. Here S. springs from two separate origins, on one side European S., on the other the African religions. The source of the first stream is to be found in the USA, and dates from 1848 (the Fox sisters). It was, however, the Frenchman Allan Kardec (Léon H. D. Rivail) who worked out the doctrine (1854) which is influential in Brazil at the present time. The central idea is that communication with discarnate spirits is possible, and that there are varied forms of continued existence in different worlds. This form of S. has been found in Brazil from 1865 onwards, and considerably extended its influence at the end of the century. This form is known as Kardeism.

The African stream has its source among the Negroes settled in Brazil. Its origin is Bantu. The Yoruba and the Fon have kept their own religions, while the Bantu from the Congo region and Angola have moved in the direction of new forms. The Candomblés or Voodoos have remained very near to the ancient religions, and must not be confused with the other S. of Negro origin —Umbanda or Kimbanda. This stream is characterized by a ritual *syncretism with Roman Catholicism.

The two forms of African S. are not very different from one another in the matter of rites and worship. However, the Umbanda is more dynamic in character, and better adapted to modern methods, while the Kimbanda, remaining nearer to the African origins, is losing ground.

The African influence in the popular form of S. lays stress on the importance of rites (initiation, sacrifices, singing and dancing). Umbanda is characterized by dancing accompanied by spirit possession and by the large number of statues (borrowed for the most part from the RC veneration of saints). It is possible here to identify also survivals of Amerindian influence (from the pre-Columbian population).

The two streams of this form of mediumistic religion have joined, and now in Brazil form a kind of continuum from the world of the proletariat up to the level of the intellectuals. Powerful federations have come into existence, especially in the large cities. They possess important means of communication—magazines, radio and television programmes, and an impressive network of charitable and medical services.

Since 1940 the progress of S. in numbers of adherents has been considerable. Officially 2% of the population has registered itself as belonging to these movements, but certainly the actual proportion is higher, since it is by no means rare for the same person to be both RC and Spiritist.

The growth of S. on the popular level, and this is the form which is most widely extended, is a phenomenon of city life. It must be understood as meeting a need for psychological and social integration, strongly felt by populations of rural origin, which have carried out a mass migration to the great cities.

See also VOODOOISM.

F. HOUTART

R. Bastide: 'Le Spiritisme au Brésil' in *Archives de Sociologie des Religions* XXIV (1967), pp.3–16, *Les Religions Africaines au Brésil* (Paris 1960); C. P. de Camargo: *Aspectos Sociologicos del Espiritismo en Saô Paulo* (Fribourg 1961); V. Lanternari: *The Religions of the Oppressed* (London 1963).

STEPHENS, THOMAS (c.1547–1619), an English *Jesuit, was the first English member of his society to become a missionary, and may have been the first Englishman to reside for any length of time in India. He arrived in India in 1579 and spent the greater part of a long life of service in the island of Salsette in the neighbourhood of Bombay. Here he made himself master of the Konkani language, of which he wrote a grammar; but is chiefly famous for his lengthy poem the *Kristu Purāna*. This enormous work in 10,962 strophes is written in a fairly simple, though poetic, style. It contains a summary of the OT, a life of Christ, and an introduction to Christian teaching. In spite of the date at which it was written, it has been found permanently useful for the work of Christian instruction. It was edited by J. S. Saldanha (Mangalore 1907) with biographical introduction, English summary of the text and vocabulary. S. died in Goa in 1619.

STEPHEN NEILL

G. Schurhammer: 'Thomas Stephens 1549–1619' in *The Month* NS XIII (1955), pp.197–210; *DNB* Suppl. iii, 355; *LTK* IX, 1054; *NCE* XIII, 702.

STERN, HENRY AARON (1820–1885), was born at Unterreichenbach, near Gelnhausen, Germany. His parents were strict Jews. After a commercial training he came to London in 1839, where he was converted through the LSPCJ, and was baptized in 1840. In 1844 the society sent him to Iraq and Persia, where he travelled widely and made some converts. In 1853 S. became head of the society's mission at Constantinople, where he ministered to Jews who were persecuted and demoralized through the Crimean war. In 1856 he became one of the few Europeans to penetrate to the interior of S. Arabia. In 1860 he visited King Theodore of Ethiopia, who gave permission for J. M. *Flad's work among the Falashas (Ethiopian Jews), provided that converts were baptized in the Ethiopian church. From 1863 to 1868 S. was imprisoned and ill-treated by the king, who felt that he had been offended by the British government. From 1870 S. worked as senior missionary of his society in London. He was outstanding as a discoverer of opportunities for missionary work and as a leader and organizer.

JOHN GOODWIN

A. A. Isaacs: *Biography of the Rev. Henry Aaron Stern, D.D.* (London 1886); H. A. Stern: *Wandering among the Falashas in Abyssinia* (London 1862); *DNB* LIV, 197.

STEWART, JAMES (1831–1905), was born in Edinburgh, Scotland. As a divinity student of the Free Church of Scotland he became interested in mission work in Africa. With a view to prospecting for a mission station he joined David *Livingstone in Central Africa (1862–64). In 1867 he was appointed to the staff of Lovedale, the pioneer educational and missionary institution in South Africa, and was its principal 1870–1905. Convinced that Africans would value more what they paid for, he insisted that all pupils pay fees. When Africans in the Transkei Territory asked for 'a child of Lovedale', he urged that they collect £1,000 as a contribution. Ultimately they collected £4,500, and Blythswood Institution was opened. On Livingstone's death S. inaugurated a scheme for a mission in Central Africa—Livingstonia, begun in 1875. Later he founded Kibwezi (now Kikuyu) mission in East Africa. He long advocated university education for Africans, and before his death left a blue-print of what later became the University College of Fort Hare. A missionary statesman, he wrote several books, the best-known being *Dawn in the Dark Continent* (1902), a missionary classic, and *Lovedale Past and Present* (1887), a powerful defence of African education.

R. H. W. SHEPHERD

R. H. W. Shepherd: *Lovedale, South Africa: The Story of a Century 1841–1941* (Lovedale 1940); J. Wells: *Stewart of Lovedale* (London 1909).

STRATEGY FOR MISSION. The NT reflects certain strategic ideas. The mission to Israel and the mission to the Gentiles were assigned as the sphere respectively of the Jerusalem apostles and of Paul (Gal.2). Paul worked out the plan of planting the church in each of the main cities of the Roman world, and was largely successful in putting this plan into effect.

The modern missionary enterprise, by contrast, has been a scene of chaos. Roman Catholic effort tended to follow political interests rather than spiritual ideas, except in so far as the *Jesuits were inspired by the idea of worldwide evangelism. The first serious attempt to guide and co-ordinate effort came with the foundation of the

*Propaganda in 1622. Much difficulty was still caused by the privileges earlier granted to the orders, and by the rivalries between them; but Rome patiently and steadily gathered the threads into the hands of the central authority and, by the system of apostolic delegates directly representing the pope in each area, brought all missionary enterprise increasingly under control and direction. The effectiveness of this control is seen in the manner in which, after the expulsion of all missionaries from China, immense RC forces have been concentrated on Africa, with a view to making it by the end of this century a mainly RC continent.

Protestant missionary work has nothing comparable to show. One society after another entered the work without consultation with others, and the result was overlapping, competition and waste of effort. The acceptance of the principle of *comity helped to mitigate these evils. The tendency elsewhere has been in the direction of closer co-operation and fellowship. The foundation of the *IMC (1921), and of *National Christian Councils in many countries, for the first time made it possible for the Protestant world to look at its task as a whole. In some areas, such as theological training, and Christian literature, planning on a worldwide scale has proved possible. But the IMC was never given any executive authority or power of direction, and it is still the case that some of the largest and most active Protestant societies enter into fields where others are already successfully at work. At the same time many opportunities have been lost, as in the mass movement areas in India, because the necessary forces were not released to serve where they could be most useful. It is not yet clear whether the *Division of World Mission and Evangelism of the *WCC will be able to work more effectively in the direction of strategic thinking; the new regional organizations seem to hold out new possibilities. What is needed is a regular system of surveys, careful assessments of needs and opportunities, flexibility and an adventurous spirit in the churches.

Full strategic thinking will be possible only when the RC and Protestant forces are able to work together in full harmony. This is still a distant ideal; but the great improvement in relationships in recent years gives reason to hope that the old rancours and rivalries are now a thing of the past.

STEPHEN NEILL

R. P. Beaver: *Ecumenical Beginnings in Protestant World Mission* (New York 1962); N. A. Horner: *Cross and Crucifix in Mission, a Comparison of Protestant-Roman Catholic Missionary Strategy* (Nashville 1965).

STUDD, CHARLES THOMAS (1861–1931), the son of wealthy parents, was born in England and educated at Eton and Cambridge. An outstanding cricketer, he was for two years named as England's best player. In 1885 he went to China as leader of the 'Cambridge Seven' whose outgoing stirred the university world. S. remained in China with the *CIM until 1894; he gave away his entire inheritance of £40,000 to Christian causes, and lived henceforth by 'faith' principles (see FAITH MISSIONS). In 1888 he married Priscilla Stewart, who shared closely in his work. Invalided home to England, S. worked there and in the USA as evangelistic preacher and individual counsellor. From 1900 to 1906 he did pastoral work at Ootacamund, India. In 1913 he went to north-east Congo, where he remained for practically the whole of his last eighteen years. Here he founded the Heart of Africa Mission and the *Worldwide Evangelization Crusade. S's biographer describes his heroic standards, which meant 'living in native-built houses, plainest of food, no holidays, no recreations, complete absorption in the one task of saving the heathen'. Before S. died at Ibambi he had 40 missionaries working with him, and the African church which he had founded was evangelizing tribes hitherto untouched.

NORMAN P. GRUBB

N. P. Grubb: *C. T. Studd, Cricketer and Pioneer* (London 1933; reprint, Fort Washington, Pa. 1965).

STUDENT CHRISTIAN MOVEMENT, THE (SCM), is the *World Student Christian Federation (WSCF) in its particular national embodiments. The aim of the individual SCMs has been evangelistic and missionary—the uniting of students in Christian purpose. In the process the SCMs have been ecumenical pioneers.

The impact of D. L. *Moody through the *Northfield Conferences and the decisive influence of the *SVM motto, 'The evangelization of the world in this generation', provide the key elements in the emergence of the SCMs. The SVM usually has been an integral part of the SCM and has stimulated in each one missionary purpose, study and recruitment.

In the USA, college *YMCAs and *YWCAs were part of the SCM from its inception in the 1880s; but elsewhere YMCAs and YWCAs, with programmes reaching far beyond the student world, have usually operated separately from but co-operatively with the SCMs. Often the same leaders have served both.

SCM founders regarded students as strategic keys to world evangelization. They confronted the meaning of Christian division and saw the relation between mission and unity. They stood in the evangelical tradition, but were open to all—High Anglicans, Orthodox and Roman Catholics —prepared to accept the WSCF's Basis (trinitarian and evangelistic). Thus SCMs developed in Orthodox and predominantly RC lands and by the first world war had spread to each continent.

This broad inclusiveness in the SCM always involved free, vigorous discussion on the essentials of faith and enabled such SCM men as J. R. *Mott and J. H. *Oldham, decisively to shape Edinburgh 1910, by bringing the High Anglicans fully into the ecumenical stream. They also brought younger SCM leaders, among them William Temple, John Baillie and Otto Dibelius, to Edinburgh as stewards. All future *IMC conferences had SCM delegates.

Through the WSCF Western SCMs early recognized and responded to the importance of Asian and African Christian students and regularly involved them and speakers from their homelands in SCM conferences. This outreach became an SCM hallmark.

In recent years SCMs have emphasized special forms of frontier work in various parts of the world. The mission within the university has loomed large in thought and action. By 1969 certain of the European SCMs were badly divided by conflicting convictions about Christian life in a revolutionary world.

Since the second world war, the *IVF in Britain, Canada, the USA and elsewhere has grown rapidly. More conservative biblically and theologically, it has operated apart from the SCM.

See also STUDENT CONFERENCES.

W. RICHEY HOGG

T. Tatlow: *The Story of the SCM of Great Britain and Ireland* (London 1933); C. P. Shedd: *Two Centuries of Student Christian Movements* (New York 1934); R. Rouse: *The World's Student Christian Federation* (London 1948); R. Rouse and S. C. Neill, eds.: *A History of the Ecumenical Movement* (London 1954), pp.341–45; 599–612.

STUDENT CONFERENCES. Although it did not invent them, the *SCM so utilized and refined conferences that through them it made a distinct contribution. On the six continents where it has taken root the SCM has used conferences to make clear its purposes and to appeal to the student mind. Conferences have provided arenas for new ideas, occasions for Christian dialogue, and opportunities for SCM advance. Some have created bursts of new life, and all have been training grounds for SCM leaders. For eight decades they have confronted one student generation after another with the meaning and challenge of God's mission. Their cumulative impact has been enormous.

The American Intercollegiate *YMCA had been growing for nine years when Luther Wishard and C. K. Ober persuaded Dwight L. *Moody to invite to his Mt. Hermon School near Northfield, Massachusetts the movement's *first* student conference. Thus, in the summer of 1886 more than 250 students from across the USA and from many denominations came to spend a month with Moody. In that conference was born the *SVM with its 100 Volunteers. So great was the ensuing response that Moody agreed to invite conferences annually, and from 1887 they met in Northfield. The fame of these *Northfield Conferences spread widely. Not only did foreign students studying in the USA attend, but also students and professors came from Europe—among them Nathan Söderblom, Karl Fries and Henry Drummond. Collegians everywhere heard of 'The World's Student Christian Conference', and through the SVM, SCM and *WSCF it was soon reproduced around the world.

The SVM Quadrennial Conferences through most of their history confronted successive generations of students with the challenge of vocational decision for mission in other lands. Within 50 years (1889–1939) they accounted for more than 25,000 university graduates—the great majority being North American—entering that service and largely explain why by 1937 English-speaking persons accounted for 87% of the Protestant missionary force in Asia, the Pacific, Africa and Latin America. SVM conferences convened in Europe, but the SVM watchword there never had the wide acceptance that it did in Britain and North America.

Conferences provide the landmarks in WSCF history. Vadstena, 1895, had marked its founding. Each successive conference was planned and located for a particular strategic purpose. Tokyo 1907, arranged by the Japanese SCM for the WSCF, reflected the superb capability of Asians in world Christian partnership. The WSCF's universal missionary purpose hastened its ecumenical inclusiveness. Constantinople 1911 marked the full entry of the WSCF into the world of Eastern Orthodoxy. It had the blessing of the Ecumenical Patriarch, involved such men as Archbishop Germanos, and initiated Protestant-Orthodox encounter—a relationship fostered by

*Mott and with incalculable consequences. Henceforth the WSCF welcomed all Christian students who accepted its Basis. Peking 1922 emphasized international and inter-racial concern, focused on the equal partnership of all churches in world mission, and insisted upon full understanding by Christians of other religions. Peking was the last of the WSCF's world gatherings. Thenceforth its representative but much smaller General Committee met at different centres throughout the world.

Jointly sponsored by major ecumenical bodies, and with the WSCF participating, other *World Conferences of Christian Youth have been held. These include Amsterdam 1939; Oslo 1947; and Kottayam, South India 1952. Yet in recent years the large student conferences have been regional, e.g. the All-Africa Christian Youth Assembly, Nairobi 1963, and the Asian Christian Youth Assembly, Dumaguete City, Philippines, 1964–65.

W. RICHEY HOGG

J. R. Mott: *Addresses and Papers of John R. Mott*, Vol. II—*The World's Student Christian Federation* (New York 1947); R. Rouse: *The World's Student Christian Federation* (London 1948); C. P. Shedd: *Two Centuries of Student Christian Movements* (New York 1934); H.-R. Weber: *Asia and the Ecumenical Movement* (London 1966).

STUDENT FOREIGN MISSIONS FELLOWSHIP OF THE INTERVARSITY CHRISTIAN FELLOWSHIP, THE.

The SFMF began in 1936 with a blaze of missionary interest among students in American Christian colleges and Bible institutes. Robert C. McQuilkin of Columbia Bible College was one of the key leaders. Three years later the IVCF, led in the USA by C. Stacey Woods, began its ministry in secular schools with one of its goals also being the promotion of foreign missions. In 1945 the two movements merged and IVCF through its SFMF now has two main fields of missionary ministry among students: (a) that in Christian schools, with approximately 100 SFMF chapters, and (b) that in secular schools, including schools of nursing, totalling approximately 650 chapters.

The SFMF ministry includes the organizing of area missionary conferences and the large triennial international missionary convention which, in recent years, has convened on the campus of the University of Illinois (USA) and has attracted between 5,000 and 10,000 delegates. In addition the SFMF produces missionary materials, conducts an annual Missionary Camp, arranges for an itinerant ministry of selected missionary speakers, and engages in a ministry of counselling through correspondence and personal contacts.

The SFMF is a faith interdenominational agency that recruits missionary candidates for all boards. The *New Mandate* and *His* magazines stimulate missionary commitment. The parent organization is a member of the *EFMA, and both agencies maintain headquarters at 130 North Wells, Chicago, Illinois 60606, USA.

HAROLD LINDSELL

STUDENT VOLUNTEER MOVEMENT. The Student Volunteer Movement for Foreign Missions (SVM) arose in the USA in 1886, and from it emerged the Student Volunteer Missionary Union (SVMU) in Britain in 1892. The SVM(U)'s watchword, 'The evangelization of the world in this generation', stated its purpose, and to that end it sought to enrol university students for worldwide mission. Its remarkable results helped to shape Protestant missions from 1890 to 1940, drew churches together in mission, and became probably the most decisive factor leading to *Edinburgh 1910.

In 1886 at *Moody's Mt. Hermon Student Conference, Robert P. *Wilder, a missionary's son, was the chief figure in launching the SVM with 100 volunteers, among them John R. *Mott. The SVM grew steadily, and several thousand each year signed its pledge, 'It is my purpose, if God permit, to become a foreign missionary'. Only a minority went overseas, but the

others became a missionary force in their homelands. In 1888 Mott became chairman and Robert E. *Speer travelling secretary of the SVM. Wilder's 1891–92 tour among British universities led to the SVMU's founding, and from it soon came the British *SCM. The SVM spread to Holland, Germany, Switzerland, Scandinavia, Australia and also into Japan, China and India.

Beginning in 1891 SVM Quadrennial Conventions regularly assembled up to 4,000 students. Within four decades nearly 4,000 SVMU members went to Asia or Africa under their mission societies. By 1939 the SVMs had recruited some 25,000 missionaries, the majority of them North Americans.

The SVMs brought university students into mission as never before—most notably in Germany—raised standards for candidates, greatly enlarged the missionary force and launched mission studies. The SVM(U) steadily produced mission books and study programmes. These spread in Britain and North America to the churches. The *National Council of Churches annual nationwide mission studies in the USA root back, through the Missionary Education Movement, in the SVM.

The SVM's watchword provided great power into the 1920s and also shaped the whole SCM. But from 1922, when the SVMU dropped it, the watchword declined in importance. Many misunderstood its intent. A call to duty, not a prophecy, it envisioned neither the conversion nor the christianization of the world, but declared the responsibility of Christians in each generation to proclaim the gospel to the whole world in that generation. Many misinterpreted its method and supposed it meant flooding the world with westerners. Yet its basic premise held that only an *indigenous church and ministry in each land could accomplish the task. It asked western churches to provide the missionaries needed (tripling the then existing Protestant force of 15,000) to build national churches for their basic job of evangelization. Today the SVMs have little discernible existence, except as the SCMs of which they are a part continue the pattern of Quadrennial Conferences.

W. RICHEY HOGG

J. R. Mott: *The Evangelization of the World in This Generation* (New York 1900); *Addresses and Papers of John R. Mott*, Vol I, *The Student Volunteer Movement* (New York 1946); R. P. Wilder: *The Great Commission: The Missionary Response of the SVM in North America and Europe* (London 1936).

STUDENTS, CHRISTIAN WORK AMONGST. In a large variety of ways, Christians have addressed themselves to giving the gospel to students and in helping Christian students to grow in the faith. Prominent have been several organizations, begun chiefly in the latter half of the 19th century and continuing into the 20th century. To name only four: the *World Alliance of YMCAs was organized in 1855; the *World YWCA dates its founding from 1894; the World's Christian Endeavour Union came into being in 1895; the*WSCF was inaugurated in 1895. All four were represented widely. Of the four the WSCF, as its name indicates, was directed primarily to students. Its founder was John R. *Mott. It arose from his vision of making effective the watchword of the SVM, 'The evangelization of the world in this generation'. By that was meant the presentation of the gospel to all members of each generation the world around. Mott was convinced that if that were to be accomplished attention must be directed to students, as the future leaders of their respective countries. He therefore became an evangelist to students in country after country and sought to bring into being in every land student Christian movements. The WSCF was made up of these movements. Mott was its first General Secretary and then its Chairman.

See also STUDENT CHRISTIAN MOVEMENT; STUDENT FOREIGN MISSIONS FELLOWSHIP OF THE IVCF.

KENNETH SCOTT LATOURETTE

R. Rouse: *The World's Student Christian Federation* (London 1948).

STUDIES OF NON-CHRISTIAN RELIGIONS. See COMPARATIVE STUDY OF RELIGIONS.

SUCHANOV, CYRIL (1741–1810), a Russian Orthodox missionary in Siberia, began as a layman his activity among the Tungus people in the district of Dauria, which lies on the borders between Russia and China. Self-taught, S. obtained an adequate knowledge of the Tungus language. He did not, however, preach, but attempted to win disciples for Jesus Christ through an exemplary and unpretentious life. On his journeyings among the nomads he carried his few possessions with him in a knapsack. In 1776 he built his first church, and settled the nomads who had become Christians in the neighbourhood. Together with instruction in the Christian faith he imparted to his new Christians skills in handicrafts and in agriculture. Finally S. accepted ordination at the hands of the bishop of Irkutsk, in order that the new Christians might be able to take part fully in the life of the church. He so deeply won the love of his people that they came to be called after him—the Suchanov Tunguses. S. is the classic example of the personal initiative and the charismatic call, which have always played a notable role in the life of Russian Orthodox missions.

JOSEF GLAZIK

J. Glazik: *Die russ.-orth. Heidenmission* (Münster 1954), pp.88ff.

SUDAN, THE. The name S. is an abbreviation of the Arabic '*Bilad as Sudan*' meaning the land of the blacks. It originally denoted Africa south of the Sahara, stretching from the Atlantic to the Red Sea and the Indian Ocean. In the present context it refers to the Independent Republic of the Sudan, formerly the Anglo-Egyptian Condominium. It stretches from the Nubian desert in the north on the Egyptian and Libyan borders, through the swamps of the Sudd region of the Upper Nile, to the Immatong Mountains of Equatoria, and the Nile-Congo Divide in the south, on the Kenya, Uganda and Congo borders; from the Red

Sea, Eritrea and Ethiopia in the east, to Chad, the Central African Republic and the Congo (Kinshasa) in the west. It is the largest country on the continent of Africa, being nearly 1,000,000 sq.m. in area. It has a population of about 13,000,000 people. The country gained its independence on 1 January 1956.

In the north, *Islam is the dominant religion amongst the people who are mainly of Sudanic-Arab stock. In the south the dominant religion is *animism amongst tribes mainly of Nilotic and Nilo-Hamitic stock. It is presumed that Christianity first reached S. through travellers like the Ethiopian Eunuch of the Acts of the Apostles, who was a servant of Candace (or Queen) of Merowe, which is in the present Northern S. By the 4th century A.D. Christianity had begun to spread up the Nile from Egypt, and was encouraged by the Emperor in Constantinople, Justinian (d.565), and his wife Theodora. By the latter part of the 6th century a certain Bishop Longinus was sent to consolidate the work of the earlier missionaries in Nubia and Makuria, and was responsible for the conversion of the more southerly Kingdom of Aloa, whose capital, Soba, was not far from the present capital city of Khartoum.

With the movement of Islam across North Africa, the church in the Northern S. became isolated and eventually disintegrated. By the 12th century A.D. probably the only traces left were the remains of some church buildings, and certain Christian superstitions. The weakness of that early church was the fact that it did not penetrate deeply into the heart and life of the people, as its bishops and priests were foreigners, and its liturgical language and literature were in a foreign tongue.

It was not until the middle of the 19th century that some intrepid Roman Catholic missionaries entered S. at a time when explorers and other adventurers were finding their way into the heart of Africa via the Nile. During the period of the Mahdiya, towards the end of the 19th century, little was left of these pioneer efforts. The beginning of the 20th century saw the Condominium rule established in S. following the defeat of the Khalifa's forces in 1898. This ushered in a new period of Sudanese church history. Once again Christian missionaries entered S. with the approval of the authorities. In the north no direct evangelism or proselytising was permitted, but educational and medical work was started in Khartoum, Omdurman and other towns by missionary societies of the RC (Italian), Anglican (British) and Presbyterian (American) churches. In the south these missions were encouraged to open up work amongst the pagan tribes, being given separate 'spheres'. There were no limitations on evangelism, and schools and hospitals, followed later by agricultural and technical work, were established in many parts of the southern provinces. It was from these pioneer efforts that the church in S. began to grow and become *indigenous, with its own bishops and priests, its vernacular prayer book and liturgy, and the holy Scriptures translated into the main tribal languages, of the church areas of the south. Other, interdenominational missions (the *SIM, the *SUM and the Africa Inland Mission) entered the field of evangelism. Today the RC church reckons to have a membership of about 300,000, the Anglican (Episcopal) church about 150,000, the Church of Christ on the Upper Nile (Presbyterian) about 7,000 and the other missionary churches smaller numbers.

During the military régime, from 1958 to 1964, foreign missionaries were steadily withdrawn from the south owing to government restrictions, and the church came under increasing pressure from the authorities. Finally, in February 1964, all remaining foreign missionaries were summarily expelled from the south, thus leaving the church temporarily isolated and bereft of all foreign helpers. Then in July 1965 came the massacres in the south under a new civilian government, which led to a mass exodus of southerners as refugees into neighbouring African states. These included Sudanese bishops, clergy and church workers, many of whom narrowly escaped death. Several leading Christians were killed, with others, during that tragic period. In 1970 the Sudanese bishops and clergy, who were outside the borders of S., continued to minister to the spiritual needs of the tens of thousands of refugees. All the theological students were being trained in colleges of east and west Africa and Lebanon, since the theological colleges in S. were destroyed in 1965, together with many of the parish churches in the south. Following this, the remaining clergy left their parish centres and went into hiding with their people. At the time of writing, only in the three Southern Province headquarters and three or four District headquarters have things returned so far to anything like normal. The general church life in the south has been completely disrupted, but the work and witness of the church continues. In the northern towns the churches are free to continue their normal activities; Christian schools and a hospital in Omdurman play their part in the life of the country unimpeded. The Sudan Council of Churches, whose membership consists of representatives of ten churches—Catholic, Protestant and Orthodox—was founded in 1965, arising out of an earlier Northern Sudan Christian Council. This council is affiliated with the NECC and the *AACC, an indication of the unique place which the Sudan holds, belonging both to Africa and to the Near East.

OLIVER C. ALLISON

O. C. Allison: *A Pilgrim Church's Progress* (London 1966); K. D. Henderson: *Sudan Republic* (London 1965); R. Herzog: *Sudan* (Bonn 1958); H. C. Jackson: *Pastor on the Nile. Some Account of the Life and Letters of L. H. Gwynne* (London 1960); *BM* II, 796–801; *NCE* XIII, 773f.; *WKL*, 1404f.

SUDAN INTERIOR MISSION. A society founded in Canada in 1893 to evangelize the interior of Africa between the Sahara and the equator. In 1893 W. Gowans, T. Kent and R. V. *Bingham proceeded north from Lagos but were halted by sickness; only Bingham lived to return home. He organized a mission board on conservative evangelical lines but without the official support of any denomination. Missionaries convinced of a divine call set out in faith that money for their support would be forthcoming. In 1901 a station was established at Patigi on the Niger. The missionaries preached to Muslims and pagans, translated the Scriptures, and eventually founded hospitals and schools. There were few converts until 1908, when some hundreds from the Yagba tribe joined the church at the Egbe station. Similar results followed among other tribes in N. Nigeria and in Dahomey, Ghana, Upper Volta and Niger.

Branches of the SIM were formed in USA, UK, Australia, New Zealand, South Africa and Switzerland. Work was begun in Ethiopia in 1927, in Aden (1947), and in the Somali Republic (1954); from 1937 to 1964 SIM worked in E. Sudan (Republic of the Sudan). *Indigenous churches founded by the mission include the Evangelical Churches of W. Africa, the Fellowship of Ethiopian Evangelical Churches, and the Church in the E. Central Sudan. In 1968 SIM had 1,311 missionaries, medical work including twelve hospitals and eleven leprosaria, colleges, schools, printing presses and bookshops. Its periodical *African Challenge* is widely circulated, and its radio station ELWA in Liberia broadcasts to all Africa. SIM is a member of *IFMA.

JOHN GOODWIN

J. H. Hunter: *A Flame of Fire* (Toronto 1961).

SUDAN UNITED MISSION. A society founded in Great Britain in 1904 for work in Western, Central and Eastern Africa immediately south of the Sahara. This area, where numerous pagan tribes were subject to Muslim influence, had recently become open to Christian missionaries. The founders of SUM were members of the Baptist, Congregational, Methodist and Presbyterian churches, soon to be joined by Anglicans and others. In 1904 H. K. W. *Kumm and two other missionaries established a station at Wase in N. Nigeria. Since then more than

100 tribes have been reached with the gospel, accompanied by medical and educational work. There have been converts in each tribe, including a few from among Muslims. Already before the first world war most of the direct evangelism was being done by Africans. The first African ministers were ordained in 1938.

Branches of the SUM were founded in America (1906), South Africa (1907), Australia and New Zealand (1911), Denmark (1912), Norway (1922), Canada (1924), Switzerland (1950) and France (1961). Evangelical Christians of several denominations joined in the work, notably Evangelical United Brethren (USA), Lutherans and Reformed.

In 1968 SUM had 600 missionaries, with 63 stations in Nigeria, thirteen in Cameroon and twelve in Chad. Missionaries worked in Eastern Sudan (Republic of the Sudan) from 1913 to 1962. The self-governing Evangelical Church, covering all areas pioneered by SUM, was constituted in 1955. In 1968 it had 261 African ordained ministers, 3,095 evangelists and 122,125 baptized members, with 491,200 persons attending Christian worship. SUM is a member of *IFMA.

JOHN GOODWIN

J. L. Maxwell: *Half a Century of Grace* (London 1954).

SUFISM describes the mystical tradition in *Islām. The probable derivation is from *sūf*, the rough wool worn by ascetics, including Christian hermits. One of the first *sūfīs*, Hasan of Basra (642–728) was criticized for wearing *sūf* in imitation of Jesus. Rābi'a al- 'Adawiyya, the famous woman mystic (752–801), explored the doctrine of divine love. In previously Buddhist N.E. Persia, Ibrāhīm b. Adham (died c. 776–783) renounced his life as a prince to become an ascetic; Abū Yazīd of Bistām (died c. 874) was notorious for his ecstatic doctrines of becoming lost in God. Junayd of Baghdād (died c. 910) developed the idea of dying to oneself in oneness with God; Hallāj died as a martyr in 922 for implying God's incarnation in man and for

exclaiming in supreme ecstasy 'I am the Truth'.

The emphasis of S. had shifted from asceticism to gnosis, from an impatience with external ritual to a search for communion with God and for the ultimate, and often esoteric, Truth. From the 10th century onwards the path of S. was analysed by theoreticians: Qushayrī (died c. 1040) describes the stages of the soul's approach to God starting with repentance and asceticism and ending with gnosis, love and constant yearning. The moderate S. of Ghazālī (1058–1111) in his last years shows this spirituality in an orthodox setting; orthodoxy was to reject the pantheism of Ibn al-'Arabī (1165–1240) who had, nevertheless, the widest appeal of any *sūfī*. Of mystical poetry the Persian work of Rūmī (1207–1273) is best known and still inspires the seances of the Whirling Dervishes.

The dominant phenomenon of mediaeval Islām became the institutionalized *sūfī* order (*tarīqah*) led by 'saints'. These orders were more effective than armies and governments in propagating Islām in Anatolia, India and Africa. Their popular appeal, individualism and esotericism became overlaid by hierarchical controls and formal observances, and brought S. into disrepute.

JOHN B. TAYLOR

A. J. Arberry: *Sufism* (London 1950); J. M. Abun-Nasr: *The Tijaniyya. A Sufi Order in the Modern World* (London 1965); M. Smith: *Readings from the Mystics of Islam* (London 1950). *ERE* XII, 10–17; *NCE* XIII, 778–81.

SUH SANG-YUN (So Saw, c. 1849–1926), pioneer Korean evangelist, was one of the earliest Koreans to receive Protestant baptism. In medicine trade across the Manchurian border he had met (1878) Scots Presbyterian missionaries *Ross and Macintyre and became their main help in translating the first Bible portions into Korean (Luke, John, 1881). In 1883 Ross sent S. into forbidden Korea as BFBS colporteur. Though arrested and his Scriptures confiscated, S. escaped with ten copies to Sorai, his family home on the west coast. There (c. 1884–85) he secretly converted and gathered together Korea's first group of worshipping Protestants. By then the first Protestant missionaries began to arrive, but S. remained hidden until 1886 when he asked H. G. *Underwood for baptism for his converts in Sorai. This village, where 50 to 58 families were soon Christian, set patterns of indigenous evangelism and self-support for all Korea. S's brother Suh Kyung-Cho was in the first class of Presbyterian pastors (1907). S. became evangelist and helper in Seoul but spent his later years in Sorai which he had made 'the cradle of Protestant Christianity in Korea'.

SAMUEL H. MOFFETT

L. G. Paik: *History of Protestant Missions in Korea 1832–1910* (Pyongyang 1929), pp. 46–51, 130f., 143f.

SULAWESI. See INDONESIA.

SUMMER INSTITUTE OF LINGUISTICS. See WYCLIFFE BIBLE TRANSLATORS.

SUNDAR SINGH, SĀDHU (1889–1929), was born in a well-to-do Sikh family in the Panjab, and learned much that was good from his pious mother. But he found nothing to satisfy him in his own religion; and, hating Christianity as the religion of the foreigner, on 16 December 1904 he burned a Bible as a gesture of defiance. Three days later he underwent a profound experience in which he became convinced of the truth of the gospel of Jesus Christ. He was baptized on 3 September 1905. From 1909 to 1911 he was a student in St. John's Divinity School in Lahore; but this was a life for which he was not fitted, and he left in order to become a *sādhu*, a wandering preacher of the gospel. He preached in many areas of India, always with acceptance. His sphere was enlarged in 1920 when he visited England, and in 1922 when he spoke in a number of European countries. At first he spoke through an interpreter, but gradually, as his knowledge of English improved, he began to use the English language. S. had long been interested in the Himalayan countries, and especially in Tibet. His tales of miraculous experiences in these regions, of a large number of Hindu holy men who had secretly accepted the Christian faith, of a *rishi* 300 years old whom he had met in the Himalayas, raised doubts as to his veracity. No one, however, who met him had any doubts as to his sincerity. Wherever he went, this young man with his orange robe, his deep life of devotion, and extreme simplicity of utterance, left a deep impression on all who heard him. But it seems almost certain that many of the things which he related had taken place in a dreamlike state of inner concentration, rather than in the outward world of day and night. In 1929 S. left for a further journey in Tibet, and was never heard of again. Nothing whatever is known of this journey, and no trace has ever been discovered of S. It is to be supposed that somewhere in the mountains he met his end.

S. wrote much in a number of languages, always with the single aim of bringing home to his readers the glory and the nearness of Christ. His books have been translated into almost all western languages, and are still widely read. He left behind him a memory of goodness, but no movement. There have been other Christian *sādhus*; some of these have been rogues, and others simple, good men; but none of them has come anywhere near the stature of the original Christian *sādhu*.

STEPHEN NEILL

B. H. Streeter and A. J. Appasamy: *The Sādhu* (London 1921); A. J. Appasamy: *Sādhu Sundar Singh* (London 1968); A. J. Appasamy, ed.: *The Cross is Heaven, The Life and Writings of Sādhu Sundar Singh* (World Christian Books, No. 13, 2nd ed., London 1957); *LTK* IX, 1168f.; *RGG* VI, 526f.

SUNG, JOHN SHANG-CHIEH (1901–1944), was born in Hinghua, Fukien, South China, and died in the Western Hills near Peking, North China, of cancer and tuberculosis.

One of ten children of a Chinese Methodist pastor, JS as a boy was influenced by revival movements. He graduated BSc at Ohio Wesleyan University, and PhD in chemistry (Ohio State University). Passing through a difficult period in his personal faith, he enrolled at Union Theological Seminary, New York, went through severe emotional nervous strain, and spent six months in a mental hospital, returning to Hinghua at the end of 1927. In the following year he began his association with Andrew Gih and the Bethel Band, a mainly indigenous revivalist and evangelistic organization. This lasted till 1934, and took JS on mission to almost every part of China, resulting in revival of many local churches, and many new converts. After the separation, JS continued his mission in China, and also to the Chinese in South East Asia.

As a man, JS appeared bad-tempered and arrogant at times. As a Bible exegete, he indulged in fantastic explanations. Yet he moved thousands to faith in God through Jesus Christ, and to active participation in mission. His anti-intellectual bias and his diatribes against 'the social gospel' have, however, left their marks on South East Asian Chinese churches to this day.

JOHN FLEMING

L. T. Lyall: *John Sung—A Biography* (London 1954).

SUPPORT OF MISSIONS. See FINANCIAL SUPPORT FOR MISSIONS.

SUPRANATIONALITY OF MISSIONS. During the first world war, Christian missionaries of different nations were interned because they were 'enemy aliens' in the country in which they were working. Missionary bodies, believing that the church is a community transcending national boundaries, called to proclaim the gospel to all nations, began to propound the idea of the supranationality of missions, one of the earliest uses of the term being in a statement in 1915 of the Conference of Swedish Missionary Societies. The term was a questionable one in the context of international law; it could lead to a missionary being treated as having no nationality. The World Alliance for International Friendship through the Churches expressed the core of the idea in 1919 in terms of religious liberty : 'Freedom to carry the gospel of Christ to all nations is essential to the life of the church ... Whatever political control is found necessary should be exercised in a way that interferes as little as possible with the religious work of missionaries.' The League of Nations mandates legally recognized the principle of missionary freedom. The continuance of this line may be seen in the work of the *CCIA to secure, after the second world war, the safeguarding of religious freedom, including the freedom to propagate one's faith, in the UN Declaration of Human Rights and in the constitutions of new nations.

The second world war made Christians very aware of the peril of the demonic elements in *nationalism, and the concept of supranationality was invoked again at the *Whitby (1947) meeting of the *IMC. It saw the matter in terms of 'citizenship in the Kingdom which is not of this world and the citizenship of the land of their birth or adoption'; and of 'the Church ... seen as an ecumenical fellowship within which great differences are brought together—racial, national, cultural, economic—but which by its very existence is a token of a Kingdom in which differences have been overcome'; and of 'belonging to Christ' meaning 'at the same time responsibility for and solidarity with the world and our fellow men, along with a sense of being strangers and sojourners in the world and in our nation'. Here the concept of supranationality is both a new form of the older debate about the indigenous and the universal aspects of the church and an anticipation of more recent discussions of the relation of the church to human communities.

In theory the Roman Catholic church is completely supranational. In practice it has found itself no less subject to the stresses of the modern world than other churches. In the first world war Pope Benedict XV was deeply suspected of pro-German leanings; controversy still rages as to the part played by Pope Pius XII in the time of the Third Reich in Germany and of the second world war. RC missionaries were interned, no less than Protestants, by the combatants on both sides. RCs certainly have a stronger sense than Protestants of belonging to one great international corporation; but they do not for that reason cease to be citizens of their own country, and carry with them wherever they go certain characteristics of church and social life in that country.

In recent times RC missionaries have solved the problem for themselves by taking out citizenship in the country in which they work (e.g. Fr Vincent *Lebbe in China).The Second *Vatican Council again and again stressed the supranational character of the church (especially in the document *de Ecclesia*) as the divinely appointed home for all nations. The too close alliance between church and colonial powers in the 19th century (especially in China) is now seen to have been a disastrous mistake. Increasingly in their utterances the popes have come to address themselves to all the nations of the world, and not only to the Christian part of it.

RONALD K. ORCHARD AND
STEPHEN NEILL

W. R. Hogg: *Ecumenical Foundations* (New York 1952), pp.187–89; R. K. Orchard: *Out of Every Nation: A Discussion of the Internationalizing of Missions* (London 1959); C. W. Ranson: *Renewal and Advance* (Report of Whitby meeting, IMC, London 1948), pp.219–21.

SURINAM. See CARIBBEAN.

SWAIN, CLARA A. (1834–1910), was the first woman missionary doctor in the world. Born in Elmira, New York, USA, she grew up in nearby Castile. In 1869 she graduated from the Woman's Medical College in Philadelphia. Responding to an urgent plea for a woman doctor in India, she became one of the first two missionaries sent out in 1869 by the newly formed Woman's Foreign Missionary Society of the Methodist Episcopal Church. In Bareilly,

North India, she began work on the morning of her arrival and was soon so swamped with patients that a hospital became imperative. A Mogul ruler, the Nawab of Rampur, though an opponent of Christianity, was so impressed by her work that he donated for her use a tract of 40 acres, including a palatial residence, which in 1872 became the first women's hospital in Asia. Other buildings followed, the first units in the fine modern medical centre which bears her name. After two terms at Bareilly, in 1885 CS became a physician in the palace of the Rajah of Khetri, where until 1895 she laboured to bring healing and the gospel to an area untouched by Christianity. She spent her last years in Castile, New York, returning to India only once in 1906 at the time of the 50th Jubilee of Indian Methodism.

DOROTHY CLARKE WILSON

A Glimpse of India, Extracts from the Letters of Dr Clara A. Swain (New York 1909); D. C. Wilson: *Palace of Healing, The Story of Dr Clara Swain and the Hospital She Founded* (New York 1968).

SWAZILAND, bordering South Africa and Mozambique, was a British High Commission Territory in Southern Africa until it obtained independence in 1968. Sometimes called by its Swazi name Ngwane, it is a kingdom of 6,704 sq.m. of mountainous terrain, with a population (1967) of 385,000, including 10,000 Europeans. Its economy is inextricably linked with that of South Africa, and in 1967 46% of its land was owned by Europeans. The majority of the population remain animists. A Roman Catholic prefecture apostolic was formed in 1923, and by 1966 the single diocese of Manzini had 28,300 Catholics. At least ten Protestant missions are at work, with a total community of about 26,000; these include the African Evangelical Church (*SAGM), Bantu Evangelical Church (*Evangelical Alliance Mission), Church of the Nazarene, Anglican Diocese of Swaziland, Evangelical Lutheran Church (Southeastern region), Full Gospel Church of God, Methodist Church of South Africa,

Seventh-day Adventist Church and Swedish Alliance Mission. *African independent churches have gradually increased in numbers since 1904, and numbered in 1966 thirty bodies with 30,000 adherents.

DAVID B. BARRETT

BM II, 819f.

SWEETMAN, JAMES WINDROW (1891–1966), entered the Methodist ministry in 1915 and spent much of his life between 1919 and 1946 in India. From 1934, when he was appointed as a lecturer at the *Henry Martyn School, Lahore, the MMS released him for full time work on the Christian approach to Muslims, a task for which he had long been preparing himself through patient private study. His work was not confined to the instruction of Christians in sympathetic understanding of *Islam; his effective communication with Muslims is illustrated in autobiographical examples in his pamphlet *The Bible in Islam* (London 1953). From 1934 to 1946 he was editor of *News and Notes* (*India*) where further details of his activities are recorded.

In 1947 he was invited to take up the newly created chair of Islamics at the *Selly Oak Colleges, Birmingham. He built on academic foundations laid by Dr Alphonse Mingana and he fostered the inter-religious sensitivity for which Lootfy Levonian had worked at Selly Oak. He introduced missionary candidates of many denominations to a sense of priority for Christian mission to Muslims; to those who offered themselves for more specialist training as Islamists he gave guidance which has borne fruit throughout the Muslim world. The tradition in Islamics which he developed at Selly Oak has reached a stage where post-graduate degrees in Islamics are being undertaken by both Muslim and Christian students. Despite life-long ill-health, through which his wife nursed him and supported him, he undertook many responsibilities such as that of Advisory Editor to *The Muslim World* and Assessor to the Missionary Council of the Church Assembly. In 1953 he carried out a strenuous tour through India and Pakistan, serving the needs of churches of many denominations in their outreach to Muslims. His chief preoccupation, however, was with his monumental work, *Islam and Christian Theology*, of which three volumes appeared (London 1945, 1947, 1958), a fourth volume being still in the press when he died. He thus covered the origins and the scholastic development of Islamic theology in its relationships with Christian thought; his projected fifth volume of critical reconstruction remains unwritten, but his extensive research material for this is available, with all his other voluminous unpublished papers concerning Christian-Muslim relations, in the Selly Oak Colleges library.

JOHN B. TAYLOR

SYMBOLISM arises from the ability of the brain, like a computer, to register a permanent association between one remembered experience and another. Animals can be trained to link the sound of a bell with the sensation that food is near. The bell becomes a *sign*, indicating the nearness of the food. It is not a natural sign, such as the smell of meat, but an artificial sign which has to be learnt. Every human language is a system of artificial signs—sounds we can hear or writing we can see or feel. Human society depends on signs of many different kinds but all of them are a sort of language. We use mathematical and scientific signs for our calculations; signs which direct and warn us as we travel; uniforms to indicate a person's profession, flags to show nationality, emblems to indicate different religions, and so on. Signs may be objects, such as a crown; sounds such as a whistle; or actions such as bowing. But the function of a sign is always to *indicate* or *represent* something else. And sometimes it actually brings into effect what it represents. Among some people, for example, sharing a meal actually turns enemies into allies. This is called an *effective sign*. The Christian *sacraments are effective signs.

But the power of the mind to associate one remembered experience with another goes further than this. A wedding ring is more than a sign indicating marriage. It brings together the experience of human love with the thought of gold, which is precious and cannot rust, and the shape of a circle, which has neither beginning nor end. So the ring is a *symbol*, which enlarges our understanding of married love by linking together these separate ideas or pictures. Metaphors, poetic images and myths work in the same way as symbols; they all *enlarge our understanding* of the things they represent. Some ideas and experiences, particularly those we call 'spiritual', can hardly be understood at all except through symbols.

The most powerful and universal symbols arise from man's oneness with nature or from his dreams. Blood symbolizes life; water death, but also the unconscious, or the great chaos from which new life emerges; and so on.

If we take myths and symbols literally, or fail to grasp what they represent, we shall misunderstand our own religion and misjudge the beliefs and rituals of others.

JOHN V. TAYLOR

ERE XII, 134–51.

SYNCRETISM arises in the course of presenting Jesus Christ as sole Lord and Saviour to men of other religions living in cultures not moulded by the biblical revelation. By translating the gospel into local languages, and adapting or accommodating to local ideas and customs, these are absorbed into the life of the church. Many such elements have, however, been intimately related to another religion, and it is often difficult to incoporate them without also absorbing their previous religious associations and meanings. Those local ways that can be adopted without such associations make possible a cultural S. or synthesis; for example, local dress, musical instruments, building methods and styles. Other local practices and concepts more closely associated with religion may be 'taken possession of' by Christ, given a new or transposed meaning, and so be baptized into the church to enrich its life, and plant it more firmly in local soil. These cultural syncretisms lead to genuine *indigenization.

If what is drawn from local sources retains its original religious meaning, and is merely amalgamated with other Christian elements, we have a religious S. (See the Canaanite altar and grove of Gideon's father, Jud.6:25–32.) This is a hybrid or mixture in which Christ through the Scriptures does not control all elements, and at best it is only partly Christian. When the Christian elements are themselves interpreted and transformed in a pagan direction, it becomes again a pagan religion, although now enriched by Christian borrowings. (See Simon wanting to add the Holy Spirit to his powers, Acts 8:19.)

Current examples of such extreme S. occur where Jesus Christ becomes merely another great teacher or is replaced by a local founder as messiah; where ecstatic behaviour is the main gift of the Holy Spirit who may also be confused with other spirits; where dreams, visions, or angels become the main channels of revelation, and prophecy only a new form of divination or witchfinding; where baptism becomes a purification or healing ceremony, holy water rites replace the Lord's Supper, and Christian conduct is the observance of a set of tabus.

Since the various forms of S. may not be easily identified one must (1) keep studying how the Bible deals with these matters; (2) be patient where efforts at indigenization have produced some religious S.; (3) respect an earnest spiritual search behind even the neo-pagan syncretisms with the Christian religion.

HAROLD W. TURNER

W. A. Visser't Hooft: *No Other Name* (London 1963); H. Kraemer: *Religion and the Christian Faith* (London 1956), chs. 24–25; M.-L. Martin: *The Biblical Concept of Messianism and Messianism in Southern Africa* (Morija, Lesotho 1964), especially pp.158–61, 179–85; *ERE* XII 155–57; *WKL*, 1416–19.

SYRIA, or the Syrian Arab Republic, includes 71,000 sq.m., and has a population of 5,652,000 (1967). The name S. was used until 1920, and even later, to include what is now known as Lebanon. The history of the development of mission work in S. before 1920 is thus much the same as that in Lebanon.

The great majority of the population is Muslim, although Christians have lived in S. since the 1st century, the Orthodox patriarchates of Antioch dating their founding from St. Peter. There are about 300,000 Orthodox (Greek, Syriac, Armenian and *Nestorian), and over 150,000 Catholics. Catholic missions may be said to date from the brief visit to the area of St. Francis of Assisi in 1219. Even earlier, in 1181, a first step was taken to bring the whole of the eastern Maronite church under Rome, a growing movement that was finally confirmed in 1516. The Chaldean church ('Nestorian Catholic') was established by movements in the 16th century and again in the 17th century, the Armenian Catholic in the 15th and the 18th centuries. The Greek Catholic or Melkite church was founded in 1724, the Coptic Catholic in Egypt in 1732, and the Syrian Catholic in 1783. Each of these Uniate churches represents a branch of an eastern rite that has come under the authority of Rome (see EASTERN CHURCHES, LESSER OR SEPARATED).

Protestants number about 10,000, of whom the majority belong to the Evangelical Synod of Syria and Lebanon or to the Union of Armenian Evangelical Churches of the Near East. The former grew out of the work of three mission groups, the Syria Mission of the Presbyterian Church in the USA in Hums, Hama, Aleppo and the Jezirah, the Danish Mission to the Orient in Nebk and Karyatain, and the North America Reformed Presbyterian Mission in the Latakia area. The work and property of these missions since 1959 has for the most part been given into the hands of the national synod.

The Union of Armenian Evangelical Churches is especially strong in northern S., where Armenian refugees from Turkey settled in great numbers after the first world war. L'Action Chrétienne en Orient works especially with the Armenian Union in Aleppo and in the Jezirah but also with the synod, assisting the work of the churches with funds and occasionally with personnel. The Armenian churches have their own elementary and middle schools, in addition to Aleppo College, in which they have a share.

In Damascus, the Irish Presbyterian Jewish Mission is no longer active, but the National Evangelical Church of Damascus carries on as the fruit of its work and the work of the other missions. Founded in 1842, the Irish Mission extended its work outside Damascus, from Bludan to the Hauran, and was the originator of work in the Nebk area which later was taken over by the Danish Mission to the Orient. The co-operation of Presbyterian and Lutheran missions in their early beginnings was notable. The British Syrian Mission has withdrawn from Damascus after long service in education in St. Paul's School.

The SDA, the Church of the Nazarene and the *CMA have some work continuing.

Restrictions on evangelism have made mission work extremely difficult. Foreign societies are generally suspect. Syrian nationals are not permitted to change their legal registration from Muslim to Christian.

HARRY G. DORMAN ,JR

H. H. Jessup: *Fifty-three Years in Syria* (New York 1910); G. H. Scherer: *Mediterranean Missions* (Beirut n.d., MS); F. J. Bliss, ed.: *The Reminiscences of Daniel *Bliss* (New York 1920); *The News Bulletin of the Near East Christian Council*, quarterly, Cairo, Beirut, 1926–1967; *BM* II, 820–27; *NCE* XIII, 894f.

SYRIAN CHURCHES, INDIA. The Syrian Christian community in India founded in Kerala, South India, was governed for centuries by bishops from Syria and used Syriac in worship; hence the name Syrian. It is now entirely Indian in race.

The community numbers $3\frac{1}{4}$ million; divided ecclesiastically between Orthodox Syrian Church (Malankara) in India (formerly called Jacobite), the *Mar Thoma

Church (Reformed), the Romo-Syrians (three rites and hierarchies), *CSI, and certain Protestant groups.

All Syrians believe that St. Thomas the Apostle first preached the gospel in India, 52 A.D. The first certain reference to the Kerala Church is in Cosmas Indicopleustes (535 A.D.). He speaks of a bishop appointed from Persia, i.e. from the East Syrian Church (*'Nestorian').

The first Europeans to contact the church in modern times were the Portuguese at the beginning of the 16th century. In 1599 Aleixo de Menezes Archbishop of Goa went to Kerala to subjugate the SC to Rome, following contacts by *Jesuits. He made priests renounce Nestorian heresy and the Patriarch of Babylon, corrected their Liturgy of Addai and Mari and put Jesuit bishop Francis Roz over them. But there was much discontent. In 1665 a Jacobite bishop arrived in Kerala and was welcomed by the anti-Roman party who had been strengthened by the Dutch expulsion of the Portuguese in 1662. From this time there were two effective churches in Kerala, the Romo-Syrians headed by an Indian bishop, and what had become the Jacobite church.

The British succeeded the Dutch as the foreign trading interest in 1795. Evangelical officials became interested in the Jacobite church and persuaded the local bishop to accept *CMS help with the education of his clergy. The missionaries also translated the Bible into Malayalam, the vernacular.

After 20 years the uneasy alliance broke up. The missionaries remained in Kerala to care for their converts from the out-castes and were joined by a number of Syrian families (now in the CSI).

Some Syrians strongly influenced by evangelical ideas remained in the church, however. Their leader, Abraham Malpan, revised the liturgy and protested against unscriptural practices. His nephew was consecrated in Syria by the patriarch as Mathew Athanasios. On his return in 1843 the church split in two, the reforming party recognizing Athanasios, the conservatives the reigning Metropolitan. Lawsuits for the possession of church property started. Patriarch Peter himself arrived in 1857 to settle the dispute. He consolidated patriarchal authority and consecrated new bishops. He excommunicated Athanasios, who had already consecrated his nephew Thomas Athanasios to succeed him. Most of the lawsuits were decided against the reformers who had to build new churches and organize themselves afresh under Thomas Athanasios. This church, claiming to be the continuing ancient church is called the Mar Thoma Church.

Within the Jacobite church a dispute between adherents of the patriarch (Jacobite) of Antioch and a party wanting local autonomy divided the church for 60 years. Full integration of the two parties took place in 1964. The church is now autocephalous under a Catholicos and is known as the Orthodox Syrian Church in India.

The Syrians' liturgy was Christian but their customs *caste Hindu. They were literate and pioneers of western education. Today they are engaged in commerce and education throughout India, Pakistan, in Malaya, East Africa and the Persian Gulf. Some Syrians have been ministers of central government or governors of states. They now own about 30 colleges of degree standard and many schools. The worship of Syrians is now mostly in Malayalam.

LESLIE BROWN

L. W. Brown: *The Indian Christians of St. Thomas* (Cambridge 1956); C. P. Mathew and M. M. Thomas: *The Indian Churches of St. Thomas* (Delhi 1967); E. M. Philip: *The Indian Church of St. Thomas* (Nagercoil 1950); E. Tisserant: *Eastern Christianity in India* (London 1957).

T

TAHITI. See PACIFIC ISLANDS.

TAIWAN (FORMOSA) is an island of 13,900 sq.m. and 12,500,000 people, about 80% of whom are Taiwanese, descendants of early Chinese immigrants. About 2% are mountain tribes of the Malayan race, and the remaining 18% are mainland Chinese who came to Taiwan after 1945. Most of the people are nominal Buddhists mixed with *Taoism, *Confucianism and superstitious *animism. *Ancestor worship with sacrificial offerings in many festivals is very popular; but today these are more social than religious affairs. Materialistic *secularism is very widespread among the city-dwellers. Politically, T. has been a part of China for several centuries. But it was briefly occupied by the Dutch in the 17th century (1624–61), and again by the Japanese for 50 years (1895–1945). Both Roman Catholic and Reformed churches came to T. during the 17th century, but both died out soon after the Chinese took power over the island. The RC church reopened its mission in 1859. After the second world war more than 400 priests and 300 sisters were sent in for the extended mission works. It now claims a community of almost 300,000, with one archdiocese, six dioceses, 362 organized churches and 935 chapels. On the Protestant side, the Presbyterian Church of England broke ground in the south in 1865, and the Presbyterian Church in Canada started its work in the north in 1872. Up till 1950, the Presbyterians were almost the only Protestant denomination in T. Both missions carried on in spite of many difficulties, in the fields of evangelism, medicine and education. In 1880, after only eight years' work, the Canadian missionary, G. L. *Mackay, could report 20 chapels in the north. In 1885, after 20 years, there were 29 national workers in the south. In the following year, the south began its own outreach by opening three stations in the Pescadore islands. During the first decade of the Japanese occupation, church membership doubled. Significantly enough, the greatest gains in T. coincided with periods of stress and strain during the two world wars. The first presbytery was organized in the south in 1896, and in the north in 1904. In 1912, both presbyteries united to form one synod for the whole island. The return of T. to China in 1945 gave them the great opportunity for consolidation and expansion. In 1951, the General Assembly was formed with two synods and eight presbyteries, and that same year it joined the *WCC. The evangelization of the mountain tribes after the war has been called 'the twentieth century miracle' because of its tremendous results. The Presbyterians alone have 411 mountain churches with 77,563 members among them now. In order to celebrate the centennial, during 1954 to 1965, the Presbyterian church committed itself to the Double-the-Church movement, which was very successful. It is now in the New Century movement, which puts more emphasis on the quality of the church rather than quantity alone. The Presbyterian church is an independent, self-governing church. Missionaries from five mission boards are completely integrated within the church. It now has 417 organized churches, 464 chapels and 174,955 members (1968 annual report). After the war, with the inrush of people from the mainland, more than 60 mission bodies of different denominations and some Chinese indigenous churches came to T. Among the new mission efforts, the Baptists, the Lutherans, the Methodists, the SDA and the Holiness groups are the strongest; but there are also smaller groups such as the Assemblies of God, the Quakers, the Mennonites and the Mormon sect, etc. Among the indigenous groups, the Little Flock and the True Jesus Church are the two most successful ones, both having originated on the mainland. The formation of a Council of Churches has been proposed by the major denominations, and it is in the stage of negotiation. A degree of inter-mission co-operation is brought about by the Taiwan Missionary Fellowship. In 1965, 21 Protestant churches and groups joined together with the Presbyterian church for the celebration of the centenary of Protestant Christian witness in T. They all hope to enter 'into the second century together'. The whole Protestant church altogether numbers about 354,773 (Taiwan Christian Yearbook, 1968), which is about 3% of the whole population.

LIEN-MIN CHENG

E. Band: *Working His Purpose Out* (London 1947); L. Dickson: *These My People* (Grand Rapids 1958); C. H. Hwang: *Joint Action for Mission in Formosa* (Geneva 1968); H. MacMillan: *First Century in Formosa* (Taipei 1963); H. K. Tong: *Christianity in Taiwan: A History* (Taipei 1961); *BM* II, 240–45; *NCE* XIII, 916f.; *WKL*, 1421–23.

TAKAYAMA, JUSTUS UKON (c. 1553–1615), born in the province of Settsu (Osaka Prefecture), Japan, was the son of Takayama Dario Hidanokami. Baptized in 1563 he became the most outstanding personality among the Christian lords of the Christian Century (1549–1650). Following his father's example he used his position, wealth and cultural talents for the propagation of the faith. A brilliant general, he served under Nobunaga and Hideyoshi and successively became lord of Takatsuki (1573) and Akashi (1584). In 1587 Hideyoshi made him face the alternative of denying the faith or losing both his fief and his position in the army. Ukon went into hiding first on the island of Awaji, then on Shodoshima and in Kyushu. In 1588, at the request of Hideyoshi he returned to Kyoto and was sent into exile to Kanazawa where, for some time, he lived in poverty. Though he was gradually rehabilitated he never again played an important role in public affairs. In 1614 he was banished from Japan and died on 5 February 1615, shortly after his arrival at Manila.

JOSEPH J. SPAE

J. Laures, SJ: *Takayama Ukon und die Anfänge der Kirche in Japan* (Münster 1954).

TAMBARAM 1938. See CONFERENCES, WORLD MISSIONARY.

TANGANYIKA. See TANZANIA.

TANZANIA. In 1964 the newly independent states of Tanganyika (1961) and Zanzibar (1963) united to form the Republic of T. This country of 363,708 sq.m., made up of 125 different ethnic groups has a population (1967) of 12,231,342.

Of the population, between 40% and 45% follow traditional African religions (*animism). Approximately 20–25% are Muslims, but the majority of these also practise traditional animistic rites. The Christians number about 30% of the population and continue to grow consistently in numbers at the rate of 7–10% annually.

The first mission attempts were made by the Roman Catholic Portuguese who held the coastal towns in the 15th–16th centuries. They made little impact on the Arabs and local population and all traces of their work vanished when the Arabs reconquered the coast in 1730. Although David *Livingstone and *CMS missionaries *Krapf and Rebmann explored T. earlier, it was not until 1863 that RC *Holy Ghost Fathers began work in Zanzibar and on the mainland in 1868. The Anglicans (*UMCA) also started in Zanzibar in 1864 and began permanent work on the mainland in 1875. The Lutherans (*Berlin Mission III) likewise arrived in Zanzibar in 1886, but transferred their work to the mainland in 1887.

The Holy Ghost Fathers were followed by the *Benedictines (1887), the Consolata Fathers (1920), the *Capuchins (1921), the Passionists (1933), the Pallotine Fathers (1940), the Rosminians (1945) and recently some *Maryknoll Fathers, Salvatorians, Camillion Fathers, Priests of the Precious Blood and *Jesuits. The RC church has two archdioceses in T. with 23 dioceses. The dioceses carry out joint work through the secretariat of the T. Episcopal Conference.

The Anglican (UMCA) coastal mission

work was later extended inland by the British CMS and is now supported mainly by the CMS of Australia. The eight Anglican dioceses in T. are a part of the Province of East Africa.

The Evangelical Lutheran Church of T. is the largest Protestant church in the country. The early foundations were laid by the German mission societies: Berlin III (1886), Berlin I (1901), *Bethel (1889) and *Leipzig (1893). The (American) Augustana Lutheran church began work in 1922 and the Swedish Lutheran church in 1939. During and after the second world war the German mission work was administered by the National Lutheran Council of America and supported by Lutheran churches of America, Sweden, Denmark, Norway and Finland. In 1963 seven separate synods and dioceses united to form the Evangelical Lutheran Church of T.

The *Moravian work began in 1891 and now has the two largest Moravian provinces in the world located in T. The *Friends Society (British) began work on Pemba Island in 1898. SDA (German) came in 1906, the AIM 1909 and the *Mennonites 1934. Following the second world war came Baptists (American Southern), *Salvation Army, *Pentecostals, Assemblies of God, Church of Christ, Elim and Brethren. No national independent or prophetic groups have originated in T. nor has any significant schism taken place.

On the basis of the most recent reports, the estimate of church membership for 1967 is: RCs 2,400,000; Lutherans 500,000; Anglicans 300,000; Moravians 80,000; Africa Inland Church 35,000; Pentecostals 35,000; SDA 30,000; Baptists 3,000; others 20,000; which makes a Christian community of approximately 3,360,000.

In 1936 the major Protestant churches organized the Tanganyika Missionary Council which later became the Christian Council of T.Through the CCT churches co-ordinate or work jointly in student and youth work, education and welfare, literature publication, radio, Sunday school and women's work. On behalf of the CCT and the *WCC, the *Lutheran World Federation sponsors a large welfare service in aid of some 36,000 African refugees. Two papers, *Target* (English) and *Lengo* (Swahili) are produced jointly by churches in T. and Kenya.

In recent years there have been particularly cordial relations between Protestant and RC Christians. Yearly joint meetings are held between the CCT and the T. Episcopal Conference and occasionally joint prayer services and evangelistic meetings are conducted. All churches in the country use the same Swahili version of the Bible.

Serious discussions toward union have been going on since 1961 between the Anglican, Lutheran, Methodist, Moravian and Presbyterian churches of T. and Kenya. An Interim Basis of Union has been published and general agreement has been reached except on the issue of the nature and significance of succession in the ordained ministry.

The churches in T. which pioneered in educational and medical services today still administer more than half of the schools and hospitals in the country. This is done with financial subsidy and supervision from the government under a very cordial and co-operative working arrangement. The lack of pastors and local financial support hinders the church from expansion and in giving an effective witness in the growing urban centres. All the major denominations have become independent, self-governing churches with national leadership in the majority. However, 3,000 overseas missionaries are still at work in T. and it appears it will take some years before local workers will be able to replace them. The church continues as a vital spiritual force in the country and plays an important role in the building of this new nation.

LLOYD W. SWANTZ

C. J. Hellberg: *Missions on a Colonial Frontier West of Lake Victoria* (Lund 1965); J. P. Moffett: *Handbook of Tanganyika* (Dar-es-Salaam 1958); R. Oliver: *The Missionary Factor in East Africa* (2nd ed., London 1965); L. W. Swantz: *Church, Mission and State Relations in Pre- and Post-Independent Tanzania*, Occasional Paper 19, Syracuse

University (Syracuse 1967); *BM* II, 827–33; *NCE* XIII, 932; *WKL*, 1423–25.

TAOISM is one of the three religions of China, the name coming from the Chinese word *Tao* (Way). While *Confucianism emphasized social responsibility, and looked at the world from a commonsense standpoint, the *Tao* was essentially a way prescribed by heaven. Although T., as it was traditionally understood, provided an ethical way for man to follow, it was much more concerned to turn man from what was human or belonged to the everyday world to what lay beyond or was spiritual. Its language was the language of poetry and mysticism.

The *Tao* is understood as the ultimate ground of all definite existences, the basic source of unity, in which all contradictions and distinctions of existence can be finally resolved. In its ethical teaching, T. emphasized a *yielding acceptance*, the absence of strife or coercion, leading to spontaneous action which was effortless and inexhaustible. The teaching of T. is attributed to Lao-tzu (born 604 B.C.), and tradition attributes the book *Tao te ching* (The Way of Virtue) to him. In that writing the *Tao* is represented as *eternal* and *nameless*:

The *Tao* that can be spoken about
Is not the eternal *Tao:*
The name that can be named
Is not the eternal name.
Nameless, it is the basis of heaven and earth;
When named, it is the mother of all things.

While popular T. incorporated numerous deities, representing natural objects, historical persons, professions, parts of the human body, etc., together with a host of superstitions, fortune-telling, astrology and *magic, Christian missionaries were able to use the concept of *Tao* as a means of introducing Christ as the *Word*, eternal and yet present in the world, 'unknown' and yet 'known' in his incarnate life.

RAYMOND J. HAMMER

H. G. Creel: *Chinese Thought* (London 1962); W. E. Soothill: *The Three Religions*

of China (London 1929); W. T. De Bary, ed.: *Sources of Chinese Tradition* (2 vols., New York 1960); *ERE* XII, 197–202.

TAUFAAHAU (also Siosi, King George I, c. 1798–1893), native ruler of Haabi Island in the Tonga group, was converted to Christianity in 1830 and was baptized. The chief of Vanau Island, Ulukalala, on his death bed willed his domain to T. Back of this was a struggle which had been going on between the chiefs of the various islands to unite them under one ruler. T. did this as a Christian by opposing the ancient faith. The anti-Christian chiefs were centred on the island of Tongatabu. Catholic missionaries, forbidden to land on Haabi, settled on Tongabatu where they won the allegiance of the disaffected nations. War ensued which by 1852 was won by T. Shortly afterwards the governor of French Oceania, having sent representatives to investigate the events in Tonga, signed a Convention with Taufaahau acknowledging the independence of his kingdom and his right to rule. Previously, T. had promulgated a code of laws for his people, with the advice, but not the entire approval, of the missionaries; in 1862 he established a parliamentary form of government and became a constitutional ruler. In his later years one of the missionaries, Shirley Baker, became his prime minister; using his authority he urged the king to free his people from entanglements with western powers. A break with the Australian Conference of the Wesleyan Methodist Church occurred, and in 1880 the Free Church of Tonga, an independent state church was established. The influence of T. spread to Samoa, Fiji and Urea.

J. LESLIE DUNSTAN

G. G. Findlay and W. W. Holdsworth: *The History of the Wesleyan Methodist Missionary Society* (London 1921–1924).

TAYLOR, JAMES HUDSON (1832–1905), was born at Barnsley, Yorkshire, England, son of a chemist. At seventeen T. underwent a deep conversion experience, followed by a vivid call to China, a closed empire except for treaty ports. In Hull and London, while evangelizing the poor and disciplining himself to depend on God alone for his needs, he trained as a doctor but sailed unqualified as the first agent of the short-lived Chinese Evangelization Society. Landing in Shanghai in 1854, and soon reacting against the attitude of the few missionaries already in China, who clung to the international settlement and regarded the Chinese as inferiors, he tried to reach the vast inland and identified himself with the Chinese by adopting their dress. The failure of the Chinese Evangelization Society to send his money threw him back on faith, and in 1857 he severed the connection.

T. was small, sandy haired, musical, imaginative, highly affectionate, with a strong sense of fun; and driven by a tremendous awareness of heaven and hell, of Christ's present reality and of the Chinese need for him. Though in some ways slow to mature, his character and spirit ran deep, his dedication was intense and he was a great man of prayer. In Ningpo T. met Maria Dyer. They married (1858) despite violent opposition from older missionaries. She was his greatest help until her death in 1870. Invalided home in 1860, T. qualified as a surgeon and translated the NT into Ningpo dialect. Increasingly burdened for inland China, now accessible by treaty, and finding no encouragement from established societies, he dared on 24 June 1865 to 'pray for 24 willing, skilful labourers', the nucleus of the *China Inland Mission.

CIM was the first truly *interdenominational mission and the first to accept men and women without college training. To avoid diverting funds from established societies, T. applied his principle of faith and never appealed. ('God's work done in God's way will never lack supplies'.)

The first party sailed in 1866 and established a base at Hangchow. Surviving internal strains and opposition from other missionaries, the CIM took the gospel to inland provinces. In 1868 the Ts and others survived a serious riot at Yangchow, which the British government used as a pretext for a display of the 'gunboat policy' which

20

T. hated. In the subsequent distress he underwent a profound spiritual experience.

T's aim was to bring the gospel to every province as quickly as possible. T. emphasized *identification (all missionaries wore native dress) and sought, not always successfully, the growth of *indigenous churches. T. established a new principle that the mission's general director should be based on the field, not at home, and despite indifferent health, hardship and dangers he travelled extensively in China. He also went back and forth to Europe (and later America), for he considered it equally his duty to keep the needs of China's evangelization before the home churches, and to help deepen their spiritual life as the surest way to encouraging missionary vocations; T. was an ardent supporter of the *Keswick Convention. T. issued appeals for prayer, and for recruits by definite numbers: e.g. for 70, among which proved to be the famous Cambridge Seven (1885), and for 100 (1887).

By 1895 CIM had 641 missionaries, being about half the entire Protestant force in China. Its example had led many other missions to press forward, and T. frequently encouraged these to reap the benefits of CIM pioneering. T's impact was far wider than on CIM, through his writing and speaking, his example of faith, unselfish promotion of all evangelical missions, and his personal character, the influence of which continued to grow since his death, partly through the official *Biography* by his son and daughter-in-law, Dr and Mrs Howard Taylor (see the shortened version, London 1965). This, though inaccurate in certain respects, is a spiritual classic. In old age T. kept the CIM together through the *Boxer Rising; one of his last policy decisions was to refuse *compensation for losses sustained. In 1901 he retired from the direction, and in 1905 died suddenly at Changsha, capital of the last province to be opened.

JOHN POLLOCK

J. C. Pollock: *Hudson Taylor and Maria* (London 1962); Dr and Mrs Howard Taylor: *Hudson Taylor in Early Years* (London 1911),

Hudson Taylor and the CIM (London 1918); *RGG* II, 663.

TAYLOR, WILLIAM (1821–1902), was born in Rockbridge County, Virginia, USA, of Scots-Irish parents, was converted at 20 at a Methodist camp meeting, taught school for a while, began preaching in 1841, and was then constantly on the move till his retirement in 1896. T. worked in the Baltimore Conference of the Methodist Episcopal Church till 1846; was missionary to the gold-diggers in California 1849–56; evangelist in eastern USA 1856–62; in England and Australia 1862–66; in South Africa 1866; invited by J. M. *Thoburn to India 1870–75; with D. L. *Moody in England 1875; in South America 1877–84; bishop for Africa 1884–96. T., basing all his work on the idea of self-support, brought conflict with the missionary society and severe hardship on many of his missionaries. He led his church to open work all over India, to start work on the west coast of South America, to go beyond the Afro-American English speaking groups in Liberia—especially on the Kru coast—and to start work in Angola and Mozambique. The self-support did not work well, so at T's retirement all his work was taken over by his church. T. was a colourful, controversial figure who permanently influenced the work of Methodism on four continents.

PER HASSING

W. Taylor: *Story of My Life* (New York 1896); *DAB* XVIII, 345f.

TCHAD. See CHAD.

TEACHERS, TRAINING OF INDIGENOUS. Despite emphasis on education from the beginning, Protestant missions only slowly made provision for the training of national teachers. When training was instituted, a single seminary usually taught pastors, teachers and evangelists together. As late as his *Centennial Survey of Foreign Missions* (1902), J. S. Dennis lists 'theological and training schools' together, and the notes indicate large numbers had the dual function. This remained the case in the South Pacific until recently. Example, Rongorongo Training Institution, Gilbert Islands. However, the pressure of vast elementary school systems demanded better teachers, and the new women's missionary societies towards the end of the 19th century added 'normal departments' to their new high schools for girls. This led boys' high schools to do the same. McTyeire School, opened by Laura A. Haygood in Shanghai in 1892, is a good example of such a high school. But more than this was necessary, and special 'normal schools' began to be founded about the middle of the 19th century. Lahainaluna High School (1831) was in 1949 turned over to the Hawaiian government by the *ABCFM to be the normal school for the islands. C. T. H. Stagg of the *LMS established in Madagascar in 1862 a Normal School with a three-year course. After 1900 such schools multiplied. The majority were denominational schools aimed at local area needs, such as the American Methodist vernacular Normal School at Moradabad, India (1907), and the LMS normal schools at Martandam (Tamil) and Warkala (Malayalam) in South India; Hankey, S. Africa; Mbereshi, Northern Rhodesia, and Hope Fountain in Southern Rhodesia.

However, greater resources were needed, and many union teacher training schools were founded. An outstanding example is St. Christopher's Training College, Madras, 1923, jointly founded by 12 British, Canadian and USA missions. This led to a companion school for men, Meston College, established by six missions in 1937. Another example is Central China Teachers' College, in Wuchang, 1921.

Beach and St. John's 1916 survey reports 238 normal schools with 6,058 students; Beach and Fahs in 1925 record 297 with 11,442 students; and Parker's *Statistical Interpretative Survey* of 1938 gives 260 with 14,626 students. The largest numbers were in India and China. In 1955 there were still 108 such schools in India.

After governments largely took over existing elementary schools or founded their own systems following the second world war and independence, the demand for teachers produced by the church schools continued. *Christian Education in Africa*, the report of the Salisbury Conference of 1962–63, stresses the importance of church teacher training so as to ensure that Christian influence may permeate government elementary schools.

The rise of high schools and normal schools in their turn demanded a still higher grade of national teacher, and this was an important factor in the development of Christian higher education through *colleges and universities.

R. PIERCE BEAVER

TEACHING OF MISSIONS. See MISSION STUDIES IN THEOLOGICAL EDUCATION.

TEAM MINISTRIES. In the western church from the middle ages onwards, the tradition grew up of having parishes staffed primarily by a single clergyman as vicar or rector, and this pattern has spread to much of the Protestant world on all continents. By the 20th century, however, the growing impact of secularization and urban industrial society on the parochial machinery had caused in many areas a total failure in ministry, the single priest or minister becoming isolated and overwhelmed in a task increasingly irrelevant to secular life around him. In such areas or situations numbers of similar parish units, often of different denominations, have been restructured to produce group ministries in which all the clergy, and often laity too, work as a team jointly responsible for the whole area. Technically, a team ministry is a partnership of shared responsibility characterized by commitment to each other's support for a definite period of time, for example five years. TMs have been particularly successful in areas where the church's failure has been most marked, e.g. in the inner-city areas of large metropolitan regions. Famous examples are: in North America, East Harlem Protestant Parish, New York, and West Side Christian Parish, Chicago; in Britain, the East Manchester

Group, and the South Ormsby experiment (Lincolnshire); in Europe, the *Mission de France*; and there is a very large number of others. Several notable ecumenical Protestant/Catholic TMs also exist. The TM appears most successful either where the existing structure of the ministry has failed under the pressure of modern life, or where a quite new situation allows the church no precedents to fall back on. Examples of the latter are the new universities of Asia and Africa, in several of which TMs have had marked success; one case is the ecumenical Chaplaincy Centre of University College, Nairobi (Kenya), run by a team ministry of four clergy and five lay lecturers, with both Protestant and RC co-operation.

DAVID B. BARRETT

TECHNOLOGY AND MISSION. Tremendous recent increase in technology—the totality of the means employed to provide objects necessary for human sustenance and comfort—has provided mission with tape recorders, airplanes, refrigerators, radios, automobiles, bicycles, mill-made cloth, ball point pens, paper and books, printing presses, flash lights, and countless other objects. Missionaries are often the first to use these. They disseminate them effectively and use them in the propagation of the gospel. The new technology, however, soon becomes an unnoticed necessity. The bicycle, a startling innovation in 1900, is 'old hat' everywhere today.

In addition, some recent technology does more than provide objects. It pyramids the processes for producing such objects and for planning vast enterprises such as the Pan-American Highway or a great new sea port. The computer enables tremendous amounts of information to be stored and recovered instantaneously. When fed the right kind of information, it 'keeps account' of the current state of any enterprise and reports it back to management when desired.

Such technology, potentially extremely important, has yet to be understood and used by missions, which too frequently do not see the task as a whole and are concerned only about a very small segment of it. Research and information centres, which will help missions plan their enterprises in the light of the whole and keep them aware of current developments and priority ratings are a variety of technology which Christian mission will undoubtedly use in the years immediately ahead to its very great benefit.

DONALD A. MCGAVRAN

THAILAND (formerly SIAM) is a kingdom of South-east Asia, in area 200,000 sq.m., with over 30 million population, of whom 70% are literate, and more than 3,000,000 expatriate Chinese.

State-established Thēravāda (Hinayana) *Buddhism claims 94% of the population. There are 23,000 Buddhist temples and 236,000 monks and novices. A small minority of Muslims lives in the south. The total number of Christians is less than 1%: 130,000 Roman Catholics and 32,000 Protestants. The king is the protector of all religions and there is a high degree of religious *liberty.

Thai ethnic roots trace back 2,000 years to China. T. emerged as a nation in the 13th century and was discovered by the west in the 16th century. Waves of Portuguese, Dutch, British and French brought firearms, commerce, missions. The first RC priests visited Siam in 1511, and in 1555 two *Dominican priests took up residence in Ayuthia. They were martyred ten years later. A few *Franciscans and *Jesuits (1607) followed. In 1662 Bishop de la Motte of the *MEP established the present Mission of Siam. In 1666 a seminary for the national clergy was established at Ayuthia. By 1680 there were only 600 Thai Catholics with larger numbers of Chinese, Vietnamese, and Japanese. Current policy calls for efforts to integrate Catholics of foreign origin with the Thai people through their schools. Prominent among the bishops of Thailand was Bishop Pallegoix (1841–1861), scholar and close friend of the Buddhist monk who later became King Mongut (Rama IV). Since the second world war the mission of Siam has been greatly broadened with missionaries from many nations and congregations. The Sacred Hierarchy was established on 18 December 1965, with two Thai archbishops and one other Thai among the seven suffragan bishops.

The first Protestants, the Rev. K. F. A. *Gützlaff, MD, an independent German, and the Rev. Jacob Tomlin, *LMS, arrived in 1828 to work with the Chinese. Shortly Presbyterians, Congregationalists and American Baptists arrived. The Rev. John Taylor Jones, repatriated to Siam from Burma, organized the first Protestant church in East Asia in 1837.

From 1840 until 1940 the American Presbyterians carried most of the Protestant work in T. The early missionaries introduced the first printing press, the first smallpox vaccine, the first modern surgery and permanent hospital, the first leprosarium and the first modern schools. They brought the sewing machine, credit unions, the Thai typewriter and the Thai dictionary. During this period five hospitals, 54 schools and 50 churches were founded. It took the Protestants 20 years to convert the first Thai.

Preparation for the formation of an *indigenous Thai church began with the Siam *National Christian Council in 1930; the first General Assembly of the Thai United Church took place four years later. The 11th General Assembly, in 1966, drew 140 delegates from all over the kingdom. The Moderator of the Thai church is the Rev. Charoon Wichaidist, the General Secretary, the Rev. Wichien Wattakicharoen and the Treasurer, Mr. Suty Gunankara.

This church functions entirely under a Thai General Assembly, a Thai General Council and Thai administrators. Relationships with those missionaries who serve under them as colleagues is warm and friendly. Relationships with those unaffiliated groups who prefer the older missionary patterns are somewhat more complicated.

The following are those groups now integrated with or affiliated with the (United Protestant) Church of Christ in Thailand: (1) United Presbyterian USA, arrived 1840.

It has 76 *fraternal workers, and has founded educational and medical institutions, printing presses and agricultural projects, most of which are still in operation, and are fully integrated with the Thai church. (2) The United Christian Missionary Society (*Disciples of Christ), arrived 1903. It has seventeen missionaries; its institutions are fully integrated with the Thai church. (3) American Baptist Mission, re-entered T. in 1952. It has 32 missionaries and engages in tribal work among Karens. Between 1833 and 1893 it carried on work with Chinese in T. It is affiliated with the Thai church. (4) Marburger Mission (German Lutheran), arrived 1953. It has 20 missionaries and is fully integrated with the Thai church. (5) The United Church of Christ in the Philippines, (6) Presbyterian Church in Korea, (7) the United Church of Christ in Japan (Kyodan) and (8) the Church of South India each had two missionaries in 1968.

The Church of Christ in Thailand is a member of the *EACC, whose administrative office is in the headquarters building of CCT, 14 Pramuan Road, Bangkok. It also deals directly with *Church World Service and the *WCC. CCT has 130 churches and a membership of about 24,000; 40 schools with 23,000 students; a theological seminary, two Bible schools, seven hospitals with 2,000 patients, two rural programmes, two university centres and an extensive scholarship programme.

The following are groups not associated with CCT: (1) Roman Catholics, arrived 1511. There are almost 300 priests, 100 brothers and over 900 nuns; 38 churches, 140 schools, three hospitals, various other institutions, and about 130,000 adherents. (2) *Overseas Missionary Fellowship, arrived 1951. It has 230 missionaries, working mostly with tribes, and has formed 30 groups of 800 members. (3) *Christian and Missionary Alliance Mission, arrived 1929. There are 73 missionaries, 59 churches, 85 groups and 1,500–2,000 members. (4) Southern Baptists, arrived 1949. They have 58 missionaries, eleven churches, seventeen groups, 876 members and 1,500 Sunday

School attendants. (5) Seventh Day Adventist Church of Thailand, arrived 1918. There are 51 missionaries, eight churches, four groups and 1,374 members. Other bodies with work on a smaller scale are: (6) *Worldwide Evangelization Crusade, (7) Finnish Free Mission in Thailand (*Pentecostal), (8) Japanese Independent Missionaries, (9) Church of Christ (Texas), (10) *New Tribes Mission, (11) Christian Brethren (English), (12) American Churches of Christ Mission in Thailand, (13) Swedish Free Mission (Swedish Pentecostal), (14) Free Christian Mission (Scandinavian), (15) Christian Literature Crusade, (16) Thailand Child Evangelism Fellowship, (17) Slavic and Oriental Mission, (18) Thailand Bible House (American Bible Society, serving all Christians), (19) Christ Church (a Church of England congregation), (20) *YMCA, and (21) *YWCA.

RAY C. DOWNS

R. C. Downs: 'Thailand: A Struggling Church in a Stable Land' in G. H. Anderson, ed.: *Christ and Crisis in Southeast Asia* (New York 1968), pp.29–54; K. E. Wells: *History of Protestant Work in Thailand, 1828–1958* (Bangkok 1958); *BM* II, 846–51; *NCE* XIV, 1f.; *WKL*, 1438f.

THEOLOGICAL EDUCATION: SEMINARIES AND BIBLE SCHOOLS. TE was recently defined by a group of North-east Asian theologians as 'an intensive and structured preparation of men and women of the church for participation in the ministry of Christ in the world'.

There are probably over 1,500 Protestant, Orthodox and Roman Catholic schools in Africa, Asia, Latin America, the Caribbean and Oceania, whose primary purpose is to offer such preparation. Two hundred of these schools are the RC 'major seminaries', which provide at least six years of philosophical and theological schooling for graduates of secondary training, which is often undertaken in a 'minor seminary'. Another dozen of these schools belong to Orthodox churches, and are located primarily in the Middle East. The remainder of the schools serve the Protestant churches.

Titles employed by Protestant schools vary even within a single nation: 'theological school', 'theological college' and 'theological seminary' are used without distinctive meaning, but generally refer to a relatively high academic level of training. Less frequently and precisely employed are such titles as: 'theological faculty', 'pastors' training college', 'theological community' and 'training institute'. 'Bible school' and 'Bible institute' in some situations denote lay training programmes, but in others, notably Latin America, and in churches founded by conservative evangelicals, these terms describe ordination training as well. Protestant theological education is conducted at every academic level from primary to doctoral courses.

Although a small number of theological schools was established in the 19th century, most were created in response to the emphasis in this present century upon *indigenous church leadership. Some of the earliest schools still function. The Orthodox Theological Seminary of India still uses its first building dedicated in 1815 in Kottayam. *Serampore College, begun by William *Carey and others in 1818, today serves as the hub of a common degree and examination system used by schools throughout India. Established by the Baptists in 1843, Calabar Theological College of Jamaica retains its identity within the recently constituted United Theological College of the West Indies. Most Protestant theological schools, however, have been established since the end of the second world war, and are supported by a single church or mission agency.

Progress. Widespread concern for the weaknesses of the schools was mobilized by the *Tambaram meeting of the *IMC in 1938, but the second world war delayed most attempts at improvement. By the 1950s, however, the development of TE was being given higher priority in the financial and personnel decisions of churches and mission agencies. The *TEF was created by the IMC in 1958. As an educational foundation the TEF has aided Protestant and Orthodox schools in such matters as faculty strengthening, curriculum, libraries, textbooks and buildings. Through such co-operative agencies and by direct assistance, the churches have in recent years considerably improved the housing, libraries and operating budgets of many theological schools.

A higher level of instruction has been attempted. Sometimes this is made possible through the creation of an entirely new school, such as the Pacific Theological College, Fiji, or the *Faculté de Théologie protestante* at Yaoundé, Cameroon, which from a wide geographical area draw students who are often graduates of local theological schools. More frequently, however, higher academic levels have resulted from internal factors such as better qualified teachers, better students and greater expectations of churches regarding the preparation of their ministers. Although entrance standards in the last decade have become more stringent, enrolment in theological schools generally increased within the same period.

A growing number of universities has become associated with TE. Nearly 30 Protestant and RC universities now sponsor departments of theology, while departments of religion treating Christianity as well as other faiths are today found in about fifteen government and private universities. Other theological schools have recently moved to a location near a university: Trinity College in Ghana; Immanuel College in Ibadan; the *Ecole de Théologie évangélique* at Kinshasa, Congo; Tokyo Union Theological Seminary and Japan Lutheran Theological College and Seminary; the Theological Community of Mexico City, and the United Theological College of the West Indies.

Considerable attention has also been given by schools to the development of theological books printed in the language of instruction. Most areas now possess programmes administered by local committees which seek to provide a basic range of books suitable for study. Although these programmes primarily translate internationally significant books, they have also encouraged original writing. A number of theological journals written by *younger church scholars have also developed in recent years.

Within the decade between 1958 and 1968 nearly a score of theological school associations were created, and today these embrace nearly every higher theological school in the Protestant and Orthodox churches. About half of the associations cover international regions such as North-east Asia or the Middle East, the other half are national associations. Both types provide occasions for regular consultation between schools, as well as joint projects such as textbook programmes and research studies; they encourage fellowship and understanding between teachers of different church backgrounds.

Weaknesses. A fundamental problem of the theological schools is their large number. The financial and teaching resources of the world church are claimed by so many different schools that few institutions have achieved significant academic strength or have given outstanding service to their churches. The better academic programmes, such as those of the *Facultad Evangélica de Teología* of Buenos Aires, United Theological College of Bangalore, Tainan Theological College of Taiwan and the Doshisha School of Theology of Kyoto, are found to be almost invariably a result of joint planning between several churches and mission agencies. Federations of existing schools have therefore been an important feature of the 1960s: the Federal Theological Seminary of Southern Africa, the United Theological College of Madagascar and the Andhra Christian Theological College are examples. The creation of new, single denomination schools, however, still outpaces the number of mergers seen elsewhere.

Teaching in many schools, moreover, tends to be mechanical and imitative of a pattern inherited from a western country. Those who perform this teaching are frequently overworked, ill-trained, and, in Africa and the island nations, mostly foreign. These teaching handicaps make even more serious the basic difficulty today confronting TE throughout all nations of the world: that of the gap between teaching and the life and culture in which the church is to carry out its mission. Current uncertainties about the nature of ministry and about the interpretation of Christian mission also affect the theological schools, although sometimes beneficially.

With the decided increase in recent years, however, of competent national instruction, and of national church concern for common action in TE, there may arise a new concentration of teaching resources and a new direction of these towards the mission of the church.

JAMES F. HOPEWELL

Y. Allen, Jr: *A Seminary Survey* (New York 1960); C. W. Ranson: *The Christian Minister in India* (London 1946); W. Scopes, ed.: *The Christian Ministry in Latin America and the Caribbean* (Geneva 1962); B. Sundkler: *The Christian Ministry in Africa* (London 1960); 'Theological Education Tomorrow' in *Study Encounter* III (1967), pp.166–201.

THEOLOGICAL EDUCATION FUND, THE, was launched by the *IMC at Ghana in 1957, on the initiative of Dr C. W. Ranson, for the advancement of theological training in Asia, Africa and Latin America, the circumstances and needs of which had been disclosed in a series of expert surveys. There were initial resources of $4,000,000 contributed by J. D. Rockefeller, Jr, and eight mission boards of USA, with later contributions from Australia, Canada and Scotland. The fund, set up as a service of IMC (later *CWME of *WCC) with an autonomous committee, was authorized to use the money on a five year (later extended to seven) plan to develop and strengthen indigenous theological education, to stimulate local responsibility for the training of the ministry, to encourage creative thinking, and to provide a higher standard of scholarship and training suited to the needs of the churches to be served. One million dollars was reserved for the development of theological literature and the improvement of libraries. From 1958 to 1965 the fund was used in making 23 major grants to institutions, on the basis of prolonged and careful investigation; in inaugurating programmes of text books in 20 languages; in strengthening over 300 libraries, and in special projects of recruitment and training. In 1963 CWME at Mexico extended the life of the fund to 1970, authorizing the raising of a further $4,000,000 on an international basis, and under a mandate reaffirming the main objects and instructing concentration, in this second phase, on the seminary as a Christian community; strengthening the faculty and student body; re-thinking the curriculum; improving the tools; and post-seminary training. The present director is Dr J. F. Hopewell at 27 Marylebone Road, London, N.W.1., England.

MARCUS WARD

Y. Allen, Jr: *A Seminary Survey* (New York 1960); *Five Years: A Report from the Theological Education Fund, 1958-1963* (New York and London 1965).

THEOLOGY OF MISSION is concerned with the basic presuppositions and underlying principles which determine, from the standpoint of Christian faith, the motives, message, methods, strategy and goals of the Christian world mission.

Until the *Jerusalem meeting of the *IMC in 1928, it was largely taken for granted that the *Great Commision of Christ (Matt.28:19) was the only basis needed for the missionary enterprise. The missionary obligation was considered a self-evident axiom to be obeyed, not to be questioned. Critical rethinking that began at Jerusalem, 1928, was carried further in *Re-Thinking Missions* (New York 1932), the report of the *Laymen's Foreign Missions Inquiry edited by William Ernest *Hocking, and in Hendrik *Kraemer's important book, *The Christian Message in a Non-Christian World* (London 1938). The discussion reached a high point at the *Tambaram-Madras meeting of the IMC in 1938, centring on the issues of *continuity-discontinuity and Kraemer's so-called 'Biblical realism'. The *Willingen IMC meeting, 1952, gave new impetus to the study but was unable to adopt an agreed statement on 'The Missionary Obligation of the Church'. By the time of the *Ghana IMC assembly, 1957-58, the missionary enterprise was asking itself the most radical question in its history, 'What is Christian mission?' In the period following the integration of the IMC with the *WCC (1961), intensive effort went into a fundamental reformulation of the TM. Three points are especially important for understanding contemporary TM: the basis, the scope, and the task of mission.

Basis: The source of mission is the triune God who is himself a missionary. God's mission is to redeem this world and restore it to a unity of purpose with the divine will and way. The Bible, which is missionary literature from beginning to end, witnesses to God's revealing and redeeming activity as Father, Son and Holy Spirit, from the event of Creation onwards. In Jesus Christ, interpreted by Christian faith, the meaning of history comes into focus, the total activity of God becomes coherent, and the deepest needs of human existence are fulfilled. The church as the confessing people of God is the sign and steward of God's mission in the world and for the world. Mission is participation in the promise and purpose of God between the coming of Christ and the fulfilled kingdom of God.

Scope: In this 'post-Constantinian' age of church history, mission is no longer understood as outreach beyond Christendom, but rather as 'the common witness of the whole church, bringing the whole gospel to the whole world' (*CWME-WCC, *Mexico City, 1963). Christians are called to mission in six continents, for the missionary task is essentially the same in all countries. The home base of mission is wherever the church is, and every church must be both a sending and a receiving church. Mission inevitably means crossing frontiers, but these are not only geographical; they are ideological, religious, cultural, social, economic and racial.

Task: Evangelization is humanization. The goal of mission is the new man, the new humanity in Jesus Christ (cf. WCC

*Uppsala Assembly, 1968, Report of Section II). Through witness and service to men, assisting them in their struggles for justice, peace and dignity, Christians share in God's mission of restoring men to their true, God-intended nature, thereby enabling them, through the power of the Holy Spirit, to grow into 'mature manhood, to the measure of the stature of the fulness of Christ' (Eph.4:13).

Conservative evangelical Protestants, in particular, would demur from certain of these formulations, preferring instead to emphasize the distinctiveness of mission, proclamation, and individual conversion in Asia, Africa and Latin America (three continents view), as over against the larger concepts of witness, presence, and social evangelism in six continents.

A similar tension prevails in contemporary Roman Catholic TM. The Second *Vatican Council, in the 'Decree on Missionary Activity', reaffirmed the traditional Christendom notion of missions as the church's activity in the non-western world. But the 'Constitution on the Church' of the Second Vatican Council begins with the words, 'Christ is the light of all nations', and describes the church in terms of the universality of its mission. Vigorous discussion continues among RC missiologists in formulating their TM.

See also: AIM OF CHRISTIAN MISSIONS; CONTINUITY AND DISCONTINUITY; GOSPEL; MESSAGE FOT HE MISSIONARY; MOTIVES; THEORY OF MISSIONS; TRINITARIANISM.

GERALD H. ANDERSON

G. H. Anderson: *Bibliography of the Theology of Missions in the Twentieth Century* (New York 1958; 3rd ed. 1966); G. H. Anderson, ed.: *The Theology of the Christian Mission* (New York 1961); J. Blauw: *The Missionary Nature of the Church* (London 1962); J. C. Hoekendijk: *Kirche und Volk in der deutschen Missionswissenschaft* (München 1967); N. A. Horner, ed.: *Protestant Crosscurrents in Mission* (Nashville 1968); H. Kraemer: *Religion and the Christian Faith* (London 1956); H. J. Margull: *Theologie der missionarischen Verkündigung* (Stuttgart 1959; Eng.
20*

tr., *Hope in Action*, Philadelphia 1962); S. C. Neill: *The Unfinished Task* (London 1957); L. Newbigin: *The Relevance of Trinitarian Doctrine for Today's Mission* (London 1963); D. T. Niles: *Upon the Earth* (London 1962); T. Ohm: *Machet zu Jüngern alle Völker* (Freiburg 1962); R. K. Orchard: *Missions in a Time of Testing* (London 1964); 'Christliche Mission, Begründung und Ziel' in RGG3, IV, 974–80; L. Wiedenmann: *Mission und Eschatologie* (Paderborn 1965).

THEORY OF MISSIONS. Mission theory describes what mission, its chief ends, governing principles and methods essentially are. Each theory, rising from biblical and theological grounds, is formed in the light of what seems necessary and possible at that particular period. The warp of theory is biblical; the woof is contemporary conditions. Thus *Zinzendorf's mission theory was that since all Jews must become Christian before Gentile nations can be discipled, missionaries should work for a few individual converts. In this theory both the biblical base and the very difficult conditions facing mission in 1730 are apparent. Thus theories of mission are formulated, modified, and discarded as theologians wax and wane, and history flows on through new country.

Theories of Christian mission are weak in Reformation writing. Protestant nations had, as yet, no colonial world. They interpreted *ta ethnē* ('the heathen') as nations within Christendom. The *Great Commission was supposedly fulfilled. The best Roman Catholic expression of mission came from Cardinal Brancate, c. 1680, who defined mission as the church's duty to send missionaries, and saw missionary life in terms of vocation.

A Protestant theory of mission appears c. 1590 in the writings of Adrian Saravia (1531–1612) who, holding the Great Commission still binding on the church, said missionaries required spiritual equipment, sense of call, and authority from the church. Justinian von *Welz, c. 1664, urged the establishment of a missionary society, comprised of 'promoters', 'conservers' and 'missionaries'.

When Protestant missions emerged, they came from *Pietism, not from Lutheran or Calvinistic orthodoxy. Pietist missionaries, after first holding a civilizing theory, swung over to the more biblical view that mission is evangelism. The theory of evangelizing by civilizing, a hardy perennial, still appears today in new forms.

The most important theoretical document leading to modern missions was *Carey's Enquiry, 1792. He related the geographical and technological advances of his day to the Great Commission. He assembled statistical data of the distribution of religions, and argued the practicability of the church evangelizing paganism. Contemporary statements by Boyle and Horne and Carey's views ushered in the period of great missionary societies. The missionary society theory, necessary in its day, 150 years later opened the door to mission as an essential function of the whole church.

Two notable contributors to mission theory in the last century were Henry *Venn and Rufus *Anderson. Venn's concept of the euthanasia of the mission was far ahead of his contemporaries. Anderson stressed discipling the nations and multiplying churches, 'each complete in itself, with presbyters of the same race'. Both men are well worth reading today.

More recently John *Nevius, G. *Warneck, Sidney Clark, Roland *Allen, John *Mott and H. *Kraemer have made important contributions to missionary theory.

Many theories of mission are abroad today. This century opened with one dominant—that mission is the establishment of self-governing, self-supporting, self-propagating churches. In 1933 *Hocking published his theory that, the era of church planting being over, reconception of religions is mission. In missions to unresponsive populations a common theory is that mission is proclamation to all men—whether they become responsible members of Christ's church or not. Recently an omnibus theory—that mission is dialogue

with other religions, christianization of the social order, kindly service to men, or even 'Christian presence'—has become popular in some circles. When mission is defined as everything Christians do outside their local congregations and specially when the ultimate salvation of all men is assumed, the concept of mission becomes still more clouded. By contrast, the *church growth theory of missions teaches that, while mission biblically is a broad enterprise, winning men to Christ, multiplying sound churches, and discipling nations is always a chief and irreplaceable purpose of mission. Growth is a test of the church's faithfulness.

Each theory is woven out of theology and circumstance and directs the expenditure of large church resources.

DONALD A. MCGAVRAN
AND ALAN R. TIPPETT

THEOSOPHY. The name means literally 'knowledge of divine matters'. It is associated especially with 'the most serious and most successful of all modern attempts to establish a new religion' (G. West: The Life of A. Besant [London 1929], p.2). Mme H. P. Blavatsky (1831–1891), who had been brought up in the Russian church but became a Buddhist, collected a great deal of material from Hindu, Buddhist and mediaeval Jewish literature. She linked all this with the idea of evolution. The result seems to many readers to be a mixture of speculation, myth and magic, but to her followers it is 'the synthesis of science, religion and philosophy'. In 1875 Mme Blavatsky with H. S. Olcott founded the Theosophical Society in New York and in 1878 moved to India. The society spread to Britain, Germany and other European countries, and Australasia. From 1891 Mrs A. Besant (1847–1933) became leader of the society; she stressed the importance of social service and of freedom of thought. In 1895 a separate American society was formed, led by W. Q. Judge; and after 1927 many theosophists followed J. Krishnamurti in ceasing to belong to the society as an organization.

Theosophists think of God and the universe as essentially one (pantheism). Man to them is an expression of God's being, and can come to know God directly 'through any religion or through his own unaided efforts' (A. Besant). They believe in *reincarnation as a means of progress to higher spiritual life; their 'Masters' are religious teachers 'who have climbed up the ladder of evolution till they have reached perfection in humanity . . .'. These include the Christ (whom theosophists think of as originally a mere man), the Buddha and many others. Some have claimed that one or more of the 'masters' have spoken to them through dreams, visions or spiritualistic experiences. Many theosophists are vegetarians. Some groups meet together for worship, others for meditation, discussion or study.

In Europe, N. America and Australasia T. has appealed mainly to men and women who are dissatisfied with the forms of Christianity familiar to them. In Asia it is evidently most at home since it is so closely akin to *Hinduism and *Buddhism. From the early days in India a number of Christian missionaries have naturally spoken against it as a rival of Christianity. After the first world war T. spread to West Africa, where belief in reincarnation was common ground with the indigenous *animism and *polytheism. Groups have also been formed in Egypt, Singapore, Persia and elsewhere.

Active theosophists throughout the world are probably to be numbered in tens of thousands (e.g. the English Section of the Theosophical Society had 2,656 members in 1965). Many converts to T. seem to lapse after a time. The individualism of the doctrine prevents theosophists from organizing themselves as a missionary community. Its *syncretism deprives them of what is distinctive in Christianity or in most other religions. Many Christians, however, can respect their tolerance and their tradition of social service. There are probably few places in the world today where T. competes with the Christian mission on any large scale.

JOHN GOODWIN

A. Besant: *The Ancient Wisdom* (Adyar, Madras 1897); T. Besterman: *Mrs Annie Besant: A Modern Prophet* (London 1934: a sympathetic but critical study by a former theosophist); H. P. Blavatsky: *The Secret Doctrine* (London 1888–1897); J. N. Farquar: *Modern Religious Movements in India* (2nd ed., London 1929); *ERE* XII, 304–15; *NCE* XIV, 74; *WKL*, 1454f.

THOBURN, JAMES MILLS (1836–1922), was born in St. Clairsville, Ohio, USA, of Scots-Irish parents, and graduated from Allegheny College, Meadville, Pennsylvania, at 21. In college he experienced conversion and the call to preach, was ordained in the Methodist Episcopal Church in 1859 shortly before going as a missionary to North India. T's career was long and distinguished. He was the co-founder of *The Indian Witness*, 1871; started Methodism in Burma, 1879; in Malaysia, 1885; in the Philippines, 1899. He became the first missionary bishop of his church in Asia, 1888, was the first of his church to see the significance of the *mass movements, supported education for both boys and girls, and promoted medical and social work. He influenced the organization of the church in America and India, where he helped to form the Central Conference, was one of the main promoters of the *deaconess work and wrote the laws governing it into the Methodist book of *Discipline*. He helped to change the method of collecting money for missionary support. T. had a positive evaluation of the religions of India, wrote several books and numerous articles. One of the greatest missionaries of his church, he retired in 1908.

PER HASSING

W. F. Oldham: *Thoburn—Called of God* (New York 1918); J. M. Thoburn: *My Missionary Apprenticeship* (New York 1884); *DAB* XVIII, 418–20.

THOMAS, JOHN (1806–1870), was born in Wales and was sent by the *CMS to India in 1836. He served as a missionary at Megnanapuram, Tinnevelly District, in South India. He found a wilderness and left a garden. The great church of St. Paul, with its spire 192 feet high, is a monument to his diligence and imaginative vision. His greatest service to the church in India was his championship of the idea of a simple village ministry for village people. The tradition had been one of almost European standards for Indian priests, with the result that foreign missionaries outnumbered ordained Indians by eighteen to one. In face of much opposition T. persuaded the authorities that the right method was to take the best of the village catechists, give them a biblical training in their own language, and then ordain them. The first class of six men was formed in 1846; the first ordination took place in 1851. The success of the scheme was so great that it continued in operation for forty years. One of those so ordained was the father of Bishop V. S. *Azariah, who later applied in his diocese of Dornakal exactly the methods that had been worked out by T. 80 years before. When T. died, his body was carried to the grave by eleven Indian clergymen, all of whom had grown up under his supervision.

STEPHEN NEILL

P. Appasamy: *The Centenary History of the Church Missionary Society in Tinnevelly* (Palamcottah 1923); E. Stock: *History of the Church Missionary Society*, II, 180f.; 542f. The memoir of the Rev. John Thomas by A. H. Grey-Edwards is not a satisfactory work.

THOMAS CHRISTIANS. See INDIA; SYRIAN CHURCHES, INDIA.

THOMPSON, THOMAS (c. 1708–1773), was probably born at Gilling, Yorkshire, England. In 1745 he resigned his position as fellow and dean of Christ's College, Cambridge, to become a missionary of the *SPG. He was sent to Monmouth County, New Jersey, where he worked until 1751. His contacts with Negro slaves led him to think of the conversion of the peoples of West Africa. The SPG agreed to send him to attempt this work, and in 1752 he settled at Cape Coast (Ghana). Through the co-operation of Cudjo, a friendly chief, he

preached and taught among Africans. He baptized a number of them and sent three African boys to England to be educated. T. made little progress in learning the language of the area and returned to England owing to ill health in 1756.

T. is notable as the first Protestant missionary to West Africa, and the first Anglican missionary to any part of Africa. One of the boys whom he sent to England was Cudjo's son, Philip Quaque, who became the first non-European since the Reformation to receive Anglican ordination. In 1765 Quaque returned as the SPG's 'Missionary, Schoolmaster and Catechist to the Negroes on the Gold Coast in Africa', where he laboured faithfully until his death in 1816.

JOHN GOODWIN

T. Thompson: *An Account of Two Missionary Voyages* (first published in London 1758; reprinted in facsimile with Introduction and Notes, London 1937).

THOMSON, JAMES (DIEGO—1788–1854), was born in Creetown, County of Kircudbright, Scotland. Having served as co-pastor with J. A. Haldane of Leith Walk Tabernacle, Edinburgh, and after training briefly at the BFBS school at Borough Road, London, he went, on his own initiative, to Buenos Aires (1818) to establish monitorial schools and distribute Scriptures. Argentine (1818–21) and Chile (1821–22) where he was made director of elementary education, both granted him honorary citizenship. In Perú (1822–24) T. organized public education, and arranged for the translation of the NT in the Quechua language; in Bogotá (1825) he encouraged leading statesmen and RC clergy to organize the short-lived Bible Society of Colombia. T. married in England, then went as official agent of the BFBS to Mexico (1827–30); the Antilles (1831–38) and Canada (1838–42), where he graduated Doctor of Medicine from McGill University (1842). After deputation work in England and Scotland (1843–44), he succeeded George Borrow as the Bible Society's agent in Spain, where his wife died (1848). In 1849 he left the Bible

Society and gave himself to Protestant work in Portugal and Spain. Most important is his *Letters on the Moral and Religious State of South America* (London 1827).

DONALD R. MITCHELL

J. C. Varetto: *Diego Thomson* (Buenos Aires 1918).

THOMSON, JOHN FRANCIS (1843–1933), was born in Scotland but brought to Argentina by his parents in 1851. At the age of fourteen, he experienced a religious conversion under the preaching and personal influence of a distinguished pioneer Methodist minister, Dr William Goodfellow. T. soon felt called to the ministry and Dr Goodfellow and other leaders saw in him the talented and consecrated 'man of the hour' to begin the first Protestant preaching of the gospel in Argentina in the language of the people T. received a thorough academic preparation at Ohio Wesleyan University (USA) from 1862 to 1866. Returning at the age of 24, he preached the first formal Protestant sermon in Spanish in the old First Methodist Church on 25 May (the national Independence Day), 1876, to a capacity audience including judges, lawyers and doctors as well as the common people. T's ardent, eloquent, polemical preaching was very successful in its day. He also pioneered the Protestant work in Montevideo, Uruguay, and his public ministry in the two countries lasted more than 50 years.

IRA E. SHERMAN

J. C. Varetto: *El Apostol del Plata* (Buenos Aires 1943).

THREE-SELF MOVEMENT. Three-self is a characteristic Chinese abbreviation for 'self-support, self-government and self-propagation'. The Chinese Christian Three-Self Patriotic Movement is the officially recognized organ representing Chinese Protestantism under the communist government in China. In July 1950 40 Chinese Christian leaders met and put out a Manifesto calling for complete independence from western churches and mission boards. Then in April 1951 about 150 Chinese Christians, chosen to be broadly representative of all the larger denominations, met in Peking under government auspices and set up a preparatory committee for what they called the Chinese Christian Three-Self Reform Committee. The official organization, with a constitution and officers, was effected by a conference of 232 delegates which met in Peking in July 1954. A second nation-wide conference was held in Shanghai in January 1961.

This organization has in effect replaced the *National Christian Council as the spokesman for Chinese Protestantism. The latter body was deemed unsuited to the new era: It had been organized by 'imperialistic' missionaries, and moreover the large wing of conservative Christians had refused to join it. This new movement, sidestepping the liberal-conservative controversy and appealing to patriotism, with in fact the official *imprimatur* of the People's Government, has been able to bring about almost 100% at least nominal participation by all Chinese Protestant groups.

At first the movement disclaimed any intention of meddling with any of the internal affairs of any denomination. The word 'Reform' in the title was changed to 'Patriotic' in 1954 to avoid any suggestion of doctrinal interference. But as time went on the movement became more and more powerful. Branches were organized in every province, and even in every larger city where more than one denomination was at work. These were all under the supervision of the national and provincial commissars of religion.

In the summer of 1958, at the height of the Great Leap Forward in economic organization, the movement took a step which practically if not officially did away with all the separate denominations. All Protestant worship was consolidated into a few centres, four in Peking, between 20 and 30 in Shanghai, etc., and the church property thus released was in many cases as a patriotic expression ceded to the government for public use. The details of this consolidation of worship seem to have been worked out locally, resulting in considerable diversity from place to place. No attempt has yet been made to crystallize this new situation in a corresponding church organization which shall include all of Chinese Protestantism, but that is clearly the direction in which the movement's activities are pointing.

FRANCIS P. JONES

K. Hockin: *Servants of God in People's China* (New York 1962); F. P. Jones: *The Church in Communist China* (New York 1962); *Documents of the Three-Self Movement* (Asia Department, DOM, NCCC, 475 Riverside Drive, New York); L. T. Lyall: *Come Wind, Come Weather* (Chicago 1960).

TIBET. A country in the Western Himalayas, extending from the borders of Afghanistan to those of Nepal. It is 470,000 sq.m. in area and has a population of about 3,000,000. In this traditionally 'forbidden territory', improved physical communications in recent years have been counterbalanced by disturbed political conditions which have kept the country closed to Christian work.

Strictly speaking, there is no Christian work in central Tibet today. The *Moravian church exists in Ladakh Province, a Tibetan-speaking area but independent of Lhasa. This province became part of the state of Jammu and Kashmir in 1846. Owing to the conflicts on the Kashmir-Pakistan and Kashmir-China borders, even the work in this province has suffered severe setbacks. Many members of the Moravian community (the only Christian community there) have left Ladakh and have made their homes in Kashmir and Uttar Pradesh in India. Missionaries are no longer given entry permits and this has resulted in the hospital at Leh being closed. Church activities also, especially in Leh, the capital of Ladakh, have come almost to a standstill. In 1960 it was estimated that the Moravian church among Tibetans in Ladakh and other areas on the borders of present-day T. had three places of worship—at Leh, Shey and Khalatse, with a total community of 197. These are small results of years of strenuous

and devoted work, but in the words of one of the Moravian pioneers, 'In the kingdom of God, results are not counted but weighed'.

At the present time the Anglican diocese of Amritsar is giving temporary spiritual oversight to the Moravian Christians in Kashmir, and a Moravian Tibetan pastor who has taken Anglican orders is an assistant priest in Srinagar. In 1956 the Moravian Ladakh Church became a constituent member of the United Church of Northern India, Punjab Synod.

During the years (the first pioneers arrived in 1855) the Moravian church has carried on educational and industrial work as well as the medical work already mentioned. An able Tibetan Christian, the Rev. E. Phuntsog, is in charge of Bible revision and other important literature work, especially among Tibetan refugees. These refugees, especially those in Rajpur, U.P., are encouraged to learn various handcrafts and so to adjust themselves to their new surroundings. In this work, two women missionaries of the *Evangelical Alliance Mission (Chicago) are co-operating with the Moravian church.

HENRY LEFEVER

J. E. Hutton: *History of Moravian Missions* (London 1922); *On the Roof of the World* (Winston-Salem, N. Carolina 1966); E. Wilson: *Work among the Tibetans* (London 1965). *NCE* XIV, 151f.

TILAK, NĀRĀYAN VĀMAN (1862–1919), was born a Chitpawān Brahman, the highest sect of the Hindus of Western India. When eighteen years of age he was married to a girl who was then eleven. Always an eager and passionate lover of knowledge, he read widely in English and Sanskrit, as well as in his native Marathi. T. was to some extent familiar with Christian teaching, but was not attracted by it, nor by the Christians whom he had observed. His first real interest was aroused by an unknown European whom he met in a train in 1893, and who asked him to read the NT. When he reached the Sermon on the Mount, he found that all his doubts had been removed and that he was in heart a Christian. He was baptized on 10 February 1895. T. was of too restless a temper ever to settle in one employment for long. He wore himself out in a varied ministry of teaching, lecturing and writing, and above all in the composition of hymns, an art of which he was master; a large part of the hymns in the Marathi hymnbook are from his pen. Although T. had never received formal theological training, it was agreed in 1906 that he should be ordained a pastor of the American Presbyterian Mission, but he never held a regular pastoral charge. He combined the deepest affection for his missionary friends with radical criticism of everything in missionary policy or practice which seemed to him to degrade or weaken Indian Christians.

STEPHEN NEILL

L. Tilak: *I Follow After* (tr. J. L. Inkster, London 1950); L. Tilak: *From Brahma to Christ* (World Christian Books No. 9, London 1956); *RGG* VI, 899.

TIMOR, PORTUGUESE, an overseas province of Portugal since 1951, includes the eastern half and the enclave Ocussi-Ambeno in the western Indonesian half of the largest of the Nusa Tenggara Islands in the Malay archipelago. It is 7,332 sq.m. in area, and has a population of 556,859. The inhabitants, predominantly of palaeo-mongoloid stock, practise tribal *ancestor worship. There are some Muslims in the coastal areas. In 1555 the *Dominican Anthony of Taveira visited PT, baptizing. Dominicans came again in 1562, arriving from Solor, the Indonesian island north of T., which served as the centre of European missionary and colonial activity in the whole area of the Lesser Sunda Islands for over a century. Ecclesiastically PT like Solor belonged to the diocese of Macao, China. The retreat from the conquering Dutch in 1641 of the bishop of Malacca to PT led to renewed Christian activity. The Dominican mission period came finally to an end in 1754, chiefly owing to Dutch Protestant progress. For all of Flores, Solor and T. only eight Dominicans and four churches maintained themselves in 1804. The arrival of priests of the *OMI in 1816 marks a new

attempt to penetrate the territory. In 1940 PT was elevated to be a suffragan diocese of Goa, India. There are thirteen parishes, 29 diocesan and twelve regular priests. With 122,167 RC Christians more than 70% of the population remains to be reached with the gospel. No Protestants are resident in PT.

LOTHAR SCHREINER

BM II, 851f.; *NCE* XIV, 165f.

TING LI-MEI (c. 1875–c. 1937), Chinese Presbyterian pastor, born in Shantung Province, who gave inspiring leadership to the Student Volunteer Movement for the Ministry in the early part of the 20th century. His soul had been kindled by sufferings experienced in the *Boxer uprising of 1900. During a religious revival at Shantung Union College in 1909 more than a hundred students responded to T's charismatic appeal for young men who would pour out their lives for the church. The fire spread to other schools. New and old bands of volunteers united in 1910 to form the Chinese SVM, somewhat on the pattern of Christian student movements in North America and Europe. The *YMCA Student Department gave guidance and encouragement. T. resigned from the pastorate of his local church to become travelling secretary for the national organization. Everywhere his profound insights into the Scriptures, intense evangelistic spirit, radiant personality, and compelling presentation of China's need for educated ministers left an unforgettable impression. Twelve years later it was reported that 1,570 students had enlisted, 530 for full-time ministry, and 136 had already become pastors. The mantle of T. fell on younger shoulders, while he returned to his home and work in Shantung.

F. W. PRICE

Various sources in MRL, New York.

TOGO is a West African republic forming a narrow strip of 21,853 sq.m. between Ghana, Dahomey and Upper Volta. Population in 1967 was 1,724,000. A RC prefecture apostolic was erected in 1892;

Catholics in 1965 numbered 303,864 in four dioceses. The largest Protestant church is the *Eglise Evangélique du Togo*, served by the *North German Missionary Society (Bremen), *Société des Missions Evangéliques de Paris* (*PEMS) and the *United Church Board for World Ministries (USA); total community in 1965 numbered 45,000. The second large body is the *Eglise Méthodiste* (MMS) with almost the same size constituency. Other missions and churches are the Southern Baptist Convention, *Assemblées de Dieu* and *Eglise Apostolique*. The total Protestant community numbers 96,944. Since 1940 *African independent churches have gathered about 1,000 adherents among three of the country's tribes.

DAVID B. BARRETT

R. Cornevin: *Le Togo* (Paris 1967); H. W. Debrunner: *A Church between Colonial Powers* (London 1965); J. Schramm: *Togo* (Bonn 1962); *BM* II, 852–55; *NCE* XIV, 186f.

TOLERANCE. See LIBERTY, RELIGIOUS.

TONGA. See PACIFIC ISLANDS.

TORRANCE, DAVID WATT (1862–1923), was born at Airdrie, Scotland, and qualified MB, CM at Glasgow University in 1883. In the following year the Jewish Mission Committee of the Free Church of Scotland sent him to found the 'Sea of Galilee Medical Mission' at Tiberias, Palestine. The area was considered the most neglected and unhealthy in the whole country; but, after Jerusalem, Tiberias was deemed second in importance of the four Jewish holy cities; its population was 6,000, of whom 3,500 were Jews. T. became 'the first (Protestant) physician to heal and teach on the shore of the Lake of Galilee'. He built the first Christian hospital there—geographically the world's lowest, 682 feet below sea level. In 1900 the number of inpatients was 296, of whom 115 were Jews, 130 Muslims and 51 Christians. Many were influenced by Christianity as taught and practised by T. and his colleagues; but very

few openly professed conversion, which for Jews meant persecution and for Muslims death. T. worked heroically until Turkey entered the first world war; then he had to depart hurriedly to Britain, losing all his possessions. After service in the RAMC he returned to the looted mission in 1919 and carried on bravely with failing health. 'Torrance of Tiberias', admired by Arab and Jew, died at Safed and was buried in the hospital garden at Tiberias.

HERBERT W. TORRANCE

W. P. Livingstone: *A Galilee Doctor* (London 1923).

TOTALITARIANISM. The term is modern and came into general use only in connection with claims made by Adolf Hitler and the Nazi state in Germany to supreme and unquestionable authority over every aspect of human life and conscience. But the concept is much older than that. Every religion which claims universality must in some sense be totalitarian in its claims. This is seen most clearly in *Islam, which admits of no distinction between the sacred and the profane. In the Qur'ān God has revealed his will for the whole of man's life—social, political and economic as well as religious. It is the duty of every Muslim to strive to put the will of God everywhere and in all ways into effect; an Islamic government exists only to be of service to the Islamic cause. Those who are not Muslims may be tolerated in an Islamic state, but they lack the essential qualification for true citizenship. Rather a similar claim seems to have been made in recent times by the Buddhists of Ceylon; their desire seems to be that in that island of several races and religions, there should be one people, one government, one language, one culture, and one religion, the religion being of course, *Buddhism, and everything else being controlled by its relation to the dominant faith.

In one sense the Christian faith is no less totalitarian than any other. It claims that Jesus Christ is Lord, that there are no autonomous realms that may claim to be exempt from his dominion and that the faith is to be put into practice in every area of human life. But by slow degrees, and in part through their own experiences as a minority in many lands, Christians have learnt the limits within which this ideal can be put into practice, and have come to value the idea of a pluralistic society. Since there must be no coercion in matters of belief, and all minorities must have full freedom to worship or not to worship according to their conscience, absolute unity of belief and uniformity of practice are not to be expected. This involves, however, a separation between the realms of the religious and the secular such as was hardly known before the 18th century.

Other religions are now being faced with the same problem. In Pakistan, for instance, religious *liberty is guaranteed to all under the constitution, and non-Muslims have almost the same rights of citizenship as Muslims. This situation involves for faithful Muslims much painful re-thinking of the relationship between faith and life.

Christians are expected to honour and obey the government under which they live, provided that nothing is commanded contrary to the will of God. But, from the time of King Nebuchadrezzar it has been clear that on occasion obedience to God may involve disobedience to man (Dan. 3). To discern the exact point at which inevitable conflict begins is very difficult; for this the special guidance of the Holy Spirit is needed.

See also ABSOLUTENESS OF CHRISTIANITY.

STEPHEN NEILL

On totalitarianism in Germany, see especially J. S. Conway: *The Nazi Persecution of the Churches* (London 1965).

TOURNON, CHARLES THOMAS MAILLARD DE (1668–1710), papal legate to the court of Peking, was born at Turin, Italy. A gifted young cleric, he was selected by Pope Clement XI for the difficult task of bringing peace to the Chinese church harassed by dissensions and of winning over the emperor to the church's view on the Chinese *Rites. In 1701 he was named Patriarch of Antioch and Visitor General with ample powers. In India he intervened in the quarrels concerning the Malabar rites, condemning sixteen items by his decree of 23 June 1704. In 1705 he arrived at Peking where Emperor Kang-hsi received him with exceptional honours, but insisted on a favourable interpretation of the Chinese rites. T., knowing that the pope had decided the matter in the opposite sense, wanted to evade an open clash, but gradually relations grew tense. Kang-hsi not only refused to accept T. as superior of all missions in China, but demanded of each missionary a declaration in favour of the customs followed by Matthew *Ricci as condition for a permit of further stay in China. T. was sent home, but while at Nanking he published on 25 January 1707 a mandate prescribing strict observance of the papal decision of 20 November 1704. The incensed emperor relegated T. to Macao to be held as hostage by the Portuguese. A few months before his death, T. was elevated to the dignity of a cardinal.

BERNWARD H. WILLEKE

Enciclopedia Cattolica XII (1954) 384–85; F. Rouleau: 'Maillard de Tournon, Papal Legate to the Court of Peking' *Archivum Historicum Societatis Iesu* XXXI (1962), 264–322; *LTK* X, 285f.; *NCE* XIV, 217f.

TOWNSEND, HENRY (1815–1886), was born at Exeter, England. He was sent by the *CMS to Sierra Leone as a catechist in 1836. In 1840 he married Sarah Pearse of Exeter, who thereafter accompanied him in Africa. T. went in 1842 to Abeokuta, where Egba ex-slaves from Sierra Leone had discovered their relatives. Ordained in London in 1844, T. returned to found the CMS Yoruba Mission at Abeokuta in 1846. He began to print Christian literature in Yoruba in 1854 and in 1859 founded the first Yoruba newspaper. Local politics caused T., like all Europeans, to be excluded from Abeokuta from 1867 to 1875, but the church which he had founded continued to prosper. Meanwhile he directed the Yoruba Mission from Lagos. After a final year in Abeokuta he returned to England in 1876. His 40 years' service in West Africa was a unique record for a

European missionary in the 19th century. T. was described as 'a firm, wise and prudent father to his people'. Though he fostered self-support, he did not share H. *Venn's vision of indigenous African leadership; and he made it clear that he would not accept any direction from S. A. *Crowther as bishop. His *paternalistic methods, however, were acceptable, successful and, at the time, inevitable.

JOHN GOODWIN

G. Townsend: *Memoir of the Rev. Henry Townsend* (London 1887).

TRAINING, MISSIONARY. See PRE-PARATION OF MISSIONARIES.

TRANSLATION WORK. All TW needs to be faithful to the spirit of the original, and as close to the form of the original as is consistent with the language into which the translation is made. This is particularly true of Bible translation. A translated novel, for instance, may be read only once; but a Bible will be read over and over again, and much preaching and teaching will be based upon it. Its very words will often be regarded as sacrosanct.

Many translators have therefore felt it their duty to keep as close to the original as possible, translating word for word in many places, regardless of the idioms of the language into which they were translating. Often, indeed, this has brought literal translations into the accepted usage of another language.

Others have felt it more important to reproduce the spirit than the letter. They have ignored the syntax and style of the original, in order to communicate the meaning more expressively. In English, the two attitudes are represented by, say, the Revised Version and the New English Bible. Their respective translations of Lk.4:37 read as follows: 'And there went forth a rumour concerning him into every place of the region round about' (RV); 'So the news spread, and he was the talk of the whole district' (NEB).

The RV faithfully follows the Greek word for word. The NEB disregards the Greek wording, and represents its meaning in vivid modern English. A translator who does not know Greek needs both these versions to guide him. The first will give him his groundwork, but it is not the spoken language of today. The second will be the model for his own efforts, but the two idioms in it will probably not be translatable as they stand. He must find equivalent idioms that can be developed naturally from the Greek or from a close translation.

Another difficulty arises from the fact that the Bible was written in Mediterranean countries, in the midst of their agricultural and social life. An Eskimo translator finds all references to agriculture difficult. Bread is a commodity that is not known in many tropical countries. Customs of greeting differ. Terms such as 'justification' do not have the background that they had for Paul. The danger of substituting some other food for bread is that it deviates from the original. The danger of retaining the Greek or English word is that it is incomprehensible. Translators must throughout use the *closest*, *natural* equivalent; but to work that out in practice is always difficult.

Translation work today is done at all levels. There are still a number of languages spoken by few people, which have never been learnt by a foreigner, and which have to be reduced to writing before Scriptures can be translated. In other languages some translation work has already appeared, and NTs and Bibles are being completed. In the major languages the need is very often for revision. The style of a language changes. Orthography is altered. Scholarship develops. National translators arise who can translate more idiomatically than the pioneer foreigner. Revision, however, needs great care. People become closely attached to a long-standing version, however imperfect it may be.

Much original TW has been done by individuals. Standard translation, however, is best done by a representative and balanced committee, working on the drafts of a chief translator. They are wise if they use as many dictionaries, concordances, commentaries and other translations as possible—and if they keep in touch with the common man outside. The main *Bible Societies have translations departments which guide translators in their work and check it carefully before recommending it for publication. In this way everything is done to ensure the accuracy and acceptability of the printed word.

See also BIBLE TRANSLATIONS AND VERSIONS.

HAROLD K. MOULTON

W. Barclay: *The New Testament: A New Translation* (London 1968), section: 'On Translating the New Testament', pp.307–351; R. A. Knox: *On Englishing the Bible* (London 1949); E. A. Nida: *Bible Translating* (New York 1961), *God's Word in Man's Language* (New York 1952); J. B. Phillips: *The New Testament in Modern English* (London 1958), Foreword, pp.ix–xiii; *The Bible Translator* (quarterly journal, United Bible Societies, London).

TRANSMIGRATION AND REINCARNATION are terms which refer to the doctrine, found chiefly in *Hinduism and *Buddhism, that individual souls exist everlastingly, passing from one bodily existence after another in a continuous cycle of rebirth (*samsāra*), their condition in each existence being determined, for good or ill, by the merit or demerit of their conduct (*karma*) in previous existences.

T., as distinct from R., may embrace other than human forms of existence and its effect has sometimes been to emphasise the unity of all forms of life.

The doctrine is not found in the earliest Hindu scriptures, the hymns of the Rigveda with their positive attitude to life. In spite of the fact that T. attempts to point to a life beyond the grave it has not traditionally been associated with joyous hope but rather with pessimism and life-weariness. Salvation is release (*moksha*) from the everlastingness of the cycle of life, death and rebirth. Modern Hindu scholars, however, emphasize the moral element of the doctrine, implying as it does that there is no un-merited happiness or unhappiness.

In later Buddhism, notably in the teaching of Santidevas (c. 700 A.D.), the doctrine is relieved by faith in the ultimate attainment of the goal of Buddhahood. If the numerous stages of *samsāra* are stages on the road to heavenly bliss (*nirvāna*) then they are related to that goal. So modern Mahāyāna Buddhists can say '*samsāra* (i.e. history) is *nirvāna*'. But this attitude, though hopeful, ignores the question of the future destiny of the sinful and the ignorant. Another difficulty in the Buddhist concept of T. is that of reconciling the doctrine with the teaching that the self is to be distinguished from personality. Though the self will continue in further bodily existences, there is no enduring personality and it is difficult therefore to know what it is that is reborn and how what is reborn can be affected by past deeds 'in the body'.

In Christianity the doctrine has been universally condemned, e.g. at the Council of Lyons in 1274 and of Florence in 1439, which affirmed that souls go immediately on death to heaven, purgatory or hell. The doctrine lingers in certain Christian deviations, notably Spiritualism and *Theosophy. From the standpoint of orthodox Christian teaching the belief is at variance with that of the resurrection of the body. Perhaps the chief defect of the doctrine of reincarnation is its emphasis on 'salvation by works'. So in Hinduism it was superseded by the belief that salvation comes not through meritorious acts but through spiritual insight and loving devotion.

HENRY LEFEVER

Articles 'Transmigration' in *ERE;* R. E. Hume: *Thirteen Principal Upanishads* (London 1921); F. Spiegelberg: *Living Religions of the World* (London 1957); Article 'Metempsychosis' in *ODCC*, p.892.

TRANS-WORLD RADIO (INTERNATIONAL EVANGELISM, INC.). See BROADCASTING, CHRISTIAN.

TRIBAL CONVERSION. The term is used in connection with the adhesion of entire sociological groups or tribal peoples to the Christian faith. An early example is the conversion of the Franks. In recent periods of missionary work, such conversions have taken place among the adherents of *primitive religions, notably in Uganda and Ruanda, among the Hovas of Madagascar, among tribal peoples in India, among the Bataks in Sumatra and the Toradja in Celebes, and in all parts of the Pacific Islands. In a number of lands the chieftain was converted, and his people followed him into the faith. Elsewhere, the traditional religion was so shaken by individual conversion that in the end whole tribes were converted.

There have also been areas in which missionaries have deliberately used the method of TC. For the adherents of primitive religions, religion is entirely a communal affair. Anyone who abandons the religion of the tribe is at the same time separating himself from the community. When folk are so closely bound to their society, it is very hard to win them as individuals for Christian faith. In consequence, such men as Christian *Keysser, Bruno *Gutmann and Traugott Bachmann set themselves to bring about TC. To some extent this same method has in recent years been recommended by Donald McGavran. When this method is followed, the tribe as a whole must be influenced by the gospel until it is ready as a whole to accept the Christian faith. Those who have been won as a result of individual conversion must wait for baptism, and thus they become the best missionaries to their own people. TC is never followed by mass baptisms of the tribe; it creates the condition under which it is possible for the individual to be baptized. But, since the tribe has declared its willingness to accept the Christian faith, it is the Christian community which assumes direction of its levels. In TC the gospel and the life of a people are brought into close relationship with one another, with the result that an *indigenous church comes into being. This close connection has been the object of criticism on the part of a number of observers, notable among them J. C. Hoekendijk. The danger, when churches have come into being in this fashion, is that

as a result of decisions taken as a group, they may fall victim to influences entirely different from those of the gospel.

See also PEOPLE MOVEMENTS.

GEORG F. VICEDOM

J. Bachmann: *Ich gab manchen Anstoss* (Leipzig 1957); B. Gutmann: *Afrikaner Europäer in nächstenschaftlicher Entsprechung* (Stuttgart 1966); J. C. Hoekendijk: *Kirche und Volk in der deutschen Missionswissenschaft* (München 1967); G. F. Vicedom: *Church and People in New Guinea* (World Christian Books No. 38, London 1961).

TRIBALISM in religious matters, as in political, has taken on the unfavourable meaning of the attitude and outlook that places the interests of a particular tribal group above the general welfare. As such it is constantly being fought by governments and church leaders. In many parts of the world, Africa for example, the tribe has been for centuries past and to a large degree still is today the main psychological, social, economic and even governmental reality. 'Tribe' is defined variously by the various disciplines but is generally used for a cluster or group of people sharing a common name, language, culture, territory, tradition of common descent, ideological unity and consciousness of belonging. When missions entered regions with numerous tribal groups, the principle of *comity ensured that the form of Christianity that grew up in a given tribe was usually different from that in its neighbours. Furthermore, if one tribe became largely Roman Catholic, its rivals thereupon tended to embrace a Protestant denomination, as has happened in numerous areas. Missions also contributed unwittingly to the growth of T. by sponsoring the various factors that have increased tribal consciousness: the learning of tribal languages, evolution of orthographies, reducing the vernacular to writing, production of grammars and dictionaries, vernacular scripture translations, tribal ethnic studies and so on. One result has been the growth of tribal political parties, welfare societies, tribal voluntary associations of all kinds (especially in the cities), and tribal *independent (separatist) churches. Cases of the latter which employ the name of their tribe in the title of their church are found in at least 60 African tribes. Although such tribal organizations are not necessarily tribalistic, elements in them are often responsible for T. when it appears.

DAVID B. BARRETT

TRINIDAD AND TOBAGO. See CARIBBEAN.

TRINITARIANISM is not formulated as an explicit doctrine in the NT. The threefold Name appears in the Pauline 'grace' and in the baptismal formula (Matt.28:18), which many scholars regard as reflecting the practice of the later church. Attentive study of the Pauline letters shows that the threefold Name is often just below the surface (e.g. 1 Cor.12:4–6; Eph.3:14–19). However, the name Triad, or Trinity does not seem to have been used till near the end of the 2nd century.

The doctrine as formulated (mainly) by the Cappadocian fathers was needed in order to state the truth of the gospel in a form which protected it from the misunderstandings of the classical world. That world accepted as axiomatic a disjunction between the inner world of pure reason and the outer world of things. It also took for granted a hierarchy of beings extending up through creatures and man to semi-divine beings and finally to the Source of all. In this context Christ was easily interpreted as a semi-divine being, the story of the incarnation as a myth which merely reflected eternal reality, and the Holy Spirit as one of the varieties of religious experience. The trinitarian doctrine 'provided the basis for a radically new and unclassical account of the structure and content of experience' (C. Cochrane: *Christianity and Classical Culture* [London 1944], p.237), in which this dichotomy was overcome.

In subsequent centuries the interpretation of the doctrine has tended to oscillate between an emphasis upon the distinct functions of the three 'Persons' which bordered on tritheism, and an emphasis on the unicity of the Godhead which made the 'Persons' mere aspects or modes of the divine activity. More often the doctrine has been—among practical Christians—reverently ignored.

Its importance for missions may be suggested in the following points. (1) Jesus Christ cannot be introduced to those of another religion simply as 'God'. He can only be introduced as the Son of the Father. (2) The sovereign freedom of the Holy Spirit over as well as within the church is the starting point of missionary renewal. (3) The church's mission is the clue to world history, but is subject to the Father who over-rules all things according to his will.

See also THEOLOGY OF MISSION.

LESSLIE NEWBIGIN

L. Hodgson: *The Doctrine of the Trinity* (London 1943); P. May: *The Doctrine of the Trinity* (Serampore 1955); L. Newbigin: *Trinitarian Faith for To-day's Mission* (London 1963, Richmond, Va. 1964).

TROLLOPE, MARK NAPIER (1862–1930), born in London, England; died at sea outside Kobe, Japan. In 1890 he sailed with C. J. Corfe, first Anglican bishop of Korea. Through pastoral work in Seoul and Kanghoa he became closely familiar with the life of the country. He helped in the revision of the Korean New Testament in 1893 and edited other translations and grammatical works. In 1897 he baptized the first adult converts of the English Church Mission. After working in England from 1902 to 1911 he became bishop of Korea, which in 1910 had been annexed by Japan. By 1911 there were 5,000 Korean Anglicans. T. worked for the upbuilding of existing congregations, the encouragement of self-support and self-government, and the provision of an indigenous ministry. In 1926 he consecrated the cathedral at Seoul, which became the most notable church building in the Far East. He co-operated with the Japanese government in educational and medical work and persuaded the Japanese, at least in some measure, to respect Korean national feeling. T's interest in Korean culture, and his collection of a great library of Korean literature, made him unique among western missionaries in the country during his time. Though he had had very few missionaries to help him, he left a church thoroughly trained and capable of self-extension.

JOHN GOODWIN

C. Trollope: *Mark Napier Trollope, Bishop in Corea* (London 1936).

TROTTER, ISABELLE LILIAS (1853–1928), was born in London, England, and died in Algiers. A talented artist, she gave up a promising art career to serve as a missionary in North Africa among Muslims. She was also active among underprivileged working women in London (1869–79), through the *YWCA.

LT began missionary work in Algeria in 1888. She founded the Algiers Mission Band (AMB), a non-denominational missionary organization welcoming into its fellowship workers from several countries and various denominational backgrounds, one of the earliest ecumenical missionary groups in North Africa. Under LT's leadership the AMB established work in coastal, mountain and desert areas of Algeria, where it continues today.

LT did considerable writing and translation work, illustrating her books with sketches from Algerian life: for example, *Parables of the Cross; Parables of the Christ Life; Between the Desert and the Sea* (Marshall Brothers Ltd., London). Her mystic faith expressed in parable language appealed strongly to Arabs.

Lover of beauty, strong believer in prayer, a humble, joyous Christian, with keen mind and deep love for people, her talents were all dedicated to making Christ known to North Africa. Her strictly disciplined life and ability to overcome obstacles were exemplified in her own life by one of her sayings: 'Things that are impossible with men are possible with God'.

GLORA WYSNER

C. E. Padwick, ed.: *Master of the Impossible.*

Sayings from the Letters and Journals of Lilias Trotter of Algiers (London 1938); B. A. F. Pigott: *I. Lilias Trotter, Founder of the Algiers Mission Band* (London and Edinburgh 1930).

TRUMBULL, DAVID (1819–1889), was a pioneer missionary to Chile and to the west coast of South America. His ancestors are traced back to the Puritans and Pilgrims of New England. Upon finishing studies at Yale College and Princeton Seminary he was sent in 1845 by the Foreign Evangelical Society to serve as chaplain to the sailors of the world who passed through the Port of Valparaiso, Chile. His 'parish' gradually widened to include the foreign colonies in that city and other cities along the Pacific coast and finally to the people of Chile as a nation.

T. considered himself an apostle of the Reformed tradition and in this spirit preached expository sermons of the Scriptures, founded Union Church in 1847, organized the Valparaiso Bible Society, an orphans' home, a school for the common people, the *YMCA and a temperance society. His distinctive contribution to the nation was to advocate religious toleration, thus opening the way for the rights of minorities, and to bring about social and moral amelioration. When the reforms he advocated were written into the constitution, and in fulfilment of his promise, T. became a Chilean citizen in 1886.

The Evangelical Movement initiated in Chile by T. was incorporated, at his request, by the United Presbyterian Church in 1873. Dr Robert E. *Speer writes of him as one of the six missionary statesmen of the world of missions, and Margarette Daniels includes him as one of the twelve 'Makers of South America'.

IRVIN PAUL

M. Daniels: *Makers of South America* (New York 1916), pp.185–202; R. E. Speer: *Studies of Missionary Leadership* (Philadelphia 1914), pp.181–234.

TSIZEHENA, JOHN (1840–1912), was a young Malagasy aged 25 when baptized in 1865 at the Anglican *CMS mission in Vohemar, Madagascar. He became ill and was dying when suddenly he revived, to hear God's call to evangelize the pagan Antankarana to the north. With no support from the Anglican mission he began at Namakia in 1885, taking with him the Malagasy Bible which had been translated 50 years earlier. With no other resources, this untrained layman created in a few years a strong *indigenous body variously known as Mission Lord Church, the Diocese of the North, or the Northern Church of Madagascar, which soon became noted for its fidelity to Anglican worship, including its litanies. After years of waiting in vain for mission help, his zealous followers lost patience with Anglican procrastination in Tananarive and consecrated John as bishop with the title Lord Bishop of the North, D.D. A year before his death in 1912, he was visited by the Anglican missionary bishop from the south and agreed to place his church henceforth under Anglican control; he himself was allowed to continue as bishop, but his clergy had to undergo Anglican ordination after training. In 1967 the church formed part of the Anglican diocese of Madagascar and had 4,000 baptized members. T's almost unknown work is typical of the indigenous initiative in evangelization by which much of the church in Africa and Madagascar was planted in the 19th and 20th centuries.

DAVID B. BARRETT

G. L. King: *A Self-made Bishop: the Story of John Tsizehena, 'Bishop of the North, D.D.'* (London 1933).

TUCKER, ALFRED ROBERT (1849–1914), born at Woolwich, England, was the son of artists, and had exhibited at the Royal Academy when in 1878 he was called to ordination. He took a degree at Oxford, was ordained in 1883, and in 1890, enquiring of *CMS concerning missionary service, was asked to become bishop of Eastern Equatorial Africa. Consecrated the same year, he travelled to Uganda, which he found in a state of semi-war. He persuaded the Imperial British East Africa Company to

continue control in Uganda till the British government could be prevailed upon to declare a protectorate (ratified 1894). T. early realized that European missionaries could not cope with the flood of enquirers, and in 1896 ordained Baganda priests. He drew up the constitution of the Native Anglican Church in the conviction that national Christians and missionaries should have equal status, and before resigning in 1912 saw missionaries and African evangelists working amongst almost every tribe. Though never fluent in an African language, T. was a missionary statesman who saw further than others who had more understanding of local languages and customs. He was one of the first missionary leaders to see that the *indigenous church should be one within which missionaries could serve, in contrast to the view originating with Henry *Venn, which favoured missionaries withdrawing and leaving the church to look after itself. Returning to England in 1908, T. became a canon of Durham Cathedral and died in June 1914.

DAVID B. BARRETT

A. P. Shepherd: *Tucker of Uganda, Artist and Apostle* (London 1929); *DNB* (1912–1920), 533f.

TUCKER, JOHN TAYLOR (1883–1958), was born in Fremington, Devon, England. Upon graduation from the Congregational College, Montreal, Canada, in 1912 he went to Angola under the Congregational Foreign Missionary Society of Canada (now a part of the United Church of Canada) and served with the *ABCFM in West Central Africa for about 35 years. He became principal of Currie Institute at Dondi, Angola, in 1914. Later he was the first missionary in that country to help prepare men for the Christian ministry. At one time he was the treasurer of the Angola mission of his church.

In 1922 he was appointed a member of the Phelps-Stokes Commission investigating the educational needs in West and South Africa.

Through his efforts the Angola Evangelical Alliance of several missionary bodies was formed, and he was elected its first full-time secretary in 1946. For a time he was the representative of all the Protestant mission bodies on matters related to the Portuguese government. He performed this service a little later in Lisbon, Portugal, for all Protestant missions in the Portuguese empire, while serving as director of the *Liga Evangelica de Accão Missionária e Educational*.

Noteworthy of his missionary efforts were his evangelistic zeal, love for the people, wise counsel, timely reproof, practical help, and vision for the growing church. Besides many translations and articles he left four books including: *Angola, The Land of the Blacksmith Prince* (London 1933).

ROBERT T. PARSONS

TUNISIA. A republic of North Africa, in area 63,378 sq.m., with a population of 4,458,000, of whom the great majority are Arab and Berber Muslims. Of the 65,000 Jews estimated by the UN in 1965 the great majority left the country during the three following years. The ancient church was wiped out by invading Arabs in the 7th century; Roman Catholicism re-entered with the French and Italian settlers of the 19th century. Earlier attempts at evangelization, which had no permanent result, include visits by *Franciscan friars in 1219 and by Raymond Lull in 1292 and 1314. French Lazarists worked 1645–1829, *Capuchins 1665–1891, and *Jesuits until their expulsion in 1880. Cardinal *Lavigerie re-established work in Carthage, of which he was named Archbishop in 1884. Franciscan Missionaries of Mary established a convent in 1886; Fathers of Zion and Sisters of Zion worked among Jews. In 1964 the Vatican reached an agreement with the government (the first of its kind made with a Muslim state) by which the RC church has a recognized status.

Protestant work was begun at the end of the 19th century by the *North Africa Mission, but was suspended by government order in 1963. The Methodist Church and the CMJ and a few smaller groups have maintained limited work. Direct evangelism is forbidden. The church has not as yet taken deep root among Muslims or Jews.

The government is attempting to make *Islam relevant to the needs of the people. There has been a great increase in educational opportunities since 1956.

An Inter-church Council of member bodies of the *WCC was organized in 1964 by the Reformed, Methodist, Anglican, Greek Orthodox and Russian Orthodox churches.

See ALGERIA.

GLORA M. WYSNER

BM II, 857–63; *NCE* XIV, 341.f.

TURKEY, with a rapidly growing population of 34 million, covers 301,380 sq.m. (3% in Europe). A secular republic, its constitution recognizes no established religion and affirms civil and human rights. Although 98% are Muslims, the religious pattern has become the social and political force of modern *nationalism. Of the Christian community of 230,190, the majority are Orthodox, with Protestants numbering 17,396 and Roman Catholics 24,774. Christianity antedated *Islam. Here is the territory of Paul's missionary journeys and the seven churches in Revelation. Here is the scene of the early ecumenical councils, the uniting creed of Nicaea, and the first serious schisms which brought into being the Ancient Oriental, Greek Orthodox, and the Uniate Churches. On the European side of Istanbul still resides the Ecumenical Patriarch of Constantinople.

Smyrna (now Izmir) was the first base for *Fisk and Parsons sent to the Bible lands in 1819 by the *ABCFM with 'two grand inquiries: What good can be done? By what means?' The initial objective was to give the gospel to Jews and Muslims by working with and through reformed, revitalized Orthodox churches. Emphasis on personal knowledge of the Bible and its teachings failed to avoid conflicts on rites and ceremonies, and in 1846 the first Armenian Protestant church was organized by a group 'cast out of the church'. The second period of missionary endeavour was in co-operation with Armenian and Greek Protestants. Across the land a growing, independent Armenian Evangelical Church had flourishing churches, printing presses, hospitals and schools at all levels.

After the first world war when the larger part of Greek and Armenian Christians were forced to leave, missionaries continued work with Turks in educational and medical institutions and through publication work. As a new democracy grew, Protestant cultural values in modern education and social ideas were welcomed. Witness to the truth of the gospel has been mainly in emphasis on the worth of the individual and his responsibility in society, and in the active hope that barriers of misunderstanding between Christianity and Islam since the Crusades and even from the beginning of Islam can be bridged. Protestant *comity arrangements of the 1870s still linger, and major western representation is by the American Bible Society, the BFBS, and the ABCFM, now the United Church Board for World Ministries. Shortage of personnel and funds has reduced institutional work to three high schools, a hospital, a clinic and a publication department.

RC institutions, located largely in Istanbul, include five primary schools (for non-Turkish citizens), five middle schools and six high schools. They are staffed and supported mainly by the Carmelite, Lazarist and *Jesuit orders with Italian, French, German, Dutch and Austrian faculties. Several RC hospitals in Istanbul serve both the foreign and local Christian and non-Christian communities. Both Uniate and Latin-rite churches are found in T.

During the 1930s for nearly ten years the late Pope John XXIII served as Papal Nuncio in T. Since the Second *Vatican Council RCs have co-operated with Orthodox and Protestants to express the ecumenical nature of the church.

MARGARET R. BLEMKER

W. E. Strong: *Story of the American Board* (Boston 1910), pp.80ff.; *American Board Annual Report* (1846), p.244.; *BM* II, 863–71; *NCE* XIV, 344–46.

TURKS AND CAICOS ISLANDS. See CARIBBEAN.

U

UCHIMURA, KANZO (1861–1930), is relatively unknown outside Japan, and yet his influence in Japan has been greater than that of any other Japanese Christian. He preached to the largest congregations in Japan, and more than 600 attended his sermons and Bible lectures in Tokyo. Amongst his disciples were two presidents of Tokyo University, eminent scientists, politicians and educationalists. His writings still are sold in tens of thousands, whilst eight titles are included in a popular paperback series. Among them is *How I Became a Christian*, the story of his conversion in March 1878 at the newly established Agricultural College in Sapporo. A 27-volume collection of his selected works was published in 1953–55 and over 200,000 copies have been sold.

U. is best known as the founder of the *Non-Church Movement, not because he wished to deny the church in the NT sense, but because he rejected the denominationalism imposed from abroad, and wished to promote a truly Japanese form of Christianity. Despite his strong patriotism he clashed with the political authorities over his refusal to bow at the reading of the newly issued Rescript on Education (in 1890) and also attacked the social evils of Japan – 'feudalism, corruption, and chauvinism'. In his later years he was less antagonistic, emphasizing far more personal faith and Adventist hopes.

RAYMOND J. HAMMER

R. P. Jennings: *Jesus, Japan and Kanzo Uchimura* (Tokyo 1958); *WKL*, 234f.

UEMURA, MASAHISA (1859–1925), was one of the most prominent leaders in Japanese Protestantism. From 1890 there were three schools of thought – traditionalism, modernism and the moderating position. As a Calvinist, U. was the chief exponent of the traditional position. He emphasized the gospel as an objective, historical revelation as against the seemingly subjective interpretations of liberalism.

Converted in his youth, he was one of the leaders of the *YMCA after its foundation in 1880. Together with *Uchimura and Kozaki he opposed the growing *nationalism centred in an emphasis on the emperor, which led to the passing of the Imperial Rescript on Education in 1890. He demanded freedom of conscience – the freedom to recognize God above all earthly rulers. (In later life, however, he was less concerned with matters of social life outside the church.)

His controversy with Ebina Danjo c. 1900 was most significant, when he stood out as the exponent of orthodoxy over against a growing Unitarianism, and stressed the full divinity of Christ. 'We believe in Him, are united to Him and depend on and entrust ourselves to Him in life and death.'

In 1904 – apart from his work as pastor of the largest Presbyterian church in Tokyo – he founded a Presbyterian seminary, and till his death expressed a strong independence of foreign influences and emphasized the need for strong Japanese leadership in the church.

RAYMOND J. HAMMER

Katsuhisa Aoyoshi: *Dr Masahisa Uemura. A Christian Leader* (Tokyo 1941).

UGANDA is a country of about 91,000 sq.m., with a mainly agricultural population of 8,000,000. To the south and west live Bantu-speaking peoples mostly organized into highly centralised kingdom states. Their traditional religions possess a clear concept of God but give a good deal of attention to various divinities and spirits and the sacral position of the king. To the north and east live Nilotes, Nilo-Hamites and Sudanic peoples. It is impossible to generalize about their traditional religions; in some, reverence of the ancestors predominates; in some the central concept is that of *jok*, an all-pervading spirit force focused in certain occurrences and rituals.

We must turn to Buganda to trace the course of events. *Islam brought by Swahili and Arab traders from the coast found a good response at the Buganda court. The high pre-literary culture and organization of Buganda also caught and fascinated the interest of European explorers and missionaries. In 1877 the *CMS began work and in 1879 the *White Fathers. These competing religious influences acted as catalysts on a society already subject to change from internal pressures. The first converts were young men in training at court as future leaders. In 1885 and 1886 the threat they presented to the conservative elements, coupled with the danger of foreign political interference, led to the martyrdom of at least 150 of them. In 1888 plans to exterminate all Christians and Muslims miscarried and they formed a coalition to overthrow the Kabaka. After a brief period of Muslim power a Christian revolution was effected. Then the Roman Catholics (associated with the French White Fathers) and the Protestants (associated with the British CMS) fell out with one another and a settlement partly based on religious differences was imposed by British officials, the churches and the Muslim community being given extensive land holdings and recognized as part of the Bugandan establishment. The English-speaking *Mill Hill RC mission was introduced in an effort to reduce tensions.

The decade 1894–1904 saw a rapid expansion of Christianity in which African initiative played a large part. Much informal teaching went on and both missions employed hundreds of *catechists who pioneered before Europeans arrived in new areas. The role of chiefs in supporting teachers and influencing their subjects was great. Both missions had difficulty in coping with the masses who flocked into the church, with too little instruction and pastoral care. The period 1895–1901 saw Christianity introduced throughout the Bantu kingdoms and Busoga; by 1914 Acoli, Teso and Bukedi were entered, whilst catechists had reached Lango and Kigezi. West Nile was

entered by the AIM and the Verona Fathers in 1917, and Karamoja by the BCMS and the Verona Fathers in the 1930s. Except in West Nile, Anglican work in non-Bantu areas had been hampered by lack of staff. Both churches concentrated on the education, secular and religious, of an élite. The first Anglican nationals were ordained in 1893, the same year that the Catholics opened their first minor seminary. In 1913 two Ugandans became the first East African RC priests; the first African RC bishop of modern times, Joseph Kiwanuka, was consecrated in 1939, and the first Anglican bishop in East Africa, Aberi Balya, in 1947. The early attitude of respect, though largely lost under the influence of *colonialism, was written into the constitution of the Native Anglican Church, giving greater responsibility to Africans than was found elsewhere before independence. Educational requirements for Anglican clergy were, however, relatively low. Great efforts are being made to remedy this, and five are now university graduates. African Catholic sisterhoods were also early established; the novitiate for the *Bannabikira* was opened in 1908. Today the RC Church has 270 indigenous priests, 120 brothers and 1200 sisters; the Anglicans 500 indigenous clergy.

In the early days, particularly of the Anglican mission, learning to read and receiving Christian instruction were so closely linked that the expressions 'reader' and 'Christian enquirer' were synonymous. Until 1924 all education was in mission hands; and as well as schools which have developed into today's leading secondary schools, there was a network of 'bush' schools. From 1924, when the Phelps-Stokes Commission first recommended grants-in-aid, until 1964, mission and government worked in close alliance. In 1964 government took over the administration of all schools.

The Catholic hierarchy was erected in Uganda in 1953, and in 1961 the Anglican Church in Uganda, Rwanda and Burundi became a Province of the Anglican

Communion. An increasing number of bishops are now Africans. A Joint Christian Council was set up in 1964 representing Anglicans and Catholics, and it has undertaken joint social action. In the 1930s a revival movement in the Anglican church, whose members are known as *Balokole* (saved ones), spread from Rwanda, bringing much needed new life to many. The danger that this would develop as a *separatist church has been avoided. The canonisation of 22 Catholic Uganda martyrs in 1964 profoundly stirred the RC church and was marked by public celebrations, renewed dedication and evangelism, together with recognition of the many martyrs who professed the Anglican form of the Christian faith. Catholic Action and the Legion of Mary are strong. Today the RC church claims 2,400,000 members. Total membership of the Church of Uganda (Anglican) is about 1,500,000. The more recently introduced Seventh Day Adventists and Pentecostalists number perhaps 10,000. The African Greek Orthodox Church numbers some 6,000. There are a few small 'break-away' or 'prophetic' churches but they have not the significance they have in other parts of Africa. The *Baha'i have some thousands of adherents. There are about half a million Muslims, mainly Shafi Sunnis, and Ugandan Islam is vigorous and increasing. The non-African population is less than 1.5%. This includes some Americans and Europeans, but consists mainly of people from Bharat/ Pakistan who have taken Ugandan citizenship. They include Ismaili, Ithna-asheri, Bohra and other Muslims, as well as Sikhs, Hindus and Parsees, and some Goans who have been a constant support to RC work.

NOEL Q. KING
M. LOUISE PIROUET

H. Berger: *Uganda* (Bonn 1964); A. Cook: *Uganda Memories* (Entebbe 1947); J. F. Faupel: *African Holocaust* (rev. ed., London 1965); H. P. Gale: *Uganda and the Mill Hill Fathers* (London 1959); A. Luck: *African Saint: The Story of Apolo Kivebulaya* (London 1963); R. Oliver: *The Missionary Factor in East Africa* (rev. ed., London 1965); J. K. Russell: *Men Without God?* (London 1966); J. V. Taylor: *The Growth of the Church in Buganda* (London 1958); H. B. Thomas and R. Scott: *Uganda* (London 1935); *Catholic Directory of Eastern Africa* (Tabora, 1969 edition); *Uganda Journal* (published by the Uganda Society, P.O. Box 4980, Kampala, carries articles on many relevant topics); F. B. Welbourn: *East African Rebels* (London 1961); *BM* II, 655–61; *NCE* XIV, 326f.; *WKL*, 1489f.

UNDERWOOD, HORACE GRANT (1859–1916), was born in London, England, but migrated to America and in 1881 graduated from New York University. After further theological studies he was accepted by the Presbyterian Board of Missions for service in Korea, and arrived in Chemulpo in 1885. The following year in Seoul he opened the first Christian orphanage, which later became a school for boys. In 1888 U. established the Korean Tract Society and began the translation of the NT books; in 1889 he published a Korean grammar and dictionary, followed by the first Korean hymnal. In 1891 he persuaded his church to adopt the *Nevius plan of self-propagation, self-government and self-support for newly established churches. Although in the 1890s he encountered serious political opposition to evangelism, he found some Koreans ready for Christian leadership, especially in education. U. worked when he could with the government, and gained its approval for the 'Jesus Hospital' which he founded in 1895 for victims of a cholera epidemic. He initiated in 1896 a public observance of the birthday of the Korean king, the largest assembly of people ever held under Christian auspices until that time. Much later he served effectively in promoting understanding between Japanese officials and Korean Christians during the early years of 'occupation' by Japan.

U. fostered co-operation between different Christian bodies: in 1892 he secured general approval for a *comity plan allocating areas to several denominations for evangelistic outreach. Between 1901 and 1905 he arranged the co-ordination of many Christian schools and promoted the establishment of Union Medical College in Seoul, which with Severance Hospital and the Nurses Training School was later merged with Chosen Christian University, to form what is now Yonsei University in Seoul. He brought into being the Pierson Bible Institute in 1912–13 and urged united theological training, which was achieved at Yonsei University 50 years after his death.

THOBURN T. BRUMBAUGH

L. H. Underwood: *Underwood of Korea* (New York and London, 1918); H. A. Rhodes, ed.: *History of Korea Mission, Presbyterian Church – U.S.A., 1884–1934*; (Seoul 1934); *DAB* XIX, 113.

UNEVANGELIZED AREAS. An area is unevangelized when its people have no opportunity to hear the gospel in such a way that they can accept it. To be evangelized men must have a real chance to become responsible members of Christ's church.

Four main kinds of UA exist – whole countries, whole tribes, sections of countries and sections of cities. A few whole countries, such as Tibet, Afghanistan and Saudi Arabia, remain unevangelized. The gospel is proclaimed around the edges. Sometimes at the centre secret believers and visitors commend Christ quietly. Perhaps two thousand small tribes remain unevangelized.

Thousands of sections of countries remain unevangelized. Churches have been established at centres; but around many centres hundreds or thousands of outlying villages are without church, Christian or Bible, never visited by a messenger of the good news.

Many growing cities, too, are full of UAs. In whole wards men have no way to hear the gospel. Square mile after square mile are full of people living in ignorance of Jesus Christ. The campuses of many universities are unevangelized. The few Christians there neither sound forth an understandable evangel nor disciple the pagans.

Which UA should be approached first? Some hold that numbers are the sole criterion. The larger the numbers of unevangelized, the better their claim to attention. Across the years and the continents, however, it has generally been held that, in answering the question, both 'movement into Christian faith' and 'importance of the population' must be taken into account. Importance alone is not enough. The Romans in the year one were vastly more important than the Jews – but were not moving to Christian faith and could not be won to Christian faith until a strong church of scores of thousands had been established among the Jews. Those who will accept the Lord and be formed into the churches now always have high priority: the more vigorous and powerful they are, the more influential they are likely to be in the coming spread of the Christian religion.

Potential Christian nations of to-morrow have very high priority. Liberia, Korea, Ghana, Ethiopia, Northeast India, Taiwan, Chile and some others display this double criterion of willingness to become disciples and strategic importance.

Certain resistant UAs are so important that Christian mission must continually experiment, not to 'reach' them, but to baptize them; not to 'work among' them but to multiply churches in them. Student populations, so largely unevangelized, are a case in point. Ways must be found of bringing hundreds of students to become disciples of Christ in reproductive churches of his. 'Student work' is not the goal. The goal is so to evangelize students that multitudes of them become vital Christians.

DONALD A. MCGAVRAN

UNEVANGELIZED FIELDS MISSION, a non-denominational *faith agency, founded in London, England, in 1931 with fields in Congo and Brazil, was established in North America that same year by the Rev. and Mrs. E. J. Pudney.

By 1967 UFM was supporting more than 400 missionaries in France, the Ivory Coast, Guyana, Haiti, the Dominican

Republic, Egypt, Papua and Irian, as well as the Congo and Brazil; it also had work among the Spanish-speaking people of the southwestern USA. Apart from its main work of evangelization, the agency trains nationals, plants *indigenous churches, and conducts medical and educational institutions.

The mission has headquarters in Bala-Cynwyd, Pennsylvania, USA; London, England, and Melbourne, Australia. The annual income for all headquarters is over a million dollars. It holds membership in the *IFMA.

HAROLD LINDSELL

UNION MOVEMENTS, MISSIONARY AND CHURCH. The mission-field has always been the seed-bed of Christian union. By the circumstances of their work the missions have always been driven to co-operate in a great many enterprises, notably in the translation of the Bible. The principle of *comity enabled them to avoid rivalry and unnecessary competition. The development of councils in the lands of the *younger churches, and of conferences in the west, set co-operation on a new basis. But, although actual church union was often talked about in the 19th century, achievement had to wait till the 20th century.

The first notable union was that between the Presbyterians and Congregationalists in South India (1908), through which the South India United Church came into being. Since that date unions have been so numerous that in this article it is not possible to give more than a small selection; for the full list reference must be made to the works referred to at the end of the article.

(1) *Three types of Union.* (*a*) The *Church of South India (1947). This union is significant for a number of reasons; among others, that it is the only union in which so far Anglican churches have found themselves able to join, in this case with Presbyterians, Methodists, Congregationalists and the *Basel Mission (partly Lutheran). The first proposal was made

in 1919; 28 years were spent in working out all the problems. Because this work was so carefully done, and because the union has proved successful, *The Scheme of Church Union in South India* has exercised an immense influence both on other plans for union, and on the thinking of the church in general. One remarkable feature of this scheme is the provision of an interim period of at least 30 years, during which the process of unification should be completed.

(*b*) The Church of Christ in China (1927) followed a different plan, and, with a very brief confession and a somewhat loose organization, was successful in drawing together eight Protestant denominations, including the Baptists. Living for the most part widely separated from one another, the denominations continued to act very much as they had always done; but those who served in that church declared that it was much more than a federation, and that the sense of belonging to a single church was growing all the time.

(*c*) The Church of Christ in Japan (*Nippon Kirisuto Kyodan*) was unique in taking its origin (1941) not from Christian conviction but from government action. The government, wishing to have to deal only with a smaller number of Christian bodies, during the second world war practically compelled all the Protestant bodies to join together in what was rather an administrative union than a church. Those bodies which refused to join were legally dissolved. As soon as the war ended, Anglicans, Lutherans and some Presbyterians withdrew; but other Presbyterians remained with the Methodists and the Congregationalists to form what is still the largest Protestant body in Japan. The church has been able to develop a confession of faith – this it had not been able to do during the war years. It has held together as a church, and has taken a leading part in all the social and evangelistic concerns of the Japanese churches.

(2) *Some current negotiations.* Discussions about church union are going on in almost every country in the world. A few

examples must suffice to illustrate the process.

(a) In North India and Pakistan, starting in 1929, five churches set to work to create a union, using large parts of the South India *Scheme* as the basis for their work. What was expected to be an almost final form of their Scheme was published in 1951. One fundamental change was that, wishing to avoid the interim period of the South India plan, they introduced a ceremony for the unification of the ministry with the laying on of hands, to be observed at the inauguration of union. This led to much debate and disagreement; but it seems that agreement has at last been reached, and that the *Scheme* in its finally revised form may be accepted by the churches. It is hoped that the decisions may be taken in time for the Union to come into being in 1970.

(b) In Nigeria, Anglicans, Methodists and Presbyterians had produced a plan, following very closely the South India *Scheme*. All was ready for union to take place in 1965, when a sudden hostile reaction on the part of some Methodist groups, accompanied by threats of legal action, led to the postponement of the union *sine die*. Great care had been taken to inform the constituents of what was being done; but successful opposition on the part of a very small minority is a possibility with which it is always necessary to reckon. The immediate dispute has been settled by agreement, but on terms which make it unlikely that union can be brought about in the course of the next few years.

(c) In East Africa discussions between Anglicans, Methodists, Presbyterians, Lutherans and Moravians have been broken off, largely because of the Lutheran insistence that all forms of church organization are optional, and because of the failure of the Anglicans to convince them of the desirability of the historic episcopate as part of every church order. Friendly co-operation is to continue, and discussions with a view to church union have been renewed, with a deeper consideration of the theological issues involved.

(3) It seems certain that the movement for church union will continue to grow in strength throughout the Christian world. But it is not certain that the movement will continue in its present form unchanged. Already voices have been raised, questioning whether the production of united churches in restricted areas, according to the method so far followed, is really the right method. Does this mean simply the production of a number of new denominations unrelated to one another? Is not the world confessional body the right organ for discussion with a view to union, especially now that the Church of Rome has entered into the picture? The proposal for a merger of the Presbyterian World Alliance (1875) with the International Congregational Council (1891) is something new in ecumenical history. It may be that the Spirit which for 50 years worked in the direction of local unity is now moving in another direction.

STEPHEN NEILL

R. Rouse and S. C. Neill, eds.: *A History of the Ecumenical Movement 1517–1948* (London 1954); S. C. Neill: *Towards Church Union 1937–1952* (London 1952), *The Church and Christian Union* (London 1968); B. G. M. Sundkler: *The Church of South India* (London 1954); and the periodical reports published by the *WCC in the *Ecumenical Review*; WKL, 1498–1513.

UNION OF SOUTH AFRICA. See SOUTH AFRICA, REPUBLIC OF.

UNION OF SOVIET SOCIALIST REPUBLICS. The revolution of 1917 not merely liquidated the Tsarist state, it also brought to an end the Russian Orthodox State Church. Organized missionary activity was no longer possible, since the new rulers were hostile to missions as one of the instruments through which the imperialists had exercised their power. The policies of the new government in regard to 'nationalities' during the early phase of Bolshevism, were agreeable to many of the non-Russian elements in the population, which regarded missionary activity as one of the means used for their 'Russification'. This resistance was strongest among the Islamic peoples of Russia.

At the same time, Christians of the missionary areas seem to have held fast their Christian faith with no less devotion than other Christians. As evidence for this it is possible to mention the fact that in the new organization of the eparchies of the Russian Orthodox church, account is taken of the various nationalities. Thus the Eparch of Cheboksary takes his title from the Chuvash people, the Eparch of Ufa from the Bashkirs and so on. This can serve as evidence that members of these races make up so large a part of the population of the eparchy that the name of each race has been taken up into the official title of the eparchy. Moreover it seems to be of importance that in the Constitution of the Eparchies we find the names of cities which are the centre of areas of settlement of the non-Russian peoples. (See V. Alexeev: *Russian Orthodox Bishops in the Soviet Union 1941–1953*, New York, n.d.). Precise details about the former missionary areas are given in the *Annuaire du Monde Musulman*, where the number of Tartar Christians in the Middle Volga is given as 100,000.

These indications are all the more significant in that the adherents of all religions and confessions in the course of Soviet history have repeatedly been exposed to violent persecutions, which in many cases have been closely related to changes in social organizations, or to large changes within the communist party structure. Thus the fight against the kulaks (the prosperous peasants), the introduction of the collective economy (1929), the great purges which followed on the murder of Kirov (1936) were in each case followed by a religious persecution -- members, and especially leaders, of religious communities were classed as reactionaries who should be liquidated.

During the second world war a change took place in the relationship between the Soviet authorities and the religious communities. Freedom of religious worship was granted not only to Orthodox Christians, but also to Jews, Muslims and Buddhists. At the same time Article 124 of the Constitution of Soviet Russia and Article 13 of the party programme remained in force; under these anti-religious propaganda is firmly established by law, whereas all religious activity with a view to winning new members, including religious education within the sphere of the confessions themselves, is forbidden.

In consequence the establishment by the Moscow Patriarchate of a missionary council (1949) must be regarded with some suspicion, especially as the primary object which it sets before itself is not the evangelization of the non-Christian peoples, but the conversion of the Balts, the Letts, the Esthonians, the Lithuanians and other non-Orthodox Christians.

Since 1956 the atheistic propaganda carried on by the communist party has been considerably strengthened; and the revision of the Constitution which was carried through in 1967 has made it easier than it was before for the state to interfere in the life of the church. The attitude of Bolshevism towards Christian missions is unmistakably seen in the *Soviet Encyclopaedia*, in which the following definition occurs: 'Mission is one of the forms of religious and political activity, which are carried out by ecclesiastical organizations. It carries on propaganda, in order to convert men to the faith. In the Middle Ages, as in the present, Christian missions have been an instrument of aggression, and of the oppression of coloured races. In our time missionaries are employed as secret agents of espionage and sabotage in the service of the imperialist powers'.

JOSEF GLAZIK

J. S. Curtiss: *The Russian Church and the Soviet State 1917–1950* (Boston 1953); J. M. Bochenski and G. Niemeyer: *Handbuch des Weltkommunismus* (Freiburg 1958), pp.517–68; W. de Vries: *Kirche und Staat in der Sowjetunion* (Munich 1959); B. Stasiewski: '*Sowjetische Religionspolitik*' in *Hochland* LII (1960), pp.315–24.

21

UNIQUENESS OF CHRISTIANITY. The enterprise of missions would be absurd if there were not something in Christianity which is not to be had otherwise. But the gospel does not require us to believe that everything outside of Christianity is of the devil. The NT shows us the developing understanding of the church about the uniqueness of Christ in the context of Jewish faith. It gives only intermittent guidance about his relation to other religions. The church of the first three centuries, fighting for its life, often regarded pagan religion as the work of the devil, but was glad to acknowledge the presence of the *logos* in the great pagan philosophers. The rise of *Islam confronted the church with what could only be seen as a terrible enemy to be resisted at all costs. The Jews were seen as those who had rejected Christ, the Christians forgot that in this respect the Jews were simply the representatives of humanity. When, after many centuries, Christendom came into close contact with other great religions, the contact was vitiated by all the evils that go with *colonialism. It is in relatively modern times that the relation of Christianity to other religions can be considered in the context of a shared world.

The *World Missionary Conference (1910) claimed that Christianity was unique but (1) distinguished between real Christianity and the actual beliefs and behaviour of Christians; (2) claimed that there were many evidences of the work of the Holy Spirit in non-Christian religions which missionaries must cherish. The *Jerusalem meeting of 1928 sought to define further these 'values' in the non-Christian religions, but was challenged by H. *Kraemer with the question: 'What is the value of these values?' The 1938 meeting (*Tambaram) was introduced by Kraemer's book *The Christian Message in a Non-Christian World*, which claimed that not Christianity but the gospel was absolutely unique and *sui generis*. In his acute criticism of Kraemer, A. G. Hogg of Madras insisted that God does reveal himself to the devout faith of the non-Christian, and that what is unique in the gospel is not the occurrence of revelation, but its content. Clearly it is impossible to make a total dichotomy between revelation as an act of God and human faith as the response, since if there is no response there is no effective revelation. In some sense, therefore, Christianity (and not only 'the gospel') is involved in the question of uniqueness.

Recent discussion of the matter has been greatly influenced by: (1) the growing intermingling of people of all races in a common secular culture; (2) wider diffusion of the *comparative study of religions; (3) the idea propagated in the papal *Encyclical *Suam Ecclesiam* of religions as concentric circles having the RC church at the centre and others at increasingly remote distances; (4) the acute bad conscience of western man, who wishes above all to avoid any claims to superiority for what is thought to be his. To this it may be added that the Hindu belief that all religions are differing roads to one reality is becoming increasingly the unchallenged axiom of modern educated people.

An answer to the question of the uniqueness of Christianity relevant to the present situation will probably only be discovered as the church is able to demonstrate in practice that in Christ is to be found the unique possibility of meaningful action in secular history. The question of the uniqueness of Christianity is not just a question of the comparative study of religions; it is the question whether Jesus Christ is the clue to the meaning of world history, and therefore to our involvement in it.

See also CONTINUITY AND DISCONTINUITY; THEOLOGY OF MISSION.

LESSLIE NEWBIGIN

A. G. Hogg: *The Christian Message to the Hindu* (London 1947); H. Kraemer: *The Christian Message in a Non-Christian World* (London 1938), *Why Christianity of all Religions?* (London 1962); N. Macnicol: *Is Christianity Unique?* (Oxford 1935); L. Newbigin: *A Faith for this One World?* (New York 1961).

UNITED ARAB REPUBLIC. See EGYPT.

UNITED BIBLE SOCIETIES, THE. A world organization of Bible Societies which was established in 1946, after a conference of Bible Society and church leaders held in Haywards Heath (England) at the invitation of the American Bible Society and the BFBS. It is not an executive body but a fellowship of Bible Societies, with the following aims: (1) To encourage the co-ordination and extension of efforts and to develop patterns of effective co-operation among Bible Societies. (2) To facilitate the exchange of information among the Bible Societies, in policies as well as in technical problems, and to encourage the harmonization of policies and techniques. (3) To supply to societies such helps and services as can more easily be provided centrally. (4) To collect, assemble and diffuse information on world trends, on religious developments and on the various aspects of and progress in the effective use of the Bible in the churches' life and witness. (5) To represent the Bible Societies movement among the international Christian organizations. (6) To arrange for any emergency service that may be needed on specific occasions.

The UBS has a permanent Committee on Translation, which fulfils the aims of the UBS in the field of translation and meets at least once a year. It publishes *The Bible Translator*, a quarterly journal devoted to the problems of translation which is now in its twentieth year. It has also published six volumes in a series of Translators' Aids.

Membership in the UBS is open to national societies actively concerned with the wider circulation of the Scriptures, rooted in the life of their people and of their churches and effectively administered by an autonomous national committee. National committees still working under the administrative control of 'mother' societies are eligible for associate membership. The steady growth in the number of members reflects the concern of the Bible Society movement for societies to be closely related to the life of the local churches in the areas where they function. At the end of 1968 there were 27 member societies and eight in associate membership.

The Council, on which every member society is represented and has one vote, is the supreme governing body of the UBS. The last meeting of the council, held in the USA in 1966, adopted a number of far reaching changes. In future the council will meet once in six years in connection with the meeting of a General Assembly representing churches as well as Bible Societies.

Its business will be carried out during the interim by means of regional conferences in each of the following four regions: Africa, the Americas, Europe and Asia-South Pacific. In addition it will be served by a general committee, formed predominantly by the election of representatives from the regional conferences, and an executive committee which will meet at least once a year.

In 1963 the President of the UBS, Dr F. D. Coggan, the Archbishop of York, launched in Tokyo on behalf of the Council a worldwide campaign calling for the trebling of Scripture distribution figures by 1966. Although in many areas the goal was not reached, the campaign resulted in a significant increase in world circulation. The Council, meeting in 1966, called for a continuation of the campaign with special emphasis on the Bible as the Book for new readers, especially young people in schools and colleges and new literates.

In addition to *The Bible Translator* the UBS publishes *The UBS Bulletin* (a quarterly magazine of information) and two news sheets, the fortnightly *News and Views* in English, and *Nouvelles Bibliques* in French which appears eight times a year. Yearly statistics of Scripture distribution and translation are issued by UBS headquarters in London.

W. J. CULSHAW

UNITED BOARD FOR CHRISTIAN HIGHER EDUCATION IN ASIA, THE, has its origin in joint conferences in New York in 1918–19 by agencies supporting Christian colleges in China. A Central Office of the China Union Universities was set up in 1922 and a Permanent Committee for the Co-ordination and Promotion of Christian Higher Education in China appointed in 1925. This became in 1928 the Committee for Christian Colleges in China. The boards of some colleges in 1932 formed the Associated Boards for Christian Colleges in China. Remaining duplication was eliminated in 1947 by the founding of the United Board for Christian Colleges in China, which supported all thirteen institutions. When contact with the colleges ceased in 1950 new responsibilities were accepted in East Asia and in 1955 the name was legally changed to the UBCHEA. Twelve American mission boards, six colleges with overseas programmes, the Community Churches, and a few British societies participate. Support is given to Satya Watjana Christian University in Indonesia, Silliman in the Philippines, Philippine Christian College, Tunghai University in Taiwan, Chung Chi in Hong Kong, and Yonsei University and Medical Centre in Korea. Expenditures for the year ending 30 June 1966 were $1,012,957. Income is from gifts of mission boards, foundations, and the general public, and from endowment. Address: 475 Riverside Drive, New York, N.Y. 10027, USA.

R. PIERCE BEAVER

UNITED BRETHREN MISSIONS. The United Brethren in Christ, issuing out of the *revival movements of the 18th century in the USA, was organized in 1800 by Philip Wm. Otterbein (1726–1813). The Home, Frontier and Foreign Missionary Society was organized in 1853 and the Woman's Missionary Association in 1875. The first overseas mission was attempted in Sierra Leone in 1855 and soon afterwards permanently effected at Shenge by the Rev. D. K. Flickinger. The neighbouring Mende Mission was taken over from the American Missionary Association in 1882. The Sierra Leone Conference in 1966 reported 186 churches, 310 preaching points and 12,712 communicants. The WMA took the initiative in beginning work in south China near Canton in 1889 and on

the island of Luzon in the Philippines in 1901. The churches arising from these efforts were incorporated into the Church of Christ in China (1919) and the United Church of Christ in the Philippines. The UB and Evangelical Churches united to form the *Evangelical United Brethren Church in 1946. (Evangelical missions: Japan, 1876; China, 1889; Puerto Rico, 1899; and 1926 joined in the *SUM in Nigeria). Brazil was the first new mission after the union (1949). The Division of World Missions (601 Riverview Avenue, Dayton, Ohio 45406) in 1966 reported 145 missionaries in all fields. The EUB Church and the Methodist Church merged in 1968 to form the United Methodist Church and their mission work has been integrated.

A division among the UB occurred in 1889 over the adoption of a new constitution. The United Brethren in Christ, Old Constitution, with its Parent Missionary Society and Woman's Missionary Association, claims to continue the original church and mission agencies. Headquarters in Huntingdon, Indiana. Missionaries in 1962 numbered 44 at work in Honduras, Jamaica, Sierra Leone and Hong Kong.

R. PIERCE BEAVER

Annual Reports of the Boards; *The Evangel*, 1881–1946; A. W. Drury: *History of the Church of the United Brethren in Christ* (rev. ed., Dayton, Ohio 1931); P. H. Eller: *These Evangelical United Brethren* (Dayton, Ohio 1950).

UNITED CHRISTIAN MISSIONARY SOCIETY. See CHRISTIAN CHURCH (DISCIPLES OF CHRIST).

UNITED CHURCH OF CHRIST, USA, MISSIONS. In July 1961 the General Synod of the UCC formally established two 'instrumentalities' to serve as the arms of the church's mission overseas and in the homeland. Responsible for the mission abroad, the United Church Board for World Ministries succeeded to the work of the *ABCFM of the Congregational-Christian Churches and the

Board of International Missions of the Evangelical and Reformed Church as well as the World Service agencies of the two united denominations. With its principal offices in New York City, the UCBWM in 1966 reported more than 500 missionaries in some 32 countries. The board participates in the operation overseas of 171 schools, 34 colleges, fifteen seminaries, 62 hospitals and clinics, five publishing houses, nineteen social service centres, thirteen agricultural institutes and in many local congregations. From 80% to 85% of the work of the UCBWM is shared with overseas agencies of other churches and church-related institutions, and by co-operating with various ecumenical organizations the board supports the Christian presence in nearly every nation on earth.

The United Church Board for Homeland Ministries co-ordinates the home mission of the UCC, and its work is divided for administrative purposes into six divisions: Christian Education, Church Extension, Evangelism, Health and Welfare Services, Higher Education and the American Missionary Association, and Publication. Included in its many important tasks is a religious, educational and medical ministry to the American Indians and in Puerto Rico.

The two boards are free to plan and develop their respective programmes, but they do so under the purview of the General Synod and its Executive Council which correlates their work, publicity and promotion.

PETER G. GOWING

The United Church of Christ: History and Program (New York 1965); D. Horton: *The United Church of Christ* (New York 1962).

UNITED CHURCHES. This article deals only with the problem presented to the Christian world by the 20th century phenomenon of UCs.

In the past, many *younger churches, such as the Methodist Church of Southern Asia, have been related to only one denomination and one mission board in the west. As

younger churches have become independent, they have automatically belonged to the confessional group from which they took their origin, and in many cases have sought and obtained membership in the official world organization of that confession.

But when a UC has come into existence, none of these conditions holds any longer. The *CSI has to deal with missionary societies of four different denominations. It is the aim of its members to retain close relations with all the churches in the west which have contributed to their existence. But they belong to a different order of existence. A bishop of the Church of South India may be invited to take part in a meeting of the 'wider episcopal fellowship' which the Anglican Communion is gradually gathering round itself; but is not an Anglican bishop, and has no admission to the purely Anglican Lambeth Conference. Such a UC clearly cannot adhere to any of the world confessional organizations, which exist only to unite geographically separated churches of one confessional type. An entirely new situation, without precedent, has been brought about.

On the whole the western churches have been slow to realize the change that has taken place. After the formation of the (united) Church of Christ in Japan, the American mission boards which had had most to do with the growing churches in Japan, formed the Inter-board Committee for Christian work in Japan, so that all the assistance which went to Japan from the USA should go from a single body to the church, and not from an existing denomination in America to a denomination which had ceased to exist in Japan. It is greatly to be regretted that no such organization has been formed in the west for aid to the CSI; the continued relationship to a number of missionary societies in Britain is one of the features which has delayed or impeded the completion of the unity of the church in India.

Where is a united church at home in the Christian family? All the existing UCs are deeply interested in the worldwide *ecumenical movement, and feel a special responsibility by example and admonition to stimulate the less progressive western churches to be aware of their failures and to take more seriously the challenge to Christian union. Their contribution is of notable value. It has been observed at ecumenical gatherings that the Communion Service of the CSI is the most acceptable in the world, and that a wider range of Christians of diverse professions can take part in it without violation of conscience than in any other.

The UCs are deeply interested in one another, and desirous to learn from one another both of progress and of problems in the field of Christian union. Should they then seek to create a world fellowship of UCs, thus adding one more to the already long list of world denominational organizations? A separate meeting for the representatives of UCs was held at the *Amsterdam Assembly of the *WCC in 1948, but no suggestion has been made that this should become a permanent feature of the Christian world scene. The UCs find that they have quite enough to do in strengthening and developing their own inner unity, in spreading the spirit of unity in the area in which they exist, in drawing others into the fellowship, and in bearing witness in the wider ecumenical context. They seem to have no wish to burden themselves with yet one more organization with a special and limited aim.

The number of UCs is already large, and seems likely to become much larger in the future. The United Church of Christ in the USA belongs to no confessional family. If the Consultation on Church Union in that country leads to the merger of a number of Protestant denominations, the whole world situation of the churches will have been changed. It is impossible to predict the future. But it seems clear that the tension between denomination and unity, between confessional organization and ecumenical act, will be one of the major problems of the Christian churches for the next 50 years.

See also UNION MOVEMENTS, MISSIONARY AND CHURCH.

STEPHEN NEILL

UNITED METHODIST CHURCH. See EVANGELICAL UNITED BRETHREN MISSIONS; METHODIST MISSIONS.

UNITED PRESBYTERIAN CHURCH, THE, in the USA, administers missionary work through its Commission on Ecumenical Mission and Relations, with headquarters at 475 Riverside Drive, New York, N.Y. 10027. Representatives of the UPC are 'partners in mission' in 23 countries beginning in Lebanon in 1823, India 1834, Iran 1835, Thailand 1840, Hong Kong 1844, Pakistan 1849, Rio Muni 1850, Egypt 1854, Colombia 1856, Brazil and Japan 1859, Chile 1873, Cameroon 1879, Guatemala 1882, Korea 1884, Venezuela 1897, Philippines 1899, Sudan 1900, Ethiopia 1920, Iraq 1924, Ecuador 1945, Indonesia 1951, Taiwan 1952 and Nepal 1953.

Some 1164 *fraternal workers serve in the self-governing churches in all these lands where there is a total Christian community of 2,653,438. Expenditures from the USA for all the programmes of assistance in 1965 were $8,653,700.

A wide variety of services include co-operation with other denominations in at least nine countries. The services are in the following areas: evangelism, family service, councils of churches, *theological education, study centres of religion and cultures, work with rural pastors, Christian education and literature, industrial programmes and radio broadcasting. Participation in personnel and funds is to be found in educational institutions from nursery schools to university systems, from agricultural extensions, technical institutes, medical schools and language learning institutes. In several areas exchanges have recently been established between RC and Protestant bodies.

Current problems include co-operation with Pentecostal churches, the development of a completely independent church as in

Chile; the long-term problems of church support; new efforts to meet the challenges at universities among student groups; new programmes among the working classes of the cities; daily efforts in many areas to clarify the roles of the fraternal workers (missionaries) and the workers of the self-governing churches. Assistance is given to local leaders of the church as they struggle with the problems of personal and academic freedom; as they seek new understandings between the church and government; and as they seek to discover why in some countries they have apparent opportunities as a church but they have difficulties in making the proper contacts.

ROBERT T. PARSONS

UNITED SOCIETY FOR CHRISTIAN LITERATURE, THE, is the oldest British interdenominational Christian literature society. Founded in 1799 as the Religious Tract Society, the group was in 1804 instrumental in the establishment of the British and Foreign Bible Society. The present title was adopted in 1935 on the society's amalgamation with the Christian Literature Society, India and Africa, and the Christian Literature Society for China.

Originally concerned almost exclusively with the publication of literature for Great Britain, and later for Africa and Asia, the functions of the society were reorganized following the union of 1935. Home publishing interests were centred on the Lutterworth Press, London, though still remaining under the direction of the USCL, which devoted its own resources to the development of its overseas commitments. Besides the publication of books and the granting of financial assistance for local publishing by missions and Christian councils throughout the world, the work of the society now embraces the training of Christian writers, journalists and artists; the provision of bookshops and mobile means of book distribution and assistance to local groups in the creation of Christian magazines and newspapers.

The society was closely associated with the Feed the Minds Campaign of 1964–

67, and is now one of the partners with *SPCK, the Archbishop of York's Fund, and the Christian Literature Council of the *Conference of Missionary Societies in Joint Action for Christian Literature Overseas. This gives permanent expression to the joint presentation throughout Great Britain of worldwide Christian literature needs.

D. RIDLEY CHESTERTON

UNITED SOCIETY FOR THE PROPAGATION OF THE GOSPEL, THE, was formed by the merger in 1965 of the Society for the Propagation of the Gospel in Foreign Parts and the Universities' Mission to Central Africa. The SPG was founded in 1701 by the Rev. Thomas Bray, who had been sent to inspect the unsatisfactory state of church life in the American colonies: the society's aim was to provide a remedy, both by ministering to English settlers overseas and by propagating the gospel among the heathen with whom the settlers might come into contact. The first missionary sailed to North America in 1702. Its work spread to the West Indies (1712), South India (1750), Gambia (1751), Gold Coast (1752), Canada (1759), Australia (1793), Calcutta and South Africa (1821), Ceylon (1840), Burma (1859), Madagascar (1864), Japan (1873), North China (1874), Korea (1890) and Polynesia (1903).

The UMCA was founded in response to an appeal made by David *Livingstone at Cambridge University in 1857. Cambridge, Oxford, London and Durham Universities (with Dublin for a time) formed committees, and resolved to establish in Central Africa stations which would promote 'true religion, agriculture, and lawful commerce, and the ultimate extinction of the slave trade'. Five missionaries and their bishop arrived near Lake Nyasa in 1861. Disaster followed, but in 1864 a headquarters was established at Zanzibar, and work increased on the mainland. In 1896 the diocese of Zanzibar was divided to make Nyasaland a separate diocese, and the area of work has been further expanded and sub-divided into six dioceses (1966).

SPG and UMCA agreed in regarding mission as the responsibility not of the societies but of the local churches. They saw their task as helping the church to mobilize its resources of manpower and money, and to help British Christians to take their due responsibility in helping the life of the church overseas. They saw no reason to carry out this work in separation and therefore became a single society in 1965.

The resulting society continues the work formerly done by SPG and UMCA, and assists the church in over 60 dioceses in the Anglican provinces of the West Indies, West, Central, East and South Africa, India, Pakistan and Ceylon, and Japan; and in Madagascar, Mauritius, Singapore and Malaya, Borneo, Korea and Polynesia. It is supported by the churches of England, Wales and Ireland, and encourages informed prayer for the church abroad, seeks offers of service, and acts as a channel for financial help. In 1966 it accepted 129 missionaries for service abroad, and its income was just under one million pounds.

JOHN WILKINSON

A. E. M. Anderson-Morshead and A. G. Blood: *The History of the UMCA*, (3 vols., London 1955–1962); C. F. Pascoe: *Two Hundred Years of the S.P.G.* (London 1901); H. P. Thompson: *Into All Lands, History of SPGFP 1701–1950* (London 1951).

UNITED STATES OF AMERICA: INDIAN AND NEGRO MISSIONS.

(a) *Protestant*. Thomas Mayhew and his son, Thomas, Jr, began in 1642 on Martha's Vineyard and Nantucket Is. a mission to the Indians, which the family continued for five generations. John *Eliot, pastor at Roxbury, began preaching in 1646 and led in the creation of fourteen towns of 'Praying Indians'. The Stockbridge Mission was founded by John Sergeant in 1734, and David *Brainerd's short ministry at Cranberry, N.J., provided lasting inspiration. The New England missionaries went to the Iroquois but success was limited to the Oneidas, who were largely converted by Samuel Kirkland, beginning in 1766. Motivation was the glory of God and compassion. Methods, which provided the model for later foreign missions, included preaching and teaching, nurture through worship, catechization, and vernacular literature; organization of churches with the training of Indian pastors and workers; and the gathering of converts into towns where they were taught arts and crafts of civilization. Eliot's Massachusetts Bible was a notable achievement. The work was supported by local gifts, grants by the legislatures, and funds and supplies from the New England Co. (London 1649) and the Society in Scotland for the Propagating of Christian Knowledge (1709).

The Anglican mission to the Mohawks was begun at the request of the governor of New York and supported by the *SPG. The entire tribe was converted through the efforts of Sir William Johnson and Chief Joseph Brant, and, loyal to Britain, moved to Ontario after the Revolution. Heroic Moravian missions, beginning in Georgia in 1735 and on the NY-Connecticut border in 1740, because of harassment by settlers moved by stages across Pennsylvania into Ohio and finally, after the terrible massacre at Gnadenhütten, into Ontario.

Meanwhile the importation of African slaves brought another large pagan element. Mistresses of plantations were good teachers and evangelism was largely a parish activity. Elias Neau opened a catechetical school at New York under the SPG in 1705, and Dr Bray's Associates founded a more general school in 1760. The latter society also had schools in Savannah and Philadelphia. The Virginia Revival of 1773–76 and the Great Awakening of 1799 swept Negroes en masse into the Baptist and Methodist Churches. Negroes largely converted themselves, but the Methodists under Bishop Wm. Capers about 1829–55 conducted a special mission with 26 stations and 32 preachers. Mission boards concentrated on education. Thus Avery College was founded in 1849 and Lincoln University in 1856. The most extensive work was by the

American Missionary Association (1846, Congregationalist), among whose colleges are Fiske, Hampton, Atlanta, Talladega and Tougaloo. Samuel Hopkins and Ezra Stiles in 1773 founded at Newport, R.I., a society to send freedmen missionaries to Africa, but the Revolution ended it. When the American Colonization Society (founded 1817) undertook the settlement of freedmen in Liberia Baptist and Methodist missions accompanied it.

Many missionary societies were founded between 1787 and 1820 for work with Indians and frontier settlers, but their Indian missions were generally not successful because of the pressure of white settlement. The foreign mission boards, beginning in 1810, assumed responsibility, but about 1860–80 handed the missions over to the home mission boards. The US government in 1818 established an 'Education Fund' and relied on mission boards to conduct schools connected with the missions. The most notable missions before the Civil War were those of the American Board to the Cherokees and Choctaws. The government's removal policy destroyed most of the fruits of these efforts, excepting for the Cherokees and Choctaws. After the Civil War President U.S. Grant adopted a 'Peace Policy', which assigned specific reservations to certain boards both for nomination of agents and for the conduct of mission and school work. Mission work was greatly stimulated, and at this time the Episcopal Church began its large mission programme. All partnership with government ended in the 1890s because of politics and new ideas about church-state relations.

Fourteen member boards of the Home Missions Council in 1909 formed the Committee on Indian Affairs (now Indian Dept. of the National Council of Churches), and the National Fellowship of Indian Workers was founded in 1935. *The World Missionary Atlas* of 1925 reported a combined total for 21 boards of 483 churches with a community of 35,174 and communicants 31,932. There has been no complete census since then. Indian churches are now

likely to be integrated into presbyteries, associations, etc., with white churches. The largest Indian mission programmes are those of the Episcopal Church and the United Presbyterian Church in the USA. As the Indians leave the reservations for the cities the Christians are either integrated into white churches or are lost. Cook Christian Training School at Tempe, Arizona, is probably the most important school. The churches maintain it co-operatively through the Indian Department of the National Council of Churches, and the students come from many tribes. Graduates go on to higher study or become lay workers in the churches. See also ALASKA; and for missions to the Polynesians of Hawaii, see HAWAII.

R. PIERCE BEAVER

(b) *Roman Catholic*. With the gradual extension of the USA to its present limits, the RC church in the States found itself the heir to the much earlier missions of the French and Spaniards in northern New York, California and elsewhere; but many of these missions had been devastated by war and by the advance of the white man, and little was left on which to build. For a hundred years RC work among the Indians was widespread and registered little success. The first effort was probably that made by Bishop John Carroll, who in 1791 sent a Sulpician priest to minister, at their earnest request, to a small group of RC Indians in Maine. This small mission was maintained for more than a century.

The great period of RC missions to the Indians began in 1875 with the formation of a special Bureau of Catholic Indian Missions, a renewed interest of the Federal Government in Indian education, and generous help especially from the *Jesuit, *Franciscan and *Benedictine orders, with the co-operation of many sisterhoods. Between 1875 and 1900 the number of RC Indians grew from 25,000 to 50,000, the schools from seven to 60.

With the increasing integration of Indian into the general population, there is less need for specifically Indian work; nevertheless the RC church still maintains work in 40 reservations in the North, Mid-west and Western areas of the country.

During the colonial period of American history, a small number of RC Negroes were to be found, but almost all in Louisiana, which had been under French influence, and in Maryland, of which the first proprietor, Lord Baltimore, had been an RC. After independence little was done by the RC church, and in consequence the vast majority of American Negroes are Protestants (Baptists predominating). Only after the end of the Civil War did the RC church devote itself in any strength to the Negro problem, and even then progress was very slow. The first Negro priest was ordained in 1886 in Rome; the first ordination in the USA itself took place as late as 1891. A great step forward was taken in 1920 when the *SVD inaugurated a seminary for the training of Negro candidates for their community at Bay St. Louis (Miss.). Between 1935 and 1965 the number of RC Negro priests in the USA grew from six to 159. A priest of partly Negro origin, James A. Healy, was appointed bishop of Maine in 1874; but only in the 1960s was it found possible to appoint the first RC bishop of full Negro blood. A number of RC bishops have taken a strong line against racial distinction, and have spoken out very plainly against segregation.

It is reckoned that at the present time, of the 19 million Negroes in the USA, between 750,000 and one million are RCs.

EDITORS

R. P. Beaver: *Church, State, and the American Indians* (St. Louis 1966), *Pioneers in Mission* (Grand Rapids 1966); R. F. Berkhofer, Jr: *Salvation and the Savage: an Analysis of Protestant Missions and American Indian Response, 1787–1862* (Lexington 1965); A. S. Foley: *God's Men of Color* (New York 1955); J. T. Gillard: *The Catholic Church and the American Negro* (Baltimore 1930); G. Hinman: *The American Indian and Christian Missions* (New York 1932); W. Kellaway: *The New England Company 1654–1776* (New York 1962); G. E. E. Lindquist: *Indians in Transition* (New York 1951), *New Trails for Old, a*

Handbook for Missionary Workers among the American Indians (New York 1951); A. T. Vaughan: *New England Frontier, Puritans and Indians 1620–1675* (Boston 1965); *The Indian Sentinel* (journal of the Catholic Indian Bureau, Washington, DC, 1916–); *NCE* I, 402–08; *NCE* X, 299–314.

UNITED WORLD MISSION, INC., was founded in 1946 in Dayton, Ohio USA, by Sidney Correll (along with seventeen evangelical pastors) as a non-denominational *faith missionary agency. It supports somewhat fewer than 100 missionaries in eighteen countries. Its workers are engaged in evangelism, literature distribution, radio broadcasting and church planting. Ancillary enterprises include orphanages, schools, and medical and nursing stations. More than one hundred national churches have been established, staffed by as many national pastors and workers. The mission publishes *United World Mission Reports*, a quarterly, and has headquarters located in St. Petersburg (Box 8000), Florida, USA. It is a member of *EFMA. Its annual income is in excess of $550,000. Dr Correll is president and general director.

HAROLD LINDSELL

UNIVERSALISM. Belief that eventually all persons will receive God's forgiveness and be saved. Origen (185–254) taught this doctrine, as following from belief in God's unbounded love. Other early universalists were Gregory of Nyssa (c.332–c.398) and John Scotus Erigena (c.800–c.880). On the contemporary scene we must distinguish between belief in the doctrine as defined here and the tenets of any one of the various Universalist churches and associations which exist in various countries. In some of these churches, as in the USA, U. has come to stand for a very general moral idealism and liberal religion with stress on freedom of belief, rather than on any specific doctrine or system of doctrines.

Belief that all persons will finally be saved is maintained by many people, including several distinguished theologians, whose basic doctrinal positions are much more conservative than those of the present Universalist churches. Among such theologians must be mentioned especially Emil Brunner and Nels Ferré.

The doctrine of universal salvation is defended both by appeal to belief in God's limitless love and also to more specific teachings of Scripture. Among the passages more commonly employed are the following: Jn.12:32; 1 Cor.15:22; 2 Cor.5:19; Eph.1:10; 1 Tim.2:3,4,5; Titus 2:11; 2 Peter 3:9; 1 Jn.2:2. Of course much biblical teaching is also cited in opposition, along with the dominant creeds and traditions of Christendom.

Universalist beliefs were among the several influences which motivated the strong *anti-missionary movement in the USA about 1820–40. Even when universalist ideas are taught by missionaries and other vigorous supporters of Christian missions, such ideas are often viewed as inimical to missionary earnestness. If all people are to be finally saved in any case, then why should any Christians give up the comforts of home and friends to carry an often unwanted gospel to strange lands? Universalist defenders of missions reply that if a person truly loves his distant neighbours and treasures the Christian faith he cannot do otherwise than take part in sharing the faith with those who do not have it. Failing to do this would show either a lack of real love for Christ or a lack of love for humanity, and hence the absence of genuine Christian faith.

L. HAROLD DeWOLF

H. Ballou (1771–1852): *A Treatise on the Atonement* (15th ed., Boston 1959); H. E. Brunner: *Eternal Hope* (Philadelphia 1954); N. Ferré: *The Christian Understanding of God* (New York 1951); ERE XI, 529–35; NCE XIV, 452.

UNIVERSITY MISSIONS. Increased participation by highly trained graduates in Christian missionary work was one of the characteristic features of the second half of the 19th century. Most of these graduates served in the general missionary societies, but a number of societies specially

linked to one university came into being. (1) Under the inspiration of the great Bishop B. F. Westcott, three of whose sons later served in India, the Cambridge Mission to Delhi was founded in 1877. It has been served by a number of men of great distinction, two of its heads having become Metropolitans of the Anglican Church in India. (2) The Oxford Mission to Calcutta, joined later by the Sisterhood of the Epiphany, dedicated itself mainly to work among students, and to the publication of a valuable weekly *The Epiphany*. (3) The third of the Anglican group was the Dublin University Mission, founded at Hazaribagh, Bihar, in 1891, with a branch in Fukien, China. (4) In the USA the connection between the universities and missions has always been close. In 1880 a number of graduates of Oberlin desired to go together to China in the service of the *ABCFM. Five missionaries entered into service in 1881 and 1882. After the death in the *Boxer troubles of two missionaries and five children, graduates of Oberlin, desiring to continue the tradition of 'Oberlin in China' formed the Shansi Memorial Association in memory of the martyrs. (5) The Yale Foreign Missionary Society (1902) chose Changsha in Hunan as the field of its operations, and carried on an extensive work until the communist take-over in 1949 made further work by foreign missionaries in China impossible.

In the present era, when a large proportion of missionary candidates has had university training, the need for special university missions seems no longer to be strongly felt, though the Anglican missions referred to above still maintain their special witness.

STEPHEN NEILL

UNIVERSITIES' MISSION TO CENTRAL AFRICA. See UNITED SOCIETY FOR THE PROPAGATION OF THE GOSPEL.

UPADHYAYA, BRAHMABANDHAV (1861–1907), whose original name was Bhawani Charan Banerji Uphadhyaya, was born in a Kanauj Brahman family not far from Calcutta. In early years he was in touch with Keshub Chunder Sen and Swami Vivekhānanda, and was thus led to consider seriously the claims of Christ. On 26 February 1891 he was baptized by an Anglican missionary, though without the intention of joining any Christian body. Later in the same year he was persuaded to be conditionally baptized by a Roman Catholic priest, taking the name Theophilus, which he Indianized in the form of Brahmabandhav. B. was convinced that the missions in India had done great harm by failing to take seriously the spiritual tradition of India. The Vedānta should be accepted as having prepared the Indian mind for the gospel, and a specifically Indian form of Christianity developed. These and other ideas were set forth with great eloquence in the periodical *Sophia*; but the adventurous views set forth were not to the mind of the hierarchy in India, and *Sophia* fell under ecclesiastical censure on 20 October 1900. The same fate befell another paper *The Twentieth Century* with which B. planned to replace *Sophia*. In later years, B. became occupied with the more extreme forms of *nationalism, and at the time of his sudden death in 1907 was about to stand his trial for seditious activity. He maintained till the end that, in spite of ecclesiastical disapproval, he remained a faithful Christian. His activities were premature, and his manner provocative; it is, however, sad that better use could not be made of the great talents which he wished to devote to the service of Christ and of India.

STEPHEN NEILL

A. Väth, SJ: *Im Kampf mit der Zauberwelt des Hinduismus* (Berlin and Bonn 1928); *LTK* X, 538f.

UPPER VOLTA is a landlocked republic of 105,879 sq.m. immediately south of the Sahara in French-speaking West Africa. The population of 5,054,000 (1967) is nearly half composed of the large Mossi tribe, which has resisted *Islam for four centuries but is now rapidly accepting this

faith. Roman Catholic missions have had marked success, adherents increasing from 4,339 in 1925, to 39,435 in 1945, and to 194,958 Catholics in 1965, with the first African cardinal in West Africa. Protestant missions entered in 1925 with the arrival of Assemblies of God (USA) missionaries; they were later joined by French *Assemblées de Dieu* workers, and have a strong national-led church of 24,000 total community, almost all Mossi. Other missions include the Upper Volta Mission (Evangelistic Tabernacle, Vancouver), Evangelical Christian Church of Mali and Upper Volta (3,000 adherents; served by the *CMA), Evangelical Churches of West Africa (*SIM) and the *WEC. The Protestant community (1966) was 31,159.

DAVID B. BARRETT

W. Fischer: *Ober-Volta* (Bonn 1962); *BM* II, 440–44; *NCE* XIV, 474.

UPPSALA 1968. See ASSEMBLIES, ECUMENICAL.

URBAN MISSION. The vast proliferation and growth of cities across the world in the 20th century, with the attendant problems caused by continuously changing and expanding urbanization and industrialization, have produced a mass of new thinking and experiment on the *theology of mission, evidenced in a large body of literature in a score of languages. UM is the term used to refer to the church's task in contemporary urban society, seeking answers to the problems of what urban culture is, who urban man is, what Christian ministry means in this context, etc. A classic statement of this position is given in Cox (see below). *Industrial Mission* is a more specialized aspect of UM focused on what goes on inside factories, plants, etc. The pioneer Sheffield Industrial Mission began in 1944 in that city's steel industry, to be followed by missions in Bristol, Birmingham and numerous other industrial complexes in Britain. Because of the intractable nature of the problem and the extreme apathy often encountered, the number of projects begun only to be soon abandoned rises each year. Meanwhile the French Catholic worker-priest experiment aroused fierce controversy until it was suppressed in 1962 after some priests had asked permission to marry and others had joined the communist party. In the USA the largest has been the Detroit Industrial Mission (1956) which concentrated on the vast Ford Rouge car factory complex. Countless other missions have sprung up across the world, from Tokyo to Nairobi and Latin America. The movement is largely interdenominational, and although led mainly by clergy is heavily lay-centred and often opposed by the institutionalized churches. It has coined an extensive theological vocabulary of its own, such as the Japanese *shoko uku dendo* ('sharing the joy that is within you with the one who works next to you') for occupational evangelism in factories. The basis of UM is a theological attempt to hear what God is saying through urban and technological society, and consists of the following emphases: (1) a frank recognition of the past failure of the church in the urban milieu, exemplified in the historic estrangement of the working classes in post-Christian Europe; (2) a positive affirmation that urban society and industrialization are good in themselves, even that 'technology is the major act of God in the 20th century'; and (3) a radical strategy of planning for missionary engagement, of involvement in urban and metropolitan renewal under secular auspices, and of the leadership of ideas and clarification of issues. The classical statement of this strategy is in Wickham (see below), chapter VI. Both UM and Industrial Mission recognize frankly that they are only exploratory ministries and that years or decades will be necessary before the impact of their mission will be seen.

DAVID B. BARRETT

H. Cox: *The Secular City* (London 1965); G. Velteu: *Mission in Industrial France* (London 1968); E. R. Wickham: *Church and People in an Industrial City* (London 1957).

URUGUAY, a republic and the smallest independent state in S. America, lies on the Atlantic coast between Brazil and Argentina. Area: 72,172 sq.m. Population (est. in 1968): 2,818,000, most of whom are of Spanish and Italian descent, with a number of various European extraction and 11% of mixed European and Amerindian or Negro race. Spanish is almost universally spoken, and the literacy rate is 80%. U. was discovered by the Spaniards in 1516, but ownership of the territory was long in dispute between Spain and Portugal, and afterwards between Argentina and Brazil. U. became independent in 1830.

*Jesuit missionaries entered U. in the 17th century but did not succeed in establishing permanent work. From an early date most of the population was at least nominally Catholic but the church was not strong. This was due in part to wars, which were frequent until 1911, and in part to a shortage of clergy and missionaries. It was not until 1878 that the diocese of Montevideo was created. During the 19th and 20th centuries anti-clericalism has been a considerable force, though seldom extreme or bitter. In 1838 the *Franciscan convents were suppressed by the government, and their property confiscated on the ground that it was being wasted through lack of recruits. Jesuits were re-admitted soon after 1836, expelled in 1859 and admitted again from 1865. The 1830 constitution of U. provided for religious toleration, and the RC church was established until the separation of church and state in 1918. The total RC community is estimated at 2,220,000 (WCH 1968), and in 1960 there were 688 priests, 477 churches, 237 church schools and 45 charitable institutions (W. S. Rycroft and M. M. Clemer: *A Factual Study of Latin America* [New York 1963]).

The first Protestant missionary to preach in Spanish in U. was J. F. *Thomson, an Argentinian of Scottish birth. In 1870 he founded an 'Evangelical Mission' in Montevideo and won an immediate response. In 1877 Thomson was joined by T. B. Wood from the USA, and in 1878 their growing work was incorporated into the

Methodist Episcopal Church. Other Protestant missions entered U. from the USA, and after the first world war Pentecostalists began to outnumber the Methodists. The *YMCA, which has its South American headquarters in Montevideo, has done notable work among educated young people. The total Protestant community in 1968 was 39,690. The Methodists numbered 3,591; denominations claiming more than 4,000 were the Assemblies of God; Church of God (Cleveland); German Evangelical, La Plata Synod; *SDA; and Southern Baptist Convention. These, together with other groups, had a total of 288 national full-time workers and 120 fraternal workers (WCH 1968). Most churches have schools and philanthropic institutions, and there is a united evangelical hospital.

EDITORS

W. J. Coleman: *Latin-American Catholicism. A Self-Evaluation* (New York 1958); J. L. Mecham: *Church and State in Latin America* (rev. ed., Chapel Hill, N.C., 1966, pp.252–61); *Los 80 Años de la Iglesia Metodista en el Uruguay, 1878–1958* (Montevideo 1958); *BM* II, 893–98; *NCE* XIV, 495–97; *WKL*, 1521f.

V

VALIGNANO, ALESSANDRO (1539–1606), was born at Chieti in Italy, joined the Society of *Jesus in 1566, and in 1573 was appointed Visitor, i.e. Chief Superintendent, of all the Jesuit missions in the Far East. He consolidated the work of Francis *Xavier in India. He elevated the mission in Japan to the status of a Vice-Province. From Macao he organized the mission in China. V. encouraged Matthew *Ricci in his 'translation' (adaptation) of the Christian message into Chinese. He gave the impulse for the admission of Chinese and Japanese Christians to the priesthood and to the religious orders; he founded the colleges in Macao, Nagasaki and Arima for their training. V. spent the years 1579–82, 1590–92 and 1598–1603 in Japan. From 1583 to 1587 he was provincial in India, and journeyed back and forth between Goa, Macao and Japan. The principles of missionary work laid down by him are still valid today.

JOSEF GLAZIK

J. F. Schütte: *Valignanos Missionsgrundsätze für Japan* I:1–2 (Rome 1951, 1958); J. Wicki, ed.: *Historia del principio y progresso de la Compañía de Jesús en las Indias Orientales* (Rome 1944); *LTK* X, 605f.; *NCE* XIV, 522.

VANDERKEMP, JOHANNES THEODORUS (1747–1811), was born at Rotterdam, Holland, the son of a Lutheran professor of theology. He lost his first wife and only child in a drowning tragedy. VdK received his medical degree in 1782. At first he rejected the Trinity and Godhead of Christ but not the doctrine of original sin. After experiencing a spiritual revolution he prepared himself as a pioneer missionary and became co-founder of the Netherlands Missionary Society (1797). On 31 March 1799 he arrived in Cape Town as a representative of the NMS. Starting work among the slaves he later worked among the Xhosa until accused by them of conspiracy.

His only convert here was Sarah, a Hottentot woman. He subsequently worked among the Hottentots in the Graaff-Reinet area. From here he moved to Bota's Place near Algoa Bay and in 1803 settled at Bethelsdorp, which was intended to be an industrial institution. Not much was done in this respect nor in instilling proficiency in agriculture. The land was brackish and sterile. Far-sighted in the question of communication, VdK in 1804 printed a catechism, *Principles of the Word of God for the Hottentot Mission*, the first South African book to be printed here. Bethelsdorp was not only seen by the Dutch colonists as a hostile institution of a hostile government, but the Xhosas and Hottentots even attacked it physically. VdK was early in conflict with colonial opinion on the race issue and also refused to co-operate with both the Dutch, and later British, authorities. Emotional, brilliant, eccentric, intensely proud, with personal hardships often self-inflicted, he nevertheless left an indelible mark on the pages of South African history. He associated himself to such an extent with the indigenous people that he chose to share the Hottentot manner of living. Insisting on strict discipline in church matters he did not readily admit persons to membership of the church. Evangelists went out from Bethelsdorp as early as 1806. His marriage, at the age of 60, to a 17-year-old Malagasy slave girl aroused the strong disapproval of the colonists. When he died on 19 December 1811, Cape Town gave him a large funeral attended by huge crowds. He became known as a protagonist of racial justice, although often tactless, an evangelist who stood for what he considered to be the universal principles of the gospel of Jesus Christ. The issues he raised are still largely unresolved.

GERHARDUS C. OOSTHUIZEN

A. D. Martin: *Doctor Vanderkemp* (London 1931); J. C. du Plessis: *A History of*

Christian Missions in South Africa (London 1911).

VATICAN COUNCIL II AND MISSIONS. The bishops from Africa and Asia, eager to have liturgical rites rendered more easily intelligible to their people, were largely responsible for the stand taken by the Second Vatican Council (1962–65) in favour of introducing the vernacular in the liturgy. They also played an important role in having the document on the Jews expanded into a 'Declaration on the Relationship of the Church to Non-Christian Religions', in which – besides *Judaism – mention is made of *Hinduism, *Buddhism and *Islam. The 'Decree on the Church's Missionary Activity' states that missionary activity is concerned with 'the task of preaching the gospel and planting the church among peoples or groups who do not yet believe in Christ'. Non-Catholic Christian groups, or churches, are not called an object of mission work, but instead are invited to take part in dialogue, as indicated in the 'Decree on Ecumenism'. Further clarification on the stand of the Catholic church toward non-Christian and non-Catholic Christian religions is contained in the 'Declaration on Religious Freedom'.

RALPH M. WILTGEN, SVD

W. M. Abbott, gen. ed.: *The Documents of Vatican II* (New York 1966); J. Schütte, ed.: *Mission nach dem Konzil* (Mainz 1967); R. M. Wiltgen: *The Rhine Flows into the Tiber: The Unknown Council* (New York).

VAZ, JOSEPH (1651–1711), was born at Sancoale near Goa and died at Kandy, Ceylon. He was the son of Christian Brahmins and was educated by the *Jesuits at Goa. In 1676 he was ordained priest and soon achieved fame as an ascetic, preacher and confessor especially at Kanara, near Goa, where he worked from 1681 till 1684. In 1685 he became head of a community of Indian priests who lived according to the rule of the Oratory of St. Philip Neri (Oratorian). When he heard of the pitiable conditions of the Catholics in Ceylon, he wished to go there, but the Calvinistic Dutch would not allow him to enter. He disguised himself first as a slave and later as a beggar and succeeded in entering Ceylon, where he reorganized the Catholic missionary activity with such great fervour and success that he obtained the much deserved title for himself of 'the Apostle of Ceylon'. His cause of beatification was introduced in 1737 and re-opened in 1935.

A. MCCORMACK, MHM

S. G. Perera: *Life of the Venerable Father Joseph Vaz* (Galle 1953²); *LTK* X, 645; *NCE* XIV, 580.

VELLORE CHRISTIAN MEDICAL COLLEGE AND HOSPITAL, SOUTH INDIA, was founded in 1900 by Dr Ida S. *Scudder, of the Arcot Mission of the Reformed Church, USA, in one room of her father's bungalow. The flood of patients led to the building, in 1902, of the Mary Taber Schell Hospital with 40 beds. In 1906 Dr Scudder began visits to nearby villages, setting up roadside clinics. Relying first on untrained assistance, in 1909 she began training Indian women for the lower grade of nursing and in 1918 for the Diploma of the Licenced Medical Practitioner, University of Madras. In 1924 a new 267 bed hospital was built and by 1932 the nucleus of the Medical College had been established on a site four miles away. In 1942 the college passed the stringent tests for recognition to offer the MB, BS degrees of Madras. In 1947 men students were admitted. By now it had become a union institution in which 60 churches and missions from ten countries join with the church in India. There is now an annual intake of 60 students, in equal numbers of men and women, from all religions and communities and including some from outside India. Today there are approximately 1,000 beds and some 3,500 patients are treated daily. The total staff is nearly 2,000 of whom about 50 are from overseas. These include 300 doctors and 300 nurses, some in both categories doing postgraduate training. By 1966 Vellore had produced 768 medical and 563 nursing graduates, with 68 having post-graduate degrees.

MARCUS WARD

D. C. Wilson: *Dr Ida* (New York 1959), *Take My Hands* (London 1964).

VENEZUELA, a South American republic, bounded on the north by the Caribbean Sea, on the east by Guyana, on the south by Brazil, and on the west by Colombia. Area 352,143 sq.m. Estimated population nine million. The coast of V. was first sighted by Columbus in 1498. The Spanish conquest followed, and in 1500 the area was proclaimed to be the captain-generalcy of Caracas. Independence of Spain was declared on 14 July 1811, but was not finally recognized by Spain till 30 March 1845. In the last thirty years V. has been transformed by the discovery of oil and natural gas, which account for 21% of the gross natural product and make of Caracas one of the most expensive cities in the world.

With the Spaniards arrived the missionaries. But, though the first mass was said in 1513 and a bishopric was founded at Coro in 1531, the ferocity of some of the inhabitants, the wandering habits of the majority of the Indian tribes, and the deadly climate of part of the country, made the work of evangelization extremely slow. There were few mass conversions of the kind reported from other Latin American countries, and even at the end of the 18th century the first work of superficial christianization can hardly be said to have been accomplished. But today the vast majority of the inhabitants are nominally members of the Roman Catholic church. There are 23 dioceses, the archbishop of Caracas being the primate of V. Toleration for all religions is guaranteed by the Constitution, but practice does not always correspond to the letter of the law.

Though sporadic efforts had been made before by representatives of the British and American Bible Societies, the arrival of Dr Theodore S. Pond and his wife in March 1897 marks the beginning of consecutive Protestant missionary work in V. The Ponds

had come from Colombia, sent by the Board of Foreign Missions of the Presbyterian Church. Among the evangelical Christians who met them were Mr and Mrs Joseph Norwood, Bible Society agent, and Dr Heraclio Osuan, founder of the still existent Colegio Americano in Caracas.

Though conditions had been favourable at the outset, religious opposition soon made work slow. Activities were centred at the school and the Redentor Church, organized in 1900. Another early founder was the Rev. Gerard A. Bailly, of the *CMA, who opened work in Caracas in 1898 and organized 'Sion' Chapel in 1903. Later the Rev. and Mrs David Findstrom, of the Swedish Evangelical Free Church, established work in central V. In 1906 the Rev. T. J. Bach and the Rev. John Christiansen of the Scandinavian Alliance Mission founded work in Maracaibo. The Rev. G. F. Bender opened work under a Pentecostal mission in Barquisimeto, while in 1910 Mr and Mrs Stephen Adams began work for the Plymouth Brethren.

Today there are an estimated 35,000 evangelicals. Half belong to some branch of the Pentecostal persuasion and the rest are related to Southern Baptist, Baptist Mid-Missions, Lutheran and Anglican churches, as well as those already mentioned

ROBERTO E. SEEL AND EDITORS

K. G. Grubb: *The Lowland Indians of Amazonia* (London 1939); C. A. Phillips: *A History of the Presbyterian Church in Venezuela* (Caracas 1958); *BM* II, 899–904; *NCE* XIV, 597–99; *WKL*, 1527f.

VENIAMINOV, INNOKENTI (1797–1879), from 1868 Metropolitan of Moscow, was noted as a missionary to Alaska and Siberia. He was born, as John Popov, in the district of Irkutsk, but took the name V. after his first bishop. In 1823 he went to the Aleutian Islands as missionary, studied the local language with great zeal, and in 1829 extended his activity to Alaska. In 1839 he presented to the Holy Synod a plan for extensive missionary work, and as bishop of Kamchatka and Russian America, he was entrusted with the carrying out of this plan. At his ordination as monk he took the name Innokenti.

In the course of extended journeys he founded many mission stations, in East Siberia as well as in other areas, and in 1852 as archbishop transferred his residence to East Siberia. After the signing of the treaty of Aigun (1858), by which the eastern districts as far as the Sea of Japan were surrendered to Russia, he took in hand a new organization of church life in Russia's far eastern provinces. He settled in the Amur region, without, however, neglecting the other areas for which he had been responsible. Later, as metropolitan of Moscow he tried to bring home to the Russian church as a whole the sense of missionary responsibility. V's literary works include a number of linguistic researches. His best known book is *A Guide to the Kingdom of Heaven* (22nd ed., 1881). His collected works have been published in three volumes (1886–1888), and his letters, also in three volumes (1879–1901).

JOSEF GLAZIK

J. Glazik: *Die russ.-orth. Heidenmission* (Münster 1954), pp.145–66, with references to sources.

VENN, HENRY (1796–1873), was the son of John Venn, rector of Clapham, England. In 1819 he became a fellow of Queens' College, Cambridge, and in 1841 Chief Secretary of the *CMS, in which capacity he served until the end of 1872. On almost any reckoning V. was the outstanding European missionary leader, thinker and administrator of the 19th century. An Anglican of firm evangelical principles he was none the less irenic in mind and ecumenical in spirit. His great preoccupation was with the establishment of principles upon which the as yet largely unplanned missionary work of the church might best be forwarded. Living as he did at a time when Britain was the undisputed industrial leader of the world, its greatest commercial power, and its most rapidly expanding empire, he was of necessity a man of his own age, sharing its enthusiasms and its limitations. Yet he saw beyond the horizons of his own time and lived and worked for a vision of the future. This vision was expressed in a phrase, almost identical with that coined by Rufus *Anderson, his American contemporary, who was secretary of the *ABCFM – the vision of an *indigenous church 'self-supporting. self-governing and self-extending'. Where, as yet, Christian communities in Asia and Africa consisted of only a handful of Christians he planned so to strengthen them that they might as soon as possible be in a position to determine their own policies, be independent of foreign aid, and be themselves missionary communities. To this end he projected as a plan of development a growth in responsibility from the bottom upward, seeking to foster small local councils and from these to call out local leadership until it should be possible for a 'native' ministry to take over completely from the foreign missionary. Far ahead of his time he looked for and planned for the 'euthanasia of the mission'. This did not mean he foresaw an end to the service of the foreign missionary, but only an end to his control of the local church. Undoubtedly V. failed to allow for the tendency for power structures to establish themselves. No less surely he shared to the full the optimism of the Victorian age, and saw the development of the future as one of uninterrupted progress. Events were to prove him wrong in this particular or that, but the broad perspective of his mind increasingly influenced the future of the missionary movement. Asians and Africans today recognize in him a pioneer of that pattern of church relationship which they themselves pursue.

MAX WARREN

W. Knight: *Memoir of the Rev. H. Venn* (London 1880); E. Stock: *The History of the Church Missionary Society*, I, 367–504, II (London 1899); M. Warren, ed.: *To Apply the Gospel – Henry Venn* (Grand Rapids 1970); *DNB* LVIII, 208; *RGG* VI, 1254.

VERBECK, GUIDO FRIDOLIN (1830–98), was born of godly parents in Zeist,

Holland, and reared under Moravian influence. Educated at Utrecht in engineering, he was also a gifted linguist, musician and poet. V. emigrated to the USA and while ill was called to the gospel ministry. After graduation from Auburn Seminary ordination and marriage, V. was accepted by the Board of Missions of the Reformed Church in America, for service in recently opened Japan, and located at Nagasaki, treaty port for Dutch merchants. While Christianity was still prohibited, he had some notable converts and influenced students who later rose to national leadership. In 1869 V. was called to Tokyo to head the incipient Imperial University and his counsel was often sought by ministers of state. Subsequently he was attached to the government in an advisory capacity and translated the constitutions and legal codes of many western countries and was decorated by the Emperor. The last two decades of his life were devoted to fruitful preaching, teaching theological students, lecturing at the Peers School, preparation of a hymnal and Christian literature and Scripture translation. Modest and unassuming, courageous in the right, V. had the stature of a giant among the pioneer missionaries.

GORDON K. CHAPMAN

W. E. Griffis: *Verbeck of Japan* (London 1901); C. W. Iglehart: *A Century of Protestant Christianity in Japan*, (Tokyo 1959), pp.32–34, 40–50; *DAB* XIX, 248f.

VICARS APOSTOLIC. This extraordinary rank within the Roman Catholic hierarchy had its origin in the 17th century due to Portugal's claim to the right to name residential bishops for her colonies. Both her failure to supply enough bishops and her unwillingness to permit them to administer mission work effectively caused Rome to circumvent Portugal's claim. This was done by sending titular bishops to the Far East to administer territories outside the effective control of Portugal, until such time as circumstances would permit their erection into dioceses. Today vicars are titular bishops who rule a

mission territory known as a vicariate, which is considered as not yet sufficiently developed to enjoy the status of a diocese. In their own territory they normally enjoy the same rights and privileges as residential bishops, the prinicipal difference being that the latter have ordinary, proper jurisdiction, the vicars ordinary but vicarious authority, that is, authority received from the pope.

RONAN HOFFMAN

F. J. Winslow: *Vicars and Prefects Apostolic* (Washington 1924).

VIETNAM, NORTH. A republic of S.E. Asia, in area 60,156 sq.m., and with a population estimated at 20 million. It covers the former French territories of Tongking and Annam to the 17th degree of latitude. Mahāyāna *Buddhism has been predominant, at any rate until the establishment of the communist régime, with minorities adhering to *Taoism and tribal religions. The first missionaries were *Jesuits who began work in Tongking in 1615. Alexander de *Rhodes, SJ, founder and apostle of the Annamese church, arrived in 1627. A first group of seven priests was ordained in connection with the *Jesuits soon after 1668. After a period of adversity the *MEP had established permanent Christian work in 1666. As they began to penetrate Annam they were joined by Dominicans from the Philippines (the 2nd apostolic vicariate of Tongking was set up in 1679). Persecutions occurred in 1698, 1712–20 and 1773. *Pigneau de Béhaine, vicar apostolic of West Tongking, supported French political influence in 1787. After severe persecutions religious freedom and peace in Vietnam were secured in 1874. (See also VIETNAM, SOUTH, for events up to 1954, when about one million RCs, including an estimated 66% of the priests and 75% of the RC population of Hanoi, and Protestants of North Annam fled to South Vietnam because of suppression believed to be expected from the Ho régime.) The RC hierarchy, established in Vietnam in 1690, included ten dioceses of North Vietnam: all have bishops, of whom six were confirmed by the Vatican after 1956. All the 300–400 clergy are Vietnamese.

Ten seminaries have been re-opened after the 'exodus' of 1954, with about 100 priests in training. The archbishop of Hanoi, appointed in 1962, is the Most Rev. Trinh Nhu Khue. The faithful number between 700,000 and one million. The church, suffering through the wars which have followed the second world war, is functioning, but silent.

LOTHAR SCHREINER

A. Launay: *Histoire de la mission de Tonkin*, Vol. I, 1658–1717 (Paris 1927); D. Paquette: 'Religious persecutions in North Vietnam', *Asia* XII (Hong Kong 1960), 11–18; Tran-minh-Tièt: *Histoire des Persécutions au Vietnam* (Blois 1955).

VIETNAM, SOUTH, a republic since 1954, in area 65,948 sq.m., and with a population of 16 million, covers the former French territories of Cochin-China and Annam to the 17th degree of latitude. Mahāyāna *Buddhism is established, with strong minorities of the syncretist Cao-dai sect (1·5 million), *Taoism, tribal religions, and the indigenous Hoa-Hao sect. *Franciscans from Manila reached Cochin-China in 1583. *Jesuits followed in 1615, with Alexander de *Rhodes in 1624, who was expelled in 1645. With the arrival in 1666 of the apostolic vicars *Pallu and Lambert de la Motte, the *MEP established Christianity permanently. They were joined by Dominicans from the Philippines. The missions co-operated with arriving French commercial and political forces during the 18th century. After *Pigneau de Béhaine, apostolic vicar, secured with French military help the reinstatement of an exiled king of Cochin, Christianity was received more easily. The number and zeal of the missionaries as well as the weakness of Buddhism led to strong Christian communities. Christianity had been persecuted from time to time since 1664; in the 19th century revived Buddhism undergirded by local rulers reacted violently, during the years 1832–41 for religious reasons, and 1856–62 against European political and military interference. Thousands of Christians were put to death, including Th. Vénard, J. *Hermosilla and 115 Vietnamese priests. These persecutions were among the severest of modern church history. There was a 50% increase of RC membership between 1900 and 1935. With six minor and three major seminaries the area has proportionately the strongest indigenous RC priesthood in S.E. Asia, 1,532 Vietnamese besides about 400 foreigners. Nine out of eleven sees are headed by Vietnamese, the first having been consecrated in 1933. The RC community is 1,456,258 strong. Their ministry in education, medical work and rural uplift make Vietnam one of the best RC missionary achievements in Asia-Africa. Owing to French preference towards RCs the *CMA was admitted to North and Central Annam only in 1911. Permission to evangelize among the tribal peoples followed in 1929. The Evang. Church of Vietnam, organized in 1927, but CMA-controlled until the second world war, stands out for its self-support and thrust thanks to the 'leader-method' of R. A. Jaffray. Spread over 43 provinces, chiefly among mountain tribes, there are 343 local churches with a community of 45,000, 104 Vietnamese ministers and more than 200 lay workers. Nine missionary couples of the indigenous church were sent out to the tribes in 1954. Hitherto isolated, the Evang. Church of Vietnam is affirming ecumenical fellowship offered through the *EACC-ACS. The Bible has been translated into Vietnamese and Annamese. American CMA staff numbers 118. Also at work are the *OMF, SDA, *WEC and small groups from other missions.

From 1954 onwards the Mennonites pioneered in relief work in South Vietnam. With the escalation of the war, other Protestant churches working through *Church World Service, Lutheran World Relief and the Mennonite Central Committee set up an agency called Vietnam Christian Service, to provide greater resources and services to those in need. Additional relief work was carried on by

Asian Christian Service of the *EACC, and Catholic Relief Services. Christians were planning to co-operate in a major programme for rehabilitation and reconstruction after the war.

LOTHAR SCHREINER

R. De Roeck: 'Vietnam, Cambodia and Laos' in G. H. Anderson, ed.: *Christ and Crisis in Southeast Asia* (New York 1968), pp.55–80; H. E. Dowdy: *The Bamboo Cross* (New York, 1964); F. Irwin: *With Christ in Indo-China* (Harrisburg, Pa. 1937); G. H. Smith: *Victory in Vietnam* (Grand Rapids 1965); *BM* II, 905–12; *NCE* XIV, 661–63.

VIRGIN ISLANDS. See CARIBBEAN.

VOCATION, MISSIONARY. All Christians are called to be witnesses to Christ (Acts 1:8), *some* are called to be evangelists (Eph. 4:11). All Christians are called to share in the priesthood and mission of the people of God (1 Pet. 2:5,9), *some* are called to be in the full-time service of the church as its ministers or its missionaries.

The calling to be a missionary usually means service overseas or, as in the case of some Indian missionaries, among a people and in an area different from one's own. This involves a willingness to learn another language, to enter into the thinking and culture of another people, to renounce all personal ambition, and to accept a salary or allowance just sufficient to cover the cost of fairly simple living in that place.

As with the calling to the ordained ministry, the missionary vocation has to be tested and the candidate adequately prepared. This is normally the responsibility of the sending church. God's call may come at any age. Some hear it as children, others when their own children have grown up. For some the calling is unmistakably clear from the first; for others it is tentative and less certain. At one time the majority of missionaries felt their calling to the people of another land to be lifelong; today, with the growth

of the church in all the world and the rise of so many independent countries – some with governments suspicious of missionaries if not hostile to them – such service is often for shorter periods.

In Protestant churches, as distinct from the RC church, most missionaries have been married. An important part of their witness has been through the love of a Christian family and the hospitality of a Christian home. Roman Catholics with their celibate communities of priests, lay brothers, and nuns, have demonstrated the power of Christian community life. Both kinds of witness are needed. But among Protestants and in certain spheres of work there is a need for more unmarried missionaries of both sexes. The missionary vocation is always part of God's total calling of a man or a woman which will include the vocation to marriage or the single life.

DOUGLAS WEBSTER

D. N. Sargent: *The Making of a Missionary* (London 1960); D. Webster: *What is a Missionary?* (London 1955).

VOICE OF THE ANDES. See BROADCASTING, CHRISTIAN.

VOLTAIC REPUBLIC. See UPPER VOLTA.

VOODOOISM is a *syncretistic form of religion, which is practised principally in Haiti. The name is derived from the Ewe (E. Togo, Dahomey) word *vodu*, which is used to denote a divinity or a spirit. The word and the practice were brought by slaves from the Guinea Coast to Central America. Here the complex manifestations of West African *primitive religion, perhaps enriched by Red Indian concepts, were combined with magical practices to produce an individual religion. In this the spirits (*lao*), the dead, and twins, play a special part. The spirits can show themselves to men, or reveal themselves in dreams and in ecstasy. The ritual is many-sided (e.g. libations, sacrifice, dancing, rites of initiation, marriage to a divinity, the cult of the dead). Characteristic is the close association between Voodoo beliefs and certain Christian ideas which were taken from the Roman Catholic church. This is evident from a number of rites. Latin formulae were used; the Lord's Prayer, the Confession, and the *Ave Maria* were recited. Holy water was used. The consecrated Host was much sought after, the liturgical calendar taken over, and pilgrimage practised. At the same time the original Christian sense was distorted by being fitted into the pattern of a primitive religion, and above all of *magic.

The RC church treats V. as an enemy, and this attitude is expressed in expositions in the catechism, and in requiring special oaths to be taken against it. The Protestant churches take an equally rigid view of the matter. In them Christians feel themselves protected against the influence of V., which can be a serious matter in the case of conversion from V. In spite of the official rejection by the churches, there is an everpresent danger that V. may live on just under the surface. Popular Catholicism, and the emotional atmosphere of some of the Protestant sects (e.g. the *Pentecostalists) provide an open door for this return.

See also SPIRITISM.

ERNST DAMMANN

M. J. Hershowitz: 'African Gods and Catholic Saints in New World Negro Belief' in *American Anthropologist* XXXIX (1937); A. Métraux: *Le Vaudou Haitien* (4th ed., Paris 1958); *NCE* XIV, 752f.

W

WADDELL, HOPE MASTERTON (1804–1895), was born in Dublin, Ireland. In 1829 the Scottish Missionary Society in Edinburgh sent him with his wife (née Jessie Simpson) to Jamaica. He did notable pastoral work during the critical period before and after the liberation of the slaves. In 1845 he persuaded the United Secession Church in Scotland to sponsor a mission from Jamaica to Calabar. In 1846 he reached Calabar with five companions and, with the agreement of the local rulers, founded the mission. Living among the people, preaching and teaching, they began to win converts. By 1854 their school had 150 children on roll. W. travelled inland and did translation into Efik, printing, and rudimentary medical work. Combining patience with vigorous and plain speaking he attacked inhumane customs, particularly the ritual murder of slaves, and overcame the opposition of a number of Africans and European traders. When his chief supporter, King Eyo Honesty II of Creek Town, died in 1858 there was no ritual murder at the funeral. In the same year W. left Calabar owing to ill health. He had laid the mission on firm foundations, seen an indigenous church planted, and made a valuable contribution to social progress. His name is commemorated in the Hope Waddell Institution where African leaders, including Dr Francis Ibiam, have received their education.

JOHN GOODWIN

H. M. Waddell: *Twenty-nine Years in the West Indies and Central Africa* (London 1863).

WAKE ISLAND. See PACIFIC ISLANDS.

WALLIS AND FUTUNA ISLANDS. See PACIFIC ISLANDS

WALSH, JAMES ANTHONY (1867–1936), bishop, co-founder of the Catholic Foreign Mission Society of America (*Maryknoll). Born in Cambridge, Massachusetts, USA, of Irish-American parents, W. was solidly devout without ostentation, had a keen intellect, great organizing ability and the Irish sense of humour. In 1886 he entered St John's Seminary, Brighton, Massachusetts, founded only two years previously by French Sulpician priests. The rector, Abbé Hogan, had been a friend of Father Théophane Vénard, who at the age of 31 had been beheaded by the natives of Tongking (now part of Vietnam). The Abbé possessed some letters from the young martyr which he read to his students. To W. they were incendiary letters, kindling a fire in him that would sweep the globe.

On 20 May 1892, James Anthony Walsh was ordained to the priesthood. After working in St Patrick's parish, Roxbury, until 1903, he was made archdiocesan director of the Society for the Propagation of the Faith. He conceived the idea that there ought to be a Catholic foreign missionary seminary in the USA, and with this in mind he started a magazine called *The Field Afar* in January 1907. He and a kindred soul, Fr T. F. Price went to Rome in 1911 where Pope Saint Pius X received them and their plan with welcome and approval. In time the headquarters of the society which they founded came to be located on a hill near Ossining, New York, and was called Maryknoll. The new Catholic Foreign Mission Society drew priests from other dioceses as well as students for the seminary of which W. was head. The first four priests left for China in 1918. In a few years the society was worldwide. On 29 June 1933, at Propaganda College in Rome, W. was consecrated bishop. He then resumed his duties at Maryknoll, in constant contact with the numerous houses at home and abroad until his death on 14 April 1936.

W. had been born into a church whose Catholics, a small minority in Protestant America, were mostly concerned with keeping their own faith. He left them with a wider vision, a greater charity, and a stronger faith.

SISTER M. JULIANA, MM

R. A. Lane, ed.: *The Early Days of Maryknoll* (New York 1951); D. Sargent: *All the Day Long* (New York 1941); 'In Memoriam, Bishop Walsh of Maryknoll', *The Field Afar*, Maryknoll Magazine, V (May 1936); *DAB* XXII, 691–93; *NCE* XIV, 781f.

WAR AND MISSIONS. The Christian mission is a mission of peace. It is, therefore, self-evident that it must at all times be opposed to every kind of war, and that its operations will be gravely hindered and imperilled by war. But, within this generalization, it is possible to make some distinctions.

(1) A state of continuous tribal war makes the foundation and the maintenance of missionary work almost impossible. The ceaseless inter-tribal wars of Africa, and later the ever-recurring struggle between Boers and African races in South Africa, led constantly to the destruction of mission stations and to the overthrow of work that had patiently been brought into being. Similarly the 18th century in India, the period of the gradual dissolution of the Mogul empire, was much less favourable to Christian missions than either the 16th or 17th, when Mogul rule was still able to supply large areas in India with peace and order. The restoration of order by colonial powers made possible the resumption and wide extension of missionary work.

(2) Some wars, however, have at least temporarily appeared to aid the Christian cause. The Spanish wars of conquest in the western world opened the door to the christianization, however superficial, of the many peoples of Latin America. The missions had long awaited the opportunity legally to enter China, and always in vain. The Opium war of 1840 and its successor of 1856 finally broke down the resistance of the Chinese to the presence of foreigners in their midst; and missionaries, like traders and diplomats, took advantage of the new freedom to enter and establish themselves in China. But many later students are of the opinion that the gospel was almost fatally prejudiced from the start in these countries by the accident that it entered as a consequence of the success of Christian arms.

(3) An entirely new situation arose with the two world wars of the 20th century. The Christian faith had enjoyed something of a reflected prestige from the growing importance of the west throughout the entire world. Western culture has at many points been deeply suffused with Christian ideas. Christian concepts of the value of the individual person, of freedom and responsibility, proved deeply attractive to a great many thoughtful people in non-Christian countries, who came to realize that these pleasing political and social ideas were in the last resort inseparable from the gospel in which they had their origin. Many missionaries tended to stress this aspect of western culture; while never going so far as to identify the gospel with it, they were inclined to think that the acceptance of the gospel could produce in the east something like western society as they knew it.

The two world wars entirely and permanently destroyed the prestige of the west. Non-Christians had before their eyes the spectacle of respected missionaries being interned and in a number of cases ill-treated by fellow Christians who happened to have become their enemies. Destruction of life and property was on an immense scale. Unscrupulous propaganda was circulated. Millions of soldiers became acquainted with the most sordid side of western existence. But worst of all was the evident fact that nations with a thousand years of Christian teaching behind them had failed to control their passions and had set the whole world ablaze for the satisfaction of less than admirable ambitions.

This at the time may have seemed to be a disaster; but in the end it proved to be a great advantage. Once and for all it was made clear that the Christian mission was not identical with the western colonial enterprise, and was not dependent on it. The western churches are now on the whole penitent churches; their claims are more modest, and they are willing to recognize that they stand under the judgment of God at least as much as the non-Christian peoples to whom they speak. At the same time, history since the end of the second world war has made it clear that guilt has not lain wholly on the side of the western peoples, and that the end of *colonialism has not meant the solution of all problems of human justice and peace.

In point of fact, the number of Christian missionaries of all churches and confessions has increased more rapidly since 1945 than in any previous period of Christian history. Their work has become more widely extended and has taken deeper root. New methods of co-operation with *indigenous churches have been devised. Some missionaries have accepted naturalization as citizens of the countries in which they work. There is a deeper sense of international responsibility and of the obligation to work for peace. It is not possible to say that the world will be spared the great calamity of a third world war; one of the forces working against such a calamity is without doubt the presence, in every country of the world, of the international Christian mission.

See also ORPHANED MISSIONS.

STEPHEN NEILL

WARNECK, GUSTAV (1834–1910), was born in Naumburg, Germany, and, after the completion of his theological studies and some years in pastoral work, became successively Mission Inspector at Barmen (1871), pastor of Rothenschirmbach, and professor of the science of missions at Halle (1896). His first great contribution to the missionary enterprise was the foundation in 1874 of the journal *Allgemeine Missionszeitschrift,* the aim of which was the objective and scientific discussion of missionary topics. Of similar character was the Mission Conference of Saxony, founded by W. in 1879. This found imitators in the areas of all the German regional churches; the deepest influences were exercised on the minds of the pastors, but the aim was also to draw into fellowship the various missionary societies in each area. The missionary co-operation which had been promoted in this way found organized expression in the German Protes-

tant Committee (*Ausschuss*) which was brought into being in 1885 on the basis of proposals put forward by W., and which has found its successor in the German Missionary Council (*Missionsrat*). W. exercised a decisive influence on all the continental missionary conferences. To the Centenary Conference on Foreign Missions held in London in 1888 W. sent an article in which were foreshadowed with singular exactness plans that were brought into effect only with the foundation of the *IMC in 1921.

W. is generally regarded as the founder of Protestant science of missions. He was not the first to deal with missionary problems in a scientific manner, but he was the first to produce a vast systematic treatise on this subject, the *Evangelische Missionslehre,* which appeared in five volumes between 1892 and 1903. His *Sketch of the History of Protestant Missions from the Reformation to the Present Day* (1892) was reprinted ten times; the book on missionary science appeared only once. The reason for this is that this scientific work was essentially directed to practice, and entered so deeply into practical details that, though it was a pioneer work, it is marked by the period to which it belongs. The work is based on Scripture and experience, but it is carried out in such a fashion that in many cases the validity of the basic Scriptural exposition is established from the practical experiences. This peculiarity is linked to another, the fact that the dominant understanding of mission is as education; both world history and mission history display themselves before the eyes of W. as 'a divine process of mission as education'. He sees a certain parallelism between the history of the world and that of the missionary enterprise, since developments in world history—world trade, the policies of colonial annexation—have brought in 'a period of the opening of doors to the gospel'. On one side W. stresses the independence of missions over against the policies of colonial governments, and on the other strenuously rejects the slogan of the *SVMU, 'the evangelization of the world in this generation'.

This linking of Scripture with experience,

and the prevailing understanding of mission in terms of divine education are seen most clearly in the fact that the task of mission is held to be both 'the extension of the kingdom of God', and also 'the founding of the church', which is not to be understood simply as 'the invitation addressed to individuals to become believers'. Although the first stage is that of the conversion of individuals, the aim must be the development of 'people's churches', which should lead to such a christianization of whole peoples that at the end of the process we find 'not a general world-wide church made up simply of believing members, but rather such a victory of Christianity that paganism is everywhere overcome, and that every people lives in such a Christian atmosphere that the knowledge of the truth and the acceptance of salvation are mediated to every member of the race'. Yet on the other hand, the little flock represents 'the special harvest of missionary labour unto eternal life'.

Alongside the foundation of the church upon the Word of God stands its incorporation into the life of the peoples. 'The Christian faith does not destroy but transfigures the particular character of a people.' This is, on the one hand, the proclamation of the need for independent, *indigenous churches, though limited by the 'educational' point of view; but on the other side the door is opened to the danger of the 'divinization of a people', not so much through concentration on the idea of the church, as from the lack of an eschatological dimension in the understanding of the church.

W. HOLSTEN

J. Dürr: *Sendende und werdende Kirche in der Missionstheologie Gustav Warnecks* (Basel 1947); J. C. Hoekendijk: *Kirche und Volk in der deutschen Missionswissenschaft* (München 1967); S. A. Teinonen: *Gustav Warneckin Varhaisen Lähetystorian Teologiset Perusteet* (with summary in English, Helsinki 1959); *EKL* III, 1734; *RGG* VI, 1547; *WKL*, 1570f.

WARNECK, JOHANNES (1867–1944), a son of Gustav W., was born in Dommitsch,

Saxony, Germany. He was a missionary with the Batak church in Sumatra from 1892 to 1906, first as a pioneer for four years on the island of Samosir in Lake Toba, then as teacher, and from 1898 director, at the Rhenish Mission's seminary for preachers at Sipoholon (1896–1906). In 1908 W. was appointed to the home staff of his society, with responsibility for its work in Indonesia. The first lectureship in missions at the Bethel Theological School was conferred on him in 1912. Succeeding L.I. *Nommensen as Ephorus W. went back to Sumatra in 1920 to lead the church until 1931. He directed the *Rhenish Missionary Society in Wuppertal-Barmen from 1932 to 1937, and continued with literary work during his retirement. W's influence is outstanding in four respects.

(1) He promoted a training that was thoroughly practical, as well as academic, for the indigenous ministry. During his first term in Sumatra W. built the new seminary at Sipoholon-Tarutung, revised its syllabus systematically and produced text books and NT commentaries. In the late 1920s, together with H. *Kraemer and others, W. supported new plans for educating ordinands at the university level. Their efforts resulted in the opening of the United Theological Seminary at Djakarta in 1934.

(2) Following on Nommensen's work with its emphasis on the expansion of the Batak church, W. recognized that concentration and guidance towards self-government were of crucial importance. He wrote a new constitution for the church, which thereby became legally recognized as an autonomous religious body in 1930. The constitution defines the Batak church as an indigenous body and ensured a majority of nationals on the governing board: seven Bataks, together with three Europeans. But autonomy for him depended on the 'inward quality', which is not man-made, but has to grow from a 'nucleus of true Christians', who are the 'ferment' within the mass congregations.

(3) W's research into the language, literature and beliefs of the Bataks contributed considerably to the scientific know-

ledge concerning this Indonesian people (*Die Religion der Batak*, 1908).

(4) As a prolific writer W. spread a deeper understanding and a wider appreciation of the missionary cause generally and deepened the relations between mission churches in Indonesia and the interested public in central Europe. In *Die Lebenskräfte des Evangeliums* (1908, 7th ed. 1922; Eng./Amer. ed. *The Living Christ and Dying Heathenism*, 1909, 2nd ed. 1954) he unfolded a broad psychological perspective of the religious evolution of 'animist' peoples, who first, he observed, grasp the message of Christ's domination over the spirit-world, before they come to understand the message about sin and grace. Following his father's doctrine of missions, he combined in his scholarly work and his leadership both conservative Lutheran pietism and a sympathetic evaluation of 'primitive' religions. He understood these in terms of the 19th century's theory of animism, which he effectively popularized.

LOTHAR SCHREINER

J. Warneck's autobiography: *Werfet eure Netze aus* (Berlin 1938); *RGG* VI, 1547f.

WARNSHUIS, ABBE LIVINGSTON (1877–1958), American missionary to China and ecumenical pioneer, was born at Clymer, New York, of Dutch ancestry. Educated at Hope College, Michigan, and New Brunswick Seminary, he was ordained in 1900 in the Reformed Church in America and appointed to Amoy, where he arrived in the year of the *Boxer rebellion. W. played a leading part in educational developments in the Fukien Province and in the events which resulted in the formation of the Church of Christ in China. Under pressure from John R. *Mott in 1916 W. became National Evangelistic secretary of the body which became the *National Christian Council of China. Again at Mott's suggestion, in 1920 W. left China to become the first American secretary of the *IMC, which he served for 21 years, being responsible for much of the organization of the council's meetings in *Jerusalem, 1928, and *Tambaram, 1938. He carried much of the responsibility for the international wartime operation known as the *'Orphaned Missions' service of the IMC. His retirement in 1942 was only the prelude to a long period of service, first on behalf of the European churches in their reconstruction needs, and secondly in the extension of this relief and rehabilitation work to Asia. More than any other person, he became the architect of *Church World Service, the great service agency of the American churches.

NORMAN GOODALL

N. Goodall: *Christian Ambassador* (London 1963).

WELZ, JUSTINIAN VON (1621–1668?) was born into the family of an Austrian nobleman who had to leave his country for the sake of his Lutheran faith. Little is known about his early years. He did however, experience a sudden conversion, inspired chiefly by the study of the Bible and of ascetic-mystical literature. In 1664 W. published three books, all of them for reasons yet to be accounted for devoted to a passionate appeal to Protestant Christianity to engage in world mission. W. offered nothing less than a detailed blueprint of a mission society, somewhat along the lines of the cultural and scientific societies of his age but unique in its consistent direction to foreign missions. While a number of theologians were prepared to support the bold layman, he was unable to win the approval of the authorities of the churches; he associated himself with spiritualist enthusiasts and lost his life as a freelance missionary in the Dutch colony of Surinam. It was only after the missionary revival in *Pietism that his vision was at least in part realized.

H.-W. GENSICHEN

F. Laubach, 'Justinian von Welz', *Evang. Missionszeitschrift*, Vol. XXI (1964), pp. 158–65; J. A. Scherer: *Justinian Welz* (Grand Rapids 1969); *RGG* VI, 1634f.

WESLEY, JOHN (1703–1791). The influence of W. on the modern missionary movement has been consistently underrated, probably on account of its indirect nature. Yet the man himself, the forces which were to find focus in his ministry, and the movement which he founded were of inestimable importance in creating the background of religious conviction in which what Latourette has called the 'Great Century' emerged. The religious awakenings of the 18th century, expressive of a long dormant evangelical tradition, brought new life to the Protestantism of Great Britain, enabling it to become more vigorous, active, and widespread than any other branch of the church, including the Roman Catholic, in expanding the Christian faith. Of this evangelical movement the Methodist *revival was the most vivid and effective manifestation and W. the outstanding leader.

The fact that the new Protestant missionary movement was largely the outgrowth of the Evangelical Revival in its broadest sense should not be allowed to obscure the particular influence of W. and his Methodists. It is not merely that the stress on personal conversion and holiness of life produced a sense of social responsibility and zeal for mission far removed from the attitude, e.g. of William *Carey's critics. There is also, perhaps more importantly, the element in W. of conscious unbreakable conviction that God had commanded him to proclaim the good news of salvation in Christ to all whom he could reach and had appointed him to care for the souls converted under his preaching and that of his fellow workers.

Even before his evangelical conversion a sense of priestly obligation sent W. to Georgia as servant of SPCK (1735–37). The failures here and the experience of teaching a little Negro cabin-boy on the sad journey home were the first steps in the journey to that religious experience to which can be traced the worldwide Methodist movement and all that this has meant for the wider mission. W. was never himself to take direct part in 'foreign' mission yet the Great Awakening of America, with all that was to mean for the expansion of the church, was to a great extent the result of the revival he led in his homeland. There were Methodist missions from Britain to the American colonies in the 1760s and it was in this context that W. was led to ordain Thomas *Coke and others, under an evangelical compulsion stronger than his ingrained loyalty to church order.

Typical of W's indirect influence on missions is the story of Nathaniel Gilbert. This planter and lawyer of Antigua came into a transforming and contagious religious experience through hearing W. when on a visit to England. On his return to Antigua he preached to his slaves, established a Methodist church, and made Antigua, in 1760, the first centre of Protestantism among the Negroes of the West Indies. What Gilbert began was consolidated and enlarged by Coke, commissioned by W. to take the lead in carrying the gospel overseas, in America, the West Indies, and beyond. The mission was directed in particular to those of other than European descent, with the result that Methodism became the first church of the black Christians. The work was carried out by others but the enthusiasm and the enterprise were kindled by W. Thus, long before BMS, *CMS, *LMS and other societies came into being W's Methodists had been engaged in spreading the faith. Before W's death the Conference was organizing help for Coke and other workers overseas and although the WMMS did not emerge as an official organ of Conference till 1817 it was there *in nucleo* under W. It was W's rediscovery and practice of the great evangelical certainties—that all men can be saved; and know that they are saved, and saved to the full—which more than any other factor created the climate out of which the modern missionary enterprise sprang and in which it was to flourish.

MARCUS WARD

J. E. Rattenbury: *Wesley's Legacy to the World* (London 1928); M. Schmitt: *The Young Wesley: Missionary and Theologian of Missions* (London 1958); E. W. Thompson: *Wesley, Apostolic Man* (London 1957).

WEST INDIES. See CARIBBEAN.

WEST INDIES MISSION, INC., was

founded in 1928 by Elmer V. Thompson, an American, and B. G. Lavastida, a Cuban. They opened the Cuba Bible Institute in 1928, and from it came the impulse to evangelize the West Indies Islands as a whole. The mission has emphasized establishing *indigenous churches and training nationals for leadership. It has engaged in specialized ministries such as medical work, radio, orphanages, and literature distribution. The mission has established 350 national churches. In 1966, 210 missionaries were supported by the agency. The annual income now exceeds $500,000 a year. The mission publishes a bimonthly, *Whitened Harvest*. International headquarters are at 832 S.W. 23rd Avenue, Miami, Florida 33135 (USA). It is a member of *IFMA.

HAROLD LINDSELL

WESTON, FRANK (1871–1924), was born in South London; his father was a strongly evangelical tea-broker in Mincing Lane. Achieving a first-class theology degree at Trinity College, Oxford, W. did parish work from 1893 to 1898 at the college mission at Stratford, where he was ordained, and St. Matthew's, Westminster, both in the London diocese. In 1898 he fulfilled his undergraduate ambition to serve in Zanzibar, and within four months of his arrival wrote an *Open Letter* in which he pointed out that the chief obstacle to mission was the Englishman's consciousness of race superiority. After ten years of teaching work he was consecrated Bishop of Zanzibar in 1908, and thenceforth travelled on foot for nine months of each year. Africans and Europeans alike admired him. He founded the Community of the Sacred Passion, and the first sisters arrived from England in 1910. In 1913 he took issue with the *Kikuyu Conference and with his brother bishops of Uganda and Mombasa. He accused them of 'the grievous faults of propagating heresy and committing schism', threatened to put Zanzibar out of communion with their dioceses and appealed to the Archbishop of Canterbury. Davidson's pronouncement, accompanied by the report to him of the Lambeth Consultative Committee, was

delayed till 1915 by the outbreak of war. It upheld W's objections, without condemning his brother bishops. In 1917 W. attended the next Kikuyu Conference. He acted as President of the Anglo-Catholic Congresses of 1920 and 1924 and died four months after his return to Zanzibar. W's devotion, energy and determined defence of catholic principle left a long-lasting impression on his diocese.

JOHN WILKINSON

H. M. Smith: *Frank, Bishop of Zanzibar* (London 1926); *DNB* (1922–1930), 902f.

WHITBY 1947. See CONFERENCES, WORLD MISSIONARY.

WHITE, JOHN (1866–1933), was born at Dearham, Cumberland, England, of farmer parents, was trained for the Methodist ministry at Didsbury College, ordained, and sent by the Wesleyan Methodist Missionary Society to Transvaal, Africa, in 1892, and to Rhodesia in 1894, where he served with distinction till retirement in 1932. W. was general superintendent of his church, 1901–1926 and 1926–30, started the Waddilove Training Institution in 1898 and was its governor till 1932. He died in Birmingham, England. W. came to Rhodesia shortly after the British occupation of the country and became a public figure almost at once. During the Shona rebellion, 1896–97, he proved himself a friend of the Africans and an able spokesman for their human rights. After the rebellion he published a courageous letter exposing the weakness of the British administration, which made him very unpopular with the European settlers. Throughout his career he was a fearless and intelligent spokesman for the Africans in matters of education, land policy, social welfare and political rights, being far ahead of the political thinking of his time. African events of the 1960s proved the validity of his remarkable insight.

PER HASSING

C. F. Andrews: *John White of Mashonaland* (New York and London 1935).

WHITE FATHERS OF AFRICA, THE. The Society of Missionaries of Africa, popularly known as the White Fathers because of their white robes and hooded capes, was founded in 1868 by Charles *Lavigerie, Archbishop of Algiers. Its 3,600 priests and brothers come from Europe, the USA and Canada.

Although L. formed the first community of WF to care for the thousands of Arab children left homeless by a severe typhoid epidemic and famine in Algeria, his aim was to carry on missionary work throughout the continent. The first mission stations were set up in the Kabylia Mountains and on the northern edge of the Sahara. In 1878, after several attempts to cross the desert and found missions further south, they moved into eastern and central Africa, and can now be found in seventeen African countries.

L. gave detailed instructions to the first missionaries sent to the interior of the continent. They were to settle in a centrally located spot, gather together orphans and ransomed slaves to create the nucleus of a Christian community, and cultivate the friendship of the local tribal leaders. Prospective converts were progressively instructed over a four-year period. From the beginning they also trained Africans as *catechists to assist in their work.

A severe persecution of Christians in Uganda from 1885 to 1887 resulted in the martyrdom of about 150 Ugandans. Twenty-two of the Catholics among them were canonized in 1964, thus making them the first African saints of modern times. Despite such early persecutions, the work of the WF in Central Africa has been more successful than in any other part of the continent.

The WF have focused their attention especially on parishes, and on the training of an African clergy. The parishes and the dioceses are gradually being placed under the direction of the African clergy. The WF remain to work under them, and ultimately withdraw completely from one diocese to begin in another.

RONAN HOFFMAN

W. Burridge: *Destiny Africa* (London 1966) G. D. Kittler: *The White Fathers* (New York 1957); *NCE* XIV, 894f.

WHITEHEAD, HENRY (1853–1947), the elder brother of A. N. Whitehead the philosopher (1861–1947), was fellow of Trinity College, Oxford, 1878–83, principal of Bishop's College, Calcutta, 1883–99, and became Anglican bishop of Madras in 1899. He was one of the first church leaders in India to realize the importance of the *'mass movements' among the depressed classes, which in the northern parts of his diocese were bringing many thousands of people into the church every year. Whereas many Indian church leaders viewed these movements with anxiety and suspicion, W. was convinced that they were a God-given opportunity for the church. Convinced that the time had come for the Indian church to assert its independence, he was largely instrumental in securing the appointment and consecration of V. S. *Azariah (1912) as the first Indian Anglican bishop. W. played a leading part in the early stages of the discussions which led to the formation of the *CSI; but he died on 14 April 1947, just five months before that church came into being. In the later years of his long life he endured much suffering; but spent his time in almost ceaseless intercession for the country to which he had given almost 40 years (1883–1922) of service.

STEPHEN NEILL

No memoir of Whitehead has been written, but there is a good deal of autobiographical material in his book *Indian Problems in Religion, Education, Politics* (London 1924).

WILDER, ROBERT PARMELEE (1863–1938), was born in Kelhapur, India, the son of a missionary. When he was twelve years old his parents returned to the USA and made their home in Princeton, New Jersey. W. graduated from Princeton in 1886. That summer he attended a student Christian conference at Mt Hermon, Massachusetts, led by Dwight L. *Moody. There he was the centre of a group which by the end of the gathering swelled to 100 who had decided to become foreign missionaries. The following year W. travelled through the colleges, universities and theological seminaries of the United States recruiting for the Movement. He early spread the Movement to the British Isles and the continent of Europe. During most of the decade 1892–1902 he was in India as a missionary among students. Ill health forced him to leave. After recuperating, he became an evangelist to students in the British Isles and the European continent. He served for a time with the *YMCAs of North America, for several years was General Secretary of the *SVM and in his mid-sixties became secretary of the newly organized Near East Christian Council. His later years were spent quietly in Norway among his wife's people.

KENNETH SCOTT LATOURETTE

R. B. Wilder: *In This Generation: The Story of Robert P. Wilder* (New York 1941).

WILLIAMS, CHANNING MOORE (1829–1910), was born in Richmond, Virginia, USA. Upon completing his theological studies in 1855, he sailed for Shanghai with a colleague, John Liggins. As Japan was reopened to foreigners, the two were posted by the PECUSA to Nagasaki in 1859, becoming the first Protestant missionaries in that country. W. began to work with expatriates, and slowly won the confidence of a few Japanese, despite lingering government antagonism. In 1866 he was appointed bishop of China and Japan. After living in China for several years he returned to Japan, basing himself in Osaka. In 1874 he finally convinced his board to separate China from his jurisdiction, and he was named Bishop of Yedo (Tokyo). By circumstance he was a pioneer; constructing the first Protestant church building in Japan; founding Rikkyo University and St Luke's Hospital, Tokyo; translating the Book of Common Prayer into Japanese. By inclination he was more interested in sound, thorough training than in broad, rapid growth. By nature he was shy, pious and unpretentious, which caused a later bishop in Japan to note, 'The Japanese still revere him not only as the founder of their church but still more as its patron saint'.

A. THEODORE EASTMAN

Hisakazu Kaneko: *A Story of Channing Moore Williams: the Bishop of Yedo* (Tokyo

1965); M. Minor: *Pioneer Missionary in Japan: Channing Moore Williams* (New York 1959); *DAB* XX, 250f.

WILLIAMS, JOHN (1796–1839), pioneer and martyr missionary to the islands of the South Pacific. Born in Tottenham, England, into a 'working-class' home of fervent evangelical piety, he had little formal education and was apprenticed at the age of fourteen to a London ironmonger. In his eighteenth year W. experienced a powerful conversion, at a time when the churches were stirred by dramatic news of the first English missionaries to the South Seas. This, together with his reading of the voyages of Captain James Cook, kindled his missionary ambition. In 1816 he was ordained to the Congregational ministry and commissioned —with Robert *Moffat of Africa fame—for service with the *LMS. At the age of twenty and with a nineteen-year-old wife he sailed for Tahiti in the Society Islands (the voyage lasting a year). King Pomare of Tahiti had recently been baptized and a strong movement towards Christianity was under way; but W. was restless to preach the gospel where it had not been heard. In 1818 he settled in Raiatea and won the confidence of King Tamatoa. Here he combined 'teaching of the arts and sciences' with his evangelism, and assisted the king to fashion a code of laws for the island 'in the light of the word of God'. The Christian community grew rapidly and set itself immediately to evangelize other islands as yet unvisited. Early effect was thus given to one of the greatest features of W's work—his conviction that the gospel must be transmitted through indigenous witnesses. Between 1823 and his death W. made pioneer voyages to other island groups, notably to the Hervey Islands (now known as the Cook Islands), Samoa, Tonga and the New Hebrides, evangelizing, educating, and training indigenous teachers to continue the work. These voyages involved the hazards of little-explored waters in frail vessels, as well as danger to life from hostile islanders. It was in an attempt to take the good news to the island of Erromanga that W. was murdered by cannibals. In addition to his dedication and heroism, W. possessed great natural gifts, manual skills and a wide-ranging mind. During years crowded with movement he did remarkable linguistic work, including the translation of the NT into Raratongan. His *Narrative of Missionary Enterprises in the South Sea Islands* (1837) is a classic of exploration. His martyr-death and adventurous life continue to quicken Christian dedication in others—as symbolized by a succession of missionary ships which, ever since his death, have borne his name. The latest (voyaging in the South Seas in 1968) is the *John Williams VII*.

NORMAN GOODALL

B. Mathews: *Williams the Shipbuilder* (London 1915); C. Northcott: *John Williams Sails On* (London 1939); E. Prout: *Memoirs of the Life of the Rev. John Williams* (London 1843); *DNB* LXI, 423; *RGG* VI, 1725.

WILLIAMS, SAMUEL WELLS (1812–1884), missionary Sinologist and diplomat, was born at Utica, New York, USA, son of a printer. At 21 he was sent by the *ABCFM to start a mission press at Canton. There he rapidly mastered the spoken and written language. W. printed and later edited *The Chinese Repository*, a scholarly English journal (1832–51), wrote aids for students of Chinese, and prepared Christian litera-ture. He also learned to interpret Japanese. On furlough he published *The Middle Kingdom* (1848), for many years a standard text on Chinese history and culture. In 1855 he was appointed secretary and interpreter to the American legation at Peking and assisted in negotiating the Treaty of Tientsin (1858–60) with its tolerance clause for missionaries and converts. Nine times he was chargé d'affaires. His second great work of scholarship, the *Syllabic Dictionary of the Chinese Language*, came off the press in 1884. Retiring at New Haven (1885) he lectured, revised his writings, supported pro-Chinese causes, and modified some disparaging judgments of early missionary days. A man of extraordinary learning, industry and perseverance, along with Christian conviction and character, he made a unique contribution to the planting of Protestant Christianity in East Asia.

F. W. PRICE

F. W. Williams: *The Life and Letters of Samuel Wells Williams* (New York and London 1889); *DAB* XX, 290f.

WILLINGEN 1952. See CONFERENCES, WORLD MISSIONARY.

WILSON, JOHN (1804–1875), was born at Lauder in Berwickshire, Scotland. After ordination in the Church of Scotland, he went to Bombay in 1829. A brilliant linguist, he preached in houses and in the streets, founded schools, debated with Hindu, Moslem and Parsee apologists, edited a monthly magazine—said to be the earliest Christian periodical in India—and travelled widely, preaching, observing, talking with all sorts of people. In Bombay City, W. founded a small congregation of converts in 1831 and in 1832 a school which, although not his earliest, was the first clear antecedent of the famous college over which he later presided and which now bears his name. These twin activities of evangelism and education were carried on together through-out his career, informed by intimate knowledge of Indian literature, history and social custom. Notable among his services to learning is his contribution to the work of deciphering the edicts of the Buddhist Emperor Asoka, engraved on the rock of Girnar in Western India. Others who carried on this work gratefully acknow-ledged that he had shown the way. W. became President of the Bombay Asiatic Society, DD of Edinburgh, Fellow of the Royal Society, first Vice-Chancellor of Bombay University, Moderator of the General Assembly of the Free Church of Scotland. He was respectfully consulted by governments on education and other matters, but declined a government appoint-ment because he wished 'to be only a missionary'.

A. J. BOYD

G. Smith: *Life of John Wilson* (London 1878); *DNB* LXII, 113.

WITCHCRAFT arises from belief in a supernatural power, which as a rule is brought into play to produce some harmful effect. It belongs to the same area of understanding as the belief in *māna*, and is practised by individuals who know what methods of action are needed to bring about the effects of W. The consequences of its application are to be seen in nature (failure of the rain, sterility, death of cattle) or among men (sickness, untimely death, misfortune). Certain individuals—witches and witch-doctors—are regarded as being in special degree bearers of the powers of witchcraft. In many languages there is a special term for witch-doctors, by which they are sharply distinguished from other possessors of magical powers, e.g. in Zulu *umthakati*, in Swahili *mchawi* or *mloji*, as against in the one case *inyanga*, in the other *mganga*. W. is generally feared, regarded as anti-social, and in scientific language classified as black magic. Its effects may be inhibited by the use of magical countermeasures (white magic). In practice the term W. is also used of supernatural activity with a beneficent purpose. When used so generally W. becomes equivalent to any form of magical activity (see MAGIC).

All participation in W. is forbidden for Christians, inasmuch as it calls in question the sovereignty of God. In times of fierce temptation the Christian can console himself with the knowledge that through Christ the power of W. has been radically broken. The post-Christian Kitawala movement has attempted to eradicate W. by violent methods.

In the *younger churches the tendency to believe in the reality of W. is strong and widespread. Its effects are believed to be seen especially in sickness, but also in other misfortunes such as failure in an examination or ill-success in love. The result is seen in a confusion of religious ideas. In the so-called Zionist movement in Africa the axis has shifted further in the direction of belief in W., inasmuch as this is often associated with manifestations of demon-possession among sick-people. Only belief without compromise in the liberation wrought by Christ is

strong enough to guard men against the threat of W., and this needs to be strengthened by unwearied spiritual care.

ERNST DAMMANN

H. Debrunner: *Witchcraft in Ghana* (Kumasi 1959); *NCE* XIV, 977-79.

WOLFF, JOSEPH (1795-1862), was born at Weilersbach, Bavaria, Germany. His father was a rabbi, but W. while still a boy questioned the Jewish faith and left home. In 1812 he was baptized at Prague in the RC church. He studied at the *Propaganda in Rome with the hope of becoming a missionary, but was expelled in 1818 owing to his unorthodox views. In 1819 he joined the Church of England and prepared for work with the LSPCJ. Between 1821 and 1837 W. travelled in Europe, Egypt, Palestine, Syria, Mesopotamia, Persia, Afghanistan, Turkestan, India, Arabia and Ethiopia. An able linguist, bold preacher and ready debater, he was generally welcomed by Jews, though some were hostile. Other peoples in remote places robbed, beat and imprisoned him; many times he narrowly escaped death. He returned to Turkestan in 1843–44. The rest of his life was spent in pastoral work in England.

W's zeal, energy, learning, charm and generosity made him a great pioneer. Everywhere he went he distributed the Scriptures and in many places converted small companies of Jews to Christianity. Although he never organized a church, he prepared the way for permanent missions which others established afterwards.

JOHN GOODWIN

H. P. Palmer: *Joseph Wolff, His Romantic Life and Travels* (London 1935); J. Wolff: *Travels and Adventures of the Rev. Joseph Wolff* (London 1861).

WOMEN IN MISSIONS. Women have had an important part in missionary work since the beginning of the church. Priscilla and her husband Aquila explained the faith to Apollos at Ephesus (Acts 18:24–8). English nuns helped Boniface evangelize Germany in the eighth century. English Quaker women carried the gospel to North

22

America, the West Indies, Greece and Turkey in the 17th century.

The hardships of missionary life in the Middle Ages meant that in most cases no place at all was found for women. The beginning seems to have been made when *Marie de l'Incarnation brought the first group of Ursuline sisters to Quebec in 1659. Their first task was to open a school for Indian girls. From that time on, the work of RC fathers and brothers has been supplemented at every point by that of nuns and other religious women. These women have in their turn brought into being indigenous sisterhoods in the countries in which they have worked.

On the Protestant side wives accompanying missionary husbands became the pioneers of missionary work for women in the educational, medical and evangelistic fields. Some letters from Frau *Ziegenbalg, wife of the first Protestant missionary in India, have been published by Prof. A. Lehmann in *Alte Briefe aus Indien*.

But grave doubts were felt and expressed as to the desirability of sending young unmarried women to engage in missionary work overseas. The formidable Bishop Daniel Wilson of Calcutta (d. 1858) expressed the opinion that, if sent, they would all be married off within the year. Undeterred by raised episcopal eyebrows, British Christians formed in 1834 the Society for Promoting Female Education in the East, to be followed in 1852 by the Indian Female Normal School and Instruction Society. This later became the Zenana Bible and Medical Mission (now the Bible and Medical Missionary Fellowship), to be followed in 1880 by the Anglican CEZMS. It is true that many of the women who served these societies did marry; it does not always follow that they were lost to Christian witness in non-Christian countries.

A parallel course of events took place in the USA. The Women's Union Missionary Society of America was formed in New York in 1860, and sent out its first representative to Peking in 1868. In 1861 the undenominational Women's Missionary Society of America took India as its principal field.

Many denominational societies for women were formed in the same period. Most of these today form part of the mission board, in which men and women work together in the total mission programme.

It was a major revolution when women, including the wives of missionaries, came greatly to outnumber men in the western missionary enterprise. It was not long before women in the *younger churches came to play a leading role in missionary work. Most famous of all is Pandita *Ramabai of India; but outstanding names could be cited from every part of the world.

Women now travel in every direction in the service of Christ—from east to west, from north to south, for example Koreans to Nepal, Filipinos to Sarawak, Japanese to America. They work in many new patterns of mission, e.g. literacy, radio, public health and village welfare. Many are working in ecumenical teams.

See also WOMEN'S WORLD DAY OF PRAYER.

EDITORS

R. P. Beaver: *All Loves Excelling* (Grand Rapids 1968); D. C. Wilson: *Palace of Healing* (New York 1968).

WOMEN, STATUS AND OPPORTUNITIES OF. The missionary movement opened avenues of service to women in the 18th and 19th centuries at a time when the church offered few opportunities for them to use their leadership talents or their abilities to serve. With their deep concern to make Christ known and with growing social concerns, they gave themselves wholeheartedly to organizing women's missionary societies in most of the leading denominations (see WOMEN IN MISSIONS). Through study, prayer and raising of funds, women used their talents and became leaders. When churches failed to give them opportunities they worked through their own organizations and became leaders in movements for peace, suffrage, abolition of slavery and women's rights. Women throughout the world are indebted to these dedicated souls.

In the early organizations the work was carried on by volunteers. It was not until the early 20th century that the major responsibilities were given to paid executives. Many of the early leaders, women of wealth, had sufficient time and funds to travel abroad to learn about work and plan for it. However, many women, with very limited funds, tithed their money and found numerous ways to support the work.

Women leaders in Africa, Asia and Latin America are indebted to these pioneer women who had vision, dedication and courage, to plan for schools, medical work, training centres, that have made it possible for them to develop their talents and to become leaders in their own countries. The training some of them have had makes it possible for them to be given places of responsibility in their own developing countries. As yet, not many have been given the leadership in the *ecumenical movement they are capable of exercising. Some are finding more opportunities for Christian service outside the church than under church leadership.

Christian schools, from kindergarten to advanced university work, have helped to raise the status of women throughout the world. Literacy has opened a whole new world to illiterate women, while Christian literature and Christian women's magazines have helped them to grow spiritually and given them new insights into family life.

With new opportunities for travel, ecumenical contacts are more frequent, the joy of Christian fellowship and understanding is deepened and women realize more how much all women are indebted to Christian missions.

GLORA M. WYSNER

E. T. Culver: *Women in the World of Religion* (New York 1967).

WOMEN'S WORLD DAY OF PRAYER, THE,

has been observed annually until 1969 on the first Friday in Lent, but thereafter on the first Friday in March. It is a united expression of women's concerns in the Christian mission throughout the world and of their belief in the power of prayer. Observance of the day began in the USA in 1887; the first prayer groups in other countries started in 1890; these united in 1919.

Missionaries took the programme overseas and representative worldwide participation began in 1927. Although it was begun by Protestant women, Roman Catholic and Jewish women are now participating in some areas in this important service.

Each year a different country assumes responsibility for composing a service of world prayer, which is then translated in various countries and adapted according to cultural needs. Braille editions are produced by the John Milton Society (see BLIND, MISSIONS TO THE). In 1930 Dr Helen Kim became the first Asian woman to prepare the service.

Offerings taken on the day are used for ecumenical projects of both national and international scope, for women's Christian colleges, women's and children's magazines, literacy programmes and projects concerned with Christian home life.

GLORA M. WYSNER

R. P. Beaver: *All Loves Excelling* (Grand Rapids 1968).

WORLD ALLIANCE OF REFORMED CHURCHES

('World Presbyterian Alliance'). The 'Alliance of Reformed Churches throughout the world holding the Presbyterian Order' was organized in 1875 and held its first general council 1877 (Edinburgh). Constituency: 102 autonomous churches in 69 countries, total membership 55 million. Sixty-three churches also belong to the *WCC; 60 are *younger churches'. They share the Calvinist tradition, via the continental 'Reformed' line and the 'Presbyterianism' of John Knox and of some of the English-speaking peoples. WARC merger with the International Congregational Council (projected 1970) will broaden the family to include its third, 'Congregationalist' branch.

Calvinist churches since the 16th century have shown remarkable diversity. As 'confessional' bodies they subscribe to over 60 different Reformed confessions. Common emphasis on the preached word is practised in liturgies that range from 'high' to 'low'. Representative government excludes neither bishops (Hungary) nor congregational decision-making. Established or folk churches share Calvinism with free and minority churches, many with a history of persecution.

The WARC was produced by the 19th century missionary movement. 'Distribution of missionary work' and 'the combination of church energies' (Constitution 1877) were a continuing preoccupation of the early General Councils (cf. *Proceedings*). 'Progressive' missionary policies were encouraged: church unions should come early, it was felt in 1877, 'while zeal for evangelizing makes differences appear insignificant'. (In 1966 WARC member churches participated in over 30 church union negotiations with more than 90 different partners. Only four of the 30 were exclusively intra-Reformed. Across the union tables sat 22 Anglican, sixteen Methodist, fifteen Congregationalist, fourteen other Reformed, seven Disciples of Christ and five Lutheran bodies, as well as others). The WARC has encouraged western churches to let churches they have planted become *autonomous as quickly as possible. Religious *freedom has been a major concern.

Organization. The WARC was the first world body set up on the conciliar pattern later adopted e.g. by the *WCC. General Councils meet every four or five years; an executive committee meets annually. Headquartered in Edinburgh until 1948, it moved to Geneva to implement a policy of full cooperation with WCC and other ecumenical agencies.

Departments and committees: finance; theology; women's work; co-operation and witness; information. *Staff:* general secretary (Dr Marcel Pradervand); assistant general secretary; secretaries for theology and information. *Regional Committees* (without staff) are organized in Europe and North America. *Address:* 150 route de Ferney, 1211 Geneva 20, Switzerland.

LEWIS WILKINS

Proceedings of General Councils (1st, Edinburgh 1877 to 19th, Frankfurt 1964); *Reformed and Presbyterian World* (published under various titles, 1879ff.); *Bulletin* of the Department of Theology; *Reformed and Presbyterian Press Service.*

WORLD ALLIANCE OF YMCAs, THE, unites most of the national YMCAs. In the decade following George Williams' founding of the first Association in London in 1844, YMCAs spread rapidly among workers and students in Europe, Britain and America. Henri Dunant in Geneva (later instrumental in founding the Red Cross) and others urged a world movement of YMCAs. Thus was founded in Paris in 1855 the World Alliance of YMCAs. It united those who regarded 'Jesus Christ as their God and Saviour according to the Holy Scriptures'. That basis, later adopted by the *WSCF, *World YWCA, *Faith and Order and the *WCC, represents one of the many contributions of the World Alliance of YMCAs to the *ecumenical movement. Encouraging close relations with the church and seeking to produce for its ministry men with world vision, it still insists upon lay control and encourages lay witness. Its missionary thrust, especially in Asia, has been notable. It helped to produce national SCMs and the WSCF and maintained close relations with them. Yet it has worked chiefly among non-students—soldiers, sailors, railwaymen, young men in business and industry, and rural youth. Other major endeavours include prisoners of war, displaced persons and refugees, migrants, literacy, physical education, boys' work. Strong Protestant evangelical and missionary concern produced the World Alliance. Yet in the 20th century members included Roman Catholics, Orthodox, and also non-Christians. Problems of self-understanding and purpose loom large. Headquarters are at 37 Quai Wilson, Geneva, Switzerland.

W. RICHEY HOGG

C. P. Shedd: *History of the World Alliance of YMCAs* (London 1955); *WKL*, 238–41.

WORLD CHRISTIAN BOOKS is an enterprise sponsored by the *WCC and supported by various bodies interested in the work of Christian literature, and by missionaries, with a view to producing books of serious theological content, but in a style simple enough to be readily understood by those whose own language is not English, and translated without too much difficulty. From the start the series has been international and inter-confessional, the writers of the 60 books which have so far appeared representing ten nations and twelve confessions. Translations of at least one book have been recorded in over 50 languages, and also in Braille. The latest enterprise is a series of concise dictionaries. That on the Bible has already appeared. The present dictionary is the second in the series. Plans have been made for a dictionary of religions as the third. It is the wish of the committee to move out also into what is sometimes called the third level, even simpler books based on a strictly controlled vocabulary, and on the level to be understood and used by the village catechist; but funds and personnel for this venture are not at present available.

STEPHEN NEILL

Occasional *Newsletters* available at the World Christian Books office, 2 Eaton Gate, London, S.W.1.

WORLD CONFERENCES OF CHRISTIAN YOUTH. Three World Conferences of Christian Youth have been held: in Amsterdam in 1939, in Oslo in 1947, and in Kottayam (India) in 1952. All three were a common undertaking of the ecumenical church bodies and world youth organizations.

The purpose of the WCCY at Amsterdam was to give young people an opportunity to consider the results of the world conferences on *Life and Work (Oxford) and *Faith and Order (Edinburgh), both held in 1937, and to make their own contribution at this creative stage of the *ecumenical movement. Thirteen hundred participants attended. The German delegates were not allowed to take part by their government. The programme included two features which were unprecedented in large ecumenical meetings. The first was the bible-study in relatively small groups, the second was the worship according to the different liturgical tradi-

tions. Since the conference met under the shadow of war (the war broke out four weeks later) the central theme 'Christus Victor' became a common confession of faith over against the powers of hatred and destruction. The intensive experience of fellowship in Christ helped many to remain faithful during the years of trial which followed. Two sentences from the conference statement sum up what Amsterdam 1939 meant for the youth generation of that time: the first is: 'many of us have discovered the Bible afresh and in so far as we have allowed God to speak to us, He has become a living God, declaring a living message for our lives and generation'. The second is: 'In war, conflict or persecution, we must strengthen one another and preserve our Christian unity unbroken'.

The WCCY in Oslo was the first world conference after the war, and was characterized by the spirit of reconciliation and the desire for a radical renewal in the life of church and society. The German delegation was the first large group of Germans to come to Norway after the years of occupation. A dramatic element in the meeting was the common declaration of the delegations from Indonesia and the Netherlands about the acute conflict between their countries. There were 1,265 participants. The main theme was: 'Jesus is Lord'. Oslo made it clear that young people desired to play their own specific role in the ecumenical movement and to accept responsibility for leadership in their own organisations.

The WCCY in Kottayam (South India) was a smaller conference (300). Almost half of the participants came from Asia. One of the new features of the conference were the large daily meetings at which conference delegates addressed the people of Kerala. The whole conference also participated in the celebration of the St. Thomas-festival (1900 years after the arrival of the apostle in India). The theme was: 'Christ the Answer'. The Kottayam meeting helped many western young people to discover Asian Christianity. It was also important in promoting closer relations among Asian Christians and thus helped to prepare the way for the creation of the *East Asia Christian Conference.

W. A. VISSER'T HOOFT

D. G. M. Patrick, ed.: *Christus Victor: The Report of the First World Conference of Christian Youth* (Geneva 1939); P. G. Macy, ed.: *The Report of the Second World Conference of Christian Youth* (Geneva 1947); *Footprints in Travancore, A Report of the Third World Conference of Christian Youth* (New York 1953); *WKL*, 1590–92.

WORLD CONFESSIONAL FAMILIES. A world-wide denomination is a new phenomenon of the late 19th century. As a result of the dispersion of the white races through the world and the success of missionary work, all the main denominations have found themselves in this situation of world-wide expansion, and with no organization to hold together the scattered churches which felt related to one another through a common confessional allegiance or historical origin. New organs had to be created to express this sense of unity, to restore it if it had been lost, or to create it, if it had never existed.

The RC church and the Orthodox, which have no world organization of the kind described in this article, are not treated here. The main such organizations in other parts of the Christian world are the following, in chronological order of formation:

(1) *The Alliance of Reformed Churches throughout the World holding the Presbyterian system* (1875): total membership 55 million in 69 countries; see WORLD ALLIANCE OF REFORMED CHURCHES. Ninety-five per cent of the 'Reformed' family of churches are members. This WCF holds a world meeting about once in five years, and through its department of co-operation and witness finds ways to give expression to common concerns.

(2) *The World Methodist Council* (1881, but till 1951 known as the Ecumenical Methodist Council: total membership about 40 million) does not legislate for the member churches or invade their autonomy, but exists to serve them and to promote the wisest use of Methodist resources in the

Christian mission. It arranges a world exchange of preachers.

(3) *The Old Catholic Union of Utrecht* (1889) holds together the Old Catholic Churches in Holland, Germany, Austria and other countries. The governing body in this union is made up of the bishops of the various churches.

(4) *The International Congregational Council* (1891: total membership 6 million), mainly in the USA, Great Britain and associated countries.

(5) *The Baptist World Alliance* (1905: total membership 50 million) is 'a voluntary fraternal association for promoting fellowship and co-operation among Baptists'. The Alliance serves as a forum for discussion based on the work of four permanent study commissions; it is also a channel for corporate action, and holds a World Congress once every five years.

(6) *The World Convention of the Churches of Christ* (*Disciples*: 1930) exists to represent member churches in world situations, and to encourage theological study and deeper understanding. Not more than half the churches of this persuasion are members of its World Convention.

(7) *The Friends' World Committee for Consultation* (1930).

(8) *The International Association for Liberal Christianity and Religious Freedom* (1930), in the main the organ of the Unitarian and Universalist Churches. Close co-operation between these bodies and other parts of the *ecumenical movement is excluded by the basis of the WCC in its present form.

(9) *The *Lutheran World Federation* (1947, but building on the earlier Lutheran World Convention of 1923: total membership about 60 million) is a free association of Lutheran churches, organized not to exercise churchly functions or to legislate for its member churches, but to develop fellowship and co-operation between them. Many Lutheran churches adhere to the Federation but some of the largest remain outside it. This is the the strongest and best organized of all the WCFs.

(10) *The Anglican Communion* (total

membership about 40 million) differs from other world denominations in that all Anglican churches throughout the world are automatically part of the Anglican Communion. This unity from 1867 onwards was expressed in the Lambeth Conference of Anglican bishops, which held its tenth session in 1968; it has been strengthened since 1958 by the appointment of one bishop as central executive and by a committee on missionary strategy.

(11) *The Salvation Army* has from the start been so strictly centralized, with extensive powers in the hands of the Generals, that with its worldwide extension all that was needed was the expansion of an existing organization and not the creation of any new organ of unity

Since 1962 representatives of most of these WCFs have met with some regularity in Geneva, under the auspices of the *WCC, for mutual consultation and advice.

The 20th century has been marked by an increase of confessional consciousness and denominational loyalty. This could menace the development of the ecumenical sense. But several of the world organizations have declared that their intention is exactly the opposite—to bring into the ecumenical consensus the full strength and riches of the inheritance which they have built up in separation.

A new significance has been given to the WCFs by the entry of Rome into the ecumenical arena. Naturally Rome prefers to talk to a worldwide fellowship rather than to an individual church; most of the commissions appointed to carry further the ecumenical work of the Second *Vatican Council have been appointed on this worldwide basis.

Proposals have been made for a merger between the Presbyterian and the Congregational organizations though without involving all the local churches necessarily in union. This is a proposal without precedent in the Christian world; if it is finally accepted in 1970, a new situation will have been brought about. It is certain that in future local churches will find it difficult to take further action in any ecumenical

sense, without considering the effect of their actions on all other churches within the confessional fellowship.

H. A. HAMILTON AND EDITORS

R. Rouse and S. C. Neill, eds.: *A History of the Ecumenical Movement, 1517–1948* (2nd ed., London 1967); H. E. Fey, ed.: *History of the Ecumenical Movement, 1948–1968* (London 1970).

WORLD COUNCIL OF CHRISTIAN EDUCATION, THE, was organized at the fifth World Sunday School Convention held in Rome in 1907 as the World Sunday School Association. The world office is presently located at the Ecumenical Centre in Geneva with an office in London and another in New York. It consists of 71 member units – churches, councils, councils of Christian education and Sunday school associations throughout the world; two regional committees—European and North American; and four affiliated regional organizations—the *AACC, the *EACC, the Latin American Evangelical Commission of Christian Education, and the *NECC.

The WCCE meets in Quadrennial Assembly and works through its Board of Managers having interdenominational and international representation. It is the common instrument for its interdependent world constituency for enlisting and providing resources in thought, personnel, counsel, material, finances, training events and co-operative projects wherever needed for the development of more effective educational programmes and competent leadership. It is also engaged in curriculum development for church and day schools and co-operates with the *WCC in areas of common educational concerns. It publishes the quarterly *World Christian Education*.

RALPH MOULD

WORLD COUNCIL OF CHURCHES, THE. The plan to establish a World Council of Churches was worked out at a meeting of 35 leaders of various sectors of the *ecumenical movement just before the two world conferences of *'Life and Work' (Oxford) and *'Faith and Order'

(Edinburgh) in 1937. It was widely felt that these two movements should be brought together since the issues of unity and those of witness in face of the needs of the world were closely related. At the same time the situation was ripe to give a more definite shape to the ecumenical work of the churches and to create a body which would be truly representative of the participating churches. The two world conferences approved the plan in principle. Thus it became possible to call in 1938 a conference in Utrecht to elaborate a draft-constitution. This constitution was sent to the churches together with a letter of invitation. It was hoped to hold the first official assembly in 1941, but this proved impossible because of the second world war. In the meantime the Provisional Committee of the World Council of Churches (in process of formation) had to take responsibility for the ongoing ecumenical work to which were added the new tasks growing out of the war (prisoners of war, refugees, *inter-church aid). The inaugural Assembly took place in *Amsterdam in 1948, and approved the constitution worked out at Utrecht.

That constitution describes the WCC as a fellowship of churches. It does not legislate for the churches. And according to a well-known phrase of Archbishop William Temple: 'Any authority that it may have will consist in the weight which it carries with the churches by its own wisdom'. The WCC has a basis of membership. The Utrecht conference had decided to take over the basis of the Faith and Order movement: 'churches which accept our Lord Jesus Christ as God and Saviour'. This basis remained unchanged until 1961 when it was developed as follows: 'churches which confess the Lord Jesus Christ as God and Saviour according to the Scriptures and therefore seek to fulfill together their common calling to the glory of the one God, Father, Son and Holy Spirit'. A church which desires to join the WCC must declare in writing that it accepts this basis. The principal authority in the Council is the Assembly. Every member church is entitled to send at least one representative to the Assembly. Larger churches have more representatives. The schedule of allocation of seats is worked out by the Central Committee which must give due regard to such factors as numerical size, adequate confessional representation and adequate geographical distribution. The Central Committee has also been instructed to urge the churches to include both men and women, both laymen and clerical persons in their delegations. The Assembly elects a Presidium. At the moment the Council has six Presidents. The Assembly also appoints the central committee which meets ordinarily every year and carries out the policies decided upon by the Assembly. This central committee appoints its own officers and an executive committee which meets ordinarily twice annually. The General Secretary, the Associate General Secretaries and the heads of departments are appointed by the central committee, other staff members by the executive committee.

The World Council has held four *Assemblies. The first took place in Amsterdam in 1948. The number of churches represented was 147. There were 351 delegates and 258 alternates. The main theme was: 'Man's Disorder and God's Design'. The Message of the Assembly contained the phrase: 'We intend to stay together'. The churches had found each other again after the tragic years of war and rejoiced in their newly found solidarity. It was decided that the WCC and the *International Missionary Council should be considered as being in association with each other. Plans were made for the work of the Council in many different fields.

The second Assembly was held in Evanston (USA) in 1954. The number of churches participating was 140 and the number of official delegates 502. The theme on which a carefully chosen commission had worked for three years was: 'Christ, the hope of the world'. This theme led to searching theological discussion concerning the nature of the Christian hope. The message stated: 'We thank God for his blessing on our work and fellowship during these six years. We enter now upon a second stage, To stay together is not enough. We must go forward together'.

The third Assembly took place in New Delhi (India) in 1961; 174 churches were represented by 582 official delegates. The theme was: 'Jesus Christ, the light of the world'. This time there had been widespread participation in the preparation of the Assembly. The study booklet on the theme had been translated into 30 languages and between 600,000 and 700,000 copies had been sold. The Assembly approved the integration of the WCC and the IMC. Thus all the main streams of the ecumenical movement had come together in one body. Owing to the joining of a number of Orthodox churches and churches from Africa the message could say: 'We rejoice and thank God that we experience here a fellowship as deep as before and wider.' One of the most notable statements of the Assembly was the declaration on the Unity of the Church, which sought to define the nature of the unity which the churches seek together.

The fourth Assembly met at Uppsala, Sweden, in 1968, with 704 delegates from 235 member churches. The theme of the Assembly was 'Behold, I make all things new'. Concern for issues of peace, youth, racial and social justice, and world economic development dominated the discussions. Pope Paul VI sent warm personal greetings and RC participation included fifteen delegated observers and two platform speakers. Nine RC theologians were elected to the Faith and Order Commission. In its message the Assembly said, 'With people of all convictions, we Christians want to ensure human rights in a just world community . . . The ecumenical movement must become bolder, and more representative'.

The story of the WCC is a story of growth and expansion. There is in the first place the geographical expansion. The Council has become increasingly a *world* council. By the time of the New Delhi Assembly the Council had twice as many member churches in Asia, Africa, and Latin America as entered the Council at the

first Assembly in Amsterdam. This is reflected in the activities of the Council. Its work of inter-church aid was at first almost wholly centred on Europe; today its main work is done in Asia, Africa and Latin America. Again at the World Conference on Church and Society (Geneva, 1966) nearly one half of the delegates came from those three continents. There is in the second place the expansion with regard to the confessional scope of the Council. Here we must note especially the growing participation of the Orthodox churches. At present nearly all Orthodox churches are members of the Council. At the fourth Assembly in Uppsala there were 140 representatives of Orthodox churches. Thus the Council has an unique opportunity to build new bridges between eastern and western Christianity which have been separated from each other for a thousand years. The presence of many churches living in communist countries also means that the Council can help to overcome the tensions existing between the communist world and other countries. The Roman Catholic church is not a member of the Council, but since the setting up of the Secretariat for Unity in the Vatican there is a regular exchange of official observers at important meetings. In 1965 the Vatican and the WCC agreed to set up a joint working group which meets regularly to discuss common concerns and to prepare proposals for common study or action which are then submitted to the appropriate authorities on each side.

In the third place the scope of the WCC's activities has grown very considerably. From its parent bodies the Council had inherited the concern with study on social questions (which became later the department on Church and Society), the concern with unity in Faith and Order, and the work among youth. The first new activities became the service for refugees and inter-church aid which were brought together in one division, now the largest division of the Council. Soon after the war the Ecumenical Institute was started as well as the department for laity and that for co-

22*

operation among men and women. Under the auspices of the IMC and the WCC a *Commission of the Churches on International Affairs was set up. Evangelism also became an important concern. At the time of the Evanston Assembly all departments were brought together in three divisions (Study, Ecumenical Action, Inter-Church Aid World Service and Refugees). And at New Delhi, with the integration of the WCC and the IMC, the *Division of World Mission and Evangelism was added.

The WCC is not the definitive answer to the problem of Christian unity. It is rather an instrument which helps the churches to move forward on the road to full unity and, as long as that unity does not exist, to act together in all matters except those in which deep differences of conviction compel t hem to act separately.

See also ECUMENICAL MOVEMENT, THE.

W. A. VISSER'T HOOFT

The First Six Years. A report of the Central Committee of the World Council of Churches on the activities of the Departments and Secretariats of the Council (Geneva 1954); *From Evanston to New Delhi 1954-1961. Report of the Central Committee to the Third Assembly of the World Council of Churches* (Geneva 1961); *New Delhi to Uppsala 1961-1968. Report of the Central Committee to the Fourth Assembly of the World Council of Churches* (Geneva 1968); *The First Assembly of the World Council of Churches* (London and New York 1949); *The Evanston Report. The Second Assembly of the World Council of Churches 1954* (London 1955); *The New Delhi Report. The Third Assembly of the World Council of Churches, 1961* (London 1962); *The Uppsala Report. The Fourth Assembly of the World Council of Churches, 1968* (Geneva 1968); P. A. Crow, Jr: *The Ecumenical Movement in Bibliographical Outline* (New York 1965); E. Duff: *The Social Thought of the WCC* (New York 1956); H. E. Fey, ed.: *History of the Ecumenical Movement, 1948-1968* (London 1970); D. P. Gaines: *The World Council of Churches* (Peterborough, New Hampshire 1966); R. Rouse and S. C. Neill, eds.: *A History of the Ecumenical Movement,*

1517-1948 (2nd ed., London 1967); *The Ecumenical Review* (quarterly, 1948ff.); *WKL*, 1046-69.

WORLD DOMINION MOVEMENT. This name broadly indicates the work of the Survey Application Trust and the World Dominion Press. The Movement began in 1916: the periodical *World Dominion* was first published in 1923 (later to become *Frontier*), and the Trust was formally set up in 1924. S. J. W. Clark, the donor, died in 1930, and Dr T. Cochrane, the Rev A. McLeish, the Rev Roland Allen and Dr R. Cochrane assumed responsibility.

The Press has been a pioneer of missionary and church surveys. Other works, often by Roland Allen, were issued on 'the indigenous church' question. One of its major publications through the years has been the several editions of the *World Christian Handbook*. In 1931 the Trust moved to the Mildmay Conference Centre.

The Trust made numerous grants to evangelistic projects. It wound up its operations for all effective purposes on 30 June 1968.

KENNETH GRUBB

WORLD EVANGELICAL FELLOWSHIP. The WEF was formally constituted at an international conference held in Holland in 1952. It professed to be the successor to the World Evangelical Alliance dating from 1846, a movement that was regarded by some as no longer adhering firmly to its original aims (see EVANGELICAL CHURCHES).

The WEF arose out of extended world trips by J. Elwin Wright, and later by Clyde W. Taylor of the National Association of Evangelicals with which it has close ties. National bodies known as 'alliances', 'associations', 'councils' and 'fellowships' have been founded in many parts of the world and have allied themselves voluntarily with WEF which is international, interdenominational and ecumenical. It represents conservative evangelicals around the world to assure them of a voice on matters of common concern and in the conservation of evangelical missionary activity. World conferences of WEF meet periodically. Its international office is at 36 Crossburn Drive, Don Mills, Ontario, Canada.

HAROLD LINDSELL

WORLD FELLOWSHIP OF HEBREW CHRISTIANS, THE. There are no statistics on the number of Jews who have become Christians. The reason is that the main policy has been to integrate converted Jews into the Christian congregations and churches in order that they should not be treated in any way differently from other church members. The International Hebrew Christian Alliance, however, tries to hold together 'Hebrew Christians' all over the world in national groups in order to present to the Jewish people a united testimony of their faith in Jesus Christ as the Messiah. Such groups are especially strong in America, Great Britain and Israel. The Hebrew Christian Alliance claims that a Christian of Jewish origin is still a Jew, and their aim is also to create Hebrew Christian congregations or churches, where this is possible. Headquarters are at 19, Draycott Place, London, S.W.3, and at 100 W. Chicago Avenue, Chicago, Ill. 60610.

GÖTE HEDENQUIST

WORLD GOSPEL CRUSADES, INC., was founded in 1949 by Mrs Charles E. Cowman (author of the devotional classic *Streams in the Desert*). Its purpose is the evangelization of the world through the mass media of communication—i.e. literature distribution, radio and television broadcasting, and united evangelistic campaigns.

As a non-denominational service arm of the church, the mission does not build churches or establish institutions. It maintains distribution centres in the USA, Mexico, Brazil, Argentina, Spain, and Africa (Burundi). The international headquarters are Upland (Box 3), California, USA. It holds associate membership in *EFMA and publishes a monthly period-

ical, *Crusades*. Dr C. Mervin Russell is president.

HAROLD LINDSELL

WORLD GOSPEL MISSION, THE, was founded in 1910 by the National Holiness Association. It was created to 'establish, maintain and conduct interdenominational missions and missionary work in home and foreign fields, and to spread scriptural holiness largely through a properly qualified national ministry'. WGM uses evangelistic, medical, educational, industrial and other means of witness to accomplish an evangelistic end.

The agency operates in Kenya, Burundi, Egypt, Lebanon, India, Taiwan, Japan, Bolivia, Honduras, Mexico, Haiti, Brazil and the USA. As of October 1966 the mission supported approximately 250 missionaries on an income exceeding $1,200,000. The mission publishes *Call to Prayer for Missions*, is a member of the *EFMA and has its headquarters at 123 West Fifth Street, Box 948, Marion, Indiana, USA.

HAROLD LINDSELL

WORLD MISSIONARY CONFERENCES. See CONFERENCES, WORLD MISSIONARY.

WORLD RADIO MISSIONARY FELLOWSHIP, INC., founded in 1931, is a society organized on *faith mission principles which operates station HCJB, 'The Voice of the Andes', at Quito, Ecuador, broadcasting to Latin America and by shortwave to other parts of the world. In 1961 HCJB-TV likewise became the pioneer missionary telecaster. The mission also carries out a medical ministry, operating several hospitals and clinics in Ecuador. Principally a USA society, it has a branch office in Toronto and representatives in other Commonwealth countries. The staff is largely concentrated in Quito, but missionaries are stationed in Brazil, Panama, Uruguay and Europe. Staff in 1966: 137 on the field (six not US) and ten in home office. Income in 1966, $1,133,725. Headquarters: Box 691, Miami, Florida

33147. Periodical: *Call of the Andes*. Member of *IFMA and *EFMA and of Pan-American Christian Network.

R. PIERCE BEAVER

WORLD STUDENT CHRISTIAN FEDERATION, THE. Through the WSCF the *Student Christian Movements (SCMs) of each nation express their universality. The WSCF is the SCMs at work on a world scale.

WSCF achievements are considerable. Its conferences have pioneered much in mission and unity. It has bound Christian students and professors together throughout the world, enabling those in east and west to gain fuller appreciation of one another. It has probed new theological thought and experimented with new working forms in mission. Through books, its quarterly, *Student World* (1908 ff.), and meetings it has provided substantial theological training in the meaning of faith and mission for tens of thousands who would otherwise have remained untouched. It has nurtured and proved many missionary and ecumenical leaders for the church.

The WSCF emerged in 1895 from the famous Vadstena Castle meeting in Sweden. Through John R. *Mott's vision and drive, five SCMs—North America, Britain, Germany, Scandinavia and 'Mission Lands' —formed the WSCF, which immediately began founding around the world other national SCMs. The aim was to claim students—the future leaders of their nations—for Christ and for the evangelization of the world. The *SVM's motto shaped the first twenty years of the WSCF.

The WSCF was the first worldwide, representative, non-Roman Christian agency built upon independent national organizations. Each of these was free to work out its own patterns so long as they conformed to the Basis of the WSCF, affirming faith in 'Jesus Christ as God and Saviour according to the Holy Scriptures'. It gave ecumenical training to several generations of Christian statesmen who knew that the whole united human family is required to show forth the full meaning of Christ's

gospel. Fresh from their 1907 Tokyo Conference, the most widely representative gathering to that time, top WSCF men became the key planners for Edinburgh 1910. Their SCM experience enabled them to bring in the High Anglicans—a fact which gave decisive form to the organized *ecumenical movement. The WSCF steadily lifted student thinking to encompass the world Christian community. It pointed national SCMs to foreign students studying in their midst and provided a crucial ministry to many who later in their homelands achieved positions of national prominence. At Constantinople in 1911 the WSCF opened membership in its national movements to all Christian students who would accept its Basis (trinitarian and evangelistic). SCMs developed in the Near East and the Orthodox world, thus paving the way for entry of the Orthodox into larger co-operation.

Over the years WSCF emphases changed. By the first world war concern for social action had expressed itself. In the 1930s new interest centred on the Christian message for the world. By the second world war the meaning of the university was a prime question, and the mission in the university was a strong concern. By the 1950s in the post-Christendom age, when the old ecclesiastical structures appeared inadequate the 'Life and Mission of the Church' came to the fore. Since 1960 the varied forms of mission in a technological and revolutionary society have been explored in study and experiment, and the meaning of responsible 'Christian presence' has been probed.

The WSCF's greatest contribution to the worldwide church is in those it has trained and projected into major leadership. The list includes many women and is long, but several examples must suffice: Bishop *Honda of Japan, Bishop *Azariah who was instrumental in the founding of the *CSI, T. Z. Koo of China, Nathan Söderblom of Sweden, J. H. *Oldham and William Temple of Britain. It provided the chief training ground for Mott's chairmanship of the *IMC (in process of formation 1910–21, and subsequently until 1943) and for W. A. Visser't Hooft's general secretaryship of the *WCC (in process of formation 1938–48, and subsequently until 1966).

W. RICHEY HOGG

J. R. Mott: *Addresses and Papers of John R. Mott*, Vol. II: *The World's Student Christian Federation* (New York 1947); R. Rouse: *The World's Student Christian Federation* (London 1948); *Student World*, quarterly (Geneva 1908ff.); *WKL*, 236–38.

WORLD SUNDAY SCHOOL UNION. See WORLD COUNCIL OF CHRISTIAN EDUCATION.

WORLD VISION, INC., founded by Bob Pierce and incorporated in California, USA, in 1930, is a service organization having for its basic objectives (1) Christian social welfare service, (2) evangelistic outreach, (3) Christian leadership development, (4) emergency aid, and (5) missionary challenge. It is not a missionary sending organization but has more than a dozen representatives overseas. A number of children's homes are operated, and in some 25 countries Christian enterprises of various kinds are given financial grants. Pastors' conferences are held around the world. *World Vision Magazine* is published monthly. The annual income for 1967 was approximately $6,000,000. World Vision is a member of *EFMA. Its home offices are located at 919 West Huntington Drive, Monrovia, California 91016, USA.

HAROLD LINDSELL

WORLD YWCA. The Young Women's Christian Association started in the mid-nineteenth century. Among the national movements which eventually came together to form the World YWCA, there were two main streams, the one emphasizing *prayer* and the other *service* for young women. By prayer and service, rather than by preaching, the movement has made its contribution to the outreach of the Christian church in about 70 countries of the world. The World YWCA, founded in 1894, with headquarters now situated at 37 Quai Wilson, Geneva, endeavours 'to build a world-wide fellowship through which women and girls may come to know more of the love of God as revealed in Jesus Christ for themselves and for all people, and may learn to express that love in responsible action'. The movement is concerned with the whole of the life of women and girls, and this broad conception leads it into many different kinds of activities; into concerns like education and vocational training, leadership development, international understanding and peace, the struggle against racial discrimination, the eradication of illiteracy; and into undertakings such as the setting up of hostels, clubs, nurseries, camps, refugee and emergency services. A number of YWCA projects in developing countries receive support from *Inter-Church Aid and Technical Aid sources.

National associations of the YWCA are formed when a group of women in a particular country themselves decide to form a YWCA and are able to meet the conditions of affiliation, including the acceptance of the Christian basis and purpose of the World YWCA.

Leadership and financial assistance from abroad is available to developing associations through the Mutual Service and International Voluntary Service schemes, by means of which the World YWCA is able to organize the sharing of resources among many different countries throughout the world.

It is the purpose of the association to serve *all* women and girls and to have activities and services open to all, irrespective of religious belief. Thus in countries where the dominant faith is other than Christian, those of other faiths form the bulk of the membership and often take responsibility for aspects of the programme, participation in any religious activities being entirely voluntary.

The interdenominational character of the YWCA was a characteristic from its beginning and led to the Association playing a leading role in the early stages of the *ecumenical movement. It has developed from Protestant origins into a fully inter-confessional body. Roman Catholics, Orthodox and Protestants of various denominations now work together in the legislative and executive bodies of the World YWCA.

ELIZABETH PALMER

Constitution of the World Young Women's Christian Association (latest edition 1968); *World YWCA Statements of Policy, 1895–1967; Christian Unity: Ecumenical Outlook and Practice in the YWCA* (1965); *The YWCA Serves the Community* (1961); *The Responsibility of the YWCA for Education* (1968); *An Open Door? Report of a YMCA/YWCA Consultation on the task of the two Movements in countries where the dominant faith is other than Christian* (1966). All published by the World YWCA, 37 Quai Wilson, 1201 Geneva, Switzerland. *WKL*, 241–43.

WORLD'S MISSIONARY COMMITTEE OF CHRISTIAN WOMEN, THE, was the first international, interdenominational representative ecumenical organization. It was formed by the resolution of the women who attended the Centenary Conference on Foreign Missions at London in 1888 on the initiative of the 32 USA and four Canadian representatives. Nine societies in the British Isles, seven in Canada, two in the USA and one in Honolulu became members, all being foreign mission societies, although home mission societies were also invited. The objectives were '1. for special prayer; 2. for united effort for other objects as, for example, the legal relief of twenty million widows in India; 3. for the arrangement of any general conference that may be deemed desirable'.

The achievements of the committee include a weekly (Sunday) hour of intercessory prayer for missions; annual distribution of a news report of each member society; the conference of women's missionary societies held in connection with the Woman's Congress of Missions at the Columbian Exposition in Chicago in 1893; the women's work programmes of the Ecumenical Missionary Conference in New York in 1900; and the highly successful

(American) Central Committee for the United Study of Missions. The leading spirit of the committee, Miss Abbie B. Child, died suddenly in 1902, and the organization then rapidly declined.

R. PIERCE BEAVER

R. P. Beaver: *All Loves Excelling: American Protestant Women in World Mission* (Grand Rapids 1968).

WORLD'S PARLIAMENT OF RELIGIONS, THE, organized in Chicago in connection with the Columbian Exhibition, was opened on 11 September 1893 by the Rev J. H. Barrows, later notable as a Christian lecturer in India. Representatives of eight religions were present, and among those on the platform at the opening meeting was Cardinal Gibbons, archbishop of Baltimore. The Parliament made a deep impression on the western world, as the first occasion on which representatives of the eastern religions were made welcome in the west, with full equality to the Christian representatives. The most striking figure in the Parliament was the young Bengali Narendranath Datta, who had taken the name Swami Vivekānanda. With great eloquence he put forward the claim that Hinduism is the mother of religions, and that the west has much to learn from the ancient wisdom of the east. He seems to have been the inventor of the mythology of the 'materialistic west' and the 'spiritual east'. His address at the final session contained the words: 'The Christian is not to become a Hindu or a Buddhist, nor a Hindu or a Buddhist to become a Christian. But each must assimilate the spirit of the others and yet preserve his individuality and grow according to the law of growth.'

STEPHEN NEILL

J. H. Barrows, ed.: *The World's Parliament of Religions* (2 vols., Chicago 1893); *The Life of Swami Vivekānanda* (Calcutta, 5th impression, 1955).

WORLDWIDE COMMUNION SUNDAY is an American innovation in the church year, now extensively adopted. It was originally in the early 1930s a promotional device of the Board of Foreign Missions of the Presbyterian Church in the USA intended to assure the missionaries of the love and support of the members of the churches. When Dr Jesse N. Bader, a minister of the Disciples of Christ, in 1936 became secretary of the Department of Evangelism of the Federal Council of Churches, he secured consent of the Presbyterians to extend the practice to all denominations and their missions as a means of fostering ecumenical unity, fellowship, and evangelism. The Federal Council gave the day official status and called for the first general observance on the first Sunday in October in 1940. Thereafter that was to be the annual date. The council began providing literature for the observance in 1941. Co-operation of the Provisional Committee of the *WCC was sought. Geneva disliked the proposal as being sentimental, but it was vigorously promoted by Dr Henry Smith Leiper of the USA Conference of the WCC as an effective symbol of unity. Non-liturgical churches speedily adopted the observance, while the liturgical churches took it up more slowly. Missionaries carried it far abroad. After American involvement in the war began in 1941, the observance of the day became a powerful assertion of unity in Christ across all man-made barriers and divisions.

R. PIERCE BEAVER

WORLDWIDE   EVANGELIZATION CRUSADE, THE, was founded in 1913 by C. T. *Studd. International and interdenominational, its objective is 'to evangelize the remaining unevangelized parts of the world in the shortest possible time, beginning with the heart of Africa'. In 50 years it has established *pioneer work in 37 areas; in eleven countries of Africa, four of Latin America, India, Pakistan, Indonesia, Thailand, Japan, Korea, Taiwan and Vietnam, where it has founded churches with their own national leadership, established Bible schools, translated the Scriptures, opened leprosy and medical centres and given elementary education. In 1941 the Christian Literature Crusade was started by Kenneth

R. Adams as a branch of WEC and has become an independent Crusade with 75 literature centres in 28 countries. The total staffs of the two Crusades number 1,100. No mention or solicitation of funds is made, but all needs have been supplied by faith in God alone. WEC is affiliated with *EFMA and publishes the periodical *Worldwide*. Headquarters in UK are at Bulstrode, Gerrards Cross, Bucks.; and in USA at P.O. Box A, Fort Washington, Pa. 19034. Offices are maintained also in Germany, Australia and New Zealand.

NORMAN P. GRUBB

N. P. Grubb: *After C. T. Studd* (London 1939).

WORLDWIDE   PRAYER   AND   MISSIONARY UNION, INC., is a fund-raising, forwarding and information agency founded by the Rev C. L. Eicher in 1931. It is intimately but unofficially related to the missionaries of the *CMA, and serves many others, such as members of the *Missionary Aviation Fellowship, *Far Eastern Gospel Crusade, and the Ramabai Mukti Mission. It also raises and forwards funds for independent missionaries; in 1966 these were four couples and three single women. The 1965 income was $99,725. The periodical of the Union is the monthly *Missionary Newsletter*. Headquarters: 6821 North Ottawa Ave., Chicago, Illinois 60631, USA.

R. PIERCE BEAVER

WORSHIP AND MISSION. Christian worship is the worship of God the Father through Jesus Christ in the power of the Holy Spirit. Essentially the Christian mission has as its primary purpose to persuade men so to worship. It is not that Christian missionaries go to persuade men to worship. That men already do in an infinite variety of ways. Indeed the fact that man is a worshipping being is one of the fundamental facts about humanity which at once establishes the unity of mankind and holds out the possibility that all men may yet become one in a worship which is worship in Spirit and in truth.

The Christian is not concerned to deny

that worship other than Christian worship is a genuine activity of the human spirit. Still less is he concerned to deny that God will hear and accept all prayer addressed to him, whatever ideas of God a man may have. No Christian is entitled to impose limits upon the mercy and loving-kindness of God. It is part of the mystery of the divine charity that God may even be found by those who do not seek him (Isaiah 65:1).

But the task of the Christian church in its mission is, through its worship, to help men to discover God, as revealed in Jesus Christ. If this is to be possible at all worship has to be seen as the life activity of Christians and not only as an occasional activity. When the apostle bids his readers offer themselves to God in worship (Romans 12:1) he uses a word which had a profoundly secular meaning before ever it acquired an ecclesiastical one. The Greek word here used for worship is *latreia*. In its basic meaning this refers to any occupation by which one earns one's daily bread. All one's life therefore is meant to be full of worship. Hence it is that in the missionary movement, as in the long tradition of the church, the attempt has been made to relate all life to the Giver of life.

Only in that context is the specific activity of ministering and receiving the Word and the Sacraments safe from a dangerous distortion.

One great problem has confronted the missionary movement and to this day it remains a problem despite every effort to solve it. Christianity is a religion rooted in history. The traditions of the faith, the way of worship, the very manner of praying and the setting in which corporate prayer is made, all these are highly valued by Christians. How then is this central activity of the Christian Church to be 'translated' into the idiom of a new culture? For long it was the tacit, if not explicit, assumption of most western missionaries that the shape of a church building with which they were familiar in their own land must be reproduced in Asia or Africa. A traveller by air from Bangkok to Rangoon will find himself looking down on a typical English country church set in the midst of Burmese rice fields. Only recently has it come to be widely recognized that some variant of Gothic architecture is not the only possible setting for Christian worship. Similarly it is only slowly being realized that the liturgical details of western Europe are not sacrosanct.

It is when a church is rooted not only in the long tradition of the past but also in the very soil of the local culture that it is able to interpret worship both in liturgy and in work as a reasonable service which relates religion to life.

See also INDIGENIZATION; WORSHIP, INDIGENOUS.

MAX WARREN

J. G. Davies: *Worship and Mission* (London 1966); D. J. Fleming: *Heritage of Beauty* (New York 1937), *Each with his own Brush* (New York 1938), *Christian Symbols in a World Community* (New York 1940); T. S. Garrett: *Worship in the Church of South India* (London 1958); A. Lehmann: *Afroasiatische Christliche Kunst* (Berlin 1966; Eng. tr., *Christian Art in Africa and Asia*, St. Louis, Mo. 1969).

WORSHIP, INDIGENOUS. Prayer and devotion are a universal but also an intensely personal human response. They find their expression, therefore, in a person's mother-tongue, partly because this is the 'language of the heart', and partly because most men first learn to worship as little children. Hence the Protestant insistence on vernacular versions of the Bible and of all forms of prayer.

But this principle extends far beyond the mere use of words. Music is a kind of language; so are gestures, rituals and symbolic acts, and various art forms. All these forms of expression are the 'vernacular' of a particular culture or ethnic group, and they differ from one group to another. It follows that every Christian group can best worship 'in spirit and in truth' when all the outward forms of sight and sound and action come naturally to its members because they are already familiar features of their cultural background. This is what is meant by IW.

So in the seventh century Pope Gregory

instructed Mellitus, his missionary in England, that the pagan temples were not to be destroyed but 'purified from devil-worship and dedicated to the service of the true God'. A thousand years later the Jesuit, Robert de *Nobili was accused of schism because he encouraged converts in India to christianize such customs as the daily application of ashes. During the years of western *colonialism the spread of Christianity was almost always accompanied by European outward forms. But recently many churches, including the Roman Catholic, have grown bolder in adopting indigenous forms. There have been a few good examples of church buildings in traditional national styles in Japan, Hong Kong, Indonesia, India and Iran. Indigenous styles of song and musical accompaniment are fairly widely used, though still with too many echoes of western hymn-tunes. Instances of ceremonial dancing incorporated into Christian festivals have been cited from Latin America, Northern Uganda, Pakistan, Indonesia and the Pacific. Among indigenous ritual acts one might quote the complete prostration of the worshippers in several *African Independent Churches, the *Church of South India's form of the kiss of peace, and the removal of shoes at the church doors in Japan, India and other Asian countries.

But time as well as place is involved. Something archaic from one's own tradition may be more alien than something imported. To be truly indigenous, worship must be contemporary.

If we think of these indigenous expressions as a kind of vernacular, we should remember, too, that language differences sow disunity, and a *lingua franca* is often essential. For the sake of both unity and truth, Christian worship must retain certain basic features which remain constant in every place and every generation. For the true church in every place is universal as well as local. Every church is in its world yet not of it. The new solidarity of the human race makes a merely localized Christianity inadequate.

Worship, like ethics, theology and ministry, must be universal if it is to be true, but it must be related to a given situation if it is to be authentic and creative. The church is like a great tree whose roots, fastened deep in the Eternal, give it its universal and worldwide validity, but into which many branches from a great variety of stocks have been grafted. These branches —the local churches with their different cultural backgrounds—draw upon the vitality and strength of the main stem, but the fruits they bear still carry the peculiar and recognizable characteristics of the stocks from which they came.

See also INDIGENIZATION; WORSHIP AND MISSION.

JOHN V. TAYLOR

WYCLIFFE BIBLE TRANSLATORS, INC., founded in 1934 by L. L. Legters and W. Cameron Townsend, is a specialized agency engaged in linguistic and translation work in nineteen countries. Overseas, W's 2,150 workers are known as members of the Summer Institute of Linguistics, a scientific and educational organization which enters a country only by invitation. Working under government contract they make scientific surveys, reduce languages to writing, produce grammars, primers, and other basic educational tools; and, of course, they translate the Scriptures.

Technically speaking, W. translators are not missionaries but professional linguists. As such they do not engage in gospel preaching or church planting, though churches have come into existence as an indirect result of their work.

Most of the 419 tribes in which they are working now have at least one portion of the Scriptures, while fifteen tribes possess the entire NT. The aviation wing of WBT, known as Jungle Aviation and Radio Service, operates 29 planes in seven countries. A network of 254 radio stations provides all jungle stations with two-way radio communications.

The Summer Institute of Linguistics trains some 550 linguists annually in the USA, Britain, Germany, Australia and

New Zealand. In its 32 years of existence it has provided intensive linguistic training for 12,000 missionaries now serving under 123 boards in all parts of the world.

One of the fastest growing mission agencies, W. personnel has increased in the past ten years from 550 to 2,150. Present projections call for a membership of 8,000 by 1985. Headquarters address: P.O. Box 1960, 219 W. Walnut, Santa Ana, California 92702, USA.

J. HERBERT KANE

E. F. Wallis and M. A. Bennett: *Two Thousand Tongues To Go* (New York 1959) is regarded as the official history of WBT

X

XAVIER (XAVER), FRANCIS (1506–1552), one of the greatest missionaries of all times, was born in the Basque country and died on the small island of Chang-Chuen-Shan off the coast of China, which he was hoping to penetrate with the gospel. In 1533 X. attached himself to Ignatius Loyola and became one of the first six members of the Society of *Jesus. In 1541 he was sent to India as papal legate and representative of the king of Portugal. Landing at Goa on 6 May 1542, X. gave himself for a few months of strenuous effort to raising the moral and Christian standards of Goa; but then travelled to the Coromandel Coast to look into the affairs of the Parava (Bharetha) fisher folk, who had been baptized in 1534 as a condition for their receiving the help of the king of Portugal against the northern robbers by whom their life was made a misery. Nothing had been done for their spiritual welfare. In spite of his ignorance of the difficult Tamil language, and the lack of suitable helpers, X. was successful in securing a very rough translation of the Creed, the Lord's Prayer and the Ten Commandments, and was able to create the outlines of a Christian church, outlines which were to be filled in by a succession of able Jesuits, through whose labours the Paravas were to be constituted a stable Christian community.

A large part of X's time in the years 1542 to 1547 was spent at or in the neighbourhood of Malacca, the easternmost of the great ports of the Portuguese, from which it seemed possible that great developments in evangelization might be expected in what is now Eastern Indonesia. Continuous residence in this area was interrupted by visits to Goa, in the course of which X. was brought into contact with some Japanese converts and was fired with the idea of making his way to Japan. This country was reached in 1549. Up till that time Europe had hardly known anything of Japan, and it is significant that X. and his companions were the first Europeans to reside in that area and to send home reliable information as to the situation in the Far East. The difficulties were immense. The fathers, used to the tropical climate of South India and Malacca, had had no idea of the severity of Japanese winters and suffered terribly from the cold. It soon became clear that their Japanese companions were so ill-instructed in the culture of their own country as to be a menace rather than a help in the attempt to communicate Christian truth in a wholly unfamiliar and difficult idiom. The missionaries had no knowledge of the religious system of the country, and were gravely perplexed at the political situation, which seemed to consist of a multiplicity of minor principalities with little central control. But despite all the difficulties they held on, holding discussions with princelings, with Buddhist monks and with anyone they could encounter. Some listened with attention, and the beginnings of a Japanese church came into existence.

As a result of this contact with the Japanese civilization a remarkable change took place in X's own attitude to the non-Christian world. During his time with the almost wholly illiterate Paravas and the depraved mixed population of Goa, he had accepted the view then generally prevalent in Europe of the *tabula rasa*—first all 'heathen' ideas must be exterminated, and then alone can the seed of the gospel be sown. In Japan, however, he could hardly find words too good for the qualities of the Japanese people, their nobility, the excellence of their civilization and their ability to grasp the deepest truths of the gospel. He had, indeed, no mercy for the aberrations of the Buddhist monks whose abandonment of marriage had, as he saw it, led them into extremities of homosexual vice. But his high estimate of the Japanese people and of their culture as an introduction to the Christian way of life remained unaltered.

After nearly three years in Japan, X. felt that the time had come to return to Goa to see to the affairs of other regions of his vast jurisdiction in the east. But his frame was exhausted through his austerities, and through exposure to endless labours in unfavourable climates. He died within sight of the shores of China, which was still wholly resistant to penetration by the Christian gospel. His body was brought to Goa. It was not long before X. was canonized (in 1622), to become perhaps the most popular of all the saints who have laboured in Asia.

A number of the letters of X. have fortunately been preserved. They reveal him as a man of intense, almost sentimental, human affection; but also as a man of affairs, with a shrewd awareness of the limitations of human nature, and of the possibilities of a situation. Of his utter devotion to the cause of Christ, and of his love for souls there can be no doubt at all. But he was to the end a man of the middle ages. He was untouched, like his master Ignatius, by any of the currents of the Renaissance and the Reformation. It was natural to him to write to the king of Portugal, urging the introduction of the Inquisition into Goa, and also to write to the king that he must bring pressure to bear on his governors to be the prime instruments in the evangelization of the subject peoples—by methods which would not commend themselves in the 20th century. The zeal and apostolic fervour of X. remain as a model and an inspiration to all subsequent ages; it would be strange if four centuries had not taught us many things which he did not know as to the Christian manner of approach to strange and unfamiliar peoples.

STEPHEN NEILL

J. Brodrick: *Saint Francis Xavier* (London 1952; a racy account by one who unfortunately lacked the knowledge of Asia, which is almost essential for the production of such a work); E. A. Robertson: *Francis Xavier* (London 1930); G. Schur-hammer: *Franz Xaver* (2 vols., a third to follow: Freiburg 1956, 1963); G. Schurhammer and J. Wicki: *Letters of St. Francis Xavier 1542–1552* (in the original languages, Rome 1944–1945; an accurate English translation of these letters with elucidation is much to be desired); *LTK* IV, 247f.; *NCE* XIV, 1059f.; *RGG* VI, 1853.

XAVIER, JEROME (1549–1617), was born at Beire, Spain, and entered the Society of *Jesus 1568. He arrived at Goa, India, 1581; in 1584 became rector of the college of Bassein; in 1586 rector of the college of Cochin; in 1592 superior of the Professed House at Goa; was chosen to conduct the third Mogul mission to the court of the emperor Akbar in 1594, and arrived at the court in Lahore on May 5, 1595. He returned to Goa in 1614 and acted as rector of St. Paul's College till his death in 1617.

The success of the third Mogul mission—which lasted till the death of the last Jesuit in 1803—is mainly due to the missionary methods employed by X. This method consisted of four stages. (1) The first stage was a thorough preparation through the study of the language of the court, Persian; of the environment including the religions of the empire, *Islam and *Hinduism; of the religion of the Emperor Akbar, the Divine Monotheism; and finally *adaptation to the religious and cultural feelings of the population. The creation of a Christian literature written in Persian—though this was continued throughout the whole stay in the mission—may also be considered to have been a preparation for other activities. (Main works: *Life of the Lord Jesus, Fountain of Life* (a comparison of Christianity with Islam and Hinduism), *History of the Apostles*, the *Duties of Kingship*, a Portuguese translation of the Qur'ān, parts of the Holy Bible, several catechisms and translations of parts of the works of Roman philosophers.) (2) The maintenance of good relations with the emperors Akbar and Jahangir (mainly through introduction of western art). (3) Oral disputes with the Muslims at the court as well as at other places. (4) Full display of Christian religious life (liturgy, ceremonies, exhibition of pictures). This direct approach to Islam was made possible by the religious tolerance of the emperors Akbar and Jahangir. As this policy changed after the death of Jahangir, the results X. hoped his successors would see did not appear.

A. CAMPS, OFM

A. Camps: *Jerome Xavier S. J. and the Muslims of the Mogul Empire, controversial works and missionary activity*, (Schoneck-Beckenried 1957), 'Persian Works of Jerome Xavier', *Islamic Culture* XXXV (Hyderabad-Deccan 1961), 166–76; E. Maclagan: *The Jesuits and the Great Mogul* (London 1932); *LTK* X, 1284f.

Y

YAMAMURO, GUMPEI (1872–1940), was born in Okayama-ken, Japan. He was converted at the age of fifteen and early dedicated himself to serve the poor. Y. received his education under *Niijima at Doshisha University. He became the first Japanese officer of the *Salvation Army in 1895 and later served as Territorial Commander. As a popular evangelist he preached some 10,000 times and won many souls to Christ. His communication of the gospel was simple and clear and well adapted to the Japanese mind. Y's ready pen produced many books and pamphlets, the most popular of which, *The Common People's Gospel*, has reached the 499th edition. He was early recognized as a courageous pioneer of social welfare projects which enhanced the reputation of the SA. Widely revered for his saintly life, his prayer list included more than 800 names remembered regularly before the 'throne of grace.' The SA admitted him to the Order of the Founder in 1937 and he was 'promoted to glory' in 1940.

GORDON K. CHAPMAN

N. Ebizawa, ed.: *Japanese Witnesses for Christ* (WCB No. 20, London 1957), pp.62–90; M. & N. Prichard: *Ten Against the Storm* (New York 1957), pp.43–53.

YEMEN. See ARABIAN PENINSULA.

YMCA. See WORLD ALLIANCE OF YMCAs.

YOUNGER CHURCHES. The expression 'younger churches' seems to have come into regular use only at the time of the second *World Missionary Conference (Jerusalem 1928), and, as soon as invented, to have been disliked by the members of the churches so described, as implying a stigma of inferiority. But no satisfactory substitute has been devised, and the term continues to be widely used.

It is, however, hard to say exactly what is covered by the term; it cannot be interpreted only in chronological or geographical terms. Perhaps the best definition is that a 'younger church' is 'one which exists as a minority in the midst of a non-Christian majority the culture of which has never at any time been deeply influenced by the Christian gospel'. If this is accepted, the only exception seems to be the ancient church of the *Thomas Christians in southwest India, which fulfils all the other conditions, but can hardly be described as 'younger'.

All the missions have dimly realized that the people they have been allowed to convert would one day wish to gather themselves into churches, and that these churches would one day attain to such a measure of maturity as to be able to meet all needs, material and spiritual, from their own resources, and to be no longer dependent for anything on the churches from which they first received the gospel. But few had any clear vision of this goal, or of the means by which it was to be attained. The formulation, by Henry *Venn and Rufus *Anderson in the middle of the 19th century, that churches must be self-governing, self-supporting and self-propagating, was a great step forward. But at the end of the century there were few areas in which the problem had been seriously tackled; the history of the 20th century is largely that of the discovery, the creation or the liberation of the YCs.

The problem has been dealt with in various fashions.

(1) For the Roman Catholic church there can in one sense be no problem. There can be no 'younger church'; every convert at baptism is admitted to the one church which has always existed. In spite of this view, the RC church has been very casual in provision for the churchly character of these new Christian groups; areas have been left for long periods without bishops, and it has therefore been impossible for anyone to be

ordained, unless he could afford the long and dangerous journey to a European country. The organization of this church is highly centralized; the history of its missions has been largely that of increasingly rigid and effective control from the centre. Recognition of the reality of the more distant churches has come in three stages: (a) the creation of the hierarchy (India 1886, West Africa 1950, South Africa 1951, etc.), after which the area concerned is no longer under the *Propaganda in Rome, control being wholly exercised by an apostolic delegate, who is the direct representative of the pope himself; (b) the creation of local episcopal conferences, with a measure of responsibility and freedom of decision within limits strictly laid down by Rome; (c) the creation (1966) of a central episcopal synod in Rome to help the pope in the government of the church: by this means the more distant areas may be able to obtain direct representation in the central councils of the church.

(2) It might be thought that the Independent (Congregational) or Baptist system under which each Christian congregation is a church wholly independent of any other, was the ideal one for producing genuine independence at an early date. The matter was, however, not quite so simple as this. Some criterion had to be established by which to judge whether a group of Christians had reached the point at which they could be regarded as a church. In many areas the criterion chosen was that of self-support, and self-support was interpreted as meaning the payment of the local ministers. This was harmful in two ways. It created an unhappy division between self-supporting congregations and those which were not yet self-supporting; and it identified spiritual maturity with a measure of economic prosperity. Various methods have been found of overcoming these difficulties, but usually at the cost of sacrificing some part of the Independent principle itself.

(3) The Methodist churches have tended to work on a highly centralized system. For British Methodists, membership of 'Conference' was a privilege greatly valued by those who could only very rarely attend a conference. In the American Methodist Church, all the bishops of the church were formerly chosen at General Conferences as bishops of the church, and not simply as of that area to which they might be allocated. This system has been deeply modified for two reasons. First, the growing spirit of *nationalism in Asia and Africa has made it inevitable that political freedom should be reflected also in the freedom of the churches from any semblance of outside control. Secondly, the definition of an *autonomous church reached by the *WCC ruled out from membership large Asian and African churches, which were really self-governing, on purely technical grounds. The only solution seemed to be to create autonomous churches and conferences, which would no longer maintain the existing close links with the centre.

(4) For the Anglican churches the unit of independence is the Province, which must be constituted of at least four dioceses, and which has the right to write its own constitution, to elect its own bishops, and to revise its own constitution. The nature of an independent Province was shown when the church in New Zealand attained its independence in 1852; but developments elsewhere were very slow. Large parts of the church remained legally parts of the Church of England, or were under the superintendence of the Archbishop of Canterbury as quasi-metropolitan. But now almost the entire Anglican world is organized in provinces, with the exception of some scattered dioceses which cannot easily be grouped together. The Lambeth Conference of Anglican bishops stands as a symbol of a world-wide unity which is deeply felt though not always clearly expressed.

(5) The Presbyterian and Reformed churches seem to have had less difficulty than others in providing a form of independence which can be attained at an early stage. The basis is generally geographic, and sometimes racial. Size is not held to matter greatly so long as a group shows a certain measure of stability. Thus in Indonesia at least ten independent Reformed churches came into being, none with

any necessary relation to any other, and without any official focus of unity. This method has been made workable only by the strong sense of duty and local responsibility which the Reformed churches have developed in their members from the time of Calvin on.

Space forbids detailed consideration of all the confessions in the Christian world. It is hoped that these five, taken as types, cover most of the ground (see also AUTONOMOUS CHURCHES).

The work of liberation has been carried out on a gigantic scale; but this does not mean that all problems have been solved. Three may be specially mentioned:

(1) In a number of cases the nature of the church concerned was defined in such narrowly racial terms as to exclude the possibility of any co-operation by missionaries, since as foreigners they could not work inside the church, and did not wish to work outside it, for fear of creating a rival organization.

(2) Very few YCs are as yet fully independent financially. In many areas it is felt that the independence granted is really a sham, and finance is controlled from the west, directly by a mission treasurer, or indirectly through the conditions on which financial grants are made available.

(3) To many YCs independence has brought a sense of helplessness and isolation. In such a situation, where is the unity of the church to be descried? In general, four types of unity can be discerned, all of which are of comparatively recent origin:

a. Corporate union with churches of other confessional origin which exist in the same area.

b. A link to the new regional organizations, such as the *EACC and *AACC, which have come into being since 1958.

c. Direct membership in a *world confessional family, the growing importance of which is a feature of 20th century church history.

d. Direct membership in the WCC. This is eagerly desired by almost all YCs. But, there is at the same time grave dissatisfaction that the ecumenical organization is so overpoweringly western. The YCs are small, but they consider themselves to be the first fruits and the representatives of great populations. For the *Tambaram Conference (1938) John R. *Mott made the very salutary rule that at least half the delegates from the various countries must be nationals. Nothing like this proportion was observed again until the Geneva Conference (1966) on Church and Society, at which *older and younger churches enjoyed about equal representation.

The distinction between older and younger churches will in course of time cease to have any meaning. It is certain that the influence of those which now can be called YCs will increase in all ecumenical concerns with the passing of the years.

STEPHEN NEILL

P. Beyerhaus: *Die Selbständigkeit der jungen Kirchen als missionarisches Problem* (Wuppertal-Barmen, 3rd ed. 1967); P. Beyerhaus and H. Lefever: *The Responsible Church and the Foreign Mission* (London 1964).

YOUTH CONFERENCES. See WORLD CONFERENCES OF CHRISTIAN YOUTH.

YOUTH FOR CHRIST INTERNATIONAL is an interdenominational organization specializing in teenage evangelism. Born in North America out of the large youth rallies of the early '40s, YFCI was organized in 1945 with Torrey Johnson as its first president. Almost immediately YFC spread to evangelize teen-agers in foreign countries; it currently ministers in 54 nations.

Its outreaches: (1) Saturday night youth rallies are geared to evoke teen-age commitments to Christ. In North America 256 cities have chartered YFC programmes; overseas there are more than 300 rally centres. (2) On-campus activities include 3,000 high-school clubs, designed to mature the Christian teen-ager and equip him to reach his peers. (3) Eight national youth magazines are bolstered by other literature aimed at both Christian growth and evangelism. (4) *Lifeline* annually ministers to

13,000 delinquent and near-delinquent boys and girls in 130 cities through summer camps, year-round counselling, and three rehabilitation homes. (5) Leadership training for youth evangelism aims at filling not only YFC personnel needs, but aiding church youth workers in effective communication. (6) Overseas outreaches for youth include Teen Teams (4–7 teen-agers sent abroad for four-month tours of intensive evangelism) and Y-2 (college-graduated couples in 24-month assignments overseas). (7) Conventions and camps, especially during summer and holiday seasons, gather large numbers of teen-agers for concentrated spiritual learning.

YFCI is supported by faith through contributions; North American personnel number over 1,000. Overseas personnel total 500, including 40 North Americans.

YFCI's headquarters are at North Main Street, Wheaton, Illinois, USA. YFCI is a member of *EFMA.

HAROLD LINDSELL

YUI, DAVID Z. T. (YU JIH-CHANG, 1882–1936). National Secretary of the *YMCA in China for sixteen years and Chairman of the *National Christian Council for ten years, he exerted a dynamic influence in government and educational circles as well as in the Christian movement. Son of a Christian minister in Hupeh Province, he studied at Boone and St. John's universities, then earned an MA degree at Harvard. Returning to China he served in a few government positions but declined many large political and business offers, in order to devote his energies to the building of Christian character and the salvation of his country. He represented Chinese people's organizations at the Washington Disarmament Conference of 1921, and in 1932 travelled abroad to arouse support for China in her struggle against Japanese aggression. He was active in the Institute of Pacific Relations, and a prominent member of the Chinese delegation at the *Jerusalem Conference of the *IMC in 1928. As Chairman of the NCC of China he guided the member missions and church bodies

through a revolutionary decade, stressing responsible Chinese leadership, a relevant Christian message and continuous efforts toward church unity. He won the confidence and support of both liberals and conservatives. Far-seeing administrator, magnetic personality, tireless worker, his health broke when he was only 50. His death in 1936, a year before the Sino-Japanese war, was widely mourned.

F. W. PRICE

H. L. Boorman, *Biographical Dictionary of Republican China* (New York 1967).

YUN, TCHI-HO, Baron (1865–1945), Korean nobleman and Methodist leader, as a youth became interpreter to the first American minister to Korea (1883). When a palace coup forced his grandfather, the minister of war, from power Y. sought asylum in Shanghai (1885). Greatly impressed by Young Allen, head of the Anglo-Chinese College, he became a Christian (1887). In the USA for further study (1888–1893) at Emory and Vanderbilt universities he urged Southern Methodists to open work in Korea, which they did in 1896. From 1895 to 1906 Y. served his country with distinction as diplomat, spokesman for reform and vice-minister of education, but Korea's loss of independence turned his energies into religious work from 1906 to 1920. He was principal of the Anglo-Korean School (1906–11), delegate to *Edinburgh (1910), and General Secretary of the Korean *YMCA (1915–20). Imprisonment (1911–1915) for alleged independence activity made him a popular hero. He was twice called from retirement, first for negotiations that united northern and southern Methodist mission work in the *autonomous Methodist Church of Korea (1930), and again as first Korean president of Chosen Christian College (now Yonsei University), 1941–44. A nephew, Po-Sun Yun, in 1960 was elected second president of the Republic of Korea.

SAMUEL H. MOFFETT

J. S. Ryang, ed.: *Southern Methodism in Korea* (Seoul 1927), pp.14–43ff.

YWCA. See WORLD YWCA.

Z

ZAMBIA, formerly Northern Rhodesia, is a land-locked, central African country, 290,587 square miles in extent, bounded on the north by Congo, Lake Tanganyika and Tanzania, on the east by Malawi, on the south by Mozambique and Rhodesia, on the west by Angola, with a 1963 population of 3,540,000 (1968 estimate: 4,014,000), of whom 72,000 were Europeans and 11,200 Asians. The capital, Lusaka, has 154,000 inhabitants. The official language is English. The Africans are Bantu speaking, divided into 73 tribes with 30 different languages. The largest tribes are the Bemba, Ila, Lozi, Lunda, and Ngoni. Economically Zambia is dependent on copper, discovered in 1895 and developed by British, South African, and American capital. Agricultural products are also important.

The Bantu-speaking population replaced earlier Bushmen, some of the tribes invading Zambia in the 19th century. Portuguese travellers explored the country in the 19th century and the missionary David *Livingstone discovered the Victoria Falls in 1855; he died at Lake Bangweolo in 1873. In 1890 British protection was extended first over Barotseland and then over all of Zambia. The administration and development of the country was turned over to the British South Africa Company directed by Cecil Rhodes after whom the country was first named. The Company ended the slave trade by 1910. Its rule came to an end in 1924, the country being ruled by the British Crown until it became part of the Federation of Rhodesia and Nyasaland, 1953–63. In 1964 Zambia became an independent republic with Kenneth Kaunda its first President. From 1966 onwards the country faced serious economic difficulties because of its opposition to the Smith government in Rhodesia.

The religion of the Bantu-speaking tribes includes belief in a Supreme Being, veneration of the ancestors, a spiritualized conception of nature; practice of *magic and *witchcraft. *Islam has not penetrated perceptibly in Zambia. The first Christian approach to reach Zambia was made by the *LMS from Botswana in 1859, and by the *UMCA from the east coast in 1861, both of which failed because of illness and natural disasters. Roman Catholic attempts by *Jesuits during the years 1879–85 also failed. Frederick Stanley *Arnot of the Plymouth Brethren visited chief Lewanika of Barotseland in 1882–84, and in 1884 François *Coillard, one of the greatest of the pioneer African missionaries, of the *PEMS, managed to obtain permission from Lewanika to start work among the Lozi. The LMS made new attempts from the east coast and reached Zambia in 1885, and in the same year came the Presbyterians from Scotland. Then followed in fairly quick succession the Primitive Methodist Church, 1890; the RC order of the *White Fathers, 1891; the DRC of South Africa, 1899; the Nyasa Industrial Mission, 1905; the SDA, 1905; the Brethren in Christ, 1906; the *SAGM, now the Africa Evangelical Fellowship, 1910; the Wesleyan Methodist Missionary Society, 1912; the South African Baptist Missionary Society, 1914. The Christian churches have experienced a healthy growth during the 20th century, with a Protestant community of more than 450,000 and a RC population in excess of 500,000.

There are three theological training centres, of which the United Church Ministerial Training College at Kitwe is an ecumenical undertaking. The whole Bible has been translated into the Bemba and Lozi languages and the NT into at least four others. As early as 1908 the missionaries came together in an ecumenical missionary conference which in time was reorganized as the Zambia Christian Council. In 1958 the Mindolo Ecumenical Centre was established where conferences of different kinds could be held and training could be

677

given in writing, journalism, art, home-making, and agriculture. The Africa Literature Centre is located at Mindolo, which also served as the first headquarters of the *AACC, later moved to Nairobi. The churches originating from the LMS, the PEMS and the Methodist and Presbyterian churches formed the United Church of Zambia in January 1965. This new church is now negotiating a further union which may include the Zambia work of the Anglican Church, the African Reformed Church and the Presbyterian Church of Southern Africa.

The churches pioneered in education for Africans with a growing amount of government aid. In 1958 it was estimated that 90% of the rural and 50% of the urban children were attending primary schools. The aim at present is primary schooling for all children to the age of 13. In 1963 there were 5,280 students in secondary and 682 in trade schools. A university was founded at Lusaka in 1966. The churches also pioneered hospitals and health services, but now the government and mining companies provide most of the facilities.

The churches face problems of divisions from within, such as the large Lenshina movement which broke away from the main stream of Christian tradition and resisted Kaunda's government. The need is to build an ecumenical, trans-tribal Christian unity fit to serve the new nation.

PER HASSING

P. Bolink: *Towards Church Union in Zambia* (Franeker, Holland 1967); L. H. Gann: *A History of Northern Rhodesia: Early Days to 1953* (London 1964); K. Kaunda: *Zambia, Independence and Beyond* (London 1966); R. I. Rotberg: *Christian Missionaries and the Creation of Northern Rhodesia 1880–1924* (Princeton 1965); J. V. Taylor and D. Lehmann: *Christians of the Copperbelt* (London 1961); *NCE* XIV, 1110f.

ZAMORA, NICOLAS (1875–1914), was born in Manila, the son of Paulino Zamora who was exiled by the Spanish for independent religious convictions, and the grandnephew of Jacinto Zamora, martyred nationalist priest. Z. left graduate law studies at the University of Santo Tomás to join the revolution against Spain, rising to the rank of lieutenant colonel. Following American occupation of the Philippines and the beginning of religious liberty, Z. and his father were among the first Protestant converts. In time Z. became well known for his evangelistic messages and decided to enter the ministry. On March 10, 1900, Z. was ordained by Methodist Bishop James M. *Thoburn as the first Filipino Protestant minister. After theological study in Shanghai he returned to the Philippines under appointment as itinerant evangelist. In 1903 he was assigned as the first Filipino pastor of Knox Memorial Methodist Church in Manila. Owing to various factors, including nationalistic grievances, Z. established on February 28, 1909, La Iglesia Metodista en las Islas Filipinas (the 'IEMELIF'), a church completely free of foreign resources and direction, although remaining Methodist in discipline and doctrine. As General Superintendent of the IEMELIF, Z. led what has become the largest (more than 20,000 members) indigenous Protestant church in the archipelago. His life was tragically cut short at the age of 39 during a cholera outbreak.

RICHARD L. DEATS

G. H. Anderson, ed.: *Studies in Philippine Church History* (Ithaca, NY, 1969); R. L. Deats: *The Story of Methodism in the Philippines* (Manila 1964), *Nationalism and Christianity in the Philippines* (Dallas 1969).

ZANZIBAR. See TANZANIA.

ZEN BUDDHISM. The word 'Zen' is the Japanese form of the Chinese 'Ch'an', itself derived from the Sanskrit word 'Dhyana', which means 'meditation'. ZB is, therefore, that sect of *Buddhism, which emphasizes meditation as the way to achieve the *enlightenment* (in Japanese, *satori*) which Sākyamuni is supposed to have gained when he became the *Buddha* (i.e. 'the enlightened one'). Zen claims to be original Buddhism, but there is undoubtedly a strong Taoist influence to be seen in its development in China.

The legendary founder, Bodhidharma (died in A.D. 528), is supposed to have brought the teaching from India to China, where a succession of teachers was established. The teaching was taken from China to Japan by Eisai (1141–1215) and Dōgen (1200–1253), and it is in Japan that this form of Buddhism now flourishes. Zen aspires to a profound spiritual awakening, which begins with self-knowledge. 'One who has not seen into one's own nature is not to be called a wise teacher' (D. T. Suzuki: *Zen Buddhism*, p.87). Instead of dependence on the Buddhist Sūtras, Zen stressed the leap from doubt and uncertainty to the place of enlightenment. A Chinese teacher, Yuan-chan (died in 1827) describes his experience: 'The whole outlook changed . . . The whole universe . . . appeared quite different . . . and was now seen to be nothing else but the outflow of my own inmost nature which in itself remained bright, true and transparent'. Included in the *satori* experience are a sense of authority, a beyondness, a feeling of ecstasy. Through it the Zen disciple is believed to find his fundamental unity with being itself and to overcome any feelings of dividedness or separateness. The experience is not to be found by seeking; it cannot be acquired or cultivated. The enlightenment comes, we are told, with a shattering suddenness, and the *Koan* (or puzzle), often used at meditation, is simply a key to the limitations of logic. Nor is *satori* to be confined to the meditation hall; it passes out into all the situations of life, and fills all experience with meaningfulness. The response is one of 'infinite gratitude to all beings in the past, infinite gratitude and service to all beings in the present and infinite responsibility to all beings in the future' (R. F. Sasaki: *Zen: A Religion*, p.21). *Satori* has often been compared with the Christian experience of *conversion*, but there are profound differences. In Zen there is a total lack of any idea of a *personal* meeting with the *other*. There is no sense of dependence, no doctrine of grace. The enlightenment does not come from outside, but only from within man. The small, selfish ego is delivered through its own efforts, when it realises that its *self-ness* is not the ultimate truth of existence.

RAYMOND J. HAMMER

H. Dumoulin: *A History of Zen Buddhism* (London 1963); D. T. Suzuki: *Zen Buddhism* (New York 1956); *NCE* XIV, 114–17.

ZIEGENBALG, BARTHOLOMÄUS

(1682–1719), was born in Pulsnitz, Saxony, Germany. In youth his faith was shaped by *Pietism, and for a time he studied under A. H. Francke at the University of Halle, the centre of this movement. But his education was incomplete and his health weak when he was called to missionary service. With H. Plütschau he went to Copenhagen, where they were ordained. On 9 July 1706 they arrived at the Danish colony of Tranquebar as the first Protestant missionaries to India. Some landmarks: 1707, first baptisms; 1708–09, four months' imprisonment by the governor; 1712, printing press established; 1715, Tamil NT printed; 1714–16, 'deputation work' in Europe; 1719, death at Tranquebar.

Z. studied Tamil thoroughly. He worked on a dictionary and published a grammar. He wrote, printed and spread Tamil literature with remarkable effect and produced the first translation of the NT into any Indian language. He learnt from the Tamil of the *Jesuit missionaries, but his style was less literary. Z. studied the Indian culture and Hindu religion. He sent manuscripts, e.g. one on *The genealogy of the Malabar gods*, to Halle. But the friends at home refused to print them. In seeing the need for missionary research in religions, Z. was ahead of his time.

He started schools (India's first girls' school), mainly to educate co-workers, and orphanages. He opened a seminary to train teachers and eventually pastors, expecting a time when Europeans would no longer be needed. His plans to have missionaries sent out as candidates to be trained and ordained at Tranquebar were only partly realized.

All institutions needed money (22 helpers had to be paid in 1712). Z. also supported poor Christians. This was criticized by Wendt, the Copenhagen Mission Secretary. He wanted an 'Apostolic mission'; the missionaries should only preach and not get involved in externals; in these the Indian church should stand on its own legs; no 'European Christendom' should be planted. This sounds modern; so does Z's answer: The care for souls demands also the care for bodies. A Christianity which refuses such service is not of the right kind. Z. found that his opposition to *caste prevented more conversions; but he was tolerant enough of caste to win a good number of caste converts.

Z. was a 'Royal Danish missionary' with a salary from the treasury of King Frederick IV. But the opposition of the colonial authorities, and the support from private circles of friends make him a link between the earlier colonial missions and later society missions. Co-operation with the *SPCK made his work one of the earliest ecumenical ventures.

Much of what Z. did, whether right or wrong, seems obvious to us. But he had to find the paths on which generations of missionaries could follow.

See also DANISH-HALLE MISSION.

D. WINKLER

E. Beyreuther: *Bartholomaeus Ziegenbalg* (Madras 1955); C. B. Firth: *An Introduction to Indian Church History* (Madras 1961), pp.127–34; E. A. Lehmann: *It Began at Tranquebar* (Madras 1955); *RGG* VI, 1907.

ZINZENDORF, NIKOLAUS LUDWIG VON (1700–1760), received decisive impulses, not so much for his thinking as for his missionary activity, from August Hermann Francke, in whose institutions at Halle he resided from 1710 to 1716. In 1722, with refugees from Moravia, he founded the colony of Herrnhut. On 21 August 1732, this young community sent out its first missionaries (including J. L. *Dober) to the West Indies and to Greenland. By the date of the death of Z. these had been followed by another 300 missionaries. For Z. mission is always an enterprise of the community. Through this understanding of the problem

he is directly linked to the earliest period of the Christian church. The missionaries of the community are lay folk, whose task it is to bear witness to Christians and non-Christians alike. The basis of Z's missionary thinking is the Bible, in which he finds Christ and Christ alone. His concern is 'the enthronement of the Lamb of God as the sole creator, sustainer, redeemer and sanctifier of the entire world, and the catholicity of the doctrine of his passion as a comprehensive theology both in theory and in practice'. Herein the missionary motive as well as the aim of mission is set forth.

Since we live here in the realm of the cross and not yet in the realm of glory, nothing more is possible for us in this epoch than the bringing into existence, everywhere in the world and even among the remotest nations, of congregations of 'first-fruits' as an earnest of the completion of the harvest. To this end countless messengers to the non-Christians go in every direction under the sun. Yet even in this area, it is the aim of the work of Z. to be a work of following. He wishes to go only to places 'where the Holy Spirit has already gone before'. Through this comprehensive theology, of which Christ alone is the centre, every form of confessionalism can be avoided. Z's missionary work cannot be considered in isolation from his other aims: For him, world-wide church and congregation, mission and *diaspora* ('dispersion') are one single entity. He understands the church of Christ as a whole in this epoch as 'the realm of the cross'; but that means as *diaspora*, as the scattered community. Thus his reconciling labours, directed towards closer fellowship among the denominations, the gathering together of faithful believers in the different confessions in the old world as well as in the non-Christian world, serves the purpose of the manifestation of the church, the community of God. He therefore understands the unity of the children of God among Christians and non-Christians, which has been brought into being during his life-time, as a sign, a symbolic representation of the Church of

Christ as a whole. Z's permanent contributions to the understanding of the Christian mission are recognition of the Christian community as the bearer of responsibility for mission; missionary preaching as the proclamation of the cross; the organic unity of Christian community and mission, world-wide church and scattered community (*diaspora*).

HEINZ MOTEL

E. Beyreuther: *Der Junge Zinzendorf* (Marburg/Lahn 1957), *Zinzendorf und die sich allhier beisammen finden* (Marburg/Lahn 1959), *Zinzendorf und die Christenheit* (Marburg/Lahn 1961); A. J. Lewis: *Zinzendorf, the Ecumenical Pioneer* (London 1962); *EKL* III, 1905ff; *LTK* X, 1376–78; *RGG* VI, 1913–16; *WKL*, 1633–35.

ZOROASTRIANISM, one of the ancient religions of Iran, officially approved from A.D. 211 to 640, and still surviving, though with only a small number of adherents. It is now generally held that Zoroaster (Zarathustra) lived in the sixth century B.C., and that he was a teacher of genuinely prophetic power. His system is dualistic: on the one hand stands the wise Creator of the world, Ahura Mazda, with his seven divine spirits; on the other the evil spirit Angra Mainyu together with his six attendant spirits. The world is the scene of the perpetual conflict between the two. But Z. appears to have believed that, through the intervention of a Saviour, 'the bridge of decision' would be built, over which all men would ultimately pass into the world of eternal bliss, and that thus the final triumph of the good would be assured. The ethical teachings of Z. are pure and of an almost Christian standard.

The small but wealthy and influential community of the Parsis, in and around Bombay, originally refugees from Iran, have maintained the Zoroastrian faith until the present day. A small number of Parsis have become Christians; the family of the Sorabjis in particular having added distinction to the annals of the Christian Church in India.

STEPHEN NEILL

J. H. Moulton: *The Treasure of the Magi* (London 1917); G. Smith: *The Life of John Wilson* (London 1878); R. C. Zaehner: *The Dawn and Twilight of Zoroastrianism* (London 1961).

ZUMARRAGA (CUMARRAGA), JUAN DE (1476–1548), was born at Durango, near Bilbao, Spain, and died in Mexico. He entered the OFM (*Franciscans) and later became a local, then provincial superior. He was proposed by Charles V as first bishop of Mexico, and sent there in 1528, without being consecrated a bishop, which made his position very difficult. In 1530 he was nominated by Rome first bishop of the newly erected diocese of Mexico—in 1533 was consecrated bishop—and in 1546 became first archbishop of Mexico. He was a great missionary and defender of the rights of the Indians against the Spaniards. He organized the building of churches, convents, hospitals and schools for boys and girls; he fostered agriculture, handicrafts and simple industries. One of his great achievements was the foundation of the Colégio Santa Cruz en Tlatelolco in 1536, to create an Indian élite, and train an indigenous clergy. With the first project success was obtained, but the almost insurmountable difficulty of celibacy created doubt about success with the latter. Another great achievement was the setting up of the first printing press in the New World with the help of John Cromberger of Seville (1539) to print religious literature and especially Sacred Scripture in the Indian languages, thus showing views which were far ahead of general Catholic opinion of his time.

A. MCCORMACK, MHM

R. E. Greenleaf: *Zumarraga and the Mexican Inquisition* (Washington 1961); J. García Icazbalceta: *Don fray Juan de Zumárraga primer obispo y arzobispo de Mexico* (4 vols., Mexico 1947); J. Specker: '*Die Einschatzung der H. C. Schrift in der Spanisch-amerikanischen Missionen*' in *Neue Zeitschrift für Missionswissenschaft* (1962), pp.250ff.; *LTK* X, 1412f.; *NCE* XIV, 1137f.

ZWEMER, SAMUEL MARINUS (1867–

1952), missionary to Muslims, was born in Vriesland, Michigan, the son of Dutch immigrants to the USA. He was educated at Hope College and New Brunswick Seminary, and immediately after the completion of his studies in 1890 he set out with a pioneer band of missionaries for Arabia. Work was begun first in Basrah and then Bahrein and Muscat before the enterprise was finally adopted by the mission board of the Reformed Church in America, from whose congregation the mission had come. Z. was an excellent preacher and zealous evangelist, ever reaching out to and exploring new areas of Arabia. He gradually made the whole field of missions to Muslims his concern. In 1912 he was invited to Cairo to help in the production of literature for Muslim missions and to give leadership in the field as a whole. Soon he was travelling widely and constantly over the entire Muslim world. His great interests were in evangelistic speaking, personal work and writing. Wherever he went he found Muslims to whom he could present, individually or in groups, the Christian faith. He organized numerous conferences on work for Muslims, and in 1911 began *The Moslem World*, a scholarly journal, which he edited for 36 years and which has continued to be the major forum of thought on Muslim-Christian relations. From 1929 to his retirement in 1937 he served as Professor of Christian Missions and History of Religions at Princeton Seminary in New Jersey. A steady stream of books flowed from his pen not only during his years of teaching but also through the earlier years of missionary activity. Among his better known works were *Arabia, the Cradle of Islam* (1900), *Islam: A Challenge to Faith* (1907), *The Muslim Christ* (1912), *Across the Moslem World* (1929), *The Origin of Religion* (1935) and *The Cross Above the Crescent* (1943). In all he wrote some 37 books and was a joint author of another dozen. Many of these went through numerous editions and translations.

CHARLES W. FORMAN

J. C. Wilson: *Apostle to Islam. A Biography of Samuel M. Zwemer* (Grand Rapids, Michigan 1952); S. M. Zwemer and J. Cantine: *The Golden Milestone* (New York 1938); *RGG* VI, 1949; *WKL* 1636f.